International Encyclopedia of Information and Library Science

International Encyclopedia of Information and Library Science

Second edition

Edited by John Feather and Paul Sturges

Routledge
Taylor & Francis Group

LONDON AND NEW YORK

First published 1997
Second edition published 2003
by Routledge
11 New Fetter Lane, London EC4P 4EE
Simultaneously published in the USA and Canada
by Routledge
29 West 35th Street, New York, NY 10001

Routledge is an imprint of the Taylor & Francis Group

© 1997, 2003 Routledge

Typeset in Times by Taylor & Francis Books Ltd
Printed and bound in Great Britain by TJ International Ltd, Padstow,
Cornwall

British Library Cataloguing in Publication Data
A catalogue record for this book is available from the British Library

Library of Congress Cataloging in Publication Data
International encyclopdia of information and library science/edited by
John Feather and Paul Sturges. – 2nd ed.
Includes bibliographical references and index.
1. Information science–Encyclopedias. 2. Library science–Encyclopedias.
I. Feather, John. II. Sturges, R. P. (Rodney Paul)
Z1006 .I57 2003
004′.03–dc21   2002032699

ISBN 0–415–25901–0

Contents

Consultant editors

Christine Borgman
University of California at Los Angeles, USA
(American Consultant Editor)

Lynne Brindley
British Library, UK

Michael Koenig
University of Long Island, USA

Tamiko Matsumura
Tokyo, Japan

Julie Sabaratnam
National Library of Singapore

Peter Vodosek
Hochschule der Medien, Stuttgart, Germany

Trevor Wood-Harper
University of Salford, UK

Contributors

Alastair J. Allan
University of Sheffield, UK

J.L. Alty
Loughborough University, UK

James D. Anderson
Rutgers State University of New Jersey, USA

John Ashman
Glasgow University, UK

Raymond G. Astbury
Retired

David Avison
ESSEC Business School, France

K.G.B. Bakewell
*Professor Emeritus, Liverpool
John Moores University*

David R. Bender
*Retired Executive Director, Special Libraries
Association*

Raymond Bérard
*École Nationale supérieure des sciences de
l'information et des bibliothèques, Villeurbanne,
France*

H.S. Bhola
Emeritus Professor, Indiana University, USA

Alistair Black
Leeds Metropolitan University, UK

Barry Bloomfield
Deceased, formerly of the British Library, UK

Andrew Booth
University of Sheffield, UK

R.T. Bottle
Deceased, formerly of the City University, UK

Ross Bourne
Retired, formerly of the British Library, UK

Russell Bowden
Retired

Alan Brine
Loughborough University, UK

Peter Brophy
Manchester Metropolitan University, UK

Christine S. Bruce
Queensland University of Technology, Australia

Philip Bryant
Retired

Allan Bunch
Freelance writer/designer, Peterborough, UK

Juan Miguel Campanario
Universidad de Alcala, Spain

James V. Carmichael, Jnr
*University of North Carolina at
Greensboro, USA*

Kenneth E. Carpenter
Harvard University, USA

David Carr
University of North Carolina at Chapel Hill, USA

Roderick Cave
Retired

Tony Cawkell
Citech Ltd, Iver, UK

Andrew Chadwick
Royal Holloway, University of London, UK

Helen E. Chandler
*Retired, formerly of Liverpool
John Moores University, UK*

Michael Chaney
Loughborough University, UK

Liz Chapman
Taylor Institution, University of Oxford, UK

Robert W. Clarida, Esq
*Partner, Cowan Liebowitz and Latman,
New York, USA*

Michèle Valerie Cloonan
Simmons College, USA

Nigel Clubb
*National Monuments Record, English Heritage,
UK*

John Y. Cole
*Director, Center for the Book, Library of
Congress, USA*

Michael Cook
*Centre for Archive Studies, University of
Liverpool, UK*

Alan Cooper
Library Association, UK

Gary Copitch
Manchester Community Information Network, UK

Sheila Corrall
University of Southampton, UK

Penny Craven
Independant consultant

Claire Creaser
*Library and Information Statistics Unit,
Loughborough University, UK*

M.J. Crump
British Library, UK

J.E. Davies
Loughborough University, UK

Maurice Davies
Deputy Director, Museums Association, UK

James Dearnley
Loughborough University, UK

Michael Dewe
Retired

Neil F. Doherty
Loughborough University, UK

Harry East
City University

Tamara Eisenschitz
City University, London, UK

Kai Ekholm
Helsinki University, Finland

David Ellis
University of Wales, Aberystwyth, UK

Hilary Evans
Mary Evans Picture Library, UK

John Feather
Loughborough University, UK

Tom Featherstone
Retired

Stephney Ferguson
University of the West Indies

Rosa Maria Fernandez de Zamora
*Biblioteca Nacional, Universidad Nacional
Autonoma de Mexico*

Guy Fitzgerald
Brunel University, UK

Michael P. Fourman
University of Edinburgh, UK

Maurice Frankel
Campaign for Freedom of Information, UK

Marcia Freed Taylor
University of Essex, UK

Thomas J. Froehlich
Kent State University, USA

John Furlong
*Director of Legal Research and Education,
Matheson Ormsby Prentice, Dublin, Ireland*

Brian K. Geiger
University of North Carolina, Chapel Hill, USA

Ekaterina Genieva
*M. Rudomino Library for Foreign Literature,
Russia*

Alan Gilchrist
CURA Consortium, UK

Peter Golding
Loughborough University, UK

Deborah L. Goodall
Universtiy of Northumbria at Newcastle

G.E. Gorman
Victoria University of Wellington, New Zealand

Ellen Gredley
*Queen Mary and Westfield College, University
of London, UK*

José-Marie Griffiths
*Doreen A. Boyce Chair and Professor, University
of Pittsburgh, USA*

Matthew Hall
Aston University, UK

Sigrún Klara Hannesdóttir
National and University Library of Iceland

Stevan Harnad
*Centre de Neuroscience de la Cognition (CNC),
Universite du Québec à Montréal, Canada*

Janet Harrison
Loughborough University, UK

K.C. Harrison
Retired

R.J. Hartley
*Department of Information and Communications,
Manchester Metropolitan University, UK*

Ross Harvey
Charles Sturt University, Australia

Peter Havard-Williams
*Deceased, formerly of the University
of Botswana*

Robert M. Hayes
*Professor Emeritus, University of California at
Los Angeles, USA*

Mark Hepworth
Loughborough University, UK

Sheila Hingley
Canterbury Cathedral, UK

Birger Hjørland
*Royal School of Library and Information Science,
Copenhagen, Denmark*

Peter Hoare
Formerly of the University of Nottingham, UK

Susan Hockey
University College London, UK

Edward G. Holley
*Professor Emeritus, University of North Carolina,
Chapel Hill, USA*

Bob Hook
English Heritage, UK

Christopher J. Hunt
*Retired, formerly of the University of
Manchester, UK*

David Huxley
Manchester Metropolitan University, UK

Peter Ingwersen
*Royal School of Library and Information Science,
Denmark*

Kalervo Järvelin
University of Tampere, Finland

Nimal Jayaratna
Curtin University of Technology, Australia

Srećko Jelušić
University J.J. Strossmayer in Osijek, Croatia

Rosalind Johnson
Freelance Consultant, UK

Simon Jones
Loughborough University, UK

W.A. Katz
State University of New York, USA

Stella Keenan
Retired

Don Kennington
Capital Planning Information Ltd, UK

Shaban A. Khalifa
University of Cairo, Egypt

Anis Khurshid
Pakistan

Margaret Kinnell
DeMontfort University, Leicester, UK

Joyce Kirk
University of Technology, Sydney, Australia

Michael Koenig
*College of Information and Computer Science,
University of Long Island, USA*

Hannele Koivunen
*Counsellor for Cultural Affairs, Ministry of
Education, Science and Culture, Docent at
the Helsinki University, Finland*

Christine M. Koontz
Florida State University, USA

Kathleen Ladizesky
Retired, UK

Monica Landoni
University of Strathclyde, UK

Derek G. Law
*Head of the Information Resources Directorate,
University of Strathclyde, UK*

Yves F. Le Coadic
*Conservatoire National des Arts et Métiers,
France*

Peter W. Lea
*Department of Information and Communications,
Manchester Metropolitan University, UK*

Diane Lees
Bethnal Green Museum of Childhood, UK

Ben Light
*Information Systems Research Centre, University
of Salford, UK*

Paul A. Longley
University College London, UK

Peter Johan Lor
*National Library of South Africa, Professor
Extraordinary, Department of Information
Science, University of Pretoria*

Mary Niles Maack
*Department of Information Studies, University of
California at Los Angeles, USA*

Scott McDonald
University of Sheffield, UK

Alan MacDougall
King's College, London, UK

Kevin McGarry
Retired

Cliff McKnight
Loughborough University, UK

Paul Marett
Legal author and Barrister

Ivo Maroević
University of Zagreb, Croatia

Geoffrey Martin
University of Essex, UK

Stephen W. Massil
Hebraica Libraries Group, London, UK

Graham Matthews
University of Central England, Birmingham, UK

Kingo Mchombu
University of Namibia

Jack Meadows
Loughborough University, UK

Elizabeth A. Melrose
*North Yorkshire County Library Service,
UK*

Michel J. Menou
*Department of Information Science,
City University London, UK*

Anne Morris
Loughborough University, UK

Ian Murray
Loughborough University, UK

Musila Musembi
Kenya National Archives

Eisuke Naito
Tokyo University, Japan

Alisande Nuttall
MDA, UK

Ann O'Brien
Loughborough University, UK

Pat Oddy
British Library, UK

Sherelyn Ogden
Minnesota Historical Society, USA

Robert E. Oldroyd
University of Nottingham, UK

Charles Oppenheim
Loughborough University, UK

David Orman
*John Rylands University Library of Manchester,
UK*

Elizabeth Orna
Orna Information and Editorial Consultancy, UK

Jim Parker
Registrar of Public Lending Right, UK

Nicola Parker
University of Technology, Sydney, Australia

John Pateman
*Head of Libraries and Heritage, London Borough
of Merton, UK*

David Pearson
Victoria and Albert Museum, UK

J. Michael Pemberton
University of Tennessee, Knoxville, USA

Jean Plaister
Retired

Niels O. Pors
*Department of Library and Information
Management, Royal School of Library
and Information Science, Denmark*

Martine Poulain
University of Paris, France

Alan Poulter
University of Strathclyde, UK

Ronald R. Powell
Wayne State University, USA

Derek J. Priest
Formerly of the University of Manchester, UK

Carol Priestley
*Director, International Network for the
Availability of Scientific Publications (INASP),
UK*

Lyndon Pugh
Managing Editor, Multimedia Information and Technology, UK

Claire Raven
Manchester Community Information Network, UK

Pamela S. Richards
Deceased, formerly of Rutgers State University of New Jersey, USA

Mickey Risseeuw
Formerly of the International Translation Centre, Netherlands

Louise S. Robbins
University of Wisconsin-Madison, USA

William H. Robinson
US Congressional Research Service, Library of Congress, USA

Ian Rogerson
Retired, formerly of Manchester Metropolitan University, UK

Michael Roper
Former Keeper of the Public Records, UK

Hermann Rösch
Fachhochschule Köln/University of Applied Sciences, Germany

Diana Rosenberg
Adviser on Books and Libraries, UK

Ian Rowlands
Centre for Information Behaviour and the Evaluation of Research (ciber), City University, London, UK

Julie Sabaratnam
National Library of Singapore

Goff Sargent
Loughborough University, UK

Ross Shimmon
Secretary General, IFLA, The Hague, Netherlands

Deborah Shorley
University of Sussex, UK

David Slee
University of Hertfordshire, UK

Geoffrey Smith
Libraries and Book Trade Consultant, UK

Inese A. Smith
Loughborough University, UK

Kerry Smith
Curtin University of Technology, Australia

Linda M. Smith
Nottingham Trent University, UK

Marek Sroka
University of Illinois, USA

Derek Stephens
Loughborough University, UK

Valerie Stevenson
Faculty Information Consultant, Social Sciences and Law, University of Aberdeen, UK

Frederick Stielow
Wayne State University, USA

Penelope Street
University of Liverpool, UK

John Sumsion
Loughborough University, UK

Elaine Svenonius
Professor Emeritus, Department of Information Studies, UCLA, USA

Susan G. Swartzburg
Deceased, formerly of Rutgers State University of New Jersey, USA

Mohamed Taher
Ontario Multifaith Center, Canada

Anne Taylor
British Library, UK

James Thomson
Retired, formerly of the University of Birmingham, UK

Takashi Tomikubo
National Diet Library, Tokyo, Japan

Briony Train
University of Central England in Birmingham, UK

Daniel Traister
University of Pennsylvania, USA

Gwyneth Tseng
Retired, formerly of Loughborough University, UK

Robert Usherwood
University of Sheffield, UK

John van Loo
University of Sheffield, UK

Sherry L. Vellucci
St John's University, New York, USA

Waldomiro Vergueiro
University of São Paulo, Brazil

Giuseppe Vitiello
University of Venezia, Italy

Bill Webb
Retired

Sylvia P. Webb
Consultant, UK

Sheila Webber
University of Sheffield, UK

Darlene E. Weingand
Professor Emerita, University of Wisconsin-Madison, USA

Gernot Wersig
Freie Universität Berlin, Germany

R.H.A. Wessels
Jupiter Bureau, Netherlands

Martin White
Managing Director, Intranet Focus Ltd, UK

Andrew Whitworth
University of Leeds, UK

Wayne A. Wiegand
Florida State University, USA

Glenys Willars
Libraries and Information Service, Leicestershire County Council, UK

Francis Wilson
University of Salford, UK

T.D. Wilson
Professor Emeritus, University of Sheffield, UK

Kate Wood
Retired, formerly of the Library Association, UK

Susi Woodhouse
President, International Association of Music Libraries (United Kingdom and Ireland Branch)

Hazel Woodward
Cranfield University, UK

Irene Wormell
Swedish School of Library and Information Science

Patricia Jane Wortley
Retired

Zimin Wu
De Montfort University, UK

Penelope Yates-Mercer
City University, UK

Illustrations

Preface

Librarianship is as old as libraries themselves, and they can be traced amid the ruins of ancient Nineveh. Information science is one of the new stars in the academic firmament; its basic concepts have only reached their semi-centenary, and its name is more recent than that. These two disciplines, the ancient and the modern, have been yoked together, not always comfortably, in the names of academic departments, degree courses and even professorial chairs. The link is not wholly artificial. In some important respects, the discipline of information science grew out of the practice of librarianship, while the theories that information scientists, and their close colleagues in cognitive science and the sociology of knowledge, have developed are now underpinning our conceptual understanding of how information is garnered, ordered and delivered, a process that lies at the heart of the librarian's work. As a consequence, librarianship can be argued to have become a subfield of a broader discipline to whose development it made a major contribution; this line of argument suggests that information science, with its strong theoretical base and conceptual framework, now overarches the entire domain. There are, of course, other views. Among both academics and practitioners there are proponents of the idea that information systems, or information management, or informatics or, to some extent, knowledge management offer a distinctive conceptual foundation to the discipline. We have sought to give full and objective exposure to these claims in this revised edition.

The *International Encyclopedia of Information and Library Science* (IEILS) takes a broad sweep across this domain. In planning and designing it, and now in revising it for a second edition, we have taken information itself as the basic unit of the currency in which we are trading. *IEILS* seeks to expound the theory of information, how it is collected, stored, processed and retrieved, and how it is communicated to those who seek it. Much of this work still takes place in or through libraries and is undertaken by men and women whose professional designation is 'librarian'. Consequently, the management and organization of libraries, and the skills and techniques of librarianship, form a significant part of the book. It is, however, fundamental to our understanding of the field, and to the design of this book, to recognize that libraries and librarianship are only one part of the information world. In the few years that have passed since we planned the first edition, that has become even more apparent.

At the most mundane level, not all information is sought from, or provided by, librarians and libraries. In the developed world, a multiplicity of agencies, from voluntary organizations to government departments, have the provision of information as part of their mission; in less developed countries oral transmission remains the dominant mode. Other collecting and disseminating institutions – museums and archives, for example – share some (but by no means all) of the characteristics of libraries. Information is disseminated by broadcasters and by publishers; dissemination is facilitated by sophisticated telecommunications systems at one end of the scale, and by the age-old human skill of speech at the other. These agencies and agents use an almost bewildering variety of media and formats to attain their end: hand-written documents, printed books, sound recording, photography and digitized data storage are only a sample. Where do we draw the lines? How do we define the discipline to which this book is a guide? What is the epistemology of the subject?

The essence of the matter is that we are concerned with information that has been brought under control in a way which makes it accessible and therefore usable. Raw data is the building block, and knowledge is the construct; information is the cement. The effective management of information allows it to be stored by means that permit it to be systematically and efficiently retrieved in a format that will facilitate the tasks of the end-user. For the user, however, information is a tool, a means not an end. It may facilitate work or leisure, necessity or luxury, education or entertainment; the concern of the information professional is to ensure that the user's reasonable demands are met.

The management of information, however, incurs costs of which both provider and recipient must be aware. How these costs are met is the subject of more discussion now than for many decades past, but even defining them has caused problems. The mensuration of the cost and value of information is far from being a precise science. Part of the cost of information provision lies in the creation, distribution and storage of information media; part lies in the provision of institutions and systems through which information is accessed; part lies in employing the skilled workers who manage the institutions and design and operate the systems; and we must try to assess the opportunity costs of the absence of information or of the failure to provide it. Information provision can never be wholly separated either from the sources from which the information is derived or from the mechanisms through which it is supplied.

Effective provision, however, requires a clear understanding of information itself; the theory of information may not be the daily concern of the practising professional, and yet without a clear conceptual understanding of our basic commodity it is doubtful whether we can fully exploit its potential. Why and how users seek information can never be convincingly explained outside a clear conceptual framework. Similarly, information provision can never be effective without proper systems of communication; an understanding of the means by which human beings convey facts, ideas and emotions therefore takes its place among our concerns.

Two other factors now come into play: the communication of information to end-users is a social act, and it is a social act that is, in large part, determined by the availability of methods of communication which can convey the information effectively to that user. The social dimension of information is of increasing importance in the self-proclaimed information societies of the West and the newly industrialized countries of the Pacific Rim. Governments, which might doubt the priority that is to be accorded to the provision of libraries, can have little doubt that information policy is one of their proper spheres of activity. Public policy may constrain or control the flow of information, through censorship or by a state monopoly of the means of distribution and supply; or it may facilitate it through the absence of such controls and, more actively, by the encouragement or even the provision of the systems and institutions that are needed. In either case – and in the majority that fall between these two extremes – the world of information has a political and legal dimension that cannot be ignored.

Finally, we turn to the tools that are used for the management and dissemination of information. The technology of information storage and retrieval, and the technology of communication, are the last of the boundary markers of our domain. The use of technology by information providers antedates the invention of the computer by more than a century, but it is, of course, the computer that has transformed almost everything with which *IEILS* is concerned. Even our understanding of information itself has changed as we have contemplated how we are to communicate with machines whose logic is perfect but which, for the most part, have no means of making an alogical decision. The linkage of computing and telecommunications – which, in the strictest sense, is the definition of information technology – will surely be the late twentieth century's most influential legacy, for it has changed the paradigms of human communications at least as much as the invention of printing, and perhaps as much as the evolution of language itself. No account of the information world could be complete or even remotely adequate if it did not recognize and expound the profundity of the impact of technological change.

It is on this understanding of the discipline of library and information science that we have built *IEILS*. We make no pretence of having given equal treatment to every topic; we have made judgements on their relative significance, and have designed the book so that those of greatest significance are given the most space; they are indeed the foundations on which the book is built. There are therefore twelve articles, each written by leading scholars in the field, which come to grips with the central issues. These are:

- Communication.
- Economics of information.
- Informatics.
- Information management.
- Information policy.
- Information professions.
- Information society.
- Information systems.
- Information theory.
- Knowledge industries.
- Knowledge management.
- Organization of knowledge.

Each of these is supported by many other articles, again written by specialists, which deal with specific topics, and these again by short entries that define the basic concepts, activities and objects of the information world. In this way, and uniquely, *IEILS* is not merely a series of dictionary definitions of terms, but a collection of essays, covering the whole broad sweep of library and information science, each of which can stand alone, but each of which is strengthened by the companion pieces that stand alongside it.

The revision of *IEILS* has involved a number of interconnected activities. Some entries have been retained in their original form, although even in many of those the citations and readings have been updated. Some have been revised by their original authors. A few have been heavily revised by the editors themselves, and these are duly indicated. A significant number have been replaced by wholly new entries both by named contributors and by the editors. The definitions have been both revised and augmented, and many more now have bibliographical references.

Most important of all, the revision has taken account of the developments of the last decade. The first edition was planned in 1991, commissioned in 1992 and largely written in 1993–5. For this edition – on which the work began in 2000 – we have added dozens of entries that relate to the Internet and the World Wide Web (including new entries on both of those topics), as well as a significant new entry on information systems and supporting entries in that domain. At the same time, we have augmented the entries in some other parts of our domain, notably the cultural industries including museums. We have also increased the coverage of various regions of the world through geographical entries, which have also taken account of the great changes of the last decades, especially in Central, Eastern and Southeastern Europe. At the same time we have tried to reflect the emergent social and economic issues that surround the theory and practice of information work, in both the developed and the less developed countries at the beginning of the twenty-first century.

These changes of content, however, are within the structure that we devised for the first edition, which seems to have served users well. We have constructed an apparatus of references and indexing terms. The basic definitions, most of which are unsupported by bibliographical references, will send the user by means of cross-references or 'see also' references to another entry, often one of the twelve major articles, in which the term is either further defined or put into a broader context, or both. The shorter signed articles similarly have cross-references between themselves and to the twelve major articles, but they can also, for some purposes, stand alone. All have either bibliographical references or lists of further reading (using an abbreviated format), and most have both, for any book of this kind must refer beyond itself into the wider literature on which is it based. Finally, the twelve major articles are fully referenced and have detailed lists of readings. They are cross-referenced to articles that give fuller – although usually less contextual – accounts of some of the topics with which they deal, often in passing. The whole work, therefore, is knitted together by these twelve major articles, and, despite its conventional alphabetical order, is far more than a mere listing and exposition of terms.

This structure was possible only because of a systematic choice of headings, and a judgement of their relative importance. We have indicated the theoretical basis on which our judgement was formed, and it was that which essentially dictated both the pattern of the book, and the selection of the subjects of the major articles. For the other articles, however, we combed the literature to seek out appropriate topics and ideas, and the terms commonly used to describe them. Our preliminary listings were refined by a further search in the literature of both this and related disciplines, and the results were then considered in conjunction with our Editorial Advisory Board. It was only then that a final, or almost final, version emerged, on the basis of which the signed articles were commissioned.

It was at this stage that we compiled a list of additional terms that needed further definition, and began the process of selecting terms that would be indexed. The definitions were the joint responsibility of the editors, although with much assistance from some of those listed in the Acknowledgements. The result is, we believe, a comprehensive but intellectually consistent work of reference, written by experts and driven by a clear vision of the discipline that it explains.

Acknowledgments

The first and greatest debt of the editors is to the authors of this book, for without them it would not exist. We have drawn on our professional contacts and perhaps even exploited our friendships throughout the world to assemble our team. One of the greatest pleasures of the task has been to share in the knowledge, enthusiasm and commitment of the contributors. Each contributor of a signed article is responsible for the content of his or her work, although we have augmented the citations and readings in some entries which have been carried forward unchanged from the first edition, and in a few cases we have indicated that we are responsible for a substantial revision.

A reference book is always a collaborative effort between editors, authors and publishers. The members of our Advisory Editorial Board, and our American Consultant Editor, played a larger part than they may realise in the early stages of the planning of the revision. Mark Barragry, formerly Senior Reference Editor of Routledge, was a strong supporter of this book when it was first suggested. His successors, and especially Dominic Shryane, have been equally helpful. We thank Wendy Styles not only for compiling the index but also for saving us from a gross error. We are indebted to many colleagues at Loughborough, some of whom have lived with this book for as long as we have. A number of them are contributors, but many others have also been sounding-boards. We are grateful to Adam Warren for his help in dealing with issues which arose out of copy editing, and to those authors who responded so quickly to him. Finally, we must thank Claire Sturges for bibliographical research, painstaking work on the proofs and all her other support during the making of this book.

How to use this book

To find information on a particular subject first look for the term in the alphabetical listing. If you find a simple definition that does not wholly satisfy your needs, follow through the cross-references (in CAPITALS in the text) or 'see also' references (at the end of the entry), which will lead you to a more detailed account, often embedded in a major article that will provide the full context for the subject. If the term does not appear as a heading, turn to the index, which contains hundreds of additional terms, as well as incidental references to terms also used as headings.

For a general introduction to a topic turn first to the most relevant of the twelve major entries (listed on p. xix). If none seems relevant, use the index to identify which of them deals with a key term or concept in the subject in which you are interested. From the major entry, you should then, through the cross-references and 'see also' references, be able to find more specific details of any aspects of the topic that seem particularly relevant to you.

Abbreviations

AACR	Anglo-American Cataloguing Rules
AALS	Association of American Library Schools
AATA	Art and Archaeology Technical Abstracts
ABLISS	Association of British Library and Information Science Schools
ACCOPI	Access Control and Copyright Protection for Images
ACE	Automatic Computing Engine
ACM	Association for Computing Machinery
ACPM	Australian Common Practice Manual
ACQNET	Acquisitions Librarians Electronic Network
ACRL	Association of College and Research Libraries
ACURIL	Association of Caribbean University, Research and Institutional Libraries
ADI	American Documentation Institute
ADSL	Asymmetric Digital Subscriber Loop
AF2I	Association des Intermédiaires en Information
AFAS	French Association for Sound Archives
AFLI	Arab Federation for Libraries and Information
AFNOR	Association Française de Normalisation
AGM	Annual General Meeting
AI	Artificial Intelligence
AIBA	Agricultural Information Bank for Asia
AICCM	Australian Institute for the Conservation of Cultural Materials
AID	Associative Interactive Dictionary
AIIP	Association of Independent Information Professionals
AIRS	Alliance of Information and Referral Systems, Inc.
ALA	American Library Association; Associate of the Library Association; Australian Library Association
ALIA	Australian Library and Information Association
ALISE	Association for Library and Information Science Education
ALP	Advancement of Librarianship in the Third World Programme (IFLA)
ALPAC	Automatic Language Processing Advisory Committee
ALPSP	Association of Learned and Professional Society Publishers
ANSI	American National Standards Institute
API	American Petroleum Institute
APPM	Archives, Private Papers and Manuscripts (USA)
ARIST	Annual Review of Information Science and Technology
ARL	Association of Research Libraries
ARLIS/NA	Art Libraries Society of North America

ARLIS/UK & Ireland	British and Irish Art Libraries Society
ARMA	Association of Records Managers and Administrators; American Records Management Association
ARSC	Association for Recorded Sound Collections
ASEAN	Association of Southeast Asian Nations
ASI	American Society of Indexers
ASIS	Ameslan Society for Information Science
ASK	Anomalous State of Knowledge
ASLIB	Association for Information Management (previously the Association of Special Libraries and Information Bureaux); Association of Special Libraries
ASM	American Society for Metals
ASTM	American Society for Testing and Materials
ATM	Asynchronous Transport Mode
AV	Audiovisual
BAILER	British Association for Information and Library Education and Research
BANSDOC	National Bangladesh Scientific Documentation Centre
BARC	Bangladesh Agricultural Research Council; Bhabha Atomic Research Centre
BBC	British Broadcasting Corporation
BBS	Bulletin Board System
BIDS	Bath Information and Data Services
BINT	Biuro Innostranoi Nauki i Tekhnologii [Bureau for Foreign Science and Technology]
BIRS	British Institute of Recorded Sound
BL	British Library
BLDSC	British Library Document Supply Centre
BLISS	British Library Information Science Service
BLR&DD	British Library Research and Development Department
BM	British Museum
BNB	British National Bibliography
BPP	Books Presentation Programme
BSI	British Standards Institution
BT	British Telecommunications plc
BTEC	Business and Technician Education Council
BUBL	Bulletin Board for Libraries
CAB	Citizens' Advice Bureaux
CAD	Commission on Archival Development; Computer-Aided Design
CADIST	Centres d'Acquisitions et de Diffusion de l'Information Scientifique et Technique
CAL	Computer-Assisted Learning
CARICOM	Caribbean Community
CARISPLAN	Caribbean Information System for Planners
CAS	Chemical Abstracts Service; Current Alerting Services
CAS-IAS	Current Alerting Services – Individual Article Supply
CAT	Computer-Assisted Translation
CB	Citizens' Band
CBS	Columbia Broadcasting System
CCT	Compulsory Competitive Tendering
CCTA	Central Computer and Telecommunications Agency
CCTV	Closed-Circuit Television
CD	Compact Disc
CDCR	Center for Documentation and Communication Research
CD-I	Compact Disc – Interactive
CD-R	Compact Disc – Recordable
CD-ROM	Compact Disc – Read-Only Memory

CEC	Commission of the European Communities
CEE	Central and Eastern Europe
CEIS	Caribbean Energy Information System
CEN/CENELEC	Joint European Standards Organization
CENID	National Centre for Information and Documentation (Chile)
CERN	European Centre for Nuclear Research
CESSDA	Committee of European Social Science Data Archives
CHI	Computer–Human Interaction
CIA	Central Intelligence Agency
CICI	Confederation of Information Communication Industries
CISTI	Canada Institute for Scientific and Technical Information
CITED	Copyright in Transferred Electronic Data
CITRA	Conférence Internationale de Table Ronde des Archives [International Conference of the Round Table on Archives]
CIX	Commercial Internet Exchange
CLA	Children's Libraries Association
CLAC	Centres de Lecture et d'Animation Culturelle en Milieu Rural
CLR	Council on Library Resources
CLSCP	Copyright Libraries Shared Cataloguing Programme
COM	Computer Output Microfilm
COMLA	Commonwealth Library Association
CONSAL	Congress of Southeast Asian Librarians
COPICAT	Copyright Ownership Protection in Computer-Assisted Twinning
CORMOSEA	Committee on Deposit Material on Southeast Asia
COSLA	Convention of Scottish Local Authorities
CPD	Continuing Professional Development
CPU	Central Processing Unit
CRLIS	Current Research in Library and Information Science
CRS	Computerized Reservation Systems
CSCW	Computer-Supported Co-operative Work
CSMA	Carrier Sense Multiple Access
CSMA/CD	Carrier Sense Multiple Access with Collision Detection
CTI	Computers in Teaching Initiative
CURL	Consortium of University Research Libraries
DAT	Digital Audio Tape
DBA	Documentation, Library and Archives Department of UNESCO
DBMS	Database Management Systems
DBS	Direct Broadcasting by Satellite
DCC	Digital Compact Cassette
DCE	Data Circuit-terminating Equipment
DDC	Dewey Decimal Classification
DES	Data Encryption Standard
DIN	Deutsches Institut für Normung
DIP	Document Image Processing
DOS	Department of State; Disk Operating System
DRTC	Documentation Research and Training Centre
DSE	Deutsche Stiftung für internationale Entwicklung
DSP	Digital Signal Processor
DSS	Decision Support Systems
DTE	Data Terminal Equipment
DTI	Department of Trade and Industry
DTP	Desktop Publishing
EAGLE	European Association for Grey Literature Exploitation

EBLIDA	European Bureau of Library, Information and Documentation Associations
ECHO	European Commission Host Organization
EDI	Electronic Data Interchange
EIIA	European Information Industry Association
EIRENE	European Information Researchers Network
ELBS	Educational Low-priced Books Scheme
EPIDOS	European Patent Information and Documentation Systems
EPLA	East Pakistan Library Association
EPO	European Patent Office
EROMM	European Register of Microform Masters
ES	Expert Systems
ESAIRS	European Space Agency Information Retrieval Service
ESPRIT	European Strategic Programme for Research in Information Technologies
ESRC	Economic and Social Research Council
ESTC	Eighteenth-century Short-Title Catalogue
ESTC-NA	Eighteenth-century Short-Title Catalogue North America
ETC	Enhanced Throughput Cellular
ETS	European Telecommunications Standards
EU	European Union
EUCLID	European Conference of Library and Information Departments
EUSIDIC	European Association of Information Services
FAIS	Foreign Affairs Information System
FBI	Federal Bureau of Investigation
FDDI	Fibre Distributed Data Interface
FIAC	Federation of Independent Advice Centres
FID	Fédération Internationale d'Information et de Documentation/International Federation for Information and Documentation
FIDA	International Archival Development Fund
FID/CAF	FID Regional Commission for Western, Eastern and Southern Africa
FID/CAO	FID Regional Commission for Asia and Oceania
FID/CLA	FID Regional Commission for Latin America
FID/CNA	FID Regional Commission for the Caribbean and North America
FID/NANE	FID Regional Commission for Northern Africa and the Near East
FID/ROE	FID Regional Commission for Europe
FLA	Fellow of the Library Association
FOI	Freedom of Information
FOIA	Freedom of Information Act
FSU	Former Soviet Union
FT	Financial Times
FTE	Full-Time Equivalent
FTP	File Transfer Protocol
G7	Group of Seven
GATT	General Agreement on Tariffs and Trade
Gb	Gigabyte
GCI	Getty Conservation Institute
GCS	Global Cataloguing Service
GDP	Gross Domestic Product
GDSS	Group Decision Support Systems
GILS	Government Information Locator Service
GIS	Geographic Information System
GUI	Graphical User Interface
GUIDE	Graphical User Interface Design and Evaluation
HCI	Human–Computer Interaction

HDTV	High Definition Television
HEA	Higher Education Act
HF	Human Factors
HMSO	Her Majesty's Stationery Office
HSE	Health and Safety Executive
HTML	HyperText Mark-up Language
IR	Information and Referral
IAMIC	International Association of Music Information Centres
IAML	International Association of Music Libraries
IARIL	International Association of Rural and Isolated Libraries
IAS	Individual Article Supply
IASA	International Association of Sound Archives
IASSIST	International Association for Social Science Information Service and Technology
IATUL	International Association of Technological University Libraries
IBBY	International Board on Books for Young People
IBI	Intergovernmental Bureau of Information
IBICT	Brazilian Institute for Information in Science and Technology
ICA	International Communications Association; International Council on Archives
ICSU	International Council of Scientific Unions
ID	Identification
IDA	Integrated Digital Access
IDRC	International Development Research Centre
IEC	International Electrotechnical Commission
IEEE	Institute of Electrical and Electronics Engineers, Inc.
IFDO	International Federation of Data Organizations
IFLA	International Federation of Library Associations and Institutions
IHAC	Information Highway Advisory Council
IIB	International Institute of Bibliography; Institut International de Bibliographie (now FID)
IIC	International Institute for the Conservation of Art and Historic Artefacts
IIC-GC	International Institute for Conservation – Canadian Group
IIR	Intelligent Information Retrieval
IIS	Institute of Information Scientists
IK	Indigenous Knowledge
ILA	Indian Library Association
ILL	Interlibrary Loan/Lending
IM	Information Management
INIST	Institut de l'Information Scientifique et Technique
INPADOC	International Patent Documentation Service
INSDOC	Indian National Scientific Documentation Centre
IPA	International Publishers Association
IPC	Institute for Paper Conservation
IR	Information Retrieval
IRC	Internet Relay Chat
IRM	Information Resource(s) Management
IS	Information Superhighway
ISAD(G)	General International Standard Archival Description
ISBD	International Standard Bibliographic Description
ISBN	International Standard Book Number
ISDN	Integrated Services Digital Network
ISDS-SEA	International Serials Data System – Southeast Asia
ISI	Institute for Scientific Information
ISMN	International Standard Music Number

ISO	International Standards Organization
ISRN	International Standard Recording Number
ISSN	International Standard Serial Number
IT	Information Technology
ITC	International Translations Centre
ITU	International Telecommunications Union
JANET	Joint Academic Network
JASIST	Journal of the American Society for Information Science and Technology
JELIS	Journal of Education for Library and Information Science
JLA	Japan Library Association
JPRS	Joint Publications Research Service
JSC	Joint Steering Committee for Revision of AACR
Kb	Kilobyte
KBMT	Knowledge-Based Machine Translation
KGB	Komitet Gosudarstvennoi Bezopasnosti [State Security Committee]
KLA	Korean Library Association
KWAC	KeyWord and Context
KWIC	KeyWord in Context
KWOC	KeyWord out of Context
LA	Library Association
LAB	Library Association of Bangladesh
LAC	Library Association of China
LAN	Local-Area Network
LAP-B	Link Access Procedure – Balanced Protocol
LAPL	Library Association Publishing Limited
LASER	London and Southeast Regional Library Bureau
LAUK	Library Association of the United Kingdom; now the Library Association
LC	Library of Congress
LCC	Library of Congress Classification
LCCDG	Library Collections Conservation Discussion Group
LCMARC	Library of Congress Machine-Readable Cataloging
LCSH	Library of Congress Subject Headings
LED	Light-Emitting Diode
LINC	Library and Information Co-operation Council
LIP	Library and Information Plan
LIS	Library and Information Science/Service(s)/Studies/Sector
LISA	Library and Information Science Abstracts
LISC	Library and Information Services Council
LML	Liaquat Memorial Library
LOEX	Library Orientation Instruction Exchange
LP	Long-Playing Record
LSCA	Library Services and Construction Grant
MA	Master of Arts; Museums Association
MAD2	Manual of Archival Description, 2nd edn (UK)
MADAM	Manchester Automatic Digital Machine
MALA	Madras Library Association
MALMARC	Malaysian MARC
MAN	Metropolitan-Area Network
MARC	Machine-Readable Cataloguing
MAT	Machine-Aided Translation
Mb	Megabyte
MDA	Museums Documentation Association
MeSH	Medical Subject Headings

MHz	Megahertz
MIDI	Musical Instrument Device Interface
MIInfSci	Member, Institute of Information Scienists
MIMOS	Malaysian Institute of Microelectronic Systems
MIP	Modern Information Professional
MIS	Management Information Systems
MIT	Massachusetts Institute of Technology
MLA	Medical Library Association
MLS	Master of Library Science/Studies
MMI	Man–Machine Interaction
MMS	Man–Machine Systems
MPC	Multimedia Personal Computers
MPhil	Master of Philosophy
MPM	Multimedia Presentation Manager
MS-DOS	Microsoft Disk Operating System
MSS	Management Support System
MT	Machine Translation
MUSE	Music Search
MWSS	Microsoft Windows Sound System
NACAB	National Association of Citizens' Advice Bureaux
NACSIS	National Centre for Scientific Information Systems
NAG	National Acquisitions Group
NARA	National Archives and Records Administration
NASA	National Aeronautical and Space Administration
NATIS	National Information System
NBC	National Broadcasting Corporation
NBLC	Nederlands Bibliotheek en Lektuur Centrum [Dutch Centre for Public Library Literature]
NBS	National Bibliographic Service
NCIP	North American Collection Inventory Project
NCL	National Central Library
NDLP	Netherlands Library Development Project
NEPHIS	Nested Phrase Indexing System
NGO	Non-Governmental Organization
NHS	National Health Service
NIDOC	National Information and Documentation Centre
NII	National Information Infrastructure
NISO	National Information Standards Organization
NLB	National Library for the Blind; National Library of Bangladesh
NLG	National Libraries Group
NLLST	National Lending Library for Science and Technology
NLM	National Library of Medicine
NLSFBPH	National Library Service for the Blind and Physically Handicapped
NNLM	National Network for Libraries in Medicine
NORDBOK	Nordic Literature and Library Committee
NORDINFO	Nordic Committee on Scientific Information and Documentation
NOSP	Nordic Union Catalogue of Scientific Periodicals
NREN	National Research and Education Network
NSA	National Sound Archive
NSDD	National Security Decision Directive
NSF	National Science Foundation
NSTP	New Straits Times Publications
NTA	National Telecommunications Agency

NTE	Network Terminating Equipment
NTIA	National Telecommunications and Information Administration
NTIS	National Technical Information Service
NUC	National Union Catalog
NUCMC	National Union Catalog of Manuscript Collections
NVQ	National Vocational Qualification
NWICO	New World Information and Communication Order
OCLC	Ohio College Library Center; Online Computer Library Center
OCR	Optical Character Recognition
ODA	Open Document Architecture
OECD	Organization for Economic Co-operation and Development
OED	Oxford English Dictionary
OLE	Object Linking and Embedding
OMB	One-Man Band
OMG	Object Management Group
OOS	Occupational Overuse Syndrome
OPACS	Online Public-Access Catalogues
OPL	One-Person Libraries
OSB	Order of St Benedict
OSI	Open Systems Interconnection
OSS	Office of Strategic Studies
PAC	Preservation and Conservation Core Programme (IFLA)
PAD	Packet Assembly/Disassembly Device
PANSDOC	Pakistan National Scientific and Technical Documentation Centre
PARC	Palo Alto Research Center
PASTIC	Pakistan Scientific and Technical Information Centre
PBWG	Pakistan Bibliographical Working Group
PC	Personal Computer
PGI	Programme Général de l'Information/General Information Programme
PGP	Pretty Good Privacy
PhD	Doctor of Philosophy
PIIC	Public Interest Immunity Certificate
PIN	Personal Identification Number
PINFET	PIN Field Effect Transistors
PLA	Pakistan Library Association
PLR	Public Lending Right
PNB	Pakistan National Bibliography
PPRG	Publicity and Public Relations Group
PRECIS	Preserved Context Indexing System
PRO	Public Records Office
PSS	Packet Switching System
PSTN	Packet-Switched Telephone Network
PTT	Posts, Telegraphs and Telephones
PULINET	Provincial University Library Network
QA	Quality Assurance
R&D	Research and Development
RAD	Rules for Archival Description (Canada)
RAM	Random-Access Memory
RAMP	Records and Archives Management Programme (UNESCO)
RATER	Reliability, Assurance, Tangibles, Empathy and Responsiveness
RBU	Répertoire Bibliographique Universel
RCRC	Rural Community Resource Centre
RENBU	National Network of University Libraries (Argentina)

RGA	Readers' Guide Abstracts
RIdIM	Répertoire Internationale d'Iconographie Musicale
RILM	Répertoire Internationale de Littérature Musicale
RIPM	Répertoire Internationale de la Presse Musicale
RISM	Répertoire Internationale des Sources Musicales
RLG	Research Libraries Group
RLIN	Research Libraries Network
RLS	Regional Library System
RMS	Records Management Society
RNIB	Royal National Institute for the Blind
Rpm	Revolutions Per Minute
RSI	Repetitive Strain Injury
SAA	Systems Applications Architecture
SARBICA	Southeast Asian Regional Branch of the International Council on Archives
SCECSAL	Standing Conference of East, Central and Southern African Librarians
SCONUL	Standing Conference of National and University Libraries
SDI	Selective Dissemination of Information
SGML	Standard Generalized Mark-up Language
SIG	Special Interest Group
SIGLE	System for Information on Grey Literature in Europe
SILAS	Singapore Library Automation System
SINASBI	National System of Library Information
SISA	School of Information Studies for Africa
SL	Source Language
SLB	Section of Libraries for the Blind
SMEs	Small and Medium-sized Enterprises
SNA	Systems Network Architecture
SNB	Singapore National Bibliography
SPSS	Statistical Package for Social Science
SQL	Structured Query Language
STM	Scientific, Technical and Medical (book publishing)
STS	Science, Technology and Society
STUDIO	Structured User Interface Design for Interaction Optimization
STV	Share the Vision
SWIFT	Society For Worldwide Interbank Financial Communications
TCP/IP	Transmission Control Protocol/Internet Protocol
TDF	Transborder Data Flow
TFPL	Task Force Pro Libra
TL	Target Language
TLTP	Teaching and Learning Technology Programme
TNAUK	Talking Newspaper Association of the United Kingdom
TQM	Total Quality Management
TREC	Text Retrieval Evaluation Conference
TRIPS	Trade-Related Aspects of Intellectual Property Rights
TV	Television
UAI	Universal Availability of Information
UAP	Universal Availability of Publications Programme (IFLA)
UBC	Universal Bibliographic Control
UBCIM	Universal Bibliographic Control and International MARC
UCL	University College London
UDC	Universal Decimal Classification; Universal Dataflow and Communications
UE	User Education
UGC	University Grants Commission

UIA	Union of International Associations
UIMS	User Interface Management System
UK	United Kingdom
UKMARC	United Kingdom Machine-Readable Cataloguing
UMIST	University of Manchester Institute of Science and Technology
UNESCO	United Nations Educational, Scientific and Cultural Organization
UNIMARC	Universal Machine-Readable Cataloguing
UNISIST	United Nations Information System in Science and Technology
URL	Uniform Resource Locator
USA	United States of America
USSR	Union of Soviet Socialist Republics
UWI	University of the West Indies
VAN	Value-Added Network
VAT	Value-Added Tax (EU countries)
VDT	Visual Display Terminal
VDU	Visual Display Unit
VINITTI	All-Union Institute for Scientific and Technical Information
VMS	Voice Mail Systems
VOD	Video On Demand
VR	Virtual Reality
VRAM	Video Random Access Memory
WAIS	Wide-Area Information Server
WAN	Wide-Area Network
WARC	World Administrative Radio Conference
WHO	World Health Organization
WIMPS	Windows, Icons, Mouse, Pull-down menus
WIPO	World Intellectual Property Organization
WORM	Write Once Read Many
WTI	World Translations Index
WWW	World Wide Web
WYSIWYG	What You See Is What You Get

A

ABSTRACT

An abstract is a summary of the essential content of another, longer, document. An abstracts service is a form of current bibliography in which contributions to periodicals, other collections and sometimes books are summarized. They are accompanied by bibliographical citations to enable the publications to be traced, and are frequently arranged in classified order. They may be in the language of the original or translated. Abstracts may be indicative, mainly directing the reader to an original item with relevant content; informative, giving much information about the original, summarizing the principal arguments and giving the principal data; or evaluative, when they comment on the quality of the original. A general abstract is one that covers all essential points in an article, and is provided where the interests of readers are varied and known to the abstractor only in general terms. A selective abstract contains a condensation of parts of an article known to be directly related to the needs of the clientele and is prepared by a librarian or information officer (1) for the executives, research workers and specialists within an organization or those normally making use of library services, (2) in response to a request for a literature search or (3) to keep the staff of an organization informed of developments revealed in the daily periodical press, documents or reports. An author abstract is one written by the author of the original article.

SEE ALSO: abstracting and indexing services; communication; organization of knowledge

ABSTRACTING AND INDEXING SERVICES

Serial publications that analyse on a continuing basis the contents of a whole range of periodical and other titles relating to a common discipline or to a particular category of material. They are published in printed format, in electronic DATABASES on CD-ROM, or are accessible via remote HOSTS, such as DIALOG and DataStar, now part of the Thomson Corporation.

Arrangement

Printed indexing services typically make this information accessible by an alphabetical arrangement in the body of the text of subject headings, under which appear the bibliographic references to the documents relating to that subject. Author and other indexes provide additional access points. Abstracting services extend the bibliographic information by providing a synopsis (ABSTRACT) of the cited document. Printed abstracting services differ in their arrangement from indexing services in that the documents are usually grouped in classified order on which a sequential numbering system is superimposed for identification via a subject index. Their electronic counterparts afford the greater flexibility of both FREE-TEXT SEARCHING of terms or controlled searching of the database fields.

History and purpose

HISTORY

The first indexing service, *An Index to Periodical Literature*, the forerunner of the *Reader's Guide to Periodical Literature*, was published in 1802 and was the work of William Frederick

Poole, one of the pioneers of bibliography, who recognized that periodical articles were being overlooked due to a lack of an effective indexing service. A significant later nineteenth-century title is *Index Medicus* (1879–), the innovation of Dr John Shaw Billings, a work that, however, underwent a number of subsequent changes of title. *The Times Index*, although historically significant in that it dates back to 1790, was originally an index to a single newspaper, and only in 1974 could it be regarded as an indexing service, when it incorporated a number of newspapers of the Times Newspaper Group. Indexing services developed over the twentieth century to cover broad subject disciplines. Examples include *Art Index* (1929–), *Bibliographic Index* (1937–), *Biography Index* (1946–), the resumed title of *Index Medicus* and *Cumulative Index Medicus*, from 1960 under the auspices of the National Library of Medicine, *British Humanities Index* (1963–) and *Current Technology Index* (1981–), retitled from its predecessor, *British Technology Index*, to reflect its international coverage.

Originally, abstracting services developed to aid research scientists in keeping abreast of an exponential growth in scientific journal publications. In contrast to the broader scope of indexing services, abstracting services focused on comparatively narrow subject areas. An early broad-based abstracting service was *Science Abstracts*, first published in 1898, but by 1903 this needed to be subdivided. The modern publications deriving from *Science Abstracts* are *Physics Abstracts*, *Electrical and Electronic Engineering Abstracts* and *Computer and Control Abstracts*. The giant in this category is *Chemical Abstracts* (1907–), with abstracts of over 170,000 articles from more than 12,000 periodicals. From their origin as a service to the scientific community, over the twentieth century the number of abstracting services has grown to cover a range of subjects and the estimated number of abstracting and indexing services today is around 1,450 publications.

Many abstracting services are now available online, through providers such as Cambridge Scientific Abstracts (CSA) (www.csa.co.uk), and some have ceased paper publication altogether. The advantages in terms of search facilities are considerable. Moreover, some services allow libraries to build in links to their own catalogues or to electronic DOCUMENT DELIVERY services. It has been argued that traditional abstracting services may eventually be outmoded because more efficient searches can be made using powerful SEARCH ENGINES (Jasco 2000).

PURPOSE

The main purpose of abstracting and indexing services is to help researchers overcome the difficulties of tracing potentially useful articles scattered over periodical and other literature. Abstracts are of especial benefit as they provide an overview of the article and thus aid researchers in their selection of what they consider worth reading. There are three types of abstract: indicative, informative and combined. The indicative abstract is similar to a table of contents; the informative abstract aims to supply sufficient detail to allow the reader to gain an accurate understanding of the document as a whole; and the combined abstract focuses in its informative detail on the new information, such as the findings and conclusions of research. Abstracts that are sufficiently informative can supply enough detail to keep busy professionals up to date with current research and practice without their having recourse to the original documents, which may be either too time consuming to read or written in a foreign language. Thus, informative abstracts also help overcome the language barrier. The art of abstracting is complex, and is best performed by trained information professionals. Attempts at automatic abstracting have so far given unsatisfactory outcomes, although experimentation will no doubt continue (Craven 2000).

Bibliographic control

Within the scope of this article only a few representative examples can be provided. For a comprehensive list of current indexing and abstracting services the reader is directed to *Ulrich's International Periodicals Directory*, published annually by R.R. Bowker. Here the titles of abstracting and indexing services are listed alphabetically at the start of the classified section, with cross-references to the main entries, which may also be accessed via the title and subject indexes. Other bibliographies that include indexing and abstracting services, and which in addition are annotated, are the regularly updated *Walford's Guide to Reference Material*, published by the LIBRARY ASSOCIATION (7th edn, 1996–8), and E.P. Sheehy's *Guide to*

Reference Books, published by the AMERICAN LIBRARY ASSOCIATION.

Indexing and abstracting services in library and information science

Library Literature (1934–), published by H.W. Wilson, is an author and subject index providing exhaustive coverage of librarianship periodicals. In addition it covers books, pamphlets, other selected periodical articles of relevance, films, filmstrips, microtexts, library school theses and research papers. A further feature is a citations listing of individual book reviews. It is now entitled *Library Literature and Information Science*, and is available online from the publishers (www.hwwilson.com).

   Library and Information Science Abstracts (*LISA*) (1969–, formerly *Library Science Abstracts*, 1950–68), published by Bowker Saur, abstracts articles from over 500 journals and papers from major English-language conference proceedings. *LISA* processes material from approximately sixty different countries and provides English-language abstracts of source documents that have been published in up to thirty-four foreign languages. From 1994 books have been indexed on a regular basis and book reviews have been assigned their own section to assist browsing. *LISA* is available through the services offered by CSA. *Information Science Abstracts* (1966–) offers abstracts of articles from around 700 journals. The larger proportion of abstracts is from technical literature and deals with various aspects of computer systems and software. It is a service that is particularly appropriate for systems specialists. An enhanced version became available through DIALOG and Silver Platter in 2001.

References

Craven, T.C. (2000) 'Abstracts produced with computer assistance', *Journal of the American Society for Information Science* 51: 745–56.
Jasco, P. (2000) 'A look at the endangered species of the database world', *Information World Review* 164: 72–3.

Further reading

Lea, P.W. and Day, A. (eds) (1990) *Printed Reference Material and Related Sources of Information*, 3rd edn, Library Association, pp. 142–6 (news and current events); pp. 174–82 (periodicals); pp. 185–203 (reports, theses, conferences, literature); pp. 183–203 (indexes).

SEE ALSO: bibliographic control; Bradford, Samuel Clement; communication; indexing; organization of knowledge; scholarly communication

HELEN E. CHANDLER

ACADEMIC LIBRARIES

Libraries attached to academic institutions above the secondary or high school level, serving the teaching and research needs of students and staff.

Types of academic library

In addition to UNIVERSITY LIBRARIES other libraries at tertiary level are classed as academic libraries and have certain features in common. The libraries of tertiary colleges and of smaller or vocational colleges have similar functions to university libraries, but because of their size not all factors apply to them. Most academic libraries face severe problems because of growth in student numbers and declining financial resources; these were partly addressed in Britain by the Follett Report (Joint Funding Councils' Libraries Review Group 1993), which has led to recognition of the problems at government level and the provision of some additional funding to support the development of learning and teaching resources and the maintenance and accessibility of research collections. Increasingly, information needs are met by a variety of agencies in the institution, of which the library is only one; CONVERGENCE of library and computing services has led in many cases to the establishment of a single 'information services' unit.

Purposes

Academic libraries have a primary obligation to meet the information needs of the members of their institution. Functions outside this, such as availability to the general public, are secondary, though FEE-BASED SERVICES are becoming significant. Academic libraries therefore always have two purposes:

1   Providing for the educational needs of students, both those arising directly from the curriculum and those of a more general nature.

2 Supporting the teaching staff in their need for up-to-date material required for their teaching role.

In most universities, a third purpose can be added:

3 Providing for research (where the institution undertakes this), both higher-degree work and research activity of academic staff.

Numerically the students' needs are paramount, and this aspect of work predominates in most academic libraries; but depending on the mission of the institution the other purposes – especially the support of research – are also of great importance.

Meeting needs

STUDENTS

Students' needs are largely predictable and the librarian should ensure that adequate numbers of books, journals and other information sources are available within the appropriate subject areas. This now involves co-ordination of library and computing resources, including experiments in the DIGITAL LIBRARY and the hybrid library (see HYBRID LIBRARIES). The growth in project-based work and dissertations calling for research means that students often want a wider variety of material than the library can provide, and provision must be made for interlibrary loan (see INTERLIBRARY LENDING) or access to collections elsewhere; but for basic student material the library should be more or less self-sufficient. Teaching staff must therefore be involved in the selection, but not exclusively: librarians have direct experience of students' use of the library and can often better judge the whole range of literature and the number of copies needed. The widespread adoption of student-centred learning (partly as a strategy for dealing with the growth of student numbers) has made new demands on librarians and libraries. In addition to providing relevant materials and high-quality advice on information searching, libraries have to provide space for group study and a significant number of public access work-stations.

TEACHING STAFF

The library must support a high standard of teaching in the institution, providing up-to-date and wide-ranging material. Teachers may have their own specialized personal collections of books and journals but still rely on the library for material not in their immediate field of interest or too expensive for them to purchase. A good teacher is not restricted to what is already known about, and a lively acquisition policy on the part of the librarian can enhance the quality of teaching. CURRENT AWARENESS services are helpful in ensuring that teaching staff are up to date in their own and in related fields; such provision must include helping teaching staff to remain abreast of new electronic resources, websites and discussion lists in their disciplines.

RESEARCH

Providing for research needs is the most difficult and the most expensive part of an academic library's work. In most fields the primary medium for research is the scholarly journal; in many disciplines in the humanities and social sciences, however, the library contains the basic material of research, whether in the form of historical source material (including rare-book and archive collections), literary works or published statistical data. Libraries outside major research institutions often find it impossible to acquire and house substantial collections across whole disciplines, and have to be more selective. However, alternatives to print-on-paper are now commonplace, particularly with the greater availability of electronic data, whether held locally as CD-ROM or accessed over the INTERNET, and with improved DOCUMENT DELIVERY services. In turn, this needs to be supported by the provision of ABSTRACTING AND INDEXING SERVICES; these also are now typically provided online by giving access to the appropriate commercial databases.

Services

Special services have developed to serve users of academic libraries. USER EDUCATION of all kinds is essential as information sources become more complex and as students move into new fields of study. Intensive use of lending services is characteristic of academic libraries, particularly short-loan collections, to ensure rapid circulation of heavy-demand texts, and self-service photocopiers are heavily used. Long opening hours are desirable, and growth in part-time and mature students, who cannot always use the library during the normal working day, requires more flexibility. In universities and colleges that offer distance-learning programmes, some of them internationally, the library and associated network services have to make appropriate provision for this group of students as well. The right balance in use of staff resources is necessary to ensure that all users are best served. Networked integrated systems have allowed libraries to offer fuller services in all parts of the institution and to interface with campus information systems, giving wider access to catalogues and circulation data, as well as to electronic information sources, even outside the library.

Administration

The organization of an academic library depends on its size and range of activities; a library operating on several sites, while aiming to meet the same needs, cannot easily be managed in the same way as a more compact library. Automated systems help in providing equitable levels of service across the whole institution and to distant users, but they are only fully effective when all library staff have the appropriate expertise to exploit them both for users and for administrative purposes. Use of subject specialization also varies, but most libraries provide services tailored to the needs of different subject groups. Budgetary allocation is normally under the librarian's control, within funds allocated by the institution, but consultation with different interest groups is desirable, through a committee structure or in other ways. Monitoring the library's activity is important, both as a measure of performance for internal management, and for external purposes such as statistical series and 'political' arguments within the institution or more widely.

References

Joint Funding Councils' Libraries Review Group (1993) *Report* (chairman: Sir Brian Follett), Higher Education Funding Council.

Further reading

Baker, D. (ed.) (1997) *Resource Management in Academic Libraries*, Library Association Publishing.
Coughlin, C.M. and Gertzog, A. (1992) *Lyle's Administration of the College Library*, 5th edn, Scarecrow Press [standard, traditional work on running smaller college libraries – US context].
Dower, L. (ed.) (1997) *Gateways to Knowledge. The Role of Academic Libraries in Teaching, Learning, and Research*, MIT Press.

SEE ALSO: archives; libraries; rare-book libraries; university libraries

PETER HOARE

ACCEPTABLE USE POLICY

The acceptable use policy (AUP) is an organization's expression of the limits within which it expects or requires staff, members or the public to restrict their use of computer and network facilities for which the organization has responsibility. This is generally set out in a document to which users may be asked to formally assent by signing a declaration, or clicking an appropriate box when the AUP is presented electronically. Within an organization the AUP will concentrate on defining the permitted limits for personal use of facilities, but is also likely to specify the types of site that should not be accessed and the types of message that should not be exchanged. For libraries and other organizations providing public access, the AUP is likely to contain rules concerning booking terminals, the time limits for sessions, age limits, printing and downloading, etc. In policies for any type of user there are likely to be reminders both about legal restrictions on use and the avoidance of disruption or harassment to fellow users and staff. The chief concern in many AUPs is to prevent users accessing pornography and other 'harmful' categories of material such as sites inciting hatred or violence. AUPs are often used in association with FILTERING systems and their enforcement requires monitoring of use, usually via software systems provided for that purpose.

Further reading

Criddle, S. (*c.* 2000) 'Internet acceptable use policies' (www.earl.org.uk/policy/issuepapers/internet.html).
Sturges, P. (2002) *Public Internet Access in Libraries and Information Services*, Facet Publishing.

ACCESSIONS

The process of adding material, whether it be purchases, gifts or exchanges, to the stock of a library. The records of this process are now typically integrated into a library's integrated management system, often enhancing a record made or bought when the item was ordered, which will eventually become the permanent record in the catalogue.

SEE ALSO: libraries

ACCREDITATION OF LIS SCHOOLS

The procedure operated by national LIBRARY ASSOCIATIONS for approval of institutions offering programmes leading to professional qualifications in library science. Accreditation is generally accepted as an indicator of educational quality, and it is often used by employers as assurance of the adequate preparation of prospective employees. This process is in addition to that used by institutions themselves, and external educational agencies, for the approval of programmes of study.

SEE ALSO: information science education; library education

ACQUISITIONS

The operations involved in selecting, ordering and receiving materials for libraries. It includes budgeting and dealing with outside agencies such as LIBRARY SUPPLIERS and publishers. The objective of the acquisitions staff is to obtain material as quickly and as economically as possible in the interests of potential users, and to provide information on the status of all requests.

Selection

Acquisitions work begins with selection and may be conducted by specialist SUBJECT LIBRARIANS considering publisher and supplier information, or by teams of librarians looking at stock on approval. In all libraries a proportion of purchases will be made following requests and advice from library users. Selection should be made following a clear policy as described in COLLECTION MANAGEMENT. The acquisition of periodical material is described in SERIALS LIBRARIANSHIP.

'Acquisitions' has traditionally implied the buying of newly published books but there are many different formats needed for libraries. Purchasing procedures need to include FILM, ELECTRONIC BOOKS, MULTIMEDIA and MICRO-FORMS. Different types of material such as GOVERNMENT PUBLISHING or output from small presses must be bought as well as material from other countries. Arrangements need to be made to buy out-of-print and second-hand books. Some books, such as annuals or monograph series, can be bought on standing order. Some items can be obtained by EXCHANGE PROGRAMMES and some material will come as DONATIONS TO LIBRARIES.

Pre-order checking

Staff always need to check existing stock and orders before placing a new order, to avoid duplication and to verify details. It follows that acquisitions staff need to have a familiarity with CATALOGUES. Some libraries purchase expensive items co-operatively via consortia agreements, and, for those that share resources in a system of co-operation, checks on existing stock and orders will need to be wider, but are often simplified by online access. Checks also need to be made on those materials recently arrived in the library that may fall between the order file and the catalogue. In ACADEMIC LIBRARIES reading lists for students pose extra checking problems but if received in a timely fashion greatly help in the provision of stock.

Having checked current holdings it is important to verify and enhance request details. The information sources here are library suppliers, publishers, trade bibliographies (see TRADE BIBLIOGRAPHY) and national bibliographies (see NATIONAL BIBLIOGRAPHY). There are specialist bibliographies or catalogues available for many subjects and geographical areas, and data from online Internet suppliers is also useful.

Ordering

There are many sources of supply available to libraries, the most obvious being booksellers who specialize in the area, known as library suppliers. Consideration needs to be given to the variables of speed, accuracy and service before choosing a supplier. It is not good practice to place all orders with one supplier, although academic libraries may have a percentage of business with their campus bookshop. Tendering for total supply for libraries is negotiated in some places to maximize discount. A range of suppliers will be needed for second-hand, antiquarian, specialist subject or format, or international supply, and for these the Internet is increasingly useful for information and supply.

Apart from setting up accounts with suppliers, acquisitions staff need to keep up good communication to ensure smooth supply. Suppliers require clear information on requirements such as servicing (jacketing, insertion of security triggers, labelling), invoicing, reporting and how to handle urgent orders. They also need specific information on author, title, edition, binding, number of copies and the INTERNATIONAL STANDARD BOOK NUMBER or other identifier.

Acquisitions staff commonly set up brief catalogue records for online systems at the order stage. Online placement of orders is possible and publishers' catalogues, supplier databases and library catalogues can also be accessed via the Internet.

Receipt

With reliable suppliers there should be few problems, but checks are always necessary on accuracy/condition of goods and invoicing. Good relationships with suppliers will allow for returns and credit, as well as cancellation of orders.

Suppliers will report on items they are unable to supply (out of print, not yet published, publication abandoned) and the library can decide on action. Acquisitions should claim outstanding orders as a matter of routine.

Urgent orders or those reserved for specific users should be dealt with promptly, but there should be no significant delays between receipt of material, announcement of arrival and cataloguing.

Operational statistics on items ordered, received and paid for will need to be collected. Regular reports will also be needed on money spent and funds committed.

Budgeting and finance

Acquisitions work revolves around the management of a budget divided into funds to cover different subjects, materials or formats. As material is ordered a price commitment is made against the relevant fund so that the library knows how much money may be left to spend in the financial year.

Responsibility for the budget, which is likely to be held by acquisitions on behalf of the Library Director, means that there is a requirement to understand basic accounting methods and to liaise with institutional accountants and auditors. Checking and authorizing payment of invoices, credits and reporting on tax liability, as well as checking supplier statements of account and estimating future commitments, are all part of acquisitions work. Online systems preferably need to be able to communicate between the library and the finance office.

In times of budget constraint acquisitions is often the first area to be cut, causing orders to be stockpiled or cancelled. Conversely, in times of unexpected affluence acquisitions may benefit.

Professional development

Acquisitions staff can keep in touch with publishing and the BOOK trade by attending book fairs such as those in Frankfurt or London. Meetings and training courses where matters of current concern can be discussed are run by the AMERICAN LIBRARY ASSOCIATION and in the UK by the National Acquisitions Group (NAG). Both of these organizations have drawn up codes of ethics for acquisitions staff. Electronic mail lists and journals provide support, information and discussion for acquisitions staff, suppliers and publishers.

Further reading

AcqWeb (1994) (www.library.vanderbilt.edu).
Against the Grain (1989) Charleston, SC (quarterly).
The Bookseller (1859) Whitaker (weekly).
Chapman, L. (2001) *Managing Acquisitions in Library and Information Services*, Library Association.
Library Collections, Acquisitions and Technical Services (1977) Pergamon (quarterly)
Schmidt, K. (ed.) (1999) *Understanding the Business of Library Acquisitions*, 2nd edn, ALA.

SEE ALSO: accessions; book trade; collection management; digital library; grey literature; library suppliers; national bibliography; subject librarian

LIZ CHAPMAN

ADVICE SERVICE

An activity aimed at enabling citizens and consumers to obtain their rights, exercise responsibilities and access services. It is essentially locality-based, available free of charge to all users and covers all subjects, and a means of countering social exclusion (see SOCIAL EXCLUSION AND LIBRARIES). In practice the majority of advice work enquiries relate to social security, housing, fuel, consumer, financial, employment, immigration and family matters.

Elements

Advice work covers a range of activities, the main ones being:

- Information-giving, which involves the transfer to a client of simple or complex information obtained from other sources.
- Advice-giving, which is information tailored to individual need – a more complex process that can involve the fairly neutral activity of setting out a course of action or options through to evaluation of available services and help with choosing.
- Referral, the act of directing clients to another agency or facility where they can get further help, which may involve making direct contact with that agency, arranging an appointment and sometimes escorting the client to the agency.
- Action, which can range from simple help with filling in forms and writing letters on the client's behalf to mediation between people in dispute and representation ('advocacy') at tribunal hearings
- Feedback, the reporting and transmission of information, obtained through the advice work process, on how policies, programmes, services or procedures are working in practice and what gaps exist in provision.

Models

Unlike community work and social work, advice work has little theoretical base. Nevertheless, Thornton has identified 'three major schools of thought among advice workers', which she characterizes as the 'professional', the 'community' and the 'counselling' approach.

The 'professional' approach is often found in longer-established advice centres. In this model advice work is an activity comparable to the traditional professions, such as medicine or the law. The advice worker is the 'expert' who is being consulted about an essentially technical problem. The focus is on the user's problem; technical excellence is pursued. An adviser's skill can be measured by the despatch with which s/he 'solves' problems. The 'client' is

dependent on the advice worker for her/his expertise....

The 'community' approach to advice work emerged in the 1970s and finds its origins in community work theory applied to advice work....The underlying principles are those of equality and collectivity. The dependent expert/client relationship is rejected, and instead advice workers are now required to relate to service users in ways that emphasize the equality of the relationship and enable the user to deal with her/his problem her/himself or (better yet) collectively with others in the same position. Collective solutions are more highly valued than individual ones....

The third approach arrives in the advice spectrum through the medium of specialist agencies, often those providing a range of services to a particular user group. It can be particularly helpful where the user group is traditionally and institutionally disadvantaged, because unlike the two approaches...above, it is person-centred rather than problem-centred. Advisers are likely to spend more time with each user than in either of the other types of centre. What might be defined as the 'advice' issues (practical rather than personal) are dealt with in a counselling framework and this offers the user the opportunity to work out an approach to her/his difficulties. There is a greater emphasis on the interpersonal skills of the adviser.

(Thornton 1989)

Organization

Most advice work takes place in advice centres or, in the USA, information and referral (I&R) centres and is carried out mostly by a mixture of paid professionals, paraprofessionals and volunteers. Paid workers tend to provide continuity of management and supervision, handle the more difficult problems or provide specialist advice in particular areas. Volunteers, suitably trained, are responsible for handling the bulk of enquiries and other aspects of advice work, such as outreach.

The National Association of Citizens' Advice Bureaux (NACAB), established in the UK during the Second World War, has by far the most highly structured system for advice work and has become the model for other, mainly British Commonwealth, countries. It includes mandatory initial and ongoing training, staff assessment, standards for bureau operation and an extensive and regularly updated information base to ensure accuracy and consistency of advice-giving. The three basic tenets of the CAB service are independence, impartiality and objectivity, and confidentiality.

Since the 1960s in Britain there has been a growth in other advice centres offering a different style of operation or covering more specialized areas, such as housing, fuel, consumer law, employment, legal rights, money and immigration. Many of these are represented by the Federation of Independent Advice Centres (FIAC), an umbrella organization that arranges training courses on advice work and issues guidelines on good practice (Thornton 1989). A government agency, the National Consumer Council, has taken a strong interest in advice services over the years and has issued a set of guidelines on minimum standards for local advice services (National Consumer Council 1986). New services provided through the Internet, such as the personal health advisory services provided by NHS Direct in the UK (www.NHSdirect. nhs.uk), now supplement traditional face-to-face services.

I&R services in the USA developed out of the profusion (and confusion) of new social service programmes in the 1960s with similar aims to CABs but lacking their structure and centralized support. Umbrella organizations, such as the United Way of America and the Alliance of Information and Referral Systems, Inc. (AIRS), have issued a variety of materials on programme development and staff training, and published jointly national standards for information and referral (United Way of America 1983).

Initially, advice work was concentrated on urban areas but there has been a growing interest in ways of delivering such services to rural populations. The British Community Information Project and the National Consumer Council have been instrumental in researching options.

Advice work has not escaped the intrusion of new technology and computers feature strongly in the work of many advice services, particularly for file organization and maintaining statistical records, and as an aid to performing benefit calculations. Again, the National Consumer Council and the British Community Information Project have played an active role in promoting such use.

References

National Consumer Council (1986) *Good Advice for All: Guidelines on Standards for Local Advice Services*, National Consumer Council.
Thornton, C. (1989) *Managing to Advise*, Federation of Independent Advice Centres, pp. 9–10.
United Way of America (1983) *National Standards for Information and Referral Services*, United Way of America and the Alliance of Information and Referral Systems, Inc.

Further reading

Kempson, E. (1981) *On the Road: A Guide to Setting Up and Running a Mobile Advice Centre*, London: Community Information Project.
Levinson, R. (1988) *Information and Referral Networks: Doorways to Human Services*, New York: Springer Publishing Company.
Levinson, R. and Haynes, K. S. (eds) (1984) *Accessing Human Services: International Perspectives*, Beverley Hills, CA: Sage Publications (Social Service Delivery Systems vol. 7) [examines CAB and I&R models in detail and other systems worldwide briefly].
Ottley, P. and Kempson, E. (1982) *Computer Benefits? Guidelines for Local Information and Advice Services*, London: National Consumer Council.
Steele, J. (1991) *Information Management in Advice Centres*, London: Policy Studies Institute.

SEE ALSO: community information

ALLAN BUNCH

AFRICA

This region comprises the more than fifty African states that are unified, if at all, by an enduring legacy of colonialism or foreign occupation. African countries vary in size from the enormous expanses of Sudan and the Democratic Republic of the Congo to small island states in the Atlantic and Indian Oceans. In population they vary from Nigeria's more than 100 million and Egypt's nearly 70 million, to just a few thousand. Most are extremely poor, with average annual incomes in countries like Burkina Faso and Sierra Leone being amongst the very lowest in the world. Despite notable exceptions, their populations tend to be thinly spread throughout the rural areas. The majority of people are dependent on subsistence agriculture, and are highly vulnerable to the famines and natural disasters that occur with frequency in the tropical climates of the region. There is an enormous diversity of languages and cultural traditions within many of the countries themselves, as well as in the continent as a whole.

Although sectors of some countries, most notably South Africa, are highly developed, in general the information infrastructures and library and information institutions of the region reflect low levels of national development. Modern library and information work is still a pioneer activity in most of the region, despite the fact that the countries of the Mediterranean fringe have a documentary tradition going back for thousands of years.

History

It is important to be aware that written records have a much longer history in Africa than in Europe. Clay tablets have been found in parts of Egypt dating back to before 3000 BC. The various different ages of Egyptian civilization produced a wealth of documentation and the Maghreb as a whole can also show riches that include Berber inscriptions, Greek and Roman books, Vandal wooden tablets from the fifth and sixth centuries, and great quantities of Arabic literature after the Muslim conquests and conversions of the seventh century. Whether or not ancient Egypt had many libraries, as opposed to archives and ceremonial collections, the Ptolemaic period certainly produced one of the world's most famous libraries: that of Alexandria. There were Roman libraries scattered through the Mediterranean provinces, and the Arabic and Ottoman periods had a comparative abundance of libraries created for mosques, universities and palaces.

The story of modern libraries is the story of the effects of colonization, which were suffered by every African country (except Ethiopia, if we ignore the brief Italian occupation of the 1930s). Control of the continent fluctuated between many European powers until the first half of the twentieth century when, for a while, Britain, France and Portugal were the main external forces. In the Maghreb, French, Spanish and Italian linguistic influence did not supplant a powerful Arabic written culture, and Egypt, which fell in the British sphere of influence, remained an important centre for Middle Eastern, Islamic and secular Arabic culture, with comparatively large and significant libraries. In sub-Saharan Africa, settlers and Christian missionaries were chiefly responsible for giving orthographies to African languages so that the Bible and other religious writings could be made

widely accessible. This did not mean that sub-Saharan Africa had sufficient books in African languages to form libraries. The first libraries in the region seem to have been on its geographical fringes: in the Sahara itself, with mosque libraries in cities like Timbuktu and Djenne in the sixteenth century; along the east coast in trading communities like Mombasa, Zanzibar or Kilwa; and in South Africa, where in 1761 a small public library was set up by European settlers.

In fact, during the colonial period, which ended for most African countries in the 1960s, administrations paid little attention to library and information services for the general population. Libraries (often for the exclusive use of white people) were sometimes set up where there were large numbers of settlers, as in Kenya, Zimbabwe and Algeria. It was not, however, until preparations were being made for the independence of some of the British colonies that much attention was given to more accessible information and library facilities. In Ghana, for instance, the Ghana Library Board was established in 1950, seven years before independence. Several former British colonies, such as Tanzania in 1963, also passed legislation to set up and support library services very early in their independent existence. In francophone Africa, the pattern of library provision in the colonial period was usually more tentative, though Morocco, Tunisia and Algeria show an Arabic tradition overlain by French colonial influences. Some of the most positive initiatives in francophone Africa were in the former Belgian colonies, but independence does not seem to have brought quite the same enthusiasm or opportunities as in English-speaking Africa. Likewise, the Portuguese colonies could only show a few old-established libraries like the Biblioteca Municipal de Luanda (1873) and a network of early twentieth-century research libraries.

The information environment

Indigenous African culture was, and is, richly oral, with history, religion, medicine, geography and works of the imagination, nowadays often referred to together as indigenous knowledge (IK), held in the human mind. Africa's oral society should most definitely not be treated as if it were a problem for those wishing to create effective information institutions. It does, however, raise a set of questions that have not needed to be answered in countries, such as those of Europe and North America, where large proportions of the population were both literate and print-oriented before libraries were widely available. One issue is that of how governments and their agencies communicate with citizens. Newspapers, despite low literacy levels, are a popular source of information, but they are often government-controlled or censored, and their economic base is frequently precarious. Newsprint is cripplingly expensive, advertising revenue is limited and unreliable, and distribution networks seldom stretch much beyond the cities, even if sufficient copies could be printed to sell more widely. Radio is more or less ubiquitous, but receivers and batteries are expensive in relation to people's incomes and it is unrealistic to claim that access to radio is truly universal. What is more, use of radio by governments as an information medium is not merely unidirectional (top down) but usually clumsy and ineffective. Not every country has a television service, and, where there is one, the signal often does not reach far beyond the main centres of population. Ownership of receivers is also very low, with just a few thousand sets in many countries. Local programme content is rare and not of a high standard, so much of what is broadcast is the cheaper product of the US broadcasting export trade. Satellite transmission is in the process of transforming the scope of television reception, but at present this, too, has a comparatively limited audience in Africa.

Problems of information service in Africa

In practice, most formal information services suffer from crippling problems, and few realize their full potential. Budgetary constraints affect LIBRARIES, public BROADCASTING, extension services, other information agencies and infrastructural services in virtually every African country. The availability of printed material of all kinds is severely limited because of shortages of paper, limited printing capacity and underdeveloped distribution channels. National publishing industries that produce fewer than one hundred titles per year are the norm. Although Egypt produces about 10,000 titles, in sub-Saharan Africa, apart from South Africa with about 2,500 titles, only Nigeria reaches a figure of 1,000 titles per year. CENSORSHIP is often one of the most efficient activities of government, and the suppression of

unacceptable opinion or information is frequently brutal. Imported publications are expensive in local terms, and foreign currency to purchase them is severely rationed in most countries. Import dues and customs restrictions also contribute to the expense. Locally produced GREY LITERATURE is a resource of more than usual value when conventional publishing is so weak, but is often even more difficult to acquire in some African countries than it is in other parts of the world because of practices such as officials retaining copies in the hope of personal profit.

Postal services, both internal and external, tend to be slow and unreliable. Likewise, internal telephone communications are often very inefficient, although satellite links to other countries are usually highly effective. Levels of access to telephones have been extremely low, with seldom more than an average of one telephone line per hundred inhabitants and more commonly one per each thousand people. The deregulation of telecommunications in many African countries and the licensing of new cellular networks is, however, transforming the situation. The number of mobile subscribers is expected to exceed those with fixed connections during 2002 and better telecommunications access opens the way for better online access. Computers, whilst almost ubiquitous in banks, businesses and government offices, are relatively expensive to buy in the first place, and to maintain and to run subsequently. Whilst the endemically unreliable electrical supply of most African countries may no longer provide quite the same threat to computer files as it used to, it does make effective use of computers somewhat difficult. Despite this, the number of home computers and of computer literate people is rising at a swift rate. There now seem to be genuine indications that some sectors of African society are entering the information age, but this also serves to increase the divide between information haves and have-nots

Library and archive services

SPECIAL LIBRARIES

The first sector in which consistent, positive library developments can be observed across the continent is that of SPECIAL LIBRARIES and documentation centres. Geological libraries, beginning with that at Khartoum, Sudan, in 1904, and agricultural libraries, such as the Forestry Department Library and Herbarium, Entebbe,

Uganda, also in 1904, were often the earliest to be founded. In 1910 administrative libraries were required by law in the former Belgian Congo, and the number of special libraries of various types across the continent increased steadily, although not swiftly, thereafter. Today special libraries and documentation centres continue to be important and comparatively flourishing institutions. Many form part of government ministries, parastatals and NGOs, and are thus able to appeal for support very directly to the decision-makers. They serve small but influential clienteles, whose activities can be seen as affecting the economic prospects of the country. Although the libraries need expensive imported monographs and journals, their most significant stock is probably grey literature, which is difficult, but not expensive, to acquire. They often have useful links with overseas institutions that may supply materials as gifts or exchanges. Special libraries increasingly exploit online access and the resources of the World Wide Web, and this tends to raise the profile of information work within the institution.

ACADEMIC LIBRARIES

The academic library (see ACADEMIC LIBRARIES) has a long pedigree in Africa and some of the world's oldest universities are found there. Al-Azhar University, Cairo, was founded in 970 and Quarouine University in Fez, Morocco, in 1400. However, in sub-Saharan Africa few academic libraries, such as those at Fourah Boy College, Sierra Leone (1827), and Liberia College, Monrovia, Liberia (1862), date from as long ago as the nineteenth century. Most African universities and their libraries were founded in the period since the Second World War. African countries have invested extremely high proportions of their public revenue on education and this has included at least one university in almost every state. Many of these have sizeable and sometimes architecturally impressive library buildings, which express the vision of the founders of the important role that the library would play in the university. The sad reality is that the expense of developing and maintaining collections to support teaching and research has proved beyond the resources found in most African countries. Up-to-date, well-selected and well-cared-for collections are the exception rather than the rule, so that researchers and teachers lack the essentials for progressive scholarship, and students are

often forced to rely exclusively on their own lecture notes. SCHOOL LIBRARIES frequently suffer even greater degrees of deprivation, some existing in name only. The possibility that electronic information services may open up a new form of access for the staff and students of educational establishments, replacing conventional library service almost entirely, seems like one of the most hopeful possibilities in many cases.

NATIONAL AND PUBLIC LIBRARIES

These two forms of library are deliberately linked, since the arrangements in many African countries are different from those in other parts of the world. National library (see NATIONAL LIBRARIES) services are not usually a national research collection rooted in legal deposit acquisitions, as would be expected elsewhere, though such libraries do exist. For instance, the former Khedive's Library of 1870, in Cairo, which is now the national library of Egypt, has a great wealth of Arabic books and manuscripts assembled from various neglected earlier collections. There are also more recent stirrings. A fine modern national library building was opened in Windhoek, Namibia, in 2001, and in 2002 the Ugandan government drafted a law instituting a national library. However, by far the most significant national library development, and probably the most significant library project in twenty-first century Africa, is the new library of Alexandria. Work towards this joint project of the Egyptian government and UNESCO began in 1995 and its official inauguration was in April 2002. It is to be both a modern national library and a centre for Egyptian and regional studies.

Much more commonly, national libraries take the form of a national public library service, with a central headquarters co-ordinating branches in various parts of the country. Some services do have LEGAL DEPOSIT collections, but in other cases the depository centre might be the national archives, the national university or a separate bibliographical agency. The NATIONAL BIBLIOGRAPHY, where it exists, may emanate from any of these institutions. Perhaps of all the types of library to be found in Africa, national/public libraries have had the hardest struggle to adapt to need. The European or North American model of the public library (see PUBLIC LIBRARIES) is posited, first and foremost, on the existence of a large well-schooled population of adult readers.

Whereas in Africa, where such a group hardly existed until recently, the public library tends to be marginalized. It is seen to best advantage in communities, like the high-density suburbs (townships) of Bulawayo, Zimbabwe, where the number of readers is high and the stock reasonably well adapted to their needs. Simple observation shows that the demand for public libraries is strongest amongst children of school age, but very few libraries recognize this by gearing their collections and services, at least for the medium term, to this manifest need.

ARCHIVE SERVICES

Although one or two countries, notably Mauritius, had archive services during the nineteenth century, the main period of development probably began with the setting up of services in French colonies: Senegal and Niger in 1913, and Benin in 1914. The Portuguese possessions were also quite advanced: a National Historical and Research Centre was founded in Angola in 1933, and the Historical Archives of Mozambique in 1934. The first major service in a British colony was founded in the then Rhodesia (Zimbabwe) in 1935. This particular service has since been something of a leader, as the Central African Archives for the Rhodesias and Nyasaland (after 1946), and now as the National Archives of Zimbabwe. Archives in Africa have tended to be quite outward-looking information institutions, rather than stressing their purely historical function. Whilst libraries have struggled because of, among other things, lack of material to provide for users, archives have naturally been the recipients of a constant flow of documentation from their parent bodies. Several of them, such as the National Archives of Zambia and of Zimbabwe, have also been designated for the receipt of legal deposit copies of published materials. Recognizing the value of much of what they hold for immediate practical purposes, services like those of Kenya and Zimbabwe have promoted use of their collections by planners and businessmen, as well as researchers and academics, to good effect.

PROFESSIONAL ACTIVITY AND EDUCATION FOR
INFORMATION AND LIBRARY WORK

More than half of the African states now have some form of library and information association. At first, such organizations were regional, with the West African Library Association, founded in 1954, the pioneer. The member countries dissolved this is 1962, and single-country associations are the norm, although some countries, like Nigeria and South Africa (because of its apartheid legacy), have more than one. The membership of most associations may be small, but they do succeed in carrying out a range of professional activities despite their difficulties. Journals such as the *Botswana Library Association Journal* and *Maktaba* from Kenya are important sources of professional development information, as are the meetings, seminars and conferences that the associations organize. An outstanding example of the latter is the biennial meeting of the Standing Conference of East, Central and Southern African Librarians (SCECSAL), which since the early 1970s has provided marvellous opportunities for the exchange of professional information and opinion to library personnel from the English-speaking eastern half of the continent. African librarians also provide a growing input to the activities of international organizations such as the International Federation of Library Associations (IFLA), at conferences, on committees and through programmes such as IFLA's ALP (Advancement of Librarianship in the Third World). This complements the activities of development organizations with African programmes, such as Germany's Deutsche Stiftung für Internationale Entwicklung (DSE), or Canada's International Development Research Centre (IDRC), which have organized many valuable programmes and publications. African librarians, particularly those of Nigeria, are now prolific writers on professional topics and their articles will be found throughout the literature.

All this has been achieved in a comparatively short time, whilst coping with difficulties of the kind outlined above. Much is owed to the progress in LIBRARY EDUCATION that has been achieved during this time. The University of Ibadan began the first African programme, at non-professional level, in 1950, followed by a programme at professional level in 1960, but before then, and since, great numbers of African librarians have studied in Britain, France, the USA, Russia and elsewhere. These graduates of foreign institutions have provided staff for a whole series of schools subsequently established across the continent. Some had a regional function, like the school set up at Dakar in Senegal in 1962 for francophone Africa, the school set up in

Morocco with UNESCO assistance in 1974, or the East African School of Librarianship established at Makere University in Uganda in 1963. More recently, the School of Information Studies for Africa (SISA), set up at the University of Addis Ababa with considerable financial assistance from the IDRC, has claimed a continent-wide role. Increasingly, the schools are beginning to be staffed by teachers with degrees, including PhDs, from African universities and the potential for an educational agenda generated from within the region becomes stronger all the time.

New directions for information work in Africa

One consistent theme from writings and public statements by African librarians is the need for an agenda for library and information work that derives from the distinctive needs of Africa's people. Those needs already include, and will increasingly include, the provision of electronic information via networks or from stand-alone systems like CD-ROMs. There is also a clear need for conventional libraries, documentation centres and archives, particularly for planning, research and education. However, what is only now being fully addressed is the need for better information for those within the oral culture that is still so much part of the African way of life. Add to this the poverty, geographical dispersion and cultural and linguistic isolation of the individuals and groups who could benefit from better information on farming and small-scale industry or health and hygiene, and there is clearly a need that conventional forms of service have not answered. At present there is more analysis of the problem and intellectual exploration of possible solutions than there are practical steps to solve it. However, experiments with simple reading rooms providing shelter, light and a few essential printed materials are widespread, and indeed amount to a fully fledged system in some countries like Tanzania and Malawi. Multifunction centres, such as the Centres de Lecture et d'Animation Culturelle en Milieu Rural (CLAC), are being tried under the aegis of IFLA's ALP programme in francophone countries such as Benin, Senegal, the Ivory Coast and Burkina Faso. Rural Community Resource Centres (RCRC) also exist on a semi-experimental basis in Sierra Leone and other West African countries. Such centres – acquiring

materials whether oral, printed or in some other form, and disseminating information orally, pictorially, on tape, through drama, dance and song or any other viable form, including print – offer exciting possibilities for a new form of information work to address an old and intractable set of problems.

Further reading

Amadi, A.O. (1981) *African Libraries: Western Tradition and Colonial Brainwashing*, Scarecrow Press.

Issak, A. (2000) *Public Libraries in Africa: A Report and Annotated Bibliography*, INASP.

Sitzman, G.L. (1988) *African Libraries*, Scarecrow Press.

Stilwell, C., Leach, A. and Burton, S. (eds) (2001) *Knowledge, Information and Development: An African Perspective*, University of Natal.

Sturges, P. and Neill, R. (1998) *The Quiet Struggle: Libraries and Information for Africa*, 2nd edn, Mansell.

Wise, M. (ed.) (1985) *Aspects of African Librarianship: A Collection of Writings*, Mansell.

SEE ALSO: agricultural documentation and information; communication; communication technology; development co-operation in support of information and knowledge activities; distance learning; information policy; Islamic libraries; library associations; mass media; Middle East; oral traditions

PAUL STURGES

AGRICULTURAL DOCUMENTATION AND INFORMATION

Agriculture-related publications form a substantial literature. Over 300 reference works in agriculture, fisheries, forestry, horticulture and food were listed in *Walford's Guide to Reference Material* (Mullay and Schlicke 1993), including major guides to the literature, as well as directories, dictionaries, etc. Numerous secondary services for agriculture are described by Keenan and Wortley (1993). *Current Contents Agriculture* provides details of journal contents immediately after publication.

A characteristic component of agricultural literature is non-conventional material. Authors like Hutchinson and Martin (1994) and Posnett and Reilly (1986) have demonstrated how it can be handled. Methods of dealing with extension literature are described by Johnson (1988) and by Mathews (1987). Advisory leaflets and trade literature abound at demonstrations and agricultural shows and are important for updating farmers. A very large organization like FAO generates enormous numbers of reports, working papers, etc.

Information exchange networks are discussed by Nelson and Farrington (1994). Niang (1987) has drawn attention to the importance of documentation networks (like those in Zaire and Senegal) and the exchange of information and experiences. The International Association of Agricultural Information Specialists (IAALD) is the professional association with worldwide membership. IAALD, like FAO library, CAB International and IDRC, has had a significant role in training. There have been many initiatives to assist in the provision of agricultural information for developing countries. Olsen and Kennedy-Olsen (1991) described their core agricultural literature project. FAO and CAB International have SDI and document delivery services. Fisher *et al.* (1990) listed agricultural information resource centres worldwide.

Computers have brought significant changes in the way that researchers, farmers, publishers and information specialists work. Drew's *Guide to Internet/Bitnet Resources* (1994) showed their great potential.

References

Drew, W. (1994) *Not Just Cows: A Guide to Internet/Bitnet Resources in Agriculture and Related Sciences. World Wide Web Version*, SUNY College of Agriculture and Technology.

Fisher, R.C. *et al.* (1990) *Agricultural Information Resource Centres: A World Directory*, IAALD/CTA.

Hutchinson, B.S. and Martin, D.J. (1994) 'Building an information resource on famine mitigation: A lesson in accessing non-conventional literature', *Quarterly Bulletin of IAALD* 39: 305–11.

International Union List of Agricultural Serials, CAB International.

Johnson, R.M. (1988) 'Extension literature in UK agriculture: Its bibliographic control', *Quarterly Bulletin of IAALD* 33: 99–104.

Keenan, S. and Wortley, P.J. (comps) (1993) *Directory of Agricultural Bibliographic Information Sources*, Technical Centre for Agricultural and Rural Cooperation, CTA.

Mathews, E. (1987) 'Bibliographic access to state agricultural experiment station publications', *Quarterly Bulletin of IAALD* 32: 193–9.

Mullay, M. and Schlicke, P. (eds) (1993) *Walford's Guide to Reference Material*, 6th edn, vol. 1, *Science and Technology* 63, Agriculture and livestock, pp. 553–95, Library Association.

Nelson, J. and Farrington, J. (1994) *Information Exchange Networks for Agricultural Development*, CTA.

Niang, T. (1987) 'The CTA's Q and A service: For whom and for what?', *Quarterly Bulletin of IAALD* 32: 104–5.

Olsen, W.C. and Kennedy-Olsen, J. (1991) 'Determining the current core literature in the agricultural sciences', *Quarterly Bulletin of IAALD* 33: 122–7.

Posnett, N.W. and Reilly, P.M. (1986) 'Non-conventional literature in tropical agriculture and a national bibliography: An assessment', *Quarterly Bulletin of IAALD* 31: 27–33.

Further reading

Frank, R.C. (1987) 'Agricultural information systems and services', *Annual Review of Information Science and Technology* 22: 293–334

Lendvay, O. (1980) *Primer for Agricultural Libraries*, 2nd edn, PUDOC for IAALD [also French, Portuguese and Spanish editions].

Niang, T. (1988) 'Improving the diffusion of scientific and technical information in ACP countries', *Quarterly Bulletin of IAALD* 33: 170–1.

Wortley, P.J. (1981) 'Tropical agriculture', in G.P. Lilley (ed.) *Information Sources in Agriculture and Food Science*, Butterworths, pp. 357–406.

PATRICIA JANE WORTLEY,
REVISED BY THE EDITORS

ALGORITHM

Instructions for carrying out a series of logical procedural steps in a specified order; now used especially in computing and related disciplines.

ALPHABETIZATION RULES

Alphabetization rules govern the arrangement of words (as in the entries in a catalogue (see CATALOGUES)) in an order primarily determined by the position of their constituent letters in the alphabet. The principle of alphabetization, once established, is both simple and highly adaptable. Its purpose is to allow systematic reference to bodies of material too large or complex for effective casual access. It can be used alone, as it generally is in the INDEX of a book, but it can readily be combined with other modes of CLASSIFICATION. Its widespread and enduring use suggests that it is particularly well suited to the processes of the human eye and brain.

The technique of strict alphabetization (taking account of every letter in sequence, and thus placing analyst before analytical) appears to have been invented by the Greeks. By the third century

BC it was used in compiling bibliographies (see BIBLIOGRAPHY) relating to, and therefore conceivably in the arrangement of, the library attached to the Temple of the Muses at Alexandria. There is, however, no striking evidence of its use in the Roman world. The Romans acquired alphabetical lists in Greek texts, but seem to have made no consistent use of the principle and to have been content with first-letter indexing. The practice is notably absent from the documented organization of the army, the most potent and sophisticated of Roman institutions. Under the circumstances, it is probably significant that the Romans appear to have had no consistent names for the letters of the alphabet, which were probably memorized in the form of voiced syllables, rather than in the rhythmic chants of ancient Greece and modern Europe.

The precarious survival of LITERACY in the early Middle Ages greatly reduced the volume of written material in use. Except in England, where there was a vernacular literary tradition that the Normans destroyed, literacy remained a matter of Latinity and confined to the clergy. At the same time the oral tradition (see ORAL TRADITIONS) in the barbarian societies of the West gave even the literate a capacity for memorizing and recalling verse and prose (especially verse), which it is difficult now to imagine.

The need for aids to recall and study was correspondingly reduced. Libraries were rare, and commonly small: even in the thirteenth century a shelf of nine books could constitute a library for a Cistercian abbey. The clergy were provided with service books, but constant repetition made both the liturgy and the prescribed lessons from the Vulgate familiar to the least accomplished reader. Scholars consulted more complex texts, thematically arranged, with a similar assurance. Library catalogues, correspondingly, were commonly shelf-guides, or finding-lists from which the completeness of the collection could be checked, rather than surveys of scholarship. When authors' names were alphabetized, as they sometimes were, it was by initial letters.

However, as the power of the papacy and the scope of the canon law grew, so the written records of the international church multiplied. The clergy developed their literary and administrative skills, and lent them to kings and other laymen. Accumulations of intricate and unfamiliar material demanded new styles of reference and management. Early in the fourteenth century records in the English exchequer were classified and registered, to be filed in boxes distinguished by symbols and icons that illiterate messengers could recognize.

About the same time papal clerks were compiling indexes both to current and to some older records in order of initial letters. There are some isolated examples of a similar but more tentative arrangement in accounts kept in France fifty years earlier, but we do not know how the practice spread. The records of the Husting Court of London include registers of documents that show the clerks progressing in the course of the fourteenth century from symbols to initial letters in the margin marking names in the text, and then to compiling an alphabetical list of testators arranged in the chronological order of their probate.

Individuals probably developed more elaborate schemes of their own at all periods, but the subject still needs research. However, account books and manuals of practice from Italy suggest that mercantile houses there, the most accomplished and sophisticated region of Europe, did not progress beyond first-letter indexing during the Middle Ages. It was the advent of printing, and the multiplication not only of texts but also of kinds of texts, that stimulated the exploitation of full alphabetical order.

The availability of cheap paper for indexing slips probably also played its part. Parchment was expensive in the Middle Ages, and was sparingly used. From the late fifteenth century paper was abundant, and the change encouraged the spread of informal written memoranda. Intensive indexing is made much simpler, and on any large scale is only possible, if the entries can be reviewed and manipulated individually. There was, however, no mechanical sorting until Herman Hollerith devised his machine in the 1880s.

The full alphabetical index therefore emerged as the printed book established itself as an engine of scholarship. Alphabetization also came into its own as a guide to the contents of the greatly expanded libraries that printing made both possible and necessary to the advancement of learning. Thomas James's first catalogue of the Bodleian Library (1605) was an early and notable work of a kind that has, with the BIBLIOGRAPHY, sustained two revolutions in humane learning, science and technology in the course of four centuries.

In modern libraries the formal assessment of accessions has largely given place to reference to bibliographical databases, a practice anticipated by the cataloguing service that the LIBRARY OF CONGRESS made available to subscribers over several decades. Alphabetical sorting itself can similarly be left to the computer, though the card catalogue still needs individual attention. Those and other devices, however, have extended rather than displaced the basic principles of alphabetization, which are well into their third millennium.

Further reading

British Museum (1940) *Guide to the Arrangement of Headings and Entries in the General Catalogue of Printed Books.*
Daly, L.W. (1967) *Contributions to a History of Alphabetization in Antiquity and the Middle Ages,* Collection Latomus, 90, Brussels.
Martin, G.H. (1990) *The Husting Rolls of Deeds and Wills: Guide to the Microform Edition,* Cambridge.

SEE ALSO: organization of knowledge

GEOFFREY MARTIN

AMERICAN LIBRARY ASSOCIATION

As the oldest and largest of LIBRARY ASSOCIATIONS in the world, the American Library Association (ALA) works to promote and improve librarianship and library service.

The ALA was founded in 1876, the year of the USA's centennial. Responding to the call of such early library leaders as William Frederick Poole, Melvil DEWEY and Justin Winsor, ninety men and thirteen women, from as far away as Chicago, Illinois and England, gathered in Philadelphia, in October. At the end of their conference they voted to form the ALA. From these humble beginnings, by 1995 the Association had grown to 56,954 members and had an endowment valued at $5,493,000 and an annual budget of $28,731,000.

The organizational structure of the ALA has been aptly described as 'an association of associations'. The ALA is divided into eleven divisions. Each division represents a different type of library or library service and each maintains its own executive director, officers, programmes and budget. Furthermore, there are discussion groups, round tables and committees within both the Association and the divisions. The Association has ties to fifty-three independent state and regional library associations, called chapters, and to twenty-four national and international affiliates, such as the Medical Library Association and the Canadian Library Association, which have purposes similar to those of the ALA. The Association is governed by a council consisting of 175 members, including one hundred elected at large. It is managed by an executive board comprised of the elected officers and eight members elected by council. The ALA Executive Director and a staff of about 250 work in the main Chicago office and other offices in Washington, DC, and Middletown, Connecticut.

According to its charter, the ALA was founded for 'the purpose of promoting library interests throughout the world'. To fulfil this mission the Association has established certain goals and priorities, including improving library and information services, ensuring appropriate legislation and funding, protecting intellectual freedom and strengthening the library profession.

The ALA has sought to increase public use and support of libraries since its first conference in 1876. In 1975 the Association gained an important public relations tool when it assumed control of National Library Week (NLW), a week in April dedicated to promoting libraries. The ALA has made NLW the cornerstone of its year-round campaign to increase public visibility of libraries and librarianship.

NLW also plays an important role in the Association's political activities, which are largely the responsibility of the ALA Washington Office. Two of that office's achievements have been the passage of the Library Services Act (1956), which secured federal aid for PUBLIC LIBRARIES, and the Library Services and Construction Act (1964), which improved LIBRARY BUILDINGS and services. Every year during NLW the Washington Office co-sponsors Legislative Day in order to give librarians an opportunity to meet with federal legislators.

The ALA has also been politically active in its long-standing effort to protect intellectual freedom. In 1939 the Association adopted the Library Bill of Rights, its own version of the First Amendment to the US Constitution. In 1953 the ALA, in co-operation with other organizations, issued the 'Freedom to Read Statement', largely in response to the attempted CENSORSHIP of library materials by Senator Joseph McCarthy.

Today the Office for Intellectual Freedom co-ordinates efforts to encourage libraries to shelve and circulate materials representing different points of view.

Another goal of the ALA is to encourage professional innovation and improvement. One way it works to meet this goal is by accreditation of library schools. Since the Association began accrediting library schools in 1924, the Masters in Library Science (MLS) has become the standard degree for library professionals, with many schools now also offering the Doctor of Philosophy (PhD) degree. Today the ALA's Committee on Accreditation is the sole agency authorized by the US Government to evaluate and accredit graduate programmes in library science.

The ALA also works to help improve the profession through its publishing programme, one of the largest programmes for library-related materials in the world. The enormously popular *Guide to Reference Books* – a standard reference source since 1902 – is just one of many books published by ALA. The Association also publishes numerous periodicals, including *Booklist*, a selection journal covering print and non-print materials, and *Choice*, a book review journal for ACADEMIC LIBRARIES.

In order to honour individuals and institutions for innovation and achievement in the profession, the ALA has established an extensive awards programme that covers numerous and diverse areas such as authorship, library architecture and public relations. Probably the best known of the awards are the prestigious Newbery Medal and Caldecott Medal, both given annually to distinguished authors of children's literature.

In almost all of its activities the ALA has worked mainly within the USA, despite its self-proclaimed international scope. Nonetheless, since its inception the Association has maintained an interest in international librarianship. In 1877 a number of US librarians were in London for the formation of the LIBRARY ASSOCIATION (LA) of the United Kingdom. Fifty years later, in 1927, the ALA helped establish the International Federation of Library Associations (IFLA). During the periods 1943–9 and 1956–72, the ALA dedicated an office to international relations. Working through the Committee on International Relations and the International Relations Round Table, numerous committees and boards continue to promote library interests around the world.

The ALA holds two conferences each year. The Midwinter Meeting is usually held in January and is dedicated to business matters. The Annual Conference, held in June, is devoted to educational and professional programmes and attracts thousands of people from around the country and abroad. The main ALA headquarters are located at 50 E. Huron Street, Chicago, IL 60611, USA.

Further reading

ALA Handbook of Organization and Membership Directory, 1994–5.
Holley, E. G. (1976) 'ALA at 100', *The ALA Yearbook (centennial edition).*
Sullivan, P. (1976) *Carl H. Milam and the American Library Association*, HW Wilson.

SEE ALSO: freedom of information; information professions; library education

BRIAN K. GEIGER AND EDWARD G. HOLLEY

AMERICAN SOCIETY FOR INFORMATION SCIENCE AND TECHNOLOGY

The mission of the American Society for Information Science and Technology (ASIST) is to advance information professionals and the field of INFORMATION SCIENCE.

ASIST is a non-profit professional association boasting around 4,000 members. The membership is drawn from a variety of disciplines, including LIBRARIANSHIP, computer science, management and chemistry. ASIST aims to provide methods of communication and continuing education for information professionals, encourage research and development in the information science field and increase public awareness of the information science discipline.

History

ASIST owes its origins to the American Documentation Institute (ADI), which was chartered as a non-profit organization in March 1937. Originally, membership was confined to nominated representatives of affiliated organizations and government agencies. In 1950 the ADI first published its journal *American Documentation*, and in 1952 individual members were admitted to membership. With advances in computer technology in the 1950s and 1960s, membership of the ADI increased rapidly – by 1967 the Institute had over 2,000 members. To reflect changes in its activities a vote was taken in 1967 to change the name of the ADI to the *American Society for Information Science*; ADI became ASIS on 1 January 1968. A further change occurred in 2000 when the name became American Society for Information Science and Technology (ASIST) to recognize the changing interests of the membership.

Publications

ASIST produces two well-respected publications in the information science field. The *Bulletin of the American Society for Information Science and Technology* covers news of the Society as well as opinions and analysis of present and future advances in the field. The *Journal of the American Society for Information Science and Technology* (*JASIST*) aims to be the leading publication on current research and theoretical work on future information science developments. In addition to its publications, ASIST has a thriving student membership and offers members participation in twenty Special Interest Groups (SIG).

Further reading

American Society for Information Science and Technology (www.asis.org).

SEE ALSO: information science

JAMES DEARNLEY

ANGLO-AMERICAN CATALOGUING RULES

A set of rules for the standard description of all materials which a library may hold or to which it may have access, and for the formulation of standard forms of names and titles to provide access to and grouping of those descriptions.

The *Anglo-American Cataloguing Rules* (*AACR*) is the dominant bibliographic standard regulating descriptive cataloguing in the English-speaking world. First published in 1967, *AACR* marked a departure from previous cataloguing rules, which had grown haphazardly into mere compilations of regulations to handle specific bibliographic cases. The second edition of *AACR*, which appeared eleven years later in 1978, was an even more radical departure from this tradition, due largely to the pioneering work of its principal editor, Michael Gorman. By using a set of principles derived from the International Standard Bibliographic Description (ISBD) and by explicitly covering all library materials, the rules are able to produce neutral cataloguing that is not dependent on either the physical form of the item being catalogued or the country or institution where the cataloguing takes place.

AACR falls into two parts. Part 1 is concerned with the creation of a BIBLIOGRAPHIC DESCRIPTION of the item being catalogued and consists of a chapter giving general rules applicable to all materials, followed by chapters covering the differing physical forms taken by communicated information and knowledge: sound recordings, music, graphic materials, cartographic materials, computer files, for example. Each chapter, regardless of the medium with which it is concerned, follows the principles of the ISBD by grouping the elements of the description into eight discrete areas. These areas are given in a set and invariable order in the bibliographic description and are separated from each other by prescribed punctuation. The effect of application of the rules is to produce a standard pattern that is recognizable to catalogue users and which enables the easy exchange of records created by different agencies.

Part 2 gives rules for the choice and form of access points. These headings provide access to the bibliographic descriptions from the name of a person or corporate body related to the item and from the standard title of the work, of which the physical item may be one of many manifestations. The first chapter in Part 2 is concerned with the choice of a main entry heading. Although no longer required in a fully developed automated catalogue, where all access points are of equal value, the concept of a main entry is still of practical use in single-entry listings of library materials and is enshrined in all of the major MACHINE-READABLE CATALOGUING (MARC) formats used to communicate computer-readable bibliographic records. The chapter on choice of main entry also marks the abandonment by *AACR* of the concept of corporate authorship, whilst continuing to recognize that on certain occasions main entry under a corporate name is the most useful way of retrieving an item description.

Further chapters give rules for the creation of headings for personal names, corporate names and geographic names. It is a fundamental principle of *AACR* that the form of name on which the heading is based is that by which the person or body is commonly known or identified. When the name has been chosen, the rules then provide guidance on choice of the entry element of the name and on additions that may be needed to distinguish the name from an otherwise identical heading for another bibliographic identity. A separate chapter deals with the creation of a uniform or standard title for a work that may have had many manifestations differing in form and content. For example, the work commonly known as *Othello* may have been published not only under several different titles, but also as a film and as a sound recording, as well as a video recording of a stage production. Linking the descriptions of all these distinct physical items to a single standard title facilitates access to all manifestations of the work that are available to the library user. Finally, there are chapters containing rules for the creation of references from variant and differing forms of the name or uniform title.

AACR is a living standard, and is responsive to changes and developments in media and the ways in which knowledge and information are communicated. The creation and maintenance of *AACR* is a matter of international collaboration. The content of the rules is the responsibility of the Joint Steering Committee for Revision of *AACR* (JSC), which consists of representatives from the AMERICAN LIBRARY ASSOCIATION, the LIBRARY ASSOCIATION, the BRITISH LIBRARY, the LIBRARY OF CONGRESS, the Australian Committee on Cataloguing and the Canadian Committee on Cataloguing. Numerous committees and institutions at the national level in the anglophone countries feed suggestions and proposals for change to *AACR* into the JSC machinery. Changes that are agreed by the JSC are published at irregular intervals by the three *AACR* publishers: the Library Association, the American Library Association and the Canadian Library Association. The Committee of Principals exercizes executive responsibility for all matters connected with *AACR* on behalf of its author bodies.

References

Anglo-American Cataloguing Rules (1988) 2nd edn, Library Association Publishing.
ISBD(G): General International Standard Bibliographic Description (1977) IFLA International Office for UBC.

Further reading

Gorman, M. (1978) 'The Anglo-American cataloguing rules, second edition', *Library Resources and Technical Services* 22: 209–26.
Maxwell, M.F. (1989) *Handbook for AACR2 1988 Revision*, American Library Association.

SEE ALSO: organization of knowledge

PAT ODDY

ANOMALOUS STATE OF KNOWLEDGE

A model for INFORMATION RETRIEVAL based on the assumption that the formulation of a query by a user signifies the recognition by the enquirer of some anomaly (or incompleteness) in their state of KNOWLEDGE. The anomalous state of knowledge (ASK) model is based on the understanding that, given such an anomaly, the user is probably unable to state precisely what is needed to resolve the lack of information. The model tries to describe the user's ASK with respect to a given query rather than requiring the user to state the query precisely. The ASK can then be used to formulate an appropriate search strategy.

Further reading

Belkin, N.J. (1982) 'ASK for information retrieved, part I: Background and theory'; 'part II: Results of design study', *Journal of Documentation* 38: 68–71, 145–64.

SEE ALSO: information seeking research; information theory

ARCHIVAL DESCRIPTION

The creation of an accurate representation of a unit of description and its component parts, if any, by the process of capturing, collating, analysing and organizing any information that serves to identify archival material and explain the context and records systems that produced it.

Archival description is the equivalent in archivology to cataloguing in librarianship. There are important differences of principle and practice between these two fields, and in the relative importance of description in professional practice. The above definition from the General International Standard Archival Description (ISAD(G)) makes use of important concepts underlying archival management.

- The principle of representation. Because original archival materials cannot be organized for direct physical access by users (they are usually kept in boxes in closed storage areas) they have to be managed and retrieved by using representations. These representations have to contain the right data to allow for their effective use in the various functions of management.
- The unit of description: the basic unit in archival management is taken to be the group (FONDS in international usage; also often termed COLLECTION). Most often a group is a large body of materials that can be subdivided into subordinate entities. It would be normal, therefore, for an archive group to have a description representing the whole group, followed by a number of interlinked descriptions of its components.
- Generally, archival descriptions must contain information on the provenance, background and context of the materials. It is in principle not possible to describe archival materials in terms of their contents and physical form alone. Provenance information includes a history of the administration or activity that caused the archives to be created and explains how they were used during the period when they were current records.

Archival descriptions therefore reflect the principles of provenance and original order, contain elements that correspond to the recognized levels of arrangement, and conform (ideally at least) to national and international standards.

Levels of arrangement and description

Levels of arrangement are the physical sets into which archival materials are sorted after analysis. These levels are transformed into levels of description when representations are made of these organized materials. Archival descriptions can be set in the context of an internationally recognized hierarchy of levels, summarized as follows:

MANAGEMENT GROUPS

These are groups brought together in description for convenience, e.g. municipal archives, private papers.

GROUPS (INTERNATIONALLY 'FONDS')

These are the whole of the documents, regardless of form or medium, organically created and/or accumulated and used by a particular person, family or corporate body in the course of that creator's activities and functions (ISAD(G), glossary).

SUBGROUPS (INTERNATIONALLY 'SUBFONDS')

These are a subdivision of a fond containing a body of related documents corresponding to administrative subdivisions in the originating agency or organization or, when that is not possible, to geographical, chronological, functional or similar groupings of the material itself. When the creating body has a complex hierarchical structure, each subgroup has as many subordinate subgroups as are necessary to reflect the levels of the hierarchical structure of the primary subordinate administrative unit (ISAD(G), glossary).

CLASSES (INTERNATIONALLY 'SERIES')

These are documents arranged in accordance with a filing system or maintained as a unit because they result from the same accumulation or filing process or the same activity; have a particular form; or because of some other relationship arising out of their creation, receipt or use (ISAD(G), glossary).

ITEMS (INTERNATIONALLY 'FILES')

These are the physical units of handling and retrieval (MAD2, glossary).

PIECES (NOT USED INTERNATIONALLY)

These are basic single, indivisible documents. Levels that are not appropriate to particular cases (since all archives are by definition unique) may be left unused. However, the level definitions remain valid even when left unused. For example, there may be a group that contains no subgroups or classes, only items. In this case there will be a description of the group, followed by linked descriptions of items. The hierarchy of levels must remain linked to the level definitions; the levels are absolute and not relative. Extensive consultation has demonstrated that these levels of arrangement and description are observable in all societies. Fuller explanation of this usage is in Cook (1993).

The purpose of description

Archival descriptions are used for all the purposes of an archives service. Particular purposes demand particular types of description. Therefore descriptions have many forms. An archives service puts these together as systems of finding aids.

Traditionally, archival finding aids are used to establish administrative and/or intellectual control over the archives, these two categories comprising the whole range of activities from physical conservation to exploiting the content.

Archival description standards

At the time of writing, there are four national description standards available in English. These are the *Manual of Archival Description*, 2nd edition (*MAD2*) for Britain; *Archives, Private Papers and Manuscripts* (*APPM*) for the USA; *Rules for Archival Description* (*RAD*) for Canada; and the *Australian Common Practice Manual* (*ACPM*). Other national standards are listed in *Toward International Descriptive Standards for Archives* (1993). The International Council on Archives (ICA), through its Ad Hoc Commission on Archival Description, has produced ISAD(G), referred to above, which was adopted at the International Congress on Archives, Montreal, 1992, and published by the ICA in 1994. Work on further international standards (initially on authority records) is continuing. Technical standards that apply to archives are listed in Walch (1994).

References

Cook, M. (1993) *Information Management and Archival Data*, Library Association Publishing.
Cook, M. and Procter, M. (1990) *Manual of Archival Description*, 2nd edn, Gower.
Rules for Archival Description (1992, in progress) Ottawa: Bureau of Canadian Archivists.
Toward International Descriptive Standards for Archives (1993), papers presented at the ICA Invitational Meeting of Experts on Descriptive Standards, National Archives of Canada (4–7 October 1988), Ottawa: K.G. Saur.
Walch, V.I. (comp.) (1994) *Standards for Archival Description: A Handbook*, Chicago: Society of American Archivists.

Further reading

Australian Common Practice Manual (1992, in progress), Australian Society of Archivists.
Hensen, S. (1989) *Archives, Personal Papers and Manuscripts: A Cataloging Manual for Archive Repositories, Historical Societies and Manuscript Libraries*, Chicago: Society of American Archivists.
International Council on Archives (2001) *ISAD(G) – General International Standard Archive Description*, ICA.

SEE ALSO: catalogues; information professions

MICHAEL COOK

ARCHIVAL LIBRARY

A library whose principal function is to preserve, in perpetuity, the documents that it contains. It may be an entire institution, or part of a larger library or other institution. NATIONAL LIBRARIES and the larger RESEARCH LIBRARIES usually undertake some function of this kind.

SEE ALSO: libraries

ARCHIVES

Archives is a plural noun with a variety of meanings. It refers to both a type of repository and the written materials held there. Technically, these are the records of enduring value of an institution, but the phrase has also come to embrace manuscript collections of personal papers.

The term was originally synonymous with LIBRARIES and a copying tradition that literally defined the birth of history. Scribal enterprises helped codify the words of the gods and served as civic monuments, as well as the more mundane functions of recording business transactions, entertainment and government enactments. The printing press eventually intervened to alter this comfortable model. Archives strove to continue the traditional roles, while libraries became separate institutions for published materials.

Our present conceptions are largely based on a nineteenth-century Western model. The expanding bureaucracy of the modern nation-state combined with scholarly interests and cultural motives to redefine an often secretive institution into a public institution. The founding of the French Archives Nationales and later of the

PUBLIC RECORD OFFICE in the UK helped set off a minor fad for NATIONAL ARCHIVES.

In the 1830s, the French went on to form the first modern archival training centre at the Ecole des Chartes. This school drew on the scholarship of PALAEOGRAPHY and diplomatics with a focus on authenticating documents. In the 1840s, the French codified one of the two key archival principles, *Respect des Fonds*. The Prussians followed to take the lead with Added Order. They formalized the French doctrine into their *Provenienzprinzip*. The ARCHIVIST would maintain records physically together and retrieve them by their PROVENANCE or agency of creation. In the 1880s, they produced the second and allied postulate of *Registraturprinzip*, or Original Order. Records would maintain their arrangement. Instead of library CLASSIFICATION and re-slotting into rigid TAXONOMIES, archivists had adopted relativistic and Aristotelian approaches. These techniques were widely disseminated through the 1898 Dutch manual of Muller, Feith and Fruin, and the British Sir Hilary JENKINSON's 1937 volume.

The USA had developed a hagiographic interest in manuscripts and signatures in the early nineteenth century. However, US interests in modern collecting were delayed until the early twentieth century. Southerners looked to state archives for celebratory aspects to a culture lost during the Civil War. The LIBRARY OF CONGRESS (LC) played a significant role in both manuscripts and modern archives. In the early twentieth century, its Manuscripts Division contributed the Register – a work diary or booklet with narrative history/summary and inventory that became the basis for archival description. LC's immediate post-World War Two efforts looked to holdings information through the *National Union Catalog of Manuscript Collections* (NUCMC).

Members of a budding historical profession were also lobbying for access and the PRESERVATION of public records. Their influences culminated in 1934 with the founding of the National Archives and Records Administration (NARA) and the subsequent opening of the NATIONAL ARCHIVES OF THE UNITED STATES. The new agency would borrow from LC and adapt Registers into institutional Inventories. NARA eschewed diplomatics, but partially adopted European practices to the US scene. The synthesis was a pragmatic school of archival management, which was best reflected in the later publications of T.R. SCHELLENBERG.

NARA also quickly begat the Society of American Archivists (SAA), the major professional association. During the Second World War, the agency also gave birth to the practice of RECORDS MANAGEMENT, a field that remained with archives until a political split in the 1970s. NARA's National Historical Publications and Records Commission pushed documentary editing and took the lead in identifying the location of archives. With the assistance of the State Department and UNESCO's RAMP projects, such US approaches spread around the world after 1945.

In the 1960s and especially the 1970s, the number of institutions expanded and US archivists professionalized. NARA set SAA free, and US archivists sought an identity separate from historians. Registers and inventories spread as a quasi-standard, generically encompassed by the term FINDING AID. Governmental largesse spread with the National Endowment for the Humanities and other funders. The US Bicentennial accelerated interest in the documentary heritage. Businesses and universities embraced the trend. Formerly sacrosanct temples to the establishment also added new hues. Special collections on minorities, trade unions and other non-elites rose to prominence. Significantly, too, Americans launched graduate education courses. Generally taught by practitioners, classes were housed first in history departments. Library schools entered the picture in an uneasy alliance, but their MLS degrees would rise to become the major professional credential.

The US field reached a level of maturity in the 1980s. Multicourse archival education concentrations with regular faculty lines appeared. Diplomatics entered with an Italian slant by way of Canadian education programmes. An Academy of Certified Archivists appeared to attempt to define professional criteria. NARA, which had been reduced to a subsidiary federal agency, gained its freedom from the Office of Management and Budget. Automation also reared its head. With some trepidation, archivists adopted a new MARC-AMC (Archival and Manuscripts Control) format and parallel *APPM Guidelines* to catalogue finding aids into library bibliographic systems. Also, the PC-revolution helped set the stage for another potential redefinition of the field in the era of the Web.

During the 1990s, the Web stimulated a wave of standardization and globalization. The Bureau of Canadian Archivists issued its *Rules for Archival Description*. The International Council on Archives produced the general *ISAD(G)* guidelines and *ISAAD* set for authority records. American archivists turned to SGML for their finding aids. Despite mislabelling as a Web technology, the resulting *Encoded Archival Description (EAD)* provided significant descriptive standards to unify an idiosyncratic field.

The information highway is also eliminating the age-old problem of identifying repositories. Researchers are gaining online access to finding aids. Most importantly, archival materials are being democratized and made widely available through digitization. The Web's HTML and XML protocols reduce the age-old problem of locating archives, as well as potentially solving migration problems for electronic records and other PRESERVATION dilemmas.

Yet, significant research on information storage and retrieval techniques for archives, the use of artificial intelligence and advanced SEARCH ENGINES, and even the most basic analysis of users is only beginning. Additional forms of description are needed to capture interactive media. Outside forces must also be recognized. The term has expanded into the verb 'to archive' as a synonym for long-term computer storage. In addition, scholars and citizens are creating their own digital archives independent of the experts, and 'heritage tourism' is rising on the economic scene.

In sum, archives are undergoing another redefinition. Their potential for information management, education and as cultural icons has stood the test of time. Archives will continue during the era of the information highway as they have since the dawn of history.

Further reading

The key sources will now be found on the Web:
ACA (http://certifiedarchivists.org).
EAD (www.loc.gov/ead).
ICA (ISAD(G) and ISAAD) (www.ica.org).
NARA (www.nara.gov).
NUCMC (http://lcweb.loc.gov/coll/nucmc).
SAA (www.archivists.org).
UNESCO Portal (www.unesco.org/webworld/portal_archives).

SEE ALSO: archival description; information professions; library education

FRED STIELOW

ARCHIVIST

Information professional whose role is to establish and maintain control, both physical and intellectual, of records that are judged to have permanent value.

Professional archivists are first really identifiable in the nineteenth century, when great accumulations of ARCHIVES arising from government and other administrative activity began to be seen as requiring specialist care. The first two schools to train archivists, the École Nationale des Chartes, in Paris, and the Bayerische Archivschüle, München, were both founded in 1821. Education for archive administration revolved around an appreciation of the organic nature of the archive accumulation, and concentrated on the selection of records for retention as archives, their PRESERVATION and the preparation of findings aids. Expertise in the historical sciences (such as PALAEOGRAPHY) has, until comparatively recently, been very strongly stressed, but the modern archivist is much more a manager of collections, personnel and budget than the old scholarly image, and shares the librarian's concern to make collections available and to encourage their effective use. Membership of the Society of American Archivists in the USA, the Society of Archivists in the UK or equivalents in other countries is the basic test of membership of the profession.

Further reading

Dollar, C.M. (1993) 'Archivists and records managers in the information age', *Archivaria* 36: 37–51.

SEE ALSO: information professions

ART LIBRARIES

Libraries whose primary function is to identify, acquire, organize and provide access to information relating to all aspects of the visual arts.

Context

Traditionally art libraries have been seen to stand apart from all other types of library. There are three main reasons for this: first, the huge scope and heterogeneous nature of the fields encompassed in the broad term 'visual arts' (taken here to include not only traditional fine art and art history but also design, architecture, crafts and other related topics); second, the diverse and frequently unpredictable needs of art library users; and, third, the bewildering physical variety of the materials handled. (In his much-quoted article on the subject, Fawcett (1975) expands on these differences at some length.) For these three reasons, which are considered in greater detail below, the development of art libraries has historically been independent of the mainstream and art librarians have always regarded their professional role as fundamentally different from that of their colleagues in other areas of librarianship.

Historical development

Although it could be argued that art libraries have existed for well over 300 years, the term as we currently understand it was probably first applied to the San Francisco Art Association's library, founded in 1871 and followed by a number of similar institutions throughout the USA in the latter part of the nineteenth century. By 1908 Jane Wright, Librarian of Cincinnati Art Museum, was making an impassioned plea for art libraries to be taken as seriously as public libraries (Wright 1908). Art libraries have continued to flourish ever since, especially throughout Western Europe and North America, and the period since the mid-1960s has seen particularly vigorous growth. It is no coincidence that the British and Irish Art Libraries Society (now ARLIS/UK & Ireland) was founded in the United Kingdom in 1969 and its North American equivalent, the Art Libraries Society of North America (ARLIS/NA) in 1972. As with many other types of library, development elsewhere in the world has been far more patchy.

Types of art library

The term 'art libraries' here includes small museum or art college libraries, special or professional practice libraries, the art sections of public libraries or larger academic libraries and the largest autonomous libraries that, although nominally attached to larger institutions, are of national or international significance in their own right (for example, the National Art Library of the UK based at the Victoria and Albert Museum in London).

Professional guidelines

Although there are inevitably wide variations in practice, guidelines covering stock, staffing and the general management of art libraries, published by both ARLIS/UK & Ireland (1990) and ARLIS/NA (1983), have in the past helped art librarians devise their own dedicated standards as appropriate. Such guidelines (now badly in need of updating) emphasize above all the need to respond sensitively to the widely varying needs of users, who range from art historians or curators, professional architects and designers to practising artists, art students and members of the general public. For many of these users the foremost need is for visual references rather than written information, and it is for this reason above all that art librarians develop and exploit their collections in very different ways from their colleagues in other areas of librarianship.

Art information resources

As well as the books and periodicals that can be expected to form the bulk of all paper-based library collections, art libraries may, in response to the needs of their readers, stock a wide range of other printed material: exhibition catalogues, printed EPHEMERA, artists' books, PATENTS and registered designs, and other more or less GREY LITERATURE. The BIBLIOGRAPHIC CONTROL of such items has always caused particular difficulties, many of which remain broadly unsolved today. In addition art libraries frequently stock a large variety of AUDIOVISUAL MATERIALS, such as illustrations, photographs and slides, microforms, films and video-recordings, all of which are especially valuable for the provision of visual references so often sought. The acquisition, storage and exploitation of material of this nature is inevitably problematic and requires specialist knowledge and experience. Art libraries can also serve as ARCHIVES for unique items such as plans, drawings, artwork and trade samples, all of which demand special treatment.

The ICT context

Meanwhile the rapid technological advances of recent decades have been of particular benefit to art libraries. Much relevant material has been available in digital format for the past several years and the Internet is now an essential tool in most areas of the visual arts, as the electronic transmission of high-quality images becomes ever easier. The potential for innovation in this field remains tremendous.

Professional co-operation

The historical isolation of art librarianship from the mainstream of the profession has encouraged energetic co-operation among art librarians, both formal and informal, at local, national and international levels. The energetic professional societies that flourish all over the world bear witness to this generous spirit of practical collaboration. ARLIS/UK & Ireland and ARLIS/NA continue to be extremely active in the areas of bibliographical control and there is an ever growing number of similar societies elsewhere in the world. The International Federation of Library Associations (IFLA) Art Libraries Section provides an international focus, and its traditional meeting immediately prior to the annual IFLA Conference ensures that as far as possible art librarians speak with a common voice to their professional colleagues and governments, as well as to the world at large.

References

Fawcett, T. (1975) 'The complete art librarian', *ARLIS Newsletter* (UK) 22 (March): 7–9.
Guidelines for Art and Design Libraries: Stock, Planning, Staffing and Autonomy (1990), ARLIS/UK & Eire.
Standards for Art Libraries and Fine Arts Slide Collections (1983), occasional papers no. 2, Art Libraries Society of North America.
Wright, J. (1908) 'Plea of the art librarian', *Public Libraries* (November): 348–9.

Further reading

The 'Annual bibliography of art librarianship' published in the *Art Libraries Journal* provides a comprehensive record of recent writings on relevant topics from all over the world.

SEE ALSO: image retrieval; picture libraries

DEBORAH SHORLEY

ARTEFACT

Anything made by human invention and workmanship: an artificial product. They are collected in museums, and occasionally occur in LIBRARIES and ARCHIVES, because of their KNOWLEDGE content. Museum objects include artefacts in addition to naturally occurring items; all books and documents, including multimedia products, are also artefacts. The value of an artefact is generally for its information content, although some are also of aesthetic or cultural interest.

SEE ALSO: museology; museum; museum documentation

ARTIFICIAL INTELLIGENCE

Artificial Intelligence (AI) is:

> concerned with the study and creation of computer systems that exhibit some form of intelligence: systems that learn new concepts and tasks, systems that can reason and draw useful conclusions about the world around us, systems that can understand a natural language or perceive and comprehend a visual scene, and systems that perform other types of feats that require human types of intelligence.
>
> (Patterson 1990)

AI, as a separate computer discipline, started in the 1950s, although its roots, the study of intelligence and COGNITIVE SCIENCE go back much further. During the 1950s it was realized that electronic computers could have a much wider application: they could handle symbols and logic, and not just numbers. Much of the impetus for the early AI work stemmed from the Dartmouth Conference of 1959 in the USA. Some progress was made in the UK but the Lighthill Report of 1969, which was sceptical about the value of AI, effectively stopped all government funding for several years (Barrett and Beerel 1988). The early work concentrated on formal reasoning methods and on general problem solving. However, the thrust of AI research changed direction in the mid-1970s when it was realized that systems needed to be made much more specific and that knowledge was a more important issue than problem solving. Another milestone in AI research was reached in the early 1980s when the Japanese announced their plans to build a so-called 'fifth-generation' computer having natural-language capabilities, and processing and reasoning capabilities far greater than any developed so far. This spurred researchers and funders in both the USA and Europe into action. Since then AI has grown rapidly and today encompasses many different areas of research, including knowledge-based systems – of which EXPERT SYSTEMS are the most well known – natural language understanding, machine vision, computer games, robotics, automatic programming and computer-assisted learning. It is also an interdisciplinary field involving not only COMPUTER SCIENCE, but also mathematics, linguistics, philosophy, psychology and cognitive science.

The application of AI techniques to information and library work peaked in the late 1980s and early 1990s, mostly in the expert-systems field. Success has not yet been achieved, because much of the work either has been theoretical or has resulted in the production of a prototype; very few commercial systems have been developed. Investigations have covered a broad spectrum of topics including ONLINE information retrieval, reference work, cataloguing, CLASSIFICATION, INDEXING, abstracting (see ABSTRACTING AND INDEXING SERVICES) and document selection.

Online information retrieval is probably the most researched topic. Many efforts have been made to simplify the process of searching and different approaches have been adopted (see Haverkamp and Gauch 1998). Some have concentrated on improving the interface design, while others have prototyped intelligent information retrieval (IIR) systems to explore new and better ways to store, describe and retrieve documents. Several researchers have also developed prototype systems to aid one or more 'intelligent' – rather than just procedural – aspects of the searching process such as identifying DATABASES, constructing search statements, modifying SEARCH statements and interpreting results.

Reference services were developed in the late nineteenth century to help readers find relevant and pertinent information sources. As the number of information sources has grown so too has the demand for reference services. Expert systems are seen by some researchers as a possible way of meeting this extra demand and freeing staff for other duties. Preliminary work has been done on identifying the rules of reference, modelling the reference process, constructing user models and identifying the types of knowledge that expert systems need to contain. Some prototypes have also been built to give advice in specific areas such as horticulture, agriculture, patents and US government sources.

The costly and time-consuming process of cataloguing material has been identified as one area that could benefit from the use of knowledge-based systems techniques. Three directions of research have emerged: the development of advisory systems that give users guidance on which rule to use, prototype systems that go beyond this and create records, and attempts to automate the whole process using optical character recognition.

Some progress has been made in the field of INDEXING. A number of indexing prototypes have been built that attempt to analyse the subject content of documents and suggest associated subject relationships. A few commercial systems are also now appearing. Reuters, for example, use AI techniques to index news stories automatically. Some progress has also been made in developing systems that help to classify documents.

Producing an ABSTRACT can be extremely time consuming. Not surprisingly, attempts have been made to apply AI techniques to aid the process. Much of the research has concentrated on the practicalities of extracting and aggregating sentences and evaluating different techniques. Although much still remains to be achieved, advances in the fields of linguistics and natural language make automatic abstracting an interesting and promising research area.

Research papers coupling document selection with AI appeared in the 1990s. A few prototype systems have been built to aid journal selection and monographs. Further progress in this field, however, will probably be dependent on gaining direct access to publishers' electronic catalogues.

Although much progress has been made already, the AI library field is still very young. No doubt future library users will be able to discuss their information needs with intelligent interfaces using natural language and be presented on demand with relevant references based on some kind of user modelling, abstracts and a synthesis of the contents of selected documents. Libraries will become knowledge warehouses accessed via networks; even the physical browsing of shelves may also be a thing of the past as users opt to use intelligent virtual reality programmes. AI is an exciting discipline and one that will help steer the INFORMATION SOCIETY of the future.

References

Barrett, M.L. and Beerel, A.C. (1988) *Expert Systems in Business: A Practical Approach*, Chichester: Ellis Horwood.

Haverkamp, D.S. and Gauch, S. (1998) 'Intelligent information agents: Review and challenges for distributed information sources', *Journal of the American Society for Information Science* 49(4): 304–11.

Patterson, D.W. (1990) *Introduction to Artificial Intelligence and Expert Systems*, London: Prentice Hall.

Further reading

Artificial Intelligence. (http://library.thinkquest.org/2705/ Accessed 30 May 2002.)

Morris, A. (1992) *The Application of Expert Systems in Libraries and Information Centres*, London: Bowker Saur.

Weckert, J. and McDonald, C. (eds) (1992) 'A special issue on artificial intelligence, knowledge systems, and the future library', *Library Hi Tech* 10: 37–8.

Zainab, A.N. and De Silva, S.M. (1998) 'Expert systems in library and information services: Publication trends, authorship patterns and expressiveness of published titles', *Journal of Information Science* 24(5): 313–36.

SEE ALSO: informatics; information management; organization of knowledge

ANNE MORRIS

ASSOCIATION FOR LIBRARY AND INFORMATION SCIENCE EDUCATION

The Association for Library and Information Science Education (ALISE) is a not-for-profit corporation, organized and existing under the laws of the State of Delaware, USA, with a mission to promote excellence in research, teaching and service for library and INFORMATION SCIENCE EDUCATION. An elected Board of Directors governs the organization and consists of President, Past President, Vice-President/President-Elect, Secretary-Treasurer and three Directors. An Executive Director is *ex officio* to the Board. Programmatically, ALISE operates through standing committees and special interest groups (SIGs) that represent a fluid range of interests, such as research, curriculum, teaching methods, continuing education, gender issues, library history, preservation education, youth services, doctoral students and international library education. ALISE publishes the *Journal of Education for Library and Information Science* (*JELIS*), a refereed research-based quarterly journal.

History

The first recorded gathering of representatives from library schools in North America took place in 1907 at the AMERICAN LIBRARY ASSOCIATION conference. This group organized into a Round Table of Library Schools and held regular meetings until 1915, when twenty-five interested individuals representing nine schools met and voted to form a more permanent organization: the Association of American Library Schools (AALS). The Association operated under this name until 1983, when the name was officially changed to the Association for Library and Information Science Education (ALISE).

The Association's primary purpose was fellowship and the discussion of issues facing professional education, such as the recruitment of faculty, curriculum and instruction, internal matters of professional education and the role of professional education in higher education and in the university.

Goals

These areas of interest are represented in the five goals of the Association that were officially adopted in 1989:

1 To articulate the scope of the field and relationship to other fields and the requirements thereof.

2 To formulate and promote positions on matters related to library and information science education.

3 To promote the local, national and international development of library and information science education.

4 To foster the strength of institutional members within the university and the profession.

5 To support the professional growth of its individual members.

Policies

Policies and position statements of the Association are organized into three categories and represent significant professional consensus on major topic areas:

EDUCATIONAL MATTERS

• The role of graduate programmes in library and information science education.

- The accreditation process.
- Guidelines for student field experiences.
- Standards for the development of sixth-year programmes.
- The PhD in library and information science.
- The role of ALISE and its member schools in continuing education.
- Continuing library and information science education.

GOVERNMENTAL RELATIONS

- Elements of a federal legislative programme for LIS education in the USA.
- Access to government information.
- Higher Education Act, Title II-B.

ORGANIZATIONAL MATTERS

- Practitioner/ALISE membership education-related communication.
- Affiliation between ALISE and other groups.
- Endorsement of joint sponsorship of projects and activities.
- Distribution of questionnaires or other materials to ALISE members.
- External sponsorships.

Membership

ALISE is a dynamic organization and the membership categories of the Association have changed over time: current categories include personal members (open to anyone having an interest in the goals of the Association); institutional members (schools in the USA or Canada that offer a graduate degree in library and information science, or cognate field, which is accredited by the appropriate authority); and international affiliated members (schools outside the USA and Canada that offer a programme to educate students for practice at the professional level, as defined by the country in which the school is located).

Conference

ALISE presents an annual conference each year, structured around a theme. Each ALISE Vice-President/President-Elect establishes priorities (which must be approved by the Board) for his/her year as President and also recommends a theme for the conference in that year. In recent times conferences have included such themes as intellectual diversity, international interdependence, relationship of schools to parent institutions, politics of higher education and matters of changing curriculum and research. The conference is also a centre for the recruiting and interviewing of prospective faculty members.

Awards

A variety of awards are presented at the annual conference, following a competitive process. These awards are presented for research (the ALISE Research Award for proposed research, the Research Paper Competition, the Hannigan Research Award and the Doctoral Student Dissertation Competition) and for individual achievement (Professional Contribution to Library and Information Science Education, the Award for Teaching Excellence and the ALISE Service Award).

Liaison

In order for ALISE to serve as a means of communication between the ALISE community of educators and individual practitioners and organized practitioner groups, formal liaison relationships are maintained with the following groups: American Association of School Libraries, AMERICAN LIBRARY ASSOCIATION, ALA Accreditation Study, ALA International Relations Committee, ALA LAMA Statistics Section, ALA Committee on Education, AMERICAN SOCIETY FOR INFORMATION SCIENCE AND TECHNOLOGY, Association of Records Managers and Administrators, Coalition on Government Information, Documentation Abstracts, Inc., International Federation of Library Associations (IFLA) (including the Sections on Education and Training, Statistics, and Information Technology, as well as the US Members Committee), Network Advisory Committee, Office of Educational Research and Improvement, Society of American Archivists, and Special Libraries Association.

Further reading

Davis, D. (1991) 'Seventy-five years of education for the profession: Reflections on the early years', *Journal of Library and Information Science Education* 32 (fall–winter): 157–77.

Sineath, T. (1991) 'Trends in library and information science education: An overview', in *Proceedings of the International Conference on New Frontiers in Library and Information Services*, Taipei, p. 799.

SEE ALSO: accreditation of LIS schools; continuing professional development; library education

DARLENE E. WEINGAND

AUDIOVISUAL MATERIALS

A generic term to describe information CONTENT held in storage and transmission media, and formats that use images and sound rather than, or sometimes in addition to, textual matter. This includes: audio CD, records and tapes; photographs, slides, film and video; and formats that combine two or more of these such as tape–slide displays. Many of the formats are now completely outmoded, but some libraries, especially RESEARCH LIBRARIES and academic libraries, still retain them, and must therefore keep equipment on which they can be played in working order if at all possible. The term, however, is still quite useful, and has not been entirely displaced by MULTIMEDIA, which is often – wrongly – used as a fashionable synonym for it.

AUTHOR

The person, persons or corporate body responsible for the writing or compilation of a book or other work, usually in textual form. The author is usually distinguished from an editor, translator, copier, etc., although these are sometimes treated as authors for purposes of cataloguing. In a wider sense the concept of authorship can include artists, composers of musical works or photographers who are creators of original CONTENT. An author is legally responsible for a work, and also acquires the COPYRIGHT in it.

The idea of authorship rests in turn on the concept of originality, whereby it is maintained that individuals may produce written or unwritten contributions to human knowledge or ideas, whether through scientific investigation, scholarship or philosophical exploration, which are uniquely their own. Originality is the root of an individual's claim to the role of author. It is the underpinning for the legal concept of INTELLECTUAL PROPERTY, which in turn is central to the operation of the KNOWLEDGE INDUSTRIES, CULTURAL INDUSTRIES and LIBRARIANSHIP and INFORMATION SCIENCE.

The medieval view of the writer was as a collector, continuator, interpreter and contributor. Writers paid tribute to the authority of earlier texts, did not make claims to originality and frequently did not attach their names to the texts of which the modern interpretation would regard them as author. Subsequently it has come to be widely accepted that individuals may have unique inspirations, can make totally fresh discoveries and should therefore be recognized as creators, and, indeed, be rewarded accordingly. The reality of claims to be original is much more complex than this might suggest.

Ideas are potentially original in the sense that they are new and unique. However, it is almost impossibly hard to identify ideas that meet this criterion. It is much more common for ideas to be original in the sense that they have been arrived at independently by an individual but are not entirely new or unique to that individual. In recognition of the near impossibility of identifying totally original ideas to protect, intellectual property law in the English legal tradition awards copyright to works on the grounds, not that they are original, but merely that they are not copied. Thus it only excludes works that are based on plagiarism, and protects in turn against a range of unauthorized copying including piracy. The continental tradition of law takes a more exalted view of authors as creators and concentrates on their moral rights first and foremost.

Further reading

Foucault, M. (1979) 'What is an author?', in J.V. Hariri, *Textual Strategies: Perspectives in Post-structuralist Criticism*, Cornell University Press.

SEE ALSO: copyright; intellectual property; publishing

AUTHORING SYSTEMS

Used both in optical media, as a general term for the hardware and software needed for authoring interactive compact discs, and in computer-aided learning, to indicate a computer system capable of executing an authoring language.

SEE ALSO: computer-assisted learning in library and information science

AUTHORITY FILE

1   A list of all personal and corporate names, titles of anonymous works and the headings

for series cards that are used as headings in a catalogue. The entries are made when a heading is first established. It gives subject cataloguers a record of the form that has already been used in the catalogue.

2   A list in classified order of classification symbols or numbers that have been allocated to books, with their corresponding index entries.

SEE ALSO: catalogues

B

BANDWIDTH

The capacity of a cable or wireless network to carry data, measured in bits per second (bps), often described as narrow or broad. BROADBAND has the highest capacity.

BARCODE

A visual code representing alpha-numeric symbols arranged in a series of vertical parallel lines or bars, representing data. It is read by a barcode scanner as digital signals for entry in a computer database. It is used in many forms of automated library circulation systems, as well as in many other contexts such as supermarket (and indeed bookshop) checkouts.

SEE ALSO: information and communication technology

BAREFOOT LIBRARIAN

A library or information worker providing informal, community-based services, usually in rural areas. A term given prominence, almost incidentally, by Wijasuriya (1975) in relation to Southeast Asia, and used by him to signify professionals with a rural rather than urban orientation. It has since been used to refer to non-professional or paraprofessional helpers recruited in the community to staff READING ROOMS or rudimentary libraries and information centres. This is exemplified by the practice of Tanzania Library Service, which hires local residents with a minimum of primary-level education, gives them short training courses and pays them a monthly honorarium. The term echoes similar ones referring to other providers of services in rural areas, such as the Chinese barefoot doctors (Cheng 1988).

References

Cheng, T.O. (1988) 'Barefoot doctors', *Journal of the American Medical Association* 259: 3,561.
Wijasuriya, D.E.K. (1975) *The Barefoot Librarian*, Bingley.

Further reading

Yocklunn, J. (1988) 'The barefoot librarian: A model for developing countries?', *Libraries Alone* 1: 13–20.

SEE ALSO: information professions

BERNE CONVENTION

The International Convention for the Protection of Literary and Artistic Works, known as the 'Berne Convention', was adopted by an international conference held in Berne, Switzerland, in 1886. It was designed to protect in as uniform a manner as possible the rights of authors in their literary and artistic works. It was revised in Paris in 1896, and again in 1908, 1928, 1948, 1967 and 1971. The USA, although bound by the Universal Copyright Convention since 1955, joined only in 1988. The protection of the Berne Convention applies to authors who are nationals of any of the countries of the Union established by the Convention, for their works, whether published or not, and also to authors who are nationals of non-Union countries for their works first published in one of those countries. The duration of the protection provided by the Berne Convention is determined by national law. Works published in any signatory state are protected in all other signatory states on the same terms as books first published there. Historically, this has typically been for the author's lifetime and fifty years thereafter, but in the European Union it is now seventy years.

SEE ALSO: copyright

BERNERS-LEE, TIM (1955–)

The inventor of the WORLD WIDE WEB and its various component parts and more recently developer of the SEMANTIC WEB.

Born and brought up in London, he took his degree in Physics from Queen's College, Oxford, in 1976. During six months in 1980 as consultant software engineer at CERN, the European Particle Physics Laboratory in Geneva, Switzerland, he developed a program that he called Enquire for his own use. This provided the conceptual basis for his proposal, in 1989, of a global HYPERTEXT project using the INTERNET, to be known as the World Wide Web. For this he developed the mark-up language HTML (see MARK-UP LANGUAGES), the addressing system of UNIFORM RESOURCE LOCATORS (URLs), the PROTOCOL HTTP and the first WEB BROWSER (Mosaic). The Web was introduced on the Internet in 1991 and has provided the means by which it has become a medium accessible to all, rather than a specialized tool for an elite. In 1994 he joined the Massachusetts Institute of Technology, from where he directs the World Wide Web Consortium, which seeks to move the Web forward through the development of standards. His achievements have been recognized by the award of many honours, including Fellowship of the Royal Society (2001).

Further reading

Berners-Lee, T. (1999) *Weaving the Web*. San Francisco: Harper.
World Wide Web Consortium (www.w3.org/).

BESTERMAN, THEODORE (1904–76)

Bibliographer and Voltaire scholar.

Born in Poland and, after his family had moved to London, educated mostly at home. During the 1930s he worked for ASLIB, estab-lishing the *Journal of Documentation* in 1945 and planning the *British Union Catalogue of Periodicals* (BUCOP). From 1945 to 1949 he was head of the department for the international exchange of information at UNESCO. He later became a prolific Voltaire scholar, first at the Institut et Musée Voltaire, created in Voltaire's own house, Les Délices, in Geneva, and officially opened in 1954. He later moved his Voltaire publishing activities to England and established in Oxford the Voltaire Foundation, which he bequeathed to the University.

His interest in the discipline of bibliography followed his own compilation of published author bibliographies, and he published *The Beginnings of Systematic Bibliography* in 1935. His *magnum opus*, *World Bibliography of Bibliographies and of Bibliographical Catalogues, Calendars, Abstracts, Digests, Indexes and the Like*, was first published in 1939–40, revised in 1955–6 and revised again in four volumes with a separate volume of index in 1965–6. Compilation of this immense work set high standards of scholarly dedication, and involved the personal handling of more than 80,000 volumes in the Library of Congress and the British Museum Library. His enormous contribution to enumerative bibliography is recognized by the LIBRARY ASSOCIATION through its Besterman Medal, awarded annually for an outstanding bibliography or guide to the literature published in the United Kingdom during the year. There is an annual Besterman Lecture at Oxford University, usually delivered by a distinguished scholar with interests in eighteenth-century French bibliography.

Further reading

Cordasco, F. (ed.) (1992) *Theodore Besterman, Bibliographer and Editor*, Scarecrow Press.

SEE ALSO: bibliography

BIBLIOGRAPHIC CLASSIFICATION

Bibliographic classification may be defined as a set of organizing principles by which information is arranged, usually according to its subject matter. The subject divisions identified are generally assigned a coded notation to represent the subject content. Individual items are placed within the appropriate subject area, either as an arrangement of physical items or they are described in a catalogue or database.

Theoretical considerations

Bibliographical classification groups 'things' together by seeking out similarities or likenesses within them. These 'things' may be either concrete or abstract and may be discerned either intuitively or by conscious reasoning. Classification also shows the relationships between 'things'; this exposition of the subject content usually leads to a formal structure such as a bibliographic classification scheme (Buchanan 1979). Originally, bibliographic classification was closely linked to scientific and philosophical classification – at a time when it was possible to equate knowledge with the printed product in which it appeared. There is a constant tension in bibliographic classification between the one-dimensional linear order that is necessary for useful shelf arrangement and the more complex, multidimensional set of relationships that exist between concepts in real life. Thus, a truly effective bibliographic classification scheme may need to reveal links and relationships that are impossible to show when books are placed on shelves.

Components of a bibliographic classification scheme

The central part of any scheme is the classification schedules. This consists of the systematic arrangement of the subject concepts according to the fundamentals of the particular scheme. Thus, in the DEWEY DECIMAL CLASSIFICATION (DDC), where there are ten main classes, the schedules are a detailed listing of elements within these classes. There is normally an alphabetical arrangement or index that acts as a verbal entry mechanism to the schedules showing the links and relationships between terms and concepts. The novel device that characterizes bibliographic classification is the notation (coding system) devised to represent the subject concepts. A code or notation (usually called the classification number or classmark) is used as a shorthand version of the subject concept. It may be written on the book to facilitate retrieval from the shelves or it may act as an access point in a catalogue or database. The notation may consist of numbers, letters, symbols or a combination of these. In DDC, the notation is almost totally

numerical, e.g. the classification number for a book about 'tennis' is 796.342 (where the decimal point acts simply as a separator between three digits with no mathematical value).

Bibliographic classification – approaches and schemes

Most major library classification schemes have their origins in the nineteenth century and reflect either (1) an ideology that thought it possible to represent the whole world of knowledge or (2) a pragmatic attempt to group similar documents together on the shelves of a major library. The DDC and the LIBRARY OF CONGRESS CLASSIFICATION Scheme (LCC) have elements of both of these considerations and both are widely used throughout the world. The 'world of knowledge' is divided into suitable classes, and new subject concepts may be added to each class when necessary. These schemes are referred to as enumerative schemes. Seriously dated in their fundamental conceptual approach to knowledge, they survive because libraries can still make them work effectively for shelf arrangement. The UNIVERSAL DECIMAL CLASSIFICATION (UDC) is a development of DDC that allows for more complex relationships to be shown with less enumeration.

It was, however, with the development of FACETED CLASSIFICATION by S.R. Ranganathan (1892–1972) that an innovative approach appeared. In faceted classification, subjects are analysed into 'their component elemental classes' rather than by starting with the whole world of knowledge and dividing it up into useful segments. Thus, a concept is classified by assembling its component elemental classes, e.g. the activity of building may be composed of the facets 'thing built', 'building materials', 'method of building', etc. This leads to a more rigorous, as well as a more economical, approach to devising schemes. Faceted schemes work best in small-scale focused subject areas. In the UK, the Classification Research Group was responsible for much research and development in this area in the latter half of the twentieth century.

Bibliographic classification as a tool in information retrieval

With the advent of ONLINE public access catalogues (OPACS), cataloguing, indexing and classification data have increasingly been bought in by libraries from specialized cataloguing agencies and as a result a diminishing amount of in-house classification now takes place. This has resulted in consolidation around the larger enumerative classifications (DDC and LCC) as the data for these schemes predominates in automated records.

Recent experience has shown that very few online catalogue searches involve classification, as the notational code is now too great a barrier to users. The main function of bibliographic classification is, therefore, the systematic arrangement of physical objects (often referred to as 'marking and parking'). In public libraries, there is also some disenchantment with the usefulness of classification. In many cases, popular material, e.g. fiction, cookery, war, gardening, etc., may be arranged in loose categories similar to arrangements in bookshops, using the approach usually described as CATEGORIZATION, rather than a formal classification scheme On a more positive note, classification has recently found a significant role in the organization of digital information on the Internet and in knowledge-based systems. Increasing dissatisfaction and frustration with excessive recall and lack of precision from SEARCH ENGINES has led to a renewed interest in a structured approach to information organization and retrieval. Hierarchical classification schemes, in particular DDC, have been used as the framework for organizing selected resources in directory indexes and on PORTALS AND GATEWAYS, as a scheme such as DDC provides a ready-made and tested information structure. Bibliographic classification systems (as well as the use of a THESAURUS) are also currently in vogue as the subject foundation for TAXONOMIES in KNOWLEDGE MANAGEMENT systems.

References

Buchanan, Brian (1979) *Theory of Classification*, Bingley.

Further reading

Chan, L.M. (1994) *Cataloging and Classification: An Introduction*, 2nd edn, New York: McGraw Hill.
Meadows, J. (2001) *Understanding Information*, Saur.
Taylor, A. (1999) *The Organization of Information*, Libraries Unlimited.

SEE ALSO: Dewey, Melvil; indexing; information retrieval; organization of knowledge; Otlet, Paul-Marie-Ghislain

ANNE O'BRIEN

BIBLIOGRAPHIC CONTROL

The means and methods by which publications are listed on a systematic basis in bibliographic files. In this context, 'publications' include not only printed books and serials (i.e. journals, magazines, annuals, newspapers, etc.) but also works in other media, e.g. microforms, computer files, audio cassettes, OPTICAL DISKS.

Bibliographic control covers a range of library and information disciplines. These may include the following: BIBLIOGRAPHIC DESCRIPTION, subject access by CLASSIFICATION schemes, subject access by controlled vocabulary subject headings, name authority control and coding for MACHINE-READABLE CATALOGUING (MARC). A variety of systems and schemes have been developed for these disciplines. Those in common use in the English-speaking world include the following.

Description

The provisions of the International Standard Bibliographic Descriptions (ISBDs), developed and published by the INTERNATIONAL FEDERATION OF LIBRARY ASSOCIATIONS (IFLA) and covering most media and bibliographic conditions, have been incorporated in the ANGLO-AMERICAN CATALOGUING RULES (AACR 1988). A description will record the physical and identifying characteristics of a publication, including title, imprint and pagination/size/binding information.

Classification schemes

Schemes in common use include the DEWEY DECIMAL CLASSIFICATION, the LIBRARY OF CONGRESS CLASSIFICATION and the UNIVERSAL DECIMAL CLASSIFICATION. Characteristically, alphabetical and/or numeric notation, which may reflect subject hierarchies, is used to represent the overall subject of a publication both for linear arrangement in published bibliographies and catalogues, and for library shelf arrangement.

Subject headings

These may or may not complement the use of a classification scheme in a bibliographic file. In order to maintain consistency, subject headings employ a controlled vocabulary with references to broader and narrower terms within a subject hierarchy and from unused or non-preferred terminology. Lists of subject headings may also be referred to as thesauri. Those lists in common use include *Library of Congress Subject Headings* (often used in research libraries) and *Sears List of Subject Headings* (mostly used in smaller libraries). In the UK, the BRITISH LIBRARY has used, successively, its PRECIS and COMPASS systems, not only for subject access within its bibliographic records but also as a subject index to the *British National Bibliography*.

Name authorities

Authority control ensures that names (personal and corporate names, series and uniform titles) are always presented in precisely the same form, mostly for the purposes of linear arrangement in bibliographies and catalogues but also for overall consistency within the bibliographic file. Lists of authority-controlled names are produced by the British Library, the LIBRARY OF CONGRESS and other bodies.

Machine-readable coding

Where bibliographic information is manipulated through automation, the various bibliographic elements may be individually coded to facilitate access and enable particular routines, such as linear filing, to take place. The most common system in use is MARC, based on ISO 2709 (ISO 1981); this is manifested in various national formats such as UKMARC and USMARC, and in IFLA's international format UNIMARC.

The use of standards in bibliographic control is intended to impose overall consistency on the records contained in bibliographic files. These files may include individual library CATA-LOGUES, UNION CATALOGUES representing the holdings of more than one collection, current and retrospective national bibliographies as produced by national bibliographic agencies, selective bibliographies based on author, subject or other topic for the purposes of scholarly research and in- and out-of-print trade bibliographies (see TRADE BIBLIOGRAPHY) produced by and for the BOOK TRADE. Bibliographic control may, therefore, be independent of particular library collections.

Access to bibliographic files may be either pre-co-ordinated or post-co-ordinated. The former is represented by printed or microform bibliographies and catalogues, and traditional card catalogues housed in cabinets; the latter by online files and those in CD-ROM format.

Until the 1960s co-operative cataloguing in bibliographic control was spasmodic and to a large extent impractical. However, the development by the Library of Congress in the 1960s of the MARC format has subsequently enabled co-operation to take place on an international basis and led indirectly to the establishment by IFLA of its programme for Universal Bibliographic Control (UBC). While not tied to automated processes, the UBC programme facilitated greater sharing of bibliographic data through its development of appropriate standards such as the ISBDs and UNIMARC, and hence the ultimate target of a global network of bibliographic data.

References

AACR (1988) *Anglo-American Cataloguing Rules*, 2nd edn (1988 revision), Ottawa: Canadian Library Association; London: Library Association Publishing Limited; Chicago: American Library Association.

ISO (International Organization for Standardization) (1981) *Documentation: Format for Bibliographic Information Interchange on Magnetic Tape*, 2nd edn, Geneva: ISO (ISO 2709–1981).

Further reading

Anderson, D. (1974) *Universal Bibliographic Control: A Long-term Policy, a Plan for Action*, Pullach bei München: Verlag Dokumentation.

Davinson, D. (1981) *Bibliographic Control*, 2nd edn, London: Bingley.

Gredley, E. and Hopkinson, A. (1990) *Exchanging Bibliographic Data: MARC and Other International Formats*, Ottawa: Canadian Library Association; London: Library Association Publishing Limited; Chicago: American Library Association.

SEE ALSO: bibliographic description; bibliography; classification; libraries; Machine-Readable Cataloguing; organization of knowledge; Universal Bibliographic Control and International MARC

ROSS BOURNE

BIBLIOGRAPHIC DESCRIPTION

Description of library materials to facilitate retrieval, as specified, for instance, in the

ANGLO-AMERICAN CATALOGUING RULES. A description will typically include areas such as: title and statement of responsibility, edition, physical description, series, standard number, etc. Each of these areas is likely to be further divided into a number of elements, which vary according to the type of material.

In a specialist sense, the term 'bibliographic (or, more often, 'bibliographical') description' is applied to the very detailed description of the physical and bibliographical characteristics, printing and publishing history and visual manifestation of early printed books associated with the work of Fredson BOWERS and his followers.

Further reading

Bowers, F.T. (1948) *Principles of Bibliographical Description*, Princeton, NJ: Princeton University Press.
Chan, L.M. (1994) *Cataloging and Classification: An Introduction*, 2nd edn, New York: McGraw Hill.

SEE ALSO: bibliography

BIBLIOGRAPHIC INSTRUCTION

Also known as USER EDUCATION. It is widely practised in academic and special libraries, and less often in public libraries. It begins with orientation programmes for new users and can go on to include training in the use of the whole range of catalogues, bibliographies, collections and online services that the library offers. The term is falling out of use and is being replaced by training in INFORMATION SKILLS as part of a programme in which users, especially students, are initiated into the skills of INFORMATION LITERACY.

BIBLIOGRAPHY

The systematic listing and analytical study of books, manuscripts and other documents.

A bibliography is compiled with the intention of providing comprehensive coverage of its chosen field. This field might be defined chronologically, geographically, by subject, by author or by format of publication, or by some combination of one or more of these. This form of bibliography is known as enumerative bibliography, a term which encompasses almost all bibliographies. There are three types of enumerative bibliography that are commonly distinguished:

- Author bibliographies.
- Subject bibliographies.
- National bibliographies.

Author and subject bibliographies are self-explanatory. A NATIONAL BIBLIOGRAPHY is a record of the publications of a country, typically published by its national library (see NATIONAL LIBRARIES). In some countries works about the country and/or works by authors resident and/or born in and/or ethnic nationals of the country are also included.

Bibliographers, as the compilers of bibliographies are normally known, seek to achieve comprehensive coverage as well as complete accuracy. In practice, the former is extremely difficult to attain. Even a superficially simple task such as the compilation of a list of the works of a dead author can be complicated by such things as fugitive pieces published in magazines, unpublished works that have survived in manuscript, anonymous, pseudonymous and unacknowledged work, and so on. The bibliographer must also decide whether to include, for example, translations of the author's works into other languages, second and subsequent editions, works about an author or adaptations of the author's works (a short story as a play, for example, or a play as a musical). All of this precedes key decisions about the form and content of entries, the level of detail to be provided, the order of the bibliography, the provision of indexes and the like. With subject bibliographies, or bibliographies that purport to record the whole printed output of a particular country or a particular period of time, the issues become even more complicated.

Not all bibliographies are retrospective. Some, including national bibliographies, are serial in nature: they are published at regular intervals (usually annually) and record new works in their field of coverage, usually with a separate listing of works from previous years that have been accidentally omitted. It is increasingly common for bibliographies to be published in electronic formats. This allows for greater currency, and also for more frequent updating.

Underlying the compilation of bibliographies lies a substantial body of theory and practice about the forms of entry. It is the essence of a bibliography that entries should be uniform with each other, to achieve consistency in the record. The International Standard Book Description, which has, either as a whole or in part, been adopted by most national bibliographies, was designed to achieve international uniformity. It has been a particular concern of UNESCO, through its PGI programme, and of IFLA, through its UNIVERSAL BIBLIOGRAPHIC CONTROL AND INTERNATIONAL MARC (UBCIM) Core Programme, to prescribe and, where possible, to enforce uniform standards of this kind.

Bibliography is also the study of books. In this sense it is used in the rather specialized applications called historical and analytical bibliography. Historical bibliography is a broader subject than the term suggests. In addition to being concerned with the compilation of bibliographies of older books, historical bibliographers are also scholars of the history of the book trade and of book production, of the history of reading and the use of books and the history of the book as a physical and cultural object. In recent years the phrase has been partly displaced by other terms such as 'history of the book' or simply 'book history'. Analytical bibliography is also a historical study, based upon the assumption that books, especially those printed by hand before the first quarter of the nineteenth century, contain a great deal of evidence about their own production. Bibliographers analyse the typography, printing and format of the book, and thus claim to reveal its printing history, and even, in some cases, to cast light upon the history and authenticity of the text that it contains. The term descriptive bibliography is used for bibliographies that give extended descriptions based on a full bibliographical analysis. Bibliography became a major field of endeavour for some literary scholars in the middle decades of the twentieth century, and was particularly influential in the development of new and more accurate styles of editing literary texts for scholarly use.

Bibliography, both as a word and as an activity, is of Greek origin. It was practised in the ancient world and in medieval Europe but became more common after the middle of the sixteenth century, when the rapid proliferation of printed books forced librarians and scholars to develop more effective systems of BIBLIOGRAPHIC CONTROL. CATALOGUES were developed as another response to the same need, but catalogues record only the contents of a single library or designated group of libraries, while bibliogra-

phies seek to be a comprehensive record of the items they record, regardless of the current location of any particular item listed. In other words, bibliographies, although based upon the physical description of objects, are independent of any particular object or repository of objects.

Further reading

Adams, T.R. and Barker, N. (1993) 'A new model for the study of the book', in N. Barker (ed.) *A Potencie of Life. Books in Society*, London: The British Library.

Besterman, T. (1935) *The Beginnings of Systematic Bibliography*, Oxford: Oxford University Press.

Krummell, D.W. (1984) *Bibliographies. Their Aims and Methods*, Mansell Publishing.

Stokes, R. (1982) *The Function of Bibliography*, 2nd edn, Gower.

SEE ALSO: Bowers, Fredson Thayer; organization of knowledge

JOHN FEATHER

BIBLIOMANIA

A mania for collecting and possessing books. The term was popularized (and perhaps coined) by Thomas Frognall Dibdin (1776–1845), an author and bibliographer who made book-collecting a fashionable aristocratic pursuit in early nineteenth-century England. He used the word in the title of his *Bibliomania* (1809), one of his many bibliographic publications.

SEE ALSO: private libraries

BIBLIOMETRICS

The use of mathematical and statistical methods to study documents and patterns of publication. It is a core methodology of INFORMATION SCIENCE, practised by pioneers such as S.C. BRADFORD long before the term itself was coined in the late 1960s. Bibliometrics can be divided into 'descriptive' and 'evaluative', both of which can, in turn, be further divided by 'productive count' (geography, time and discipline) and 'literature count' (reference and citation). The term replaced the older and narrower term statistical bibliography. Bibliometrics is now understood as part of the larger domain of INFORMETRICS.

SEE ALSO: citation analysis; scientometrics

BIBLIOTHÈQUE NATIONALE DE FRANCE

The National Library of France. Questions concerning the site, organization, mission, status and readers of the National Library have been asked throughout its history. The history of the Royal Library, which became the National Library during the French Revolution, was marked by all of these questions and can be read in that light. The notions of ACQUISITIONS and stock development, of CONSERVATION and PRESERVATION, of communication and of the transmission of heritage have only emerged gradually.

A long story

If Charlemagne and his descendants showed any interest in manuscripts and collected a number of them, their holdings were usually scattered at their deaths. Charles V, in the second half of the fourteenth century, installed his 'librairie' in the Louvre and enhanced it. From the reign of Louis XI onwards, the Royal Library was passed down from generation to generation. The processes of transmission and improvement were unevenly implemented, and the Royal Library never stopped being moved from one place to another following the moves of the capital of the kingdom. During its first centuries of existence, the Library was located in Blois, in Fontainebleau, in various areas of Paris and many other sites in royal residences.

The final foundation act was the work of François I: the Montpelier Decree of 28 December 1537 initiated LEGAL DEPOSIT. The dual purpose of this edict was well understood in France and abroad; it was a sign both of reverence for books and of the fear of their power. The Royal Library was gradually enriched by the operation of the Decree. Little by little, 'Library Science' emerged, describing how to organize the treasures they acquired. The *Advis pour dresser une bibliothèque*, by Gabriel Naudé, published in 1627, was the first evidence of this phenomenon.

Colbert settled the Royal Library in the Vivienne district of Paris, where it stayed until recently. He had great ambitions for the Library: 'we need to choose a site to build a large and superb Library without any equivalent in the whole world', he wrote. In the eighteenth century the French Royal Library was one of the wealthiest and most important in the world. Abbé Bignon was one of the major forces behind this incomparable expansion. By 1741 the collections of the Library had multiplied twofold, with 135,000 printed books and 30,000 manuscripts.

The French Revolution, and the disruptions it brought about, affected the Royal Library. The new 'National' Library was created, with more than 250,000 books thanks to the confiscation of the collections of the clergy and the aristocracy.

The nineteenth century was the century of all types of expansion: collections, readers, buildings. The architect Henri Labrouste built the new hall for printed materials, and the major catalogues were initiated. In the twentieth century the Library was prey to inflation, to the need for protecting all publications and to the growing numbers of readers; it realized that it did not have the means to fulfil its mission.

A new library

A new institution was born in January 1994: the Bibliothèque Nationale de France, a merger of the Bibliothèque Nationale and of the projected Bibliothèque de France, announced in 1988 by the President of the Republic, who wished to see France graced with a 'great library, perhaps the greatest in the world' at the disposal of all and open to the newest technologies.

Gradually, after much thought and sometimes tumultuous discussions between politicians, administrators, professionals and users, the project was modified, clarified and stabilized. The building was designed by Dominique Perrault in a rectangular shape. The aisles surround a huge garden and are punctuated with four towers ('four books open on the city'). The space open to the public is organized on two floors.

At the garden level the Library is dedicated to researchers and specialists who need to use heritage holdings, amounting to some 10 million volumes. They have 400,000 volumes on open access at their disposal. The upper garden library is a research library (see RESEARCH LIBRARIES) more widely open to the public. It offers standard collections on open access that amount to 350,000 volumes. The two libraries are divided into four subject departments: philosophy, history and social sciences; political science, law and economics; literature and arts; science and technology; and each of them includes an audiovisual department. The 10 million volumes are kept in the stacks surrounding the reading rooms, and a quarter of them are kept in the towers.

Professional issues

The building and opening of the Bibliothèque Nationale de France marks the beginning of many important projects in librarianship. After a century of shortage of funds, new resources allow significant increases in acquisitions. Besides documents received through legal deposit, purchases are expected to amount to 80,000 volumes a year compared with the previous 15,000.

These funds are dedicated to supplying foreign materials, and to enhancing the scientific and technical collections. Audiovisual holdings have significantly increased and diversified: 6,000 hours of sound recordings, 1,000 hours of moving images and 100,000 digital images are expected to be acquired annually.

The bibliographic database of the Library, BN-opale, now has 2 million records and is to be completed by a retrospective conversion of the whole collection (5 million records are being processed). The French Union Catalogue is being implemented and will provide access to the main collections of academic, research and public libraries; there will be 13 million records by the opening day.

Reading conditions have been improved by human and technological services: work stations allow readers to find reference material, to reserve a seat or to consult and order a document. Computerized reading stations allow access to a corpus of digital texts (100,000 at the time of opening) and provide the facility to modify these texts freely.

The preservation and storage conditions of documents are enhanced thanks to a policy of restoration, reproduction and protection supported by additional resources. A new technical centre located in the suburbs of Paris, at Marne-la-Vallée, has been added to the processing workshops. It is devoted to storage and to the processing of documents. Finally, the old library in Rue Richelieu is now a specialized department for Manuscripts, Maps and Plans, and Engravings, and the site of a project for a National Library of Arts.

After building one of the biggest libraries of the end of the twentieth century, and after having reasserted in various ways its interest in the development of all types of libraries, France has to make sure in the long term that its new National Library actually fulfils the mission of enhancement and renewal that has been assigned to it. For the current position, see the Library's website at www.bnf.fr.

Further reading

Balayé, J. (1988) *La Bibliothèque Nationale des origines à 1800*, Droz.

Bibliothèque de France, bibliothèque ouverte (1989) IMEC [describes the main concepts of the Bibliothèque de France].

'Bibliothèque Nationale, Bibliothèque de France: où en sont les grands chantiers?' (1993) *Bulletin des bibliothèques de France* 38(3) [the state of the art on some important issues].

Blasselle, B. and Melet-Sanson, J. (1990) *La Bibliothèque Nationale: Mémoire de l'avenir*, Gallimard.

Cahart, P. and Melot, M. (1989) *Propositions pour une grande bibliothèque*, La Documentation française [the first report on the 'grande bibliothèque' project].

Gattégno, J. (1992) *La Bibliothèque de France à miparcours: de la TGB à la BN bis*, Le Cercle de la Librairie [analyses the initial project and the subsequent changes].

Histoire des bibliothèques françaises (1988–92), sous la direction d'André Vernet, Claude Jolly, Dominique Varry, Martine Poulain. Promodis-Le Cercle de la Librairie, 4 vols [the most recent and the most detailed history of French libraries; includes several papers on the Bibliothèque Nationale].

Programme général de la Bibliothèque de France (1993) (March).

SEE ALSO: national libraries

MARTINE POULAIN

BIBLIOTHERAPY

Therapy using reading materials in order to help a client solve emotional, mental and social problems. It is used by librarians, counsellors, psychologists, social workers and teachers, with or without a support group. The process of bibliotherapy is sometimes described as including three phases: identification of the reader with the character in the book, catharsis and insight. One example is the Reading and You Scheme (RAYS) in Kirklees, UK, in which the public library service, in partnership with local primary healthcare groups, accepts referrals from doctors, community psychiatric nurses and social workers. The service's bibliotherapists work with individual clients and discussion groups, seeking to introduce a complement to the medical and psychiatric therapy that they are receiving.

BODLEY, SIR THOMAS (1545–1613)

Founder of the Bodleian Library, Oxford University, England.

Educated at Oxford and later a Fellow of Merton College, he lectured in Greek and natural philosophy but left in 1576 to learn foreign languages by travelling across Europe. From 1585 to 1596 he was in the diplomatic service, but after retiring he directed his attention to the collecting of books and the developing of a great academic library (see ACADEMIC LIBRARIES) at Oxford University.

This library, which had existed since the fourteenth century, and had been augmented and rehoused by Humfrey, Duke of Gloucester, in the fifteenth century, had been despoiled during the Reformation. Bodley proposed to restore the library room and assemble new collections in it. His offer was accepted in 1598, and Thomas James was appointed as the first Librarian. The library opened in 1602. His great success in acquiring books for the library led to a need for expansion. The year 1610 marked the opening of the Arts End extension, which Bodley supervised and financed. On his death in 1613 Bodley left his fortune to the library, in part to build the storage extensions he had proposed and which now form the Old Schools Quadrangle, which is still the heart of the library.

Bodley was not merely a library benefactor; he also had strong views on library organization. He imposed a cataloguing and CLASSIFICATION system on James and kept a careful eye on ACQUISITIONS. He was, however, very open-minded. His library was not just for Oxford, but also for 'the whole common-wealth of learning', and (contrary to popular belief) was never narrowly theological (and certainly not solely Protestant) in its holdings. He identified the elements that made his work for the library possible as: his knowledge of literature, the ability to finance the project, friends to call on for assistance and the leisure in which to work.

Further reading

Philip, I. (1983) *The Bodleian Library in the Seventeenth and Eighteenth Centuries*, Oxford: Clarendon Press, pp. 1–22.

SEE ALSO: academic libraries

BOOK

An object that is container for written, printed or graphic information. Whilst there have been other forms of book, notably the scroll, for the last two millennia in the West the term has been used to refer to the codex, consisting of sheets of vellum, parchment, PAPER or other material sewn or stapled and enclosed within protective covers. By extension, the word also refers to the material contained within this object. A definition designed to distinguish the book from other written forms, such as pamphlets, for library purposes was attempted by a UNESCO conference in 1964. This described a book as a non-periodical printed publication of at least forty-nine pages, exclusive of cover pages.

The book has come to have an iconic status, having become a symbol for religious traditions (the 'people of the book') and even for civilization itself. In the late twentieth century, the word was used is such contexts as 'talking book' (sound recordings to provide services for the visually impaired) and ELECTRONIC BOOKS. These MULTIMEDIA formats are fundamentally different objects from the book, but the use of the word in this context reinforces its perceived cultural significance.

SEE ALSO: book trade

BOOK CLUB

1   A method of publishing by issuing books to members of a society, at a lower price than the 'trade' editions. The books have usually been published before and are reprinted for this purpose. Distribution is by mail and the royalties from book club sales are seen as providing extra profits to both publisher and author.

2   In the seventeenth and eighteenth centuries the term was used to describe a club whose members bought books for their joint use, often meeting regularly to discuss the contents.

SEE ALSO: book trade

BOOK DESIGN

The process of planning the typography, illustration and external features (jacket and binding) of a book. It is both aesthetic and utilitarian. A well-designed book is both easy to read and agreeable to look at.

Further reading

Williamson, H. (1983) *Methods of Book Design*, New Haven, CT: Yale University Press.

SEE ALSO: publishing

BOOK FAIR

An exhibition of books and of book-making, sometimes including talks by authors, illustrators, booksellers and publishers. Although some book fairs are intended for the general public (especially those mounted by antiquarian and second-hand booksellers), most are aimed at the BOOK TRADE itself.

The Frankfurt Book Fair, which can trace its origins to the fifteenth century, is the most important international means of selling books and INTELLECTUAL PROPERTY rights, and of promoting international sales and the translation of books into other languages. Fairs are held in many cities, including, for example, Moscow, London and Harare.

SEE ALSO: book trade

BOOK JOBBER

In US usage, a wholesale bookseller who stocks many copies of books issued by different publishers and supplies them to retailers and libraries. There are two types of jobber: (1) those who stock mainly current textbooks, trade and technical books, and (2) those who stock only remainders. The equivalent UK booksellers are called LIBRARY SUPPLIERS.

SEE ALSO: book trade

BOOK PRODUCTION

The art and craft of making books, including BOOK DESIGN, choice and use of materials, illustration, printing and binding.

SEE ALSO: book trade; publishing

BOOK SELECTION

The process of choosing books for inclusion in a library with a view to providing a balanced increase to the stock. Book selection is a key professional skill for librarians, but they work closely with users to ensure that the collection is developed in a relevant and appropriate way. This is especially the case in ACADEMIC LIBRARIES and SPECIAL LIBRARIES, where book selection is often virtually a joint process.

SEE ALSO: acquisitions; collection management

BOOK TRADE

The commercial activities involved in the production, distribution and sale of books and other printed products.

The three principal components of the book trade are PUBLISHING, printing and bookselling. They are normally undertaken as separate activities by different companies, although in some countries, especially in the developing world, two or more of the functions may be combined in a single organization.

Publishing is the main operational element in the trade. A publishing company (which may be a large multinational corporation or a single individual) obtains the COPYRIGHT in books from their authors and then makes arrangements for their production and sale. This process involves negotiations with authors leading to an agreement embodied in a legal contract; the editing of the submitted work, including, if appropriate, requiring the author to make alterations suggested by authoritative independent readers employed by the publisher; the design of the printed book; the management of the production processes; and the marketing, promotion and sale of the book. The capital for all of these activities is provided by the publisher. Some of the work may be undertaken by agents rather than employees of the publishing house, especially design, copy-editing and proof-reading; all the production processes are normally undertaken by other companies on behalf of the publisher.

The production process is in three stages: typesetting, printing and binding. The word 'typesetting' is now an anachronism in the production of almost all books. Metal type is no longer used, since authors are required to submit their work in word-processed form, and the digital files can be used to drive the computers that produce the photographic output which is used to print the book. Nevertheless, the word is often used to describe the process of copy generation that is the first stage of the physical production of a book. If the text is keyboarded by the publisher rather than the author, this is normally undertaken by a specialist company; in any case, such a company will be involved in converting the author's files into an appropriate form for printing, and in generating display pages (such as the title page) and other technical aspects of copy generation. The output, after proof-reading and correction, is transferred photographically onto metal plates that are then sent to the printer. The printer produces the number of copies required by the publisher. These copies are then bound. Printing and binding may be undertaken by the same company, but some publishers will prefer to seek separate estimates for the two operations and commission the work accordingly. The finished product is sent to the warehouse, either of the publisher or of a distribution company chosen by the publisher.

While the editorial and production work has been in progress, the publisher's marketing and sales team have been at work. Books are typically listed in catalogues and advertised in the trade press up to six months before publication date, with a view to maximizing the sales at the time of publication. Publishers sell their books to retail and wholesale booksellers, not to the individual consumer. In addition, there are specialized markets such as BOOK CLUBS and LIBRARY SUPPLIERS. In the United Kingdom the consumer book market is dominated by a small number of bookselling companies with a widespread network of branches throughout the country, all carrying similar, but not identical, stocks. There is no wholesaling system for hardbacks; the publishers deal directly with the bookshops. Paperbacks are sold through wholesalers, and are typically found in a far wider range of retail outlets, the majority of which (such as newsagents and stationers) are not primarily bookshops. In some other countries, most notably the USA, there is a more highly developed system of wholesaling ('jobbing' in the USA) for both hardbacks and paperbacks. Book clubs buy either copies of the book or the rights to it, for sale to their own members at a price normally significantly lower than the usual retail price of

the publisher's edition. The advantage to the publisher is either the sale of large numbers of copies of the book or the income generated by the sale of the book club rights. Library suppliers are in the business of selling books to libraries, to whom they often offer additional services such as inserting marks of ownership or security devices, putting the books in special bindings (for paperbacks, for example) or even, in some cases, cataloguing and classification services. Throughout the world, bookshops now face a serious challenge from online bookshops. The first and now the largest of these was Amazon, which opened for business in 1995 (www.amazon.com). There was already some online bookselling, but it was the success of Amazon (in terms of the volume of business that it transacted) that really drew attention to this new technique in the book trade. As e-commerce expanded in the late 1990s, many traditional booksellers including Barnes and Noble in the USA (www.barnesandnoble.com) and Blackwell in the UK (www.blackwell.co.uk) also developed significant online operations.

In addition to these core areas of the book trade, there are many peripheral and related activities, some undertaken by persons and organizations involved in the book trade itself. Some library suppliers also act as agents for the publishers of learned journals (SERIALS agents). Many shops that sell books also sell magazines and other printed products, and, increasingly, computer software and audiovisual media. A few companies specialize in export sales, especially in the major English-language publishing countries, which command a global market for their products.

The book trade is international in every respect. Booksellers are to be found in all countries, and publishers in most. In practice, however, publishing is dominated by a small number of global corporations, and by works in the English language. There is a vast imbalance of trade between the industrialized countries and the developing world for books and other printed matter, as there is in many manufactured goods. This has significant educational, cultural and political dimensions like other aspects of the uneven development of the INFORMATION SOCIETY.

In some countries the activities of the trade are carefully monitored by the state for purposes of social or political control, or to protect or encourage indigenous cultures and languages. In the democracies, however, such regulation of the trade is considered to be unacceptable, although a number of aspects of INFORMATION LAW impinge on how the trade works. There are some restrictions on the international flow of books through the trade, although these have substantially diminished since 1989.

Further reading

Altbach, P.G. (1987) *The Knowledge Context: Comparative Perspectives on the Distribution of Knowledge*, State University of New York Press.

Coser, L.A., Kadushin, C. and Powell, W.W. (1985) *Books. The Culture and Commerce of Publishing*, University of Chicago Press.

Dessauer, J.P. (1994) *Book Publishing. The Basic Introduction*, revised edn, Continuum.

Feather, J (forthcoming) *Publishing: Communicating Knowledge in the Twenty-first Century*, K.G. Saur.

SEE ALSO: author; fiction; knowledge industries

JOHN FEATHER

BOOLEAN LOGIC

A branch of mathematical logic devised in 1847 by the mathematician George Boole and which has been applied to probability theory and to the algebraic manipulation of sets (collections of items that share some common characteristic). Amongst other disciplines it is used in electronics, as a basis for digital circuit design, and in library and information science as the most common method of searching electronic DATABASES such as CD-ROMS, ONLINE databases and library CATALOGUES (OPACs).

Boolean logic and information retrieval

Most INFORMATION RETRIEVAL systems work on the principle of text matching, whereby a search term (a word or a two- or three-word phrase that the user wishes to look up) is input and the retrieval system returns a set of records from the database (these might be documents or references to documents) that contain the term in question.

In practice, however, few search topics can be adequately expressed by a single word or short phrase, and Boolean logic is used as a means of combining brief search terms (which are all that can be matched successfully against stored text)

in order to put a more complex or detailed search expression to the database.

Most information retrieval systems offer three Boolean connectors (Boolean operators) to link search terms: AND, OR and NOT. These are usually explained using Venn diagrams.

Venn diagrams

Suppose in a database a certain number of items (such as documents) contain the term 'X' and a different number contain the term 'Y'. In a Venn diagram these two sets of documents are represented by two circles that overlap when some documents contain both terms.

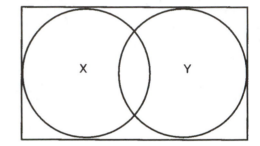

Figure 1 Venn diagram

In the next three sections, the search expressions shown on the left (called search statements) retrieve those documents which lie in the shaded area of the corresponding Venn diagram.

The AND connector

Potato AND blight   AND narrows the retrieval

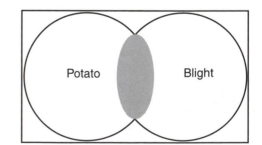

Figure 2 The AND connector

Documents that contain BOTH terms – 'potato' AND 'blight'.

AND is used to link separate concepts to build up a compound search topic, e.g. the 'design' of 'kitchen appliances' for the 'physically handicapped' (three concepts).

The Boolean AND connection is sometimes referred to as: intersection (∩) or conjunction (∧). This terminology and the corresponding notation come from two branches of mathematics that have close links with Boolean logic: set theory and propositional logic, respectively.

The OR connector

Woman OR female   OR broadens the retrieval

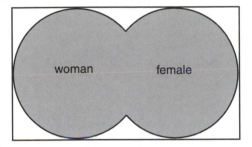

Figure 3 The OR connector

Documents that contain EITHER the term 'woman' OR the term 'female' OR both

OR is used to link together synonyms, lexical and morphological variants, and terms that are close in meaning in the context of a particular search.

The OR connector is often overlooked by novice users of electronic information retrieval systems (Sewell and Teitelbaum 1986), yet it can be essential for successful retrieval because the words and phrases used to describe the same subject in different documents can vary enormously. Thus the searcher should anticipate common variants to each search term and join them with the OR connector BEFORE using the AND connector, as illustrated by the following Boolean search formulation for information on all aspects of BSE (mad cow disease) in relation to the European Union:

Mad cow disease OR bovine spongiform encephalopathy OR BSE
European Union OR EU OR EC OR EEC OR European Community
1 AND 2

Alternative terms and notation for OR are: union (∪); disjunction (∨).

The NOT connector

promotion   NOT narrows the
NOT advertising   retrieval

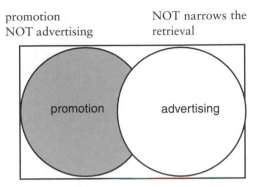

Figure 4 The NOT connector

Documents that contain the term 'promotion' but NOT the term 'advertising'

The obvious use of the NOT connector is to avoid retrieving irrelevant documents. For example 'promotion NOT advertising' might be used to exclude items concerning the promotion of goods and services from a search on job promotion. There is, however, some danger in doing this because useful items can be eliminated too. More helpfully, NOT can be used to remove from a subsequent set those items that have already been retrieved, to avoid the nuisance and possibly the cost of viewing them a second time.

Alternative terms and notation for NOT are: complement (–); negation (~).

Complex Boolean search statements

Brackets can normally be used to prioritize the processing of a Boolean search statement:

(pollution OR contamination) AND (ocean OR sea)

If a search statement contains two or more different Boolean connectors it almost certainly needs brackets to ensure that the logic is unambiguous.

Problems with Boolean retrieval and some solutions

To satisfy a query, search terms simply have to be present anywhere in the matching DATABASE records according to the specified Boolean relationship. Thus, in a bibliographic database, a record containing the word 'school' in the title and 'libraries' in the abstract will be retrieved by the search expression

school AND libraries

regardless of whether or not it is really about school libraries (which is presumably what the searcher had intended). To combat this problem, many information retrieval systems provide positional as well as Boolean connectors, to allow searches for phrases and for words in close proximity to each other.

Despite the fact that they are extremely widely used, Boolean-based retrieval systems are criticized on other grounds, notably that:

- Boolean logic is not intuitive and easy for most people to use correctly (possibly because it can conflict with conventional English locution, as illustrated by the query 'find the names of the Oxford AND Cambridge colleges' and its equivalent Boolean search expression, 'Oxford OR Cambridge').
- Boolean logic is unable accurately to represent some queries, leading to imprecise retrieval (to illustrate simply, the Boolean expression 'teaching AND French AND schools' can retrieve items concerning 'teaching French in schools' as well as 'teaching in French schools', and more).
- Boolean relationships are too rigid: items belong to a set or they do not, hence items are retrieved or they are not retrieved, whereas, in reality, documents have different degrees of relevance and usefulness to each query and searcher.

More philosophically, many queries to information retrieval systems are vague and ill defined because the searcher is engaged in problem solving, seeking new information on a topic that they may only partially comprehend (Belkin *et al.* 1982). Arguably, it is unhelpful to apply a formal system of logic in this situation (Belnap and Steel 1976).

To combat searchers' unfamiliarity with Boolean logic, some CD-ROMs use 'form filling' or other techniques for query input, which disguise the underlying Boolean-based retrieval. Information retrieval researchers have developed alternatives to the Boolean retrieval model, notably document clustering (where a cluster of measurably similar documents is assessed for similarity

with a query); term weighting (where indexing terms are 'weighted' according, usually, to their frequency of occurrence in a database and 'fuzzy' or partial matching between indexing and search terms is possible); and probabilistic retrieval (which ranks documents in decreasing order of probable relevance to a query). Despite their promising performance in the research environment, few alternative retrieval models have been implemented in operational systems because of the cost, effort and computer-processing overheads involved in applying them to very large databases.

References

Belkin, N.J., Oddy, R.N. and Brooks, H.M. (1982) 'ASK for information retrieval: Part I. Background and theory', *Journal of Documentation* 38(2): 61–71.

Belnap, N.D. and Steel, T.D. (1976) *The Logic of Questions and Answers*, New Haven: Yale University Press, p. 11.

Sewell, W. and Teitelbaum, S. (1986) 'Observations of end-user online searching behavior over eleven years', *Journal of the American Society for Information Science* 37(4): 234–45.

Further reading

Pao, M.L. (1989) *Concepts of Information Retrieval*, Englewood, CO: Libraries Unlimited, pp. 176–89.

SEE ALSO: information retrieval; organization of knowledge; relational database

GWYNETH TSENG

BOWERS, FREDSON THAYER (1905–91)

Bibliographer and literary scholar, best known for his editorial work, and for his theoretical work on historical and descriptive BIBLIOGRAPHY and textual criticism.

He edited the annual *Studies in Bibliography* from 1948 until his death, and under his editorship it became one of the most prestigious bibliographical journals in the world. His *The Principles of Bibliographical Description* established itself as indispensable to all who were concerned with the exact description of printed books, as soon as it was published in 1949. Bowers offered a complete analysis of the descriptive principles that guide a bibliographer. From these principles he developed the methods by which each part of a book can be described according to a standard system that can be generally understood. He also edited a large number of literary works, including Thomas Dekker, Stephen Crane and Christopher Marlowe.

If some of his theories are now questioned and his methods of textual analysis seem rather outmoded, he nevertheless remains a towering presence in bibliographical studies. His intellectual rigour and his relentless pursuit of truth and accuracy set a standard to which many of his successors have aspired.

Further reading

Tanselle, G.T. (1993) 'The life and work of Fredson Bowers', *Studies in Bibliography* 46: 1–154.

SEE ALSO: bibliography

BOX LIBRARIES

Boxes containing standard sets of books catering for different tastes and supplied in developing countries by community development organizations to community centres in rural areas, for circulation from village to village. The idea goes back at least to the itinerating libraries of Samuel Brown (1779–1839) in nineteenth-century Scotland. Book Box service, as provided by National or Public Library services, is a more 'official' version of this concept. Also sometimes referred to by other terms, such as Suitcase Libraries or Home Libraries.

SEE ALSO: barefoot librarian; lending libraries; rural library services

BRADFORD, SAMUEL CLEMENT (1878–1948)

Born and educated in London, he spent his whole professional life in the Science Library at South Kensington. Bradford had no professional qualifications in librarianship, but founded the British Society for International Bibliography and his eminence in information science was recognized by his election as President of FID in 1945.

Bradford was an avid proponent of the UNIVERSAL DECIMAL CLASSIFICATION (UDC) and of the utility of abstracts of scientific literature. He found that no more than half the scientific

articles published were listed by the abstracting and subject-indexing periodicals, as the editors concentrated upon the periodicals devoted to their special subjects, ignoring material in other journals and non-periodical material such as books, pamphlets or patents. His work on the scattering of useful articles on a given subject throughout the mass of current published material is now known as Bradford's Law of Scatter. To address this problem he advocated comprehensive subject indexing of books and non-book materials by scientific libraries, using UDC.

He is regarded as one of the founding fathers of the formal study of information flows.

Further reading

Bradford, S.C. (1948) *Documentation*, London: Crosby Lockwood.
Gosset, M. and Urquhart, D.J. (1977) 'S.C. Bradford, Keeper of the Science Museum Library 1925–1937', *Journal of Documentation* 33: 173–9.

SEE ALSO: abstracting and indexing services; bibliometrics; information science

BRAY, THOMAS (1656–1730)

Promoter of libraries.

Born in Shropshire, and a graduate of Oxford, he entered the ministry of the Church of England. When asked to serve in Maryland, he accepted the position on the understanding that the bishop would provide for the establishment of parochial libraries for ministers going to the colony. He later developed plans for providing parochial libraries throughout England and Wales, with funds provided by the clergyman and the congregation. The congregation would have the right to borrow books from these libraries because of their financial contribution. This plan was soon further developed by the Society for the Promotion of Christian Knowledge, which he founded in 1698.

During his time in the USA (1700–6) he founded thirty-nine libraries, and he was also responsible for the foundation of eighty libraries in England and Wales. His ideas on library development were set out in *An Essay towards Promoting All Necessary and Useful Knowledge both Divine and Human in All Parts of His Majesty's Dominions* (1697), and he also wrote extensively on religious topics. The libraries founded under his direction, and after his death by the Associates of Dr Bray, were small (usually under 1,000 volumes) and tended not to have funds attached for their care and development, but were, nevertheless, the fruits of a comprehensive view of the value of libraries in the community. In 1708 he persuaded the British parliament to pass an *Act for the Better Preservation of Parochial Libraries in that Part of Great Britain Called England*, which, although ineffective, was an early example of LIBRARY LEGISLATION.

Further reading

Gray, S. and Baggs, C. (2000) 'The English parish library: A celebration of diversity', *Libraries and Culture* 35: 414–33.

SEE ALSO: library legislation

BRITISH LIBRARY

The national library (see NATIONAL LIBRARIES) of the United Kingdom.

History

The British Library was formed in 1973 by the British Library Act of 1972. It brought together various bodies at its foundation and was supplemented, in later years, by the addition of the British National Bibliography, the India Office Library and Records, and the National Sound Archive. Until 1997 it continued to exist in the various buildings across London that had housed its constituent parts. From the opening of the new British Library building at St Pancras, the London collections and services (with the exception of the Newspaper Library) have been largely brought together on a single site. The research and development function has been devolved to Re:source, the Council for Museums, Archives and Libraries.

While the London services are offered from the St Pancras building, two external, London repositories have been retained for overflow stock. A new CONSERVATION studio is being built on the site and will replace the bindery that remained at the British Museum. The Newspaper Library remains at Colindale. Half of the Library's staff of about 2,300, and a significant part of its collection, is based at Boston Spa, Yorkshire, where not only document supply but the cataloguing of most of the intake of acquisitions and many of the IT operations take place.

Structure

The Library's structure has evolved over the years since its foundation in 1973 as it has increasingly sought to create a single corporate whole from its constituent parts. The latest structure demonstrates, in addition, the determination to play a central role in the provision and archiving of electronic texts. Scholarship and Collections is responsible for collection development and exploitation of all collections and collection management (preservation and cataloguing); Operations and Services is responsible for all services, bringing together services to remote users and reading rooms, and for services to science technology and industry; a directorate of E-Strategy and Programmes leads the development of services and collections on the Web. Directorates of Marketing and of Finance and Corporate Resources (Human Resources, Estates and IS) support these others.

Collection

Although of relatively recent foundation the Library traces its roots back to the foundation of the British Museum Library in 1753 and the collection reflects this. The Library's collection covers all known languages and every age of written civilization. The breadth and historical depth, in particular, make it of worldwide significance. The Library is the beneficiary of LEGAL DEPOSIT legislation which ensures that UK publications are deposited. However, about £14 million is also committed each year for the addition of overseas material and other formats such as manuscripts and electronic material that are not received by legal deposit. In the year 2000–1, 526,903 items were received by deposit, 70,133 items were donated, and 243,412 items, as well as 1.7 million patents, were purchased for the collection. Since 1 January 2000, a scheme of voluntary deposit of electronic material has operated with UK publishers. Legal deposit of such material awaits legislation.

Services

Since the Collection Development Initiative of 1995–6, the collection has been viewed as a single resource. Services designed for remote users and those for the reading rooms are being devised as a unity. The requirement to order items to be delivered either remotely or to the reading rooms (depending on the nature of the material) represents a single need for ordering on the Web. The Library delivers 8.3 million items a year (4.9 million of them in reading rooms and 3.4 million to remote users). The Library produces the NATIONAL BIBLIOGRAPHY of all items published in the UK. Services to the general public are provided through the exhibitions programme, and the lectures and publications of the Library. The education section also provides increasing access for schools as well as content geared to the national curriculum.

Electronic media allow the Library to widen both the scope of services and the audiences to whom they are delivered. On the scholarly side this has led to projects such as the DIGITIZATION of the Beowulf manuscript, with the University of Kentucky, and the digitization of the Gutenberg Bible (Mainz *c.* 1455) in association with Keio University, Japan, funded by NTT Japan. The Library's Turning the Pages software has been used on several key treasures to provide the experience of turning the pages of illuminated manuscripts and other texts so as to allow visitors to the galleries to see more than a single opening of the books. The large digitization projects, funded by the New Opportunities Fund of the national lottery, will further extend the range of material available in electronic form.

Funding

While the Library earns a greater proportion of its spend than any other national library, government remains the single most important source of funding. In the financial year 2000–1 total spend was £111 million (Grant in Aid £82.3 million).

Further reading

The British Library Annual Report and Accounts 2000–01 (2001) British Library.
Day, A.E. (1998) *Inside the British Library*, Library Association.
Harris, P.R. (1998) *A History of the British Museum Library 1753–1973*, British Library.

M.J. CRUMP

BROADBAND

The term used to describe wide BANDWIDTH network connections using various advanced technology systems such as ISDN and satellite-based systems. The minimum speed for broad-band is 512 Kbps, but some providers are already offering up to 2 Mbps. The installation of broadband capacity is a high priority, both for providers and for many businesses and governments, to increase the facilities for e-commerce and other applications demanding reliable high-speed connections to the INTERNET.

BROADCASTING

A method of transmitting sound or pictures, using electromagnetic waves, to large, heterogeneous audiences. Broadcasting is normally taken to mean radio (originally called 'wireless' to distinguish it from wired telegraphy and telephony) and television. It may be distinguished from the less common term 'narrowcasting', which denotes the sending of messages by similar technologies to identified and discrete groups of receivers, as in citizens' band (CB) radio or closed-circuit television (CCTV).

There has been much dispute about the 'inventor' of radio and television, and undoubtedly the emergence of these dominant MASS MEDIA of the twentieth century owes its birth to the work of many individuals and organizations. Crucial, however, was the theoretical and laboratory work of the physicists James Maxwell in Scotland and Heinrich Hertz in Germany. Nonetheless it was the arrival of the Italian Guglielmo Marconi in Britain, in 1896, which marks the take-off point in the story. Initially taken up with enthusiasm only by amateurs (closely licensed by the Post Office) and the navy, Marconi's transmissions attracted considerable attention from potential investors, including electrical receiving apparatus manufacturers. In 1922 six of these combined to form the British Broadcasting Company (BBC) with John (later Lord) Reith as its General Manager. In the USA rapid growth in radio led to dispute over its appropriate use. Lee De Forest, inventor of the Audion vacuum tube, became a leading advocate of widespread public access to the new medium, and is credited with concocting the word broadcasting to encompass this vision. He later proclaimed himself 'disgusted and ashamed' of the direction his 'pet child' had taken (McChesney 1993: 88).

Essentially two models of broadcasting emerged from this early period. In the USA the basis was commercial, with blocks of air time sold to advertisers and the formation of major corporate organizations – the National Broadcasting Company (NBC) in 1926 and Columbia Broadcasting System (CBS) in 1928 – as programme and transmission sources. The Federal Radio Commission (later Federal Communications Commission) created by the Radio Act of 1927 provided a regulatory underpinning, but the essential driving force and organizing principle was commercial entertainment as a medium for advertising. This model also became the basis for broadcasting in most of Latin America, and in some areas of the Far East. By contrast, in Britain in 1926 the BBC became a Corporation with its legal basis in a Royal Charter and with an independent Board of Governors, its mission to provide information, entertainment and education to a high standard as a public service. This formulation, 'a masterpiece of calculated imprecision' (Burns 1977: 15), creating a body at arm's length from the state but nevertheless protected from commercial determination, was repeated variably throughout Europe, and in many other parts of the world. Funding was derived either directly from government or, as in Britain, from an unusual form of hypothecated poll tax, the licence fee. A variant on this structure, with broadcasting firmly in the public sector, and indeed under direct government control, was developed most obviously in communist Eastern Europe, and in many Third World countries after national independence.

Television had a faltering history in the first half of the century. Laboratory experiments by Paul Nipkow in Germany and, later, by Vladimir Zworykin, in Russia, had demonstrated the possibilities. (Zworykin later went to the USA and became a key figure in the development of the Radio Corporation of America, the company that bought out American Marconi and gave birth to NBC.) In Britain the Scot, John Logie Baird, took television from the laboratory, and against much scepticism persuaded the BBC to experiment with transmissions from 1929. Real development required the arrival of the cathode-ray tube, and transmissions soon petered out for lack of interest, while the Second World War halted further progress.

In the post-war period television soon became the dominant medium. In Britain the BBC had grown rapidly during the war, with under 5,000 staff in 1938 and over 11,000 in 1945. Audience exposure to US style programmes during the war, together with a concerted lobby from manufac-

turers, advertisers and others, built up momentum for commercial broadcasting, and it was the creation of the advertising-based commercial television network in 1954 that led to a very rapid expansion in television ownership, from 10 per cent of homes in 1950 to 90 per cent of homes in 1963. Radio-only licences disappeared in 1971. In the USA television mushroomed from about a million households in 1948 to 90 per cent of the population in 1954, with 377 stations in operation. The recognition by the Hollywood moguls, that television was not a threat but an opportunity, saw the creation of the mass-manufactured serials and recycling of film stocks that were to become the staple diet of the world television market. Between them radio and television have come to occupy prime place in people's leisure time. In the UK in the 1990s adults watched television on average between twenty-five and thirty hours a week, and spent about twenty hours a week listening to radio. With the growing use of recorded videotapes, watching television no longer only means watching broadcast programmes, while radio listening has been sustained, and even increased, as a form of media consumption with the growth of 'in car entertainment'.

Internationally, radio and television have spread very unequally. The introduction of the transistor in 1948 held out hopes that radio would become a cheap, mobile and crucial contributor to social and economic development. Yet after the 'lost decade' of the 1980s the broadcasting map was very uneven. UNESCO figures published at the end of the century showed that in 1997 the developed world had nearly eight times as many radios per capita as the developing world, and over twenty times as many television sets. Africa, with just sixty televisions per 1,000 inhabitants in 1997 and just 216 radios, illustrates how far some regions have been left behind. In North America the equivalent figures showed an increase greater than total ownership in Africa. Many smaller and poorer countries import the majority of their programming, especially for television, leading to complaints of 'cultural imperialism', and the call, much promoted by UNESCO, for a 'New World Information and Communication Order' (UNESCO 1980).

Major new technological initiatives, such as High Definition Television (HDTV), Direct Broadcasting by Satellite (DBS), cable distribution and digital transmission, may change the face of broadcasting, though as yet the changes have been slower than many have predicted. Broadcast programmes are now distributed not just terrestrially, but also increasingly via cable television and satellite, and even the Internet. However, these are new means for distributing broadcasting rather than alternative mass media. The major debates within broadcasting are likely to be about the implications of such changes for the social role and public regulation of technologies increasingly integrated with computing and telecommunications, and which have come to dominate people's lives to a degree totally unprecedented.

References

Burns, T. (1977) *The BBC: Public Institution and Private World*, London: Macmillan
McChesney, R.W. (1993) *Telecommunications, Mass Media and Democracy*, New York: Oxford University Press
UNESCO (1980) *Many Voices, One World: Report of the MacBride Commission*, London: Kogan Page for UNESCO

Further reading

Barnouw, E. (1966) *A Tower in Babel*, New York: Oxford University Press. [This and later volumes, *The Golden Web* (1968) and *The Image Empire* (1970), may be considered the US equivalents of Briggs. His summary volume, *Tube of Plenty: Evolution of American Television* (1992), New York: Oxford University Press, is also valuable.]
Briggs, A (1985) *The BBC: The First Fifty Years*, Oxford: Oxford University Press. [Briggs's authorized history may be read in much greater detail in the five volumes so far published by OUP of his *History of Broadcasting in the United Kingdom*.]
Dunnett, P.J.S. (1990) *The World Television Industry: An Economic Analysis*, London: Routledge.
Hendy, D. (2000) *Radio in the Global Age*, London: Polity Press. [A comprehensive and informed descriptive and analytical account of a medium that refuses to give way to the dominance of television.]
Thussu, D.K. (2000) *International Communication: Continuity and Change*, London: Arnold. [Critical and informed account, mainly of broadcasting, telecommunications and related sectors, with relevant theoretical and empirical material.]

SEE ALSO: cable television; communication technology; cultural industries; film; information and communication technology; knowledge industries; mass media; PTT; telecommunications

PETER GOLDING

BROWSING

The traditional use of the term is to describe casual investigation of the contents of a collection of books or documents, possibly with some subject in mind, but equally possibly for 'interesting' material. This normally takes the form of looking along the shelves of a library, the means by which large numbers of library users select books to borrow. Similar SERENDIPITY can, however, be exercised in browsing through a periodical or a reference book.

Since the mid-1990s, the term has come to be associated with the WORLD WIDE WEB, and in particular with the use of software called a WEB BROWSER. The user can then scan (or 'surf' (see SURFING)) the Web in a manner that is analogous to browsing through a collection of documents or other objects. Ideally, a DIGITAL LIBRARY is structured in a way that facilitates browsing.

SEE ALSO: communication; reading research

BULLETIN BOARD

Originally a place on which public notices were displayed. It is now, however, used as the generic descriptor of a computer-based information service. Information is sent to an editor, who posts it on the electronic bulletin board. Access is usually by the Internet, using either a specific address or through a UNIFORM RESOURCE LOCATOR on the WORLD WIDE WEB. In the UK, for example, the Bulletin Board for Libraries, BUBL (www.bubl.ac.uk), has become an invaluable information source.

Some general-purpose bulletin boards are operated by commercial service companies, such as CompuServe and Delphi in the USA, but many are operated by common interest groups, such as people using a particular type of personal computer or sharing an interest in a particular hobby or political issue. The major INTERNET SERVICE PROVIDERS typically provide facilities for groups to set up their own bulletin boards and other means of sharing information and communicating with each other.

SEE ALSO: communication

BUSH, VANNEVAR (1890–1974)

Electrical engineer and inventor who worked on the development of mechanical, electromechanical and, latterly, electronic calculating machines or analogue computers, which led directly to the development of the digital COMPUTER. Amongst many other projects, he also worked on the development of the typewriter and the microfilm scanner.

Born in Everett, Massachusetts, and a graduate of Tufts College, he worked first for the General Electric Company, then in the Inspection Department of the US Navy. He took doctoral degrees from both Harvard and MIT in 1916, and taught at Tufts and then MIT (1919–38). From 1940 he directed the war-related research projects undertaken by the US government, including the Manhattan Project, as Director of the Office of Scientific Research and Development. Afterwards he remained active as an adviser to many governmental agencies and boards on matters of scientific manpower, organization and policy. His best-known contribution to INFORMATION SCIENCE was the 1945 paper 'As we may think'. In this enormously influential paper he achieved what is still regarded by many as the most convincing forecasts of the impact of INFORMATION TECHNOLOGY.

References

Bush, V. (1945) 'As we may think', *Atlantic Monthly* 176: 101–8.

BUSINESS INFORMATION SERVICE

This term is used in several different contexts, and can cover services that provide information *about* business and others providing information *for* business (though there is a broad overlap between these two types of service).

Business information may be defined either as any information that a business needs in order to operate (including, for example, technical information) or as information relating specifically to companies, markets, products and management topics. The term 'company information' refers to company profile data (e.g. address, financial data, personnel), although it may be taken to mean other information such as news stories or stockbroker reports. 'Market information' *either* refers to stock market data *or* information about a specific market sector (e.g. the market for mineral water). A 'market', in

the latter context, can be defined as potential customers who are interested in obtaining a particular product or service, have the means and authority to obtain it, and who can be addressed as a group when developing marketing strategy.

The type of business information offered by a business information service will be influenced by factors such as: the mission of the information supplier, the needs of the target market, competition, the information to which the supplier has ready access and the expertise of its staff. Services may include compilation and dissemination of databases, DOCUMENT DELIVERY services, publications, CONSULTANCY and advice, provision of training, CURRENT AWARENESS services and compilation of specialist reports. The medium in which the information is supplied will increasingly be electronic (e.g. via a public website or a newsfeed into the INTRANET). The Internet is changing businesspeople's information habits, and has changed the market for some products (such as news), but people and organizations are still important information channels for business, and print also still has a place.

A wide range of organizations provides business information services. There are commercial information providers, pricing, delivering and packaging their products in many different ways to meet the needs of particular market segments. For example, company information publishers Dun and Bradstreet (D&B) sell individual credit reports to businesses, produce printed directories and CD-ROMs, mount databases on hosts like DIALOG and on the Web, and form partnerships that will help them embed their information products in business processes. Mergers have led to some strong business information providers such as the North American Thomson Corporation (DIALOG, Gale Group, WestLaw, etc.) and the Swedish Bonnier Affärsinformation (ICC, Hoppenstedt, etc.). Whilst there is much excellent business information free on the Internet, publishers are still experimenting with pricing models and in 2001–2 some valued free sources (such as the *Financial Times*) imposed charges or withdrew services.

There are some private-sector INFORMATION BROKERS, or information consultants, specializing in business information. These range from the French SVP (*'Il y a toujours quelqu'un qui sait!'*)

and the *Financial Times*'s Ask FT service to one- or two-person brokerages that will normally focus on the specialist skills of the people who have set up the business. Some services focus on competitive intelligence (collection and analysis of information about competitors and their business strategy). Competitive intelligence professionals are expected to be more skilful at extracting information from people, organizations and published sources, and to add value by analysing the information rather than just presenting it.

Information professionals, including specialists in competitive intelligence, patents and so forth, may be employed in in-house information centres or units. The service they supply is likely to have a growing emphasis on negotiation with information suppliers for provision of networked information, design of effective delivery of information to the desktop and on developing strategies that enable end-users to make the best use of enterprise information portals (see PORTALS AND GATEWAYS), intranets or KNOWLEDGE MANAGEMENT systems. Thus the company's business information centre may deliver support, training and advice in the use of networked products (including free sources on the Internet), but staff will still have to be adept in using a wider range of business information services themselves.

In the public sector, business information services may be supplied by the library and information sector, and by those with a mission to support business. There are some information brokers or consultants based in PUBLIC LIBRARIES, although in the UK there has been a decline in the number of priced services after a peak of interest in the late 1980s–early 1990s. Nevertheless, access to the Internet has meant that public librarians can use their information skills to help businesses access free or inexpensive information. The provision of business information services from public sector libraries is more common in the UK and USA than it is in some continental European countries such as France and Germany. One of the causes of this is the greater strength and importance of local chambers of commerce in the latter countries, which has led chambers (rather than local libraries) to take the lead in information provision. Businesses are also likely to turn to trade associations,

business associations (such as the UK's Federation of Small Businesses or the US's National Business Association) and advisers such as accountants and banks.

There have been a number of initiatives to help small and medium-sized enterprises (SMEs). The European Commission has funded several types of European Information Service, some of which are aimed specifically at business (e.g. the Euro Info Centres) and some of which include business in their remit (e.g. the Rural Information Carrefours). In the UK, there has been a succession of initiatives aimed to help, in particular, small business and exporters, with frequent rebranding and restructuring of the services. These include the Small Business Service, Business Links (providing a range of advice and information to small businesses in England), Invest Northern Ireland and the Business Information Source network in the Highlands and Islands of Scotland. Some, but not all, of these units have qualified library and information professionals on their staff.

Further reading

Blakeman, K. (2002) *Business Information on the Internet* [online], RBA Information Services. www.rba.co.uk/sources/index.htm.

Burke, M. and Hall, H. (1998) *Navigating Business Information Sources,* Library Association Publishing.

Business Information Source network: www.bis.uk.com/.

Business Links: www.businesslink.org/.

http://europa.eu.int/comm/relays/index_en.htm.

European Commission (2002) *Relays: Europe at your fingertips.* Luxembourg: The Commission.

Federation of Small Businesses: www.fsb.org.uk/.

Invest Northern Ireland: www.investni.com/.

Lavin, M.R. (2002) *Business Information: How to Find It, How to Use It,* 3rd edn, Oryx Press.

Lowe, M. (1999) *Business Information at Work,* ASLIB/IMI.

Marchand, D. (2000) *Competing with Information,* John Wiley.

National Business Association: www.nationalbusiness.org/.

Sabroski, S. (2002) *Super Searchers Make It on Their Own,* CyberAge Books. [The Super Searchers series includes titles focusing on various types of business information professional, including tips and source lists.]

Small Business Service: www.sbs.gov.uk/.

Society of Competitive Intelligence Professionals: www.scip.org/.

Special Libraries Association Business and Finance Division: www.slabf.org/.

KEY JOURNALS

Business Information Review; *Business Information Testdrive*; *Business Information Alert*; *Business Information Searcher*. [There are also a good number of relevant, practical articles in *Free Pint* (www.free-pint.com), *Searcher*, *Econtent* and *Online*.]

SEE ALSO: European Union information policies; fee-based services; information professions; market research; trade literature

SHEILA WEBBER

BYTE

The space occupied in a computer memory by one character or by one space; it consists of eight binary digits. The memory of many computer systems, and particularly of personal computers, is organized and addressed in terms of bytes.

SEE ALSO: information and communication technology; kilobyte; megabyte

C

CABLE TELEVISION

Television that is broadcast through fixed cables rather than by wireless transmission. The system has been in use in the USA since the 1940s to provide good-quality reception to places that could not be served adequately by domestic antennas. Developments in Europe were slower, partly because of strict government controls over broadcasting licences, and partly because of the higher quality of typical broadcast signals. As the markets were deregulated in the 1980s, cable television did grow in Europe, however, and a number of channels began to be broadcast in several countries. The UK market was particularly stagnant, as the UHF transmitter network improved reception via antennas, and government regulations prevented the introduction of new channels. In 1980 a small number of pilot services were licensed as the ITAP Report on Wideband Cable Systems (1981) suggested that IT-based services could be financed by the private sector. This led to the setting up of the Hunt Committee, whose report proposed a liberal framework of regulations to encourage private investment. Programmes are transmitted via coaxial cable or by fibre-optic links. The latest generation of BROADBAND fibre-optic cables will allow multipurpose interactive use. It is through this mechanism, where television is merely one part of the CONTENT carried by the cable network, that cable is getting a share of the domestic market.

Further reading

Winston, B. (1998) *Media, Technology and Society. A History from the Telegraph to the Internet*, London: Routledge, pp. 305–20.

SEE ALSO: broadcasting; knowledge industries

CARIBBEAN

Although the term Caribbean in its geographical context can be said to describe all the lands washed by the Caribbean Sea, traditionally it has come to be applied to the Antillean island chain that stretches from latitude 23.50° to 10° north and between longitude 85° and 59° west. These Caribbean islands include many territories with historical, political, linguistic and cultural affiliations that are as varied as their past, which has been greatly influenced by the relationships of the pre- and post-colonial era. English, French, Dutch and Spanish are the main languages but local languages such as Papiamento (in the Dutch Islands) and Creole (in the French Islands) are also spoken.

However, the English-speaking Caribbean, a cohesive subregion, is the area of concern, and here the term Caribbean refers to those island territories comprising Anguilla, Antigua/Barbuda, Barbados, the Bahamas, the Cayman Islands, Dominica, Grenada, Jamaica, St Kitts/Nevis, St Lucia, Montserrat, St Vincent and the Grenadines, Trinidad and Tobago, and the Turks and Caicos Islands, as well as the mainland territories of Belize and Guyana. These former colonies of Britain have now become independent states or have some form of limited self-government as Associated States of Britain. The independent territories have formed themselves into an economic grouping known as the Caribbean Community (CARICOM) but the shared historical experience has resulted in many cultural and economic similarities, and their people share a common bond and participate in many co-operative activities at both governmental and non-governmental levels.

Generally speaking, the libraries of the Caribbean promote the use of international standards by subscribing to the principles of Universal Bibliographic Control (UBC), and the use of ANGLO-AMERICAN CATALOGUING RULES (AACR2) and International Standard Bibliographic Description (ISBD) for different categories of information materials is the norm in libraries that are staffed by trained professionals.

Public libraries

PUBLIC LIBRARIES, introduced by the British from as early as the mid-nineteenth century, exhibit varying stages of development. These range from comprehensive island coverage incorporating mobile and static units that offer service in both urban and rural areas, in Jamaica, to a single unit in the island of Anguilla. These government-supported libraries provide free services and many are housed in well-designed buildings, offering reference and lending services to the population at large as well as special services to some institutionalized groups in their communities. Many serve as centres for LEGAL DEPOSIT where such legislation is in force and these also maintain collections of the national imprints, although the arrangements are far from perfect and there are some serious problems (Peltier-Davies 1997).

National libraries

Although the term national library (see NATIONAL LIBRARIES) is incorporated in the names of many Caribbean library systems, the traditional national library as defined by Humphreys (1966) exists only in Jamaica. There the National Library of Jamaica, established in 1979 and based on the collections and staff of the former West India Reference Library, houses an impressive collection of Caribbean material and serves as the national bibliographic centre, while performing most of the functions associated with traditional national libraries (Ferguson 1996).

Special libraries

Early SPECIAL LIBRARIES date back to the turn of the century, which saw the growth particularly of medical, agricultural and legal libraries. Gener-

ally speaking, however, development of other types of special libraries in the Caribbean really began in the 1960s and can be attributed to the emphasis placed on the diversification of the economies from primary products to service and manufacturing industries with the advent of political independence in that decade. These libraries, although commonly associated with government ministries and departments, are also to be found in many semi-government entities, such as statutory bodies and public sector corporations, as well as in private-sector organizations involved in business, manufacturing, mining and service industries. Special libraries led the way in LIBRARY AUTOMATION in the region (Renwick 1996).

Academic libraries

ACADEMIC LIBRARIES exist at the University College of Belize, at the University of Guyana and on the three campus territories of the regional University of the West Indies (UWI). The UWI libraries use OCLC for cataloguing support and are located at Mona in Jamaica, Cava Hill in Barbados and St Augustine in Trinidad and Tobago. Academic libraries are also to be found in professional schools such as those associated with law in Jamaica and in Trinidad and Tobago or in theological seminaries. A few US offshore university installations also operate academic libraries in some islands such as Antigua and St Vincent. Depending on the curricula in each institution, these libraries carry significant holdings either in the arts and humanities, the social sciences or the natural sciences. The Medical Branch of the University of the West Indies Library on the Mona Campus is the centre for a Caribbean Medical Literature Indexing Project (MEDCARIB), while the law library on the Cave Hill Campus, which is well known for its collection of Caribbean and other English materials, is the centre for the West Indian Case Laws Indexing Project (WICLIP). All these academic libraries support resource-sharing both nationally and regionally.

College libraries

These serve other tertiary institutions such as teachers' colleges and special institutions such as the College of the Bahamas, the Sir Arthur Lewis College in St Lucia and the College of Arts, Science and Technology in Jamaica. Their development is uneven, ranging from well-staffed libraries in functional buildings with comprehensive collections designed to meet the needs of faculty and students, to small collections housed in makeshift accommodation and operated by paraprofessionals. Recently, however, the degree-granting and university-associated status achieved or desired by some colleges has stimulated the development of the better libraries, some of which now approximate to international academic standards.

School libraries

SCHOOL LIBRARIES are unevenly developed and varied in their administration. In some territories a basic service is provided by the Ministry of Education, either independently or through the public library. In others, however, the school library service can only be described as rudimentary, based on the initiatives of the school with support from community groups such as parent–teacher associations. The tendency is for a national service at the primary-school level with the secondary schools developing their libraries individually.

Library associations

Active LIBRARY ASSOCIATIONS have existed for several decades, uniting people with an interest in library work and serving the library and information profession in the larger territories of Barbados, Jamaica, Guyana and Trinidad and Tobago, but their fortunes have waxed and waned in the smaller territories. Worthy of note, however, is the regional Association of Caribbean University, Research and Institutional Libraries (ACURIL), which was established in 1969 and in which most of the territories are actively involved. This association links not only all the English-speaking territories of the Caribbean but also the Dutch-, French- and Spanish-speaking territories as well. ACURIL has held an annual conference each year since its inception and plays an important role in continuing education and co-operative activities for library and information professionals of the region.

Education and training

Prior to 1971 librarians gained professional qualifications either by sitting external examinations of the LIBRARY ASSOCIATION in Britain or by attending library schools in that country or in North America. The education and training of librarians (see LIBRARY EDUCATION) is now carried out by the regional school, which is the Department of Library Studies of the University of the West Indies and is located at the Mona Campus in Jamaica. This school, which was established in 1971, offers, at the undergraduate level, a three-year programme leading to the Bachelor of Arts Degree (Library Studies major). From 1973 to 1989 it offered a twelve-month Postgraduate Diploma programme. Since then, however, the postgraduate programme has been upgraded to a fifteen-month programme that incorporates ten semester courses and a research paper leading to the Master of Library Studies (MLS). Three months of compulsory fieldwork is an integral part of all three programmes. An MA in Library and Information Studies for those holding a BA in the subject was introduced in 1998. An MPhil, obtained by research and thesis, has existed since 1996. The department sees itself as having a regional as well as a national role. Special short continuing-education courses for information professionals in the field, as well as basic training for support staff, have also been organized as part of the school's outreach programme. A few people still continue to qualify or to upgrade their professional knowledge overseas. Expertise in the Caribbean has been developed on a broad basis as a result of this influence and also through involvement in international activities. For details of the school, see http://dlis_pde.uwimona.edu.jm/.

Information networks

A relatively recent development in the region has been the growth of specialized information networks that serve a variety of sectoral interests. Examples of these include the Caribbean Energy Information System (CEIS), with its focal point in Jamaica, the Caribbean Information System for Planners (CARISPLAN), with its focal point at the subregional Secretariat of the Economic Commission for Latin America and the Caribbean (ECLAC), which is based in Trinidad and Tobago. These information networks are characterized by co-operatively built automated databases with the emphasis on documents and other information material produced in the region. Online access is possible to some regional databases such as the CARISPLAN database, and also to international databases such as DIALOG, from the larger territories. The introduction of the INTERNET on the Mona Campus of the UWI and the emergence of network servers such as AMBIONET, in Trinidad, and CARIBBEAN ONLINE, in Barbados, initiated networking in the region in the early 1990s. Services developed significantly in the second half of the decade, and there are examples of regionally based Internet Service Bureaux and other infrastructural support (Miles and Bromberg 2000).

Information technology

Computer application is gradually being introduced in the region's libraries, where the CDS/ISIS software developed by UNESCO for microcomputers is emerging as the standard, mainly because it is available free of charge to developing countries. It is used primarily by the national documentation centres and special libraries that serve public sector institutions and organizations. Other software for integrated library applications has been introduced in some libraries, largely in the special library sector.

International links and relationships

International links are maintained by librarians and information professionals in the region through membership and active participation in international professional associations such as IFLA, FID and the Commonwealth Library Association (COMLA), which, except for a brief period, has had its headquarters in Jamaica since it was established in 1972.

References

Ferguson, S. (1996) 'Defining a role of a new national library in a developing country: The National Library of Jamaica 1980–1990', *Alexandria* 8: 65–74.
Humphreys, K.W. (1996) 'National library functions', *UNESCO Bulletin for Libraries* 20(4): 158–69.
Miles, K. and Bromberg, S. (2000) 'Filling an information gap for the Caribbean', *Business Information Alert* 12: 1–3.
Peltier-Davies, C. (1997) 'Public libraries as national libraries – the Caribbean experience', *Alexandria* 9: 213–38.
Renwick, S. (1996) 'Access to information in the English-speaking Caribbean', *Third World Libraries* 6: 20–8.

Further reading

Amenu-Kpodo, N. (1993) 'Commonwealth Library Association', *World Encyclopedia of Library & Information Services*, 3rd edn, ALA, pp. 220–21.
Blackman, J. (1993) 'Barbados', *World Encyclopedia of Library & Information Services*, 3rd edn, ALA, pp. 103–4.
Blake, D. (1997) 'The Commonwealth Caribbean', in *Information Sources in Official Publications*, Bowker Saur, pp. 77–91.
Douglas, D. (1981) 'British Caribbean', in M. Jackson (ed.) *International Handbook of Contemporary Developments*, New York: Greenwood Press, pp. 567–94.
Ferguson, S. (1993) 'Jamaica', *World Encyclopedia of Library & Information Services*, 3rd edn, pp. 405–6.
Johnson, I.M. and Medina, A.F. (2000) 'Library and information studies in Latin America and the Caribbean', *Focus* 31: 61–70.
Jordan, A. and Commisiong, B. (1993) 'Trinidad & Tobago', *World Encyclopedia of Library & Information Services*, 3rd edn, ALA, pp. 818–19.
Vernon, L.S. (1993) 'Belize', *World Encyclopedia of Library & Information Services*, 3rd edn, pp. ALA, 108–9.

STEPHNEY FERGUSON, REVISED BY THE EDITORS

CARNEGIE, ANDREW (1835–1919)

Industrialist and philanthropist who made new LIBRARY BUILDINGS available to hundreds of communities all over the world. His enormous financial donations paid for 2,509 library buildings throughout the English-speaking world, including 1,679 public library buildings in 1,412 communities, and 108 academic library buildings in the USA. He also donated an even larger total sum to other philanthropic ventures, including more than 7,000 church organs to the Carnegie Endowments for International Peace.

He was born in Dunfermline, Scotland, to a poor family and, despite receiving little formal education, he prospered in the USA and built up the Carnegie Steel Company. He sold this at the age of sixty-six and devoted his retirement to systematic philanthropy. For library services, his donations came at an important time. Both in the USA and Britain the need for library buildings was desperate, as towns and cities that founded services would seldom commit sufficient funds to house collections appropriately. His initiative stimulated other library benefactions and encouraged communities to fund their libraries to better levels. In 1956 financial assistance from the Carnegie Corporation helped the AMERICAN LIBRARY ASSOCIATION to formulate Public Library Standards, which confirmed much of the improvement that his donations had encouraged in the first place.

Further reading

Bobinski, G.S. (1969) *Carnegie Libraries: Their History and Impact on American Public Library Development*, Chicago: American Library Association.

SEE ALSO: donations to libraries; public libraries

CATALOGUES

Generically, a catalogue is any list, register or enumeration. Bibliographically, a catalogue is a list, whose entries identify, describe and relate information resources, hereafter referred to as *documents*.

Objectives

The objectives of modern catalogues have developed over time. The earliest Western catalogues listed manuscripts that were owned by an individual, usually royal or noble, or an institution such as a monastery or college, and served an inventory function. Gradually systematic order was introduced into the lists to permit locating documents by author, and catalogues assumed a finding function, using formal systems of alphabetization (see ALPHABETIZATION RULES); then, when the need for comprehensive and retrospective information arose, catalogues adopted a collocation function: to bring together all the editions of a work, all the works of an author and all the works on a given subject; they thus assumed the character of a bibliographic tool (Pettee 1936). The objectives of a bibliographic-tool catalogue were stated implicitly, in the middle of the nineteenth century, by Sir Anthony PANIZZI in his call for a full and accurate catalogue that would collocate like items and differentiate among similar ones. Charles Ammi CUTTER in 1876 made the first explicit statement of the objectives of catalogue; Seymour Lubetzky modified these in 1960 to underscore the concept of work, and in this form they were adopted in 1961 by the International Conference on Cataloging Principles. In 1998 the objectives were once again modified by IFLA in *Functional Requirements for Bibliographic Records* to explicate the finding, identifying, selecting and obtaining functions of catalogues.

Objects of bibliographic records

Up until the twentieth century, the documents described in catalogue entries consisted primarily of books and manuscripts. Gradually different non-book materials came to be regarded as entities embodying information and, thus, subject to bibliographical description: first serials, then musical scores, maps, films and videos, sound recordings, two- and three-dimensional representations, computer files and, now, documents in digital form.

Domains of catalogues

For the most part, the domain of documents referenced by a given catalogue has been, and continues to be, a single institution, such as a library. Catalogues describing the holdings of more than one library, called UNION CATALOGUES, were envisioned as early as the thirteenth century (Strout 1957: 10), but not until seven centuries later did they begin to be implemented at local and national levels. Today libraries are beginning to develop interfaces to their in-house catalogues to provide access to information from the Internet, including indexes to periodicals, catalogues of other libraries and full-text documents.

Physical forms

The mechanics of catalogue construction are a function of technology. One of the first catalogues, a Sumerian tablet found at Nippur, dating around 2000 BC, was carved in stone (Strout 1957: 5). For most of their long history catalogues have consisted of handwritten entries in list, sheaf or book form, inscribed on the prevailing medium for writing: after stone, there was papyrus, parchment and paper. 'Printed' entries began to appear with the invention of the typewriter in the first part of the nineteenth century, although the writing out of entries in 'library hand' continued well into the twentieth century. The use of cards as carriers for catalogue entries dates from 1791 (Strout 1957: 17), but did not become widespread until the end of the nineteenth century. The mass printing by typesetting machines and distribution of catalogue cards from a central source dates from 1901, when the LIBRARY OF CONGRESS began its card distribution programme. In the middle of the twentieth century there was a flurry of interest in catalogues in the form of microfiche and micro-film, but these have become all but eclipsed by the advent of catalogues in electronic form. For the most part these are ONLINE public access catalogues (OPACS), but they may also be carried by a magnetic or silicon storage medium, such as CD-ROM, magnetic tape or disk. Increasingly catalogue entries in machine-readable form (MARC) are being created co-operatively and distributed from a centralized source.

Arrangement of entries

In traditional (non-electronic) catalogues, how entries are arranged determines the type of access available to the user. Normally entries are arranged by author, title, alphabetic subject and classified subject. Several types of catalogues are definable in terms of these arrangements: DICTIONARY CATALOGUES, which interfile author, title and alphabetic subject entries in one sequence; divided catalogues, which separate author and title entries into one sequence and alphabetic subject entries into another; and CLASSIFIED CATALOGUES with subject entries arranged by the notation of a classification system. Entries in online catalogue displays need to be arranged methodically if catalogue objectives are to be met, with the added constraint that the arrangement must be consonant with computer filing. For the most part, the sort keys used are the traditional ones, but some online catalogues sort by non-conventional data elements such as date of publication and type of media.

Cataloguing rules

Separate codes of rules are used: (1) to describe the physical and publication attributes of documents and provide author and title access to them; and (2) to provide subject access to documents. The most extensively used code of rules for descriptive cataloguing is the ANGLO-AMERICAN CATALOGUING RULES (AACR), 2nd edn (1988) Deriving from the ninety-one rules developed by Panizzi, AACR are becoming increasingly reflective of co-operation and standardization efforts carried out at an international level. Translated into many languages, the present code is becoming something of a *de facto* standard. There has been less acceptance of a standard to provide subject access to information. In the Anglo-American community the

LIBRARY OF CONGRESS SUBJECT HEADINGS and accompanying Subject Cataloging Manual are used for alphabetic-subject access. The DEWEY DECIMAL CLASSIFICATION is a widely used standard for classified subject access to bibliographic information.

The future of catalogues

Future catalogues might be expected to develop along present economic, political and technological trends: widening of catalogue domains beyond library walls; incremental advancement toward universal bibliographical control, as this is realizable by international standardization and the sharing of bibliographic records; adaptation of codes designed for card catalogues to the online environment; development of formalisms for describing and accessing digital documents; automation of the creation of catalogue entries, to the extent this is possible.

References

Pettee, J. (1936) 'The development of authorship entry and the formation of authorship rules as found in the Anglo-American code', *Library Quarterly* 6: 270–90.
Strout, R.F. (1957) 'The development of the catalog and cataloging codes', in R.F. Strout (ed.) *Toward a Better Cataloging Code*, Chicago: University of Chicago Press, pp. 4–25.

Further reading

Svenonius, E. (2000) *The Intellectual Foundation of Information Organization*, Cambridge, MA: MIT Press.

SEE ALSO: bibliographic control; bibliographic description; MARC; organization of knowledge

ELAINE SVENONIUS

CATEGORIZATION

The practice of organizing library collections in broad categories, as opposed to detailed CLASSIFICATION. The term particularly refers to this practice for fiction, but can apply to other materials, for instance in SCHOOL LIBRARIES.

CATEGORIZATION OF FICTION

The physical arrangement of FICTION into divisions or reader interest categories, often known as genres. The rationale behind categorization is that it is a user-oriented approach to library organization and improves access to popular material. In the USA the term CLASSIFICATION tends to be used to mean categorization. However, in the UK, fiction classification schemes are identified with a more theoretical approach, for example analysing and representing the content of fiction books in a classified catalogue whilst the novels themselves remain in an alphabetical order on the shelves.

Categorization versus alphabetical arrangement

The arrangement of fiction in a single sequence, alphabetically by author, was long held to be the only possible method of shelf presentation in PUBLIC LIBRARIES. There are certain organizational advantages for the library in that the order is easy to follow, there is only one place for the books to be reshelved and, if the author is known, it is easy to find a book. Such a presentation, however, makes the assumption that readers select books by referring to the names of the authors. READING RESEARCH suggests otherwise. The majority of readers who use public libraries are not looking for a specific author or title. For example, 69 per cent of readers at libraries said they searched for fiction by type or kind (Spiller 1980). Even those who do look for specific authors are often unable to find those known authors on the shelves. In such cases the alphabetic sequence is of little use in enabling readers to discover new authors or in guiding them to similar books.

McClellan (1981) was one of the first to note that the habit of arranging fiction in alphabetical order presents the majority of readers with a daunting choice and that this serious mismatch between the level of service and the needs of the reader was damaging to the library's effectiveness. This led to experimentation with alternative arrangements such as categorization by subject matter, which was shown to satisfy hidden and unstated preferences of readers for previously unseen types of books. Some of the first British public library authorities to use this approach, applied to both fiction and non-fiction, were Cambridgeshire, Hertfordshire and Surrey, and their experiences have been described by Ainley and Totterdell (1982).

Choosing categories

In practice, shelf categorization breaks down the A–Z sequence by grouping books with similar contents together under one heading. Any library wishing to adopt categorization as a means of arranging its fiction stock needs to decide what categories to use and how many categories of subdivisions are helpful. There are no definite answers to these questions and too many categories can be as unhelpful for the reader as one alphabetic sequence. Research in the USA (Harrell 1985) surveyed forty-seven libraries and found twenty-six different fiction categories in use. However, all libraries used three categories: science fiction, westerns and mysteries. In the UK the categories used to establish PUBLIC LENDING RIGHT payments for adult fiction are romance, mystery and crime, historical, westerns, war, science fiction, fantasy and horror, and short stories (Sumsion 1991).

When choosing categories, library staff need to take into account their readers' interests and trends in publishing, which may identify new categories such as feminist fiction. A practical guide as to whether a new category is viable is whether there is sufficient material to support the section. Categorization is also a useful technique to use on a short-term basis to promote areas of stock. For example, Kent County Library Service took an innovative approach to combining the theory of fiction categorization with good display techniques to set up a number of browsing areas in which stock was arranged under a number of themes, such as 'books made into films' or 'bestsellers – past and present', to help readers choose their fiction.

Criticisms of categorization

The major practical problem of categorization is that it does not allow more than one placing. It has also been criticized (Dixon 1986) as being relevant only to some types of fiction, most of which are recognizable from the cover or publisher (such as Mills and Boon for romance, Collins for crime), and for being carried out inconsistently and not being maintained, as well as for discouraging readers from using the whole fiction collection and for encouraging a lazy approach by staff to the fiction service. A US study (Baker 1988) found that users at larger libraries were very much in favour of fiction categorization, saying it made their selection easier and quicker, and enabled them to become familiar with other novelists in a particular genre.

References

Ainley, P. and Totterdell, B. (eds) (1982) *Alternative Arrangement: New Approaches to Public Library Stock*, London: Association of Assistant Librarians.

Baker, S.L. (1988) 'Will fiction classification schemes increase use?', *Reference Quarterly* 27: 366–76.

Dixon, J. (ed.) (1986) *Fiction in Libraries*, Library Association, pp. 162–6.

Harrell, G. (1985) 'The classification and organisation of adult fiction in large American public libraries', *Public Libraries* 24(1): 13–14.

McClellan, A.W. (1981) 'The reading dimension in effectiveness and service', *Library Review* 30: 77–86.

Sear, L. and Jennings, B. (1989) 'Novel ideas: A browsing area for fiction', *Public Library Journal* 4(3): 41–4.

Spiller, D. (1980) 'The provision of fiction for public libraries', *Journal of Librarianship* 12(4): 238–64.

Sumsion, J. (1991) *PLR in Practice*, Registrar of Public Lending Right, p. 137.

Further reading

Goodall, D. (1992) *Browsing in Public Libraries*, Library and Information Statistics Unit, Loughborough University [describes eight studies of English public library use, focusing on fiction selection from the point of view of the reader].

Kinnell, M. (1991) *Managing Fiction in Libraries*, Library Association [Chapter 7, by L. Sear and B. Jennings, on organizing fiction for use, is excellent].

SEE ALSO: organization of knowledge

DEBORAH L. GOODALL

CD-ROM

A computer-based information storage and retrieval medium based on laser-technology and a strong, highly resistant 4.75 in.-diameter OPTICAL DISK. CD-ROM (Compact Disc – Read Only Memory) is one of the most popular and familiar of computer-based media. It can hold the equivalent of about 250,000 typewritten pages, or 500,000 catalogue cards or 500 high-density floppy diskettes. Its capacity ranges between 500 and 680 million characters (Mb) depending on the type of CD used. It uses the same technology as the audio CD for recording and reading data, and can have full MULTIMEDIA functionality. CD-ROM players have become standard microcomputer peripherals, and CD writers with which users can record (or 'burn') their own CDs are becoming increasingly common.

CENSORSHIP

Prohibition by political or religious authorities and their agencies of the production, distribution, circulation or sale of material in any medium or format whose content or presentation is considered to be politically, religiously or morally objectionable or otherwise harmful to individuals and society.

The concept of censorship

The concept of censorship tempts us to approach it with a moralistic black-and-white attitude. A common fallacy in censorship research has been in concentrating on specific literary cases, forgetting the general context. Censorship has in most countries been an essential part of political and cultural history, publishing, reading history and library policy.

Classical, 'hard censorship' mostly appears as a concrete, visible drama (burning of books, purification of libraries) and can be described as discontinuation of the information or literary chain. Modern censorship ('soft censorship') is more latent, and appears more intertwined with the processes of publication and tends to form permanent structures and systems (self-censorship). While the target of classical censorship was the book, modern censorship targets the reader.

We can also speak of official and unofficial censorship, political and religious censorship, direct and indirect censorship. We can define macrocensorship that refers to the governmental level (official orders, policy) and microcensorship that refers to the local decisions (local removals from collections). We can also speculate on market censorship that appears as commercial selection of materials.

Censorship can take on preventive roles (precensorship) by monitoring beforehand the materials to be published and read. It can also take the form of guidance, giving instructions to publishers and readers, and thus securing the implementation of the policy (post-censorship). Censorship has both concrete and symbolic effects, by demonizing instead of banning a book or an author.

History of modern library censorship

Libraries were heavily censored in Nazi Germany (1933–45) (Stieg 1992). Public libraries are institutions whose purpose is to collect, maintain and distribute cultural material. When their cultural content is defined politically, the social role of libraries becomes emphasized and we can even detect features of a political institution in them. Public libraries in Nazi Germany were harnessed to ideological work. Stieg's study has valuable information on general book censorship and the librarian's mental adjustment to the change. In the 1930s, the library system of Nazi Germany was a microcosm of the whole state, where politics became the only standard, and where political values controlled the whole moral code, beliefs, attitudes and social behaviour.

Similar developments had taken place in the Soviet Union after the 1917 revolution. V.I. Lenin and Nadezha K. Krupskaja defined a strategy for Soviet libraries to fight against reactionary forces. Libraries should support the class struggle and act as a vehicle spreading the international communistic movement. In the Soviet Union, strictly political BOOK SELECTION led to the creation of closed collections called *spetshrans* (*spetsialnoe hranilistse*). These hidden collections were used until the late 1980s in the Soviet Union itself and in most of the countries of CENTRAL AND EASTERN EUROPE. In 1985 the *spetshran* of the Lenin Library alone had over a million items, with 30,000–35,000 books added yearly.

In the Soviet Union, politics and censorship were never open but they were faceless and all-embracing: the term *omnicensorship* describes the situation prevailing in the Soviet Union, where in addition to the author's self-censorship the book had to pass through the publisher's censorship and also tight library inspection.

Censorship is not confined to totalitarian states. There is a classic and much discussed research study into book selection and censorship in Californian public and school libraries (Fiske 1960), designed to discover whether some external body imposed restrictions on librarians or whether librarians themselves limit their activity so that a citizen's right to versatile collections becomes threatened. The conclusion was that Californian librarians themselves act as the most active censors of their own library collections. There was not much external pressure to remove or include certain books in the library; instead, when making acquisitions, librarians themselves estimated what books would probably arouse indignation in clients and school authorities, and these books were not acquired. According to librarians, the best way to avoid book removals and censorship disputes was not to acquire controversial books for the library at all.

The authoritarian role of librarians has been the subject of further research (Busha 1972). It was determined that the best-educated librarians in the biggest libraries were the least authoritarian. But there is a contradiction: librarians can support non-censorship in principle but may still participate in censorship as a part of a security procedure.

In 1953 200 libraries supported by USIA (United States Information Agency) were investigated and censored by Joseph McCarthy, Roy Cohn and David Schine. They reported that in European USIA libraries there were 30,000 books of allegedly communistically biased writers. Works of forty writers were removed from the libraries, including books by Sinclair Lewis and Dashiell Hammett. In the 1980s the censorship by supporters of Christian fundamentalism in the USA received much publicity. Salinger's *Catcher in the Rye*, Judy Bloom's books and even Vonnegut's *Slaughterhouse 5* were banned in many school libraries.

Usually the unofficial 'soft' forms are awarded the label of censorship. For instance US library censorship in the 1980s typically followed this pattern:

1. Inquiry.
2. Expression of concern.
3. Formal complaint.
4. Attack.
5. Censorship (official removal of the material by governmental order).

The newest and most difficult form of censorship takes place on the Internet. The so-called digital or network censorship mostly happens by blocking, filtering and pre-censoring materials on the Internet. Though the persons usually targeted are the children, network censorship can prevent any user from accessing certain materials. Filtering by searches for particular terms or words can have hilarious results, such as blocking pages containing words like Dick Van *Dyke*, describing Al Gore and Bill Clinton as a *couple* or giving recipes containing chicken *breast*.

References

Busha, C.H. (1972) *Freedom versus Suppression and Censorship. With a Study of the Attitudes of Mid-western Public Libraries and a Bibliography of Censorship*, Littleton.

Fiske, M. (1960) *Book Selection and Censorship*, Berkeley: University of California Press.

Stieg, M.F. (1992) *Public Libraries in Nazi Germany*, Tuscaloosa and London: University of Alabama Press

Further reading

Blanshard, P. (1956) *The Right to Read. The Battle Against Censorship*, 2nd edn, Boston.

'Censorship', in *Encyclopaedia Britannica* (www.britannica.com).

Ekholm, K. (2000) *Kielletyt kirjat 1944–46 [Banned books in 1944–1946]*, Jyväskylä.

Kasinec, E. (1998) 'Reminiscences of a Soviet Research Library', in *Books, Libraries, Reading and Publishing in the Cold War. Livre, edition, bibliothèques, lecture durant la guerre Froide. La Table Ronde Histoire des Bibliothèques d'IFLA. 11 et 12 Juin 1998*, Paris.

Sturges, P. (1998) *Freedom of Expression and the Communication Networks*, Strasbourg: Council of Europe.

SEE ALSO: freedom of information; information law; information policy; Russia and the former Soviet Union

KAI EKHOLM

CENTRAL AMERICA

Central America consists of Guatemala, El Salvador, Honduras, Mexico, Nicaragua, Costa Rica and Panama; the total population is more than 136 million, of whom some 101 million are in Mexico. These seven countries constitute a complex and multicultural society. Costa Rica has the lowest illiteracy levels, and Guatemala the highest. Countries of various sizes have faced continuous economic, political and social crises that have caused different and unfair development levels. This uneven situation is also evident in the information services sector. Some of them handle many documentary resources, and use the most advanced technology for their library services, while others are lacking them. However, significant changes have been experienced since the late 1990s, due to greater support from the governments, as well as to a greater awareness of the need to use information, and a change of attitude towards co-operation in sharing resources especially within Central America.

Academic libraries

The ACADEMIC LIBRARIES are those that have reached the highest levels of development, in response to the demand for higher education across the region. A great number of these libraries, in both public and private institutions, have been able to automate their services, to hold important collections recorded according to international standards such as the ANGLO-AMERICAN CATALOGUING RULES (AACR) and MARC, to offer ONLINE public-access catalogues (OPACS), to access the most advanced information systems, have websites and, in some cases, publish electronic documents. The Universidad de Colima, Mexico, has produced a great number of CD-ROMs for regional libraries. Some libraries have started with the DIGITIZATION process of their holdings, such as the COLMEX (El Colegio de México) and the UNAM (Universidad Nacional Autónoma de México) libraries.

The increase in the co-operative work to ensure access to information resources has been outstanding; such is the case of the libraries of CSUCA (Consejo de Universidades Centroamericanas), which has led to the establishment of online co-operative catalogues and services, as with the one for the Instituto Interamericano de Administración de Empresas (www.incae.ac.cr) serving Costa Rica and Nicaragua, and the efforts of the Comite de Cooperacion de Bibliotecas Universitarias de Guatemala. The online catalogue of the UNAM library system, LIBRUNAM, integrated by 140 libraries, has had great influence on the academic libraries of Mexico and other countries (www.dgbiblio.unam.mx). In Mexico, the Amigos group, whose head is the COLMEX library (www.colmex.mx), has been working with US libraries in order to improve interlibrary lending.

Library associations

In all the countries there are one or more LIBRARY ASSOCIATIONS, whose aim is the improvement and development of information services, the training of library staff and to achieve greater recognition for the profession. According to the *Directorio de Asociaciones de Bibliotecarios y Profesiones Afines de America Latina y el Caribe*, published by IFLA in 1998, the six Central American countries (other than Mexico) have only one association or college, while Mexico has eleven associations and one college.

The AMBAC (Asociación Mexicana de Bibliotecarios, AC, www.ambac.org), the one with the highest membership in the region, has been responsible in the last forty-five years for the organization of the Jornadas, the most important national discussion forum, and their *Memorias* constitute an important source of information on the development of the library profession. Mexico also has the Colegio de Bibliotecarios, representing librarians with university degrees. The outstanding Colegio de Bibliotecarios de Costa Rica has attained a high degree of recognition from government and academic authorities, and has established that professional librarians should be in charge of publicly financed libraries. Also in this country AIBDA (Asociación Interamericana de Bibliotecarios y Documentalistas Agrícolas) has wide influence on SPECIAL LIBRARIES in Latin America (www.iicanet.org/aibda/). The Asociación Panameña de Bibliotecarios has also earned the recognition of academic and governmental authorities.

These associations have worked out a code of professional ethics, and published the proceedings of their congresses, serials and bulletins, although sometimes at irregular intervals.

The II Seminario Latinoamericano de asociaciones de Bibliotecarios was held in Mexico City in 1999, sponsored by IFLA, UNAM and AMBAC, in which sixteen countries participated and analysed the professional problems, the present status of the associations and the future actions that were needed to address international issues.

Library education

All Central American countries, with the exception of Honduras, have one or more library schools, generally as a part of a university, where professional librarians are educated at technician, bachelor and master levels. Although a significant number of professional librarians have been educated in these institutions, this is not enough considering the potential demand of existing libraries and information centres in the region. Also, there is a low recognition of the library profession, evidenced by the poor wages offered to these professionals.

Costa Rica has three schools: one of them linked to the Universidad Nacional, another as a part of the Universidad de Costa Rica and the third established in the Universidad Estatal a Distancia in which they offer distance library education. In Guatemala, the library school of the Universidad de San Carlos was established in 1948. Panama also offers library science studies in three university schools. El Salvador and Nicaragua have one school each. The CABCE (Centro de Actualización Bibliotecologica de Centro America), located in Costa Rica, organizes a diversity of continuous education programmes, and is sponsored by the Mellon Foundation.

In Mexico there are six schools offering undergraduate studies in librarianship. In Mexico City there is the Colegio de Bibliotecología of UNAM and the ENBA (Escuela Nacional de Bibliotecnomia y Archivonomia), and both have four-year programmes, although their curricula are different; ENBA also has a distance education programme for librarians. Postgraduate studies are only provided by UNAM; there has been a Master's degree since 1970. UNAM's doctorate in Library Science and Information Studies, which began in 2000, is the first in the Spanish-speaking Latin American countries.

It is worth mentioning that library science studies have been strongly influenced by the USA.

Library research and publications

In the UNAM, the CUIB (Centro Universitario de Investigaciones Bibliotecologicas) was established in 1981, as a forward-looking institution to encourage library science research. It has had a wide influence in Latin America. Its twenty-six research members are working in areas related to theoretical and practical problems faced by the organization and transmission of information and the provision of library services, in the country as well as in the Latin American region. Thus, a number of seminars, courses and publications on reading promotion, training of librarians, COLLECTION DEVELOPMENT, library services to the indigenous communities, universal bibliographic control, bibliographic and documentary heritage, INFORMATION POLICY, problems of the INFORMATION SOCIETY and others have been organized. CUIB has an outstanding role in the academic advancement of librarians due to its courses, seminars and diplomas, in which national and foreign specialists take part. CUIB has the most important professional publishing programme in the region. Its periodical,

Investigación bibliotecológica. Archivos, bibliotecas, documentación, is published in printed and electronic formats.

The library schools, academic libraries and the associations also publish important documents, but still the scarcity of professional literature in Spanish to support library education is a serious problem.

National libraries

The Central American NATIONAL LIBRARIES are supported by the cultural or the education governmental authorities of each country, except in the case of the National Library of Mexico, which since 1929 has been a part of the UNAM.

In the 1990s these libraries, together with those of all Latin America, Spain and Portugal, joined together to form the ABINIA (Asociación de Estados Iberoamericanos para el Desarrollo de las Bibliotecas Nacionales de los Países de Iberoamérica), which has promoted a better knowledge of the development achieved by these libraries. It has also carried out joint research into their common problems, including co-operative projects related to PRESERVATION, digital libraries (see DIGITAL LIBRARY) and UNION CATALOGUES. The Central American national libraries have joined together to obtain foreign financial support to encourage the improvement of their services. Nicaragua and Guatemala have received special support from Sweden to enhance their collections, to conclude their national bibliographies and to microfilm historic documents, and from Spain to improve their SERVICES FOR VISUALLY IMPAIRED PEOPLE.

The national libraries of Costa Rica and Panama are in a better situation. The latter has the support of the Fundación Biblioteca Nacional de Panamá as a provider of financial resources for its institution (www.binal.ac.pa).

All national libraries benefit from LEGAL DEPOSIT to develop their collections, and to ensure the preservation and diffusion of their bibliographic and documentary heritage. The Biblioteca Nacional de México has an outstanding position, holding the more important bibliographic and documentary heritage in the region, being the American country in which the first printing house was established in the sixteenth century (http://biblional.bibliog.unam.mx).

Mexican and Nicaraguan representatives are part of the regional committee for the Memory of the World programme of UNESCO.

Public and school libraries

In Central America in general, PUBLIC LIBRARIES also act as SCHOOL LIBRARIES, because most of the educational institutions have not developed effective library services; this is true even in Mexico. Public libraries in Guatemala and Nicaragua have received special support from Sweden, Spain and the USA for the improvement of their services, especially for children. El Salvador's libraries have had a rather peculiar development because of the continuous earthquakes suffered in this country.

In some countries, public libraries have had significant improvements to their services, in some cases supported by the national libraries. This is the case in Panama with its sixty-nine public libraries, and in Costa Rica, with sixty libraries.

In Mexico, the Dirección General de Bibliotecas (Públicas) has achieved a significant increase in library services all over the country, in which 6,000 public libraries of various sizes have been established, although most of them have holdings and are intended to support basic school students. Some libraries have begun to offer services through the Internet. Mexican and Central American public libraries face the serious problem of unqualified personnel and extremely low wages.

In spite of the fact that the greatest part of Central American countries and the central and southern regions of Mexico have a high percentage of indigenous population, they have not developed special collection policies or library services for these communities.

Special libraries

Among the SPECIAL LIBRARIES in the region, the agricultural and medical libraries and information centres have had the most notable development. The Instituto Interamericano de Cooperación para la Agricultura has its headquarters in Costa Rica; its library has a great influence all over the region (www.iicanet.org). In the same field, the International Maize and Wheat Improvement Centre library, established in Mexico, is famed for its information services all over the world (www.cimmyt.mx).

The libraries of hospitals and health centres have established a valuable information system in Mexico, whose head is Centro Nacional de Información y Documentación sobre Salud (http://cenids.insp.mx/cenids/).

In these countries, especially in Mexico, there are also important special libraries and information centres on art, literature, history and energy resources using all electronic resources and international databanks to give support to their users. The private Biblioteca Gallardo, with a collection of ancient and valuable books, the most important in El Salvador, was practically destroyed during the January 2001 earthquake.

Central American countries were represented at the Primer Encuentro Iberoamericano de Bibliotecas Parlamentarias, which took place in Mexico City in 1994, supported by IFLA, where they learned about the information services required by the parliamentary bodies.

Further reading

Fernandez de Zamora, R.M. and Budnik, C. (2001) 'Bibliographic Heritage of Latin America', *Alexandria* 13: 27–34.
Memoria (2001) *Encuentro Latinoamericano sobre Atención Bibliotecaria a Comunidades Indígenas*, México: UNAM.
Memoria (2001) *II Seminario Latinoamericano de Asociaciones de Bibliotecarios y Profesionales Afines*, México: IFLA, UNAM.
Polo Sifontes, F. (2001) *The Development of National Libraries in Central America*, Boston: IFLA-CDNL.

ROSA MARIA FERNANDEZ DE ZAMORA

CENTRAL AND EASTERN EUROPE

The Central and Eastern European (CEE) countries considered in this entry include Albania, Bulgaria, the Czech Republic, Hungary, Poland, Romania, Slovakia and the former Yugoslavia.

Economic and political transition

The collapse of communism and the dissolution of the Soviet Union resulted in major economic and political changes in Central and Eastern Europe in the early 1990s. One of the most important changes was the creation of new states such as the Slovak and Czech Republics, and the countries that emerged from the former Yugoslavia, namely Bosnia-Herzegovina, Croatia, Macedonia, Slovenia and Yugoslavia (i.e. Serbia and Montenegro). While the Czechs and Slovaks

divided their country peacefully, the Southeastern European countries of the former Yugoslavia went through a decade of civil wars.

Yugoslav civil wars did not spare libraries. In 1992 Serbian forces set fire to Bosnia's National and University Library in Sarajevo. An estimated 90 per cent of the Library's collection (including 155,000 rare books and 478 manuscript codices) was destroyed (Riedlmayer 2001). One of the few Bosnian libraries that escaped destruction during the 1992–5 war was the Gazi Husrev-bey Library in Sarajevo. Library staff saved the collection by relocating it eight times during the war (Peic 1999).

In addition to political changes, the CEE countries have been undergoing economic reforms that in some cases have resulted in more competitive and free-market economies. There is already a growing gap between the Czech Republic, Hungary, Poland and Slovenia, countries that have reformed their economies extensively, and Albania, Bulgaria, Romania and most of the former Yugoslav republics, countries that have failed to attract foreign direct investment and are falling behind in economic reforms (Smith 2000: xii).

The current economic situation and possible future enlargement of the European Union will have a major influence on the development of library and information services in the region. Once the more prosperous countries reintegrate their economies into the Western European market they will be able to spend more on their cultural and educational institutions. There is a danger that the poorer countries, especially in the Balkans, will end up on the outside of a newly integrated Europe.

Library and information services and systems

Since the early 1990s the CEE countries have struggled to provide sufficient funds for social programmes, including cultural and educational ones. After the collapse of communism most of the CEE countries cut subsidies for libraries and state-run publishing companies. Consequently, many libraries, especially PUBLIC LIBRARIES, were closed or consolidated as 'they were at the bottom of the list of governmental priorities' (Krastev 1996: 62).

Since the mid-1990s the economic situation has improved, at least in some CEE countries.

For example, the Czech Republic, Hungary, Poland and Slovenia can now afford to spend more on cultural and educational institutions. There has also been external support provided by Western Europe through PHARE and TEMPUS (European Union programmes designed to help CEE countries with their economic and social restructuring) and by US foundations such as the Andrew W. Mellon Foundation and the Soros Foundation. A large part of this support has been used for LIBRARY AUTOMATION and the development of ONLINE public-access catalogues.

NATIONAL UNION CATALOGUES

Libraries, in conjunction with universities and research institutes, are Internet pioneers in Central and Eastern Europe. The development of the World Wide Web and the implementation of integrated library systems provide the user with access to the CEE library catalogues as well as information about their collections and services. The creation of national UNION CATALOGUES is one of the best examples of the latest technological developments in some CEE libraries.

As of mid-2001 the Czech Republic, Slovenia and Poland have already developed or have begun the implementation of national union catalogues.

The CASLIN Union Catalogue of the Czech Republic was created on the basis of the CASLIN (Czech and Slovak Library Information Network) Project in the late 1990s. There are over thirty Czech and Moravian libraries that participate in the CASLIN Union Catalogue by contributing new cataloguing records or using the existing ones for cataloguing purposes. In 2000 there were almost 600,000 monograph records and approximately 60,000 foreign serials records in the CASLIN Union Catalogue. The participating libraries must observe established standards for record processing (e.g. UNIMARC, ISBD, AACR2, UNIVERSAL DECIMAL CLASSIFICATION (UDC)). It should be mentioned here that some records produced by the Czech National Library (one of the major CASLIN participants) are now occasionally being loaded into the OCLC database. In the near future the CASLIN Union Catalogue will also include records of Czech periodicals that will be merged with the existing catalogue of foreign serials.

COBISS (Co-operative Online Bibliographic System and Services) is Slovenia's national union catalogue and its major gateway to information resources. It provides the participating 244 libraries (including the National Library of Slovenia) with 'conditions, necessary for shared cataloguing at a national level, including bibliographies and the automation of local functions' (Seljak 2000: 12). As of May 2000 the COBISS National Union Catalogue contained over 1.7 million monographic and serials records of print and non-print materials. Some records originally created by the Slovenian National Library in the COBISS system can now also be found in the OCLC database. While the COBISS system and catalogue is mainly used by the Slovenian libraries, some Bosnian and Croatian libraries have joined (or rejoined) it recently. This is a very positive development, as the countries of the former Yugoslavia work to re-establish cultural, economic and political relations.

The COBISS system also functions as the main gateway for Slovenian libraries and their users to access information resources. Patrons can get access to foreign bibliographic databases such as OCLC WorldCat, ERIC, the Library of Congress name AUTHORITY FILE and many others.

By mid-1997 eleven Polish libraries already had catalogues available through the Internet. The implementation of VTLS by some major Polish libraries had 'a considerable effect upon the creation of bibliographic and cataloging standards fitted for the online environment' (Sroka 1997: 191). One of the most important standards first adopted by the VTLS Consortium of Polish libraries and later by the National Library was the USMARC format for the transfer of bibliographic data.

The main authority file (abbreviated in Polish as *ckhw*) has become a basis for the creation of the National Union Catalogue (referred to as NUKat). The catalogue should be operational by the end of 2001. The participants of the NUKat project include twenty-one VTLS libraries, fifty-four Horizon libraries and the National Library. As of June 2001 the main authority file consisted of 460,333 records (including 340,799 personal and corporate names and 50,803 subject headings). The NUKat National Union Catalogue will make those records (as well as bibliographic records) available to participating libraries and thus will greatly enhance bibliographic and cataloguing standards in Polish libraries.

National libraries' websites

Since the Internet made its way to the region many CEE national libraries have been using Web technology to advertise their collections and provide access to their online catalogues. Well-designed websites can attract a whole new category of virtual users interested in CEE libraries.

By mid-2001 eight CEE national libraries had websites. Most of them had a corresponding English version, but the English-language site was usually lacking some information from the original version. Only the Hungarian National Library could be accessed in another language (German) in addition to English. Most of the sites had links to either Web-based OPACs or telnet OPACs. Only the Polish National Library and the Hungarian National Library provided access to their national bibliographies.

The accessibility and performance of some CEE national library websites are hindered by the lack of an accurate English version, poorly organized staff directories and the lack of a site search engine. By improving their websites the CEE national libraries may attract even more foreign virtual users. These websites can be traced through the Gabriel gateway (Gabriel 2001)

Library education

Many CEE library schools have been undergoing organizational and curricular changes. Their biggest challenge is the development of a new model of library studies that would combine more traditional book-based and bibliographic studies with modern information technology.

For example, the University of Warsaw Institute of Information Science and Bibliological Studies tries to reconcile two orientations, namely bibliological studies and information science. On the other hand, the International Centre for Information Management Systems and Services in Toruń (created in 1997 as a self-supporting school of librarianship and information management for Central and Eastern European students) challenges the traditional model of library education in Poland. The school focuses exclusively on the latest developments in information technology and library management.

The Institute of Information Studies and Librarianship at Charles University in Prague offers a variety of courses ranging from retrospective bibliography to information science and information management.

The curriculum of the Department of Library and Information Science of the Eotvos Lorand University in Budapest includes courses in both the history of bibliography and information science.

The CEE library schools are now teaching more topics such as computer technology, library management, library automation, etc. There is a decreasing demand for traditional subjects such as history of libraries, history of the book, etc. The trend towards modern library education will continue as the CEE library schools revise and update their curricula in line with developments in US and Western European library studies. Many of the schools have websites that can be found through the website of the Royal School of Library and Information Science in Denmark (www.db.dk/dbi/internet/schools.htm).

Future trends

More than ten years after the fall of communism, Central and Eastern Europe is a greatly diversified region. The Czech Republic, Hungary, Poland and Slovenia are more advanced in their economic reforms than other CEE countries. As they can afford to spend more on education, their libraries and library schools are in the forefront of library automation and educational reforms. The greatest challenge facing the countries of the former Yugoslavia (Slovenia being an exception) as well as Albania, Bulgaria and Romania is bridging the economic gap between Southeastern Europe and Central Europe. A chronic political crisis and a lack of economic reforms experienced by many Balkan countries will have a negative impact on the development of libraries and information services in that region.

That is why it is crucial for the future development of Southeastern European libraries to maintain co-operation with the West and former Communist countries (especially Slovenia). An interesting example of the co-operation between Bosnian libraries and Western European and US libraries is 'CUPRIJA' (a bridge) – a group of librarians who are helping to reconstruct the National and University Library in Sarajevo and reconstitute its holdings, especially the collections of Bosniaca (www.soros.org.ba/cuprija/index.html).

As the co-operation between CEE libraries and Western Europe and the USA increases, the need for stricter standards for the transfer of bibliographic data will become even more important. Some CEE libraries are already using USMARC or UNIMARC in their bibliographic databases. The Czech National Library and the Slovenian National Library are contributing records to OCLC. The CEE cataloguing standards need to be revised and updated so that more CEE cataloguing records can be used by global bibliographic utilities (e.g. OCLC WorldCat etc.).

References

Gabriel (2001) [For URLs and information about Central and Eastern European national libraries see the homepage of 'Gabriel – Gateway to Europe's National Libraries' (http://portico.bl.uk/gabriel/en/welcome.html).]

Krastev, D. (1996) 'Libraries in transition', in M. Kocójowa (ed.) *Libraries in Europe's Post Communist Countries*, Krakow: Polskie Towarzystvo Bibliologiczne, Oddzial w Krakowie, pp. 61–4.

Peic, S. (1999) 'Sarajevo: Coping with disaster', in P. Sturges (ed.) *Disaster and After*, Taylor Graham, pp. 151–60.

Riedlmayer, A. (2001) 'Convivencia under fire', in J. Rose (ed.) *The Holocaust and the Book*, Amherst: University of Massachusetts Press, pp. 266–91.

Seljak, M. (2000) 'COBISS: National Union Catalogue', *New Library World* 101(1,153): 12–20.

Smith, A. (2000) *The Return to Europe*, New York: St Martin's Press.

Sroka, M. (1997) 'Creating bibliographic and cataloging standards and developing cooperation in Polish academic libraries after the implementation of VTLS', *Information Technology and Libraries* 16(4): 182–92.

SEE ALSO: European Union information policies; Nordic countries; Russia and the former Soviet Union

MAREK SROKA

CHAIN INDEXING

An alphabetical SUBJECT INDEX system, originally devised by S.R. RANGANATHAN. A list of terms is taken from the terms used in a CLASSIFICATION scheme. For each item (which might be a monograph, a paper in a journal or some other entity), either the most precise term, or the broadest term, is assigned. The chain is then created by going from this term to the broadest term that describes the item. The chain might thus run *farming:agriculture:technology*. Any of the terms

can be used as the heading in the index, and the other headings then follow in order. The entry might thus take one of these three forms:

> *farming:agriculture:technology*
> *agriculture:technology*
> *technology*

This can also be presented in the reverse order, beginning with the broadest term, but no link in the chain can be omitted between the first term chosen and the end of the sequence.

SEE ALSO: organization of knowledge

CHAOS THEORY

The study of phenomena that appear random, but which in fact have an element of regularity that can be described mathematically. First identified by the meteorologist Edward Lorenz in 1960, chaotic behaviour has been found to exist in a wide range of applications, such as the incidence of medical conditions or weather patterns. Katsirikou and Skiadis (2001) argue that the volume of resources, variety of technologies, number of different providers and interfaces available in LIBRARIES constitute an instance of chaotic behaviour. Chaos theory can therefore provide useful approaches to the management of information.

References

Katsirikou, A. and Skiadis, C.H. (2001) 'Chaos in the library environment', *Library Management* 22: 278–87.

Further reading

Alligood, K. *et al.* (eds) (1996) *Chaos: An Introduction to Dynamical Systems*, New York: Springer.

Haywood, T. and Preston, J. (1999) 'Chaos theory, economics and information: The implications for strategic decision making', *Journal of Information Science* 25: 173–82.

CHILDREN'S LIBRARIES

Services to children and young people aged from birth to adolescence provided by public library (see PUBLIC LIBRARIES) authorities in most countries. Ages of formal transfer to adult services vary between 11 and 18 years, with 14–16 the usual period of transition. Ease of access to targeted lending and reference materials in a variety of formats, study space, specialist staff and promotional programmes are common elements in well-founded services.

Service origins

EARLY LIBRARIES

Prior to 1850 in the UK, few library services were available to children, other than those provided in day and Sunday schools. A similar situation existed in other developed countries. Books were mostly provided through class teaching and rudimentary SCHOOL LIBRARIES. The earliest public library service to youths was at Manchester in 1862, when a separate reading department for boys, with its own stock of literature, was opened. There were around forty libraries throughout England and Wales by 1891 that had special collections for children. Similar moves were taking place in the USA, where the first children's library opened in Brookline, Massachusetts, in 1890. So rapid were developments that, in 1901, the Children's Library Association (CLA) became a section of the AMERICAN LIBRARY ASSOCIATION (ALA).

In the UK, services were rudimentary at first: opening hours took little account of children's needs and poorly educated individuals were often appointed as librarians. Few children were even allowed direct access to the books, until 1906, when a children's reading room was opened at the new Islington Central Library. Schemes of public and school library co-operation were common in this period; these evolved into the schools library services, largely provided by public libraries in England and Wales. These acted as agents for local education authorities to support school libraries and ensure children's libraries were not used by children and teachers simply as textbook repositories. Links between public and school libraries have not developed in the same way in other countries.

TRANSATLANTIC COMPARISONS

Some of the best early public library services for children, with spacious buildings, customized equipment, furniture and well-qualified staff, were found in the USA. Specialist training was instituted there in 1898. However, in the 1920s advances in library work with teenagers were being developed in the UK. A pioneer intermediate library opened at Walthamstow in 1924 with over 4,000 volumes, and the Carnegie United Kingdom Trust provided book grants to youth clubs in 1926. As the quality and quantity of CHILDREN'S LITERATURE increased in the 1930s and 1940s, book stocks were enhanced by new authors, although there were still concerns about the range of titles being provided. In 1936 the first modern reviewing journal, *Junior Bookshelf*, modelled on the US *Horn Book Magazine*, was published, and surveys of children's reading began to be considered important. A more professional approach to service delivery was also evident in the LIBRARY ASSOCIATION's greater interest in children's work; the Association of Children's Librarians was established as their Youth Libraries Section (later Group) in 1945. In commitment to young adult services, however, they lagged behind the USA somewhat; there, as early as 1929, the Young People's Reading Round Table had been founded as part of the CLA.

Professional approaches to children's services

Since 1945 there has been increasing professional commitment to children's and youth services, with the IFLA complementing the work of national associations by defining standards of basic provision and establishing a philosophy for children's services. In 1963 IFLA issued a Memorandum on Library Work with Children, drawn up by the Sub-Committee of the Public Libraries Section (IFLA 1965). This remains a definitive statement of purpose, although a revised edition is currently being prepared (www.ifla.org/VII/s10/scl.htm#3). The ALA produced its *Standards for Children's Services in Public Libraries* in 1964 (Chicago ALA), and emphasized the need for non-book materials, then an uncommon feature of provision in most other countries. The Library Association guidelines, which were not produced until 1991, have reflected the increasing focus on the child as user and the importance of targeting services more carefully to ensure individual needs are met. Intellectual, language, social and educational development are the focus for provision, with emphasis on the need for adequate materials, including books, periodicals, audiovisual media and computer equipment and software. Specialist staff and effective training for all public library staff in serving children and young people are regarded as essential, although there is concern at the reduction in the number of specialist posts and the loss of children's work from library school curricula (Shepherd 1986).

Standards of service

Much of the work on delivering effective services is now directed to measuring the quality of services and identifying the relevant performance indicators. Basic provision has not been established in most countries and the emphasis therefore remains on maximizing scarce resources and ensuring children's needs are accurately identified so that they may be more effectively met.

References

International Federation of Library Associations, Committee on Library Work with children (1965) *Library Service to Children*, 2nd edn, Stockholm: Biblioteksjanst Lund.

Shepherd, J. (1986) 'A crisis of confidence: The future of children's work', *International Review of Children's Literature and Librarianship* 1: 22–32.

Further reading

Barker, K. (1997) *Children's Libraries: A Reading List*, Library Association (available at www.la-hq.org.uk/directory/prof_issues.html).

Ellis, A. (1971) *Library Services for Young People in England and Wales 1830–1970*, Pergamon Press.

Library Association (1991) *Children and Young People: Library Association Guidelines for Public Library Services*, Library Association Publishing.

Walter, V.A. (1992) *Output Measures for Public Library Service to Children: A Manual of Standardised Procedures*, American Library Association.

SEE ALSO: public libraries

MARGARET KINNELL

CHILDREN'S LITERATURE

Books and other materials in an increasingly diverse range of formats, including audio cassettes and CD-ROM, which contain narrative texts written for children and young adults. The breadth of scope implied by this has caused much critical controversy about what constitutes a children's book, given that concepts of childhood and adolescence have shifted over the centuries.

Development

THE EARLY PERIOD

Children's books written for entertainment did not emerge as a commercially viable specialism until the 1740s. Before then, children and young adults read widely in adult popular literature, in the school books published from Caxton's time and in books of courtesy like *The Babee's Book*. Children learnt to read from crudely produced ABCs and hornbooks. From these emerged the battledore, a folded piece of cardboard popular until the mid-nineteenth century. Illustrated alphabets were rare before the eighteenth century, but Comenius's *Orbis sensualium pictus*, first published in English in 1659 and the earliest illustrated encyclopaedia for children, was known throughout Europe. This exceptional text served to highlight the lack of suitable material for child readers.

ORIGINS OF THE CHILDREN'S BOOK TRADE

When John Locke wrote his *Thoughts Concerning Education* in 1693 he therefore reiterated others' concerns that children should have 'some easy, pleasant book', as well as school texts and the flimsy chapbooks that contained old tales from the oral tradition (see ORAL TRADITIONS). Thomas Boreman and Mary Cooper were among the earliest publishers to supply such material – *The Gigantick Histories* (1740–3) and *Tommy Thumb's Pretty Song Book, Voll 2* [sic] (1744) just pre-dated John Newbery's more successful and sustained publishing and bookselling venture. His most famous books are *A Little Pretty Pocket-Book* (1744) and *The History of Little Goody Two-Shoes* (1765); he is acknowledged as the first publisher to make a business of importance from the children's trade. The mid-eighteenth century was a turning point in children's BOOK PRODUCTION. Changed attitudes to childhood, wider LITERACY and better educational opportunities created the conditions for publishers to specialize in children's books (Plumb 1975). By the end of the nineteenth century production techniques were improving, coloured illustrations were becoming widely available and a great range of titles was being issued. Cross-cultural influences were also important. Fairy tales, *Robinson Crusoe* and the moral tales inspired by the educational philosopher Jean-Jacques Rousseau appeared in most of the European languages; they also crossed the Atlantic.

NINETEENTH-CENTURY EXPANSION

Morality and instruction were the main themes of much of children's literature through to the nineteenth century and beyond – Isaac Watts's

Divine Songs (1717), for example, was a staple of Victorian nurseries. More lighthearted and amusing tales also became increasingly available. The Grimms and Hans Andersen were early on translated into English and joined the numerous versions of Charles Perrault's fairy tales that were first famous in England as *Histories, or Tales of Past Times. Told by Mother Goose.* Illustrated books proliferated as mechanical production techniques were introduced and pictures often assumed greater significance than text. From the mid-century, serious artists, who included Randolph Caldecott, Walter Crane and Kate Greenaway, turned to children's literature as a creative outlet and made the modern picture book. (The Library Association Greenaway Medal was instituted in 1955.) Authorship was also being pursued more intensely. Lewis Carroll's *Alice's Adventures in Wonderland* (1865) changed the whole cast of children's literature with its extended fantasy narrative (Darton 1982) and adventure and school stories were becoming more significant. Thomas Hughes's *Tom Brown's School Days* (1857) and Frederic Farrar's *Eric, or Little by Little* (1858), for example, developed characterization and storyline, and presaged the modern novel, and by the turn of the century E. Nesbit was achieving genuine warmth and humour in her extension of the range of domestic stories. Periodical literature, too, offered greater variety and amusement, with plentiful illustrations and vivid stories. *Little Folks* (1871–1933) was a magazine for children which included W.G.H. Kingston and Mrs Ewing among its early contributors and retained a lively naturalness until its demise. A less patronizing tone was increasingly evident in writing for children.

Modern children's books

From the beginning of the twentieth century up to the 1940s children's books grew in importance as the number of juvenile titles increased by around 70 per cent and the paperback became successful. The Library Association established its Carnegie Medal in 1936, with Arthur Ransome's *Pigeon Post* the first winner. This was also the period when many 'classics' and enduring characters first appeared, including *The Wind in the Willows*, Rupert Bear, Winnie-the-Pooh, the Hobbit, Biggles, Just William and Mary Poppins. Media involvement began with radio broadcasts of serial readings. After 1945 internationalism

was heightened as the quality and quantity of books improved in the UK, the USA and across Europe. The International Board on Books for Young People (IBBY) and its Hans Christian Andersen Medal have been catalysts for translation and exchange. Major writers, among them William Mayne, Lucy Boston, Philippa Pearce and Peter Dickinson, are now widely known overseas, although fewer international authors have been translated into English. Successful exceptions include Paul Berna, Dick Bruna and Astrid Lindgren. The impact of Canadian, Australian and New Zealand writers has been influential in challenging the dominance of an English perspective in children's books, as has multinational publishing. Films, television and computer media now complement as well as compete with more traditional formats, although books are retaining their appeal.

References

Darton, F.J.H. (1982) *Children's Books in England: Five Centuries of Social Life*, Cambridge, UK: Cambridge University Press.

Plumb, J.H. (1975) 'The new world of children in eighteenth century England', *Past and Present* 67: 64–95.

Further reading

Hunt, P. (ed.) (1995) *An Illustrated History of Children's Literature*, Oxford: Oxford University Press.

Whalley, J.I. and Chester, T.R. (1988) *A History of Children's Book Illustration*, London: John Murray.

SEE ALSO: book trade; publishing

MARGARET KINNELL

CILIP

Since April 2002, the Chartered Institute of Library and Information Professionals (CILIP) has been the successor to the LIBRARY ASSOCIATION and the INSTITUTE OF INFORMATION SCIENTISTS, and the chief association for the INFORMATION PROFESSIONS in the UK. Similar bodies recognizing the CONVERGENCE between librarians and information scientists have been created elsewhere, notably the Australian Library and Information Association (ALIA) and the Library and Information Association of South Africa (LIASA), but none have included such a large and venerable association as the Library Association. A new association, also intended to include ASLIB, had been proposed by Saunders (1989), but on that occasion the obstacles had proved too great to be overcome. A Charter and Bylaws for the new association were agreed in 2001, but the period April 2002 to March 2005 is intended as a transitional period in which matters like new local branch arrangements, a new framework of qualifications and a new CODE OF PROFESSIONAL CONDUCT will be developed.

References

Saunders, W.L. (1989) *Towards a Unified Professional Organization for Library and Information Science and Services: A Personal View*, Library Association Publishing.

Further reading

Library and Information Update (April 2002–). CILIP website (www.cilip.org.uk).

CINEMA

The general term for motion pictures, the industry that produces and distributes them, the art form that they embody and (in the UK) the place in which they are exhibited to the general public. The US term for the last is movie theater.

SEE ALSO: film; mass media

CIRCULATING LIBRARY

Although this can mean any library that lends books for use outside the building, in common usage it is reserved for a commercial library where payment has to be made for the use of books. Borrowers, unlike the users of SUBSCRIPTION LIBRARIES, do not have joint ownership of the books and other materials. Such libraries were first established in England in the late seventeenth century, but reached their apogee in the nineteenth century in the rival companies of Mudie and W.H. Smith. They were also common in the USA in the eighteenth and nineteenth centuries, and in some other parts of the then British Empire. A few commercial circulating libraries survive (including one in India), but for the most part their role has now been inherited by PUBLIC LIBRARIES. The principle, however, underlies the commercial video lending libraries that became ubiquitous towards the end of the twentieth century.

Further reading

Griest, G.L. (1970) *Mudie's Circulating Library and the Victorian Novel*, David & Charles.
Skelton-Foord, C. (1998) 'To buy or to borrow? Circulating libraries and novel reading Britain, 1778–1828', *Library Review* 47: 348–54.

SEE ALSO: history of libraries

CIRCULATION SYSTEM

A method, either manual or electronic, of recording loans of documents and other media from a collection by linking unique borrower and bibliographic data. A system will normally provide the means to identify overdue loans and to recall loans required before the due date. Circulation systems are central to the wider concept of 'access services', a term now sometimes used to include other areas of library operation such as reshelving, interlibrary loan (see INTERLIBRARY LENDING) and current periodicals.

Non-electronic systems

The earliest method of recording loans was to write borrower and item details in a ledger. Cancelling a loan, let alone checking the whereabouts of a particular item, becomes difficult with even a small number of loans. The Brown issue system, widely used in libraries before automation was common, physically links a card taken from the book with a ticket surrendered by the borrower. The cards, inserted in the ticket pocket, are filed in order, allowing checks on books; the number of tickets allocated to each borrower limits their total loans. No statistics, other than a gross loan count, are possible as the borrower–book link is destroyed when the book is returned and its card replaced. Multipart slips (two- or three-part carboned slips), on which book and borrower information is recorded, offer a wider range of query facilities as the slips can be separated and filed in book, borrower or date order, but more filing is involved for both issues and returns. Slips may be saved for manual analysis. Photocharging offers a quick method of collecting loan data, by photographing book label and borrower ID together, but the processing of the data is the same as for any other manual system.

Manual methods become both staff- and space-intensive as issues increase. They are susceptible to human filing error, and checking for overdue items can be difficult unless loan periods are fixed (for example at the end of an academic term). The provision of any sort of statistical data, other than a raw count of transactions, is strictly limited. However, manual systems can still be effective in collections where circulation is low or where automation is too expensive.

Electronic systems

Advances in computer technology since the early 1970s have led to the introduction of automated circulation systems in many libraries. Increased accuracy of circulation records has improved access to collection material and electronic data capture has made the service quicker and easier for borrowers. Data capture, from both document and borrower, is by means of electronic coding, using optical character recognition, magnetic coding or, most frequently, bar-coding. Each borrower number is unique, as is each document number, although the latter may be based on INTERNATIONAL STANDARD BOOK NUMBER or library accession number. Different bar-coding systems exist, often leading to incompatibility between commercial systems.

The linked borrower and document numbers are stored electronically in a database and may be sorted to provide either printed lists of borrower loans, items borrowed, overdue loans, etc., or an online interrogation facility on a terminal linked to the database. Early systems were offline – that is, not connected directly to the database. In an offline system data is collected and stored, usually on magnetic tape, and this is used to update the database at regular intervals, for example overnight ('batch-processing'). Bibliographic information may be added at this stage. Printouts of the previous day's transactions will be produced and copies of the entire loan database, sorted by document number and borrower number, will be printed less frequently, perhaps weekly. This type of system can usually provide printed letters for overdue or recalled items and fairly detailed circulation statistics.

The next stage in development was online access to the database, doing away with large printouts, although updating was still batched, usually overnight, so the current day's transactions could not be viewed. Interrogation of the database is through a query function, removing the need to page through lists. The most recent

systems operate in real time, with the database updated immediately a loan transaction occurs. Many are linked to an ONLINE public access catalogue, which provides the circulation system with bibliographic data and the catalogue with current access information. These are known as integrated library systems.

Functions

Various types of collection will have different circulation requirements. For example, ACADEMIC LIBRARIES will usually want to include a short-loan collection (one-day loan or less) for undergraduate course material and require an efficient recall process for reserved material. PUBLIC LIBRARIES need to cope with items incurring hire charges, such as music and videos, and to record loans from mobile libraries (see MOBILE LIBRARY) and to housebound readers. SPECIAL COLLECTIONS of rare material on closed access may require a circulation system to record in-house use. There are, however, core features that are now expected from an automated circulation system. An integrated system should offer the variety, choice and ease of operation needed to implement a collection's policies and regulations. These will include variable borrower categories (reflecting different privileges), variable document categories (reflecting different loan policies), variable loan periods and variable fines. Reliability is essential, with some form of standby provision should the main system go down. Because of DATA PROTECTION legislation, security of data is important: any public access query facility must only be available to the authorized borrower, and security is achieved by using personal identification numbers (PINs) in conjunction with borrower ID or by electronically scanning the borrower card.

Statistics have become increasingly important for collection management. If loan data is archived, sophisticated systems should be able to provide virtually unlimited analysis. This is particularly valuable when linked to bibliographic data, giving detailed profiles of a collection's use. In practice, such analysis often requires specialist expertise and can be extravagant with processing time, sometimes interfering with the more essential operations of the circulation system or ONLINE public-access catalogue (OPAC). Accuracy and consistency of loan data are important in the recording of sample loans for the PUBLIC LENDING RIGHT scheme, and accounts information, particularly of hire charges, may be required for auditing purposes.

Future developments

Self-service is a major current development in integrated systems. Reservations are possible on OPACs and self-service issue points have been installed in some collections. The concept of virtual access has already reached libraries. Music and video can be accessed on the Internet and some universities are already offering tuition online. Following the trend from holdings to access, the future will bring a greater use of online access to documents and less borrowing of original material, thus diminishing the importance of circulation systems.

Further reading

Paietta, A.C. (1991) *Access Services: A Handbook*, McFarland & Company (Chapter 1).
Preece, B.G., and Kilpatrick, T.L. (1998). 'Cutting out the middleman: Patron initiated inter library loans', *Library Trends* 47: 144–57.
Sapp, G. (ed.) (1992) *Access Services in Libraries: New Solutions for Collection Management*, Haworth Press.

PENNY CRAVEN

CITATION ANALYSIS

Citations and reasons for citing

Citations are notes placed in the main text of an academic publication that give a bibliographic reference to published work which has been used or quoted by the author. The principle underlying the indexing of citations is as follows: if one document cites another document, they bear a conceptual relationship. The references given in a publication link that publication to previous knowledge. This is the basic idea that led to the development of citation indexes, published by the Philadelphia-based Institute for Scientific Information (ISI) (www.isinet.com). In addition, journal-to-journal citation data are compiled by the ISI and published in the *Journal of Citation Reports* (*JCR*). Citation analysis is the study of citations to and from DOCUMENTS, of the authorship of such documents and of the JOURNALS in which the documents are published.

The issue of why AUTHORS cite other authors has been widely discussed among scholars. The different functions of citations are:

1   Giving credit (i.e. identifying antecedents and original publications in which a fact, idea, concept or principle was first published).
2   Previous work (i.e. identifying general documents related to the topic; presenting previous results or announcing future work; commenting, correcting or criticizing previous work; identifying methodology, equipment, etc.).
3   Authority (i.e. substantiating claims and persuading readers; authenticating data and other results, or identifying the results by others supporting the author's work).
4   Social factors (i.e. citing prestigious researchers; citing work by the author's graduate students, fellows and co-workers to increase their visibility; 'perfunctory' citations).

Citation data obtained from ISI databases reveal that citation distributions are very skewed: the majority of papers cite relatively few journals and authors.

Evaluation of research performance

Citation analysis has been used for the evaluation of research performance. Among other outcomes, this has led to the study of rankings of journals, university departments, research institutions and individual scholars and scientists. The starting point of this approach is that citations, even negative ones that refute or correct the work cited, are a measure of influence in science: the more often an article is cited the more it is known to the scientific community. The whole academic community acts as a big set of peers to recognize, by means of citations, the value of a given contribution and the decisions of this jury can be studied using citation indexes.

Citation analysis can be used to identify the most frequently cited journals relevant to a given field. As has been noted in many studies, in a given area or discipline, a few core journals receive many citations and the rest receive far fewer citations. This pattern has been also identified with individual authors and through other approaches to analysis.

When used to study research performance, all

publications or a sample, covering a given time period, are selected. Typically, research papers published in primary sources (academic journals) are used as units of analysis. Next, citations to these documents are collected from citation indexes to be analysed to discover the most cited authors or articles and the antecedents or core documents in a given field or discipline.

The work that has been done demonstrates that there is a correlation between most-cited authors and the judgement of peers on their academic excellence, eminence and visibility. However, raw citation counts should be used with care for evaluating the quality of scientific work done by individual scientists. For example, is a scientist who has received 200 citations half as qualified as one receiving 400 citations? Citation analysis cannot replace experts that read and evaluate the work done by others within the same field; it essentially complements other evidence.

Structure of science

Dynamic mapping of science using citation indexes has been pursued for more than thirty years. The starting point is that citations from paper to paper or from journal to journal provide indicators of intellectual linkages between subject areas, organizations or individuals. Research approaches used in this field study co-citations (one document is cited by two other documents) and bibliographic coupling (two documents are cited in another document).

The clustering of citation matrices has been pursued for the purpose of obtaining comprehensive and dynamic maps of science from which the natural structural units of science can be shown.

Different analytical units and methodologies have been used. Thus, there are networks of authors, references, citations, institutions and journals. Studies at different levels (i.e. word, article, journal and so on) and using different methodologies (cluster analysis, factorial analysis, graph analysis, NEURAL NETWORKS, multi-dimensional scaling) are found in the readings at the end of this entry. And there are even authors who have integrated multiple sources of information in literature-based maps of science to visualize semantic spaces and networks. Among the various units of analysis listed above, journals merit special attention from researchers.

The results of studies carried out with the above methodologies have been used to identify science and discipline maps, research fronts, networks of scientific journals, epistemological and conceptual networks, INVISIBLE COLLEGES or author NETWORKS.

Some problems and caveats

Potential limitations for citation analysis are:

1   Not all significant journals are covered by the ISI in the citation indexes.
2   Some informal influences are not cited. Alternatively, repetition of errors of detail reveals secondary or tertiary citing, i.e. documents that have been cited without having been read.
3   There are different kinds of citations (positive citations, self-citations, negative citations).
4   Citation indexes include only printed journals, and, in some research fields, a significant part of publication is done in ELECTRONIC JOURNALS.
5   Important and influential discoveries are often incorporated by 'obliteration' in the common knowledge of a given discipline, and the original paper reporting is not often cited.
6   Errors can be misleading (e.g. errors may occur in the year, volume and/or page numbers of a citation; names can be misspelled; there can be inconsistent use of initials by authors; homonyms can be confused; and so on).

Further reading

Case, D.O. and Higgins, G.M. (2000) 'How can we investigate citation behavior? A study of reasons for citing literature in communication', *Journal of the American Society for Information Science* 51: 635–45.
Cronin, B. (1984) *The Citation Process*, London: Taylor Graham
Seglen, P.O. (1992) 'The skewness of science', *Journal of the American Society for Information Science* 43: 628–38.
White, H.D. and McCain, K.W. (1998) 'Visualizing a discipline: An author co-citation analysis of information science, 1972–1995', *Journal of the American Society for Information Science* 49: 327–55.
[See also many articles at the Web page of Eugene Garfield (http://garfield.library.upenn.edu).]

SEE ALSO: Garfield, Eugene; invisible college;

research in library and information science; scholarly communication

JUAN MIGUEL CAMPANARIO

CLASSIFICATION

The systematic organization of books, serials and other documents in all media by their subject matter. The subject divisions identified are generally assigned a coded notation to represent the subject content. Classification schemes in libraries, or BIBLIOGRAPHIC CLASSIFICATION, are used both as the basis of the SUBJECT CATALOGUE and a SUBJECT INDEX, and for the arrangement of the items on the shelves.

SEE ALSO: organization of knowledge

CLASSIFIED CATALOGUES

A library catalogue (see CATALOGUES) in which the entries are arranged in the order of the CLASSIFICATION scheme used by the library. Such catalogues are now being replaced by automated catalogues with a wide range of search facilities, but they still exist in many older academic libraries.

CLOSED ACCESS

A part of the library where books and other items are stored to which only staff have direct access. Once common in all libraries, closed access is now typically used only for RARE BOOKS, SPECIAL COLLECTIONS, manuscripts, ARCHIVES and other material of exceptional financial or artefactual value. In libraries in RUSSIA AND THE FORMER SOVIET UNION, and in CENTRAL AND EASTERN EUROPE, closed access was common until the late 1980s as a means of CENSORSHIP, since it allowed control of access to materials. Closed access necessitates the provision of a catalogue or library indicator that informs the reader which books are available and also directs the librarian to the fixed shelf position at which the book is to be found.

In archive administration, archives that are not available to the general public due to the existence of a confidentiality restriction are 'closed'. They are said to be 'open' when the period of restriction has expired.

CODE OF PROFESSIONAL CONDUCT

A set of standards of ethical behaviour expected of individual members of a professional association. Codes are issued by professional bodies to establish and encourage the highest possible standards of conduct by their members in their performance of professional duties. A code will usually outline grounds and procedures for complaints. In the library and information world professional codes normally indicate those actions that may be regarded as contrary to the aims, objectives and interests of professional associations and/or the professions of LIBRARIANSHIP and INFORMATION SCIENCE.

History

It is argued that until 1800 ethics had nothing to do with formal codes of conduct because a true professional, being a gentleman, did not need formal instructions about how to behave (Baker 1999). In the nineteenth century the established professions debated the issue, while during the early part of the twentieth century a number of newer professional groups started to develop codes of conduct. The INFORMATION PROFESSIONS came rather late to the discussion. The need for librarians to maintain ethical standards was first mentioned in 1903 by Mary W. Plummer, who observed 'Doctors, lawyers and ministers, college professors, officers of the army and navy, have a certain code which presupposes that they are gentlemen, and wish to remain so....Librarians and educators in general have their code still to make' (Plummer 1903: 208).

However, despite intermittent discussions the AMERICAN LIBRARY ASSOCIATION did not adopt a Code of Ethics until 1938. The years that followed were dominated by war and later, in the USA, by McCarthyism. This tended to concentrate minds on intellectual freedom issues, and the ethical concerns of librarians of that period are reflected in the American Library Association's *Library Bill of Rights* and *Freedom to Read Statement*. In Britain the library profession's concern with these matters resulted in a LIBRARY ASSOCIATION statement on censorship, published in 1963. This document appeared a year after Foskett's often quoted but misunderstood *The Creed of the Librarian – No Politics, No Religion, No Morals* (1962). The issue of

CENSORSHIP is closely related to matters of professional conduct, as is that of FREEDOM OF INFORMATION, and it was perhaps more than a coincidence that the Library Association set up working parties to consider all three topics. As a result the Library Association, after much discussion and consultation, adopted a Code of Professional Conduct in 1983. Clearly, with the unification of the Library Association and IIS (Institute of Information Scientists), the two organizations will need to work together to produce one Code for the Chartered Institute of Library and Information Professionals (CILIP).

There was a revival of interest in the subject in the 1980s as professions responded 'to societal pressure stemming from the Watergate years and increasing public skepticism…about professional privilege' (Vosper 1985: 74) The literature of the period includes references to ethics from places as far apart as France, South Africa, Scandinavia, Singapore, Poland and the USA (Usherwood 1989). A code of ethics for information professionals in Portugal was adopted in 1999.

Areas of concern

Codes of professional conduct set out rules designed to safeguard the standard of service provided to clients and to regulate relationships within the library and information professions. It is possible to identify several areas of concern: the competence of the librarian or information worker, the question of discretion and respect for a client's PRIVACY, professional independence and intellectual freedom, the impartiality of the library and information professions, financial ethics and the integrity of members. Froehlich (1997) links ethical and legal concerns, and includes copyright in his survey for IFLA.

The moral and ethical questions facing librarians and information workers have been complicated by political, economic and technological developments. The introduction of commercial ideas, such as competitive tendering for public libraries and other council services, together with the increased use of consultants and contracts has resulted in codes of conduct for local government that cover such subjects as professional standards, confidentiality, relationships, hospitality and sponsorship.

Any consideration of professional ethics causes one to explore a series of responsibilities and relationships. These include a professional's relationship to the client, to the employer and/or governing authority; the relationship with other members of staff and with other library and information services; the relationship to LIBRARY SUPPLIERS, trade unions, publishers and commercial organizations; and the individual's relationship to her or his profession. There is also the need to consider areas of personal conflict, for example between religious and professional value systems. There is, for instance, potential for conflict when a librarian or information worker is asked to provide information dealing with a topic about which she or he holds strong beliefs.

Interpretation

Although such issues are common to many professional codes of conduct, their interpretation by individual associations is sometimes significantly different. For instance, there is a difference of emphasis between the Library Association (1999) and the Library Association of Singapore (1992) on the issue of duty to the client and employer. The Singapore code states that 'The librarian must give complete loyalty and fidelity to the policies set by the governing authority', while the Library Association's code says that, 'In all professional considerations, the interests of clients within their prescribed or legitimate requirements take precedence over all other interests'. It goes on to say, in the guidance notes that accompany the code, that 'it would certainly constitute unprofessional conduct for a librarian to refuse to supply information or knowingly to supply erroneous or misleadingly incomplete information to a legitimate client at the behest of the librarian's employer'. There are also differences between the British and US positions on the promotion of material the purpose of which is to encourage discrimination on grounds of race, colour, creed, gender or sexual orientation. These differences reflect the tension in trying to accommodate two ethical concerns: intellectual freedom and social responsibility.

There are differences, too, in the way that the professional associations enforce codes. The Library Association's Code of Professional Conduct goes further than others in the profession by having a procedure whereby a member who fails to comply with the requirements of the code can be expelled, suspended, admonished or 'given appropriate guidance as to his or her future conduct'. This can affect an individual's ability to practise in those organizations that require chartered librarians – that is, professionally qualified members of the Library Association.

Professional codes of conduct are not, however, mainly about the disciplining of members; rather they are a formal recognition of the profession's responsibilities with regard to a number of important issues. It may be argued that a code is only a statement of what is already being done. Even if this is so, good habits need reinforcing and this is an important function of professional codes. Last but by no means least, they are a public proclamation of library and information workers' individual and collective professional concern for service, standards and practice.

References

Baker, R. (1999) 'Codes of ethics: Some history' (www.iit.edu/departments/csep/perspective/persp_v19_fall99_2.html) [accessed 10 August 2001].

Foskett, D.J. (1962) *The Creed of the Librarian – No Politics, No Religion, No Morals*, LA Reference, Special and Information Section, North Western Group Occasional Papers no. 3.

Froehlich, T.J. (1997) *Survey and Analysis of the Major Ethical and Legal Issues Facing Library and Information Services*, München: K.G. Saur (IFLA Publications 78).

Library Association (1999) *The Library Association's Code of Professional Conduct and Guidance Notes*, 3rd edn, London: Library Association.

Library Association of Singapore (1992) Constitution: Code of ethics (www.las.org.sg/constit.htm#ethics) [accessed 14 August 2001].

Plummer, M.W. (1903) 'The pros and cons of training for librarianship', *Public Libraries* 8(5) (May: 208–20).

Usherwood, B. (1989) 'Ethics of information', in J.E. Rowley (ed.) *Where the Book Stops. The Legal Dimensions of Information. Proceedings of the Institute of Information Scientists Annual Conference 1989*. ASLIB.

Vosper, R. (1985) 'Commentary on the code', in J.A. Lindsey and A.E. Prentice (eds) *Professional Ethics and Librarians*, Phoenix, AZ: Oryx Press.

Further reading

Alfino, M. and Pierce, L. (1997) *Information Ethics for Librarians*, Jefferson, NC: McFarland.

SEE ALSO: information ethics

BOB USHERWOOD

CODEN

1 A code assigned to a document or other library item, which generally consists of four capital letters followed by two hyphenated groups of Arabic numerals, or of two Arabic numerals followed by two capital letters, or of some similar combination.

2 More particularly, the American Society for Testing and Materials (ASTM) coden is intended to provide a unique and unambiguous permanent identifier for a specific periodical title. It uses five-letter codes as a substitute for full or abbreviated titles of periodicals in processing and storing bibliographical data. These can be found in many computer-based information handling systems. The first four letters of each coden have some mnemonic relation to the title, and the fifth letter is arbitrary. The ASTM Coden system was transferred in 1975 to Chemical Abstracts Service (CAS).

SEE ALSO: periodical

COGNITIVE SCIENCE

The discipline that studies the internal structures and processes that are involved in the acquisition and use of knowledge, including sensation, perception, attention, learning, memory, language, thinking and reasoning. Cognitive scientists are to be found among researchers in the areas of cognitive psychology, philosophy, linguistics, COMPUTER SCIENCE and cognitive neuroscience. They propose and test theories about the functional components of cognition based on observations of an organism's external behaviour in specific situations. The findings of cognitive science underlie much theoretical thinking in INFORMATION SCIENCE.

SEE ALSO: informatics; information theory; organization of knowledge; systems theory

COLLECTION

A planned accumulation of selected artefacts. The term is used in MUSEUMS as well as in libraries. In the latter it includes not only books and other printed matter, but also all information materials. A collection might consist of the whole contents of the institution, and is used in this sense in such phrases as COLLECTION MANAGEMENT or COLLECTION DEVELOPMENT. It can also, however, refer to a designated part of the whole, sometimes known generically as SPECIAL COLLECTIONS, or to a particular group of materials on a specific subject or accumulated by or about a named individual. More broadly, it can also be taken to include all the information resources to which a library has access, including those available through physical and virtual NETWORKS.

COLLECTION DEVELOPMENT

The process of planning a library's programme for ACQUISITIONS and disposals, focusing on the building of collections in the context of the institution's COLLECTION MANAGEMENT policy.

SEE ALSO: information management

COLLECTION MANAGEMENT

'Collection management' is a broad term that has replaced the narrower 'collection building' and 'COLLECTION DEVELOPMENT' of former decades. In its present manifestation collection management includes:

- Planning and funding.
- Collection development.
- BOOK selection.
- ACQUISITIONS.
- Provision of access.
- Use.
- Maintenance.
- Evaluation.
- PRESERVATION.
- Weeding.

It thus encompasses the activities traditionally associated with collection development – the selection and acquisition of library material – but is also far more comprehensive: it also includes the systematic maintenance of a library's collection, covering resource allocation, technical processing, preservation and storage, weeding and discarding of stock, and the monitoring and encouragement of collection use.

Collection development

A term sometimes used synonymously with collection management, collection development is in fact a specific subset of the broader activity of collection management. Collection development focuses on the building of library COLLECTIONS, ideally following guidelines already established and articulated in the library's written collection development policy. It involves the formulation of a systematic general plan for the creation of a library collection that will meet the needs of that library's clients and incorporates a number of activities related to the development of the library's collection, including the determination and co-ordination of relevant policies, assessment of user needs, studies of collection use, collection evaluation, identification of collection needs, selection of materials (the identification of information resources appropriate to a particular field, and the choice of what to acquire or provide access to from within it), planning for resource sharing, collection maintenance and weeding.

COLLECTION POLICIES

A library collection is an assemblage of physical information sources combined with virtual access to selected and organized information sources. Such collections are often managed according to two types of policies. A collection management policy can be viewed as a statement guiding the systematic management of the planning, composition, funding, evaluation and use of library collections. It is thus a global statement about a library's collections, of which the collection development aspect is but a single component. A 'collection development policy' is a statement of general collection-building principles that delineates the purpose and content of a collection in terms relevant to both external audiences (such as readers and funders) and internal audiences (or staff). Collection development policies are formal, written statements that provide clear and specific guidelines for the selection, acquisition, storage, preservation, relegation and discard of stock. The guidelines should be formulated in relation to the mission of the individual library, and the current and future needs of its users. The policy statement should cover all subject fields and all formats of information.

Collection development policies assist in ensuring the adoption of a consistent, balanced approach to selection, evaluation and relegation, and help to minimize personal bias in these activities. They can be invaluable in helping to differentiate between those collecting priorities that must be supported at all costs and those that are to be developed only as funding permits. They can also lead to improved communication between the library and its users, and to an increased understanding of the library's objectives by the administrators whose decisions influence resource allocation. If collection development policies are to be effective, it is important that they allow for a degree of flexibility in the collection-building process and that they are reviewed on a regular basis.

Collection evaluation

Collection evaluation is defined as the process of measuring the degree to which a library acquires the materials it intends to acquire in accordance with stated parameters (usually in a collection development policy). It is concerned with how 'good' a collection is in terms of the kinds of materials in it and the value of each item in relation to the community being served. It is also the process of getting to know the strengths and weaknesses of a collection using techniques which are likely to yield valid and reliable results.

Collection evaluation consists principally of two types of approaches. The first is use- and user-centred, meaning that concentration is on the individual user as the unit of analysis, with 'user' being defined as the person using the materials in the collection. The second is collection-centred, meaning that the evaluation techniques focus on examination of the collection in terms of its size, scope, depth and significance. Measures of use seem to be the most broadly useful means of evaluating a collection, and widely accepted indicators of use include the following:

- Number of loans per capita.
- Items on loan per capita.
- Loans per item per annum.
- Percentage of items borrowed/not borrowed.
- Proportion of interlibrary loans to total loans.
- Ratio of interlibrary loans received to interlibrary loans lent.
- A 'needs-fill' measure of whether users find what they seek.
- User satisfaction with stock.

By definition collection-centred evaluation involves the evaluation of a collection. Collection-centred measures include size, rate of growth, the quality of the collection when compared with agreed external standards, and citation analysis. In the digital age libraries no longer have 'a' collection. Instead they consist of a hybrid collection: a physical collection of print, MULTI-MEDIA and digital objects complemented by access to the emerging worldwide VIRTUAL LIBRARY. Clients should not need to know whether an item is held locally or merely available on demand: if they want a particular piece of information, their library can access it for them. The result of this is that use- and user-centred evaluation methods are increasingly the assessment methods of choice. Accordingly, evaluation now tends to focus on techniques of user or client evaluation: usage studies, client surveys, DOCUMENT DELIVERY studies and availability studies.

In the recent past a most popular collection-centred approach to evaluation was the CONSPECTUS method. This was devised in the USA by the Research Libraries Group and was successfully adopted or modified for use in many countries. The method is based on a set of codified descriptions that record existing collection strengths and current collecting intensity. However, many have been deterred from using the full Conspectus methodology because of the level of detail it requires, and it seems to have gone into decline as a popular approach to describing collections, at least outside the USA.

A properly conducted collection evaluation exercise is a demanding and time-consuming process, and it will usually be undertaken with a view to understanding the strengths and weaknesses of the collection, with the aim of producing something better by retaining and enhancing the strengths, and reducing or eliminating the weaknesses. In other words evaluation of a collection should lead to a more objective understanding of the scope and depth of the collection, and provide a guide for collection planning, budgeting and decision making.

Resource allocation

The ways in which libraries allocate their resources vary widely. Some divide them according to material type; others use a discipline-based approach. With the advent of electronic publishing libraries have begun to include within the collection management budget not only the costs of material they add to their own stock, but also the costs of providing access to information stored elsewhere. Library managers in pursuit of objectivity will sometimes calculate their budgets on a formula basis, but it is questionable whether a formulaic approach is really any more objective a method of allocating resources, since subjective opinion will almost certainly influence the weighting factors used.

Technical processing

For the library's collections to be made accessible to library users it is important that the technical processing activities of the library are carried out efficiently and effectively. Acquisitions, BIBLIO-GRAPHIC CONTROL, CLASSIFICATION, storage, preservation and DISASTER PREPAREDNESS PLANNING all come into play and contribute to the overall management of the library's collections. Decisions taken by a technical processing department can have a major impact on whether the clientele find the library easy to use, so it is important that staff working in these departments keep user needs in mind when devising procedures for processing the collections.

Weeding, relegation and disposal

Weeding is the process of removing material from OPEN ACCESS and reassessing its value. It is a generic term, which includes both relegation and discarding. Once an item has been removed it can be relegated or transferred to storage in another area under the control of the library, designed for less regular use, perhaps one operated jointly with partner institutions. Other material may be sold, or discarded – permanently removed from the stock of the library.

Positive reasons for weeding include a belief that there is an optimum size beyond which the collection should not be allowed to grow and a conviction that with the passage of time some of the items in any library lose some or all of whatever value they originally had, and become a distraction to users rather than an asset. The classic rule is that the criteria for weeding should be essentially those used in the first place for selection – in fact, weeding has often been referred to as deselection.

Criteria for weeding, relegation and disposal vary according to the type of library, but will include publication date, acquisition date, physical condition, circulation history and continued relevance (this last often based on professional judgement exercised in conjunction with the library's collection development policy). For many libraries lack of space is a principal factor motivating relegation and disposal. Developments in OPTICAL DISK technology may make DIGITIZATION an increasingly attractive option for those whose problems are primarily space-related. Computerized library housekeeping systems can provide management information relating to stock management. Such information will make it easier to apply mechanistic criteria to the weeding and relegation process, although professional judgement will still sometimes need to be exercised if over-simplistic application of the rules is to be avoided.

Further reading

Clayton, P. and Gorman, G.E. (2001) *Managing Information Resources in Libraries: Collection Management in Theory and Practice*, London: Library Association Publishing.

Collection Building (1981–) Emerald/MCB (quarterly).

Gorman, G.E. (ed.) (2000) *International Yearbook of Library and Information Management, 2000–2001: Collection Management*, London: Library Association Publishing.

Gorman, G.E. and Miller, R.H. (eds) *Collection Management for the 21st Century: A Handbook for Librarians*, Westport, CT: Greenwood Press.

Jenkins, C. and Morley, M. (eds) (1999) *Collection Management in Academic Libraries*, 2nd edn, Aldershot: Gower Publishing.

Library Collections, Acquisitions and Technical Services (1977–) Elsevier (quarterly).

Spiller, D. (2000) *Providing Materials for Library Users*, London: Library Association Publishing.

SEE ALSO: digital library; hybrid libraries; libraries; organizational information policies; user studies

G.E. GORMAN

COLON CLASSIFICATION

Designed by S.R. RANGANATHAN, this is based on the CLASSIFICATION of any subject by its uses and relations, which are indicated by numbers divided by a colon ':'. It was the first example of an analyticosynthetic classification, in which the subject field is first analysed into facets, and class numbers are then constructed by synthesis.

Ready-made class numbers are not provided for most topics but are constructed by combining the classes of the various unit schedules of which the scheme consists. It has proved particularly popular in India and has inspired classification researchers in many parts of the world.

SEE ALSO: faceted classification; organization of knowledge

COMMUNICATION

'Communication' is a word with many meanings: the *Concise Oxford Dictionary*, for example, lists six. When examined more closely, however, these various definitions can be reduced to two basic entities: the process of communication and the message communicated. The study of communication typically involves both elements.

Communication is obviously fundamental to any kind of social activity. It therefore forms a topic for study by a very wide range of disciplines – from science, medicine and technology through law and the social sciences to the humanities. Nor, of course, is communication limited to human beings. In this wider context, what we mean by communication has to be looked at more closely. The only way of telling that one animal has certainly communicated with another is by showing that the interaction has somehow changed the behaviour of the latter. (Even for human beings, this can be an enlightening way of examining communication.) Animal communication also draws attention to the limits imposed on communication by the senses. Some animals can hear sounds that we cannot; some can see colours invisible to us. In fact, humans rely primarily on two senses – sight and hearing. Touch, smell and taste not only convey less information than these, but are also not easily communicable in a quantitative form (though the preceding definition of communication includes everything from quantitative information to emotion). Even in conveying emotions, however, sight and hearing play a fundamental part. The most important reason for this is the distinctive human reliance on language.

Although speech and writing are by far the most important means of human communication, they face a major obstacle – incompatible languages. Coping with different dialects in the same language can be a stumbling block, but the

serious problems obviously arise with different languages. Only a minority of most populations study foreign-language material in any depth. Speakers of major languages can find so much material in their own language that, specialists apart, they rarely need to look elsewhere. Translated works help to bridge the language barrier, but the effort of moving from one language to another still represents a brake on the process of communication. It can also involve considerable cost: thus a large part of the budget of the European Union is expended on providing the same information in the different official languages. One much-debated solution is to choose a particular language to be used for international communication. Such a proposal faces a number of difficulties, not least national pride in one's own language. A less contentious way forward is to invoke the power of the computer. MACHINE TRANSLATION, though far from perfect, has made great strides in recent years, as have speech recognition and synthesis.

The communication process

Imagine a simple form of human communication: two people talking to each other over the telephone. First, the speaker has to work out what to say, and say it clearly. Then the speech must be converted to electricity, which is transmitted and reconverted at the other end. Finally, the listener must hear and understand what has been said. This apparently simple process involves elements of importance to a wide range of disciplines: psychology, linguistics, sociology, engineering and so on.

The question of people talking over the telephone was first examined in detail from a mathematical viewpoint half a century ago. The resultant publication by SHANNON and Weaver in 1949 has become a classic, and has influenced thinking about communication across most of the disciplines involved. Their discussion, as Figure 5 indicates, contained one additional element – the box marked 'noise'. This represents any type of interference that affects reception of the signal. In the original work on telephones, the word 'noise' could be taken literally. The type example was crackling in the earpiece, which drowned out some of the conversation. As the model has come to be used more widely, so 'noise' has been reinterpreted as anything that hinders reception

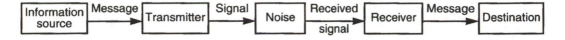

Figure 5 The Shannon–Weaver model

of a message. For example, something may be missed because the attention of the listener has been diverted. It is also possible to talk about 'semantic noise', meaning by that any way in which the meaning of a message becomes distorted during the process of communication. For example, the speaker may use words with which the listener is not acquainted.

The Shannon–Weaver model represents communication as a linear flow process. This is obviously only a partial reflection of how communication works. It does not, for example, include feedback. In a telephone conversation, the speaker becomes the listener and the listener the speaker, in turn. Conveying meaning often depends on this interaction to reduce misunderstandings. Again, messages may be filtered through more than one information source. Thus, the recipient of a telephone message may pass some of its contents on to a colleague.

The message communicated

Messages are made up of signs, entities that refer to something other than themselves. (The word 'symbol' is sometimes used in much the same sense.) A road sign showing a speed limit is an example of communication via signs in two senses: its shape and layout are signs indicating that it is an instruction to drivers, whilst the number emblazoned on it is a further sign representing the maximum permissible speed. In order to convey meaning, signs must be organized into a system – called a 'code' – which relates the signs to each other in a way that can be interpreted by the receiver of the message. Take road signs again as an example. A speed limit sign has a specific physical format that relates it to the whole group of road signs that must be obeyed by a driver (as distinct from signs that provide information or give a warning). The number on it involves another code, whose interpretation depends on our understanding of the numerical system in current use. Designing a speed limit thus requires encoding two sets of signs. The driver has the task of decoding these signs in

order to comprehend their significance. Errors can easily occur in this process, depending on the background of the recipient. For example, someone accustomed to seeing road signs denoting speeds in kilometres per hour may misunderstand signs in another country that uses miles per hour.

The study of signs and codes is called 'SEMIOTICS'. There are, correspondingly, semiotic models and theories that can be used for looking at message transfer. One simple model, for example, is based on a triangular interaction (see Figure 6). It reflects the fact that a person receiving a message is likely to have direct knowledge of the object that is being signified, as well as of the sign that represents it. Interpretation for an individual will then depend on the interaction between these two types of knowledge. For example, the word 'stream' is likely to invoke a different picture for people living in a flat country as compared with those living in mountains. Models help in the discussion of communication by concentrating attention on the aspects that are most important and by providing a framework for analysis. Inevitably, any one model is limited in its scope. For this reason, many communications models exist: the important thing is to choose an appropriate one for the particular needs at hand. A problem is that, with so many theories in circulation, any individual theory is used but rarely, which can make intercomparisons difficult. One survey of basic textbooks on communication found that there was little overlap between the theories described in each. Over three-quarters of the theories were mentioned in only one of the books.

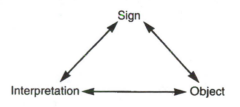

Figure 6 Triangular interaction

Technology and communication channels

For many years past, one of the distinctive features of human communication has been the growth in the number and diversity of the communication channels available. Recent developments have related almost entirely to digital channels (i.e. ones that operate in terms of bits). Obvious examples of this are the appearance of digital television and digital mobile telephones. Digital channels have a number of virtues (such as a better ability to handle noise), but their particular interest is their computer-related capabilities. A digital television can be used for teleshopping, while a mobile phone can send and receive text as well as oral messages. Two types of channel can be used for transmission – either some kind of cable, or the atmosphere. Traditionally, these were deployed for different types of message. The atmosphere was used for transmitting messages aimed at a wide audience, as with radio and television. Cable was used for personal messages, as with telephone calls. Nowadays, digital messages of all kinds can go via either route. For example, telephone calls may go either via cable or through the atmosphere, and the same is true of television programmes. The sorts of message transmitted by the various channels are likewise changing. For example, a computer network can be employed to look for particular categories of news. The items retrieved can then be used to construct an individually personalized newspaper. As all this reflects, a key characteristic of digital channels is that they support interactive communication, whether with computers or other human beings.

In some ways, there are parallels between human and computer handling of information. Each has sensors to accept incoming information, methods for internally handling and storing the information, and devices for outputting information to the external world. Correspondingly, it is necessary to see how the computer system can best be adapted to the human system (usually referred to as HUMAN–COMPUTER INTERACTION). To give one example, humans often react differently to the provision of information on-screen and on the printed page. So it seems generally to be easier to read long pieces of text on paper than on-screen; the requirements for easily legible text may be different between screen and paper; colour, too, must be used in a different way.

For communication, however, it is not the individual computer that is important, but the totality of networked computers. The combination of computers and NETWORKS is usually called information technology. The significance of the growing role of information technology is not simply its ability to handle large quantities of information very quickly, but also its power to reorganize the way we look at information. For example, in terms of effort by the sender it makes little difference whether a message is sent to an individual colleague locally or to large numbers of contacts worldwide. Information technology is here blurring the dividing line between personal communication and mass communication. Electronic discussion groups demonstrate a different aspect of this blurring process. In such discussions, any participant can put up a query, and any other can reply. Here, large numbers of people are involved in the communication process, but it is still possible to have individualized interaction. As this suggests, electronic communication may draw the boundaries between information activities in different places from written communication. Indeed, it has been suggested that electronic communication has a number of characteristics in common with oral communication. For example, text and graphics can be ontinually manipulated by a computer, so that it may never be possible to point to a definitive version, as one can for printed text or graphics. In some ways, this is analogous to storytelling, where the theme may stay the same but the details may change at each retelling. Thus, the use of information technology represents not simply a new communication channel, but a new set of possibilities for handling information.

Communication options

Just because information is provided via a communication channel, this does not mean that it will necessarily be absorbed by recipients. Many channels, especially nowadays the INTERNET, transmit so much information that it is impossible for any individual to sift through it all. This information overload acts as another source of noise in the system. Although relevant items may exist, they can often be hidden in the flood of irrelevant items. The difficulty lies not only in the flood of information currently appearing, but also in the stores of past information that can increasingly be accessed.

Though the Internet provides an obvious example of these problems, they also afflict other channels. Thus keeping up with the flood of fiction available is a major concern for public libraries, while maintaining access to all the research journals available is equally a matter of concern for UNIVERSITY LIBRARIES. One consequence is that all libraries have had to become more efficient in their handling of material. Developments down the years have ranged from the growth of interlibrary loan schemes to the automation of library CATALOGUES. The rapid expansion of global information and communication obviously depends in part on the growth of world population. It has, however, been aided and abetted by the growth of mechanical methods for collecting, storing and disseminating information. For example, a single remote-sensing satellite examining the earth produces a greater quantity of data than all the ground-based surveys of the earth throughout history put together. Clearly, with such a vast information store, communication in the future will rely increasingly on electronic assistance.

The use of particular information sources depends not only on the likelihood of retrieving relevant information from them, but also on the relative convenience of the communication channels through which they can be accessed. Given the choice, many information users prefer a convenient channel providing lower-quality information to a less convenient channel providing higher-quality information. The question, of course, is what makes a communication channel 'convenient'. Physical proximity is certainly one factor. Not surprisingly, more distant channels are less likely to be tapped than nearby ones. But 'distant' here can mean something very limited indeed. On a university campus, for example, a library that is twenty minutes' walk away from the office will be used less frequently on average than a library that is two minutes' walk away. Even smaller obstacles can impede informal communication. For example, communication between people working on different floors of a building is typically worse than communication between people working on the same floor. In recent years, the obvious example of this rule – that distances to the communication channel must be small – has been the use of computers for communication. The level of usage of electro-nic mail drops unless the computer terminal is actually on the desk of the sender/recipient.

Although the impact of distance on use is most evident for communication channels, it is often possible to discern a distance-related factor in the choice of the information sources themselves. For example, local telephone calls typically predominate over calls to people further afield. Here, the cause is not necessarily convenience: cost and the location of colleagues are likely to be more important. In looking at communication in these terms, however, it is often necessary to look at questions of time as well as distance. People usually consider the speed of interaction when choosing communication channels. Something that needs an immediate response may be answered by fax or ELECTRONIC MAIL, whereas a message that is less urgent may be replied to by ordinary mail. Hence, distance is only one of the factors involved when individuals select communication channels: speed, cost, etc. also influence their choice.

One consequence of these selection factors is that communication channels are as likely to complement each other as to be in competition. Effectively, different channels create niches for themselves that exploit their distinctive characteristics. The idea of a 'niche' comes from evolution. Darwinian evolution is often thought of as depending on vigorous competition, leading to survival of the fittest species. In practice, what happens is that organisms tend to find specific niches in the environment: the better they fit into these, the more limited the competition that they face. Something similar happens in communication. Take NEWSPAPERS as an example. Most countries publish a range of different newspapers. An examination of these makes it clear that they are not all competing with each other for readers. Some may limit themselves geographically. A Los Angeles newspaper is not in direct competition with one published in New York. Most limit themselves by aiming at a particular audience. There are, for example, upmarket broadsheets and downmarket tabloids. Some newspapers appear on Sunday only, and so on. The main point about niche creation is that it works reasonably well so long as the environment remains stable. For organisms, rapid environmental change can have a catastrophic result if they fail to adapt quickly. In communication, the introduction of information technology has been the equivalent of a rapid environmental change.

The question is how traditional communication channels will reposition themselves (i.e. find new niches) in the new electronic environment. That such repositioning is occurring is illustrated, for example, by the rapid growth of electronic publishing.

Communication in groups

Communication is essentially a group activity, one-to-one communication simply being one end of the chain. For this reason, many studies of communication examine how it works in particular groups, communities or organizations. The communication links between individual members form a 'network', the exact nature of which affects the way communication occurs within the group. Indeed, the differing networking patterns of different groups means that for some communication purposes each group can be thought of as having an identity of its own, separate from that of its constituent members.

Consider, as an example, a commercial firm. It has its own goals, which have a long-term validity regardless of changes in personnel, and its own organization, which typically imposes a hierarchical structure on the activities of these personnel. Communication in such a firm is traditionally expected to be vertical, starting with the managing director at the top and passing through various levels to manual labour at the base of the organizational pyramid. Employees obtain instructions from the level above, and pass on their own instructions to the level below. An efficient firm also arranges for information to flow back upwards again, so providing feedback. Otherwise, plans made at the top may be frustrated by unrecognized problems further down the hierarchy.

This picture of a hierarchical network usually fits fairly well the way in which formal communication (e.g. office memos) works within the firm. However, to concentrate solely on formal communication is to omit the equally important flow of informal communication. People operating at the same or nearly related levels in the hierarchy often pass information horizontally via conversation. Someone like the managing director's secretary, who may appear to rank fairly low in the formal communication hierarchy, can play an important role in the flow of informal communication. Most organizations contain people who are recognized by their fellow employees as important sources of information although their apparent position in the hierarchy may not seem important. Such people are often labelled 'gatekeepers', because they help control and direct the flow of information. This applies to external information coming into a firm as well as to the information generated within it. The GATEKEEPER function depends on the inclination of the individuals concerned and their range of contacts: if they leave the firm, their replacements may well not act as gatekeepers. Reorganization of the firm can also affect the way that gatekeepers operate. For example, moving from a low-level building to a high-rise building can reduce their contacts, and so their effectiveness.

The network pattern within a group obviously depends on the way in which the group is organized. For example, there may be one leader to whom all the information from other members flows, or, alternatively, each member may pass on information to all the other members simultaneously. Each pattern has its own advantages and disadvantages. Thus, information may be transmitted and recorded more accurately with the first type of network, but all the participants, apart from the leader, tend to find their communication activities less satisfying. On the contrary, participants enjoy the second type of network more, but their information may be less carefully transmitted and recorded.

The nature of the interaction between participants can also depend on the communication channel employed. Nowadays, much information within organizations is handled by computers, and circulates via an INTRANET. Introducing computers changes the nature of the communication network. For example, a computer network can readily make all kinds of information available to any member of an organization. This acts to flatten the traditional hierarchical flow, since information no longer needs to cascade down from the top to the bottom of the organization. It also affects the role of gatekeepers, since it enhances everyone's ability to access information directly. The changes are most evident in firms that allow staff to work from home, keeping in touch via electronic networks (teleworking). Managers in such firms can find it difficult to redefine their communication roles, while the staff at home miss informal exchanges of information over coffee. Computer-mediated communication is also increasingly affecting education. It is seen, in particular, as an essential base for

DISTANCE LEARNING. However, online interaction between teachers, students and information sources alters both teaching and learning processes in ways that are still being investigated.

One important aspect of communication is how it can be used to introduce new ideas. Within a group, such ideas may be introduced by gatekeepers and accepted by the more information-conscious members. If the ideas prove interesting enough, most of the members in the group then take up the idea. The remaining members either absorb the idea more slowly or may never accept it at all. These kinds of reaction have been discerned, for example, in the acceptance of a new drug by the medical profession or the acceptance of a new type of communication channel by the public at large. However, the way in which innovations are accepted can be greatly influenced by the beliefs and preconceptions of each of the individuals concerned. It is a commonplace of media studies that what people take from any branch of the media depends on what they bring to it. A political programme on television may be watched by people from both the left and the right of the political spectrum. Both are likely to find in it confirmation of their beliefs, and both may complain that it is biased in favour of the opposing side.

Structuring communication

From their earliest days, human beings develop expectations about the way communication works and about the information environment that the communication channels reveal. Children acquire a reasonably extensive vocabulary quite early. A 3-year-old may know a thousand words, which should be compared with the fact that most people can get through their everyday life with a vocabulary of only 5,000 words. But the ability to apply this vocabulary and to understand the subtleties of communication takes much longer. For example, many children cannot use abstract terms correctly and creatively until they are in their teens. For this sort of reason, CHILDREN'S LITERATURE is often aimed at particular age ranges, and written accordingly. The ability to use language, whether in terms of oral fluency or of literacy, obviously varies not only with age, but also from individual to individual. This is reflected in the provision of formal sources of information as well as in informal conversation. For example, the range of daily newspapers available caters for varying degrees of literacy. Tabloid newspapers are aimed at less sophisticated readers: they typically have simpler syntax and a greater emphasis on pictures than the upmarket broadsheet newspapers. In fact, the whole layout of the newspaper, from the size of the headlines to the typeface used, can be related to the expected target audience. Equally, there are differences not only in the way in which news is presented, but also in what news is communicated. Tabloid newspapers contain many fewer mentions of science and finance, for example, than broadsheets. The interaction between the medium, the message and the target audience extends across all types of information. It can be illustrated in some detail by looking at the appearance and function of an ordinary research journal

Scholarly articles tend to be structured in a standard way, which derives from their role as communication channels for research. First comes the title. This is formulated so as best to catch the attention of its intended audience. It should, for example, contain all the key words that might be expected by a potential reader, so that it will be retrieved efficiently from an automated list of articles. Next come the names of the authors, together with their institutional affiliations. The ordering of names can be significant here, since it is often supposed that the first-named author will have contributed most to the article. The expectation that the authors will have an institutional rather than a personal address reflects the fact that research is now a highly professionalized activity. The inclusion of addresses also allows readers who have queries about the article to get in touch directly with the author(s). Under the authors' names may come an indication of when the article was received and/or accepted for publication. This date is part of the regulatory activity of the scholarly community. Its inclusion gives the authors some protection if they need to defend their priority in publishing a new idea or result. After these introductory elements, there is an ABSTRACT summarizing the contents of the article. Like the title, this abstract may appear in other printed or automated listings that provide a guide to the original research literature. It is customary to refer to such listings as secondary communications, which draw attention to this primary research literature.

The body of each article is usually also structured in a standard way. It may, for example, have successive sections labelled introduction, methodology, results, discussion and so on. Most scholarly articles also include – often at the end – a list of other publications that have been used in the process of putting together the new contribution. These citations form a network linking the new publication to previous research that has been formally communicated to the research community. By tracing such networks, it is possible to form some idea of how research is linked, in communication terms, not only with current contributions, but also with past developments.

Not all the communication characteristics of the research community can be derived purely by scanning individual articles. Some are reflected in other parts of the journal. For example, the end-pages of each issue often call attention to another aspect – quality control. Here are listed editor(s), and referees may be mentioned, too. It is particularly important that research information should be reliable, since it is used as the basis for further research. Assessment by experts, together with their advice on how to improve work, is seen as an essential way of implementing control over the dissemination of research information. Indeed, a scholarly journal can be seen as a printed artefact reflecting what is regarded as acceptable practice by the research community.

Although an article in a scholarly journal is a particularly good example of a structured communication, readers always have prior expectations regarding the way in which information will be presented to them via any formal source. For example, a reader will expect anything described as a 'novel' to be a book, divided into chapters and probably with few illustrations. Equally, someone interested in news about (say) microcomputers will usually look at computer magazines. They will expect such magazines to have colourful covers, often featuring a picture of computing equipment. The cover will also announce the main features to be found inside. On opening the magazine, these main articles will be found to be accompanied by various shorter snippets of news, but much of the space will be occupied by advertising. These expectations help, in the first place, with the choice of reading matter. A glance at the cover and a quick skim through a computer magazine, for example, is usually sufficient to decide whether or not it is worth purchasing. Similarly, standard placement of items inside (e.g. the editorial) allows rapid retrieval of the category of information that most interests the individual reader.

The point can be put in another way. The presentation of information in a standard way assists its rapid retrieval when browsing. Browsing is one of the most important ways in which readers seek information. It is essentially a sampling process, in which salient features of the text and graphics are scanned until the reader is satisfied that the desired amount of information has been gathered. For example, readers of scholarly journals often flip through the pages of a newly received issue to see if anything catches their attention. They will typically glance at the title, authors and abstract first. If these seem interesting, they may next look at the introduction and conclusion, and at some of the diagrams or other graphics included. If these also prove interesting, the greater part of the article may then be read with attention. Such selective reading is the norm rather than the exception. Even with a novel, readers will skip paragraphs that strike them as boring.

BROWSING might be labelled 'undirected' reading. The reader is looking for any item of interest, but does not know ahead of time what the item will be. In 'directed' reading, in contrast, the reader knows what information is required and is actively seeking it. For example, a cook who has it in mind to produce a particular dish may search through a selection of cookery books to find the appropriate recipe. Different types of reading matter have differing probabilities of being used for directed reading. A dictionary or an encyclopaedia is typically consulted when a particular piece of information is required, whereas novels usually are not. This difference affects the way the information in the source is structured. An encyclopaedia, for example, besides having its contents arranged alphabetically, may also have various indexes to allow readers to pin down quickly the precise piece of information they need. Even the physical shape and size of a publication can relate to its expected communication function. For example, a 'coffee table' book, as the name implies, is not meant to be read on a train.

Oral communication has always ranked on a

par with formal sources as a means of transmitting information. Surveys of researchers, for example, show that discussion with colleagues is ranked as of top importance for acquiring relevant information, alongside journals and books. The choice between oral and print sources of information depends on a range of factors – the type of feedback sought, the currency of the information and so on. But the nature of the information can also be important. Thus, craft knowledge – how to make something – is often difficult to transmit fully via text and pictures. It may be better picked up on the basis of on-the-job discussions. Equally, complex concepts – such as mathematical equations – nearly always have to be written down if they are to be properly understood and manipulated. It follows that formal and informal sources of information often prove complementary in their information provision. Indeed, even for information dealing with the same topic, people seem to require exposure to it via a variety of channels in order to perceive its full significance. Impact can vary with context as well as with channel. People watching a television programme by themselves may assess it differently from people who watch in a group, for the group discussion may modify their opinions.

The nature of oral information transfer at a group meeting depends critically on the size of the group. A few people together can have a fairly unstructured, interactive discussion without much difficulty. They simply observe a few conventions. For example, it is normally regarded as bad manners to interrupt a speaker in the middle of a sentence. As the size of the group increases, so the need for structure grows. Thus, talks at conferences are scheduled for a specific place and time, audiovisual aids are laid on, etc. At the same time, the feedback element that characterizes oral discourse decreases with group size. There is rarely time for more than a few questions at the end of a conference talk. The ubiquity of radio and television nowadays means that mass communication is concerned as much with the spoken as with the written word. Again, the different channels tend to be complementary rather than competitive. Many people read daily newspapers and listen to both radio and television. From the broadcast information they may obtain the most up-to-date news, whilst from the printed information they may obtain a more detailed analysis.

Limitations on communication

The obvious restriction on use of communication channels relates to economic problems. People in developing countries often find it difficult to buy books, both because they cost too much and because the distribution system is inefficient. Similarly, telephone networks in many such countries serve only a minority of the population and do not necessarily do so very efficiently. Radio is a widely used channel in developing countries: it is relatively cheap (for group purchase) and does not presume a literate audience. Unlike the telephone, however, it does not permit two-way communication. A key question now is whether the growing use of information technology will increase, or decrease, the communication gap between the haves and the have-nots.

In developed countries, a different debate is under way. This concerns COPYRIGHT, and the effect that electronic channels may have on it. The problem relates to the 'copy' part of the word 'copyright'. Copying a printed book takes time, and is not necessarily cheap. Copying an electronic document, on the contrary, is rapid, and the costs are trivial. Commercial providers of electronic information are therefore demanding stricter controls on copyright for networked information. This is opposed by many users, who believe both that communication via the Internet (and any successor) should be as free as possible of control and that, in any case, such control will prove to be very difficult to impose. The outcome from this debate will affect users in both developed and developing countries.

Further reading

Communication Research (www.communication research.org/).

Crystal, D. (1997) *The Cambridge Encyclopaedia of Language*, Cambridge: Cambridge University Press.

Freeman, R.L. (1999) *Fundamentals of Telecommunications*, Wiley-Interscience.

McQuail, D. and Windahl, S. (1993) *Communication Models*, Longman.

Pemberton, L. and Shurville, S. (eds) (2000) *Words on the Web: Computer Mediated Communication*, Intellect.

Rutter, D.R. (1987) *Communicating by Telephone*, Pergamon Press.

Schiffman, H.R. (2000) *Sensation and Perception*, John Wiley.

Shannon, C. and Weaver, W. (1949) *The Mathematical Theory of Communication*, University of Illinois Press.

Tubbs, S.L. and Moss, S. (2000) *Human Communication*, McGraw-Hill.

SEE ALSO: broadcasting; e-commerce; economics of information; Geographic Information Systems; information and communication technology; mass media; oral traditions; PTT; scholarly communication; telecommunications; translations

JACK MEADOWS

COMMUNICATION TECHNOLOGY

The design and application of systems and equipment for sending or exchanging data by electrical means between two or more distant stations.

SEE ALSO: information and communication technology

COMMUNICATIONS AUDIT

The process whereby the communications within an organization are analysed by an internal or external consultant, with a view to increasing organizational efficiency or effectiveness. In contemporary practice, this is often part of a broader process of INFORMATION AUDIT. Communications auditing is largely oriented towards human behaviour, as even technical specifications for computer-based systems need to respond to the needs and motivations of employees using them. They therefore use techniques such as interviews and questionnaires that elicit personal responses to institutional structures. The practice has its origin in the early 1950s, but has been transformed by the application of INFORMATION AND COMMUNICATION TECHNOLOGY.

Further reading

Booth, A. (1988) *The Communications Audit: A Guide for Managers*, Gower [out of date in terms of technology, but still useful for concepts].

SEE ALSO: information management

COMMUNITIES OF INTEREST

Communities of interest and communities of practice form naturally on the INTERNET through the freedom to publish information that it gives to individuals, and the searchability of the WORLD WIDE WEB. For example, academics can communicate and share research with greater ease across national boundaries and between institutions in ways that extend the concept of the INVISIBLE COLLEGE; groups following a particular hobby can link up to share their interests; and wider-based support groups for people who suffer from particular disabilities or other problems become possible. Such virtual communities become sources of specialized information and advice, and as such form an important part of networks of referral and information service.

COMMUNITY INFORMATION

Community information is the information that people and their dependents need or want in order to live their everyday lives. It can enable individuals and groups to make informed decisions about themselves and the communities in which they live, and participate more effectively in the democratic process. In this sense it can have a positive impact on preventing social exclusion (see SOCIAL EXCLUSION AND LIBRARIES). Community information relates to areas such as housing, transport, benefits, health and recreation, and includes such things as bus timetables, the locations of doctors' surgeries and details of events and activities. Characteristically, community information is ephemeral and takes the form of leaflets, posters, pamphlets or an electronic form that can be updated more easily than formally published material. Community information can also be a term applied to information that records the feelings, activities and identity of a distinct community. Collections of stories from or about a particular community, memories of a geographical area or documented discussions about issues pertinent to a particular group could also be considered to be 'community information'.

The 'communities' that need and use this type of information fall into two main categories: COMMUNITIES OF INTEREST and geographical communities. This distinction is important when determining the information needs of a particular community and effective methods of disseminating and maintaining community information. The former refers to communities that share a common interest or characteristic, for example, a group with a particular medical condition or one that shares a common heritage. The boundaries of geographical communities may be determined by agencies external to them, as in the case of wards and districts, for example. In practice, communities tend to define their own boundaries, which may or may not coincide with formal definitions. Examples of electronic community information provided on a geographical basis might be www.healthprofile.org.uk, www.cheetham.info or www.seamless.org.uk.

Sources of community information

Community information may be information about an organization that can help people in particular circumstances. For example, a public library (see PUBLIC LIBRARIES) may signpost an individual to an advice agency. Community information is also useful factual information generated by a number of agencies, organizations and individuals across all sectors, public, voluntary, community and private. Central government, for example, provides information about the National Curriculum for primary and secondary education, local authorities make available information relating to more localized education provision and the voluntary sector in many cases provides information about subjects such as bullying, youth issues and educational opportunities outside the mainstream. This broad range of sources enables users to find information through the means that is most appropriate and accessible to them. However, the variety of sources can act as a barrier to access. There can be significant degrees of overlap and contradiction between, leaving users with feelings of 'information overload'. Communities may find it difficult to make sense of the information available to them and to evaluate effectively the quality and accuracy of the information.

Electronic community information

Increasingly, community information is being presented electronically. This is advantageous to both providers and users for a number of reasons. Organizations can more easily share information collections, therefore helping to eliminate duplication and anomalies. METADATA schemes enable users to search for and find information more effectively and XML (extensible mark-up languages) standards allow providers to share electronic community information easily. The classification of electronic community information is evolving in order to accommodate the variety of metadata schemes but as yet conforms to no recognized protocols.

As people's access to INFORMATION AND COMMUNICATION TECHNOLOGY increases, so does the potential for community information to take the form of online participation and debate. This may be through discussion forums, online advice or chat, e-mail lists, etc. It may serve to equip users with the means to make decisions at a personal, local, national or international level.

The provision of community information in an electronic format means that, potentially, users can access the information from their own homes. This removes barriers people may have when communicating with institutions. Users in remote and rural locations can access information without having to make prohibitive journeys to a physical venue. Specific skills are still required in order to access information via a personal computer, mobile telephone or Internet television, but increasingly the skills issue is being addressed by a range of training initiatives, for example, the government's UKOnline programme (www.ukonline.gov.uk). Language and literacy problems can be minimized by developing audio-based community content online. People who do not read English or other written languages can use the Internet to access information spoken in these languages. People who are housebound may also benefit from accessing electronic community information from their own homes.

A distinction can be drawn between organizations and individuals *creating* community information and those which fulfil an *enabling* role in terms of promoting *access* to that information. 'GATEWAYS' or intermediaries have traditionally been advice agencies and libraries, and both continue to play an important role in the delivery of community information. Increasingly and in addition, community information is provided electronically by a range of organizations using a variety of mechanisms including online databases and portal sites, for example, www.mymanchester.net, a portal site facilitated by a community information network in Manchester, UK.

The provision of community information

The provision of community information by some agencies constitutes a 'top-down' approach, where the information flows vertically from the provider down to the user. Judgements are made about the information needs of communities and the most effective methods of meeting those needs. Whilst this approach can maximize skills within an organization, ensure that information is co-ordinated effectively and draw upon economies of scale (as in the creation of bus timetables, for example), it can also lead to the creation of information that is irrelevant to particular communities, which is inaccurate or out of date by the time it is disseminated. A 'top-down' approach can result in the tendency to present community information in a way that reflects the structure of an organization rather than the needs of a user group, and it often ignores the importance of community information in the form of memories, documented discussions, stories etc.

An alternative model for community information is a 'bottom-up' approach, whereby a community develops the capacity to create, maintain and disseminate information that it considers relevant. This process enables information to flow much more fluidly between agencies and users with potential users in many instances becoming providers themselves. An example might be in the creation of information about local events and activities. This approach is potentially more sustainable as relevant skills are developed and retained within the communities that need the information. Similarly, as there is less distance between the information and the users of it, the information is likely to retain its accuracy and currency.

The quality of community information

Issues associated with the quality of information differ from other areas of information provision. Information from a self-help group for diabetes sufferers, for example, could hold equal status as that originating from the National Health Service.

Community information enables individuals to make informed decisions relating to themselves, their dependents and their communities, and can promote participation, social inclusion and access to the democratic process. A variety of mechanisms have evolved to disseminate community information effectively and in a timely and accessible way, with perhaps the most effective and sustainable being a community-centred, 'bottom-up' model.

Further reading

Leech, H. (1999) CIRCE: Better Communities through Better Information, Library and Information Commission.

Nicholas, D. (2000) Assessing Information Needs: Tools, Techniques and Concepts for the Internet Age, ASLIB.

Pantry, S. (ed.) (1999) Building Community Information Networks: Strategies and Experiences, Library Association Publishing.

Sokvitine, L. (2001) 'Cataloguers may yet inherit the earth', State Library of Tasmania, 22 May 2001 (www.service.tas.gov.au/papers/catinherit4.htm).

SEE ALSO: advice service; communication; community librarianship; e-government; electronic public-information services; telecentres

CLAIRE RAVEN AND GARY COPITCH

COMMUNITY LIBRARIANSHIP

The provision of library and information services of special relevance to a particular community, at community level. Provision focuses particularly on social, domestic, health or educational facilities, details of local cultural activities, clubs and societies, and the range of local authority or governmental services. PUBLIC LIBRARIES have long accepted this as a major responsibility, providing COMMUNITY INFORMATION and meeting facilities, but it may also be provided via a special unit set up by a local authority, a voluntary agency or an advice group. Community librarianship has come to have a higher profile in recent years as a mechanism by which libraries can contribute to overcoming problems of social exclusion (see SOCIAL EXCLUSION AND LIBRARIES).

Further reading

Black, A. (1997) Understanding Community Librarianship, Aldershot: Avebury.

SEE ALSO: community information; social exclusion and libraries

COMPUTER

An electronic device that can accept, store, process and retrieve data following the instructions contained in a pre-written program that has been installed into its memory. Conceptually, computers were envisioned in the nineteenth century, but the first machines that were capable of the full range of operations of preprogrammed data storage, processing and retrieval were not built until the 1940s (Winston 1998: 166–88). Since then there has been rapid and continuous progress in their development, in their capacity, in their functionality and in their ability to communicate with each other. Computers are now ubiquitous, and are of particular importance in all aspects of information management including librarianship. The digital electronic technology on which modern computers are based is also used by many forms of communications device, both for voice communications, and for broadcasting.

References

Winston, B. (1998) *Media, Technology and Society*, London and New York: Routledge.

SEE ALSO: communication; informatics; information and communication technology; information management

COMPUTER-ASSISTED LEARNING IN LIBRARY AND INFORMATION SCIENCE

The rapid pace of change in the library and information science (LIS) curriculum is leading to the more extensive use of information technology (IT) in all aspects of LIS education. Students on LIS courses must, on completion of their chosen course of study, have a broader range of IT-based skills. LIS curricula now require that students be highly IT literate, and will include such diverse areas as HTML programming, electronic publishing and ONLINE searching. These are only a few of the topics in which LIS students are educated.

In the early 1980s computer-assisted learning (CAL) packages were created by academics to aid them in the teaching of students. This was especially so in INFORMATION RETRIEVAL, as both TELECOMMUNICATIONS and HOST database charges were prohibitive, and prevented excessive use of online teaching methods. CAL packages were created to avoid these charges. These conditions have now changed. Through the introduction of CD-ROM, and of access to databases via JANET in the UK and similar academic networks in other countries, the cost of searching has been significantly reduced. Furthermore the host providers, such as DIALOG, now provide online tutorials that enable students to familiarize themselves with the database, and how to search it. So, although real-time searching may, on occasion, still be expensive, it is possible for students to practise using databases and refining searches before going online, thereby minimizing any costs incurred.

These reasons mitigate against the creation of specialist CAL packages, especially in comparatively small disciplines like LIS. The cost of producing them, in terms of staff time and material costs, is disproportionate to the lifespan of the product before revisions to the software are necessary. A package is likely to need updating within two years of its creation.

The only noteworthy CAL package still being used in LIS education is CATSKILL. Produced by the UK LIBRARY ASSOCIATION this allows students to learn cataloguing skills. The product has been in use since the mid-1990s and is based on the MARC format and the ANGLO-AMERICAN CATALOGUING RULES. It maintains its currency by focusing on cataloguing skills and standards, not technology.

The rate of change in IT and the rapid redundancy of technology have led to the flooding of the market with software training packages that can instruct students in general IT literacy. Departments of LIS have generally chosen to use industry standard software and training packages without the need to create CAL packages internally. Students can, therefore, prepare themselves using the very tools they will use in the work environment following the completion of their studies. The growth in the number of these packages available makes it impossible for any printed directory to remain current once published.

LIS departments are now able to purchase products by established IT training providers to use as part of their teaching. Products include training on word processing, spreadsheets and databases. Particular emphasis is being given in higher education to the European Computer Driving Licence (ECDL) syllabus, which is maintained and supported by the British Computing Society. This can give students a foundation in

IT, from word processing through to networks. This programme is supported by commercial software recommended by ECDL. Products, such as Electric Paper, are now available and enable students to learn independently.

The development of the INTERNET has increased the possibilities for developments in education. By using free and available technology, including HTML and Internet browsers, resources can now be made available more readily for students. Academics can prepare resources for students, which can be accessed via the Internet. These range from reading lists, through to assignments being made available online. There have also been some developments in the use of Computer-Assisted Assessment (CAA) and further growth can be predicted for the future.

The familiarity of students with the Internet has led to an explosion of information available via the medium. Service providers, including publishers and libraries, are now more confident in making their materials available electronically over the Internet. This encompasses library catalogues, electronic journals, online tutorials and other resources to support students.

Librarians, themselves the products of LIS education, are providing online training for students via the Internet. Examples of guides to plagiarism, citation and information skills, to name but a few, can be found on university websites. These have been created by librarians to aid students in their learning across all subject disciplines.

UK higher education has sought ways to widen participation. To this end both part-time and distance learners have been targeted. This has led to the advent of managed learning environments (MLEs) in higher education institutions and is giving a new dimension to CAL. Students are now able to log on remotely to systems that provide support and materials for their chosen course of study. The Department of Information Science at City University has been adapting this technology to develop their courses. The use of MLEs will gradually increase over the coming years, and some aspects of learning and teaching will be given over to more electronically based solutions. CAL packages, as developed in the 1980s, have ceased to be used, but with the increase in the use of Internet technology a new electronically based environment for education is being created.

Further reading

JISC (2001) 'Managed Learning' Environments (www.jisc.ac.uk/mle/).

Stephens, D. and Curtis, A. (2001) 'Use of Computer Assisted Assessment by staff in the teaching of information science and library studies subjects' *ITALICS* 1 (www.ics.ltsn.ac.uk/pub/italics/index. html).

SEE ALSO: information science education; library education

ALAN BRINE

COMPUTER CRIME

A term used to describe both crimes directed at computers and networks, and crimes committed through the agency of computers. Some definitions are even more inclusive than this. The Royal Canadian Mounted Police, for instance, describe it as 'Any illegal act which involves a computer system, whether the computer is an object of a crime, an instrument used to commit a crime or a repository of evidence related to a crime'. They associate it with telecommunication crime, which they describe as 'the fraudulent use of any telephone, microwave, satellite or other telecommunication system' (Computer Crime 1999).

Does computer crime exist?

In fact, there is a strong case for denying the existence of computer crime as such and arguing that media and popular excitement concerning it is an example of 'moral panic'. This line of argument would hold that all the so-called computer crimes are examples of previously identified types of offence and are capable of being dealt with by existing laws. Much of the public concern relates to security of credit cards. The credit card companies deny that details of cards are ever stolen from within their systems, arguing that the problem occurs when details are stolen in the real world. Successful prosecutions of computer-related offences under existing law have, however, proved very difficult to obtain. An exception is the death sentences against the Hao brothers in 1998 for hacking into the computer system of a state-owned Chinese bank, and transferring money to bank accounts under their control. However, computer-related crimes do usually share sufficient characteristics, in addition to the fact that they are usually difficult to prosecute, to make it worthwhile to discuss them as a category of crime. Despite such doubts, it is commonly accepted official practice to treat computer crime as a distinct category, and issue statistics and estimates of its volume. The UK Audit Commission, for instance, has regularly issued such estimates, whilst admitting that many offences involving computers are never reported, usually because the victims fear consequent public loss of confidence in their systems.

Fraud

Much computer crime is, in fact, merely fraud that takes advantage of the facilities offered by computers. The massive and complex corporate fraud in the Equity Funding affair has sometimes been quoted as the first major example of computer fraud (Seidler *et al.* 1977). However, although the firm, and therefore the fraudsters, employed computers, there was virtually nothing in the whole case that originated in, or relied on, the computer. Three categories of computer fraud are usually identified, but the first two, input and output fraud, are arguably not computer crime as such. An input fraud involves creating false data to enter into a computer system so as to obtain some sort of profit or advantage for the person concerned. A fairly typical offence consisted of an employee reactivating retired colleagues' records so that their 'salaries' could be directed to bank accounts she controlled. Output fraud is much less common, or significant, and involves manipulating data at the point of output from a computer. Thus, a case of (input) fraud by a bank manager also included suppressing other incriminating records that the computer would generate. Only the third category, program fraud, actually involves the computer as an essential tool of the fraud. A new program is introduced into a system, or an existing program modified, so as to achieve some fraudulent aim. A retail accounting system that could conceal a proportion of transactions so as to reduce tax liability is often cited as a classic example.

Other offences

There are various other types of offence that are commonly committed in the computer environment. Invasions of PRIVACY, ranging from reading someone else's e-mail to examining confidential files on the medical, financial or business affairs of others, are typical. They usually involve stealing passwords or bypassing password protection. Eavesdropping, often to obtain business intelligence, through the agency of bugging devices clandestinely attached to computer systems or the use of equipment that can pick up electromagnetic radiation at a distance, is also said to be widely practised. Sabotage of computers, usually through the introduction of viruses but occasionally through direct damage to the machinery, seems mainly to be done as a demonstration of programming and network expertise, or, in the latter type of case, as a means of obtaining temporary relief from the drudgery of routine computer-based employment. Theft of software, although an enormously profitable and common infringement of COPYRIGHT, for practitioners of PIRACY and major unlicensed users alike, is also practised by advocates of the sharing of software as a common good rather than a proprietorial product.

Hacking

Indeed, a great deal of the type of activity described above is attributable to the activities of enthusiasts who make unsanctioned use of networks and the access they give to other people's computers. Their activities follow from and overlap with those of the phone phreaks who have delighted in cheating the telephone companies by finding ingenious methods of making free calls. A distinction is generally made between hackers, who test their technical abilities and ingenuity against computer systems in this way, and crackers, whose intentions are malicious. However, the activities of either can result in disruption and expense to those whose systems prove vulnerable. The imagination and persistence with which they pursue this type of activity on networks is well captured in Clifford Stoll's enthralling account of his encounters with hackers (Stoll 1990). When hackers have been apprehended for alleged offences, they have on occasion successfully argued that they acted without malice and in the grip of an obsession or addiction. Kevin Mitnick, whose major coups included hacking into the North American Air Defence Command's main computer in 1982, successfully avoided imprisonment in 1989 on the grounds of 'impulse disorder', and could cite the lack of any personal profit from his activities in support.

Responses

The laws that have been used, or suggested for use, to prosecute computer-related crime in Britain include: the Theft Act, 1968, for theft of electricity; the Criminal Damage Act, 1971, for introduction of viruses; and the Forgery and Counterfeiting Act, 1981, for the presentation of a false password. However, it was the failure of the prosecution of the hackers Gold and Schifreen under the forgery laws in 1988 that was largely responsible for the introduction of the UK Computer Misuse Act of 1990. This introduced into British law the three offences of unauthorized access to computers, unauthorized access with intent to commit a crime and unauthorized modification of the contents of a computer. Very few prosecutions have, however, been brought under the Act, and if it has had an effect at all it has been merely as a deterrent. In 2001 the Council of Europe, a Europe-wide policy forum not to be confused with the European Union, approved a Convention on Cyber Crime designed to harmonize laws on Internet crime. (Convention 2001) Although the convention will only come into force if and when countries formally sign up to it, its inclusion of a very wide range of offences (copyright infringement, child pornography, malicious hacking, etc.) has aroused fears amongst civil liberties groups.

References

Computer Crime (1999) 'Can it affect you?' (www3.sk.sympatico.ca/rcmpccs/cpu-crim.html) [accessed 2 April 1999].

Convention on Cyber Crime (2001). http://conventions. coe.int/Treaty/EN/projets/FinalCybercrime.htm [accessed 23 November 2001].

Seidler, L.J., Andrews, F. and Epstein, M.J. (1977) *The Equity Funding Papers: The Anatomy of a Fraud*, Wiley.

Stoll, C. (1990) *The Cuckoo's Egg*, Bodley Head.

Further reading

Bowcott, O. and Hamilton, S. (1992) *Beating the System: Hackers, Phreaks and Electronic Spies*, Bloomsbury.

Chaney, M. and MacDougall, A.F. (1992) *Security and Crime Prevention in Libraries*, Ashgate.

Clark, F. and Diliberto, K. (1996) *Investigating Computer Crime*, CRC Press.

Clough, B. and Mungo, P. (1992) *Approaching Zero: Data Crime and the Computer Underworld*, Faber.

Tapper, C. (1989) *Computer Law*, Longman.

Wasik, M. (1991) *Crime and the Computer*, Oxford.

SEE ALSO: computer security; crime in libraries; encryption; information law; security in libraries

PAUL STURGES

COMPUTER SCIENCE

All the activities concerned with the complete or partial automation of problem-solving strategies using some form of automatic system (usually known as a computer). Currently such systems are invariably implemented using electronic signal processing, but this need not always be so (for example, early computer-like implementations such as Babbage's Analytical Engine were based upon mechanical properties, and future systems may be chemically or biologically based). The term computer is usually restricted to systems that operate using a stored 'program' or set of instructions describing the computations to be carried out. The system that actually executes the problem solving (or computation) is known as the computer or 'HARDWARE' and the stored program (or programs) is collectively known as the 'SOFTWARE'. Using the stored program approach, the same hardware can be used to solve many different problems by loading and executing different programs. Activities may be theory-based (for example examining the power, limits and costs of the process of computation), design-based (design of hardware, languages, applications, interfaces) or efficiency-based (the efficiency of ALGORITHMS, representations or the efficient storage and retrieval of information).

Acceptance of the term 'computer science'

The term 'computer science', whilst used quite generally, is not completely accepted. Opinions differ as to whether the subject is a science, or whether it is closer to an engineering discipline. In reality, it is probably best described as a cross-discipline subject. Other terms in use include computer (or computing) engineering, computing and computer studies. On the continent of Europe, and increasingly in the UK, the term 'INFORMATICS' is often used.

Broad aims and coverage

Computer science covers all activities associated with computation, from hardware design (that is the design of the computational engine) to the evaluation of the effectiveness of computer applications in the field. The current content of the discipline can be broadly separated into ten subject areas. These are:

- Architectural methods.
- Operating systems.
- Numerical and symbolic computation.
- Programming languages.
- Algorithms and data structures.
- Software methodology and engineering.
- Databases, knowledge management and information retrieval.
- ARTIFICIAL INTELLIGENCE and robotics.
- Human–Computer Interaction (HCI).
- Graphics and visualization.

Three extensions to these subject areas – high-performance scientific computing, bio-informatics and quantum computing – are currently of increasing interest in the community.

Each of these subject areas can be understood from three viewpoints – theory, abstraction and design (ACM 1991). Theory is concerned with axioms and theorem proving (for example, computability and proving program correctness). Abstraction is concerned with data collection and modelling, and the interpretation of results. Design involves the engineering aspects of computer science including requirements analysis, design rationale and implementation, methodologies, testing and analysis.

Subject areas in more detail

ARCHITECTURAL METHODS

This area focuses on the overall design of the essential components of computing systems – processors (serial or parallel), memory organizations, communications software and hardware, systems distribution and software/hardware interfaces. Key objectives include the design of systems that are predictable, reliable, safe and efficient. Architectural research has increasingly focused on distributed systems and their interconnection, and the transmission of complex media between systems. High-performance scientific computing, for example, involves the interconnection of powerful remote computers using high-speed communication lines.

OPERATING SYSTEMS

This area covers the development of control mechanisms (usually in software) that allow for the efficient use of multiple computing resources such as processor time, disk space, communications facilities and memory, by concurrently executing programs. In recent times such control systems have been extended to cover distributed or 'grid' systems (that is, processors and memory distributed geographically, connected by high-speed communication lines).

NUMERICAL AND SYMBOLIC COMPUTATION

A highly mathematical area concerned with the efficient solution of equations using either symbolic (i.e. algebraic) or numeric (i.e. approximation) techniques. Work in this area has resulted in highly reliable and efficient packages of mathematical routines for science and engineering research workers.

PROGRAMMING LANGUAGES

Programming languages are notations for instructing virtual machines on how to execute algorithms. Many different types of programming language exist that are appropriate for solving particular problems. The four main classes of language are procedural (such as FORTRAN, PASCAL or BASIC), functional (such as LISP, ML and HASKELL), object-oriented (examples include SMALLTALK, EIFFEL, JAVA and C++) and logic programming (PROLOG).

ALGORITHMS AND DATA STRUCTURES

This area is concerned with the development of efficient methods for solving specific problems (algorithms) and how data is organized (and accessed) in computer memory or in secondary storage.

SOFTWARE METHODOLOGY AND ENGINEERING

This area is concerned with the specification, design and development of large software systems. Techniques and approaches include requirements and systems analysis, good programming practice (step-wise refinement, structured programming), verification and validation techniques for showing that programs actually do what they have been designed to do, and testing techniques. Safety, security, reliability and dependability are key goals.

Databases, knowledge management and information retrieval

This area is primarily concerned with the organization of, and access to, data on secondary storage (disks, tapes, floppy disks or CD drives). Database techniques attack the problems of storing and accessing large amounts of highly structured data in an efficient and flexible manner. Such large collections of data will usually be accessed by many terminals at local and remote locations, so that security, integrity and privacy are major issues. More recently, the storage and retrieval of multimedia data has become important. This involves not only new storage techniques but also new retrieval mechanisms in which elements of the media themselves are used as search strings. The development of the WORLD WIDE WEB has also had a major impact in database and INFORMATION RETRIEVAL research.

ARTIFICIAL INTELLIGENCE AND ROBOTICS

Artificial intelligence has two main goals – the simulation of human intelligent behaviour in computer systems, and the testing of possible models of human behaviour. Key aspects include knowledge representation, inference, deduction and pattern recognition. Early successes involved the creation of expert systems (systems storing representations of expert knowledge). Other techniques include neural networks and genetic algorithms. With the introduction of object-oriented programming and the INTERNET, the development of software agents has become an important research area.

HUMAN–COMPUTER INTERACTION

The field of HCI is mainly concerned with the efficient transfer of information between persons and computers. It is the study of how human beings and computers interact. It involves the conception, design, implementation, and evaluation of the effects of user interfaces and tools on those who use them. A key design principle is user-centred design, where the needs, capabilities and limitations of the intended users are properly taken into account during the design process. More recently, the implications of group working and the effects of the organizational environment have also become a focus for research.

Recent developments

There used to be a clear distinction between hardware and software (that is, the machinery that carried out the computation and the set of instructions for that computation). Recently such distinctions have become blurred. First, there was the development of microprogramming that provided a bridge between hardware and software, allowing computers to emulate other computers based on different hardware. Second, the development of programming in Silicon has resulted in a form of hardware programming (or 'firmware').

The object-oriented paradigm has been enthusiastically adopted in many application areas and the language JAVA is now widely used, partly because it is platform independent, meaning that JAVA programs can be passed and executed across dissimilar computers. This makes it ideal for Web-based applications.

Another important development has been the adoption of software-agent technology. Such agents are autonomous, proactive and have some limited social awareness. Some problems can now be solved efficiently using collections of co-operating agents that, if built using languages such as JAVA, may be spread across dissimilar and remote computers.

Quantum computing (or quantum information processing) exploits quantum mechanical effects for computation and information transfer. Although in its early stages, this research has already yielded cryptographical methods for unconditionally secure information transfer.

References

ACM (1991) *Computing Curricula*, Report of the ACM/IEEE–CS Joint Task Force.

Further reading

Bacon, J. (1998) *Concurrent Systems: Operating Systems, Database and Distributed Systems, an Integrated Approach*, 2nd edn, Addison-Wesley.

Date, C.J. (1999) *Introduction to Database Systems*, 7th edn, Addison-Wesley.

Russell, S.J. and Norvig, P. (1994) *Artificial Intelligence, a Modern Approach*, 1st edn, Prentice-Hall.

Schneider, F.B. and Rodd, M. (2001) *International Review of UK Research in Computer Science*, IEE.

Silberschatz, A., Galvin, P.B. and Gagne, G. (2001) *Operating Systems*, 6th edn, John Wiley & Sons.

Sommerville, I. (2000) *Software Engineering*, 6th edn, Addison-Wesley.

SEE ALSO: information and communication technology

J.L. ALTY

COMPUTER SECURITY

The term includes the policies, practices and technology necessary to preserve computers, NETWORKS, software, data and communications from accidental or malicious damage. The extreme vulnerability of digital information itself has been further compounded by the increasingly networked computer environment. Theft, intrusion, ESPIONAGE and malicious damage can be carried out from distant sites, and the consequences of data errors, fire and natural disasters can have far-reaching effects. The majority of companies will admit that security breaches occur every year, and that many of these can be regarded as serious. The consequences of serious failures in security are capable of crippling or destroying the computerized organization. Surveys suggest that public confidence in the security of systems for banking, commerce and other transactions is low. At the same time, there are many computer security products on the market, and the services of security consultants can be used in the creation of comprehensive protection for the organization's facilities. Despite this, computer security is widely neglected. This shows itself both in organizational information policy-making (see ORGANIZATIONAL INFORMATION POLICIES) and the observation of existing sets of security rules.

Types of security

The physical security of computer systems needs to be protected first of all through protection of the areas in which they are located. Environmental protection of computer facilities begins with restricted human access to relevant areas, or the whole, of computerized premises. Identity cards, passwords, door codes, restricted access to keys and alarm systems are amongst the methods by which this can be achieved. Video surveillance is increasingly used to deter those who might offer a threat to computer and other property and facilities, and as a means of identifying those who might have attempted or succeeded in some form of physical intrusion. Physical security also includes protection of power supply, heating, ventilation and lighting systems. Power failures, excessive heat and humidity, water damage, fire and excessive quantities of dust and dirt (whether airborne or introduced by people) can all cause irretrievable damage.

The security of computer hardware itself then follows. Theft of computers or computer chips is common and increasingly easy as systems become more and more compact and portable. Malicious damage to hardware is also a potential problem. Both of these are initially combated by protecting the areas in which hardware is located, but also security cables can be used to attach computers to walls and immovable objects. Drive locks can also be employed to prevent unauthorized use of hardware. Smart-card technology also controls access by holding encrypted passwords, IDs and, if required, biometric means of identification, based on voiceprints, fingerprints, iris recognition and other unique data about authorized users.

Software security is needed to protect against both indiscriminate damage of the kind caused by viruses, and the more specific abuses that can be inflicted by people either within or outside the organization. Virtually all organizations experience virus attacks, and protect against these by attempting to prevent employees introducing data and software from unauthorized sources, and running virus protection software and firewall systems. Firewalls enforce access control between networks, or individual sectors of a system, by controlling connections, authenticating users, filtering data and creating security logs for audit purposes. ENCRYPTION is also widely used as a software solution for the protection of data security. Information, which might be e-mail messages or other files that are to be communicated, is scrambled in a manner that only the intended receiver can decrypt.

Finally, however, a system is only as secure as the people who have access to it. An organization that is strongly concerned with security will need to screen potential employees for dishonest claims in their applications and curriculum vitae, and evidence of personal history that might suggest unreliability. It is quite common to conduct extensive security checks where sensitive posts are concerned, making use of credit rating agencies, legal records and even the services of private investigation agencies. The sensitivity of particular posts needs to be thoroughly assessed and the duties that are allocated to employees may need to be segregated so that the duties of one employee will provide a cross-check on the work of another. Important though such precautions may be, it is arguably much more important that there is good training of all employees with computer access in good security practice. This will include, as a priority, protection of their passwords and other access facilities, and the regular backing up and secure storage of data.

Security policy

Computer security is essentially a matter of organizational policy, and like all such areas it calls for a thorough process of policy making, including appropriate research and consultation. Identification of the resources to be protected and an assessment of risks and threats are essential starting points. The organization's policy should set out the conclusions drawn from this broad analysis, but then the policy must be backed up by guidelines on procedures and the standards to be applied. Lines of responsibility within the organization are particularly vital and at the apex of the system there should be a security administrator or team to take responsibility for the area. Large companies and government agencies frequently employ computer security consultants, sometimes referred to as 'ethical hackers' to test their systems and procedures so as to identify problems. Finally, such is the speed of change in the field and the scale of the problems that occur that even a thoroughly protected organization will need a contingency plan so as to respond to some unanticipated disaster

Further reading

Gollmann, D. (1999) *Computer Security*, Wiley.
Information Management and Computer Security (1992–) ISSN 0968–5227.
Shim, J.K, Qureshi, A.A. and Siegel, J.G. (2000) *The International Handbook of Computer Security*, Glenlake Publishing.
White, G.W. *et al.* (1996) *Computer Systems and Network Security*, CRC Press.

SEE ALSO: computer crime; data protection; disaster preparedness planning; security in libraries

PAUL STURGES

CONCORDANCE

An alphabetical index of words in a document or set of documents, each word present in the text being an index entry.

CONSERVATION

The PRESERVATION of materials by the physical and chemical treatment of them and through preventive care. The purpose of conservation is to stabilize materials, to retard their further deterioration and to maintain them in a condition as close as possible to their original form. In general no attempt is made to restore materials to look as they did originally. Although previously the term 'conservation' implied primarily treatment, it now often is defined more widely and includes preventive care practices. Conservation treatment is carried out by professionally trained conservators or conservation technicians who work under the supervision of a conservator. These conservators are also familiar with preventive care practices and how to implement them.

Physical treatments that are invasive destroy much of the physical evidence in an object, evidence that can tell how, and frequently where, the object was produced. Such evidence in books and manuscripts is essential for bibliographers, and scholars of the history, technology and production of the book. Conservators are trained to avoid invasive treatments and, when they are necessary, to save all physical evidence found within a book, such as sewing thread and material from the covers.

A number of outstanding book and paper conservators and educators have been trained in apprenticeship programmes in the UK and in continental Europe. Only slowly, over the past forty years, as conservation evolved from a craft to a profession, did training programmes develop within academic institutions. Today book and paper conservators are trained in rigorous programmes that combine theory with practice in treatment. Programmes offer undergraduate and/ or postgraduate certificates or degrees. To enrol in a conservation training programme a student must have specific credentials in art history or the humanities and in science, especially chemistry, and demonstrate superior manual skills. In addition to their academic training, conservators spend one or more years in internships in their specialties before reaching full professional status. At that point a conservator may elect to go into private practice or join a conservation department within a library, archive or museum.

Many senior conservators are Fellows of the International Institute for the Conservation of Art and Historic Artefacts (IIC) and/or their national professional organizations, such as the International Institute for Conservation – Canadian Group (IIC–CG), the Australian Institute for the Conservation of Cultural Materials (AICCM), or the American Institute for the Conservation of Art and Historic Artefacts (AIC). Many book and paper conservators are also members of the Institute of Paper Conservation (IPC), which recently developed an accreditation programme.

Today's conservators are generous with their time and knowledge, sharing the results of research and solutions to conservation problems with their colleagues. The IIC journal, *Studies in Conservation*, and the Australian and American journals deal with conservation in all fields and often have excellent articles on book, paper and photograph conservation, as well as on research into environmental concerns such as light damage. *Restaurator*, published in Munich, is an international journal for the preservation of library and archival material. IPC publishes an annual journal, *The Paper Conservator*, with refereed papers, and the AIC Book and Paper Group issues an unrefereed *Annual*. Both publish current research and treatment reports of considerable interest, not only to conservators but also to librarians and archivists. The *Abbey Newsletter*, published in Austin, Texas, USA, also provides current information about conservation research. *Art and Archaeology Technical Abstracts* (AATA), published by the Getty Conservation Institute (GCI) in association with IIC, provides printed and online abstracts of the conservation literature. The latest tool for communication among conservators is the Internet, which carries debates about theory and treatments on various 'listservs' with active participants from around the world.

Libraries, ARCHIVES and MUSEUMS contract for conservation treatment with conservators in private practice in lieu of, or in addition to, treatments undertaken in-house. In addition to treatments, conservators frequently undertake surveys to determine the physical condition of library and archival collections, and of the environment in which the collections are stored. These surveys help librarians, archivists and curators create environments that will preserve collections, for it is useless to treat a damaged book or document if it is returned to conditions that contribute to its deterioration. A professional conservator knows a great deal about the physical nature of the materials and how to remedy harmful environmental conditions, often at little cost. More and more, conservators are asked to assist in establishing an environmental monitoring programme in an institution or to implement other preventive care measures.

A professional conservator will explain treatment options to librarians and archivists but will not appraise materials, which is against the profession's ethical code of practice. A conservator will assess the damage to a book or document and will prepare an estimate for treatment, explaining what treatment will be undertaken. Conservators keep detailed treatment records, with photographic documentation before, during and following treatment for valuable items. For treatment of entire collections, such as a large collection of documents, less detailed treatment records are kept to minimize cost.

This represents a recent shift from single item to collections conservation. Technological and economic developments have caused conservators to view their work in new ways and to change their approach to preservation. They strive to make the most effective use of new technologies to preserve not just single items, but entire collections. Today book and paper conservators frequently treat groups of documents, photographs or books to stabilize them, and a subspeciality of collections conservation is emerging. In the USA a recently formed Library Collections Conservation Discussion Group (LCCDG) meets at the annual meeting of the American Institute for Conservation, and a number of articles on collections care have appeared in the literature.

Conservation as a profession has evolved from the craft of restoration. Today its focus is as likely to be on the preservation of entire collections as on the treatment of single items, and activities are as likely to include preventive care practices as complex treatment procedures. The goal, however, remains the same – to extend the useful life of library and archival materials for future generations.

Further reading

Merrill-Oldham, J. and Schrock, N.C. (2000) 'The conservation of general collections', in P.N. Banks and R. Pilette (eds), *Preservation Issues and Planning*, Chicago and London: American Library Association, pp. 225–47.

Stewart, E. (2000) 'Special collections conservation', in P.N. Banks and R. Pilette (eds), *Preservation Issues and Planning*, Chicago and London: American Library Association, pp. 285–307.

SEE ALSO: bibliography; paper; preservation; special collections

SUSAN G. SWARTZBURG, REVISED AND UPDATED
BY SHERELYN OGDEN

CONSOLIDATION OF INFORMATION

The restructuring of existing public knowledge into the form of a text or other form of message, so as to make it available to those whose circumstances would otherwise effectively deny them access to this knowledge.

Whilst this is essentially a process that is already used in all kinds of circumstances (BROADCASTING, journalism, etc.), it has been discussed amongst information scientists because of its potential for information services in less developed countries. Weak local publishing industries, poor availability of imported books and journals, and unsatisfactory access to online information all lead to a call for alternatives. Repackaging, or, more correctly, provision of consolidated information, is often offered as such an alternative. The consolidation process, as described by Saracevic and Wood (1981), begins with the study of potential users, selection of primary information sources and the evaluation of their information content. Analysis of content to permit restructuring (condensation, rewriting, etc.) and packaging or repackaging of the restructured information can then follow. The diffusion or dissemination of the packages should be accompanied by feedback from users to enable evaluation and adjustment of the process to take place.

This process is in the first place, of course, totally dependent on the availability of information content to repackage. This content can be derived from published material, from raw data collected by research institutes and government statistical services, from GREY LITERATURE, from information acquired electronically via online services and networks, and indeed from the people's own corpus of indigenous knowledge. Given the existence of suitable materials to consolidate, for an effective process to follow there are three main requirements: first, that information materials such as books and journals, or grey literature, should be collected or accessed and their content organized efficiently; second, that there should be the capacity to research the content and create new information packages from it; and, third, that these new products should be disseminated effectively.

National and public library services, national and local archives, and national institutes of research are all capable of contributing to the acquisition of source materials. However, the point is made very strongly by Saracevic and Wood that the information consolidation unit proper needs a host organization that contains subject experts. The work needs to be done by people who have a full understanding of both the message they must repackage and the audience for which it is intended. Specialized research institutions in particular subject areas provide the necessary technical expertise in interpreting the source materials, rewriting and re-presenting the information for different media of communication, whilst a broad-based service, such as a library or archive, does not. Sturges (1994) cites the Botswana Technology Centre as an example of a subject specialist institution performing this function effectively. To complete the chain, institutions are required that are able to mediate the delivery of information, in the context of places and situations accepted by the public. Extension and adult education services, broadcasting corporations, libraries and other informal information services whose personnel understand their public are amongst the various suitable institutions.

The ultimate product of the consolidation process may be a printed leaflet, such as the Technical Bulletins on *Better Care for Your Car Battery, An Easier Way to Make Tomato Crates* or *Protecting Your Home against Lightning* from the Botswana Technology Centre. It can be a verbal message passed on by the central management of an Agricultural Extension Service to the extension workers at their regular training sessions, so that they can disseminate it to farmers who they will visit in their homes or meet in groups for practical demonstrations of farming improvements. It can be the content of a radio broadcast, whether as a simple announcement, part of a documentary programme or embedded in a fictional serial directed at the rural community, such as Kenya's *Ndinga Nacio*. It can be the health education songs and playlets performed in villages by the Malawi Ministry of Health's Katemera Band. It can be a CD-ROM product, a file available via the INTERNET or whatever product the community at which it is aimed will best absorb, but essentially it will embody the original knowledge, from whatever source, transformed by expert hands into something more appropriate to prevailing circumstances.

References

Saracevic, T. and Wood, J.B. (1981) *Consolidation of Information: A Handbook on Evaluation, Restructuring and Repackaging of Scientific and Technical Information*, UNESCO.
Sturges, P. (1994) 'Using grey literature in informal information services in Africa', *Journal of Documentation* 50: 273–90.

SEE ALSO: dissemination of information; social exclusion and libraries

PAUL STURGES

CONSPECTUS

A tool to enable libraries to describe their existing collection strengths and current collecting interests. It was conceived in 1979 in the context of library co-operation and the more effective sharing of resources, originally within North America. Codes are allocated to a collection to indicate collection strength, linguistic and geographical coverage and intellectual level. The data was made available through RLIN. In 1983 Research Libraries Group and the Association of Research Libraries in the USA joined forces to work on the North American Collection Inventory Project (NCIP), to provide data online about the collections of a large number of libraries. NCIP has been growing steadily.

Interest in Conspectus has grown outside North America. In Australia the National Library has accepted Conspectus methodology and there has also been much interest from the university and the state libraries. The National Library of Scotland and the BRITISH LIBRARY have also been active. After the first meeting of the Conference of European National Librarians

in 1987, the National Libraries Conspectus Group was established, with representatives from the National Libraries of France, Germany, Holland, Portugal and the United Kingdom.

SEE ALSO: collection management; library co-operation; research libraries

CONSULTANCY

Consultants are widely used as a means to address some particular need experienced by the organization without increasing the salaried staff establishment. The practice has been a growth industry since the 1980s, and has grown even more rapidly as companies in the 1990s sought to divest themselves of all but their core function. The information sector of the economy uses consultants for a wide range of services, which can include planning, research, INFORMATION AUDIT and system and database design. The distinction between the consultant and the INFORMATION BROKER is seldom a clear one, since people describing themselves as consultants are frequently engaged to find information, conduct online searches or provide document delivery. However, used strictly the term consultant should refer to someone whose services go much beyond information provision. Consultants are expected to be able to offer a detached and objective view of the organization's needs and problems, and, for their fee, to recommend and, on occasion, implement fresh solutions.

Further reading

Vickers, P. (1992) 'Information consultancy in the UK', *Journal of Information Science* 18: 259–67.

SEE ALSO: fee-based services; information professions; research in library and information science

CONTENT

The term describes the INFORMATION that INFORMATION SYSTEMS and MASS MEDIA carry, and thus makes an important distinction, which is not always made clear, between the medium and the message. The CULTURAL INDUSTRIES and KNOWLEDGE INDUSTRIES produce a flow of data, text, images, moving images and MULTIMEDIA combinations of these, and there is an enormous heritage of artistic, scholarly, popular, technical and scientific material in established forms, some of which is undergoing or likely to undergo DIGITIZATION. This is content, and its exploitation is the reason why INFORMATION AND COMMUNICATION TECHNOLOGY has gone so far towards creating an INFORMATION SOCIETY.

In terms of information systems, content is regarded both as information structured in some way, as a DATABASE or (comparatively) unstructured text. Content objects are discrete bodies of information and thus the building blocks of any provision of content to users. They are described as having certain levels of granularity. Thus the finest grained objects are individual documents, graphics, audio clips and similar individual items in other formats. Coarser granularity is represented by collections, such as sites, applications and databases, consisting of fine-grained objects. The business of acquiring content for media distribution is highly profitable and has resulted in the emergence of enormous content-based companies such as AOL Time Warner. They acquire marketable content from many sources, and vigorously defend intellectual property rights.

Further reading

Sturges, P. (1999) 'The pursuit of content', *Education for Information* 17: 175–85.

CONTINUING PROFESSIONAL DEVELOPMENT

Continuing professional development (CPD) is the acquisitions of professional skills and knowledge beyond those required for initial qualification and learned in formal programmes of education. It is an activity strongly promoted by library and information associations, which typically make provision for it by providing seminars and workshops, and perhaps through their publications. It involves a systematic approach to staff development and continuing education, usually consisting of a programme of learning opportunities made available over a period of time. The intention is to ensure that information workers continue to acquire and adapt their skills and knowledge to a swiftly changing professional environment. Increasingly, professionals are expected to take responsibility for their own CPD as they plan the enhance-

ment of their skills and the development of their careers.

Further reading

Dawson, A. (1998) 'Skills of the archive labour pool', *Journal of the Society of Archivists* 19: 177–87.
Evans, J. (1996) 'Continuing professional development', *Education for Information Services: Australia* 13: 37–42.
Prytherch, R. (2002) *The Literature Review: State of the Sector Project*, London: Library and Information Commission (report no. 166).

SEE ALSO: information professions; information science education; library associations; library education

CONTRACTS FOR INFORMATION PROVISION

Contracts determine the ground rules of the relationship between the provider and the client in imaginative and useful ways. An understanding of the role of contract is essential to everyone, at whatever level or in whatever type of organization, concerned with the provision of information. The importance lies not only in the ability of the contract to set out the basic 'work for money' agreement, but also in the way it enables disputes to be avoided or, if that is not possible, at least contained. They need not be regarded as mechanisms for keeping clients at arm's length, though they can do this. More properly they should be regarded as a marketing tool that allows the needs of the client to be identified, structured relative to fees and targeted to fit need so that the client gets no less than required but no more. Nowhere is this more important than in relation to INTELLECTUAL PROPERTY rights.

Contracts for information provision need no special format, which means that they can be entered into verbally or in writing. The major problem with oral contracts is that there is no proof as to their content or existence. If, for example, A had carried out work for B as the result of a telephone call, then there is a verbal contract between A and B. If, however, B subsequently reneges, there is little that A can do. Even if A can convince a court that work was carried out in expectation of a fee, the court is likely to impose what it believes to be a reasonable fee.

This is hardly satisfactory; in effect the parties (or more exactly the party who carried out the work) have abdicated the right to negotiate a professional fee for services rendered.

Written contracts, on the other hand, prove the existence of a relationship but present different problems, namely, what terms to include and how to interpret them. The latter question cannot be answered here but some indication is given below of the types of term that will be useful. Even a precisely drawn contract cannot cover every eventuality, but at the worst it can act as the foundation for a court action and at best it can stimulate realistic formal negotiation that allows parties to be aware of whether they are asking favours or enforcing rights so as hopefully to allow the parties to continue an ongoing business relationship. The contract has many other advantages too, which the following review will highlight.

Entry

One must avoid verbal contracts, for the reasons stated above, yet it would be unrealistic to expect every commission for a client to have a formal written contract associated with it. However, if the provider adopts a standard business contract, which has been designed to cover a range of possible circumstances, stratifying the types of service to be provided through different levels of user licence, each with variations on the restrictions imposed in keeping with appropriate fee structures, in much the same way as an insurance policy has different schedules attached, then this can be used as a reference document for all transactions. All that is then required, whether the client approaches in writing, fax or simple telephone call, is an indication, at the time of the contact, that the provider is dealing on their standard terms of business followed immediately by the completion of a standard confirmatory letter referring to and incorporating the appropriate provisions of the reference document. A contract has been made and the detailed terms evidenced in writing; it is still better if a copy of the standard terms is sent simultaneously, and it can even be printed on the back. The letter can also detail the name of the client, information requirements, purposes for which information is required and the appropriate sections of the reference contract.

Defining the relationship

Liability for either party under the contract results from a failure to meet the terms; consequently, the way in which the terms are drafted will to a large degree determine the existence of liability. The contract must clearly stipulate what is being provided in return for the fee, but equally must delineate what has not been provided. This latter element is important not only as a marketing device to establish a pathway to greater value-added fees, relative to the client's needs, but also in recording the use for which the information was provided so as to set limits on the professional standard that the provider must achieve in the event of any subsequent action for negligence. Provided that this standard is established, a provider who uses 'best practice' is unlikely to fall foul of a claim for negligence. Such a clear definition of purpose is also useful, particularly where the provider is an intermediary using copyright or other information gained from another, to establish what rights of further use and distribution the client may have. If the provider is an intermediary (for example, is acting as a HOST) such definition must match the provider's contract with the source of information so that it is clearly within the remit allowed for the use of that information, e.g. is the provider's further dissemination of that information a breach of copyright or confidence?

Exclusion of liability

The first point to make is that a carefully drafted contract will substantially diminish the probability of liability in the first place. It will define clearly and precisely what the parties must do to fulfil their obligations, so that disputes of the 'who should do what' variety should not happen. But, even when things do go wrong, the contract can cater for minor failures or incursions by including a graduated scale of agreed damages payable by the parties on the occurrence of specified events, such as lateness, all the way to the rights of the parties on termination of the agreement. It is also useful, in order to avoid potentially costly court appearances, to include an arbitration clause. When it does become necessary to consider exclusion it is wise to bear a number of key points in mind:

1 It is usually acceptable to exclude all liability for the acts of another.

2 It is not usually acceptable to attempt a total exclusion of one's own liability; the courts will usually view an attempt to do so as unfair. Much more acceptable is a limitation of liability. This can include quite strict limitations if one is dealing with another business party of equal bargaining power. The position taken by the court is that such parties will, like the provider, have lawyers advising and so must be assumed to know what they are doing.

3 Where the other party with whom one is contracting can be viewed as a consumer, then any attempt to exclude liability will be totally disallowed or highly constrained either by the Unfair Contract Terms Act 1977 or, more recently, the Unfair Terms in Consumer Contracts Regulations 1994, which put into effect the EU Directive on Unfair Terms in Consumer Contracts 1993 and came into effect on 1 July 1995. The regulations go so far as to allow pre-emptive strikes against unfair terms.

The end of the contract

The contract ends when each of the parties has fulfilled its obligations. This will end the relationship between the parties, unless some term is included for renewal. Where a party has broken an obligation under the contract, where there has been a breach of warranty or minor term, the contract will not necessarily end but damages may be payable. These may either have been previously agreed by the parties, as suggested above, or be imposed by the court. Where there has been a breach of a major term, a condition, the contract will end, unless the innocent party waives his rights and treats it as a breach of warranty. The contract can make this right explicit. Damages may be payable here too. When the court assesses damages it does so on two bases. First, do the damages claimed 'arise naturally from the breach' or are they too remote (for example has the client lost contracts as a result of the provider's failure)? Second, the court will assess the amount payable, which must be commensurate with loss but may be more than just the contract price. The party claiming has a duty to mitigate loss.

Further reading

Downes, T.A. (1991) *Textbook on Contract*, Blackstone Press.

Major, W.T. (1990) *Casebook on Contract Law*, Pitman.

Slee, D. (1991) 'Legal aspects of information provision', in *The Information Business, Issues for the 1990s*, Hertis Information and Research.

SEE ALSO: liability for information provision

DAVID SLEE

CONVERGENCE

1 The coming together of technologies and media, both technically and industrially; thus fibre-optic cables can deliver television, voice communications, interactive computing or viewdata systems. Group media ownership (e.g. of newspapers, motion picture products, complete broadcasting systems) is becoming common as a consequence of the technological developments.

2 The coming together of library and computing services in universities, both managerially and operationally. There is a lively professional debate on the benefits and potential pitfalls of the convergence of libraries and computing services, within the context of a rapidly changing technological and learning environment, not least in relation to the wider developments in virtual learning environments.

3 The integration of access methods to local information and remote-site information, where the remote-site information typically refers to remote online bibliographic information.

Further reading

Sidgreaves, Ivan *et al.* (1995) 'Library and computing services: Converge, merge or diverge?', *The Journal of the University College and Research Group* 42: 3–9.

SEE ALSO: information professions; knowledge industries

COOKIES

A cookie is a very small text file that is placed on a user's hard drive by a Web page server, when the user visits a particular site. It functions as a means of identification and can be read by the server that placed it so as to record the user's comings and goings, usually without their knowledge or consent. The companies that use them describe them as a helpful means of personalizing the service that they provide to users when they return to a site. Their contention is that this is in the interests of both the company and the user, but cookies are widely regarded as a tool of excessive covert SURVEILLANCE by the commercial sector.

COPYRIGHT

A legal concept that concerns rights to copy. Copyright protects the labour, skill and judgement that someone – AUTHOR, artist or some other creator – expends in the creation of an original piece of work, whether it is a so-called 'literary work', a piece of music, a painting, a photograph, a TV programme or any other created work.

Acquiring copyright

Copyright is an automatic right in the UK; there is no need to register with any authority, and putting © is not essential, although the case is different in many other legal systems. Remarks at the start of books along the lines of 'All rights reserved. No part of this publication may be photocopied, recorded or otherwise reproduced, stored in any retrieval system, etc.' are not necessary to gain copyright protection, and indeed have no validity in British law. The Copyright, Designs and Patents Act (1988) and its related Statutory Instruments determine what may or may not be reproduced or photocopied.

Who can own copyright?

The owner of copyright can be an individual or an organization; in the latter case, an employee who creates something as part of the course of his/her normal duties passes ownership of the copyright to his/her employer. UK law uses the word 'author' in its broadest sense, to apply to, say, not only a novelist but also a playwright, composer, photographer, artist and so on. Any works originated by a corporate body that show no personal author are protected as 'anonymous works'. Copyright can change hands by assignment. A novelist or an author of a learned article

typically assigns to a publisher the right to reproduce copies of his/her work.

The law gives rights of protection not only to originators but also to those who create particular physical formats for general distribution or sale, such as publishers of printed books, producers of audiovisual media and providers of broadcasting services. Certain rights are also given to performers of plays and other works.

It is important to note that copyright is a negative right. It does not give someone the right to copy items; it gives the owner the right to prevent others copying items. No one is obliged to give such permission if they do not want to do so. An author (and his/her heirs) is granted a monopoly for a finite period. After the period, copyright ends and the materials are said to 'fall into the public domain'; they are then usable without restriction by third parties.

Copyright can only occur provided a work is 'fixed' or recorded in some form. Thus, for example, a speech or a telephone conversation is not copyright unless it is in some fixed format, such as a tape recording or a transcript. Care should be taken not to confuse copyright with LEGAL DEPOSIT, which is also known as copyright deposit.

Originality

A work must be original to be regarded as copyrightable. Under current UK law its degree of originality need not be large. 'Original' implies 'not copied'. Works can overlap by coincidence. Thus, if two people take a photograph of the Houses of Parliament from the same spot, both own the copyright in their respective photographs even though the images might be identical.

There is no copyright in a fact, such as the closing share price for a company, the temperature in London today, the capital of a country or bibliographical citations, even if the fact is original.

Restricted acts

The copyright owner has the right to prevent others from selling, hiring out, copying, performing in public, broadcasting on radio or TV, or amending ('adapting') the copyright work. These acts are the so-called restricted acts. Just because someone owns the copyright, this does not necessarily mean he/she can produce copies at will – for example if the work breaks national security law, or if it infringes someone else's copyright. It is possible for a work to be original copyright and yet infringe someone else's copyright. This sort of situation is not uncommon in INTELLECTUAL PROPERTY law. Infringement of copyright occurs if someone does one of the restricted acts without the copyright owner's permission. He/she can be sued for this. Except in extreme cases, the penalty for this is payment of financial damages to the aggrieved party.

International treaties

Copyright law is governed by international treaties, the most important of which are the BERNE CONVENTION and the Universal Copyright Convention. These allow for basic minimum laws in all countries that are parties to the particular treaty, and allow for reciprocal protection for nationals from other signatory countries. If there is a question about a copyright, it is the local law that applies. The origins of the work are immaterial. The crucial question is the country in which the act is perpetrated.

Acts of parliament, statutory instruments and European Union directives

Copyright is regulated by law (statute law, interpreted in particular cases as appropriate) and by contracts. The major UK statute is the Copyright, Designs and Patents Act 1988. This Act should never be consulted in isolation, but considered in relation to the many Statutory Instruments of relevance. The Act is not the only piece of primary legislation that affects British copyright law. European Union Directives in the field have been issued, and will continue to appear. A Directive, once passed by the Council of Ministers, becomes law in the member states two years after approval.

The different types of copyright

Literary works, dramatic works (plays), pieces of music, artistic works (paintings and sculptures), sound recordings, films, TV broadcasts and radio broadcasts are the most important materials protected by copyright.

The term Related Rights is used to cover rights that, while they are not concerned with copying and other copyright restrictions, apply to copyright materials and are linked to the duration of copyright. These rights include public rental or hire, public lending, so-called moral rights and so-called neighbouring rights. This last term includes rights such as performing and broadcasting rights, recording rights and film distribution rights.

Any item may take several material forms. Each of them will enjoy a separate copyright. For example, in the case of a book there will first be an unpublished manuscript (regarded as 'written' whether produced in handwriting, typed or word processed) and a published volume. There may be a radio broadcast of the works as well, or other adaptations or forms, such as a cinema, film or magazine serialization.

Literary works

The library and information community is mainly concerned with text and numbers, so-called literary works. These include handwritten documents, books, pamphlets, magazines, the lyrics of songs, poetry, learned journals and tabular material such as statistical tables or railway timetables, as well as computer programmes and data in machine-readable form. There is no implication that this is quality literature.

There is a special type of literary work called a compilation. This is a collection of works, each of which may or may not be subject to individual copyright. The compilation enjoys its own copyright because skill and effort were expended selecting and organizing the collection. A compilation therefore includes a directory, encyclopaedia, anthology or database, whether in written, printed or electronic form.

The owner's ability to prevent others from doing certain acts is limited in various ways. For example, copyright in a literary work lasts for seventy years beyond the author's death. The 1988 Act states that third parties are permitted to copy small portions of a literary work without prior approval under a provision known as fair dealing. There are also special provisions for libraries to make copies on behalf of patrons, as long as the patrons sign appropriate copyright declaration forms.

Copyright is a complex area of law, and one which abounds with misunderstanding. In several areas of relevance to librarians, experts disagree about their interpretation of the Act. Non-specialists should read one of the standard texts on the subject and/or consult a copyright lawyer if they are in any doubt about what they are or are not permitted to copy.

Further reading

Copyright, Designs and Patents Act 1988 (1988), London: HMSO [Chapter 48 – a typically unreadable piece of legislation – is reproduced in full in Oppenheim, Phillips and Wall 1994].

Cornish, G. (1990) Copyright: Interpreting the Law for Libraries and Archives, London: Library Association [although now slightly dated, a very user-friendly and reliable overview of typical questions that arise in libraries].

Oppenheim, C., Phillips, J. and Wall, R. (1994) The ASLIB Guide to Copyright, London: ASLIB [comprehensive looseleaf account of copyright law, with an emphasis on user needs and requirements; reproduces relevant pieces of legislation].

Wall, R.A. (1993) Copyright Made Easier, London: ASLIB [despite its title, not a particularly easy book to read; should be read with caution, as the author makes statements from time to time that are not supported by the legal profession].

SEE ALSO: book trade; broadcasting; communication technology; information policy; intellectual property; trade marks

CHARLES OPPENHEIM

CRIME IN LIBRARIES

Ranges from theft of books, other library materials and personal belongings of staff and users, to damage to books, library buildings, fittings and equipment, and violent attacks on staff and users, and other anti-social behaviour on library premises.

Descriptions of Persians looting papyri from Egyptian libraries and images of fifteenth-century chained libraries indicate that crime in libraries is not new and that its most obvious manifestation has been the theft of library stock. Accounts of notorious biblioklepts from centuries past are well documented (Thompson 1968; Stuart 1988). However, many other forms of criminal activity now prevail in libraries, mirroring changes in the wider society of which libraries are a part. All types of library are affected; none are immune.

Comprehensive, accurate statistics on library crime are not readily available, since published crime statistics are not normally recorded to this level of detail. However, several studies (Lincoln 1984; Burrows and Cooper 1992) have begun to address this and supplement anecdotal accounts and estimates. Serious interest in and approaches to crime in libraries gathered momentum in the USA in the 1960s, with libraries in the UK beginning to address crime in the 1970s as, coincidentally, electronic security systems became more widely available. It would seem that much theft in libraries is opportunistic, although several notorious thieves (librarians among their number) have systematically stolen books and removed maps and illustrative plates. Reasons for theft range from BIBLIOMANIA, building collections at home, to selling stolen property for financial gain – sometimes, especially with rare books, to order.

Traditionally, librarians have recourse to library rules and regulations, together with the civil and criminal law of the land (and, perhaps, local codes) under which to prosecute offenders. However, prosecutions appear limited as it can be difficult to prove in law, for instance, that someone who has not returned a borrowed book intended to remove it permanently from the library. Similarly, some librarians may not wish to publicize instances of theft for fear of drawing attention to weaknesses in security and their own lackadaisical behaviour. Others have felt that relatively small fines meted out by courts have not justified lengthy administrative procedures, and that this time and effort might be better spent on prevention if library theft is apparently not treated as seriously as, say, theft from supermarkets. Those cases that have been taken to court would seem to be where major large-scale theft has been uncovered. In the UK one notorious case was that of Norma Hague, who stole fashion plates from various major libraries, causing damage estimated at £50,000; in the USA the case of Stephen Blumberg, who stole 25,000 volumes from libraries, has been widely reported (Jackson 1991). Without going to law, PUBLIC LIBRARIES have traditionally barred persistent offenders from library entry or access to services. ACADEMIC LIBRARIES additionally can recommend non-promulgation of degree awards or other institutional penalties, at least so far as students are concerned.

To the outside world, libraries are quiet, orderly institutions. However, since the 1970s or so this has increasingly not been the case, with libraries facing a growing range of criminal activity – including theft of personal belongings from individuals (staff and users) and theft of equipment (televisions, video recorders, computers, etc.); attacks on buildings, including vandalism, arson, graffiti and terrorism; and violence, aggression, general nuisance, physical abuse and harassment of staff and users. Commonly identified problem patrons include unruly gangs of young people, drunks, eccentrics and those involved in activities such as importuning and drug abuse in areas of the library such as toilet facilities.

Each library is recommended to adopt security measures relevant to its own circumstances. Security marking of equipment and property marks in books are commonplace. Strong rooms, electronic security pads and magic eyes and beams are for those with expensive, rare book collections, but many busy lending libraries now at least have security systems with books triggered to deter theft, and building security systems; and some have panic buttons for staff to summon rapid assistance. Where fines for delayed return of books are not a sufficient deterrent, some libraries have occasional fines amnesties in an attempt to encourage the return of overdue books; others have employed Book Recovery Officers to call at readers' home addresses to recover long-overdue books and this kind of service has been found to more than pay for itself.

Professional bodies and advisers place great emphasis on devising and deploying preventative measures against crime. A library policy and strategy on dealing with crime is strongly recommended, as is adequate training of staff in its implementation. Thought must be given to the location of the library (those in inner-city areas and rural sites are both prone to crime) and its internal design and layout. Surveillance can be undertaken through security patrols and by video cameras but this can be costly. Advice should be sought from Police Crime Prevention Officers and Health and Safety Officers. Some crime can be designed out through planned layout of library furniture, avoiding hidden corners and increasing lighting and staff visibility, but there is sometimes a conflict between security measures and access and use of stock. There are costs but these should be set against potential savings and the damaging effects of crime on service and morale.

References

Burrows, J. and Cooper, D. (1992) *Theft and Loss from UK Libraries: A National Survey*, Police Research Group, Crime Prevention Unit Series Paper no. 37, Home Office Police Department.

Jackson, M. (1991) 'Library security: Facts and figures', *Library Association Record* 93(6): 380, 382, 384.

Lincoln, A.J. (1984) *Crime in the Library: A Study of Patterns, Impact and Security*, R.R. Bowker.

Stuart, M. (1988) 'The crime of Dr Pichler: A scholar-biblioklept in Imperial Russia and his European predecessors', *Libraries and Culture* 28(4): 401–26.

Thompson, L.S. (1968) *Bibliokleptomania*, Peacock Press.

Further reading

Chadley, O.A. (1996) 'Campus crime and personal safety in libraries', *College and Research Libraries* 57: 385–90.

Chadwick, W.E. (1998) 'Special collections library security: An internal audit perspective', *Journal of Library Administration* 25: 15–31.

Chaney, M. and MacDougall, A.F. (eds) (1992) *Security and Crime Prevention in Libraries*, Ashgate.

Lincoln, A.J. and Lincoln, C.Z. (1987) *Library Crime and Security: An International Perspective*, Haworth Press.

Nicewarmer, M. and Heaton, S. (1995) 'Providing security in an urban academic library', *Library and Archival Security* 13: 9–19

SEE ALSO: computer crime; copyright; data protection; espionage; forgery; health and safety; intellectual property; liability for information provision; official secrecy; preservation; security in libraries

GRAHAM MATTHEWS

CULTURAL INDUSTRIES

A term used to describe the commercial activities that promote or facilitate the use of culture in the broadest sense. It thus includes PUBLISHING, cinema and almost all BROADCASTING. It also includes many other activities such as entertainment, sport and many aspects of cultural heritage in general, including access to much of the built and natural environment such as historic houses and national parks. There are several parallel concepts such as entertainment industries, KNOWLEDGE INDUSTRIES, creative industries and CONTENT industries. The concept of content industries became particularly common in the European Union in the 1990s.

History of cultural industries

The concept of cultural industries was created by members of the Frankfurt School of social sciences working in Los Angeles, and was embodied in the *Dialectic of Enlightenment*, by Theodor Adorno and Max Horkheimer, originally published in 1944 (Horkheimer and Adorno 1972). Walter Benjamin believed that multiplied and industrially produced cultural industries could function as a source of enlightenment to the masses. Unlike him, Adorno and Horkheimer criticized the phenomenon of cultural industries as a passive mass culture. Adorno himself described mass culture as 'the bad social conscience of high culture'. According to them, the cultural industries can be traced back to the European cultural monopolies at the beginning of the twentieth century. The history of the cultural industries during the twentieth century reflects the continuing debate between these two ways of approaching the issue: the positive attitude to cultural industries as a democratic force, and the negative attitude that identifies an increasing cultural passivity among the masses.

The proportion of immaterial exchange in the economy is continuously on the increase and it is evolving into a central growth factor for national economies in the future. At a global level, this development is already visible. Competitiveness is increasingly dependent on the level of control and knowledge of the international market of cultural significances. Successful products are charged with symbolic value, be they intangible goods or traditional commodities. Culture is the innovation reserve for this immaterial production. Cultural industries provide new economic opportunities for creativity in a world where immaterial exchange, and in particular the exchange of cultural significances, is a rapidly growing area, and of important potential for the innovation of economy both at national and international levels.

As a form of exchange of symbols and social meanings cultural industry is by no means new; on the contrary, it is an ancient action concept of human communities. In the long run, however, the focus is shifting more and more from commodity production to production of symbols.

The future will see a shift of focus from the INFORMATION SOCIETY towards the society of meaning, which emphasizes production of signification, or meaning industries. Cultural industries may also be considered from an ecological point of view as an alternative form of sustainable development to support living and material culture, as a key element of social and economic development that results in social inclusion, environmental protection and the reduction of poverty.

Definitions

The concept of cultural industries is problematic, because it combines two separate spheres, traditionally far apart from each other: artistic creativity and economic production. This combination forces us to evaluate the points of convergence and the section surfaces of these two spheres in a new light; therefore, the concept of cultural industry may function as a producer of new questions and solutions. In addition, the concept is well adapted for describing the increase of immaterial exchange in the global action environment. Symbolic exchange is a typical growth area of the supranational economy in post-industrial production.

The concept of cultural industry can be defined on several levels. Existing definitions can be classified into four groups as follows.

According to the most general definition, cultural industry is production based on the meaning of contents. This general definition covers traditional commodity production marketed by cultural meaning, for instance design, clothing or any kind of brand product. According to this general definition, cultural industry is a perspective on several sectors of industry, because, in addition to the different core areas like, for instance, the entertainment industry, it encompasses sports, the clothing industry and almost every form of trade in the world, for the meanings connected to commodity production dictate demand, supply and consumption. The definition is interesting, but it easily leads to the conclusion that 'everything is cultural industry' and makes it, therefore, difficult to grasp in specific terms. On the other hand, the general definition enables us to visualize and comprehend ongoing social processes and development of perceptions in society. It enables us to determine the new infrastructure of a society of cultural industry, and the educational needs of the citizens in this environment.

On another level, cultural industry could be defined as an industry covering both the fields of traditional and modern art and culture, from artistic creation to distribution: the creative work of an artist, its further development and commercialization to a piece of work, the presentation of the work and its distribution and reception. According to this definition cultural industry covers literature, the plastic arts, music, architecture, theatre, dance, photography, cinema, industrial design, media art and other fields of creative and performing arts. It also includes the production and distribution systems of art and culture, such as publishing (books, newspapers and magazines, music in recorded and printed form), programme production, galleries, the art trade, libraries, museums, radio, television and Web-art. This definition provides an opportunity to present action proposals for new guidelines for traditional art and cultural institutions in the context of a society of cultural industry.

The third group of definitions is based on the criteria of replication and multiplication, which emphasize the role of electronic production. In this definition, the criteria for determining the extent of the cultural industry are mainly related to commercial success, mass audiences and the reproducibility of works of art. In this case cultural industry comprises cinema, television, radio, publishing activity, music industry and production of cultural content. Cultural content production can be linked with a particular field of activity. Cultural content production means producing cultural material, and then distributing and presenting it through various media in such a manner that it generates business activity. The 'culturality' of this material is determined according to the community's prevalent views of culture; it is, therefore, a variable definition.

The fourth, and the narrowest, definition of cultural industry is from the perspective of cultural entrepreneurship. In this case, the production of art and culture is seen as entrepreneurship: cultural contents are the commodities, and the value and distinction of the exchanged products are based on significances, whether the products and services are material or immaterial.

The concept of cultural industry is more a general perspective on producing and distributing creativity than an exactly definable, strictly limited operational starting point. It might be better to talk about 'producing creativity' or 'creative production' than about cultural industries. On the other hand, a concept that links the arts and culture sector to the economy as a whole and to the concept of production is useful in the sense that it questions traditional modes of thought and can, at its best, create new kinds of bridges between these areas that now are seen as separate. Creativity always involves new kinds of combinations of the existing definitions and classifications.

The concept of cultural industry is still fluid and, therefore, controversial. The concept must be redefined for each context. For example, there is a need for definitions that permit the collection of better statistics about the sector, which can in turn underpin the future planning process.

Cultural industries is an umbrella concept that combines the phenomena of creative production, such as opportunities for employment in cultural professions, differentiation of audiences and fulfilment of their diverse needs, with current cultural policy, recognizing the possibilities of creative human capital in the development of national and international innovation systems.

Value chain of the cultural industries

Cultural activity can be analysed by dividing it into different phases of action with the help of the concept of the 'value chain', used in economic theory. The value chain consists of content creation, content development, content packaging, marketing and distribution to final audience, or consumers. As regards cultural industries it is important to emphasize the importance of feedback and reformulate the value chain into the form of a circle (see Figures 7–9).

The value circle covers all the phases of cultural production, from the artist's idea to the audience or customers and the effect on them. The value circle includes content creation, development and packaging for different channels of distribution, and marketing and distribution to consumers. Actors in the various phases of the value circle include artists, producers, marketing professionals and the audience itself. The cultural industries value circle has a positive potential in society: if a society has high capacity for cultural signification it produces more and more cultural signification. Thus, cultural signification is in principle a resource with no limits.

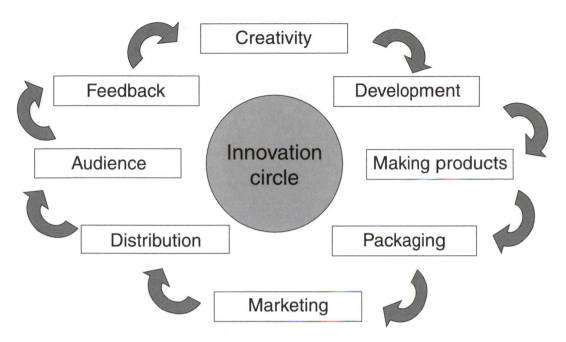

Figure 7 Value circle of the cultural information society
Copyright Hannele Koivunen, www.hanneleinen.com

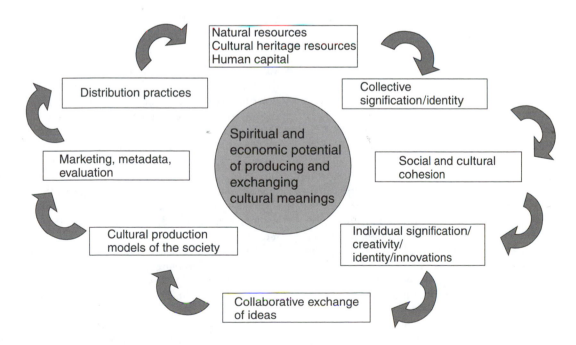

Figure 8 Value circle of cultural production
Copyright Hannele Koivunen, www.hanneleinen.com

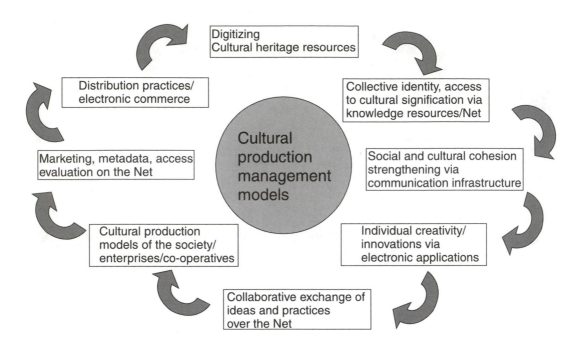

Figure 9 Electronic applications of cultural production
Copyright Hannele Koivunen, www.hanneleinen.com

Libraries and information services as cultural industries

In the value chain of cultural industries, libraries belong most evidently to the phase of distribution, but, if we consider the issue more closely, the role of libraries is more complicated, and actually libraries penetrate the whole circle. Creativity always depends on knowing the signification of the community. Library collections are a crucial resource of cultural heritage for the information society, from which all kinds of creativity get raw material. Innovations are developed as continuity from the past or in reaction to it. Libraries form an essential infrastructure for a networking information community, and for realizing the right to knowledge for citizens in the information society. Libraries also develop information and signification products for information retrieval, and have a pivotal role in the distribution of information. Through libraries new cultural products go into the value circle as feedback, and strengthen the capacity of society for new cultural production.

Library products

The core of library know-how comes from designing and creating products in the field of METADATA. Metadata can be defined as creating the knowledge of both form and content that describes various meanings of documents. Traditionally this means cataloguing, CLASSIFICATION and INDEXING bibliographic data and the information content of cultural products. The use of INFORMATION AND COMMUNICATION TECHNOLOGY has, however, added new elements to this process, and we can define three dimensions of metadata: technical surroundings, the traditional field of metadata and the added-value development of products.

The traditional field of metadata consists of cataloguing, classifying, indexing and all kinds of description for the content of documents. The dimension of technical surroundings consists of all kinds of technical solutions like standards and formats (such as the ANGLO-AMERICAN CATALOGUING RULES (AACR) or DUBLIN CORE), which are essential for distributing information, for example, on the Web. Technical solutions

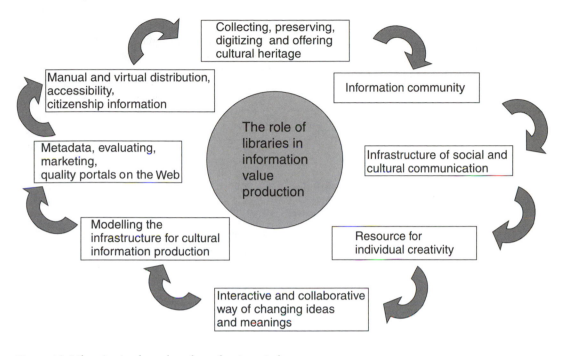

Figure 10 Libraries in the cultural production circle
Copyright Hannele Koivunen, www.hanneleinen.com

form the basis for such distribution, but very often they simultaneously intermingle with choosing content opportunities, and creating functioning metadata products. In the cultural industries, as in other sectors, post-industrial production is characterized by networking, flexible action models and the use of new technology, where technical solutions, products and services are blurred.

The field of library products development will in the future be creating more and more focused on-demand added-value metadata products. Libraries may develop metadata products creating quality portals (see PORTALS AND GATEWAYS) on the Web, and, while fulfilling classical information roles with ABSTRACTS, summaries, criticism and packaged information on different themes for special audiences and customers. Libraries have traditionally networked both locally and globally with each other, but the development of library products will increasingly be mixed with creating new kind of network solutions. We might even say that library networks form the interface and infrastructure for distributing metadata.

Further reading

Adorno, T.W. (1990) *Culture Industry. Selected Essays on Mass Culture*, London: Routledge.
Bermingham, A. and Brewer, J. (eds) (1995) *The Consumption of Culture 1600–1800. Image, Object, Text*, London: Routledge.
Bourdieu, P. (1993) *The Field of Cultural Production. Essays on Art and Literature*, Cambridge: Polity Press.
Castells, Manuel (1996) *The Information Age: Economy, Society, and Culture, vol. 1: The Rise of Network Society*, Oxford: Blackwell.
Lash, S. and Urry, J. (1994) *Economies of Sign and Space*, London: Sage.

References

Horkheimer, M. and Adorno, T.W. (1972) *Dialectic of Enlightenment*, New York: Herder & Herder.

SEE ALSO: catalogues; copyright; digital library; economics of information; European Union information policies; knowledge industries; mass media

HANNELE KOIVUNEN

CURRENT AWARENESS

A service for notifying current documents to users of libraries and information services. It can take the form of selective dissemination of information (SDI), information bulletins, indexing services or reviews of current literature. Such services are now typically provided using the Internet from such sources as Denver UnCover (www.uncweb.carl.org) and the Bath Information and Data Service (BIDS) (www.bids.ac.uk).

Further reading

Martin, P. and Metcalfe, M. (2001) 'Informing the knowledge workers', *Reference Services Review* 29: 267–75.

SEE ALSO: dissemination of information; document delivery

CURRENT CONTENTS LIST

A publication that reproduces the contents lists of periodicals in a particular subject field. *Current Contents* is a registered trade mark (see TRADE MARKS) of the INSTITUTE FOR SCIENTIFIC INFORMATION (ISI), and is used for their family of publications that reproduce the contents pages of periodicals (www.isinet.com/isi/products/cc), and is accessible through ISI's Web of Knowledge portal (see PORTALS AND GATEWAYS). Generically the phrase is used to mean any such list, including those produced non-commercially by libraries and other information agencies for their own clients.

Further reading

Jezzard, H. (2001) 'ISI launches new portal', *Information World Review* 175: 6.

CUTTER, CHARLES AMMI (1837–1903)

Librarian and developer of the most successful format for DICTIONARY CATALOGUES. His *Rules for a Printed Dictionary Catalogue* and his activity in AMERICAN LIBRARY ASSOCIATION (ALA) committees on cataloguing were extremely influential, but he also did significant theoretical work on subject access. Cutter numbers bear his name and are still much used in library catalogues.

Born in Boston, Massachusetts, he was a Harvard graduate who first became interested in librarianship as student librarian at the Harvard Divinity School. He joined the Harvard library staff in 1860, moving to the Boston Athenaeum Library in 1869 and remaining for twenty-four years. In 1876 he was associated with Melvil DEWEY in the establishment of ALA. He was an enthusiastic supporter of Dewey's projects for co-operation and standardization in librarianship. Influenced by Dewey's book CLASSIFICATION system, he developed his shelf classification system for the Athenaeum. The 'Author Tables' for this became the Cutter numbers, which are used for arranging books alphabetically by author. His eminence in librarianship was recognized by his appointment to the editorship of the *Library Journal* in succession to Dewey, a post that he held until 1893.

Further reading

Miksa, F. (ed.) (1977) *Charles Ammi Cutter: Library Systematizer*, Littleton, CO: Libraries Unlimited.

SEE ALSO: bibliographic classification

CYBERCAFÉ

A café that not only serves food and drinks, but also provides personal computers connected to the INTERNET for use by customers; it is thus sometimes referred to as an Internet café. Whilst some cybercafés do not charge customers to use the computers it is more normal for them to charge by the hour or part of the hour. It was estimated that by 2001 their numbers would be in tens of thousands rather than thousands, and they are to be found even in small and remote communities worldwide. They provide an extremely important local facility where public Internet access facilities are rare, fewer homes have computers or computers with fast network lines, up-to-date hardware and the latest browsers are uncommon. However, they are found most commonly in the industrialized countries and those parts of the world frequented by tourists and migrants who require contact with home.

CYBERNETICS

The science of the communication and control of information in machines and animals. In this sense, and for this purpose, it was developed by Norbert WIENER.

Further reading

Web Dictionary of Cybernetics and Systems (2002) (www.pespmc1.vub.ac.be/ASC/indexASC.html).

SEE ALSO: information theory; systems theory

CYBERSPACE

A term generally credited to the novelist William Gibson in 1984 in the novel *Neuromancer*. It refers to the way that users of computers and NETWORKS, particularly the INTERNET, can per-

ceive themselves as existing in a world of VIRTUAL REALITY paralleling the real world. The display of data in an artificial three-dimensional space, real-time communication and the playing of elaborate simulation and fantasy games all contribute to the illusion that people are connected in a way that transcends physical space and time. Perhaps the strongest and most persuasive expression of the idea comes from John Perry Barlow (1996).

References

Barlow, J.P. (1996) 'A declaration of the independence of cyberspace' (www.eff.org/barlow/declaration-final.html).

D

DATA

A general term for quantitative or numerically encoded information, particularly used for information stored in a DATABASE. The word is, however, frequently used in a casual way with a sense not especially different from 'information', as, for instance, in a phrase like 'biographical data'.

SEE ALSO: information; information and communication technology; information management

DATA ARCHIVES

Research facilities acting as central processors and disseminators of electronic research DATA to users, taking electronic data resulting from research projects and administrative processes in the form in which data generators find it convenient to provide it, and then processing, documenting and disseminating it (through a variety of media) in a form convenient to users. Data archives offer a variety of additional services ranging from DISSEMINATION OF INFORMATION about data, through the provision of INFORMATION RETRIEVAL resources and systems, instruction and training in data analysis techniques and methodologies, to the creation of special-purpose datasets and packages.

Development

The roots of centralized social data archives lie in the late 1950s, when millions of computer cards containing data from market research survey interviews were preserved and made available through the first data archives, or survey archives

as they were originally titled. Because the data were on cards, and could therefore be used, reused and copied long after they were collected, researchers saw the advantages of recycling the information collected and created central distributing repositories, or ARCHIVES, of machine-readable social data, to encourage this ecological approach to research data. The largest of these in the USA is the Inter-University Consortium for Political and Social Research (ICPSR) at the University of Michigan (www.icpsr.umich.edu/ORG/). In 1960, the first European data archive was established in West Germany, the Zentral-archiv in Cologne (www.gesis.org/ZA/). There are now central data service centres in most major European countries, and throughout Canada, the USA and elsewhere. Data archives are usually of two types: data dissemination services offered as part of the more traditional library, with little or no processing of the data; or data and research services offered by a separate entity or an adjunct to a social science teaching and research department, in which data are processed (cleaned), documented and manipulated to increase ease of access. Data handled by these archives generally cover all of the social sciences, although some tend to concentrate on particular disciplines or substantive areas.

The UK Data Archive at the University of Essex (www.data-archive.ac.uk/) is among the largest in Europe. Established in 1967 by the Economic and Social Research Council, the Data Archive now holds some 4,000 datasets from both national and international academic, commercial and government sources, and provides a wide variety of services. Data holdings cover the social sciences in general. In common with its international counterparts, the Data Archive is developing a number of specialist services for the research community, for example special units on historical and qualitative data, and is widening its remit to include data-based resources throughout the world.

Advantages and services

Data archives are effective in both maximizing the benefits of developments in technology and in minimizing its risks and disadvantages. As there is no single standard for storing and analysing electronic data, data archives have developed a variety of techniques for the conversion of data into an archival standard format and for disseminating them in a form required by the user. In a time of rising costs of data collection, the secondary use of data collected for other purposes – academic or administrative – becomes increasingly attractive. Data archives facilitate this process by cleaning and documenting data for more general use, and by devising and developing techniques to ease data access and retrieval. Acting as data brokers or GATEKEEPERS, archives regularly acquire data from governmental agencies and provide, on a centralized basis, the monitoring and control required for its safe and responsible use.

Archives also provide co-ordination centres for the creation, implementation and maintenance of standards of data collection, documentation and description. As computer technology develops, large numbers of data files are being created, and archives have responded by concentrating on development of techniques to assist users in locating relevant and useful data: this has included techniques for BIBLIOGRAPHIC CONTROL of electronic data files and the development of standardized data description formats. A working group co-ordinated by the UK Data Archive developed standards for the inclusion of references to computer files within the common MARC format for library catalogues in 1989, and investigated the feasibility of a union catalogue (see UNION CATALOGUES) of computer files in a British Library project. Almost all European data archives now implement the European Standard Study Description Scheme, which allows exchange of information and catalogues between the archives. Most data archives also provide sophisticated finding aids for their own collections, involving detailed and comprehensive indexing and advanced information-retrieval

systems. The UK Data Archive offers, through its BIRON catalogue, an index to all of its holdings, based on a specially constructed social science THESAURUS, and an easy-to-use retrieval system, available on the electronic networks for instant interrogation by British and international research users.

As electronic data without comprehensive documentation are of little use to researchers interested in their secondary analysis, data documentation has been a long-standing concern for data archives, who have developed guidelines for good practice and documentation standards for collectors and users of data. A more recent development, the Data Documentation Initiative (DDI), is attempting to establish an international standard and methodology for the content, presentation, transport and preservation of METADATA about datasets in the social and behavioural sciences. This will allow codebooks to be created in a uniform, highly structured format that is easily searchable on the Web, and that fosters simultaneous use of multiple datasets. Within the DDI, a Document Type Definition (DTD) for mark-up of social science codebooks is being developed, employing the eXtensible Mark-up Language (XML), which is a dialect of the more general mark-up language, SGML (see MARK-UP LANGUAGES).

Dissemination of data has traditionally been offered on a variety of portable media, including magnetic tape and CD-ROM. Most archives now offer data via electronic transfer or online access. Completion of necessary undertakings and licences can also now frequently be done online.

As archive services are increasingly becoming more WORLD WIDE WEB-based, and in response to data users' requirements for linking datasets from disparate sources, a consortium of archives has collaborated in the development of NESSTAR (www.nesstar.org/server/), an infrastructure for data dissemination via the Internet that allows users to locate multiple data sources across national boundaries. This researcher's 'dream machine' provides an end-user interface for searching, analysing and downloading data and documentation. The service is based on utilization of the DDI data and metadata structure, and is being implemented in a large number of data archives and libraries throughout the world.

Charges for data archive services vary considerably between countries; charges are usually not made for the data themselves, although individual data depositors may require that surcharges are added to defray their own data collection costs.

International co-operation

The Standing Committee on Social Science Data Archives of the International Social Science Council of UNESCO laid the groundwork for international co-operation between the world data archives in 1966. Two organizations, in which the majority of the world data archives hold institutional memberships, organize and facilitate this international effort: the Committee of European Social Science Data Archives (CESSDA) (www.nsd.uib.no/Cessda/) oversees and fosters non-raiding agreements and collaborative ventures; and the International Federation of Data Organizations (IFDO) (http://www.ifdo.org/), which includes members not only in Europe but also in Australasia, the USA, Canada, Japan and India, sets policies for collaboration and co-operation, and supports a number of common projects. The International Association for Social Science Information Service and Technology (IASSIST) (http://datalib.library.ualberta.ca/iassist/), an association of individuals working in data organizations, holds joint annual conferences with IFDO, alternating between venues in the USA and Europe.

Further reading

ICPSR (2000) *Guide to Social Science Data Preparation and Archiving*, http://www.icpsr.umich.edu/ACCESS/dpm.html.

Mochmann, E. and de Guchteneire, P. (1998) *The Social Science Data Archive Step by Step*, http://www.ifdo.org/archiving_distribution/archive_sbs_bfr.htm.

Ryssevik, J and Musgrave, S. (1999) *The Social Science Dream Machine: Resource Discovery, Analysis and Delivery on the Web*, http://www.nesstar.org/papers.

Scheuch, E.K. (1990) 'From a data archive to an infrastructure for the social sciences', *International Social Science Journal* 42: 93–111.

Silver, H.J. (2000) 'Data needs in the social sciences', in *Conference on Information and Democratic Society: 'Representing and Conveying Quantitative Data'*, Columbia University, 31 March 2000 (www.cossa.org/dataneeds.html).

Taylor, M. (1990) 'Data for research: Issues in dissemination', in M. Feeney, and K. Merry (eds) *Information Technology and the Research Process*, Bowker-Saur.

Taylor, M.F. and Tanenbaum, E.T. (1991) 'Developing social science data archives', *International Social Science Journal* 43: 225–34.

SEE ALSO: archival description; archives; catalogues

MARCIA FREED TAYLOR

DATA BANK

Usually synonymous with DATABASE but sometimes used to specify collections of non-bibliographic data or numeric data.

DATA COMPRESSION

Techniques used for the reduction of the storage space needed in a computer by the encoding of data and the reduction of redundant information. A trade-off is made between the savings in storage capacity and the increase in computation needed to achieve the compression itself and to restore the original when it is retrieved. The enormous popular success of MP3 compression for the exchange of music files is at the heart of the whole PEER-TO-PEER (P2P) movement.

Further reading

Cannane, A., and Williams, H.E. (2001) 'General purpose compression for efficient retrieval', *Journal of the American Society for Information Science* 52: 430–7.

SEE ALSO: information and communication technology

DATA MINING

Data mining is the exploration and analysis of very large volumes of data stored in a company's existing databases, or in repositories, such as DATA ARCHIVES and DATA WAREHOUSES, to discover meaningful new correlations, patterns and trends. The development of new ALGORITHMS to cope with very large datasets has made it possible to exploit information that was stored, but to all intents and purposes unusable. The process uses statistical techniques and pattern recognition technologies. It is essentially a mechanism for identifying data, on the basis of specified terms and associated terms and concepts, from a wide range of sources, so as to address complex problems.

DATA PROTECTION

According to the Standard: BS-ISO 2382 on information processing systems, data protection is defined as: 'The implementation of appropriate administrative, technical or physical means to guard against the unauthorized interrogation and use of procedures and data.'

In the context in which the term is customarily used, however, there needs to be a greater emphasis on protecting personal information. The definition of *privacy protection* in the same Standard appears more appropriate.

> The implementation of appropriate administrative, technical, and physical safeguards to ensure the security and confidentiality of data records and to protect both security and confidentiality against any threat or hazard that could result in substantial harm, embarrassment, inconvenience, or unfairness to any individual about whom such information is maintained.

Data protection extends far beyond the mechanics of DATA SECURITY and preserving personal PRIVACY. In addition to ensuring the security and confidentiality of information, it also incorporates the need for reliability, completeness and accuracy of any information, together with its fair use, in terms of the motives and behaviour of data users. This takes on particular meaning with public domain information that is clearly not private but still needs to be safeguarded against misuse. A recent investigation into UK public register information is relevant here.

Until relatively recently considerations of data protection were, to a large extent, centred on electronic data processing with its considerable potential for performing a range of operations with personal information. Early international initiatives, government policies and legislation tended to reflect this attitude. The current approach recognizes the need to safeguard personal information regardless of the medium on which it is kept or the mode of its processing. It encompasses paper-based or 'manual' records as well as a range of other manifestations of personal data including electronic images and sound. Thus data protection applies equally to the contents of a piece of paper, the use of a mobile telephone or information gathered on a CCTV surveillance system.

In 1981 the Council of Europe established a *Convention for the Protection of Individuals with Regard to Automatic Processing of Personal Data*, which became the catalyst for, and formed the model for, many nations to enact legislation. The OECD issued, also in 1981, its *Guidelines on the Protection of Privacy and Transborder Flows of Personal Data*, which also acted as a landmark for the development of policy and legislation. Though there had long been European Union interest in the issue, serious attempts to codify and regulate activity did not gather momentum until the appearance of a draft Directive on data protection in 1990. This encountered strong opposition from a range of interests, and a much revised version was presented in 1992 and achieved formal translation into European legislation in 1995. The objectives of the Directive, as encapsulated in Article 1, are two-fold. It seeks to protect fundamental rights to privacy as well as facilitate the legitimate flow of information within member states.

Article 1 Object of the Directive:

1. In accordance with this Directive, Member States shall protect the fundamental rights and freedoms of natural persons, and in particular their right to privacy with respect to the processing of personal data.
2. Member States shall neither restrict nor prohibit the free flow of personal data between Member States for reasons connected with the protection afforded under paragraph 1.

The first body to enact data protection legislation was the Lander of Hesse, in Germany, which achieved this in 1970. Sweden can claim the distinction of passing the first national data protection law in 1973. A number of countries now have legislation designed to achieve data protection in some measure. The UK Information Commissioner's website includes a page (http://www.dataprotection.gov.uk/dpr/dpdoc.nsf) that provides details of data protection and privacy authorities for the following countries (see Davies *et al.* 2000):

UK Territories:
  Guernsey, Isle of Man, Jersey.
European Union and EEA Authorities:
  Austria, Belgium, Denmark, Finland, France, Germany, Greece, Iceland, Ireland, Luxembourg, the Netherlands, Norway, Portugal, Spain, Sweden, United Kingdom.
Other Data Protection/Privacy Authorities:
  Australia, Canada, Czech Republic, Hawaii, Hong Kong, Hungary, Israel, Japan, Monaco, New Zealand, Poland, Slovak Republic, Switzerland, Thailand, Uruguay.

In the UK, the proper foundations of data protection legislation may be regarded as having been laid by the Younger Committee on Privacy, established in 1970. The Committee's Report appeared in 1972. Later, the Lindop Committee on Data Protection, established in 1976, undertook the most extensive review of the issue and its Report, published in 1978, is of considerable value as a detailed commentary on the subject. The international initiatives from the Council of Europe and the OECD, noted earlier, provided added impetus and the first Data Protection Act in the UK was passed in 1984. The legislation currently in force is the Data Protection Act 1998, which derives from the European Union Directive and covers personal data in whatever form, including paper records. The full text is available on the Web at: www.legislation. hmso.gov.uk/acts/acts1998/19980029.htm.

Its purpose is described in its preamble as: 'An Act to make new provision for the regulation of the processing of information relating to individuals, including the obtaining, holding, use or disclosure of such information.'

The Act has, as its basis, eight guiding principles. They require that personal data be:

- Processed fairly and lawfully [detailed conditions are specified].
- Obtained and processed only for specified and lawful purposes.
- Adequate, relevant and not excessive.
- Accurate and, where necessary, kept up to date.
- Not be kept for longer than is necessary.
- Processed in accordance with the rights of individuals about whom data are held [defined as *data subjects*].
- Processed under appropriate technical and organizational security measures.

- Not transferred to a country or territory outside the *European Economic Area* unless that country or territory ensures an adequate level of data protection.

The role of implementing the legislation is placed upon the Office of the Information Commissioner. The Commissioner maintains a Register of personal data-processing activity compiled from notifications submitted by data users [defined as: *data controllers*]. Operating without notifying the Commissioner is prohibited and a punishable offence unless the circumstances are covered by an exemption. The Commissioner also has powers to investigate, monitor, approve, regulate and direct the activities of data users and has responsibility for promoting good practice and disseminating information about data protection. A Data Protection Tribunal acts as an appeal mechanism for data controllers regarding decisions taken by the Commissioner.

The interests of the individual are safeguarded in the Act by several means. In many cases a person's informed consent has to be sought for data gathering and use, and a person may object to data processing in certain circumstances. A person's rights of scrutiny of data and provision for redress in the event of its inaccuracy or if it is being misused are also included. The Act also identifies a category of *sensitive personal data* for which additional safeguards are specified. Such data comprises information on a person's race, or political, religious or trade union activity as well as a person's health, sexual life or any alleged or actual criminal offences.

There is a lengthy list of exemptions to the Act's provisions, and these are generally specified in relation to the purposes to which information is put. Many are rather specialized and the degree and nature of exemption varies. Among the exemptions are information applied to:

- Protecting national security.
- The prevention of crime and offences relating to taxation.
- Health, education and social work where there are conditions on data subject access.
- Regulatory activity such as that undertaken by agencies concerned with the protection of members of the public [for example, Ombudsmen and similar 'watchdogs'].
- Journalism, literature and art as they represent

'*special purposes*' that warrant a degree of protection of expression.

- Research, history and statistics [an important provision for academic activity].
- Information available to the public by, or under, any enactment [it will be in the public domain already].
- Disclosures required by law or made in connection with legal proceedings.
- Domestic household purposes [lists of home personal contacts and addresses].

The global relevance of data protection is clearly apparent especially with the potential for transborder data flow offered by information technology. The need to assure adequate data protection across national boundaries becomes imperative. Legislation originating in European Union countries makes adequate protection beyond the European Economic Area a requirement. This has caused particular difficulty for the USA with its fundamentally different approach based on voluntary self-regulation. The situation has been resolved through the creation of a 'Safe Harbour' arrangement. Through this means organizations may affirm their compliance with prescribed controls that then enable them to operate globally. This 'self-certification' is overseen by the US Department of Commerce, which publishes a list on its website of organizations participating (www.exports.gov/safeharbor/).

There is particular relevance in data protection for knowledge managers and those directing information and library services because they have customarily played a role in ensuring the efficient handling of data. Examples where personal data feature in information and library services are numerous. They include user registration records, loan transaction files, records of information services provided, logs of database searches, Internet transactions, library catalogues containing personal authors' details, indexes of expertise and databases, sales, accounts and financial records, staff files, payroll and pension records, and survey and research data. The management of operations necessitates appropriate systems, procedures, training and supervision to ensure adequate data protection and that it is an ongoing commitment.

Reference to specific legislation has been made above. It needs to be emphasized that, in the discussion, detail has of necessity been abbreviated. There is no substitute for consulting the full text of the legislation before undertaking any related action.

References

BS-ISO 2382/8:1986.

Committee on Data Protection (1978) *Report of the Committee on Data Protection* (Chairman: Sir Norman Lindop), London: HMSO (Command Paper no. Cmnd 7341).

Committee on Privacy (1972) *Report of the Committee on Privacy* (Chairman: Rt Hon. Kenneth Younger), London: HMSO (Command Paper no. Cmnd 5012).

Council of Europe (1981) *Convention for the Protection of Individuals with Regard to Automatic Processing of Personal Data*, Strasbourg: Council of Europe (European Treaty Series no. 108).

Data Protection Act (1984) London: HMSO (Public General Acts 1984 – Chapter 35).

—— (1998), London: SO (Public General Acts 1998 – Chapter 29).

Davies, J.E., Oppenheim, C. and Boguscz, B. (2000) *Study of the Availability and Use of Personal Information in Public Registers: Final Report to the Office of the Data Protection Registrar*, Wilmslow, Office of the Data Protection Commissioner [published on the Information Commissioner's website at: http://www.dataprotection.gov.uk/dpr/dpdoc.nsf].

European Communities Commission (1995) *Directive 95/46/EC of the European Parliament and of the Council of 24 October 1995 on the Protection of Individuals with Regard to the Processing of Personal Data and on the Free Movement of Such Data*, Brussels: EC Commission (*Official Journal of the European Communities*, 23 November 1995, no. L 281, p. 31).

Information processing systems – Vocabulary – Part 08. Control, integrity and security. Section 08.06.03

Information processing systems – Vocabulary – Part 08. Control, integrity and security. Section 08.06.04

Organization for Economic Co-operation and Development (1981) *Guidelines on the Protection of Privacy and Transborder Flows of Personal Data*, Paris: OECD.

Further reading

Carey, P. (2000) *Data Protection in the UK*, London: Blackstone.

Jay, R. and Hamilton, A. (1999) *Data Protection: Law and Practice*, London, Sweet & Maxwell.

Lloyd, I. (1998) *A Guide to the Data Protection Act 1998*, London: Butterworths.

Oppenheim, C. and Davies, J.E. (1999) *Guide to the Practical Implementation of the Data Protection Act 1998*, London: British Standards Institution (BSI-DISC PD0012).

Ticher, P. (2001) *Data Protection for Library and Information Services*, London: ASLIB [ASLIB know-how guides].

SEE ALSO: information management;
information policy

J.E. DAVIES

DATA SECURITY

The sensitivity of much computer-held information (personal files, strategic business information, etc.) requires password protection and possibly ENCRYPTION to ensure that it is not capable of being accessed or interfered with by unauthorized persons. The evidence is that data security is habitually neglected by the organizations and individuals that hold data, making the activities of those who might wish to access the data – hackers, for example – that much easier. Part of the purpose of DATA PROTECTION laws is to promote positive attitudes towards data security. The issue is becoming even more important as E-COMMERCE continues to expand, bringing with it increased use of personal and corporate credit cards in online transactions.

SEE ALSO: computer security; information management

DATA WAREHOUSE

A system designed to enable improved decision making through the swift provision of appropriate information. It utilizes a collection of technologies to integrate heterogeneous information sources for online analytic processing. Organizations have invested considerable sums in creating data warehouses to counter the inefficiency resulting from the different transaction characteristics of systems already in place. In particular the problem of legacy data from outdated systems is addressed by bringing it into a common conceptual and technical framework, so as to retain it for current and future use. Within the warehouse, information can be customized and cached for particular user groups, thus increasing the speed and efficiency of access.

Further reading

Jarke, M. *et al.* (2000) *Fundamentals of Data Warehouses*, Berlin: Springer.

SEE ALSO: data mining; Geographic Information Systems

DATABASE

The term is normally applied to digital data stored in a computer or on an optical disk. It is a systematically ordered collection of information, which might be, for example, bibliographic data such as a BIBLIOGRAPHY or catalogue (see CATALOGUES), numerical or statistical material, or textual material of the kind found in a text archive, a data archive (see DATA ARCHIVES) or an ABSTRACTING AND INDEXING SERVICE. It might be assembled for personal or corporate use, but can also be assembled to be marketed commercially. Data is generally structured so that it can be sought and retrieved automatically. Access to commercially available databases is usually online on the Internet.

SEE ALSO: database management systems; economics of information; informatics; knowledge industries; organization of knowledge

DATABASE MANAGEMENT SYSTEMS

A DATABASE management system (DBMS) is a program that can input, edit and retrieve information from a database. A database is a collection of information organized into records and fields, and stored as files on a computer. Sometimes the term database is used to include the DBMS as well.

Relational, object-oriented, network, flat and hierarchical are all types of DBMS. They differ in how they organize information for storage. Retrieval from a DBMS requires a query language, a structured way for expressing search requests. Relational DBMS alone have a standard query language called SQL (structured query language).

Further reading

Ramakrishnan, R. (1998) *Database Management Systems*, WCB/McGraw Hill.

SEE ALSO: informatics; information retrieval; object-oriented technology

ALAN POULTER

DATABASES

Information collections, sharing a common characteristic such as subject discipline or type, which are published electronically by public- or private-sector database producers (usually on a commercial basis) and made available to a large public for interactive searching and information retrieval. Online databases are accessed via TELECOMMUNICATIONS or wide-area network links to remote online HOST services that normally offer many different databases. CD-ROMs are OPTICAL DISKS that are mounted locally on a PC, workstation or local-area network. In terms of their content, online and CD-ROM databases share many common features. Indeed, many databases are published in both formats. Other less commonly used formats for database distribution include diskette, magnetic tape and hand-held products.

Background

The first databases to go online in the 1970s were bibliographic, containing references to and (usually) abstracts of articles in the academic and professional literature (examples include *Chemical Abstracts* and *Medline*, which aim to cover the worldwide literature of chemistry and medicine, respectively). Since then there has been a tremendous growth in the number and scope of online databases, as well as the introduction of the CD-ROM format in the early 1980s. Worldwide, there are no accurate statistics for the total number of databases in existence. As long ago as 1997 it was possible to identify over 10,000 databases (including those on CD-ROM) (Walker and Janes 1999). The USA is by far the largest producer of internationally available databases, followed by the UK, Canada and Germany.

Coverage and updating

Online or CD-ROM databases can be found in almost all fields of human endeavour, though the majority are still geared to the academic or professional user. The largest number of databases exists in the business sector, followed by science, technology and engineering, law, health and life sciences. Although fewer databases cover the arts, humanities and social sciences, this belies the enormous wealth of electronic information that is also available in these fields. Information in online and CD-ROM databases tends to be archival in nature, though online can be rapidly updated compared to printed and CD-ROM equivalents. Some online databases that contain time-sensitive data such as stock market prices are updated in real time, though these are almost invariably very expensive to use.

Types

Online and CD-ROM databases now cover a huge range of different types of information, but the vast majority fall into one or more of the categories below.

BIBLIOGRAPHIC DATABASES

Bibliographic databases contain references to published literature, including journal and newspaper articles, conference proceedings and papers, reports, government and legal publications, patents, books, etc. In contrast to library catalogue entries, a large proportion of the bibliographic records in online and CD-ROM databases describe analytics (articles, conference papers, etc.) rather than complete monographs, and they generally contain very rich subject descriptions in the form of subject-indexing terms and abstracts.

FULL-TEXT DATABASES

These contain, in addition to a BIBLIOGRAPHIC DESCRIPTION, the entire text of documents. For example, the majority of articles from all the UK quality newspapers are available in online format, and many are also published on CD-ROM. As the full text is normally searchable, abstracts and indexing terms may not be present.

DIRECTORY DATABASES

Directory databases contain descriptive information for entities. Different directories may list organizations, individuals, electronic or printed publications, materials, chemical substances, computer software, audiovisual materials, etc.

NUMERIC DATABASES

These contain predominantly numeric data. Examples include company accounts and financial performance indicators, commodity and stock market data, statistical data of all types, including time series, and chemical or physical properties of substances.

MULTIMEDIA DATABASES

MULTIMEDIA databases contain a mix of different media such as text, audio, video and still graphics (photographs, diagrams and illustrations, graphs, charts, maps and even representations of works of art). Because of the limitations of current telecommunications networks in transmitting large graphics files, multimedia databases are more usually in CD-ROM format than on-line, though the implementation of high-speed networks will radically alter this situation in the foreseeable future.

TRANSACTIONAL DATABASES

These contain information on goods and services that the user can order electronically; they are normally online.

OTHER

Other types include dictionary databases (word definitions, glossaries, thesauri), encyclopaedias (often in multimedia format), chemical structure databases, patent and trade marks, and computer software.

Structure and searching

Database structures and search techniques still have their roots in the 1970s systems, though with considerable refinement and enhancement since then.

Each database comprises a vast number of records (typically several hundred thousand, but the largest contain several million records). Records in the same database normally (but not always) have the same structure. Records are subdivided into separately identifiable and searchable fields, as illustrated by the following (fictitious and abbreviated) company record.

Table 1 Fields in a database record

CO	TZL Group PLC
AD	St John's Drive
	Reading
	Berkshire
	RG7 9QL
TE	Telephone: 0734 999999
	Fax: 0734 888888
NO	Registered Company Number: 00000001
DE	Tour Operators
MA	Managing director: L.N. Hoult
	Secretary: B.T. Etherington
	Directors: P.M. Hill
	J.K. Paige

Searching is in accordance with the principles of TEXT RETRIEVAL. Although many online hosts have introduced easy-to-use (usually menu-driven) search interfaces, CD-ROMs are generally regarded as easier to use because of their more intuitive and guided screen displays. Some CD-ROMs provide additional software for the manipulation of subset data, particularly numeric.

Publication formats

Many online and CD-ROM databases have an equivalent printed publication, two advantages of the electronic formats being the speed of searching and convenient storage. An increasing number, however, are only published electronically.

Charging mechanisms

Online databases are normally charged on a pay-as-you-use basis, with charges being levied for the amount of time the user is connected to the database and the amount of information viewed, printed or downloaded. Connect-time and viewing charges vary considerably from database to database, from as little as nothing to over £100 per hour or per record for high-value information such as the full text of stockbroker and market research reports. Relatively few online databases are available on a subscription basis, whereas this is the main method of pricing for CD-ROMs. CD-ROM subscriptions are also highly variable, from a few pounds to several thousand pounds per annum, with additional charges for networked workstations.

References

Walker, G and Janes, J. (1999) *Online Retrieval: A Dialogue of Theory and Practice*, 2nd edn, Libraries Unlimited.

Further reading

Henderson, A. (1998) *Electronic Databases and Publishing*, New Brunswick: Transaction Publishers.

SEE ALSO: electronic information resources; information retrieval; online services; organization of knowledge; relational database

GWYNETH TSENG, REVISED BY THE EDITORS

DECISION SUPPORT SYSTEMS

Decision support systems (DSS) have been

defined as 'interactive computer-based systems that help decision-makers to utilize data and models to solve relatively unstructured problems' (Turban 1988). Sprague and Watson (1986) suggest that other defining characteristics of decision support systems are that they typically focus on the underspecified problems that senior managers face, they promote features that make them easy to use by non-specialists and they emphasize flexibility and adaptability so that they can respond to the user's requirements. Decision support systems have found a wide variety of applications including planning, forecasting, simulation and investment appraisal.

The role of decision support systems

There are many different types of computer-based systems operating in the library environment whose aim is directly to support the decision-making process. These systems are generally given the generic title of MANAGEMENT SUPPORT SYSTEMS (MSS). Decision support systems, management information systems (MIS) and managerial EXPERT SYSTEMS are the three most common types of management support system. Decision support systsems are both flexible and responsive to the user, and consequently they play an active role in the decision-making process. The user of a decision support system will be able to interrogate the system, experiment with and evaluate different strategies, and generally get a better understanding of the problem. The decision, however, will ultimately be made by combining the insights provided by the decision support system with the skills, judgement and experience of the decision-maker. This is a distinctly different role from that of both the MIS, which simply acts as a passive source of information for the decision-maker, and the expert system, where the decision is typically made on behalf of the decision-maker.

It should be noted that while the majority of decision support systems are designed to be used by a single manager, many newer systems have been developed explicitly to support the decision-making processes of a group of managers. Such systems, known as group decision support systems (GDSS), may either be used by a group of decision-makers in a single location or facilitate decision-making across a number of diverse locations by using a communications network.

Components of a decision support system

Turban (1988) suggests that such systems are typically composed of three components: the user interface, the model management system and the database management system, each of which is briefly described below.

USER INTERFACE

The user interface is the part of the system that is responsible for controlling all the communication between the system and the user. As decision support systems are invariably used by functional managers rather than by systems specialists, it is essential that the interface is clear, concise and readily understandable, often incorporating sophisticated graphics facilities. Graphics, in the form of graphs, charts and diagrams, are particularly important in decision support systems, as they help managers visualize data and relationships.

MODEL MANAGEMENT SYSTEM

A model is a representation of reality upon which experiments can be conducted in order to support more fully reasoned decisions. The decision support system may have either a single model or a model-base containing a range of different business models. The modelling tools and techniques embedded within the decision support system can range from the general purpose, such as a spreadsheet package, to the highly specific, such as a piece of forecasting, linear programming, simulation or statistical analysis software.

DATABASE MANAGEMENT SYSTEM

The database management facility will incorporate data that has been generated internally within the organization and data that is retrieved from external sources. There are a large number of commercial information services to which an organization may subscribe. These provide access to external databases, which may contain financial, economic, statistical, geo-demographic, market-oriented or commercial information that can be utilized in a decision support system application.

Applications of decision support systems

Decision support systems have found a wide variety of applications in all the functional areas of organizations. Decision support systems can, for example, be found in the areas of financial planning, sales forecasting, cash-flow analysis, corporate strategy evaluation, production planning, factory and warehouse location selection and manpower planning. Whilst the majority of applications of decision support systems are found in the commercial sector, many applications have been implemented in public-sector organizations, including libraries.

APPLICATIONS OF DECISION SUPPORT SYSTEMS WITHIN THE LIBRARY

Most of the writing on the utilization of decision support systems in libraries has concentrated on performance assessment applications (Adams *et al.* 1993; Bommer and Chorba 1982). Typically, such systems focus on identifying and analysing the current utilization of resources so that more informed decisions can be made on how resources should be allocated in the future. In addition to these performance assessment applications, however, there are a wide range of other potential applications in which decision support systems could be used in a library context. Such systems could, for example, be used to simulate the ways in which queues are serviced in a library, to determine what the optimum number of counter staff is at various times of the day. Alternatively, simulation models could be used to identify the optimal ways of laying out facilities and resources within the library so as best to service the needs of the users.

The appropriate use of decision support systems provides the potential greatly to facilitate the decision-making process, by providing a comparative analysis of the alternative courses of action facing a manager. It must, however, be recognized that decision support systems will be effective only if the systems are designed to be compatible with a manager's decision-making style and managers are educated and trained with regard to their use.

References

Adams, R., Bloor, I., Collier, M., Meldrum, M. and Ward, S. (1993) *Decision Support Systems and Performance Assessment in Libraries*, Bowker Saur.

Bommer, M. and Chorba, R. (1982) *Decision Making for Library Management*, Knowledge Industry Publications.

Sprague, R. and Watson, H. (1986) *Decision Support Systems: Putting Theory into Practice*, Prentice-Hall International.

Turban, E. (1988) *Decision Support and Expert Systems: Managerial Perspectives*, Macmillan.

Further reading

Finlay, P. (1994) *Introducing Decision Support Systems*, NCC Blackwell [this is an informative book that thoroughly explores the major applications of DSS and reviews methods for their development, validation and implementation].

SEE ALSO: economics of information; information management

NEIL F. DOHERTY

DEFAMATION

Defamation is the making of a statement that tends to reflect adversely on a person in the estimation of members of society. The word 'publication' is used to describe this process, but in the legal sense that it is communicated to someone else, not that it takes the form of a published document. Defamation can take the form either of libel, which is written, or of slander, which is oral. It is possible to take legal action for a libel on the grounds that it would cause damage, whereas slander is actionable only on proof of actual damage. This distinction, critical to the common law tradition, does not exist in Roman law. Whilst it has always been a concern in libraries and information services, the relaxed communication environment of the IN-TERNET has made potentially defamatory comment more accessible. Issues relating to liability for defamatory comment are a concern best treated as matters of INFORMATION ETHICS. The development of NETIQUETTE can be seen as, at least in part, a response to defamatory statements in electronic communication forums.

DESKTOP COMPUTER

The generic name for the typical COMPUTER now in universal use. It consists of a keyboard, a processing unit containing the hard disk and disk drives, and a visual display unit. The term is actually used principally to distinguish this device from the increasingly common laptop and palmtop computers.

SEE ALSO: personal computer

DESKTOP PUBLISHING

Desktop publishing (DTP) is the use of personal computers for interactive document composition

(Tuck 1989). Satisfactory definitions are elusive if only because DTP stands at the confluence of office work, printing and computing. The term is a misnomer as it is not really to do with publishing but with improving the quality and lowering the costs of text preparation. As it was originally developed in the 1980s, it was a combination of page make-up software running on a DESKTOP COMPUTER with a laser printer for the production of copy that was then reproduced for conventional printing. The growth in the functionality of personal computers, however, means that much of what could only be done by DTP systems can now be performed by common word-processing packages, and high-quality output can be derived from colour laser printers. DTP can be easily distinguished from electronic publishing, because DTP is designed to generate a printed product, but it is increasingly difficult to distinguish it from the highest quality of word-processed material.

Applications

DTP was devised to be used for the preparation of documents such as reports, newsletters, leaflets, posters, manuals, brochures and invoices that contain text and often graphics of various sorts and where presentation is important. For libraries and information services this facilitates better-quality documents or reduces the costs of producing high-quality materials, perhaps enabling them to produce publications where traditional costs would have been prohibitive. One of the main advantages of DTP is that it makes it relatively easy to incorporate pictures, logos, diagrams and graphs into documents. Again, much of this can now be done by word-processing packages.

Software and hardware

DTP packages arrived in the mid-1980s and were more sophisticated than word-processing packages at that time, but simpler than those used for photo-typesetting. DTP packages have facilities and characteristics suitable for different user groups, such as office/computing users (e.g. PageMaker and Ventura Publisher), designers/typesetters (e.g. QuarkXPress) and technical authorship (e.g. Interleaf). Thus there is software to enable the non-specialist to make up document pages and also software to assist designers in the graphic design process. The needs of both groups are rather different.

The hardware required includes a computer (often an Apple Macintosh or PC is used) with hard disk, graphics capability, a high-resolution screen and a laser printer. A document scanner, graphics tablet and optical character recognition software may be desirable.

Generally documents are created and edited in a word-processing package and then imported into the DTP package, where the pages are designed. Graphics, created with a drawing package, can also be imported into pre-defined frames within the page, as can images from a document scanner. Various 'style sheets' (e.g. for a newsletter or report) can be designed and stored. These specify such attributes as page size, margin sizes, columns, font styles, font sizes, headings, subheadings, etc. A key characteristic of most packages is 'WYSIWYG' (What You See Is What You Get), in which the user can see on the (high-resolution) screen the page as it will finally appear. As screen resolution is lower than printer resolution, this is not precise. The final output from the laser printer is camera-ready copy ready for reproduction.

Design

One of the main dangers with DTP for the inexperienced is design; it becomes very easy for anyone with a package to 'play around' with all the features and facilities newly at their fingertips, and the results can be disastrously evident. Published documents have a purpose, a message to communicate. Design plays a large part in achieving that purpose, and attention to the design of the documents is crucial. LIS professionals specialize in the presentation and communication of information, and DTP has provided them with a powerful tool to enhance the design of their documents, improve the presentation of the information and thus increase the communication value of them. But for those without any graphic design skills, caution should be exercised.

Developments

As DTP became more sophisticated, other issues arose and were addressed. One of the more obvious was the problems created by foreign languages, from extra characters and symbols to completely different character sets. This exemplifies the advances of the late 1990s, since not only are the diacritical marks used in many Latin alphabet languages available in word-processing packages, but so also are fonts for other scripts such as Greek, Cyrillic, Arabic and Hebrew.

The retention of the document structure and layout is often important, and in these respects DTP is related to MARK-UP LANGUAGES such as SGML, document structure standards such as ODA and publishing standards such as Adobe Acrobat. As processes have become more integrated, so the software packages at each stage have been linked in with those in other stages. Another area of development, and potential confusion, is 'desktop CD-ROM publishing' whereby ordinary users can produce (and publish) material on CD-ROM on their desktop.

A problem created for the LIS profession, but of a different nature, is that DTP and similar technologies make it easier for many people to produce and publish, often on a small scale, documents that would not previously have seen the light of day – that is, it has resulted in a growth in GREY LITERATURE. This in turn will create accessing, cataloguing and handling problems.

References

Tuck, B. (1989) 'Desktop publishing: What it is and what it can do for you', *ASLIB Proceedings* 41: 29–37.

Further reading

Carson, J. (1988) *Desktop Publishing and Libraries*, Taylor Graham [discusses the role of DTP, and includes a survey of DTP use in UK public libraries].
Hall, J. (1999) *Desk Top Publishing*, Liberty Hall.
Tuck, B., McKnight, C., Hayet, M. and Archer, C. (1990) *Project Quartet*, British Library Board (Library and Information Research Report 76) [Chapter 7 gives a general outline of DTP and relates it to document architecture and mark-up].
Yates-Mercer, P.A. and Crook. A. (1989) *The Potential Applications of Desktop Publishing in Information Services*, British Library Board (British Library Research Paper 62) [describes a survey of DTP users in information services and six case studies of potential users].

SEE ALSO: informatics; knowledge industries; publishing; reprography

PENELOPE YATES-MERCER,
REVISED BY THE EDITORS

DEVELOPMENT CO-OPERATION IN SUPPORT OF INFORMATION AND KNOWLEDGE ACTIVITIES

Agencies that offer aid and other assistance to developing countries have been involved in many activities designed to promote the development of LIBRARIES, information services and the KNOWLEDGE INDUSTRIES in general. Such agencies include international bodies such as the United Nations Development Programme (UNDP) and UNESCO, national agencies such as the British Council, and non-governmental organizations including some charitable foundations.

Publishing

Initiatives to support PUBLISHING in developing countries in the early 1990s were often sporadic and unco-ordinated. Some focused on training potential writers, others on providing workshops for editors. Development agencies discovered that the provision of modern printing units by themselves did not generate books, and the next phase of project support concentrated on preparation of manuscripts. By the late 1990s the trend changed to focus on bolstering indigenous publishing initiatives to counteract the dependence on information being provided from the 'North'. Other funders sought to get the results of their support disseminated to a wider audience. However, the flurry of new journal titles that appeared in the early 1990s did not lead to sustainable publications and the 'Volume 1, Issue 1' syndrome continued to indicate a fragile publishing environment.

By the late 1990s the development community began to appreciate that publishing only makes sense if its objective is permanent supply to its target group, and information is only useful the moment it is in the hands of readers. The publication chain has to be complete. The relationships between authorship, editorial work, publishing in the private and commercial sectors, marketing and distribution have to be considered within an overall context. Development support at the end of the decade therefore tried to concentrate efforts on a 'holistic' approach. Agencies such as those in Sweden, Denmark and Norway have made a considerable effort to work together in supporting projects with common aims and objectives. This approach has also given rise to the requirement for partners to elaborate short, medium and long-term strategic plans that can be funded collaboratively. Successful examples include the African Books Collective (ABC) and the African Publishers' Network (APNET).

Library development

Funding for large capital projects became unsustainable by the end of the 1980s and agencies revised their policies. With few exceptions, support for access to information became one element of individual project support. As a principle, this might have worked if the economic and 'political' environment had been able to sustain the foundations provided in the 1960s and 1970s. In reality, funding for information activities became *ad hoc*, and national and central libraries began to collapse during the 1980s and 1990s. As research for the *University Libraries in Africa: A Review of their Current State and Future Potential* showed (see Rosenberg 1997) – although few agencies were able to put a figure on the scale of their support to African university libraries, since aid was being channelled through a number of parallel ways – many libraries became highly, if not totally, dependent on external assistance. Between 1989–94 the level of external support was no longer a supplement to an institution's budget, but rather replaced it. Only the universities of Botswana and Zimbabwe, and the private universities in Kenya and Zimbabwe, used cash or material donations to supplement their own budget; and the University of Botswana was the only institution that could afford to turn down development support.

Support for information and knowledge activities in the twenty-first century

Virtually all new initiatives in the field of access to information and 'knowledge', particularly in Africa – whether the acquisition of computers, staff training, development of services like CD-ROM searching, e-mail, Internet access, establishment of networks and 'TELECENTRES' – are the result of outside assistance. Although a great deal of emphasis from 1995–2000 was placed on 'affordability' and 'sustainability', there is no doubt that many of these programmes were totally dependent on external funding for start-up investment. Furthermore, many institutions

found that they were unable to bear the recurrent costs of updating software or telephone line rental and call costs, and some of the heavily resource-dependent projects have now fallen into decay.

Funding for the production of information, especially at research level, has continued to be sporadic. There is considerable pressure to create viable publishing industries within developing countries, but it is difficult to support this sector without running into the problems of the high cost of production and the lack of purchasing power of libraries and individuals. Small-scale academic publishing, especially of journals, is a precarious business all over the world, but those operating from a developing-country base are particularly vulnerable. The opportunities afforded by the electronic medium provide possibilities for exposure and dissemination, which were hitherto not available. There are a few particularly well-targeted and practical programmes in this area – SciELO (Scientific Electronic Library OnLine) providing a fully electronic environment for selected biomedical journals in Latin America, and AJOL (African Journals OnLine) providing the tables of contents and abstracts of articles from scientific journals published in Africa.

Following the trend of development co-operation in the late 1990s, many agencies have given clear articulations of what types of projects might receive positive consideration for funding. In the field of information the most obvious 'good candidate' has been that which involves the use of new technology. However, the importance of training is often ignored, and the need to position electronic information as a component of a total solution, in which the print format continues to have a place, is frequently overlooked.

Another trend that has been accelerating is the willingness, indeed keenness, for funding bodies to see themselves as supporting pilot projects to 'test' or 'trial' new initiatives or approaches, again preferably at the cutting edge in the use of new INFORMATION AND COMMUNICATION TECHNOLOGY. In theory this is a positive development as small amounts of money can often facilitate a useful pilot in a specific area. The down-side is that, in many instances, the funding available for pilots is very short term in nature, and where it can take between twelve to eighteen months to get a pilot underway the completion date is often on the horizon before activity has matured to provide positive results. In fact, by the time the project really begins to take off there has often been little funding available within the host institution, the 'intermediary' or the funding body to continue those that are evaluated to be 'successful'. The host is left with a 'showcase' experiment, the 'intermediary' feels that it is letting the involved partners down and the funder has moved on to the next 'pilot' in a newer, more 'trendy' field somewhere else.

There is no doubt that the new technologies can offer tremendous potential in providing a complementary medium for provision and exchange of information, and there are several initiatives that have received external funding, and some that are low-cost indigenous initiatives, which bear possibilities for replication elsewhere. The fashion for funding high-cost technical components is running its course. As more stable communication infrastructures are in place, more development agencies are open to give consideration to the content aspects of information and knowledge sharing and provision, and, as a result, a number of information 'access' programmes have been developed in 2000–1. Some have a single aim – to provide 'free' or differentially priced access to online journals, the most significant of which at the time of writing include eIFL (the *Electronic Information for Libraries Direct*) of the Open Society Institute and HINARI (*Health InterNetwork Access to Research Initiative*) of the World Health Organization. Others have developed programmes in close collaboration with their partners and used a more holistic approach – the Programme for the Enhancement of Research Information (PERI) being described as the most developmentally mature of the activities available (Silver 2002).

Conclusion

Work in the information/global knowledge arena is going through an exciting and rapidly changing period, but the ability to be in a position to respond to the challenges seems less certain. Taking into account the above trends, development organizations see their role, quite rightly, no longer as central to identification of projects, nor 'ownership' of implementation, nor even to provision of long-term technical assistance. Their ability to disburse or attract funding for such aspects is long past. However, the supportive role of 'intermediaries' in providing advice, sharing information and in advocacy, seems to be in even greater demand. Non-governmental organizations (NGOs), with long-term practical relationships with colleagues, have fulfilled a special role in drawing the attention of the major funding and development bodies to the continued and central importance of information. The voice and experience of colleagues in developing and transitional countries must be heard so that the full advantages of the potential in the 'new information' era can be explored and implemented.

References

Silver, K. (2002) *Pressing the Send Key – Preferential Journal Access in Developing Countries*, Learned Publishing, April 2002.

Further reading

African Books Collective (ABC) (http://www.african bookscollective.com/).
African Journals OnLine (AJOL) (http://www.inasp. info/ajol/).
African Publishers' Network (APNET) (http://www. apnet.org/).
eIFL (*Electronic Information for Libraries Direct*) of the Open Society Institute (http://eifl.net).
HINARI (*Health InterNetwork Access to Research Initiative*) (http://www.who.int/inf-pr-2001/en/ pr2001–32.html) (press release only available at December 2001).
Programme for the Enhancement of Research Information (PERI) (http://www.inasp.info/peri/).
Rosenberg, D. (1997) *University Libraries in Africa: A Review of their Current State and Future Potential*, International African Institute.
SciELO (Scientific Electronic Library OnLine) (http:// www.scielo.br/).

SEE ALSO: Africa; book trade; Central America; knowledge industries; South America

CAROL PRIESTLEY

DEWEY, MELVIL (1857–1931)

Although most famous for the DEWEY DECIMAL CLASSIFICATION, Dewey, more than any other individual, was responsible for the development of modern library science.

Born in New York and educated at Amherst College, his career in librarianship began with a study of the techniques used in the best-known libraries in the northeastern US states. Recognizing the limitations of the fixed-location method of arranging library collections, Dewey devised the idea of relative location – using decimal numbers to indicate the subjects of books rather than numbering the books themselves. The Dewey Decimal Classification, the outcome of this work, was published in 1876. In the same remarkable year, the AMERICAN LIBRARY ASSOCIATION was founded, as was the *Library Journal*, under Dewey's own editorship. Dewey also established the Library Bureau, a company that developed standardized supplies, equipment and library methods under his direction.

He became Librarian at Columbia College, New York, in 1883 and developed the world's first library school there. He later became Director of the New York State Library and helped found the New York Library Association, the first of the state associations and the model for those to come, in 1890. In addition to his contributions to the techniques of librarianship and to library education, he took a strong interest in library services for the disadvantaged and in travelling libraries or bookmobiles for isolated communities. He also saw the value of acquisitions of non-book media in libraries. His contribution was recognized by award of the Presidency of the Association of State Librarians (1889–92) and of ALA (1890 and 1892–3).

Further reading

Wiegand, W.A. (1996) *Irrepressible Reformer: A Biography of Melvil Dewey*, American Library Association.

SEE ALSO: bibliographic classification; library education

DEWEY DECIMAL CLASSIFICATION

A BIBLIOGRAPHIC CLASSIFICATION scheme devised by Melvil DEWEY and first published anonymously in 1876. It has now reached its twenty-first revised edition (Dewey 1996). Knowledge is divided into ten main classes, each designated by a numeral from 0 to 9, which can then be subdivided by the addition of two numerals before a decimal point and further numerals after it. These indicate subdivisions of the broad class. It has a relative index that shows the relation of each subject that is indexed to a larger subject (or class or division). For shelving purposes the first three

letters of the author's name or of the title of the work are often added after the classification number. The published schedules have been extended and modified in successive editions. DDC as it is commonly known is widely used in public and academic libraries throughout the world.

References

Dewey (1996) *Decimal Classification and Relative Index*, 21st edn, revised by J.S. Mitchell *et al.*, Forest Press.

SEE ALSO: organization of knowledge

DIALOG

A major US HOST offering access to in excess of 12 terabytes of content. Founded in 1972, DIALOG was one of the pioneers of commercial provision of online information services. It is now part of the Thomson Corporation. Further information can be found at www.dialog.com.

SEE ALSO: electronic information resources

DICTIONARY

A list and explanation of the words of a language or the vocabulary of a particular subject. The words are arranged in the order determined by the appropriate ALPHABETIZATION RULES. A language dictionary typically gives the orthography, pronunciation and meaning of each word, and sometimes its etymology and examples of usage. A dictionary of the words in a restricted field of knowledge usually only gives the meaning, although it may be more elaborate. In information retrieval, it can be used as synonymous with THESAURUS.

DICTIONARY CATALOGUES

A library catalogue (see CATALOGUES) in which entries for authors, titles and subjects are interfiled in a single alphabetical sequence. Such catalogues were once normal in the USA, although less usual elsewhere. The National Union Catalog published by the LIBRARY OF CONGRESS is the largest and probably best-known example of a dictionary catalogue.

DIGITAL LIBRARY

What is a digital library?

The literature abounds with definitions of digital libraries. However, the definition formulated by the Digital Library Foundation and cited by Waters (1998) is particularly broad-ranging:

> Digital libraries are organizations that provide the resources, including the specialized staff, to select, structure, offer intellectual access to, interpret, distribute, preserve the integrity of, and ensure the persistence over time of collections of digital works so that they are readily and economically available for use by a defined community or set of communities.

It is interesting to note that removal of the two instances of the word 'digital' results in a good definition of a library. Deconstructing this definition yields an overview of many of the interrelated issues facing digital libraries today.

ORGANIZATION

Is there necessarily an 'organization' behind a digital library? Increasingly on the WORLD WIDE WEB, individuals are making available collections of material. Arms (2000: 80) points to the Perseus project as 'one of the most important digital libraries in the humanities' but which was started by Gregory Crane, a member of the faculty at Harvard University.

RESOURCES

Libraries have always required resources and digital libraries are no different. One of the myths of digital libraries (Kuny and Cleveland 1998) is that they will be cheaper than print libraries. However, there is no evidence for this. Shelves may be replaced by servers, thereby possibly saving some space, but the servers represent significant hardware costs and require skilled maintenance. Additionally, there are costs associated with providing and maintaining a network infrastructure.

STAFF

There has been an interesting discussion in the literature over whether the digital library needs librarians (e.g. Matson and Bonski 1997). Although some have suggested that librarians are no longer needed (so-called 'disintermediation'), the more prevalent view is that their role is changing, with terms like 'cybrarian' appearing in the literature as a reflection of this change. As the role changes, so training needs will change to include management of the technical infrastructure as well as 'the collection'. It is also likely that there will be an increased need for user training and engagement in the concomitant discussion about what services the digital library should provide.

SELECTION

This can be construed in two different senses: selecting digital material to include in the 'collection'; and selecting what is to be digitized. Part of the disintermediation argument is that with powerful SEARCH ENGINES there is little reason to select – simply make everything available and rely on the search engine to find it. However, it is widely accepted that it would be impossible (and not necessarily desirable) to digitize all the existing paper documents and so some selection is necessary.

STRUCTURE

Similar arguments to those surrounding selection recur in relation to structure, particularly concerning the power of search engines. However, such arguments fail to recognize that searching is only one mode of information discovery. BROWSING is another important mode and is difficult to achieve without some structure.

ACCESS

One of the much-vaunted advantages of the digital library is that it is accessible twenty-four hours a day, seven days a week, 365 days of the year. This ideal view ignores the frailty of computer networks and servers, and their need for maintenance. However, a digital library is more accessible for longer hours than the traditional library. What is more, there is some evidence that significant use is made of digital collections out of 'normal' office hours. This increased access to information is fine for those with the necessary technology, but half the world's population have never made a telephone call. The digital library could actually work to *widen* the gap between the information rich and the information poor.

PRESERVE THE INTEGRITY

In the digital library, preserving the integrity of the information can be seen as a technical function, making sure the files are not corrupted.

However, there are still organizational and management functions that are necessary to ensure that the process is carried out in the short term. In the long term, other issues arise.

PERSISTENCE OVER TIME

Paradoxically, it is possible to walk into Trinity College, Dublin, and read the *Book of Kells*, which was written in about AD 800, yet there are floppy disks that are only ten years old but for which we no longer have machines that can read them. Such technological obsolescence is in danger of rendering vast amounts of information inaccessible. Digital media are also subject to deterioration. As Rothenberg said, 'digital information lasts forever – or five years, whichever comes first' (Rothenberg 1995: 24). The PRESERVATION of digital information is still an active research area and one that must be a concern for the digital library.

COLLECTIONS OF DIGITAL WORKS

Although there now exist many digital 'collections', one possibility for the digital library is that it goes beyond a single collection and provides access to resources not held by the host library. Zemon (2001) discusses the role of the librarian in such portal development (see PORTALS AND GATEWAYS). Additionally, we are now seeing the emergence of digital content providers – organizations like Questia, netLibrary and ebrary – offering libraries and users instant access to large collections.

THE ECONOMIC DIMENSION

The move to digital media has created a different economic climate, one in which the journal subscription or book price has been replaced with the software licence. The implications of this change are still being worked out and new economic models are being explored (see, for example, Halliday and Oppenheim 2000).

COMMUNITY

As Borgman says, 'Digital libraries are constructed – collected and organized – by [and for] a community of users, and their functional capabilities support the information needs and uses of that community' (Borgman 2000: 42). With library budgets shrinking, collections need to be user driven, serving an identifiable need rather than being collected 'just in case'.

Some remaining issues

Comprehensive though the definition is, there are other issues involved in digital libraries. The following are examples.

STANDARDS

As the old saying goes, 'The good thing about standards is that there are so many to choose from!' However, if digital libraries are to achieve a reasonable level of interoperability, then a variety of standards are needed for different parts of the process of making information available. Such standards are emerging, for example the adoption of the Z39.50 search and retrieve protocol, the discussion surrounding the DUBLIN CORE metadata proposals and so forth.

INTERFACE

The *de facto* interface to the digital library seems to be Web-based. However, this by no means guarantees usability and there is a need to design for the user population and the tasks they wish to perform. Closely related to interface issues are the issues regarding user acceptance of digital library technology.

COPYRIGHT

The ease with which electronic documents can be copied has prompted a reconsideration of the COPYRIGHT legislation. On one hand, publishers have advocated strengthening the law in order to protect their product (and therefore their income stream). However, balanced against this is the view that copyright is a social construct that served a purpose but which may no longer do so (Samuelson 1995). Do we need it? Can we sustain it?

SCALABILITY

Most of the work done so far has been relatively small scale. It remains to be seen whether the methods and techniques will scale up to cope with large numbers of users and enormous volumes of information.

MEDIA INTEGRATION

Although there are examples of 'pure' digital libraries, traditional libraries are themselves moving increasingly toward making digital content available to their users. This has given rise to the concept of the hybrid library (see HYBRID LIBRARIES) in which digital and paper-based content coexist. Effective integration of services is a management challenge for the modern librarian.

References

Arms, W.Y. (2000) *Digital Libraries*, Cambridge, MA: MIT Press.

Borgman, C.L. (2000) *From Gutenberg to the Global Information Infrastructure: Access to Information in the Networked World*, Cambridge, MA: MIT Press.

Halliday, L.L. and Oppenheim, C. (2000) 'Comparison and evaluation of some economic models of digital-only journals', *Journal of Documentation* 56(6): 660–73.

Kuny, T. and Cleveland, G. (1998) 'The digital library: Myths and challenges', *IFLA Journal* 24(2), 107–13.

Matson, L.D. and Bonski, D.J. (1997) 'Do digital libraries need librarians? An experiential dialog', *Online*, November. (http://www.onlineinc.com/onlinemag/NovOL97/matson11.html) [accessed 31 July 2001].

Rothenberg, J. (1995) 'Ensuring the longevity of digital documents', *Scientific American* 272(1): 24–9.

Samuelson, P. (1995) 'Copyright and digital libraries', *Communications of the ACM* 38(4): 15–21 and 110.

Waters, D.J. (1998) 'What are digital libraries?', *CLIR Issues* 4 (July/August) (http://www.clir.org/pubs/issues/issues04.html) [accessed 31 July 2001].

Zemon, M. (2001) 'The librarian's role in portal development', *College and Research Libraries News* 62(7) (July/August) (http://www.ala.org/acrl/zemon.html) [accessed 31 July 2001].

SEE ALSO: information and communication technology; information professions; information society; libraries; licences; social exclusion and libraries

CLIFF MCKNIGHT

DIGITAL PRESERVATION

The PRESERVATION of digital documents for future use. Digital media are dependent on the availability of software and hardware through which the content can be read, so long-term preservation is now conceived in terms of continuous refreshment of selected files so that they are compatible with currently available equipment and systems. Despite early optimism, digitized versions are not considered sufficiently stable to be used as SURROGATEs for the originals.

DIGITIZATION

The process of converting analogue information to a digital format for storage and processing in a computer, or in COMMUNICATION the process of converting analogue signals to digital signals for transmission across digital networks such as the Internet. In library and information work, digitization is normally understood as the process of creating digital versions of analogue documents. Depending on the input methods used, this may produce an electronic file that can be manipulated as if it had been created in digital form, or it may merely be capable of retrieval. Digitization has sometimes been argued to have potential applications in the field of PRESERVATION, but in practice the preservation of digitized files themselves is often more problematical (Hedstrom 1998).

References

Hedstrom, M. (1998) 'Digital preservation: A time bomb for digital libraries', *Computers and the Humanities* 31: 189–202.

Further reading

Youngs, K. (2001) *Managing the Digitisation of Library, Archive and Museum Materials*, National Preservation Office.

SEE ALSO: document image processing; informatics; information and communication technology

DIPLOMATIC

The science of the critical study of official documents, such as charters, acts, treaties, contracts, judicial records, rolls, cartularies, registers, etc., as historical sources.

SEE ALSO: archives; palaeography

DIRECTORY

1   A book containing lists of the names and addresses, sometimes with other information added, of people, organizations or businesses, in a particular area, or with some common interest such as membership of a particular trade or profession.

2   In computing, a list of the contents of a disk or other filestore.

DISASTER PREPAREDNESS PLANNING

The process of organizing a system for coping with emergencies, and for dealing with the damage that may be caused to the library by fire, storm, flood and so on, and by man-made disasters perhaps resulting from war or terrorism. Although traditionally this has been concerned with books and other documents, it is equally important to have effective plans in place for retrieving data that is lost if a computer system is physically or electronically damaged.

Risk assessment and disaster prevention

A risk assessment may be conducted as a preliminary step towards developing a plan. This should identify what sort of problems might lead to loss or damage to the stock or breakdown of service, and what the long-term consequences might be. The principal concern of most library disaster plans is how to salvage materials following fire or flood damage, though the question of disaster prevention and the backing-up of computer systems may also be addressed.

If a library building (see LIBRARY BUILDINGS) survey is undertaken, the results should bring to light which areas are most susceptible and relate this to where the most valuable materials are kept. Periodic safety inspections may also help. Risk assessment may lead to improved building maintenance and may help prevent disasters, and it is closely related to the need to ensure adequate insurance cover is provided.

Disaster response

The first priority must be people's safety. Notices may be posted round the building telling staff and readers what to do in case of fire or other emergency. The provision of fire extinguishers or water hoses, fire escapes and other matters may be required by law. Consideration may also be given to the installation of sprinklers or other automatic fire-control systems, and staff may receive training in the use of fire extinguishers. In some countries, staff may also be given guidelines on the action to be taken in severe weather conditions and in the event of floods or earthquakes.

In larger buildings it is desirable to maintain a rota so that there is always a designated Duty Officer available to respond to emergencies and to oversee the evacuation of the building. A list may also be needed of staff who could be called upon to attend in the event of an emergency outside working hours.

Stocks may be kept of such things as polythene sheeting, paper products for absorbing water or other materials for use in emergencies. Special equipment may be kept for pumping out water and cleaning up, and basic training given to familiarize staff with the use of any special equipment. Procedures for contacting electricians, plumbers and so on need to be as clear as possible. As it is not practicable to keep everything that may be required in stock, it is recommended that lists be kept of local suppliers and other sources of assistance.

In the event of a disaster, teams may need to be organized to assist with the salvage of the stock, the whole operation being co-ordinated by a senior member of staff. A number of books have been published giving salvage guidelines, and some national libraries provide an advisory service. Many libraries and record offices have prepared their own staff manuals dealing in some detail with the salvage of water-damaged materials, usually based on a published model such as that produced by the National Library of Scotland (Anderson and McIntyre 1985).

Initial action plan

Initial action should concentrate on efforts to stabilize the condition of materials that need to be removed and prevent further damage, and on the task of rescuing as much of the damaged material as possible so as to minimize the need for future restoration or replacement. It has been found that when books are badly damaged, the combined costs of salvage and restoration are likely to be greater than the cost of replacement for books that are still obtainable, but no hasty decisions should be made in the initial stages of dealing with a disaster. Typically, guidelines will recommend that:

- The degree and character of damage should be assessed as soon as possible, and the different types of media should be distinguished (photographs, manuscripts, printed books, brittle and semi-brittle papers, coated paper), as different CONSERVATION treatment may be required.

- Priority should be given to the removal of standing water, reducing temperature and introducing controlled ventilation, so as to delay the onset of mould or to slow its growth.
- The amount of handling given to damaged materials should be minimized, and all conservation work should be avoided during the salvage operation or while working under pressure.
- No attempt should be made to lay out wet documents to dry, or to fan out wet books to air the pages inside, until the situation has been brought under control and conditions are conducive to drying; the relative humidity in the area may need to be monitored.

It is generally acknowledged that mould growth is liable to begin within forty-eight hours in warm humid conditions. Freezing is the best way of preventing mould, and can be used as a way of providing a 'breathing space', allowing time to make proper arrangements for drying, to analyse the relative costs of the different drying methods available, to prepare appropriate environmental conditions, to restore the buildings affected, to estimate full recovery costs or just to defer decisions until the value of damaged materials may be better assessed.

Recovery plan

Decisions regarding the drying of materials that have been frozen, the repair or replacement of damaged books and the restoration of damaged buildings may be dealt with separately as part of an agreed recovery plan. Points to be considered may include the following:

- The treatment of books on coated paper may not be successful unless the materials are frozen quickly while still wet.
- Freeze drying or vacuum drying may be the only practical treatment for some types of water-damaged library materials: books printed on coated paper, masses of paper stuck together, magnetic media, manuscripts with

fugitive inks, hand-coloured prints, maps, etc.

- No water-damaged material should be returned to a high-humidity environment (such as that often specified for the air-conditioned areas for ARCHIVES and SPECIAL COLLECTIONS) without having first been rehabilitated in a cool dry area and monitored for mould growth.

A reacclimatization period of at least six months has been recommended by the Library of Congress (Waters 1975). If environmental controls are available in the storage area, it is recommended that the relative humidity be set as low as 35 or 45 per cent for the first six months and then increased gradually to match the desired conditions for long-term storage.

References

Anderson, H. and McIntyre, J. (1985) *Planning Manual for Disaster Control in Scottish Libraries and Record Offices*, National Library of Scotland.

Waters, P. (1975) *Procedures for Salvage of Water-damaged Library Materials*, Library of Congress.

Further reading

Matthews, G. and Eden, P. (1996) *Disaster Management in British Libraries: Project Report with Guidelines for Library Managers*, British Library.

Matthews, G. and Feather, J. (eds) (2002) *Disaster Management in Libraries and Archives*, Ashgate.

Morris, J. (1986) *The Library Disaster Preparedness Handbook*, American Library Association [includes discussion of fire protection, safety and security, and the salvage and restoration of water-damaged materials].

Sturges, P. and Rosenberg, D, (1999) *Disaster and After: Practicalities of Information Services in Times of War and Other Catastrophes*, Taylor Graham.

SEE ALSO: computer security; health and safety; preservation

JOHN ASHMAN, REVISED BY THE EDITORS

DISCOGRAPHY

1 The study of sound recording (see SOUND RECORDINGS).
2 A list of sound recordings giving details of composer, title, performer(s), maker and maker's catalogue number, analogous to a BIBLIOGRAPHY of printed matter.

DISSEMINATION OF INFORMATION

Definition

Active distribution and the spreading of information of all kinds is called dissemination of information. It concerns METADATA as well as primary sources. This service is offered by libraries and other information agencies to defined target groups or individuals whose particular information requirements must have been previously determined. In this case the term *selective dissemination of information* (SDI) is frequently used. Its goal is to supply customers with all the latest information exclusively relevant for them. This information process has to take place at regular intervals. The evaluation criteria have to be the satisfaction of the customers. As an instrument of quality management their relevance feedback gives the opportunity to control and improve the accuracy of the service. The interest profiles of individuals or target groups stored by the provider must be checked and regularly updated. In addition, customers have the opportunity to access their individual profile data and to make changes at any time.

AIM

The VALUE ADDED for customers consists in saving of time and the avoidance of information overflow through a regular supply of current information, for scientific research or professional practice, for political, social and cultural purposes or for the cultivation of hobbies. Even customers who never would be able or willing to keep themselves informed about the latest developments can be supplied with current information. Dissemination of information is an effective means to improve the level of information and allows the making of decisions of all kinds on a well-informed basis. Charges for corresponding services usually vary considerably depending on different qualitative and quantitative levels.

Evolution

Traditionally, libraries as well as archives were restricted to gathering, classifying and providing information. SPECIAL LIBRARIES and documentation centres expanded their basic functions by adding the distribution and dissemination of information.

The transition from industrial society to INFORMATION SOCIETY will affect the traditional library functions. Most library types will have to integrate services like the dissemination of information as soon as possible. This can be achieved by supplying traditional pull services through push services that can be tailored to the individual or group information profiles.

MARKETING of libraries allows the development of appropriate services that are regularly adapted to the customers' requirements. In the past, dissemination of information offered by libraries or rather special libraries was restricted to library-owned material. Now digital media and the Internet make it possible to access sources that are located all over the world. This concept means that the well-proven INTERLIBRARY LENDING is broadened by co-operative dissemination of information. Institutions like subject gateways, subject portals (see PORTALS AND GATEWAYS) or information co-operatives of scientific and public libraries are heading in this direction and show both a clear revaluation of active dissemination of information and a preference for working collaboratively.

FORMS

Intensity and forms of dissemination of information vary. At a basic level current journals and reports or their tables of contents are circulated to those customers whose information profiles they affect (current contents). Externally generated bulletins and CURRENT-AWARENESS services that are made and offered for default profiles can be subscribed and are distributed by the library. In this particular case the library acts as a mediator.

A higher level of dissemination service is achieved if the library or a related institution generates the relevant information itself, compiles it and forwards it to the clients. All relevant sources (printed material, bibliographic and factual databases, hosts, Internet sources) are scanned and evaluated for this purpose regularly by the library. The profile-corresponding selection and compression of relevant information is also done by the library. Methodically and technically these activities have been simplified considerably through intelligent agents. Default profiles or individual information profiles can be stored there and be rendered into the search vocabulary of the respective sources. Intelligent agents, filters (see FILTERING) or PUSH TECHNOL-OGY assistants facilitate a drastic improvement of dissemination of information. However, they do not replace the work of highly qualified information specialists by any means. Conception, maintenance and management of these instruments belong to their tasks.

An appropriate methodology of generation, description, maintenance and adaptation of individual profiles of interest is basic to effective dissemination services. Internet portals for example provide checklists, thus enabling their customers to describe their focal interests. With an extensive THESAURUS, customers tend to select too many descriptors. In order to avoid this, it is more often offered to customers as a way to describe their interest fields using common terms. Afterwards, information specialists convert these non-standardized descriptions into controlled vocabulary to produce exact information profiles. Avoiding uncertainties requires purposeful feedback from the client and ideally a proper REFERENCE INTERVIEW. Interest profiles can be personalized or be tailored to a target audience. Where the interests of numerous customers coincide, a default profile is recommended that can be distributed in the form of an information bulletin. Heterogeneous profiles require personalized dissemination services. In large institutions and information co-operatives a combination of both alternatives can be offered. Individual relevance feedback allows the successive personalization of what were initially default profiles.

The content of dissemination of information services can include metadata and primary sources, hypotheses and validated information, published and informal material. Metadata should be detailed and include annotations, abstracts and so forth so that customers are enabled to judge whether, for example, the ordering of digital or printed material with resulting costs is worthwhile.

Dissemination of information in former times occurred through newsletters, information bulletins or individual messages in printed form. Today such bulletins and newsletters are offered online in combination with personal notification by e-mail.

Whether printed or digital, the extent of the information provided per issue must not be too great so that the clarity is not impeded and customers can use the added value of this regular push service immediately and without large expenditure. User-friendly structuring of all material is, of course, a basic condition for that.

State and perspectives

Dissemination of information in the academic sector is usually offered by libraries. The trend to produce such services co-operatively is obvious. Commercial providers too are venturing into this market although their customers are for now mainly enterprises. Lately dissemination of information has gained immensely in importance as an instrument to increase the customer relationship regarding e-commerce. Customers define their individual profile, e.g. within the context of Internet portals, in order to be supplied with specific information. Thus created personalized data can be used for effective one-to-one marketing. In the economic sector personalized and role-based push services are used, to supply employees with exactly the information they need to do their jobs. Personalization proves to be a basic constituent of the information society. Libraries too integrate this trend into new conceptions and services, and they even establish new institutions for this purpose; dissemination of information receives a considerably increased value within the framework of subject gateways, library portals and virtual libraries (see VIRTUAL LIBRARY).

Further reading

Hamilton, F. (1995) *Current Awareness, Current Techniques*, Gower.
Murch, R. and Johnson, T. (1999) *Intelligent Software Agents*, Prentice Hall PTR.

SEE ALSO: current awareness; current contents list; information service; portals and gateways; virtual library

HERMANN RÖSCH

DISTANCE LEARNING

Distance learning (also known as 'distance education' and 'open learning') in library and information studies covers both the professional qualification and further education of library and information sector (LIS) workers. Distance learners are not required to attend the institution offering the course of study; they learn from a location of their choice, often at the time of their choosing. The effects of barriers such as geographical isolation and personal and work commitments are thus minimized. Distance learning in LIS using the postal system was proposed as early as 1888 by Melvil DEWEY. It is now firmly established in mainstream LIS education, increasingly complementing and replacing face-to-face teaching and learning.

Delivery modes

Distance learning can be thought of as a continuum, ranging from broadcast modes of delivery of learning material, to full interactivity between learner and teacher.

Traditional distance learning attempts to replicate classroom teaching by sending teaching staff to students at remote locations and offering radio and television broadcasts and short-term residential schools. These are usually supplemented by print material, audio-cassette and video material and home lab kits. There is little or no formal peer-to-peer communication. Interactivity between student and teaching staff is increased through techniques such as telephone tutoring and interactive video (video-conferencing).

Currently, the widespread adoption of INFORMATION AND COMMUNICATION TECHNOLOGY and the Internet allows greater interactivity, transforming distance learning with peer-to-peer communication in multiple modes. Asynchronous tools such as e-mail, online forums, newsgroups and electronic submission of assignments, and synchronous learning using desktop interactive video, online chat and MOO (Multi-user Object-Oriented domains) are used. The WORLD WIDE WEB is used as a delivery mechanism for learning materials, supplementing or replacing print material, and as an information resource, providing resource-based learning opportunities.

Popularity of distance learning

Distance learning is becoming increasingly popular with LIS workers and students. It offers greater flexibility for students who may be isolated by distance, by family circumstance or by employment constraints (such as shift workers). The distance learning mode is also increasingly popular for continuing and further education for similar reasons: it allows skills and knowledge to be updated in one's own time, free from workplace constraints such as lack of study leave, and it can be planned and undertaken around family and social responsibilities.

Constraints

Distance learning faces technological, resource and pedagogical constraints. Technological constraints include limited student access to information and communication technology (e.g. high charges for Internet access) and lack of infrastructure and resources (e.g. poor technology support by the teaching institution). Resource constraints include limited library provision of services to distance learning students.

The pedagogical issues are less significant as more distance learning takes place, but some still need to be addressed. Chief among them is how to encourage regular peer-to-peer and faculty-to-student communication, an essential part of effective learning. To ensure that students maintain high levels of self-discipline and commitment it is essential to create and maintain an active community of learners. To this end mechanisms such as online forums and newsgroups are used. The pastoral care aspects of education assume greater prominence in effective distance learning. Scepticism about whether distance learning is as effective as face-to-face learning is dissipating rapidly.

Large distances and sparse populations

Large distances and sparse populations have been the incentive in some countries to provide distance learning in LIS. Australia's large land mass and widely dispersed population has resulted in most of its thirteen LIS schools offering distance learning. Charles Sturt University's School of Information Studies (http://www.csu.edu.au) has offered courses solely in this mode for two decades, moving from traditional print-based mail packages to Web-based subjects supplemented by CD-ROM. All courses are fully supported by interactive Web mechanisms such as forums and e-mail.

South Africa provides another example of a country where distance learning is offered as an effective way to counter the constraints of distance. The University of South Africa (www.unisa.ac.za) has a long history of offering distance learning in LIS. It is currently implementing Internet-based services and its students have access to learning centres throughout the country.

Need to increase education opportunities

Elsewhere, the incentive for distance learning has been the need to rapidly increase the number of citizens participating in formal education at all levels. In India, distance learning in LIS was offered in 1985 by the University of Madras, followed in 1989 by the Indira Gandhi National Open University (IGNOU). One decade later, at least twenty-five institutions offered distance learning LIS programmes to about 4,000 students. IGNOU provides self-instructional print material supplemented by video and audio programmes (which are also regularly broadcast by the National TV Network and All India Radio), counselling sessions at study centres throughout India and satellite-based teleconferencing (http://www.ignou.edu).

Thailand, like India, has rapidly moved to providing education to populations who have traditionally not had access to universities. Sukhotai Thammathirat Open University has offered distance learning LIS programmes since 1989, using mailed material (textbooks and workbooks) supplemented by audio-cassettes, radio and television programmes. Optional tutorials are offered and counselling support is available. There is a compulsory residential period.

Offering greater study choices

Another principal driver of distance learning has been the flexibility it offers to learners whose personal and work commitments prevent them from attending campus. European countries are starting to offer distance learning opportunities in LIS, such as the programmes of the University of Wales Aberystwyth (http://www.dil.aber.ac.uk) and the Swedish School of Library and Information Studies at Göteborg University and Högskolan i Borås (http://www.hb.se/bhs/bhs-eng).

Of the fifty-six American Library Association-accredited masters programmes in LIS in August 2001, thirty-six offered some form of distance learning. Of these, twenty-three were primarily involved in delivering courses at satellite sites and thirteen with delivery via the Internet. This represents a change over the last decade from primarily face-to-face delivery, to most schools supplementing face-to-face teaching with off-campus instruction. There is also an increasing move towards full degrees being available through distance learning.

Conclusion

Distance learning is now accepted as a mainstream delivery mode, although concerns still exist about some pedagogical issues. It is one of several avenues available for library and information studies education, both for gaining professional qualifications and for continuing professional development activities. Its popularity suggests that it may eventually eclipse other methods of delivering learning to the LIS profession.

Further reading

Distance Education Clearinghouse Website (2001) (http://www.uwex.edu/disted/definition.html) [provides a wide range of definitions of distance learning and distance education].

Julien, H., Robbins, J., Logan, E. and Dalrymple, P. (2001) 'Going the distance', *Journal of Education for Library and Information Science* 42: 200–5.

SEE ALSO: computer-assisted learning in library and information science; information professions; information science education; library education; object-oriented technology

ROSS HARVEY

DOCUMENT

A record that contains information CONTENT. In common usage it still normally means a piece of paper with words or graphics on it. In library and information work, the term is however used to mean any information-carrying medium, regardless of format. Thus books, manuscripts, videotapes and computer files and databases are all regarded as documents.

DOCUMENT CLUSTERING

Clustering involves grouping together descriptions of documents by their similarity to each other. INFORMATION RETRIEVAL systems have used clustering of documents and queries to improve both retrieval efficiency and retrieval effectiveness. Document clustering is reflected in the methodologies of some of the newer searching techniques, such as DATA MINING, which are being developed to facilitate more efficient and focused searching for documents on the WORLD WIDE WEB. Recent work has included the creation of automated clustering systems (Roussinov and Chen 2001), which seem likely to be the way of the future.

References

Roussinov, D.G. and Chen, H. (2001) 'Information navigation on the Web by clustering and summarizing query results', *Information Processing and Management* 37: 789–816.

DOCUMENT DELIVERY

Definitions for document delivery vary, but it has come to mean the provision of material that may be retained by users. This is in contrast to INTERLIBRARY LENDING, which is the lending of an item by one library to another. This distinction has, in some instances, led to a physical division of operations within single libraries. Occasionally, too, the term interlending is regarded as encompassing both traditional interlending and document supply operations, with the phrase document delivery (or, increasingly, docdel) being used to refer exclusively to electronic document delivery, often regarded as being a faster and more sophisticated method of satisfying requests for material. The vast majority of traditional and electronic document delivery is run as a mediated service, with the library being involved in the processing, ordering and (sometimes) receipt and delivery of documents. Unmediated document delivery, by way of contrast, allows the individual library user to order and receive a document direct from the supplier. This can be beneficial to library users and to libraries by reducing the amount of administration involved in the process, thus speeding up the supply of material, though the process is not as unproblematic as this bald summary implies.

Document delivery can be proactive or reactive depending on the users and their requirements. In the early 1990s Current Alerting Services – Individual Article Supply (CAS-IAS) was launched, which provided a mechanism for alerting end-users and librarians to the existence of new article titles. In CAS-IAS services a DATABASE is constructed, culled from the tables of contents from significant journals that are in active use. Interrogating this database enables individuals to identify titles of particular relevance to their research, and to place an order online for the article itself. These CAS-IAS services differ from formal interlending and document delivery because a royalty payment is made to the copyright holder (the publisher) in order to comply with national copyright laws. As such, these integrated services tend to be more expensive than interlending or centralized document delivery services.

As a reactive measure, document delivery represents an alternative strategy that can be used by librarians according to budgetary requirements. It is a feature of collection development that the growth in materials budgets has in general been insufficient to allow the continued acquisition of the full range of journals that library users require, particularly given the continued growth in information output. As journals are cancelled, the prices of other journals are raised by a factor greater than overall inflation in order to compensate publishers for loss of earnings, forcing librarians to cancel additional titles. Such economic pressures, combined with the rapid increase of information available electronically, has led to a change in the role of libraries, with the traditional model of owning as much material as possible being replaced by a global approach to providing access to that material via document delivery.

A key factor in document delivery is its susceptibility to economic and technical trends. It is therefore a less stable activity than interlending, which relies heavily on librarians' expertise, but it has the advantage of being able to adapt more quickly to new developments. It is also an area of library work that both concerns and attracts commercial suppliers, whether publishers or distributors.

The key players

The BRITISH LIBRARY Document Supply Centre (BLDSC) dominates the UK scene for document delivery. It receives over 3.8 million requests each year, over a million of which are from outside the UK; 89 per cent of these are satisfied from BLDSC's own stock. Three-quarters of the requests received by BLDSC are made electronically. Most of the orders are dispatched by mail, and delivery to UK clients usually takes between twenty-four and forty-eight hours.

Similar services operate in France (INIST), in Germany (Hanover, Cologne), in Canada (CISTI) and in other counties that have adopted the BLDSC model as their basis. The adoption of a centralized approach has been stimulated by the apparent efficiency of a dedicated source for document delivery, though in many instances this requires some sort of (usually) governmental subsidy. Such subsidies are often regarded as part of the government's support for education and the national research effort.

In the USA, OCLC has taken a dominant role in providing an interlibrary lending subsystem to its library management system, thus facilitating the creation, sending and tracking of document delivery and ILL requests for materials included on World Cat (OCLC's Online Union Catalogue), which provides access to the combined resources of over 6,700 libraries, totalling over 43 million records. Around 18,000 libraries are part of the OCLC network, and the ability to find articles or books required within this vast library system is an attractive option, particularly as there is no charge for such transactions in many instances.

The growth in demand for document delivery has resulted in an increased number of options being available to libraries in terms of commercial document suppliers and the range of services they provide. These include UnCover, ISI's Current Contents Online database, Current Citations Online from Ebsco Subscription Services and Swetscan from Swets Blackwell. The British Library's own contributions include Zetoc, an electronic table of contents service that provides access to the British Library's Electronic Tables of Contents (ETOC) database. OCLC has developed its own Article First and Contents First databases while the Research Libraries Group uses its CitaDel system in a similar way.

Technological developments

The rise in the 1990s of ELECTRONIC JOURNALS available via the World Wide Web posed a challenge to traditional docdel. Such journals are in some cases refereed, some are freely available and some of them command a price. Most importantly, many do not have a printed equivalent from which a document request might otherwise be satisfied. A further development in the UK electronic journals environment has been the National Electronic Site Licence Initiative (NESLI), established by the Joint Information Systems Committee (JISC). Intended as a service designed to promote the widespread delivery and use of electronic journals in the UK higher education and research community, NESLI is an initiative intended to address the many issues that at present hinder the most effective use of, access to and purchase of electronic journals in the academic library community. A model licence is an idealized version of a licensing contract that gives both libraries and vendors a basis for evaluating and negotiating contracts that will be fair and profitable to all parties. Document delivery is a particularly contentious issue for vendors of electronic information and a clear definition of terms is one of the most valuable functions model licences can perform in supporting the needs of the library's ILL and document delivery functions.

The future

The nature of document supply will inevitably change as an increasing amount of material becomes available only electronically. There are a number of issues and challenges for libraries to contend with: access remains a major issue facing libraries and the debate over copyright law and its application is likely to continue as libraries and publishers attempt to deal with the implications of new technologies, new formats for information and improved networks of communication. The interoperability of equipment and software, and the development of standards for the delivery of information for both traditional library-based interlending and commercial suppliers are further issues of concern. In addition to these, other factors will need to be considered as document delivery continues to evolve: the cancellation rate on printed journal subscriptions threatens to drive many specialized journals out of existence; and the increasing number of commercial suppliers affords users an ever-increasing choice of potential sources of supply. There is also the increasing possibility of a changing marketing model as publishers move away in the future from the page fidelity approach of current scientific, technical and medical (STM) journals to a truly electronic version where content takes precedence over printed appearance.

Reviewing research in the area of document delivery is useful and allows the identification of future trends. In the UK, FIDDO (Focused Investigation of Document Delivery Options) was a major Electronic Libraries Programme (eLib) project aimed at providing information about other projects, document suppliers and trends, and had, as one of its major objectives, to supply relevant, up-to-date information to library managers. Other such projects concerned with the future of document delivery were EDDIS (Electronic Document Delivery: the Integrated System), SEREN (Sharing of Educational Resources ·in an Electronic Network), LAMDA (London and Manchester Document Access), JEDDS (Joint Electronic Document Delivery Software) and Infobike. Similar projects have been undertaken in other countries: Australia has been very active in exploring the possibilities of new technologies for document delivery and the REDD (Regional Document Delivery Project), JEDDS and LIDDA (Local Interlending and Document Delivery Administration) websites give useful information on this work. In the USA, NAILDD (North American Interlibrary Loan Document Delivery Project) was initiated to promote developments that will improve the delivery of library materials to users at costs that are sustainable for libraries.

Increasingly, libraries operate in a global environment and document delivery has a key role to play within this. As libraries move from a traditional model where they are the resource centre and purchase items, to an access-based model with items being purchased at time of need, this role becomes even more critical. It is likely that document delivery will become more streamlined, more integrated and less reliant on library staff mediation as suppliers move towards providing direct electronic access to the end-user. The need for a library-based document delivery department will remain but it is likely that its role will change. Though much attention is focused on document delivery as the salvation of librarians in meeting their responsibilities for 'just in time' information for their clients, the document delivery process is by no means without its problems. The question of whether a fair balance can be reached between those who provide the source articles and those who order them through a document delivery process is one that must be solved if real progress is to be made.

Further reading

Braid, A. (1994) 'Electronic document delivery: Vision and reality', *Libri* 44: 224–36.

Brown, D. (2001) 'The document delivery disgrace', *Library Association Record* 103(10): 610–11.

Davies, E. ·and Morris, A. (1998) 'Weighing up the options for document supply: A description and discussion of the FIDDO project', *Interlending and Document Supply* 26: 76–82.

Finnie, E. (1998) *Document Delivery*, ASLIB.

Gould, S. (ed.) (1997) *Charging for Document Supply and Interlending*, IFLA.

Interlending and Document Supply, MCB University Press [a specialist journal in the field].

Morris, A. and Blagg, E. (1998) 'Current practices and use of document delivery services in UK academic libraries', *Library Management* 19: 271–80.

Morris, A., Jacobs, N. and Davies, E. (eds) (1999) *Document Delivery Beyond 2000*, Taylor Graham.

Orman, D. (ed.) (1997) *Evolution or Revolution? The Challenge of Resource Sharing in the Electronic Environment*, The British Library.

Vickers, P. and Martyn, J. (1994) *The Impact of Electronic Publishing on Library Services and Resources in the UK: Report of the British Library Working Party on Electronic Publishing*, The British Library Board (Library and Information Research Report 102).

SEE ALSO: collection management; current awareness

PENELOPE STREET AND DAVID ORMAN

DOCUMENT IMAGE PROCESSING

The DIGITIZATION by scanning of information from paper or DOCUMENTs in other media (such as MICROFORMS). The data can then be processed and stored in a computer.

DOCUMENTATION

The librarians' lexicon in Anglophone countries tends to make less and less use of the term 'documentation', as evidenced in the professional literature, and to give preference to the term 'INFORMATION SCIENCE'. While the word 'documentation' is almost equivalent in semantic content, both in English and in French, there is however a noticeable discrepancy in the usage of this term: the English term covers a narrower area of concepts and practices than its French counterpart. As early as 1951, the Documentation Committee of the Special Library Association (SLA) gave a rather qualified definition: 'Documentation is the art comprised of (a) document reproduction, (b) document distribution, (c) document utilization' (Kent and Lancour 1972: 264). While debating the setting up of a documentation section under the umbrella of the SLA, members indeed pointed out that 'documentation is procedural in nature as opposed to substantive' (Kent and Lancour 1972: 265).

The French term 'documentation' is still a popular word and very much used by the profession. It encompasses several concepts and thus totally embraces the whole field of information science. It covers a full range of activities related to document acquisition (see ACQUISTIONS) and selection, evaluation of materials, CLASSIFICATION schemes, storage and DOCUMENT DELIVERY, as well as the technical procedures linked to these activities. It also implies an activity such as search strategy and designates a comprehensive amount of documents related to one topic as well as the tasks performed by the staff in charge.

It is of paramount importance to stress that in French-speaking countries the very characteristics of documentation/resource centres on the one hand and of LIBRARIES on the other hand are traditionally clearly marked. This distinction also applies to the training the staff receive, as well as to the duties and responsibilities they are involved in. The mission of libraries, generally speaking, is to give access to primary resources, the bulk of the latter still being the printed book. Documentation/resource centres differ from libraries because of the greater diversity of documents they hold. Printed books account for a limited amount of their holdings, whereas periodicals and GREY LITERATURE constitute their strength. This includes PhD theses, in-house reports, conference proceedings, patents, drawings, maps, plans, statistical records, photographs and audiovisual materials, among other things. One must stress other elements specific to these centres: the diversity of the public/clients they cater for (depending on their field of expertise), the complexity of the queries as well as the irreplaceable added value as complementary information to primary resources. Information scientists are facilitators and the essential interfaces between users/patrons and their resources. While the centres are responsible for the management of their resources, they also provide informed advice on the contents of the materials they hold and provide services and products specifically designed and developed for the public they serve.

However, the sharp demarcation between the missions of libraries and of documentation/resource centres has tended to become less and less noticeable even in France. This trend is particularly true in the case of ACADEMIC LIBRARIES, which tend to follow the pattern of English-speaking countries where there exists no clear-cut distinction between librarianship or library science and information science. Such is the case because activities such as information storage, retrieval and search are based on the principles established for LIBRARIANSHIP.

Interestingly enough, few international organizations have kept the term 'documentation' in the wording of their names with the exception of FID (the now defunct International Federation for Information and Documentation), thus reflecting its French-speaking Belgian origins. The various changes made through time to the name of the latter organization reflect the change of conceptualization in the field of what professionals mean by the term 'documentation' in French-speaking countries. The name 'Institut International de Bibliographie' was chosen at the time of its inception in Brussels in 1895. In 1931 the name changed to 'Institut International de Documentation', becoming 'Fédération internationale de Documentation' in 1937. It is only as late as 1988 that it came to be known under its present name. While the Universal Bibliographic Repertory and the UNIVERSAL DECIMAL CLASSIFICATION remained for a long time the most visible aspect of its activities, both Paul OTLET and Henri La Fontaine, the two men who started this organization, had indeed privileged connections with Belgian political life and an internationalist perspective of what documentation was all about. The Palais Mondial in Brussels was built to host the Institut International de Bibliographie, which was to be a national library, a museum and an international university. It marked the peak of such a vision, a utopian plan marred by the devastation of the First World War.

The term 'documentation' is more and more either qualified (if used) or replaced by the term information, as evidenced by the various changes that have occurred in the course of time to the name FID. Thus the French professional organization ADBS (Association des Documentalistes et Bibliothécaires Specialisés) has kept its acronym, but makes itself known by the more up-to-date expression Association des Professionnels de l'Information et de la Documentation (Professional Association of Information and Documentation). The change in usage of the term 'documentation' is not only to be accounted for by Anglo-Saxon influence, but also by the development of new technologies. The latter have broadened information scientists' field of expertise, thus allowing for the emergence of new needs by businesses and organizations, needs which can be met thanks to new computer-based tools (strategic information services, database management and INFORMATION ENGINEERING). Therefore, the challenge for librarians and information scientists in this information age is to redefine their roles and extend their boundaries of knowledge.

References

Kent, A. and Lancour, H. (eds) (1972) *Encyclopaedia of Library and Information Science*, vol. 7, Marcel Dekker

Further reading

ADBS chart (http://www.adbs.fr/adbs/actu/html/charte.htm).

d'Olier, J.H. and Paillard, M.-F. (1997) 'Documentation', in *Encyclopaedia Universalis* vol. 7, pp. 598–605.

Sutter, E. (1997) 'Documentation', in S. Cacaly (ed.) *Dictionnaire encyclopédique de l'information et de la documentation*, Nathan, pp. 187–91.

Rayward, W.B. (1994) 'The International Federation for Information and Documentation (FID)', in W.A. Wiegand and D.G. Davis (eds) *Encyclopaedia of Library History*, Garland Press, pp. 290–4.

SEE ALSO: information professions; information theory; special libraries

RAYMOND BERARD

DOMAIN NAME

Whilst in common parlance a domain is a geographical area controlled by a particular ruler or government, it also refers to a sphere of activity or knowledge. In relation to the INTERNET, however, a domain refers to a set of sites with NETWORK addresses distinguished by a common suffix, such as .de (Germany, geographical) or .com (commercial, category). A domain name consists of the specific name of a site followed by a category, followed in turn by a country (except in the case of US sites) as with lboro.ac.uk (Loughborough University, an academic site in the UK).

The selection and protection of domain names is a major consideration in E-COMMERCE, and international responsibility for this is taken by the Internet Corporation for Assigned Names and Numbers (ICANN). ICANN is a non-profit corporation that handles the allocation and management of the domain name system, a function previously performed under US Government contract by various other bodies.

Further reading

Internet Corporation for Assigned Names and Numbers (www.icann.org).

DONATIONS TO LIBRARIES

Gifts of books or other material to a library, normally intended to be added to its stock; also used for gifts of money, equipment or buildings. From the earliest times donations were one of the principal ways in which libraries added to their stock. In many cases libraries were established by the gift or bequest of a private collection of books or manuscripts, for example to a college or church. Only rarely, however, were such gifts supported by provision for continuing funding, so that libraries of this kind often became fossilized.

One notable donation was the refounding of the university library at Oxford by Sir Thomas BODLEY in 1598 by the gift of his own books and the cost of a librarian; this led to many other donations, which set the Bodleian Library on its highly successful path. The gift of the rich library of King George III to the nation by his son George IV in 1823 immeasurably strengthened the rare book collections of the British Museum (now part of the BRITISH LIBRARY).

Similar large donations to public or research libraries have long been recognized as an important source of specialized material, and libraries often contain special collections named after donors. Individual donations of more recent material, for example an author's own books, or special items felt to merit permanent preservation in a public collection, are regularly received by libraries of all kinds. Librarians usually accept such gifts of books with gratitude, and in many cases these gifts represent books that the library wishes to acquire but lacks the resources to purchase. In the case of scholarly donors, the material may well complement existing strengths and include valuable out-of-print works. Gifts of subscriptions to periodicals can also usefully extend a library's range.

Libraries often have a section within the ACQUISITIONS department concerned with the acknowledgement and handling of donations, including assessment of their value to the library in relation to the cost of processing and storage. (Such a department will often also handle exchanges (see EXCHANGE PROGRAMMES), which have some similarities to donations but are essentially acquisitions paid for in kind; they have even more cost implications than donations.)

Donations can, however, cause problems beyond those associated with checking, cataloguing and housing a large volume of material. They may duplicate stock already held by the library, or may be in a field in which the library has no interest. In the case of periodicals, the library needs to be assured that parts will be received regularly. There may be problems of space to accommodate a large collection, or the material may be in need of expensive conservation. A donor may place stipulations on the gift, for example requiring the collection to be kept as a unit or even requiring it to be kept in a specified location. Individual books or serials may be distributed free to libraries by government agencies or bodies wishing to secure free publicity; in such cases the librarian must guard against the dangers of unbalanced propaganda.

Such considerations make it desirable for the librarian to discuss the terms of a gift or bequest with the donor wherever possible. Most donors are happy for the library to dispose of material that it does not require, and are glad to see their material going to a more appropriate home. The involvement of FRIENDS OF THE LIBRARY can be useful both in soliciting donations and in helping donors to understand the library's real needs.

In some cases benefactors have given money rather than books, often to provide endowment funds either for purchasing or for specified posts. LIBRARY BUILDINGS, too, have often been built at the expense of a benefactor. An outstanding example is Andrew CARNEGIE, who began funding library buildings in 1886 with the gift of $1 million for a central library and seven branches in Pittsburgh. Carnegie extended his benefactions to Britain, and many library buildings funded by him and his trustees still survive. His gifts, however, laid a responsibility on the local authorities to stock and maintain the library, which meant that not all his offers were accepted – another example of the hidden costs that can underlie donations of all kinds.

Further reading

Chapman, L. (1989) *Buying Books for Libraries*, Bingley [stresses the problems caused by donations].

Magrill, R.M. and Corbin, J. (1989) *Acquisitions Management and Collection Development in Libraries*, 2nd edn, American Library Association [Chapter 11 (pp. 216–33) deals with gifts and exchanges].

PETER HOARE

DUBLIN CORE

A METADATA initiative intended to allow users of the WORLD WIDE WEB to search for ELECTRONIC INFORMATION RESOURCES and information about resources in other formats in a way analogous to using a library catalogue (see CATALOGUES). It offers a resource discovery mechanism based on fifteen descriptive elements. These are:

- Title (the name given the resource).
- Creator (the AUTHOR or institution responsible for creating the CONTENT).
- Subject (the topic of the resource).
- Description (text outlining or providing an ABSTRACT of the content).
- Publisher (those responsible for making the resource available).
- Contributors (those who supplied elements of the content).
- Date (when the resource was made available).
- Type (a CATEGORIZATION of the content).
- Format (digital or physical manifestation of the content).
- Identifier (an unambiguous reference to the resource, e.g. UNIFORM RESOURCE LOCATOR or INTERNATIONAL STANDARD BOOK NUMBER).
- Source (an original resource from which the content is derived).
- Language.
- Relation (reference to any related resource).
- Coverage (extent or scope of the content).
- Rights (information on copyright status).

The Dublin Core Metadata Initiative began in 1995, after a workshop in Dublin, Ohio, and continues as an open forum working to promote acceptance and use of metadata standards and practices generally, and the Dublin Core elements in particular. Its activities include working groups, workshops, conferences, liaison on standards and educational efforts.

Further reading

Dublin Core Metadata Initiative (http://dublincore.org).

E

E-COMMERCE

At a basic level this refers to selling goods and services via the INTERNET, using Web pages. In this sense there is little basic difference between e-commerce and catalogue sales or the use of television shopping channels, in that awareness of the product may be obtained at a distance, but delivery is likely to be via POSTAL SERVICES and other means of delivery to the purchaser's actual address. E-commerce is, however, distinct in that the methods for ordering (by ELECTRONIC MAIL) and paying (by ELECTRONIC DATA INTERCHANGE) are fully integrated with the means of advertising. It can also involve the delivery of specifically electronic products. For instance, access to pornographic images and text is the most traded category of e-commerce.

The concept of e-commerce is now subsumed within a broader concept of e-business in which the Internet, INTRANETS and EXTRANETS are used to create and transform business relationships. E-business can not only increase the speed of service delivery, and reduce the cost of business operations, but also contribute to the improvement of the quality of goods and services through the effective transfer and sharing of information with customers, within organizations and between organizations.

E-GOVERNMENT

In broad terms, electronic or e-government can refer to the use of INFORMATION AND COMMUNICATION TECHNOLOGY (ICT) in politics at the global, state, party or civil societal level. A narrower definition, dominant in most political systems, refers to the impact of the Internet and related network technologies on the values, processes and outcomes of central and local government, and their administrative structures, with the objective of providing public access 'to information about all the services offered by ... Departments and their agencies; and enabling the public to conduct and conclude transactions for all those services' (UK National Audit Office 2002: 1). Although the term is sometimes considered to be synonymous with 'e-democracy', this is misleading. An analytical distinction should be drawn between the two on the grounds that, unlike e-democracy, the dominant model of e-government to date has not often involved the development of direct forms of political deliberation and decision-making through electronic referendums and similar devices.

E-government emerged as an agenda for general reform of the public sectors of liberal democratic political systems during the early 1990s. The Clinton Presidency in the USA led the way with its 'National Performance Review' of the Federal bureaucracy (US National Performance Review 1993). It was the explosion of Internet use in the mid-1990s, however, which gave impetus to the idea, and countries such as the UK, Canada, Australia and New Zealand soon followed suit with their own versions. In the UK, the Labour Party, elected in 1997, put 'electronic service delivery' at the centre of its programme for 'Modernising Government' (UK Cabinet Office 1998), claiming that all public services would be online by 2005 – a target greeted with much scepticism by the IT industry and political commentators alike.

In common with other programmes of organizational reform, the claims made about e-government differ quite substantially, but can be divided into two main schools.

According to one, far-reaching, perspective, the principal aim is to use ICTs, especially the Internet, to open up the state to citizen involvement. The ubiquity of network technologies offers the potential to increase political participation and reshape the state into an open, interactive, network form, as an alternative to both traditional, hierarchical, bureaucratic organizations and more recent, market-like forms of service delivery based on the 'contracting out' of public-sector activities, often termed the 'New Public Management'. Proponents of this perspective argue that widespread use of the Internet means that the traditional application of ICTs in public bureaucracies, based around inward-facing mainframe computer systems that originated in the 1960s, should now be superseded by outward-facing networks in which the division between an organization's internal information processing and its external users effectively becomes redundant. Government becomes a 'learning organization', able to respond to the needs of its citizens, who are in turn able to influence public bureaucracies by rapid, aggregative feedback mechanisms like e-mail and interactive websites.

A second, less radical, school of thought suggests that e-government does not necessarily require greater public involvement in shaping how services are delivered, but instead indirectly benefits citizens through the efficiency gains and cost savings produced by the reduction of internal organizational 'friction', chiefly via the automation of routine tasks and disintermediation. Networks are also at the core of this perspective, but it is the ability of the Internet and intranets to 'join up' and co-ordinate the activities of previously disparate government departments and services that is seen as its most attractive feature. In this view, citizens are perceived mainly as the 'consumers' of public services like healthcare information, benefits payments, passport applications, tax returns and so on. This has been the dominant model in those countries that have taken the lead in introducing e-government reforms.

E-government is not without its critics. Some suggest that changes are limited to a 'managerial' agenda of service delivery more consistent with the New Public Management and that the opportunities offered by the Internet for invigorating democracy and citizenship might be missed (Chadwick and May 2003). Other criticisms are: that the conservatism of existing administrative elites will scupper any prospects of decisive change; that issues of unequal access (both within and between states) to online services are being neglected; that large corporate IT interests are exercising an undue influence on the shape of e-government due to their expertise; that traditional face-to-face contacts with public services, especially those associated with welfare systems, cannot be satisfactorily replaced by web-based communication; that the cost savings promised by reforms have been slow to materialize; and that disintermediation of traditional representative bodies (parliaments, local councils) may occur, to the detriment of democracy.

Whatever the claims made for e-government, perhaps its most significant feature from the perspective of the information sciences is that the Web browser and the Internet, with their associated standards, protocols and file formats, brought together under the umbrella of the World Wide Web Consortium (W3C), will form the foundation of public sector use of ICTs for the foreseeable future. The most popular ways of transferring data across the Internet – from secure transactions, to compressed graphics, video and sound – will be used by governments from now on. The days of large-scale, often Byzantine, tailor-made systems that rapidly date are perhaps coming to an end. Networks are easier to build and maintain than ever before, and it is much simpler for governments to interface their internal networks with the outside world.

References

Chadwick, A. and May, C. (2003) 'Interaction between states and citizens in the age of the Internet: "e-government" in the United States, Britain and the European Union', *Governance* 16(2).

UK National Audit Office (2002) *Better Public Services through E-Government*, HC704–1, HMSO.

US National Performance Review (1993) *Re-Engineering through Information Technology: Accompanying Report of the National Performance Review*, GPO.

Further reading

Barney, D. (2000) *Prometheus Wired: The Hope For Democracy in the Age of Network Technology*, University of Chicago Press [a well-written account].

E-Governance resources: www.rhul.ac.uk/sociopolitical-science/e-governance).

Egovlinks (www.egovlinks.com).

Margolis, M. and Resnick, D. (2000) *Politics as Usual: The Cyberspace 'Revolution'*, Sage [for a very sceptical view].

SEE ALSO: information society

ANDREW CHADWICK

EAST ASIA

The region is comprised of China (the People's Republic of China: PRC), Japan, Korea (the Republic of Korea, the Democratic People's Republic of Korea) and Taiwan (the Republic of China). Hong Kong has been a Special Administrative Region of PRC since 1997. A distinctive feature of the region is the size of the population, political tensions and economic development. The huge population is a major information market for IT and ICT services and products. Nations in East Asia have been a good information market and they will continue to be so. Factors that may inhibit further development, especially of the INTERNET, include language-processing capability, character set and encoding standards, weak NATIONAL BIBLIOGRAPHY databases, and bibliographic utilities.

Writing systems and Chinese characters

The writing systems of East Asia are based on Chinese characters (scripts) that have been developed since around the third century BCE. Chinese logographic (ideographic) characters have meanings and readings of each character that evolved through the ages and with geographic variations. The Chinese character set, however, is stable in its logographic and semantic features so that written materials could be commonly assimilated across the region. Thus the languages of China, Japan and Korea are different but all use the Chinese characters following their own conventions. However, the characters have evolved in China, Japan, Korea and Vietnam with variations in shape and meaning according to the needs and conventions of local language.

In China, the government introduced a simplified character set in 1956 as part of its national literacy policy. This had a great impact on character conventions in neighbouring countries. The shapes of the simplified characters keep the original forms of radicals so people in Korea and Japan are able to identify the original character.

In Korea, printing by movable type was invented in CE 1234. Hangul, the Korean phonetic alphabet, which originally had twenty-eight characters, was established by Sejong the Great of the Yi dynasty in CE 1443. Hangul became the Korean national characters after the Second World War. There are variations of Hangul between South and the North Korea.

It is believed that Wang In, a Korean monk, took the *Analects* of Confucius and the *Thousand Characters Text* – a primer of Chinese characters – to Japan in CE 285. Local developments derived phonetic symbols of forty-eight Kana, based on the Japanese pronunciation of Chinese characters, and this became the basic component, together with Chinese characters, of the Japanese writing system.

The total number of Chinese characters is supposed to be about 100,000. Variant shapes exist in each language. New Chinese characters are constantly created by combining radicals for personal names, especially in Hong Kong. However, the number of domestic creations of Chinese characters in Korea and Japan are less than 100 in each language after 1,700 years. Learning Chinese characters up to the level needed for newspaper reading (3,000 characters in the case of the Japanese language) is a lengthy business.

ROMANIZATION (TRANSLITERATION)

Romanization or transliteration of Chinese, Japanese and Korean has been practised for a long time. For example, the *Vocabulario da Lingoa de Iapan*, a Portuguese–Japanese dictionary was compiled and published in 1603 by Jesuit priests stationed in Japan. The dictionary has entries of transliterated Japanese words of the period. Other Christian missionaries devised transliteration schemes for languages in East Asia during the seventeenth and eighteenth centuries, which could then be used for printing.

The modern transliteration schemes were created during the nineteenth century. The Wade–Giles system for Chinese, the McCune–Reischauer system for Korean and the Hepburn system for Japanese are famous and widely used examples. These schemes are applied not only for language training but also for filing catalogue (see CATALOGUES) entries in libraries. Each language has its own filing order but when Western names and domestic names are filed together, romanization is the inevitable choice. A transliteration scheme based on pronunciation, however, can be unsatisfactory, not least in whether it is developed by native speakers or non-native speakers. In an attempt to produce generally acceptable schemes, modern governments in East Asia introduced new revised schemes during the nineteenth and twentieth centuries. The Kunrei method for Japanese was introduced in 1937 and 1954, the Pin Yin method for Chinese in 1958 and the latest scheme for Korean in 2000. In the case of Korean, there have been several revisions of the scheme and a mixed version is now commonly used.

COMPUTER CHARACTER SET STANDARDS

Computer diffusion in East Asia has been phenomenal, especially since 1995. Computer development work was started in the 1950s in each country. Until around the mid-1970s, national language support was unavailable because of the scripts and the large number of characters in the East Asian languages. Encoded character sets had to be developed to facilitate natural language processing; these were used with Western products in the early stages of development. Although the conventions by which the characters are used in the three languages differ from each other, their fundamental characteristics are the same. In particular the Chinese character set is open-ended, i.e. new characters can emerge by government policy, by voluntary addition or by mistake. Thus it is impossible in theory to get a complete set of Chinese characters in each language.

In the last thirty years of the twentieth century, effort was devoted to establishing standard character codes and sets in three languages. During the 1970s, all three countries established national standards for a computer character set in one byte based on ASCII, and followed this with the development of national standards of domestic Chinese characters in two bytes. They are Japanese JIS C 6226 in 1978, Chinese GB 2312 in 1980, Chinese (Taipei) CNS 11643 in 1986 and Korean KS C 5601 in 1987. CCCII code created in Taiwan in 1980 became the East Asian Common Character (EACC) for the US Research Libraries Group (RLG) and others, and then became ANSI Z39.64: 1989.

In the computer industry, *de facto* standards are common practice. Big 5 was developed in Taiwan in 1984 for Chinese characters, and the Shift JIS code was developed for Japanese personal computers during the 1970s. Both standards are in widespread use.

The publication of the Unicode 1st edition in 1980 and UCS (Universal Character Set: ISO 10646) in 1993 had an impact on the computer industry, its customers and governments in East Asia, and indeed on worldwide users of Chinese characters and the East Asian languages. The three governments made tremendous efforts to harmonize the development of the Unicode, ISO/UCS and national standards for computer character sets. At the beginning of the twenty-first century, it seems that the technical harmonization has been achieved. The next step is the change over to the Unicode/UCS environment among users. It is estimated that a company-wide changeover of the character code in a big company would need investment in a scale of several million (US) dollars.

NATIONAL MARCS AND BIBLIOGRAPHIC UTILITIES

Developing the capacity of natural language processing in Chinese characters made it possible to create and maintain national bibliographic databases (MARC) in the national languages of East Asia. The standards are the China MARC, the Japan MARC and the KOR MARC. Housekeeping, technical processing and CIRCULATION SYSTEM control all started during the 1970s.

The National Diet Library (NDL), Tokyo, was founded in 1948 and is the national parliamentary library controlled by the legislature (www.ndl.go.jp/e/index.html). It started computerization of its operations in 1970. Prior to the publication of Japan MARC in 1981, a cataloguing system for Japanese materials (1977) and a printed weekly list of publications (1978) were implemented by NDL. The Japan MARC is UNIMARC compatible and covers 2.7 million catalogue records since 1864. The Web OPAC (see OPACS) of NDL holdings is a very popular website. The second NDL, the new Kansai-Kan, is due to be opened in 2002 in Nara near Osaka.

The National Library of China (known as The Beijing Library) was established in 1909; it now holds some 23 million items (www.nlc.gov.cn/english.htm). It started computer utilization in the middle of the 1980s and established the China MARC in 1990. China MARC format is IFLA UNIMARC compatible, and was established as a cultural professional standard (WH/T 0503–96) in 1996. The China MARC database covers 1.1 million bibliographic records of Chinese books published since 1979.

The National Library of Korea (NLK), Seoul, was established in 1945 and holds 4.1 million items (www.nl.go.kr/eng/index.php3). It started computerization of bibliographic services in 1976, backed by a government plan for computer applications for administration. KOR MARC printed-card distribution was started in 1983. The KOR MARC format is a national standard (KS X 6006–2), is USMARC compatible, covers 1.8 million bibliographic records and is operated on the KOLIS system (KOrean LIbrary System), based on the Windows system. NLK has run the Korean Library Information Network (KOLIS-NET) since 1991. The DIGITAL LIBRARY Programme was started in 1998 and holds 59 million pages of scanned images.

Bibliographic utilities were developed in the region during the 1980s and 1990s. They are NII/NACSIS (Japan) (www.nii.ac.jp/index.html), KERIS (Korea) (www.keris.or.kr/eng/eng.html) and CALIS (China) (www.calis.edu.cn). A common feature is that these three organizations were all established primarily for academia and maintained by government funds as not-for-profit organizations. In 1984, a shared cataloguing system was installed in Japan, which became NACSIS-CAT. It was designed as a RELATIONAL DATABASE system based on the entity-relationship model. As of 2001, 1,200 libraries in 900 universities among 1,200 higher-education institutions in Japan were participating in NACSIS-CAT, which now contains 6.1 million bibliographic records and 58.6 million records of holdings. NACSIS was transferred to the National Institute of Informatics (NII) in 2000. NACSIS/NII offers an online shared cataloguing system, and an interlibrary loan requests system, ELECTRONIC JOURNALS, scanned journal articles and OPACS.

In 1994, the Korea Research Information Centre was established by the Ministry of Education and transformed into the Korea Education and Research Information Services (KERIS) in 1999. The mission of KERIS is the development, management and provision of education and research information at the national level through (1) management of the Research Information Sharing Union, (2) management of the integrated retrieval system, (3) digital thesis collection and dissemination, (4) the development of a research information database, and (5) the management of the INTERLIBRARY LENDING system (L2L). In 2001, 155 university libraries were participating in the KERIS system with a total of 5.4 million bibliographic records.

In 1998, the China Academic Library and Information System (CALIS) was established with funding from the government; seventy university libraries participated, with core subject-centres at Beijing University, Tsinghua University, the China Agriculture University and the Beijing Medical University as well as seven regional subcentres covering the whole country. The mission of CALIS is shared cataloguing, interlibrary lending, DOCUMENT DELIVERY, document DIGITIZATION, providing an Internet portal (see PORTALS AND GATEWAYS), running an electronic-journal licensing consortium (see ELECTRONIC JOURNALS), and so on.

Bibliographic utilities in East Asia share common obstacles such as COPYRIGHT legislation and copyright clearance mechanisms for document delivery as well as multimedia database creation. Network governance has been a standing issue among organizations such as national libraries, national science and technology information centres, and academia. All of these institutions are affected by population structure, the price rise of publications in general and the price rise of online and printed journals in particular, licensing copyright clearance issues, professional education and training, and competence in developing new services.

Further reading

CALIS (2002) (www.calis.edu.cn/).

Gong, Y. and Gorman, G.E. (2000). *Libraries and Information Services in China*, Scarecrow Press.

Inoue, Y. (2000) 'People, libraries and the JLA committee on intellectual freedom in libraries', *IFLA Journal* 26: 293–7 [deals with a range of ethical and professional issues in relation to librarianship in Japan].

Lee, P. and Um, Y.A. (1994) *Libraries and Librarianship in Korea*, Greenwood Press.

National Diet Library (2002) (www.ndl.go.jp/e/index.html).

National Library of China (2002) (www. nlc.gov.cn/english.htm).

National Library of Korea (2002) (www.nl.go.kr/eng/index.php3).

Negeshi, M. (1999) 'Trend of electronic libraries in Japan, with emphasis on academic information services', *ICSTI Forum* 31 (www.icsti.org/icsti/forum/fo9907.html#negeshi) [a list of selected electronic library sites in Japan, including links].

NII [Japan] (2002) (www.nii.ac.jp/index.html).

Oshiro, Z. (2000) 'Cooperative programmes and networks in Japanese academic libraries', *Library Review* 49: 370–9.

EISUKE NAITO AND TAKASHI TOMIKUBO

ECCLESIASTICAL LIBRARIES

Libraries that are part of, or associated with, the Christian churches, and their institutions and activities.

The Middle Ages

Within seventy years of the death of Jesus Christ, the religion he founded was relying on the written word for its survival and transmission. The writing and copying of books was central to the Christian tradition, and hence great importance was attached to the storage and protection of collections of them. Collections of liturgical and other Christian texts are found in association with all the various traditions that developed in the Middle East, North Africa and Europe in the first four centuries of the Common Era. After the collapse of the Roman Empire in the West in the early fifth century CE, all institutional libraries were ecclesiastical for over 600 years. They were usually attached to cathedrals or monasteries and comprised collections of MANUSCRIPT books stored near to study areas or altars where they were used, rather than in library buildings. They contained standard works: the Bible and its commentaries, the works of the church fathers, lives of the saints and liturgies. Chronicles, canon law and other secular subjects were introduced gradually. In the early Middle Ages, books were produced in monastic scriptoria but after the founding of universities in the thirteenth century a lay BOOK TRADE emerged to supply their libraries.

From this time LITERACY and libraries were no longer monopolized by the Church, but ecclesiastical libraries continued to be of importance. The fifteenth century saw the founding of the Vatican Library by Pope Nicholas V, but lay libraries, particularly those of humanist scholars, also became increasingly common. The Reformation and the invention of printing produced an expansion of book ownership at all levels of society and a decline in the fortunes of traditional ecclesiastical libraries. In England the dissolution of the monasteries (*c.* 1540) brought about the dispersal of manuscript books from cathedrals and other religious houses. Cathedral libraries were re-established under Protestant deans and chapters but in a diminished form.

Early modern period

The seventeenth century saw an enormous expansion in ecclesiastical libraries despite religious wars on the Continent and civil war in Britain. In Catholic Europe the Society of Jesus was prominent in establishing libraries (as it was in the Asian and American colonies of Catholic powers, notably Spain), old-established abbeys renewed their collections and buildings, and two libraries were founded by cardinals, the Ambrosiana in Milan (1609) and the Mazarine in Paris (1643). In Britain, cathedral libraries, after suffering losses in the Civil War, were refunded with large donations of money and books from the higher clergy. Sir Christopher Wren was associated with the design of two new cathedral libraries, at Lincoln where a library was built between 1674 and 1676, and at St Paul's where a library in the upper west end was included in the rebuilt cathedral.

In 1610, Archbishop William Bancroft bequeathed his books to his successors at Lambeth Palace to form a public library, and a library was added to Sion College, a meeting place for London clergy, in 1630. Individuals also founded libraries in the seventeenth century that were either intended for the use of the clergy, or contained a high proportion of religious and theological literature, such as the library set up by Archbishop Thomas Tenison in St Martin-in-the-Fields, London. In Ireland the library of Trinity College, Dublin, had been enlarged in 1661 by the addition of Archbishop James Ussher's books and in 1701 Archbishop Narcissus Marsh founded what has been described as Ireland's first public library in Dublin.

Parish libraries

Parish churches since the late Middle Ages had begun to acquire small collections of books for the improvement of their parishioners; the texts were often chained to desks in churches. In the mid-sixteenth century the Reformation brought destruction of Roman Catholic books but also a series of injunctions ordering the placing of copies of the Bible, and other books, such as Erasmus's *Paraphrases* and John Foxe's *Martyrs*, in parish churches.

The late seventeenth century saw the

beginnings of the parochial library movement. Individuals often gave books, or money for books, to parishes for the use of either the incumbents or the parishioners, including that left to Grantham by Francis Trigge in 1589 and to Reigate by Andrew Cranston in 1701. The name of Thomas BRAY (1656–1730) is forever associated with the movement by the Society for Promoting Christian Knowledge to supply libraries to poor parishes. By the time of Bray's death about sixty-five 'Bray libraries' had been established.

A number of parish libraries were chained. Chaining had begun to be used in the later Middle Ages as a way of confining reference works and popular books to a library. Hereford and Wells cathedrals still have chained collections, but in most other libraries the chains were removed in the late seventeenth century, exceptions being the parochial library at Wimborne Minster (founded 1685) and All Saints church, Hereford (founded 1715).

In Scotland James Kirkwood instigated a similar campaign to that of Bray in 1704, when libraries were ordered to be placed in parishes throughout the Highlands. As in England individuals also gave book collections to parishes and, as in England, their content was mainly theological. A notable example was the Leighton Library of 1,300 volumes, given for the benefit of the clergy of Dunblane and opened in 1688. The Bray movement spread to the English colonies in North America, and similar drives towards the creation of libraries for clergy and laity can be found in the Protestant countries of Northern Europe, especially in Scandinavia.

Nineteenth and twentieth centuries

Parish libraries continued to be founded into the nineteenth century, but as literacy spread other subjects began to jostle with theology for popularity and the predominance of Anglican libraries was challenged. The Society of Friends had a library in the City of London from 1673 and the Baptists also, from 1708. The non-conformists were very keen to present sound and wholesome literature to a wide audience of readers and this could be found at the Unitarian library in the West End of London and the Methodist Library at Brunswick Chapel (founded 1808). Dr William's Library, set up in 1729 under the will of a Presbyterian minister Daniel Williams, has now gathered in a number of these non-conformist collections.

The twentieth century saw a decline in the fortunes of ecclesiastical libraries with historic and modern collections struggling for survival. There has been a trend towards amalgamation, for example the removal of parish libraries to larger repositories. Reading religious literature is not part of popular culture as in the past. Greater need for security, the use of information technology and shrinking funds are just three of the problems that now face ecclesiastical libraries at the beginning of the twenty-first century.

Further reading

Bloomfield, B.C. (1997) *A Directory of Rare Book and Special Collections in the United Kingdom*, 2nd edn, Library Association Publishing.

Ker, N.R. (1964) *Medieval Libraries of Great Britain*, 2nd edn, *Supplement* (1987), Royal Historical Society. [Various cathedrals have now produced histories with chapters on their libraries.]

Perkin, M. (forthcoming) *Directory of Parochial Libraries*, 2nd edn, Bibliographical Society.

SEE ALSO: monastic library

SHEILA HINGLEY

ECONOMICS OF INFORMATION

Information: definition, economic roles and economic properties

DEFINITION OF 'INFORMATION'

The economics of information will be considered within the following definition:

Information is that property of data that represents and measures effects of processing of them.

Processing includes data transfer, selection, structuring, reduction and conceptualization. For data transfer there is an accepted measure of the amount of information (the SHANNON or 'entropy' measure), but it is inappropriate for more complex processing in which value, economic or otherwise, is important (Arrow 1984: 138). Hayes (1993) has proposed measures for some of the other levels of processing.

In that definition, 'data' is taken as equivalent to physical 'recorded symbols', exemplified by printed characters; by binary characters in magnetic, punched or optical form; by spoken words; or by images. Whatever the physical form may be, it becomes a recorded symbol when it is interpreted as representing something.

It is therefore necessary to recognize both physical and symbolic aspects of both entities and processes. The following matrix (Table 2) illustrates with examples of economic contexts:

Table 2 Matrix of entity and process

Entities	Processes	
	Physical	*Symbolic*
	Agriculture	Data input
Physical	Manual labour	Data storage
	Personal services	Data output (e.g. reports)
	Sports	Intellectual games
Symbolic	Performance arts	Writing and composing
	Classroom lecturing	Programming and mathematics

This matrix will be used to summarize the macroeconomic structure of national economies in distributions of the workforce among types of industries and types of processes. It will also be used to summarize the micro-economic distribution of costs within industries.

Each of the two dimensions, though shown as a dichotomy, is a spectrum reflecting the relative importance of the two polar positions. For example, 'consumption' is a mix of physical and symbolic: one needs food to live, so it is a physical entity and consumption is a physical process, but one uses food to represent a lifestyle and both entity and process become symbolic – what Veblen (1899) called 'conspicuous consumption'. As one moves in economic development from subsistence through capital formation, to capital control, to social control, the role of capital shifts from physical to symbolic.

For the processing dimension, the spectrum is exemplified by the types of data processes. Data transfer is essentially physical, involving the movement of signals. Selection is a mixture of physical and conceptual, decisions being symbolic but selection itself being physical. Analysis

is symbolic and can remain so, though it is likely to be translated into physical realizations in display formats. Data reduction is almost purely symbolic, levels such as conceptualization even more so.

There can be transition from quadrant to quadrant in the matrix. An example is the transition of persons from manual labour into sports, and the conversion of what may have been simply physical effort into a game. As another example, concepts may be made real through artistic performance, and physical products may be derived from artistic performances.

ECONOMIC ROLES OF INFORMATION

The writings of the economists concerning information almost universally focus on its role in decision-making. (Some relevant references include Von Neumann and Morgenstern 1952; Arrow 1984; Laffont 1989; Philips 1988). But information clearly is important in operational management beyond use in decision-making. This role is supported by management information systems. Furthermore, information is a result of environmental scan to ensure that there is knowledge of external reality in decision-making.

Information can serve as a substitute for physical entities. 'TELECOMMUTING' replaces the movement of people with the transmission of data. Exploration through imaging replaces exploration through surgery.

Information is used to influence and persuade. Advertising serves buyers wanting to learn about products and vendors wanting to sell them. It subsidizes a wide range of information media.

Information is essential in education, serving the process of learning, supplementing interaction with teachers and providing (in books, media and DATABASES) much of the substance. It may be an educational objective in itself, since among things to be learned are the tools for access to and use of information.

Information is the substance of cultural enrichment, entertainment and amusement. People are willing to pay for it, which is the basis for the entertainment industries. In the matrix of Table 2, these are represented by 'writing and composing', 'sports' and 'performing arts'.

Information can be a product, a commodity – something produced as a package. And information can be a service. Indeed, the majority of 'business services' (the national economic account that includes consulting) are information based. Information can be a capital resource, especially for companies that produce information products and services. For them, databases are the means for producing copies for distribution, the source for derivative products and services, and the basis for developing new products and services. They are likely to be the major capital investment, more important than equipment or buildings.

GENERAL ECONOMIC PROPERTIES OF INFORMATION

Given its definition and roles, information is an economic entity with both costs and values, and people differ in their perceptions of the balance between the two. Beyond that, though, information has more specific properties of economic importance.

- While information is represented in physical form, that form can be changed without changing its content.
- In contrast to physical goods, intellectual goods can be created with limited physical resources, and frequently as a by-product of other operations. Information is easily and cheaply transported. The first copy represents most of the costs in creation, and reproduction costs are relatively small. As a result, it can be produced and distributed with minimal depletion of physical resources.
- There is an evident and direct relationship between physical goods and the materials used in producing them. One knows exactly how much steel is needed to produce a car. But there is no comparably direct relationship between any kind of good – physical or symbolic – and the information used in its production. The value of research, market information or advertising is uncertain, at best probabilistic, and much of the value is potential rather than actual.
- There is a complex relationship between the time of acquiring information and the value of it. For some, the value lies in immediacy – yesterday's stock information may be worthless tomorrow. For others, the value is likely to be received in the future rather than the present.
- Persons differ greatly in perceptions of the value of information, in kinds of use, in ability and willingness to use, in assessments of costs and in ability to pay. Typically the distribution of use of information is highly skewed, with small percentages of users frequent in their use

and the great majority infrequent.

- Use of information is affected by the distance users must travel to get access to it. The theory states that the use of any facility decays as the distance increases, as a function of the cost of travel; if the cost is linear, the decay is exponential and if the cost is logarithmic, it is quadratic. This theory applies to information resources (Hayes and Palmer 1983).
- An accumulation of information has more value than the sum of the individual values because it increases the combinations that can be made. The information and communication technologies (see INFORMATION AND COMMUNICATION TECHNOLOGY) have greatly increased the ability to make combinations. The number of databases, their size, the means for processing and relating them, the ability to use them – all are growing exponentially.
- There are immense economies of scale. Combined with the value in accumulation, this provides strong incentives for sharing information, especially since, once available, it can be distributed cheaply, which makes sharing easy.
- Information is not consumed by being used or transmitted to others. It can be resold or given away with no diminution of its content. Many persons may possess and use the same information, even at the same time, without diminishing its value to others. All these imply that information is a public good.
- However, there is the need to invest in the creation, production and distribution of information and that implies a wish to recover the investment. Furthermore, there may be value associated with exclusivity in knowledge, so there must be an incentive to make it available to others. This implies that information is a private good.
- Most information products and services lie somewhere between pure private goods and pure public goods, and the same information may alternate as a public and private good at different stages of information processing and distribution.
- Given that mixture of public and private good, private rights must be balanced with the rights to use the information. COPYRIGHT is one means of doing so, and the copyright clause of the Constitution of the USA embodies this balance: 'The Congress shall have the power...to promote the progress of science and the useful arts by securing for limited

times to authors and inventors the exclusive rights to their respective writings and discoveries' – progress implying use and rights implying protection.

The macroeconomics of information

BACKGROUND

In *The Information Economy* (1977), PORAT added an 'information' sector to the usual three sectors of national economies – agriculture, industry and services. As a basis for economic assessment, Table 3 provides a comparison of the distribution of workforce among sectors (the 'information sector' and the other three combined as 'non-information sectors') and functions for economies at three levels of development (Hayes 1992).

In 1998, the percentage of the US workforce employed in the information industries was about 32 per cent, much greater than 22 per cent in 1990 and the 20 per cent shown in Table 3 for 1980, so there has been a substantial increase in information even in the economy of the USA.

Within the information sector, information functions can be classified into four groups: management functions, support functions (primarily clerical in nature), equipment functions (hardware and software), and substantive functions (involved in the production and distribution of information). Information industries can be classified into four categories (see Table 4):

NATIONAL POLICY PLANNING

Nations and corporations can gain economic

Table 3 Illustrative levels of development for information economies

Full-scale development, representing economies like that in the USA in the 1980s			
	Category of function		
Category of industry	*Non-information functions*	*Information functions*	*Organization total*
Non-information sectors	50%	30%	80%
Information sector	6%	14%	20%

Substantial development, representing most other industrialized economies			
	Category of function		
Category of industry	*Non-information functions*	*Information functions*	*Organization total*
Non-information sectors	60%	25%	85%
Information sector	6%	9%	15%

Limited development, representing most peasant-based economies			
	Category of function		
Category of industry	*Non-information functions*	*Information functions*	*Organization total*
Non-information sectors	80%	14%	94%
Information sector	3%	3%	6%

Table 4 Categories of organizations in the information sector of the economy

Categories	Examples
Information production	Research and development Authoring and composing
Information distribution	Publishing and libraries Television and movies
Information transactions	Telecommunication Banking and brokerage
Information equipment	Computer hardware and software Telecommunications

values from an information-based economy, but balancing them are barriers (see below):

Values from use of information

- Better workforce, better trained and more capable of dealing with problems.
- Better product planning and marketing, based on more knowledge about consumer needs.
- Better engineering, based on availability and use of scientific and technical information.
- Better economic data, leading to improved investment decisions and allocation of resources.
- Better management from improved communication and decision-making.

Barriers to use of information

- Costs are incurred in acquiring information.
- It is likely that the return is over the long term, while the expenditure is made immediately.
- Except for the information industries themselves, information is not directly productive.
- Rarely are results clearly attributable to the information on which they were based.
- Accounting practice treats information as an 'overhead' expense, subject to cost-cutting.

The barriers can deter companies from making investments in information resources. That does create opportunities for information entrepreneurs, but there will be risks for them. On balance, the benefits would seem to outweigh the barriers, so macroeconomic policies should try to alleviate the barriers to information development, encourage information entrepreneurs, assure that information resources are available when needed and prepare managers to use information. The implications for national policy planning are shown below.

National policy implications

General economic policies

- Encourage entrepreneurship.
- Shift from low technology to high technology.
- Shift from production of physical goods to information goods.

Develop the 'information economy'

- Encourage effective use of information in business.
- Provide incentives for information industries.
- Develop information skills.

Management of information enterprises

- Establish technical information skills
- Develop information support staff skills

The micro-economics of information

INCOME TO THE PROVIDERS OF INFORMATION PRODUCTS AND SERVICES

The revenues for the information industries in the USA in 1990 and 1998, as percentages of gross national product and absolute dollars, are shown in Tables 5 and 6 (*Statistical Abstract of the United States* 1993, 2000):

Of special importance is the steady year by year increase, for the past decade, in expenditures for 'Business Services', reflecting growing use of information in the economy.

THE COSTS OF INFORMATION

Costs occur in the following stages of information production and distribution:

1 Information must be created, by generation and processing of data; these are authoring functions.
2 It must be assessed for publishability; these are editorial functions.
3 It must be processed for the generation of a master; these are composition functions.
4 Products and/or services will be produced.
5 The products and services will be marketed.
6 They will be distributed. The stages exemplify the schematic used in the definition of information (see Table 7)

Table 5 US distribution of revenues in percentages of GNP and absolute dollars I

Information industries	US data for 1990		US data for 1998	
Transaction industries	4.9%	$274 billion	7.1%	$629 billion
Hardware and software industries	3.4%	190 billion	7.6%	665 billion
Production and distribution industries	14.0%	783 billion	17.7%	1,545 billion
Total for information industries	22.3%	1,147 billion	32.4%	2,839 billion
Gross National Product	100.0%	$5,600 billion	100.0%	$8,750 billion

Table 6 US distribution of revenues in percentages of GNP and absolute dollars II

Details of production and distribution	1990		1998	
Book publishing	0.3%	$15 billion	0.3%	$29 billion
Journal publishing	0.3%	15 billion	0.3%	30 billion
Entertainment	3.2%	180 billion	3.8%	330 billion
Formal education	7.0%	392 billion	6.9%	601 billion
University research and development	0.4%	21 billion	0.3%	27 billion
Business services	2.9%	160 billion	6.0%	528 billion
Total	14.1%	$783 billion	17.6%	$1,545 billion

The costs for authoring, editorial and composition will be treated as capital investments; those for production, marketing and distribution as delivery costs. In practice, the costs of authoring usually are borne by authors, compensated for by royalties and thus part of the costs of sales for the publishers

Today, three forms of distribution need to be recognized: (1) printed and film, (2) magnetic tapes (VHS-VCR) and OPTICAL DISKS (CD-ROM and DVD), and (3) electronic. For the first two, distribution is by a combination of wholesale distributors, retail outlets and libraries. For electronic, by television (broadcast, cable and satellite) and the Internet.

Table 7 Information production and distribution processes

Entities	Processes	
	Physical	*Symbolic*
Physical	Production Distribution	Marketing
Symbolic	Composition	Creation Editorial

Table 8 provides a qualitative summary of the relative importance of each form of distribution for several types of information. In that summary, 'primary' means that the form is the initial means for distribution, the major source of income and the basis for recovering most if not all of the capital investment; 'secondary' means the form is a significant alternative means for distribution; 'tertiary' means that the form is speculative, with income still too small to be significant; blank means the form is of no substantial significance. The assessment for books with respect to non-print distribution and for scholarly journals with respect to CD-ROM distribution may be too pessimistic, but the facts are that the current income from them is minuscule.

For distributors and retail outlets, capital investments are primarily in physical plant, though there will be some in inventory. Those for libraries are in physical buildings and equipment, but most significantly in their collections and associated technical processing. Delivery costs for distributors, retail outlets and libraries are largely for staff. (For all retail establishments in 1997, capital expenditures represented about 20 per cent of total costs, and staff 80 per cent.)

Table 8 Importance of forms of distribution

	Forms of distribution		
Types of information	*Printed/film*	*Magnetic/optical*	*Television/Internet*
Books	Primary	Tertiary	Tertiary
Scholarly journals	Primary	Tertiary	Secondary
Software		Primary	Secondary
Databases		Secondary	Primary
Motion pictures	Primary	Secondary	Secondary
Television		Secondary	Primary

For the Internet, capital investments are in hardware and software for processing and communication. Delivery costs are for staff and communication access charges. Unfortunately, any estimates for Internet costs are uncertain. First, costs occur at several points – communication services, network backbones, domain servers, INTERNET SERVICE PROVIDERS and user facilities. The costs for network access are largely independent of actual use, being connection charges related to bandwidth and reflecting anticipated demand. Second, the rate of growth of the Internet is so rapid that data on one component of operations, reported at one point in time, cannot be compared with data for another component, reported at another point in time. Third, there are mixtures of funding – public, institutional, advertising and individual users – and many of the costs are subsidized, buried in other accounting categories.

Complicating the assessment of Internet costs is the fact that many of them are borne by the users instead of by the producers and/or distributors. The costs of local storage and printing are borne by the user, and they are not negligible. Users spend time in accessing, downloading and managing the digital files.

Despite those difficulties, one analysis (Hayes 1999) estimated that the yearly delivery costs for access to a DIGITAL LIBRARY on the Internet would be distributed 25 per cent for communication, 50 per cent for staff and 25 per cent for amortization of equipment.

THE MICRO-ECONOMICS OF BOOK PUBLISHING

The text of a book is usually the creation of an author. The return on that investment is usually derived from royalties, typically 10 per cent of the list price of the book. For scholarly and professional books, there usually is no royalty. Less than 1 per cent of authors actually get published and only half of those are really successful (Hartwick 1984).

Estimates can be made of the costs for print-form distribution. Table 9 simplifies and generalizes from data reported by Dessauer (1981), Bingley (1966) and Machlup (1962), showing costs of print-form distribution as percentages of list price. Data are not available to make comparable estimates for CD-ROM or Internet distribution, and sales of 'electronic books' are still minuscule (Streitfeld 2001).

Table 9 Costs of print-form distribution as percentages

Royalties	10%
Capital costs	30%
Editorial	5%
Composition	25%
Delivery costs	30%
Production	14%
Distribution	16%
Discount	30%

Editorial functions include locating and encouraging authors, working with them in creating suitable manuscripts and assessing the value, marketability and suitability for production. The functions in production management include copy-editing, formatting and organizing the content, and managing composition or transition to the production master. To these must be added overhead and general administrative costs covering the wide range of corporate costs–benefits, space, supplies, etc.

The functions in production are those necessary for a marketable, distributable product – printed, bound and warehoused. Books must be marketed and distributed. In practice, these functions are shared between the publisher and the seller or distributor, with the former primarily responsible for promotion and the latter for selling. The costs for the seller or distributor are covered through a discount, typically in the order of 30 per cent of the list price.

Of these, the operating expenses and composition (30 per cent of the total) are here treated as capital investments; those for production and distribution (again, 30 per cent of the total), as costs for delivery.

THE MICRO-ECONOMICS OF SCHOLARLY JOURNAL PUBLISHING

A typical research faculty member spends between 20 and 50 per cent of the year in research; beyond that personal time, funded by academic salary, there may well be added costs funded by grants or contracts. The outcome averages two or three published research articles per year, each of perhaps twenty pages. For research faculty the rewards for such creativity are rarely, if ever, derived from income from the publication itself; instead, they come from academic advancement, tenure and scholarly reputation.

Again, estimates can be made of the costs for print-form distribution, but data are not available to make comparable estimates for CD-ROM or Internet distribution. Table 10 summarizes and simplifies detailed estimates of functional costs (see King and Tenopir 1998).

Table 10 Estimates of functional costs as percentages

Capital costs	61%
Editorial	32%
Composition	29%
Delivery costs	39%
Production	26%
Distribution	13%

Note that the composition costs are substantially greater than for books, reflecting the more complex nature of scholarly journal publication. The costs for editorial work, composition, graphics and G&A will be taken as capital costs; all others, as delivery costs. Note that there are no costs for royalties (since few scholarly journals pay the authors) or for discounts to distributors (since subscriptions are handled by the publishers).

THE MICRO-ECONOMICS OF DATABASES AND DIGITAL LIBRARIES

Databases and digital libraries include digitized text, numerical data files, images, reference databases and bibliographic catalogues. They have become, through the Internet, a widespread means of electronic publication. There are no data on which to estimate the distribution of costs between capital and delivery functions.

Beyond the costs of the producer and distributor, there will be costs incurred by the users or by information intermediaries – reference librarians, INFORMATION BROKERS or information entrepreneurs. In King et al. (1983), the staff time for an average search was estimated at about fifty minutes; at a professional salary of $15 per hour plus overhead at 100 per cent of direct costs, that would be a cost of $25. The estimated direct costs of searching a reference database are shown in Table 11.

The royalties represent the payment to the database producer to cover their capital investment and costs in storage and delivery; the other costs, including that for the intermediary, at $25, are for delivery.

THE MICRO-ECONOMICS OF MOVIES AND TELEVISION

The creation of a motion picture is a complex interaction among producers, directors, writers, actors, cameramen, set designers and crew. The costs are huge – multimillion-dollar budgets in the case of movies, hundreds of thousands for a television programme, tens of thousands for an episode in a television series. The tangible results are a master negative or magnetic tape. From that master come the distribution copies for

Table 11 Estimated direct costs of searching a reference database

1985	Royalties	$38	Computer	$35	Telecom	$5
1978	Royalties	$20	Computer	$50	Telecom	$10

presentation in theatres and on the television screen.

Vogel provides pictures of the distribution of costs at break-even (see Table 12).

Table 12 Distribution of costs at break-even

	Motion picture	Television
Production costs	20%	40%
Distribution costs	80%	60%

Source: Vogel (1986: 101–25)

THE VALUES OF INFORMATION IN USE

Value of information to individuals

The value of cultural enrichment, entertainment and amusement as uses of information is demonstrated by the willingness of people to pay for them. Motion pictures, television, theatre and the arts, sports – these are all major, multibillion-dollar industries, supported both by consumers of them and by advertisers.

As shown in Table 13, Vogel (1986: 11) estimates time and expenditures by adults in 1981 in selected leisure activities. They represent over half of the waking time of a person and nearly 3 per cent of the Gross National Product (GNP). By any measure, that is a substantial commitment of time and resources!

The other major individual use of information

Table 13 Time and expenditures by adults in 1981 in selected leisure activities

	Hours per person/year	Expenditures ($ millions)
Television	1,511	$21,600
Radio	1,196	5,900
Newspapers	200	19,500
Records and tapes	190	6,900
Magazines	135	9,000
Leisure books	70	4,100
Movies	11	3,000
Spectator sports	10	2,300
Cultural events	4	1,300
Miscellaneous	25	7,500
Total	3,352	$81,100

Source: Vogel (1986: 11)

is for education and personal development. *Statistical Abstract of the United States* reported in 2000 that the total expenditure in 1998 for formal education, both public and private at all levels, was $601 billion. Thus, expenditures for formal education represent about 7 per cent of the GNP.

Beyond that are those for industrial training. A study by the Research Institute of America reported that more than $30 billion was spent in 1986 (about 0.7 per cent of the GNP) for formal employee training but that an additional $180 billion was spent for on-the-job training. *Fortune* (1993: 62–64) uses the figure of $30 billion as the magnitude of formal industrial training programmes in 1993. The American Society for Training and Development (ASTD 1999) reported that expenditures for formal employee training in 1995 were $55.3 billion (again about 0.7 per cent of the GNP). Consistently for the past decade, hours for informal on-the-job training have been from two to three times that for formal training (*Statistical Abstract* 2000).

Value of information services to professionals

It has been estimated that professionals spend nearly 60 per cent of their time communicating and working with information (Carroll and King 1985). They incur costs in obtaining information and in using it, but it has been estimated that the direct benefits to them are as much as ten times those costs. More important than direct benefits, though, are increases in productivity measured by results produced (reports, management publications, research plans and proposals, presentations, consultations and substantive advice).

Value of information in commerce and industry

Business and commerce need information in support of operational management, business planning and decision-making. Information is essential for product development, marketing, financial management and manufacturing operations.

In view of the importance of information to business, a business plan should identify the role of information in support of the business objectives, so that any potential investor can assess the extent to which it has been recognized. Information is important for support of product research and development, for access to finance, for marketing, for knowledge of government regulations, for use of industry standards and for management of personnel. The returns to profitability from investment in information are real and large (Hayes and Erickson 1982).

References

Arrow, K.J. (1984) *The Economics of Information*, Cambridge, MA: Harvard University Press (vol. 4 of *The Collected Papers of Kenneth J. Arrow*).

ASTD (1999) *American Society for Training and Development: State of the Industry Report*, Arlington, VA: American Society for Training and Development.

Bingley, C. (1966) *Book Publishing Practice*, London: Crosby, Lockwood & Son.

Carroll, B. and King, D.W. (1985) 'Value of information', *Drexel Library Quarterly* 21 (summer): 39–60.

Dessauer, J.P. (1981) *Book Publishing: What it Is, What it Does*, New York: R.R. Bowker.

Fortune (1993) 127(6) (22 March): 62–4.

Hartwick, J.M. (1984) *Aspects of the Economics of Book Publishing*, Ontario: Queens University, Institute for Economic Research.

Hayes, R.M. (1999) *Economics of Digital Libraries* (http://www.ime.usp.br/~cesar/simposio99/hayes.htm).

—— (1993) 'Measurement of information and communication: A set of definitions', *Information and Behaviour* 4: 81–103.

—— (1992) 'A simplified model for the fine structure of national information economies', in *Proceedings of the NIT '92 Conference*, Hong Kong, 30 November–2 December 1992.

Hayes, R.M. and Erickson, T. (1982) 'Added value as a function of purchases of information services', *The Information Society* 1(4) (December): 307–38.

Hayes, R.M. and Palmer, S. (1983) 'The effects of distance upon use of libraries: Case studies based on a survey of users of the Los Angeles Public Library, Central Library and branches', *Library and Information Science Research* 5(1): 67–100.

King, W. *et al.* (1983) *Key Papers in the Economics of Information*, White Plains, NY: Knowledge Industry Publications.

King, D.W. and Tenopir, C. (1998) 'Economic cost models of scientific scholarly journals', ICSU Press Workshop, Keble College, Oxford, UK, 1998 (http://www.bodley.ox.ac.uk/icsu/kingppr.htm).

Laffont, J.J. (1989) *The Economics of Uncertainty and Information*, Cambridge, MA: MIT Press.

Machlup, F. (1962) *The Production and Distribution of Knowledge in the United States*, Princeton, NJ: Princeton University Press.

Philips, L. (1988) *The Economics of Imperfect Information*, New York: Cambridge University Press.

Porat, M.U. (1977) *The Information Economy: Definition and Measurement*, Washington, DC: US Department of Commerce, Office of Telecommunications.

Statistical Abstract of the United States (1993, 2000) US Department of Commerce.

Streitfeld, David (2001). 'E-book saga is full of woe – and a bit of intrigue', *Los Angeles Times*, 6 August 2001.

Veblen, O. (1899) *The Theory of the Leisure Class*, Chicago: Macmillan.

Vogel, H.L. (1986) *Entertainment Industry Economics*, New York: Cambridge University Press.

Von Neumann, J. and Morgenstern, O. (1952) *Theory of Games and Economic Behaviour*, Princeton, NJ: Princeton University Press.

Further reading

Bowker Annual of Library and Book Trade Information (1988), New York: R.R. Bowker Company.

Burns, C. (1986) *The Economics of Information*, Washington, DC: Office of Technology Assessment, US Congress.

Bysouth, P. (ed.) (1987) *The Economics of Online*, London: Taylor Graham, Institute of Information Scientists.

Dizard, W.P. (1985) *The Coming Information Age: An Overview of Technology, Economics and Politics*, 2nd edn, New York: Longman.

Egan, B.L. (1991) *Information Superhighways: The Economics of Advanced Public Communication Networks*, Boston: Artech House.

Galatin, M. and Leiter, R.D. (eds) (1981) *Economics of Information*, Boston: Nijhoff.

Hayes, R.M. (2001) *Models for Library Management, Decision-Making, and Planning*, New York: Academic Press.

Kingma, Bruce R. (2000) *Economics of Information: A Guide to Economic and Cost-Benefit Analysis for Information Professionals*, 2nd edn. Englewood, CO: Libraries Unlimited

McCall, J. (ed.) (1982) *The Economics of Information and Uncertainty*, Chicago: University of Chicago Press.

Machlup, F. and Leeson, K. (1978) *Information through the Printed Word: The Dissemination of Scholarly, Scientific and Intellectual Knowledge*, New York: Praeger.

Martyn, J. (1983) *The Economics of Information*, London: British Library.

Parker, M.M. (1988) *Information Economics: Linking Business Performance to Information Technology*, Englewood Cliffs, NJ: Prentice Hall.

Rubin, M.R. (1983a) *Information Economics and Policy in the United States*, Denver: Libraries Unlimited.

—— (1983b) *The Information Economy*, Denver: Libraries Unlimited.

Rubin, M.R. and Huber, M.T. (1986) *The Knowledge Industry in the United States*, Princeton, NJ: Princeton University Press.

Shapiro, Carl and Varian, Hal R. (1999) *Information Rules*, Boston, MA: Harvard Business School Press.

Wolpert, S.A. (1986) *Economics of Information*, New York: Van Nostrand Reinhold.

SEE ALSO: book trade; communication; consultancy; cultural industries; information; information management; information professions; information society; intellectual property; knowledge industries; mass media; scholarly communication; transfer of technology

ROBERT M. HAYES

ELECTROCOPYING

Copying of a print or other work from hard-copy form to a machine-readable form, and to another machine-readable form or back to hard copy as required. A list of forms that electrocopying might take, includes:

- Re-keying for electronic storage.
- Optical scanning.
- Transmission from one computer to another (via a network or by datacasting).
- Computer printout.
- Transmission by fax to a computer.

Electrocopying offers flexibility of format, improved access potential and opportunities for rights owners to develop new sources of revenue. At the same time it has been widely seen as creating threats to rights owners who can become less able to control distribution of their works, and can consequently suffer loss of revenue and damage to the integrity of the material.

Further reading

Barrow, E. (1998) 'Digitisation: issues and solutions', *Learned Publishing* 11: 259–263.
Cornish, G. 'Electrocopying' (http://www.niss.ac.uk/education/hefc/follett/wp/).

SEE ALSO: digitization

ELECTRONIC BOOKS

The result of integrating classical BOOK structure, or rather the familiar concept of a book, with features that can be provided within an electronic environment is referred to as an electronic book (or e-book), which is intended as an interactive DOCUMENT that can be composed and read on a computer. From the conceptual side, it is an attempt to overcome the limitations of paper books by adding a series of useful features that are made possible through the nature of an electronic environment. The main features of electronic books are that they are dynamic, reactive and can be made available in different formats and/or editions in a short time. For this reason the translation from paper to electronic environment is not appropriate for every type of publication and for every type of reader: the process of reading and the tasks readers are attempting to complete have a central role in judging the suitability of this translation. In any case the cognitive overhead that results from the special environment chosen (i.e. the computer) represents a valid reason for carefully considering the appropriateness and the method of realizing this conversion. The fact that technology is able to represent documents on the screen is not a sufficient reason for translating every piece of paper into electronic format.

It is important to define different kinds of use corresponding to different types of document. These range from ancient manuscripts to modern examples of hyperliterature.

Examples of electronic books

A conceptual distinction can be made between electronic books that implement the book metaphor in different ways. It is possible to delineate a hierarchy starting from those that imitate the paper book in all its physical components to the so-called cyberbooks that do not have anything in common with the paper book apart from being a tool to present information to readers. Among the book imitators it is useful to identify additional subclasses each of which focuses on a different aspect of the book metaphor and gives greater or lesser emphasis to the features inherited from the paper book.

This classification covers the following classes:

- Page turners.
- Scrolling books.
- Portable books.
- Multimedia books.
- Hypermedia books.
- Cyberbooks.

PAGE TURNERS

Page turner books can be divided into those that imitate the original paper book, and those that have no paper counterpart and imitate the general idea of a book, i.e. the book metaphor. Among those which have a paper counterpart there are different levels of closeness, from those that maintain all the visual features of the original book by using a picture of the original pages, to those that use a graphic template to imitate the original book but do not allow the reader to interact with it in the same way as a paper book. An interesting example of a page turner book is the Mercury project. It is based on the idea of a full-text electronic library (Arms and Michalak 1990) and has been developed at Carnegie Mellon University. The project aims were to demonstrate that current technology (high-speed networks, high-resolution screens, multimedia facilities), and the techniques for processing electronic documents, make it possible to build such libraries. Mercury is also evaluating a number of different approaches for acquiring and storing documents (e.g. scanning documents and saving them as images or capturing documents in machine-readable format). Very similar to the Mercury project is CORE (Chemistry Online Retrieval Experiment) (Lesk 1991), which has produced a prototype for the storage, searching and displaying of primary scientific journal data in electronic form together with related graphical information such as tables, graphics, etc. *The Visual Book* (Landoni 1997) represents a particular interpretation of the electronic book, based mainly on the visual aspects of the real book, its physical features, such as dimensions, thickness, page form and general design style.

SCROLLING BOOKS

Scrolling books are ones where text is presented according to a scroll metaphor.

This was the classic way to write text on parchment and in modern times this metaphor is very close to that used in word processor environments. This strategy lets the designer determine the page size based on the space available and dimension of the screen. The page, as a logical and physical unit, no longer exists, nor does any reference to page numbers or to the page sequence. The text scrolls almost without any physical limitation. As a result the electronic scrolling book is portable on different platforms and does not have any dependency on screen dimension. However, readers lose one of the classical and fundamental keys to accessing information in a book, the page number, and they can easily get lost in the flow of information. The book metaphor is kept in its logical structure. The information is presented according to a book-style hierarchy, made of chapters, subchapters, paragraphs and sections. Another important observation is that information in this class of electronic book is made of text and graphics, even if there may be some hypertextual features such as the presence of links to browse the electronic book. This is still a very traditional way of interpreting the concept of a book in electronic terms and for this reason it is closely related to the paper book. Examples of scrolling books with more sophisticated hypertextual interfaces are Dynabook and Superbook (Egan *et al*. 1991). Both of these provide full-text indexing, links, navigation and orientation through a dynamic table of contents and a multiwindow text display. An interesting aspect of these two systems is the fact that they provide the capability for automatically importing text that is available electronically in different formats. The HyperTextBook (Crestani and Melucci 1998) is a good example of a well-targeted experiment in creating electronic books with particular attention to the book structure. A further step in the development of successful scrolling books is represented by the WEB Book project (Wilson 1999), where the same textbook used in Crestani and Melucci's experiment was redesigned by following an adaptation of Morkes and Nielsen's guidelines in order to maximize its overall usability.

PORTABLE BOOKS

Portable books are becoming more and more common, as appropriate technology has developed. They imitate the book as a portable tool for providing information. A side problem is that they have to deal with limitations in screen size and resolution and efficiency, but these are all technological rather than conceptual aspects. Portable books are divided into hardware and software applications. Hardware devices are usually in the shape of slates; to use a metaphor borrowed from the history of writing, they tend to be light and simple to interact with, and provide high resolution and possibly colours to make reading a pleasant enough experience. The idea is that they provide a tool for reading – the container – where users can visualize and read any sort of content in the appropriate format.

The software applications, also known as e-book readers, provide extra functionalities such as annotations, bookmarks, different fonts and colours to help users in their reading/scanning process. They can sit on a number of different platforms ranging from desktop computer to palmtops (hand-held devices) as well as on specific hardware for portable e-books.

The area of portable electronic books has received a boost in 2001 from the interest showed by Microsoft. A series of brand new products has just hit the market.

These all share the same philosophy and could

be better named *portable electronic book readers*. E-books have to be light, provide high resolution, support basic functionalities (bookmarks and search), allow a certain level of customization, conform to reasonable standards and possibly take advantage of the Web phenomenon. There are no assumptions on the kind of audience, nor on the usage of the e-books available to read through these e-books viewers.

MULTIMEDIA BOOKS

Multimedia books represent a further step away from the paper book. The contents of such books are no longer simply electronic text or pictures but a mixture of different contributions such as video, sound, animation, text and pictures. It is no longer possible to keep this sort of enriched form of information inside the physical border of a classical book. That is why the electronic environment is the natural one for this class of book. They still borrow essential features from the book metaphor by either imitating its physical appearance or keeping the same logical structure. The metaphor is enlarged to consider this new form of information as generic book contents and to organize it in the new book container according to new needs and presentation paradigms (Barker *et al.* 1994; Barker 1996).

HYPERMEDIA BOOKS

HYPERMEDIA books present textual material and integrate it with other related sources, such as video, sounds and pictures, and provide the reader with alternative reading/browsing paths. The resulting book is an augmented version of the original. Hypermedia books inherit all the problems related to the use of HYPERTEXT and hypermedia, such as orientation problems and the risk of confusing users with too much information. A rich subset of hypermedia books are those, now ever more common, which are available on the World Wide Web. Another group of electronic books that are widely available are those on tape where actors read for the reader/listener pieces from classical literature.

CYBERBOOKS

Cyberbooks are completely free from any physical/conceptual dependence on the paper book, as they have only appeared in electronic form. In this context the term book is used in its broadest sense as a repository for information. On the other hand they depend very much on the dynamic nature of their context, the computer. In this sense they can be defined as active books with which readers can interact. They are part of an alternative new line in modern literature, called post-modern literature, which closely integrates computer culture with the classical human one.

From paper to electronic books

After this brief survey on existing examples of electronic books it is time to introduce some considerations on one of the crucial issues related to their production, that is how to define if a publication is suitable for electronic translation, on the assumption that not all of them are. An electronic environment allows changes and updating of original information, provides different views/readings of the same document, integrates multimedia sources of information, permits interchange of data and offers software support online. All these facilities, while being useful for some types of publication, are not appropriate for every kind of book; different kinds of reading requirements make electronic translation more or less useful for the reader. In particular, books that are commonly read in their entirety and in a linear way are not as suited to electronic translation.

On the other hand, publications that are consulted rather then read, such as reference books, suggest a different kind of reading that is geared to problem-solving, and are more suited to electronic support. The reader of these types of publication is more involved in using their contents than in simply reading them. The electronic support plays an important and meaningful role by offering the user more facilities; the crucial issue is to choose which are the most relevant and how to include them in the electronic-book design.

Before translating existing paper books from paper to electronic form the designer should consider whether the user will prefer it to the paper version containing the same information; this can happen in the following situations:

- If its paper version does not completely satisfy the reader.
- If there is no paper version and the electronic version can solve problems of dissemination.
- If reading from the screen is not a problem, i.e.

the book is going to be 'used'.
- If the electronic environment is easily available to the user.

Future developments

There is already a great number of electronic books available on the market or in prototype but still it is not clear why and for whom they have been created.

Electronic books should be produced only when they can provide added value to the paper counterpart. A well-founded initial *choice* is crucial for future electronic books. After the decision to produce an electronic book has been made, particular attention has to be paid to *representation*, by following the example of the traditional PUBLISHING process that has focused on the improvement of the typographical techniques in order to get a better presentation for information. And finally additional functionalities have to be provided so that electronic books can exploit better the potentiality of their electronic media. In this way electronic books will turn into *enhanced* versions of paper books, not just empty book-similes.

Electronic books can undoubtedly share the same space and even the same audience of paper books as long as they are properly designed and implemented. As Jay Bolter (1991) wrote, 'Printed books could remain abundant or even super abundant, as they are now, and will lose their status as the defining form of symbolic communication.'

References

Arms, W.Y. and Michalak, T.J. (1990).'Carnegie Mellon University', in C. Arms (ed.) *Strategies for Libraries and Electronic Information*, Bedford, MA: Digital Press.

Barker, P. (1996) 'Living books and dynamic electronic libraries', *The Electronic Library* 14: 491–501.

Barker, P., Richardson, S. and Benest, I.D. (1994) 'Human–computer interface design for electronic books', in D.I. Raitt and B. Jeapes (eds) *Proceedings of the Online Information 94, 16th International Online Information Meeting, London 6–8 December*, Oxford: Learned Information, pp. 213–92.

Bolter, J.D. (1991) *Writing Space: The Computer, Hypertext, and the Mediation of Print*, Lawrence Earl-baum Associates.

Crestani, F. and Melucci M. (1998) 'A case study of automatic authoring: From a textbook to a hyper-textbook', *Data and Knowledge Engineering* 27: 1–30.

Egan, D.E., Lesk, M.E., Ketchum, R.D., Lochbaum, C.C., Remde, J.R., Littman, M. and Landauer T.K. (1991) 'Hypertext for the electronic library? CORE sample results', in *Proceedings of Hypertext '91, San Antonio*, New York: ACM Press, pp. 299–312.

Landoni, M. (1997) 'The visual book system: A study of the use of visual rhetoric in the design of electronic books', PhD thesis, Glasgow: Department of Information Science of the University of Strathclyde.

Lesk, M. (1991) 'The CORE electronic chemistry library', in A. Bookstein, Y. Chiaramella, G. Salton and V.V. Raghavan (eds) *Proceedings of the 14th Annual International ACM/SIGIR Conference on Research and Development in Information Retrieval (SIGIR91)*, New York: ACM Press, pp. 93–113.

Wilson, R. (1999) *The Importance of Appearance in the Design of WEB books*, Glasgow: Department of Information Science of the University of Strathclyde (MSc dissertation).

SEE ALSO: digital library; Human–Computer Interaction; information and communication technology

MONICA LANDONI

ELECTRONIC DATA INTERCHANGE

Electronic data interchange (EDI) is a method for conducting business transactions across networks, with the exchange of invoices, orders and other documentation carried out in a standardized manner between the computers of trading companies. A major objective is, by standardizing and simplifying, to shorten the time between ordering and delivery. There are now tens of thousands of companies using EDI throughout the world. The European Union supported its expansion in the mid-1990s through a number of cross-border pilot projects, designed to show that it can benefit both small and large businesses. EDI is a critical tool for E-COMMERCE, not least in the book trade and hence in the process of library supply.

Further reading

Harris, R. and Sillman, M. (1996) *Electronic Data Interchange: Implementation Guide*, HMSO.

ELECTRONIC DOCUMENT DELIVERY

Electronic document delivery (EDD) is the transfer of information from publisher or library to user by electronic means. EDD can be used as a tool for a DOCUMENT DELIVERY system.

Further reading

Morris, A., Woodfield, J. and Davies, J.E. (1999) 'Experimental evaluation of selected electronic document delivery systems', *Journal of Librarianship and Information Science* 31: 139–44.

ELECTRONIC FUNDS TRANSFER

The transmission of electronic messages recording financial transactions directly from the computer of the initiating institution to that of the receiving institution, so that a transaction can be accounted for immediately. Where the transaction is captured at point of sale, such as at a supermarket checkout, this is described as 'electronic funds transfer at point of sale' or, more commonly, EFTPOS. The system is increasingly used in the retail BOOK TRADE, partly because it can also be valuable as a stock control system.

ELECTRONIC INFORMATION RESOURCES

Electronic information resources (EIR) have their origins in experimental computer systems developed for the storage and retrieval of bibliographic data during the 1960s. By the end of that decade some of the major bibliographic databases (such as Chemical Abstracts and Index Medicus) were available in magnetic tape versions that were searchable in offline batch mode. During the 1970s and 1980s, the increasing availability of this machine-readable data together with the emergence of both real-time interactive computing and computer networks enabled the online information industry to emerge. Initially the major scientific bibliographic databases became available in machine-readable form. Commercial vendors, many of whom have now ceased to exist, aggregated the databases and made them available for searching. The interaction used an interface that now appears arcane, consisting as it did of a command language that required learning and a set of incomprehensible error messages. There was a rapid increase in the number of bibliographic databases available, extending into the social sciences and humanities, and into medium-sized

mission-oriented databases. Bibliographic databases were followed by factual databases. Generally these were highly structured and contained material such as chemical properties but there were also encyclopaedias and newspapers. The users of these databases were normally trained information professionals within academic and commercial organizations, searching on behalf of their clients.

During the 1980s, ACADEMIC LIBRARIES began to transfer from card CATALOGUES to online public-access catalogues (OPACS). The significance of this development was that for the first time most of the searches were undertaken by END-USERS, and system designers started to design their systems with this in mind. At about the same time as OPACs became widely available, the CD-ROM emerged as an information delivery vehicle. CD-ROMs freed the database suppliers from the grips of the online service providers and the constraints of their connect-time charging mechanisms. Suppliers of CD-ROM information products experimented by making available many different types of information through this medium. Suppliers came and went. However the significant contribution of the CD-ROM was that it enabled the suppliers to develop far more user-friendly interfaces, These could be used by searchers who were not information professionals. The widespread availability of CD-ROM products, together with the appearance of OPACs, created a marked increase in the searching of electronic information resources by professional workers of all descriptions. The searching of electronic information resources had moved once and for all beyond the province of the information professional.

Throughout this period, the information that was publicly available was provided by commercial producers who had subjected the information to appropriate quality-control mechanisms. Furthermore the normal method of retrieval was the creation of a query statement containing criteria that the sought items must match. Usually this consisted of terms that had to be present, linked together by Boolean operators or other facilities provided by the search software. These facilities might have been made explicitly available to the searcher or they might have been implicit, for example through the use of search boxes. The search partitioned the database into those items that met the search criteria and those that did not with the assumption that the former were relevant whilst the latter were not.

Since the late 1960s, INFORMATION RETRIEVAL researchers have developed a variety of alternatives to the Boolean retrieval model. Rather than partitioning the database into retrieved and not retrieved, these attempted to rank the items in the database such that the searcher was presented with items in the order of decreasing relevance. There was only very limited adoption of these approaches by either CD-ROM producers or the online information vendors.

The emergence of the WORLD WIDE WEB has enabled a revolution in electronic information resources. This environment differs from the earlier situation in that:

- The available information is not restricted to text but includes large numbers of images, audio and MULTIMEDIA items so that it is more appropriate to think of them as information objects rather than documents.
- The information available is an amorphous mass to which anyone can add if they have even a limited knowledge of HTML and thus the available information is no longer subject to quality-control mechanisms prior to publication.
- The information is not structured to facilitate retrieval, but through the hypertext links it is structured to facilitate browsing and easy moving between information objects. Links can all too readily be broken.
- The Web browser environment has continued the trend towards user-friendly interfaces that was initiated by the development of CD-ROM and Windows.

In addition to enabling this vast uncontrolled mass of information objects to be made available, the Web also provides access to quality-controlled electronic information resources from the traditional information aggregators such as Dialog. Further it provides a vehicle whereby an increasing number of electronic versions of formal publications, such as electronic versions of refereed journals, is accessible. Finally it offers access to an expanding range of quality-controlled information such as electronic journals and newsletters of which there has never been a print equivalent. From the perspective of the searcher, the situation has become vastly more complex.

Alongside considerable change in the type and scale of available EIR, there has been an even more remarkable change in the users of these resources. Use of EIR has moved from being an esoteric activity undertaken by information professionals, and a slowly increasing band of other professional people, to an action undertaken every day by countless millions around the world.

The surge in the availability of electronic information, coupled with the attractiveness of Web-based interfaces, has further enhanced the notion that information seeking in the electronic age is a simple process. The reality, of course, is that the plethora of information sources means that effective retrieval of the best available information has become even more complex. On the one hand the INTERNET serves simply as an access mechanism to the quality-controlled information products made available by information aggregators such as Dialog, or publishers such as ISI and the major academic publishers such as Elsevier. On the other hand the Web enables anyone to make available resources on any topic with no regard to the quality or validity of that information.

A range of tools has been developed to enable retrieval of material from the Web. These include a large number of SEARCH ENGINES, directories, GATEWAYS and portals (see PORTALS AND GATEWAYS).

The search engines automatically create huge databases of items on the Web. The indexing and updating of these databases is done automatically by software. It is often forgotten that even the largest of these search engines, such as Google and Alta Vista, provide access to but a small proportion of the resources available on the Web. Based on the assumptions that these search engines will often be used by unskilled searchers, these search engines often make use of the IR research techniques of the 1960s as the basis for providing the user with output that has been ranked by presumed relevance to the input query. A common problem with such systems is that the user can be faced with thousands if not millions of references. A further problem is that they may well direct the user to old or redundant sites. Given that these search engines are based upon databases that are automatically created, and thus there is no quality control on the material indexed, the searcher is often faced with a large proportion of irrelevant material of doubtful quality. An inescapable conclusion is that the searcher must become increasingly competent in the judgement of the quality of electronic information resources.

An alternative approach to that of the search engine is the directory approach where access is provided to a much smaller set subset of the Internet that has been chosen by human selectors who have considered the quality of the website and then provide access to the information via a structured hierarchy (in effect a controlled vocabulary). This approach reduces considerably the number of items drawn to the searcher's attention and increases the relevance of the items, but this is achieved at the expense of marked reduction in the number of items retrieved. Yahoo! is the pre-eminent exponent of this approach. However, this clear distinction is slowly disappearing as search engines experiment with directory access and directories incorporate search engines.

A less well-known approach is the subject gateway exemplified in the United Kingdom by gateways such as SOSIG (www.sosig.ac.uk) for the social sciences and EEVL (www.eevl.ac.uk) for engineering. Useful as these gateways are in providing access to quality-controlled resources selected for their relevance to higher education, the reality is that they offer access to only a minute proportion of the resources available on the Web and they remain lightly used.

The emergence of this new information landscape has caused information professionals to work together with other professional groups to consider the METADATA requirements of the new landscape. Whilst initiatives such as DUBLIN CORE are of potential importance, it remains to be seen whether they can have a significant impact in the unordered world of the Web.

Information professionals face a challenging future tackling a range of problems created by the new information landscape. Amongst these are:

- Developing approaches to electronic archiving which ensure that quality information objects remain accessible over time.
- Developing simple to use yet effective mechanisms to allow users with a range of skills to access the information that they require. Since this has not been mastered successfully for text and research in areas such as content-based

image retrieval and music retrieval, this remains a considerable challenge.

- The successful integration of electronic information resources to developments in digital and hybrid library research.
- Understanding the relationship between electronic information resources and the rapidly developing virtual learning environments and managed learning environments.

In summary there has been a vast increase in complexity of electronic information resources. The challenge is to make them accessible in useful ways for a hugely enlarged community, many of whom are inevitably unskilled in the use of the resources.

Further reading

American Library Assocation (2002) *Guidelines for the Introduction of Electronic Information Resources to Users* (http://www.ala.org/rusa/stnd_electron.html) [visited 24 June 2002].

Large, A., Tedd, L. and Hartley, R.J. (1999) *Information Seeking in the Online Age: Principles and Practice*, Bowker Saur.

Marchionini, G. and Komlodi, A. (1998) 'Design of interfaces for information seeking', in M. Williams (ed.) *Annual Review of Information Science and Technology (ARIST)* 33: 89–130 [despite its title, it covers much relevant material and offers access to the research literature].

R.J. HARTLEY

ELECTRONIC JOURNAL ARCHIVES

Peer-reviewed journals

There currently exist at least 20,000 peer-reviewed journals, across all scholarly and scientific disciplines, published in most of the research-active nations and tongues of the world. The (at least) 2 million articles that appear in them annually are only accepted after they have successfully met the quality-standards of the particular journal to which they were submitted. There is a hierarchy of quality standards across journals, from the most rigorous ones at the top – usually the journals with the highest rejection rates and the highest 'impact factors' (the number of times their articles are cited by other articles) – all the way down to a virtual vanity press at the bottom.

The responsibility for maintaining each journal's quality standards is that of the editor(s) and referees. The editor chooses qualified experts ('peers') who then review the submissions and recommend acceptance, rejection or various degrees of revision.

In the past, journals were not concerned with archiving. Their contents appeared on paper; the journal's responsibility was the peer review, editing, mark-up, typesetting, proofing, printing and distribution of the paper texts. It was the subscribers (individual or institutional) who had to concern themselves with the archiving and preservation, usually in the form of the occupation of space on library shelves, occasionally supplemented by copying onto microfiche as a back-up. The main back-up, however, was the (presumably) preserved multiple copies on individual and institutional library shelves around the world. It was this redundancy that ensured that refereed journals were archival and did not vanish within a few days of printing, as ephemeral newspapers and leaflets might do.

In recent decades, journals have increasingly produced online versions in addition to on-paper versions of their contents. Initially, the online version was offered as an extra feature for institutional subscribers, and could be received only if the institution also subscribed to the paper version. Eventually, institutional site-licences to the online version alone became a desired option for institutions. For approximately the same price as a paper subscription, online LICENCES offered much wider and more convenient access to institutional users than a single paper subscription ever could do.

Archiving

This new option raised the problem of archiving again, however: Who owns and maintains the online archive of past issues? In paper days, it was clear that the subscriber owned the 'archive', in the form of the enduring paper edition on the shelf. But with digital texts there is the question of storing them, upgrading them with each advance in technology and in general seeing to it that they are permanently accessible to all institutional users online.

If the journal maintains the online archive, (1) what happens when an institution discontinues its subscription? No new issues are received, of course, but (2) what about past issues, already paid for?

And (3) are publishers really in a position to become archivists too, adding to their traditional functions (peer review, editing, etc.) the function of permanent online archiving, upgrading, migration, preservation and search/access-provision? Are these traditional library and digital library functions now to become publisher functions? There is not yet a satisfactory answer to any of these questions, but the means of implementing them, once we decide on what the correct answers are, have meanwhile already been created.

Implementing online archiving

First, a means was needed to make the digital literature 'interoperable'. This required agreeing on a shared METADATA tagging convention that would allow distributed digital archives to share information automatically, so that their contents were navigable as if they were all in the same place and in the same format. An unambiguous vocabulary had to be agreed upon so that digital texts could be tagged by their author, title, publication date, journal, volume, issue, etc. (along with keywords, subject classification, citation-linking and even an inverted full-text index for searching).

These 'metadata' tags could then be 'harvested', both by individual users and by SEARCH ENGINES that provided sophisticated NAVIGATION capabilities. In principle, the outcome would be as if each of the annual 2 million articles in the 20,000 peer-reviewed journals were all in one global archive.

This shared metadata tagging convention has been provided by the Open Archives Initiative (OAI) (http://www.openarchives.org) and is being adopted by a growing number of archives, including both journal archives and institutional archives. The OAI convention, however, does not answer the question of who should do the archiving: journals or institutions.

Another growing movement, the Budapest Open Access Initiative (BOAI) (http://www.soros.org/openaccess/) is likely to influence this outcome. To understand the form this may take, we have to distinguish two kinds of archives: 'open archives', which are all OAI-compliant archives, and 'open-access archives', which are not only OAI-compliant, but access to their full-text contents is free.

The case for online archiving

Explaining why and how free online access is the optimal and inevitable solution for this special literature (of 20,000 peer-reviewed journals) goes beyond the scope of this article, but it is based on the fact that this literature differs from most other literatures in that it is without exception all an author give-away: none of the authors of the annual 2 million refereed articles seeks royalties or fees in exchange for their text. All these authors seek is as many readers and users as possible, for it is the research impact of these articles – of which a rough measure is the number of times each is cited – that brings these authors their rewards (employment, promotion, tenure, grants, prizes, prestige). It is not subscription/licence sales revenue that brings authors these rewards: on the contrary, these toll-based access-barriers are also impact-barriers, and therefore at odds with the interests of research and researchers.

Hence, from their authors' point of view, the optimal solution for archiving is that the archives should be open-access archives. There are two ways to achieve this. One is that (1) the journals should add archiving to their existing services and make the contents of their archives open-access.

This is on the face of it a rather unrealistic thing to ask from journals, for it asks them to take on additional expenses, over and above their traditional ones, and yet to seek no revenue in exchange, but instead give away all their contents online. It becomes somewhat more realistic if we anticipate a future time when there is no longer any demand for the on-paper version, and so it, and all its associated expenses, can be eliminated, by downsizing to only the essentials.

It has been estimated that if journals performed only peer review, and nothing else, becoming only quality-control service-providers and certifiers, then their expenses per article would be reduced by about 75 per cent. The average revenue per article is currently $2,000 (the sum of all subscription, licence and pay-per-view income, mostly paid by institutions). But this still leaves $500 per article to be recovered, somehow: How to do it if the text is given away for free?

We will return to this question in a moment, noting only that it is still futuristic, becoming relevant only when there is no longer enough demand for the paper version to cover all the costs it had in the past. There are conceivably sources for covering a cost of $500 per article, including research grants and other possible sources of institutional or governmental subsidy in the interest of open access to research. But there is another possibility, not calling for subsidy.

The second way to achieve open-access archives – an immediate rather than a future-contingent way like (1) – is (2) through the author/institution self-archiving of all peer-reviewed articles in institutional eprint archives. Institutions create open-access eprint archives for all of their own peer-reviewed research output (http://www.eprints.org). This provides immediate open access to the entire peer-reviewed journal literature for all would-be users, everywhere.

While the on-paper versions continue to be sold and bought, that continues to be the 'true' archive, and all publication costs are covered the old way (through subscription and licence payments to journals). But if and when the day arrives when there is no longer any demand or market for the publisher's paper version, institutions will already have the 100 per cent annual windfall savings out of which to redirect the 25 per cent needed to cover the peer review costs for their own annual research output. And at that point the interoperable, OAI-compliant institutional eprint archives will also become the true archives of the peer-reviewed journal literature.

Further reading

Harnad, S. (2001) 'The self-archiving initiative', *Nature* 410:1,024–5.(http://cogprints.soton.ac.uk/documents /disk0/00/00/16/42/index.html).

Odlyzko, A.M. (2002) 'The rapid evolution of scholarly communication', *Learned Publishing* 1: 7–19 (http:// www.si.umich.edu/PEAK-2000/odlyzko.pdf).

SEE ALSO: citation analysis; digital library; scholarly communication

STEVAN HARNAD

ELECTRONIC JOURNALS

A journal that is available in electronic form through an ONLINE host. Electronic journals have existed experimentally since the late 1970s, but it was only in the 1990s with the mushroom growth of the INTERNET and the development of the WORLD WIDE WEB that they became comparatively common. The great benefit of electronic journals is that the user can access directly the individual paper or article which s/he requires, typically from a desktop workstation, without having to find a part or volume in a library and then find the specific item.

Despite their obvious advantages to users, however, electronic journals have developed rather more slowly than the technology would have allowed. There has been significant resistance among academics – perhaps surprisingly most notably in the scientific community – partly because of a belief that the traditional techniques of journal editing were being ignored. In particular, there was suspicion that papers were not fully refereed; as a result, electronic journals commanded less prestige than traditional printed journals, good papers were not submitted to them and something of a vicious circle was created. Only now is this being broken (Anderson *et al.* 2001). Moreover, there is a concern that electronic journals may have only a limited lifespan; the creation of ELECTRONIC-JOURNAL ARCHIVES is an important step forward in overcoming this suspicion.

From the perspective of the publishing industry, electronic journals present a different, but equally significant, problem. Traditionally, journal publishers have sold their products on subscription, mainly to ACADEMIC LIBRARIES, although also to some in other sectors. Subscriptions to electronic journals are differently structured, with the end-user being charged for each access to a paper. In practice, libraries buy a licence, typically on an annual subscription basis, to give access to the journal for all its own registered users. Although this system works well, it is forcing the publishers to reconsider their approach to journal publishing, and especially to the cost of subscriptions to journals in all formats.

Despite all the current issues, however, it seems likely that electronic journals will become the normal mode of SCHOLARLY COMMUNICATION in many disciplines (not only in the sciences) in the not too distant future.

References

Anderson, K., Sack, J., Kraus, L. and O'Keefe, L. (2001) 'Publishing online only peer-reviewed biomedical literature: Three years of citation, author perception, and usage experience', *Journal of Elec-*

tronic Publishing 6 (www.press.umich.edu/jep/06–03/andreson.html).

Further reading

Journal of Electronic Publishing (www.press. umich.edu/jep/).
Tenopir, C. and King, D.W. (2000) *Towards Electronic Journals*, Special Libraries Association.

SEE ALSO: book trade; communication; electronic books; serials librarianship

ELECTRONIC LIBRARY

An organized collection of electronic DOCUMENTS. The term DIGITAL LIBRARY is now normally preferred.

ELECTRONIC MAIL

A method of sending messages, data files, etc. by electronic means from one computer with network access to another. The receiving terminal is usually equipped with a storage area, or mailbox, in which the messages are deposited. Users can read their incoming messages on-screen when they choose and, if they wish, print them out or download them on to a disk. Its advantages over postal services are speed and reliability; and over telephone communication, the availability of a message received at any time in a permanent and convenient form. Files of substantial size can be sent via e-mail almost as easily as the informal exchanges that are encouraged by the user-friendliness of the medium. The earliest use of e-mail seems to have been in 1972, after which the now-familiar conventions (such as the use of the symbol) and EMOTICONs were quickly developed. It has become the ubiquitous means of communication for INTERNET users throughout the world, and indeed has been argued to have been one of the drivers for the expansion of the Internet in the 1980s and 1990s. The use of e-mail, however, still raises important issues in information transfer, arising from its lack of security. Solutions to this that are being explored mainly involve new methods of data ENCRYPTION.

Further reading

Palme, J. (1995) *Electronic mail*, Artech House.

SEE ALSO: communication; computer security;

information and communication technology; information management

ELECTRONIC PUBLIC INFORMATION SERVICES

Information available directly to the general public through electronic systems.

For most of history, access to information has been the preserve of the few. In more recent times, the public has had the MASS MEDIA to augment word of mouth, but most information sources remained in the hands of the specialists.

Prestel was the first significant publicly accessible information system. This was developed in the 1970s by Fedida and Malik, and used a standard telephone line to connect to a central computer. The display, intended for a domestic television, consisted of 'frames' (screens) of information, but these were severely limited both as to the amount of text displayed (forty character per line) and the quality of graphics. Effects such as colour change were achieved with hidden characters between words, and the graphics were composed of 'graphic characters' – groups of coloured squares ('pixels') that together could be arranged to form a picture. Although undoubted talent was employed by designers to create the frames, the graphics were crude and angular.

The technology became known generically as 'viewdata', but, unlike the similar French MINITEL system, Prestel was not a popular success. In part, this was due to competition from TELETEXT, which supplied 'pages' that looked similar to viewdata frames, but did so using spare capacity in the television picture signals.

Teletext services were normally free, and no phone connections were involved. Decoders and handsets became routinely included in nearly all standard televisions sold. Most television broadcasters, including terrestrial, satellite and even cable services, ran teletext services. The information carried covered television-related topics such as programme times, news and magazine-style content, but also a wide range of data such as stock market prices, weather forecasts and travel information. Commercial television also carried advertising.

In the 1980s and 1990s, viewdata had something of a revival. Political pressures on national and regional governments to become more open resulted in many of them seeking ways to widen the distribution of information about their activities. One of the solutions commonly adopted was the development of local viewdata systems. These were accessed via microcomputers located in public buildings, especially libraries. In many cases the viewdata frames were held on the microcomputers themselves, rather than on a central computer, removing the need for telephone connections. Another popular solution was to update the frames held on the microcomputers via a single telephone connection in the middle of the night.

Microcomputers modified to show only a specific viewdata service were called 'kiosks'. In a more rugged version, kiosks were also placed in open public areas such as streets and bus stations.

These methods, and various custom solutions, were adopted by other public bodies to provide information on employment services, travel, tourism and health.

The development of the INTERNET and, more particularly, the WORLD WIDE WEB, drew even more organizations to publish information in electronic form. In the late 1990s, those local authorities that had developed viewdata systems began to abandon them in favour of this more sophisticated medium. Beside the advantages of improved display and organization of information, the new websites could be accessed by a much larger section of the population either at home or in the workplace.

Local government sites tended to supply details of their services and contact information, as well as community information for the area they served. However, the growth of Web-based information brought about a broadening of the type of material carried and the technology used to display it. GEOGRAPHIC INFORMATION SYSTEMS (GIS), for instance, might be used to display COMMUNITY INFORMATION, such as the location of schools, overlaid on a map of the area.

Increasingly during this period of development, local authority reports and minutes were being published on the Web, and a number of authorities broadcast their council meetings live via their website (webcast).

Other information providers included national and local newspapers. The BBC, who maintained a website in support of its broadcast programmes, also provided public information about a number of British cities, and included the use of cameras to monitor city traffic conditions ('Jam-Cams').

A number of UK central government departments developed their own websites, and the Central Computer and Telecommunications Agency (CCTA) not only published guidelines in this area, but also acted as a 'portal', linking most government and related sites.

There was a major increase in central government interest in this technology following the election of the 1997 Labour government. A white paper was produced on 'Modernising Government'. In this, all government services were to be provided electronically where practical, to give a round-the-clock service. The concept became known as e-government, and included information about government services and other more interactive features, such as online form submission. A set of standards known as the Government Interoperability Framework (e-GIF) was developed to underlie the initiative and ensure working compatibility between government sites. This made HTML, XML and related protocols standard for display and data structures, and provided for an extension of the DUBLIN CORE system of METADATA.

The government reasoned that Internet access via computer ownership alone was unlikely to become universal within a reasonable period of time. There was fear of a developing 'digital divide' causing 'social exclusion' of those without access to electronic services. Four platforms were therefore included in e-GIF. These were Internet browsers, public kiosks, WAP phones and digital television.

Digital television was planned to supersede analogue BROADCASTING within the first decade of the twenty-first century, and carried with it the ability to provide sophisticated, interactive text-based services. Broadcasters were already using this to augment programmes in a way that teletext had been unable to do. At the start of the century, a number of local authorities, housing associations and trusts grouped together provide a means of communicating directly with tenants, and supply interactive services using this technology.

Another group that it was feared would be isolated were those with visual disabilities. Government guidelines were published to establish appropriate Web design that was as inclusive as possible. A new portal, UK Online, was opened to create an easy access to government and related Web facilities without demanding significant search skills.

Even so, some continued to argue that such technological solutions required skills that were not universal. Surveys had shown that people preferred to talk to human beings rather than use machines. As a result, some authorities turned to call-centre technology. This allowed members of the public to speak over the phone to trained operatives who had access to various electronic tools, and were able to mediate between the data and the client.

Further reading

Modernising Government (www.cabinet-office.gov.uk/moderngov).
Office of the E-Envoy (www.e-envoy.gov.uk).
Society of Public Information Networks (SPIN) (www.spin.org.uk).
UK GovTalk (www.govtalk.gov.uk).
UK Online Portal (www.ukonline.gov.uk).

SEE ALSO: e-government; videotex

GOFF SARGENT

EMOTICON

Said to be based on a contraction of 'emotion icon', but, whether that is the actual origin or not, the term refers to the smiley faces that punctuate the ELECTRONIC MAIL communication, chat and newsgroup postings of many INTERNET users. They consist of a short sequence of letters and symbols that when viewed by tilting the head to the left emulate a facial expression. They are used to reinforce the feeling that a message is intended to convey, and can be taken as a means of communicating in the spirit of NETIQUETTE.

EMPIRICISM AND POSITIVISM

Empiricism is the view that experience, observation or sense data are the only or the most important way of acquiring knowledge, both in ordinary life and in science. Although empiricism can trace its origin to Aristotle, modern empiricism developed like classical rationalism from different ways of drawing epistemological lessons from the scientific revolution consummated by Newton. Together, rationalism and empiricism constitute the two main tendencies of European philosophy in the period between scholasticism and Kant. Empiricism is connected to British thinking, rationalism to Continental thought (Garrett and Barbanell 1997: ix).

POSITIVISM's central claim that science is the highest form of knowledge and that philosophy therefore must be scientific, that there is one scientific method common to all science, and that metaphysical claims are pseudoscientific, was in conflict with the empirical tradition.

The logical positivists of the mid-twentieth century tried to reconcile the two positions. They also attacked metaphysics but brought in the empiricist tradition. They argued that sensory knowledge was the most certain kind of knowledge and that any sentence not directly about sensory experience should be translatable into observational sentences. Those sentences that could not be so translated were rejected as meaningless. This view implied that knowledge is divided into theoretical and observable knowledge, and that theoretical concepts and sentences must be defined in observational terms. Good science consists of *a priori* logic and cumulated sense data, and is value free. All science can be united and reduced to physics.

Positivist assumptions have influenced the use of statistics in the social sciences, including LIS. Positivistic views implicitly treat research as a mechanical, purely logical process. Typical of positivism is also its anti-realism. Research is seen as reports of correlation between observational variables. Underlying cause is regarded as metaphysics and thus ignored. The same applies to knowing the essence or nature of something. Positivism is closely related to behaviourism, the view that all knowledge about psychological phenomena must be studied by observing the behaviour of organisms (e.g. users in LIS). The principle of methodological individualism implies that positivists reduce the study of all collective phenomena, e.g. institutions, ideologies and social norms, to the study of attributes of individuals.

The strength of positivism is its methodology for eliminating kinds of errors related to the researchers' subject. By applying control groups, experiments, statistical methods, etc. subjectivity is eliminated and intersubjective data are established. In this regard it is opposed to HERMENEU-TICS, which find it impossible to eliminate subjectivity, but which try to explicate the subjective presumptions as much as possible.

One could say that the relative strength of positivism compared to hermeneutics is its methodology for processing empirical data, while its relative weakness is its methodology for considering theoretical and conceptual aspects concerning what data to consider relevant in the first place. Positivism produces intersubjective controlled data, but such data are often criticized for being trivial or even ideologically biased by more hermeneutically or critically oriented researchers. Positivists can, for example, provide reliable data about correlations between race and intelligence. They tend to ignore, however, the different conditions in which races have to develop their intelligence in the society.

In popular myth positivism is regarded as quantitative science. This is not so. Both quantitative and qualitative research can be positivist or non-positivist. Neither is positivism 'hard science' or objective science. Positivism is an EPISTEMOLOGY that has been declared dead, but it still continues to dominate many research areas. Many shortcomings can be avoided by applying other approaches, of which critical realism and hermeneutics are very important. Such alternatives are more concerned with observations as manifestations of different layers of reality or underlying causes and mechanisms that cannot always be translated into observational terms. They regard methods as something that are not universal and *a priori*, but must be specified in relation to the specific object of research. They have also undercut the motivations for behaviourism and methodological individualism.

Positivism has been called 'the invisible philosophy of science' because its adherents regard it as the solely scientific approach and tend to avoid or ignore philosophical problems. It is not regarded by itself as a school or a paradigm, merely as a science. This is the reverse of, for example, hermeneutic or feminist epistemology that recognize and label their approach as one among others.

Empiricism and positivism in LIS

If we regard LIS as a field of research, we should regard the strength and weaknesses of different epistemologies and try to apply the best ones. Positivist assumptions have dominated in, for example, many kinds of user studies and experiments in IR. It has produced large amounts of fragmented data of dubious relevance. The problem is not that such studies are empirical or quantitative, but that they suffer from other shortcomings from the positivist inheritance. Mainstream information science can benefit from the discussions about the shortcomings of positivism.

There is another important implication for LIS. LIS is about selecting, organizing, seeking and intermediating information and knowledge. Most of that information is produced by implicit positivist norms, which affects its quality, value, organization, language, etc. Hjørland (2000) summarizes a description of how the definition, delimiting and structure of the social sciences rest upon positivist views, which are currently in crisis, and why the classification of this area seems anachronistic. If LIS is to find principles of classification, information seeking, etc. for this area, it must go through an analysis of implicit positivistic norms.

References

Garrett, D. and Barbanell, E. (eds) (1997) *Encyclopedia of Empiricism*, London: Fitzroy Dearborn Publishers.

Hjørland, B. (2000) 'Review of Wallerstein (1996) *Open the Social Sciences*, Stanford, CA: Stanford University Press I', *Knowledge Organization* 27(4): 238–41.

Further reading

Alston, W.P. (1998) 'Empiricism', in *Routledge Encyclopaedia of Philosophy, Version 1.0*, London: Routledge.

Kincaid, H. (1998) 'Positivism in the social sciences', in *Routledge Encyclopedia of Philosophy, Version 1.0*, London: Routledge

SEE ALSO: epistemology; information theory; philosophies of science; research in library and information science

BIRGER HJØRLAND

ENCRYPTION

The encoding of data that is to be transmitted through telecommunications systems so that only authorized users can read it. Encryption is normal for all data transmitted across the Internet with decryption software being built into the recipient computer's system and programs. There are various Data Encryption Standards that are widely used for this purpose. Encryption is an essential element in protecting the confidentiality of transmitted data, and is especially important in commercial uses, where sensitive personal data is involved (such as in health informatics systems), and for government data.

Further reading

Soh, B.C. and Young, S. (1998) 'Network system and World Wide Web security', *Computer Communications* 20: 1,431–6.

SEE ALSO: data security; espionage; privacy; surveillance

ENCYCLOPEDIA

A DATABASE or REFERENCE BOOK containing information on all subjects, or limited to a special field or subject, arranged in systematic (usually alphabetical) order. The form lends itself ideally to multimedia and interactive formats, and on CD-ROM was one of the first genres to be produced in the form of ELECTRONIC BOOKS.

END-USER

Distinguishes the user for whom an INFORMATION AND COMMUNICATION TECHNOLOGY product or information service is designed, from the developers, installers, administrators, system operators, information scientists, librarians and service personnel who are, in some sense or other, also users. It reflects the fact that most information technologies and services involve a chain of interconnected product components and human activities at the end of which is the user, but 'end' is still generally redundant. Its usefulness is in distinguishing between users who require a finished product or service (end-users), and intermediaries who might use a product that has not been fully tested for development purposes or handle raw or unprocessed information on behalf of an end-user.

ENTERPRISE RESOURCE PLANNING

Enterprise Resource Planning (ERP) SOFTWARE is mostly recognized as standard package software, usually sourced from one vendor, which provides support for a wide range of core business processes in a variety of organizations.

The origins of ERP software

ERP software evolved from Manufacturing Re-source Planning (or Materials Requirements Planning) (MRP) software. MRP software began to be introduced into organizations throughout the 1960s. At this stage the software was used to provide support for work in manufacturing-based organizations. The software could help people manage production through the use of electronic records such as stock held that were linked to bills of materials and work in progress. For example, an organization that made cars may need thousands of different parts to go into making that car – the record of this would be the bill of materials. Therefore in order to satisfy an order for a car, they would need to make sure they had all the parts in stock. The MRP soft-ware would therefore enable personnel to check stock levels and work in progress at the organi-zation and calculate what parts they might need to make or order to fulfil the order for the car. MRP software was then developed further into MRPII software and this included functionality relating to the management of finance in an organization. ERP software is merely a further evolution of the idea of using IT to help in the management of resources, but on an enterprise scale. ERP software therefore provides support for other areas such as human resources and distribution services.

The rationale for ERP software adoption

Much of the rationale for the adoption of ERP software to support organizational business pro-cesses is inextricably linked with legacy informa-tion system (Legacy IS) problems. Legacy IS can be viewed as the inter-related organizational and technological situation. Very simply, organiza-tions were having problems with their Legacy IS, and ERP software was seen as a way of over-coming these difficulties.

From a technical perspective, many people in organizations were using IT-based standard soft-ware or custom-developed systems that had been implemented generally at least a decade before, and these often presented organizations with a number of problems. They had usually been developed and/or maintained over a number of years by different people leading to high levels of entropy and complexity. These changes were sometimes not very well documented: meaning that dealing with problems, developing the soft-ware or performing routine maintenance was becoming a resource-intensive activity. Further-more, throughout the 1990s the year 2000 (Y2K) problem emerged and this required people in organizations to have very good knowledge of the workings of the software they used in order that they could take corrective action.

Inextricably linked with the technological viewpoint of the Legacy IS problem was the organizational one. Strategies had shifted for many organizations from local to global, and IT support was required to co-ordinate this. Tied to the internationalization of markets was increased global competition in many areas and consequently there was a requirement to stream-line operations and become (more) customer-facing. This translated for many into a move from a functionally based organization towards one that was process oriented. However, be-cause of the problems of their Legacy IS, people in organizations found it very difficult to get their software to support new strategies and for some it was impossible. Consequently, the adop-tion of standard software, especially ERP soft-ware, was seen as the preferred remedial strategy.

The ERP software response and its potential implications

As ERP software is standard software, many organizational members saw this as an opportu-nity to implement a new IT (and sometimes organizational) infrastructure that would wipe away the existing problems. ERP software was bought pre-coded (pre-programmed/pre-built) and like much standard software was fully documented. This translated into a decision to outsource maintenance and development work to a third party with the idea that this would be taken care of by an ongoing service contract and future upgrades. ERP software was also Y2K compliant, had multilingual and multicurrency capabilities, and supported a process-oriented organization structure. The overwhelming view was that the software dealt with Legacy IS problems and, consequently, the market grew tremendously throughout the 1990s.

During the 1990s there was rhetoric about the need for ERP software and it is only really since the late 1990s that a more realistic view of it has emerged. ERP can be a very good solution for organizations, yet many have found that they cannot fully capitalize on its status as standard software. This is because organizations can be very different in terms of their functionality requirements (what they want a piece of software to do). Organizations will somewhat change the ways that they work in line with the ERP software in order to maximize the benefits of its adoption. That is, they will not tailor the software, and thus can keep taking upgrades and do not have to undertake unnecessary maintenance themselves. However, some organizations have found it absolutely necessary to tailor the software as certain functionality, critical to the organization, is missing from the standard software. This customization, or modification, varies in nature. Ultimately, however, it leads to increased maintenance activity that has the potential to put organizations in the problematic position they first chose to remedy by implementing ERP software.

Further reading

Holland, C.P. and Light, B. (1999) 'A critical success factors model for ERP implementation', *IEEE Software* 16: 30–6.
Klaus, H., Rosemann, M. and Gable, G.G. (2000) 'What is ERP?', *Information Systems Frontiers* 2: 141–62.
Light, B. (2001) 'The maintenance implications of the customisation of ERP software', *The Journal of Software Maintenance: Research and Practice* 13: 415–30.
Markus, M.L. and Tanis, C. (2000) 'The enterprise system experience – from adoption to success', in R.W. Zmud (ed.) *Framing the Domains of IT Research: Glimpsing the Future through the Past*, Pinnaflex Educational Resources, pp. 173–207.

SEE ALSO: information systems; organizational information policies

BEN LIGHT

ENUMERATIVE BIBLIOGRAPHY

A list of documents, ideally comprehensive, compiled on some predetermined basis, which can be geographical, chronological or topical. It can also be confined to the work of a single author or works in a particular genre.

SEE ALSO: bibliography

EPHEMERA

Ephemera has been described as the 'minor transient documents of everyday life'. The concept encompasses the poster or leaflet of political activity or theatrical promotion; the packaging or containers of commercial products, such as the plastic bag or cigarette packet; personal mementos like the business or birthday card, or the printed aspects of popular culture, such as the seaside postcard, record sleeve or comic. As well as by private collectors, MUSEUMS and record offices, ephemera is collected by all types of library, both generally or in particular formats, or because of its place or subject associations. Major UK collections include the John Johnson Collection in the Bodleian Library and the Robert Opie Collection at the Museum of Advertising and Packaging, Gloucester. Public library LOCAL STUDIES COLLECTIONS in particular usually contain much ephemera for their locality, such as election literature, posters, programmes and handbills.

Value of ephemera

Interest in ephemera, and in particular that of the private collector, are met by the Ephemera Society, founded in 1975 by Maurice Rickards, of which there are offshoot associations in Austria, Canada, Australia and the USA. It publishes a quarterly journal, *The Ephemerist* (1975–), and a *Handbook and Dealer Directory*. In 1993 Rickards's own collection, housed in over one hundred custom-made boxes, was transferred to the University of Reading to form part of the newly created Centre for Ephemera Studies in the Department of Typography and Graphic Communication (www.rdg.ac.uk/Acadepts/lt). Such a centre, with its symposia, workshops and publications, has helped to overcome the possible undervaluing of ephemera, for it is part of the documentary evidence for the study of society, both past and contemporary. Its particular value is that it records the transactions and concerns of everyday life, grassroots opinions and aspects of popular culture – information that may not be found elsewhere. It is also useful as a source of illustration, and for the contribution it can make to the history of printing, graphic design and the use of language. In many libraries, however, it may only be collected for its current information rather than its long-term value.

Problems of definition

While the definition offered at the beginning of this entry gets to the heart of the matter and has the virtue of brevity, it does not wholly adequately define it. Indeed, given ephemera's many forms, it is unlikely that any satisfactory definition could be agreed upon by all those interested in its collection. Makepeace (1985) discusses the various definitions that have been put forward and provides a checklist of items that might be called ephemera. Collecting libraries should, therefore, consider how it is to be defined in their own context, bearing in mind its various types, the collecting activities of other institutions and the need to distinguish it from miscellaneous OFFICIAL PUBLICATIONS, minor publications and GREY LITERATURE (which may escape bibliographical listing), and from material that can usually be seen as belonging to distinct categories, such as photographs, newspapers, periodicals and stamps. Where formerly libraries may have been principally concerned with the retrospective collection of surviving items of ephemera, which were often treated with the bibliographical and CONSERVATION considerations given to rare books, such a definition was perhaps unnecessary. However, now that there is an increasing awareness of the need to collect contemporary items in a proactive way because of their documentary value, potentially low survival rate and likely future high cost as collectables, this becomes a more central concern.

The problems of ephemera

Even with a 'definition' of ephemera, the collection, organization, storage and exploitation of a collection of contemporary printed ephemera poses a number of difficulties for the librarian that, unless taken into consideration, may limit the impact of what is collected and curtail its use and usefulness. These have been summarized as problems of excess and access (Clinton 1981): the large amount of contemporary material that is available for collection; the need for better, particularly subject, access to individual collections at the local level and awareness of collections and their contents at the national level. Failure to consider these issues of 'excess and access' by individual libraries can result in unfocused, haphazard collections from a restricted range of acquisition sources, which are

given minimal processing for INFORMATION RETRIEVAL and may also be subject to inadequate conservation and unsuitable storage.

EXCESS

Because of the sheer quantity of printed ephemera it is unlikely (and probably unnecessary) that libraries will be able to collect comprehensively, except in some well-defined areas, and there are dangers of both duplication and omission by libraries and other institutions collecting within the same geographical area or subject field. Solutions to these problems demand an understanding of the present collecting position in a given area, the existence of collection policies for ephemera within its libraries and other institutions, and a framework for a co-operative scheme for its collection.

A research project carried out in Wales (Dewe and Drew 1994) found, however, that even where libraries had collection policies and collected ephemera, it was not necessarily dealt with in such documents or it was dealt with in insufficient detail. At the national level, for example, the National Library of Wales was found to have no formal policy or machinery for collecting ephemera but did acquire it from a variety of sources. The outcome of the project was a set of guidelines (which could act as a model for other regions) that made proposals for the effective collection of ephemera at the national and local levels in Wales, particularly by public library local studies libraries, and stressed the leadership and collecting roles of the national library.

ACCESS

A somewhat different solution to the problem of ephemera was suggested earlier (Pemberton 1971), through the creation of a National Documents Library, at the then British Museum, and the compilation of a National Register of Collections by the proposed National Documents Library. The first suggestion was not pursued by the BRITISH LIBRARY, although its role as a collector of ephemera has been the subject of internal discussion. However, the idea was taken up in a more modest way by the National Library of Scotland, which, although collecting ephemera for some years, adopted a policy on the collection and treatment of current Scottish ephemera only in 1985, although this is not done on a co-operative basis with other Scottish libraries. The second suggestion was investigated and something similar to the National Register of Archives advocated (Clinton 1981), but this was not proceeded with either. In Australia, however, the State Library of New South Wales has published a *Directory of Australian Ephemera* (Robertson 1992), and one of the outcomes of the Welsh project was the proposal for the compilation of a UK directory. While they do not meet the suggested detailed subject approach of a national register, in the absence of this register such directories help publicize the existence, availability and broad scope of collections.

Because of its slightness and varied size, ephemera is usually housed separately from other material and may be arranged by a mixture of format and broad subject groupings; for example, posters are often kept together, and leaflets, programmes, small notices and similar items can be filed together within appropriate subject groupings. Rarely do such arrangements cater for detailed subject access to the material, and the allocation of resources for fully documenting individual items of ephemera, even though they are to be retained permanently in many instances, does not appear a priority. Depending upon the nature of the collection, better subject access may be obtained by libraries classifying material according either to a scheme already in use, e.g. DEWEY DECIMAL CLASSIFICATION, or to an in-house one. The National Library of Scotland has devised such a scheme based on nine major subject categories plus three format categories, all with appropriate subdivisions. Material is not catalogued, but classified by the nature of the organization producing the material, regardless of subject content, and the year of accession is added to the class mark so that material is stored chronologically in its boxes. Thus, without the index that had been proposed, broad subject access is provided to potentially useful material.

Removing barriers

Since the early 1960s, the importance of ephemera as part of a nation's documentary heritage has gradually been recognized in the UK and conditions are being created (through collection policy formulation and local information plans, for example) to assist its wider and improved collection. This needs to be followed by better management in terms of its organization and access and PRESERVATION. In Australia, the issue of collecting responsibilities within its three-tier library structure – national library, state and public libraries – is one of current professional debate (Dewe and Drew 1993). The way forward for the documentary heritage of Australia, including ephemera, emphasizes distributed responsibility for its collection and national bibliographical accessibility through the Australian Bibliographic Network.

References

Clinton, A. (1981) *Printed Ephemera: Its Collection, Organisation and Access*, Bingley.

Dewe, M. and Drew, P.R. (1994) *A Collection Policy for Printed Welsh Ephemera: A Report and Guidelines*, University of Wales, Aberystwyth, Department of Information and Library Studies.

—— (1993) 'The collection of printed ephemera in Australia at national, state and local levels', *International Information and Library Review* 25: 123–40.

Makepeace, C.E. (1985) *Ephemera: A Book on its Collection, Conservation and Use*, Gower.

Pemberton, J. (1971) *The National Provision of Printed Ephemera in the Social Sciences*, University of Warwick.

Robertson, A. (comp.) (1992) *Directory of Australian Ephemera Collections: A Listing of Institutions and Individuals in Australia Collecting Ephemera*, State Library of New South Wales.

Further reading

Collection Management, (2001) 25: 37–80 [three papers from a conference on ephemera in archives].

Price, L.O. (1997) 'The preservation of ephemera', *Popular Culture in Libraries* 4: 35–46.

Rickards, M. (2000) *Encyclopedia of Ephemera*, British Library/Routledge.

—— (1978) *This Is Ephemera: Collecting Printed Throwaways*, David & Charles.

SEE ALSO: collection management

MICHAEL DEWE

EPISTEMOLOGY

The science of organizing ideas in their exact correspondence with outward things or KNOWLEDGE; the study of the nature and vitality of knowledge. Epistemology underlies the theory of knowledge and is thus the philosophical foundation of INFORMATION THEORY.

SEE ALSO: sociology of knowledge

ESPIONAGE

In general terms, the illegal gathering of secret information of any kind, often by means of agents or MONITORING devices.

Rival powers have been seeking strategically important information about one another since the beginning of recorded history. This information, when used for decision-making, is called 'INTELLIGENCE'. The connection between intelligence-gathering and libraries is fairly new, having several preconditions: first, the realization by the political and military sectors that knowledge, specifically scientific and technical knowledge, can win wars and economic dominion; second, the existence of a well-established network of publications serving as international vehicles of this knowledge; and, third, the development of libraries from storehouses into points of access and delivery of published information. All of these conditions existed by the third decade of the twentieth century.

The First World War, with its mustard gas and Zeppelin air raids, demonstrated the importance of applied science to the military, and for the first time attention was focused on library collections as a means of monitoring strategic enemy activity. Great Britain, until 1914 dependent on Germany for strategically important optical and chemical imports, established in 1916 a government Department of Scientific and Industrial Research, with libraries and documentation centres for each branch of industry to monitor publications – German publications included – in these fields.

In the battle for economic survival during the interwar years, Germany's Weimar government subsidized two new institutions to bolster German scientific intelligence-gathering: the Notgemeinschaft der Deutschen Wissenschaft (predecessor of today's Deutscher Forschungsgemeinschaft), which financed an acquisitions centre at the Prussian State Library to co-ordinate and subsidize the collection of specialized foreign literature for Germany's libraries; and the German government-founded Reichszentrale für wissenschaftliche Berichterstattung, a centre for the photo-reproduction of foreign journals that in the 1930s and early 1940s was located in the library of the Technische Hochschule in Berlin. But the most ambitious scientific and technical intelligence-gathering programme of the interwar years was that of the Soviet Union, whose Bureau

for Foreign Science and Technology (BINT) maintained an outpost in Berlin from 1920 to 1928 to publish Russian translations of the newest Western science and disseminate them to Soviet libraries.

By 1939 a new information technology, microfilm, was in use in European and US RESEARCH LIBRARIES and it would play an important role in scientific intelligence-gathering in the coming war. The Germans used it in supplying their scientists with copies of US and British journals through the Reichszentrale; after 1942 German subscribers to the *Referatenblatt*, a periodical index of enemy journal articles, could receive microfilms of the originals from Berlin. Many of the Allied journals were supplied to the *Referatenblatt* by German agents in Lisbon. After the land route to Portugal was cut off by the invasion of Normandy in June 1944, the Germans tried novel means to ensure the supply. In November 1944 two German agents were landed by submarine on the coast of Maine in an unsuccessful mission to proceed with their microfilm camera to New York Public Library and photograph technical journals for dispatch to Germany. The Germans also developed the 'microdot', a much-reduced microfilm that could contain an entire issue of a technical journal and be secreted in the 'period' hole punctured in paper by a manual typewriter. Microdots were used by the Germans to send copies of Allied publications from Mexico to Berlin.

On the Allied side, the British were the pioneers in the use of microfilm for scientific espionage. In 1941 the Association of Special Libraries (ASLIB) established a service to deliver to British libraries microfilm copies of strategic German journals cut off by the British continental embargo. In 1942 the US Office of Strategic Services (OSS) began to contribute to the ASLIB service journals collected clandestinely by OSS agents operating on the periphery of the Reich. From 1943 on, these journals were reprinted by photo-offset by Edwards Brothers of Ann Arbor, Michigan, under licence from the US Department of Justice, which had seized the journals' copyrights. By the end of the war, reprints of 116 journals published within the Reich were available to US and Commonwealth libraries by subscription from Edwards Brothers.

Some of the intelligence-gathering techniques developed during the Second World War were adapted for Cold War use. In 1946, for example, the acquisitions activities of the OSS were taken over by the Office of Technical Services, which eventually evolved into today's US National Technical Information Service (NTIS).

There were also many new initiatives taken in both the Western and Soviet camps that affected libraries. In the USA in 1950 the National Science Foundation was established; it oversaw a translation (see TRANSLATIONS) programme of Soviet scientific works. In England, one of the arguments used to rally support for the opening of the National Lending Library for Science and Technology in 1962 was the undersupply of Soviet journals in British libraries. The most grandiose system of all for gathering enemy scientific intelligence was the Soviets' All-Union Institute for Scientific and Technical Information (VINITTI), founded at the Soviet Academy of Sciences in 1952. Not yet signatories of the international copyright convention, the Soviets during the 1960s were able to use new photo-duplication technologies to disseminate heavily censored versions of Western scientific journals to their libraries and laboratories.

The logical outgrowth of the increased importance of libraries in intelligence-gathering was their emergence as targets for counter-intelligence activities (counter-intelligence being the protection of strategically important information). In the Soviet Union this protective process began even before publication, with editorial censorship and the alteration of maps and charts. In the West, counter-intelligence focused on the point of use, namely the library. Thus in the 1980s the US Federal Bureau of Investigation launched its 'Library Awareness Program', which sought (unsuccessfully) to recruit librarians' help in identifying suspicious use of freely available library materials.

In recent decades large corporations have used intelligence-gathering techniques to learn of competitors' products and services. The fields of 'technology watching' and 'business intelligence', of which industrial espionage is but one aspect, have become discrete disciplines, with their own journals and specialists. Like all forms of intelligence-gathering activities, those of the business world rely greatly on libraries.

Further reading

Richards, P.S. (1994) *Scientific Information in Wartime: The Allied–German Rivalry 1939–1945*, Stamford, CT: Greenwood.

SEE ALSO: military intelligence; Russia and the former Soviet Union; scholarly communication

PAMELA S. RICHARDS

EUROPEAN UNION INFORMATION POLICIES

European Union (EU) information policies are made throughout the EU institutions and their administrative units, and address a number of areas. EU information policies include guidelines and legislation concerned with economic and industrial competitiveness, DATA PROTECTION, COPYRIGHT, INTELLECTUAL PROPERTY, PRIVACY, ELECTRONIC PUBLIC-INFORMATION SERVICES, E-GOVERNMENT, DIGITIZATION, PRESERVATION, and education and lifelong learning. EU information policy also covers issues relating to the transparency of the EU's own administration and decision-making processes, and the ease of access to EU information by Europe's citizens. EU information policy is not solely concerned with the EU member states, but also with the candidate countries for EU membership. Although EU information policy was previously made in a fragmented fashion, there has been significantly greater dialogue and cohesion since the reform of the European Commission in 2000. This is an area that changes rapidly, with substantial amounts of information available only on the Internet.

The EU is managed by five main institutions. The European Commission (EC) is made up of twenty Commissioners appointed by the national governments of each member state. It carries out EU policies, implements the budget, verifies application of EU law by member states and brings forward proposals for new legislation and activities. The Council of Ministers comprises government ministers from each member state. It discusses proposals put forward by the EC, suggests amendments and ensures that national interests are represented. The European Parliament (EP) consists of 626 members (MEPs) democratically elected from the member states. The EP adopts legislative proposals and the budget, normally through the co-decision process with the Council of Ministers. It also exercises democratic supervision over all EU executive activities, including the activities of the EC. The European Court of Justice has the task of interpreting EU law, mainly through cases brought by individuals and firms or member states against the EU institutions, by one EU institution against another or by the EC against a member state. The Court of Auditors monitors all financial transactions in the EU.

What is the EU policy on information?

EU INFORMATION POLICY is complex, but can be seen to have two basic themes. These are the importance of information services to the European economy, and the importance of information services to the citizens of Europe's civil society.

The EU aims to implement its information policies in several ways. It aims to encourage research, to establish a framework of regulations and standards designed to generate competitiveness and encourage economic growth, and to support the development of applications and content that will enable all European citizens to become stakeholders in the INFORMATION SOCIETY. It looks at issues of closer co-operation between EU institutions in all information and communication matters, and examines ways of bringing EU information to citizens.

The EU aims to make Europe the most competitive and dynamic knowledge-based economy in the world, capable of sustaining economic growth with more and better jobs, and with greater social cohesion. A major building block in achieving EU information policy goals is the *e*Europe initiative. Launched in December 1999, the subsequent *e*Europe 2002 Action Plan of June 2000 set out a roadmap to achieve *e*Europe's targets. The Action Plan identified three main objectives: a cheaper, faster secure Internet; investing in people and skills; and stimulating the use of the Internet.

In seeking to establish a cheap, fast and secure Internet, the EU identifies the need to provide cheaper and faster Internet access for all citizens by means of the liberalization of telecommunications regulations, and the availability of low-cost, high-speed networks. Faster Internet access for students and researchers will ideally be made available, and secure networks and smart cards developed. In the interests of social inclusion, the EU sees these developments as being made available to all citizens, including those in remote and less developed areas.

Investing in people and skills is crucial to getting people into jobs and encouraging economic competitiveness. The EU actively encourages the deployment of the Internet in schools to prepare students for working in the information economy. It encourages member states to invest in education and training, including lifelong learning, in order to stimulate digital literacy among employees and to create employment opportunities. Participation for all citizens in the knowledge-based economy is crucial to full social inclusion. The EU recognizes the importance of educating people in making use of electronic access to public information, and the opportunities offered by electronic participation in decision-making processes.

Stimulating the use of the Internet is vital to EU information policy, both for the economy and for the information needs of the citizen. The EU aims to promote measures to accelerate electronic commerce, provide electronic access to public services, address the issues of healthcare online, provide European digital content for global-wide networks and develop intelligent transport systems. Consumer confidence and issues of copyright and data protection need to be addressed in order to fully achieve the objective of encouraging Internet use in all areas of public and private life.

*e*Europe is not the only EU information policy initiative. The linked *e*Learning initiative seeks to mobilize the educational and cultural communities, as well as the economic and social players in Europe, in order to speed up changes in the education and training systems for Europe's move to a knowledge-based society. Additionally, the EU also funds programmes researching information issues. These include the eContent programme and the Information Society Technologies (IST) Programme.

Further reading

*e*Europe (http://www.europa.eu.int/information_society/ eeurope/index_en.htm).

eEurope 2002: Creating a EU Framework for the Exploitation of Public Sector Information (2001) (http://www.cordis.lu/econtent/psi/home.html).

eContent programme (http://www.cordis.lu/econtent/).

*e*Learning (http://europa.eu.int/comm/education/elearn ing/index.html).

EU Information Society policies (http://www. europa.eu.int/pol/infso/index_en.htm).

Information Society (2001) (http://www.europa.eu.int/ scadplus/leg/en/lvb/l24100.htm).

Information Society Technologies (IST) Programme (http://www.cordis.lu/ist/).

SEE ALSO: business information service; economics of information; research in library and information science; telecommunications

ROSALIND JOHNSON

EVIDENCE-BASED HEALTHCARE

Evidence-based healthcare advocates the collection, interpretation and integration of valid, important and applicable evidence. Such evidence may include symptoms or perceptions reported by the patient, physical signs observed by the clinician and findings derived from rigorously conducted research. Irrespective of its origin, the best available evidence, moderated by sensitivity to a patient's circumstances and preferences, is harnessed to improve clinical decision-making.

This model of clinical KNOWLEDGE MANAGEMENT therefore promotes research evidence in making decisions that affect the health of individual patients or whole populations. In doing so, evidence-based healthcare seeks to address information overload (requiring clinicians in internal medicine to read nineteen articles per day every day of the year to keep-up-to-date) and information delay (a ten- to fifteen-year delay between publication of research findings and their promotion as routine practice in textbooks). It also acknowledges the inevitability of information decay (deterioration of a clinician's knowledge from the time of their qualification), unless practitioners develop life-long learning strategies for replenishing that knowledge.

The rise of evidence-based healthcare

Evidence-based medicine first emerged from McMaster University, Canada, in the early 1990s. Whereas the statistical focus of its predecessor, clinical epidemiology, seemed detached from direct patient care, evidence-based medicine demonstrated increasing sophistication in applying research at the bedside. The paradigm soon encompassed specific branches of medicine such as psychiatry and dentistry, and related domains such as nursing, pathology and pharmacotherapy. By the mid-1990s a broader term, evidence-based healthcare, was a portmanteau for wide-ranging activities promoted within and outside medicine.

The late 1990s saw evidence-based healthcare spread to contiguous fields such as education, social services, human resource management and criminology. This attests to the potential of the model for any profession with a substantive knowledge base and a requirement for informed decision-making. An even broader term, evidence-based practice, captures the commonality of approaches across a broad spectrum of professional endeavour.

The process of evidence-based healthcare

Evidence-based healthcare emphasizes four requisite information processes: problem specification (focusing the question), searching the literature, filtering search results and critical appraisal (assessing retrieved items for validity, reliability and applicability). These processes may be conducted by intermediaries, such as librarians or information officers, on behalf of busy clinicians or, increasingly, by end-users themselves. They are followed by clinician-specific tasks such as applying the results to individual patients and evaluating clinical and professional performance.

Impact on health information management

The impact of evidence-based healthcare on the information profession is threefold. First, librarians are involved in the production of evidence, searching across multiple databases to retrieve rigorous studies for use in developing practice guidelines or systematic reviews. Such reviews efficiently summarize the literature addressing a given question. They aim to be systematic, explicit and reproducible and thereby minimize bias. Review methods are quality assured by guidance produced either nationally, by the UK NHS Centre for Reviews and Dissemination at the University of York, or internationally, by the Cochrane Collaboration. The Cochrane Collaboration is an international organization dedicated to the production, maintenance and dissemination of systematic reviews of healthcare. The Campbell Collaboration, a recent sibling of its Cochrane namesake, has similar objectives but is targeted at systematic reviews of education, legislation and social care. Systematic reviews and guidelines are very resource-intensive and are typically supported by information workers associated with an academic research unit, a professional organization or a regional or national health technology assessment agency.

Second, librarians working for local health organizations provide services, training and resources to enable staff to address specific clinical questions. This clinical orientation has led to the resurgence of librarians attached to clinical teams (clinical librarians) and even to a new role – the *informationist*. Librarians are learning how to break down a clinical question into its component parts, typically using a Patient Intervention Comparison Outcome (PICO) anatomy. They are also becoming familiar with methodological filters – groups of search terms associated with rigorous research studies – as developed by McMaster University. Many librarians participate in critical appraisal skills programmes that utilize specially developed checklists to ensure that essential criteria are addressed when evaluating research. Specialist value-added evidence databases augment traditional bibliographic products such as MEDLINE. These include the Cochrane Library (for systematic reviews and randomized controlled trials), the Database of Abstracts of Reviews of Effectiveness, Best Evidence (a database of one-page critically appraised summaries) and the NHS Economic Evaluation Database (for cost-effectiveness studies). The rise of evidence-based healthcare has coincided with the growth of the Internet with an increasing number of tools and resources bypassing traditional publishing routes to become available directly via the World Wide Web (see, for example, Netting the Evidence at www.netting theevidence.org.uk).

Finally, involvement by librarians in evidence-based healthcare has led to interest in evidence-based librarianship. Such cross-fertilization of an overtly biomedical model to librarianship poses many challenges. Librarianship requires a more accommodating definition of evidence and the development of new tools (such as checklists) and databases to accommodate different models of working. Rigorous research is less plentiful while established evidence-handling techniques need to be translated or adapted to apparently incompatible domains.

Wider impact of evidence-based healthcare

Evidence-based healthcare has had a pervasive impact on health information management. The examples above are directly attributable to the paradigm but more tangential links lie in products of an evidence-based era such as the UK National Electronic Library for Health and the National Health Service's telephone (NHSDirect), and Web-based (NHSDirectOnline) enquiry services. Given the progress of evidence-based healthcare over little more than a decade, its inexorable rise seems destined to continue for many years to come.

Further reading

Eldredge, J.D. (2000) 'Evidence-based librarianship: An overview', *Bulletin of the Medical Library Association* 88: 289–302.

Gray, J.A.M. (2001) *Evidence-Based Healthcare: How to Make Health Policy and Management Decisions*, 2nd edn, Churchill-Livingstone.

Sackett, D.L., Richardson, W.S., Rosenberg, W.M.C. and Haynes, R.B. (2000) *Evidence-Based Medicine: How to Practice and Teach EBM*, 2nd edn, Churchill-Livingstone.

Trinder, L. and Reynolds, S. (eds) (2000) *Evidence-Based Practice: A Critical Appraisal*, Blackwell Science.

ANDREW BOOTH

EXCHANGE PROGRAMMES

A means of acquiring printed materials that would otherwise be unattainable either because of financial restrictions or because they are not available through established trade channels. It is known that, as long ago as the seventeenth century, exchange of publications was taking place, as when the Royal Library of France received English, German and Chinese publications in exchange for duplicates. Formal exchanges of sets of public documents between governments are generally termed 'official exchanges', while the informal arrangements among learned associations and institutions involving the interchange of all types of publications are deemed to be unofficial (Einhorn 1972).

Establishing an exchange programme is a relatively time-consuming process. A suitable supplier has first to be identified, then contacted, and if a successful agreement is negotiated supply of publications can consequently be expected. The administrative process has been considerably speeded up with the development of electronic communications since the 1980s.

Items that are used for exchange by either party can be their own publications, duplicates received from elsewhere or titles that have been purchased for the purpose of the exchange. An exchange can be set up as:

- A one-for-one exchange, where similar monetary worth can be surmised.
- A block exchange, where several titles are thought to be of roughly equivalent value.
- Open exchange, where no definitive value can be established and materials are supplied as and when they are published.

It may be said that exchange is a form of barter that is hard to quantify as usually no real values are available. In this case the worth of an exchange item can only be realized in the use made of it.

An important area of exchange has been between the West and RUSSIA AND THE FORMER SOVIET UNION and the other former socialist countries of CENTRAL AND EASTERN EUROPE. Following the Second World War, information from the Soviet Union was of great significance and interest to the West, particularly that contained in scientific publications. This, with the accompanying growth of Soviet Studies in universities, led to extensive exchanges of publications. The two basic elements that influenced the establishment of strong exchange agreements were (1) the unavailability of publications from the communist countries on the market, leaving exchange as the only way for Western libraries to obtain some publications, and (2) the weak currencies of the communist countries, which encouraged a willingness among institutions there to develop reliable exchange programmes in exchange for Western publications. Since the early 1990s, the market has become more open. This, however, is not a speedy process and it will be several decades before the need for exchanges with the region will vanish.

Exchange programmes of materials in the languages of EAST ASIA, particularly those from China and Japan, also play an important part in library ACQUISITIONS. Again, this system is necessary as many research publications are not for sale, due to government regulations.

The basis for exchange programmes changes with the economic and political climate at any time. For example, during the communist period many libraries in the USSR and Eastern Europe were supplied with several copies of each publication from the state publishing houses. These

were ideal for use in their exchange programmes. In most of these countries this supply of multiple copies is no longer forthcoming. Since the 1990s, although large libraries with sufficient funds have been able to continue with exchange programmes, many smaller libraries are finding it difficult. In the West, exchange librarians are always conscious of the need to monitor the cost-effectiveness of exchange programmes versus purchasing. Electronic document delivery is also beginning to have an impact on exchange programmes, which may now be seen as less necessary than was formerly the case.

UNESCO has always promoted international exchange of publications and the UNESCO *Handbook on the International Exchange of Publications*, first compiled in the 1950s, was a comprehensive work on the subject published in one volume and in four languages. At a time when library exchanges were developing, this publication explained the exchange process in detail and highlighted the value of such transactions between nations. For those wishing to initiate exchange agreements, *The World of Learning*, published annually, contains useful addresses, and a publication with proven contact addresses is *East–West Links. Directory of Information Providers in the Former Soviet Union and Central-Eastern Europe* (Hogg and Ladizesky 1996).

References

Einhorn, N.R. (1972) 'Exchange of publications', *Encyclopedia of Library and Information Science* 8, New York: Dekker, p. 283.

Hogg, R. and Ladizesky, K. (1996) *East–West Links. Directory of Information Providers in the Former Soviet Union and Central-Eastern Europe*, British Library Document Supply Centre.

The World of Learning (annual) Europa.

United Nations Educational Scientific and Cultural Organization (1964) *Handbook on the International Exchange of Publications*, 3rd edn, Paris: UNESCO.

Further reading

Deal, C. (1989) 'The administration of international exchanges in academic libraries: A survey', *Library Acquisitions: Practice and Theory* 13: 199–209 [a useful survey citing several valuable items for additional reading].

Zilper, N. (1986) 'Assessment of contemporary research materials exchanges between American and Soviet Libraries', in M. Tax-Choldin (ed.) *Libraries and Information in Slavic and East European Studies: Proceedings of the Second National Conference of*

Slavic Librarians and Information Specialists, New York: Russian Publishers, pp. 486–503.

SEE ALSO: collection development

KATHLEEN LADIZESKY

EXPERT SYSTEMS

Computer programs that solve problems or give advice, with explanations when appropriate, by employing a reasoning mechanism using stored knowledge and data relating to a specific problem situation.

General applications

As a practical implementation of research into ARTIFICIAL INTELLIGENCE, expert systems (ES), also described as knowledge-based systems, have been developed as an attempt to propagate, via a computer program, the knowledge and skills of experts who are engaged in tasks such as diagnosis, interpretation, prediction, instruction, design and monitoring. Through the development of such systems, organizations seek improved and consistent performance at places where relevant expertise is not otherwise accessible. ES have evolved from initial attempts to emulate intelligent behaviour on a computer (by capturing and representing the knowledge of experts using HEURISTICS), to include relatively straightforward applications, which take advantage of easy-to-use expert system development packages. As artefacts embodying knowledge they can be regarded as potential sources of information and advice for the library user, accessed over local and public NETWORKS.

SEE ALSO: organization of knowledge

EXTRANET

A private NETWORK using the Internet PROTOCOL to share a company's information with suppliers, partners, customers or other businesses. An extranet can be viewed as an INTRANET opened to a wider range of users so as to provide a company with an effective forum for work on projects, obtaining bids, sharing of news, joint training programmes and ongoing communication over co-operation. Security is crucial so that firewalls, ENCRYPTION and other network and COMPUTER SECURITY features are essential.

F

FACETED CLASSIFICATION

1 A scheme of BIBLIOGRAPHIC CLASSIFICATION based on the analysis of subjects according to a set of fundamental concepts, usually personality, matter, energy, space, time. All modern schemes of classification are faceted to a certain degree, e.g. they provide tables of constant numbers for divisions relating to time and space. A classification scheme that allows the classifier to build up a description of a particular document from various unit schedules can be called 'faceted', 'synthetic' or 'analytic-synthetic'.

2 Classification schemes whose terms are grouped by conceptual categories and ordered so as to display their generic relations. The categories or 'facets' are standard unit-schedules and the notation for the terms from these various unit-schedules is combined as appropriate, in accordance with a prescribed order of permutation or combination.

SEE ALSO: organization of knowledge; Ranganathan, Shiyali Ramamrita

FARRADANE, JASON (1906–89)

British information scientist and founder member of the INSTITUTE OF INFORMATION SCIENTISTS.

His career was devoted to the scientific approach to information handling, a theme he sketched out in his paper at the Royal Society Scientific Information Conference in 1948. Education for INFORMATION SCIENCE was not available in Britain until he established courses at Northampton College of Advanced Technology (now City University, London). He was the first editor of the *Bulletin of the Institute of Information Scientists* and editor in chief of *Information Storage and Retrieval*.

His chief theoretical contribution was to relational analysis, which he developed during the 1960s as a counter to the artificiality of existing CLASSIFICATION and INDEXING systems. From his study of the psychology of thinking he derived nine categories of relations to express the relationships between concepts in documents. Due to their complexity, however, relational indexing structures did not lend themselves easily to contemporary computer applications and have thus remained rather as a theoretical development.

Further reading

Yates-Mercer, P.A. (1989) 'An appreciation of Jason Farradane', *Journal of Information Science* 15: 305–6.

SEE ALSO: information science education

FEE-BASED SERVICES

Fee-based services are those that offer to provide a range of information on demand in return for payment. They may be provided as one part of a range of library and information services, other parts of which may be offered without a direct charge, e.g. as within a public or academic library setting, or could be the sole activity, or part of a range of commercial services, available from companies operating in the private sector. These could include a number of different types of organization ranging from societies and associations to independent INFORMATION

BROKERS and large information PUBLISHING companies.

Why they exist

However large and comprehensive the collection of information and related service provision maintained by an organization may be, it is unlikely to be self-sufficient in terms of its ability to provide the total information requirement of that organization at all times, either in terms of subject coverage or format, or often in terms of timeliness. Private individuals also have the need from time to time for specialist information, not necessarily work-related and not always readily available from local or free sources, including those available on the Internet. Both groups will therefore want to be able to meet their specialist needs as they arise and the only means could be by purchasing a tailor-made information product from a reliable information provider. Therefore the first reason is likely to be market demand.

A second reason for the initial existence, but not always continuance, of fee-based services, is pressure from senior management, who in turn may be responding to corporate, or local and central government, policies. Library and information services may be perceived as having considerable commercial potential, either as a unique or specialist collection in a particular subject area, or as serving a given geographical region. However, to develop a viable commercial service requires thorough market research and resource planning by those who will be running it, as well as long-term support and commitment by the parent body.

The providers

These cover a range of organizations across the public and private sectors, including NATIONAL LIBRARIES, PUBLIC LIBRARIES, educational institutions, membership associations, information brokers, specialist consultants, MARKET RESEARCH organizations, database producers and publishers. Private companies may also make their own internal information service available to external clients on a fee-paying basis. In public and national libraries fee-based services are often set up as autonomous units with their own separate budgets, and run alongside the free core services. Staff may be employed specifically to work within the fee-based service, or may take on duties elsewhere in the organization. Staff

expertise and knowledge will be a key element of any fee-based service. One area in which a considerable number of fee-based services have been successfully set up is that of business information (*Where to Buy Business Information* 1999). Services may be listed on websites, in brochures and sometimes, as in the case of local services, via the local press.

How they operate

Having established that there is a market for a fee-based service, those putting a fee-based service in place have to set out a policy and procedures for its effective and efficient operation (Webb and Winterton 2002). Consideration will have to be given to appropriate delivery methods, as well as to information sources, to meet expressed user needs. The user should then be able to see a detailed statement of what is available, where and when, what it will cost and whether the provider accepts liability for, or guarantees the accuracy of, the information provided. There may be a standard charge for certain services, e.g. photocopying, online searching or an individual quotation given for each job. Charges will vary according to the amount of time taken, the expertise and level of staff involved, the sources used and the overall pricing policy. Users, or clients, may have a choice of payment methods, e.g. payment in advance, subscription, payment on delivery, or in arrears by invoice or credit card.

What is provided

As noted above, a large number of fee-based services provide business information of various kinds, including company, financial and related legal information, as well as carrying out market research. Also on offer across a range of subject areas are monitoring and alerting services, abstracting and indexing, mailing list maintenance, mail shots, translation services, fax and e-mail bureaux, arrangement of conferences, training, DESKTOP PUBLISHING, economic and statistical forecasting and commentary, report writing and a variety of research services. Information can be provided at regular intervals, as with current awareness services, or on a one-off basis, and in various formats, e.g. as a printed document or in electronic form. Delivery can be by post, courier or electronic means. Speed and confidentiality are likely to be key determinants in the choice of delivery method. Other fee-based services could involve the buying-in of information expertise, rather than just information itself, as is indicated by some of the services listed above.

The users

There are a number of organizations that do not have their own internal library or information resource. Although most will have access to the Internet they may not have the time or the expertise to benefit fully from its use (Pedley 2001). Nor will all the information required necessarily be available directly. Such organizations could rely heavily on the use of a range of external information providers for various purposes. Money saved through not supporting an internal service becomes available for the purchase of information from an outside service. Other organizations, even those with an in-house information service, choose to make occasional or regular use of external services to complement their own resources. The third category would cover individuals who require information for their own private purposes. They may obtain some information from a free source, which might then refer them on to a fee-based service for more detailed research. In order to be able to take advantage of such services, potential users need to be aware of their existence. Therefore directories, lists and reviews of services, as well as providers' own brochures, need to be widely available. Professional groups, associations and publishers could help identify specialist consultants.

References

Pedley, P. (2001) *The Invisible Web*, London: ASLIB.
Webb, S.P. and Winterton, J. (2002) *Fee-Based Services in Library and Information Centres*, London: ASLIB.
Where to Buy Business Information (1999) East Grinstead: Bowker-Saur

SEE ALSO: business information service; consultancy; information professions; liability for information provision

SYLVIA WEBB

FIBRE-OPTICS

Thin strands of highly transparent glass or plastic that will carry DATA in the form of pulses of laser light. They carry BROADBAND signals that sup-

port a wide range of services to the home and workplace.

SEE ALSO: information and communication technology

FICTION

Imaginative writing that usually takes the form of novels and short stories.

The value of fiction

We may live in an INFORMATION SOCIETY but we also need to satisfy people's imaginative needs. Fiction is an art form that possesses a unique personal quality not found in other media. Nothing can replace the one-to-one communication between the author and the reader through the printed word, nothing can simulate that interweaving of text and imagination that is the experience of reading: the British novelist Margaret Drabble denies that novels are a frivolity, a luxury or an indulgence, contending that they are in fact a means of comprehending and experiencing and extending our world and our vision. At a time of increasing concern about LITERACY levels, the potential for PUBLIC LIBRARIES to promote imaginative reading is very great.

The fiction industry

In 1999 108,000 books were published in the UK. Fiction was by far the largest category, accounting for some 9,700 titles. That is equivalent to more than twenty new novels for every day of the year. Sales of fiction account for almost a quarter of the total estimated value of the book sector.

The incredible array of choice means that it can be difficult to keep up to date with or to discover new novelists. Reviews of new titles are featured in many newspapers; however, many books are never reviewed at all. Most academic texts tend to concentrate on established writers; however, *The Novel Today* (Massie 1990) provides a manageable introduction to contemporary British fiction. *The Good Reading Guide* (McLeish 1988) is also very accessible. It contains short features on some 300 authors, describing the kinds of book they write and suggesting books that might make interesting follow-ups.

What do people like to read?

Surveys by Euromonitor (Mann 1991) have consistently shown that fiction accounts for over two-thirds of the books being read at any one time. The most popular categories of fiction are romance and crime/thrillers (each accounting for about 15 per cent of all books being read), modern novels and historical novels (each accounting for about 9 per cent), and war/adventure books and classic titles (each accounting for about 5 per cent). By contrast, the most popular non-fiction subject is biography, accounting for 6 per cent of all books being read. The Euromonitor surveys also consider how people obtain the books they read: over one-third of the books currently being read had been bought (including purchases through book clubs), about one-third had been borrowed from libraries and probably less than one-fifth had been borrowed from friends or relatives. The rest were gifts or were already in the home.

Fiction in public libraries

Fiction is very popular in public libraries, accounting for 326.2 million loans during 1990–1 (Sumsion and Fossey 1992). The stock is heavily used: adult fiction accounted for 38 per cent of active lending stock in 1991 but for 58 per cent of book issues. The government-funded PUBLIC LENDING RIGHT (PLR) pays a royalty to authors for the loans of their books from public libraries and the PLR listings indicate the most popular authors. In 1993 the leading five authors were all fiction authors: Catherine Cookson, Agatha Christie, Danielle Steel, Dick Francis and Ruth Rendell (PLR 1993). The PLR data also demonstrates the diversity of the public's taste in literature, showing, for example, that the classics are still widely read. The PLR lists were used in the compilation of *Who Else Writes Like?* (Huse 1993). This is a readers' guide to fiction authors based principally on a list of popular authors, to which a number of librarians and fiction specialists have added other names and alternative authors whose genre and writing style are very similar.

Promoting fiction reading

There has been much debate about whether libraries exist to give people the books they want or the books that those in authority believe the people need. The best approaches to fiction promotion should make no judgements about what is 'good' or 'bad' reading but encourage creative reading and help readers decide for themselves what they want to read next. They should also take into account the findings of READING RESEARCH. Goodall (1991) describes successful fiction promotions carried out by several UK library authorities. Libraries can also learn from the BOOK TRADE in promoting fiction; for example, the annual awarding of the Booker Prize has now become a major media event and winning the Prize can increase sales of a book dramatically. There are also benefits to be gained by joint fiction promotion schemes, which can involve publishers, booksellers and book suppliers as well as library authorities. A strikingly successful example of such co-operation in the UK is the 'Well Worth Reading Scheme' (Kempthorne 1991).

References

Goodall, D. (1991) in M. Kinnell (ed.) *Managing Fiction in Libraries*, Library Association.

Huse, R. (ed.) (1993) *Who Else Writes Like? A Readers' Guide to Fiction Authors*, Library and Information Statistics Unit, Loughborough University.

Kempthorne, B. (1991) 'Still well worth reading about: Well Worth Reading – the third chapter', *Public Library Journal* 6(6): 157–61.

McLeish, K. (1988) *Good Reading Guide*, Bloomsbury.

Mann, P.H. (1991) in M. Kinnell (ed.) *Managing Fiction in Libraries*, Library Association.

Massie, A. (1990) *The Novel Today: A Critical Guide to the British Novel 1970–1989*, Longman.

PLR (annual press release available in January from PLR, Bayheath House, Prince Regent Street, Stockton-on-Tees, Cleveland TS18 1DF).

Sumsion, J. and Fossey, D.R. (1992) *LISU Annual Library Statistics 1992*, Library and Information Statistics Unit, Loughborough University.

Further reading

Kinnell, M. (ed.) (1991) *Managing Fiction in Libraries*, Library Association.

SEE ALSO: book trade

DEBORAH L. GOODALL

FID

The FID (International Federation for Information and Documentation), formed in 1895 and effectively dissolved in 2002, was an international professional association of institutions and individuals involved in developing, producing, researching and using information products, information systems and methods, and in the management of information.

Membership and structure

FID membership included National, International, Institutional, Sponsoring, Corporate and Personal Members from nearly 100 countries. It was governed by a General Assembly and Council, and there were strategic groups to advise the Council on membership, liaison and training. Operational advice groups worked with the Secretariat on conferences and congresses; marketing and public relations; projects; publications; training issues; and product development.

There were six regional commissions – for Western, Eastern and Southern Africa (FID/CAF); Asia and Oceania (FID/CAO); Latin America (FID/CLA); the Caribbean and North America (FID/CNA); Northern Africa and the Near East (FID/NANE); and Europe (FID/ROE). Its range of professional concern could be seen through its committees, which covered classification; education and training; information for industry; information policies and programmes; intellectual property issues; social sciences documentation and information; and the Universal Decimal Classification (UDC). Special interest groups dealt with archives and records management; banking, finance and insurance information; environmental information; executive information systems; information for public administration; roles, careers and development of the modern information professional; quality issues in the information sector; and safety control and risk management. There was also a Corporate Members network and a task force on global information infrastructures and superhighways.

Professional programme, activities and publications

FID had seven main programme areas, covering professional development; business, finance and industrial information; information policy; information science; information and communication technology; information processing and products; and information management. FID's functions and activities focused on education and training; conferences and seminars; publications and projects; personal networks; and consultancy services. It operated two international clearing houses for education and training, and information policy issues. Publications included the *FID News Bulletin, Education and Training Newsletter, International Forum on Information and Documentation* and a series of Occasional Papers.

Universal Decimal Classification

When FID was formed as the Institut International de Bibliographie (IIB) in 1895 by Paul OTLET and Henri La Fontaine, one of the objectives was to create a Répertoire bibliographique universel (RBU), which resulted in the development of the UNIVERSAL DECIMAL CLASSIFICATION (UDC). UDC is a numerical system for the classification and retrieval of information. It is maintained by a not-for-profit Consortium of Publishers of UDC together with the FID and is widely used internationally for scientific and technical information as it is not dependent on any one alphabet or language. In March 1993 the UDC Consortium completed the compilation of the first authorized machine-readable version of the UDC schedules.

Tokyo Resolution

To mark its 100th anniversary, FID developed perhaps its last notable contribution, the Tokyo Resolution on a Strategic Alliance of International Non-Governmental Organizations in Information. This resolution was intended to be a manifesto for future decades that would strengthen the collaboration between information-oriented non-governmental organizations (NGOs) and associations in the information age. It expressed deep concern with global problems; open and unrestricted access to information; universal human rights; universal literacy, lifelong learning, education and training; the importance of change; the information gap between various countries and societies; and the need for NGO collaboration, consultation and strategic planning. Its high ideals and sense of the realities of the INFORMATION SOCIETY are a fitting memorial to an organization that played an important role in the world of information work for over 100 years.

The end of FID

A deepening financial crisis that resulted in failure to pay debts, staff salaries and operating costs gradually brought FID to a point at which the Secretariat had to be closed down and its office furniture auctioned off in 2002. The existing Council's terms of office expired at the end of 2001 and no elections were held to replace them. Although FID was not dissolved as a legal entity at this time, it effectively ceased to exist. Its archive continues to be held by the Royal Library at the Hague, Netherlands, and will be safeguarded by the UDC Consortium.

Further reading

Goedegebuure, B.G. (1994) 'Celebrating FID's centennial – the Tokyo Resolution', *FID News Bulletin* 44: 115–17.

SEE ALSO: information professions; library associations

STELLA KEENAN, REVISED BY EDITORS

FILE TRANSFER PROTOCOL

A file transfer protocol (FTP) provides facilities to transmit data and files between host-specific formats and networked standard form. This permits file transfer to take place between otherwise incompatible systems across a network.

SEE ALSO: information and communication technology

FILM

Sequential still photographic images on celluloid that give the illusion of movement when projected. Also referred to as motion pictures and movies.

History

Primitive moving pictures were available before the invention of photography, in the form of, for example, optical toys based on the phenomenon of persistence of vision. The actual inventor of film is uncertain. Thomas Edison invented the kinetoscope in 1890 but this was not strictly speaking a projected film system. There are many other candidates, including the Lumière brothers in France (1895) and William Friese-Greene in England (1889). However, the problems with the precise definition of what constitutes projected film and complications such as the amount of work done for Edison by William Dickson make

a definitive date and inventor almost impossible to ascertain (Happé 1971).

The novelty of early film meant that initially even the most basic short documentary topic would be successful, but the new medium soon developed more complicated narrative systems. Black-and-white silent film established itself as the major entertainment medium of the early twentieth century. At the same time it began to provide a unique social and historical documentary record of the period.

Although there had been many earlier experiments with sound, a practical sound system was not actually introduced until 1927, and from that date silent film was made virtually redundant. Various forms of colour film were also available (including hand tinting) before the Technicolor three-colour process was used in 1935. Colour very gradually increased in popularity but did not dominate feature film production until the 1960s. Other developments have ranged from short-lived gimmicks (for example 3D film) to more significant alterations such as the introduction of Cinemascope in 1953, which changed the ratio of feature films from 1.33:1 to 2.35:1.

Increasing interest in films as an art form led to greater interest in preservation and to the founding of national bodies such as the British Film Institute (founded 1933) and the American Film Centre (founded 1938), and co-operation through the Fédération Internationale des Archives du Film (FIAF), founded in 1938.

The study of film as a serious art form has also led to the creation of a vast body of historical and theoretical writing.

Formats

There have been various minor film formats but the most commonly used have established themselves as suitable for certain specific uses. Most feature films have been shot on either 35 mm or 70 mm film. Because of the great cost of cameras and projectors for the larger formats, smaller 16 mm film has been normally used for educational and short films. A large 16 mm film hire system was established, which also made feature films available in this format for educational and non-professional bodies. Home use of film was normally in 8 mm until 1964, when Super 8 mm became available.

The latter use of film has virtually been superseded by videotape, which is also now the most common method for the storage of non-archival film collections. ARCHIVES may also make videos available for viewing rather than expensive film duplicates or rare originals. Although there are larger tape formats available for professional broadcast quality, the most common videotape format for library or home use is the half-inch VHS videocassette. Although VHS became the predominant format in the 1980s, there are still problems of incompatibility due to national variations in broadcast standards. Equally it does not have a long enough life to make it suitable for archival purposes.

However, the comparative robustness of video-cassettes, combined with their low cost and easy operation, has meant that they have made films more accessible to their audience than ever before. It seems likely that video tapes will in turn be replaced by the OPTICAL DISK format known as DVD, a high-quality multimedia digital format increasingly used for the commercial distribution of feature films for home use. Indeed, as digital cameras make inroads into the traditional market for still photography, it is possible that the whole medium of film will eventually disappear or least be superseded for all normal purposes.

Preservation and storage

Early film stock was nitrate-based, which means that it is unstable and subject to both natural deterioration and spontaneous combustion. Much early film has been lost in this way and many archives have been engaged in a race to duplicate nitrate film on to safer acetate stock before it is destroyed. Nitrate and acetate film have to be stored separately and both are normally held on circular cans, which can be bulky and difficult to store. Handling can easily damage film and to minimize risk film always needs to be projected by someone who is professionally qualified.

The cost of film and the difficulties of storage have made large collections impractical for all but the most affluent of libraries or archives. Where rare or original films are held there is also a tension between the need for PRESERVATION and the provision of reasonable access for library users. DVD shares both the qualities and the faults of all digital objects in this respect.

Classification and cataloguing

There is no widely recognized 'purpose-built' CLASSIFICATION system for film. Existing systems such as Dewey or UDC are sometimes used in preference to individually designed systems. Collections may be filed in an order that is deemed more appropriate, for example alphabetically by title for feature films or in date order for news film.

The cataloguing of film has been described as 'probably more expensive and demanding than any other form of information source' (Kent *et al.* 1971: 108).

There are several codes available, including the ASLIB Film Production Librarians' Group Film Cataloguing Rules (1963) and the ANGLO-AMER-ICAN CATALOGUING RULES. Feature films in particular cause problems in relation to authorship. As well as the director's there may be important contributions from scriptwriters, producers, actors, cinematographers, art directors and designers. Indexing all the relevant names or providing one-word plot summaries or stock shots can obviously be very time-consuming, and can be particularly aided by computerized systems (Tucker 1988). Although documentary film may normally involve fewer personnel it may include many subjects worthy of index entries. Film libraries that hold short stock shots of numerous subjects require easy access through indexing even though the extracts may have no obvious title or 'author'. In all of these cases there is a need for catalogues to be able to review films in some detail.

References

Happé, B.L. (1971) *Basic Motion Picture Technology*, Focal Press.

Kent, A., Lancour, H. and Daily, J.E. (eds) (1971) *The Encyclopedia of Library and Information Science*, vol. 20, Marcel Dekker Inc., p. 108.

Tucker, G. (1988) 'The STRIX system in HTV Film Library', *Audio Visual Librarian* 14: 82–3.

Further reading

Harrison, H.P. (1973) *Film Library Techniques*, Focal Press.

SEE ALSO: broadcasting; cultural industries; knowledge industries; multimedia librarianship; preservation

DAVID HUXLEY

FILTERING

Filtering is most commonly used to refer to the employment of software packages designed to identify and block access to INTERNET content, although it also applies to the same process in any networked environment. This process is dependent upon the MONITORING of usage, which raises privacy issues. Although the term filtering is invariably used as if it meant filtering and blocking to exclude content, it is worth remembering that it can be applied with equal validity to filtering to select content through RECOMMENDER SYSTEMS.

Filtering software

Access to content can be filtered across a whole network, within a specific organization, at the computer of a family or an individual or by a provider of public access facilities. Software products that can achieve this are widely available and are often referred to, by the name of one of the early entrants into the market, as 'Net Nannies'. Other products that are, or have been, available are Cyber Patrol, Cyber Sitter, Net Shepherd, Smart Filter, Surf Watch and Websense. In the first place, all of them depend on accurate monitoring of usage. They will keep track of what happens on a network or an individual computer, recording keystrokes, time and date, name of program executed and the specific workstation on which activities occur. As an example, Surfcontrol publicizes its Cyber Patrol software as a secure and customizable means to protect children from websites that contain pornography, incitement to hatred, depictions of violence and a range of other disturbing or unacceptable content. The company also points out that it has integrated this into a range of systems and applications such as firewalls, proxy servers, search engines and ISP services, so as to offer systems protection against security breaches and inappropriate internal usage.

Filtering software identifies and blocks content on the basis of one or more criteria. It can block on the basis of:

- A 'stop list' of named sites. Someone, usually the supplier, has to create and update the list, but users can generally customize the list themselves. The software can also usually be set to exclude all sites except those specifically allowed.
- Particular words, parts of words and particular types of images (such as those with patches of flesh-tone colour). This approach is also dependent on the creation and management of a list, in this case of unacceptable words.
- Ratings that have been applied to a site. This can be done by the owners of the site, or by some third-party agency, according to an agreed system. Metadata facilities for a rating to be applied to a site exist, in the form of the Platform for Internet Content Selection (PICS). PICS will support whatever ratings system is chosen, but the dominant system is that of the Internet Content Ratings Association (www.rsac.org).

The basic technical case and rationale for filtering was well put by Paul Resnick, then Chair of the working group that developed PICS (Resnick and Miller 1996). If a filtering product is to be applied, making a good choice is vital. Apart from the publicity material put out by suppliers of filtering products, there are also good numbers of product reviews available. Schneider (1997) is the most systematic, but Heins and Cho (2001) collate reports on nineteen different products, including all the best-known ones. Schneider suggests a seven-stage process prior to operating filtering that includes an assessment of needs, testing products and adjusting the product that is actually purchased and installed.

Ethics of filtering

Whilst the individual's choice to filter, or not, is entirely their own concern, the most common use of filtering is to circumscribe children's access to Internet content. Many parents are not only afraid of bad effects on their children from certain kinds of WWW text, graphics and video, but also of the danger that they will exchange messages with potential corrupters. It is for these reasons that filtering systems are frequently advertised as permitting parents to control their children's Internet use. When a child's Internet access is via school facilities, parents generally expect the school authorities to act *in loco parentis*, and this generally means restricting access by some method, most usually filtering. Schools have well-defined objectives concerned with student learning, and filtering can be seen as merely ensuring that access to resources is appropriately focused on a set of learning objectives.

Some parents, however, are wary of imposing their own views on their children through filtering. There is a body of international law and statements of principle on children's rights, including the United Nations Convention on the Rights of the Child. Its provisions apply to young people up to the age of eighteen and set out in detail how the law should both protect and respect their rights. In particular, Article 13 affirms that the right to freedom of expression (including the rights to seek and receive information) applies to children as well as adults. Article 17 then goes on to specify that states should ensure that children have access to information and material from a diverse range of sources and media, including books published for children. This Article then goes on to call for 'appropriate guidelines for the protection of the child from information and material injurious to his or her well-being'. Examples of guidelines and sets of rules for safe Internet use that parents can teach to their children can be found in various places on the Web, for example Guidelines for Parents (www.missingkids.com).

The question of filtering generally arises where there is any kind of public responsibility for access, for instance in the work or office context. Pornographic images and text from the Internet are sometimes blatantly displayed or circulated in office e-mail systems with a clear intention of giving offence to colleagues (particularly women colleagues). Managers have an obvious responsibility to prevent this, so that employees can carry out their duties without gratuitous interference. Monitoring and filtering the company's system are obviously attractive forms of intervention. They seem capable of preventing the occurrence of this kind of delicate managerial problem, and allow management to argue that reasonable care has been taken. Disciplinary measures, including dismissal in one or two high-profile cases, have taken place. More difficult ethically are cases involving files of pornographic material left on the hard disks of computers used by an employee that might also be used by colleagues. Such cases have also attracted disciplinary measures, on the grounds that an unsuspecting discoverer has been harassed. It could well be claimed that in such cases the person responsible for the computer had not harassed anyone, but had suffered an invasion of privacy. Their real offence was personal use of company facilities.

Filtering in libraries

Many information professionals reject any filtering of public-access facilities, such as those found in libraries and information centres, on principle as the introduction of a form of CENSORSHIP. This is the argument adopted by the American Library Association. There are also practical objections to the filtering of public-information facilities. Experience shows that systems make virtually no distinction in blocking between what is legal and what is not. This can often disadvantage those who need access to content that is legal, such as that on safe sex or sexual health, particularly if they are too diffident to insist on their entitlements. At the same time, there is strong pressure for filtering in libraries particularly from pressure groups in the USA (Family Friendly Libraries, Library Watch, Enough is Enough, Coalition for the Protection of Children and Families, etc.) that exist almost entirely to promote filtering. Burt (1997) has put a cogent case for filtering in libraries along similar lines. In the UK there is an industry body, the Internet Watch Foundation, which favours filtering and encourages the reporting of objectionable content for possible police action.

Practice in libraries is similarly polarized. Many libraries do filter, but others do not. Baseline data on the prevalence of either approach is lacking (Willson and Oulton 2000). What is common in both cases is the existence of an ACCEPTABLE USE POLICY (AUP). These documents form a kind of contract between library and user, setting out, amongst other things, what may be accessed and what may not. Users are often asked to sign as evidence of their assent to the policy. A copy of the AUP may be handed to each user, it may be displayed in the form of a poster or it may appear on screen at the beginning of each Internet session, sometimes requiring a reaffirmation of acceptance. Examples of AUPs are widely available from library websites, and there are collections assembled for the use of those drafting or revising their own policies such as *Acceptable Use Policies: A Handbook* (www.pen.k12va.us/go/VDOE/technology/AUP/home/). Filtering may have a role in the policy, but in other cases the assent of users to the policy, coupled with a certain amount of supervision of the access points, may be considered sufficient action on the part of library management.

References

Burt, D. (1997) 'In defense of filtering', *American Libraries* 28: 46–8.

Heins, M. and Cho, C. (2001) *Internet Filters: A Public Policy Report*, National Coalition Against Censorship (www.ncac.org/issues/internetfilters.html).

Resnick, P. and Miller, J. (1996) 'PICS: Internet access controls without censorship', *Communications of the ACM* 39: 87–93.

Schneider, K. (1997) *A Practical Guide to Internet Filters*, Neal-Schuman.

Willson, J. and Oulton, T. (2000) 'Controlling access to the internet in UK public libraries', *OCLC Systems and Services* 16: 194–201.

Further reading

Sturges, P. (2002) *Public Internet Access in Libraries and Information Services*, Facet Publishing.

PAUL STURGES

FINDING AID

The term normally used by archivists as a general description of the calendars, indexes, catalogues and similar tools provided in record offices and archives.

SEE ALSO: archival description; archives

FIXED LOCATION

A method of assigning a specific position to a book in a library, in relation to other books and perhaps to a specific shelf. A mark is assigned which identifies that position. Absolute and unchanging fixed locations are normally only found in older libraries and collections that are kept in their original rooms or buildings. This is known as a shelf mark or class mark, the latter term reflecting the fact that CLASSIFICATION numbers (sometimes abbreviated in the case of complex FACETED CLASSIFICATIONS) are often used to derive the location mark. Fixed location is normally associated with CLOSED-ACCESS libraries. The mark is recorded in the catalogue, which must be consulted before the book can be retrieved. Subject retrieval of any book kept in a library organized on this system is achieved by the existence of an index to the catalogue or with the assistance of subject bibliographies.

FLOPPY DISK

The ubiquitous portable electromagnetic disk storage medium independent of and external to the computer in which it is used. Originally made in 8 1/4 in.- and 5 1/4 in.-diameter size and mounted in flexible plastic envelopes, floppies are now 3 1/2 in. in diameter and maintained in rigid plastic, with a metal sliding cover to protect the disk surface.

FONDS

A term used by ARCHIVISTS for a group of documents emanating from a distinct and single source. It is similar to the use of the term collection in the context of SPECIAL COLLECTIONS in RARE BOOK LIBRARIES and MANUSCRIPT LIBRARIES. Although the word is most common in European usage, it is also used by Anglophone archivists to imply something that is a more significant unit than a mere collection of documents. The principle of *respect du fonds* is central to all rules concerning the arrangement of the contents of archives, where it is considered vital not to disturb the context that establishes and supports the PROVENANCE of documents.

SEE ALSO: archival description; archives

FORGERY

Fabrication or alteration of a document with the intent to injure the interests of another. Document forgery is exemplified by the production of fake currency notes. Text forgeries include such classics as the *Donations of Constantine* (which allegedly conferred secular authority on the Pope), the 'Shakespeare' plays written by William Henry Ireland and the epistles of 'Phalaris'. A more esoteric form of forgery, of interest to bibliographers, is the creation of fake first editions of real works, a practice probably invented and certainly perfected by Harry Buxton Forman and Thomas James Wise.

SEE ALSO: bibliography; book trade

FREE-TEXT SEARCHING

Searching in which all aspects of the records in a database may be searched for terms chosen by the user, rather than terms occurring in a predetermined controlled vocabulary.

FREEDOM OF INFORMATION

A statutory right of access by the public to official information, particularly in the form of a Freedom of Information (FOI) Act, has existed in the USA since 1966 and in Australia, Canada and New Zealand since 1982, but Britain has only had an equivalent statute since 2000. Other European countries with FOI laws include Finland (enacted in 1951), Norway and Denmark (1970), Holland and France (1978). Sweden has had such legislation for more than 200 years: its Freedom of the Press Act of 1766 required that official documents should 'upon request immediately be made available to anyone'.

FOI laws

Under FOI laws applicants specify the information to which they seek access, and must be supplied with copies of relevant documents or records within a fixed time. The right is not absolute. FOI laws typically exempt information whose disclosure would be likely to harm defence, foreign relations, national security, law enforcement, the commercial activities of the government or third parties and personal privacy. Applicants who believe that information has been improperly withheld may appeal either to the courts or, in some countries, first to an Ombudsman, commissioner or tribunal. The legislation is seen as a means of improving the accountability of government, preventing secrecy being used to avoid embarrassment or legitimate criticism. Because the legislation gives the citizen a direct right of access to official information it empowers the individual, allowing people to make more informed choices and to play a greater role in influencing decisions and exposing the policy-making process to more effective scrutiny.

UK experience

The UK experience has been revealing, because it sets proponents of open government against a deeply ingrained tradition of official concealment. Slow and uneven progress towards greater freedom of information was made in the form of a number of limited disclosure statutes, many of which resulted from private member's bills or European legislation. The Consumer Credit Act 1974 allows individuals to see credit reference agency files on themselves. The DATA PROTEC-TION Act 1984 provides access to personal information held on computer. The Local Government (Access to Information) Act 1985 provides access to local authority meetings and connected documents. The Access to Personal Files Act 1987 allows individuals to see manually held social work and housing records on themselves. The Access to Medical Reports Act 1988 allows people to see a medical report written by their doctor for an insurance company or employer. The Education (School Records) Regulations 1989 allow access to school records. The Access to Health Records Act 1990 provides access to manually held health records. The Environmental Information Regulations 1992 provide access to environmental information held by public authorities.

At the same time, there was repeated pressure for comprehensive FOI legislation in the form of private member's and ten-minute rule bills in the House of Commons. Notably, Mark Fisher's Right to Know Bill (1992) proposed not only a general right of access to information held by public authorities, but also a right to certain private sector information. It also sought to reform the 1989 Official Secrets Act, in particular by providing that anyone charged with making an unauthorized disclosure of protected information should be able to argue that the disclosure was justified in the public interest. The bill, which had all-party support, completed its committee stage in the House of Commons before being talked out in July 1993.

Instead of a statutory right, a Code of Practice on Access to Government Information was introduced in April 1994. The code committed government departments and certain other bodies to releasing information on request, subject to fifteen broad categories of exemption. Exempt information may be released if the public interest in openness outweighs any harm that may result. Departments are also required to publish internal guidance affecting the public and to reveal the facts and analysis that have led to major policy decisions. Complaints about non-compliance with the code can be made, via an MP, to the Parliamentary Ombudsman, who can investigate and recommend disclosure. Not surprisingly, this failed to satisfy the demand for FOI rights equivalent to those in other democracies.

The Labour government of 1997 was elected with a manifesto pledge to enact a FOI law. This pledge it redeemed, after considerable further debate, with the Freedom of Information Act 2000. To a certain extent the Act merely drew together existing rights under the 1994 Code of Practice and the other legislation mentioned above. The Act obliges 'public authorities' both to respond to requests for information, and to adopt and maintain a publication scheme. An Information Commissioner (formerly the Data Protection Commissioner, and now responsible for both measures) is responsible for approving publication schemes. There are exemptions to the Act, but few of these are absolute, most being subject to a 'public interest test' by which a decision must be made as to whether the public interest in withholding information is greater than in disclosing it. A major consequence of the Act is that each public authority will now have an enormous incentive to create an integrated RECORDS MANAGEMENT system so as make its publication scheme possible and to facilitate responses to information requests. The scope and complexity of this has been cited by the government in delaying full implementation of the Act until 2005, the last permitted date. However, some will see this as yet another manifestation of official resistance to openness.

Further reading

Birkinshaw, P. (1988) *Freedom of Information: The Law, the Practice and the Ideal*, Weidenfeld & Nicolson.

Campaign for Freedom of Information (1994) *Open Government Briefing No. 1, Testing the Open Government Code of Practice*, CFI.

SEE ALSO: information policy

MAURICE FRANKEL, REVISED BY THE EDITORS

FREENET

A generic term that describes an organization which makes Internet access available without charge to all users. Freenet facilities are widely used by individuals, but are also of importance in the provision of unofficial COMMUNITY INFORMATION.

FREEWARE

Copyright software that is offered as a contribution to the common good for use by individuals and non-profit organizations at no charge. It is quite distinct from non-copyright SOFTWARE programs that are in the public domain. Since the copyright is asserted, its programming cannot be incorporated directly into new products that may be developed by a user of the freeware product. The software is not intended to be sold, issued under licence (see LICENCES) or otherwise distributed in a commercial enterprise, and such bodies are expected to contact the creator to negotiate costs and terms of use. Freeware is also distinct from SHAREWARE, though both share the ethos of the OPEN-SOURCE movement.

FRIENDS OF THE LIBRARY

Associations of persons, often informal but sometimes constituted as separate legal bodies, devoted to supporting individual libraries or groups of libraries, by providing political, moral, volunteer and financial assistance.

The phrase is first recorded in the title of La Société des Amis de la Bibliothèque Nationale et les Grandes Bibliothèques de la France, founded in 1913, although there were numerous preceding informal associations organized to support private and corporate libraries and book clubs, and individual friends of libraries have existed since the formation of libraries themselves. (The most famous in the United Kingdom is, perhaps, Sir Thomas BODLEY, who revived the library now named after him.) The Friends of the Bodleian was founded in 1925, as was the Friends of Harvard University Library, and David Eugene Smith formed the Friends of Columbia University Library in 1928, while in the United Kingdom this was followed by the Friends of the National Libraries in 1931. By this date similar bodies existed for the libraries of Yale, Princeton and Johns Hopkins universities, and in 1935 the AMERICAN LIBRARY ASSOCIATION founded its Friends of Libraries Group and issued its first advisory leaflet *Remember the Library*, a title with admonitory overtones. (The LIBRARY ASSOCIATION, and its successor body CILIP, have not so far followed suit by attempting to mobilize these bodies.)

By 1978 a directory of such organizations in the USA listed more than 20,000 such groups throughout the country, while New York State alone listed 238 similar bodies in 1982, the earliest dating from 1929. In 1979 they all banded together to form 'Friends of Libraries USA', a co-operative lobbying organization that provides advice to member societies and seeks to promote concerted policies for the benefit of libraries, particularly in relation to tax privileges.

In the United Kingdom bodies of friends exist for many major university and research libraries – including, for example, Cambridge, Edinburgh, London and Lambeth Palace – and they can be fissiparous. For example, the Friends of the Bodleian has spawned separately constituted 'American Friends', 'German Friends', 'Japanese Friends' and 'South African Friends'. The BRITISH LIBRARY belatedly formed its friends organization in 1989, and public libraries in the United Kingdom are now following suit with bodies such as the 'Friends of Lorn Libraries and Museums' (1991).

Friends usually comprise devoted readers and patrons with some assistance, outside normal working hours, from professional librarians employed in the library. They are often recognized as charitable bodies with tax-exempt status, and membership normally carries no special privileges, but requires payment of a membership fee and/or annual subscription, support for the library and all its activities, a duty to influence opinion and improve the public relations and PROMOTION of the library and its image, and, most frequently, the obligation to assist in raising funds on its behalf. Funds raised in this way are not normally used to finance the basic activities of the library in the provision of buildings, payment of staff and the purchase of books, but to supplement income, to provide extra facilities and equipment for readers and staff, to assist with pump-priming cash for innovations, to raise money for special purchases of expensive books and other library materials, and to catalogue or publish catalogues of special donations (see DONATIONS TO LIBRARIES), other acquisitions or exhibitions. These groups often organize lectures, tours of the library and meetings with the professional staff, visits to neighbouring libraries, the publication of a library newsletter and other social and community activities. It is increasingly recognized that groups of friends may provide volunteers to supplement professional staff in giving informal guiding (see GUIDING AND SIGNS) and assistance for users of the library or occasional visiting groups of students. The organizing committee, or directing board, often embodies *ex officio* representatives of the library management to help and advise it.

Further reading

Brewer, F.J. (1961) 'Friends of the library and other benefactors and donors', *Library Trends* 9: 453–65.

Day, A.E. (1976) 'Friends of the National Libraries', *New Library World* 77: 219–21.

Dolnick, S. (ed.) (1990) *Friends of Libraries Sourcebook*, 2nd edn, American Library Association.

Friends of the Bodleian (1925–) *Annual Report*.

Friends of the National Libraries (1931/2–) *Annual Report*.

Furber, K., Gwyn, A. and McArthur, A. (1975) 'Friends of the library', *College and Research Libraries* 36: 272–82.

Krummel, D.W. (ed.) (1980) *Organizing the Library's Support: Donors, Volunteers, Friends*, Urbana Champaign, IL: Graduate School of Library Science.

Munch, J.B. (1988) 'College library friends groups in New York, New Jersey and Connecticut', *College and Research Libraries* 49: 442–7.

Wallace, S.L. (ed.) (1962) *Friends of the Library: Organization and Methods*, American Library Association [see also her summary article in the *Encyclopedia of Library and Information Science* (1973), vol. 9, pp. 111–31].

BARRY BLOOMFIELD

FUZZY LOGIC

A method of representing smoothly variable (analogue) functions on digital computers. It is a multivalued logic that deals with uncertainty and imprecision in knowledge representation by using softer boundaries between the logic values. Fuzzy predicates would include 'small' and 'large'; fuzzy quantifiers would include 'most' and 'some'; fuzzy truth values would include 'very true' and 'mostly true'. Rules can be written for the execution of statements such as 'if the patient's temperature is high and there are other symptoms of fever, then treat with aspirin'. Thus fuzzy logic has applications in TEXT RETRIEVAL and EXPERT SYSTEMS.

G

GADAMER, HANS-GEORG (1900–2002)

German philosopher whose system of philosophical HERMENEUTICS, derived in part from the concepts of Wilhelm Dilthey, Edmund Husserl and Martin Heidegger, was widely influential, not least upon information science.

Educated in the humanities at the universities of Breslau, Marburg, Freiburg and Munich, he earned his first doctorate at Freiburg in 1922. He took a second doctorate under Heidegger at Marburg in 1929, and lectured there in aesthetics and ethics, being named Extraordinary Professor in 1937. Two years later he was appointed Professor at the University of Leipzig. He subsequently taught at the universities of Frankfurt am Main (1947–9) and Heidelberg (from 1949). He remained there until his death, becoming Professor Emeritus in 1968.

Gadamer's most important work, *Wahrheit und Methode* (1960; translated as *Truth and Method*, 1975), is considered by some to be the major twentieth-century philosophical statement on hermeneutical theory (the nature of understanding and interpretation). His influence spread through his many pupils, prominent among whom was Jürgen HABERMAS.

Further reading

Warnke, G. (1987) *Gadamer: Hermeneutics, Tradition and Reason*, Cambridge: Polity Press.

GARFIELD, EUGENE (1925–)

Information scientist and originator of published citation indexes.

Born in New York City and educated at Columbia University in Chemistry and Library Science, he very quickly went on to found a tiny company, producing the predecessor to *Current Contents* in a converted chicken coop. Whilst running the company, which took the name INSTITUTE FOR SCIENTIFIC INFORMATION (ISI), he studied for a PhD in Structural Linguistics from the University of Pennsylvania. In this he applied modern linguistics to the indexing of chemical information. In the same year, 1961, he published the first citation index that covered a broad spectrum of science literature, in this case in genetics.

ISI became a major information company, based on the success of *Current Contents* and *Science Citation Index*. However, citation indexing is not merely a means of providing researchers with bibliographical information but also a 'tool for quantitative investigation of the sociology of scientific disciplines. Citation behaviour as a means of acknowledging intellectual debt reveals the intellectual influence of ideas and the structure of communication within and across disciplines. If information about citations is cumulated in a convenient and searchable way, such as that provided by the ISI's citation index databases, then empirical study becomes possible in ways not possible before. Citation studies in information science research owe almost everything to the ideas and work of Garfield.

Further reading

Cronin, B. and Atkins, H.B. (2000) *The Web of Knowledge: A Festschrift in Honor of Eugene Garfield*, Medford, NJ: Information Today.

SEE ALSO: citation analysis; current contents lists

GATEKEEPER

Someone, not necessarily an information professional, who facilitates the transfer of information by informal methods, such as sending notes or mentioning publications, or recommending people with special knowledge to colleagues. A gatekeeper is the type of person to whom others gravitate to discuss ideas or look for help in finding material from the literature. Librarians use professional knowledge, skills and competencies to the same ends and can thus work highly effectively by identifying gatekeepers and working through them.

Further reading

Sturges, P. (2001) 'Gatekeepers and other intermediaries', *ASLIB Proceedings* 53: 62–7.

SEE ALSO: communication; information professions; sociology of knowledge

GATEWAY

A term used, primarily in the academic community, for a browser giving access to Web-based information resources. The more common term for this tool is portal (see PORTALS AND GATEWAYS).

SEE ALSO: information and communication technology

GATEWAY LIBRARY

A term sometimes used in the USA for HYBRID LIBRARIES in which both physical documents and digital objects are provided for users.

GAZETTEER

Geographical DICTIONARY listing and locating, usually by means of grid references, the names of places or features, and frequently also providing a varying amount of descriptive, geographical, historical or statistical information.

GEOGRAPHIC INFORMATION SYSTEMS

Definition

Everyone has their own favourite definition of a Geographic Information System (GIS: often termed Geographical Information Systems outside the USA), and there are very many to choose from. According to Longley *et al.* (1999), GIS is:

- A software product, acquired to perform well-defined functions (*GIS software*).
- Digital representations of aspects of the world (*GIS data*).
- A community of people who use these tools for various purposes (the *GIS community*).
- The activity of using GIS to solve problems or advance science (*doing GIS*).

Table 14 describes some different definitions of GIS, along with the types of users who might find them useful.

Table 14 Different definitions of GIS and types of users

A container of maps in digital form	The general public
A computerized tool for solving geographic problems	Decision-makers, community groups, planners
A spatial decision support system	Management scientists, operations researchers
A mechanized inventory of geographically distributed features and facilities	Utility managers, transportation officials, resource managers
A tool for revealing what is otherwise invisible in geographic information	Scientists, investigators
A tool for performing operations on geographic data that are too tedious or expensive or inaccurate if performed by hand	Resource managers, planners

Source: Taken from Longley *et al.* (2001: 10)

History and development

The first GIS was the Canada Geographic Information System, which was designed in the mid-1960s as a computerized map measuring system. In a separate development in the late 1960s, the US Bureau of the Census developed the DIME (Dual Independent Map Encoding) system, which provided digital records of all US streets and supported automatic referencing and aggregation of census records. Critically, early GIS developers recognized that the same basic needs were present in many different application areas, from resource management to the census.

GIS did not develop as an entirely new area, however, and it is helpful to think of GIS as a rapidly developing interdisciplinary meeting place. Amongst the contributors to the field, the separate needs of cartographers and mapping agencies led to the use of computers to support map editing in the late 1960s, followed by the widespread computerization of mapping functions by the late 1970s. Military needs have also been of sustained importance throughout the development of GIS – initially arising out of the development of military satellites in the 1950s, right through to the later development of Global Positioning System (GPS). Most military applications have subsequently found use in the civilian sector. The modern history of GIS dates from the early 1980s, when the price of sufficiently powerful computers fell below $250,000 and typical software costs fell below $100,000. In this sense, much of the history of GIS has been technology-led.

GIS architecture

Today's GIS is a complex of software, hardware, DATABASES, people, procedures and NETWORKS, all set in an institutional context (Figure 11).

An effective network, such as the Internet or the INTRANETS of large organizations, is essential for rapid communication or information sharing. The Internet has emerged as society's mechanism of information exchange, and in a typical GIS application will be used to connect ARCHIVES, clearing houses, digital libraries (see DIGITAL LIBRARY) and DATA WAREHOUSES. Recent years have seen the development of methods for searching this storehouse, and the development of software that allows the user to work with data in remote Internet locations. GIS hardware fosters user interaction using the WIMP (Windows, Icons, Mouse, Pull-down menus) interface, and takes the form of laptops, personal data

- **Hardware**
- **Software**
- **Data**
- **People**
- **Procedures**
- **Network**

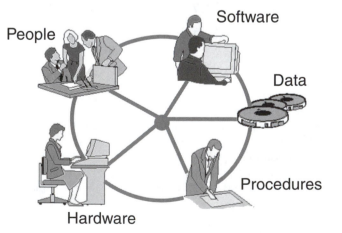

Figure 11 Six parts of a GIS
Source: ESRI

assistants (PDAs), in-vehicle devices and cellular telephones, as well as conventional DESKTOP COMPUTERS. In many applications, the user's device is the *client*, connected through the network to a *server*. GIS software is created by a number of vendors, and is frequently packaged to suit a diverse range of needs – ranging from simple viewing and mapping applications, through software for supporting GIS-oriented websites, to fully-fledged systems capable of advanced analysis functions. Some software is specifically designed for particular classes of applications, such as utilities or defence applications. Geographical databases frequently constitute an important tradable commodity and strategic organizational resource, and come in a range of sizes. Suitably qualified people are fundamental to the design, programming and maintenance of GIS: they also supply the GIS with appropriate data and are responsible for interpreting outputs.

GIS and GIScience

Geographic information systems are useful tools, but Longley *et al.* (2001: Chapters 1 and 2) demonstrate that their usage raises frustrating and profound questions. How does a user know that the results obtained using GIS analysis are accurate? What principles might help a GIS user to design better maps? How can user interfaces be made readily understandable to novice users? These are all questions of design, data and methods that are stimulated by our exposure to GIS or to its products, and GIS use can beg almost as many questions as it answers. Resolution of these questions is central to the emergent field of *geographic information science* (GISc) (Goodchild 1992), which studies the fundamental issues arising from the creation, handling, storage and use of geographically referenced information.

Today, GIS remains fundamentally a subject concerned with creating workable real-world applications. But the advent of GISc has brought heightened awareness that effective use of GIS requires sensitivity to, and depth of understanding of, all aspects of geographic information. It also brings the recognition that the intellectual heart of this young but fast-developing discipline lies in understanding core organizing principles, techniques and management practices, rather

than mastering much more transitory software systems or following current academic fashions. Above all, GIS is a very exciting area of activity, which has very much to offer students interested in tackling geographical problems in the real world.

References

Goodchild M.F. (1992) 'Geographical information science', *International Journal of Geographical Information Systems* 6: 31–45.
Longley P.A., Goodchild M.F., Maguire D.J. and Rhind D.W. (eds) (1999) *Geographical Information Systems: Principles, Techniques, Management and Applications*, New York: Wiley.

Further reading

CASA (1999) 'The GIS timeline' (www.casa.ucl.ac.uk/gistimeline/) [an excellent summary of the history of GIS].
Longley P.A., Goodchild M.F., Maguire D.J. and Rhind D.W. (2001) *Geographic Information Systems and Science*, Chichester: Wiley.

SEE ALSO: map

PAUL A. LONGLEY

GESNER, CONRAD (1516–65)

Humanist scholar and bibliographer. Although others had done important work before him, Gesner's project for the *Bibliotheca Universalis*, a bibliography of everything ever published in the European languages of scholarship, was on such a monumental scale as to justify identifying him as the most significant early pioneer of the subject.

Born in Zurich, he was appointed as Professor of Greek at the newly founded University of Lausanne in 1537. Four years later he left for a chair in Physics and Natural History at the Collegium Carolinum in Zurich, where he remained for the rest of his life. He was the author of seventy-two works published in his lifetime and left eighteen more unfinished. They cover a wide range of disciplines, including botany, zoology, philology, cookery, geology and mineralogy.

Although the *Bibliotheca Universalis*, which was issued in four folio volumes, fell far short of its hoped-for comprehensiveness, it was still a massive achievement. Two abridgements quickly appeared (1551, 1555), supplements were issued as early as 1555 and expanded new editions were assembled by his pupils Josias Simler (1574) and Johann Jacob Frisius (1583). Gesner's entries include not only author and title information, but also in many cases imprints, chapter and section headings or other contents descriptions, and occasional critical annotations. In many ways the project for Universal Bibliographic Control began with Gesner.

Further reading

Besterman, T. (1936) *The Beginnings of Systematic Bibliography*, Oxford University Press.

GOPHER

A computer facility, or navigational aid, for searching out specific content from the INTERNET. The gopher allows the user to search the Internet using free-text search terms. Although they were of great importance in the 1980s and early 1990s, gophers have been largely replaced in common usage by WEB BROWSERS.

GOVERNMENT PUBLISHING

The production of a form of OFFICIAL PUBLICATIONS by a government printer or publisher, or by government departments and agencies themselves, for information, educational or historical purposes. Notoriously hard to trace and obtain, they are a classic form of GREY LITERATURE. In many countries, government documents are now made available electronically, thus making a major contribution to E-GOVERNMENT.

GRAPHIC USER INTERFACE

Graphic User Interface (GUI) is the generic term for a mechanism that enables people to communicate with computers based on graphics rather than solely on text. It is also known by the acronym WIMPS (Windows, Icons, Mouse, Pulldown menus), after the four key elements of these interfaces. Screen graphics are used to display windows, icons and menus, and a mouse or similar pointing device is used to select them. This type of interface was developed by Xerox and first commercially exploited in the form of the Apple Macintosh PERSONAL COMPUTER in the 1980s, followed by the development of the now ubiquitous Microsoft Windows software. GUI is now the normal means of interface with computers for all but the most technical of users.

SEE ALSO: Human–Computer Interaction; information and communication technology; Windows

GRAPHICS

Generically the term is used to describe diagrams, drawings, etc. that give a visual representation of a person, place or phenomenon. In computing the term has been adopted with the sole specific meaning of information 'drawn' on screen, rather than displayed as lines of text. It may consist of lines, curves and shapes entered as freehand drawings (with a mouse or graphic tablet), copied by means of a scanner or generated by software (for example, bar charts). Graphics are now a familiar feature to all computer users.

GREY LITERATURE

Publications that are not available through normal BOOK TRADE channels. Examples of grey literature are reports, doctoral dissertations and conference proceedings. It is very difficult, however, to give a conclusive definition of grey literature. Organizations working with these documents therefore prefer to give not a definition but a general description. It will be clear that some dissertations and conference proceedings are indeed available through normal bookselling channels. Government reports are often available through booksellers and subscription agents. The above definition is therefore clearly not watertight, but it is in practice a useful one.

Who is publishing grey literature?

Among the authors of grey literature there are many whose parent body or funding institution feels that there is no serious need to publish in journals. They do not seek a high citation rate; financing of their future projects does not depend on it. Their prime objective is to disseminate the information as quickly and inexpensively as possible to a sometimes-restricted group of people or organizations that might be interested in it. They want to avoid the considerable delay involved in journal publication.

The development of INFORMATION AND COMMUNICATION TECHNOLOGY, especially such products as DESKTOP PUBLISHING, makes it easy to bring the publication process under one's own control. The main types of body that issue grey literature are research institutes, universities, international, national and local authorities, and industrial firms. There are, of course, other reasons for publishing grey. Some reports are published grey because they have commercial value. Even if this commercial value is no longer present, industry tends to keep this material confidential. Other reasons for publishing grey are that the content is expected to be of interest to only a very limited group of people or that it is too long or too short for normal commercial publication. There may be other reasons. The fact is, however, that most of the grey literature that is handled by libraries and DATABASE producers is produced by established bodies and organizations.

The quality of grey literature

Organizations that produce grey literature cannot afford to issue low-quality reports if they value their reputations. One could consider internal quality control to have nearly the same selective effect as a peer review in 'white' literature. Traditionally, quality research is supposed to be published 'white'. Much of the grey literature, however, will never be published 'white' because of the reasons mentioned. Moreover, database producers that enter grey documents in their databases may have selection criteria, of which quality is a principal one. Admission onto a database will be permitted only if it is acceptable in the view of subject specialists. So the quality of grey documents should not be considered to be a problem for the user of grey literature databases.

Document delivery

Many grey documents are disseminated as a matter of routine to sister institutions and governing bodies. Here we see the first real problem of grey literature, the dissemination pattern. The small print runs are distributed very selectively, with poor publicity. Because of the interdisciplinary nature of research, grey literature will reach only a proportion of interested researchers. Even if a researcher hears that a report in the field exists, it is often very difficult to trace the publishing organization; if it is located, it can be very hard to obtain a copy. In many cases, the number of copies produced is so small that only

a few are available to meet requests. Moreover, most of these organizations have no staff experienced in, or concerned with, document delivery. A visit to the library will therefore often be fruitless for a researcher. Since the acquisition of grey literature is difficult, many libraries prefer to acquire only 'white' literature.

Bibliographic control

Grey literature is not commonly entered into general databases. The producers of databases such as Biosis and Medline can hardly cope with the extensive output of journal literature, and, because of this, and the difficulties of collecting grey literature, they have excluded it from coverage. Special attention to grey literature has, however, been given by the producers of specialized international databases in the field of technology. Many users of these databases are themselves producers of grey literature who recognize its value. Because grey literature is difficult to acquire, some of them have established national centres in countries that produce grey literature in their subject area. From the above, one might imagine that the BIBLIO-GRAPHIC CONTROL and availability are managed quite well. All researchers need to do is to search the specialized database relevant to their subject field and they will find all the grey literature they need. There are, however, two further problems: the interdisciplinary nature of research and the costs involved in database publishing. To be comprehensive, a national centre needs to cover publications of organizations other than those in its subject area. Furthermore, the costs of the acquisition and database publication of one record describing a grey document are so high that limits have to be imposed on input. For these reasons the coverage of grey literature on related subject fields will be limited. In the end, the researcher will find only a selection of the existing grey publications in the chosen database.

Grey literature databases

The most important grey literature databases are SIGLE and NTIS. SIGLE (System for Information on Grey Literature in Europe) is produced by EAGLE (European Association for Grey Literature Exploitation) (Wood and Smith 1993). EAGLE has members and national SIGLE centres in Belgium, the Czech Republic, France, Germany, Hungary, Italy, Luxembourg, the Netherlands, Spain and the UK. Annually 41,000 records are added to SIGLE from all fields of science and technology. NTIS, a service of the US Department of Commerce, is producing a database mainly in the field of technology and related sciences. Annually 75,000 records are added to the database. It can be accessed at www.silver-platter.com/catalog/sigl.htm.

Electronic grey literature

Personal communication has always been an excellent means of information exchange in frontier research. Next to contacts in meetings and writing, the researchers quickly adapted to the use of electronic NETWORKS. The number of specific discussion files is increasing tremendously. Users who do not belong to the in-crowd of a specific file will remain unaware of existing information. In view of the interdisciplinary nature of information this is most undesirable. In fact these networks confront the user and the information professional with a new type of 'grey' document. As for the printed 'grey' documents, bibliographic databases are needed to make this electronic information available to a broader public. Measures should be taken for quality control and storage. The exponential growth of informal communications using the Internet has both increased the quantity of grey literature and diversified its formats. The use of a search engine (see SEARCH ENGINES) to search for almost any term will reveal electronic grey literature emanating from a multitude of sources. The more formal manifestations include e-prints, some in formal archives, various kinds of net-base directories and websites, often running into hundreds.

References

Wood, D.N. and Smith A.W. (1993) 'SIGLE: A model for international co-operation', *Interlending and Document Supply* 21(1): 18–22.

Further reading

Alberani, V. and De Castro, P. (2001) 'Grey literature from the York Seminar (UK) of 1978 to the year 2000' *Inspel* 35: 236–47.
Farace, D. (1993) *Proceedings of the First International Conference on Grey Literature*, Amsterdam: Trans-Atlantic.
Wessels, R.H.A. (1994a) 'The importance of international cooperation for grey literature availability', *Alexandria* 5(3): 185–92.

—— (1994b) 'Infrastructure of scientific and technical information', in *World Infrastructure 1994*, London: Sterling Publications Limited, pp. 93–4.
—— (1993) 'Libraries and publishers; Competitors or complements', *NVB-WB Cahier 5*: 50–5, Den Haag: NBLC (in Dutch).

SEE ALSO: bibliographic control; document delivery; government publishing; knowledge industries; official publications; publishing

R.H.A. WESSELS

GUIDING AND SIGNS

Guiding is the process of matching library/information service users with their information and other needs and requirements without the need for staff assistance.

Signs are the static, physical resources used to communicate the required information to users in order to achieve effective guiding.

Guiding

The fundamental aim of a good library guiding system is to answer the question: 'Where do I go to find…?' A library and information service guiding (or wayfinding) system enables users first to orient themselves within the service quickly, efficiently and without stress. It then directs them, following the rule of general to specific, to the correct destination for their information requirements, identifies that destination and explains, to a greater or lesser extent, the nature, scope and content of the particular resource to which the guiding system has conducted them. If the system operates successfully, users' information requirements are satisfied comprehensively and without the need to consult library/information service staff. Good guiding maximizes self-help, thus freeing staff resources for more cost-effective work. It also promotes positive user perceptions of efficient, confident and successful libraries/information services.

Signs

Signs are the means by which successful guiding is achieved. They are a static, impersonal method of communicating information and should meet the following criteria for maximum effectiveness: clear, consistent and visually co-ordinated; arranged logically and sited at appropriate locations, following a sequence which leads from the general to the specific; visible and easy to use;

aesthetically pleasing and professional looking in order to reinforce corporate image and an impression of an efficient service; flexible, adaptable and inexpensive to maintain.

TYPES OF SIGN

There are two basic categories of signs for libraries and information services: signs that direct users to specific destinations and signs that explain the features of individual resources. Content and location of all categories of sign are fundamental considerations in implementing a successful scheme.

DIRECTIONAL SIGNS

Directional signs range from all-inclusive resources such as library directories to signs that identify individual destination points (e.g. 'Enquiry Desk'). Floor plans and directional symbols (e.g. arrows) are included in this category.

EXPLANATORY SIGNS

Explanatory signs contain general information (e.g. opening hours), more precise information on individual aspects of the library service (e.g. how to use a workstation) or instructions on emergency procedures. Warning signs (e.g. 'No Smoking') are also included in this category.

CONTENT OF SIGNS

The minimum amount of information consistent with the successful transmission of the intended message is required. Signs should be clear and simple to use and aimed at communicating the full message to the maximum number of potential users. Language and terminology should be clear, concise, unambiguous and jargon-free. Formal consistent language should be used, but phrased in a welcoming style. Cultural and ethnic issues must be taken into account and gender-specific language avoided. Diagrams are useful devices to use when written language is inappropriate.

LOCATION OF SIGNS

Signs should be located at appropriate decision points identified by a survey of traffic flow routes.

DESIGN OF SIGNS

The production of library signs to professional standards is the norm. In-house production of signs should be limited to temporary notices required to meet immediate or short-term needs (e.g. training courses, meetings, etc.). Advice from external design consultants should be procured. Sign panels should be of standard sizes and formats, readily visible but not excessively obtrusive and fixed in a manner appropriate to the location (i.e. flat wall-fixings, ceiling suspensions or wall projections). There are many materials and designs available for sign panels and they should be selected on the basis of their suitability for individual circumstances in consultation with professional design consultants. Colour-coding should be used sparingly, standardized throughout and utilizing strong shades only – a sizeable proportion of the population is colour-blind. Consistency is the principal consideration in sign design but, this notwithstanding, signs should be reasonably adaptable and flexible in order to be able to absorb changes. The legibility of the typeface used for signs incorporates the following considerations: style of lettering (e.g. seriffed or non-seriffed letter faces – Helvetica is a popular style); size and positioning of letters and words; use of upper- and lower-case letters; roman or italic typeface; and thickness, or weight, of the print. The complex nature of libraries/information services renders the use of symbol signs such as pictograms (e.g. lavatory signs) generally inappropriate, although arrow signs (preferably left and right directions only) are used. Symbols can be confusing and the principles of visibility and consistency are particularly important if they are selected for use; standard symbols such as those produced by the ISO are recommended.

Managing library guiding and signing

A systematic management approach to library signing and guiding is required, with a fully formulated schedule of activities from initial conceptualization of a project to full implementation and subsequent continuous review. A thorough study of the guiding requirements of potential users of the service should be conducted in order to establish a firm basis for the enterprise. The project should be accorded an appropriate degree of professional status by the appointment of a senior member of staff to manage the scheme, and professional design consultants should be engaged to advise on the proposed undertaking. A reputable firm should be contracted to produce and install the signs.

In-house production of signs should observe the same principles of professional appearance, consistency and aesthetics as professionally produced signs; the senior professional appointed to manage the guiding system for the organization should also co-ordinate the production of these signs. A sign manual for the organization should be drawn up for future reference purposes.

Further reading

Pope, L.G. (1982) 'Library signs and guiding', unpublished MLS thesis, Department of Library and Information Studies, Loughborough University of Technology [an illustrated comparative study of three library guiding schemes; also considers the principles of library signing and guiding].

Reynolds, L. and Barrett, S. (1981) *Signs and Guiding for Libraries*, Clive Bingley [the standard text on library signs and guiding; comprehensive and well illustrated].

SEE ALSO: user studies

MICHAEL CHANEY

GUTENBERG, JOHANN
(1395–1468)

Regarded in the West as the inventor of printing with movable type, but it must be noted that in EAST ASIA, Korea in particular, printing had a longer heritage. Gutenberg's invention does seem to have been an independent technical achievement. It took place between 1440 and 1450, in somewhat shadowy circumstances, but its significance in the history of world civilization is not seriously disputed.

Evidence about his life is extremely fragmentary and unfortunately there is no printed book that actually bears his name, despite the reliable attribution of several masterpieces of printing to him. It is unlikely that Gutenberg had any direct knowledge of the printing techniques that had been developed in China and Korea. In any case, his invention was fundamentally different. The key to it was a method of casting metal types, each bearing one letter or other character, identical to each other and reusable. He adopted the form of press used by bookbinders (and perhaps vintners) to make his impressions.

Gutenberg himself produced few books and soon lost his investment. His invention, however, was taken up by others, and knowledge of it spread (largely through Germans) to the Low Countries, Italy and France, and gradually to the outlying parts of Europe. By the 1480s printing was well established, and by 1500 the commercial production of manuscript books in the West had almost ceased.

Further reading

Scholderer, V. (1970) *Johann Gutenberg*, British Museum.

SEE ALSO: book

H

HABERMAS, JÜRGEN (1929–)

German philosopher and sociologist whose critical appraisal of Western institutions and rationality draws on influences from Kant, Marx and other key figures in the philosophical tradition as well as the outstanding sociological theorists. His work has proved applicable in a wide variety of fields including EPISTEMOLOGY and HERMENEUTICS, and has influenced ideas not only in economics and public policy, but also on the theory of INFORMATION SYSTEMS, INFORMATION theory and on our understanding of the INFORMATION SOCIETY.

Born in Dusseldorf, he studied in Gottingen, Zurich and Bonn, obtaining his doctorate in 1954. He was assistant to Theodor Adorno at Frankfurt (1956–9) and is often referred to as a second-generation member of the Frankfurt School of philosophy. He has held posts at a number of institutions in Germany and the USA, notably with GADAMER at Heidelberg and once again at Frankfurt where he succeeded Adorno.

His theory of communicative action (also the title of his most important work, *The Theory of Communicative Action* (2 vols, trans. Thomas McCarthy, Boston, 1984 and 1987) is based on truthfulness, critique and the development of rational consensus. His approach has never been detached from everyday reality and he has always promoted discussion on matters of public concern.

Further reading

White, S.K. (ed.) (1995) *The Cambridge Companion to Habermas*, Cambridge University Press.

HARD COPY

Used in a cluster of closely related senses as a record on card or paper, to distinguish it from a record on microfilm or magnetic tape; a printed copy of machine output in readable form; or, more generally, human-readable copy produced from information held in a form not easily readable.

HARD DISK

A disk storage medium on which the recording surfaces are rigid, in contrast to a FLOPPY DISK, where the recording surface is flexible. It may be housed within the case of the computer (internal hard disk) or within its own case (external hard disk). The storage capacity of hard disks is increasing all the time; indeed they are often configured on a server in a way that makes two or more disks appear to be a single object, thus theoretically providing unlimited space. Capacity up to 400 gigabytes is not unknown, although it is still uncommon.

HARDWARE

The physical components of a COMPUTER system, consisting of four elements: the processor that executes the programs; the memory that stores programs and data; the peripherals, used to store data longer term and to exchange commands and information with users; and the input/output devices that interconnect the above. It is perhaps easier to think of it as those parts of a computer that are not software.

HEALTH AND SAFETY

Information work generally involves the use of a computer, which means that information workers should be aware of the possible adverse health effects of using such technology and how risks can be reduced, and be conversant with government legislation on the issue.

Possible adverse health effects

Numerous allegations have been made about the health implications of using visual display units (VDUs), arousing much media attention. Over the last ten years an increasing number of VDU operators have complained of muscular aches and pains, eye discomfort and visual fatigue, stress and, in a few cases, skin rashes. Concerns have also been raised about radiation emissions and the possible adverse effects VDUs may have on unborn foetuses and epilepsy sufferers.

VDU operators report a high incidence of muscular discomfort, particularly in shoulders, neck, hands and wrist. Pain may also occur in the back and legs. Most of the recent publicity has been focused on repetitive strain injury (RSI), which is being increasingly referred to as work-related upper-limb disorders (WRULDs). WRULDs cover a variety of complaints but all result in the operator experiencing pain in the joints, usually in the fingers but possibly also in the wrists, elbows or elsewhere, which may be temporary at first but, if unchecked, can result in permanent damage. Generally, muscular discomfort is influenced by three factors: the length of time operators have to adopt a fixed position, the intensity of computer use and the design of the workstation.

Eye discomfort and visual fatigue can be caused by a number of factors. These include glare on the screen, a poorly contrasted and unstable screen display, too long being spent working at a VDU and the user not having the correct eye appliances for computer work (Morris and Dyer 1998).

Occupational stress can occur in any type of employment. In VDU work it can be linked to poor job design, particularly where jobs are either too pressured or are monotonous; inflexible working procedures; inadequate supervision; poor training; and inappropriate management style. Poor environmental conditions (such as depressing décor, inadequate space, bad lighting, excessive noise and poor heating), unergonomic workstation design and unfriendly software can also contribute to stress.

Skin rashes, which may take the form of occasional itching to reddening (*erythema*), giving the appearance of sunburn, are thought to be caused by a combination of low humidity levels and the presence of high levels of static. Increasing the humidity levels and treating carpets with antistatic fluids have been found to alleviate most problems.

The suggestion that VDUs emit harmful radiation is now largely discounted. Recent legislation does not require VDUs to be tested for emissions (HSE 1992a). Similarly, it is now generally believed that VDU use is not associated with adverse pregnancy outcomes (Brent *et al.* 1993).

Epilepsy is not caused by VDU work but the use of a VDU can cause seizures for those suffering from a rare form known as photosensitive epilepsy. Consequently, it is inadvisable for sufferers of this rare condition to work with VDUs.

Reducing health risks and legislation

Many of the health risks can be reduced with careful choice of equipment and software, ergonomic workstation design and improved job design. Guidance in assessing and reducing health risks is given in the UK Health and Safety (Display Screen Equipment) Regulations 1992. Essentially the Regulations require employers to:

- Assess and record the identification of hazards, the evaluation of risks and the extent of health risks.
- Comply with the minimum requirements for workstations covering equipment, the environment and the software interface.
- Provide eye and eyesight tests, and pay for the cost of special corrective appliances needed for VDU work.
- Provide adequate health and safety training in the use of workstations.
- Provide employees with adequate information on all aspects of health and safety relating to their workstations and the Regulations.

Other UK legislation includes the Health and Safety at Work Act 1974 (HSC 1992), and the more recent Regulations – the Management of Health and Safety at Work Regulations 1999 (HSE 1999), the Workplace (Health, Safety and Welfare) Regulations 1992 (HSE 1992b) and the Provision and Use of Work Equipment Regulations 1998 (HSE 1998). The ergonomics of design and use of IT in offices is also covered in the British Standard, BS EN ISO 9241–5-1999.

The issues are, of course, universal, and similar legislation or recommendations exist in most industrialized countries. The European Union has taken a particular interest in the subject under the broad umbrella of its concern for social actions relating to health in the workplace, through the European agency for Safety and Health at work. Its Risk Assessment for Display Screen Equipment is a particularly useful source (http://europe.osha.eu.int/good_practice/risks/msd/risk_links.asp?id=3). In the USA, the Department of Labor has overall responsibility for this field, through its Occupational Safety and Health Administration; the relevant documents can be found at www.osha.gov/STLC/computerworkstation/index.html).

References

Brent, R.L., Gordon, W.E., Bennett, W.R. and Beckman, D.A. (1993) 'Reproductive and teratologic effects of electromagnetic fields', *Reproductive Toxicology* 7: 535–80.

British Standards Institution (1999) *Ergonomics Requirements for Office Work with Visual Display Terminals (VDTs)*, BS EN ISO 9241–5-1999, BSI.

Health and Safety Commission (HSC) (1992) *A Guide to the Health and Safety at Work etc. Act 1974*, HSE Books.

Health and Safety Executive (HSE) (1999) *Management of Health and Safety at Work, Approved Code of Practice*, HSE Books.

—— (1998) *Provision and Use of Work Equipment Regulation, Approved Code of Practice and Guidance*, HSE Books.

—— (1992a) *Display Screen Equipment Work, Guidance on Regulations*, HSE Books.

—— (1992b) *Workplace Health, Safety and Welfare, Approved Code of Practice*, HSE Books.

Morris, A. and Dyer, H. (1998) *Human Aspects of Library Automation*, Gower [gives detailed guidance and advice specifically directed at LIS practitioners].

Further reading

Health and Safety Executive (HSE) (2002) *Working with VDUs* (www.hse.gov.uk/pubns/indg36.pdf).

SEE ALSO: Human–Computer Interaction; information and communication technology; information professions

ANNE MORRIS

HEALTH SCIENCE LIBRARIES

Libraries that support the information needs of the education, research, management and practice of healthcare. The library's users include students, teachers, research scientists, health service managers, planners and epidemiologists, doctors, nurses and paramedical staff and the consumers of healthcare, patients and carers. Libraries with a healthcare interest will therefore be found in government departments, health authorities, primary, community and acute (hospital) services, higher-education institutions, research institutes, drug companies, PUBLIC LIBRARIES and the voluntary sector (Ryder 2002). The literature and information support, which is now required by this variety of user, extends beyond biomedical and health sciences to economics, ethics, engineering, statistics, law, management theory, the behavioural sciences and knowledge management.

History and development

Collections of medical books are known to have existed in ancient Egypt, China, Greece and Rome (Norman 1991), and some of them were preserved in the medieval monasteries of Western Europe. A catalogue of Dover Priory (1389) lists 118 medical books, including Hippocrates, Galen and Rhazes. Medical libraries in their own right begin to be seen with the establishment of medical schools in the ancient universities. For example, Florence (1287), Paris (1395) and Aberdeen (1495) are known to have had special medical collections.

The major spur to the growth of medical libraries in the United Kingdom was the creation of medical corporations (Royal Colleges) and medical societies in the seventeenth and eighteenth centuries. London, Edinburgh and Dublin were all major centres of teaching and a myriad of institutions were founded in each city, many with their own libraries. In London, eighteen societies agreed to merge as the Royal Society of Medicine in 1907, the prime mover for this being Sir John MacAlister, the Society's first Secretary and Librarian, later to be President of the LIBRARY ASSOCIATION (Godbolt and Munford 1983). The Society's library is now one of the primary medical libraries in the UK, with 250,000 volumes and 2,000 current periodicals.

In the USA, the National Library of Medicine (NLM) played a critical part in the development of medical library services. Founded in 1836 from the library of the Surgeon-General's Office, it owes much of its success to its Librarian, John Shaw Billings (1836–1913), who created the Index-Catalogue of the Surgeon-General's Office (vol. 1 published in 1880), as well as originating the monthly *Index Medicus* in 1879, the precursor of so many index and abstract publications.

The first half of the twentieth century was characterized by consolidation in the higher-education sector, with universities in the UK and the USA concentrating on COLLECTION DEVELOPMENT and co-operative schemes. The 1980s and 1990s were characterized by major external changes in higher education and healthcare provision. These required a clearer vision for library services, more flexible and assertive attitudes, stronger co-operative and multidisciplinary networks, the exploitation of technological developments and the adoption of management skills to demonstrate accountability and quality. From the mid-1990s, health science libraries have responded to the growth of the Internet and electronic publishing by developing their own electronic profile within organizational INTRANETS and marketing services to the user's own desktop.

Health and education service changes

Organizational changes first emerged in Britain in the 1960s within the National Health Service (NHS), when statutory obligations for postgraduate medical education led to a major increase in the number of postgraduate libraries in general hospitals. The immediate impact of this was that the number of staff providing library services to NHS personnel rose by 72 per cent (to 1,302 staff) between 1978 and 1985 (NHS Regional Librarians' Group 1987). This, in turn, led to the recognition of a strategic co-ordinating role at the regional level and the appointment of a number of 'Regional Librarians' (Forrest and Carmel 1987).

Healthcare reform has been a major driver for change with a succession of reorganizations and official directives, many of which have stressed 'the need for extensive, comprehensive, accurate and up-to-date information (of all types) to support the work of NHS staff at all levels, and in addition to provide information for healthcare consumers' (Brittain 1993). Such an information-rich environment has obviously provided opportunities for information professionals, and the

publication of Information for Health (NHS Executive 1998), the NHS Information Strategy, embedded library and information services as a core NHS function by stating that 'better care for patients, and improved health for everyone, depend on the availability of good information, accessible when and where it is needed' with Trusts tasked to 'provide every NHS professional with online access to the latest local guidance and national evidence on treatment'. The establishment of Workforce Development Confederations (Department of Health 2000) will introduce further managerial and organizational changes to health libraries in the UK.

The transfer of nurse education to the higher-education sector (UKCC 1986) and the emphasis on continuing professional development in nursing have had major implications for the provision of information services to nursing. Basic nurse training has moved from a hospital-based apprenticeship to an academic, research-oriented education. The number of nursing schools has been dramatically reduced as they merge and are integrated into university faculties. Within medical teaching, the reduction in the amount of factual content to be learned and the application of student-based learning principles (General Medical Council 1993) will require closer liaison with curriculum planners and a greater emphasis on emerging networked learning environments.

The Follett Report (Higher Education Funding Council 1993) provided a significant milestone for the state of health science libraries in British higher education in the mid-1990s. It was argued that pressure from rising student numbers, shortage of accommodation and high inflation in book and journal prices could be alleviated by addressing a more central and strategic institutional role, clarifying objectives and exploiting new information technology. The resulting Resource Discovery Network (http://www.rdn.ac.uk/about/) is a 'free Internet service dedicated to providing effective access to high quality Internet resources for the learning, teaching and research community', which hosts the major UK Internet health and medicine resource catalogue, OMNI (http://omni.ac.uk/).

The NHS Research and Development Strategy has been the impetus for a number of initiatives 'to secure a knowledge-based health service in which clinical, managerial and policy decisions are based on pertinent information about research findings and scientific and technological advances' (Department of Health 1991). These include the Cochrane Library, the NHS Centre for Research and Dissemination and ultimately the National Electronic Library for Health (http://www.nelh.nhs.uk) where librarians have played a critical role in undertaking systematic reviews and critically appraising the literature. In particular, the librarian's role in supporting evidence-based practice, clinical effectiveness and training in critical appraisal has given added value to the profession's status (Booth and Walton 2000). The concept of knowledge management, with the differentiation between explicit and tacit knowledge, is now encouraging health librarians to enhance their roles by identifying new strategies to support organizational development (Booth 2001).

These changes have produced a professional sector that is highly conscious of its image, its need for continuous learning and its responsibility to develop the next generation of health science information workers (*Health Libraries Review* 1995). In the USA, the Medical Library Association (MLA) has published *Platform for Change* (Medical Library Association 1992), which outlines the knowledge and skills required for the twenty-first century. In the UK, the Library Association has developed the Framework for Continuing Professional Development, which is being used by individual health science librarians as a tool to assess and plan professional development, as well as by employers to undertake training needs surveys and to demonstrate commitment to professional development.

Professional co-operation

Perhaps more than in any other UK library sector, staff working in health science libraries have set up a proliferation of associations, subject groups, networks and pressure groups. Each one undertakes meetings, conferences, resource sharing, publishing and representative activities. The Library Association Health Libraries Group (http://www.la-hq.org.uk/groups/hlg/index.html) is the largest, with over 2,300 members, and amongst other activities it organizes an annual conference and publishes the *Directory of Health Library and Information Services* (Ryder 2002). Other groups include the University Medical School Librarians Group (http://www.umslg.ac.uk/umslg.html), Consumer Health Information Consortium (http://omni.ac.uk/CHIC/), Medical In-

formation Working Party (http://library.bma.org.uk/miwp/miwp.htm), University Health Science Librarians (http://www.sbu.ac.uk/lis/uhsl/executive.html), the SCONUL Advisory Committee on Health Services (http://www.sconul.ac.uk/health/index.htm) and the NHS Regional Librarians Group (http://www.nthames-health.tpmde.ac.uk/rlg/index.htm).

The establishment, in 1995, of a UK 'Health Panel', arising from the initiatives of the Library and Information Co-operation Council (LINC) with representatives of many of the above groups, is an attempt to minimize the fragmentation and speak with 'one voice'. This group has been reconstituted as the Health Libraries and Information Confederation (http://wwwlib.jr2.ox.ac.uk/linchealth/) with a particular remit to influence policy makers.

In the USA, national co-ordination and leadership are more effective with the clearer roles of the NLM and the MLA. The NLM provides the national framework for resource sharing through the National Network for Libraries in Medicine (NNLM), and in research and development through the National Centres for Biomedical Communications and Biotechnology Information. The MLA (http://www.mlanet.org/), the professional body for medical librarians, with over 5,000 members, is responsible for accrediting professional competence, sets standards on quality of service and undertakes a major programme of training and staff development.

Supra-national professional organizations exist in Africa, South America, Asia and in Europe (http://www.eahil.org/). As well as offering an often rare opportunity for professionals to meet at conferences, these organizations undertake important practical work, such as the compilation of the African and Latin American Index Medicus (collecting much 'fugitive' information) and the production of local catalogues and union lists through which ILL requests can be satisfied locally. Finally, the International Federation of Library Associations (IFLA), through its Biological and Medical Sciences Section (http://www.ifla.org/VII/s28/sbams.htm), provides a forum for addressing global issues. In particular it organizes the five-yearly International Congress on Medical Librarianship. In 1995 this was held in Washington, DC, and in 2000 was held in London, where it attracted over 1,400 participants (http://www.icml.org). In 2005, the Congress will be hosted in São Paulo, Brazil.

References

Booth, A. (2001) 'Managing knowledge for clinical excellence: Ten building blocks', *Journal of Clinical Excellence* 3: 187–94.

Booth, A. and Walton, G. (2000) *Managing Knowledge in Health Services*, Library Association.

Brittain, M. (1993) 'Information and the health of the nation', *ASLIB Proceedings* 45: 53–60.

Department of Health (2000) *A Health Service of all the Talents: Developing the NHS Workforce*, Department of Health.

—— (1991) *Research for Health*, Department of Health.

Forrest, M. and Carmel, M. (1987) 'The NHS Regional Librarians' Group', *Health Libraries Review* 4: 160–3.

General Medical Council (1993) *Tomorrow's Doctors: Recommendations on Undergraduate Medical Education*, GMC Education Committee.

Godbolt, S. and Munford, W.A. (1983) *The Incomparable Mac. A Biographical Study of Sir John Young Walker MacAlister (1856–1925)*, Library Association.

Health Libraries Review (1995) 13(1) [theme issue on Continuing Professional Development].

Higher Education Funding Council (1993) *Joint Funding Council's Library Review Group Report (Chair: Sir Brian Follett)*, Higher Education Funding Council for England.

Medical Library Association (1992) *Platform for Change. The Educational Policy Statement of the MLA*, Medical Library Association.

NHS Executive (1998) *Information for Health: An Information Strategy for the Modern NHS 1998–2005*, Department of Health.

NHS Regional Librarians' Group (1987) *Census of Staff Providing Library Services to NHS Personnel 1985*, NHS RLG.

Norman, J.M. (ed.) (1991) *Morton's Medical Bibliography: An Annotated Checklist of Texts Illustrating the History of Medicine* (Garrison and Morton), 5th edn, Scolar Press.

Ryder, J. (2002) *Directory of Health Library and Information Services in the United Kingdom and Republic of Ireland*, 11th edn, Library Association.

UKCC (1986) *Project 2000: A New Preparation for Practice*, United Kingdom Central Council for Nursing, Midwifery and Health Visiting.

Further reading

Booth, A. and Walton, G. (2000) *Managing Knowledge in Health Services*, Library Association.

Bulletin of the Medical Library Association (quarterly journal of the Medical Library Association).

Carmel, M. (ed.) (1995) *Health Care Librarianship and Information Work*, 2nd edn, Library Association Publishing.

Health Information and Libraries Journal (quarterly journal of the Library Association: Health Libraries Group).

SEE ALSO: evidence-based healthcare; special libraries; university libraries

JOHN VAN LOO

HERITAGE SITES AND MONUMENTS INFORMATION

The information base that supports our knowledge and understanding of heritage sites and other historic monuments, buildings and landscapes is a complex and specialized field of activity. It is essential, however, if we are to understand them as fully as possible.

Monument inventories

The desire to identify, record, understand, explain and enjoy the heritage of our historic sites and monuments is characteristic of a society that values its history and culture. The creation of information about the historic environment through archaeological and architectural survey and the dissemination of information is central to this desire. Structured, accessible and properly referenced records of the historic environment, including archaeological sites, the built environment and historic landscapes, are maintained at an international level and, in many countries, at a national, regional and/or local level. They may be known as inventories, records, lists or registers of sites and monuments or of the historic environment. In some countries, separate inventories of archaeological sites and historic buildings are held. In other countries, including the UK, there are trends to integrate these records as holistic records of the historic environment.

Inventories of sites and monuments are established for the purposes of protection, conservation, planning, education and leisure. They may focus on monuments, buildings and landscapes with statutory designations and/or protection, but they may also include records of destroyed monuments and/or monuments at risk. They may contain the evidence to support assessments of archaeological and/or architectural potential when new developments are considered in an environmental planning framework. They may be detailed or summary, selective or comprehensive and be topographically or thematically based. Monument inventories will only be effective for their purpose if they are dynamic, being updated systematically as new knowledge comes to light.

At an international level, lists of World Heritage Sites of outstanding universal value are maintained by the United Nations Educational, Scientific and Cultural Organization (UNESCO) (see www.unesco.org/whc). At a national level, monument inventories are usually curated by government or other public bodies. Increasingly they are likely to be computerized, at least at index level. They may have access to the functionality of spatial (geographical) information systems and imaging technologies as well as holding primary ARCHIVES such as surveys, reports, photographs and measured drawings. The survey material that supports monument inventories is often captured in digital form (see below) and may be archived digitally. Monument inventories in some countries will still consist of hard-copy records, such as index cards, often supported by overlays depicting the locations of monuments on a map-base. In a growing number of countries, monument inventories are being Web-enabled, with user-interfaces incorporating educational and interpretative material. Concerns have been expressed in some countries, including the UK, that uncontrolled access to monument data can aid treasure hunters and burglary, however.

For an example of a national inventory, see the US National Register of Historic Places (www.cr.nps.gov/places.html). For a state-based example in Australia, see www.heritage.nsw.gov. au. In Europe, the EU-funded Council of Europe project, European-Heritage Net (www.european-heritage.net) provides signposting to the existence of national monument inventories. In the UK, the Historic Environment Information Resources Register (HEIRNET) provides information about monument inventories and other relevant resources (see www.ads.ahds.ac.uk/catalogue/HEIRNET/html). The national inventories for England, Scotland and Wales are known as National Monuments Records (see www.english-heritage.org.uk, www.rcahms.gov.uk/canmore. html and www.rcahmw.org.uk/nmrw/collecting. html, respectively), while in Northern Ireland the inventory is maintained by the Environment and Heritage Service (www.ehsni. gov.uk/BuiltHeritage).

For a national photographic record of statutory listed historic buildings being developed by English Heritage, see www.imagesofengland.org.

uk. In England and Wales, many local authorities maintain local intensive Sites and Monuments Records (see HEIRNET above and/or membership of the Association of Local Government Archaeological Officers (www.algao.org.uk)). For Scotland, see membership of the Association of Regional and Island archaeologists (www. scotlink.org (click on /members2000/aria)).

Data standards

A number of organizations have developed and published data and other standards for monument inventories, including the International Committee for Documentation of the International Council of Museums (ICOM/CIDOC) and the Council of Europe. For a national standard and a thesaurus of monument types developed by English Heritage, see www.rchme. gov.uk/midas.

Public and private archives

Inventories are structured records created for heritage purposes. Many historic public and private archives also contain information that will help inform the documentation and interpretation of the historic environment, but have not been created specifically for that purpose. These will be found in national, regional and local archive institutions, as well as the archives of companies, institutions and estates. These may include government and private records of land management and transfers, taxation and wills, design, construction and transport. For an international list of archive repositories, see www. unesco.org/webworld/portal_archives.

For a national list of archive repositories in England, Wales, Scotland and Northern Ireland, see www.archivesinfo.net/uksites.html. Historic records of architects' firms, including architectural drawings, are often deposited in architectural libraries and museums. For members of the International Confederation of Architectural Museums, see www.icam-web.org (click on 'about'). The British Architectural Library is an example of a national institution holding historic architects' records (see www.riba-library.com). In Scotland, the National Monuments Record holds historic records of architectural practices (see above). There is a trend for archives repositories to make their catalogues available online. For the English strand in the UK archives network, see the A2A (Access to Archives) database (www. a2a.pro.gov.uk).

Surveys of heritage sites and monuments

Monument inventories usually consist of high-level records of a large number of items.

Detailed surveys of individual historic buildings and archaeological sites are also made for a variety of reasons. They can be undertaken to obtain a fuller understanding of the development of the building or site; for the purpose of academic study; to inform planning decisions or to support historical research. Records made for other purposes (such as insurance plans or land surveys) can be valuable sources of material to inform this process of understanding and their use forms a part of the compilation of more detailed surveys for inventory purposes.

Much attention has been given to the methodologies of compiling a record for the purposes of historical analysis. It is helpful to define different levels or intensities of recording. Most records will combine a written description and analysis with a visual record made by drawing and photography. It is, however, not possible to prescribe forms and levels of record for all circumstances, and it is often necessary to vary the content of a record to provide elements to supplement existing surveys or reflect particular aspects of the site or building. Whilst surveys of archaeological sites and historic buildings vary in detail, there is an increasing awareness of the need to look at the relationship between buildings and their setting and, conversely, archaeological/topographical features in relation to the present above-ground structures.

Written survey reports

The simplest level of survey is essentially a descriptive visual record, supplemented by the minimum of information needed to identify the site or building's location, age and type. It is typically used when the aim is to gather basic information about large numbers of buildings or sites for statistical sampling, for a pilot project, identification for planning purposes or for protection, and whenever resources are limited and much ground has to be covered in a short time. With buildings, this type of survey is made from exterior inspection only, though the interior may sometimes be seen. Pro forma recording forms are often used. Limited summary analysis is possible by this method, which can be of use in the wider context in understanding the overall morphology or evolution of a site or settlement. It is often useful to produce a sketch plan to supplement the map base.

At the most complex end of the spectrum, a fully analytical survey will include all the elements of the simplest, with the addition of a systematic written account of the building or site's origins, development and use. The record should include an account of the evidence on which the analysis has been based, allowing its validity to be re-examined. It will also include all visual records required to illustrate the site or building's appearance and structure, and to support a historical analysis. The information will mostly have been obtained through a close examination of the site or building itself, but should relate it to the wider typological, stylistic or historical context and importance. It should also include the results of documentary research and be fully supported by comprehensive measured surveys and photography.

Most surveys lie somewhere between these two extremes, but should always include elements of description and analysis, clearly distinguished, and adequate visual support material. This can take the form of photographs, sketches or full measured surveys.

Photographic survey

A photographic survey offers a full visual record, and can be compiled considerably quicker than a measured survey or illustrative sketch. It is the primary means of record in aerial survey, linked closely to a map base to identify, locate and depict historic sites and landscapes. In building survey, photography is routinely used for illustrative purposes and is the most practical means of recording a building that has complex decoration or historic furnishing. It is also of primary importance in recording townscapes or identifying spatial relationships between rooms in a building or visual elements in a designed landscape such as a park or formal garden. A photographic record should always include basic location information and captions indicating which element of the site or buildings is shown or the direction in which the photograph is taken.

Survey drawings

Surveys are made by direct measurement using either hand survey methods with tapes and rods or by Total Station Electronic Distance Measuring (EDM) equipment on larger and more complex sites. Measured surveys may be augmented by other techniques designed to record detail, such as photogrammetry and rectified photography. The advantages and disadvantages of each of these processes must be understood before they are employed in the course of recording. The use of GPS (Global Positioning System) equipment, based on a constellation of satellites, gives high levels of accuracy in positioning sites and is of particular use in the survey of archaeological landscapes. The scale of drawings derived from a survey should be appropriate to the subject surveyed – typically 1:100, 1:50 or 1:20 for buildings and up to 1:500 or 1:1,000 for landscapes. Scales and north points should always be included. The use of a standard convention set aids comparison of different sites and buildings.

Digital survey data

Survey information is now often produced in digital form, whether as a word-processed file, an EDM survey of a site or a CAD drawing. Whilst in theory it is possible to store all such material in digital form, the pace of change in computer hardware means that some storage formats have already become obsolete, and it may be necessary to transfer data between different types of media to ensure their continued readability. It is therefore advisable to hold a hard copy of all data deposited in digital form. Whilst the digital record can provide information not susceptible to reproduction on paper (e.g. three-dimensional views, or the ability to examine minute areas of a drawing in close detail), the paper archive at least ensures the currency and accessibility of most of the information.

Further reading

Council of Europe (2001) *Guidance on Inventory and Documentation of the Cultural Heritage*, Council of Europe.
—— (1999) *Core Data Standards for Archaeological Sites*, Council of Europe.
English Heritage (2000) *Informed Conservation*, English Heritage.
International Committee for Documentation of the International Council of Museums (1995) *Draft International Core Data Standard for Archaeological Sites and Monuments*, ICDICM.
Morris, R.K. (ed.) (2000) *The Archaeology of Buildings*, Tempus.
RCHME (1998) *Recording Archaeological Field Monuments: A Descriptive Specification*, Royal Commission on Historical Monuments in England.
—— (1996) *Recording Historic Buildings: A Descriptive Specification*, 3rd edn, Royal Commission on Historical Monuments in England.

SEE ALSO: archival description; Geographic Information Systems

NIGEL CLUBB AND BOB HOOK

HERMENEUTICS

Hermeneutics is the art of interpretation. The word goes back to the Greek god Hermes, who was thought to have delivered the messages of the gods to human beings. Hermes translated the messages into human speech and thus became a symbol of the task of translation between different orders, times and places.

The oldest development of hermeneutics was connected to the interpretation of the Bible, of laws and of other difficult texts. Some have argued that the interpretation of the Bible must always be literal because the word of God is explicit and complete. Thus literal interpretation is one kind of hermeneutic interpretation. Others have insisted that the biblical words must always have a deeper 'spiritual' meaning because God's message and truth is self-evidently profound. Thus, for example, *allegorical interpretation* interprets the biblical narratives as having a second level of reference beyond those persons, things and events explicitly mentioned in the text. A particular form of allegorical interpretation is the typological, according to which the key figures, main events and principal institutions of the Old Testament are seen as foreshadowing persons, events and objects in the New Testament.

In the long and important history of hermeneutics only a few contributions can be mentioned here. Friedrich Schleiermacher (1768–1834) developed hermeneutics into a single discipline, embracing the interpretation of all texts, regardless of subject and genre. At each level of interpretation we are involved in a hermeneutical circle: we cannot know the correct reading of a passage in a text unless we know, roughly, the text as a whole; we cannot know the text as a whole unless we know particular passages. We cannot fully understand the text unless we know the author's life and works as a whole, which requires knowledge of his texts. We cannot fully understand a text unless we know about the whole culture from which it emerged, but this presupposes knowledge of the texts that constitute the culture. In the latter 1800s Wilhelm Dilthey (1833–1911) sought to defend the humanities against the growing competition from the sciences. He thought that hermeneutics could be developed into a humanistic method that could produce objective knowledge.

In the twentieth century Martin Heidegger (1889–1976) and Hans-Georg Gadamer (1900–2002) are the most important contributors. Heidegger distinguishes three modes of people's involvement with their surroundings:

- An everyday mode of practical activity.
- A reflective problem-solving mode.
- A theoretical mode.

In picking up a hammer to nail something, hermeneutic understanding is already at work. Pre-understanding can be put into words, but by this action the original hermeneutical relation between person and world is reified. Knowledge is always perspectival and situated. There is no escape to an absolute view without presuppositions. Human knowledge is always an interpretative clarification of the world, not a pure, interest-free theory. It is a mistake of Western science to believe that methods can construct a platform above the knower's historical situation. One can, however, become aware of one's own prejudgements through an interaction with others and with documents.

Philosophy of science

Some philosophers have seen POSITIVISM as the philosophy of the natural sciences and hermeneutics as the philosophy of the humanities. Although there may be a kernel of truth in this standpoint, it represents too simplistic an understanding. Kuhn (1970 [1962]) can be seen as a hermeneutic interpretation of the sciences because it conceives of scientists as governed by assumptions that are historically embedded and linguistically mediated activities organized around paradigms that direct the conceptualization and investigation of their studies. Scientific revolutions imply that one paradigm replaces another and introduces a new set of theories, approaches and definitions. According to Mallery et al. (1992), the notion of a paradigm-centred scientific community is analogous to Gadamer's notion of a linguistically encoded social tradition. In this way hermeneutics challenge the positivist view that science can cumulate objective facts. Observations are always made on the background of theoretical assumptions: they are theory-dependent.

Library and Information Science

Because hermeneutics is about interpretation of texts, it is in a way an obvious method for LIS. Research methodologies have been dominated by views that take the laboratory as a model. It should be obvious for LIS to defend a method, which makes the library a model for research.

Research in Library and Information Science has been dominated by a positivistic view. Among the few researchers who have pointed to the shortcomings of positivism and tried to inform LIS on hermeneutical alternatives are Benediktsson (1989), Budd (1995), Capurro (1985), Cornelius (1996), Hansson (1999) and Winograd and Flores (1987). Hermeneutics may at first glance seem disappointing for positivistic-minded and technology-oriented researchers. Hermeneutics does, however, make room for human interpretation that cannot be automated. Thereby it makes room for using people in information work as well as for developing qualitatively better information systems and services. In this connection there is a problem, however, in that researchers with knowledge of both hermeneutics and information retrieval are extremely rare.

References

Benediktsson, D. (1989) 'Hermeneutics: Dimensions towards LIS thinking', *Library and Information Science Research* 11: 201–34.

Budd, J.M. (1995) 'An epistemological foundation for library and information science', *Library Quarterly* 65: 295–318.

Capurro, R. (1985) 'Epistemology and information science', lecture given at the Royal Institute of Technology Library, Stockholm, Sweden (also available at: www.capurro.de/trita.htm#III. Hermeneutics and Information).

Cornelius, I. (1996) *Meaning and Method in Information Studies*, Norwood, NJ: Ablex.

Hansson, J. (1999) *Classification, Libraries and Society: A Critical Hermeneutic Study on 'Klassifika-*

tionssystem för Svenska Bibliotek' (the SAB-System), Borås, Sweden: Valfrid.

Kuhn, T.S. (1970 [1962]) *The Structure of Scientific Revolutions*, Chicago, IL: University of Chicago Press.

Mallery, J.C., Hurwitz, R. and Duffy, G. (1992) 'Hermeneutics', in S.C. Shapiro (ed.) *Encyclopaedia of Artificial Intelligence*, vol. 1, 2nd edn, New York: John Wiley & Sons. pp. 596–611.

Winograd, T. and Flores, F. (1987) *Understanding Computers and Cognition: A New Foundation for Design*, New York: Addison-Wesley.

Further reading

Inwood, M. (1998). 'Hermeneutics', in *Routledge Encyclopedia of Philosophy*, Version 1.0, London: Routledge.

SEE ALSO: Kuhn, Thomas S.; philosophies of science

BIRGER HJØRLAND

HEURISTICS

A set of techniques for problem-solving that accepts the goal of finding a good solution, but perhaps not the best possible solution. Heuristics functions may be based on trial and error, exploring potential solutions, looking at their outcomes and revising the procedure. A heuristic technique is precisely that likely to be employed by the user of LIBRARIES when searching for information or a document. The search is modified as it progresses, each piece of information or document found tending to influence the continuing search. Heuristics are often employed in ARTIFICIAL INTELLIGENCE systems.

SEE ALSO: information-seeking behaviour

HISTORICAL BIBLIOGRAPHY

A branch of BIBLIOGRAPHY dealing with the history and methods of book production, including the study of printing, binding, paper-making, illustrating and publishing. In recent years historical bibliography has tended to be subsumed into the broader study of the history of books, but its basic techniques and a knowledge of its principal findings are still essential to rare book librarians.

HISTORY OF LIBRARIES

The history of libraries resides within boundaries defined by its literature. Although LIBRARIES as

institutions have existed for thousands of years, serious and systematic study of their history came largely in the first decades of the twentieth century after formal LIBRARY EDUCATION had found a home in colleges and universities. Here library school students and scholars benefited from a nurturing research environment, and many were encouraged to explore the origins of library institutions. As a result most library history has been written either by library students completing thesis and dissertation requirements for advanced degrees, or by library and information science educators and some practising professionals influenced by a reward structure the academy extended to its members for publishing results of their research. Much excellent work has been done, although it seems to be somewhat isolated from the mainstream of academic endeavour in some departments (Black and Crawford 2001).

The scope of library history literature has not spread itself evenly across the world, or even within particular societies in particular regions of the world. The literature of library history largely reflects a Western bias. Several factors explain this skewed coverage. Because libraries have been mostly concerned with collecting the printed products of literate societies, oral societies (like many African cultures) that did not evolve a history of library institutions had no reason to generate a literature of library history. In addition, native cultures colonized by imperial powers had little incentive to study institutions imposed upon them by a dominant group that defined the role these institutions would play in the process of subjugating native populations. Also, societies in which formal library studies are largely late twentieth-century phenomena had not had adequate time to develop a substantial literature.

The literature of library history also reflects a white heterosexual male middle- to upper-class perspective, because libraries were generally supported and staffed by these people. Only in the last quarter of the twentieth century did library historians begin to explore the role that women, the working classes and ethnic and racial minorities had on libraries, both as employees and as users. Finally, the literature of library history has tended to glorify rather than critically analyse library institutions and their services. Research focused mostly positive attention on the profession's leaders and interpreted library history largely independently of the sociocultural environments in which libraries operate.

But within these narrowed confines, library history has nonetheless enjoyed a prosperous existence. Several serials (*Libraries and Culture*; *Library History*; the *Japanese Journal of Library History*) provide important conduits for library history articles. Good compendia exist in library history encyclopaedias and handbooks (Wayne A. Wiegand and Donald G. Davis, Jnr's *Encyclopedia of Library History*, 1994; Fritz Milkau's *Handbuch der Bibliothekswissenschaft*, 1955; and Alan Kent, Harold Lancour and Jay Daily's multivolume *Encyclopedia of Library and Information Science*, 1968–). Library history bibliographies include Sharon Chien Lin and Martha C. Leung's *Chinese Libraries and Librarianship: An Annotated Bibliography* (1986) and Donald G. Davis, Jnr and John Mark Tucker's *American Library History: A Comprehensive Guide to the Literature* (1989). There are several good histories of libraries within countries (for Italy, see Enzo Bottasso's *Storia della biblioteca in Italia*, 1984; for India, A.K. Ohdedar's *Growth of the Library in Modern India, 1489–1836*, 1966; for Germany, Wolfgang Thauer and Peter Vodosek's *Geschichte der öffentlichen Bücherei in Deutschland*, 1990; for Spain, Hipolito Escolar Sobrino's *Historia de las bibliotecas*, 1990; and for France, the multivolume *Histoire des bibliothèques françaises*, 1988–92). Unfortunately, however, as of this writing no comprehensive textbook covering world library history exists.

Model biographies of library leaders include Edward G. Holley's *Charles Evans: American Bibliographer* (1963) and W.A. Munford's *Edward Edwards: Portrait of a Librarian, 1812–1886* (1963). Exemplary histories of particular library institutions include Phyllis Dain's *New York Public Library: A History of Its Founding and Early Years* (1972), Doris C. Dale's *The United Nations Library: Its Origins and Development* (1970), Maria Siponta de Salvia's *The Vatican Library and Its Treasures* (1990) and Edward Miller's *That Noble Cabinet: A History of the British Museum* (1973). Good works that cover types of library institutions include Mohamed Makki Sibai's *Mosque Libraries: An Historical Study* (1988) and Raleigh Skelton's *Maps: A Historical Survey of Their Study and Collecting* (1972). Except for the USA and the United Kingdom, however, the history of library associations has received little attention. And remarkably little library history attempts to measure the impact of any library on its user populations.

The generally positive approach to library history was directly challenged in 1973 when Michael Harris published 'The purpose of the American Public Library: A revisionist interpretation of history'. The essay countered conventional thinking by hypothesizing that elite groups organized and funded US public libraries to help control working and immigrant classes. Many library historians initially dismissed the argument, but its basic tenet persisted and in the USA ushered in a revisionist literature that included Dee Garrison's *Apostle of Culture: The Public Librarian and American Society* (1979) and Rosemary Ruhig DuMont's *Reform and Reaction: The Big City Public Library in American Life* (1977).

In part, revisionism was finally able to penetrate library history literature because its practitioners increasingly began to research larger volumes of relevant primary source materials, rigorously to apply a greater variety of research methods to their data and to adopt research models and paradigms developed in cognate disciplines. And with the emergence of 'book' or 'print culture history' in the latter decades of the twentieth century, library historians were offered an opportunity to carve out a niche in a broader interdisciplinary area already pushing beyond a traditional Western white male middle-class heterosexual perspective that approaches its subject from the 'top-down/inside-out', to a more encompassing multicultural worldview that includes analysis from the 'bottom-up/outside-in'. Recent work has encompassed issues of gender (Kerslake and Moody 2000), and broader social issues (Black 2000).

References

Black, A. (2000). 'Skeleton in the cupboard: Social class and the public library in Britain through 150 years', *Journal of Information, Communication and Library Science* 7: 17–26.

Black, A. and Crawford, J. (2001). 'The identity of library and information history: An audit of library and information history teaching and research in departments and schools of library and information studies in Britain and Ireland', *Library History* 17: 127–31.

Kerslake, E. and Moody, N. (2000) *Gendering Library History*, Liverpool: John Moores University and Association for Research in Popular Fiction.

Further reading

'Library history research in the international context: Proceedings of an International Symposium, 1988' (1990) *Libraries and Culture* 25: 1–152.

Manley, K.A. (ed.) (2002) A special issue of *Library History* (18(1)) in honour of Peter Hoare.

Wertheimer, A.B. and Davis, D.G. (eds) (2000) A special issue of *Libraries and Culture* (35(1)) for the fiftieth anniversary of the Library History Round Table.

SEE ALSO: ecclesiastical libraries; Islamic libraries; oral traditions; women in librarianship

WAYNE A. WIEGAND

HOST

A computer that can provide services to a number of simultaneous users, frequently at remote locations as well as those situated at the host site. In library and information work the term has two main manifestations: ONLINE host and NETWORK host.

Online host

A host computer that provides the public at large with access to software and independently produced electronic databases for the purposes of selective retrieval of information. Users access the remote service via terminals or PCs connected via a TELECOMMUNICATIONS or WIDE-AREA NETWORK link. In the vast majority of cases the service is provided commercially to registered users only, either on a subscription basis or (more usually) according to the amount of individual use measured in terms of the time for which the user is connected (connect time) and/or the amount of information viewed, printed or downloaded.

Additional services offered by online hosts may include document ordering; ELECTRONIC MAIL; downloading arrangements; communications, search interface and accounting software; selective DISSEMINATION OF INFORMATION (SDI); current awareness services; and gateways to other systems.

DIALOG is the largest online host in the world. Internationally, there are hundreds more, including CompuServe, DataStar DIALOG (Europe), Dow Jones, ESA-IRS, FIZ Technik, FT Profile, InfoPro Technologies (BRS and Orbit Online), Mead Data Central, NewsNet, QL Systems and Questel, to name a small but well-known selection of the larger hosts.

Network host

Any computer that provides network applications (such as electronic mail or file transfer) over a wide area network such as the INTERNET or JANET. The host may be linked directly to the network or via a gateway on an intermediate computer or network server.

A direct network connection can be provided for members of an organization either through its centralized computing service or (in the case of the Internet) through any number of distributed PCs or workstations on a LOCAL-AREA NETWORK (LAN). Of the two, the former scenario is more common, as provided in many academic institutions, where access to JANET and/or the Internet is via the university computing service. In this case, the local systems administrator will normally control what network applications are supported and how they are implemented on the host. Where each PC, workstation or LAN server is actually an Internet host in its own right, users may obtain access to the full features of the network and may (in theory at least) control the software they choose to use for network access.

At an institutional level, indirect connections to a network via an intermediate host may be a convenient way to access services without taking out a separate and possibly very expensive subscription. One example is the gateway provided by major online hosts' electronic mail services (such as DIAL-MAIL and Data-Mail on DIALOG and DataStar respectively) to the Internet (for delivery of messages to Internet sites). Indirect connections, however, may not (depending on the sophistication of the gateway) offer the full range of network facilities. The operating procedures may not be entirely seamless either.

Where the network host is not the user's desktop computer, access to it can be via:

- A modern and dial-up telephone line
- A dedicated or multiplexed serial connection
- A local area network link.

Further reading

Majka, D.R. (1997) 'Remote host databases: Issues and content', *Reference Services Review* 25: 23–35.

SEE ALSO: electronic-journal archives; knowledge industries; World Wide Web

GWYNETH TSENG

HOT SPOT

An area on the computer screen, such as a word or part of a graphic, that the user can activate by indicating it with the mouse pointer and clicking, in order to follow a link to an associated unit of information. It is the essential principle of HYPERTEXT, and the basis for the links that allow the user to move around the WORLD WIDE WEB and elsewhere on the INTERNET by clicking on links.

HUMAN–COMPUTER INTERACTION

Computer Interaction (HCI) is a generic term that describes all the activities concerned with the research, design, analysis, development, implementation and evaluation of the interactions across the interface between computer applications and human beings (often called users or operators) who are interacting with the application. The main emphasis of HCI activity is on designing safe, reliable and usable systems, thus there has been an increasing emphasis on 'user-centred' design (as opposed to 'technology-centred' design) where the requirements, objectives and limitations of the intended users drive the design of the interface. HCI has wide applicability, covering HARDWARE Design (specific input and output devices, and their characteristics), Interface Engineering (the actual design of the interface and its relationship with the whole system design) and Social and Organizational Issues (such as group working or management structures).

Evolution of the term 'HCI'

The original term used was Man–Machine Interaction (MMI), which came into prominence in the 1970s as computer processing power and memory became available for supporting interface design, initially through an alliance of computer scientists and psychologists. The term has fallen out of favour because of its gender-specific implications. Two other related terms are MMS (Man–Machine Systems) still in common

use in the process control area, and Human Factors (HF), which evolved out of ergonomics. However, both these terms have wider application than HCI (or MMI), since they cover interactions with machines and systems, rather than with computers alone. In the USA, HCI is often known as Computer–Human Interaction (CHI).

The technology of the interface

Human–Computer Interaction is achieved through a variety of communication media. Examples of different media include:

Output media   text, graphics, sound, music, speech, colour, animation, still pictures, moving video.
Input media   text (keyboard, handwriting), gesture (mouse, pen, data glove, eye-movement), audio (voice or sound).

Output media are currently more closely attuned to human information processing characteristics. Input media are still rather primitive, requiring training and output feedback for effective use.

Each medium of communication is actually a language made up of a set of allowable symbols (or lexicon), rules for combining these symbols (syntax) and common usage rules (pragmatics) to which meaning (semantics) is assigned. For example, the symbols, syntax, semantics and pragmatics of moving video are derived from practices in the cinema or used on television. Media are often used in parallel on the same interface. They can be combined in an unsynchronized or synchronized manner (e.g. sound and moving pictures). In the synchronized case the combination may often form a new medium.

Most interfaces involve a collection of media, often in use at the same time. The term 'multi-media interface' however is usually reserved for interfaces involving at least the use of text, colour, graphics, animation, sound or video.

HCI research areas

The HCI designer needs to be familiar with human psychological and physiological abilities and limitations, current interface technologies, task analysis techniques, evaluation strategies, the rules of social interaction and organizational or environmental influences. HCI is therefore of a multidisciplinary nature, bringing together a number of disciplines including COMPUTER SCIENCE, psychology, ergonomics, ethnography, linguistics, social psychology, artificial intelligence and engineering. For convenience, HCI can be divided into the following research areas.

INPUT–OUTPUT DEVICES

Although building input and output devices is mainly an electronic engineering activity, the HCI interest is in the specification of such devices and their evaluation.

SOFTWARE ARCHITECTURES, TOOLS AND TECHNIQUES

There is a considerable HCI interest in designing architectures that support human–computer communication. Early attempts included User Interface Management Systems (UIMS), which tried to separate out the presentation, dialogue and task aspects of the application. In the 1990s there was a significant move towards the use of Direct Manipulation Interfaces utilizing Graphical User Interfaces (GUIs). OBJECT-ORIENTED TECHNOLOGY has also had a major impact on recent architectural approaches. Many tools and techniques have been developed to assist HCI designers (screen formatting, interaction analysis, the standard 'look-and-feel' approaches, interface creation, etc.) but better tools are still needed. Tools for creating interfaces using object-oriented techniques have become commonplace. Recently, sets of co-operating software agents have been suggested as a way forward towards the creation of intelligent and/or adaptive interfaces. Such interfaces can anticipate the user and make allowances for human frailty.

DESIGN METHODOLOGIES AND DESIGN RATIONALE

There is a need for HCI design methodologies. Multimedia developments have provided a large choice of media but design guidelines are practically non-existent. Some informal guidelines do exist (Browne 1994), but these are incomplete and need interpretation. The 'look and feel' of an interface is now an important issue and involves consistent representations across the whole interface. These are provided by toolkits supported by documents (style-guides).

Design rationale is a relatively new research area. It involves the recording of design decisions as they happen, in a structured way, so that later changes may be checked against the original rationale. An example of a design rational is QOC (Maclean *et al.* 1991).

COMPUTER-SUPPORTED CO-OPERATIVE WORK (CSCW)

This involves the support of simultaneously co-operating users (usually in remote locations) who are endeavouring to reach a common objective. Examples might include a video conference, shared use of word processors or shared drawing packages. In such situations ethnography can offer useful analysis tools.

USABILITY

Usability is the next most important goal after utility. HCI workers define usability in terms of effectiveness, learnability, flexibility and user satisfaction. (Shackel 1990). One technique that has been explored for improving the match between a computer and a user is the user model. User models are static (or dynamic) representations of the user that can be interrogated to develop a systems view of the user (preferences, weaknesses, habits, etc.). Currently, user modelling is still rather primitive.

INTERACTION STYLES AND DIALOGUE DESIGN

Interaction with the user has usually been supported by some form of metaphor or interaction style. In command line processing, the user provides commands (with parameters) and the computer reacts by carrying out the commands. For inexperienced users, menus are used that limit choice and give a sense of closure. Other metaphors used include form filling and direct manipulation (Shneiderman 1983) where users manipulate graphical objects on the screen mimicking the actions required. The desktop metaphor, where many aspects of the interface are portrayed as actions on a desk, is an example of direct manipulation. As a consequence, Graphical User Interfaces have become popular. Another important principle used in direct manipulation interfaces is WYSIWYG – What You See Is What You Get, implying a one-to-one relationship between, say, printed output and screen content.

Dialogue design involves the structure of the interaction across a set of commands, manipulations, etc. and is concerned with conversational styles, consistency and transitions.

USE OF MULTIPLE MEDIA

With the development of powerful personal computers, a large variety of media have become available to the designer. There are hopes that the use of such media will provide a more natural interface for the average user and greatly improved interfaces for users with disabilities. However, there is a serious lack of effective guidelines as to their use and, at the present time, there is much experimentation in progress (for example, on the World Wide Web). Development of guidelines and design methods will become important since we are moving into a world where end-user technology is becoming highly mobile and powerful. Although heavily used in human–human communication, auditory media are rarely used in HCI.

EVALUATION AND EXPERIMENTATION.

Because HCI is still a fairly new research area, evaluation (usually by experimentation) is important. There are two radically different approaches – the detailed, carefully controlled laboratory experiment, and the longitudinal study, where actual users are observed in the normal setting carrying out normal tasks. Both approaches have their place. Proper evaluation is important because, too often, changes are introduced into commercial packages without any justification or user-checks whatsoever. Evaluation is also essential for assessing the capabilities and limitations of new input–output devices.

References

Browne, D. (1994) *Structured User Interface Design for Interaction Optimisation (STUDIO)*, Prentice-Hall [the STUDIO Design Methodology].

Maclean, A., Bellotti, V.M.E. and Moran, T.P. (1991) 'Questions, options and criteria: Elements of design space analysis', *Human Computer Interaction* 6: 201–50.

Shackel, B. (1990) 'Human Factors and Usability', in J. Preece and L. Keller (eds) *Human–Computer Interaction, Selected Readings*, Prentice-Hall, pp. 27–41.

Shneiderman, B. (1983) 'Direct manipulation: A step beyond programming languages', *IEEE Computer* 16(8): 57–69.

Further reading

Dix, A., Finlay, J., Abowd, G. and Beale, R. (1998) *Human Computer Interaction*, Hemel Hempstead, UK: Prentice-Hall.

Hellander, M., Landauer, T.K. and Prasad, V.P. (1998) *The Handbook of Human Computer Interaction*, North-Holland.

Laurel, B. (ed.) (1990) *The Art of Human–Computer Interface Design*, Addison-Wesley [a collection of interesting papers in HCI research].

Norman, D. (1990) *The Psychology of Everyday Things*, Basic Books [a very interesting and readable book on interface design issues].

Raskin, J. (2000) *The Humane Interface: New Directions for Designing Interactive Systems*, Addison-Wesley.

J.L. ALTY

HYBRID LIBRARIES

The first identified use of the term hybrid library was by Sutton (1996). However, it was almost simultaneously coined by Rusbridge (1998), then Programme Director of the Electronic Libraries (eLib) Programme in the United Kingdom, who popularized the term and with whose name it is now associated (JISC 1997). Although largely confined to higher education, it is likely that the concept will spread to other types of library.

The term has been used rather loosely in the literature – even as a synonym for digital libraries (see DIGITAL LIBRARY). Two distinct interpretations are in common usage, the first location-dependent and the second collection-dependent. In the first, *a* hybrid library may be described as a physical library in which seamless, integrated access is provided to all the resources available to that library, irrespective of medium or location – sometimes known as a one-stop shop. As a separate strand of definition *the* hybrid library is used more specifically to describe the integration of electronic services into a more coherent whole, irrespective of their location. A similar meaning is conveyed by the term GATEWAY LIBRARY, sometimes used in the USA, while the process involved is often if jocularly referred to as 'clicks and mortar' and appears to be in the process of being superseded by the interest in, and increasingly commonly used term, personal portals. In the latter case it is often associated with the Distributed National Electronic Resource (DNER), which provides a range of shared services – middleware, content, resource discovery, etc. – which can be assembled to meet local needs.

It may seem a statement of the obvious that a library will provide access to many different types of media, but the essential element of hybridity is that the user is presented with simple and unified access. Rusbridge (1998) identifies four classes of resource that must be brought together: legacy resources, that is existing non-digital resources; traditional resources, that is legacy resources which also exist in digitized form; new resources that are born digital; and future resources that will incorporate access methods. Although some work is required to combine technologies, the hybrid library is seen much more as embodying cultural rather than technological change. Whether the hybrid library is seen as a sort of staging post towards truly electronic libraries or whether the idea will develop in its own right is as yet unclear.

The term was introduced into general parlance by a call for demonstrator projects by the UK Joint Information Systems Committee (JISC) in March 1997 (JISC 1997). Five projects were funded: Agora, which is building a standards-based broker system; BUILDER, which covers institutional issues; HEADLINE is about information landscapes and the set of resources of interest to the user; HYLIFE is about different client groups and types; MALIBU is about management implications and the development of models.

By 2000, the term was sufficiently embedded into both usage and practice that the University of Birmingham could be awarded a contract for the development of Hybrid Information Management Skills for Senior Managers (Birmingham 2000). The concept has also found favour in the Asia-Pacific region, again in higher education, and is seen as a key building block in enhancing the relationship between library and university.

References

Birmingham, University of (2000) *HIMSS Project* (www.himss.bham.ac.uk/Documents/OfficialDocs/PBSummary.html).

JISC (Joint Information Systems Committee) (1997) *Electronic Information Development Programme: E-Lib Phase 3*, Circular 3/97 at www.jisc.ac.uk/pub97/c3–97.html.

Rusbridge, C. (1998) 'Towards the hybrid library', *D-Lib Magazine* July/August (www.ariadne.ac.uk/issue26).

Sutton, S. (1996) 'Future service models and the convergence of functions: The reference librarian as technician, author and consultant', in K. Low (ed.) *The Roles of Reference Librarians, Today and Tomorrow*, New York: Haworth Press.

Further reading

Bundy, A.A. (1999) 'Partner in learning and research: The hybrid university library of the 21st century' (www.library.unisa.edu.au/papers/hybrid.htm).

e-Lib Phase 3 websites: AGORA (http://hosted.ukoln.ac.uk/agora/scope.html); BUILDER (http://builder.bham.ac.uk); HEADLINE (www.headline.ac.uk/); HYLIFE (www.unn.ac.uk/~xcu2/hylife/summary.htm); MALIBU (www.kcl.ac.uk/humanities/cch/malibu/).

New Review of Academic Librarianship (1989) A special issue (vol. 4) on hybrid libraries.

Oppenheim, C. and Smithson, D. (1999) 'What is the hybrid library?', *Journal of Information Science* 25: 97–112.

Pinfield, S. and Dempsey, L. (2001) 'The Distributed National Electronic Resource (DNER) and the hybrid library', *Ariadne* 26 (www.ariadne.ac.uk/issue26/dner/intro.html).

Rusbridge, C. and Royan, B. (2000) 'Towards the hybrid library: Developments in UK higher education', Paper 001–142-E, 66th IFLA Council and General Conference, Jerusalem (www.ifla.org/IV/ifla66/papers/001–142e.htm).

SEE ALSO: electronic-journal archives; university libraries

DEREK G. LAW

HYPERMEDIA

A generic term now widely used for multimedia applications of the HYPERTEXT principle. This permits the user to follow associative links between units of information by clicking on a HOT SPOT with a mouse. Web-delivered documents are the most familiar form of hypermedia.

HYPERTEXT

The concept of hypertext was developed by Ted Nelson in 1960. He envisioned a computer-based system that would reproduce what he called 'non-sequential writing', i.e. the associative rather than logical way in which human minds work. In effect, this was to be a form of electronic browsing, which allowed the user movement from one 'page' to another, to move between index and text, and to have the electronic equivalent of a finger in a page while looking at another page (or book, or picture, or any other information-varying object). A working system was developed in 1967, but Nelson himself became obsessed with developing a system called Xanadu, which was to be a *de facto* universal library, to which he gave the name 'docuverse'. Xanadu was impractical, and in any case unattainable with the software then available, but the hypertext idea was not forgotten, and when Tim BERNERS-LEE began to develop the information system that was to become the WORLD WIDE

WEB he reverted to Nelson's idea. As a result, the Web is, in effect, the universal hypertext system that Nelson had envisaged. The essential principle of hypertext – the ability to move without interruption from one information resource to another – is fundamental to conducting searches on the Web.

Further reading

McAleese, R. (ed.) (1999) *Hypertext: Theory into Practice*, revised edn, Exeter: Intellect.
Nelson, T. (1987) 'All for one and one for all', in *Hypermedia '87 Proceedings*.

SEE ALSO: information and communication technology; organization of knowledge

I

ICON

A small symbol on a display screen, such as the wastebasket (or trashcan) for deleting files, which represents a resource or a function provided by a computer application, hypermedia program or GRAPHIC USER INTERFACE.

IFLA

IFLA (International Federation of Library Associations and Institutions) is the international body representing the interests of library and information services and their users. Founded in Edinburgh, Scotland, in 1927 on the occasion of the fiftieth anniversary of the UK LIBRARY ASSOCIATION, IFLA now has nearly 1,800 members in over 150 countries. The Federation was registered in the Netherlands in 1971. The Royal Library of the Netherlands in The Hague provides facilities for its headquarters.

Aims

The Federation is an independent, international, non-governmental, not-for-profit organization. Its objectives are to:

- Promote high standards of provision of library and information services.
- Encourage widespread understanding of the value of good library and information services.
- Represent the interests of its members.

Core values

A set of core values are embodied in the Statutes of the Federation, including the belief that people, communities and organizations need free access to knowledge for their well-being, and that the provision of high-quality library and information services help guarantee that access.

Membership

The original members of IFLA, national LIBRARY ASSOCIATIONS, remain at the heart of the organization. Individual library and information services and all kinds of organizations in the library and information sector, ranging from major national libraries and research institutes to school libraries, may join as Institutional Members, with special provision for one-person units. Individual practitioners may join as Personal Affiliates, with special provision for students. More than thirty corporations in the information industry have formed a working relationship with IFLA under the Corporate Partners scheme. In return for financial and 'in-kind' support, they receive a range of benefits, including opportunities to present their products to a worldwide audience.

Relations with other bodies

Good working relationships have been forged with important international bodies whose interests overlap with those of IFLA. UNESCO recognizes IFLA with Formal Associate Status. The UN has accorded it observer status, as has the World Intellectual Property Organization (WIPO), the World Trade Organization (WTO) and the International Standards Organization (ISO), whilst the International Council of Scientific Unions has granted IFLA associate status. In turn, IFLA has offered consultative status to a number of bodies, including the INTERNATIONAL COUNCIL ON ARCHIVES (ICA) and the International Publishers Association (IPA). IFLA is a founder member, along with the ICA, the International Council on Museums (ICOM) and the International Council on Monuments and Sites (ICOMOS), of the International Committee for the Blue Shield (ICBS). The mission of the ICBS, the cultural equivalent of the International Committee of the Red Cross, is to collect and disseminate information and to co-ordinate action in situations when cultural property is at risk.

General Conference

Up to 3,000 library and information specialists meet in August in a different host country each year at the IFLA conference, the biggest international gathering of its kind. They meet to exchange experience, debate professional issues, see the latest products of the information industry, conduct the business of IFLA and experience something of the culture of the host country. In addition, many of IFLA's professional units and core activities hold a range of professional meetings, seminars and workshops around the world.

Governance

The General Council, consisting of delegates of voting Members, is the highest organ of the Federation. Under new Statutes adopted by the Federation's Council held in Jerusalem in 2000, it elects the President-elect and members of the Governing Board by postal ballot. It also meets every year during the annual conference, when it considers general and professional resolutions that, if approved, are usually referred to the Governing Board or Professional Committee for action. The Governing Board is responsible for general policy, management, finance and external relations. It consists of the President (in the chair), the President-elect, ten elected members and nine members of the Professional Committee. The Professional Committee directs the planning of IFLA's professional activities and monitors their progress. To this end, it adopted a series of professional priorities in January 2001, which all IFLA professional units use as the basis of their strategic plans.

Professional units

The Sections are the primary focus for the Federation's work in:

- A particular type of library and information service (for example National Libraries or School Libraries).
- An aspect of the practice of library and information science (for example Document Delivery and Interlending, or Management and Marketing).
- A specific region (there are three regional sections covering Africa, Asia & Oceania, and Latin America & the Caribbean).

Three regional offices located in Dakar, Senegal, Bangkok, Thailand, and São Paolo, Brazil support the regional Sections.

All IFLA members are entitled to register for one or more of the forty-five Sections of their choice. Once registered, voting members have the right to nominate specialists for the Standing Committee of those Sections. The Standing Committee is the key group of professionals who develop the programme of the Section, including research activity, publications and its contribution to the annual conference programme. Discussion Groups have also been established to cater for new or relatively ephemeral subjects, which do not require the establishment of a Section. All these units are grouped into eight Divisions, which are represented on the Professional Committee.

Core activities

Issues common to library and information services around the world are the concern of IFLA's six core activities. The Advancement of Librarianship (ALP) core activity has a very wide remit, dealing with the broad range of issues specific to the developing world. Others cover current, internationally important, matters:

- Copyright and other Legal Matters (CLM).
- Free Access to Information and Freedom of Expression (FAIFE).
- Preservation and Conservation (PAC).
- Universal Availability of Publications (UAP).
- Universal Bibliographic Control and International MARC (UBCIM).

Each core activity is hosted by a national library

or other institution in a different part of the world.

Publications

IFLA Journal is published five times a year. Each issue covers news of current IFLA activities, together with in-depth articles selected to appear to reflect the variety of the information profession. Four titles are published each year in the monograph series published for IFLA by K.G. Saur of Munich, Germany. Recent titles include *The Public Library Service: IFLA/UNESCO Guidelines for Development* and *Delivering Lifelong Continuing Professional Education across Space and Time*. The IFLA Professional Reports Series, published by IFLA HQ, features reports of professional meetings and guidelines to best practice. Recent titles include: *Proceedings of the Pan-African, Pan-Arab Conference on Public and School Libraries* and *Camel Library Services in Kenya, a Report on the Assessment of Non-motorized Mobile Libraries*. The website IFLA-NET (www.ifla.org) has rapidly become a prime source of information not only about IFLA, but also about a broad spectrum of library and information issues.

Resources

About 80 per cent of IFLA's income is derived from membership fees. Other sources of income include sales of publications, contributions from the corporate partners and grants from foundations and government and international agencies. Twenty donors, including libraries and individuals, contribute to the core activities fund and seven institutions provide accommodation and infrastructure for the core activities and IFLA's Headquarters. Several hundred library and information professionals contribute their time, expertise and financial resources to the realization of IFLA's professional programmes.

Further reading

Website (www.ifla.org).

ROSS SHIMMON

IMAGE RETRIEVAL

The identification and retrieval of visual images from DATABASES.

This is a significant and growing problem in INFORMATION RETRIEVAL. Conventional systems of INDEXING and searching are geared to CATALOGUES or textual databases, in which BOOLEAN LOGIC or FREE-TEXT SEARCHING will take the user to relevant items with comparative ease and accuracy, using authors, titles, keywords and so on, or through complete searches of the file. Visual images, however, need a different kind of indexing and retrieval system if they are to be comparably accessible. Essentially two approaches have been developed. The traditional approach is to assign indexing terms, which may relate to specifically visual features (such as shape), but are more usually a more conventional indexing term assigned to describe the subject of the contents of the image. Such systems have been evolved over many decades as means of indexing and cataloguing visual documents such as prints, photographs, architectural drawings and so on. For digital files, however, systems are being developed in which the image can be retrieved using key visual indicators such as colour, texture and shape. These more sophisticated systems are likely to become of increasing importance as the number of such databanks itself increases. (Gudrum *et al.* 2001).

Image retrieval is still a significant problem that is being addressed through research and experimentation in a number of countries. It is particularly important in ART LIBRARIES, but equally relevant to work in local studies librarianship (see LOCAL STUDIES COLLECTIONS), rare book librarianship (see RARE BOOK LIBRARIES), the documentation of HERITAGE SITES AND MONUMENTS INFORMATION, and other fields, from medicine to engineering, in which visual images are important conveyors of information. The related and complex issues around the sophisticated retrieval of moving images are also the subject of research, although these systems are still at a comparatively early stage of development (Sandom and Enser 2002).

References

Gudrum, A.A., Rorvig, M.E, Jeong, K-T. and Suresh, C. (2001) 'An open source agenda for research linking text and image content features', *Journal of the American Society for Information Science* 52: 948–53.

Sandom, C.J. and Enser, P.G.B. (2002) *VIRAMI: Visual Information Retrieval for Archival Moving Imagery*, London: Library and Information Commission (Report 129).

SEE ALSO: multimedia librarianship; picture libraries

Further reading

Chu, H. (2001) 'Research in image indexing and retrieval as reflected in the literature', *Journal of the American Society for Information Science* 52: 1,011–18.

INCUNABULA

Books printed before the year 1501; the literal meaning is 'cradle books'. Although such books are rare and usually valuable, they are not really different from those printed in 1501 and the years immediately afterwards. Nonetheless, they have been treated as a separate group since the late eighteenth century and incunabulists have developed their own techniques for studying them, as well as compiling large catalogues and bibliographies.

Further reading

Hellinga, L. and Goldfinch, J. (eds) (1987) *Bibliography and the Study of Fifteenth Century Civilization*, British Library.

SEE ALSO: rare-book libraries

INDEX

An organized grouping of terms intended to facilitate access to a document or collection of documents in any medium or format. It is normally alphabetical. The most familiar form is the index to a book or series of books, indicating at what place or places topics, places or persons are mentioned by page number or some other indicator of location. The term is also used to describe a finding aid to the position of material in a library collection, more or less synonymously with catalogue (see CATALOGUES). Although the principles of analysis used are identical, however, an index entry merely locates a subject, whilst a catalogue entry also includes descriptive specification of a document concerned with the subject.

SEE ALSO: organization of knowledge

INDEXING

Analysing the contents of a document (book, pamphlet, audiovisual or machine-readable item, etc.) or collection of documents and translating the results of the analysis into terms for use in an INDEX – an organized grouping of such terms to allow location and retrieval of information.

Kinds of index

Indexes may include entries for a range of categories, including personal, corporate and geographical names; subjects; titles of works; first lines; quotations; abbreviations; acronyms and initialisms; citations; numbers; and dates. Examples of indexes include an index to CLASSIFIED CATALOGUES in a library or other collection, an index to a group of periodicals and an index to an individual periodical, book or other document. Although indexes, other than numerical and date indexes, are usually arranged alphabetically, there are examples of classified and alphabetico-classed indexes such as *Index to Theses Accepted for Higher Degrees in the Universities of Great Britain and Ireland* and *Engineering Index*.

Purposes of indexes

The main purpose of an index is to facilitate the speedy location of specific items of information. The index rearranges the material, bringing together scattered references to a topic. A good index indicates what is not in a document and so is a valuable aid to selection. It can also limit wear and tear on a document, because it saves a reader from having to flip through the complete text each time a piece of information is sought.

Standards for indexing

The ISO standard on indexing (British Standards Institution 1996) usefully defines the function, type and features of indexes and gives advice on content and general organization, arrangement of entries in indexes and presentation of indexes. This derives from an earlier British standard (British Standards Institution 1988) which it replaces.

Features of a good index

Accuracy is an obvious requirement of an index and the index should normally be comprehensive – though certain limitations on comprehensiveness may be allowable if clearly explained. Terms should be used consistently and consistency is more likely to be achieved if a reliable thesaurus is used, indexing decisions are systematically recorded and work on the same index done by more than one indexer is carefully co-ordinated (British Standards Institution 1988: clause 4.4). There should be enough 'see also' cross-references to connect related items in the index. 'See' references should be used for synonyms and alternative forms of name, but in the case of a book index it is often more economical, as well as being more helpful to the user of the index, to make additional entries rather than 'see' references.

The computer and indexing

Computers have long been used to produce some forms of index, including string indexes like the entries in *Current Technology Index* and the subject index entries produced for the *British National Bibliography* between 1971 and 1990 using PRECIS (the Preserved Context Indexing System). Programs are now also available for book indexes.

Indexing societies

The Society of Indexers was formed in 1957 and three other national societies are now formally affiliated to the British society: the American Society of Indexers (formed in 1968), the Australian Society of Indexers (formed in 1976) and the Indexing and Abstracting Society of Canada/ Société canadienne pour l'analyse de documents (formed in 1977). The twice-yearly journal the *Indexer* is the official journal of all four societies. The British society has published five monographs in a series of open-learning units and more are in progress.

The Cataloguing and Indexing Group of CILIP is also obviously interested in indexing. The Group publishes a quarterly journal, *Catalogue and Index*.

Awards for indexers

In 1960 the LIBRARY ASSOCIATION instituted the Wheatley Medal, so called in honour of Henry B. Wheatley (1838–1917). It is awarded annually to the compiler of the most outstanding index first published in Britain during the preceding three years. The Society of Indexers established an occasional award for outstanding services to indexing in 1977 and designated it the Carey Award in memory of the Society's first President, Gordon V. Carey (1886–1969). The H.W. Wilson Company Index Award, presented by the American Society of Indexers on behalf of the well-known index publishers, was inaugurated in 1979. The Australian Society of Indexers presented its first Medal, intended to promote standards of excellence in indexing in Australia, in 1988.

The future of indexing

Although some indexes to individual documents and to collections are still produced manually, the future is likely to see increasing use of computers. Wellisch (1991) considers the possibility of indexes to individual documents being integrated into DATABASES. He refers to experiments in the USA and Sweden aimed at achieving this and points out that such a development would make back-of-the-book indexes available to a much wider community as well as challenging indexers to achieve the highest standards of quality with regard to comprehensiveness and specificity of indexes (Wellisch 1991: 407).

References

British Standards Institution (1988) *British Standard Recommendations for Preparing Indexes to Books, Periodicals and Other Documents*, 3rd edn, British Standards Institution (BS 3700: 1988).
Wellisch, H.H. (1991) *Indexing from A to Z*, H.W. Wilson Company.

Further reading

Cleveland, D.B. and Cleveland, A.D. (1990) *Introduction to Indexing and Abstracting*, 2nd edn, Libraries Unlimited.
Lancaster, F.W. (1991) *Indexing and Abstracting in Theory and Practice*, University of Illinois, Graduate School of Library and Information Science.
Mulvany, N.C. (1994) *Indexing Books*, University of Chicago Press.

SEE ALSO: alphabetization rules; classification; information retrieval; organization of knowledge; standards specifications

K.G.B. BAKEWELL

INFORMATICS

Informatics is the science of information. It studies the representation, processing and communication of information in natural and artificial systems. Since computers, individuals and organizations all process information, informatics has computational, cognitive and social aspects.

Used as a compound, in conjunction with the name of a discipline, as in medical informatics, bioinformatics, etc., it denotes the specialization of informatics to the management and processing of data, information and knowledge in the named discipline.

Terminology

The French term *informatique*, together with various translations – *informatics* (English), *informatik* (German) and *informatica* (Italian, Spanish) – was coined by Dreyfus, in March 1962 (Dreyfus 1962), and refers to the application of computers to store and process information (see also Bauer 1996). The morphology, *information* + *-ics*, uses 'the accepted form for names of sciences, as *conics*, *linguistics*, *optics*, or matters of practice, as *economics*, *politics*, *tactics*' (*Oxford English Dictionary* 1989); *informatics* encompasses both science and practice. Phonologically, informatics combines elements from both 'information' and 'automatic', which strengthens its semantic appeal. This new term was adopted across Western Europe, and, except in English, developed a meaning roughly translated by the English 'computer science' or 'computing science'. Mikhailov *et al.* advocated the Russian term 'informatika' (1966) and the English 'informatics' (1967) as names for the 'theory of scientific information' and argued for a broader meaning, including study of the use of information technology in various communities (e.g., scientific) and of the interaction of technology and human organizational structures.

> Informatics is the discipline of science which investigates the structure and properties (not specific content) of scientific information, as well as the regularities of scientific information activity, its theory, history, methodology and organization.
>
> (Mikhailov *et al.* 1967)

Usage has since modified this definition in three ways. First, the restriction to *scientific* information has been removed, as in *business informatics* or *legal informatics*. Second, since most information is now digitally stored (Lesk 1997; Lyman

and Varian 2000), computation is now central to informatics: Gorn (1983) defines informatics as computer science + information science. Third, the processing and communication of information have been added as objects of investigation, since they are now recognized as fundamental to any scientific account of information.

In the English-speaking world the term informatics was first widely used in the compound, 'MEDICAL INFORMATICS', taken to include 'the cognitive, information processing, and communication tasks of medical practice, education, and research, including information science and the technology to support these tasks' (Greenes and Shortliffe 1990). Many such compounds are now in use.

A June 2002 web search (Google 2002) found 'informatics' and various compounds occurring more or less frequently, with the numbers of documents returned for each term given in parentheses: informatics (1,100,000), bioinformatics (691,000), medical informatics (151,000), health informatics (52,800), museum informatics (19,500), nursing informatics (15,600), geoinformatics (11,100), neuroinformatics (9,180), social informatics (6,840), business informatics (6,610), dental informatics (2,850), molecular informatics (2,630), environmental informatics (2,580), legal informatics (1,640), chemical informatics (1,230), mobile informatics (492), protein informatics (408) and library informatics (303). Some informatics specializations are named in other ways: for example, what might be called science informatics (1,710) is more usually called *e-science* (17,700); bioinformatics is often called *computational biology* (347,000).

Each of these areas studies representations and uses of information, which may be peculiar to each field of application, but draw on common social, logical and computational foundations. They all involve the use of computing and information technologies to store, process and communicate information. They all also address the interaction of technology with the production and use of information by individuals and organizations; they develop software, systems and services that aim to help people interact with information, both efficiently and effectively.

The scope of informatics

What these areas have in common is informatics: the focus on information and how it is represented in, processed by and communicated between a variety of systems. Representations include paper, analogue and digital records of text, sounds and images, as well as, for instance, the information represented in a gene and the memories of an individual or an organization. Processing includes human reasoning, digital computation and organizational processes. Communication includes human communication and the human–computer interface – with speech and gesture, with text and diagram, as well as computer communications and networking, which may use radio, optical or electrical signals.

Informatics studies the interaction of information with individuals and organizations, as well as the fundamentals of computation and computability, and the hardware and software technologies used to store, process and communicate digitized information. It includes the study of communication as a process that links people together, to affect the behaviour of individuals and organizations.

Informatics as a science

Science progresses by defining, developing, criticizing and refining new concepts, in order to account for observed phenomena. Informatics is developing its own fundamental concepts of communication, knowledge, data, secrecy, interaction and information, relating them to such phenomena as computation, thought and language, and applying them to develop tools for the management of information resources.

Informatics has many aspects. It encompasses, and builds on, a number of existing academic disciplines: primarily ARTIFICIAL INTELLIGENCE, COGNITIVE SCIENCE and COMPUTER SCIENCE. Each takes part of informatics as its natural domain: in broad terms, cognitive science concerns the study of natural information processing systems; computer science concerns the analysis of computation and the design of computing systems; and artificial intelligence plays a connecting role, producing systems designed to emulate those found in nature. Informatics also informs, and is informed by, other disciplines, such as mathematics, electronics, biology, linguistics, psychology and sociology. Thus informatics provides a link between disciplines with their own methodologies and perspectives, bringing together a common scientific paradigm, common engineering methods and a pervasive stimulus

from both technological development and practical application.

Informatics builds on a long tradition of work in logic, which provides an analysis of meaning, proof and truth. It draws on probability and statistics to relate data and information, and on the more recent tradition of computer science for abstract models of computation and fundamental notions of computability (What can be computed?) and complexity (How do we deal with the space and time requirements of a computation scale as we consider problems of different sizes?). Combining these traditions enriches them all, since they share a common interest in information.

The science of information provides a new paradigm of scientific analysis, which concentrates on the processing and communication information rather than focusing on the electrical, optical, mechanical or chemical interactions that embody this activity. Focusing on information provides novel accounts of long-standing phenomena, even in physics (Frieden 1998). Informatics provides accounts of the representation, processing and communication of information, the conceptual basis for applying computing and information technologies to develop new tools for the management of information in diverse areas, and also the basis for beginning to unravel the workings of the mind.

We illustrate the scope and nature of informatics with a brief account of one area in which informatics is contributing to library and information science. With essentially all information becoming available online, libraries will focus increasingly on selection, searching and quality assessment. The contribution of informatics to this enterprise is to provide and apply appropriate techniques for the representation, processing and communication of information. We now give an account of some of these techniques, with a focus on textual information.

Representation

The Web was designed as an information space, with the goal that it should be useful not only for human–human communication, but also that machines would be able to participate and help. One of the major obstacles to this has been the fact that most information on the Web is designed for human consumption. [...] The Semantic Web approach [...] develops languages for expressing information in a machine processable form.

(Berners-Lee 1998)

Data on the WORLD WIDE WEB makes digital representations familiar to us all. Texts, images and sounds are represented by digital encodings, as patterns of bits. Standards such as ASCII, Unicode, JPEG, TIFF, WAV and MP3 allow for the encoding, storage, exchange and decoding of multimedia information. These representations may be indexed and retrieved as individual files, but they are, to varying degrees, opaque to software agents searching for information.

Text files are stored as unstructured sequences of characters. Dividing a text into words, sentences and paragraphs is mostly straightforward. Finding keywords in a text file is straightforward, and some search engines incorporate shallow linguistic knowledge that extends keyword search. For example, 'stemming' determines the morphological root of a given word form, thus relating singular and plural forms of a noun, and different moods and tenses of a verb. Searching for swan using stemming finds swans, and searching for goose should find geese (see FREE-TEXT SEARCHING).

We can also search for content in other media. Finding keywords in recorded speech is much harder than searching a text file: it is both more expensive in computing resources and less accurate. Finding images with specified content, simply by examining the image automatically, is even harder (see IMAGE RETRIEVAL).

Extracting information from texts requires deeper linguistic analysis. For example, searching news reports to glean information about company takeovers – who is being taken over, by whom, what price is being paid, for what – requires a grammatical analysis of individual sentence structures. More complex information – such as finding arguments that support a particular decision – demands more global analyses of meaning. Text files form a small fraction of society's data storage (Lyman and Varian 2000). However, texts are rich in information that is not represented elsewhere, so it is important to make this information accessible. If texts are stored in ways that make grammatical and rhetorical structures transparent, then it becomes easier for automated tools to access such information.

METADATA

The simplest way of making searching easier is to attach an electronic 'catalogue card' to each document. Such data about data is called 'META-DATA'. For example, the DUBLIN CORE is a metadata standard which specifies a set of required and permitted elements for such a catalogue card. The Resource Description Format (RDF) is a general standard for such metadata.

Metadata allows software agents to find, retrieve and process data. Just as books in a library are made accessible by the catalogue, so information on the Web is made accessible by metadata.

The SEMANTIC WEB is a project that aims to provide a common framework for such efforts, by having data on the Web defined and linked in such a way that it can be used by machines not just for display purposes, but for automation, integration and reuse of data across various applications, so that tomorrow's programs can share and process data even when these programs have been designed totally independently.

STRUCTURED DATA

Digital documents allow, in principle, much richer automated processing – content selection, information extraction, price comparisons or document clustering. To facilitate this, data is structured; documents are given internal structure. There are many different formats for structured data, some simple in their description, others complex and rich. Many COMMUNITIES OF INTEREST (biologists, engineers, geologists, businesses) are designing new formats to allow them to put machine-understandable data on the Web. This will allow data to be shared and processed by automated tools as well as by people.

RELATIONAL DATA

Relational databases represent information by representing relations between entities (such as the relation between book and author, or the relation between book and publisher). Rather than exchange whole databases, query languages such as SQL allow users to retrieve, from the database, information about specified entities. Relational databases are appropriate for representing uniformly structured data, where all entities of a given type can be represented by specifying a given collection of relations (every part has a price, every employee has a manager).

But these are ill adapted to the open-ended nature of information on the Web, where we may find that one manager also plays in a band, and so have to represent the fact that she plays the saxophone.

MARK-UP

One common form of structuring is mark-up. Mark-up originated as a means of structuring text; before the computerization of the printing industry, mark-up was annotation written by a copy editor on a manuscript, to indicate structure (chapter, heading, paragraph, etc.) and style (italic, bold, etc.). Mark-up now refers to sequences of characters, known as tags, inserted in a text or word processing file. The original use of mark-up was to indicate how the file should look when printed or displayed. Mark-up is now often used to describe a document's logical structure, or as a format for describing an abstract logical structure, so-called 'semi-structured data' – a replacement for the representation of structured data by traditional relational databases.

Standard frameworks for mark-up, such as SGML (Standard Generalized Mark-up Language) and XML (eXtensible Mark-up Language), have been adopted by many metadata initiatives, including the semantic Web, where XML mark-up is used to structure the metadata attached to a document. An example of SGML mark-up is the HyperText Mark-up Language HTML, *lingua franca* of the World Wide Web.

A general mark-up language such as XML can be applied to encode content and structure for applications that go far beyond the original purposes of mark-up for typesetting and display. Mark-up can be used to tag entities in a document (addresses, prices or names), to tag logical roles (author, publisher), to tag logical connections, for example linking a price to an entity, or to tag phrases and parts of speech in order to indicate a text's detailed grammatical structure. Applications of XML are found everywhere: in bioinformatics and linguistics, in business-to-business applications, in cataloguing and indexing and in scholarly annotation of ancient texts.

Mark-up languages define the scope of what can and cannot be expressed in mark-up. For example, XML provides controlled flexibility and allows us to represent semi-structured data that does not fit well in the relational mould. XML tags come in pairs, < author >...< /author >, which act as 'named brackets'. These brackets must be properly nested, thus an XML document has a hierarchical structure in which each layer of the hierarchy consists of text, interspersed with elements from the layer below tagged with names (such as 'author'). This allows a mixture of structure and free text.

Most applications require further restrictions. For example, HTML is defined by a document-type definition (DTD) that specifies which elements may occur in an HTML document (headings, paragraphs, lists, etc.), and structural rules (for example, list elements occur within lists) that an HTML document must follow. A DTD can specify as many constraints on the structure as are needed for a particular application, or as few. Thus, an author element might require a surname, allow any number of forenames and permit nothing else.

From a scientific perspective, XML and the structures it allows us to express represent just one of many possibilities for structuring data. The science underlying XML provides an understanding of the ways in which data may be structured. It provides query languages and algorithms for retrieving data in response to a query. It provides the conceptual framework for understanding how structure may be specified, for example by a DTD, and algorithms for checking that a document conforms to a specified form. It provides the basis for assurances of the integrity and provenance of data, and so on.

Processing and communication

Processing is the transformation of data from one form to another. Information is data interpreted, organized and structured. For example, the English documents on the Web form a large dataset; when we use a SEARCH ENGINE to count the numbers of documents containing a given search term it finds on the Web, we extract information from this data. The ability to collect, aggregate and organize data allows us to create and represent information. Knowledge is information that has been analysed so that inter-relationships are identified, formalized and represented. Thus processing can extract information from data, and transform information into knowledge. These results must then be communicated effectively to the user.

NATURAL-LANGUAGE PROCESSING

Today (2002), machines are widely used for document retrieval. Future software agents will use Natural-Language Processing (NLP) tools to extract relevant information from documents in response to user queries, to create summaries tailored to the user's needs, and to collate, assemble and present information derived from a multitude of sources.

Human readers see structure in texts: words, sentences, paragraphs, documents, etc. They attribute meanings to documents and structure these meanings – as facts, arguments and conclusions, and so on. Representing, processing and communicating structures and meanings in ways that make these easily accessible to machine processing, so that users can easily access information relevant to their needs, are key issues for informatics.

Automated text-processing tools can tag parts of speech and annotate grammatical links: the connection between verb, subject and object; the connection between a pronoun and the phrase it refers to. Deeper linguistic processing can disambiguate word senses. Such tools are components of natural-language understanding. They convert texts into machine-accessible sources of information and provide the basis for a variety of information processing applications.

For example, current document retrieval systems, using keyword search, allow users to find documents that are relevant to their needs, but most leave it to the user to extract the useful information from those documents. Users, however, are often looking for answers, not documents. Information extraction tools, based on natural-language understanding, find and extract information from texts. Such tools, already used, by intelligence analysts and others, to sift through large amounts of textual information, will become commonplace. DOCUMENT CLUSTERING is another application that draws on natural-language technology. By examining patterns of word occurrences, together with syntactic and semantic structures, it is possible to cluster documents by topic or to search for documents similar to a given example.

Automated natural-language generation is also being applied, to new forms of information delivery. Machine-generated text can be used to present information tailored to the user (Oberlander *et al.* 1998). Such tools will be applied to present information derived from database queries, information extraction and data mining. Tools for document clustering will be linked to natural-language generation to provide automatically generated summaries drawing on a variety of sources.

Natural-language processing is one example demonstrating the way in which informatics relates to longer-established disciplines. It relies on computer science for underlying software and hardware technologies, and for algorithms that make this processing feasible. It draws on logic and linguistics for appropriate representations of linguistic and semantic structures, on machine-learning techniques from artificial intelligence for tools that extract from large text corpora information on the words and concepts relevant for a particular domain, and on cognitive science and psychology for an understanding of how people process and react to information.

These disciplines are drawn together, in informatics, by the common purpose of understanding how language can communicate information between human users and a formal representation stored in a machine. This marriage of computational and theoretical linguistics with cognitive psychology and neuroscience has generated new tools, and has also thrown new light on human communication.

It is clear that information, and hence informatics, must play a pivotal role in any analysis of human communication. Informatics is also transforming other areas of science: it provides a new paradigm for analysing complex systems, as compositions of simpler subsystems that process and communicate information. Long-standing challenges to scientific analyses, are being transformed by the new paradigm. For example, in biology, informatics provides not just tools for data-processing and knowledge discovery, but also a conceptual framework for studying the information stored and communicated by genes and processed by biochemical cycles that 'run the genetic program' to produce structure and form.

In cognitive science it provides the conceptual tools needed to develop models of the connection between cognition and the observed structure and function of the billions of neurons that make up the brain. It also provides the technologies that allow us to observe and analyse the structure and operation of the living brain in ever greater detail and to test our models by simulation of very much simplified subsystems which, despite their relative simplicity, are complex beyond analytical analysis.

Looking forward

The technologies underlying the digital storage, processing and communication of information are improving relentlessly. Since 1965 these improvements have followed 'Moore's Law': for a given price, both processor speeds and memory capacity double every 18–24 months (Moore 1965). Communication BANDWIDTH follows a similar pattern of growth, but doubles in 12 months or less (Poggio 2000). These rates of exponential growth are predicted to continue, and so processing speed and memory capacity will increase by a factor of 100, and communication bandwidth by a factor of 1000 or more, every ten years.

The combination of digitization and global connectivity makes data available in unprecedented volume. It is estimated that humanity creates more than an exabyte of data each year (Lyman and Varian 2000). Nevertheless, it will soon be technologically possible for an average person to access virtually all recorded information. The availability of cheap processing will make it increasingly feasible to restructure data into knowledge on demand. New technologies are being developed to automatically organize this material into forms that can help people satisfy their information needs quickly and accurately, realizing, and even surpassing, Vannevar BUSH's prescient vision of the 'Memex' – 'a device in which an individual stores all his or her books, records and communications, and which is mechanized so that it may be consulted with exceeding speed and flexibility' (Bush 1945). These technologies are indeed 'creating a new relationship between thinking man and the sum of our knowledge'.

By 2025, if Moore's law continues to apply, we will have, in our pockets and on our desktops, computers that each have the raw computing power of the human brain, computers linked to each other by a telepathic communication network. We currently have little idea of how we might structure and program such devices to achieve what we humans find straightforward, but already today's machines extend our capabilities by performing tasks we find impossible. We can be sure that technological changes will continue to revolutionize the ways we manage, share and analyse data, and will provide new ways of transforming data into information and knowledge.

References

Bauer, W.F. (1996) 'Informatics and (et) informatique', *Annals of the History of Computing* 18(2) (http://www.softwarehistory.org/history/Bauer1.html).

Berners-Lee, T. (1998) *Semantic Web Roadmap* (http://www.w3.org/DesignIssues/Semantic.html).

Bush, V. (1945) 'As we may think', *Atlantic Monthly* 176(1) (July): 101–8 (http://www.theatlantic.com/unbound/flashbks/computer/bushf.html).

Dreyfus, P. (1962) 'L'informatique', *Gestion*, Paris, Juin 1962, pp. 240–1.

Frieden, B.R. (1998) *Physics from Fisher Information: a Unification*, Cambridge University Press.

Google (2002) (http://www.google.com/search?q=informatics).

Gorn, S. (1983) 'Informatics (computer and information science): Its ideology, methodology, and sociology', in F. Machlup and U. Mansfield (eds) *The Study of Information: Interdisciplinary Messages*, pp. 121–40.

Greenes, R.A. and Shortliffe, E.H. (1990) 'Medical informatics: an emerging discipline with academic and institutional perspectives', *Journal of the American Medical Association* 263(8): 1114–20.

Lesk, M. (1997) *How Much Information Is There In the World?* (http://www.lesk.com/mlesk/ksg97/ksg.html).

Lyman, P. and Varian, H. (2000) 'How much information?', *The Journal of Electronic Publishing* 6(2) (http://www.press.umich.edu/jep/06-02/lyman.html).

Machlup, F. and Mansfield, U. (eds) (1983) *The Study of Information: Interdisciplinary Messages*, John Wiley & Sons.

Mikhailov, A.I., Chernyl, A.I. and Gilyarevskii, R.S. (1966) 'Informatika – novoe nazvanie teorii naunoj informacii', *Naučno tehničeskaja informacija* 12: 35–9.

—— (1967) 'Informatics – new name for the theory of scientific information', *FID News Bull.* 17(2): 70–4.

Moore, G.E. (1965) 'Cramming more components onto integrated circuits', *Electronics* 38(8): 114–17 (http://www.intel.com/research/silicon/moorespaper.pdf).

Oberlander, J., O'Donnell, M., Knott, A. and Mellish, C. (1998) 'Conversation in the museum: experiments in dynamic hypermedia with the intelligent labeling explorer', *New Review of Hypermedia and Multimedia* 4: 11–32.

Oxford English Dictionary (1989) second edition, Oxford University Press.

Poggio, A. (2000) 'Information and products', in *Englebart's Colloquium, The Unfinished Revolution* (Stanford http://www.bootstrap.org/colloquium/session_10/session_10_poggio.jsp).

Further reading

Association for Computational Linguistics (ACL) website (www.aclweb.org/).

Cole, Ron *et al.* (eds) (1998) *Survey of the State of the*

Art in Human Language Technology, Studies in Natural Language Processing, Cambridge University Press; ISBN: 0521592771 (http://cslu.cse.ogi.edu/HLTsurvey).

Cover, Robin (ed.) (2002) *XML Cover Pages* (www.oasis-open.org/cover/sgml-xml.html).

Graves, J.R. and Corcoran, S. (1989) 'The study of nursing informatics', *Image: Journal of Nursing Scholarship* 21: 227–31 (www.nih.gov/ninr/research/vol4/Overview.html).

Martin, W.J. (1988) *The Information Society*, London: ASLIB.

Musen, Mark A. (1999) 'Stanford medical informatics: Uncommon research, common goals', *MD Computing* (January/February): 47–50 (http://camis.stanford.edu/MDComputing.pdf).

Shortliffe, E.H., Perreault, L.E., Wiederhold, G. and Fagan, L.M. (1990) *Medical Informatics: Computer Applications in Health Care*, Addison-Wesley.

Social Informatics (www.slis.indiana.edu/si/concepts.html).

Text Retrieval Conference (TREC) (http://trec.nist.gov/).

SEE ALSO: artificial intelligence; communication; computer science; database; database management systems; Human–Computer interaction; hypertext; indexing; information and communication technology; information retrieval; information science; information systems; knowledge management; knowledge-based companies; machine translation; mark-up languages; metadata; neural network; relational database; search engines; software; string indexing; World Wide Web

MICHAEL P. FOURMAN

INFORMATION

Information is data that has been processed into a meaningful form. Seen in this way, information is an assemblage of data in a comprehensible form capable of communication and use; the essence of it is that a meaning has been attached to the raw facts. The conceptual distinction between information and knowledge is therefore rather unclear, although the two terms tend to be used in somewhat different contexts. Increasingly, information is the word that is applied in the broad professional and technical context represented in such phrases as 'information technology' or 'information retrieval' or 'information management'. It is thus used in a general sense to encompass all the different ways of representing facts, events and concepts in both digital and analogue systems, and in all media and formats.

INFORMATION AND COMMUNICATION TECHNOLOGY

The term is used here to describe the design and applications of systems and equipment for exchanging data by electrical means between two or more stations. There are now many kinds of telecommunication networks used for a diverse range of purposes.

Major events in the history of communications technology

In 1747 William Watson, using a crude electrical generator, showed that electricity could be conducted along a wire 2 miles long.

The first transatlantic cable of gutta-percha-insulated copper strands was completed in 1858. A ninety word message, sent by Queen Victoria to President Buchanan, which took over an hour to be correctly received, cost about £600 at today's prices.

Alexander Graham Bell's telephone, invented in 1876, was constructed from a diaphragm of gold-beaters skin that moved under the control of a soft iron armature fixed to its centre when current flowed through an adjacent electromagnet. The circuit was completed by a battery and another similar telephone.

Eventually very large 'PTTs' were formed to supply reliable almost unchanging telephone service that called for a large capital investment, but advancing technology eroded their foundations. PTTs were not well suited to adopting new technology – one reason why organizational and regulatory changes to the Packet Switched Telephone Network (PSTN) were put in hand in many countries.

Two post-war events initiated major advances in communication technology. They were the publication of SHANNON's seminal paper and the introduction of the transistor a few years later. The transistor and the later development of integrated circuits enabled complex technology and coding development to proceed in the direction of achieving the theoretical channel capacity.

The lack of inexpensive wideband channels is a major constraint. In ascending order of cost, electrical communication channels are formed from copper pairs, coaxial cable, optical fibre and satellite links. Fibre, satellite and wireless channels have the widest BANDWIDTH.

In 1991 – nearly 250 years after Watson's experiment – the INTERNET became available to the general public. Telecommunications then entered a new epoch.

Data transmission

A basic electrical communication system consists of a source, an interconnecting communications channel and a sink. Often a similar source/sink device is used serving either as a transmitter or as a receiver at both ends of the channel. In such a system 'communication' is normally synonymous with 'telecommunication'.

The data signalling method may be analogue, where the signal varies in proportion to the source data – the method adopted when the telephone system was designed. Alternatively it may be digital, where data is sent as coded sequences of signal impulses, the code may be read and processed by a computer, and the signals are less likely to be confused with noise. These and other advantages now usually make digital transmission the preferred choice.

A general requirement when data is to be sent and received using the human senses is to work at a rate corresponding to the human assimilation rate. When the telephone network, the PSTN, is used for its designed purpose – the exchange of speech signals – its bandwidth, about 2.5 KHz, is adequate for the purpose. But methods have been devised for using it for data transmission. In this case a modem (MOdulator DEModulator) is used at either end of the line to convert generated or received signals into a form suitable for transmission or reception.

MODEMS

Modems are available that will work at speeds up to the limits imposed by the transmission channel. Almost all small computers are fitted with modems these days, enabling them to be plugged into a telephone line to exchange data with other machines. See also the Standards section below. The data rate limit is much higher than appears to be the case from the telephone network's performance for speech transmission. A simplified explanation of how this is achieved is explained in a later section headed Channel capacity.

Current modem developments have been towards new compression systems, sophisticated modulation schemes with more bits per symbol, improved methods of error correction and the addition of functions such as telephone answering machine control. The complexity required for these functions is embodied in mass-produced chips so prices have dropped. Modem chip sets are now available to provide a wide range of performance alternatives and different functions. Slightly increased prices have been accompanied by far higher speeds so transmission time costs have dropped substantially.

Compression

One way of increasing the data rate is to compress the transmitted data, pass the reduced amount of data through the transmission link, and decompress it before use at the receiving point. The time taken and transmission costs will be reduced. A form of DATA COMPRESSION was introduced by Samuel Morse who noted the size of the stocks of letters and hence their frequency of occurrence, when visiting a local printing house. He designed the Morse code accordingly with E as '.' and Q as '_ _ . _'. This general principle is still used, but the modern equivalent is 'run length coding' where long strings of binary noughts and ones are represented by short codes.

Compression is particularly useful for colour picture data where there may be large areas – such as blue sky – where the repeated transmission of single picture elements (PIXEL) may be replaced by a code indicating that the same data repeated per pixel may be replaced by an instruction 'keep repeating a blue pixel until further notice'.

This, and other methods of taking advantage of redundancy – data that may be omitted without appreciably reducing the information content – can be very effective. There is a marked trend towards greater use of images particularly over the Internet. Dial-up access without data compression is slow; a wideband channel with compression the fastest. For example it would take twenty-three minutes to send an uncompressed 24-bit 1,600 × 1,200 pixel colour picture at 33 Kilobits per second (Kbps) over the PSTN. The same picture compressed twenty times and sent over a high-speed leased line at 25 Mbps would take 0.09 seconds. Motion video pictures require yet more bandwidth because while a few seconds may be tolerable before a still picture can be viewed, delays in reproducing the sequence of picture frames required to display motion need to be very small.

CHANNEL CAPACITY

Nyquist showed in 1928 that the maximum possible signalling rate in a communication channel with a bandwidth W is 2W. If the bandwidth of a telephone channel is 2.5 KHz a maximum signalling rate of 5,000 elements per second is possible. If one signalling element is conveyed as a simple 'on-off' function, contains one unit of data, or bit, and the channel is used for data transmission, the maximum rate is 5,000 bps (bits per second).

The transmission rate may be increased by representing the number of bits per signalling element as different power levels of the element. The receiver then has to distinguish between those different values in the presence of noise (random impulses present in all communication channels) instead of simply having to detect whether the signal power is 'on' or 'off'. Further increases in bit rates require a large number of small changes in signal power that become comparable with noise level changes, and bit errors become likely.

The adequacy of a noisy channel for transporting data – the channel capacity – was defined by Shannon in 1948. Shannon devised an equation for calculating the capacity (C) of a given channel taking account of its bandwidth, signal power and noise level. 'C' represents the amount of data that a channel can carry at some arbitrarily small error rate. Since ideal coding cannot be realized, very small, but not zero, error rates are achievable. The Shannon equation represents a performance yardstick and indicates how one parameter may be traded for another. Bandwidth – the range of frequencies that a channel will accommodate – is related to the bit rate of data.

Applied channel capacity

The PSTN provides an entry point into customers' premises. When used for data transmission the bit rate may be increased by introducing the Integrated Services Digital Network – likely to be superseded by ADSL (Asymmetric Digital Subscriber Loop) proposed by Valenti from Bell research in 1991. ADSL embodies methods to raise channel capacity by frequency-response

equalization and noise-reducing multi-subchannel modulation to reduce the effect of cross-talk, interference and impulsive noise. Each of the numerous subchannels accommodates as many bits as noise allows.

The data rate could be up to two megabits per second (Mbps) or more for over 90 per cent of the 'local loop' in the UK. About forty-two pages per second of typical text would be transmitted at this rate, compared with about 1.35 pages per second over a 64 Kbps ISDN channel. To increase transmission rates still further, leased lines having a wider bandwidth than the PSTN are available. They may employ coaxial cable, or fibre-optic cable (see FIBRE-OPTICS) of yet greater bandwidth. Such lines are used by CABLE TELEVISION companies for transporting television signals. Many subscribers are connected to cable TV in industrialized countries. Cable companies may also use downstream 'wireless' transmission BROADCASTING, to avoid cable-laying. Distribution via wide bandwidth satellite channels is another possibility. Different upstream paths for both of these systems via a different medium – e.g. telephone line – are usually necessary.

The rate of connection of affordable data transmission channels to data users has been much slower than the development of the means of creating and receiving large volumes of data – particularly image data. Images in colour are in general use on Internet sites for sales purposes, to make the sites more interesting and attractive, and quite frequently in order to increase information content and presentation by adopting visualization techniques. The telephone system has been pressed into service for the purpose, for which it was not designed. Attempts are being made to extend the system's capacity as already mentioned.

Techno-political issues

DEREGULATION

The first major global application of communications technology was the PSTN – still the most widely used system for data transmission. Although this article is about technology, something must be said about the associated politics that has had such a strong effect on the course of its development.

Nearly all countries originally chose a controlled monopoly to administer the system but the copper cable 'local loop' or 'last mile' part of it from exchanges out to customers is a severe data bottleneck. The telephone network is ubiquitous. The number of globally connected locations is enormous – in 1990 it was estimated that nearly 1,000 million telephones were in use – indicating far more connections than for any other type of network. It is owned by the incumbent monopolies – the Post, Telegraph and Telephone (PTT) administrations – and represents a huge investment. PTT operations change very slowly. Governments or their agencies have set about monopoly deregulation. Deregulation started in the USA, and was gradually taken up by the UK and then Europe in the belief that competitive services would stimulate change. In August 1993 there was an EC White Paper for Growth followed by plans submitted in June 1994 by commissioner Bangemann to liberalize telecommunications by 1998. The reforms proposed by the Commission are slowly being adopted.

POLITICAL ISSUES AND THE LOCAL LOOP

Higher speeds are realizable over the phone network by adopting ADSL. 'Unbundling' (enabling competition) of the local loop has been decreed by the telecommunications regulator. The attitude of the FCC (Federal Communication Commission) in the USA might affect UK users. It is believed that if ever there was an optimal time to build a new local loop that time is now. However, federal policy and industry dictate otherwise.

Telecommunications policy in the UK does not run smoothly. The politics of the local loop are an important current issue. The charges levied by the largest service provider (BT) are perceived to be high, and slow access to exchanges needed by ADSL competitors has discouraged progress. BT earns revenue from its wideband leased lines available for private rental. After the regulatory agency, OFTEL, was asked to investigate prices, it concluded that they were reasonable, but after the investigation BT reduced the rental charge for some of their lines by 75 per cent. It was reported that BT had extended the range of ADSL outwards from its exchanges. BT was also asked by OFTEL to reduce the annual ADSL rental it charges competitors. It cut it by half. It is hoped that the UK will now no longer be one of the slowest countries in Europe to adopt ADSL.

There is another way of bypassing the local loop. AT&T thought about introducing radio ('wireless') connections in 1997 but did not pursue the idea. In 2000 a US company called Terabeam proposed to do it using diffuse laser beams. Cable also has possibilities – using the services of a local telecommunications company that may have lower access and line rental charges than the major national and international providers.

FIBRE-OPTICS

Fibre-optics was invented in England by Kao and Hockham at STC in 1966 but it was the US company Corning who exploited the invention. Fibre-optic cables are in widespread use for long-distance communications. In 1988 a UK advisory council (ACOST) proposed that a very large investment should be made to construct a nationwide fibre-optic network. A refusal was followed by a report from a House of Commons committee that said that this was a golden opportunity missed.

As speeds have increased so has the use of fibre-optic interconnecting cable. For FDDI – the Fibre Distributed Data Interface – an American Standard (ANSI) X3T9.5 was agreed in 1990 for operations at up to 100 Mbps. A particular requirement is the connection of LANs, which may be working at relatively slow bit rates, to an interconnecting fibre main 'backbone' cable for fast transmission over relatively long distances.

FDDI stations use cheap Light-Emitting Diodes (LEDs) for the transmitting element and PIN Field Effect Transistors (PINFETs) for reception. An FDDI network contains two contra-rotating rings for increased reliability.

The replacement of the narrowband exchange-to-customer cable – the 'Local Loop' discussed earlier – by a wideband fibre-optic cable would enable transmission speeds through this major part of the telephone network to be greatly increased.

In 1989 it was claimed that all-fibre systems had arrived but connections between remote terminals and subscribers' homes remained twisted pair. But more than a dozen manufacturers were said to be developing equipment to replace this final kilometre.

Ten years later fibre to the home remains a controversial subject that has not fulfilled the earlier optimism. From 1998 onwards contradictory opinions rather than news of large-scale installations seem to have been the rule. It was then believed that solving the last-mile problem for electrical signals by cost-effective all-optical systems would remain elusive for many years. The magazine *Fiber Exchange* carried an article that illustrated the ongoing controversy: 'Many forecasters think fiber to the home and business won't be a significant market for another three to five years.' Companies in the business think this is wrong and 'claim they have the customer interest to prove it'.

Standards and protocols

A standard is an attempt to establish a set of recommendations to be agreed between participants so that information may be exchanged without the introduction of incompatible system problems. A PROTOCOL is a set of standardized rules for conducting telecommunications traffic.

The CCITT division of the International Telecommunications Union (ITU known as the 'ITU Standardization Sector' since March 1993) and the Bell Telephone Company made 'recommendations' independently in the early days, but latterly international standards have been set by the CCITT/ITU. For many years a 'standard' called RS232 (adopted by the CCITT as V24) sufficed to describe the interconnections between terminal and modem. It is still widely used.

Modems usually conform to 'V series' CCITT standards so that any pair of modems having the same V number should work together. Performance advances include higher speeds (over the PSTN in particular), compression, error correction and lower prices. Higher speeds are mainly achieved by data compression and working at more bits per baud; susceptibility to noise increases accordingly. Error correction reduces the effects of noise. Compression enables more data per bit to be transported.

Most error detecting/correcting systems are based on the automatic addition of extra bits to a block of a given number of data bits at the transmitter to enable a checking procedure to be carried out at the receiver. When an error has been detected, the offending sequence of data bits will be automatically corrected at the receiver, or (in simpler systems) the receiver will demand a retransmission of the offending sequence.

The difficulties caused by incompatibilities between different computers attempting to intercommunicate prompted the OPEN SYSTEMS INTERCONNECTION (OSI) model that was agreed upon

with great difficulty in the period 1976 to 1986. Information from a sender is presented to a recipient exactly in the manner intended by the sender, regardless of machines, software or *en route* variations. It requires that a user's source data be accompanied by control data, put there preferably automatically, in the expectation of encountering a number of 'managing' devices along the way to deal with particular functions, each device reading the segment of data addressed to it. Each takes the appropriate action to route onward the unchanged message. Finally, the terminating device must be able to interpret the instructions addressed to it so that the message is correctly reproduced.

IBM's SNA (Systems Network Architecture), with at least 20,000 users – among them being the largest organizations in the world – was well established before the OSI proposals. In 1984 a deal was negotiated between IBM and the EC. IBM agreed to publish details of their SNA protocols. In 1988 IBM announced its support for OSI and later included OSI-compatible protocols within its Systems Applications Architecture (SAA).

The Transmission Control Protocol/Internet Protocol (TCP/IP) was introduced in the 1970s by the US Department of Defense for the same reasons that OSI was introduced in Europe. TCP/IP has the same objectives as in the OSI model but the complexity of OSI, and the availability of ready-to-use TCP/IP systems, reduced OSI's chances of widespread adoption. The remarkable growth of the Internet with a very large number of users the world over has resulted in the adoption of TCP/IP in spite of European ambitions to develop a specifically European Internet supported by European standards.

Networks and systems

INTRODUCTION AND TYPES

A telecommunications network is a system consisting of communicating devices, such as terminals, an interconnecting medium, such as cable, and a means of establishing paths through the medium. NETWORKS cater for people with information-intensive occupations, establishing communicating paths through the medium between communicating devices. The main driving forces have been the arrival of compact, powerful, cheap technology and the need for business 'communications'.

The network needs to be transparent so that messages may be exchanged with users unaware of the complexity of the intervening medium and of the routing procedure. When one user communicates with another in a different organization, say overseas, using equipment and networks supplied by a different manufacturer, the objective of standards is that, in spite of these differences, messages may be satisfactorily exchanged.

Network types include:

Enterprise Network – a general-purpose network of any type within a large organization.

Information Superhighway (see below).

Integrated Services Digital Network (ISDN) – a network that provides end-to-end digital connectivity to support a wide range of services, including voice and non-voice, to which users have access via a limited set of standard multipurpose interfaces. There are 'Basic Rate Access' (2 × 64 Kbps 'B' channels for data or voice) or Primary Rate Access (30 B + 1 Data channel (Europe), 23 B + 1 D channel (USA)). The re-laying of cables from subscribers to local exchanges is not necessary since the system has the necessary bandwidth.

Internet – a global publicly accessible network (see below).

Local Area Network (LAN: see also below) – a short-distance network designed for data exchange between terminals and computers. A network adaptor card in the terminal is required. It contains the necessary intermediate components that work with 'driver' software – that is, software designed to work with the network being used – often to IEEE standards in order to satisfactorily connect the machine to the network.

Metropolitan-Area Network (MAN) – a 'Super LAN' fibre-optic ring operating at 10 Mbps or more over an area of about 50 Kms.

Mobile Network (see below).

Wide-Area Network (WAN) – any type of long-distance network.

Wireless Local-Area LAN (WLAN) – a WLAN contains access points to the network using a spread spectrum radio link connecting users up to about 300 metres away or infrared connection points for line-of-sight users. Spread spectrum involves hopping between a number of frequencies during communication.

LAN OPERATING PRINCIPLES

The most popular LAN systems in use today are Ethernet and Token Ring.

Ethernet, a LAN Contention system, uses Carrier Sense Multiple Access with Collision Detection (CSMA/CD) transmission. Message data travel in packets round a single cable and are captured only by the station to which they are addressed. All stations listen and only transmit when the cable is clear. In the event of two stations transmitting at once, one or other jams the network, waits for a period of time of random length and then tries again.

In Token Ring systems, supported by IBM and others, empty data packets circulate and a station wanting to transmit detects one, enters an address and data, and empties the packet after reception when it next comes round. All stations examine all packets, accepting only those addressed to them.

NETWORK INTERCONNECTIONS

Several types of devices and software are in use.

A router interconnects networks that use identical protocols. It can handle several connection paths and adopts those with the lowest cost paths.

A brouter is a router that includes some of the functions performed by a bridge.

A bridge is used to connect networks with dissimilar protocols. Bridge functions have been substantially increased and some will connect LANs to WANs and manage traffic patterns.

A GATEWAY is the most sophisticated of the interconnecting devices. It is used to interconnect two networks with different architectures and may have to handle different protocols. It could be used, for example, to interconnect a network running on an IBM protocol, and another running on a non-IBM protocol.

THE INTERNET

In 1991 the Internet became available commercially as an extension of its use by the research departments of corporations under a general agreement of use for research and educational purposes. As early as 1993, domains, such as departments within a company, containing 5.5 million people having ELECTRONIC MAIL addresses, were searchable. One of today's estimates puts the number of Internet pages at 550 billion worldwide. The efficiency of the software used by the search engine Google (see SEARCH ENGINES), and the scale of operations, is demonstrated by a search. Google took 0.3 seconds to find the 26,000 pages containing the phrase 'Internet Growth' out of the 1,388 million pages of the World Wide Web – a major part of the Internet – which it covers (August 2001).

There have been three phases of Internet activities – the research phase (up to the mid-1980s), the academic club phase (mid-1980s to early 1990s) and the public communications phase (early 1990s onwards). Valovic, formerly editor of *Telecommunications Magazine*, writes: 'up to 1991 the Internet was the world's best kept secret as a behind the scenes academic network'. But then there was 'a breakthrough that was going to massively transform communications and most other areas of human endeavour including business, education, science and entertainment' (Valovic 2000) This comment is not an exaggeration. According to Odlyzco, head of mathematics research at AT&T laboratories, Internet backbone traffic is doubling every year (Odlyzco 2000).

THE INFORMATION SUPERHIGHWAY

The objective of an Information Superhighway is to provide a global universal telecommunication network to provide entertainment and information. In September 1993 the Clinton administration in the USA published a nine-point agenda to encourage the construction of the highway. This White House agenda aimed to ensure that it would be available to all at affordable prices. Vice President Gore broadened the concept to a Global International Infrastructure in the hope that all governments would join in. We must 'work toward our goal of connecting every classroom, library, hospital, and clinic to the NII by the year 2000', said Gore (Gore 1994).

A project of this kind is likely to be constrained by:

- Existing telecom regulatory conditions.
- Interconnecting existing disparate networks.
- Developing inexpensive easy-to-use television set top boxes for service selection and user interaction.
- Copyright problems.
- Supply of risk capital.

- Uncertainty about information service needs and markets.
- Standardization requirements.
- The formation of alliances between competitive suppliers.
- Change inhibited by lifestyle and expenditure patterns.

THE GRID OF LEARNING

The Superhighway idea burned brightly for a time but it became overshadowed by the success of the Internet's WORLD WIDE WEB (WWW) and by less generalized networks. In fact the WWW is now often called the Information Superhighway. The arrival of a new UK government in 1997 prompted several proposals from departments or agencies for data highways. Suggestions for New Libraries, People's Networks and 'Grids of Learning' were made. Schools, public libraries and a 'University for Industry' would be interconnected. The purpose of the system would be to bring about 'revolutionary changes' that would provide:

> [U]ndreamed of increases in the quantity and quality of detailed information and knowledge…an information superhighway which should not just benefit the affluent….by 2002 all schools, colleges, universities and libraries, and as many community centres as possible should be connected to the Grid.

Most of the costs, totalling about £500 million, would be incurred over a five-year period.

JANET and SuperJANET

The UK possesses an inter-university high-speed network with overseas connections called SuperJANET – originally established as the Joint Academic Network (JANET), an X25 packet-switched network. It interconnected several major packet-switching exchanges in the UK, which in turn connected to a number of universities and research establishments. It was soon upgraded to work at 2 Megabits per second (Mbps) over most of its links.

Established by the Computer Board in 1984, by 1990 over 130 institutions were connected to it and to the Internet using the TCP/IP protocol. JANET users are not charged for access, although they may be charged by some of its available services. The network was used by libraries mainly for calling up another library's Online

Public-Access Catalogue (about 50 OPACS were connected), for document requests via the British Library's ARTtel DOCUMENT DELIVERY service or for connecting to the International Packet Switched Service (IPSS) and accessing online databases. Library networking is widely used, encouraged by the UK Office for Library Networking at the University of Bath.

SuperJANET was first discussed in 1989, and in 1992 British Telecom was awarded a contract to provide and operate this new fibre-optic network working at up to 622 Mbps. Super-JANET first used the Asynchronous Transfer Mode (ATM) protocol – agreed between the CCITT and ANSI for fast switching over future wideband networks. ATM uses a packet-switching technology that can handle streams of data both at constant bit rates, such as audio and video data, and at variable bit rates. In mid-2001 SuperJANET 4 was introduced – a substantial advance – using the IP protocol. It consists of loops running at 2.5 Gbps interconnecting major cities with further connections out to Metropolitan-Area Networks. By mid-2002 the backbone will be uprated to run at 10 Gbps or 20 Gbps. Work is also in progress to develop the Grid of Learning system over the SuperJANET network. Meanwhile the rate of transmission over links to the USA has been increased to 930 Mbps.

Mobile communication systems and devices
Since 2000, there have been rapid developments in mobile communications. Major players – mainly telephone incumbent organisations – have had to pay very large sums of money for rights to use suitable parts of the frequency spectrum, a scarce resource under governmental control. In the UK, Vodafone, BT and others paid out over £22 billion. In Belgium three bidders paid the minimum possible amount of 150 million euros. A fourth available licence was not sold. Licensees believe that there will be a huge increase in the numbers of users, although some of the companies that bought expensive licences have since found themselves in financial difficulties. There has already been a very large take-up by consumers who very quickly see the value of what they are willing to pay for a particular service. Perhaps this last comment does not apply to parents who pay for their children's exchange of text messages – a major application.

GPRS (General Packet Radio Service) is a faster version that transfers data in packets, to be followed by UMTS (Universal Mobile Telecommunications Service) – a high-quality global service network for mobiles in which a take-everywhere terminal, usable in all environments, public and private, is used. It is claimed that UMTS will enable high-quality broadband information commerce and entertainment services at data rates of up to 2 Mbps.

WAP (Wireless Application Protocol) is a global open-standard protocol for use directly between hand-held devices without the need for a separate computer. It will enable portable computers to access the Internet.

An intercompany intermachine initiative called Bluetooth has been developed for special services – for instance between users' digital cameras. The service operates at low power but at high bit rates. It is claimed that it may become an integrated part of company IT systems.

The outlook

By August 2001, the hitherto steady growth of information and telecommunication technology and their applications was overshadowed by several problems. The economic downturn seemed to have started with the collapse of Internet companies following unrealistic optimism and investment. Deregulation in the USA encouraged competition that has increased beyond the capacity of markets to support new entries. Frequency spectrum auctions required by organizations for their third-generation mobile services have prompted borrowing on a large scale.

It has been estimated that accumulated debt in the telecommunications sector may now be at least $250 billion. At the end of July 2001, JDS, a very large supplier of optical and other communication components in the USA, lost over $50 billion in the year ending June and announced huge job cuts. This enormous loss followed losses reported by several other well-known companies such as Nortel (nearly $20 million in the second quarter of the year) and Vodafone (over $8 billion in a full year). Financial problems at Marconi (GEC renamed) and BT have been well publicized. Corning – a major supplier of fibre-optic cable and components – expected 2001 demand to be half that of the year 2000.

No doubt the area will continue to grow as before but the above-mentioned near-recession may last for some time. Larger organizations will survive but a number of smaller companies will not.

References

Gore, A. (1994) 'Innovation delayed is innovation denied', *Computer* 27: 45–7.

Nyquist, H. (1928) 'Certain topics in telegraph transmission theory', *Transactions of the American Institute of Electrical Engineers* 47: 617–44.

Odlyzco, A. (2000) 'Internet growth: Myth and reality, use and abuse', *IMP Magazine*: 1–9.

Shannon, C.E. (1948) 'A mathematical theory of communication', *Bell System Technical Journal* 27: 379–423, 623–56.

Valovic, T. (2000) *Digital Mythologies: The Hidden Complexities of the Internet*, Rutgers University Press.

Further reading

Cawkell, T. (1997) 'The information superhighway: A review of some determining factors', *Journal of Information Science* 23: 187–208.

Vetter, R. J., Spell, C. and Ward, C. (1995) 'Mosaic and the World-Wide Web', *Computer* 27: 49–57.

SEE ALSO: communication; European Union information policies; informatics; information policy; information society; information systems

TONY CAWKELL

INFORMATION AND REFERRAL SERVICE

Describes the active mode of information service, of the type traditionally provided by SPECIAL LIBRARIES. The attention of users is drawn to information held by the library or information agency in anticipation of demands they might make. Preparation and circulation of news-sheets, literature surveys, reading lists, abstracts, etc. are used for this purpose, and in cases where the immediate resources of the service are insufficient users will be referred to specialist organizations for further help.

INFORMATION ARCHITECTURE

Designing, organizing, labelling and creating site maps, CONTENT inventories and NAVIGATION systems for websites and INTRANETS to help people find and manage information more successfully. Two main approaches can be distin-

guished: top-down, which focuses initially on the information content, and bottom-up, which takes user needs as the starting point. The term is older than the WORLD WIDE WEB, having been coined in 1976 by Richard Saul Wurman as the title of a conference in Philadelphia. He subsequently began to call himself an Information Architect.

Further reading

Rosenfeld, L. and Morville, P. (1998) *Information Architecture for the World Wide Web: Designing Large Scale Websites*, O'Reilly.

INFORMATION AUDIT

(1) In its most precise sense an information audit is that process by which a physical verification and examination of the total information assets within an organization takes place, to ensure that information resources which have been acquired by an organization can be accounted for and located. (2) It is now common practice to define the information audit much more widely, to include the initial examination of resources as described above, resulting in an inventory of information resources, then building on that to explore the way in which information flows, and KNOWLEDGE is shared throughout an organization: the mechanisms and channels used, the information needs of the organization's members and the staffing requirement in terms of knowledge and skills to ensure that the organization's total intellectual capital is managed and exploited to maximum efficiency.

Aim and purpose

The information audit in its broadest sense is seen as a valuable management tool and part of continuous management review to assist in the process of achieving maximum effectiveness of information provision and use. Although often instigated and conducted by library and information service (LIS) staff, it is not limited to the consideration of LIS resources only. Its intention is to establish the total information resource and knowledge base to which an organization and all its constituent parts have access, of which they can make use and from which they can benefit. The information audit also offers a framework from which to develop a knowledge audit (Webb

1998). It aims to consider not only what information is available, but also the means by which information and knowledge are gathered and disseminated throughout the organization, the systems and procedures required for this and the way in which such activities are managed and co-ordinated. The information audit can form the base from which an organizational information policy (see ORGANIZATIONAL INFORMATION POLICIES) can be developed (Orna 1999). It also provides the platform for long-term LIS strategic planning and service development.

Preparation and planning

What will be needed in advance of the audit itself will be a clear profile of the organization, its current and planned activities and objectives, towards which any future information and knowledge management policy and operation can be directed. Each organization will be different in terms of sector, activities, objectives, structure and management style, therefore the profile will assist in the choice of audit methods and techniques to be used; the design and content of questionnaires and checklists, and the desired mix of the user sample. Those conducting the audit must identify precisely what it is necessary to investigate, drawing up appropriate checklists of items to be audited – for example, printed materials held such as books, journals, reports and subject files; electronic sources such as both internal and external databases and networks; CD-ROMs; audiovisual material; and other non-print material. Checklists should also cover related equipment and systems in use, their quantities and location. Questionnaires or interview schedules will have to be prepared at this stage as the basis for subsequent user and usage surveys, and consideration given to appropriate methods of communication to be used. Decisions will also be required on the amount and type of operational statistics required in support of the final analysis and recommendations.

The process

Following the initial planning, the first step in the information audit is to carry out a thorough investigation of the information sources and related means of access and retrieval that exist throughout the organization. If this involves arranging visits to other departments and offices, and discussion with individuals, then it is appro-

priate to combine this first step with the next part of the process, the information needs analysis (Webb 1996). This will consider the information each person needs in order to carry out their work effectively, what they currently use and where and how it is obtained, e.g. externally or internally, through the LIS or from other departments or sources. It could also provide details of information and knowledge which that individual might contribute to the total organizational resource. In addition there should be discussion of perceived future needs in terms of both information and service provision, i.e. not only what information is likely to be required but also, for example, whether current awareness services would be helpful and what means of information delivery would be most convenient to the user, e.g. print or electronic, general or specific (e.g. via the LIS website or individually delivered).

Communication

Gathering this information requires some form of user survey, usually either by face-to-face interview or by the circulation of a questionnaire. Both methods should take as little of the user's time as possible. This is likely to generate a greater response, as is adequate preparation and understanding by all those involved. The LIS website offers a useful means of publicizing the audit and confirming the schedule. It would also provide a channel for questionnaire delivery and post-audit feedback. If the interview method is chosen, an outline of the structure with a checklist of questions should be drawn up by the person who will be conducting it, and appointments made with a cross-section of staff at all levels and representative of all functions of the organization. In order to ensure maximum co-operation from individuals and departments, appropriate communication of its objectives will need to be made beforehand. The purpose and style of the investigation should be put forward in positive terms, emphasizing the ultimate benefits and the value of the user's participation, allowing adequate time for individuals to prepare their response. When the audit has been completed there should be feedback to those who have participated as well as wider dissemination of the results to inform senior management, whose commitment will be essential to future developments.

Use and benefits

Information audits also involve reviews of systems and procedures, analysis of operations, costing and budgetary reviews, and LIS staff training and development needs assessment. Where an organization is pursuing a quality management policy, the quality manuals and related procedures can act as a valuable source of reference, often suggesting new approaches and solutions to what might have been viewed as longstanding problems.

As a management technique the information audit has a lot to offer, particularly if it is used on a regular basis, rather than as a one-off activity. It can act as a monitoring mechanism, providing regular feedback on the quality of both the information itself and its provision; it will assist in short- and long-term financial and management planning; it can help shape overall organizational policy. To achieve this will involve setting up follow-up procedures and activities to ensure: continued two-way communication with users; wider information sharing; ongoing staff development in terms of renewing skills and keeping up to date in subject knowledge and sources, as well as in professional practice; and continuous awareness of and involvement in the activities of the organization as a whole.

References

Orna, E. (1999) *Practical Information Policies: How to Manage Information Flow in Organizations*, Aldershot: Gower.
Webb, S.P. (1998) *Knowledge Management: Linchpin of Change*, London: ASLIB.
—— (1996) *Creating an Information Service*, 3rd edn, London: ASLIB.

Further reading

Thornton, S. (2000) 'Information audits', Chapter 5 in A. Scammell (ed.) *Handbook of Information Management*, London: ASLIB.

SYLVIA P. WEBB

INFORMATION BROKER

A generic term used to describe individuals or organizations selling a range of information services, of which information broking is one. Information broking is the sale of expertise in determining the availability of information from one or more sources, and delivering it in response to a specific request. The information retrieved is certifiable in an already published medium, and is not derived by the information broker through primary research. Information broking is not the collecting of information for general dissemination, nor does it involve any process that alters the information itself. It is an intermediary function that matches information to a request from a third party, for a fee. An example of information broking is the retrieval of documents identified from a literature search of ONLINE, CD-ROM or printed sources held in a private or public collection.

Problems of definition

The diverse and fragmented set of individuals and organizations that act as information brokers are constantly evolving and redefining the nature of their services. Consequently, information broking may be a greater or lesser activity than the provision of other information services and products, which can include information consultancy, the outsourcing of information and library services, market research, publications, project work and seminars. In the UK, this situation has resulted in the generic application of the term information broker to many varied organizations and professionals that offer information services for a fee, and which may or may not describe themselves as information brokers. Other titles used include information consultant, fee-based information service, business research centre, one-stop information shop and infomediary. The individuals and organizations acting as information brokers are considered to fall into two categories. First, the independent individuals or firms that set up in business specifically as information brokers are characterized by some commentators as being the 'pure' information brokers (Wolff-Terroine 1992), and in the USA make up the group of practitioners for whom the term 'information broker' is reserved (Johnson 1994). Second, the term 'fee-based information service' (see FEE-BASED SERVICES) has a popular application to information brokerages operating out of larger privately or publicly owned organizations (Crawford 1988). These include information organizations, professional associations, government organizations, national libraries, academic libraries, public libraries, chambers of commerce, etc. Wolff-Terroine (1992) reports that in Europe use of the term information broker is sometimes restricted to only those who source information from online databases.

Professional associations

The equivocal parameters of the profession are evident in the diversity of organizations and interests represented by the few professional associations. The European Information Researchers Network (EIRENE), which emerged in 1989, is considered to be the principal professional association for UK information brokers, who in 1994 accounted for twenty-six of its fifty-six members. EIRENE originally set out as a networking forum for information professionals, some of whom are not information brokers and do not engage in information-broking functions. In the USA the Association of Independent Information Professionals (AIIP) was formed in 1987, and in France the Association des Intermédiaires en Information (AF2I) was established in 1991.

References

Crawford, M.J. (1988) *Information Broking: A New Career in Information Work*, Library Association.
Johnson, A.J.H. (1994) *Information Brokers: Case Studies of Successful Ventures*, Haworth Press.
Wolff-Terroine, M. (1992) 'The brokers in Europe: Are the chances of success identical for all of them?', in D.I. Raitt (ed.) *Online Information 92: Sixteenth International Online Information Meeting Proceedings, London 8–10 December 1992*, Learned Information, pp. 267–72.

Further reading

DIRECTORIES AND PUBLISHED LISTS OF INFORMATION BROKERS

Burwell World Directory of Information Brokers 1995/6 (1995) 12th edn, TFPL.
Directory of European Information Brokers and Consultants 1994 (1994) 7th edn, Effective Technology Marketing and Information Marketmakers [the most extensive source, with 146 entries based in the UK].
EIRENE Membership Directory 1994 (1994) Manchester Business School.
European Commission Host Organization (ECHO) *I'M Guide* (Telnet echo.lu).

PRACTICAL MANUALS

EUSIDIC, EIIA and EIRENE (1993) *Code of Practice for Information Brokers*, EUSIDIC.
Everett, J.H. and Crowe, E.P. (1994) *Information for Sale*, Windcrest/McGraw-Hill.
Rugge, S. and Glossbrenner, A. (1997) *The Information Broker's Handbook*, 3rd edn, McGraw-Hill.

OTHER REFERENCES

Beesley, K. (1994) 'Information entrepreneurs: UK national review', *Information Services and Use* 14: 297–306.
Hyde, M. (1993) 'Information brokerage comes of age: Profit making and professionalism (national review – United Kingdom)', *Infomediary* 6: 77–82.
Mason, F.M. and Dobson, C. (1998) *Information Brokering*, Neal-Schuman.

SEE ALSO: information policy; information professions

MATTHEW HALL

INFORMATION ECOLOGY

The study of the inter-relationships between people, enterprises, technologies and the information environment. The interaction between these elements in a local environment is treated as an ecosystem, with human beings at the centre, encompassing information strategy, INFORMATION-SEEKING BEHAVIOUR, INFORMATION MANAGEMENT and INFORMATION ARCHITECTURE. Typical ecosystems might be: a library, with its users, resources, librarians and network links; a hospital ward, with its patients, nurses, doctors, monitoring devices and record systems; or a retail company, with sales assistants, advisers, customers, customer and supplier databases, catalogues, product specifications and user manuals.

Further reading

Davenport, T.H. and Prusak, L. (1997) *Information Ecology*, Oxford University Press.

INFORMATION ENGINEERING

The engineering approach applied to INFORMATION SYSTEMS. At its broadest, the term refers to engineering disciplines covering a spectrum from software engineering and systems engineering to electronic engineering. It also has the narrower, but well-known, meaning of a specific method for the development of organizational information systems primarily associated with James Martin. This method begins with enterprise modelling and carries through to the generation of program codes for the system.

SEE ALSO: computer science

INFORMATION ETHICS

Broadly characterized, information ethics is the study of ethical considerations that arise in the storage, processing, retrieval and use of information, INFORMATION SYSTEMS and INFORMATION AND COMMUNICATION TECHNOLOGY. 'Information ethics' as a field of study arose with the convergence of many ethical concerns of traditional disciplines such as management and information systems, and library and information science, particularly with the emergence and rapid growth of online information systems and services, and of the INTERNET. For example, privacy and confidentiality have long been a concern of both BUSINESS INFORMATION SERVICES and library CIRCULATION SYSTEMS, and both fields have common interests in the security of such systems in public-access, online, networked environments. So too libraries and newspapers which have both been concerned with intellectual freedom and the balance of COPYRIGHT with fair-use doctrines, and these concerns have heightened with the rapid deployment of information sources and services on the Internet.

Two perspectives on information ethics

Information ethics can be approached from two perspectives: (1) its role as information *ethics* as an ongoing critique in contrast to established ethical customs, norms and practices with respect to information, information systems and information technologies, which it critiques and strives to improve; and (2) its subject domain relative to other related domains of applied ethics, e.g. computer ethics, cyberethics.

The first approach emphasises the word 'ethics' in information *ethics*. In this view, articulated by Rafael Capurro, the Director of the International Center for Information Ethics (ICIE) (http://icie.zkm.de/research), ethics is seen as both descriptive theory and an emancipatory theory. As a descriptive theory it analyses the power structures of different societies and traditions. As an emancipatory theory, ethics is contrasted with established moral and legal customs, norms and practices, which it continuously, critically evaluates. In the latter view, ethics is seen as a vigilant force, trying to make sure that the institutionalized ethical norms of a society, in established practices, customs and/or laws, are constantly checked for continuing to adhere to ethical values or promote genuinely ethical behaviour at both the individual and collective level.

In the second approach, information ethics has evolved into at least two frameworks, either (1) as a metadiscipline seen to encompass a variety of related applied disciplines or (2) as another distinct discipline in relation to the other related disciplines. The view (1) that information ethics is a metadiscipline is taken by the Center for Information Ethics. Information ethics is seen as an applied ethics that deals with ethical questions 'particularly' in MASS MEDIA (media ethics), in COMPUTER SCIENCE (computer ethics), in the biological sciences (bioinformation ethics), in the library and information science field (library ethics), in the business field (business information ethics) and regarding the INTERNET (cyberethics). Such a view may be overreaching in its claims by arbitrarily appropriating disciplines by definition. Particularly problematic is the inclusion of one of the sciences (bioinformation ethics) but none of the others. While there has been dramatic growth of genetic information in the recent past, and this is fraught with many ethical concerns, ethical issues in the use of information and information technologies exist in the other sciences. Whether bioinformation ethics or science research ethics is or is not in the purview of information ethics, Capurro nonetheless sees information ethics as an inclusive domain, embracing many sub-domains, a kind of metaethics that embraces or draws upon many fields.

A second view (2) sees information ethics as another kind of applied ethical domain, sharing in and related to other fields, such as computer ethics and cyberethics. Martha Montague Smith, in her article on 'Information ethics' in *The Annual Review of Information Science and Technology* (*ARIST*), embraces this view, arguing that:

> Issues in computer ethics overlap those of information ethics with emphasis on high standards for hardware and software design; the management of secure systems, including maintaining data accuracy and integrity; the protection of privacy from the point of view of the systems administrator; and the ethics of competition.
>
> (Smith 1997: 339–40)

Others see overlaps between cyberethics and information ethics or see computer ethics evolving into cyberethics (Sullivan 1996).

Information ethics and computer ethics

A clear approach to information ethics unfortunately cannot be posed by a simple contrast with computer ethics, with computer ethics supposedly concentrating on the technical means of communication and networking, while information ethics focuses on the content of such communication. While there are some examples that support this distinction (e.g. inadequate software testing as an issue in computer ethics but not in information ethics, and intellectual freedom as an issue in information ethics and not in computer ethics), there are many areas that are not so clear (e.g. copyright infringement by making unauthorized perfect digital copies; security and the protection of privacy) and the distinction is not rigorously maintained by different writers. Deborah G. Johnson takes the view that computer ethics may eventually disappear. In her view, as information technology becomes more and more commonplace and pervasive in everyday life, its distinctive nature will fade and the issue of the ethical problem involved in an information technology context would take priority, e.g. in discussions of privacy, the heart of the discussion would lie on the principles of privacy, and information technologies would be but one aspect of the problem among others for a particular context (Johnson 2001). In a related view, some prognosticate a future where both terms disappear. For example, Krystyna Gorniak-Kocikowska argues that local ethics (ethics associated with the local environment, whether regional or national or philosophical) will be superseded by a global ethic evolving from today's computer ethics (Gorniak-Kocikowska 1996). In a contrasting view, Luciano Floridi takes the approach that information ethics is a macroethics that could serve as the philosophical foundation for computer ethics. In his approach, this macroethics would not be useful to solve specific computer ethics issues but would provide the grounds for moral principles that would then be able to create problem-solving procedures in computer ethics (Floridi 1999). Finally, there are other proponents such as Walter Maner who maintain that computer technologies in fact have created a set of unique ethical problems that would not have come about without the emergence of computers. To illustrate his case, he uses the example of a hospital system in Washington, DC, which broke down on 19 September 1989 because its calendar calculations caused an overflow of a counter in memory, a technical problem of computer architecture that would not have occurred in a manual system. He maintains that computer ethics would retain its character over time, when dealing with those issues essentially related to computer technology (Maner 1996). In sum, the status of information ethics *vis-à-vis* computer ethics is muddled.

Principles of information ethics

While the distinction between computer ethics and information ethics may not be clear, several have tried to articulate principles of information ethics. For example, Richard W. Severson in *Principles of Information Ethics* sees respect for privacy, respect for intellectual property, fair representation and non-malfeasance as constituting a core set of principles of information ethics (Severson 1997). For related and/or additional principles, see the ICIE site and Thomas J. Froehlich's *Survey and Analysis of Legal and Ethical Issues for Library and Information Services*. The latter work establishes five general ethical principles, some potentially competing and conflicting, which are then applied in the context of libraries and information centres. For example, one principle asserts that we must respect the autonomy and rights of individuals. Another one avows the need to seek social harmony. The action of buying a particular resource for a patron by a collection developer in a library, such as a book on cultivating marijuana, would manifest the former principle, but, at the same time, it may conflict with the second principle, because its appearance in the library may alienate other patrons and may not promote long-range social goals (Froehlich 1997).

Pervasiveness of information ethics

In both approaches, information ethics is conceived to be broad in scope. The *Journal of Information Ethics*, inaugurated in 1992 and edited by Robert Hauptman, asserts that it deals with 'ethics in all areas of information or knowledge production and dissemination' including library and information science, education for information professionals, technology, graphic display, database management, privacy, censorship, government information and peer review, among others. Many important organizations, such as the United Nations Educational, Scientific and Cultural Organization (UNESCO) take the position that information ethics is a part of global justice, founded in the Universal Declaration of Human Rights, particularly Article 19, which asserts that 'Everyone has right to freedom of opinion and expression; the right includes freedom to hold opinions without interference and to seek, receive and impart information and ideas through any media and regardless of frontiers'. Among many programmes, The UNESCO Observatory of the Information Society (www.unesco.orgwebworld/observatory/index.shtml) frequently addresses issues in information ethics, and UNESCO periodically holds seminars on information ethics and related issues in the information society. Among its aims, it seeks to promote 'principles of equality, justice and mutual respect in the emerging Information Society'. UNESCO tracks issues of global justice, and particularly those with a focus on freedom of access, INTELLECTUAL PROPERTY rights, freedom of expression, transborder privacy and cybercrime.

Information ethics has also emerged in the curriculum. Several schools of library and information science have courses or lecture series in information ethics. One of the longest standing, the School of Information Sciences at the University of Pittsburgh, inaugurated in 1989 a lecture series on Information Ethics, under the direction of Rev. Stephen Alamagno and Dean Toni Carbo.

In sum, information ethics is a rapidly growing and multifaceted phenomenon, related to but distinct from computer ethics and a variety of other related fields. It is extensively addressed in many venues, has a journal and websites devoted to it, is the subject of many conferences and has taken a place in the curriculum of many schools.

References

Floridi, L. (1999) 'Information ethics: On the philosophical foundation of computer ethics', *Ethics and Information Technology* 1: 37–56.

Froehlich, T. (1997) *Survey and Analysis of Legal and Ethical Issues for Library and Information Services*, G.K. Saur.

Gorniak-Kocikowska, K. (1996) 'The computer revolution and the problem of global ethics', in T. Bynum and S. Rogerson (eds) *Global Information Ethics*, Opragen, pp. 177–90.

International Center for Information Ethics (ICIE) (http://icie.zkm.de/research) [contains extensive bibliography].

Johnson, D. (2001) 'Computer ethics in the 21st century', Keynote Address delivered at the 4th ETHICOMP International Conference on the Social and Ethical Impacts of Information and Communication Technologies, Luiss Guido Carli University, Rome, Italy, 6–8 October.

Maner, W. (1996) 'Unique ethical problems in information technology', *Science and Engineering Ethics* 2(99): 137–54.

Severson, R.W. (1997) *Principles of Information Ethics*, M.E. Sharpe.

Smith, M. (1997) 'Information ethics', in M. Williams (ed.) *The Annual Review of Information Science and Technology* 32: 339–66.

Sullivan, P.F. (1996) 'Ethics in the computer age', in J. Kizza (ed.) *Social and Ethical Effects of the Computer Revolution*, McFarland & Company, pp. 288–95.

UNESCO (2002) 'Legal and ethical issues. Infoethics' (www.unesco.org/webworld/public_domain/legal.html).

UNESCO Observatory of the Information Society (2002) (www.unesco.org/webworld/observatory/index.shtml).

Further reading

Hauptman, R. (1992–) *The Journal of Information Ethics*.

Information Ethics at the School of Information Sciences at the University of Pittsburgh (www2.sis.pitt.edu/ethics/).

United Nations World Summit on the Information Society (www.itu.int/wsis/), scheduled for Geneva, 2003.

SEE ALSO: data protection; freedom of information; information law; information society; medical informatics

THOMAS J. FROEHLICH

INFORMATION LAW

Information law refers to the body of statutes, regulations and court decisions through which governmental entities control public access to, and use of, collections of otherwise unprotectable INFORMATION. The term 'information law' does not encompass the protection of sensitive personal information, which is governed by human rights and PRIVACY laws, nor the protection of information expressed in the form of original prose, music, images or other types of authorship, which is covered by COPYRIGHT law. Rather, the subset of 'information' regulated by information law is factual, non-proprietary matter that belongs to no single person, yet has economic value by virtue of being compiled and distributed in a timely, convenient manner. Information law seeks to provide a monetary incentive for commercial enterprises to compile and distribute such information, and in so doing to ensure the greatest possible public access. This entry will describe the various legal theories under which US law protects information, and will then discuss the general features of the specialized DATA PROTECTION legislation being adopted in other countries under the 1996 EU database directive.

Contract law

The most direct way to protect factual information is simply for the provider to require users to agree not to copy it. Most data providers impose mandatory terms and conditions on access, often in the form of a 'shrink-wrap' or 'click-wrap' licence (see LICENCES) restricting the uses that the user may make of the information. These agreements are generally binding and enforceable, provided that they are truly voluntary.

In one leading case, *ProCD v Zeidenberg* (1996), a US appeals court found that a clearly visible shrink-wrap licence printed on a box containing a CD-ROM telephone directory was enforceable, because the user's conduct in opening the package could be interpreted as indicating agreement with the terms and conditions. Since *Zeidenberg*, several other courts have extended the analysis to the online environment, finding valid contracts when the user makes a clear, affirmative manifestation of assent (see *Caspi v The Microsoft Network* (1999) ('click-wrap' agreement held enforceable) and *Register.com v Verio, Inc.* (2000) (upholding 'query-wrap' agreement that bound any user submitting query to plaintiff's site)).

In *Pollstar v Gigmania Ltd.* (2000), one California court even allowed a contract claim based on a 'browse-wrap' agreement, where the user did nothing more than visit the plaintiff's website. Under similar circumstances, however, a New York court held in *Specht v Netscape Communications Corp.* (2001) that Netscape's 'browse-wrap' agreement, represented by a single small box of text inviting the user to review and agree to the terms before downloading or using the software, did not give rise to an enforceable contract. Users were able to download the software without viewing the licence terms, noted the court, and might not even be aware that a licence agreement existed, since the 'invitation'

box was inconspicuous. Further, the court found that downloading itself is:

> [H]ardly an unambiguous manifestation of assent. The primary purpose of downloading is to obtain a product, not to assent to an agreement. In contrast, clicking on an icon stating 'I assent' has no meaning or purpose other than to indicate such assent.

Thus, an information provider may generally rely on written terms of use as a way of protecting its data, but only if the terms are clearly visible to the user before access is permitted, and if the user affirmatively agrees to be bound.

Trespass to chattels

The ancient common law doctrine of trespass to chattels can also protect information in the online environment. Defined as unauthorized interference with one's 'possessory interest' in tangible property, trespass has provided a basis for prohibiting the use of robot Web-searching technology to retrieve publicly available information from the Web, and various other perceived commercial abuses of the computer equipment used by data providers. Under this theory, the law does not directly protect the information itself, but only the computer on which it resides.

In *eBay Inc. v Bidder's Edge, Inc.* (2000), the trespass theory was invoked to prohibit so-called 'DATA MINING', whereby the defendant's automated search program repeatedly visited the eBay site, and various other auction sites, to permit potential bidders to locate items without having to visit each site. The court essentially held that any use of data gathered in this manner was improper, because to gain access the user had to occupy BANDWIDTH on the provider's computer network. The defendant's continual searching, entailing more than 100,000 visits per day to the eBay site, 'diminished the quality or value of eBay's computer system' even though there was no physical damage to the network. Where a user makes less invasive visits to gather publicly accessible data from a provider's computer, however, the trespass theory is not likely to provide a basis for protecting the information (see *Ticketmaster Corp. v Tickets.com, Inc.* (2000)).

Under the trespass theory, it is ironic that intangible facts, circulating in the ethereal realm of CYBERSPACE, may find their most effective protection in an ancient doctrine designed to prevent the unauthorized use of physical personal property. Futurist John Perry Barlow remarked in 1993 that intellectual property law was doomed because it governed tangible objects rather than information *per se*, 'the bottles not the wine', to use his analogy; but as the *eBay* decision demonstrates, the law can still be very useful for those who own the bottles.

'Hot news' misappropriation

Arising from the 1918 US Supreme Court decision in *International News Service v Associated Press*, the common law doctrine of misappropriation originally prohibited a competitor from selling its own rewrites of Associated Press news reports in a manner that deprived AP of its rightful window of exclusivity. The doctrine can still be used to protect so-called 'hot news' where the value of the information is ephemeral. Under the 1997 appeals court decision in *Nat'l Basketball Assn. v Motorola, Inc.* (1997), involving NBA basketball scores delivered to subscribers through a real-time pager network, a misappropriation claim for unauthorized sale of information requires the provider to establish five elements: (1) the information was gathered at some cost to the provider, (2) the information is time sensitive, (3) the rival provider is free-riding (i.e. not engaged in its own capital-intensive activity), (4) the parties are direct competitors, and (5) the rival's activity would 'substantially threaten' the provider's incentive to continue collecting the information. In the online context, such a misappropriation claim was recently allowed to proceed in *Pollstar v Gigmania, supra*, where plaintiff alleged that defendant's rival website copied time-sensitive rock concert information from plaintiff's site.

Computer Fraud and Abuse Act

Enacted in 1984 chiefly to protect computerized financial and medical information, the Computer Fraud and Abuse Act ('CFAA') can also address other forms of alleged information theft. The CFAA provides that it is a crime to 'intentionally access a computer without authorization or exceed authorized access, and thereby obtain ... information from any protected computer if the conduct involved an interstate or foreign communication'. It is also a violation to 'intentionally access a protected computer without authoriza-

tion and as a result of such conduct cause damage'. The statute then defines 'protected computer' in a way that arguably encompasses every device with an Internet connection, and defines 'damage' as 'any impairment to the integrity or availability of data...that causes loss aggregating at least $5000 in value during any one-year period'.

In the first of several cases to raise the CFAA in the Web context, the courts found that online services were damaged under the Act when their facilities or customer lists were used by third parties to propagate SPAM e-mail transmissions (see *Hotmail Corp. v Van$ Money Pie Inc.* (1998) and *AOL, Inc. v LCGM, Inc.* (1998)). In *Register.com v Verio Inc., supra*, however, a federal court in New York applied the statute more broadly, enjoining an Internet services company from using robots to gather WHOIS information about Register.com's customers even though, as an ICANN-accredited domain name registrar, Register.com is obligated to provide this information to the public on request.

EU directive and implementing statutes

Unlike the patchwork of US federal and state laws described above, the laws of many other countries are specifically drafted to protect information. In 1996, the European Parliament issued a directive to harmonize DATABASE protection in its member states, and many nations have since adopted legislation to implement the terms of the directive. As with the theories discussed above, the assumption underlying the directive is that data providers make a significant financial investment in aggregating and distributing factual information, and this investment should be protected.

The directive defines 'database' very broadly, to include collections of works, data or other materials that are systematically or methodically arranged and can be individually accessed. Significantly, this definition encompasses both hardcopy and electronic databases, so even conventional printed collections of data such as telephone directories fall within the scope of the law.

For databases exhibiting no copyrightable creativity, such as collections of raw numerical data, the directive creates a new form of protection, premised on protecting the data provider's 'quantitatively substantial investment in either the obtaining, verification or presentation of the contents'. Such protection lasts for fifteen years after completion or publication of the database, but can be renewed indefinitely in fifteen-year increments when 'substantial new investment' is made in updating and verifying the database.

Extraction and reuse prohibitions

The heart of the directive is the command that Member States shall provide for a right to prevent acts of extraction and/or re-utilisation of 'the whole or of a substantial part...of the contents of that database'. Extraction means the 'permanent or temporary transfer of all or a substantial part of the contents of a database to another medium by any means or in any form'. Reutilization means 'any form of making available to the public all or a substantial part of the contents of a database by the distribution of copies, by renting, by on-line or other forms of transmission'. Public lending is not considered a form of extraction or reutilization.

Under these definitions, the extraction and reutilization rights are only violated with respect to 'all or a substantial part of a database'. But it is important to note that repeated and systematic extraction or reutilization of even insubstantial portions of a database may violate the directive if they conflict with the normal exploitation of the database or unreasonably prejudice the legitimate interests of the provider. Many small-scale uses are expressly deemed non-infringing, such as photocopying of non-electronic databases for private purposes, teaching or non-commercial research, but member states have the option of limiting these exemptions to particular types of educational or research institutions.

References

AOL, Inc. v LCGM, Inc., 46 F. Supp. 2d 444 (E.D. Va. 1998).
Caspi v The Microsoft Network LLC, 323 N.J. Super. 118 (N.J. App. Div. 1999).
Directive 96/9/EC of the European Parliament and of the Council and of 11 March 1996 on the Legal Protection of Databases.
eBay Inc. v Bidder's Edge, Inc., No. C-99–21200 RMW (N.D. Cal. May 24, 2000).
Hotmail Corp. v Van$ Money Pie Inc., 47 U.S.P.Q.2d 1020 (N.D. Cal. 1998).
International News Service v Associated Press, 248 U.S. 215 (1918).
Nat'l Basketball Assn. v Motorola, Inc., 105 F.3d 841 (2d Cir. 1997).
Pollstar v Gigmania Ltd., No. CIV-F-005671 REC SMS (E.D. Cal. Oct. 17, 2000).
ProCD v Zeidenberg, 86 F.3d 1447 (7th Cir. 1996).
Register.com v Verio, Inc., 126 F. Supp. 2d 238 (S.D.N.Y. Dec. 2000).
Specht v Netscape Communications Corp., No. 00 Civ. 4871 (S.D.N.Y. July 3, 2001).
Ticketmaster Corp. v Tickets.com, Inc., 2000 U.S.Dist. LEXIS 12987 (Aug. 11, 2000).

Further reading

Beutler, S. (1996) 'The protection of multimedia products through the European Community's directive on the legal protection of databases', *Entertainment Law Review* 7: 317–28.
Sullivan, A.C. (2001) 'When the creative is the enemy of the true: Database protection in the U.S. and abroad', *AIPLA Quarterly Journal* 29: 317–73.

SEE ALSO: European Union information policies; information ethics; information policy

ROBERT W. CLARIDA

INFORMATION LITERACY

Ways of seeing information literacy

Sometimes interpreted as one of a number of literacies, information literacy (IL) is also described as the overarching literacy essential for twenty-first-century living. Today, IL is inextricably associated with information practices and critical thinking in the INFORMATION AND COMMUNICATION TECHNOLOGY (ICT) environment. IL is generally seen as pivotal to the pursuit of lifelong learning, and central to achieving both personal empowerment and economic development.

IL is commonly described as the ability to access, evaluate and use information. This description is based on the view that IL is an amalgam of skills, attitudes and knowledge, a view that is compatible with the prevailing interpretation of learning in twentieth-century education systems. IL is also described as a way of learning, or as a conglomerate of ways of experiencing information use. These descriptions are aligned to seeing learning as a process, or as coming to see the world in different or more sophisticated ways. Interestingly, all our descriptions of IL have emerged from the educational sector. Each of them, however, may be readily modified for use in corporate and community contexts.

IL is closely related to the ideas of INFORMATION SKILLS and INFORMATION TECHNOLOGY literacy. Sometimes, information skills are considered to be one aspect of IL. They may also be seen as the tools that assist the development of IL, in the same way that study skills may assist the process of learning. The concepts of IL and IT literacy are usually distinguished to demonstrate the difference between the intellectual capabilities involved in using information, and the capabilities required for using technologies that deliver or contain 'information'. This distinction is also made to convey the idea that provision of ICTs and associated training in the use of hardware and software – the focus of many government, corporate and educational programmes – is only a starting point in achieving desired reforms.

A brief history of information literacy

The term information literacy was first used by Paul Zurkowski in the 1970s to bring attention to the needs of people working in the newly emerging technological environment. Since then, the concept has been taken up mainly by information specialists, and promulgated worldwide through the work of the American Library Association and the National Forum for Information Literacy. By the end of the twentieth century, IL could be said to be a truly global phenomenon, with interest evident across all continents and sectors.

Information literacy programmes

After the publication of the ALA Presidential Final Report, IL was mainly a focus for librarians in the education sector. Towards the end of the twentieth century, social, governmental and corporate attention turned more strongly towards lifelong learning and associated concepts such as learning communities, learning citizens, learning organizations and the learning society. As a result, information specialists in community and workplace settings began to take a lead in establishing an IL focus in a wider range of contexts. In all sectors, interest in IL found expression in designing and implementing learning experiences and information services that help people interact with and benefit from the world of information.

Typically, in each sector where IL has emerged as a focus, the idea has been interpreted and assigned meanings relevant to the institutional contexts and their information user groups. IL programme design has also been typically context specific, with IL concerns being adapted for learning programmes and service design. Advocacy for information literacy has also clearly involved promoting cultural change, leading to the emergence of a strong role for the information specialist as a change agent.

The roles of advocate and change agent have emerged most strongly in policy development, working with organizational gatekeepers, particularly senior management, and fostering collaboration with different parts of the organization. Successful advocacy for IL in organizations has led to the appointment of staff dedicated to IL programmes, the development of organization-wide staff development programmes and significant collaboration, both inter- and intraorganizational, and sometime crossing international boundaries.

Information literacy research

The seeds of IL research were sown by the USER EDUCATION and BIBLIOGRAPHIC INSTRUCTION movements of the 1980s. Probably the most influential investigation from this period on future IL researchers was Carol Kuhlthau's exploration of students' experiences of information use. Her adoption of naturalistic research approaches led eventually to the construction of a model describing the process of learning from information, and to the description of IL as a 'way of learning'. In the early 1990s the term information literacy became prominent and a few researchers saw their work as contributing to this area. The most notable study from the 1990s is Christina Doyle's investigation of definitions of information literacy. Her Delphi study, commissioned by the National Forum for Information Literacy, gained consensus from a range of people and led to a definition and descriptions that are widely used. IL research pursued in the mid- to late 1990s was characterized by the exploration of different paradigms and the establishment of multiple research agendas. The relational model of information literacy, developed by Christine Bruce and Louise Limberg, was the most significant research outcome from this period. The relational model is grounded in a view of IL as being about the varying ways in which people interact with information.

By the end of the twentieth century, research in practice (conducted by or with practitioners), applied research (addressing problems pertinent to practice) and pure research (investigating the nature of IL) had all emerged in the IL research agenda. Researchers adopted a range of focal interests including: information users, their skills and attributes; their experiences and perceptions; and their knowledge structures. Other foci were IL programmes and curriculum issues, for example the impact of IL on learning outcomes. Many of these studies were heavily influenced by related fields including information seeking and use research, educational, information science and communications research.

Further reading

Breivik, P. (1998) *Student Learning in the Information Age*, Oryx Press.

Bruce, C.S. (1997) *Seven Faces of Information Literacy*, AUSLIB Press.

Bruce, C.S and Candy, P. (eds) (2000) *Information Literacy around the World: Advances in Programs and Research*, Centre for Information Studies, Charles Sturt University.

Loertscher, D. and Woolls, B. (1999) *Information Literacy Research: A Guide for Researchers and Practitioners*, Hi Willow Research and Pub.

Oman, J.N. (2001) 'Information literacy in the workplace', *Information Outlook* (June): 33–43.

Spitzer, K., Eisenberg, M. and Lowe, C. (1998) *Information Literacy: Essential Skills for the Information Age*, ERIC Clearinghouse on Information and Technology, Syracuse University.

SEE ALSO: information-seeking behaviour; information society

CHRISTINE S. BRUCE

INFORMATION MANAGEMENT

The application of management principles to the acquisition, organization, control, dissemination and use of information relevant to the effective operation of organizations of all kinds. 'Information' here refers to all types of information of value, whether having their origin inside or outside the organization, including: data resources, such as production data; records and files related, for example, to the personnel function; market research data; and competitive intelligence from a wide range of sources. Information management deals with the value, quality, ownership, use and security of information in the context of organizational performance.

Introduction

The term 'information management' is used ambiguously in the literatures of several fields: in COMPUTER SCIENCE and its applications it is used as a synonym for information technology management (Synott and Gruber 1981) or as identical to 'data management', where the emphasis is on the structures underlying quantitative data and their relationship to the design of DATABASES. In business or management studies it has similar connotations to technology management, with an emphasis on the relationship of COMMUNICATION and INFORMATION TECHNOLOGY to business performance and competitiveness (Synott 1987). In the field of librarianship and information science it is identified with the 'emerging market' for information workers (managers), whose perception of information embraces data, organizational intelligence, competitive intelligence, external information resources of all kinds and the associated technology (manual or machine) for handling these different sources. Compared with the other areas, information management in this latter context is more widely concerned with the meaning of information for the information user and with INFORMATION RETRIEVAL issues.

Information management, 'information resource(s) management' and 'knowledge management'

A further difficulty in defining information management arises out of the often synonymous use of the term 'information resource (or resources) management' (IRM), the term used by the US National Commission on Federal Paperwork in its report (1997), where 'paperwork', including electronic documents of all kinds, was defined as constituting the information in IRM. This usage appears to limit the idea of IRM, but the report goes on to say that an IRM function (in US government agencies) would incorporate a wide range of disparate activities, including RECORDS MANAGEMENT, library management, computer systems, printing and REPROGRAPHY, MICROFORMS and word-processing centres. Schneyman (1985) elaborates on this definition of IRM to cover five types of 'information resources': systems support, including computers and TELECOMMUNICATIONS; processing data, images, etc.; conversion and transformation, including reprographics; distribution and communication, including NETWORK management and telecommunications; and, finally, retention, storage and retrieval, which covers libraries, record centres, filing systems, and internal and external databases. He adds that 'IRM supports IM by providing the technical capability and overall guidance for IM to do its job', which he defines as managing the ownership, content, quality and use of information.

This expansion of the idea, of course, takes it into the difficult area of the interface between information resources, in the sense of data, documents, etc., and the technology used to manipulate, manage and transmit those resources, with the result that information technology becomes characterized as an information resource. This is a source of endless confusion in the literature so that, for example, when Strassman (1976) writes on 'Managing the costs of information' he is really discussing the problem of accounting for the costs of computer-based systems.

More recently, the term 'KNOWLEDGE MANAGEMENT' has entered professional vocabulary, confusing the situation further. In the 1990s the concept of 'knowledge management' emerged from the management consultancies as yet another of the 'methodologies' for improving organizational performance, following business process re-engineering, the learning organization, total quality management and all the other methodologies back to Taylor and 'scientific management'. Quite what is managed in knowledge management is difficult to determine, however. Certainly, it cannot be KNOWLEDGE, which is in our heads, or, as Peter Drucker has said, 'between two ears, and only between two ears' (Kontzer 2001). The first text on the subject was by the Swedish management consultant (now resident in Australia) Karl-Erik Sveiby (1990) under the Swedish title, *Kunskapsledning*. Curiously, Sveiby himself now says that he does not like the term and that it decomposes into the management of information and the management of people (Sveiby 2001).

From the INFORMATION SYSTEMS perspective, software houses have been quick to re-brand their products as 'knowledge management software', rather than groupware, information retrieval software or even e-mail. This strategy has been referred to as 'search and replace marketing'. A stock-market 'Knowledge Management Index' exists (Information Technology Toolbox,

Inc. 2002) that follows the fortunes of twenty-seven companies, none of which describes itself as a 'knowledge management' company, and only one of which has a product marketed under the knowledge management label. An examination of the company websites reveals that the majority of them are marketing some kind of database technology in the form of information retrieval systems, customer relationship management, groupware, e-commerce, intranet systems, etc. One has to conclude, therefore, that Sveiby's decomposition of knowledge management into information management and the management of people is accurate and that no new solution to the problems of managing information in organizations is presented by any of these companies.

From the information perspective, therefore, 'knowledge management' is simply a more pretentious synonym for information management.

The origins of information management

Although earlier uses may exist, information management and information resources management achieved a high visibility in the USA in the mid-1970s as a result of the work of the National Commission on Federal Paperwork, the aim of which was to seek a reduction in the costs incurred by organizations in satisfying the demands for paperwork by the federal bureaucracies. Ironically, as PORAT (1977) notes, the Commission itself required more than 100 information workers and produced a seven-volume report of almost 3,000 pages!

However, the Commission quickly moved from the position of concern over the physical volume of 'paperwork' to the real problem of 'information requirements planning, controlling, accounting and budgeting' (Commission on Federal Paperwork 1977). Porat (1977) addressed these essentially economic issues in a report for the US Office of Telecommunications Policy, noting that, in 1967, 'the total cost of informational inputs [to the federal government] was $50.5 billion'. However, Porat's definition of the 'information economy' is very wide, so that it included, for example, the research and development purchases of the government, amounting to $13.1 billion. Only $11.8 billion 'was in the form of direct purchase of goods and services from the primary information sector'. By 1970 the overall value of information inputs had risen to $62.8 billion.

In spite of the strong impetus provided by the Commission, however, the idea of information management did not appear to have penetrated very far into the governmental structure ten years later. Caudle (1988) notes that, in spite of the emphasis in the Paperwork Reduction Act on treating information as a resource, '12 of the 16 department IRM managers surveyed conceded that IRM is primarily seen as automation or information technology, including telecommunications' and that 'There is not a general perception outside the IRM unit that IRM has anything at all to do with good management'. She also found that there was even less of a perception of IRM as helpful to management at the bureau level (i.e. the level below departments in the federal government), where the idea was equated almost solely with the idea of end-user technology support services.

Caudle concluded that the realization that information is a resource 'is developing much more slowly than the Paperwork Reduction Act's designers likely intended' and, perhaps with more optimism than was justified by the research, that 'once the information technology infrastructure is in place and the IRM offices themselves become operationally mature, IRM office managers and their organizations should be ready to take further steps toward true IRM'.

In the UK, the development of information management did not receive the same impetus from government, which since 1979 has been concerned with establishing the concept of the 'market' in what was the public sector. The same attitude has prevailed towards information: thus, the report of the Information Technology Advisory Panel, *Making a Business of Information* (1983), was concerned simply to direct attention to the business opportunities in the information sector. Later, the government produced guidelines for departments on dealing with business in seeking to derive benefit from 'tradeable information' (DTI 1990).

There was an attempt, however, to introduce the fundamental concepts of information management in government departments when the Central Computer and Telecommunications Agency produced guidelines for departments, following an investigation into departmental practices (CCTA 1990). One of the main planks of the guidelines was the recognition that responsibility for information resources was diffused over different sections in most departments and that there was a need to ensure effective collaboration among the resource-holders and, possibly, the integration of these services (particularly data management, records management and library and information services) under a single director.

The Definitions Task Group of the IRM Network (1993), which operates under the aegis of ASLIB (Association for Information Management), has provided a concise description of the nature of information management and associated ideas. Clarifying somewhat the relationship between information management and information resources management, the group associates the former with the task of managing the relationship between organizational objectives, management processes and information needs in the development of an information strategy and in deriving from that strategy an IT strategy and an information systems strategy.

An information systems strategy is the definition of systems (technological and otherwise) that are needed to satisfy information needs, whereas an IT strategy defines the way in which the technology can support the systems strategy.

Information resources management is, then, defined as applying 'the general principles of resources management to identify discrete information resources, establish ownership and responsibility, determine cost and value, and to promote development and exploitation where appropriate'.

This brief account of the development of information management serves to show that a degree of consensus can be seen to have emerged, but the relationships to other managerial issues in organizations are such that considerable scope exists for confusion over disciplinary or intra-organizational boundaries.

The elements of information management

Several strands have contributed to the development of information management. First, it has its origins in a variety of fields that have had to do, traditionally, with the acquisition, organization, maintenance and use of documents: archives and records management, and librarianship and information science (especially in special librarianship and information work). Many of the areas of concern within information management have long been the concern of other professional groups in the information field, including database design and development, information storage and retrieval, and the ECONOMICS OF INFORMATION.

Second, the development of information technology, and its growing application to all aspects of information management, has been a strong formative influence. The costs of computer-based systems draw direct attention to the issues of the value of information and cost–benefit relationships in the development of information systems and services. Where the costs of such systems have previously been hidden in the work done by a wide range of organizational staff members, their sudden emergence into significance consequent upon the introduction of computers has caused organizations to view information functions in a new light.

Finally, the wide application of information ideas, developed in the business schools, widely accepted in business, given prominence in the business press and in the media generally, and applied increasingly in public-sector organizations, has resulted in the acceptance of such concepts as strategic planning, cost–benefit analysis, resource management and MARKETING.

Information requirements

All aspects of information management must be grounded in a consideration of the information requirements (or information needs) of customers or clients of the information systems and services. The study of information needs has occupied information science for almost fifty years, but other disciplines, notably computer science, have also had an interest in the area (Wilson 1994).

From the point of view of the designer of computer-based information systems, it is clearly necessary to understand what kind of reports a client needs from a system and, if possible, to know how the client intends to use the information contained in those reports. Armed with this information he or she can then try to ensure that the system delivers what is needed, when it is needed.

Similarly, providers of competitive INTELLIGENCE or those who analyse information from online information sources must be aware of the information requirements of customers if their work is to be cost-effective in satisfying users' needs.

There are, at least, the following problems with the idea of identifying information require-

ments, however. First, information requirements change according to changes in the user's environment (both the immediate work environment and the wider environment outside the organization), making last month's statement of requirements less relevant today. Second, information requirements change as a consequence of the information received, giving rise to new needs or rendering obsolete earlier expressions of need. Third, the relevance of information can be determined only by the ultimate user because it will depend on that person's subjective, interpretative response to the information – that is, on the extent to which the person can 'make sense' of the information and incorporate it into his or her knowledge base.

The information manager must therefore make the identification of information requirements a recurrent activity within the organization, seeking feedback on information provided, monitoring the organization's changing priorities and continually seeking to understand how his or her customers function in the organization.

The information life cycle

The idea of an information life cycle is derived from records management, where the idea of document life cycle is central to the overall process. That cycle is set out by Goodman:

The life cycle of records includes the following steps (sometimes referred to as 'document control'):

- design and creation of records;
- identification;
- authorization;
- verification, validation, auditing;
- circulation, access, loan, use;
- back-up procedures and disaster recovery plans;
- retention schedules and destruction.

(Goodman 1994: 135)

The life cycle will vary from organization to organization depending on the nature of the information, the means used to organize it, the extent of use and the controls put upon use.

The Commission on Federal Paperwork set out a very basic life cycle, which identified the following five stages: requirements determination, collection, processing, use and disposition, with the following comment on its relationship to information management: 'At each of these stages, information values must be estimated and measured, costed and accounted for, just as Government now does for any other resource' (Commission on Federal Paperwork 1977: 43).

The life cycle of information in the Department of State, referred to by Horton and Pruden (1988) (and slightly revised here), is rather more developed and more directly related to internal documents and records:

- Stage 1 draft/revise document.
- Stage 2 clearance or approval.
- Stage 3 formal and informal exchanges on document content.
- Stage 4 local retrieval and reuse (either manual or electronic).
- Stage 5 acquisition and indexing by a central archive.
- Stage 6 central retrieval and reuse.
- Stage 7 primary and secondary distribution.
- Stage 8 disposition, i.e. permanent retention, limited archiving or destruction.
- Stage 9 systems administration.

The last stage is not so much a stage as the overall administration of the foregoing stages, involving, for example, security classification, password control for electronic files and other housekeeping functions.

Information resources

As noted earlier, there is some confusion over the concept of information resources, mainly as a result of the inclusion of technological resources in the concept. However, most commentators regard the following as constituting information resources in organizations.

DATA

All organizations generate data about their activities. Thus, a local government department such as a housing department generates data on its housing stock, the physical state of the houses, the details of tenants and their rents, and so forth. A manufacturing company generates data on the production process, recording not only the number of items of each product manufactured in a given time, but also data on the reliability of the equipment used to produce those items, the turnover rate and sickness rate of workers, and the sales by outlet, by region and by sales person. Organizations also collect data on the state of

their markets, the economic circumstances of the country or of its exports markets, and so on. All of these data are important, and some are more important than others because they enable the firm, for example, to identify potentially profitable products, markets and export areas. In other words, some data have potential for competitive advantage and must be maintained securely and effectively if the organization is to benefit from having them available.

RECORDS

Data are very often associated with records of events, objects and persons. For example, a personnel record identifies an individual and includes many items of data that define the person – age, training level, sex, marital status, courses attended, year of entry to the organization and many more. Again, a project will have many records associated with its management and ultimate completion, including all the data associated with, for example, product design and development, prototyping, market testing and full-scale production. Much of the information in these records will be textual in character and will consist of files of reports, test results, correspondence with suppliers, etc. Records of these kinds have long been the province of records management and procedures have been evolved to ensure their effective filing, security, storage and eventual disposal. The techniques of records management are now being applied to computer-based files, under the heading of information management.

TEXT

Textual information has long been the province of libraries and information centres, concerned, as they have been, with the acquisition, organization, storage and dissemination of printed materials, most often from outside the organization of which the library or information centre formed a part, but also often including the maintenance of stores of internal reports, particularly in research-intensive organizations. With the development of OFFICE AUTOMATION systems and the creation of many more electronic documents in organizations, the producers of such systems have become increasingly aware of the need for effective information retrieval systems to underlie the database of electronic documents.

MULTIMEDIA

All the above, together with sound recordings, graphics, pictures and video, may now exist together in a single 'document'. Examples include various educational and reference sources published as CD-ROM packages, such as Microsoft's Encarta encyclopedia; but, increasingly, organizations are finding applications for MULTIMEDIA databases in which, for example, word-processed documents may have sound comments attached by readers and may include pictures, for example in a personal database, or video clips, in records held by a consumer products test laboratory. While the other information resources referred to above may exist in either paper or electronic form, multimedia records require the application of information technology.

INFORMATION TECHNOLOGY

Information technology embraces computers, telecommunications and software systems that aid the organization, transmission, storage and utilization of what might better be called the 'knowledge resources' dealt with above. The range of equipment and the variety of specialized knowledge needed for their effective control is enormous and for these reasons information technology is often dealt with by different sections in organizations. Thus, telecommunications, including telephone systems and facsimile transmission systems, are often controlled separately from the computer resources of the organization. Similarly, functional divisions of an organization often have more expertise in the matters concerning software packages (for example, for accounting purposes) than the computer managers. However, these technologies are merging, so that, for example, ELECTRONIC MAIL may replace internal paper mail systems and, in some cases, external mail systems. Similarly, computer linkages between a manufacturer and the supplying companies may obviate the need for communication by other means. Consequently, there is an argument for requiring information technology (in all of these senses) to be managed under an umbrella that also covers the knowledge resources.

To these information resources we may add EXPERT SYSTEMS and other manifestations of developments in ARTIFICIAL INTELLIGENCE, such as the 'learning' systems created through neural net technology. Systems of this kind, which draw upon other information resources and the personal knowledge of individuals, already play an important, but little documented, role in certain kinds of businesses (e.g. stock trading) and may become the principal means by which information is put to use in support of organizational objectives in the future.

The economics of information

As noted earlier, the fact that information resources have associated costs has been an intrinsic part of the idea of information management from the beginning. Indeed, the Commission on Federal Paperwork was set up to identify the ways in which the costs associated with preparing documentation to satisfy government regulations or to bid for government contracts could be reduced.

There are, however, broader issues than those of the costs of information, from the scale of the 'information sector' of the economy to the 'value' of information. All of these issues present problems.

The most basic of the problems is that of the value of information, a subject that has concerned information scientists for many years. The problem is exacerbated because value itself is used in a number of different ways both in ordinary speech and in accounting. However, there appears now to be a consensus that the value of information can only be considered in the context of its use and is therefore a user-driven concept not a producer concept. This means that the value of information can be determined *post facto* – after benefits have emerged from its use in some decision situation – but not before its use. The terms use-value and value-in-use were coined to convey this idea (see, for example, Repo 1986). Consequently, it is arguable that an information user must be prepared to bear at least part of the costs of information being provided (i.e. in Taylor's (1986) terms, those relating to the value-adding processes performed on data).

In macroeconomics, a topic of abiding interest is that of the scale of the 'information sector' of the economy. This question is most closely associated with the work of MACHLUP (1962) and of PORAT (1977), who attempted to define the information sector and determine its size relative to other sectors of the US economy.

An attempt to deal with the problems of cost–benefit relationship is given by Horton and

Pruden (1988) in their account of the method used by the US Department of State (DoS) to estimate the value of implementing information management strategies in the Foreign Affairs Information System (FAIS). The life cycle of information in the FAIS consists of nine stages, from drafting to disposal, and estimates were made of the amount of time DoS officers were involved with some aspect of this life cycle. Estimates of the likely impact of the new systems on this expenditure of time were then made, as a measure of the benefits to be derived. The kinds of headings under which benefits might be expected were:

- Improved productivity (efficiency).
- Improved quality of decision-making.
- Improved performance of tasks (effectiveness).
- Improved learning curve.
- Upgraded work-function importance.
- Automated replacement of certain manual tasks.
- The discontinuation of certain tasks altogether.
- Greater interchangeability of personnel.
- Eliminated intermediate steps.
- Greater task overlapping.
- Less need for clerical support.
- Reduced reliance on paper files.
- Greater reuse of information assets.
- Faster response time.
- Reduced turnaround time.
- Tighter security and reduced violations.
- Decreased instances of lost or missing information.

Many of these anticipated benefits would be attributable to the use of information technology rather than being related to the intrinsic character of information, but, of course, unless the information itself was of value there would be little point in investing in the technology.

Improvement in productivity is one of the potential benefits of effective information management noted above. This aspect was touched upon in the White House Conference on Productivity (Strassman 1986), where it was noted that the costs of information workers are almost entirely hidden in the overheads of businesses. Here, of course, information worker means anyone whose primary function in the organization is to process information – hence, it includes all general managers, finance department staff, personnel managers and many more.

The method proposed by the White House Conference for determining the productivity of information workers was that 'The adjusted ratio of labour-value-added (after subtracting operations labour costs) divided by information worker costs should be used as the measure of information worker productivity at the business-unit level of analysis'. 'Labour-value-added' is defined as the value-added remaining after the contributions of shareholders, suppliers and operating staff have been taken into account. However, this clearly requires the adoption by organizations of methods for determining labour-value-added, of accounting techniques that collect appropriate information, and of definitions of different categories of information worker so that the value added by subcategories may also be determined.

The 'value-added' approach to the economics of information is explored in the work of Taylor, who notes that:

Information systems, then are a series of formal processes by which the potential usefulness of specific input messages being processed is enhanced. These are the steps by which value is added to the items going through the system, however those items are defined. ... These processes add value, whether or not we have an appropriate definition of value.

(Taylor 1986: 6)

Taylor presents a 'spectrum' of value-adding processes in information systems, which he divides into organizing, analysing, judgemental and decision processes, each set of processes resulting in the transformation of data to information to 'informing knowledge' to 'productive knowledge' and finally to action. A number of the benefits described by Horton and Pruden above are clearly related to value-adding processes.

In common with others, Taylor acknowledges that the 'value' of information is not an intrinsic property but something negotiated between the system operators and the users. In other words, users of information make judgements about the value of information in the context in which they apply that information.

The tools of information management

Some of the tools of information management are those derived from the fields that have contributed to its development; for example, CLASSIFICATION and information retrieval from librarianship and information science; database design and development from computer science; the document life cycle from records management; COMMUNICATION AUDITS from organizational psychology; and cost–benefit analysis and value assessment from business management. Creating a 'toolbox' of techniques for the information manager requires, essentially, a sufficiently wide background to be able to know what exists in the contributory fields and to be able to select and integrate techniques to apply to the problem at hand. There are entries for most of these topics elsewhere in this work, but some techniques have become so particularly associated with the idea of information management that they deserve attention here.

INFORMATION AUDITS

The idea of the INFORMATION AUDIT is derived from financial audits in accounting, which, as Ellis *et al.* (1993: 134) note, are generally 'compliance' audits, undertaken to ensure that the organization is adhering to proper fiscal and legal standards in its financial management. Information audits take more the character of 'advisory' audits, which are 'more concerned with informing users of existing systems and practices and with assessing the appropriateness of existing systems, standards and practices to the organization's goal or objectives'.

Barker (1990) describes five types of information audit: those based on a cost–benefit model; those that seek to map the relationships between resources; hybrid approaches (which combine features of the first two); audits of management information; and operational advisory audits, which link organizational objective, information requirements and compliance with regulations and standards.

Following her analysis Barker devised a model information audit consisting of ten stages:

1 Establish the operational objectives and define the organizational environment.
2 Determine the information requirements for the users.
3 Inventory of the information resources.
4 Identify system failures and key control points.
5 Evaluate system failures.
6 Test key control points.
7 Generate alternative solutions for system failures.
8 Evaluate the alternatives.
9 Check conformity of the system with existing regulations and standards.
10 Propose recommendations.

The identification of information resources requires techniques akin to those of cataloguing, i.e. the resources must be described as books are described, according to a standard code of practice. The state of New Jersey adopted such a strategy in its 'InfoFind' tool, which 'describes the state's information sources and identifies the state workers who are most knowledgeable about them: the information custodians' (Stone 1988).

INFORMATION MAPPING

The term information mapping is most closely associated with the name of Forest 'Woody' Horton but has also been used by Best (1985). Best, however, uses the term in the context of introducing information technology in organizations and takes a systems analytical approach to developing an IT strategy.

Horton, who takes a view of information resources more in accord with this article, has been responsible for the development of the information audit into a highly structured tool, which he calls information mapping, for part of which he has developed a software package known as Infomapper. Both the book (Burk and Horton 1988) and the software package present a highly structured way of identifying and recording the information resources of an organization, keyed to departments and hierarchical levels, with indications of 'ownership', responsibility for updating and other matters such as purging and disposal. The book, however, goes beyond the software in setting out, in addition, graphical representations of the information resource 'map', and approaches to measuring the costs and the value of information.

Recently, information mapping has acquired another meaning, in the guise of 'knowledge mapping', by which is meant the identification of people's skills and competencies. This idea is an old one in new clothes, first arising in the personnel management literature in the 1960s (e.g. Bronstein 1965), resurfacing when mainframe computers replaced 5" × 3" cards (e.g. Hoey 1972), and having a further lease of life when desktop computer networks became common. The proponents of 'knowledge mapping', however, appear to be unaware of these earlier manifestations of the same concept. However, there is scope for further confusion, because the term is also used in cognitive science research as a way of determining what is learnt in learning tasks (see, e.g., Herl *et al.* 1999)

COMMUNICATION AUDITS

The communication audit predates information management as a tool for the investigation of communication in the field of organization theory. Emerging out of that field, it has also found a place in the management of organizations where it is used to identify barriers to communication and possibilities for improvement. In this area the tools developed by Goldhaber (1974) and Goldhaber and Rogers (1979) for the International Communications Association (ICA) have had most impact. ICA instruments have been used most in exploring communication between management and employees in organizations. The role of communication audits was explored by Booth (1986, 1988) and, more recently, by Potter (1990), who categorized communication audits as being used to measure: the effectiveness of introducing IT in an organization; interpersonal communications; communication between management and employees; the effectiveness of organizational communications; or public relations activity.

Clearly, given the increasing interest in various aspects of quality management and quality assurance, the communications audit has a significant role to play in ensuring that communication between information services and their customers is fully effective.

Information access, networks and intranets

Determining the appropriate mode and channel of communication is also part of the information manager's role and, in recent years, the emphasis here has shifted from the acquisition of information resources 'just in case' they are likely to be useful to the organization, to a concept of acquiring, or providing access to resources 'just in time' to be useful. In organizations, the responsibility for managing internally generated information and data has increasingly come to be the function of information technology divisions, with the acquisition and organization of external resources being the responsibility of the

special library or information service. However, the ubiquity of telecommunications and computer networks both in organizations and in the world at large is making this distinction less and less useful. It is probably no exaggeration to say that the greater part of information needed to understand markets and the market position of a company is now available electronically, either through specialized providers of business information such as Reuters and Dun and Bradstreet, or through publicly available sources such as the websites of newspapers and business magazines. Similarly, competitive intelligence can be 'mined' from Internet resources and the proprietary online systems (see, e.g., Halliman 2001).

Thus, more and more information is brought into organizations through organizational networks and their connection to the Internet and the local application of the technology – INTRANETS. The great advantage of intranets lies in the relative ease with which legacy databases can be given new life and easier access through the development of Web-based interfaces, as well as in the increased potential for information sharing. To some extent intranets have been hailed as the solution to almost every problem of information management in organizations, being seen as the basis for the 'virtual organization' or the main tool for 'organizational learning' (for a range of views on intranets see, e.g., Bernard 1998; Hills 1997; Blackmore 2001). Vaast (2001), in a study of intranets in French companies, found that 1995 marked the point at which they became a common phenomenon, but that their evolution within companies varied considerably. Some used the intranet as a major strategic initiative, e.g. in merging companies, or in presenting themselves as 'leading-edge' corporations; others allowed the development of departmental intranets, without any overall strategic objective for the company. In a UK study, Leow and MacLennan (2000) found a high acceptance of intranets as a central part of information strategies in banks.

Whatever the nature of development, however, there is little doubt that the intranet and connection to the Internet has drawn attention in organizations to the need to access and manage textual information as much as information systems have previously managed corporate data.

Access, privacy and security: information and the law

Information management aims to improve the effectiveness of organizations by managing information as a resource – providing access to relevant information in a timely and cost-effective manner. However, this aim carries with it the problem of determining who needs access to organizational information and data, whether the privacy of individuals needs to be protected and what levels of security need to be in place to ensure not only privacy but also the protection of competitive intelligence.

In the UK, the DATA PROTECTION Act of 1984 established the legal basis for the protection of personal data in computer files and provided citizens with the basis for ensuring that such information was accurate and protected from misuse. There have been some doubts about the extent to which the aims of the Act have been realized, particularly as the cost to the citizen of obtaining information on the data held is set by the data-holder and can be high.

In Europe generally, the European Commission's draft directive on the protection of personal data (Commission of the European Communities 1992) is intended to harmonize legislation across Europe and to require those states that have not yet produced such legislation to do so. The overall aims are very much those of the UK Data Protection Act but grounded in the European Convention for the Protection of Human Rights. The definition of personal data files, however, is wider, covering not only electronic files but also manual files, and a great deal of uncertainty and confusion exists as to its future operation regarding, for example, library catalogues and bibliographic databases that might be regarded as constituting personal data.

In the USA, the 'Poindexter Memorandum' (Systems Security Steering Group 1986) caused a violent protest when it sought to restrict access to government information on the grounds of national security. In seeking to protect what it called 'sensitive, but unclassified' information the memorandum could have led to what were regarded as wholly unjustified restrictions on access to information, and it was ultimately withdrawn.

In the past, librarians and information managers needed to think of information law almost solely in terms of copyright but, as Knoppers (1986) points out, the situation is now very different. He notes that the information manager should

- be responsible for identifying any existing information laws that affect the organization;
- serve as the 'missing link' between legal services...the human resources and management information systems departments, and operational units of the organization to coordinate their activities and ensure that information law requirements are being met on a day-to-day basis regardless of the information technology used;
- ensure that information law compliance is integrated into the systems design methodology of the organization; and
- advocate changes in information law when compliance with it inhibits the introduction of new information technologies, thereby threatening the competitiveness and viability of the firm.

(Knoppers 1986)

Information policy and information strategies

INFORMATION POLICY may be determined for any level of organization, from the international community to the individual organization. Information policy has become a subject for debate at the international level in Europe as a result of the attempts by the European Commission to aid the development of the European information industry.

As noted earlier, in the UK the focus of national policy has been on the business opportunities in the information sector and on 'tradeable information' held by government departments, which might constitute opportunities for business as well as earning income for the departments. More recently, following the US lead, a statement on the public-sector opportunities provided by the notion of the Information Superhighway (CCTA 1994) has been produced. The idea of the Information Superhighway came to prominence as a result of the Clinton administration's declaration of a national (US) Information Superhighway, building on the achievements of the Internet (National Telecommunications and Information Administration 1993).

Information management has developed out of the perception that information is crucially important to the success of business organizations and to the productivity of public sector agencies. At the organizational level, therefore, an information policy defines the overall aims and objectives of the organization in relation to information. As Lytle notes: 'Information policies relate to: (i) data, (ii) information processing equipment and software, (iii) information systems and services, and (iv) staff roles and responsibilities. Formal development of information policies recognizes information as a strategic organizational resource' (Lytle 1988). Thus an aim of policy may be to provide access to the organization's data resources for all executive and managerial level personnel directly from the workstation. Another aim may be to provide customized searching of external, online information resources for planning and marketing personnel.

Information strategy deals with how these policy aims are to be accomplished: thus, the second aim above might be accomplished in a variety of ways; for example, by training personal assistants and secretaries in online searching, by commissioning the organization's library services to carry out the searches on behalf of managers or by investing in the appropriate software 'agent' (such as SandPoint Corporation's 'Hoover') to enable the task to be performed automatically and delivered to the manager's terminal (see Hermans 1997). Each of these strategies will have different, associated costs, risks and time-scales that need to be evaluated against the anticipated benefits.

The National Health Service in the UK provides an interesting case study of the evolution of an information strategy and the role of the Internet and intranets in the strategy. In *Information for Health: An Information Strategy for the Modern NHS* (Department of Health 1998) the aim, set out by the Secretary of State for Health in the Foreword, was 'to provide NHS staff with the most modern tools to improve the treatment and care of patients and to be able to narrow inequalities in health by identifying individuals, groups and neighbourhoods whose healthcare needs particular attention'. The objectives, therefore, were not narrowly informational in character, but related directly to the central functions of the National Health Service. Subsequent developments in the NHS have been guided by this overall strategy, both in relation to the professionals working in the system, through NHSnet, which connects General Practitioners, NHSweb (see www.nhsia.nhs.uk/nhsnet/pages/about/intro/nhsweb.asp), and the development of electronic patient record systems and associated standards, and in relation to the citizen, through NHS Direct Online (see www.nhsdirect.nhs.uk/). The NHS is a huge organization and implementing an information strategy requires the development of a complex web of standards, technology and electronic resources.

An information policy may have a number of different dimensions and each dimension may have a variety of alternative strategies for its realization. Consequently, the STRATEGIC PLANNING necessary to define policy and relate strategies to the financial, personnel and other resources of the organization is no trivial task. An excellent example of this complexity is presented by Bowander and Miyake (1992) in their study of the information management strategy of the Nippon Steel Corporation. The strategy focused on sustaining the competitiveness of the company in the world market for steel and its success is said by the authors to be due to

(a) intensive scanning for new information;
(b) identifying new business opportunities using IT;
(c) rapid information assimilation through organizational learning;
(d) information fusion for generating new innovations;
(e) intensive use of information through learning by doing and learning by using;
(f) building competence for achieving new business through tie-ups and rapid commercial utilization of already available technologies; and
(g) highly forward-looking and intensive information management strategy at the firm level.

(Bowander and Miyake 1992)

While much of the focus of the paper is on the information technology strategies that were implemented to support the information strategy, it is notable that the company paid significant attention to information content and information sharing as the basis for its strategic business development.

Warning notes, however, are issued from all sides. For example, Galliers *et al.* (1994) have explored how information strategies fail and their conclusions are directly applicable to organizational information policy (see ORGANIZATIONAL INFORMATION POLICIES) and strategy. Failure is associated with: (1) the lack of a 'champion', someone at the highest level in the organization who takes upon himself or herself the task of arguing for resources, negotiating and restructuring, and otherwise setting the scene for the attainment of the policy (this is a frequently reiterated point in the literature – see, for example, Wilson 1989a); (2) a condition of rapid change in the business environment and the aims of the organization; (3) a lack of mutual understanding of the aims of the strategy and the means for its attainment on the part of the different actors in the development process; (4) a failure to provide the appropriate means for 'organizational learning' so that (3) may be overcome.

Sauer (1993) adds to these points the fact that the implementation of information systems is the product of a coalition of stakeholders. One of the stakeholders is the organization set up to develop systems and it relies upon the support of the others (who have the power to obtain resources etc.) to attain its objectives. Failure occurs when the system development organization runs out of support because of, for example, failure to meet expectations, or to deliver on time and within budget, or to deliver useful systems.

Strategic information systems

The idea that information has strategic value emerges out of the idea of information as an organizational resource and the related concept of competitive intelligence or environmental scanning (as the work referred to in the previous paragraph demonstrates). Thus, the information held in corporate databases may have strategic value in identifying new market opportunities or may itself constitute new information products. Such new opportunities and new products are strategic in the sense that they aid the competitive position of the organization and, given the tendency in the UK towards the adoption of market-oriented management in public services, today all organizations may need to adopt a competitive stance.

Again, an organization may scan the business environment for market opportunities, for threats to present competitive positions, for potential replacement products and services for those currently marketed, and for potential acquisitions. New products have recently been marketed to enable firms to scan the online databases and Internet resources for competitive intelligence. Such information is strategic information and the systems designed to acquire, store, organize and make available for use such information are strategic information systems. Choo (2001) has edited a useful series of papers on competitive intelligence and environmental scanning.

However, the use of information in strategic or competitive ways is not without its hazards, as Marx (1987) has pointed out. The case of computerized reservations systems (CRS) in the airline business is well known: American Airlines developed its CRS (known as SABRE) and agreed to carry information from other airlines. However, the system was set up in such a way as to give preference to information on American Airlines' flights. This was subsequently ruled to be unfair practice and American Airlines had to redesign its system.

Marx draws attention to other situations in which the competitive use of information and information systems may constitute unfair competition or restraint of trade or contribute to the creation of a monopoly position in an industry. All of this, of course, confirms the emergence of information as a key resource in business, to which the same legal constraints must be applied as are used to prevent monopolistic ownership of other means of production or distribution.

Education for information management

The state of education for information management is as diverse as the basis for its definitions. In the UK, the Departments and Schools of Librarianship and Information Science (LIS) have introduced information management options and, in some cases, new degree programmes in the field, and have made a strong bid within their institutions to be the lead departments in this new area. However, there is competition from the business schools (where the focus still tends to be on the strategic role of information technology and on the consequences of that role for the management of IT) and from computer science departments, which, in the early 1990s, felt the effect of declining demand for their courses and which, in consequence, have sought to broaden the basis for attracting students by offering courses in business information systems and information management.

Attempts to define the information management curriculum have been limited, but Wilson analysed the contents of key journals in the field and found the following categories:

- application areas (such as banking, local government, industry, etc.)
- artificial intelligence
- economics of information (including the information industry)
- education for information management
- information management functions (e.g. manpower aspects, strategic monitoring, etc.)
- information policy
- information systems (including database systems, decision support systems, legal aspects, organizational impact, etc.)
- information technology (with two main subcategories: management aspects and technological aspects)
- information use and users
- systems theory

(Wilson 1989b: 208)

While the attention given to each of these elements seems likely to differ, they do seem to constitute the general core of information management and, indeed, those departments of library and information studies in the UK that have created information management programmes have produced different mixes of the elements depending upon the existing strengths of the teaching staff. Since the first edition of this text, the situation has changed little: a study by Maceviçiūtė and Wilson (2002) found:

- In the economics of information, a shift to a concern with wider market economics, rather than cost–benefit relationships in the firm.
- Greater concern with organization and human issues.
- The emergence of information networking, the Internet and intranets as themes.
- Greater concern with telecommunication policies – associated with networking.
- More attention to intellectual property issues – also a consequence of networking etc.
- The proliferation of application areas for information management concepts.
- The emergence of knowledge management, as a virtual synonym for the field.

The situation in the USA is similar and appears to have changed little since Lytle (1988) noted that confusion existed over the educational base for information management and claimed that:

> The reason for the confusion is not curriculum overlap or battles in academia for the latest degree programme. The primary problem is confusion concerning what qualities and skills are required for IRM positions, whether these positions have IRM, MIS, or other titles.

Conclusion

Whether information management is a passing fancy or a new way of considering the role of information in organizational performance must await the test of time; however, there can be little doubt that the concept has had a significant impact on the thinking of professionals working in a variety of fields. Managers of computer services have become information managers (and even directors of information management services); records managers, archivists, information scientists and special librarians have changed their titles and shifted their professional orientations; and educational institutions have introduced new courses in information management in departments as diverse as computer science, business management and librarianship.

Clearly, then, changes have been set in train in several directions and acceptance of the concept, however defined, is widespread. The history of organizations, however, is full of ideas that have attained significance for a time and then fallen away, either into general acceptance within the body of management ideas or into whatever limbo exists for such things. One thinks in this context of 'scientific management', 'organization development', 'programmed-based budgeting' and the like.

If information management is to avoid this fate a number of things must happen: first, the function of information management (rather than simply the idea) must become accepted as a key part of organizational structures and processes, so that a constituency can exist as a basis for the other desiderata. In this respect, scale is a significant feature: government departments, local government structures and the National Health Service are large enough for the value of effective information management to be perceived, but the majority of manufacturing firms are small and medium-sized enterprises. As Roberts and Wilson (1987: 74) noted: 'Information management, in its information technology manifestation, is a distant and impractical idea for the majority of manufacturing firms. Most are devoid of levels of information awareness sufficiently lively to influence information behaviour and practices in a positive fashion.'

Second, a coherent educational programme or curriculum must emerge in which there is at least a core of universally recognized elements, so that the knowledge base of the information manager can be recognized by prospective aspirants to the role and by employees. In most cases, the situation remains confused, with business schools, computer science departments and departments of library and information studies adopting differing approaches to the field, and still, five years after the original publication of this work, there is little sign of the emergence of the desired cohesion.

Third, a research agenda must emerge to provide the theoretical basis for information management so that its problem areas can be identified and explored in a coherent and rigorous manner. Again, there is some indication that this is happening, in that the relevant journals are accepting papers from a wide range of sources, including library and information studies, recognizing the broad disciplinary approach necessary to the field. However, one of the key journals in the field, the *Information Management Review*, ceased publication in 1993 after only eight years in existence and it is evident that either the volume of research is insufficient to support even a small number of specialist journals or (and this is probably more likely) researchers wish to maintain their links with their parent disciplines. In the UK, the situation has been further exacerbated by the disappearance of the British Library R&D Department as a funding agency for research in the field. Researchers are now either in competition with every other discipline in bidding for resources from the research councils, or are engaged in more applied research for commercial sponsors and the various agencies of the European Commission.

References

Barker, R. (1990) *Information Audits: Designing a Methodology with Reference to the R and D Division of a Pharmaceutical Company*, University of Sheffield, Department of Information Studies (Occasional Publications Series, no. 8).

Bernard, R. (1998) *The Corporate Intranet*, 2nd edn, Wiley.

Best, D. (1985) 'Information mapping: A technique to assist the introduction of information technology in organizations', in B. Cronin (ed.) *Information Management: From Strategies to Action*, ASLIB.

Blackmore, P. (2001) *Intranets: A Guide to Their Design, Implementation and Management*, ASLIB.

Booth, A. (1988) *The Communication Audit: A Guide for Managers*, Gower.

—— (1986) *Communication Audits: A UK Survey*, Taylor Graham.

Bowander, B. and Miyake, T. (1992) 'Creating and sustaining competitiveness: Information management strategies of Nippon Steel Corporation', *International Journal of Information Management* 12(1): 39–57.

Bronstein, R.J. (1965) 'Setting up a skills inventory: How to do it on a shoestring', *Personnel* (March/April): 66–7.

Burk, C.F. and Horton, F.W. (1988) *InfoMap: A Complete Guide to Discovering Corporate Information Resources*, Prentice Hall.

Caudle, S.L. (1988) 'IRM: A look backward and forward at the federal level', *Information Management Review* 3(4): 9–25.

CCTA (1994) *Information Superhighways: Opportunities for Public Sector Applications in the UK*, CCTA.

—— (1990) *Managing Information as a Resource*, HMSO.

Choo, Chun Wei (ed.) (2001) Special issue on environmental scanning and competitive intelligence, *Information Research* 7(1). Available at: http://InformationR.net/ir/7–1/infres71.html [site visited 3 January 2002].

Commission of the European Communities (1992) *Amended Proposal for a Council Directive on the Protection of Individuals with Regard to the Processing of Personal Data and on the Free Movement of Such Data*, Commission ((92/C 311/04) COM (92) 422 final – SYN 287).

Commission on Federal Paperwork (1977) *Information Resources Management*, Washington, DC: US Government Printing Office.

Definitions Task Group (1993) *Final Report*, ASLIB/IRM Network.

Department of Health (1998) *Information for Health: An Information Strategy for the Modern NHS*, NHS Executive.

DTI (1990) *Government-held Tradeable Information Guidelines for Government Departments in Dealing with the Private Sector*, Department of Trade and Industry.

Ellis, D., Barker, R., Potter, S. and Pridgeon, C. (1993) 'Information audits, communication audits and information mapping: A review and survey', *Interna-*

tional Journal of Information Management 13(2): 134–51.

Galliers, R.D., Pattison, E.M. and Reponen, T. (1994) 'Strategic information systems planning workshops: Lessons from three cases', *International Journal of Information Management* 14(1): 51–68.

Goldhaber, G.M. (1974) *Organizational Communication*, Brown Publishing Co.

Goldhaber, G.M. and Rogers, D.P. (1979) *Auditing Organizational Communication Systems: The ICA Communications Audit*, Kendall-Hunt Publishing.

Goodman, E.C. (1994) 'Records management as an information management discipline – a case study from SmithKline Beecham Pharmaceuticals', *International Journal of Information Management* 14(2): 134–43.

Halliman, C. (2001) *Business Intelligence Using Smart Techniques, Environmental Scanning Using Text Mining and Competitor Analysis Using Scenarios and Manual Simulation*, Information Uncover.

Herl, H.E., O'Neil, H.F., Chung, G.K.W.K. and Schacter, J. (1999) 'Reliability and validity of a computer-based knowledge mapping system to measure content understanding', *Computers in Human Behavior* 15(3–4): 315–33.

Hermans, B. (1997) 'Intelligent software agents on the Internet', *First Monday* 2(3). Available at: www.first-monday.dk/issues/issue2_3/ch_123/index.html [site visited 3 January 2002].

Hills, M. (1997) *Intranet Business Strategies*, Wiley.

Hoey, P. O'N. (1972) 'Systematic utilization of human resources as an integral part of information science work', *Journal of the American Society for Information Science* 23: 384–91

Horton, F.W. and Pruden, J.S. (1988) 'Benefit: cost analysis – a Delphi approach', *Information Management Review* 3(4): 47–54.

Information Technology Advisory Panel (1993) *Making a Business of Information: A Survey of New Opportunities*, HMSO.

Information Technology Toolbox, Inc. (2002) *ITtoolbox Knowledge Management Index*. Available at: http://stocks.ittoolbox.com/ITtoolox/indices.asp?symbol=$KMDEX [site visited 1 January 2002].

Knoppers, J.V.T. (1986) 'Information law and information management', *Information Management Review* 1(3): 63–73.

Kontzer, T. (2001) 'Management legend: Trust never goes out of style', *InformationWeek.com*. Available at: www.informationweek.com/story/IWK20010604S0011 [site visited 3 January 2002].

Leow, K.M. and MacLennan, A. (2000) 'An investigation of the use of intranet technology in UK retail banks', *Journal of Librarianship and Information Science* 32(3): 135–46.

Lytle, R.H. (1988) 'Information resource management: A five-year perspective', *Information Management Review* 3(3): 9–16.

Macevičiūtė, E. and Wilson, T.D. (2002) 'The development of the information management research area: An update', *Information Research* 7(3). Available at: http://InformationR.net/7–3/ (forthcoming).

Machlup, F. (1962) *The Production and Distribution of Knowledge in the United States*, Princeton University Press.

Marx, P. (1987) 'The legal risks of using information as a competitive weapon', *Information Management Review* 2(4): 11–18.

National Telecommunications and Information Administration, National Information Infrastructure Office (1993) *The National Information Infrastructure: Agenda for Action*, NTIA.

Porat, M.U. (1977) 'The public bureaucracies', in *The Information Economy: Definition and Measurement*, Office of Telecommunications Policy, pp. 136–47; reprinted in F.W. Horton and D.A. Marchand (eds) (1982) *Information Management in Public Administration: An Introduction and Resource Guide to Government in the Information Age*, Information Resources Press, pp. 16–27.

Potter, S. (1990) 'The communications audit: A small-scale pilot study exploring communications between an information service and its customers in a pharmaceutical company', unpublished MSc dissertation, University of Sheffield.

Repo, A.J. (1986) 'The dual approach to the value of information: An appraisal of use and exchange values', *Information Processing and Management* 22: 373–83.

Roberts, N. and Wilson, T.D. (1987) 'Information resource management: A question of attitudes?', *International Journal of Information Management* 7(2): 67–75.

Sauer, C. (1993) *Why Information Systems Fail: A Case Study Approach*, Alfred Waller Ltd.

Schneyman, A.H. (1985) 'Organizing information resources', *Information Management Review* 1(1): 34–45.

Stone, N. (1988) 'InfoFind: A practical tool for managing information', *Information Management Review* 3(4): 39–46.

Strassman, P.A. (1986) 'Improving information worker productivity', *Information Management Review* 1(4): 55–60.

—— (1976) 'Managing the costs of information', *Harvard Business Review* 54 (September/October): 133–42.

Sveiby, K.-E. (2001) *What is Knowledge Management?*. Available at: www.sveiby.com/articles/Knowledge-Management.html [site visited 1 January 2002].

—— (1990) *Kunskapsledning: 101 råd till ledare i kunskapsintensiva organisationer* [*Knowledge Management: 101 Tips for Managing in Knowledge-intensive Organizations*], Stockholm: Affärsvärlden.

Synott, W.R. (1987) *The Information Weapon: Winning Customers and Markets with Technology*, Wiley.

Synott, W.R. and Gruber, W.H. (1981) *Information Resource Management: Opportunities and Strategies for the 1980s*, Wiley.

Systems Security Steering Group (1986) *National Policy on Protection of Sensitive, but Unclassified Information in Federal Government Telecommunications and Automated Information Systems*, SSSG (National Telecommunications and Information Systems Security Policy no. 2).

Taylor, R.S. (1986) *Value-added Processes in Information Systems*, Ablex Publishing.

Vaast, E. (2001) 'Intranets in French firms: Evolutions and revolutions', *Information Research* 6(4). Available at: http://InformationR.net/ir/6–4/paper109. html [site visited 3 January 2002].

Wilson, T.D. (1994) 'Information needs and uses: Fifty years of progress?', in B.C. Vickery (ed.) *Information Progress: A Journal of Documentation Review*, ASLIB: 15–52.

—— (1989a) 'The implementation of information system strategies in UK companies: Aims and barriers to success', *International Journal of Information Management* 9(4): 245–58.

—— (1989b) 'Towards an information management curriculum', *Journal of Information Science* 15(4–5): 203–9.

SEE ALSO: data protection; freedom of information; information; information professions; information science education; library education; market research

T.D. WILSON

INFORMATION POLICY

What is information policy?

Information policy is an important component in the deliberations of national governments and international public bodies, yet it is less immediately visible than other areas of public policy. When we think of health, education or housing policy, we can readily identify laws, regulations, responsible cabinet ministers, royal commissions, think tanks and other trappings and apparatus of government. To a more limited extent, the same is true of information policy. For example, we have laws and regulations that exist to regulate the processing of personal information (e.g. DATA PROTECTION), or to create the market conditions within which information products and services can be traded (e.g. COPYRIGHT), or to protect national security (e.g. OFFICIAL SECRECY). At the same time, there are broader policy aims that deal with information, not framed in purely legal terms. We have measures that are concerned with creating information infrastructures – from PUBLIC LIBRARIES, to the training of information professionals, to the provision of BROADBAND networks in higher education, as well as measures to help achieve an INFORMATION SOCIETY. Within the pages of our newspapers, we find fierce debates on the big political issues of the moment, many of which have a strong informational component, such as the introduction of compulsory identity cards or video SURVEILLANCE in our high streets and shopping centres. These highlight some interesting questions for information policy, such as: Who owns personal information? Should citizens sacrifice some privacy in the fight against crime? How should digital BROADCASTING be financed?

Information access and disclosure are critical elements in the working of participative democracies and measures concerning these aspects can be found in most areas of public policy. The 1993 UK White Paper on Open Government, for example, lists some forty Acts of Parliament and 280 Statutes, enacted since the war, which place various restrictions on the use of information, often tucked away within the small print of how the consumer credit market, for example, should be regulated (Hill 1994). To be fair, there are many examples of both legislation and government practice that conversely guarantee the availability of information to the public in areas as diverse as pollution registers, food labelling and agricultural statistics. However, if we decide to take a view, at least for the sake of argument, that we can treat 'access to information' as an independent variable in society, is it not possible to conceive of the whole apparatus of INFORMATION LAW and regulation, including public libraries, education, broadcasting, universal service, cryptography, freedom of expression and other related concepts as forming a kind of gigantic 'information ecosystem'? And, just as in natural ecosystems, is it not the case that each element is interdependent and that even relatively small changes to one component can lead to unpredictable large-scale changes in the rest of the system? It is this kind of thinking that led to a great deal of interest in the notion of 'national information policies' in the early 1970s, and to a recent, post-Internet, revival of interest.

At its highest level, information policy thus comprises all the laws, regulations and public policies that encourage, discourage or regulate the creation, use, storage and communication of information. It follows that information policy is a broad concept and the list of topics below may be taken as generally indicative of its scope (Chartrand 1986):

• Government information resource management policy and practice.

- TELECOMMUNICATIONS and broadcasting policy.
- International communications policy.
- Information disclosure policy.
- Information, confidentiality and PRIVACY.
- Computer regulation and COMPUTER CRIME.
- INTELLECTUAL PROPERTY.
- Library and ARCHIVES policy.
- Government information dissemination.

In many ways, information policy is a problematic concept intellectually. What binds together an apparently disparate and combustible mix of issues such as privacy, electronic government, access to official information, INTERNET provision in libraries, academic NETWORKS and identity cards? Information policy is an example of what a political scientist might recognize as an 'issue area', one which draws together a bundle of apparently unrelated concerns around a single (if highly ambiguous) integrating concept – in this case, the power of information to 'make a difference' in the social, cultural and economic life of the nation.

Many commentators on information policy have noted that it seems very different from other, more established, areas of public policy. The differences are not difficult to identify. Information policy differs from, say, education, housing or health policy in that:

- It is a relatively new area of policy concern.
- It involves an unusually large and diverse number of interest groups.
- Decisions about information can have an enormous impact on events and policies in other areas – the reverse is true to a much lesser extent.
- Information, in contrast with, say, labour or capital, does not fit into the traditional categories employed by policy analysts.
- Information policies are made at very different levels of the political and social structure, from the local to the global, and are remarkably interdependent

These differences are all, of course, relative. They may not be unique (i.e. exclusive) characteristics, but they certainly seem to be atypical of other areas of public and organizational policy, where the issues tend to be relatively more clear cut and the affected parties less numerous.

Of course, a wide range of forces other than public policy are relevant to a consideration of the issues affecting the creation, use, storage and communication of information. These include, among many others, the commercial strategies adopted by publishers and database providers, consumer behaviour, the influence of pressure groups and the proliferation of new information media and platforms. One of the characteristics of information policy that makes it a challenging area to study is that it simultaneously *shapes* and *responds to* the outside world. As an *independent* variable, information policy can be thought of in terms of its impact and outcomes, both on the wider environment and on the political process itself. When it is viewed as a *dependent* variable, our attention is drawn to the environmental, cultural, economic and other factors that shape and guide policy and its implementation (Rowlands 1996). This insight leads us to the view that we should define information policy as broadly and as inclusively as possible. Information policy is about much more than laws and white papers; it is better to think of it as referring to all those societal mechanisms used to control information, and the societal effects of applying those mechanisms.

Tracing the concept historically, we find the first systematic national information policies emerging in the USA in the early 1960s. Against the geopolitical backdrop of the Cold War and the space race, there was an increasing awareness that a nation's stock of scientific and technical information, and its ability to protect and manage those assets effectively, were becoming critical national security issues. If the needs of the military-industrial complex were one factor in the growing acceptance of the need for high-level information policy, the other integrating construct was the emergence of the computer, and later the network, as a readily identifiable focus and metaphor for information processing. The diffusion of INFORMATION AND COMMUNICATION TECHNOLOGY (ICT) into the fabric of society brought with it a series of thorny problems as new techniques for automatically processing data on a large scale became possible.

Historically, information policies have evolved in direct response to the emergence of specific technologies, such as print, telephony, radio or value-added and data services. Not surprisingly, the responsibility for these policies has tended to fall within the domain of whichever professional information community was most directly concerned with the particular technology involved (as librarians, computer scientists, broadcasters or information scientists). In other words, while information policy has been *technology driven*, policy analysis and research has typically been *discipline bounded*. The fragmentation of information policy research is mirrored by a fragmentation of policy-making institutions. In Britain, for example, the Department of Trade and Industry is the lead agency for developing policy in relation to tradeable information, standards and INTELLECTUAL PROPERTY; while data protection is under the jurisdiction of the Home Office; legal deposit under the Department of National Heritage; and public records under the Lord Chancellor's Department.

Prince Metternich once described early nineteenth-century Italy, then composed of a collection of regional entities, as little more than a 'geographical expression'. Such a viewpoint has some relevance to information policy and finds reflection in the long-standing debate about whether we should more properly speak of an all-embracing 'National Information Policy' or 'national information policies'. Other public policy areas, like social exclusion, are arguably just as fragmented as information policy and a coherent programme to tackle poverty might well include such diverse elements as innovations in education and training, tax reform, the restructuring of welfare benefits and action on housing.

The question of whether we speak of information policy or information policies is not merely a source of vexation for academics. Singular and plural forms represent differing worldviews. Consensual approaches to thinking about a particular issue area in ways that provide a basis for decision-making are called 'regimes'. A regime may be thought of as a framework of shared values and assumptions that sets the context within which specific laws and policies are developed. In education, for instance, there is almost universal consensus on the need to provide compulsory schooling up to age sixteen and to encourage participation in higher education, and there is a clear understanding of the benefits of high-quality education in relation to continuing economic prosperity. These values transcend party political divides and frame the debate on education policy in terms of the relative merits of the means at our disposal, rather than fundamentally questioning the ends themselves.

The legal and regulatory environment within which we capture, store, use and process information is complex and multifaceted. Indeed, taken at face value, many of our information laws and public policies appear to be rather uneasy bedfellows. Thus, we create information markets by treating information as intellectual property, while at the same time offering subsidized public library services that 'distort' the workings of the marketplace. We endeavour to make government more transparent and accountable through FREEDOM OF INFORMATION legislation, while contracting out many formerly public services to the private sector, thus placing information that was once protected by the cloak of official secrecy into the realm of 'commercially sensitive'. Similarly, when we think of some of the stories in today's newspapers, we find tensions between the rights of editors to free expression, the rights of certain politicians to safeguard their personal privacy, and the balancing wider public interest. As the list of specific information laws and regulations necessarily expands to cope with the need to respond to new technologies and applications – *inter alia*, digital signatures, consumer protection on the Internet, data encryption, 'voluntary' smart cards and so on – we can anticipate many more such dilemmas in the future (with considerable earnings potential for suitably qualified lawyers!).

What is missing, it seems, in the actuality of public policy in the UK and other countries is a clear sense of an integrating overview or 'information policy regime'. Just how do we make sense of the complex ecology of information laws, regulations, information management practices and institutional cultures that shape information transfer activities at the national level? Information professionals are key stakeholders in this debate and have a unique opportunity to play a role in the development of a coherent information policy regime.

Information policy as a process

Our understanding of this complex and fascinating topic will be very limited if we restrict our study just to the formal expressions of information policy: Acts of Parliament, green papers or discussion documents. The analysis of policy documents can be a dull and sterile activity. We would do much better to think of information policy as a dynamic process, as an interplay between various stakeholder groups, vested interests and power structures.

There are many frameworks in the academic literature to help us better understand the dynamics of policy-making. Some writers view policy-making as the reaction of a political system to external stimuli, representing politics as a kind of black box that regulates change in the outside world, a little like the thermostat that tells your central heating system when to come on or off. Others view policy-making as the result of a series of choices or bargains negotiated between stakeholders and represent it as an essentially chaotic, non-linear, process determined by shifting networks of power and influence. A review of all the frameworks potentially available for use in the context of information policy studies is beyond the remit of this encyclopedia entry, but one immediately useful and productive way of trying to understand information policy is to employ a systems approach. This recognises that policy-making comprises a series of inputs (people, ideology, expediency, information, research, investment) and outputs (wealth creation, better healthcare, access to democracy). By conceiving of information policy-making as a set of INPUT–PROCESS–OUTPUT (I–P–O) activities for organizing our thinking, we shift to the view that information policy governs a *process* (such as the storage and transmission of information) rather than a *thing* (such as technology). 'Information policy' might therefore be better thought of as a verb than a noun. Just as the I–P–O model can be used to describe how data are transformed into information and then knowledge, so too can it offer insights into

policy-making. So, rather than addressing policy issues relating to a specific advance in software or data communications (technology driven) we can switch our attention to the underlying functional aims and objectives of policy.

Conceptualizing policy as a *process*, rather than a specific outcome or event, is very useful. It helps us to understand how policy develops over time and how policy is shaped by (and, in turn, shapes) economic, cultural, organizational and social factors. Policy is not an abstract ideal; it takes place in an imperfect and sometimes confusing world. A typical representation of the policy-making process breaks it down into a series of stages and a relatively simple example of this approach is illustrated below (Figure 12).

As we move from left to right, a problem is first recognized and defined and then finds itself on a decision-maker's agenda. Alternative 'solutions' are developed, presented and rejected in favour of the option that offers the maximum net benefit (or is the most convenient, expedient or cheapest). This is then officially adopted. Implementation begins and some kind of evaluation or monitoring procedure is usually invoked so that any undesirable outcomes can be identified and mitigated against. In many cases, the results of that evaluation will require adjustments to be made earlier in the chain, perhaps resulting in a complete redesign of the policy. This is a rational and idealized model of policy-making. It conceptualizes policy as a planning activity. To a large extent, once a policy-making process gets underway, it tends to be continuous. It has been said that policy-making has no beginning and no end. This is overstating the case, since it is possible to

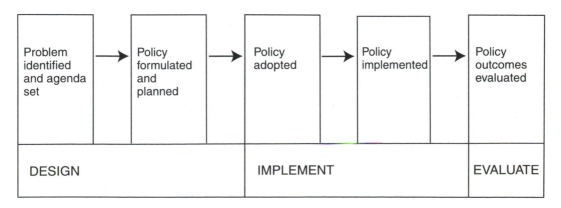

Figure 12 Staged model of the policy-making process

define reasonable starting and termination points in a pragmatic way. Within those bounds, however, the process can be regarded as continuous.

The power of the staged model is that it offers us a way of grouping a wide range of apparently disconnected decisions, phenomena, observations and data into meaningful units. It has a certain intuitive appeal that is not easily to be discounted. It also has its limitations. Many critics would immediately point out that real life, with its rough-and-tumble of politics and horse trading, is not nearly as tidy as the model suggests (Rowlands and Turner 1997). Nonetheless this is how policy-making is most often presented in the media and many policy-makers would still justify and defend their own actions, however apparently irrational at the time, in terms of this ideal framework.

Despite their apparent abstraction, theoretical models can be very powerful and can shape the course of events in the real world.

THE NORMATIVE STRUCTURE OF INFORMATION POLICY

Information policy, like public policy in general, derives its values and goals from the dominant political, economic and cultural contexts within which it is forged and developed. This point may at first seem rather obvious and unremarkable, until we reflect further on some of the implications of the staged model. Why is it, for example, that some issues capture the interest of policy-makers, while others are neglected? Is it just because of circumstances, or is it because powerful lobby groups are able to make themselves heard above the general din? Even when an issue bubbles up onto the political agenda, the ways in which it may be dealt with can vary enormously. Consider the following sequence of events:

Issue identification and problem definition – 1

Issue – people sleeping on the streets of cities.
Problem definition – vagrancy.
Policy response – tougher forms of policing.

What counts as a problem and how that problem is defined depends very much on the way that we perceive it. If we see people sleeping on the streets as a problem of vagrancy, then the policy response is more than likely to be framed in terms of law enforcement and policing.

Issue identification and problem definition – 2

Issue – People sleeping on the streets of cities.

Problem definition – homelessness.
Policy response – provide low-cost housing.

We might just as easily view the same issue as an indicator of social deprivation or a sign of failure in other policy areas such as community care – in which case the policy response will obviously be very different (we might provide low-cost housing, for example, or appropriate mental healthcare).

Information policy issues are equally ambiguous. The recent trend towards the electronic delivery of public services provides a good example. Local government has been quick to embrace electronic communications, using e-mail, the Internet and the World Wide Web. Official city websites contain a wide range of information, including 'What's On' guides to local activities, council reports and plans, tourist information and links to local community and voluntary groups. Many authorities use innovative forms of electronic communication to provide information about local services – examples include public libraries with computers hooked up to the Internet, electronic kiosks displaying pages of local information in public places like supermarkets, and videotelephony for hearing-impaired people. Simultaneously, it is possible to see these developments as informing and empowering local communities and extending democracy, as instruments to reduce administration costs and head count by re-engineering local government services, as providing a stimulus to the information industry, as a new weapon in the councils' public relations armoury, or merely as gesture politics, pandering to the technology fetishists. The truth probably lies somewhere (everywhere?) on this list, but it is not immediately evident where.

In other words, issue identification and problem definition in information policy are hardly value-free. The same is true at all points in the policy cycle, even the evaluation of policy outcomes. Economic arguments over whether information should be treated as a tradeable commodity or cherished from a public good perspective abound in the library and information science literature, perhaps in their most crystalline form in relation to intellectual property rights. The continuing creation and development of information content requires that investors be properly rewarded for their efforts.

This means conferring property rights and enabling a marketplace to develop. On the down side, these property rights may erect a barrier to the world of ideas for those who are unable to pay. This in turn necessitates a further set of public policies, such as universal service, investment in libraries, civil R&D, and education, which seek deliberately to distort the information marketplace in favour of the wider public interest. Questions of this kind, which hinge on the respective roles and responsibilities of the state and the market, and on the rights of creators and users, are ubiquitous in the professional literature.

Aside from monetary considerations, access to information and knowledge is also a function of power structures. In many situations, the widest possible access to information is seen as a 'good thing' – health promotion, information about school performance, consumer information and access to local government records being classic examples. In other circumstances unfettered access to information is more problematic – the policy advice given to ministers, personal information, information which might be prejudicial to national security or a firm's commercial position. Restrictions on the free flow of information are sometimes essential, but there is always a danger that powerful forces in society will constrict these flows to their own advantage.

Progress in our understanding of information policies depends on finding ways to make our assumptions, prejudices and values more transparent – information policy, like all aspects of public policy, is after all deeply embedded in a political and social context. Information policy-makers constantly find themselves between a rock and a hard place – just consider the following intractable dilemmas:

- Market-led *versus* state-led visions of the INFORMATION SOCIETY.
- Rights of freedom of expression *versus* rights of personal PRIVACY.
- The monopoly functions of PATENTS and COPYRIGHTS *versus* their informational aspects and the needs of users in the UK science base.
- The philosophy of open government *versus* the retention of official copyright (crown copyright in the UK) and continuing restrictive licensing practices (see LICENCES).

The tensions between the main stakeholders (information industry, government, journalists, celebrities, inventors, library users) in each case are painfully evident. Without recourse to a broader framework that makes the underlying value systems clear, how can we find a way to resolve these tensions openly and fairly?

The model shown in Figure 13 was generated automatically using a DATA MINING technique (Rowlands 1999). It relates a number of information policy concepts to one another in a two-dimensional space, depending upon how frequently pairs of concepts co-occurred in a large bibliographic database.

It is not unreasonable to suppose that closely related concepts (e.g. fish AND chips) will tend to occur together more frequently in bibliographic records than concepts that are less mutually connected (e.g. fish AND oranges). If the intensity of these relationships is represented by distance, we could construct a map that would show 'fish' and 'chips' quite close to one another, while 'fish' and 'oranges' would be much further apart.

The concepts in the information policy map appear to be reasonably coherent and probably will not come as any great surprise to anyone with more than a passing interest in the subject. Five clusters of concepts are evident and are summarized in Table 15.

The axes on the map have been set (arbitrarily) to originate from the term 'information policy'. Broadly speaking, concepts lying to the right of the origin seem to relate primarily to the direct management by the state of its own internal information resources. From the top down, these responsibilities extend from the control of sensitive official information ('Information protectionism' cluster), through the effective storage and management of official information ('Public access' cluster) to the provision of infrastructures for its wider dissemination ('Information society and infrastructure' cluster). In contrast, concepts on the left-hand side of the map seem to more closely match the state's *indirect* role as a regulator of private sector information activities. Again, scanning from the top down, we see the state first acting to constrict information flows where these are held, for instance, to be invasive of personal privacy ('Information protectionism' cluster), then creating the conditions within which market exchange can take place ('Information markets' cluster) and finally mitigating against the worst excesses of the marketplace by guaranteeing fundamental

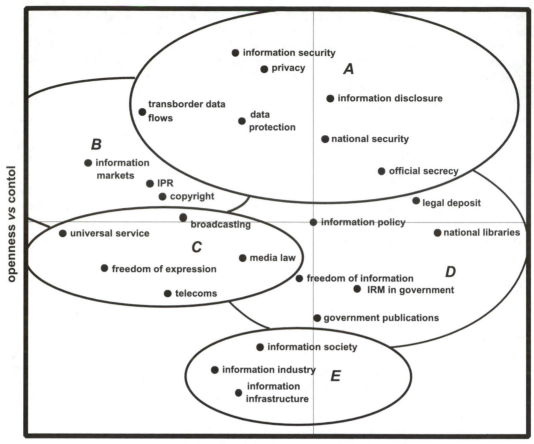

Figure 13 Information policy concepts

Table 15 Information policy subdomains

Cluster	Label	Interpretation
A	Information protectionism	Regulations and mechanisms controlling information access and disclosure in the public sphere (e.g. official secrecy) and in information markets (e.g. data protection)
B	Information markets	Laws and regulations that protect investment in the creation of information content (e.g. copyright) and enable market exchange to take place
C	Broadcasting and telecommunications	Public policies that regulate the mass media and communications, balancing commercial and citizen interests (e.g. universal access)
D	Public access to official information	Policies and regulations that frame citizens' access to information held within government (e.g. freedom of information)
E	Information society and infrastructure	Public policy measures to invest (or encourage private sector investment) in the information infrastructure, broadly defined

rights of freedom of expression and universal service ('Broadcasting and communications' cluster). For the sake of convenience, the y dimension can be summarised as expressing a spectrum between unrestricted, open (bottom) and restricted or controlled (top) information flows. The x dimension seems to indicate two distinct information policy roles for the state – as a regulator of information markets (left) and as a major gatherer and disseminator of information itself (right).

This model offers a new framework for helping us to think first and foremost about the system of values – rather than the specific laws and regulations – that underpin information policy. It may well be illustrative of aspects of the information policy 'regime' that were discussed earlier.

INFORMATION POLICY RESEARCH

It follows from all that has been said above that information policy is a multifaceted and slippery concept to get to grips with. The research literature on the topic is at the same time relatively sparse and characterized by a high degree of literary scatter – it has been estimated that academic writings on information policy can be found in the journals of more than forty disciplines, from library and information science to economics, from law to media studies. Within these writings, several distinct modes and styles of policy research can be identified:

- *Policy determination* is concerned with how policy is made, why, when and for whom.
- *Policy content* may involve either a description or a critique of a particular policy and how it relates to other, possibly earlier, policies.
- *Policy monitoring and evaluation* examines the impact of policies and how they have performed in relation to their original objectives.
- *Policy advocacy* involves research and arguments that are intended to influence the policy agenda.
- *Information for policy* is a form of analysis that is intended to feed directly into policy-making processes. This may take the form of detailed information and research or advice-giving.

In other words, research into information policy can be disinterested and followed for its own sake, or it can be undertaken in order to lobby and change the course of events. Either way, the stakes are high: information-related issues are becoming increasingly recognized as critical to many aspects of the functioning of modern societies and we need to ensure that all the roles that information plays in our lives (as an economic commodity, a social good and a private good) are recognized and supported. Are we ready for the challenge?

References

Chartrand, R.L. (1986) 'Legislating information policy', *Bulletin of the American Society for Information Science* 12: 10.

Hill, M.W. (1994) *National Information Policies and Strategies: An Overview and Bibliographic Survey*, Bowker-Saur, p. 105.

Rowlands, I. (1999) 'Some compass bearings for information policy orienteering', *ASLIB Proceedings* 50: 230–7.

—— (1996) 'Understanding information policy: Concepts, frameworks and research tools', *Journal of Information Science* 22: 13–25.

Rowlands, I. and Turner, P. (1997) 'Models and frameworks for information policy research', in I. Rowlands (ed.) *Understanding Information Policy*, Bowker-Saur, pp. 46–60.

Further reading

Braman, S. (1989) 'Defining information: An approach for policymakers', *Telecommunications Policy* 13: 233–42.

Browne, M. (1997a) 'The field of information policy: (1) fundamental concepts', *Journal of Information Science* 23: 261–75.

Browne, M. (1997b) 'The field of information policy: (2) re-defining the boundaries and methodologies', *Journal of Information Science* 23: 339–51.

Grieves, M. (ed.) (1998) *Information Policy in the Electronic Age*, Bowker-Saur.

IAN ROWLANDS

INFORMATION PROFESSIONS

A context for the information professions

The INFORMATION professions comprise all those persons directly engaged in the design, management and delivery of information, information collection and information services to communities of users. Three elements are essential in this definition: (1) engagement in the provision of information services using a collection of information developed for a community of users; (2) responsibility for the construction, management and movement of information from one situation or place to another; (3) professional decisions about INFORMATION POLICY and design for collecting, holding and providing the information. The responsibilities of an information professional may address any of these defining elements, but they are likely to appear in combinations. In many collections or organizations, a single information professional may be accountable for all of the responsibilities listed above, and more.

The most important of the definitive elements is the presence of a collection – or an array of several information collections – because a collection has multiple implications. Information professionals, for example, manage the development and maintenance of information collections. These collections may take various forms, including: the traditional forms found in a library (see LIBRARIES) or ARCHIVES, such as collections of BOOKS, JOURNALS, MANUSCRIPTS and other paper matter; research tools such as DATABASES, indexes (see INDEX), CATALOGUES and bibliographic utilities; and electronic media, including SOUND RECORDINGS, video and INTERNET resources, and the devices to use them.

The array of tools and resources might be quite vast; however, collections of this kind are finite, and most information professionals will work within acknowledged limits of content (imposed by an institution, a service community or an industry). Still, the inclusion of virtual and electronic tools and resources in any collection may make it reasonable to assume that the information collection can be conceived of as having no practical limits and as linked, at least in theory, to all other information collections, in any location. Determining and managing these extensions are also the responsibilities of information professionals.

Regardless of its size, no collection of information will be useful without multiple systems for COLLECTION DEVELOPMENT, ACQUISITIONS, BIBLIOGRAPHIC CONTROL, COLLECTION MANAGEMENT and evaluation; the professional presence in such a collection is devoted to assuring integrity in these systems.

Defining information professions

Professionals who work among information collections are typically identified as librarians, archivists or records managers, bibliographers and collection managers. It is required that they will hold undergraduate and, increasingly, graduate academic degrees in any discipline, as well as the Master's degree in either Library Science or Information Science. In research settings the Doctoral degree may be required as well. These professionals are largely concerned with constructing the definitions and determining formats of relevant and useful information; selecting new information and assuring its place in the collection; assisting its applications and uses within the community at hand; and evaluating the scope and depth of the collection, regarded as a whole over time. Among the critical values driving these responsibilities are currency, coherence, efficiency and relevance.

In practice, these responsibilities are undertaken as direct extensions of the information needs of a particular community of users, whose dependence on the collection and its services may be essential to their success. Citizens, scholars, researchers and policy-makers require current, deep and useful reservoirs of accurate information. Consequently, a grounded knowledge of a community, developed in consultation with its members, is required for appropriately responsive determinations of policy and STRATEGIC PLANNING in library and information services. Decisions regarding the housing, distribution and circulation of the collection will also fall to these professionals, but these tasks may be widely shared with peers and non-professionals as needed.

Information professionals also design systems and practices for purchasing, organizing, preserving, storing and delivering information. Among those who perform this aspect of professional responsibility are acquisitions librarians, cataloguers and serials librarians. Their primary concerns are likely to include considerations of language, TAXONOMIES and structures; accurate descriptions and details in representing and cataloguing the content of information; and the assurance of efficient purchasing paths and technical processes. Thinking among these information professionals will show a particular emphasis on solving the problems of acquiring information, establishing and maintaining standard descriptive practices, and observing consistency among technical service policies. The public service realm and the technical service realm are interdependent; neither works well without communication and collaboration with the other.

At the most advanced levels, in the most complex information collections, information professionals will also take primary responsibility for the gathering, management and movement of information, the consideration of innovations and expanding resources, and the development of systematic, co-operative relationships among distant collections. Such managers typically occupy higher offices of library administration, with titles such as library director, head of collection development, head of public services and head of technical services. In corporations, such primary information professionals may be titled chief information officer, or director of information technology. At the upper levels of responsibility in large or small information collections, professionals are charged with managing the information infrastructure, the deployment of human resources, ORGANIZA-TIONAL INFORMATION POLICIES and monitoring the rise and fall of an institution's budgetary and economic fortunes.

The most visible information professionals, however, are those whose daily work places them in contact with the users of information – youth, citizens, students, educators, business people, researchers, legislators – the human beings who create the community and the economy served by the collection. These information professionals are typically reference librarians, media specialists (chiefly in school library collections), specialists in bibliographic instruction (typically in academic collections) and circulation librarians who manage access to collected materials.

Amid this diverse array of titles and functions there are ancillary professions closely aligned with aspects of the information professions; extended definitions may include them in the situations suggested above. However, in common discourse it is unusual to consider members of the publishing industry, computer scientists, Web designers, booksellers or journalists to be members of the information professions, though each may work with information professionally. And while, to some extent, arrays of real objects may be found among information collections – typically in a section of the library identified as special collections – the primary designation of professionals who work exclusively with objects is likely to be curator, and their places of work

are likely to be museums or other cultural collections.

In these ancillary professions, the primary obligation of the practitioner is to serve other aspects of knowledge and technology than the design, management and delivery of information collections and services. It is impossible in any case to take a narrow view when defining the information professions; the field tends to expand as it is stimulated by technologies, applications and critical needs for human mediation between users and the array of informing possibilities at hand. Increasingly, traditional information resource centres now require extensive knowledge of computers, databases, DOCUMENT DELIVERY systems and BIBLIOGRAPHIC INSTRUC-TION. Larger institutions may employ webmasters or other specialists to create and monitor a presence on the WORLD WIDE WEB. Consequently, the realm of the information professional is best understood as a fluid domain where skills, practices and functions are increasingly dynamic and inclusive. Formal definitions of roles and titles – driven by the rapid evolutions of an INFORMATION SOCIETY – become increasingly provisional and tentative.

Fluidity and inclusiveness are characteristics of what Peter Drucker describes as 'the next society', which will be 'a knowledge society' (Drucker 2001: 2), where KNOWLEDGE flows freely, is available to everyone through access to education and provides all informed people with an even chance in a competitive world. The instant, global transfer of information allows the institutions of education, government, business and health to have an extraordinary reach to distant centres of knowledge, while maintaining services to a local community. In a society of this kind, there are multiple opportunities for professional work with information and its technologies, based on advanced knowledge of theory and practice, most of which must be acquired through a grounded – but extremely eclectic and combinatory – professional education.

However provisional it may be, a brief glossary of professional areas in contemporary information work will be useful. No fewer than six terms, here briefly described, are pertinent.

LIBRARIANSHIP

The area of practice, centred in libraries, devoted to the collection, organization and provision of information directly to a community, or multiple communities, of users.

INFORMATION SCIENCE

The scholarly area of study, research and theory devoted to evaluating the characteristics and processes of INFORMATION SYSTEMS, INFORMATION RETRIEVAL, INFORMATION-SEEKING BEHAVIOUR and HUMAN–COMPUTER INTERACTION.

INFORMATION MANAGEMENT

The area of practice, centred in organizations, devoted to systematic organization of information and data for storage, retrieval and transfer to users.

KNOWLEDGE MANAGEMENT

The area of practice, centred in organizations, devoted to facilitating information-based collaborations among units, based on the inter-related nature of their needs, goals and processes.

RECORDS MANAGEMENT

The area of practice, centred in organizations and institutions, devoted to assembling, maintaining and retrieving files of corporate transactions and activities over time.

ARCHIVES

A collection of permanent, preserved, original, historical records organized with pertinence to an institution's identity and growth, or field of research and activity over time.

Among these provisional definitions, we may see certain continuities. Each professional area is concerned with the collection, organization, retrieval and application of information. The collections typical of each professional area are assembled on the assumption of potential value to users. Each information professional works with files, catalogues or other records, irrespective of their content. Each area has evolved into relatively high dependence on information technology and digitization for control and access to information; and yet significant collected information is gathered, or originates, on paper and is given in face-to-face interactions.

Finally, we might say that most information professionals typically serve within the context of a larger institution or environment, embedded in a setting where communication and structure are complex and challenging to control. These roles may be further distinguished between the divi-

sions among academic, commercial or public institutions. Regardless of these differences, it is useful to note that all professionals in these areas are educated by significant exposures to similar themes in academic curricula.

Education for information professions

To understand the tasks of a contemporary information professional, and to grasp what information professionals think about in the course of their work, it is useful to examine the intentions of information education, and elements in typical graduate studies of library and information science at the beginning of the millennium.

Among the aims of such curricula, selected from the programme of one US university, these selected 'general educational objectives' may be considered exemplary intentions for an education in professional information work:

[To] Balance and integrate human and technical aspects of information systems, services and products
[To] Exhibit a strong client orientation in delivering information systems, services, and products, including an understanding of the implications of a culturally diverse society
[To] Analyze people's information requirements and match them with available technologies
[To] Analyze the flow, structure, and use of information among people and within organizations

(Drexel University 2000: 169)

Other objectives in similar institutions will include among their intentions such goals as institutional and disciplinary leadership; innovation in technology and its applications; information education for users; research and development devoted to information services and design; information architecture; and theory development. It is universal among contemporary institutions to assume great familiarity with computing, software and the transfer and presentation of information electronically; every curriculum addresses this need.

In information studies at the Master's degree level, typical curricula will emphasize competency in various combinations of the following areas:

- History and origins of knowledge; sociology of knowledge; ORGANIZATION OF KNOWLEDGE; INFORMATION SOCIETY.
- Information and its role in education, civic life and commerce; USER EDUCATION; INFORMATION LITERACY.
- COMMUNICATION; media; school libraries; storytelling; LITERACY; children's literature; popular culture.
- CLASSIFICATION; abstracting and indexing; structures of information; METADATA.
- Collection development and evaluation; community analysis.
- LIBRARY AUTOMATION; technical services and computer systems.
- Paper and electronic information tools; SEARCH ENGINES; general and special reference sources and services.
- GOVERNMENT PUBLISHING; BUSINESS INFORMATION SERVICES, HEALTH SCIENCE LIBRARIES; LEGAL INFORMATION; arts libraries.
- Development, management and evaluation of information systems and services; MARKETING of libraries.
- Information support for academic, public and special collection users.
- SPECIAL COLLECTIONS; ARCHIVES; PRESERVATION; MANUSCRIPTS; RECORDS MANAGEMENT.
- COGNITIVE SCIENCE; HUMAN–COMPUTER INTERACTION; ARTIFICIAL INTELLIGENCE.
- NETWORKS.
- MULTIMEDIA.
- Collaboration.
- INFORMATION RETRIEVAL; information design; INFORMATION THEORY; INFORMATION POLICY.
- Digital libraries (see DIGITAL LIBRARY); digitization and PRESERVATION.
- Design, use and management of DATABASES.
- Language processing.
- Software engineering; programming languages.
- CENSORSHIP; FREEDOM OF INFORMATION; INFORMATION ETHICS; INFORMATION LAW.
- Information security.
- RESEARCH IN LIBRARY AND INFORMATION SCIENCE.

This broad list is inevitably incomplete, depending on the interpretation of professional roles and responsibilities surrounding information in society and the educational mission of particular institutions. Curricular and professional practices related to information may be specifically classified by services for age groups (children and youth, young adults, adults); by disciplines and practices (law, medicine, business); by the rarity or historic importance of information (special collections, INCUNABULA); and by institutions where information is used (schools, public libraries, museums, prisons, hospitals); some practices may be directed to specific formats and the origins of information itself (multimedia, sound and video recordings; government publications).

The incomplete list of disciplinary subject matters – and its implied array of permutations – must also remind the reader that there are many kinds of professional work involved with information, many kinds of knowledge at or near the centre of the profession and several critical challenges for the field to meet, each in different domains of contemporary experience. Government, education and commerce are all dominated by questions of information and its control. Individual lives are at times overwhelmed by the tsunami of linked, telecommunicated, broadcasted and printed information at hand on any given day. Only the spoken word, perhaps because of its contemporary rarity, seems manageable in comparison to the overwhelming wave of mediated messages we receive, often unbidden.

Contemporary professional information education and practice inevitably must acknowledge an environment of change in tools and expectations. Information itself can be characterized by its great density, or by its challenging thinness and obscurity. The fluid and rapid nature of change in cultures, economies and governments means that much of what professionals know about information must be regarded as tentative and in need of confirmation. Further, it is increasingly difficult to assume narrow boundaries in information practice: interdisciplinary knowledge, and shared questions across subject matters, mean that a preparation for information work must overcome the classical limits of disciplines and knowledge.

Consequently, the information professional is required to understand more than information and its diversity. It is now necessary for the information professional to grasp the concept of a nearly infinite array of contexts, both organizational and personal. Further, in order to understand the formative concepts of information work, the professional must approach the human, interactive information search process with few assumptions, but rapidly make judgements of relevance and value in order to be helpful. A professional approach to the increasing complexity of human behaviours in relation to information problems must remain flexible, and dynamically open to change. Learning styles, research processes and information literacy are part of every engagement with information. It is fair to say that the information professions constantly require an attuned sensitivity to human cognition, an ability to map the logics of inquiry and authentic comfort in the intellectual practices of asking questions and pursuing responses to them.

If this diverse preparation for the field is necessary – and if its diversity means that no individual is likely to grasp or practice it fully, even in a lifetime – what is the meaning of 'mastery' in the information professions? How are we able to recognize professionalism in practice as a quality of mind and attitude? A professional approach to information attends to contexts as well as content, to processes as well as outcomes. As in all professions, a willingness to ask questions, contemplate an array of possibilities and become engaged in the problem-solving process offers an important model for practice. Finally, the professional is aware of constraints, and addresses the need of the information user for a response that satisfies. And yet it is also clear that, in a world of multiple and interconnected paths, there are no terminal contexts of inquiry. All professional information work remains dynamically open, and responsive to change.

Challenges of practice and promise for information professions

Describing the 'critical characteristics of the new information professional', José-Marie Griffiths (1998: 8) cites abilities required for professional success in a transformed information environment. Among them are collaboration; 'agility and flexibility' amid changing circumstances; centring on an institution's tasks, capabilities and human energies. First in her list is the ability to 'guide in the face of an uncertain future' – that is, to work willingly at an edge of knowledge and technology that may change underfoot. The metaphor, to be a guide, accepts that we work in a forested environment, where no path is worthy of long-term trust, and some paths must be created by

hand. As ever on a frontier, only the human mind – agile, flexible, collaborative – retains its authenticity and promise.

The information professional stands at the edge of the unknown every day: a new query arrives; a new program is written; a transforming capability becomes commonplace. And so it is useful to ask: How is a professional to sustain a mindful and responsible course? As always, it is important to understand the challenges of that course; several follow.

(1) A competitive information environment, in which knowledge has economic value and information makes critical differences to success and failure, carries certain risks. Increasingly, such environments can be found in every part of an information economy, corporate or academic. It is a commonplace to say that information is an industrial, economic and academic artefact, a source of social and personal power. Information professionals, whose responsibilities increasingly resemble those of medical or legal professionals, are accountable for the future robustness of such an environment, and for the well-being and security of persons who live inside it.

The pervasive nature of information, its fluidity and transformability, its extraordinary depth and completeness, does not come easily or fairly to all people. Our culture's dependence on electronic files makes the professional extraordinarily powerful, but also dependent and vulnerable. Issues of universal access, privacy and security, reasonable cost, fair policies for owners and users, and the overarching need to balance worldwide information inequities must drive a thoughtful profession in the twenty-first century. In developing countries, it is useful to recall, the essential technology is still the book, and, in such places, literacy is the essential skill.

(2) The contemporary information professional is also charged with understanding the information user, whose state of knowledge drives needs and defines literacy levels. The ability of a privileged public to interact directly with information, in libraries, homes, schools, automobiles, street corners and workplaces, inspires an obligation to advocate for information literacy and access to information tools as an issue indicative of the quality of life. All citizens deserve opportunities to learn the values and processes of access to information, and the potential effects of information skills on employment, health and independent learning. Genera-

tional disparities in information literacy, while likely to lessen over time, may always require attention. Disparities caused by economic and educational inequities may create intractable boundaries, however, and a responsive national information policy may be needed to adjust imbalances. An information professional must be a responsible advocate for such policies.

(3) The role of the information professional as a simple receiver, collector, mediator or processor of information is disappearing. Information professionals can anticipate new expansions of their work, including innovative activism as authors, synthesizers and designers of information. It is now difficult to stand outside an information problem and contribute usefully to its solution.

A projection of librarian's roles conducted in autumn 2001 (Braun 2002: 48) anticipates increases in the information specialist's roles in the creation of electronic resources and digital archiving, and slight decreases in such essential tasks as instruction, direction and evaluation of collections – still seen as the most significant things librarians do. It is likely that advances of this kind, again moved to the fore by the critical presence of technology and specialization, will require partnerships, interdependence and collaboration with such skilled partners as Web and graphic designers, information architects and content specialists.

Consequently, the study of communication and its effects on information environments, information transfer, resource development and problem solving cannot be overestimated. With such new emphases, it is likely that communication itself will become more challenging, and more likely to induce the tensions that accompany different priorities and preparations. The health of a communication environment must also be seen as a challenge to leadership.

(4) In the final decades of the twentieth century, the information professions entered, and endured, a cascade of technical, social, political, educational and economic changes, and this evolution has carried over into the twenty-first-century. Jobs and the definition of work remain in transition. Families and their access to information remain in transition. Communities and their centres of information remain in transition. The nature and permanence of emerging media are sharply divergent from the past. Languages spoken in any major shopping district may become too numerous to count. Communication is everywhere.

These are only some of the places, situations and tools influencing how people live with and encounter each other, how they teach themselves and explore their culture, and how, in every message, they express and communicate their values. Increasingly, information provision will be challenged to respond to alterations in the landscapes of civic life caused by shifting populations, changes in global economies and increasingly incomplete public educations.

Libraries and information centres, however, have always observed steady continuities amid change. People continue to ask questions. The knowledge they seek must be encountered with a full awareness of its contexts. All users are likely to require some guiding advice. And human beings continue to value literacy, and they continue to seek and read books.

Collections must be assembled, and attention must be paid to human beings. It is a professional challenge to provide assistance with a lasting sense of continuity, integrity and clarity, an adherence to ethical standards and authentic respect for others, and a desire to inspire people to overcome the challenges of their own lives. At its heart, the information profession is about the strength and courage to embrace informed change; and it is a critical characteristic of the information professions to uphold 'a commitment to the success of others' (Griffiths 1998: 10).

(5) Technology evolves rapidly, and competitively, leading to a diversity of tools, hardware, SOFTWARE, formats, platforms, applications and PROTOCOLS. The information professional is required to sustain continuously expansive competencies, and to remain steadily aware of how to evaluate new technologies as they are invented. Part of a professional vigilance, however, requires the professional to ensure that technology does not drive human inquiry, or that the inadequacies of tools do not compromise the independence of the scholar. Moreover, this rapid evolution of technology means the constant adaptation of records, or the maintenance of antiquated devices for unlocking special formats. Information professionals, aware of the speed of technical change, must be prepared to rescue information from the grip of expiring platforms.

(6) A culture of information needs to be a vigilant culture of inquiry as well. Information professionals are challenged to participate – at

their workplaces, among their colleagues and at conferences – in rigorous, systemic, critical thinking about the critical issues of assistance, confidentiality and PRIVACY, the interfaces between humans and computers, and the design of services that retain the human touch. Such vigilance is enhanced by Donald Schön's essential concept of 'reflective practice' (Schön 1983), where professional behaviours are regarded as experimental steps or 'moves', and fundamental professional acts are part of a 'conversation with the situation'. Such strategies are useful in an environment of information, where flashy immediacy tends to veil the long-term impacts of change. Information decisions are always decisions with resonant but distant consequences, and it is rare that easy or simple solutions are sufficient over time.

(7) Increasingly, it is useful to see the information professional as the singular model of thought and action for the information society, examining questions, unknowns and intentions with an eye to combining the contextual information at hand, and the new information required, in order to achieve an objective. Just as a physician or an engineer will address physical problems through a heuristic process of diagnosis and experiment, the information professional studies the given unknown, and acts with tentative steps to reduce it. The information professional is an agent of inquiry, and an instrument of change. Connections to information move a situation forward and bring its complexities under control. In an environment where specific content or knowledge must be discovered and brought to a user in order for a problem to be addressed, the information professional performs the invisible acts of process – searching, querying, communicating, connecting – that expand the possibilities of completion.

(8) Technological fluency does not always translate into educative fluency; consequently, the information professions must assure the development of a strong teaching function, which is likely to reflect the steady learning required by the evolution of tools. This link to educative acts and educative partnerships needs to be understood and supported among a wide array of potential partners.

(9) As societies and cultures become increasingly dependent on information technology and immediate access to a limitless well of knowledge, the technocracy of the computer may grow increasingly challenging to the human being. Problem solving in the domain of the information professional will continue to require a sustained human presence, an instrumental person, able to assist decisions and provide control over information tools and the interpretation of data. The information professions will be increasingly challenged to avoid reification and reduction in the face of complexity and cost. One way to remain attentive is to monitor events and issues in adjacent areas of knowledge, particularly communication, computer science, cognitive psychology and education.

(10) A lasting challenge for the information professional is to master the ambiguity of discovering an identity through service to others, in a way that also serves the sense of a professional self. Each assemblage of tools and resources brought into existence is constructed in expectation of its use, and in anticipation of a question that has not yet been asked. When the question is asked, and the assemblage of tools is put to constructive use, the information gathered disappears with the user. Consequently, an information professional must often find an identity in evanescent acts, however unclear, uncertain or unresolved they may be.

What is mastery?

The information professional knows how to interpret needs for information, how to move useful information into place and how to assure the authority and currency of the information given. As politics, economics, law and social policy initiatives increasingly address information, INTELLECTUAL PROPERTY, ownership and COPYRIGHT, the voice of the deeply informed professional will continue to be a vital one; it is not a thing a professional avoids. The information professional continuously thinks about collections, processes, languages, access to and use of information as evolving problems, never fully resolved, to be addressed steadily and thoughtfully over time. Such thinking at its best will always occur in a situation where empirical inquiry, ethical integrity and fair assessments of performance are the permanent values of information practice.

References

Braun, L.W. (2002) 'New roles: A librarian by any name', *Library Journal* 127: 46–9.

Drexel University (2000) *Drexel University Graduate Studies Catalog 2000–2001*, Philadelphia, Pennsylvania: Drexel University.

Drucker, P. (2001) 'The next society: A survey of the near future', *The Economist* 361(8,246): 2.

Griffiths, J.-M. (1998) 'The new information professional', *Bulletin of the American Society for Information Science* 24(3).

Schön, D.A. (1983) *The Reflective Practitioner: How Professionals Think in Action*, Basic Books.

Further reading

Advances in Librarianship (Annual) Academic Press.

Annual Review of Information Science and Technology (Annual).

Bowker Annual of Library and Book Trade Information, Reed Elsevier.

Criddle, S., Dempsey, L. and Heseltine, R. (eds) (1999) *Information Landscapes for a Learning Society*, Library Association.

Encyclopedia of Library and Information Science (1968–) Marcel Dekker.

Library and Information Science Annual, Libraries Unlimited.

Wilson, T.D. and Allen, D.K. (eds) (1999) *Exploring the Contexts of Information Behaviour*, Taylor Graham.

SEE ALSO: information science; information technology; libraries; organization of knowledge; philosophy of librarianship; professionalism; quality in library and information services; research in library and information science

DAVID CARR

INFORMATION RETRIEVAL

Origins and history

The early roots of information retrieval (IR) research are in the research on CLASSIFICATION and INDEXING. The origins of modern IR research can be traced back to the early 1950s when Mortimer TAUBE's Uniterm indexing system was compared in two experiments to more conventional classification and indexing systems. One of the experiments was the ASTIA–Uniterm experiment in the USA comparing uniterms and SUBJECT HEADINGS, and the other the Cranfield–Uniterm test in the United Kingdom comparing uniterms and UNIVERSAL DECIMAL CLASSIFICATION (UDC). These efforts continued in the late 1950s and early 1960s in the paradigmatic Cranfield experiments I and II, which laid the foundation of the laboratory approach to IR research (see below). The statistical approach to

IR also began in the late 1950s, when Hans Peter LUHN discovered the relationship of document word distributions to document content description: mid-frequency words are good statistical content descriptors.

The development of INFORMATION AND COMMUNICATION TECHNOLOGY has been the major driving force affecting research and development in IR from 1960 to date, from early small batch-mode IR systems to today's large Web-based systems.

IR process and systems

The IR process may be seen as a special case of INFORMATION-SEEKING BEHAVIOUR where computers are used to search, retrieve and access desired information. Within the process, a person having an information need, based on his/her work task or other activities, uses an IR system either directly as an end-user via the system's user INTERFACE, or indirectly through an intermediary, e.g. a LIBRARIAN. The information need (request) is thence represented in the IR system's query language. In order to be able to supply the desired information, the IR system has to collect and represent such information, and store the representations – full documents, their BIBLIOGRAPHIC DESCRIPTIONS or other METADATA – in a DATABASE. In addition, the IR system has to implement an ALGORITHM – a matching technique – for comparing the information need and document representations. The result of this comparison is a set of documents logically matching the query, or a ranked list of best matching documents.

IR systems are based on various retrieval models. A retrieval model determines the principles used in document and request representation, and their matching.

Based on their focus on the IR process and assumed retrieval models, the main approaches in IR research from the 1960s to the 2000s may be discussed under the headings of online bibliographic IR, best-match IR, user-oriented IR and cognitive IR.

Online bibliographic IR

Online bibliographic IR systems developed in the early 1970s. Originally they provided access to bibliographic records through a query language based on BOOLEAN LOGIC. It was frequently possible to retrieve the records through fields for intellectual indexing as well as FREE-TEXT SEARCHING in titles and abstracts. Search strategies to suit various IR situations developed. The focus was on ONLINE access, full-text indexing, and request representation and matching within Boolean logic. In the 1980s the online database industry expanded, many full-text databases in diverse subject areas emerged and in the 1990s the WWW became the common platform for online access.

Best-match IR

Best-match IR research also focused on document and request representation and matching, but developed, in contrast to Boolean logic, retrieval models that allowed for ranking the matching documents in a decreasing order of expected relevance to the request. Major best-match models (with representative systems) include the vector space model (SMART), probabilistic models (Okapi) and inference network models (InQuery).

Originally best-match IR research was strictly laboratory bound, using small test collections, but by the 1990s information technology allowed large-scale applications. Major WWW SEARCH ENGINES employ best-match retrieval models. Much of best-match IR research is based on the laboratory approach where a test collection consisting of a document database, a test request set, and a set of relevance assessments is used. The relevance assessments identify, for each request, the set of relevant documents that is of interest in retrieval. In IR experiments, the capability of IR systems or methods in retrieving the relevant documents while retaining the irrelevant documents is assessed. Major performance measures are recall and precision:

$$\text{Recall} = \frac{\text{Number of relevant documents retrieved}}{\text{Number of relevant documents in collection}}$$

$$\text{Precision} = \frac{\text{Number of relevant documents retrieved}}{\text{Number of documents retrieved}}$$

Typically, evaluation results are expressed as average precision over standard recall points, e.g. at recall points 0.0, 0.1, 0.2,..., 1.0, and as precision-recall graphs. Alternatively, recall and precision may be considered at standard document cut-off values, e.g. after retrieval 5, 10, 20, 30,..., 200 documents. To compare systems, the results are averaged across requests.

A major innovation within the best-match retrieval models was relevance feedback whereby a query may automatically be reformulated after the user's assessment of initial query results. Within the general approach of best-match IR research, methods for automatic document clustering, categorization, FILTERING and routing were also explored.

User-oriented IR

User-oriented IR research developed in the 1970s as a response to the previous approaches' focus on the system components. This research focused on persons' information needs, their expression as search tasks and the interaction between the persons and the interfaces or intermediaries of IR systems. The research drew influences from USER STUDIES and INFORMATION-SEEKING RESEARCH, often using social science research methods. The IR system setting was mainly assumed to be the Boolean online IR environment.

Cognitive IR

IR research based on the cognitive approach began to emerge in the late 1970s. Its aim is to encompass the whole IR process from document indexing to matching techniques, and from work tasks to information needs, query formulation and interaction, and to analyse these at the cognitive level as interaction of cognitive structures. Cognitive IR research was able to bridge the gap between user-oriented IR and best-match approaches, and resulted in the development of intelligent intermediary systems for IR, based on EXPERT SYSTEMS and knowledge-based systems technology.

Current trends

IR lacks a coherent body of knowledge; it is rather a collection of diverse approaches. A coherent IR theory would require models, concepts and tools for the analysis of human discourse and communication, language, and documents and collections, people, tasks and needs, IR models and techniques. The findings of such diverse areas should be synthesized together. This requirement is not met by today's approaches; it is a task of tall order indeed.

At the beginning of the third millennium, IR research explores diverse areas including:

- Retrieval models and methods such as logical and probabilistic models, language models, learning techniques and linguistics applied to IR.
- Text retrieval, including scalability issues, and mono- and multilingual IR in collections.
- MULTIMEDIA IR – image, video, speech and music IR, and IR in the WWW or hypermedia environments.
- Information extraction, question answering and summarization.
- Categorization, filtering and routing.
- News topic detection and tracking.
- IR interfaces, structured documents and novel ways of presenting search results instead of plain document listings.
- Task-based and user-oriented IR, and IR learning environments.

The concept of relevance has regained its position in IR discourse and this has led to rethinking about IR evaluation measures and methods. The denominating measures of recall and precision have been challenged for their sufficiency when interactive and/or multimedia IR systems are evaluated, when multiple types and/or levels of relevance are considered, or when performing task and/or user-oriented evaluation.

Further reading

Ellis, D. (1996) *Progress and Problems in Information Retrieval*, London: Library Association Publishing, p. 220.

Ingwersen, P. (1992) *Information Retrieval Interaction*, London, Taylor Graham, p. 246.

Sparck Jones, K. and Willett, P. (eds) *Key Papers in Information Retrieval*, ACM Digital Library (www.acm.org/dl/).

SEE ALSO: artificial intelligence; categorization; classification; cognitive science; computer; computer science; data compression; database; DIALOG; document clustering; free-text searching; Human–Computer Interaction; hypermedia; indexing; informatics; information systems; mark-up languages; neural network; organization of knowledge; text retrieval; thesaurus; virtual library

KALERVO JÄRVELIN

INFORMATION SCIENCE

A discipline that investigates the characteristics of information and the nature of the information transfer process, whilst not losing sight of the practical aspects of collecting, collating and evaluating information and organizing its dissemination through appropriate intellectual apparatus and technology.

Background

Information science is probably unique in being defined in terms of what its practitioners do, rather than vice versa. Around 1910–20 scientists were having problems finding information and other scientists started to specialize in helping them. The term 'literature chemist' and others came into use to describe them and by the 1940s the generic term 'information scientist' was being used. What they did was first described as 'information science' by Chris Hanson of ASLIB in 1956. Their attitudes, methods and backgrounds were quite different from those of the traditional custodians of information, the librarians. By 1958 a sufficient number of such individuals felt it necessary to join together and found the INSTITUTE OF INFORMATION SCIENTISTS so that specialist education and standards could be promoted.

An information scientist is anyone handling information on behalf of another and who will often have sufficient subject knowledge to evaluate much of the information passed to clients. (Normally this excludes recreational matter and information associated with formal education.) Information is transferable knowledge. It need not be alphanumeric: for example, a collection of exploded boilers and pipes could be an important information resource for a safety consultant. Having defined an information scientist and information, we can now define information science, as above. Numerous other definitions exist. Wellisch (1972) collected thirty-nine. It is also effectively defined by the Institute of Information Scientists' (IIS) *Criteria for Information Science*, which lay down guidelines for IIS approved information science courses. A new version is to be developed by CILIP.

Documentation is now almost a passé term in English, but was once a common near-synonym, as is INFORMATICS, a more recent term of Russian origin. Care should be taken in translating the French and Spanish phrases – *sciences de l'information* and *ciencias de la información* – as these have the meaning 'mass communication' and/or 'media studies'.

The dominance of scientific information in the development of information science was a demand-led phenomenon, determined by economics. Although hypothetically a literature graduate could be an information scientist in, say, a Shakespearean Research Institute, there has always been far more money available to pay science graduates to do information work in the pharmaceutical and other science-based industries. Since the mid-1980s BUSINESS INFORMATION and LEGAL INFORMATION have become increasingly important.

Despite its origins, information science is a social science because it deals with an artefact of man: information. Wersig (1993) calls it a 'postmodern science' because (like, for example, ecology) it is driven by the need to develop strategies to solve the problems caused by the classical sciences and technologies. Wersig distinguishes the classical sciences as those driven by a need to understand how the world works. Information science certainly lacks a unified theoretical structure such as one finds in the natural sciences. We are still awaiting our Linnaeus, our Mendeleyev or even our Keynes.

Initially research in information science could be regarded as at the apex of a pyramidal structure. Manufacturing industry and commerce was the base for a smaller research function. This in turn supported information departments, which, size permitting, had some capacity for R&D. Additionally a small amount of government-funded research took place in academic institutions. Since the 1970s there has been a growing contribution to R&D from the burgeoning information industry.

History

The initial dominance of scientific information, referred to above, has meant that the Royal Society's Scientific Information Conference in 1948 and its published *Proceedings* are often taken as the benchmark. The existence of an information problem in science was recognized much earlier, as is evidenced by the introduction of review journals (*Berlinisches Jahrbuch für die Pharmacie*, 1795) and abstracts journals (*Pharmaceutisches Central-Blatt*, 1830). In 1851 Joseph Henry, in his *Annual Report* as Secretary of the Smithsonian Institution, drew attention to the mounting tide of new knowledge and prophesied that it 'will begin to totter under its own weight' unless 'well digested indexes…to memoirs, papers and parts of scientific transactions and systematic works' were produced.

Information science has a history of taking techniques from the past and adapting them to present needs. *Shephard's Citations* (1871) was the ancestor of the *Science Citation Index* born in the 1960s. Jacquard's loom control cards (1801) were the forebears of punched cards – which have themselves now passed into information science history. *The* seminal event considerably predated Gutenberg. This was the production by Cardinal Hugo, aided by 500 monks, of his Concordance to the Vulgate version of the Bible. Then, as today, information science was virtually at the centre of contemporary intellectual and socio-economic activity! Some 700 years later, in 1958, aided by an IBM mainframe computer, Peter LUHN produced concordance-like indexing. The first educational programme covering all aspects of information science was run by Jason FARRADANE in 1961 at City University, London.

Literature of information science

Probably the first distinct information science literature type was the literature guide. An early example was W. Ostwald's *Die chemische Literatur und die Organisation der Wissenschaft* (Leipzig, 1919). Because of the lack of a distinct boundary between library and information science, it is not practicable to differentiate between the two in bibliometric and other studies. Such studies show the dominance of the single-author paper (characteristic of social science literature), and of English-language papers (Bottle and Efthimiades 1984). Several authors have commented on the poor quality of LIS literature; perhaps that is why it has a short half-life, of around two years (calculated from interlending data from Montanelli and Mak 1988). Although it is doubling in size about every fourteen years, as is that of chemistry, the total size of the LIS literature is only about 500,000 documents, compared with about twenty times as many in chemistry (Bottle and Efthimiades 1984).

References

Bottle, R.T. and Efthimiades, E.N. (1984) 'Library and

information science literature: Authorship and growth patterns', *Journal of Information Science* 9: 107–16.

Montanelli, D.S. and Mak, C. (1988) 'Library practitioners' use of library literature', *Library Trends* 36: 765–83.
Wellisch, H. (1972) 'From information science to informatics: A terminological investigation', *Journal of Librarianship* 4: 157–87.
Wersig, G. (1993) 'Information science: The study of postmodern knowledge usage', *Information Processing and Management* 29: 229–39.

Further reading

Bottle, R.T. (1993) 'Information, communication and libraries', in R.T. Bottle and J.F.B. Rowland (eds) *Information Sources in Chemistry*, 4ᵗʰ edn, Bowker Saur, pp. 3–10 [a brief introduction to information problems in science].
Price, D.J. de Solla (1963) *Little Science, Big Science*, Columbia University Press [the right book at the right time; it alerted scientists to the information growth problem in science – and is still well worth reading].
Vickery, B. (1999) 'A century of scientific and technical information', *Journal of Documentation* 55: 476–527.

SEE ALSO: bibliometrics; citation analysis; informatics; information professions; information science education; information theory; organization of knowledge; sociology of knowledge

R.T. BOTTLE

INFORMATION SCIENCE EDUCATION

Programmes of study designed to develop the knowledge and skills required for the provision and management of information in a complex global information and communication environment.

Programmes are of three different kinds:

1   Programmes offered either at graduate or undergraduate level. Sometimes available in modular form, they typically prepare graduates for entry to information practice and are accredited or recognized by professional associations in the information sector.

2   Graduate research programmes at Master's and Doctoral levels that normally prepare graduates for an academic career and increasingly for a practice career since the development of professional Doctorate programmes.

3   CONTINUING PROFESSIONAL DEVELOPMENT programmes or short courses. Delivered as seminars, workshops or conferences, these programmes are tailored to the needs of information practitioners and focus on a broad range of current concerns from Web design to the management and MARKETING of information services, and from copyright and regulation through to DUBLIN CORE and METADATA.

Programmes in information science

CURRICULUM

The core elements of the curriculum in INFORMATION SCIENCE are shaped by the body of knowledge on which information practice is based and the skills and attitudes required to use that knowledge effectively. The body of knowledge is informed by both information science and information practice, and is broader in scope than traditional areas of librarianship (Callison and Tilley 2001).

The philosophy of information science and its history demonstrate its interdisciplinary nature (Saracevic 1992). Some theories and concepts, such as information need, CLASSIFICATION, INFORMATION RETRIEVAL, precision, INFORMATION-SEEKING BEHAVIOUR, information utilization and information resources, are unique to information provision. Other theories and concepts from cognate disciplines such as psychology, COMMUNICATION, COGNITIVE SCIENCE, COMPUTER SCIENCE, sociology, education, philosophy and management are relevant to information provision. Examples include cognition, interpersonal communication, human information processing, HUMAN–COMPUTER INTERACTION, electronic communications, instructional design, EPISTEMOLOGY and organizational behaviour.

The field of information practice continues to diversify with a broad range of job titles for information work as new labour markets emerge in response to global, political and economic influences, particularly in the business and high-technology sectors (Kirk and Sellers 1999; Callison and Tilley 2001). These can include information officer, knowledge manager, curator, multimedia designer, librarian and competitive intelligence or information manager. Underlying these varied titles is a core of information skills focusing on the creation, dissemination and utilization of information (Bruce 1999).

Considering the scope of information science as a discipline and the breadth of information practice, it is to be expected that the curriculum will be characterized by diversity in the knowledge base on which it rests. This multidisciplinarity is also reflected in programmes being offered by departments based in very different intellectual areas including business and management, computing or communication (Feather 1997; Rochester 1997; Sutton 2001).

Funding, economic and business imperatives mean courses of study may be tailored to particular markets and learning outcomes (Rochester 1997; Callison and Tilley 2001). Information and communication skills continue to be necessary in all types of information-dependent work but entrepreneurship is beginning to be sought by employers (Johnson 2000; Curry 2000). The KNOWLEDGE MANAGEMENT area that has emerged in business and organizational development has generated specialised programmes (Todd and Southon 2000; Aiyepeku 2001). Interest in INFORMATICS and its possibilities for illuminating the social and cultural impact of technologies has increased as a consequence of exponential growth in INFORMATION AND COMMUNICATION TECHNOLOGY (Warner 2001). This is reflected in programme development (White 2001) and especially so in informatics. Examples of programme areas include Veterinary Informatics offered at the University of Strathclyde, Scotland; Informatics and Systems offered at Loughborough University; and Healthcare Information offered at the University of Sheffield. The University of Washington and Rutgers University in the USA both specialize in Informatics, and the University of New South Wales in Australia offers a programme in Health Informatics. There are also some active research groups such as the Social Informatics group at Indiana University and a similar group at the Manchester Metropolitan University.

Lifelong learning capabilities are increasingly important educational goals and they are essential for graduates competing in dynamic global job markets (Stoker 2000). INFORMATION LITERACY plays a crucial role in both lifespan learning and employability in societies where information and communication technology use has expanded exponentially and the numbers of students in post-secondary education have increased (Rochester 1997). Information professionals play a key role in developing complex information skills in all learning and teaching, workplace and community situations (Bruce and Candy 2000; Peacock 2001). Flexible learning, alternative approaches to learning design and the growing importance of the social contexts of information encourage students from disciplines other than information science to develop their information handling skills to a deeper level than is possible in the end-user-oriented short courses delivered by libraries (Feather 1997; Hornby and Andretta 2001).

In addition to developing students' knowledge, courses in information science are designed to develop students' skills, attitudes and professional ethics (Kirk and Sellers 1999). This development is supported by teaching and learning strategies used in implementing the curriculum. Among these strategies are tutorials, seminars, lectures, learning contracts, computer laboratory sessions, computer-assisted learning, online discussions, group collaboration, oral and written presentations, case studies and fieldwork. Practical work is a feature of the information science curriculum as an introduction to information practice, an illustration of the application of theoretical principles and an opportunity for career exploration and portfolio development (Yerbury and Kirk 1991).

Technological developments and widespread interest have led to the electronic delivery of some programme components to support the flexibility expected by local and international students and the business, information and knowledge management markets (Feather 1997; Alderman and Milne 2000; Tyler 2001).

ROLE OF PRACTITIONERS AND PROFESSIONAL ASSOCIATIONS

Most information science programmes rely on the involvement of practitioners to ensure courses remain relevant to information practice. Curriculum development teams frequently consist of faculty, students and practitioners. As teachers, practitioners may have roles as panellists, guest lecturers and sessional teaching staff or mentors for students.

A number of professional associations act as accreditation bodies (see ACCREDITATION OF LIS SCHOOLS), recognizing qualifications as appropriate for admission to professional membership and supporting information science education by highlighting the achievements of leading educators and students, and by organizing regular conferences as forums for the consideration of educational issues. These associations include the INSTITUTE OF INFORMATION SCIENTISTS (now part of CILIP); the Australian Library and Information Association; the AMERICAN SOCIETY FOR INFORMATION SCIENCE AND TECHNOLOGY; and the ASSOCIATION FOR LIBRARY AND INFORMATION SCIENCE EDUCATION.

INTERNATIONAL CO-OPERATION

As communication technologies reduce the impact of distance and global changes influence information development, co-operative endeavours in information science continue to be important. Universities have contributed to innovative education internationally by providing curriculum advice, programmes onshore and offshore, through the exchange of teaching and learning materials, courseware, staff exchanges and sponsorship schemes for students. Whilst developing regions vary significantly, recognition of the environmental changes Western information science education has had to embrace, and the edge information technology can offer, means that sustainable innovation and development is progressing despite resource constraints (Ocholla 2000; Rehman 2000; Aiyepeku 2001).

References

Aiyepeku, W.O. (2001) 'Grafting marketable KM skills into education for information in Africa', *Education for Information* 19: 19–33.

Alderman, B. and Milne, T. (2000) 'Designing a Web-based distance education course within a constructivist learning environment', *Education for Library and Information Services: Australia* 17: 51–61.

Bruce, C. and Candy, P. (2000) 'Information literacy programs: People, politics and potential', in C. Bruce and P. Candy (eds.) *Information Literacy around the World: Advances in Programs and Research*, Centre for Information Studies, Charles Sturt University.

Bruce, H. (1999) 'A new perspective on information education from Australia', *Education for Information* 17: 187–98.

Callison, D. and Tilley, C.L. (2001) 'Descriptive impressions of the library and information education evolution of 1988–1998 as reflected in job announcements, ALISE descriptors, and new course titles', *Journal of Education for Library and Information Science* 42: 181–99.

Curry, A. (2000) 'Canadian LIS education: Trends and issues', *Education for Information* 18: 325–37.

Feather, J. (1997) 'The future of professional education in library and information studies', in J. Elkin and T. Wilson (eds.) *The Education of Library and Information Professionals in the United Kingdom*, Mansell Publishing Limited.

Hornby, S. and Andretta, S. (2001) 'The Janus-face of information professionals', *Education for Information* 19: 35–45.

Johnson, I.M. (2000) 'Catching the tide: Environmental pressures for an emphasis on management in the library and information science curriculum', *Education for Library and Information Services: Australia* 17: 29–49.

Kirk, J. and Sellers, S. (1999) 'Education and training', in M. Line (ed.) *Librarianship and Information Work Worldwide 1999*, Bowker Saur.

Ocholla, D.N. (2000) 'Training for library and information studies: A comparative overview of LIS education in Africa', *Education for Information* 18: 33–52.

Peacock, J. (2001) 'Teaching skills for teaching librarians: Postcards from the edge', *Australian Academic and Research Libraries* 32: 26–42.

Rehman, S. (2000) *Preparing the Information Professional: An Agenda for the future*, Contributions in Librarianship and Information Science Number 93, Greenwood Press.

Rochester, M.K. (1997) *Education for Librarianship in Australia*, Mansell Publishing Limited.

Rutgers University, New Brunswick, USA (www.sclis.rutgers.edu/iti/).

Saracevic, T. (1992) 'Information science: Origin, evolution and relations', in P. Vakkari and B. Cronin (eds) *Conceptions of Library and Information Science: Historical, Empirical and Theoretical Perspectives*, Taylor Graham.

Stoker, D. (2000) 'Persistence and change: Issues for LIS educators in the first decade of the twenty first century', *Education for Information* 18: 115–22.

Sutton, S.A. (2001) 'Trends, trend projections and crystal ball gazing', *Journal of Education for Library and Information Science* 42: 241–7.

Todd, R.J. and Southon, G. (2000) 'Knowledge management: Education for information professionals in the age of the mind', *ASIS Proceedings* 37: 503–17.

Tyler, A. (2001) 'A survey of distance learning library and information science courses delivered via the Internet', *Education for Information* 19: 47–59.

Warner, J. (2001) 'W(h)ither information science?/!', *The Library Quarterly* 71: 231–42.

White, H.D. (2001) ' Computing a curriculum: Descriptor-based domain analysis for educators', *Information Processing and Management* 37: 91–117.

Yerbury, H. and Kirk, J. (1991) 'Career planning in information science education', in J. Rowley (ed.) *Information 90*, ASLIB.

Further reading

Indiana University, Bloomington (www.slis.indiana.edu/SI/index.html).

Loughborough University (www.lboro.ac.uk/departments/dils/pgprogs/pgis/pgisph.html).

Manchester Metropolitan University (www.mmu.ac.uk/h-ss/dic/research/sigroup.htm).

University of New South Wales, Sydney, Australia

(www.nsw.edu.au/programmes/completepgptog.
htm).

University of Sheffield (www.shef.ac.uk/is/courses/
modules/infpgt.html#INF6370).

University of Strathclyde, Glasgow, United Kingdom
(www.dis.strath.ac.uk/research/informan/).

University of Washington, Seattle, USA (www.ischool.
washington.edu/informatics/).

SEE ALSO: information literacy; information
management; information professions;
information skills; knowledge; library
associations; library education

NICOLA PARKER AND JOYCE KIRK

INFORMATION-SEEKING BEHAVIOUR

The complex patterns of actions and interactions
that people engage in when seeking information
of whatever kind and for whatever purpose. Like
its companion expression 'information needs', its
utility is more in its denotive than its connotive
power – to denote the presence of such activities
or patterns rather than to provide any descriptive
content. The expression is used in a wide-ranging
way to refer to any context where information is
sought, and it encompasses all forms of information seeking. In these respects, too, the expression is similar to 'information need', in that it
probably does little harm – and serves a certain
convenience – if it is used as a shorthand to refer
to activities that are then described or explained
in detail, but like the notion of 'information
need' the danger is that the expression is used as
a substitute for such description or explanation.

The concept has its home in the field of USER
STUDIES (Wilson 1994) and as such its history
may be considered to date back to the first
studies of scientific communication and information use (Royal Society 1948). Its use has also
changed in line with developments in that field.
Early references to information-seeking. behaviour would be referring to scientists' use of
formal and informal communication channels
and of a predominantly quantitative flavour.
Unpacked, the expression 'information-seeking
behaviour of scientists' would, typically, be referring to the different proportion of scientists
consulting with colleagues, using journals or
books, employing ABSTRACTING AND INDEXING
SERVICES, receiving preprints or reprints, attend-

ing conferences and their associated preferences
in terms of channel.

Over time there has been a shift towards more
theoretically grounded studies and to the application of qualitative, hybrid or methodologically
pluralist techniques. The denotation and limited
connotation of the expression has evolved in line
with these developments. In this respect the
nature and quality of what lies behind the
expression is totally dependent on the quality of
the studies themselves. The expression has as
shallow or deep a conceptualization as the
studies in which it is rooted or the actions to
which it refers. In this respect, too, it is impossible clearly to separate any historical analysis of
the use of the expression from consideration of
the associated terms 'information needs' and
'information uses'.

Nevertheless, the expression does have some
interesting internal characteristics worth noting.
The 'information-seeking' component of the expression might be thought to promise more than
it delivers in implying a level of positive activity
that might not be borne out by studies of the
individual or group, where passive 'information
gathering' might be a more accurate description
than 'information seeking'. The 'behaviour' component of the expression might also be seen as
operating a little ambiguously in having connotations of 'behaviourism'. In this respect expressions such as 'information-seeking activities' or
'information-seeking patterns' distance the notion from that of 'behaviourism' and also link the
notion philosophically closer to its true family of
concepts connected with reasons and actions, and
further from concepts of the stimulus and response group. But, again, like the notion of
'information need' the notion of 'information-
seeking behaviour' is such a useful catch-all that
these philosophical caveats are unlikely to see it
going out of fashion.

References

Royal Society (1948) *Report on the Royal Society
Scientific Information Conference*, Royal Society.
Wilson, T.D. (1994) 'Information needs and uses: Fifty
years of progress', in B.C. Vickery (ed.) *Fifty Years of
Information Progress*, ASLIB, pp. 15–51.

Further reading

Annual Review of Information Science and Technology,
vols. 1–7 (1966–72), 9 (1974), 13 (1978), 21 (1986)

and 25 (1990) [contain review chapters on information needs and uses].

Bradley, J. and Sutton, B. (eds) (1993) 'Symposium on qualitative research: Theory methods and applications', *Library Quarterly* 63: 405–527 [special issue devoted to papers describing qualitative and methodologically pluralist approaches].

Hounsell, D. and Winn, V. (eds) (1981) 'Symposium issue on qualitative approaches to the study of information problems', *Social Science Information Studies* 1: 203–56 [special issue on the potential of qualitative techniques in information studies].

SEE ALSO: information retrieval; information-seeking research

DAVID ELLIS

INFORMATION-SEEKING RESEARCH

Research on INFORMATION-SEEKING BEHAVIOUR and processes belongs to the general study of information behaviour as an important field of INFORMATION SCIENCE. Historically, the research on information seeking can be divided into three periods: 1960–85, 1986–1995, and 1996–. During the first period the research expanded and can be loosely divided into four categories of study: USER STUDIES, use studies, information behaviour studies and studies of information dissemination. The focus was on information service provision and quality. Often users were seen as scientists seeking scholarly information. Accordingly, the first proposed models of information seeking regard the user as a researcher affected by a variety of systems (Paisley 1968) later simplified by Allen (1969). Allen's model has been cited as the first theoretical foundation in later studies of information seeking. Allen, and in particular T.D. Wilson (1981), moves the research into the professional and INFORMATION MANAGEMENT domains – away from the library sphere. Wilson proposed a general model of information-seeking behaviour consisting of three basic components: the user domain, i.e. the user's experiences, including his or her tasks and social reference group; the information systems domain consisting of intermediaries and IT; and the information unit domain, containing units of information of human or documentary nature. In relation to the latter domain we observe the important distinction between seeking information from human resources, e.g. colleagues, and searching documentary systems, i.e. INFORMA-

TION RETRIEVAL (IR) systems. Wilson emphasises the crucial step away from merely descriptive studies, that is, of asking why individual users act as they act. This leads to the investigations of information needs and user-intermediary interaction, already analytically initiated by R.S. Taylor (1968).

Information need formation and development, including search interviewing, were empirically studied and modelled in an information-seeking and public library context by Ingwersen (1982) and in terms of the famous ANOMALOUS STATE OF KNOWLEDGE (ASK) concept developed by Belkin, Brooks and Oddy (1982). The central point of ASK is that a problem situation perceived by the user acts as the trigger for the recognition of the ASK by the user, leading to an information need that is variable over time according to the influence of the encountered knowledge sources (human or documentary) on the current state of knowledge.

The second period is rich in empirical studies and activity models of seeking processes. The period first saw the appearance of the famous Dervin and Nilan (1986) sense-making approach to information-seeking research, including the notion of a KNOWLEDGE gap, and the information required to bridge that gap between information situation and solution. Their approach is founded in human communication theory and has led to a vast number of empirical studies of user-centred information behaviour and seeking situations. A second important approach is the empirically based phenomenological six-phase model proposed by Kuhlthau (1991). Her phases relate explicitly to persons in working environments with perceived tasks and problems that require information in order to be solved: initiation, selection, exploration, formulation, collection and presentation. She also operates with levels of uncertainty found in the task solution process. Also during this period Ellis produced an empirically based stage-like model, consisting of eight consecutive and interacting 'features' (Ellis 1989). The work task and its complexity for decision-making becomes associated with the information-seeking process, e.g. by Järvelin (1986) and Byström and Järvelin (1995).

The third period is characterized by attempts to design comprehensive models or frameworks integrating information seeking and IR research, or to merge existing information-seeking models. We also observe the appearance of longitudinal studies of information seeking, e.g. by Wang and White (1999) and Vakkari (2001) – in both cases investigating the academic project environments. Belkin *et al.* (1995) suggest a four-dimensional 'episode' framework with the focus on sixteen information-seeking strategies that include IR interaction processes. In Ingwersen's cognitive model of IR interaction, the user's work task perception plays a central role by connecting seeking processes in the social or organizational environment to the retrieval processes. Work task or interest perception by the user is regarded as the trigger for the problem situation, a state of uncertainty, and Belkin's ASK, leading to various types of information needs (Ingwersen 1996). Increasingly, work task-based information seeking and IR are viewed in integration for the purpose of improving IR systems design and performance, also in relation to the WORLD WIDE WEB (Fidel *et al.* 1999). In a critical review Wilson analyses the central information-seeking research and the associated models, and demonstrates how some of the earlier stage-based models may be successfully combined (1999).

The research methods used during the first period are heavily dependent on quantitative descriptive surveys by means of questionnaires and interviews, despite their known drawbacks. Later, during the first and second periods, observation, diaries, critical incident and talking or thinking aloud methods, including protocol analysis, become the preferred data collection and analysis methods, attempting to explain seeking activities. Discourse analysis as well as grounded theory adds to the investigative methods in the 1990s. During this decade the central conference on information seeking in context (ISIC) was initiated and firmly established.

References

Allen, T.J. (1969). 'Information needs and uses', in C.A. Cuadra (ed.) *Annual Review of Information Science and Technology*, vol. 4, Chicago, IL: William Benton pp. 1–29.

Belkin, N.J., Brooks, H.M. and Oddy, R.N. (1982) 'Ask for information retrieval', *Journal of Documentation* 38(2): 61–71.

Belkin, N.J., Cool, C., Stein, A. and Thiel, U. (1995) 'Cases, scripts, and information seeking strategies: On the design of interactive information retrieval systems', *Expert Systems with Applications* 9(3): 379–95.

Byström, K. and Järvelin, K. (1995) 'Task complexity affects information seeking and use', *Information Processing and Management* 31(2): 191–214.

Dervin, B. and Nilan, M. (1986) 'Information needs and uses', in M.E. Williams (ed.) *Annual Review of Information Science and Technology*, vol. 21, White Plains, NY: Knowledge Industry Publications, pp. 3–33.

Ellis, D. (1989) 'A behavioral model to information retrieval system design', *Journal of Information Science* 15: 171–212.

Fidel, R., Davies, R.K., Douglass, M.H., Holder, J.K., Hopkins, C.J., Kushner, E.J., Miyagishima, B.K. and Toney, C.D. (1999) 'A visit to the information mall: Web searching behaviour of high school students', *Journal of the American Society for Information Science* 50(1): 24–37.

Ingwersen, P. (1996) 'Cognitive perspectives of information retrieval interaction: Elements of a cognitive IR theory', *Journal of Documentation* 52(1): 3–50.

—— (1982) 'Search procedures in the library analysed from the cognitive point of view', *Journal of Documentation* 38(3): 165–91.

Järvelin, K. (1986) 'On information, information technology and the development of society: An information science perspective', in P. Ingwersen, L. Kajberg and A.M. Pejtersen (eds) *Information Technology and Information Use: Towards a Unified View of Information and Information Technology*, London: Taylor Graham, pp. 35–55.

Kuhlthau, C.C. (1991) 'Inside the search process: Information seeking from the user's perspective', *Journal of the American Society for Information Science* 42: 361–71.

Paisley, W. (1968) 'Information needs and uses', in C.A. Cuadra (ed.) *Annual Review of Information Science and Technology*, vol. 3, Chicago, IL: William Benton, pp. 1–30.

Taylor, R.S. (1968) 'Question negotiation and information seeking in libraries', *College and Research Libraries* 29: 178–94.

Vakkari, P. (2001) 'A theory of the task-based information retrieval process: A summary and generalization of a longitudinal study', *Journal of Documentation* 57(1): 44–60.

Wang, P. and White, M.D. (1999) 'A cognitive model of document use during a research project: Study II: Decisions at the reading and citing stages', *Journal of the American Society for Information Science* 50(2): 98–114.

Wilson, T. (1999) 'Models in information behaviour research', *Journal of Documentation* 55(3): 249–70.

—— (1981) 'On user studies and information needs', *Journal of Documentation* 37(1): 3–15.

Further reading

Kuhlthau, C.C. (1993) *Seeking Meaning: A Process Approach to Library and Information Services*, Norwood, NJ: Ablex.

SEE ALSO: empiricism and positivism; research in library and information science

PETER INGWERSEN

INFORMATION SKILLS

Skills used in the location and interpretation of information, such as using the index of a book, locating material on library shelves, conducting an online search. USER EDUCATION within LIS institutions seeks to develop these skills in their users, so as to enable them to function more independently and effectively.

SEE ALSO: information literacy

INFORMATION SOCIETY

A term that is frequently used, but usually only vaguely defined. In general it refers to a society in which information, rather than material goods, has become the chief economic, social and cultural motor. The implication is that it is the world's richer economies, principally in North America, Europe, Japan and Australasia, who are making or have already made this transition. Daniel Bell (1976) uses the term 'post-industrial' to describe the information society. This captures well the feeling that the increasing importance of the processing of intangible information, coupled with the decline of traditional industries such as mining and manufacturing, is a historical inevitability – the next stage in the evolution of human civilization, after the industrial age.

Although observers tend to agree about general characteristics (see the list below), difficulties arise around measuring the transition to an information society. What particular information is important? How can we judge its importance, quality, validity or morality (Roszak 1986: 11–15)? These questions have not been resolved, and doubtless will not be for some time (see Webster 1995: ch. 2 for an overview). Nevertheless, we can distinguish certain significant causes and symptoms of the transition to an information society. These include:

- The development of new INFORMATION AND COMMUNICATION TECHNOLOGY, such as the INTERNET, mobile telephones, satellite communication and so on. Through vastly increasing the speed and quantity of information trans-mission, these have helped spawn a global information network.
- Large and continuing reductions in the price and availability of computers (whether in their own right, or as components in consumer goods such as cars and toys), giving individuals the ability to easily access this global network.
- The CONVERGENCE of information and communications media such as TELECOMMUNICATIONS, BROADCASTING, computing and print.
- Because of this convergence, the increasing importance and wealth of informational industries (such as advertising, MASS MEDIA, the information and communications technology sector, and education) over agriculture and primary industries such as mining and manufacturing.
- The emergence of new cultural icons and practices, for instance: the ubiquity of advertising; the fetishization of the mobile phone; the 'dot.com bubble'; global sporting events; junk mail – to name but a few symptoms of the huge increase in the importance and visibility in our everyday lives of information and communication.

Following in the tradition of Marshall MCLUHAN (1964), certain authors hold a relatively optimistic view of the consequences of this transition, particularly around the use of the Internet as a communications tool. Negroponte (1995), for instance, suggests that as the information society continues to develop, the consumer will become increasingly powerful. The enormously increased quantities of information are provoking the development of technologies through which individual consumers can filter this information, to enhance the quality and relevance of the information they pull towards them, and achieve their own personalized informational environment. Negroponte believes that this will make corporations more responsive to consumer concerns, emphasizing quality of service and advertising, rather than pure quantity and visibility. Rheingold (1993) foresees a revitalized sense of community in the information society, as physical location no longer limits social interaction. In CYBERSPACE, new communities can flourish, and potentially result in a democratization and decentralization of society as a whole.

It is true that certain historical events and developments appear to have been positively influenced by the transition to an information society. Communism's rapid collapse in the late 1980s and an increased awareness of global environmental problems like rainforest destruction could both be said to have been stimulated by the ability of populations in one country or region to view events in another, as they occur – and conversely, the increasing difficulty oppressive regimes face in preventing their citizens accessing such information. New forms of organization, social interaction, politics and even sex have developed using the Internet and other technological developments, many of which are enthusiastically defended by their converts (e.g. Rheingold 1993; Turkle 1995).

However, these authors and their kin tend to focus on discontinuities between the new information society and the earlier industrial society. It is as if the latter has gone forever, with the change to moving MEGABYTES around the globe rather than minerals having been total and irrevocable (see for instance Negroponte 1995: 4). Yet the information society is not developing from a clean slate. Rather, it is unavoidably shaped by existing social, economic and political structures, as well as the channels for communication and information dissemination that have developed under their influence.

The use of intangible, informational resources as an alternative to tangible resources such as oil, gold and grain is nothing new, even if the relative importance of the two is shifting over time. Neither resource type can become significant without the other. There are also parallels between them. Just as energy, in the form of wind and water and so on, flows through the physical environment, information flows through social networks, within which there are particular routes and channels along which it can flow more freely. Wind and water do not uniformly diffuse through the physical space available to them, and nor does information. It gathers in certain places. Sometimes its flow gets accidentally or deliberately blocked. When physical resources are concentrated and therefore controlled from one place – an oil-rich region, expensive jewellery, a Swiss bank account – we call this wealth. Such wealth also tends to equate to political power. The same processes occur with information, and there seems no reason to believe that the information society will be intrinsically more equal, and its resources more uniformly distributed. Where information is concentrated, one can deny competitors or the general public access, or control its flow, interpretation and even content. Such a GATEKEEPER role has become an indicator of power and wealth in the information society. Though traditional sources of power and wealth have in no way disappeared, they have become rivalled by the influence of information industry moguls such as Bill Gates and Rupert Murdoch.

In the information society we must also face other old issues surrounding access and use of resources, such as pollution, conservation, efficiency and deprivation. The vast amount of information now available has given rise to a form of pollution (Gore 2000: 197–204) as, with so much redundant information out there, much of it is wasted. That which does exist is now far less likely to be conserved for posterity; it is harder to envisage the writers, thinkers and artists of the early twenty-first century having collections of their e-mails published after their deaths, in the way that those of a hundred years earlier have had letters and diaries revealed. This is only one example of the concern that, paradoxically, the information society may become notable for a greater loss of information than ever before. Nor have we much sense of information efficiency – computer memory capacity increases exponentially but this merely encourages developers to write bigger and bigger applications, and games and Web designers to produce more and more complex pages. Those who must make do with older equipment or none at all, such as the poor in both the rich global North and the poorer South, are left behind in the rush to exploit this new capacity. Information deprivation is therefore emerging, just as there is material deprivation. Indeed, as the transition to the information society gathers pace, these two kinds of poverty will become interchangeable.

Even when information is freely accessible, this is no guarantee that it will be desirable. Those who wish to access information such as child pornography, incitement to racial hatred and so on now find this task relatively easy on the Internet. Nor will information always be used productively. In contrast to the optimistic portrayals of the information society remarked upon earlier, other commentators have focused more upon the negative consequences of this transition.

With people retreating into online personae, knowing people across the world better than their next-door neighbours, the information society seems dislocating and fragmented. Rather than global understanding and solidarity, it displays confusion, a multiplicity of signs and metaphors in which we can no longer discern the real from the unreal (or hyper-real: Baudrillard 1983). Blinded by the cult of information (Roszak 1986) we are far from becoming more active, aware and discerning consumers. In fact the opposite is happening, as TV channels multiply, fads and celebrities come and go with increasing rapidity, and McLuhan's putative global village becomes dominated by its shopping malls. As we negotiate this consumer-oriented, ephemeral world, business and governments watch our every step. Our PRIVACY as individuals is eroded by the use of computer technology to store and process personal data about our shopping habits, movements, cultural preferences: in short, our lives. Employers assert their right to view the private correspondence of employees, if that correspondence passed through a work e-mail account. From this perspective, the information society is far from a desirable phase in the evolution of human society.

Any synthesis between this pessimism and more positive accounts can only be achieved if it is remembered that the information society will contain both continuities and discontinuities from earlier times. In his definitive discussion of the social and political theories that can underpin ideas about the information society, Webster (1995) places the term 'information society' in quotes throughout to demonstrate its elusive nature. He acknowledges that the term is often used unproblematically in both public and academic discourse, but when doing so there is little appreciation of underlying considerations that will shape the transition to an information society. To say that information exists regardless of its social and political context (see Webster 1995: 27) may, at times, be an accurate observation. But pure information can never act upon the world without being mediated through individual minds, organizations and socio-economic structures that may be influenced by the information, but which essentially predate it. Therefore, the information society does not exist independently: it is still society, and though the flow of resources around it has become more rapid, flexible and location independent, society possesses many of the same structures and problems that it always has.

There have been radical breakthroughs in the technical realm of information and communication technologies, and the economic importance of information processing has increased to such an extent that it appears justified to state that an information society of some sort is emerging. However, to fully understand this transition requires more than just describing consequences. The information society has been developing for some decades now – perhaps even centuries – and though new technologies have accelerated its evolution, the process is far from complete, particularly when considered globally (remember that over a billion people alive today have never made a telephone call). The information society's future will be shaped by technological and economic influences, but also by social, political and cultural factors that are rather less easy to predict or direct.

References

Baudrillard, J. (1983) *Simulations*, New York: Semiotexte.

Bell, D. (1976) *The Coming of Post-Industrial Society: A Venture in Social Forecasting*, Harmondsworth: Penguin.

Gore, A. (2000) *Earth in the Balance; Forging a New Common Purpose*, London: Earthscan [Chapter 11 is particularly relevant].

McLuhan, M. (1964) *Understanding Media: The Extensions of Man*, New York: McGraw Hill.

Negroponte, N. (1995) *Being Digital*, New York: Knopf.

Rheingold, H. (1993) *The Virtual Community: Homesteading on the Electronic Frontier*, Reading, MA: Addison Wesley.

Roszak, T. (1986) *The Cult of Information: A Neo-Luddite Treatise on High Tech, Artificial Intelligence and the True Art of Thinking*, Cambridge: Lutterworth.

Turkle, S. (1995) *Life on the Screen*, New York: Simon & Schuster.

Webster, F. (1995) *Theories of the Information Society*, London: Routledge [the best summary of theoretical considerations of the issue; a revised edition is expected late in 2002].

SEE ALSO: broadcasting; censorship; communication; e-commerce; e-government; economics of information; Internet; Machlup, Fritz; mobile communications; paperless society; Porat, Marc Uri; preservation; sociology of knowledge

ANDREW WHITWORTH

INFORMATION SYSTEMS

Domain and definition

There is no agreed definition of information systems (IS) in the literature but we define it as 'the effective analysis, design, delivery and use of information for organizations and society using information technology'. Although there are information systems without computer systems (for example, the 'grapevine'), its subject matter concerns mainly the interaction of technology with organizations, individuals and society as a whole. The scope of information systems is not oriented to the technology *per se* but to the impact of its use; indeed Lee (1991) argues that the domain 'begins where COMPUTER SCIENCE ends'. Attempts to place rigid boundaries on IS have been argued to reduce the discipline's richness and value but whatever definition is used the domain clearly has a major focus on the organizational and social context surrounding the use of information technology.

Information systems as an academic discipline

IS is a fairly new discipline, with academic departments being mainly found first in the UK at the ex-polytechnics in the 1970s. However, most universities and colleges now have some form of IS programme. There are about ninety university departments teaching IS in the UK with specialist undergraduate and postgraduate programmes in information systems usually being found in Computer Science or Management departments, along with those provided by specialist departments of Information Systems. Some programmes aim to produce 'hybrid' students or managers that have IT and IS, as well as general management, skills.

Again, there is no agreed content for a programme in information systems. The main areas of difference between programmes concern the emphasis placed on technological aspects on the one hand and the organizational and social issues on the other. Hence IS academics who do not belong to an IS department are fairly equally split between Computer Science departments and management schools. In the USA, more IS academics are based in business schools. Some IS academics are fairly isolated or belong to very small groups.

Themes

IS is a rich multidisciplinary domain, where human and organizational factors are as important as technological factors. The latter include hardware, SOFTWARE, data and NETWORKS. Human and organizational factors include strategy, business processes, economic, managerial and user aspects. Computer science, engineering, mathematics and other sciences are relevant to the technological elements, whereas applied psychology, anthropology, philosophy, sociology, economics, linguistics, politics, semiotics and ethics are relevant to the more social and management-oriented aspects. Over time, there has been a slow movement away from technological factors (sometimes referred to as the harder aspects) to the organizational and social themes (the softer aspects). However the interaction of the two provides a rich and exciting domain. The socio-technical school (see, for example, Mumford 1996) places emphasis on ensuring that the impact of technology on people is positive.

Possible programme content

Although some programmes aim to address particular IT skills to meet the skills shortage in public and private organizations, the multidisciplinary aspect of information systems discussed earlier is also reflected in most academic programmes. Such a general programme in information systems might include the following aspects:

- Theoretical underpinnings of IS: information systems draws on SYSTEMS THEORY, INFORMATION THEORY and philosophy from other disciplines (see Themes above).
- Data, information and KNOWLEDGE MANAGEMENT: this relates to how raw data is converted into information (data processed for a particular purpose) through to KNOWLEDGE (the ability to use the information most effectively) including various forms of modelling, file and database organization, DATA MINING, data warehousing (see DATA WAREHOUSE) and support tools.
- Information in organizational decision-making: this looks at the nature, use and significance of information systems in organizations, and the way information provided needs to be accurate, appropriate, concise, secure, timely and relevant for the decision-maker, along with specific applications such as ENTERPRISE

RESOURCE PLANNING systems, DECISION SUP-
PORT SYSTEMS, group decision support systems
and executive IS.

- IS/IT strategy and its alignment with organizational strategy: this discusses the relationships
between the strategy for IS in organizations
and how it is aligned with business strategy,
information strategy, IT strategy and related
personnel and management strategy. In particular, it focuses on how IS/IT may enable new
ways of doing business, new organizational
forms and new strategies, for example, electronic commerce.

- Information systems design and development:
this looks at the ways in which information
systems are analysed, designed, developed and
implemented in organizations, including the
methodologies, tools and techniques supporting that development.

- INFORMATION AND COMMUNICATION TECH-
NOLOGY: this aspect includes hardware and
software both within and outside the organization, interfaces and media. Thus it will
encompass, for example, hardware devices,
systems and application software, systems
architectures, NETWORKS and communications
software.

- Management of information systems and services: this will include a discussion of the roles
and activities of personnel, specialists and
users and their relationships, and the skills,
education and training required to carry out
these roles effectively. It will also usually
examine the organization of the IT roles and
functions, including whether IS/IT might be
centralized, decentralized, federal or outsourced.

- Organizational, social and cultural impact of
IS: this looks specifically at the social, cultural
and ethical issues including impacts on the
individual, the home, the workplace, the environment and society of IS and IT. This
includes organizations in both the public and
private sectors, legal issues such as PRIVACY
and DATA PROTECTION, employment issues,
globalization and so on. A particular focus is
on change management and achieving the
benefits but mitigating the worst of the problems associated with IS/IT-induced change.

- Economic aspects of IS: this looks at the
evaluation of IS that should take place before
(referred to as a feasibility study), during and
after (post-implementation review) an infor-

mation system has been implemented. Evaluation may be broad-based, to take on board
wider cultural and social issues along with a
more conventional cost–benefit approach.

Other modules might be added to the above
list as options, for example:

- Information security and privacy.
- MEDICAL INFORMATICS (or another speciality).
- E-COMMERCE and MULTIMEDIA.
- Project management.
- Software engineering.
- Database management.
- ARTIFICIAL INTELLIGENCE and expert systems.
- Marketing and other business courses.
- IS practice and consultancy.

Some programmes demand prerequisite courses
and/or experience such as two years' computing
experience or a degree in Computer Science.
Programmes vary in regards to the proportion of
practical 'hands-on' computing, group and individual projects, amount of case study work and
so on.

Information systems in practice

IS concerns practice: it is about how information
technology is used in organizations. Typically, the
first activities in organizations that were computerized were applications at the operations level
of the firm, such as payroll, invoicing, sales order
processing and stock control, most of them
accounting-related. The word 'computerized' is
used advisedly here, for they tended to automate
clerical systems. Much of this represented an
attempt to reduce costs and speed up data
processing, but did not change the nature of
business. Earlier applications were usually developed in isolation, but there has been a more
recent interest in integrating these legacy systems,
possible using large database systems, and seen
most recently with the movement towards Enterprise Resource Planning systems, such as SAP.
Business process re-engineering, although not
necessarily driven by IT and IS, has almost
invariably been supported by them both.

IS success and failure is an enduring theme,
though the public remembers the failures, for
example, of the London Ambulance system and
Taurus for the London Stock Exchange, but is
much less aware of the successful systems that

have replaced them. Indeed the newer London Ambulance System won the BCS Information Systems Management Award for 1997 and can be considered a 'significant success' (Fitzgerald 2000).

Later applications have also concerned improving the effectiveness of management, and this has seen the development of management information systems, decision support systems, group decision support systems and executive support systems as this role continues to develop and evolve. Some are meant to support management decision-making by providing information, others attempt to automate decision-making, some aim at naïve users and yet others at experienced users. The latter may well develop their own applications, a process known as end-user development. An alternative approach is to buy or rent an application package and adapt it where necessary. Some organizations have outsourced most of their IT applications development, and IT and IS generally.

There has always been a concern about the process of developing computer applications effectively using IS development methodologies, but most recently there has been a movement away from formal approaches to enable rapid application development. Software productivity tools, known variously as workbenches, computer-aided systems engineering and developer tools, have attempted to support this process. With Web applications, this change in emphasis is particularly pronounced as companies rush to achieve a Web presence, although more complex business-to-business (b2b) Web applications require thorough development approaches and can be supported by very large databases. Some businesses see information systems as a way to gain competitive advantage (Porter and Millar 1985) or provide co-operative support, as in b2b electronic commerce. Database management applications have developed into knowledge management ones, and organizations are now gaining competitive advantage through their knowledge about how information can be used more effectively.

Before the development of microcomputers, now more usually called personal computers (PCs) or workstations (if part of a network), IT was usually associated with large mainframe computers. We now emphasize PC and distributed computing at least as much, and office applications (in particular word processing, orga-nizers, spreadsheet and file and database management), along with the use of the Internet and mobile computing, have impacted greatly on organizations. PCs have also enabled Internet use and other computer applications in the home and perhaps this experience can lead to more pleasurable as well as effective use of IT – computing need not be dehumanizing.

INFORMATION SYSTEMS RESEARCH

IS research is very varied. Topics include managing organizational change, economic aspects, productivity tools, information systems development, database modelling (and modelling in general), personal computing, office technology, competitive implications, expert systems and the impact of IT on the nature of work. Traditionally much IS research that has been published was based on the interpretation of questionnaire/surveys. This approach is often used in the sciences and can rely on statistical techniques, but the results are usually interesting and relevant only when the writer begins to interpret the information through subjective means. Some journals now publish papers with alternative approaches to IS research, including case studies, action research, HERMENEUTICS, ethnography, critical thinking, agency theory, speech act theory, structuration theory, post-modernist theory, grounded theory, feminist theory, personal construct theory and phenomenological research. The multidisciplinary nature of IS suggests that a plethora of relevant research approaches is relevant. Myers (www2.auckland.ac.nz/msis/isworld/index.html) provides an excellent overview of qualitative research in IS.

JOURNALS

The change in emphasis to both qualitative and quantitative research from a concentration on the latter is perhaps best reflected in the change of policy of the leading journal of IS: *MIS Quarterly (MISQ)*. In September 1989 it suggested that a paper:

> [I]n the Research and Theory category should...be based on a set of well-defined hypotheses, unbiased and reproducible...often [involving] the collection of considerable quantitative data through such means as laboratory experiments or survey instruments. The data are then subjected to statistical analysis.

In the March 1993 issue of *MISQ* there was a broadening of this stance as they welcomed 'research based on positivist, interpretive, or integrated approaches [though] we remain strong in our commitment to hypothesis testing and quantitative data analysis'. The present editor, Allen Lee, has bravely further expanded the methods of acceptable research (but not without opposition). Although the *MISQ* is generally recognized as the leading research journal, *Communications of the ACM* probably has the most impact, having a large circulation list (83,000), the majority being practitioners.

Other journals with an IS emphasis include (in alphabetical order) *Accounting, Management and Information Technologies*; *The Database for Advances in Information Systems*; *Decision Support Systems*; *European Journal of Information Systems*; *Information Systems Journal*; *Information Systems Research*; *Information Technology and People*; *Journal of Information Technology*; *Journal of Management Information Systems*; *Journal of Strategic Information Systems*; *Management Science*; and the *Scandinavian Journal of Information Systems*. There are also a number of online journals, such as those of the Association of Information Systems (AIS; see www.aisnet.org).

EMPLOYMENT AND INFORMATION SYSTEMS GRADUATES

IS graduates are employed in many work situations. They may perform a non-IS role in an organization that in addition requires some IS/IT knowledge and experience. On the other hand, they may be employed as the 'e-commerce expert', Webmaster, IS developer and so on. Their employment potential has been consistently high and few are tempted to start a PhD. Indeed, a particular problem regarding PhD students in IS is that they also tend to choose a non-academic life and there has always been a problem of filling academic posts at all levels.

Professional associations

The AIS is an international association for IS academics that supports conferences, PhD consortia and other activities (see ISWorld at www.aisnet.org). This is joined by national groups, such as the UK Academy for Information Systems (UKAIS). Their suggested IS syllabus helped in drawing up our section on possible course content. The UKAIS also supports confer-ences, PhD consortia, regional meetings and publishes a quarterly newsletter (www.cs.york.ac.uk/cgi-bin/ukais). Another important international group is the International Federation of Information Processing (IFIP). Its Technical Committee 8 includes information systems and this is split into several working groups (WGs). For example, WG8.1 considers information systems development methodologies; WG8.2 the impact of IS on organizations and society; WG8.3 decision-support systems; and WG8.4 e-commerce. A particularly useful site is that of IS-World at www.isworld.org.

Conferences

Relevant conferences, such as the International Conference for Information Systems (ICIS), European Conference of Information Systems (ECIS), Business Information Technology World (BIT World), the UKAIS conference, Australasian Conference in IS and regional or specialist ones have been very successful. It is generally felt that computer societies (such as the British Computer Society) emphasize the technological aspects of IS but do not focus sufficiently on the other aspects of IS relevant to IS practitioners, researchers and teachers. For this reason more specialist IS organizations, like those mentioned above, have been formed.

Books and book series

McGraw-Hill and Wiley both have international series of texts in information systems. There are a number of general texts on information systems: those by Laudon and Laudon (2002) and Kendall and Kendall (2001) are US texts that are popular, and Curtis (1995) is a UK-based text. Davis and Olsen (1985) was very influential but unfortunately is now somewhat out-of-date. References on particular topics include Banville and Landry (1989); Boland and Hirschheim (1987); Currie and Galliers (1999) and Mingers and Stowell (1997) on the domain of IS; Myers and Avison (2002) on qualitative research in IS; Connoly *et al.* (1998) on database systems; Hammer and Champy (1993) on business process re-engineering; Callon (1996) on business strategies for IT; Avison and Fitzgerald (2002) on IS development; Willcocks (1997) on evaluation; Sauer (1993) on success and failure; Zuboff (1988) on the introduction of IT; Frenzel

(1999) on IT management; and Kakakota and Robinson (1999) on e-business.

References

Avison, D.E. and Fitzgerald, G. (2002) *Information Systems Methodologies, Techniques and Tools*, 3rd edn, McGraw-Hill.

Fitzgerald, G. (2000) *IT at the Heart of Business: A Strategic Approach to Information Technology*, BCS.

Lee (1991) 'Architecture as a reference discipline for MIS', in H.-E. Nissen, R. Hirschheim and H.K. Klein (1991) *Information Systems Research: Contemporary Approaches and Emergent Traditions*, Elsevier.

Mumford, E. (1996) *Systems Design: Ethical Tools for Ethical Change*, Macmillan.

Porter, M.E. and Millar, V.E. (1985) 'How information gives you competitive advantage', *Harvard Business Review* July–August.

Further reading

Banville, C. and Landry, M. (1989) 'Can the field of MIS be disciplined?', *Communications of the ACM* 32: 48–60.

Boland, R.J. and Hirschheim, R.A. (eds) (1987) *Critical Issues in Information Systems Research*, Wiley.

Callon, J.D. (1996) *Competitive Advantage through Information Technology*, McGraw-Hill.

Connoly, T., Begg, C. and Strachan, A. (1998) *Database Systems*, Addison-Wesley.

Currie, W. and Galliers, R. (eds) (1999) *Rethinking Management Information Systems: An Interdisciplinary Perspective*, OUP.

Curtis, G. (1995) *Business Information Systems: Analysis, Design and Practice*, Addison-Wesley.

Davis, G.B. and Olsen, M.H. (1985) *Management Information Systems: Conceptual Foundations, Structure and Development*, McGraw-Hill.

Frenzel, C.W. (1999) *Management of Information Technology*, Course Technology.

Hammer, M. and Champy, J. (1993) *Reengineering the Corporation*, Harper Business.

Kakakota, R. and Robinson, M. (1999) *E-business: Roadmap for Success*, Addison-Wesley.

Kendall, K. and Kendall, J. (2001) *Systems Analysis and Design*, Prentice-Hall.

Laudon, K.C. and Laudon, J.P. (2002) *Management Information Systems: Organization and Technology*, Prentice Hall.

Mingers, J. and Stowell, F. (eds) (1997) *Information Systems: An Emerging Discipline?*, McGraw-Hill.

Myers, M. and Avison, D.E. (2002) *Qualitative Research in Information Systems: A Reader*, Sage.

Sauer, C. (1993) *Why Information Systems Fail: A Case Study Approach*, Alfred Waller.

Truex, D. and Baskerville, R. (1998) 'Deep structure or emergence theory: Contrasting theoretical foundations for information systems development', *Information Systems Journal* 8: 2.

Willcocks, L. (ed.) (1997) *Evaluating IT Investments*, Chapman & Hall.

Zuboff, S. (1988) *In the Age of the Smart Machine*, Basic Books.

SEE ALSO: informatics; information ethics; operations research; organizational information policies

DAVID AVISON AND GUY FITZGERALD

INFORMATION TECHNOLOGY

Electronic technologies for collecting, storing, processing and communicating information. There are two main categories: those that process information, such as computer systems; and those that disseminate information, such as TELECOMMUNICATIONS systems. The term can generally be understood to describe systems that combine both, but nowadays the more accurate INFORMATION AND COMMUNICATION TECHNOLOGY (ICT) is more commonly used. Whilst information technology has been the accepted term in the UK, it is not the universal term: telematics is widely used in France, and INFORMATICS is also used elsewhere in this sense.

SEE ALSO: communication; information management; information policy

INFORMATION THEORY

The strict and narrow definition is theory concerning the measurement of the quantity and quality of information.

The Shannon viewpoint

There is perhaps no other term that has become more ambiguous during the last forty years than the term 'INFORMATION'. Due to the ambiguity of the term there are hundreds or thousands of papers dealing with attempts to describe aspects, facets and components of 'information' on a level of abstraction that could be related to some understanding of 'theory'. Fairthorne (1965) therefore recommended not using this term any more. Nevertheless, 'information' still is a phenomenon that fascinates people over all the disciplines.

It perhaps all started with Claude SHANNON in 1948 when he published his *Mathematical Theory of Communication*, which included not a mathematical definition of 'information' but a measurement for the entropy of a message. His approach was inspired by the idea of optimizing the transport of signals on a communication channel between a source and a receiver. Since such channels require the coding of messages that the source intends to send, optimizing the number of signals representing a specific message sent through the channel means optimizing the coding of the representation of the message. Since the most simple and general way of achieving this is by binary code, a mathematical theory could be developed based on the binary principle that could be used in any case in which the message could be represented by discrete signs and the whole set of different discrete signs (or symbols or characters) is known. Coding could be optimized further if the discrete signs have a different frequency of occurrence or, looked at from another angle (which already goes beyond Shannon), a different probability from that in which the receiver could 'expect' a signal. Frequent signs could be coded with fewer signals; rare signs could be coded with more signals. Thus the number of signs used for the transfer of messages through channels could be optimized.

The amount of information specified by Shannon relates to the probability of signs within a restricted set of signs with known probabilities of occurrence: more frequent signs have a higher probability and therefore contain less information, while less frequent signs have a lower probability and therefore contain more information. If we look at the theory from the viewpoint of the receiver, a sign with a high probability is more likely than one with a low probability and therefore the uncertainty about the next incoming sign will be reduced less by a sign with high probability than by a sign with low probability. Shannon formalized this relation on the basis of binary coding, thus leading to his famous formula. That theory was very soon used as information theory, mainly due to its less mathematical explanation by Weaver (Shannon and Weaver 1949).

This concept was influential as an 'information theory' for several reasons:

- At the same time the concept of information was identified as one that could seriously change our view of the world. It was Norbert WIENER who discovered that our natural world consists not only of matter and energy (the physicist's view of the world) but also that information could be a third basic component if we adopt a new, post-classical view of systems and processes of control that he called CYBERNETICS (Wiener 1948). Cybernetics and

SYSTEMS THEORY were the basis of a new generation of thinking, related to information as a means of control. Shannon contributed a mathematical interpretation of information, something that is always sought by scientists and engineers.

- The mathematical theory of communication was one of the basic theories underlying the further development of data processing. The enormous impact of computers of course supported the distribution of the underlying theories.

- A major trend in the sciences after the Second World War was that they tended to adopt the cognitive model of (natural) sciences; since they had been so successful, POSITIVISM, formalization, mathematization, measurement and experimentation spread through most of the soft sciences like social sciences, the arts and humanities. Since most of the soft scientists had problems understanding the 'hard' theories of the natural world, the new concepts of systems, control and information were of enormous fascination. These theories used terms that seemed to be well known to them, the theoretical constructs looked to be rather simple and even the mathematics related to these concepts was not very difficult. So nearly everybody who wanted to be known as innovative started to play around with these concepts.

- The basic structure of Shannon's theory was his approach to communication and this had an enormous impact in itself. It provided a model of communication that related to recent theories of human communication, although it was not intended to. The classical formula of Lasswell (1948) – 'Who says what to whom on which channel with what effects' – was to some extent formalized by Shannon and Weaver, and thus a field of communication studies could emerge that in social and engineering contexts could use the same terminology and therefore could at least think that both fields meant the same phenomena. This was outlined wonderfully by Cherry (1957).

During the 1950s and 1960s the concept of 'information' and related concepts spread through different fields of scientific activity, like psychology, physiology, linguistics, biology and sociology (Dahling 1962). Unavoidably, the concepts did not remain what they had originally been. The more they were transplanted to other disciplines and contexts, the more they changed, were defined in other ways and related to other contexts and concepts. Two different developments played an important role in the process of growing confusion:

- Electronic data processing people always tended to promise more than they could deliver. So, even at a time when their machines were not able to process more than holes in paper, they started to call it information processing, which led to the establishment of the discipline that was later called INFORMATICS (especially in Europe). This created some problems, because the capacities of their machines grew considerably but they still called everything information processing. Thus, the engineering interpretation of 'information' changed with the changing capabilities of computers.
- The field of documentation was concerned with the establishment of stores of documents to be organized in such a way that someone could select something according to specific requirements. As the new technologies became available they promised to be an important tool. At the same time it became obvious that the documentation business was becoming increasingly more sophisticated. The information flood increased, the users of the stores became more specific in their needs and the new technologies required new ways of thinking. Documentation as a field of practical knowledge tended to become a field of scientific study and called itself INFORMATION SCIENCE (Borko 1968). Underlying this process was a somewhat different paradigm: it was not the paradigm of something called information being processed, but that of something called information being sought for specific reasons.

In Shannon's theory these interpretations were not incompatible: due to the known probabilities of the signs and the assumption that source and receiver used the same system of signs, the amount of information in the sign and the impacted information were more or less the same. This was not so in human contexts, where neither the assumption of coherent sets of signs nor the assumption of the identity of the original message, signs and reconstructed message were

applicable. The very notion of SEMIOTICS, which in fact became one of the most important critiques of too simple an application of information theory to human communication, led to the insight that Shannon's mathematical theory was only a theory on the syntactical level (relation of signs to signs), but with no reference to the semantic (relation of signs to meanings) and pragmatic (relation of signs to humans) levels. In consequence, some attempts were made to develop out of Shannon's theory a semantic (e.g. Bar-Hillel and Carnap 1953) or pragmatic (e.g. Yovits 1975) information theory, but these remained in the literature with no great success.

The diversification of viewpoints

At the beginning of the 1970s, when information science started to establish itself, it was faced with the problem that while nearly everybody used the term information, nearly everybody meant something different by it. The problem was complicated by the fact that most of the users of the term thought that everybody else would understand and therefore they very often did not define which kind of meaning they had in mind.

A study of the different types of meaning of information in 1971 (in detail Wersig 1971; in brief Wersig and Neveling 1975) disclosed six different types:

1   The structure approach states that the structures of the world – whether perceived by man or not – *are* information. There were some variants on this approach, such as:

- Information as the static relationship between atoms and molecules.
- Information as the relationship that may become perceptible if changes in the states of the physical objects occur.
- Information as all characteristics of physical objects.

This approach was mainly used by philosophers (e.g. Polushkin 1963).

2   The KNOWLEDGE approach states that knowledge developed on the basis of perception is information. Variants were:

- Knowledge is objectively given, whether actualized by an individual or not.
- Knowledge has to be acquired by at least

one subject.

- Knowledge serves a specific purpose (most important were the definitions of the form 'Information is of value in decision-making'; Yovits 1961).
- Information is communicated knowledge.

This approach was spread widely across disciplines but was most important in connection with decision theory.

3   The message approach continues the tradition of Shannon and Weaver: information is the message itself. Variants were:

- Information is the physical substance that is used for transmission (e.g. Graziano 1968).
- Information is the symbols produced for communication.
- Information is the unit of a physical carrier and its semantic elements (e.g. Völz 1991).

This approach was mainly used by those associated with mathematical communication theory.

4   The meaning approach states that the meaning assigned to signs or data is the information, usually connected to the conventions used in the decoding of the sign. This approach was dominant in computer science and its applications (e.g. ANSI 1966).

5   The effect approach states that information is a specific effect of a specific process, usually on the part of the recipients in a communication process. Variants were:

- Information is data produced as a result of processing data (e.g. Hayes 1969).
- Information is a change of knowledge (e.g. Kunz and Rittel 1972).
- Information is the reduction of uncertainty (e.g. Wersig 1971).

The last two variants were used mostly by behavioural scientists.

6   The process approach states that information is neither objective nor subjective, but a process. Variants were:

- Information is a process within the human mind when a problem and data are brought together (e.g. Hoshovsky and Massey 1968)
- Information is a set of actions by which

something is purposively transferred (e.g. Koblitz 1968).

This view was often adopted by information practitioners.

The cognitive viewpoint

Although information science never reached a common understanding of itself and therefore the different types of use of 'information' remained under discussion, the theoretical discussion in the discipline during the 1970s concentrated on the 'cognitive approach' (DeMey 1977; Belkin 1990), which was more or less a continuation of the 'effect approach' and continued in the 1980s and 1990s as the 'subjective approach' (Cole 1994). Some main variants that received major attention were (Ingwersen 1992):

- Information as the reduction of uncertainty as a result of communication. The uncertainty is due to a problematic situation (Wersig 1979) in which the actor has to act but does not have enough knowledge available to act rationally.
- Information as the resolution of an anomalous state of knowledge (Belkin 1975, 1977, 1978).
- Information as that which modifies subjective knowledge structure (Brookes 1975, 1980).
- Information as a meaningful message from an informant that may influence the recipient in considerations, decisions and actions (Machlup 1983).

Sometimes this led to a dual understanding that information within information science is both 'the result of a transformation of generator's knowledge structures' and 'something (a structure) that when perceived may affect and transform the recipient's state of knowledge' (Ingwersen 1992: 125). A similar duality is implicit in Buckland (1991), with his distinction between 'information-as-thing' and 'information-as-knowledge'.

One could call the developmental stage from 1948 to the 1970s the 'Shannon and Weaver phase', because most of the discussions and attempts to structure the concept of information relied on the reception of Shannon via Weaver. Although nothing remarkable happened, we seem to have entered during the 1980s a new phase of discussion of information theoretically, which can perhaps be related to several general developments:

- Information science has not reached a stage of development where it relies on a sufficiently sound theoretical and methodological base to be accepted at least as an important field of study. It is still looking for its identity (Vakkari and Cronin 1992) and one of the reasons is that its representatives have never been able to demonstrate that they are pursuing something really different from computer science, due to the strong retrieval component, which remains one of the main features of recent information science.

- The cognitive viewpoint on information, although discussed in information science, has not been developed further on a theoretical basis within the discipline. It has been adopted to some extent by computer science under the terms knowledge processing and knowledge-based systems, thus replicating the reduction of information in its cognitive facets to its automatic processing aspect with the concept of knowledge. Knowledge becomes in this context not the knowledge of the individual to which information could be set into relation, but machine-processable knowledge-representation.

- The cognitive viewpoint itself has been colonized by cognitive science, which does not try to understand cognition as it appears within humans but is concerned with cognition by means of reproducing cognition-like features on computers.

- From the other side, the cognitive viewpoint is to some extent attacked by radical constructivism, which states that knowledge is nothing more than a subjective construct; information in this context becomes unmeasurable because there are no longer any direct connections between reality, signs and knowledge (e.g. Glasersfeld 1985).

Information science, perhaps, has waited too long to establish a sound theoretical basis for a cognitive-oriented information theory; now this is adapted from communications theory (Merten *et al.* 1994; 'The future of the field I' 1993) and cognitive science (Gardner 1985), which more or less work on the cognitive paradigm but drop the concept of information as central.

Under these conditions several options for a theoretical foundation of information are considered. All of them have in common that they do not insist on only one meaning of information. There exists a position that is concerned with the situation of knowledge in our times, and that action is necessary that relates to 'information' (Wersig 1993a). The position is that something that reflects the knowledge of humans about their world exists in individuals, in human products, in organizations and in stores of different kinds. If some people call this information, they may do so. This knowledge is used – by individuals, organizations and society – but is often not available when needed. Specific kinds of activities are necessary to ensure that the knowledge that is used will be available when it is needed and in a form in which it may be used. Again people may call such activities information. Problems of this kind may be solved by different approaches: libraries, retrieval systems, multimedia systems, etc. If the problem-solving is successful, something happens with the individuals, organizations and societies that means that, if they require knowledge and they get it, they might change during this process. Again, this could be called information. In fact, this means that information theory changes from the definition of information to the definition of situations in which something like information is central.

The development of new theoretical directions

These situations relate to so many different objects – humans, documents, knowledge, computers, networks – that it is doubtful whether a common theory could be developed. Therefore the current trend in information theory is to try to make use of a broad range of theories developed for situations. The following approaches may have a future role:

- Constructivism.
- Systems theory.
- Action theory.
- Modernization theory.

CONSTRUCTIVISM

The constructivist model (e.g. Maturana and Varela 1987) may be briefly described thus: humans perceive the world through their senses and compute sensorial data by their complex neural network, thus creating their own perceptive image of the world and their self. These images guide perceptions, and thus the human notion of reality is always a subjective image. In radical constructivism, everything is regarded as being a subjective construction or reconstruction or re-reconstruction; moderate constructivism would permit some similarities between the subjective constructions and between constructions and reality. The theoretical basis for moderate constructivism is that not everything in perception is subjective because the perceptive apparatus developed by evolution is in principle working along the same lines for all individuals; perceptive machines have been developed about which we can come to similar or even the same conclusions under specific conditions. According to Oswald Wiener (1996) we all are capable of using similar rational machines in our cognitive systems. All knowledge is subjective and so is information, which could be looked at either as that which changes knowledge (or knowledge structures) or that which is changed in knowledge (or knowledge structures) (Cole 1994). This distinction is perhaps theoretically interesting, but is in fact not very important: the question of whether information exists in any case needs the observation to be made that knowledge has changed and that there is something causing this change. Both components belong together and therefore either or both could be called information.

It is worthwhile to note that this view is not a very new one; it has always been included in cognitive approaches. But these views needed the support of constructivism to overcome the dominance of 'information as a thing of its own', a view that is still alive (Buckland 1991). The evolution of the constructivist approach seems to broaden the scope and to accept different forms of constructed worlds in which, under the specific conditions, changes may occur that are caused by something, e.g. data banks, knowledge-based systems, human brains, organizational memories or virtual realities. 'Information as the change in world representations' may be the common denominator for further constructivist approaches to information theory.

SYSTEMS THEORY

Systems theory has undergone dramatic changes since the mid-1980s. Until the birth of cybernetics, systems theory was based on the approach 'the whole is more than the sum of its parts'. With general systems theory (von Bertalanffy

1950) and cybernetics, it entered a stage in which the difference between system and environment became of vital interest, and where the connections between system and environment played an important role in the background of some of the cognitive approaches, for example those formulated by Stachowiak (1965). Since the 1960s (Foerster and Zopf 1962) systems theory has been dominated by the idea of the antipoetic system that is closed against its environment, a system that is self-creating, self-reproducing, self-referencing and self-organizing, a view shared by radical constructivism.

In Luhmann's theory of social systems (Luhmann 1988) the system is a correlated set of actions in time. The system survives by generating actions that continue the system. Every time the system has different options for actions that perpetuate it, there has to be a choice. An event that chooses states of the system is called by Luhmann information – a difference that makes sense (going back to Bateson 1979). This, of course, is a broadening of Shannon and Weaver's definition: roughly in their sense, information could be considered to be a choice in favour of one sign and against all the others. If we abandon the premise of a known set of elements (signs), and replace it with an unlimited space of events that could at least be identified and isolated, we will approach Luhmann, when we retain the idea of choice. Luhmann's theory is not the only system theory and his approach cannot be used in very many real circumstances. Nevertheless his idea is generalizable: 'information as a choice for something and thus against everything else that competes'.

ACTION THEORY

The theoretical background of great influence during the 1980s, particularly in Europe, was action theory (Habermas 1981), which had been developed in sociology and which partly forms the background for Luhmann. Discussion in the information field perhaps started with the approach of an 'information man' (Roberts 1982). In the use of knowledge, man should act as in the economy: ideal-rational. This opened a discussion on the relationship between action and information. Wersig and collaborators (Wersig and Windel 1985) introduced the idea of a general relationship: every action – individual or organizational – may require knowledge that is not available in the actor. In this case a specific type of action is required, called an information action. This is the reverse of Belkin's approach: if knowledge lacks for action this is not an anomalous state of knowledge but a normal situation for every actor. The lag between them has to be closed, to rationalize actions (Wersig 1985). This has been developed by Kuhlen and collaborators (Kuhlen 1990) with the establishment of the formula 'information is knowledge in action'. This means that every actor not only needs specific knowledge for a specific action, but also needs it in a specific way, which on the one hand relates to the existing state of knowledge of the actor, and on the other hand fits the requirements of the situation of the action (e.g. in space, time, the economy, etc.). They then pick up the economic context by stating that information work takes existing knowledge and transforms it in such a way that it may more easily become information in specific actions. Information work therefore adds value to existing knowledge in order to facilitate its transformation into information (Rauch *et al.* 1994). The general idea behind this action theory of information could be called 'information as the value of knowledge in action'.

MODERNIZATION THEORY

The present development of industrialized Western countries is argued to be in a period of transition, either from modernism into post-modernism or from one stage of modernism into another stage of modernism. In either case more or less the same features play an important role: pluralism, increasing complexity, competition, fragmentation (Lyotard 1979; Wersig 1993b). Knowledge is no longer a closed set of images about reality, but dissolves into different realities: virtual realities, the virtuality of time, space and social structures. Knowledge is needed not only for action but also for orientation, the establishment of patterns, navigation through contingencies and virtualities. The universe of knowledge is split up into numerous knowledge islands, archipelagos, fragments, layers, comets, meteorites, with numerous small bridges, connections and traffic lines between them. Information in this universe would become that which provides order, orientation and navigational aid. A comprehensive theory has not yet been developed because it needs the framework of a post-modern understanding of science (Wersig 1993a, 1993b). A brief formula could be 'information as the

development of ordering structures within the ambiguous'. This view is underlined by post-modern sociologists like Zygmunt Bauman who identified uncertainty to be one of the most important features of our times (Bauman 1992).

Information and complexity

There seems to be considerable diversity in theory development, but on the other hand some kind of coherence can be seen. Behind the different approaches, a concept appears that is perhaps not one single ambiguous concept but a group of compatible concepts with a common core and fuzzy features around it. The common core is complexity:

- Constructivism is an answer to the exploration of growing complexity. We realize that we ourselves are complex and the world is becoming increasingly complex. We cannot know the complexity as such, but can only use our own complexity to reduce the complexity of the world by construction (Wersig 1996).
- Systems theory is a different but similar answer. A self-referencing system can concentrate on its own complexity and shield itself against the complexity of the world. This means using self-complexity as a means of reducing external complexity.
- Action theory draws attention to the fact that complexity does not only require cognitive reduction of action. Action requires information, but this information becomes a means of complexity reduction as a purpose of action under recent conditions. The rationalization of action is itself an important factor in complexity reduction.
- Modernization theory tries to explain why complexity is becoming increasingly important for the understanding of our present situation. Life increasingly becomes a fight within the jungle of the world's complexity and the help that is needed is reduction of this complexity by ordering patterns like individual lifestyles, patchworking or revitalising concepts of community (Sennett 1998) and embedding (Giddens 1990).

The integrated theory of information could in the near future be described as a theory of complexity reduction. This would be on the one hand a consequence of scientific and real-world developments: complexity is increasing and more and more scientific theories include the problem of complexity and its reduction, e.g. chaos theory (Briggs and Peat 1989). On the other hand this would be a further development away from Shannon and Weaver; the recent notion of complexity does not presuppose a known subset of elements and their probabilities, conditions under which uncertainty means uncertainty within a known framework. Complexity is something we know about, but which is not definable in restricted sets of elements and structures, because it is caused by unrestrictedness, unorientedness and unforeseeableness.

The reduction of this kind of disorientation would be the future of the understanding of the concept of information: 'information as the amount of complexity to be reduced or that has been reduced'. Then information will change every time it is used, not because it is a subjective concept but because it relates to the very specific understanding of complexity, the approach to complexity reduction and the kind of measurement. If complexity is defined in the Shannon way, as probability, then the measurement could be used as a specific case of complexity reduction. If there are other notions of complexity and complexity reduction other notions of information will appear.

An information theory as complexity reduction – if it is considered to be a broadening of Shannon – may require the theoretical development of some key elements:

- The base of the sender–channel-receiver communication model has to be broadened to an actor-centred communication theory as it is implied in constructivism or the model of autistic communication (Wersig 1993b).
- The discrete character-orientation of the theory has to be broadened in the direction of non-discrete, analogous and unique messages. Pictures, images and stagings as messages reducing complexities may become a core element (see Schuck-Wersig 1993). Shannon to some extent tried to deal with this problem under the heading of the continuous channel. But now we know that we have to find other solutions.
- The notion of probabilities is related to a known universe. Complexities of interest to this kind of information theory very often relate to completely or partly unknown worlds. The broadening of the concept of

probability to these worlds would either mean introducing a measurement of subjective probability (or other dimensions of subjective estimation) or giving up the idea of absolute measurements in favour of relative measurements. In other words, there is perhaps no absolute measurement of complexity (which would allow us to measure objectively its increase or reduction) but only a relative one. A relative theory of information as less or more complexity as a result of something could be the future direction of theoretical work.

But the more we think about complexity in the information age (Wersig 1996), in which the industrial society changes slowly into some kind of 'knowledge society' (Stehr 1994), the more we are forced to develop a deeper understanding of how complexity relates to knowledge structures. Knowledge structures are created from individual structures over organizational environments ('knowledge management') to societally tested, accepted and organized (by 'notification', Bühl 1984) knowledge landscapes (Spinner 1994).

New knowledge increases the complexity of knowledge structures, particularly in all the cases in which the new knowledge expands the knowledge landscape into the (so far) unknown. Complexity reduction of still expanding bodies of knowledge could be interpreted as processes of:

- Re- and metastructuring of knowledge in order to ease processes of allocating single items of knowledge (formerly known as 'CLASSIFICATION'; nowadays often called 'ONTOLOGY').
- Establishing mechanisms to adapt knowledge structures to different perspectives, approaches and levels with which the knowledge landscapes will be explored ('NAVIGATION').
- Focusing the knowledge landscape to connect simply into the need structures of actors in real life ('connectivity').

Chaos research (e.g. Briggs and Peat 1989) may be a direction where complexity reduction of knowledge structures and their connectivity into action could meet – if we could identify 'knowledge attractors', information as 'complexity reduction of knowledge structures' could be understood in terms of gravitational fields of such attractors. Respective theories are not available yet.

References

ANSI (1966) *USA Standard Vocabulary for Information Processing*, USASX3 12.1966.

Bar-Hillel, Y. and Carnap, R. (1953) 'Semantic information', *British Journal of Science* 4: 147–57.

Bateson, N. (1979) *Mind and Nature*, Dutton.

Bauman, Z. (1992) *Intimations of Postmodernity*, Routledge.

Belkin, N. (1990) 'The cognitive viewpoint in information science', *Journal of Information Science* 16: 11–15.

—— (1978) 'Information concepts for information science', *Journal of Documentation* 34: 55–85.

—— (1977) 'A concept of information for information science', Doctoral thesis, University of London.

—— (1975) 'The concept of information in informatics', in International Federation for Documentation *Theoretical Problems of Informatics* (FID 530), pp. 74–89.

Bertalanffy, L. von (1950) 'An outline of general system theory', *British Journal for the Philosophy of Science* 1: 134–65.

Borko, H. (1968) 'Information science: What is it?', *American Documentalist* 13: 3–5.

Briggs, J. and Peat, F.D. (1989) *Turbulent Mirror*, Harper & Row.

Brookes, B. (1980) 'The foundations of information science. Part 1: Philosophical aspects', *Journal of Information Science* 2: 125–33.

—— (1975) 'The fundamental equation of information science', in International Federation for Documentation *Theoretical Problems of Informatics* (FID 530), pp. 115–30.

Buckland, M. (1991) *Information and Information Systems*, Praeger.

Bühl, W.L. (1984) *Die Ordnung des Wissens*, Duncker & Humblot.

Cherry, C. (1957) *On Human Communication*, MIT.

Cole, C. (1994) 'Operationalizing the notion of information as a subjective construct', *Journal of the American Society for Information Science* 45: 465–76.

Dahling, R.C. (1962) 'Shannon's information theory. The spread of an idea', in *Studies of Innovation and Communication to the Public. Studies in the Utilization of Behavioral Science*, vol. 11.

DeMey, M. (1977) 'The cognitive viewpoint: Its development and its scope', *CC77: International Workshop on the Cognitive Viewpoint*, Ghent University, pp. xvi–xxxvi.

Fairthorne, R.A. (1965) '"Use" and "mention" in the information sciences', in L.B. Heilprin, B.A. Markuson and L. Goodman (eds) *Proceedings of the Symposium for Information Science, Warrenton, Va., Sept. 7–10, 1965*, pp. 9–12.

Foerster, H. v. and Zopf, G.W. (eds) (1962) *Principles of Self-organization*, US Office of Naval Research.

'The future of the field I' (1993) *Journal of Communication* 43(3).

Gardner, H. (1985) *The Mind's New Science*, Basic Books.

Giddens, A. (1990) *The Consequences of Modernity*, Polity Press.

Glasersfeld, E. v. (1985) 'Reconstructing the concept of knowledge', *Archives de Psychologie* 3: 91–101.

Graziano, E.E. (1968) 'On a theory of documentation', *American Documentalist* 19: 85–9.

Habermas, J. (1981) *Theorie des kommunikativen Handelns*, 2 vols, Suhrkamp.

Hayes, R.M. (1969) 'Education in information science', *American Documentalist* 20: 362–5.

Hoshovsky, A.G. and Massey, R.J. (1968) 'Information science: Its end, means and operations', in *Information Transfer*, Proc. ASIS vol. 5, pp. 47–55.

Ingwersen, P. (1992) 'Information and information science in context', *Libri* 42: 99–135.

Koblitz, J. (1968) 'Information und Dokumentation als Teilgebiet der wissenschaftlichen Information', *ZIID-Zeitschrift* 16(1): 36–43.

Kuhlen, R. (1990) 'Zum Stand pragmatischer Forschung in der Informationswissenschaft', in J. Herget and R. Kuhlen (eds) *Pragmatische Aspekte beim Entwurf und Betrieb von Informationssystemen*, Konstanz Universitätsverlag, pp. 13–18.

Kunz, W. and Rittel, H. (1972) *Die Informationswissenschaften*, Oldenbourg.

Lasswell, H.D. (1948) 'The structure and function of communication in society', in L. Bryson (ed.) *The Communication of Ideas*, pp. 37–52.

Luhmann, N. (1988) *Soziale Systeme*, 2nd edn, Suhrkamp.

Lyotard, J.-F. (1979) *La Condition postmoderne*, Éditions de Minuit.

Machlup, F. (1983) 'Semantic queries in studies of information', in F. Machlup and U. Mansfield (eds) *The Study of Information*, Wiley, pp. 641–72.

Maturana, H. and Varela, F. (1987) *The Tree of Knowledge*, Shambala.

Merten, K., Schmidt, S.J. and Weischenberg, S. (eds) (1994) *Die Wirklichkeit der Medien*, Westdeutscher Verlag.

Polushkin, V.A. (1963) 'On the determination of the concept "information"', *Naucno-Technixiskayah Informacija* 9: 6–8.

Rauch, W., Strohmeier, F., Hiller, H. and Schlögl, C. (eds) (1994) *Mehrwert von Information – Professionalisierung der Informationsarbeit*, Konstanz Universitätsverlag.

Roberts, N. (1982) 'A search for information man', *Social Science Information Studies* 2: 93–104.

Schuck-Wersig, P. (1993) *Expeditionen zum Bild. Beiträge zur Analyse des kulturellen Stellenwerts von Bildern*, Peter Lang.

Sennett, R. (1998) *The Corrosion of Character*, W.W. Norton.

Shannon, C.E. (1948) 'A mathematical theory of communication', *Bell Systems Technical Journal* 27: 379–423, 623–58.

Shannon, C.E. and Weaver, W. (1949) *The Mathematical Theory of Communication*, University of Illinois Press.

Spinner, H.F. (1994) *Die Wissensordnung*, Leske & Budrich.

Stachowiak, H. (1965) *Denken und Erkennen im kybernetischen Modell*, Springer.

Stehr, N. (1994) *Knowledge Societies*, Sage.

Vakkari, P. and Cronin, B. (eds) (1992) *Conceptions of Library and Information Science*, Taylor Graham.

Völz, H. (1991) *Grundlagen der Information*, Akademie-Verlag.

Wersig, G. (1996) *Die Komplexität der Informationsgesellschaft*, Universitätsverlag Konstanz.

—— (1993a) 'Information science: The study of postmodern knowledge usage', *Information Processing and Management* 29: 229–40.

—— (1993b) *Fokus Mensch. Bezugspunkte postmoderner Wissenschaft: Wissen, Kommunikation, Kultur*, Peter Lang.

—— (1985) *Die kommunikative Revolution*, Westdeutscher Verlag.

—— (1979) 'The problematic situation as a basic concept of information science in the framework of social sciences: A reply to N. Belkin', in International Federation for Documentation *Theoretical Problems of Informatics* (FID 568), pp. 48–57.

—— (1971) *Information Kommunikation Dokumentation*, Saur.

Wersig, G. and Neveling, U. (1975) 'The phenomena of interest to information science', *Information Scientist* 9: 127–40.

Wersig, G. and Windel, G. (1985) 'Information science needs a theory of "information actions"', *Social Science Information Studies* 5: 11–23.

Wiener, N. (1948) *Cybernetics*, Herrmann.

Wiener, O. (1996) *Schriften zur Erkenntnistheorie*, Springer.

Yovits, M.C. (1975) 'A theoretical framework for the development of information science', in International Federation for Documentation *Theoretical Problems of Informatics* (FID 530), pp. 90–114.

—— (1961) 'Information science: Toward the development of a true scientific discipline', *American Documentalist* 12: 191–7.

Further reading

Milestones in the history: Shannon and Weaver 1949; Cherry 1957; Wersig 1971; Belkin 1977.

Overviews of developments: Belkin 1990; Vakkari and Cronin 1992; Wersig and Neveling 1975.

Recent developments: Luhmann 1988 (system theory); Habermas 1981 (action theory); Lyotard 1979 (modernization theory); Wersig 1993b.

SEE ALSO: cognitive science; communication; computer science; information science; information society; research in library and information science

GERNOT WERSIG

INFORMETRICS

Informetrics is an emerging subfield in INFORMATION SCIENCE, based on the combination of quantitative studies of information flows, advanced INFORMATION RETRIEVAL and text, and DATA MINING. It has a broader scope than BIBLIOMETRICS, because it also covers non-scholarly communities in which information is produced, communicated and used. *Informetric studies* signifies the new approach to the scientific study of information flows: the improved bibliometric methods are applied not only to scientometric studies and research evaluations of science and technology (S&T), but also to the analysis of their mutual, societal, industrial and other specific relations. While bibliometrics is traditionally associated with the quantitative measurement of documentary materials, informetrics aims also to study other types of information materials, such as websites, Internet links, voice, sounds, art works, etc. Methods from the social sciences and humanities as well as experimental research in the natural sciences sense are normally applied in various contexts, serving as a base for careful validation and ensuring the scientific value of the analyses.

Informetrics is one of the rare truly interdisciplinary research fields, and the range of theoretical and methodological approaches is rich – which is the strength of the discipline.

The individual identities of *bibliometrics, informetrics, scientometrics and technometrics* are unfortunately not very clear, and there is a certain ambiguity in the terminology. At the 1987 international bibliometric conference some thought was given to changing the name of the discipline to 'informetrics' and since the end of the 1980s there is some evidence in favour of the use of this term (Egghe and Rousseau 1990). The field is becoming a scientific discipline that includes: all the statistical and mathematical analyses related to the study of information flows; evaluation of science and technology; library COLLECTION DEVELOPMENT; and documentation and information problems with strong links to the theoretical and methodological aspects of information retrieval.

Since the use of quantitative methodologies is an under-explored area of current LIS research, some information scientists have been working on the reinforcement of the link between bibliometrics and information retrieval, exploring the basic problems of ONLINE bibliometric data collection and analysis (Ingwersen and Hjortgaard Christensen 1997). In the 1990s several case studies were carried out combining online bibliometric methodologies and the use of large-scale databases in analytical works. The utilization of online bibliometric methods for trend analysis, issue management, knowledge mapping and generating business and social INTELLIGENCE is a trend that extends the boundaries of the field and signifies its multidisciplinary character (Wormell 1998, 2000). These investigations exemplify the benefits of interdisciplinary research approaches, where bibliometrics, IR and management methodologies interact in a fruitful way.

Informetrics today offers many new possibilities for LIS professionals. For those who want to explore DATABASES not only as a store of information, but also as an analytical tool, it is a way to learn how to explore online databases not only for accessing documents or finding facts, but also to trace the trends and developments in society, scientific disciplines or production and consumption. This type of information in databases is, however, visible only to the intelligent searcher and to those who have learned how to read between the lines of electronic information. Modern information technology provides a whole range of possibilities to add new value to the results of online searches, and is offering great potentialities for those who want to develop their own niches and service specialities.

Another dimension in the development of the field is the application of informetric methods to the WORLD WIDE WEB. This new emerging area of *Webometrics* elaborates on the idea of carrying out the same types of informetric analyses on the Web as are possible via a citation database. It is obvious that informetric methods using word counts can be applied here. What is new is to regard the Web as a dynamic citation network where the traditional information entities and citations are replaced by Web pages, with hyperlinks acting rather like citations (Almind and Ingwersen 1997; Ingwersen 1998; Björneborn and Ingwersen 2001). Obviously, the link structures have other functions here than those of scientific citations and references, therefore this new area needs to study such functionalities, e.g. general NAVIGATION behaviour in the electronic information environment.

Cybermetrics is an electronic journal that disseminates results from quantitative analysis of the INTERNET. Its full title is 'International Journal of Scientometrics, Informetrics and Bibliometrics' and it is published in Spain: www.cindoc.csic.es/cybermetrics. The core scientific journal of the field is *Scientometrics*, which was started in 1977 in Hungary. The International Society for Scientometrics and Informetrics (ISSI)

was established in 1993 and its biannual conferences are one of the main platforms for the presentation of progress and developments in the field.

References

Almind, T. and Ingwersen P. (1997) 'Informetric analyses on the World Wide Web: Methodological approaches to "Webometrics"', *Journal of Documentation* 53: 404–26.

Björneborn, L. and Ingwersen, P. (2001) 'Perspectives of Webometrics', *Scientometrics* 50: 65–82.

Egghe, L. and Rousseau, R. (1990) *Introduction to Informetrics. Quantitative Methods in Library, Documentation and Information Science*, Amsterdam: Elsevier.

Ingwersen, P. (1998) 'The calculation of Web impact factors. Research note', *Journal of Documentation* 54: 1–5.

Ingwersen, P. and Hjortgaard Christensen, F. (1997) 'Data set isolation for bibliometric online analyses of research publications: Fundamental methodological issues', *JASIS* 48: 205–17.

Wormell, I. (2000) 'Critical aspects of the Danish Welfare State – as revealed by issue tracking', *Scientometrics* 43: 237–50.

—— (1998) 'Informetric analysis of the international impact of scientific journals: How "international" are the international scientific journals?', *Journal of Documentation* 54: 584–605.

Further reading

Garfield, E. (1998) 'From citation indexes to informetrics: Is the tail now wagging the dog?', *Libri* 48: 67–80.

Lancaster, F.W. and Lee, Ja-Lih (1985) 'Bibliometric techniques applied to issue management: A case study', *JASIS* 36: 389–97.

Wormell, I. (2001) 'Informetrics and Webometrics for measuring impact, visibility, and connectivity in science, politics, and business', *Competitive Intelligence Review* 12: 12–23.

—— (2000) 'Informetrics – a new area of quantitative studies', *Education for Information* 18: 131–8.

IRENE WORMELL

INSTITUTE FOR SCIENTIFIC INFORMATION

The Institute for Scientific Information (ISI) is an influential multinational profit-making organization that is concerned with the production, distribution and development of secondary bibliographic and related data together with document delivery services in a wide range of subject disciplines. Its most noteworthy and enduring output is its citation indexes covering the disciplines of arts and humanities, social sciences and science.

The ISI was founded in 1958 by Eugene GARFIELD – a man of great insight and innovative skills – as a development of his earlier information consultancy organization. Over forty years later it has grown into an organization with a multimillion-dollar turnover, employing several hundred people worldwide and offering an extensive range of publications in a variety of formats. In April 1992 ISI became part of Thomson Business Information. The history and development of ISI is, to a large extent, mirrored in the history and biography of Garfield. His first venture into the commercial publishing of bibliographic information involved the creation and distribution of a regular information sheet, listing journal current contents in management.

Garfield's early experiences in investigating automated INFORMATION RETRIEVAL methods at Johns Hopkins University led him to consider alternatives to the conventional human INDEXING of research papers. He came to the conclusion that using citations as a basis for indexing offered not only an acceptable mechanism for retrieval but also in some circumstances one superior to 'conventional' indexing techniques, especially in multidisciplinary areas. Though his enthusiasm for the method was not shared by everyone, he persevered and developed the now familiar citation index.

Basically, Garfield recognized and exploited the connection between citing and cited material in scholarly publishing. A paper written on a specific topic, through its list of references, leads to related items. Thus, without the intervention and interpretation of a human indexer, a system of subject indexing 'keyed' to the subject matter of the citing papers can be constructed. What remains is a mechanical process of listing and cross-indexing cited and citing papers that does not depend upon but is greatly facilitated by computer manipulation. From these basic properties of citing and cited material, further, more sophisticated and informative patterns of relationships can be derived to analyse the dynamics of SCHOLARLY COMMUNICATION. Garfield has pioneered work in this area too.

The array of products and publications available from the ISI in both printed and various electronic formats has become extensive. They include a range of discipline-specific 'current contents' services covering topics from arts and humanities to clinical medicine and from social and behavioural sciences to engineering and technology. There is also a series of indexes for monograph, conference and review publications.

The familiar citation indexes are produced in print and a variety of electronic formats, and cover arts and humanities, social sciences and the sciences. The valuable results of bibliometric analyses conducted by the ISI are collated and published in *Journal Citation Reports*, one covering the social science journals and one covering science journals.

A comprehensive DOCUMENT DELIVERY service was developed by the ISI with several order and delivery options. Central to the ISI's operation is the formidable DATABASE maintained by the organization. This is described as the largest, most substantial multidisciplinary scientific database in the world and consists of more than 40 million source records and indexing details of around 7,000 journal titles and 6,000 books and conference proceedings. ISI adapted rapidly to changes in the 1990s, launching its *Web of Science* portal, and making its current contents service Web-deliverable in 1997. It has started a qualitative index of websites (*Current Web Contents*) as an addition to its long-established *Current Contents* service, which had its origins in ISI's first publication in 1958. Further details of activities and services will be found at www.i-sinet.com.

The contribution of the ISI to improving access to scholarly publications and to information science knowledge generally is considerable and it has had a profound influence on the thinking and behaviour of users and managers of information.

Further reading

Garfield, E. (1971) *Citation Indexing – Its Theory and Application in Science, Technology and Humanities*, John Wiley.

SEE ALSO: citation analysis; current contents list; organization of knowledge

J.E. DAVIES, REVISED BY THE EDITORS

INSTITUTE OF INFORMATION SCIENTISTS

A professional body for practitioners and theoreticians of information science, founded in the UK in 1958 and dissolved through merger with the LIBRARY ASSOCIATION, as CILIP, in 2002.

The Institute's foundation was a result of the initiative of a group of special librarians who were concerned that neither the Library Association nor ASLIB were willing to take a lead in developing training courses to equip special librarians to tackle the emerging problems of handling the rapid growth in scientific and technical information (Farradane 1970). This group, led by Jason FARRADANE, Chris Hanson and Gordon Foster, devised a constitution for the IIS that remained largely unchanged throughout its existence.

Based in London, at its peak it had over 2,600 individual information scientists, information managers and other information specialists as members. It pursued three main roles. The first was to advance the profession of INFORMATION SCIENCE through the validation of graduate and postgraduate educational courses. The second was to provide training and professional support for members through courses, conferences and publications. The third was to ensure that public and private organizations and government departments were aware of the benefits of effective INFORMATION MANAGEMENT and of the employment of information scientists, and of the implications of legislation (such as that on COPYRIGHT) on the access to and utilization of information.

Despite the fact that its membership remained small, its influence on the world of information work was disproportionately large and it entered into negotiations with the much larger (more than 25,000 members) Library Association that resulted in merger as a respected equal. CILIP, the inheritor body, arguably shows many characteristics of the Institute, although numerically dominated by former Library Association members.

References

Farradane, J.E.L. (1970) 'The Institute: The first twelve years', *Information Scientist* 4(4): 143–52.

SEE ALSO: information professions; information science education

INTELLECTUAL PROPERTY

Products of the human intellect considered as personal property, especially works protected under the law of COPYRIGHT and inventions protected by PATENTS. Other subjects include utility models, industrial designs, confidential information and TRADE MARKS.

The concept of intellectual property

Personal property may be divided into physical, tangible things and intangible, incorporeal property. Intellectual property falls into the latter category, with such things as stocks and shares or business goodwill, but it differs from other property in that rights are mostly limited in time, usually twenty years for patents and a fixed period after the author's death for copyright. Medieval authors wrote to spread their ideas or their reputation, not with any thought that they were creating property that could be defended against others. When a property right in a written work first came to be recognized, ownership by the printer-publisher was important, not that of the author. Patents originated as monopolies granted by royal letters patent, not only for inventions but also for other valuable items of commerce: the patentee's intellectual input was usually irrelevant. Eventually the creator of intellectual property was recognized as the first owner, the main exception being work produced for an employer.

What is intellectual property?

The two most important forms of intellectual property are copyright and patents. They are also the ones in which the creator's intellectual input is most obvious. Several other kinds of intangible property are usually included. Industrial innovations not satisfying the stringent tests for patentability are protected in some countries as utility models. The industrial designer's creativity merits design protection. Trade secrets are linked with other areas of confidential information. Trade marks are also considered as intellectual property. Performers' rights in their performances may be protected. In countries where copyright is narrowly defined as the author's right only, rights related to copyright, for example of a film producer or broadcasting organization, are known as neighbouring rights.

Intellectual property as economic property

Intellectual property generally has a monetary value. This can be very considerable, for a patent on a successful drug, for example, or the copyright of a best-selling novel. Creators of intellectual property are often dependent on earnings from inventions, writings or artistic work as their sole or principal means of livelihood. A publisher or film producer may own little property except copyrights. All these can be sold, or temporarily assigned, transferred as a gift or bequeathed in a will.

Intellectual property as moral property

Property can have a value beyond its pecuniary worth. The act of creativity that produces a work of intellectual property makes a special link between the creator and his or her work, especially in literary or artistic creations. The classic statement is in the famous words introducing the first French law on author's right in 1791, '*la plus sacrée, la plus personnelle de toutes les propriétés est l'ouvrage, fruit de la pensée d'un écrivain*'. France has always emphasized protection for the author's 'moral rights', particularly the rights to be recognized as the author and to object to derogatory treatment of the work. Britain saw copyright simply as economic property until moral rights were introduced in the Copyright, Designs and Patents Act 1988. In other areas of intellectual property the economic aspect is usually paramount but pecuniary loss is not always a prerequisite for legal redress.

Legal protection of intellectual property

In the United Kingdom the Patents Act 1977, Copyright, Designs and Patents Act 1988 and Trade Marks Act 1994 are the principal statutes protecting intellectual property. An owner may bring a civil action to stop infringement of a copyright, a patent, a trade mark or other intellectual property. The usual remedies are an injunction to stop illicit use and compensatory damages. Criminal sanctions are available, in particular, for illicit commercial exploitation of copyright material and fraudulent use of a trade mark. Nearly every country protects intellectual property by its law (though enforcement is sometimes poor). International conventions bind signatory states to provide minimum standards of protection and to protect the rights of each other's nationals. The most important are the BERNE CONVENTION, for copyright, and the Paris Convention, for patents.

Intellectual property and the public interest

Some people see the protection of intellectual property as a social contract under which society protects the owners' rights in return for their making their intellectual product available to the public (for suitable remuneration, of course). Others, however, see the restrictions imposed by law on the free utilization of intellectual property as undesirable, discounting the labour involved in its creation. This view is found in some countries where PIRACY is openly justified or covertly condoned, often with arguments that poverty prevents their paying high prices for imported materials, or even that it represents redress for supposed colonial 'exploitation' in the past. Widespread use of English means that authors and publishers in Britain and the USA are particular victims of copyright piracy.

The future

Modern technology has facilitated counterfeiting. The revolution in electronic storage and dissemination has meant that the old certainties of copyright in fixed paper-based works have given way before the infinite mutability of digital data. It is an open question whether the law of intellectual property will be able to cope. However, there is growing understanding worldwide of the property aspects of intellectual creations, with governments more active in enforcing rights.

Further reading

Marett, P. (1996) *Intellectual Property Law*, Sweet & Maxwell.

SEE ALSO: information policy; knowledge industries

PAUL MARETT

INTELLIGENCE

In common parlance, the capacity for understanding or the ability to perceive and comprehend meaning.

It also describes MILITARY INTELLIGENCE and other information about the affairs of a state or other corporate body, such as a commercial enterprise (business intelligence), or, indeed, an individual person, obtained to provide an advantage. Intelligence is frequently gathered clandestinely, by ESPIONAGE, as by national intelligence services.

SEE ALSO: information policy

INTERFACE

The hardware and software through which a user communicates with a computer system. The human–computer interface has progressed from the original hardware interfaces (rewiring the computer to make it perform a specific program), through batch processing (programs prepared as punch cards and processed in batches), to the command-line interface (the 'C-prompt' of DOS), to the current generation of GRAPHIC USER INTERFACES, menu-driven or with window/icon drivers.

SEE ALSO: Human–Computer Interaction; information and communication technology

INTERLIBRARY LENDING

The resources of a single library are only rarely sufficient to meet the needs of all its users. Interlibrary lending (ILL) is therefore a vital, if often small, part of most libraries' services, allowing users access to material that would not otherwise be available to them. At its basic level, ILL involves the short-term lending of an item by one library to another, generally for use by an individual user. In the 1990s, interlending began to be conflated with DOCUMENT DELIVERY. This can, in part, be seen as a move by interlending librarians to seek to raise the profile of interlending within libraries, though it should be noted that many library users regard the two activities as equivalent since both allow access to material not held in the user's own library, and both are user-initiated. Nevertheless, interlending (the lending of an item) is not the same as document delivery (the purchase of material).

Interlending arrangements vary in type and practice. They include direct transactions between two libraries; loans organized between members of a co-operating group of libraries; and nationally-organized interlending, operated either on a centralized (with material mainly being supplied from a single repository) or decentralized basis. National practices also vary. In the United Kingdom, moves towards co-operative provision began in the early twentieth century and by the 1930s Regional Library Systems (RLSs) had been formed, supplemented by what at that time was called the National Central Library (later becoming the BRITISH LIBRARY Document Supply Centre (BLDSC)) and co-ordinated by a National Committee for Regional Library Co-operation. This development was based on the principle that members of RLSs would borrow and lend within their own region, extending their search (via Regional Library Bureaux) outside the region only if an item were not available within it. In 1957 the National Lending Library for Science and Technology (NLLST) was formed to meet the needs of scientists and engineers for rapid access to the widest possible range of SERIALS. This proved the advantages of providing a large centralized stock arranged specifically for rapid retrieval of individual items. NLLST was incorporated into the British Library on the latter's formation in 1973 and eventually became known as the BLDSC. An example of such a co-operative venture in the USA is the Research Libraries Group (RLG), a non-profit organization existing to improve access to information in support of the research and learning of its member libraries' users. RLG is now an international membership alliance that includes universities and colleges, national and public libraries. Through its Shared Resources (SHARES) programme, RLG operates an effective international co-operative partnership that emphasizes generous lending and speed of supply at minimal cost.

The availability of library catalogues remotely (accelerated with the increased use of the World Wide Web in the 1990s) has prompted a steady increase in the availability of information about libraries' stock holdings worldwide, while UNION CATALOGUES such as COPAC (the merged catalogue of the Consortium of University Research Libraries (CURL)), and RLG's Union Catalog have greatly facilitated such searching. Although union catalogues recording the holdings of co-operating libraries are useful for identifying and locating items, they have sometimes proved difficult to keep sufficiently up to date for them to be accurate tools for ILL. The ability to produce electronic DATABASES out of groups of individual library CATALOGUES and union catalogues transformed the interlending scene, providing searchers with millions of references available online. Large database systems exist in most industrialized countries: OCLC and CARL in the USA, Unity and the BL catalogue along with the databases of co-operatives in the UK, SDB/ SUNIST in France and PICA in Holland are examples. Open systems interconnection (OSI) is the technology by means of which databases created on different computer systems may interact and be interrogated from within any individual system. In the USA the massive databases of OCLC and RLG, originally created for co-operative cataloguing purposes, have been put to use for interlending by libraries both inside and outside the USA. In Britain, Unity has a Web interface and utilizes Z39.50 interoperability protocols.

A direct effect of remote access to library catalogues has been to increase the number of libraries now able to make ILL requests direct to foreign institutions. From the 1990s, the IFLA Office for International Lending responded to this trend with a number of initiatives aimed at enabling international interlending to thrive. These included a twinning database so that libraries around the world could exchange information and materials; a new type of interlending payment voucher to enable international ILL to be undertaken with a minimum of administrative work; new guidelines on sending ILL requests by e-mail; a recommended list of standard response codes to ILL requests designed to overcome language barriers; and the revision of its guidelines for international interlending. The importance of international interlending within the ILL environment is now firmly recognized.

The vast growth in information about material and its location led to increased use of interlending in the mid- to late 1990s. However, DIGITIZATION and other forms of electronic provision of material (whether provided free, on subscription or for a one-off payment) have increased access to a wide range of material, and in early 2001 showed signs of leading to a decrease in interlending activity. This can be viewed in various ways, but in general terms may be regarded as resulting in interlending professionals returning to the fundamentals of their profession: using their experience and expertise to locate and obtain for their users material otherwise not available.

Further reading

Brown, D.J. (2000) *A Review of Future Developments in Inter-Library Loan and Document Delivery*, South Bank University.

Cornish, G. (1987) *Model Handbook for Interlending and Copying*, IFLA Office for International Interlending/UNESCO.

International Federation of Library Associations and Institutions (2001) *International Lending and Document Delivery: Principles and Guidelines for Procedure* (www.ifla.org/VI/2/p3/ildd.htm).

Interlending and Document Supply, MCB University Press [journal].

Jackson, M. (1993) 'Library to library: Interlibrary loan, document delivery and resources sharing', *Wilson Library Bulletin* (November): 66–8.

Pedersen, W. and Gregory, D. (1994) 'Interlibrary loan and commercial document supply: Finding the right fit', *Journal of Academic Librarianship* 20: 263–72.

DAVID ORMAN AND PENELOPE STREET

INTERNATIONAL COUNCIL ON ARCHIVES

History and objectives

The international non-governmental organization concerned with the management of records and ARCHIVES in all media and formats throughout their life cycle, founded in 1948. Initially its membership was drawn almost exclusively from the NATIONAL ARCHIVES of Europe and North America, but over the years it has become a truly international organization with members drawn from about 150 countries and including not only national archives but also many other archival institutions and individual archivists.

Its objectives are to encourage and support the development of archives worldwide, so as to preserve the archival heritage of mankind; to promote, organize and co-ordinate international activities in the fields of RECORDS MANAGEMENT and archive administration; to establish, maintain and strengthen relations between archivists and between institutions, professional bodies and other organizations concerned with the administration or PRESERVATION of records and archives or with the professional training of archivists; and to facilitate the interpretation and use of archival documents by making their contents more widely known and by encouraging greater ease of access.

Professional and technical development

ICA's work for the advancement of professional theory and practice is achieved through its sections and committees.

SECTIONS

Sections, which are self-governing groupings of archival institutions and archivists with a common interest, provide an opportunity for archival institutions and archivists outside national archives to play an active role in ICA and to contribute to professional and technical developments in their own special fields. They include sections for archival associations, archivists of international organizations, municipal archives, those involved in archival education and training, business and labour archives, archives of parliaments and political parties and university archives.

COMMITTEES

A number of expert committees undertake study and research, and disseminate their findings to the international archival community. They cover such subjects as electronic archives, archival automation, ARCHIVAL DESCRIPTION, legal matters, oral history, preservation, DISASTER PREPAREDNESS PLANNING, archival buildings and equipment, image technology, current records, archival terminology and climate history.

CONGRESSES AND CONFERENCES

Broader issues of professional concern are discussed every four years at the International Congresses on Archives, which incorporate open meetings of ICA sections and committees as well as plenary sessions and business meetings. Between Congresses the International Conference of the Round Table on Archives (CITRA), composed of the heads of national archives and of national archival associations, meets annually to discuss a topic of general interest.

PUBLICATIONS

ICA promotes professional and technical good practice through its publications. In *Archivum*, published annually, appear the proceedings of the International Congresses and volumes devoted to directories of archives, bibliographies, archival legislation and other scholarly and professional topics. *Janus* appears twice a year to disseminate the products of the work of the sections and committees. The proceedings of CITRA are published in a series of their own. In addition ICA publishes Handbooks and shorter Studies. The biannual *ICA Bulletin* includes reports of the meetings of ICA bodies and other news of interest to archivists. All members of ICA receive *Archivum*, *Janus*, the *ICA Bulletin* and new Studies.

To facilitate access to archives, ICA has supported the preparation of three series of Guides to the Sources of the History of Nations, covering Latin America, Africa south of the Sahara, and North Africa, Asia and Oceania respectively. These mainly describe sources for the history of those regions in archives in Europe and North America, but some deal with sources in one developing country that relate also to others.

International development

REGIONAL BRANCHES

To encourage the establishment, extension and modernization of records and archival systems and services throughout the world, ICA has formed ten regional branches covering the non-European regions. Each regional branch controls its own affairs, organizes conferences, seminars and other regional projects, and publishes a regional journal. The chairpersons of the branches meet annually as ICA's Commission on Archival Development (CAD).

INTERNATIONAL ARCHIVAL DEVELOPMENT FUND

A proportion of the dues of the national archives of industrialized countries is transferred to the International Archival Development Fund (FIDA) and the sum so raised is supplemented by voluntary contributions. FIDA provides aid to archives in developing countries, usually to help finance the travel of experts from outside the region to lead or speak at workshops and seminars or as consultants, or to support the participation of archivists from the poorest countries in regional activities. In addition ICA is often able to assist regional branches and archival institutions in developing countries by putting them in touch with other sources of international or regional aid, using FIDA to top up that aid when necessary and appropriate.

RECONSTITUTION OF ARCHIVAL HERITAGES

One of the concerns of developing countries to which ICA is committed is the reconstitution of their archival heritage through the provision of microform (see MICROFORMS) copies of series of archives relating to them held in archival institutions both in the former metropolitan countries and in other developing countries. The vehicle for this is the International Microfilming Programme for Developing Countries, which ICA has set up in collaboration with UNESCO.

Co-operation with UNESCO

In pursuit of its professional and international development activities, ICA works closely with the General Information Programme (PGI) of UNESCO, which, in addition to collaborating in the International Microfilming Programme for Developing Countries, has supported the establishment and activities of ICA's regional structure and other ICA projects. Perhaps the best-known fruit of this collaboration is UNESCO's Records and Archives Management Programme (RAMP), which includes the series of RAMP studies, covering virtually every aspect of records and archives work, and a number of preservation and CONSERVATION initiatives in which IFLA also has been a partner.

Further reading

Franz, E.G. (1984) 'Le Conseil international des archives, ses réalisations et son avenir', *Archives et bibliothèques de Belgique/Archief- en Bibliotheekwezen in België* 55: 3–27.
—— (1982) 'Der internationale Archivrat: Vergangenheit, Gegenwart, Zukunft', *Archivum* 29: 155–73.

MICHAEL ROPER

INTERNATIONAL STANDARD BOOK NUMBER

An International Standard Book Number (ISBN) is a ten-digit number assigned as a unique identifier to a book or other monographic publication before publication.

Background

The first Standard Book Numbering System was devised in the United Kingdom in 1967 and a brief history of its subsequent development is given in the introduction to *ISBN: International Standard Book Numbering* (1993). The description of the ISBN given here is based on the information presented in that guide, which is published by the Standard Book Numbering Agency Ltd, a wholly owned subsidiary of J. Whitaker & Sons Ltd. A current *Users' Manual* is available at www.isbn-international.org/html/userman.htm.

Function

The ISBN system was recommended for international use by the International Organization for Standardization (ISO) in October 1969 and ISO Recommendation 2108 was circulated to all its members in 1970. The purpose of this International Standard is to co-ordinate and standardize the use of identifying numbers so that each ISBN is unique to a title or edition of a book, or other monographic publication, published or produced by a specific publisher or producer. Other monographic publications include media such as audio, video, microfiche and software; however, serial publications, music sound recordings and printed music are specifically excluded as they are covered by other identification systems.

Structure

An ISBN is always ten digits in length and always divided into four parts. When printed, each part should be separated by a space or hyphen. The function of each part is as follows:

1   Group identifier: one to five digits in length. This identifies the national, language, geographic or other area in which the book concerned is published.
2   Publisher prefix: one to seven digits in length. Prefixes are allocated to publishers, principally according to their current rate of title output and/or the size of their backlist (i.e. past publications). A prefix uniquely identifies a publisher and will not be allocated to any other person or organization involved in the creation, production or distribution of a book.
3   Title number: can consist of six digits to one digit. Its length is governed by the number of digits in the publisher prefix that precedes it.
4   Check digit: one digit in length. The check digit is used to guard against a computer accepting a wrong number.

The ten digits used are the Arabic numerals 0–9; in the case of the check digit only, an X may sometimes be used.

Printing ISBNs on publications

ISO 1086: 1991, Information and documentation – Title leaves of books, specifies the locations for printing of an ISBN. In the case of printed material this shall be on the verso of the title leaf, or, if this is not possible, at the foot of the title page itself. Additional locations are at the foot of the outside back cover, if practicable, and at the foot of the back of the jacket if the book has one. Appropriate locations are also specified for monographic publications in other media.

Assignment

ISBNs are assigned by national standard book numbering agencies, e.g. the Standard Book Numbering Agency Ltd in the United Kingdom (www.whitaker.co.uk/isbn.htm) and R.R. Bowker in the USA (www.isbn.org). The agencies promote and supervise the use of the ISBN system in their own countries. They maintain master files of publisher prefix allocations and publish details of these. For a complete list of national agencies, see www.isbn-international.org/html/adgroup.htm.

Overall administration internationally

The overall administration of the international system is undertaken by the International ISBN Agency, at the Staatsbibliothek zu Berlin (Preußischer Kulturbesitz), Germany (www.isbn-international.org). The Agency has the following functions:

- To ensure the definition of groups.
- To allocate identifiers to groups.
- To advise groups on the setting up and functioning of group agencies.
- To advise group agencies on the allocation of publisher identifiers.
- To promote worldwide use of the system.
- To supervise correct use of the system.

References

ISBN: International Standard Book Numbering: Incorporating Guidelines for Numbering Software Intended for Sale by Retailers (1993) 7th revised edn, Standard Book Numbering Agency Ltd.

PHILIP BRYANT, REVISED BY THE EDITORS

INTERNET

The Internet is a metanetwork, or network of networks, which links up a global agglomeration of computer resources for public access. It began as an academic and research network, financially supported by the US government, but its phenomenal growth has brought in private and business users in great numbers.

In technical terms the Internet is distinguished by its use of particular networking PROTOCOLS. When a message is sent over the Internet, it is broken into small pieces, called packets, which travel over many different routes between the sender's computer and the recipient's computer. The networking protocol used to route the packets across the Internet is TCP/IP (Transmission Control Protocol/Internet Protocol). Use of this standard protocol enables computers using different operating systems to communicate with each other.

Interactions between computers on the Internet typically use the client/server model. The server is the computer system that contains information or resources such as Web, ELECTRONIC MAIL, DATABASES, software files, chat channels, etc. Users access those resources via client software that uses TCP/IP to deliver the item or service required. Internet technical standards are developed by the Internet Engineering Task Force (IETF) and promulgated by the Internet Society as international standards.

The number of Internet users was estimated at 195 million in September 1999, with predictions of over 300 million by 2005. These users access the Internet via commercial INTERNET SERVICE PROVIDERS (ISPs). ISPs appeared in the early 1990s in the UK (e.g. Demon, CIX) and originally offered access for a fixed fee on top of metered telephone charges. Freeserve in 1997 pioneered 'free' access in the UK, by removing the fixed fee and gaining revenue from a provider's fee for 0845 dial-in numbers. In the USA Netzero tried completely free access, with revenue coming solely from advertising, but this did not prove viable. In 2000 pressure from OFTEL, the telecommunications industry regulator, led to unmetered access flat-rate charges becoming available in the UK, having been the norm in the USA. As well, alternatives to modem access, which has reached a ceiling in terms of access speed, have appeared – namely ISDN, ADSL, cable modems and satellite. Known collectively as 'BROADBAND' these technologies offer not only faster access but 'always on' connections. Outside the home or office, cybercafés offer access for those without their own computers while Internet access is now also available via mobile phones and via televisions. In theory these changes should lead to ever more people spending longer and longer online, and having more attractive services (e.g. films on demand). In practice there have been problems in implementing the UK government's vision of 'Broadband Britain', some technical (immature technology), some commercial (market inertia) and some infrastructural (e.g. geographic limitations of cable and ADSL availability).

There is no central authority or organization that polices the Internet. Possibly because of its origins in US academic and research circles, the Internet has developed into a very open, democratic system in which free speech is respected (though not protected by international law); in theory at least, every user has an equal opportunity to be heard. The Internet has spawned a culture of co-operation and low-cost exchange of ideas, data and software hitherto unknown on such a scale. Not everything about Internet culture is worthwhile however.

Various legislative attempts to control and censor certain material on the Internet have been made, with varying degrees of success. Viruses (e.g. Sircam) have found Internet e-mail to be a fruitful dissemination mechanism. A recent development, PEER-TO-PEER systems, in which one piece of software acts as both a file SERVER and a retrieval tool, has caused concern. Napster was a peer to peer package for sharing MP3 (digitized music) files. Napster became so successful that at its height millions of users were sharing millions of music files. The problem was that many of these files contained COPYRIGHT music and eventually Napster was shut down by legal action instigated by the RIAA (Recording Industries Association of America). Hackers – individuals who exploit faults or weaknesses in Internet services and protocols usually for financial extortion – have regularly made headlines, some even taking sides in the first Internet 'infowar', fought online during the Kosovo crisis. Even well-intentioned efforts to extend the range of domain (names for computers; see DOMAIN NAME) on the Internet by ICANN (Internet Corporation for Assigned Names and Numbers) have foundered on unscrupulous business practices and litigation over name ownership.

The Internet has assumed a role as the latest in a line of MASS MEDIA, stretching back to books, newspapers, radio and television. Like these mass media, it encompasses aspects of those that come before and adds a unique feature. The Internet gives interactivity and is the first mass medium that allows the individual to interact with the mass.

Further reading

Poulter, A., Hiom D. and Tseng, G. (2000) *The Information and Library Professional's Guide to the Internet*, 3rd edn, Library Association Publishing.

SEE ALSO: economics of information; information and communication technology; information technology; networks; push technology; recommender systems; search engines; World Wide Web

ALAN POULTER

INTERNET SERVICE PROVIDER

Usually referred simply as an ISP and sometimes just Service Provider. However, ISP can also sometimes mean Independent Service Provider, which distinguishes a specialist service provider from a general telecommunications company. IAP (Internet Access Provider) is also used as a direct equivalent of ISP. It is not to be confused with providers of public access to Internet facilities such as libraries and information centres.

ISPs are companies that provide individuals and other companies with access to the INTERNET. An ISP needs TELECOMMUNICATIONS line access and this will often take the form of high-speed leased lines giving more independence from the telecommunication providers. In exchange for a payment, usually calculated on a monthly basis, the ISP provides a software package and username, and an access phone number that will allow the user to connect to the Internet and make use of its facilities. It was the appearance of ISPs that made the Internet a medium available to anyone with a computer, a telephone line and the ability to pay a regular charge.

INTRANET

The internal network of an organization, using the TCP/IP protocols. To provide an Intranet, a company must have its own LOCAL- (LAN) or WIDE-AREA NETWORK (WAN), a Web server and browsing software for users.

INVISIBLE COLLEGE

An information-sharing group such as those that have existed for many areas in science, and in other disciplines. Membership of such groups is largely dependent on personal communications and often initiated by meetings at research centres or conferences. SCHOLARLY COMMUNICATION is often facilitated by someone within the group assembling a mailing list, which can then be used to distribute a newsletter or other informal mailings. The group may then take on the status of a society, with all the apparatus of constitution and formal publications etc., by which stage its invisible college status has ended. The early stages of the development of new disciplines and subdisciplines are frequently identifiable by the existence of an invisible college. The INTERNET has greatly expanded the size and number of invisible colleges, and also their visibility, since many now take the form of mailing lists and newsgroups and other COMMUNITIES OF INTEREST.

Further reading

Noma, E. (1984) 'Co-citation and the invisible college', *Journal of the American Society of Information Scientists* 35: 29–33.

SEE ALSO: communication

ISLAMIC LIBRARIES

Introduction

Islam has a distinct and highly significant place in the history of ideas, but September 2001 created a need, both in the East and the West, for a fresh understanding of Islam and its intellectual approaches. Responses in the West can be judged from the State of Wisconsin's library initiative (2001), and *American Libraries*' results surveying the perspectives of Muslim-American librarians today (Chepesiuk 2002).

Islam as an intellectual movement and the emergence of its LIBRARIES as an area of study have already been mapped in the religious geography of the world. To understand this history, two questions must be answered: the first concerns the relationship between Islam and libraries, and the second is about the specifically Islamic elements in this. This article deals only

with the first question: the second is discussed elsewhere (Taher 1997).

What then is an 'Islamic library'? It is a library that focuses on Islamic – or Muslim – sources of information, irrespective of geographic concentration (Muslim majority/minority country), language focus or discipline orientation. Such libraries by their very nature were, from the very beginning, more public than private and, indeed, freely open to the public. This is, in effect, the untold story of the first free libraries of the world. There is an extensive literature on this history, both primary and secondary, so the present article merely highlights salient aspects.

The history of Islamic libraries has three phases, as follows:

- AD 610–1258, from the first revelation of Quran, to the destruction of Baghdad (also called the classical period).
- AD 1258–1924, from the relocation of the seat of the Caliph to other countries, to the end of the Islamic Caliphate, then seated in Turkey.
- AD 1924 onwards, a continuing evolution of this movement.

The first phase: AD 610–1258

In Islam, dissemination of knowledge is considered as worship. Based on the Prophet's emphasis on seeking knowledge, even from such distant lands as China, and in fulfilment of the religious commandment to spread knowledge, literacy, education and research gained real momentum. This process also gained impetus from external factors, such as classical literary influences from Rome, Byzantium and Persia; paper from China; and binding, calligraphy and illumination adapted by Muslims from other sources. These helped in beautifying an evolving knowledge base. The results were obvious in many ways, but more specifically in three different dimensions: first in the transmission of knowledge (Wheeler 1999); second in the development of an Islamic worldview (Sardar 1991); and third in heralding an age of scientific awakening. These processes directly inspired the Europeans' emergence from the Dark Ages. 'It was through [Islamic scholars'] work that Christian Europe received the inspiration for the Renaissance' (Lerner 1998: 69).

It became an accepted pattern for libraries to

be attached to mosques everywhere. This was because in addition to the mosque's primary religious focus as a place of worship it was the focal point of educational, political and social communication. It should be noted, however, that not every mosque had a library. It was mainly in the large mosques that books other than the Quran were also deposited. However, some mosques had several, often large, book collections (Sibai 1984: 408).

The literary and educational developments also created a felt need to have libraries in other institutions. Hence, we find libraries attached to a *madrasa* (school or college), *dargah* (or *qan-qah*, shrine), palace, research academy, university, etc.

It is pertinent to identify the terms that are used in this context. While the term *kitab* in Arabic refers to book, the place housing books was designated by its location as: *bait* (room), *khizana* (closet), *dar* (house), or in relation to activity, as *hikma* (wisdom), *ilm* (knowledge), etc. These terms are used interchangeably. Literally, the term library in Arabic is *maktabah*; in Persian/Urdu it is *kutub khana*, and in Turkish *kütüphane*. The Arabic term *maktabah* does not occur in the Quran; however, being a derivative of *k-t-b*, it does indirectly find a place in the Quran in connoting related concepts such as writing, pen, ink, papyrus, parchment, book, information, knowledge, learning, training, etc. Historians of the book have shown that papyrus was in use in seventh-century Arabia, and the papyrus codex that evolved in the same century facilitated preservation (Cook 2000: 52).

In this period Islamic libraries had royal patronage as well as scholarly involvement. It was a period that facilitated the development of industries relating to paper, ink, and later to printing, publishing, etc. It is important to ask how the infrastructure and infostructure reached a point of convergence in this culture. It can be viewed from a narrative of what the Islamic library looked like and what constituted a library in this age. The Muslim historian, al-Mukaddasi (tenth century) describes a library in Shiraz, Iran, thus:

> The library constituted a gallery by itself; there was a superintendent, a librarian, and an inspector chosen from the most trustworthy people of the country. There is no book

written up to this time in whatever branch of science but the prince has acquired a copy of it. The library consists of one long vaulted room, annex to which are storerooms. The prince had made along the long room and the store chambers scaffoldings about the height of a man, three yards wide, of decorated wood, which have shelves from top to bottom; the books are arranged on the shelves and for every branch of learning there are separate scaffolds. There are also catalogs in which all the titles of the books are entered. Only persons of standing are admitted to this library. I myself inspected this library, downstairs and upstairs, when all was still in order. I observed in each room carpets and curtains, I also saw the ventilation chamber to which the water is carried by pipes which surrounded it every side in circulation.

> (Lerner 1998: 75–6)

The royal patronage evident there was also to be found in many other sources. A master physician, Ibn Sina, reports on the focus of the collection. And as the following description shows, there is much scope for a detailed analysis of patterns of acquisition, preservation, storage and use of resources. According to Ibn Abi Usaybiya, famous biographer, it was in response to a summons from Sultan Nuh Ibn Mansur (976–97) that Ibn Sina visited the Samanids' capital, Bukhara. He reports thus:

> Having requested and obtained permission (from Sultan Nuh) to visit the library, I went there where I found many rooms filled with books which were packed up in cases (or trunks) row upon row. One room was allotted to works on poetry and Arabic philology; another to jurisprudence, and so forth, the books on each discipline being kept in a separate room. I then read the catalog of ancient authors and requested the books I needed. I saw (in this collection) books the very titles of which were unknown to most people, and which I myself have never seen either before or since.

> (Sibai 1984: 197)

There is evidence in abundance of the original research done by Islamic scholars. A number of documents survive to establish their creativity and its lasting results (UNESCO exhibition 1999;

Roper 1994). One example held by the National Library of Medicine, Bethesda, USA can be cited:

> On the 30th of November 1094 AD, a scribe in Baghdad completed a copy of an Arabic treatise by one of the most important medieval physicians and clinicians – Abu Bakr Muhammad ibn Zakariya' al-Razi, who worked in Baghdad in the previous century and was later known to Europe as Rhazes. This manuscript is the oldest volume in the National Library of Medicine and the third oldest Arabic manuscript on any medical topic known to be preserved today.
>
> (Islamic Culture and the Medical Arts 1999: 1)

In addition to libraries that were attached to a mosque, or *madrasa*, there were significant ones in research academies. Among the oldest surviving centers of learning, the best example is the Jamia Al-Azhar Library, Cairo. It started as a learning house in a mosque in AD 969, and had its first collection of reading materials within a couple of years. This is obvious from the fact that, besides being a mosque, it became – in less then a decade – a leading learning centre for religious, Arabic and metaphysical sciences. All sciences were taught at Al-Azhar in the olden times, and women attended tuition circles at the mosque.

Among the research centres and academies was Dar al-Hikma. It was founded in Cairo by the Fatimid Caliph al-Hakim (996–1021). The Egyptian historian Maqrizi in his Khitat states:

> On Saturday, the tenth day of Jumai II of the year 395 (1004 AD), the building called Dar al-Hikma was opened in Cairo. Seekers of knowledge took up their assets. Books were brought from the book-chests of the palaces (residences of the Fatimid Caliphs), and the public was permitted to enter. Anyone was at liberty to copy the book he wished, and whoever wanted to read a certain book found in the library could do so. Men of learning studied the Quran, astronomy, grammar, lexicography and medicine. More over, the building was adorned by carpets and all doors and hallways had curtains. Managers, servants, porters, and other menials were appointed to maintain the building. From the library of the Caliph al-Hakim, books which he had donated, were brought (to Dar al-Hikma). (They were) in all sciences and literatures and of

superb calligraphy such as no other potentate had ever been able to collect. Al-Hakim permitted admittance to everyone, without distinction of rank, who wished to read or consult any of the books.

> (Sibai: 1984: 187)

So influential was Islam that, in less than three centuries, libraries in urban areas facilitated free information access to all. Dr Ziauddin Sardar summarizes this remarkable process as follows:

> In one respect it is quite astonishing that in fewer than one hundred years after the hijra of the Prophet from Makkah to Medinah, the book had established itself as an easily accessible and basic tool for the dissemination of knowledge and information. However, when viewed from the perspectives of ilm (knowledge), waqf (pious endowment) and ibadah (worship), which the early Muslims put into operation at the level of individual, society, and civilization, the phenomenal spread of books and bookmen in early Islam does not look all that astonishing. Indeed when actualized at all levels of society, the conceptual matrix of Islam would work to produce the infrastructure for the dissemination of information in any society, even if it had serious flaws. The eternal concepts of Islam are for the real world: they do not operate in or have much significance for an idealized society.
>
> (Sardar 1991)

In short, this period of Islam, first, saved ancient learning from extinction, and, second, disseminated the knowledge in an enlarged and enriched form.

The second phase: AD 1258–1924

The destruction that brought the end of a glorious phase did not destroy the spirit. We find that libraries were still patronized and continued to be open to all. Many aristocrats and nobles competed with each other in building libraries. Abdur Rahim Khan-i-Khanan, the military general of Akbar the great (1542–1605), is said to have read books while travelling and in the toilet. He was reportedly fond of tracing paper, and invented a tracing paper of seven colours. He was the inventor of variegated paper also. He had his own library, with ninety-five people employed for different library and scholarly pursuits. His biographer, Maasir-i-

Rahimi, reports that scholars used this library for 'study and self-improvement'. This library was a public institution set up for the dissemination of knowledge and, as with other public libraries, some of its books disappeared. Some are preserved today at the Raza Library, Rampur, India, and at the Khuda Bhaksh Oriental Public Library, Patna, India (Taher 1997: 55). Some went abroad. In fact the British Library's Oriental Collections have their origin in the oriental-language manuscripts and printed books, and constitute probably the most comprehensive accumulation of oriental material in the world.

COLLECTION DEVELOPMENT was never limited just to Islamic theology/philosophy, and scholars continued to work in the same holistic manner as before. Muslim historians, for instance, did not simply write court chronicles or political history. A comparison of five contemporary sources that corroborate a factual report on an earthquake shows the intensity of scholarly interest that it aroused (Amateur Scientific Centre 2002).

Book hunting by individual scholars was common. The historian al-Biruni (seventeenth century) – who mastered Sanskrit, as well as Persian and Arabic – spent forty years searching for a copy of Mani's *Sifr as-Asrar*. Ibn Rushd (Averroes) (twelfth century) wanted to consult a monograph dealing with the Mutazilah philosophy, but had no access to it. Firishta (seventeenth century), another historian, visited the royal library of the Faruqi Sultans at Khandesh, India, in 1604 and from one of the books in this library he at last found the history of the Faruqi.

To get an impression of the book PUBLISHING industry, it is worth considering the state of printing. In the Ottoman Empire it was not well established:

Constantinople got its first printing press in 1726, and over the course of the eighteenth century the number of titles published in this, Islam's premier city, was only 63. Since it was closed down from 1730 to 1780 and again after 1800 it was really active for only 24 years, meaning that it turned out less than three new titles a year. It also meant that not only was the Turkish literacy rate much lower (5% as opposed to 50% in Europe), but that the Turks did not even see much need for a press. The point to be made is that Guten-

berg's invention was not only made in Europe; it succeeded there.

(Kimball 2000)

This sample, however, needs to be compared with the history of printing in the Islamic world generally (Cook 2000: 26; Taher 1997: 55).

In this age very few people set out to become librarians and bibliographers. The title for a person who managed a library was never consistent, but generally speaking in Arabic it is *warraq*, *ameen ul-maktabah*, *qayyim al-maktaba*; in Persian *kitabdars*; in Turkish *kütüphaneci*; and in Urdu *mushaf bardar*. Most of the librarians/bibliographers – e.g. the physician Avicenna or Ibn Sena (tenth century), the poet laureate Amir Khusro (fourteenth century), etc. were designated only because of their scholarship. They were conversant with both religious and secular sciences, and that brought them the status of information managers. For instance, Ibn al-Nadim, who is the first Islamic bibliographer, author of *Kitab al-Fihrist* (tenth century), could not have even imagined the value of this source. The principle duties of librarians included acquisition and preservation of resources, facilitating supplies for scholars, supervising the collation and correction of books in the collection, and co-ordinating with the library's endowment or management in administrative matters. Their contributions – as scholarly librarians – are evident in acquisition, preservation and dissemination of the Islamic literary heritage, and related scholarship.

With regard to the disappearance of libraries in this age, one point is worth mentioning. Despite the high level of bibliophilism, and the patronage that libraries enjoyed in the classical period, book burning did occur in the Muslim world. But if we trace the reasons for the loss of the great Islamic libraries, our attention is drawn by the tragic incidences of destruction of libraries by Christian crusaders, Muslim sectarianism and Mongol hordes (Lerner 1998: 78).

The third phase: AD 1924 onwards

In the third period there emerged a totally different type of library environment. These libraries not only have all the essential tools of the trade, but also are better placed to fulfil professional duties. While many Islamic libraries still exist in a less developed stage, there are a few that have developed using technological interfaces. An instance of such an advanced library is the Faisal Foundation's King Faisal Centre for Research and Islamic Studies, Riyadh, Saudi Arabia.

Interestingly, Islamic libraries are gaining importance in the professional sphere. A website provides, for the first time, some guidelines for planning and developing Islamic libraries – and, in addition to references to print resources, it also provides Web-based links (Ali 2002). The number of publications that have emerged in the last three decades in the area of Islamic libraries shows that there is a growing will among professionals to systematize the issues that relate to information access and control.

The mechanisms of cataloguing and indexing Islamic resources continue to grow – MARC 21 and DUBLIN CORE metatags are two tools that are available. It is worth mentioning that Arabic MARC is still being awaited. Library automation and virtual libraries facilitate easy access to Islamic resources. With one click, from a remote computer, it is possible to browse a Z39.50 gateway catalogue and find the required – audio, video, textual – Islamic resource including Library of Congress, Washington; British Library and School of Oriental and African Studies, London; and Chicago University Library's consortium holdings that provide access to a vast variety of resources.

Today Islamic librarians are following their predecessors in acquisition, preservation and dissemination. But today there is no synthesis of the roles of scholars and librarians: they exist as poles apart! In this frame of reference comes a message. It is from the staff of Bibliotheca Alexandria, Egypt, a replica of the ancient Alexandrian Library (historians agree that Muslims did not destroy it!): 'The library staff admit that they have no idea how to marry the library's public access mandate to its goal of becoming a center of excellence for scholars' (Veash 2002: A15). Maybe the combination of scholarship with knowledge management skills can make them scholarly librarians again.

References

Ali, S.A. (2002) 'Planning and managing special and Islamic libraries' (www.geocities.com/Athens/Rhodes/9485/) [10 April].

Amateur Scientific Centre, Pune (2002) 'Earth quake in Agra-Gwalior Region, North India, MMI 12 6th July 1505' (www.asc-india.org/gq/agra.htm).

Chepesiuk. R. (2002) 'Special news report: September 11 and its aftermath: Muslim-American librarians reflect', American Libraries (January): 40–3.

Cook, M. (2000) The Koran: A Very Short Introduction, Oxford.

Islamic Culture and the Medical Arts (1999) (www.nlm.nih.gov/exhibition/islamic_medical/islamic_01.html).

Kimball, C. (2000) 'Statistics on population and religion for the early eighteenth century' (http://xenohistorian.faithweb.com/europe/eu11b.html).

Lerner, F. (1998) 'Libraries of the Islamic world', in The Story of Libraries: From the Invention of Writing to the Computer Age, New York: Continuum.

Roper, G. (ed.) (1994) World Survey of Islamic Manuscripts, 4 vols, Al-Furqan Islamic Heritage Foundation.

Sardar, Z. (1991) 'The Civilization of the Book', in Z. Sardar (ed.) How We Know: Ilm and the Revival of Knowledge, Grey Seal.

Sibai, M.M. (1984) 'An historical investigation of mosque libraries in Islamic life and culture', PhD thesis, Indiana University.

Taher, M. (1997) Islamic Librarianship (Studies in Librarianship Series, Vol. 1). New Delhi, Anmol.

UNESCO (1999) International Exhibition On Islamic Science And Technology (http://www.unesco.org/pao/exhib/islam3.htm).

Veash, N. (2002) 'Egyptian library struggles to revive ancient glory', National Post (Toronto) (12 April): A15, library website (www.unesco.org/webworld/alexandria_new/vrml_virtual_visit.html).

Wheeler, B.M. (1999) 'Transmission of Muslim knowledge: Past traditions and new technologies', Symposium Research Papers, Islamic Information Sources, Riyadh.

Wisconsin Department of Public Instruction (2001) 'Libraries respond to national disaster' (www.dpi.state.wi.us/dpi/edforum/ef0507_3.html).

Further reading

Elayyan, R.M. (1990) 'The history of the Arabic-Islamic libraries: 7th to 14th centuries', International Library Review 22: 119–35.

Haider, S.I. (1979) 'Bibliographical heritage of Muslims', International Library Review 29: 207–18.

Inayatullah, S. (1938) 'Bibliophilism in medieval Islam', Islamic Culture 12: 154–69.

Meho, L.I. and Nsouli, M.A. (1999) Libraries and Information in the Arab World: An Annotated Bibliography, Greenwood Press.

Pedersen, J. (1984) The Arabic Book, Princeton University Press.

Taher, M. (2000) 'The book in Islamic civilization', My Islamicity (http://islamicity.cjb.net).

Wilkins, L. (1994) 'Islamic libraries to 1920', in Encyclopedia of Library History, Garland, pp. 296–306.

SEE ALSO: history of libraries

MOHAMED TAHER

J

JANET

Abbreviation of *Joint Academic NETwork*, the network linking UK universities, colleges, research councils and the British Library. It is their link to the INTERNET. Member institutions pay to belong, but ensure that access is free to users within the institution. JANET began in 1984, and was subject to a number of upgrades, which led to the creation of SuperJANET in 1992. This provided BROADBAND access through fibre-optic networks (see FIBRE-OPTICS). Improvements continue, and the proposed SuperJANET4 will offer further enhancement. It is used extensively for e-mail, to log on to remote databases, access library catalogues and send data files. Indeed it has become an indispensable component of academic life in the UK.

Further reading

www.superjanet4.net.

JENKINSON, SIR HILARY (1882–1961)

Founder of the modern archive profession in Britain.

Born in London and educated at Dulwich and Cambridge, he entered the civil service and was sent to the PUBLIC RECORD OFFICE (PRO). There he learnt the archivist's craft with medieval records, developing the principles that he was later to set out for the administration of both old and modern records. He worked in most departments of the PRO, and, amongst other achievements, helped to develop the physical care of records as a craft and science. During the Second World War he devised and directed a programme of air-raid precautions and of the temporary dispersal of records and staff to repositories outside London. He was also responsible for the development of the Records Administration Division, the PRO's most significant post-war development.

In addition to his practical work as an archivist, he taught as Maitland Lecturer in Palaeography at Cambridge (1911–35 and 1938–49), and Lecturer (from 1920) and Reader (1925–47) in Diplomatic and English Archives in the University of London. He was a founder of the British Records Association in 1932, and led the campaigns that, among other achievements, established the National Register of Archives, a nationwide network of local record offices, and also preserved many important archive accumulations from destruction. As the author of the *Manual of Archive Administration*, first published in 1922, he was a major influence on the education and training of all subsequent British archivists and fellow professionals in many other countries. He held many offices and received honours including a knighthood.

SEE ALSO: archives

JEWISH LIBRARIES

These also are proverbs of Solomon which the men of Hezekiah King of Judah copied out.
(Proverbs XXV, 1)

The library is at the heart of Jewish study and learning, and books are the lifeblood of the culture. The gloss on Proverbs XXV, 1 is that the archive commands a dynamic, texts held are for reproduction and dissemination, and are not just for lodgement. Two scrolls of the Law will serve to establish a Jewish congregation but possession of many denotes continuance and venerability – additions by gift or the support of charitable individuals commissioning a new scroll to celebrate some event or person – and offers exuberance of adornments and repletion. The Pentateuch as part of the Hebrew Bible (the TaNaKH: Torah, Nevi'im, Ketuvim = Torah, Prophets and Writings, comprising twenty-four books in total in the Hebrew canon) is read formally from the manuscript; also read from a scroll is the Book of Esther; otherwise, the prophetical readings, Ruth and the other 'scrolls', the Passover Hagaddah and psalters, *siddurim* (prayer books), *zemirot* (song-books) and 'benchers' (benedictions) are customarily read from printed editions.

Of the making of books there is no end as Ecclesiastes has it. The Jewish library starts with Pentateuch and TaNaKH, and burgeons through rabbinical commentary of Mishnah, Gemara and Talmud, Sifra, codification and Responsa, grammar and philology for super-commentary and translation (at different times into Aramaic, Yiddish, Ladino and the vernaculars of Europe, Persia and North Africa); it is compounded by the apparatus of worship and practice requiring prayer books and liturgy, benedictions and the Passover Haggadah, recensions for children and, in the past (and in Yiddish or the vernacular), recensions for women. All of these comprising 'holy writ' require care in the handling and the disposal such that faulty and damaged texts are required to be buried at the cemetery. In the past, settled communities had a '*genizah*' loft or cabinet for this purpose in the synagogue and the greatest surviving of these, the Cairo *Genizah* brought to Cambridge University Library in 1898, is researched and treasured anew amidst its own demands on modern library resources and technologies for PRESERVATION and analysis.

To the corpus of Bible, Talmud, Rashi (commentary), Psalms and Liturgy should be added legends of the Jews (through *midrash*, *aggada*, *tosephta* and other encapsulations of commentary), Kabbalah, Zohar and mystical writings, through to folktales and texts derived for edification, rounded off by poetry from Spanish Jewish poets for the sophisticated. If Chaucer's Clerk of Oxford could have had a Jewish counterpart his 'little shelf of a twenty books in black and red'

would easily be imagined from the above but what would have been characteristic of the Jewish scholar would have been the fact that he would also have carried duplicates, even triplicates of some cherished texts (accumulated by his father) in part to have something to offer by way of exchange.

The culture comes, in other words, as a library in itself and scholars have been famed for their LIBRARIES. The centres of Jewish teaching in Baghdad, in Spain and in Italy were where the congregational centres were naturally endowed with libraries so the great holocausts of Jewish literature such as the burning of Talmuds in fourteenth-century Spain and sixteenth-century Italy, and the like were the easier to enact because of the congestion of scholars' libraries that were available to be ransacked for the purpose.

From antiquity, the treasures of the scriptorium at Qumran reflect the devotion to the production of literary works inherent in the Jewish tradition, and in the Cairo *Genizah*, unique in its scope, can be seen the retentive instinct of the religious culture that sustained it. It took new strength from the invention of printing in Europe, and Hebrew printing was an early development of the new technology (requiring type cut in different standard and rabbinic alphabets), such that in Lisbon, Constantinople and elsewhere. Hebrew books were often amongst the first products of the new presses in their geographic march (so even Yiddish preceded English in the print culture of parts of western Canada in the nineteenth century). Printing brought a fruition of Hebrew book-making and empowered scholars with libraries of great strengths. To the Hebraists of the Reformation, from the Complutensian to Kennicott, the British and Foreign Bible Society (who had Hebrew types cast in India in 1817; Ricci's Plantin Polyglot brought Hebrew and Greek to China as early as 1604) and the Jewish enlightenment of the Haskalah period, the Biblical and rabbinical canon remained critical for the production of Hebrew books and the collections devoted to studying the language and the religion from whatever polemical standpoint.

The translation and printing of the Bible promoted intensively by the Reformation, and the debate over language throughout the seventeenth century, ensured the dissemination of Hebrew texts in manuscript and printed form. The great collections that remain at the universities and which came together in the British Museum from personal and official collections (Archbishop Laud, Lord Lumley and others) bespeak the intense interest in Hebraica (both among the linguists and the Christian-Platonists seeking among the mystical literature of the Jews), and also Judaica (counting the immense amount of millenialist literature of the period in general, translation of Josephus in particular, reprinted so often through the sixteenth to eighteenth centuries, and such draughts as the pamphlets accompanying the 'Jew-Bill' of 1753 in England) that inevitably went into the formation of the collections making up these libraries. A further strand, as much in evidence in Jewish as in gentile holdings, are texts of controversy between Rabbanite and Karaite Jews (a special feature of such libraries in the Russian sphere today).

This survey of the literature that makes up the religious and intellectual corpus of Jewish culture, and the basis of Jewish libraries, defines also the project of both Christian Hebraists and the philosemites and conversionists (not to speak of the defamers and antagonists) in their interest in Judaism and the Hebrew language. In the Middle Ages and at the Renaissance, Jewish libraries where they existed in any large scale were at the communal and congregational centres, as in Italy in particular. In the eighteenth century and under the development of the Haskalah, in Germany and France, collections developed taking in Jewish responses to the Enlightenment and the spread of the common humanist culture available to a people becoming free of old social and political constraints. Modern Hebrew, like Esperanto, a language of the nationalist era, inspired new matter for the Zionist era. The emergence of Yiddish from its place as a demotic and folk language in the era of migration brought about, in Whitechapel as on the Lower East Side and in Warsaw, the assimilation of Jewish and European literary culture with a profound discourse of translation – literary, political, philosophic, polemic and theatrical works bringing the wider culture to the Yiddish readership. The collections of, for example, the Whitechapel Public Library remained in use from the 1890s until the 1950s, an inspiration for Yiddish printing and reading over several generations. The academic collections of the Wissenschaft der Judentums in Germany, at Jews' College in London and the seminaries of New York and Cincinnati bear witness to the academic flowering of Jewish culture.

The early libraries in Jerusalem as the Yishuv developed prior to the formulations of Zionism and the inspiration for the Hebrew University, which predated the Balfour Declaration (1917), form the basis now of the Jewish National and University Library (JNUL) at the Hebrew University in Jerusalem.

Just as the geographico-historical progress of (Hebrew) printing marked the spread of scholarship, reading and libraries throughout Europe, the destruction of Jewry and Jewish learning in the wake of the Nazi holocaust and Soviet anti-Semitism has distorted the survival of the European-Jewish culture and its libraries.

The great repositories remain in Rome, the Escurial and Madrid, Paris and St Petersburg; in London, Oxford, Cambridge, John Rylands University Library of Manchester (JRULM) and other libraries in the UK with Middle Eastern interests; in New York and elsewhere in the USA; and in Israel where the Jewish National and University Library (JNUL) asserts for itself the function of a national and international haven for the historic collections of world Jewry. The endeavour that drove the Leo Baeck Institute from Germany to Britain and the USA and pockets in such places as Copenhagen (the Simonseniana at the Royal Library), Amsterdam (the Rosenthaliana) marks the survivors. The Mocatta Library at University College London (1905) was bombed in 1941 but has been reconstituted in part (by virtue of BM duplicates and Hebraica from the Guildhall); the Jewish Theological Seminary in New York was likewise reconstituted following a disastrous fire.

The great sales of collections that in earlier years saw the shift of bibliothecal gravity from Italy to England (when the Oppenheim collection was acquired by the Bodleian and the Almanzi MSS by the British Museum) continues today. Sales from the Sassoon collections, that of A.L. Shane and, most recently, the Beth Din Library of the United Synagogue in London have brought into temporary circulation (and the 'danger' of retention by private collectors) famous texts that may not find a home in a public library for another generation. Growth of collections is currently slow; there is small-scale purchasing of modern Hebraica at Oxbridge, JRULM and other libraries but little growth elsewhere (at Leeds, Jews' College, London, UCL for instance) and the British Library confines itself to editions of manuscripts as a core requirement only. Both the British Library and JNUL, however, opt to diversify by including glamorous texts as part of their DIGITIZATION of treasures fit for tourist and juvenile educational tours (the 'Golden Haggadah' and Maimonides MSS at the British Library, a treasury of Ketubot, marriage contracts, at the JNUL).

The residuum of this historico-geographic survey resolves in terms of library collections and heritage in the following:

Libraries in the British Isles

THE HISTORIC NATIONAL COLLECTIONS

- Bodleian, Cambridge, BRITISH LIBRARY, JRULM.
- University College London (UCL) (the Mocatta Library of the JHSE, based upon the collections of Lucien Wolf, Asher Myers, Hermann Gollancz, Moses Gaster and others, refurbished in part after war damage and losses, from BM duplicates held at the Guildhall), the Mishcon and Margulies collections; recent deposit of Rothschild material (belated transfers in the wake of the Sassoon sales).
- Cambridge with the Cairo *Genizah* and Oxford as a centre for Qumran Studies are assured of stronger prospects;
- Such places as the School of Oriental and African Studies (University of London): Israeli material, historic Judaica, Jewish music (transferred from the Guildhall School of Music and City University); Trinity College Dublin (TCD) with a token historic collection.
- The Porton Library, Leeds Public Library is the last such local studies collection of Jewish interest intact (but not kept up); the Manchester collection has been dispersed within the Central Library's general holdings (but the old subject card catalogue is retained); Whitechapel's Yiddish collections have been dispersed (to SOAS, UCL, Oxford).
- Modern collections of appeal to a Jewish readership are maintained at Westminster, Stoke Newington/Hackney, Barnet and Redbridge Public Library holdings, reflecting local concentrations of London's Jewish population;

COLLECTIONS BASED AT JEWISH INSTITUTIONS

- Jews' College (LSJS), Leo Baeck College; the Wiener Library; Oxford Centre for Jewish and Hebrew Studies at Yarnton; the Sephardi Centre at the Spanish and Portuguese Jews' Congregation, Maida Vale.
- There are also Jewish schools with appropriate libraries, synagogues and communal libraries on a small scale (nothing approaching the intensive provision of their US counterparts); also, the Scottish Jewish Archives in Glasgow and the Manchester Jewish Museum. Study centres for adult education usually muster small collections without much purpose; there is great enthusiasm for the programmes of such centres but little sense of the need to maintain libraries as part of their dynamic; despite the consolidation of efforts to sustain Jewish students at large the dispersal some years ago of the notable library at the Hillel House, London (the Jewish 'fraternity' house centre), is of a piece with the strategy of the United Synagogue in its disposal of books.

JUDAICA/HEBRAICA COMPONENTS

- Centres for German–Jewish Studies (Sussex), Leeds, Manchester, Holocaust (Imperial War Museum, Leicester University); Christian–Jewish Studies at Cambridge.
- Cambridge Colleges (W.H. Low collection at Trinity, Israel Abraham's collections at Queen's and the Oriental Faculty, Raphael Loewe's library destined for St John's), Lambeth Palace, Wellcome Institute, Durham and Exeter Middle East Studies; in Marsh's Library and at Trinity College Dublin; Hebrew editions are naturally a strong component in the Bible Society collections now at Cambridge.

JUDAICA

- The Parkes Library and the Anglo-Jewish Archive under the aegis of the Hartley Library at Southampton University.
- Anglo-Jewish archival material at Metropolitan Records, Glasgow, Liverpool and other centres; Messrs N.M. Rothschild's business archive.
- More tenuous, some Hebraica at the Liverpool Athenaeum and like establishments dating from the nineteenth century when local Jewish citizens took their places among the city worthies as professional men making gifts and deposits.

PRIVATE LIBRARIES

- Valmadonna, heir now to the Sassoon and Schocken collections and the like, strong in historic editions and manuscripts.
- A Zangwill collection, now deposited at Southampton.

Anglo-Jewry, however, at large is not a people of books. The failure of the Jewish institutions to recruit librarians at the commensurate level and to fund development of proper communal libraries exposes the strength of purpose of the United Synagogue in its recourse to its recent sales of its prime collections. This sale was grounded upon the profoundly philistine spirit of the Anglo-Jewish community. The scene contrasts with that of the USA where the major intellectual Jewish institutions of New York and New England have recently come together in a major consortium, the Centre for Jewish History, where the Association of Jewish Libraries, in parallel with the American Library Association, maintains committees and programmes at all levels of library interest, and is influential alongside the (American) Jewish Book Council in promoting books and libraries. Its Anglo-Jewish counterparts are but shadows by comparison.

The wider dereliction is reflected in the failure of a proposal to the British Library for the mounting of a major exhibition on Maimonides for his 800th anniversary in 2004; the proposal did not even reach the last six in consideration for that year. The Library does, however, promote Maimonides on a website and has digitized famous texts as public attractions. Many feel, however, that it is losing touch with scholarship and reducing acquisitions drastically.

The Mocatta Library at UCL, now absorbed into the general college Judaica holdings and the aegis of the Institute of Jewish Studies, augmented recently by Yiddish deposits, makes a respectable modern collection but is not dynamic in the field. Likewise, SOAS too. Recent academic funding through Higher Education Funding Councils' Research Support Libraries Programme projects for retrospective conversion has ensured that, across the board, Hebrew, along with other script materials, has finally been brought into the modern purview of library systems. But progress is still hampered by the failure to promote the development of a solution to the problem of non-roman character-sets in automated catalogues. SOAS has long been at fault across all its collections, lacking not only the resources but also the will to secure the necessary support to promote development in an area of what in effect is its rationale.

Further reading

Beit-Arié, M. (2000) 'The individualistic nature of the Hebrew medieval book production and consumption', in *Zion, Jerusalem*, pp. 441–51 [texts recreated for personal use; reflects the extent of literacy in Jewish society, furnishing of texts].

Encyclopaedia Judaica (1971) Jerusalem: Keter Publishing House. [The substantive article on Jewish libraries appears in: Vol. 11, cols 190–8, and includes an entry for the Jewish National and University Library at the Hebrew University.]

Friedman, P. (1980) 'The fate of the Jewish book during the Nazi era', in *Roads to Extinction: Essays on the Holocaust*, ed. A.J. Friedman, New York: Conference on Jewish Social Studies and the Jewish Publication Society of America.

Goldstein, D. (1985) *Hebrew Incunables in the British Isles: Preliminary Census*, London: British Library.

Massil, S.W. (1999) 'The books of Anglo-Jewry', in *Jewish Year Book 1999*, Valentine Mitchell, pp. xxxii–xli.

Reif, Stefan C. (1997) *Hebrew Manuscripts at Cambridge University Library: A Description and Introduction*, Cambridge: Cambridge University Press (University of Cambridge Oriental publications 52) [assisted by S. Reif and incorporating earlier work by S.M. Schiller-Szinessy, H.M.J. Loewe and J. Leveen, and including palaeographical advice from E. Engel].

Roth, C. (ed.) (1937) *Magna Bibliotheca Anglo-Judaica: A Bibliographical Guide to Anglo-Jewish History*, rev. and enl. edn, London: The Jewish Historical Society of England, University College [a revised edition of *Bibliotheca Anglo-Judaica*, compiled by J. Jacobs and L. Wolf (1888), and a catalogue of the material bearing on the study of Anglo-Jewish history that is to be found in the Mocatta Library and the allied collections housed in University College, London].

Rowland Smith, D. and Shmuel Salinger, P. (eds) (1991) *Hebrew Studies: Papers Presented at a Colloquium on Resources for Hebraica in Europe, Held at the School of Oriental and African Studies, University of London, 11–13 September 1989/11–13 Elul 5749*, London: The British Library (British Library occasional papers 13).

Sabar, S. (1990) *Ketubbah: Jewish Marriage Contracts in the Hebrew Union College Skirball Museum and Klau Library*, Philadelphia: Jewish Publication Society of America.

Shavit, P. (1997) *Hunger for words: books and libraries in the Jewish ghettos of Nazi-occupied Europe*, Jefferson, NC: McFarland & Company.

Steinschneider, M. (1852) *Catalogus Librorum Hebraeorum in Bibliotheca Bodleiana/Digessit et Notis Instruxit M. Steinschneider*, 2 vols, Berolini: A. Friedlaender.

STEPHEN MASSIL

JOINT USE LIBRARIES

A single facility, usually an actual library building, which has been jointly created by two or more organizations to serve the combined library needs of their users. Joint school and PUBLIC LIBRARIES are perhaps the most common occurrence of this type of arrangement.

Further reading

Call, I.S.B. (1993) 'Joint use libraries, just how good are they?', *College and Research Libraries News* 54(10): 551–6.

SEE ALSO: school libraries

JOURNAL

A periodical publication, particularly one issued by a society or institution and containing proceedings, transactions, reports, substantial articles and reviews of publications in a particular scholarly or scientific field. The connotation is one of quality and reliability, and the term learned journal is often used. The term has almost entirely lost its literal meaning, derived from the French, of 'daily newspaper'.

SEE ALSO: economics of information

JOURNALISM

Writing for a newspaper or magazine, but, by extension, the profession of compiling, writing for and editing newspapers and other periodicals. Sometimes used derogatively to indicate ephemeral and tendentious writing.

SEE ALSO: mass media

K

KEYWORD

A word that succinctly and accurately describes the subject, or an aspect of the subject, discussed in a document. In a permuted title index, the word from the title of a document considered to be most indicative of the subject matter, i.e. the keyword, can be used as an indexing term, permuted by one of a number of methods: KWIC (KeyWord in Context), KWAC (KeyWord and Context) or KWOC (KeyWord out of Context).

SEE ALSO: organization of knowledge

KILGOUR, FREDERICK GRIDLEY (1914–)

Librarian and founder of Ohio College Library Center (OCLC).

Kilgour was born in Springfield, Massachusetts, and studied at Harvard. He entered the Widener Library whilst still a student as a Circulation Assistant, and studied librarianship at Columbia University. His war service, from 1942 to 1945, was as Executive Secretary of the Interdepartmental Committee for the Acquisition of Foreign Publications, and after the war he was Deputy Director of the Office of Intelligence Collection and Dissemination in the Department of State. From 1948 to 1965 he was Librarian of Yale University School of Medicine. During this time he was deeply involved in one of the major early library automation efforts, the Columbia–Harvard–Yale Medical Libraries Computerization Project. Then, as Yale's first Associate University Librarian for Research and Development, between 1965 and 1967, he oversaw the University Library's first experiment in automation.

In 1967, as Director of the OCLC, he was able to build on his experience in automation at Yale. By 1971 OCLC's shared cataloguing system was available online in Ohio. Within two years it could be used elsewhere through other academic library consortia across the USA, and by 1978 it was reorganized as a national service. This breakthrough in shared cataloguing has subsequently transformed the work of academic and other libraries worldwide.

SEE ALSO: espionage; library automation

KILOBYTE

One thousand BYTES of digital data; usually written Kb.

SEE ALSO: informatics; information and communication technology

KNOWLEDGE

Knowledge is information evaluated and organized in the human mind so that it can be used purposefully. In this sense, the term can be equated with understanding.

However, it is generally used in an imprecise way to describe phenomena to which the term 'information' is otherwise often attached. The terms KNOWLEDGE INDUSTRIES, knowledge work and knowledge worker have been used since the 1960s, since they were introduced by Fritz MACHLUP and others to identify the components of what was described as a knowledge economy or knowledge society. At much the same time the same phenomena were described by PORAT as an INFORMATION SOCIETY. In a knowledge society, employment in the older forms of productivity, agriculture and industry, is replaced by knowledge-based work, which requires workers with higher levels of schooling and post-school qualifications, and in which companies may have few assets other than the knowledge resources of their workforce. Whilst the term knowledge industries has sometimes been replaced by the related, but not identical, term CULTURAL INDUSTRIES, the descriptor 'knowledge' remains significant.

KNOWLEDGE-BASED COMPANIES

Commentators identify a new type of company, built upon knowledge: typically in TELECOMMUNICATIONS, electronics, SOFTWARE or biotechnology, but also offering high-technology services to more traditional industry. Their need to bring technology-based products and services to market fast puts the premium on research, and they are therefore heavily dependent on an infrastructure of high-quality education. They also rely on the ready availability of venture capital and public start-up funding for innovation. They are also referred to as knowledge-intensive companies or learning companies.

KNOWLEDGE INDUSTRIES

The whole range of commercial and industrial activities that underlie and facilitate the compilation, distribution and sale of such products as books, databases and broadcasts. All organizations, media and formats that are capable of performing all or part of these functions are covered by this definition. They include, but are not confined to, publishing, television and radio programme origination, and the creation and hosting of databases.

Concepts: producers, products and formats

The primary producers of KNOWLEDGE are individuals who generate it through intellectual creativity based on experimentation, empirical research, observation, experience, reading or imagination. Traditional knowledge structures, such as that suggested by MACHLUP (1962), classify knowledge by a combination of the process of creation and the typology of the knowledge itself; the latter includes, for example, scientific, social and artistic knowledge. These intellectual constructs are valuable in enabling us to understand the nature of knowledge itself and its relation to information; indeed, they form the conceptual basis of INFORMATION SCIENCE as a discipline. In practice, however, all forms of knowledge can be articulated only through a system of COMMUNICATION; such systems range from human speech and gesture to sophisticated digital technologies. Whenever the communication of knowledge goes beyond simple interpersonal communications in real time (such as a conversation) or interpersonal communication over distance (via POSTAL SERVICES, for instance), it can be achieved only by using the infrastructure of support that the knowledge industries have developed.

The knowledge industries, therefore, although they are only secondary producers, are nevertheless the only channel through which knowledge can be communicated by the creator to the consumer. The longest established and still the largest group of such secondary producers are publishers. The role of the publisher is essentially that of capitalist and organizer of the communication of information and knowledge. The practice of book PUBLISHING is over 500 years old; it can be taken as typifying many of the practices of the knowledge industries as a whole, and has been used as a paradigm of them, a practice which is discussed below under 'Functions and operations'. In brief, the business of the publisher is to provide a means by which authors can reach their audience. This involves accepting unsolicited work or commissioning work for publication; the satisfactory completion of the work by the primary producer is followed by a process of editing, production (in the form of print on paper), marketing, sales and distribution. A vast international industry has grown up around these apparently simple processes.

It is convenient to distinguish between publishers and media companies, although this is a technical rather than a strictly commercial distinction. The media organizations of greatest relevance here are those involved in the production of radio and television, although the film and music industries impinge on them at various points. Such organizations have historically been typically larger than publishing houses, partly because of the very high capital costs of production. Moreover, even in countries with liberal political traditions such as freedom of the press there has typically been greater state involvement, especially in BROADCASTING, than would normally be considered acceptable in print-on-paper publishing. Media organizations therefore operate under legal and regulatory regimes that are in some respects fundamentally different from those familiar to publishers. The final producer group that ought to be distinguished is indeed the Internet Service Providers and the HOSTS that provide access to DATABASES. Such hosts are not normally the primary producers of the databases to which they sell access; in many ways, however, their function is analogous to, or at least comparable with, that of the secondary producers exemplified by publishers. They provide the essential channel of communication through which primary producer and end-user are brought together.

The distinctions, and the relationships, between different categories of secondary producers in the knowledge industries are undergoing profound change. This change is technologically driven, and is increasingly being formulated as a CONVERGENCE of formerly separate technologies and media. Perhaps the most obvious example lies in the development (which is rapid in some countries) of television programmes delivered to the home by cable rather than by broadcast signals; at the same time, telecommunications, traditionally delivered by cable, are increasingly available through wireless systems, not least in mushrooming networks of MOBILE COMMUNICATIONS systems. The two technologies – broadcasting and TELECOMMUNICATIONS – are thus brought together, opening up a wide range of commercial and social possibilities for producers and customers alike. Similarly, traditional boundaries between products and formats are eroding or being reconfigured. In the 1990s, there was a convergence not only of the technologies of knowledge production and distribution, but also of the companies that were involved in it. The whole business is now dominated by a small number of global corporations that are involved in book, magazine and newspaper publishing, in film and video production and distribution, and in terrestrial, cable and satellite broadcasting, as well as being, in some cases, major providers of content to the INTERNET, and Internet Service Providers themselves. This conglomeration of

interests is typified in such companies as News Corporation and AOL Time Warner.

Typical products of the knowledge industries include books, magazines, newspapers, television and radio programmes, and databases. It is difficult, but important, to make a clear distinction between products – such as these – and formats; for the purposes of this article, formats are understood to be merely the means by which the product is packaged and presented to the end-user.

Formats are many and various, and they are continually increasing in number as a result of technological developments. Print probably remains the most common format for the communication of information throughout the world, although it has been displaced for many purposes. It is used for books, magazines (of all kinds) and newspapers, all of which are products created by publishers. It should be noted, however, that many newspapers and some magazines would position themselves with the MASS MEDIA rather than with the more traditional products of publishing. This crossover, particularly apparent with the popular press and international mass-circulation magazines, will be explored further under 'Practice' below. Many other products that were traditionally printed are now also, or in some cases only, available as digital objects, whether as CDs or databases accessible online, often through websites. This includes such familiar products as REFERENCE BOOKS, many ABSTRACTING AND INDEXING SERVICES, BUSINESS INFORMATION SERVICES and other information for the financial services sector, and reference materials in specialized areas such as LEGAL INFORMATION and MEDICAL INFORMATICS. Indeed, the long-term future of printed reference materials must now be called into question.

Print stands clearly and separately as a long-established and widely understood medium. Indeed, the ability to read, which is fundamental to the use of printed media (with rare exceptions), has long been regarded in Western culture as the most fundamental educational attainment; its acquisition is regarded as a major indicator of both personal and national development. The other formats under consideration all differ from print, but are like each other in one fundamental respect: all require some form of apparatus to give access to them. Much of this apparatus, most obviously the television set, is so familiar as to be almost unnoticed in daily use. Its familiarity, however, should not be allowed to conceal the complexity that lies behind it in providing systems through which programmes and other information are delivered to the end-user.

The oldest form of television and radio product is the terrestrial broadcast, but in television this is being challenged and to some extent replaced by other formats. These are cable and satellite, sometimes in combination. CABLE TELEVISION is widespread in the USA and becoming more common elsewhere in the world. Cable companies provide a wide range of choice of viewing, often highly specialized (such as news, sports and movie channels), far more economically than traditional terrestrial broadcasters can do. Satellite broadcasting, based on the bouncing of signals to and from geo-stationary satellites, is increasingly common in Europe and Asia, and is comparable to cable in its ability to offer multiple channels of programming for a wide range of specialist and generalist tastes. The two can be combined: the satellite signal can be rediffused through a cable system to the end-user. The commercial element in all three television systems is paramount; until recently, television was funded through a combination of advertising and sponsorship. Some countries favoured a system of total or partial state funding; other methods include fees charged to users (such as the Television Receiving Licence in the UK) or supporter contributions (such as those for public service channels in the USA). Both satellite and cable tend towards payment by subscription; this may take the form of an annual fee to cover unlimited viewing, or a 'pay-as-you-view' system monitored by the device that decodes the signal when it is received through the cable, receiving dish or aerial.

Television was traditionally associated with mass broadcasting of programmes with wide popular appeal, but multichannel provision through cable and satellite systems has made specialized channels a reality. They include minority language channels, as well as channels for minority interests, and programming with a fairly limited appeal. At one end of the spectrum, this takes in 'art' movies; at the other, it includes shopping channels, home improvement channels and the like.

Television, however, can be used for other formats than broadcast programmes. Teletext and VIDEOTEX systems have been in use for over twenty years by the terrestrial broadcasters. There are now interactive digital systems, using both broadband cables and digital terrestrial and satellite broadcasting systems, to make the domestic television set the gateway to information services and databases, and to electronic mail and other network facilities. This has begun to take television into an area traditionally dominated by hosts rather than media organizations, providing another, and potentially the most significant, example of convergence between information and communications technologies.

Functions and operations

The knowledge industries are capital-intensive, although for the primary producers the capital is intellectual rather than financial. At the secondary level, with which this article is principally concerned, there are clear differences in capital requirements, operational arrangements and organizational structures between the various media and formats. The classic model is that of book publishing, and some of its terminology has been adopted in other areas. Although book publishing can form the basis of an analysis, it cannot stand alone or be regarded as an archetype. The paradigm is no longer applicable; in its place, a number of models must be explored under each of four key topics:

- Capital costs.
- Organization of production.
- Research and development.
- Marketing and sales.

CAPITAL COSTS

Although the knowledge industry engages in a form of mass production (of copies of books, for example), only in some very specialized applications (such as the newspaper industry) does it achieve a scale of output that allows the full cost–benefits of mass production to be obtained. More typically, there is very heavy front-end investment in a product, on which the returns are slow and fragmented. This is particularly true in book publishing, where all but a fraction of the publisher's costs are incurred before any income can be generated. A typical book, printed in 5,000 copies, must be edited, produced and marketed as a single operation; no copies can be sold until all the copies have been produced, since it is grossly uneconomic to keep the 'production line' (that is, the printing press) running on a continuing basis. Hence there can be no cost recovery, and certainly no profit, until almost all of the capital cost has been expended. Since time that elapses between the receipt of the manuscript from the author and the first sales of the book is typically of the order of nine months to one year, and the total selling time for a general trade book is about eighteen months to two years, the publisher's capital investment in any given title can be tied up for at least three years before achieving the returns on which the costing and pricing of the book was predicated. There is therefore an incentive to sell as many copies as possible as quickly as possible after publication and to have a continuous flow of many titles so that current sales can in effect provide the capital for future titles.

Book publishing is not the only manifestation of the knowledge industries in which the front-loading of capital costs is so conspicuous. The same is true in the production of television programmes and (although on a lesser scale) of radio programmes. Programme origination for both radio and television normally follows one of two routes: it is developed by an organization that combines the functions of production and broadcasting, or by a company that engages only in production and then sells or leases its product to a broadcaster. Historically, the former model has predominated, but independent production companies have become increasingly important in the industrialized countries since the early 1980s, and in both the United Kingdom and the USA now take a significant and growing share of the total market. In commercial terms, the fundamental difference between independent production companies and the broadcasting organizations is that the former retrieve their investments and make their profits by selling their products to the latter. The broadcasting organizations themselves, on the other hand, can generate revenue only by selling advertising and sponsorship time, and perhaps subsidiary rights to some programmes, as well as, in some countries and in some broadcasting organizations, through an additional fiscal input from subscriptions or taxation. Ultimately, however, all genuinely commercial broadcasting is dependent on its ability to appeal to an audience that will attract advertisers, and the organizations must produce or purchase programmes that will achieve that overriding objective.

Whatever the organization of production, the costs are high. Despite recent technological developments, discussed under 'Research and development' below, both equipment and facilities are expensive. A fully equipped studio is a multi-million-pound investment, and even the most modest programme costs many tens of thousands of pounds to make. When professional actors or presenters are used, costs increase rapidly. The technical and artistic skills needed for production are in short supply, and also consequently expensive. Independent production companies (and indeed broadcasting organizations) often draw on the large number of freelancers or small companies in the field, but, while that reduces the administrative overheads of production, it has less effect on the cost of the production itself.

In the third key area of the knowledge industries – database production and sale – the position is somewhat different from that in publishing and broadcasting, although it includes some elements that are comparable to both. The earliest commercial databases grew out of traditional publishing activities such as the production of reference books, bibliographies, indexes and abstracts. Indeed, there are significant overlaps between ownership in publishing, the mass media and the database sector. The capital investment in databases, however, is typically lower than that in conventional print-on-paper publishing of the type that it is now displacing. The costs of knowledge generation – the processes of abstracting or compiling bibliographic records, for example – remain essentially the same in intellectual terms regardless of the format of the output, but the transfer of the generated knowledge into its permanent format is significantly cheaper for database producers than it is for book publishers. No physical product is needed beyond the digitized record, which is typically generated by the primary producer, who in this case may be, for example, an abstracter or a cataloguer. Cost recovery can begin at the moment of creation if charges are directly related to use, as is typically the case with online databases, and updating of the accessible file is in real time, which is somewhat less usual. The generation of income, like the enhancement of the database itself, is in any case a more or less continuous process, with none of the waiting time that characterizes traditional publishing.

The production of off-line media for access to databases (typically a CD-ROM) inevitably involves somewhat higher costs, but, despite the greater similarities, the underlying considerations are still fundamentally different from those which apply to books. The difference partly grows out of the differences between the technologies involved. Printing is a process that can be efficiently applied only to the production of large numbers of identical copies as a single operation. The copying of digitized files, however, can take place almost instantaneously, with little advantage to be gained from continuous production of multiple copies. In effect, CD-ROMs (and indeed other media such as MICROFORMS) can be produced on an on-demand basis without any significant delay, and without incurring disproportionately larger costs than those of producing consecutive multiple copies on a continuous basis. The expenditure and the income-generation of the producers are thus brought more nearly into chronological line with each other. Moreover, updated versions analogous to the revised edition of the printed book can be produced with as little difficulty as the first 'edition' and at substantially lower costs, since the process of revision is not merely continuous, but the very essence of the enhancement and growth of the database itself.

ORGANIZATION OF PRODUCTION

A key element in any analysis of the organization of the knowledge industries lies in an understanding of their intermediary role between primary producer and ultimate consumer. The relationships thus created are primarily economic, although they are regulated within a legal framework that protects the INTELLECTUAL PROPERTY rights of the knowledge creator or primary producer and, subsequently, the capital investment of the legitimate secondary producer, such as a publisher.

The book publishing model is simple and familiar. An author writes a book, which has either been commissioned by a publisher or is submitted to a publisher for consideration. In either case, the agreement to publish ultimately takes a contractual form, in which the two parties agree on such matters as subject, length, delivery date, format and size of edition, and method of payment. For the author, the latter is typically a royalty calculated as a percentage of the publisher's income from the book, although advances against expected earnings (usually modest but occasionally, in fiction publishing, extre-

mely large) are also normally offered for titles with any realistic commercial prospects. The publishing house itself is then organized in a way that facilitates the efficient and cost-effective production of the book. Traditionally this involved a substantial number of employees engaged in such tasks as commissioning, copy-editing, design, production management, marketing, publicity and sales. In both the United Kingdom and the USA, however, the pattern changed significantly during the 1980s. Much of the work is now done by freelancers, to the extent that in some publishing houses only the core functions of commissioning, production management and marketing are undertaken on an in-house basis.

Newspapers and magazines are produced on a different basis, with an editor responsible for the contents of each issue. Staff writers are responsible for much of what appears and are retained on a salaried basis. Newspapers, however, also employ correspondents, both on a geographical and a topical basis ('our Scottish correspondent' or 'our football correspondent'), not all of whom are full-time or exclusive employees of a particular newspaper. Freelance writers are also important, especially for the magazines; they are paid for each article accepted, usually on the basis of the number of words printed. In the newspaper and magazine industry, unlike book publishing, intellectual property rights are normally assigned outright to the publisher, even when they are not generated by contracted employees.

Radio and television production have moved, in an organizational sense, in the same general direction as book publishing, with a marked increase (required or facilitated by governments in some countries, including the United Kingdom) in the number and importance of production companies that are independent of the broadcasting networks. Any production organization, however, regardless of its relationship to the broadcaster, needs access to a wide range of skills, including those of writers, designers and directors, as well as the technical skills of sound engineers, camera operators and so on. Much of this can now be supplied on a freelance basis or by small companies that specialize in, for example, sound or lighting. Even producers and directors are often employed on a freelance contract to produce a particular programme or series. Broadcasting production is a highly complex task – intensive of skilled labour, in which there is a very competitive market. Management skills of a high order are needed to achieve profitable outcomes, but increasingly these skills are applied to bringing together a large number of individuals and small companies in a particular enterprise. Mass-media production, ironically, is beginning to take on some of the characteristics of a pre-industrial cottage industry.

Again, the database industry falls somewhere between book publishing and the broadcast media. Much work is done on a freelance basis, a trend that is being reiterated by the massive expansion of public-access networks that facilitate TELECOMMUTING by freelancers, who may even be on a different continent from some of their clients. Only the hosts and producers have a formal existence as a business organization analogous to a publishing house. They function as publishing houses, commissioning, organizing, funding and distributing the databases. When the product is material as well as electronic (such as a CD-ROM), the analogy is even closer.

RESEARCH AND DEVELOPMENT

Relentless and continuous technical innovation has characterized all the communications industries since the mid-1960s, although the speed and application of the results of that innovation have varied greatly between sectors and indeed between countries. In newspaper publishing, for example, the use of computers as direct-input devices by journalists was delayed in the United Kingdom for a decade after it was commonplace in the USA; conversely, letterpress printing had almost vanished in the United Kingdom several years before offset lithography (its successor) made any serious inroads into the book printing industry in the USA.

In general, the knowledge industries have been beneficiaries rather than originators of technological innovation. All sectors of the industry have nevertheless been profoundly changed, directly or indirectly, especially by the last twenty years of development in computing. The database sector in its present form is the most obvious product of the computer age, even though it has developed out of traditional academic, technical and reference book publishing. Broadcasting production, especially for television, has also been at the forefront of the use of innovative technology. The initially electromagnetic and subsequently digital technologies of video recording have almost entirely displaced photographic media for the

creation of broadcast images. Among the consequences have been a decrease in the cost of production as well as greater flexibility in the location of programme-making. Drama of all kinds, news gathering and documentary programmes have perhaps been the major beneficiaries of the greater flexibility offered by video over film, but no field has been left untouched.

The book publishing industry, throughout the world, has always been notoriously conservative, but much of this traditional conservatism has been overcome in recent years in the industrialized countries. Authors themselves partly led the change by their insistent use of WORD PROCESSING and their consequent ability to submit work in electronic formats. In turn, this shifted some of the burden of editorial work from the publisher to the author, and can even be argued to have changed the publisher's traditional role as quality controller. Small-scale publishing has particularly benefited from the increased sophistication and decreased real costs of computing. DESKTOP PUBLISHING has made little impact on the core sectors of the industry, but has greatly facilitated the publication of commercially peripheral material that might not otherwise have found an outlet. The cultural and literary benefits of this might sometimes be questioned, but there can be no doubt that the process of print-on-paper publishing has been opened up – arguably even democratized – by technological change.

MARKETING AND SALES

It is the sale of its products that ultimately determines the fate of the knowledge industries, like any other commercial activity in a capitalist system. Here there is little homogeneity between the three sectors with which we are principally concerned.

The consumer book market still operates primarily through retail bookshops, although e-commerce is of increasing importance. Both real and virtual bookshops are normally independent of the publishing houses, although in some less developed countries it is not unusual for the same company to be involved in both publishing and bookselling, and indeed sometimes in printing as well. In more complex book trades, however, separation of functions is almost invariable. Less uniform are the trade relationships between the publishers and the booksellers. In the United Kingdom, wholesalers are virtually unknown in hardback trade, although common for paperbacks, while in the USA wholesalers (known as BOOK JOBBERS) are almost universal, as they are in Germany. In some countries, of which the USA and Australia are important examples, book sales by mail order represent a significant market sector, while in others, including the United Kingdom, France and Germany, the stock-holding bookshop still remains at the centre of the trade. The development of online bookshops, such as Amazon, and of online facilities by established booksellers is however making significant, and perhaps fundamental, changes in this pattern of trade.

In all the industrialized countries, mail-order BOOK CLUBS have also become a significant sector. The arrangement is that the publisher sells to the book club either the right to reprint the book for its members or a large number of copies for sale to members at less than the typical retail price. In the institutional sector (which represents about one-third of the total market in the United Kingdom, and rather less than that elsewhere in the developed world) specialist LIBRARY SUPPLIERS are the intermediaries between book and journal publishers on the one hand and libraries on the other. All of these channels of supply are, however, variations on a common theme: the publisher does not normally deal directly with the consumer, but works through one or more intermediaries in the wholesale or retail BOOK TRADE.

Whatever the outlets, it is always the wish of the publisher to sell as many copies as possible of each title at the time of (or better still in advance of) publication, in order to recoup costs and move rapidly into profit. Book clubs, wholesalers and library suppliers and contractors are therefore particularly attractive customers for publishers, since, despite the better discounts that they can demand, they represent mass sales at minimum cost. Publishers have the advantage of dealing almost entirely with their fellow professionals in the book world: booksellers, jobbers, wholesalers and library suppliers. Their marketing and sales operations can therefore be very precisely directed at a well-defined market.

The magazine and newspaper industries are larger and more diverse than book publishing. Newspapers tend to rely on brand loyalty to retain their readership, although they also regularly engage in service enhancements (such as exclusive stories, special offers of products and services, and so on) to maintain and to boost their circulations, as well as trying to align themselves with the social and political views of their target audience. An essentially ephemeral product, newspapers are sold through millions of outlets around the world in a consumer market in which impulse buying and irregular buying can both have profound effects on sales. Magazines are more reliant on regular subscriptions, but the mass-circulation magazines are sold through the same retail outlets as newspapers and are similarly vulnerable to shifts in public taste and perceptions. Both newspapers and magazines do advertise themselves (particularly on television), but usually only in special circumstances. Promotion through shop displays, especially using eye-catching headlines or designs, is probably more important. Wholesalers play a key role in the magazine industry throughout the world. Indeed, the mass marketing of magazines is almost entirely dependent on their ability to persuade tens of thousands of small outlets (many of which are very informal sales points rather than well-established shops) to take copies and – crucially – to display them prominently to potential customers. Newspapers are also distributed through wholesalers, although in some countries (including the USA) newspapers are typically a regional or even local phenomenon rather than being sold in a wide geographical area. Some newspapers, and many magazines, command a global market.

For the producers of material for broadcasting the market is far more limited, for it is dominated by a small number of companies and public corporations. Even where a wholly commercial system operates (most notably the USA) there is not, in the strictest sense, a free market. Licences to broadcast are jealously guarded and sparingly issued by governments, who are trying simultaneously (in most cases) to generate diversity and to restrict competition; the partly inconsistent intentions of such policies are to satisfy the interests of a large cross-section of the potential audience while protecting the investments of the broadcasting and production organizations in their expensive networks and products. The result, however, has been that independent producers still find themselves beholden to the very small numbers of national broadcasters (three networks in the USA, five national channels in the United Kingdom, for example) and a slightly larger number of less powerful regional broadcasters. The development of cable and satellite systems has made some inroads into the power of the networks over the whole broadcasting industry both nationally and globally. The satellite broadcasters in particular present serious challenges (political as well as cultural) to state monopoly broadcasters in South and Southeast Asia and the Middle East. The global market for programmes (especially those in English) creates outlets beyond the country of origin for many programmes, although the majority of these are US and are indeed produced by the major networks in that country. Indeed, there is a real fear of cultural homogenization (often a euphemism for Americanisation) of much of the world, which is reflected in attempts to sustain broadcasting in languages other than English and for minority audiences; this is particularly true in Europe where a number of aspects of EUROPEAN UNION INFORMATION POLICIES are directed to precisely this end.

The market for the broadcasters themselves is the target audience that they must reach in order to satisfy sponsors and advertisers. This is true even of non-commercial broadcasters dependent on public revenue, for they too must satisfy their ultimate paymasters (governments and thus taxpayers) in order to maintain their position. Regulatory regimes partly determine the nature of the commercial relationship between broadcaster and recipient, although they are also more concerned with maintaining allegedly desirable standards of public morality, and in some countries controlling the social and political content of programmes; quality of output is a factor in some regulatory regimes, but it is, at best, difficult to enforce.

In the database industry, marketing and sales are far more specialized, as might be expected from the nature of the product itself. Typically, the hosts and producers are marketing their services to fellow professionals in the library and information world with which this sector is indissolubly linked. Despite its massive growth, the sector is probably still producer-led rather than market-driven, for there is little real competition in the sense of competing databases that can offer the same information to potential customers.

Practice: industry structures

The convergence of information and communications technologies, and the development of new media and new formats, has inevitably created overlap between the infrastructures of superficially distinct parts of the knowledge industries. Moreover, the industries operate globally, and the very systems that have transformed them are themselves the principal mechanisms of instantaneous global communication. It is hardly surprising that the structural evolution in the industry has been as great as the technical revolution, especially when seen against a background of Western governments with an ideological commitment to free markets and the collapse of many regimes that sought to restrict the flow of information, and the creation of large free-trade areas between groups of formerly wholly distinct nation states.

The essentially international nature of the knowledge industries is neither new nor, in itself, particularly startling. The printing industry began its life with the use of an international language – Latin – and aimed its earliest products at an international learned elite for whom Latin was the common language of scholarly and theological discourse. The modern equivalent is English, the predominant language of commercial publishing, of television broadcasting and of popular music and cinema, and virtually the only language of computing and telecommunications systems. In such a climate, multinational ownership of corporations in the industry was perhaps an inevitable development, as was the dominance of individuals and corporations from the English-speaking countries.

Publishing houses have had an international presence throughout the twentieth century, to go back no further. The major British educational publishers established branches throughout the then British Empire before the First World War. Some of these eventually became independent publishing houses in their own right, retaining only the name and the implicit goodwill of their British parent. From 1960 onwards, some of the remaining subsidiaries and branches in Africa and Southeast Asia were indigenized in management, ownership and operation by the newly independent countries in which they were located. As a result, although some of the famous names of British publishing remain scattered throughout the Commonwealth, there is often little more than a nominal connection with the founding firm in Britain.

There have always been strong links between British and US publishing, for obvious linguistic and cultural reasons, even when relations between the two were not particularly friendly. Since the beginning of the twentieth century there was a steady influx of US capital into British publishing. At first this was slight and almost covert, but since about 1970 it has been extensive and very explicit. Of four of the most powerful corporations in British book publishing (Random House, Hodder Headline, News Corporation and Pearson), two are US-dominated Anglo-American companies, one is of Australian origin but is run by a man with US citizenship and is predominantly US in style and presence, and the fourth has substantial US interests. These arrangements have significance far beyond the North Atlantic. Because English is the predominant language of world publishing, especially in such key areas as science, technology, medicine, computing and business, the multinational publishers based in London and New York have a global dominance of some of the most economically, politically and socially significant, and at the same time some of the most profitable, areas of contemporary book publishing. Constructed on the firm foundation of US technological and economic strength, together with the use of a world language, Anglo-American publishing interests, whether by accident or design, are inhibiting the development of high-level publishing in much of the rest of the world.

This dominance has been sustained by commercial rather than overtly political factors, although it has certainly had, and continues to have, political consequences. On the whole, however, few attempts have been made either in the United Kingdom or in the USA to prevent the development of the multinational publishing companies. A more contentious area, which is still a matter of political debate, is that of cross-ownership between media. News Corporation is the archetype of the cross-media company. In addition to its international publishing interests, News International also owns satellite television channels, television and film production companies and important databases. Its control of content even extends to massive influence on the nature, location and timing of sporting events for which it holds global broadcasting rights. It exemplifies the multinational and international nature of the knowledge industries at the beginning of the twenty-first century. Some countries have made an attempt to legislate in this field. In some cases, as in the United Kingdom, there has

been an apparently genuine attempt to prevent undesirable monopolies being allowed to develop; in others, as in France, the equally genuine objective has been to prevent damage being inflicted on national traditions by the predominance of the English language and US culture. In both cases, success has proven elusive. The technologies have defeated the regulators.

It is the convergence of technologies that has ultimately driven the convergence of ownership. Terrestrial and satellite broadcasting and cable television services are competing for essentially the same audience. The concept of the Information Superhighway is essentially that all the various media of communication and information will be brought together on a single common carrier, commercially owned and regulated only as a commercial activity. Monopolies will inevitably develop, as they are already developing in the newspaper and television industries, if governments do not have the desire and the political will to intervene. The monopoly, however, is that of the common carrier rather than that of the provider. The network owner (especially of broadband networks) who leases 'time' and 'space' to individuals and corporations is the controller of the Information Superhighway, which will come to dominate the knowledge industries. Delivery of telephone, fax, video, videotex and electronic mail can share the same network with interactive devices for domestic and corporate transactions such as shopping, banking and share-dealing. In all of this, the transmission of knowledge and understanding is perhaps in danger of being submerged in a morass of undigested information and carefully controlled communications. The traditional secondary producers of the knowledge industries, who have been the main focus of this article, already find themselves challenged by a system of communication which facilitates direct contact between primary producers – knowledge creators – and consumers – the end-users of knowledge, a form of communication whose most familiar expression is the WORLD WIDE WEB.

In this global communications system some of the traditional providers in the knowledge industries will seem to be very small indeed; this is particularly true of the book publishers, with whom it all began. Although there is an important continuing role for the printed word in the foreseeable future, it will never again be the predominant form for the mass communication of ideas. At the same time, there will be individuals, sectors of society and even whole nations whom the knowledge industry will no longer be able to serve, or whom it will only serve as distant peripherals of its core market. Those with limited knowledge of the English language are already marginalized in business and in science, to name only two areas, and are severely restricted in their access to some of the predominant modes of popular entertainment, such as the cinema and popular music. Those with no access to information technology or with limited skills in its use are rapidly being deprived of the advantages of the information revolution. The knowledge industries are driving the development of the INFORMATION SOCIETY, and are in turn being driven by it, in a vast cycle of change and development, but they are also becoming more elitist and more exclusive as their need for human and financial capital becomes ever more insatiable. These are the challenges that the knowledge industries will face, and may address, in the new millennium.

References

Machlup, F. (1962) *The Production and Distribution of Knowledge*, Princeton University Press.

Further reading

Altbach, P.G. (1992) *Publishing and Development in the Third World*, Hans Zell.
—— (1987) *The Knowledge Context: Comparative Perspectives on the Distribution of Knowledge*, State University Press of New York.
Cronin, B. and Tudor-Silovic, N. (1990) *The Knowledge Industries: Levers of Economic and Social Development in the 1990s*, ASLIB.
Dyson, K. and Humphreys, P. (1988) *Broadcasting and New Media Policies in Western Europe*,
European Commission (1994) *Mergers & Acquisitions in the Electronic Information Industry*, Luxembourg (IMO Working Paper, 94/2).
Hartley, J., Noonan, A. and Metcalfe, S. (1987) *New Electronic Information Services: An Overview of the UK Database Industry in an International Context*, Gower.
Katz, R.L. (1988) *The Information Society: An International Perspective*, Praeger.
Luther, S.F. (1988) *The United States and Direct Broadcast Satellite: The Politics of International Broadcasting in Space*, Oxford University Press.
—— (1978) *Information through the Printed Word*, 3 vols, Praeger.
Meadows, A.J. (ed.) (1991) *Knowledge and Communication. Essays on the Information Chain*, Library Association Publishing.
Negrine, R. and Papathanassopoulos, S. (1990) *The Internationalisation of Television*, Pinter.
Rubin, R., Huber, M.T. and Taylor, E.L. (1986) *The Knowledge Industry in the United States: 1960–1980*, Princeton University Press.

SEE ALSO: communication; information professions; literacy

JOHN FEATHER

KNOWLEDGE MANAGEMENT

Basic definition

Knowledge management (KM), simply put, is the recognition that arose in the business community in the 1990s that knowledge is an important organizational asset, a 'factor of production' as economists would phrase it, in the same category with land, labour, capital and energy (Stewart 1994; Talero and Gaudette 1995) and by no means least important among them. And further, that the effective deployment of that knowledge is a key factor, perhaps *the* key factor in the post-industrial economy, in an organization's effectiveness and success (Davis and Botkin 1994).

There are scores of definitions of KM. Three classic ones are presented here. The first by Davenport (1994: 95) that 'knowledge management is the process of capturing, distributing, and effectively using knowledge' is one of the earliest and one of the simplest and most stark. The second by the Gartner Group (Duhon 1998: 9), that KM is 'a discipline that promotes an integrated approach to identifying, capturing, evaluating, retrieving, and sharing all of an enterprise's information assets. These assets may include databases, documents, policies, procedures, and previously uncaptured expertise and experience in individual workers' is illuminating because it makes very implicit the aspect of KM of including not just conventional information and knowledge units, but also 'tacit knowledge', that which is known but not captured in any formal or explicit fashion. The third definition by Ruggles (1998: 80) is that:

[K]nowledge management is a newly emerging, interdisciplinary business model dealing with all aspects of knowledge within the context of the firm, including knowledge creation, codification, sharing, learning, and innovation. Some aspects of this process are facilitated with information technologies, but knowledge management is to a greater degree, about organizational culture and practices.

This is illuminating because it emphasizes another very important dimension to KM, the emphasis upon the culture of the organization.

The development of KM

Tracing the evolution of KM is perhaps the most straightforward mechanism for delineating its components. The use of the term 'knowledge management' is a surprisingly recent phenomenon, developing only in the mid-1990s. It is the case however that the term appears to have been used first in the context of library and information work. Marchand (1985), then Dean of the School of Information Studies at Syracuse University, coined it in the 1980s as a descriptor for the final level in his stage hypothesis of INFORMATION SYSTEMS development (Koenig 1992). However, the term as presently used appears to have been re-coined more or less anonymously somewhere in the then big six accountancy and consulting firms.

In somewhat metaphorical and equestrian terms KM may be described as the intranet out of intellectual capital (Koenig 2001), intellectual capital representing the awareness that as Peter Drucker put it:

> We now know that the source of wealth is something, specifically human knowledge. If we apply knowledge to tasks that we obviously know how to do, we call it productivity. If we apply knowledge to tasks that are new and different, we call it innovation. Only knowledge allows us to achieve those two goals.
>
> (Hibbard 1997: 46)

The first blush of enthusiasm for intellectual capital centred on quantifying and measuring it. (Edvinsson 1995, 1997). Surely if it was so important, it needed to be measured. As the difficulty of measuring such an amorphous commodity as information, much less knowledge, became apparent to the business community the enthusiasm for, or at least the publication of articles about intellectual capital, subsided. Then came the emergence of the INTERNET. The business world realized that the Internet could be used to link an organization together. This was

the take-off point for KM (Koenig 1996, 1998). KM was first defined as having two components (see Figure 14).

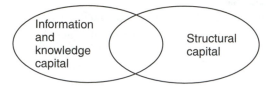

Figure 14 The two components of KM

Information and knowledge capital was of course the organization's information and knowledge, but included the informal and unstructured as well as the formal.

The structural capital was of course the mechanisms in place to take advantage of the information and knowledge capital, the mechanisms to capture, store, retrieve and communicate that information and knowledge.

Applications of Internet technology were soon extended beyond INTRANETS – the use of the Internet within an organization – to extranets that would still be private, but were used to connect an organization with its suppliers and customers. The consequence of this development was an expanded definition of KM to include the customer's knowledge and input, customer capital (see Figure 15).

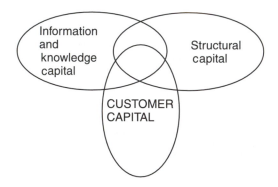

Figure 15 Expanded definition of KM

The inclusion of customer capital was also not unrelated to the popularity of TQM, or Total Quality Management, in which responding to customer need and demand was a key element.

Concurrent with intellectual capital, and very much reinforcing it, was the notion of the 'balanced score card' (Kaplan and Norton 1992). The idea here was that traditional financial reporting was too narrow in its outlook, and that in particular it focused only on the present and the past, with no thought to the future. It was argued that there should be instead a 'balanced score card' that included the traditional financial measures, but which also measured other things such as comparative product quality, customer satisfaction and turnover, things that were more indicative of current performance and better indicators of likely future performance. By traditional financial indicators, if the current balance sheet looks good, but for example customers have begun to defect to the competition, there is nothing to reveal that the situation is in fact not healthy. The idea of the balanced score card is intended to resolve that anomaly. Intellectual capital is of course one of the obvious items that should be included in the balanced scorecard.

Another version of the KM trinity is from IBM (Prusak 1998). It is very similar to the graphic shown in Figure 16, with the 'customer capital' component replaced by 'social capital'. It is now assumed that customer capital is included in all of the above, the infrastructure extended to include the customer, the knowledge resources including the customer, and the social capital embracing the relationships not just within the organization, but also with the customer (and the supplier to whom one is a customer) as well.

The concept of knowledge management continued to expand, most particularly by incorporating the notion of 'the learning organization'. Senge's *The Fifth Discipline, the Art and Practice of the Learning Organization* in appeared in 1990 and had established something of a cult following, but had not made a major impact in the business world. However, it meshed perfectly with knowledge management. The the-

sis of the learning organization is that what ultimately creates and distinguishes a successful organization is its success in creating and sharing information and knowledge, in short its success at learning. The obvious corollary is that to be successful, an organization must create a culture that fosters learning. One can say, to summarize perhaps too briefly, that the concept of the learning organization focuses on the creation of knowledge, while knowledge management, as it was originally construed, focuses on the acquisition, structuring, retention and dissemination of that knowledge. What then happened to KM is that the term was expanded to include the concept of the learning organization.

Most recently (Fishkin 2001) KM is described as a structure supported now by five columns, i.e. with five major constituents (see Figure 17).

We can reflect briefly for a moment on whether the Parthenon-like image of the structure is an unintended homage to KM as the latest temple to which the consultants lead the faithful.

KM themes and applications

Having sketched the definition and the evolution of KM, the domain can be fleshed out and to a degree mapped by briefly discussing some of the major themes running through what the business community understands as KM, and the applications that derive from those themes.

COMMUNITIES AND COLLABORATION

'Silo' is perhaps the most common buzzword in KM, as in 'How do you integrate the silos?' Silo here is a metaphor for the unit, which is too self-contained, into which stuff gets dumped and taken out of, but which has little or no communication with the other silos (products, regions, divisions, units, etc.) that constitute the organiza-

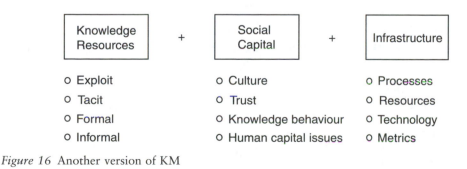

Figure 16 Another version of KM

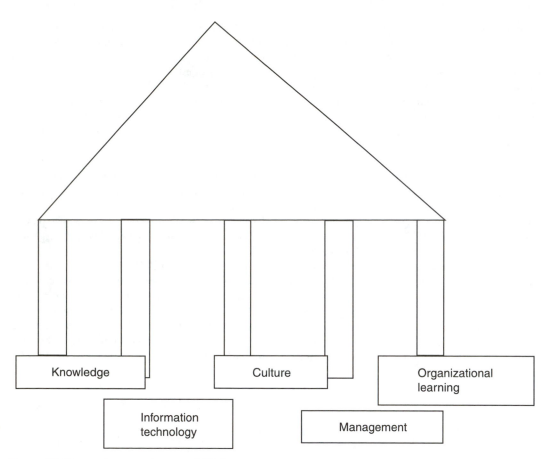

Figure 17 Five major constituents of KM

tion. The solution to the silo problem is to create communities, the common generic phrase being 'community of learning'. The most obvious reason of course is to foster collaboration and increase efficiency. Jerry Jenkins, the former president of Texas Instruments, famously remarked, 'if Texas Instruments knew what Texas Instruments knew, we would be twice as productive' (O'Dell and Grayson 2000: 1). In part the emphasis on silos is a reaction against the excesses of business process re-engineering. The silos are, if you will, what was left after business process re-engineering removed much of middle management and flattened the organization. That middle-management component had provided much of the connective tissue of the organization, providing the communication channels that kept the units from becoming silos. KM is now seen as the repair mechanism for the tears in the organization's communications fabric induced by business process re-engineering.

Most of the concrete applications of KM described to date consist of creating and supporting communities of shared subject interest and information need. These communities might be the sales representatives of a pharmaceutical company, or those persons at the World Bank and among their clients, who are interested in road transport and logistics. In some cases, as in the former, the community already to a degree exists formally and hierarchically or, as in the latter, it exists informally and horizontally. At the World Bank, for example, there are now some seventy 'knowledge areas' grouped into fifteen large sectors; at IBM there are more than 100 'competency networks'. The best-known example of such community creation is probably British Petroleum's response teams, whereby experts from around the world can be 'virtually assembled to address a problem' (Prokesch 1997: 152).

use information about your customers to establish a long-lasting and profitable relationship?

Top management support and agents of change

Another major theme is that KM is about a whole new way of operating, indeed the transformation of the organization. As such, it requires knowledge management professionals to be change agents, which in turn requires top management support. Better yet is the direct involvement of top management if the effort is to be successful.

Knowledge sharing is of the essence in KM, but knowledge sharing is to a large degree not a natural act. The encouragement of knowledge sharing requires reward, ideally both monetary and psychic, trust and a supportive corporate culture. This in turn requires examining that corporate culture and changing it where necessary. An excellent discussion is contained in Davenport and Prusak's book *Working Knowledge* (1998).

Formulae for failure and success

One of the best techniques to get a feel for the nature of KM is to examine the 'perils and pitfalls' and 'golden rules' class of articles that caution the practitioner about what not to do and what to be sure to do. KM already has several excellent articles in this genre. Fahey and Prusak delineate the eleven deadliest sins of knowledge management:

- Not developing a working definition of knowledge.
- Emphasizing knowledge stock to the detriment of knowledge flow.
- Viewing knowledge as existing predominantly outside the heads of individuals.
- Not understanding that a fundamental intermediate purpose of management knowledge is to create shared context.
- Paying little heed to the role and importance of tacit knowledge.
- Disentangling knowledge for its uses.
- Downplaying thinking and reasoning.
- Focusing on the past and the present and not the future.
- Failing to recognize the importance of experimentation.
- Substituting technological contact for human interface.
- Seeking to develop direct measures of knowledge.

Davenport (1997) similarly lists seven 'known evils':

- If we build it….
- Let's put the personnel manual online!
- None dare call it knowledge.
- Every man a knowledge manager.
- Justification by faith.
- Restricted access.
- Bottoms up!

In a later and influential article, Davenport *et al.* (1998) examine successful knowledge management projects and argue that they tend to have eight factors in common:

- Link to economic performance or industry value.
- Technical and organization infrastructure.
- Standard flexible knowledge structure.
- Knowledge-friendly culture.
- Clear purpose and language.
- Change in motivational practices.
- Multiple channels for knowledge transfer.
- Senior management support.

Careful perusal of these three articles is strongly recommended for anyone interested in KM. The names of the errors and success factors above are often cryptic and somewhat metaphoric, and reading them in context is essential.

KM versus traditional information management

Another useful way to define KM is to compare it with traditional library and information work. The view is often expressed in traditional library and information science circles that KM is just old wine in new bottles, just the new name for information resources management, which in turn was just a new name for documentation, which in turn was just a new name for LIBRARIANSHIP. There are however some real differences in emphasis, and those key differences are laid out in Table 16.

Two important pieces about KM written from the perspective of the traditional information community are Srikantaiah and Koenig's book *Knowledge Management for the Information*

Table 16 Differences in emphasis between KM and traditional library and information work

Knowledge management	*Traditional library and information work*
• The addition of and in many cases an emphasis on unstructured and informal information/knowledge	• Emphasis upon (indeed a limitation to) structured and formal information/knowledge
• Emphasis on internal information and, now, increasingly external information, but often external information that resides with supplier and customers, not in the open literature	• Emphasis on information, external to the organization, the 'literature'
• An active role in corporate culture transformation and change agentry	• Neutrality within the organization
• Information and knowledge sharing, in the context of a dense web structure	• Information and knowledge delivery, as a hub (library) and spoke structure
• A loose unformed poorly developed appreciation for information/knowledge structuring	• Syndetic structures, information structuring, taxonomies, cataloguing, classification,...
• Knowledge of the context, organization, sectoral (industry) supplier, customer	• Growing contextual knowledge, but not well recognized within the organization
• An awareness of knowledge as text, but coming from a background in non-textual information	• Information primarily as text, secondarily as numerical or graphic
• Linking knowledge-sharing with compensation policy	• Has never been involved with compensation policy

Professional (2000) and Broadbent's article 'The phenomenon of knowledge management: What does it mean to the library profession?' (1998).

A map of the domain of KM

Another approach to defining KM is to attempt to map it. Figure 18 is a somewhat expanded graphic used by IBM in their KM consultancy to help explain to potential clients what KM is and what the consultancy has to offer.

A final way to view KM is to observe that KM is the movement to replicate the information environment known to be conducive to successful R&D – rich, deep and open communication and information access – and deploy it broadly across the firm.

Given that in this post-industrial or information age, an increasingly larger proportion of the population consists of information workers, and that researchers are the quintessential information workers, and that the community has been studied in depth (Goldhar *et al.* 1976; Allen 1977; Orpen 1985; Koenig 1990, 1992, 2001; Mondschein 1990) with a substantial accumulation of knowledge about what characterizes the environment conducive to successful research, this is a very logical development. The

great irony is that there is little evidence that this body of knowledge had any direct impact on the development of KM, a classic example of the silo phenomenon. KM appears to have developed in the business community quite independently of any knowledge of the body of research about research effectiveness. Nonetheless, this definition of KM may ultimately prove to be the most straightforward and the most illuminating.

References

Allen, T. (1977) *Managing the Flow of Technology: Technology Transfer and the Dissemination of Technological Information within the R&D Organization*, Cambridge, MA: MIT Press.

Broadbent, M. (1998) 'The phenomenon of knowledge management: What does it mean to the library profession?', *Information Outlook* 2(5): 23–36.

Davenport, T.H. (1998) 'Managing customer knowledge', *CIO* 11(15): 32–4.

—— (1997) 'Known evils: Seven fallacies that can hamper development of knowledge management in a company', *CIO* 10(17): 34–6.

—— (1994) 'Coming soon: The CKO', *Information Week* 491: 95.

Davenport, T.H. and Prusak, L. (1998) *Working Knowledge: How Organizations Manage What They Know*, Woborn, MA: Harvard Business School Press.

	COLLECTING (STUFF) AND **CODIFICATION**	CONNECTING (PEOPLE) AND **PERSONALIZATION**
DIRECTED INFORMATION AND KNOWLEDGE SEARCH **EXPLOIT**	databases, external and internal content architecture information service support (*training* required) data mining best practices/lessons learned/after-action analysis **(HARVEST)**	community and learning directories, 'yellow pages', findings; facilitating tools, groupware response teams **(HARNESS)**
SERENDIPITY AND BROWSING **EXPLORE**	cultural support current awareness profiles and databases selection of items for alerting purposes/push data mining best practices **(HUNTING)**	cultural support spaces – libraries and lounges (literal and virtual), cultural support, groupware travel and meeting attendance **(HYPOTHESIZE)**

KM is an extension of the successful R&D environmnet

Figure 18 Domains of knowledge management strategy
Note: The dashed lines are intended to indicate that the boundaries are porous and overlapping

Davenport, T.H. *et al.* (1998) 'Successful knowledge management projects', *Sloan Management Review* 39(1): 43–57.

Davis, S. and Botkin, J. (1994) 'The coming of knowledge-based business', *Harvard Business Review* 72(5) (September/October): 165–70.

Duhon, B. (1998) 'It's all in our heads', *Inform* 12(8): 9–13.

Edvinsson, L. (1997) 'Developing intellectual capital at Skandia', *Long Range Planning* 30(3): 366–73.

—— (1995) 'Visualizing intellectual capital in Skandia', in *Skandia's 1994 Annual Report*, Stockholm: Skandia AFS.

Fahey, L. and Prusak, L. (1998) 'The eleven deadliest sins of knowledge management', *California Management Review* 40(3): 265–76.

Fishkin, J. (2001) 'KM and OL from an IT perspective', a presentation to the 2001 Conference Board conference: The 2001 Knowledge Management/Organizational Learning Conference: Convergence,

Application, and Infrastructure, 3–4 May, New York City.

Goldhar, J.D. *et al.* (1976) 'Information flows, management styles and technical innovation', *IEEE Transactions on Engineering Management* (February) EM-23(1): 51–61.

Hibbard, J. (1997) 'Knowing what we know', *Information Week* (20 October): 46–64.

Kaplan, R.S. and Norton, D.P. (1992) 'The balanced scorecard – Measures that drive performance', *Harvard Business Review* 70(1): 71–91.

Kleiner, A. and R.G. (1997) 'How to make experience your company's best teacher', *Harvard Business Review* 75(5): 172–7.

Koenig, M.E.D. (2001) 'Lessons from the study of scholarly communications for the new information era', *Scientometrics* 51(3): 511–28.

—— (2000) 'The evolution of knowledge management' (Chapter 3), in T.K. Srikantaiah and M.E.D. Koenig, *Knowledge Management for the Information Profes-*

sional, Medford, NJ: Information Today for the American Society for Information Science, pp. 23–36.

—— (1998) 'From intellectual capital to knowledge management: What are they talking about?', *INSPEL* 32(4): 222–33.

—— (1996) 'Intellectual capital and knowledge management', *IFLA Journal* 22(4): 299–301.

—— (1992) 'The information environment and the productivity of research', in H. Collier (ed.) *Recent Advances in Chemical Information*, London: Royal Society of Chemistry, pp. 133–43, reprinted in 'Information culture and business performance', Information Strategy Report 2, prepared for the British Library by Hertis Information And Research, 1995.

—— (1990) 'Information services and downstream productivity', in M.E. Williams (ed.) *Annual Review of Information Science and Technology 25*, New York: Elsevier Science Publishers, for the American Society for Information Science, pp. 55–86.

Liedtka, J.M. *et al.* (1997) 'The generative cycle: Linking knowledge and relationships', *Sloan Management Review* 39(1): 47–59.

Marchand, D.A. (1985) 'Information management: Strategies and tools in transition', *Information Management Review* 1(1): 27–37.

Mondschein, L.G. (1990) 'SDI use and productivity in the corporate research environment', *Special Libraries* 81(4) (fall): 265–79.

O'Dell, C. and Grayson, C.J. (2000) 'If only we knew what we know: The transfer of internal knowledge and best practice', Houston, TX: American Productivity and Quality Center.

Orpen, C. (1985) 'The effect of managerial distribution or scientific and technical information on company performance', *R&D Management* 15(4) (October): 305–8.

Prokesch, S.E. (1997) 'Unleashing the power of learning: An interview with British Petroleum's John Browne', *Harvard Business Review* (September–October): 146–8.

Prusak, L. (1998) 'Managing Principal, IBM Global Services, Consulting Group presentation to the Conference Board', paper presented at the 1998 Conference on Knowledge Management and Organizational Learning, Chicago, 16 April.

Ruggles, R. (1998) 'The state of the nation: Knowledge management in practice', *California Management Review* 40 (spring): 80–9.

Senge, P.M. (1990) *The Fifth Discipline: The Art and Practice of the Learning Organization*, New York: Doubleday/Currency.

Srikantaiah, T.K. and Koenig, M.E.D. (eds) (2000) *Knowledge Management for the Information Professional*, Medford, NJ: Information Today for the American Society for Information Science.

Stewart, T. (1994) 'Your company's most valuable asset: Intellectual capital', *Fortune* (3 October): 68–74.

Talero, E. and Gaudette, P. (1995) *Harnessing Information for Development: World Bank Group Vision and Strategy*, Washington, DC: World Bank.

Further reading

Koenig, M.E.D. (1992) 'Entering stage III – The convergence of the stage hypotheses', *Journal of the American Society for Information Science* 43(3): 204–7.

Marchand, L.A. (1983) 'Strategies and tools in transition', *Business and Economic Review* 29(5) (June): 4–8.

Prusak, L. (1999) 'Where did knowledge management come from?', *Knowledge Management* 1(1) (fall): 90–6.

SEE ALSO: information management; information professions; information society; organizational information policies

MICHAEL R. KOENIG

KUHN, THOMAS S. (1922–96)

Originator of a theory of scientific change that conflicted directly with the accepted view that scientists built on the discoveries of their predecessors in a rational sequence of development. Kuhn's perception, that change came from scientific revolutions in which 'normal science' was subverted by a new paradigm, permitted a critical view of SCHOLARLY COMMUNICATION that naturally influenced INFORMATION THEORY.

Born in Cincinnati, USA, he graduated in physics from Harvard in 1943 and, after war service in a civilian capacity, went on to obtain his Master's and Doctoral degrees in physics, also from Harvard. He taught at Harvard (1948–56), followed by the University of California at Berkeley, where he became Professor of the History of Science in 1961. He subsequently taught at Princeton and MIT, and received the George Sarton Medal in the History of Science in 1982.

The Structure of Scientific Revolutions, originally published as a contribution to an encyclopedia before it appeared as a monograph in 1962, was a scientific bestseller that was widely influential in changing the popular view of science. In it Kuhn argued that scientists generally pursued fundamentally conservative research programmes in the context of some governing paradigm such as Newtonian physics, the phlogiston theory of gases or creationist views of the origins of life forms. Change only comes when the governing paradigm can no longer satisfactorily account for new research, but the process of change meets with determined resistance that is only overturned by a revolution led by someone equivalent to Einstein, Lavoisier or Darwin. In the process, views on the validity of swathes of the literature, the reputations of individuals and institutions, and the philosophical orientation of whole disciplines require reassessment.

Further reading

Sardar, Z. (2000) *Thomas Kuhn and the Science Wars*, Totem Books.

L

LANCASTER, F. WILFRID (1933–)

Library educator and specialist in information systems and the evaluation of library services whose name is inextricably associated with the concept of the PAPERLESS SOCIETY.

Born in Durham, England, he studied at Newcastle School of Librarianship from 1950 to 1954 and began his professional career in Newcastle Public Libraries. His later career was in the USA, from 1970 on the faculty of the University of Illinois Graduate School of Library Science.

His major contributions have been principally concerned with the underlying intellectual problems and conceptual frameworks of information retrieval systems. He has worked on vocabulary control, interaction between system and user, evaluation of systems effectiveness and, in his later work, the implications of advanced information systems for the future of libraries in society. He is probably best known through the title of his 1978 book *Towards a Paperless Information Society* but his bibliography is extensive. He has also made a major contribution to the development of criteria and procedures for the evaluation of systems performance, mainly through the extension, refinement and application of concepts pioneered by the Cranfield Studies carried out in the late 1950s under the direction of C.W. Cleverdon at the College of Aeronautics, Cranfield, UK.

SEE ALSO: information society

LAW LIBRARIES

A law library may be an autonomous library building housing a distinctive collection of LEGAL INFORMATION, or a department within a larger library. In size and scope, law LIBRARIES vary from a short run of shelves in a small law firm to an important historic collection in a national library (see NATIONAL LIBRARIES) or a university library (see UNIVERSITY LIBRARIES). The users of law libraries include law students, legal academics, practising lawyers, the judiciary and the general public. Access to many law libraries is restricted to members of the institution or firm, but PUBLIC LIBRARIES usually offer a good collection of legal materials in the central library for the region.

Types of law library

The scope of the law collection and the services offered by the law library depend very much on the aims of the host organization. Academic law libraries exist primarily to support the teaching and research of the university or college. The law library can be a separate collection in its own building, or form part of a broader social sciences collection in the academic library. Typically, academic law libraries hold a comprehensive collection of legislation, case law, legal textbooks and academic law journals, supplemented by access to electronic legal databases. Law firm libraries vary in size according to the number of lawyers in the firm, and will provide a core collection of primary legal materials, current practitioners' manuals and texts, professional journals and access to electronic databases, geared to the interests of the firm. The libraries of professional societies such as the Law Society of England and Wales are only open to members, and are often large historic collections that also offer a range of information services. Court libraries are used by judges and lawyers who appear in the courts. There are a few law libraries in large businesses and industries that employ their own legal team. Public libraries in the United Kingdom usually hold a core collection of legislation, some case law, selected legal textbooks and a few law journals. In other countries, there may be dedicated law libraries open to the public, which provide more extensive services. The availability of free legal information on the Internet is increasing, which is improving access to this type of information for members of the public.

Organization

Law libraries tend to be organized rather differently from other libraries because of the categories of specialist information they hold. Some libraries group all primary and secondary legal materials by jurisdiction, while others arrange legislation, case reports, journals and books in separate sequences. Law collections within a larger library often use the cataloguing and classification schemes selected by the parent organisation, such as the Dewey Decimal or Library of Congress Classification schemes, while smaller independent libraries may use a home-grown scheme designed for a specific collection. The Moys classification scheme (Moys 2001) was designed specifically for legal materials and is used by a range of law libraries in different countries.

Law librarians

Law librarianship is recognized as a specialist branch of the library and information profession. Training in the professional use of legal materials is normally introduced as part of a general library and information science course, though there are some specialist courses in law librarianship. Most law librarians in the United Kingdom complete a general library qualification, and then receive specific training in law and legal materials in their first posts, although some choose to complete a law degree. In other countries such as the USA a legal qualification is a requirement to be a professional law librarian. Law librarians are normally responsible for the selection, purchasing and management of stock in the law library, and training users in the use of legal materials. One of the most challenging aspects of

the law librarian's job is developing the ability to answer enquiries by locating information in a very wide range of information sources, from case reports several hundred years' old, to the newest information appearing each day as the law changes. A general awareness of legal systems and current affairs is essential, and usually gained through experience on the job. Depending on the size of the library, law librarians may also require specific training and qualifications in management, finance and information technology. National associations of law librarians, such as the British and Irish Association of Law Librarians (BIALL), run training and development courses on the use of legal materials and other professional issues, provide a network of contacts and can supply information on how to become a law librarian.

Law libraries vs information centres

Law libraries, particularly in law firms, have evolved considerably over the last twenty years. The growth in electronic sources of information, in particular, means that those in charge of legal information collections may also be responsible for managing aspects of information technology within the firm or institution. Many legal information professionals work as part of a team that includes lawyers, IT specialists, marketing professionals and support staff. Some job titles have changed from law librarian to information manager to reflect the change in emphasis. As well as traditional information-handling skills, legal information professionals may require skills in KNOWLEDGE MANAGEMENT, personnel issues, budgeting, strategic planning and negotiation of contracts. In recent years there has been a trend, both in law firms and in academic libraries, to merge the library with the IT service to provide an integrated information service. This is in response to demands from library users for information delivered electronically, direct to the desktop. While the traditional law library with its imposing ranks of leather-bound volumes and quiet study areas still exists, the modern law library is likely to offer rapid and regular delivery of the latest information in a variety of formats tailored to suit the individual needs of the users.

References

Moys, E.M. (2001) *Moys Classification and Thesaurus for Legal Materials*, 4th edn, Bowker Saur.

Further reading

BIALL website (http://www.biall.org.uk).

Moys, E.M. (ed.) (1987) *Manual of Law Librarianship: The Use and Organization of Legal Literature*, 2nd edn, Gower.

VALERIE STEVENSON

LEGAL DEPOSIT

A system under which certain libraries are entitled by law to receive one or more copies of every book or other publication that is printed or published in a particular jurisdiction. It is also called copyright deposit, and indeed in some cases copyright is only established when the process of deposit is complete. Arrangements vary from country to country, but typically the national library (see NATIONAL LIBRARIES) is the principal recipient of deposit copies. Many countries, however, have more than one library that is entitled to receive a deposit copy of any or every book published in the country. In the United Kingdom, publishers are obliged to deliver a copy of each book to the BRITISH LIBRARY and also, if requested, to send a copy to the Bodleian Library, Oxford; the University Library, Cambridge; the National Library of Scotland, Edinburgh; and the National Library of Wales, Aberystwyth. In the USA, the LIBRARY OF CONGRESS is entitled to receive two copies of every item. In some countries, especially in CENTRAL AND EASTERN EUROPE, legal deposit extends to a significant number of university and public libraries.

The scope of materials that must be deposited also varies. It always includes books, periodicals and newspapers. In some jurisdictions, however, even some EPHEMERA are subject to deposit laws. MULTIMEDIA formats are more problematic. Audiovisual products, including commercial SOUND RECORDINGS and commercially produced FILM and video are subject to the law, but this is comparatively unusual. A major current issue is that of the deposit of digital products, not least in terms of how such products can be sensibly preserved and made available to users in the future.

Further reading

Jasion, J.T. (1991). *The International Guide to Legal Deposit*, Ashgate.

Larivière, J. (2000) *Guidelines for Legal Deposit Legislation*, UNESCO.

SEE ALSO: copyright; information law; information policy

LEGAL INFORMATION

Writing about the challenges facing the practice of law at the end of the twentieth century, Susskind (1996) identified a spectrum of legal information with formal sources of law such as legislation and case law at one end and human legal experts dispensing legal advice at the other.

In its broadest sense, legal information comprises all official statements of law together with interpretations and commentaries. Formal sources of legal information may be specific to a national jurisdiction, to an international jurisdiction or system or to a special non-geographic jurisdiction such as Islamic or Roman law.

Primary and secondary sources

A distinction is drawn between primary and secondary sources of law. Primary sources (broadly equivalent to formal law) include legislation and case law. Legislation includes statutes and enactments of parliamentary, executive and administrative bodies that confer rights or impose binding duties or liabilities. Case law includes judgments of courts and decisions of tribunals and other recognised judicial or quasi-judicial bodies. Primary sources of law provide the fundamental material for legal research. Secondary sources include interpretations, commentaries, texts, serials and monographs, guidance notes and other explanatory material.

Legal systems

The legal system of any jurisdiction is relevant to the sourcing of legal information. There are two main types of legal system: the civil law system derived either from Roman law through the French Code Napoleon or the German Burgelisches Gesetzbuch; and the common law system developed from the common law of England. In general, civil law systems present primary law in a consolidated and codified manner. Common law systems are less structured and also depend heavily on judicial interpretation of the law.

Legislation

Legislation in a given area may be sourced from a number of different levels. For example, statutes and enactments may require or result in secondary measures in the form of further more detailed technical regulations or rules. These may be further supplemented by official guidance notes or statements of practice on the application of the relevant law.

Case law

In all legal systems, case law (i.e. decisions of courts or tribunals) provides an important source of legal information. As well as providing a judicial or quasi-judicial decision on the facts of the case, case law (particularly in common law jurisdictions) may interpret, clarify or define aspects of legislation relevant to the case.

Legal texts

Learned and authoritative texts provide detailed commentary on primary source law and may be cited in judicial decisions. In themselves, they are also vital in providing explanatory overviews and analysis of particular subject matter, and in cross-referencing further sources of material.

Law reports and digests

Law reports comprise collected and cross-referenced sources of case law. They will usually contain a head note or summary of the relevant case or decision, together with citations and references to other relevant cases or legislation. Law digests contain summaries of case law on a subject or jurisdictional basis.

Commentaries

Commentaries include official background and briefing documents ('grey paper') together with serials and monographs. Serials in the form of academic journals and legal periodicals are a substantial source of legal current awareness.

International dimension

Primary source materials within an international dimension include international treaties and conventions and transnational legislation of bodies such as the European Union. Case law of international courts and bodies has had an increasingly significant impact on the decisions of courts at national level. In addition, courts in a common law jurisdiction system will consider relevant decisions from courts in other common law jurisdictions when deciding on cases brought before them.

Electronic sources

The development of legal information management as a recognised discipline has both broadened and challenged the boundaries of traditional law librarianship. The growth of electronic sources of law has made substantial amounts of primary and secondary source material more easily available to end-users. The use of sophisticated SEARCH ENGINES enables users to locate and retrieve legal information from online and other electronic sources. This development raises various issues about the efficiency of information retrieval, the relevance of retrieved material and the future role of the legal information professional. Substantial amounts of international and national materials are now freely available online or on a subscription basis from a range of recognized international legal information providers. The growth in the availability of legal materials online has led to the development of a number of significant legal Web portals (see PORTALS AND GATEWAYS).

Legal know-how

Many bodies, particularly in the commercial sector, now invest heavily in the attention and management of legal know-how. Know-how comprises any materials generated internally that may be of subsequent use to the organization. These would include legal commentaries, seminar papers, correspondence, opinions and other interpretations of law. In recent years within the legal sector, there has been a growth in the development of KNOWLEDGE MANAGEMENT that seeks to structure and retain both tacit and implicit knowledge held within an organization. Thus, legal information, through knowledge management, would also include the experience, skills and retained information at a personal level by members of the organization relevant to the practice and interpretation of law.

References

Susskind, R. (1996) *The Future of Law*, Oxford: Clarendon Press.

Further reading

Campbell, E., York, L.P. and Tooher, J. (eds) (1996) *Legal Research: Materials and Methods*, 4th edn, Lawbook Co.

Doyle, F.R. (1999) *Searching the Law – The States*, 3rd edn, Transnational Publishers Inc.

Germain, C. (2000) *Germain's Transnational Law Research: A Guide for Attorneys*, Transnational Publishers.

Moys, E.M. and Winterton, J. (eds) (1997) *Information Sources in Law*, 2nd edn, Bowker Saur.

Olson, K. (1998) *Legal Information: How to Find It and How to Use It*, Oryx Press.

Twining, W. (1994) *Legal Records in the Commonwealth*, Dartmouth.

Selected legal Web portals

Australian Legal Information Institute (1995) (http://www.austlii.edu.au).

British and Irish Legal Information Institute (2000) (http://www.bailii.org).

Findlaw (1994) US Materials (http://www.findlaw.com).

Hieros Gamos Web Portal (1985) International Materials (http://www.hg.org).

SEE ALSO: knowledge management; law libraries

JOHN FURLONG

LEIBNIZ, GOTTFRIED WILHELM (1646–1716)

Philosopher and librarian who developed important ideas and techniques for information science and librarianship.

Born in Leipzig, Leibniz entered the University of Leipzig at the age of fifteen. After his studies were completed he spent four years in Paris, where he was able to learn about the important libraries of the city. He then accepted a position as Counsellor and Librarian at the court of Brunswick-Luneburg at Hanover and in 1690 was also appointed Librarian of the Ducal Library at Wolfenbuttel. In Hanover and Wolfenbuttel he improved the catalogues, oversaw the construction of buildings, designed classification schemes and promoted the abstracting and indexing of scientific literature. He was an advocate of the concept of a universal library that would contain all the recorded ideas of mankind.

In addition to his contributions to librarianship, Leibniz provided important ideas and techniques for information science. He developed the binary arithmetic now generally employed in digital computers. He also provided seminal ideas for CYBERNETICS. He had plans for constructing a 'combining analytical machine' that could also handle logical operations involving alphabetical symbols.

LENDING LIBRARIES

Libraries that allow users to take books and other materials away, for the purpose of consulting and reading them at home or in another place. The concept is a comparatively recent one. Until the latter half of the nineteenth century, books were too scarce and valuable to be allowed out of the environments of libraries. Librarians saw themselves primarily as custodians of the collections placed in their charge, and, even when books were made available for loan, borrowers were subject to stringent tests and rigorous supervision. Some monastic libraries (see MONASTIC LIBRARY) of the Middle Ages did divide their manuscripts into those that could be loaned and those which remained in the library. The Vatican Library invoked the ultimate penalty of excommunication for the non-return of books, although there is no evidence to say how successful this measure was. Some of the Cambridge and Oxford colleges also loaned manuscripts for 'home reading', but again the restrictions were formidable.

The caution of these early years is understandable given the unique and precious nature of manuscripts, which made every loan a possible loss to posterity. Even the invention of printing did not significantly change attitudes, as print runs remained small and laborious. The restrictions of educational opportunities for most people also meant that the demand for books was very limited.

It was only with the increase of education, coupled with the invention of powered rotary presses in the nineteenth century, that books became cheap and numerous enough to allow libraries to relax their restrictions on lending. SUBSCRIPTION LIBRARIES had existed a century before then but reached their peak at this time. This was mainly a lending service, often through the post, for the increasingly wealthy middle classes, who could afford the subscriptions required.

Churches, voluntary societies and trade unions attempted to cater for the reading needs of the skilled working class by establishing small collections of books that were lent out to members, but it was only with the development of PUBLIC LIBRARIES in the latter half of the century that lending libraries reached a mass public. Even so, the custodial habits of librarians lingered on for a long time and admission to the lending library was often a protracted and bureaucratic process. CLOSED ACCESS to the stock was the rule for many years, a restriction that lasted, in some places, well into the twentieth century.

Access to ACADEMIC LIBRARIES remained restrictive, although the needs of students of all kinds were recognized in the UK by the foundation of the Central Library for Students, later the National Central Library, which in turn was absorbed into the BRITISH LIBRARY. The emergent county libraries offered postal loans to students and others, often building up special lending collections for this purpose. Municipal libraries tended to be more traditional and often emphasized the reference function of their service. The criteria for the allocation of material to the reference or the lending department were, as often as not, based upon the cost of the book rather than its functional nature.

The second half of the twentieth century saw enormous strides made in the development of lending libraries of all types. PUBLIC LIBRARIES established networks of branch libraries whose main function was to lend books. With the very large increase in books, many of them novels, being loaned from publicly funded libraries, there were moves, some successful, to charge for the borrowing of books. Developments in educational institutions of all kinds resulted in a growth of lending libraries in universities, colleges and schools. Traditionally, NATIONAL LIBRARIES in all countries saw themselves as the library of last resort and ultimate protectors of their countries' literary heritage. However, the part that national libraries could play in the lending of materials was exemplified in the UK by the establishment of the National Lending Library (direct ancestor of the British Library Document Supply Centre), which, with the minimum of restrictions, quickly became the largest lending library in the world. This was something of a cultural shock to many librarians, who failed to see that the dissemination of literature was just as important as its acquisition and storage.

There was also a reluctance among some librarians to embrace the new formats of communication, such as videos, records, tapes and microforms, which became increasingly available. Countries such as France, not having a tradition of public lending libraries, tended to adapt more quickly to these changes than the UK or the USA. Most public libraries took advantage of legal loopholes to subject these new materials to direct financial charges, raising again the whole question of charges for lending services.

At the beginning of the twenty-first century, the whole concept of lending libraries is being called into question. We are now in the middle of another leap forward comparable to the invention of printing in the fifteenth century, and the mass production of books in the nineteenth century. Technology now makes it possible for much of the material that in the past was loaned from libraries to be transmitted direct from suppliers to people's homes. The INTERNET is now the preferred mode of access to information in industrialized countries, but the social forms that have led to the creation of libraries are still powerful and the book has survived many forecasts of its death. Great changes are in process, but libraries, including a lending element, are likely to survive into the foreseeable future.

Further reading

Betts, D.A. (1987) *Borrowing and the Fiction Reader*, Library Association, Branch and Mobile Libraries Group

Crawford, W. and Gorman, M. (1995) *Future Libraries: Dreams, Madness and Reality*, American Library Association.

Kelly, T. (1977) *A History of Public Libraries in Great Britain*, 2nd edn, Library Association

TOM FEATHERSTONE

LESBIGAY LIBRARIANS

'Lesbigay', a post-modernist portmanteau word, succinctly labels lesbians, bisexuals and gays. The term is also sometimes employed to encompass transsexuals and others outside the heterosexual mainstream. Sexuality, which in previous eras constituted only biological assignment, now embraces identity and orientation. Usually, therefore, the term 'lesbigay' applies to self-identified lesbians, bisexuals and gays.

Homosexuality has been variously tolerated and persecuted by all cultures throughout history. Thus, Weimar Germany in the 1920s fostered a rich underground night-club culture amicable to homosexual expression, yet Heinrich Himmler made the sacking of the Magnus Hirshfeld Archives in Berlin (then a unique centre for gay research) his first official act under Hitler in 1933. In Great Britain, some writers, painters, dramatists, actors and musicians, many of whom were gay or lesbian, defied heterosexual conventions and legal strictures in the 1920s and 1930s. Sir Angus Wilson (1913–91), who served on the staff of the Department of Printed Books in the British Museum reading room for many years, satirized the hypocrisy of British attitudes towards homosexuals in *Hemlock and After* (1950) and subsequent novels well before Great Britain decriminalized homosexual acts between consenting adults in 1967.

Homosexuals in European countries have had recourse to the European Convention on Human Rights in Strasbourg since 1981, but, in the USA, only thirty-four out of fifty states had repealed antiquated sodomy laws as of 2001. The politics of consensus in the USA have necessarily given rise to legal battles that have added urgency to lesbigay activism there. US librarians, who formed the first lesbigay professional group in the world in 1970 (the Gay Task Force of the American Library Association (ALA), now called the Gay, Lesbian, Bisexual and Transgendered Round Table – GLBTRT), have focused their energies on the promotion and promulgation of lesbigay literature, the establishment of lesbigay research centres and archives, and the revision of antiquated, pejorative classification terminology and obscurantist archival practices. In 1974, the ALA adopted inclusive language for sexual orientation in its non-discrimination clauses of employment.

Since 1970, when GLBTRT awarded the first Gay Book Award, gay publishing in the USA has become a mainstream commercial concern. Whereas, between 1886 and 1969, only approximately thirty titles about homosexuality were published outside the underground lesbigay press, as of 2001, approximately 1,500 titles per year are being published for all age levels and in all genres.

The activism of the ALA GLBTRT has resulted in a greater international awareness of the importance of lesbigay publishing, libraries, archives and information services, especially since the advent of the AIDS crisis in 1981, and the proliferation of Internet sites dedicated to lesbigay concerns. There are now lesbigay archives and/or libraries in every part of the world, each with a character reflective of the local conditions that prevail. The Lesbian and Gay Archives Research Centre (NZ), for example, was unique in its incorporation into New Zealand's National Archives in 1992; it is financed by the state and occupies a government building, but retains its separate corporate identity.

With the backlash from the religious right beginning in the late 1970s, US lesbigay librarians began taking a more active role in scholarship and publication. Members of GLBTRT devised alternative classification schemes suitable for gay materials, authored essays on services to gays and lesbians, compiled bibliographies of AIDS materials relevant to public library concerns in mainstream journals and assailed in journal literature the difficult subject of lesbigay materials for youth. In 1992, a picture of lesbigay librarians marching in a Gay Day parade on the cover of *American Libraries* sparked a heated debate among some ALA members on the appropriateness of social activism among librarians, and even more controversy ensued when ALA upheld the decision to cancel a 1996 conference in Cincinnati, Ohio, after citizens there reinstated an ordinance prejudicial to lesbigay interests. Librarians also participated in the vociferous debate surrounding two of the most challenged titles of the 1990s, *Heather Has Two Mommies* and *Daddy's Roommate*, children's books about gay and lesbian parenting.

National surveys have also been conducted on the gay male stereotype and the place of social-responsibility concerns in library school curricula (Carmichael and Shontz 1996; Carmichael 1992) Further research in the late 1990s on the holdings of gay materials in major urban libraries found that public library collection management in the area had been sporadic and random (Loverich and Degnan 1999). It seems fair to surmise that while user and publishing concerns are a more comfortable subject of research than the status and condition of lesbigay librarians, research priorities among younger lesbigay librarians in the USA will continue to shift towards the professional status of lesbigay librarians. An Anglo-American conference in Liverpool in 2000 on 'Gendering Library History', which included a lesbigay essay, suggests that comparative studies may yield results fruitful to both Women's Studies and Queer Studies.

References

Carmichael, J. (1992) 'The male librarian and the feminine image: A survey of stereotype, status, and gender perceptions', *Library and Information Science Research* 14: 411–46.

Carmichael, J. and Shontz, M. (1996) 'The last socially acceptable prejudice: Lesbian and gay issues, social responsibilities and coverage of the issues in MLS/MLIS curricula, *Library Quarterly* 66: 21–58.

Loverich, P. and Degnan, D. (1999) 'Out on the shelves? Not really', *Library Journal* 124: 55.

Further reading

Carmichael, J. (ed.) (1998) *Daring to Find Our Names: The Search for Lesbigay Library History*, Greenwood. [Gay historiography and stories by GLBTRT pioneers.]

Gough, C. and Greenblatt, E. (eds) (1990) *Gay and Lesbian Library Service*, McFarland.

Kester, N. (ed.) (1997) *Liberating Minds: The Stories and Professional Lives of Gay Lesbian and Bisexual Librarians and Their Advocates*, McFarland. [Personal recollections and three essays.]

Rolph, A. (2000) 'The life and times of LiL: Lesbians in the Library', in E. Kerslake and N. Moody (eds) *Gendering Library History*, John Moore University, pp. 196–208.

Thistlethwaite, P. (1994) 'Gays and lesbians in library history', in W. Wiegand and D. Davis (eds) *Encyclopedia of Library History*, Garland, pp. 223–7.

SEE ALSO: censorship; code of professional conduct; information professions; women in librarianship

JAMES V. CARMICHAEL, JNR

LIABILITY FOR INFORMATION PROVISION

A difficult concept to define in the area of INFORMATION provision, mainly because there are so many factors that will give rise to it. At the simplest level, it is the consequence of a failure to do some act that one was bound to do; or the doing of some act that one was prohibited from doing; or the doing of some lawful act in such a manner as to render it unlawful (for example, negligently or maliciously). The legal consequences that may flow from any of these acts or omissions may be the result of the normal application of the law, in other words occurring independently of the intention of the wrongdoer. They may also flow from an agreement to provide information, made between the wrongdoer and another to provide information of a certain type, for a certain purpose, for use by the client, in a particular way. This includes an expectation as to the level of distribution of the information. The liability outcomes relating to information can be more easily seen in two categories: first, liability for the information itself and, second, liability following a contract to provide information.

Information

At the outset one must appreciate the nature of the 'product' with which one is dealing when providing information. Information is not property in its own right but it can be given some of the attributes of property in a variety of ways, each of which may potentially create a liability in relation to it.

CONFIDENTIAL INFORMATION

Information is confidential if either it has been communicated in circumstances that a reasonable person would understand to be circumstances of confidence (this would tend to be a 'one-off' type of situation, such as a business proposition) or it is the subject and substance of a confidentiality contract (probably more of an ongoing obligation, such as the information communicated to a consultant). The use of information in breach of this confidence is actionable both in its own right, as a tort, or, if a confidentiality contract has been entered into, as a breach of contract.

COPYRIGHT

It is not the information that is the problem here – in the sense of content, as would be the case for confidential information; instead it is the form into which the information is reduced for permanent record. 'Permanent form', as it is called by the current COPYRIGHT legislation, can include text, images or any other form of notation, code or language; thus, copying computer programs or materials from CD-ROM without an express licence (see LICENCES) to do so is, subject to some limitations relating to different types of copyright, an infringement. If, therefore, in providing information to a client one makes use of documents, for example by photocopying them, to which one does not personally own copyright (and this would include letters of which one is the addressee), then one is incurring liability by infringing another's copyright. Equally, if one employs individuals who one knows do this, then one is liable for authorizing an infringement.

PERSONAL DATA, WITHIN THE MEANING OF THE DATA PROTECTION ACTS

The DATA PROTECTION legislation imposes obligations on those who use or hold personal data to comply with a series of obligations relating to that data, including control of the means of obtaining data, security of storage (including network transmission) and control of those to whom the data is disclosed (including the purposes of that disclosure). Whilst a breach of the data protection rules is not in itself an offence, any serious breach, and particularly persistent breach, may result in criminal liability.

DEFAMATION

Defamation occurs where an article is published that lowers a person's reputation to the extent that the victim is exposed to 'hatred, ridicule or contempt' or is likely to be 'shunned or avoided' by right-thinking people. The definition includes all of the types of statement that one can imagine if one reads the newspapers. Perhaps of more importance in a normal business environment is a recognition that false financial data can cause a person to be shunned or avoided. There are defences: for example, a reporting of current events, qualified privilege, as well as justification and a host of others. What will destroy many of the more likely defences for an information professional is the presence of malice.

The contract to provide

As well as liability relating purely to the information itself, there are other types of liability that attach to the process of providing that information to a client. In this sphere there are two main types of liability.

CONTRACTUAL

The contract to provide information places an obligation on the provider to ensure that information of the type requested by the client is actually provided, in return for a fee. There is no particular format for the contract; it can be verbal or written, the only difference being that the latter provides a means of proof of the terms of the agreement. A failure to perform the contract will result in liability. Contractual liability is 'strict', which means that the provider cannot escape responsibility by a claim that it was not his/her fault; all that is required is an objective failure to meet the contract require-

ments. This creates a real need to ensure that all contracts are written and contain details of the information to be provided, the purpose for which it is required, the fee and of course the names of the parties. There is no need for a formal document in every instance; a standard form letter referring to a properly drawn agreement is sufficient and will act as a confirmatory letter for instructions received by telephone.

TORTIOUS

A provider of information owes a duty of care to the client, as well as to others who might reasonably be expected to act on the information. It is a duty to act reasonably (this does not mean perfectly but in a reasonably competent professional manner in line with professional 'best practice') and not to be negligent. It means providing correct and full information for the client's purposes. It is a duty that makes the contract crucial, as a means of recording details of the client's requirements in a binding agreement, the reason being that a client who wants financial background on a company may require it for the purposes of a takeover bid or simply to produce an article for an 'in-house' magazine. The responsibility of the provider would vary enormously depending on which was the case. The contract may also help limit those others to whom liability might be owed, if one suspects the client might pass the information on, by circumscribing the client's ability to disseminate the information. Also, where confidential or copyright materials are included in the information provided, this allows a forum to place notices prohibiting certain client actions, thereby potentially avoiding a claim against the provider for breach of confidence or authorizing an infringement of copyright.

Further reading

Bainbridge, D. (1994) *Intellectual Property*, Pitman.
Slee, D. (1991) 'Legal aspects of information provision', in *The Information Business, Issue for the 1990s*, IIS and Hertis Information and Research.

SEE ALSO: contracts for information provision; information law

DAVID SLEE

LIBER

Acronym of Ligue des Bibliothèques Européennes de Recherche (League of European Research

Libraries), founded in March 1971 to bring the larger libraries in Europe together in co-operation, with the intention of improving the quality of the services they provide. It actively promotes research in librarianship, seeks to facilitate international loans and exchange of publications, and publishes the biannual *LIBER Bulletin*, various monographs and a directory of bibliographic networks.

Further reading

http://www.kb.dk/liber.

SEE ALSO: research libraries

LIBRARIAN

Traditionally, and still in popular consciousness, the curator of collections of books and other information materials, administering conditional user access to these collections. In current practice, the manager and mediator of access to information for user groups of various descriptions, still initially through collections of information materials under their immediate administration, but also through the global range of available sources.

The term will be found applied to a chief librarian, often called simply the librarian; to professional librarians of different grades, distinguished by the possession of a recognized academic or professional qualification and the holding of a post with higher-level tasks and responsibilities; but also to anyone employed, or acting as a volunteer, in library work – usually more correctly referred to by some term such as PARAPROFESSIONAL, library assistant, library clerk or library messenger. Assistant librarian (as distinct from library assistant) usually refers to a professional librarian.

People who have had the care of libraries (as distinct from ARCHIVES) can be identified as early as the Greek and Roman eras (notably Callimachus, *c.* 300–240 BC, at Alexandria), in a number of other civilizations (those of the East, particularly China) and in the liberal tradition of Islamic libraries (the libraries of Baghdad in particular). Their resources may not always have been identifiable by a distinct building or room (those of the Medieval monastic libraries were not), but their curatorial role is usually quite distinct. In many cases, indeed, the role of those responsible

for libraries may have been so minimal (unlocking and locking the door to permit user access and preserve security, for instance) as almost to remove them from any useful definition of the word.

Manuals of a distinct librarian's occupation are first really apparent in the seventeenth century with Gabriel Naudé's (founder of the Bibliothèque Mazarine, Paris) *Advis pour dresser une bibliothèque* (1627) and John Durie's *The Reformed Librarie-Keeper* (1650). Librarians with a full range of professional responsibilities can be identified from about the same period – for example Thomas James, Thomas BODLEY's librarian at Oxford University, appointed in 1601. James undertook collection building and improved intellectual access through catalogue innovations, as well as creating better physical access to the collections.

The librarian's profession arguably reached a mature form in 1876 with a number of significant developments in the USA. The AMERICAN LIBRARY ASSOCIATION, the first of its kind and still the world's leading professional association for librarians, was founded at a meeting in Philadelphia. The monumental *Report on Public Libraries in the United States of America*, providing a baseline of data on libraries, was published, and attached to it was Charles Ammi CUTTER's *Rules for a Dictionary Catalog*. Melvil DEWEY's *Decimal Classification* was published, and Dewey founded a company, the Library Bureau, to provide products and services for libraries. The *Library Journal* also began publication in that year, thus completing a remarkable upgrading of professional activity and publishing.

In the twentieth century the professionalism of the librarian has continuously been expanded and enhanced, even though public abandonment of an older image has been much slower (O'Brien and Raish 1993). Twentieth-century librarians are innovative in the whole range of professional activities, and the centre of gravity in their work has shifted away from simple care of collections (except, perhaps, in archival libraries (see ARCHIVAL LIBRARY)) towards a preoccupation with the user and the user's needs. Management of libraries, with a strategic view firmly taken, has largely replaced mere administration. Librarians have also accepted new technology for CIRCULATION SYSTEMS, CATALOGUES and access to remote

TACIT KNOWLEDGE

Tacit knowledge is now the KM term typically used to describe the knowledge that is in people's heads or in their own files, as distinguished from explicit knowledge that exists in documents or databases. Current KM thinking is focused on establishing the structure and climate to enable and encourage those who have knowledge to share it. There is close to no mention of capturing that knowledge, particularly in the now rather tarnished sense of ARTIFICIAL INTELLIGENCE (AI) and the 'knowledge engineer'.

From this there have emerged two principal application areas. The first, and simplest, is the creation of organization-wide 'who knows what' directions, referred to in the KM field as 'yellow pages'. The second is the creation of 'best practices' or in the newer and more politic phrase 'lessons learned' databases. The intent is to establish systems that enable and encourage employees to submit a 'best practices' or 'lessons learned' description of how they accomplish something so that others can use it. The information may be screened and edited before it goes on the systems (particularly, for example, in pharmaceutical companies that are subject to Food and Drug Administration approval concerning what they may say about a therapeutic agent), but the knowledge typically is input by the user.

A recent phenomenon however is the creation of 'after-action teams' to interview operational personnel and capture their knowledge and insights for input into a lessons learned system. This is done not to write knowledge algorithms as in AI systems, but simply to make it easy for the user to contribute. Writing a 'lesson learned' is difficult and much too easy and tempting to push down on the priority list, while being interviewed is both enjoyable and difficult to defer.

One frustrating problem is that while KM puts great emphasis upon tacit knowledge (Hibbard 1997; Kleiner and Ruth 1997; Liedtka *et al.* 1997; Davenport 1998; Duhon 1998), there is very little reported upon in the literature that is concrete. A good system to capture and exploit tacit knowledge is inevitably rather specific to the culture and context of that organization and it is also a significant competitive advantage, not something that the organization wishes to be made public. The two most useful discussions are by Davenport (1998), who focuses on customers' knowledge, and by Kleiner and Ruth

(1997), who describe a process they call a learning history, a form of after-action reporting to capture important project-related tacit knowledge within the organization. Despite the paucity of concrete reports, tacit knowledge is heavily emphasized in the KM literature. Paying insufficient attention to tacit knowledge is (see below) Fahey and Prusak's (1998) deadly sin number five.

INCENTIVES AND REWARDS

Effective knowledge sharing requires rewarding those who input information into the system and contribute something useful. Otherwise, what motivation do employees have to contribute information that will, for example, improve the performance of other sales representatives relative to their own, thereby decreasing their own year-end bonus? Changing compensation and incentive systems however is not something that organizations do readily, or lightly; it is an undertaking fraught with peril and with unintended and often unfortunate consequences. A frequent complaint among knowledge management system implementers is how slow and difficult it is to get top management to make such changes. One aphorism heard in KM circles is that you know you really have a KM culture when the organization's compensation scheme has been changed to reflect KM.

CUSTOMER KNOWLEDGE

A pervasive theme in business discussion of KM is the importance of including the customer in the scope of KM systems so as to incorporate and leverage this expertise. This is considered key for a number of reasons:

- Customer commitment and loyalty.
- Early warning and competitive intelligence.
- Better and more timely design of new products and services.
- The synergy of collaboration.

The emphasis here is upon the exchange of knowledge, ideas and opinions, for example, not merely the transaction data currently exchanged with just-in-time inventory or supply chain management systems.

Another dimension is the use of information about customers for CRM, or Customer Relationship Management. How do you acquire and bibliographical and other resources, if not with open arms, with steady consistency.

Such development has probably been stimulated by the creation of a rival professional identity in mid-century, that of the information scientist (see INFORMATION SCIENCE), represented in the USA by the AMERICAN SOCIETY FOR INFORMATION SCIENCE AND TECHNOLOGY. Although information scientists took on a role that encompassed an even higher level of proactivity on behalf of the end-user than librarians generally felt their profession demanded, librarians have not accepted the curtailment that the existence of another profession might have implied. Today it is arguable that there is little, if any, difference between information science and many sectors of librarianship, and the term 'Library and Information Science', abbreviated as LIS or ILS, is very widely used as a consequence of this CONVERGENCE. In Britain since the late 1980s the LIBRARY ASSOCIATION and the INSTITUTE OF INFORMATION SCIENTISTS have discussed merger and this was achieved in 2002 through the founding of CILIP. A new professional identity is sought through the new association, but the sense of many members that they are actually librarians is likely to persist.

References

O'Brien, A. and Raish, M. (1993) 'The image of the librarian in commercial motion pictures: An annotated filmography', *Collection Management* 17: 61–84.

Further reading

Gurnsey, J. (1985) *The Information Professions in the Electronic Age*, Clive Bingley.

SEE ALSO: information professions

PAUL STURGES

LIBRARIANSHIP

The profession practised by those who work in libraries. The principal focus of the work of the librarian is on services to library users, but this manifests itself in many ways. It includes the selection, cataloguing and arrangement of books and other documents and information resources in all media and format; the provision of services to answer the queries of users, including giving access to information resources that are not held in the library; and the management and administration of these processes and of the library itself. In a ONE-PERSON LIBRARY these tasks are, *ex hypothesi*, undertaken by a single person. In larger organisations, there is a division by task, and perhaps also by location and hierarchy.

SEE ALSO: information professions; libraries; philosophy of librarianship

LIBRARIES

In the strict sense of the term a 'library' is a 'collection of materials organized for use'. The word derives from the Latin word '*liber*', a book. The latinized Greek word '*bibliotheca*' is the origin of the word for 'library' in the Greek, Russian and Romance languages. There is good reason to believe that the root concept of 'library' is deeply embedded in our ways of thinking about the world and coping with its problems. In its primary role as guardian of the social memory, there are many parallels with the ways in which the human memory orders, stores and retrieves the information necessary for survival. The study of library history (see HISTORY OF LIBRARIES) and its related disciplines bears witness that the instinct to preserve, the passion to collect and the desire to control have been dominant influences in the genesis and growth of the library idea in the history of civilization.

From the ARCHIVES room at Nineveh to the PUBLIC RECORD OFFICE at Kew, Surrey; from the Alexandrian Library to the LIBRARY OF CONGRESS in Washington, DC, these uniquely human attributes have been constantly at work.

The momentous advances in INFORMATION AND COMMUNICATION TECHNOLOGY (ICT) have not made the term redundant. 'Library' in information technology is used as a generic term for an ordered set of related items yielding such extended uses of the term in 'data library', 'programme library', 'routine library' and other kindred concepts. The current bibliography of librarianship contains many references to DIGITAL LIBRARY, hybrid library (see HYBRID LIBRARIES), VIRTUAL LIBRARY and other electronic extensions of the physical library, the image which usually arises in our minds when the term is loosely used. Although we may visualize a 'library' as a physical plant dedicated to storage purposes, the generic term denotes what some logicians call an 'empty category' or, as Vakkari

(1994) puts it, 'a linguistic expression that does not have content'. If I say that I work in a library I convey very little information to the reader or listener unless I supply the missing context where my skills of librarianship are being used. A random assemblage of books is not a library; order of a recognizable kind is the essence of the concept.

Returning to our basic definition of 'library', we note that the components – collection, materials, organization, use – describe interconnected and interacting parts of an operational system. Furthermore, when we analyse these components we find that they yield most of the core subjects and practical problems in the systematic study of library and information science. The initial act of collecting implies a sense of purpose and an intended or imagined user even if the user is the person who does the collecting. This kind of self-indulgence or self-glorification has resulted in many of the world's finest PRIVATE LIBRARIES and RESEARCH LIBRARIES.

The 'how', 'why' and 'for whom' questions entailed in this set of operations go to form the intellectual staple of the study of COLLECTION MANAGEMENT. A library derives its individuality from the types of materials it is designed to collect. Thus we have ART LIBRARIES, multimedia libraries (see MULTIMEDIA LIBRARIANSHIP), map libraries (see MAP LIBRARY), PICTURE LIBRARIES, toy libraries and similar collections specializing in AUDIOVISUAL MATERIALS. Advances in ICT have frequently meant changes in the physical media of communication stored by libraries. Each change in the design and shape of these media has challenged the library to rethink its design and layout, and posed problems for the students of LIBRARY BUILDINGS. Clay tablets and papyrus rolls needed different forms of storage and retrieval. In the monastic libraries, the long rooms of benches and stands gave way to wall shelving when printed books began to be published in smaller sizes. As each mass medium became popular it was seen as a potential threat to the normative book library; yet, each development in the MASS MEDIA has led to a new type of library – for example, film libraries, newspaper libraries, television libraries and multimedia librarianship.

The operations of collecting and organizing may be analysed further into the professional techniques of selection, CLASSIFICATION, cataloguing, INFORMATION MANAGEMENT and INFOR-MATION RETRIEVAL. Just as in human communication we design our message according to our image of the receiver, so also the library adjusts its purpose, content and design to its image of the user. A library intended to serve pre-school children will differ in its user approach from one designed for cosmic physicists. ACADEMIC LIBRARIES reflect the philosophy of the institutions of which they are a part; they design their collections and services to meet the educational aims and instructional objectives of the institutions they serve.

When we move outwards from the specific types of library to the wider social setting we can see how the content and purpose of the library are shaped and directed by a diversity of social concepts. A society is composed of groups of people working together to achieve common aims and satisfy basic needs. Culture is the body of knowledge, beliefs, values and skills that both initiates and results from these activities. Culture is interpreted, transmitted and disseminated by social institutions. Among these institutions are education, health, religion, law, democracy and similarly structured ways of doing social tasks. Just as human beings need information for making decisions, so also do the social agencies that implement the aims and objectives of these institutions. They need libraries for information, for recording decisions and solving problems. Education is represented in NATIONAL INFORMATION SYSTEMS by school, college and university libraries; health science libraries; the Christian religion by cathedral libraries, theological collections and other ECCLESIASTICAL LIBRARIES, and comparable institutions in other religions, such as JEWISH LIBRARIES and ISLAMIC LIBRARIES; law by LAW LIBRARIES; and the legislative process by PARLIAMENTARY LIBRARIES. Elementary social analysis will multiply examples. However, this is not a static situation: these institutions change over time. For a period of time one may predominate over the others and then slide to a lower place in the social hierarchy, thus reducing the allocation of resources to its library system. Religion was once dominant in Western Europe; then came the rise of the sciences and technologies in Europe and the USA. They produced the need for information and a consequent diffusion of science libraries, business libraries, engineering libraries and like services. The growth of institutional democracy in Britain in the nineteenth century stimulated the growth of the public library and LITERACY as well as government libraries.

A fruitful method of studying the cultural role of the library is to analyse the gradual growth in access to books and materials for all people, without distinctions of any kind. It is an important maxim in democratic philosophy that the human being develops and functions best as a responsible 'rights and duties'-bearing person; this means informed access to recorded culture. The ancient temple libraries and the medieval monastic libraries were for the select few. PRIVATE LIBRARIES, family libraries and SUBSCRIPTION LIBRARIES restrict access to their collections. Not infrequently, the librarian's role was exclusively as a conservator and librarians were consequently seen as a barrier to the use of the collection. This image is dramatically described by Eco (1983), and the legacy of this image in fiction by Taylor (1993). British public libraries began to give open access to their shelves in the latter part of the nineteenth century, more or less at the same time that public access to 'elementary' education was first provided by the state. One may usefully distinguish 'passive' access, where people may physically access the stock as borrowers and avail themselves of whatever is available regardless of need. 'Mediated' access, which provides entry to the intellectual content of the library, entails a trained staff and a suitable technology to match needs with materials and information. These developments may be observed in academic libraries as they become learning resource centres.

The decade from the mid-1980s to the mid-1990s saw the growth of what might be called 'transitive' access, in that it governs directly specific objectives. This professional philosophy is reflected in mobile libraries (see MOBILE LIBRARY), bookmobiles, services to the housebound and other outreach activities. More recently it is embodied in special collections for socially and economically disadvantaged minorities.

Problems in assigning priorities are worsened by financial pressures. Economic recessions and political policies in the USA and Western Europe in the 1980s led to reduced spending on library services and pressure to justify the existence of libraries in cost-cutting organizations. The cost of information and the pressure to participate in the market economy has led to widespread charging for services in academic and public libraries. Like any other social agency, the library is vulnerable to conflicting political philosophies. These have led to opposing positions in public library provision. One strongly held view is to target scarce resources on the less privileged in the community; the other is to emphasize value for money and competitiveness as increasing choice and therefore increasing freedom. When policies changed, and economies improved, the attempt to revive the fortunes of libraries was closely associated with a re-emphasis of their social role. Libraries are seen as safe and friendly places. They are embedded in communities and are easily accessible by all. They have therefore been used increasingly as the location for public provision of INTERNET access and other ELECTRONIC PUBLIC-INFORMATION SERVICES. The result of this has been a growing tension between the traditional perception of the library (especially of the public library) and the reality of current provision. It is far from clear that libraries do (or perhaps even can) attract the socially and economically disadvantaged to benefit from the new services that they now provide. Indeed, there is evidence that both direct Internet access from the home and provision through agencies such as Internet cafés are far more successful in giving wider network access.

Like 'the death of the book' theme with which it is so closely associated, the 'end of the library' theme has been periodically discussed in library literature. The library, in its primary sense, has habitually been identified with imaginative literature and the arts; information, in its technical sense, tends to be associated with the sciences and technologies. Although the library has traditionally been regarded as the laboratory of the humanist, library research always took place before experimentation in the laboratory. The habit of BROWSING is an inveterate part of human creativity and cognition. We enjoy it especially if it takes place in a well-guided library where the serendipity factor plays a rewarding part in human learning; better still if this learning takes place in a structured, secure and aesthetically pleasing environment. New technologies, however, and particularly the development of the WORLD WIDE WEB, have driven what is coming to seem to be a fundamental change in the processes of COMMUNICATION and research. The printed documents (and particularly journals), which are essential to research in all disciplines, are being gradually superseded by their electronic equivalents. As ELECTRONIC-JOURNAL ARCHIVES, e-print archives and the like become firmly established across the whole spectrum of scholarly and scientific endeavour, academic libraries will increasingly face pressures comparable to those already confronted by the public library system. The book storehouses of the past (an unfair description of the sophisticated institutions and service providers in almost all universities) will be seen to be increasingly irrelevant as access to a universal virtual library, symbolized by and currently embodied in the Web, becomes a reality.

Even this, however, need not presage the 'death of the library'. As a concept – an organized and accessible collection of information resources – it remains central to human activity. Developments of any kind often result in paradoxical human responses. The rapid consolidation of a global culture in a post-modern world can lead to the resurgence of local identities and concern for the continuity of local cultures. The disappearance of the built environment, historic landmarks and ancient national cultures threatens a loss of roots and identity. The heritage concept, with its emphasis on local studies, has placed the traditional public library within a mosaic of services that include MUSEUMS, tourist centres, theme parks and centres for industrial archaeology. Indeed, the CULTURAL INDUSTRIES in general, and perhaps the heritage sector in particular, may in future come to be the natural home for many services that libraries have traditionally provided. As the concept of an organized knowledge store in CYBERSPACE becomes more pervasive (and more real), its manifestations will take a multitude of forms. The future practitioners of the INFORMATION PROFESSIONS will include librarians and archivists, but also many others with related – but different – skills in the collection, management and provision of knowledge and information.

The 'library' as a formal concept remains a constant; in its actuality it is protean: ever-changing, versatile, regularly taking on new forms in response to ever-changing needs. However, no matter how flexible and adaptive it may be, 'the library' only exists as a library in the fullest sense when it is being used in accordance with its primary purpose and the capability that society designs into it.

References

Eco, U. (1983) *The Name of the Rose*, London: Secker & Warburg.

Taylor, A. (ed.) (1993) *Long Overdue: A Library Reader*, London: Library Association; Edinburgh: Mainstream Publishing.

Vakkari, P. (1994) 'Library and information science: its content and scope', in I.P. Godden (ed.) *Advances in Librarianship*, vol. 19, London/New York: Academic Press, pp. 1–51.

Further reading

Rawski, K.H. (ed.) (1973) *The Shera Festschrift: Towards a Theory of Librarianship: Papers in Honour of Jesse Hauk Shera*, Metuchen, NJ: Scarecrow Press.

Saunders, L.M. (1993) *The Virtual Library: Visions and Realities*, Westport/London: Meckler.

Williams, P. (1989) *Public Libraries and the Problems of Purpose*, Greenwood Press.

SEE ALSO: communication; library services and institutions; philosophy of librarianship; social exclusion and libraries

KEVIN MCGARRY, REVISED BY THE EDITORS

LIBRARY ASSOCIATION

The most prominent and longest lasting professional association of librarians in the United Kingdom, founded in 1877. In 1898 the Association (LAUK) was granted a Royal Charter and incorporated not as LAUK but as the Library Association (LA) (Munford 1976). In 1986 the Association, usually referred to as the LA, was granted a supplemental Royal Charter. In 2002 the Association was effectively dissolved and a new organization, CILIP, created through merger with the INSTITUTE OF INFORMATION SCIENTISTS. This article will therefore discuss the LA chiefly in terms of what the new association inherits from it.

At the time of the merger, the LA had more than 25,000 members, of whom approximately 5.5 per cent were overseas members. All members were obliged to comply with the provisions of the Charter and Bylaws, and with the provisions of the CODE OF PROFESSIONAL CONDUCT (Library Association 1985). The management of the LA was the overall responsibility of a Chief Executive, who managed a staff of seventy operating from the headquarters building in central London. The new association inherited a number of income-generating activities from the

LA, including Library Association Publishing Limited (now Facet Publishing), the *Record* (now *Update*) and the *Vacancies Supplement*, Infomatch (a professional recruitment agency) and conferences and special events.

At the time of merger, the LA's library service was no longer in its own hands, having been taken over by the British Library Information Science Service (BLISS) in 1974. BLISS houses one of the most comprehensive library and information science collections worldwide and members could exploit its resources for reference or borrowing purposes directly or by means of a postal loans service.

Among the key roles that the LA had performed for the profession were assessing and validating courses in library and information science, providing members with career guidance and its continuing professional development programme, which included the provision of around fifty short courses each year. In 1992 the LA published *The Framework for Continuing Professional Development* (CPD) to enable its members 'to keep pace with the rapid changes in the environment in which they work' (Library Association 1992).

The LA had a strong presence in international library organizations, in particular the International Federation of Library Associations (IFLA) and the European Bureau of Library, Information and Documentation Associations (EBLIDA), and it established a number of bilateral schemes of co-operation with a range of library associations.

The LA's Mission Statement asserted that 'libraries are fundamental to the maintenance of a democratic society, culture and civilisation' and therefore it was 'committed to enabling its members to achieve and maintain the highest professional standards, and encouraging and supporting them in the delivery and promotion of high quality library and information services responsive to the needs of users' (Library Association 1993). It is fully expected that CILIP will stand for exactly these values, attached to an expanded vision of the information profession.

References

Library Association (1993) *Revised Recommendations for a New Structure of the Library Association*, Library Association.
—— (1992) *The Framework for Continuing Professional Development: Your Personal Profile*, Library Association.
—— (1985) *Code of Professional Conduct and Guidance Notes*, Library Association.
Munford, W.A. (1976) *A History of the Library Association 1877–1977*, Library Association.

SEE ALSO: information professions

RAYMOND G. ASTBURY, REVISED BY THE EDITORS

LIBRARY ASSOCIATIONS

Organizations that protect the standards of library and information services provided by members to the public; establish and maintain the standards of members' performance; protect the resourcing and quality of the services to the public in which their members work; and provide services to members in return for their subscriptions.

The first library association to be established was the AMERICAN LIBRARY ASSOCIATION (ALA), which was founded in 1876, partly because of an article in *Academy* (18 March 1876) authored anonymously by an Englishman, Professor Max Müller (a former Curator of the Bodleian Library at Oxford), who proposed an international conference of librarians. This was reprinted in the New York *Publisher's Weekly* on 22 April 1876. It is generally accepted that it was this article that led to the foundation of the ALA, which was accomplished 'largely through the energy and enthusiasm of Melvil Dewey, Frederick Leypoldt, R.R. Bowker and others'. The US initiative encouraged similar interest in the United Kingdom, where Edward Williams Bynon Nicholson, then librarian of the London Institution, suggested in a letter to *The Times* (16 February 1877) that a similar conference be held in London. Support was forthcoming and the conference was held from 2 to 5 October 1877; 140 delegates from nine countries were among the 216 who attended and the LIBRARY ASSOCIATION was established (Haslam 1974).

The next association to be established appears to have been the Nihon Toshokan Kyokai (Japan Library Association), in 1892, followed in 1895 by the Swiss Librarians' Association and in 1896 by the Vereinigung Österreichischer Bibliothekare (Association of Austrian Librarians). In 1900 the Verein Deutscher Bibliothekare e.V. (Association of German Librarians) was established, and in 1905 the Danmarks Biblioteksforeng (Danish Library Association). The following year the Association des Bibliothécaires Français (Association of French Librarians) was born, followed in 1907 by the Archives et Bibliothèques de Belgique (Belgian Association of Archives and Libraries), and in 1908 by the Scottish Library Association (now part of the Library Association (UK)) and, in the Netherlands, the Nederlands Bibliotheek en Lektuur Centrum (Dutch Centre for Public Libraries and Literature; founded as the Central Association for Public Libraries). In 1910 the New Zealand Library Association and the Suomen Kirjastosueva – Finlands Biblioteksfürenung (Finnish Library Association) were established.

Thereafter came the Norsk Bibliotekforening (Norwegian Library Association), in 1913; the Sveriges Allmänna Biblioteks – Pärening (Swedish Library Association), in 1915; and the Union of Polish Librarians and Archivists (now Stuwarzyszenie Bibliotekarzy Polskich), in 1917. The year 1923 saw the establishment of the Philippine Library Association, Inc., and in 1928 the Cumann Leabharlann na h. Èireann (Library Association of Ireland) was formed. Library associations followed in Italy (1930), India (1936), Australia (1937), Canada (1946) and Spain (1949) (Fang and Songe 1990). Some of the most recent and important changes in library associations have taken place in RUSSIA AND THE FORMER SOVIET UNION and CENTRAL AND EASTERN EUROPE. There the library associations that were almost organs of the government have been re-established on democratic lines.

The International Federation of Library Associations and Institutions (IFLA) provided no focus prior to 1980 for those concerned with the operation and management of library associations. Since then a Round Table for the Management of Library Associations has been established and has undertaken much work. In 1989, under contract to UNESCO, the Round Table produced for IFLA a set of Guidelines (Bowden 1989). From the 1986 IFLA Pre-Conference Seminar in Japan came a resolution expressing concern at the poor image, weak reputation and low status of the library and information profession (see INFORMATION PROFESSIONS), with a request that IFLA undertake work to improve it. The Round Table commissioned research from the Nederlands Bibliotheek en Lektuur Centrum (NBLC). Through a questionnaire and visits to Latin America and the Caribbean and Asia, two social scientists identified some of the obstacles to improving reputation and status. The final report (Prinz and de Gier 1993) indicates clearly some of the problems that the profession generally and library associations specifically will need to address. The research helped to form the basis for an IFLA Pre-Conference Seminar held in Delhi in August 1992 and which gathered together representatives of library associations from as far apart as Vietnam, the Philippines, Namibia, St Martin and Nicaragua. Essentially the seminar agreed that one of the greatest hurdles to improved status was not only the management of library associations but also the establishment of standards for the quality of services members of the library associations provided in their workplace to the public using libraries and information services. The *Proceedings* (Bowden and Wijasuriya 1994) make interesting reading and identify through resolutions numerous actions that IFLA, FID and individual library associations need to undertake.

The UNESCO Guidelines have been used as a textbook and the basis for a number of seminars to improve the organization and efficient management of library associations, both to improve the standards of provision of services by their members and to improve the services provided by the associations to their members. In Budapest in March 1994 a seminar was held for the newly established democratic library associations in Central and Eastern Europe, bringing together librarians from Albania, Bulgaria, Moldova, Hungary, the Czech and Slovak Republics, Belarus, Latvia, Lithuania, Estonia and Russia. To facilitate their future use in seminars the Guidelines have been translated into French, Russian, Chinese, Spanish, Portuguese, Latvian, Romanian and Indonesian.

From the seminars, from the NBLC research and from the Delhi Pre-Conference Seminar Proceedings it is clear that there is a growing awareness that it is through the effective operation of library associations that the best opportunities exist for the improvement of library and information services in a country. The associations unite the profession and thus assist it in representing the interests not only of librarians but also of libraries and information services. It is clear that there is a growing awareness of the importance of establishing library associations by law, as has happened in the Philippines, and of the need for codes of conduct to indicate to members the importance of the provision of services of quality. The IFLA Round Table has embarked on work to attempt to draft a model code of conduct that can be used by associations.

Regional associations continue to undertake useful work through the Association of Caribbean University and Research Libraries (ACURIL) and, in Southern and Central Africa, the Standing Conference of East and Central and South African Librarians (SCECSAL); and particularly useful work has been done in Asia through the Conference of Southeast Asian Librarians (CONSAL). In 1992 the European Bureau of Library, Information and Documentation Associations (EBLIDA) was established to provide a focal point for library associations, libraries and librarians in the European Union, and to facilitate input into the deliberations of the European Commission and Parliament and the Council of Europe.

References

Bowden, R. (1989) *Guidelines for the Management of Professional Associations in the Fields of Archives, Library and Information Work*, Unesco (PG1–89/WS/11).

Bowden, R. and Wijasuriya, D. (eds) (1994) *The Status, Reputation and Image of the Library and Information Profession: Proceedings of the IFLA Pre-Session Seminar, Delhi, 24–28 August 1992, Under the Auspices of the IFLA Round Table for the Management of Library Associations*, IFLA/K.G. Saur.

Fang, J.S. and Songe, A.H. (1990) *World Guide to Library, Archive and Information Science Associations*, IFLA/K.G. Saur.

Haslam, D.D. (1974) 'A short history of the Library Association', *Journal of Librarianship* 6.

Prinz, H. and de Gier, W. (1993) *Status, Image and Reputation of Librarianship: A Report of an Empirical Research Undertaken on Behalf of IFLA's Round Table for the Management of Library Associations*, IFLA/NBLC.

SEE ALSO: information professions

RUSSELL BOWDEN

LIBRARY AUTOMATION

As computer-based systems have become more pervasive in all aspects of library and information work, the term library automation has become an umbrella term for the many kinds of applications that are used within the library. The various applications provide the means to input information into DATABASES that provide organized storage, and thus allow access to information (INFORMATION RETRIEVAL). Perhaps the major transformation as heralded in this volume's first edition has been the emergence of the DIGITAL LIBRARY and the hybrid library (see HYBRID LIBRARIES), resulting in the blurring of the notion of the library collection as seen as located in a physical place.

History

Dating from the 1960s the first use of library automation was the use of computers to store bibliographic data and to enable the circulation of stock. The project to place onto computer the stock of the US LIBRARY OF CONGRESS resulted ultimately in the development of MACHINE-READABLE CATALOGUING (MARC), opening up the possibility of libraries exchanging bibliographic records and encouraging co-operation between libraries. In the 1970s the library management system became the main housekeeping tool in large libraries and this trend was continued through the following two decades, leaving very few libraries without some form of system. Other fundamental developments began to bring about the convergence of the hitherto specialized library automation environment with the developments underway in the larger computer industry marketplace. These were the increasing power in the performance of the personal computer; the increasing predominance of non-proprietary software, encouraging competition but just as importantly enabling increasing exchange of data over networks; and the development of the INTERNET.

Applications

LIBRARY MANAGEMENT SYSTEMS (LMS)

A certain core functionality can be assumed, namely the provision of systems that automate the performance of the main library housekeeping functions: cataloguing, circulation, acquisitions and serials. Although typically an authority or organization will select a system supplied by a company some still develop systems in-house.

Library suppliers have continued to develop systems with the aim being to provide a more 'Windows-like' user INTERFACE, and there has been an increase in those using Windows NT as the OPERATING SYSTEM. Commonly vendors of LMS from the late 1980s onwards began to offer systems with the UNIX operating system and, although this is the standard, in an ever-evolving environment it is possible that the future will see the adoption of Linux as an alternative operating system platform for the smaller library system. The prevalence of the WORLD WIDE WEB (WWW) has led to a number of vendors developing systems that incorporate interfaces which have marked similarity with WWW interfaces. Millennium marketed by Innovative Inc. is one such example. No supplier can ignore the presence of the Internet and hence software has had to be developed that allows for the integration of local systems with the Internet. Just a few of the PROTOCOLS that can be expected to be part of any system are: TCP/IP (the Internet Protocol), Z39.50 (a protocol designed to enable the search and retrieval of bibliographic records in various formats), other forms of data exchange include MARC-formats and for the Web some systems include use of Extensible Mark-up Language (XML) (see MARK-UP LANGUAGES).

INTEGRATION

For many years it has been a goal of many systems developers to provide one single point of access to a library's resources, held on different mediums, for example, on CD-ROMs. As the development of networked computing continued through the 1980s the vision of the single point of access was only partly realized. In some cases it was considered better to keep separate the online searching of remote databases from the local access to databases offered by CD-ROM technology. In the late 1990s and into the twenty-first century, with the availability of databases accessed over the Web, both local and remote, the goal is nearer fruition, although the many parties involved in information supply and the need to safeguard contractual rights has constrained its fulfilment.

LIBRARY SYSTEMS IN THE ELECTRONIC AGE

Expectations of library users and staff have undergone a change in the age of the Internet. Users expect systems to be user-friendlier than ever before. Suppliers have reacted to this by developing 'mylibrary' software, in other words the capability for the user to personalize the interface and search for topics of particular interest. Two strands of thought have emerged in the design of systems search interfaces: first, the notion that users may start from the premise that they wish to search everything and everywhere all at once; and, second, the more traditional approach that the user starts searching

locally and only broadens the search to external sources if at first unsuccessful.

Managing library systems

Changing styles of management and the influence of political and economic agendas have impacted upon the management of library systems so that, whilst the post of systems librarian and associated systems team is often found in larger libraries, other means of managing the systems can also be employed with some organizations choosing to outsource the task of systems supply. A number of the companies who supply Library Management Systems offer a facilities management service.

Further reading

Evans, P. (ed.) (2002) *Biblio Tech Review* (http://www.biblio-tech.com/) [accessed 10 May 2002].

Cohn, M.J., Kelsey, A.L. and Fiels, K.M. (2002) *Planning for Integrated Systems and Technologies: A How-to-Do-It Manual for Librarians*, 2nd UK edn, rev. and adapted by D. Salter, London: Facet Publishing.

Electronic Library, Library Technology Reports, Online, Program and *Vine* [journals specializing in library automation].

IAN MURRAY

LIBRARY BUILDINGS

Libraries are housed in a wide variety of purpose-built or converted buildings. Soon after 1500, book collections in royal palaces, cathedrals and abbeys began to grow. Accommodation for them was at first found within those buildings but later, when NATIONAL LIBRARIES and UNIVERSITY LIBRARIES had taken root, it became evident that the rapidly growing collections required specially designed structures. The Renaissance gradually brought this about, and grandiose buildings began to appear. One of the earliest was the Laurentian Library in Florence, designed by Michelangelo and completed in 1571. From then on, buildings specifically designed for the housing of books began to be erected in other European cities and academic centres. Michelangelo was one of the first great architects to be linked with library buildings, but he was succeeded through the years by many others. However, most architects, particularly in the nineteenth century and the first half of the twentieth, concentrated on designing monumental buildings and ignored the practical needs of the libraries, which were growing more quickly than had been envisaged.

The librarian and the architect

It was not until well after the profession of librarianship had evolved and established itself that librarians began to influence the design of buildings by preparing briefs describing their technical requirements and by insisting, as far as possible, that those briefs be followed by architects in their design plans.

Even so, it has been a slow process, and instances still occur of buildings that reflect the personalities and ideas of their architects more than the librarians' practical needs. The twentieth-century renaissance in library architecture began immediately after the end of the Second World War in the USA and Scandinavia, especially Sweden and Finland. In the latter country the internationally celebrated architect Alvar Aalto designed several libraries, notably Viipuri in the 1930s and Rovaniemi in 1965.

In Britain such architects as Basil Spence, Frederick Gibberd, James Stirling, Richard Rogers, Norman Foster and Quinlan Terry have some notable library buildings to their names. The vast new BRITISH LIBRARY at St Pancras was designed by Colin St John Wilson. Built to house one of the largest and fastest-growing collections of books and other materials in the world, this is massive but has been planned so as not to be over-powering to the millions of scholars and general readers who will have recourse to it in the future. In France the new building for the BIBLIOTHÈQUE NATIONALE DE FRANCE in Paris, designed by Dominique Perrault, is also worthy of close study.

Though still imperfect, relations between librarians and architects have improved enormously. The librarian's prime task is to look as far into the future as possible. Having visualized the development of the library and having considered the possible growth of population in the area served, the librarian should prepare the brief. Discussions with the architect can then take place and agreement can be reached on a feasible plan.

Importance of the site

All this presupposes that a site has been agreed upon and that the necessary finances have been approved by the library authority. The site of any new library building is of paramount importance. It is true that dedicated scholars and users will find their way to any library if they really need to, but a building aiming to be used to maximum potential should be located in a position that is central and on the everyday axis of those who will be seeking to use its resources. The site should afford adequate car-parking space, and ideally it should also be capable of accommodating a future extension to the building.

The design plan

Every library has its own particular needs as far as interior design is concerned. The size and possible future growth of the collection are vital factors to be thought of at the pre-planning stage. However, there are some features common to the requirements of all libraries. Ease of supervision, security considerations, fire precautions, good natural lighting, efficient artificial lighting, heating and air-conditioning, facilities outside and inside the building for physically disabled users, and transfer facilities for materials, users and staff between different floor levels are just some of the factors needing detailed forethought and attention in the design plan.

Multimedia needs

Libraries once collected only manuscripts and books, with periodicals, newspapers and archives being added later. However, for some time now the information needs of users have dictated that many other media have been added to libraries – first gramophone records, and then audio-cassettes and CDs, slides and videocassettes, as well as material in microform (see MICROFORMS) and records in disk forms.

Libraries in existing premises have had to take these developments in their stride, but designers of future library buildings will have to give serious thought to the special needs both of these newer media and of their users. In fact examples of buildings of this kind already exist. The French coined the word *mediathèque* and, after the success of Richard Rogers's Centre Pompidou in Paris, more instance of multimedia centres appeared in France. The arts and media centre at Nîmes, designed by Norman Foster, is an interesting example. In Britain, attention is drawn to the Queen Mary and Westfield College library in East London, the work of Colin St John Wilson, the architect of the British Library. More recently Croydon public library, opened in 1993, pays great attention to multimedia needs.

The ideal library building, like the ideal house, does not yet exist, and probably it never will. However, there is every reason why librarians and architects should try to achieve buildings that combine all the aesthetic appeal dear to the hearts of architects with the practical requirements of librarians. Those responsible for planning and designing future libraries must learn from the past and not repeat the faults of so many existing structures. There are many lessons to be learned.

Further reading

Bisbrouck, M.-F. (ed.) (2001) *Library Buildings in a Changing Environment*, Munich: Saur.

Harrison, D. (1995) *Library Buildings, 1990–1994*, Library Services Limited.

Harrison, K.C. (ed.) (1990) *Library Buildings, 1984–1989*, Library Services Limited.

Holt, R.M. (1989) *Planning Library Building and Facilities*, Scarecrow.

Kaser, D. (1993) 'Library buildings', in *World Encyclopedia of Library and Information Services*, 3rd edn, ALA.

Leighton, P.D. and Weber, D.C. (2000) *Planning Academic and Research Library Buildings*, American Library Association.

Thompson, G. (1989) *Planning and Design of Library Buildings*, 3rd edn, Butterworths.

SEE ALSO: university libraries

K.C. HARRISON

LIBRARY CO-OPERATION

Formal or informal arrangements between libraries through which they can work together for the common benefit of their users. Few, if any, libraries can regard themselves as islands, endeavouring to keep all, or at least most, of what their users want. Throughout the centuries, communication between scholars has resulted in the lending of materials to other libraries and access being given to special collections. It was not, however, until the present century that formal schemes of library co-operation with UNION CATALOGUES, INTERLIBRARY LENDING, centralized storage and subject specialization came into being.

The LIBRARY OF CONGRESS National Union Catalog, which began in 1901, was one of the first of its kind, but most countries have developed some formalized structure for library co-operation and interlibrary loan since that time. Some are centralized systems where all co-operation is focused on one library or one union catalogue. These are rare, although they can be found in some small countries. A more common form of centralized system is the one that deals with a particular type of material – such as INIST in France, which handles only scientific and technical photocopy requests. Although much of the material supplied by the BRITISH LIBRARY Document Supply Centre (BLDSC) is in the from of photocopies of journal articles, this organization has a wider role, inherited from the old National Central Library, of co-ordinating the United Kingdom interlending structure.

Decentralized schemes of library co-operation are in fact more common and there is considerable diversity. A group of specializing libraries have a mandated responsibility to supply material in particular subject areas – the CADIST (Centres d'Acquisition et de Diffusion de l'Information Scientifique et Technique) in France, for example – or in a specific geographic area, as in the Netherlands. The pattern in the NORDIC COUNTRIES is generally to have a series of large general libraries that support either academic or public libraries, in the first instance, and then libraries of other types as a second source.

The wholesale collection and storage of materials probably reached its zenith in the 1950s with the Farmington Scheme in the USA, which divided foreign literature collecting among members of the Association of Research Libraries (ARL). Weakened budgets and lack of storage space led to its demise in 1967 and, as this and other comprehensive collection schemes became increasingly difficult to maintain, the concept of UAP, by which each country was to be responsible for making available material published in its own country, was developed by IFLA. UAP has an important part to play in international library co-operation and it must be emphasized that in theory, if not always in practice, there are no barriers to knowledge. The IFLA Section on Document Supply and Interlending is responsible, with the IFLA Office for International Lending situated at BLDSC, for the development of manuals and directories.

As it became more difficult to maintain co-operative subject specialization collections, a scheme called CONSPECTUS, which aimed to improve local and collective planning, was developed in the USA; this has been adopted in some countries, giving libraries a better understanding of their own and other libraries' collections without the vast expense of maintaining additional special collections.

From the 1960s onwards a new form of library co-operation began to appear, aimed at the sharing of cataloguing entries; these included OCLC in the USA, BLCMP and SWALCAP in the UK and Pica in the Netherlands. This development mirrored the changes that were taking place in the approach to library co-operation. Co-operation was no longer merely an adjunct to library services and a means for remedying deficiencies and meeting special needs; it became a strategy that aimed at planned relationships and services to assist a move away from 'holdings' to 'access' within libraries.

This strategy was well illustrated in reports published in the 1970s and 1980s by the Library and Information Services Council (England) on the *Future Development of Library and Information Services* and at the White House conference on Library and Information Services in 1979. The British Library strategic plan for 1989–94, *Gateway to Knowledge*, saw as its goal for the year 2000 'an integrated pattern of services based upon a single British Library collection and a range of co-operative relationships with other libraries in the UK, Europe and abroad'.

The development in the UK of Library and Information Plans (LIPs) to co-ordinate on a structured and contractual basis the services of a wide range of libraries within a geographical or sectoral area is an indication of this growing awareness of the need for sharing resources. In Canada and the USA there has been a rapidly growing phenomenon of provincial and state co-operation to meet resource-sharing objectives. Many of these new developments have been made possible by the use of new technology and the growth of networking. Union catalogues have been computerized and networks for interlibrary loan and bibliographical research have been developed. Also, in the UK the catalogues of many academic libraries are available for access via the INTERNET.

The situation is undergoing further change with the development of worldwide data communications infrastructures such as the Internet and the Information Superhighway; it is now possible to link networks and thus to access library catalogues and information systems throughout the world from a microcomputer. Full-text systems are also available and material can be downloaded, making DOCUMENT DELIVERY rather than interlibrary loan the key to the future. Unfortunately, this growth in the ability to communicate has not been matched by the freedom or ability to pay for the content of the information. It also increases the possibility of unauthorized use and raises the thorny issues of intellectual property and payment to producers.

Although the interdependence of libraries is now universally accepted and some believe that networking is the key to open vast resources of information, others are more cautious and stress the need for standards and for national and international infrastructures.

Further reading

Capital Planning Information (1989) *The Impact of Library and Information Plans on Local Cooperatives*, British Library Research and Development Department.

Fjallbrandt, N. (ed.) (1980) *Library Cooperation: Trends, Possibilities and Conditions*, IATUL.

Helal, A.H. and Weiss, J.W. (eds) (1987) *Impact of New Information Technology on International Library Cooperation: Essen Symposium*, Essen Universitätsbibliothek.

McDougall, A.F. and Prytherch, R. (eds) (1991) *Handbook of Library Cooperation*, Gower.

JEAN PLAISTER

LIBRARY EDUCATION

Library education has always coped with two sets of problems. One of them is its relationship to the profession. The other is its relationship to the academic world. To a certain degree these two types of relationships still play a fundamental role in library education. The history of library education worldwide is diverse, mirroring the state of the library movement and the educational systems in various countries.

Library education started with a very practical orientation and it has grown into a recognized academic discipline. This process has occurred at a different pace in various countries and in some places the education is still outside the university system.

Formal library education goes back to the 1880s when the first library school was established as the Columbia School of Library

Economy. In the following years, further schools were established in the USA. The University of Chicago established the first graduate school of librarianship in 1926 and from that time the education of librarians in USA has been research based and at a graduate level. Master's degrees became the recognised route for library education in the USA. The AMERICAN LIBRARY ASSOCIATION played a major role in the improvement of educational strategies. At the turn of the century the library education programmes in the USA were a source of inspiration especially for European librarians, many of whom travelled to the USA to obtain an education in librarianship.

When the Library Association (LA) was formed in 1877 in the UK, an effort to establish formal education in librarianship started. Around the turn of the century, formal education started both at University College London and at the London School of Economics. The LA played a significant role but there was some controversy about the content of the syllabus.

The educational models of the USA and the UK had a fundamental influence on education for librarianship in many countries. British models were exported to Australia and New Zealand at the beginning of the twentieth century. They also influenced education for librarianship in many parts of Sub-Saharan AFRICA and SOUTH ASIA. Models from the USA influenced the education in Canada and in Latin America and SOUTH AMERICA.

In the USA and the UK the library associations played an active role through their process of accreditation of educational programmes. This is not the case in most of the European and Scandinavian countries. Overall, in many Scandinavian and European countries library education was established in close relationship with a government department as the governing body and the library associations' influence was more advisory. Accreditation of programmes was a matter of educational monopoly. It was normal to establish education in professional schools, often outside the university system.

The real growth in library education came after the Second World War. In the UK several library schools were established at college level. The LA controlled the curriculum and conducted the examinations. During the coming decades the syllabus was increased to two years of full-time study and the basic admission requirements became the same as for universities. The period is characterized by arguments between the LA and the schools about the Association's role in accreditation and examinations. From the late 1960s Bachelor's and Master's programmes in librarianship started at various institutions and the role of the LA changed from control over examinations to accreditation of programmes and the establishment of a professional register. The acceptance and accreditation of programmes came to be based on consultation and educational guidelines.

In 1992 the UK polytechnics and a small number of higher-level colleges became universities and this further changed education for librarianship. The change placed education firmly in a more research-oriented environment and the syllabus became to an increasing extent modular in its structure. At the same time the diversity of the curricula increased. It was a response to perceived changes in the requirements of the labour market and also the development of institutional profiles for attracting students.

Traditionally the European educational system has been two-tiered, with universities and professional schools. The professional schools had a clear orientation towards the profession and they had only a limited research obligation. Many of the library education programmes were placed in these institutions, but this situation has changed a lot during the 1990s. In the Nordic countries it is now possible to take a PhD in LIS in a research-based environment. We see the same trend in many European countries. In Germany Master's programmes in librarianship and related topics have been introduced. The same is the case in many countries in CENTRAL AND EASTERN EUROPE, like Hungary.

Even though the USA and UK models have had a tremendous influence in different parts of the world it is important to note that there were educational models from the USSR system, and that these influenced, for example, library education in countries like China, which like India also has had a long history of library education.

In 2000 IFLA contributed to the development of library education by approving a set of Guidelines.

Societal changes from the 1980s onward have had consequences for library schools worldwide. The USA witnessed a closure of some library schools. In other countries there were difficulties attracting the appropriate number of students.

The profession appeared as old fashioned and this led to a rather radical diversification of the curriculum in many institutions. This diversification was a response to newly emerging job opportunities, especially in the private sector, and in some countries we see large numbers of librarians employed in new types of jobs. The struggle has been to maintain a balance between the core subjects of library education and attractive new topics.

Further reading

Elkin, J. and Wilson, T. (eds) (1997) *The Education of Library and Information Professionals in the United Kingdom*, Mansell.

Harbo, O. and Pors, N.O. (eds) (1998) *Education for Librarianship in the Nordic Countries*, Mansell.

Harris, J. (ed.) (1997) *Education for Librarianship in China*, Mansell.

Ronnie, M. (1996) *Education for Librarianship in New Zealand and the Pacific Islands*, Mansell.

Roy, L. and Sheldon, B.E. (eds) (1998) *Library and Information Studies Education in the United States*, Mansell.

SEE ALSO: information professions; information science education; South Asia; Southeast Asia

NIELS OLE PORS

LIBRARY LEGISLATION

Laws setting up and regulating individual libraries, particular categories of library or the whole library system of a state. Library legislation is also laws that define, support or delimit some particular activity or activities of libraries.

Many countries regard a comprehensive library law as an essential underpinning for library activity within their boundaries. This was particularly true of the command economies of the socialist states, particularly RUSSIA AND THE FORMER SOVIET UNION. Lenin, no doubt influenced by his librarian wife Nadezhda Krupskaya, 'considered the elevation of library work to be one of the indicators of the cultural level of a country' and expressed this straight after the Revolution in his library decrees of 1918 and 1920. Subsequent enactments, the last being the Regulation of Library Work, 1984, refined and developed the monolithic Soviet system.

A few developing countries have also achieved a very comprehensively specified legal position, Tanzania being of special interest. Even though a surprising number of former British colonies have passed library laws quite soon after achieving independence, Tanzania's is particularly inclusive. The Tanganyika Library Services Board Act of 1963 established a Board with the responsibility of promoting, establishing, equipping, managing, maintaining and developing libraries in what is now mainland Tanzania. Furthermore, this Act was replaced in 1975 by an even more comprehensive Act inspired by the NATIS concept of NATIONAL INFORMATION SYSTEMS. The 1975 Act empowered the Board to co-ordinate library and documentation services, library training, literacy campaigns, encouragement of local authorship and supervision of all types of libraries in Tanzania. Unfortunately the existence of the legal enactments has not affected the economic position of the country or its library service, which remains sadly underprovided.

It is much more common for library work to be regulated by a group of laws passed at different times for different purposes. One of the earliest modern library laws was the Act for the Better Preservation of Parochial Libraries in that part of Great Britain called England, 1708, which, as the title suggests, was designed merely to protect existing libraries, particularly those set up by Thomas BRAY. Perhaps the first national system of libraries was that of France, set up by the allocation of the revolutionary confiscations of ecclesiastical and aristocratic book collections to various national and municipal libraries. However, this cannot be attributed to a single coherent legislative enactment, though the process was largely completed by a decree of 1803. The Public Libraries Act of 1850 in Britain, despite its horrible imperfections, is probably the first real landmark in library legislation, since it was consciously designed to permit a national system of tax-supported public libraries. Subsequent amending Acts (most recently that of 1964) encouraged, and finally compelled, local government authorities to provide libraries giving a comprehensive and efficient service. Britain was, however, late with its British Library Act, 1972, which brought together a number of existing national and quasi-national services to form an outstandingly effective new library. Countries as diverse as France (1789), Russia, Brazil and Argentina (all in 1810), Belgium (1837) and Germany (1870) had already obtained their national libraries long before.

The USA, although for a long time the world's leader in library provision, nevertheless did not have major library laws until the Library Services Act 1956 provided federal funds for state public library developments, but most states already had a long tradition of high-quality library provision, usually backed by state legislation. In 1965 three Acts (the Elementary and Secondary Education Act, the Higher Education Act and the Medical Library Assistance Act) confirmed the trend of federal intervention. A Scandinavian country such as Denmark probably provides the best type of model for legal support for libraries. Its 1920 Public Library Law included a means of enforcement through a State Inspectorate for Public Libraries. It also required all primary schools (though, curiously, not secondary schools) to provide libraries for pupils. Denmark had its first modern LEGAL DEPOSIT Act in 1927 (though the practice dated back to 1697) and subsequent library legislation includes an Act setting up the Danish Royal Library School in 1956.

There is, in many countries, a tendency for important pieces of legislation relating to libraries to be concealed incidentally within other enactments. A classic example is the Local Government and Housing Act of 1989 in Britain. This gives the government the right to authorize public libraries to charge for certain facilities and services. The major principle of free public libraries is thus legally subverted in one of the countries in which it was pioneered, by a seemingly irrelevant piece of law. If nothing else, this supports the case for a comprehensive national library law that can be openly debated and that, when accepted, will assert clear and more easily defensible principles than a series of partial enactments can hope to do. In the interests of more coherent legislation relating to libraries, particularly in the emerging democracies of Central and Eastern Europe, the Council of Europe has organized a number of seminars and published a set of guidelines (Council of Europe 2000).

References

Council of Europe (2000) *Guidelines on Library Legislation and Policy in Europe: A User Guide*, Strasbourg: Council of Europe Publishing.

Further reading

Morris, R.J.B. (1977) *Parliament and the Public Libraries*, Mansell.

SEE ALSO: information policy

PAUL STURGES

LIBRARY OF CONGRESS

The Library of Congress of the USA, regarded today as the national library (see NATIONAL LIBRARIES) of the USA, occupies a unique place in US civilization. Established in 1800 as a legislative library, it grew into a national institution in the nineteenth century, a product of US cultural nationalism. Since 1950, it has become an international resource of unparalleled dimension, collecting research materials in most languages and formats. Today, with an annual government appropriation of more than $450 million, a staff of 4,600, multimedia collections totalling more than 120 million items, six overseas acquisitions offices and a range of services and programmes unmatched by any other library, it is one of the world's leading research and cultural institutions.

Reference and research services to the US Congress are still the Library's most important task. As part of the legislative branch of government, it answers directly to the US Congress – even though the Librarian of Congress is appointed by the President of the USA, subject to confirmation by the US Senate. With Congressional approval, the Library of Congress also serves members of the executive and judicial branches of the government, libraries around the world and individual scholars, researchers, artists, scientists and members of the public. Service is provided in three massive structures on Capitol Hill, the Thomas Jefferson Building (1897), the John Adams Building (1939) and the James Madison Memorial Building (1980). Storage space for the future is being constructed at Fort Meade, Maryland, twenty miles north of Capitol Hill, and a new Library of Congress Audiovisual Conservation Center is being planned in Culpepper, Virginia.

Using private funds and congressional appropriations, since 1994 the Library has made its bibliographic records and selected items from its US collections available on the INTERNET. The subsequent rapid development of its website, through which it now freely shares selected collections and exhibitions, bibliographic data and information about current legislation, copyright and its collections, services and programmes, has made the Library of Congress an increasingly important educational force. Its National Digital Library in co-operation with other institutions has digitized more than 5 million items from the historical collections of the Library and other repositories, and made them available at the Library's American Memory website. In fiscal 2000 the Library's website, one of the most heavily used in the US government, garnered close to 1 billion transactions.

The diversity of the Library of Congress is startling. Simultaneously it serves as the principal research library (see RESEARCH LIBRARIES) of the US Congress; the COPYRIGHT agency of the USA; a centre for scholarship that collects research materials in most subjects and many media, and in more than 450 languages; a public institution that is open to everyone over high school age and serves readers in twenty-one reading rooms; a government library that is heavily used by the entire US government; the national library for the blind and physically handicapped, with regional branches throughout the country; an outstanding law library (see LAW LIBRARIES), especially strong in foreign-language materials; one of the world's largest providers of bibliographic data and products; a centre for the commissioning and performance of chamber music; the home of the nation's poet laureate; the sponsor of exhibitions and of musical, literary and cultural programmes that reach across the nation and the world; a research centre for the PRESERVATION and CONSERVATION of library materials; the world's largest repository of maps, atlases, printed and recorded music, motion pictures and television programmes; and a national and international promoter of books, reading, LITERACY and libraries.

Even though it is recognized as the *de facto* national library of the USA, the Library of Congress does not have that official designation. It performs most of the functions performed by other national libraries but does defer to the National Library of Medicine (1956) and the National Library of Agriculture (1962), both part of the executive branch of government, for intensive collecting in the fields of clinical medicine and technical agriculture, respectively.

The growth of the collections of the Library of Congress is relentless. Materials arrive through an acquisitions programme that extends throughout the world and includes more than 15,000 agreements with foreign governments and re-search institutions for the exchange of research materials. Other major modes of acquisitions include copyright deposit, gifts, purchases and transfers from other government agencies. Each day about 31,000 items arrive at the Library; approximately 10,000 of them will be selected for the permanent collections.

The collections of the Library of Congress now include more than 120 million items, including more than 18 million books in the classified collections, 54 million manuscripts, 13 million photographs, 4 million maps, 4 million pieces of music and more than 0.8 million motion pictures. Its collection of more than 5,600 incunabula is the largest in the Western hemisphere. The Library also holds immense collections of newspapers, technical reports, videotapes and disks, computer programs and other audio, visual and print materials.

The Library of Congress has been shaped primarily by the philosophy and ideals of its principal founder, Thomas Jefferson, who believed that a democratic legislature needed information and ideas in all subjects in order to perform its work. In 1815 Jefferson sold his wide-ranging personal library, which encompassed many subjects and languages, to the Congress to 'recommence' the small library destroyed the previous year when the British invaded Washington and destroyed the Capitol, the Library's first home. Jefferson felt that there was 'no subject' outside the interests of Members of Congress, justifying the Congressional purchase of his personal library and the Library of Congress's future growth. His philosophy was successfully implemented in future years, most notably by Librarians of Congress Ainsworth Rand Spofford (1864–97) and Herbert Putnam (1899–1939), who together used Jefferson's philosophy to create today's Library of Congress.

The present Librarian of Congress, historian James H. Billington, was nominated by President Ronald Reagan and confirmed by the US Senate in 1987. Through his dual emphasis on developing and using new technologies and educational outreach to scholars and citizens alike, Billington has guided the Library of Congress through a period of steady growth and expansion. With the approval of Congress, in 1990 he established the James Madison Council, the Library's first national private-sector support group. In 1994 he proclaimed a new leadership role for the Library of Congress in the electronic age, announcing the establishment of a National Digital Library, a private and public sector collaborative effort to make available electronically major segments of the Library's US history collections.

Under Billington's guidance, the Library used its Bicentennial in the year 2000 to move the institution forwards on several important fronts. For example, Congress authorized eighty-four positions for the National Digital Library project, giving it permanent government support, and Madison Council chairman John W. Kluge presented the Library with a gift of $60 million as part of the Bicentennial Gifts to the Nation programme. In his annual report for the year 2000, Billington noted that, as the Library of Congress entered its third century of service to Congress, the nation and the international community, it continued to be guided by the belief of the Founding Fathers of the USA that 'free access to knowledge is the bulwark of democracy'.

Further reading

Bisbort, A. and Osborne, L.B. (2000) *The Nation's Library: The Library of Congress*, Washington, DC: Scala Books.

Conaway, James (2000) *America's Library: The Story of the Library of Congress*, Yale University Press.

Library of Congress website (www.loc.gov).

JOHN Y. COLE

LIBRARY OF CONGRESS CLASSIFICATION

The scheme of BIBLIOGRAPHIC CLASSIFICATION drawn up by Herbert Putnam in 1897. Although based in some respects on the DEWEY DECIMAL CLASSIFICATION and CUTTER's expansive schemes, it does not conform to theoretical rules for classification. It was quite explicitly compiled to meet the needs of the library's huge collection of books and is too detailed and complex for use in small libraries. It has, however, been adopted by research and university libraries throughout the world.

SEE ALSO: organization of knowledge

LIBRARY OF CONGRESS SUBJECT HEADINGS

Although the SUBJECT HEADINGS were first designed to be used in conjunction with the Library of Congress catalogue, they are widely used around the world as an authoritative list of subject headings for the CATALOGUES of many kinds of library.

SEE ALSO: organization of knowledge

LIBRARY PUBLISHING

The main aim of library PUBLISHING is to make a contribution to the fulfilment of the library's mission. Besides their most central purposes, libraries, among other activities – such as exhibitions, presentation of new books, organization of professional and scientific meetings and conferences – do publish. Since they are primary cultural and information institutions, libraries publish in order to spread information about human knowledge in the best possible way, regardless of the specific medium chosen.

Libraries mainly publish:

1   Information about their activities.
2   Works that have their source in the collections.
3   Publications that may not have their source in the collections, but could strengthen the library's position in the community.

Most libraries publish information about their activities, such as library guides, instructions for the use of the collections, plans and reports, news and bulletins for patrons and employees. Some libraries have been doing this for a long time, and some started recently. Some libraries like several NATIONAL LIBRARIES in Asia and Oceania join their efforts with others to publish news on their activities.

Publications on library buildings play a very distinctive role. They are usually meant as presents for illustrious visitors to the library, and therefore are lavishly produced, which means that they are also very expensive to publish. Most national libraries publish books on their buildings, but some university and newly built public libraries do it too.

Libraries publish material related to their collections: CATALOGUES (of the complete collection or parts of it); bibliographies (special bibliographies, retrospective bibliographies, etc.; see BIBLIOGRAPHY); books related to LOCAL STUDIES COLLECTIONS; reprints; book collectors' editions; periodicals; directories of publishers; posters;

postcards; exhibition catalogues; bookmarks; compact discs; DATABASES; portals (see PORTALS AND GATEWAYS); and so on.

Very few, if any, publishing houses could compare with the digital collections held by libraries. Even though, in the beginning, the building of digital collections did not appear to have the potential to be a major publishing activity – in fact it is. Thus, libraries decide upon a topic, select the sources, edit material selected from their collection and other sources, design it and typeset it – and publish it on a compact disc or on the Web. In such a way they aim not only to publish but also to build up the resources they can make available too, like the Czech National Library, which published a Catalogue of Arabic manuscripts with image samples in a CD-ROM and Internet version.

Libraries also publish works that are basically not different from the output of commercial publishing houses or other institutions like universities, museums or archives that have publishing programmes. They publish to fulfil their cultural, professional or scientific role more completely. This is especially so in the case of periodical publications concerned with library and information science, cultural history, the history of the book and library history. Many libraries publish magazines, historical or other professional textbooks and even fiction. Many university libraries publish guidelines for writing a Master's or Doctoral thesis. The National Library of Holland joined forces with the British Library to publish the bibliography *Incunabula Printed in the Low Countries*.

Libraries also publish catalogues of exhibitions that were held on library premises, even when these were not based upon the library's collections.

What the library is often doing in these kinds of publishing is to publish works that other publishers would not, but in countries with a developed book market the sales of those type of publications are still capable of significantly improving the library's income.

Nevertheless, it is clear that this is also a way in which the library can strengthen its public image, using publishing as part of its MARKETING plan. A good example is the public library in Šibenik, Croatia, which has established itself as an important publisher of high-quality books on the cultural history of its region that are important for Croatian history and culture generally.

An example of a library extending its basic mission in a slightly different way is *Opening the Book: Finding a Good Read*, published by Bradford Libraries in Great Britain, so as to assist its patrons' reading activities.

The type of library (school, public, etc.) greatly affects the characteristics of its publishing, much more that the national and cultural milieu does. In the spectrum from a little local library that is mainly a cultural focal point incorporating a local archive and museum, through to a major national library, great differences in approach, content and publishing can be observed.

However, libraries as mediators of cultural content learn from each other and this has led to some typical patterns emerging. Some library publishing is done according to the provisions of the law (e.g. a NATIONAL BIBLIOGRAPHY). Other publishing is done according to the library's own statutes or other regulations (e.g. a local collection catalogue, acquisitions bulletin), or on the basis of yearly or long-term planning.

Although most libraries that publish have editorial boards, publishing initiatives are generally taken upon the library director's proposals. In a number of libraries the director also acts as editor in chief.

The money needed for the expenses of publishing, mainly for printing and binding, is as a rule initially provided for in the library budget. Since a high proportion of libraries are public institutions, their annual reports reveal the amounts spent on printing and compact-disk publishing.

Most library publishing activities are carried on separately, but sometimes libraries join forces with publishing houses for projects like reprints and marketing publication in the form of calendars etc.

Library publishing is subject to trends, just like the publishing world in general. For instance, lately, several national libraries have been collecting and printing the works of their nation's most famous musicians. The Finnish national library has published the complete works of Jean Sibelius, and the Danish national library started a ten-year project to publish the works of Carl Nielsen.

Libraries also have a long and well-established tradition of printing and binding. Many of them have their own printeries and binderies with well-qualified personnel. Working with expert librarians, they can produce high-quality publications. Such publications would not be the type that requires high-quality colour printing, and they would usually be short run. But in regard to their content and binding, publications that are completely produced in a library will often receive more attention than in a publishing house, because there are not the same time and money pressures.

Further reading

Field, R. (1993). 'Library publications', in D.W. Bromley and A.M. Allott (ed.), *British Librarianship and Information Work 1986–1990*, Library Association.

SEE ALSO: cultural industries; knowledge industries

SREĆKO JELUŠIĆ

LIBRARY SECURITY SYSTEMS

A system to prevent theft, vandalism or mutilation of library collections. The costs of such systems, which typically involve electronic tagging of every document in the collection and the installation of monitoring devices at the exit points from the library, are high, but when high loss and damage rates are being sustained they can easily be demonstrated to present budgetary and operational savings.

SEE ALSO: crime in libraries

LIBRARY SUPPLIERS

Commercial organizations that supply books, other stock and associated services to libraries.

Library suppliers in the UK are a key part of the BOOK TRADE supply chain from author to reader and the parallel supply chains for other media. Unlike publishers and their distributors, wholesalers and retail booksellers, library suppliers provide a range of services to assist libraries in selection, cataloguing and classification, and processing. These services aim to provide books and other materials 'shelf ready' so reducing the work of acquisitions services in libraries and their operational costs, and reducing the time taken to make materials available for library users. In other countries wholesalers and BOOK JOBBERS provide similar services, some publishers supply direct to libraries and libraries purchase from bookshops.

In the UK the Net Book Agreement and its associated Library Licence ensured retail price maintenance and regulated the terms of business between libraries and their suppliers until 1995. Competition was through provision of supplementary services and the charges made for them. Since then competition has been by price (as discount on price, or mark-up on the cost to the supplier) and the charges made (or hidden in the discount or mark-up) for the additional services. Restrictions on public expenditure and intense competition for the business of libraries of all kinds have reduced the number of library suppliers, through mergers and closures. In the European Union, allocation of business for publicly funded libraries is subject to the requirement for competitive tendering and libraries form consortia to obtain tenders and to share expertise in their evaluation.

The main UK library suppliers export UK-published books and provide services to libraries throughout the world and, with the reduction of UK spending, this business is of increasing importance. The return on investment in the library supply industry is markedly lower than in most other industries and none of the major suppliers also operate retail bookselling businesses.

Increasingly communication between libraries and their suppliers uses electronic data interchange (EDI) services including First Edition, ELECTRONIC MAIL, the INTERNET and direct computer-to-computer links. These carry bibliographic information, orders, progress reports, invoices, information to update stock holdings on LIBRARY AUTOMATION systems and payments.

Library suppliers aim to assist librarians to select from the vast range of titles available by presenting information from publishers and other providers in timely and convenient ways. The information may be comprehensive or profiled according to the requirements of the library. The bibliographic information services provided by library suppliers to support book selection and the selection of other materials are in the form of online access to their databases, CD-ROMs, printed lists and slips, materials supplied on approval and access to showrooms and bookshops.

For newly published materials information is sent prior to their publication date so as to facilitate ordering, and also at the date of publication so that librarians can take account of reviews. The use of approval services in UK public libraries has diminished because of the high costs of the service, which are reflected in the terms of business negotiated in the tendering process.

Information on the range of titles already published is provided to assist librarians in the management of their stocks, in meeting new needs and in selecting replacements for superseded or worn books. This is done by the preparation, often in response to the library's specification, of annotated lists of available titles, access to the supplier's database and through arrangements for visits to the showrooms operated by the suppliers, to stockholding booksellers or to wholesalers.

Bibliographic data is also provided to add to library catalogues and to update catalogues. It is supplied to AACR2 and UKMARC or USMARC standards. Most suppliers outsource the preparation of the data to Bibliographic Data Services, a Dumfries-based company that also provides the British Library with Cataloguing in Publication services. The data includes DEWEY DECIMAL CLASSIFICATION and CATEGORIZATION or genre information. The library suppliers may modify the data to meet the local requirements or traditions of the libraries.

Since 1997 arrangements by which public libraries outsource selection of aspects of their stock to their suppliers have been initiated. They require the suppliers to bring their knowledge of publishing to work in partnership with the libraries, and to ensure that the aims and objectives of the libraries are achieved. The charges for these additional services offset the savings in staff time made in the libraries. It is possible that these arrangements will be extended to the management and promotion of stock.

Library suppliers also provide, in collaboration with reading development agencies, themed collections and display materials to assist librarians in the presentation and promotion of their stocks. Co-operative promotions are organized at local, regional and national level in order to support individual library services.

Libraries of all kinds make use of the services by which library suppliers provide books and other materials fully processed so that they are ready for the shelves. The insertion of date labels, spine labels, BARCODES, security tags, process stamps and book cards and pockets, and the fitting of protective sleeves for book jackets and wallets for paperbacks are charged for but assist the libraries by reducing their costs. Some suppliers also provide specially bound 'library' editions of selected titles.

Library suppliers provide, to the library's specification, regular and reliable delivery services to the main library or directly to local libraries, and use specified packaging to assist the libraries.

The major library suppliers offer comprehensive services to all types of library. Others concentrate on serving particular types of library or on supplying specialist materials. For example, books for children and young people, books and other materials in the languages of minority groups, GREY LITERATURE, maps, music, audio books, music recordings on disc or tape, video recordings on tape or DVD, prints and illustrations, and computer software. Government publications from the Stationery Office and large-print books are usually sold direct to libraries. There is a trend for libraries to pay their main suppliers to act as their agents in acquiring specialist materials, an illustration of the closer partnerships that are developing between library suppliers and their customers.

Further reading

Capital Planning Information (1996) *The Value to Libraries of Special Services Provided by Library Suppliers*, BNB Research Fund Report 77, National Acquisitions Group.

Lindley, D. (2000) 'Best value – a supplier's viewpoint', *Taking Stock 9*: 3–8.

National Acquisitions Group (1997) *Tendering for Library Supply: A Practical Guide*, 2nd edn, National Acquisitions Group.

Nettlefold, M. (2000) 'Library supply into the millennium', *Taking Stock 8*: 20–4.

Smith, G. (1999) *Outsourcing Book Selection: Supplier Selection in Public Libraries*, BNB Research Fund Report 95, Library and Information Commission.

Spiller, D. (2000) *Providing Materials for Library Users*, Library Association Publishing.

SEE ALSO: acquisitions

GEOFFREY SMITH

LICENCES

Licenses are contractual agreements, and they are used with increasing frequency to apply sets of specific terms and conditions to the supply of information products and services. Typically an information provider licenses access to intellectual property in digital form (SOFTWARE, DATABASES, ELECTRONIC BOOKS, etc.) and the licence agreement specifies not only the required payments, but also matters including number of users, locations at which use is permitted, period of validity of the licence and other restrictions on use. The right to exploit a patent is also frequently licensed out, either exclusively to a single licensee, to a sole licensee (with the licensor also retaining the right to exploit the patent) or non-exclusively to a number of competitors in a field.

Sale and licensing

In the INTELLECTUAL PROPERTY regimes of the past and under laws still in force in many countries, the sale, or assignment, of rights was the normal means by which the owners of intellectual property obtained economic benefit from their creations. Thus an author assigned the rights of a book to a publisher in return for payment, usually in the form of royalties, and the publisher sold copies of the book to purchasers who then owned their copies outright. This is often referred to as the 'first-sale' concept. Broadly speaking, it means that once an individual, or an information institution like a library, has purchased a copy of a piece of intellectual property, such as a book, that copy can then be lent, rented out, sold or given away as its owner chooses. Copying from the document is permitted according to recognized fair use, or fair-dealing, principles. Historically, it has been the purchase of pieces of intellectual property, so as to make them available to users, that has been the foundation of libraries' activities.

Licences and digital information

Digital forms of intellectual property, because of their inherent ability to be copied and transmitted at will, are seen by their creators and owners as requiring a different set of arrangements. It has become normal to make intellectual property available under licensing agreements rather than under the provisions of COPYRIGHT law. The rights specified under the terms and conditions of the licence may well be substantially different according to circumstances, the negotiating power of the two parties to the agreement and the perceived value of the product. When a major institution or consortium negotiates with a provider, they may be able to obtain very favourable deals, but the so-called shrink-wrap or click-on licence agreements may offer the individual no options. When cases relating to the validity of the shrink-wrap licence have come to court, there has been a noticeable tendency for their legality to be accepted, despite the fact that the absence of an opportunity for negotiation places the purchaser at a disadvantage in such agreements.

The terms and conditions of licences for the provision of information have shown a general tendency to exclude rights and privileges enjoyed by users under the provisions of copyright law. Thus, whilst it is permissible under copyright to photocopy a proportion of a printed book, the licence under which an equivalent digital work is obtained may specifically exclude similar use. Other examples include attempts by vendors, including Microsoft, to prevent public criticism of products by purchasers under the conditions of their licence. Furthermore, the access obtained via a licence expires after a pre-determined length of time, which will certainly be less than the periods set out under copyright law. This, in turn, allows for the possibility that material which, in print, would become part of the cultural heritage might at some time be withdrawn on the basis of a commercial calculation by the rights holder. The possible effect of this on the long-term preservation and archiving of digital resources is not clear, but it is reasonable to see it as a threat.

Legislation

Copyright holders generally employ technological solutions to protect their ability to restrict the use of digital content to what is provided for in the terms and conditions of the licences that they have granted. Such technological solutions are supported in the USA by the Digital Millennium Copyright Act, 1998, which prohibits their circumvention. Dimitri Sklyarov was arrested in 2001 under this Act because of his involvement in the development of eBook Processor, a device designed to enable the owners (or, more strictly, licensees) of digital books to transfer them to alternative reading devices. Adobe Systems claimed that eBook Processor stripped away the copy protection system from their digital books, thus enabling users to ignore the conditions of the licences in force. It is arguable that what this law does is to give legitimacy to the overturning of principles established in copyright law, which could otherwise be used to test the provisions made in many licence agreements.

The European Union's Directive on the Harmonization of Certain Aspects of Copyright and Related Rights in the Information Society, 2001, was introduced explicitly with the intention to facilitate the market in intellectual property. It was seen by libraries as likely to introduce an intellectual property regime that would effectively endorse the removal by licensing agreements of normal copyright exemptions such as those covering copying in libraries. In the event the Directive allowed member countries considerable scope in how they applied the law, thus potentially preserving many of the copyright exemptions that make it possible for libraries to provide access to information for their users. Despite this partial victory for organizations like EBLIDA (the European Bureau of Library, Information and Documentation Associations) that lobbied against the tendency of the Directive, the global trend is for the replacement of the specific provisions of copyright law as the effective means of protecting intellectual property by a regime based on licensing agreements.

Further reading

Bebbington, L.W. (2001) 'Managing content: Licensing, copyright and privacy issues in managing electronic resources', *Legal Information Management* 1: 4–12.

Harris, L.E. (2002) *Licensing Digital Content: A Practical Guide for Librarians*, Chicago: American Library Association.

IFLA Licensing Principles (http://www.ifla.org/V/ebpb/copy.htm).

Rifkin, J. (2000) *The Age of Access: How the Shift from Ownership to Access is Transforming Capitalism*, Penguin.

Veysey, G. (2001) 'IT procurement: Key steps to consider in procuring or licensing IT systems and electronically delivered content', *Business Information Review* 18: 51–6.

SEE ALSO: digital library; information law

PAUL STURGES

LITERACY

The ability to read and write in the mother tongue.

A person is literate who can with understanding both read and write a short simple statement on his everyday life....A person is functionally literate who can engage in all those activities in which literacy is required for effective functioning in his group and community and also for enabling him to continue to use reading, writing and calculation for his own and the community's development.

(UNESCO 1986)

In more theoretical terms, literacy is the ability of a person to code and decode, smoothly and effortlessly, and with understanding, a living and growing system of symbolic transformations for reality, including words, numbers, notations, schemata, diagrammatic representations and other marks, inscribed on paper or other two-dimensional surfaces (cloth, celluloid or the screen of a computer terminal), all of which have become part of the visual language of a people and thus have come to be collectively and democratically shared by both the specialist and the non-specialist (such ability having become part of the current social, economic, political and cultural demand system of a society) (Bhola 1984: 260).

Individual constructions and context-specific collective definitions

In the language of the constructivist paradigm, each learner's literacy is a uniquely individual construction. Learners acquire their literacy skills in historical, cultural and class contexts that are uniquely experienced, using individualized motivations, reading different languages and written texts, and later make different material and spiritual uses of literacy skills. Again, literacy has different meanings for members of different groups and correspondingly different acquisition modes, functions and uses (Street 1984).

On the other hand, there are collective constructions of literacy. Because of the relativities of languages, social context, text, mix of reading, writing and numeracy skills, and levels of proficiency expected in each of the three Rs, it is necessary for practitioners to develop context-specific collective definitions of literacy for implementation within the specificities of their programmes. Hence it is preferable to speak of litera*cies*, rather than of one single literacy.

Additional multiplicities of literacy

There are multiple literacies in another sense. Terms such as cultural literacy, scientific literacy, economic literacy, media literacy and environmental literacy are used to indicate more than rudimentary knowledge in a particular knowledge domain on the part of a person. The acceptance or rejection of the term dominant literacy, autonomous literacy, empowering literacy, liberational literacy or emancipatory literacy is meant to project a particular ideological position in relation to the objectives, content and process of literacy promotion. Pre-literacy, school literacy, adult literacy, family literacy, women's literacy, prison literacy, farmers' literacy, functional literacy, workers' literacy, workplace literacy and scribal literacy each indicate a level of competence or a focus on a constituency, a functional connection or a context of learning.

The essential nature of literacy

Literacy as process has two layers: surface and core. At the surface, literacy is the skill of decoding and encoding messages in a written language. At the core, literacy essentially is the process of 'symbolic transformations of reality' (Langer 1942). More than a million years ago, as part of the long evolutionary process, humans acquired the capacity to make symbolic transformation of reality and, thereby, to lend significance to their material, psychological and social world. This first culmination of human capacities of making symbolic transformations of reality gave us speech. Some 5,000 years ago, human beings invented writing systems, and literacy came to be the second culmination of the same unique human capacity to make symbolic transformations (now in writing) of reality already symbolically transformed (in speech). Thus, construed as a human fulfilment, literacy should be accepted as a human right and universal literacy seen as human destiny (Bhola 1987).

Literacy and cognition

If literacy is a second culmination of the human capacity to make symbolic transformation of reality, and ontological remaking of the human individual, then literacy should have cognitive consequences for the new literate in terms of cognitive capacities, patterns and habits. Goody (1968) suggests as much in his 'technology of intellect' hypothesis, asserting that literacy (particularly writing) enables abstract, context-free thinking and thereby changes in modes of describing, classifying, reasoning, inferring and

memorizing. Scribner and Cole (1981) suggest that the effect of literacy may not be that broadly generalizable but that changes 'specific to the range of literacy practices in particular contexts' do appear. The argument will remain on the research agenda of COGNITIVE SCIENCE for some time to come.

Literacy and culture

Literacy affects cognition and thereby culture, since culture-making is an activity of beings with cognition. Sociologists of history have posited connections between literacy, on the one hand, and history, bureaucracy and empires, on the other. Others have posited relationships between print capitalism and the emergence of imagined communities, ethnic pride and nationalism (Anderson 1991).

New literates everywhere in the world describe their journey from illiteracy in the oral tradition (see ORAL TRADITIONS) to literacy in the print culture in metaphors of power, freedom and light. In contemporary discourse there is acceptance of the potential added to the new-literate individual, enabling more effective transactions with the environment – social, economic and political. The literate participant is able to change the quality of relationships within social organizations and ethos of cultures. Literacy levels have become indicators of the knowledge capital of communications and societies, the necessary condition for innovation and modernization, for equality between genders and among castes and classes, and the litmus test of participative democracy.

The future of literacy

In the popularization of radio and television, some have seen the end of literacy and the re-emergence of an oral–electronic culture. However, the future of literacy is secure as literacy lives in the very heart of the new MASS MEDIA. Both radio and television use the grammar of print, the media narrate in printspeak and the literate get more out of media than the non-literate (Bhola 1990). The electronic information age is anchored in a global culture of print. While there are 1 billion illiterates in this world, there are over 3 billion literates. All institutions of education, socialization and governance, both sacred and secular, are based on assumptions of literacy and print (Bhola 1984).

Literacy and library

The relationship between literacy and library remains strong. In a non-literate community a public library (see PUBLIC LIBRARIES) is inconceivable. Without a good library communities may not retain literacy already acquired, may be unable to extend cultural and scientific literacies and may find it difficult, if not impossible, to engage in processes of lifelong learning. Today's library, in seeking to serve an INFORMATION SOCIETY, has changed drastically and yet remains unchanged in its essential cultural mission – as the public repository of imaginative and collective constructions of reality and as an agency to serve different publics in the intra-generational and intergenerational dissemination, utilization and validation of currently held knowledge.

The library, both in its own organization and in its information organization, uses the logic of literacy and print. While it may use new surfaces (celluloid or magnetic fields) to store marks of various kinds and to 'fetch' or 'deliver' information, it must yet be anchored in a sizeable collection in print – material that is readable by the human eye without mediation by the technology of processing, magnifying or projecting. The technologization of the library does not necessarily lead to lowered expectations of literacy. Indeed, the modern library requires higher levels of literacy and sophisticated knowledge of the conventions of print materials.

LITERACY AND THE INFORMATION SUPERHIGHWAY

The new VIRTUAL REALITY made possible by INFORMATION TECHNOLOGY is by no means a world of sensations to be experienced with the manual control of the joystick. It is a world where print/literacy remain central.

The Information Superhighway is indeed a misnomer, for it does not merely carry and delivery information, it fetches and reconfigures information on command. The two important dimensions of this new information technology are (1) interactivity, and (2) time–space convergence and cost–space convergence, through which the time and cost required to traverse distance have become unimportant. The user in interaction is able to reconfigure communication systems by using a dial-up mode for selective programming, and by choosing perspectives by selecting from among camera angles. The information environment is a world of instant communication and of virtual reality (Sawhney 1994).

Of course, only a bare minimum of literacy skills may be needed for handling the joystick to play a video game. But for significant interactions with the interactive environment one needs to be not just a reader, but also a composer and editor. The literacy skills of composing and editing are skills of the highest order.

Future challenges

Major challenges loom ahead in the new millennium. For educators, both in the developed and the developing world, the challenge lies in the universalization of literacy so that boys and girls and men and women do not merely buy and become addicted to video games but can partake of the collective inheritance of knowledge stored in libraries and embedded in DATABASES. The opportunity for lifelong education in the lives of all the people must not be left unrealized.

The prototype of the new Information Superhighway is the INTERNET, a network of networks first developed to connect university computers with government research laboratories. The choice facing modern libraries is obvious. They have to net-in or wither away on the vine of marginalization. At the same time, libraries must reach out to the communities in which they are located. Librarians will have to ensure that the unavailability of technology does not result in the social exclusion of individuals, schools, communities and societies that cannot afford to buy the necessary technology, creating yet another social divide of information haves and have-nots (see SOCIAL EXCLUSION AND LIBRARIES).

Finally, there are challenges for the managers of global-scale information environments. First, there is the technological challenge of computer hackers, who have gone beyond the excitement of disrupting computer systems of large organizations and are now engaged in COMPUTER CRIME involving the use of large computer systems for sorting and distributing stolen computer software, illicit information and pornography. There is also an ideological challenge. In building and expanding these environments, the technology must be combined with the ideology of a just and moral world order. The new Information Superhighway must lead towards a new more just and more efficient world information and communication order with the goals of 'more justice, more equity, more reciprocity in information exchange, less dependence in communication flows, less downwards diffusion of messages, more self-reliance and cultural identity, more benefits for all mankind' (MacBride *et al.* 1980: xviii).

References

Anderson, B. (1991) *Imagined Communities: Reflections on the Origin and Spread of Nationalism*, revised edn, London/New York: Verso [captures the role of print capitalism, census, map and museum in the emergence of imagined communities and manifestations of ethnicity and nationalism].

Bhola, H.S. (1990) 'Literacy in development communication: A symbiotic model for media', *Media Development* 37: 3–6.

—— (1987) 'Destined for literacy', *Educational Horizons* 66: 9–12.

—— (1984) 'A policy analysis of adult education promotion in the Third World: An account of promises made and promises fulfilled', *International Review of Education* 30: 249–64.

Goody, J. (ed.) (1968) *Literacy in Traditional Societies*, Cambridge: Cambridge University Press.

Langer, S.K. (1942) *Philosophy in a New Key: A Study in the Symbolism of Reason, Rite, and Art*, Cambridge, MA: Harvard University Press.

MacBride, S. *et al.* (1980) *Many Voices, One World: Communication and Society Today and Tomorrow*, Report of the International Commission for the Study of Communication Problems, London: Kogan Page; New York: Unipub; Paris: UNESCO.

Sawhney, H.S. (1994) 'Persisting patterns of infrastructure development', paper presented at the 19th International Association for Mass Communication Research Scientific Conference, Seoul, Korea, 3–8 July 1994.

Scribner, S. and Cole, M. (1981) *The Psychology of Literacy*, Cambridge, MA: Harvard University Press.

Street, B. (1984) *Literary in Theory and Practice*, Cambridge: Cambridge University Press.

UNESCO (1986) 'Revised recommendations concerning the international standardization of educational statistics. Adopted by the General Conference at its 20th session, Paris, 27 November 1978', *UNESCO's Standard-Setting Instruments V3, B4*, Paris: UNESCO.

Further reading

Center for Civic Networking (1993) *A Vision of Change: Civic Promise of the National Information Infrastructure*, Washington, DC: Center for Civic Networking.

Karraker, R. (1991) 'Highways of the mind', *Whole Earth Review* 70: 4–11.

Kintgen, E.R., Kroll, B.M. and Rose, M. (1988) *Perspectives on Literacy*, Carbondale, IL: Southern Illinois University Press [the perspectives discussed are theoretical, historical, educational and community; authors represented include Frederick Erickson, Paulo Freire, Shirley Brice Heath, Jack Goody, Eric A. Havelock, Carl F. Kaestle, John U. Ogbu, David R. Olson, Walter J. Ong, Daniel P. Resnick, Sylvia Scribner].

Office of Technology Assessment (1990) *Critical Connections: Communications for the Future* (OTA-CIT-407), Washington, DC: US Government Printing Office.

Purves, A.C. (1990) *The Scribal Society: An Essay on Literacy and Schooling in the Information Age*, New York/London: Longman.

Velis, J.-P. (1990) *Through a Glass, Darkly: Functional Literacy in Industrialized Countries*, Paris: UNESCO.

Willinsky, J. (1990) *The New Library*, New York: Routledge.

SEE ALSO: communication

H.S. BHOLA

LITERATURE SEARCH

A quest for literature to provide information and data that will answer a query or facilitate further research. Some librarians limit the definition to the 'intermediate stage between reference work and research, and is differentiated from both' (Prytherch 1990; see also Landau 1966). True, one may argue that finding a quick answer to a simple question is no more than 'ready reference' and does not qualify for the more demanding search process. Conversely, research questions may require many hours, days and years of work. Taken from a practical, on-the-job point of view, one can never be that certain of categories. The question on the amount of rainfall in New York may be no more than an opening shot in a broadside of queries that will lead to an extended search of the literature on climatic conditions in North America. The person posing a question does not care how it is categorized, only for the answer – whether it be short or a massive bibliography. This illustrates a major point about the literature search. First, the individual and/or the librarian must be certain as to (1) the question and its scope, and (2) the amount of material and the amount of time to expend. The second naturally follows the first, although experience indicates that some are inclined to set the time and the number of articles or books to be consulted before they undertake the modification of the original question. The search strategy is tantamount to formulating a hypothesis and testing its validity through the search itself.

Thanks to regional, national and international

networks of databases (from RLIN and OCLC to the INTERNET, Nexis and DIALOG) it is possible to sit down at a computer keyboard, type in the required subject, author or title(s) and learn what is available in every medium from books and magazine articles to dissertations and films.

The technological revolution in the literature search offers four basic improvements over the laborious book-to-book, index-to-index quest: (1) the search begins with determining what books, if any, have been published on the subject. This may be revealed by searching the catalogues of the user's own library and, thanks to OCLC, for example, what is available in all major US and Canadian libraries. Using a good search engine (see SEARCH ENGINES) on the Internet will open the catalogues of other countries. (2) Once this is determined, turning to basic INDEXes will reveal articles published about the subject. Anyone seeking periodical published information from the early twentieth or nineteenth centuries may still have to turn to printed indexes, although an increasing number are being digitized and made accessible across the Internet. (3) The ability to do searching at a workstation, instead of wandering from place to place in the library or from library to library, is the third tremendous advantage derived from the new technology, quite apart from the rapid growth of the availability of the full text of the material electronically. (4) One may quickly print out the necessary abstracts and citations, as well as modify the search process from source to source. Any involved, thorough literature search today probably starts with the use of the Internet and the World Wide Web.

So far the assumption has been that the literature search takes place in a large library with access to advanced technology. Today, this is required for the serious literature search, although the whole Internet search can, of course, take place at any network-linked computer regardless of its location. The rules are less ambitious for the individual seeking only enough material for a paper on cannibals or a talk on inflation. If one is lucky enough to be in a library with a few indexes, the problem is easy to solve. Assuming the question is clear, one turns to an overview of what has been published in the last five to ten years. The normal bibliographic checkpoints are first bypassed for the library's own catalogue. Almost always there are more than enough books in the library to meet the need. One may turn to the printed general or subject periodical index to identify pertinent articles. This usually is adequate to answer the requirements of a literature review. In practice, increasing numbers of users, especially academics and students, take a search of the Web as their starting point, all too often ignoring quality issues (to their peril).

Depending upon the philosophy of the library or the persuasion of the librarian, another intermediary step takes place in the limited literature search. An individual may find five or six books and as many articles, but have time to use only a few. Which few? The librarian familiar with reference sources and the topic will act as the intermediary and suggest what to use and what to discard. Also, the reader may have overlooked a vital source that the librarian can identify and locate. Some consider this step to be unnecessary, not even advisable; others, in an age of more and more peripheral information, consider it vital to the literature search.

Throughout the search procedure the librarian makes decisions as to whether or not this process, this source or this bit of information is relevant. The ability to do this comes from a thorough, professional knowledge of needs, a mastery of information and, as all seasoned reference librarians will admit, a sixth sense or intuition about what is likely to be right or wrong in the twisting path towards a successful literature search conclusion.

References

Landau, T. (1966) *Encyclopedia of Librarianship*, 3rd edn, Bowes & Bowes.
Prytherch, R. (1990) *Harrod's Librarian's Glossary of Terms Used in Librarianship, Documentations and the Book Crafts, and Reference Book*, 7th edn, Gower.

Further reading

Katz, W.A. (1996) *Introduction to Reference Work*, McGraw Hill [see vol. 2 and the chapters on searching].

SEE ALSO: reference interview

W.A. KATZ, REVISED BY THE EDITORS

LITERATURE SURVEY

A listing of documents, usually with full bibliographical references, on a given subject, including both older and/or current material, according to need. A thorough literature survey to establish the boundaries of a topic and acknowledge previous contributions to it is an essential feature of a research report, article or monograph. A current survey can be prepared by librarians or information officers for the information of their users, to keep them up to date with the literature.

SEE ALSO: bibliography

LOCAL-AREA NETWORK

A local-area network (LAN) is a communication NETWORK that is restricted to a small geographical area, often within a single building or group of buildings (typically an office complex or a university campus). They vary in transmission medium and in topology: optical fibres, co-axial cable or telephone wiring may be used for transmission, and topologies include bus, star and ring arrangement.

SEE ALSO: information and communication technology; intranet

LOCAL STUDIES COLLECTIONS

Local studies collections contain accumulations of books and other material in all formats 'covering the local environment in all its physical aspects, including geology, palaeontology, climatology and natural history, and in terms of all human activity within that environment, past, present and future' (Library Association Local Studies Group 2nd edn 2002). Local studies bring local people of all ages and expertise together to examine their shared heritage. PUBLIC LIBRARIES are renowned for the depth of their local studies collections, but County Record Offices, MUSEUMS, the universities and local history societies also provide local studies for many, including special interest groups, genealogists, planners, environmentalists and those involved in school curriculum work.

A few collections have remarkable antecedents, as in Manchester Chetham's Library founded in 1653. The early nineteenth century saw 'topographical' collections in libraries, the Guildhall and Warrington for example, and in the local libraries established after the 1850 Public Libraries Act. By acquiring relevant offi-

cial district records and historical sources, city librarians augmented the original donations from historians and book collectors that reflected their study of ecclesiastical or manorial history, the lives and pedigrees of landed gentry.

Over the years, local studies collections evolved from being closed, supervised collections into more accessible departments with open browsing sections. Their scope has been continually extended to support areas of investigation not considered by the early writers. Present-day students require evidence on land development, the social history of villages or factory life in industrial towns. Librarians need historic and contemporary resources to answer queries on neighbourhood businesses, folklore, births and marriages, local authors and locally printed material.

Collection policies will take account of the area and the needs of the users as well as the suitability of available material, printed and electronic. Alongside the books, PAMPHLETs and EPHEMERA, current collections in larger libraries bring together material in all formats on such diverse topics as local education, health and hospital care, environmental studies of the countryside, rural or urban transport, civic and vernacular architecture, entertainment and holiday pastimes. Resources include historic plans and MAPs, especially the Ordnance Survey editions. Local free and paid-for NEWSPAPERS may be stored and microfilmed. News-sheets, parish magazines and journals with local content may be included with census enumerators' returns, the General Register Office Index of births, marriages and deaths, trade directories, theatre programmes and sale catalogues. An important section of the collection will be illustrations of all kinds, lantern slides, prints, engravings, postcards and photographs. Non-print material is now commonplace so audio-tapes, FILM and video may be stored as well as the newer digital compilations on CD-ROM, such as *The Sheffield Time Machine*, a virtual tour of a historic city using digitized archive photographs, advertisements, film clips, sound effects and trade directory entries. Smaller branch libraries will hold lesser but useful collections of local material, which will include standard texts and specific detail about the catchment area, photocopied from other local studies files.

Recent advances in Web-based technology and lottery funding have encouraged librarians to assemble local material for digitization and display on the Internet. The Devon Library and Information Service Local Studies web-pages and sites such as *Knowsley Local History – its people and heritage* are local studies resources in their own right, promoting the local history of the region to students across the world and persuading non-library users to add their own domestic data to the various community archives. It is through e-mail and the Internet that professional contacts can be kept most easily with colleagues in other countries experiencing similar developments in local studies practice.

Even before the advent of such electronic access, use of local studies collections had grown immeasurably, in part because many adults now enjoy more leisure time and in part through the active promotion of the collections by library staff. As well as organizing library classes to familiarize schoolchildren and adults with the source material, local studies librarians work with library publishers and adult education tutors using illustrative material from the collections. In consultation with their users they may discover hitherto hidden aspects of local studies such as the history of black and Asian communities in Britain. They may mount displays, give talks to civic societies and organize events showcasing the potential use of the historic records. Libraries in both Scotland and Northern Ireland have combined to hold country-wide local studies weeks on individual themes to entertain and inform the public. Some collections are based in local studies centres alongside archive offices, while other library authorities invoke regional initiatives fostering co-operation between cultural and heritage units in order to improve the service for the whole community. In a national context, Newsplan, supported by libraries, museums, ARCHIVES and the newspaper industry, aims to conserve and microfilm the historic local newspapers of the United Kingdom with funding from the Heritage Lottery Fund.

Outside pressures on the library service – Best Value, social exclusion issues requiring collections to be accessible to the disadvantaged (see SOCIAL EXCLUSION AND LIBRARIES), DISASTER PREPAREDNESS PLANNING, standards and performance indicators – all affect the local studies department, but not always to its detriment. As local studies collections have expanded and been transformed by the use of the new media, the management of these collections remains as necessary as ever, especially where there are questions over core funding and staff deployment. Discussions with Record Offices and other repositories may help to rationalize collections, avoid unnecessary duplication and inform staff and readers. Talking books can be produced using local studies texts. A British Library pilot project archiving appropriate websites will include a local studies site, and concerns about the potential lack of an issue of record for Ordnance Survey maps are being looked at. Invariably the CONSERVATION and PRESERVATION of collections in every format is a major concern, since the development of stimulating customer-oriented services in the present must not be to the disadvantage of future generations. The tradition of local studies collections encapsulates a sense of place and the people within that place. Every effort should be directed to making this unique material, held within the local studies collections, available now and in the time to come.

References

Library Association Local Studies Group (2002) *Local Studies Libraries. Library Association Guidelines for Local Studies Provision in Public Libraries*, 2nd edn, Facet Publishing.

Further reading

Dewe, M. (ed.) (1987–91) *A Manual of Local Studies Librarianship*, 2 vols, Gower.

ELIZABETH A. MELROSE

LOTKA, ALFRED JAMES (1880–1949)

Biologist and statistician.

Born in the eastern part of the Austro-Hungarian Empire of US parents, he was educated in France, Germany, Britain and the USA. His career encompassed the chemical industry, the US Patent Office, the National Bureau of Standards, Johns Hopkins University and the statistical bureau of the Metropolitan Life Insurance Company. His achievements were recognized by the presidency of the Population Association of America (1938–9) and the American Statistical Association (1942).

His scientific work brought insights from chemistry, biology and mathematics into play in an analytical model of population. His interest in population in terms of culture and ecological influences led him into a number of related areas. Among these was the quantitative analysis of the relationship between the number of scientific writers and the number of papers they produced. Essentially, he observed that, whilst many authors produced a single paper, only a small minority produced more than a few papers. This sharp distinction between those few whose scientific contribution is at a high volume and the great number of other contributors is referred to as Lotka's Law and is one of the essential building blocks of information theory.

Further reading

Lotka, A.J. (1956) *Elements of Mathematical Biology*, New York [includes a 94-item bibliography of his papers].

SEE ALSO: information theory

LUHN, HANS PETER (1896–1964)

Information scientist and engineer. He worked on KeyWord in Context (KWIC) indexes and Selective Dissemination of Information (SDI), and pioneered the use of mechanical, and later electronic, devices for the processing of textual material.

Born in Barmen, Germany, he went to school in Germany and learned printing in Sankt Gallen, Switzerland. His first INFORMATION RETRIEVAL invention, after he had emigrated to the USA in the 1920s, was an optical coincidence system to determine which cocktails could be prepared from available ingredients. In the late 1940s he was asked by IBM to find a solution to the problem of searching chemical compounds represented in coded form, and developed a machine (the Luhn Scanner) to search files of punched cards on which these codes were recorded. The arrival of the computer offered better solutions to these problems, and his 1958 paper 'A business intelligence system' proposed an automatic method to provide current-awareness services to scientists and engineers. In 1960 the American Chemical Society adopted his KWIC method of INDEXING and published *Chemical Titles* by this method.

Further reading

Schultz, C.K. (ed.) (1968) *H.P. Luhn: Pioneer Information Scientist. Selected Works*, Macmillan.

SEE ALSO: organization of knowledge

M

MACHINE LANGUAGE

A language used within a computer, for internal communication between its related parts and for performing arithmetic and editing functions.

SEE ALSO: information and communication technology

MACHINE-READABLE CATALOGUING

A generic term for catalogue records (see CATALOGUES) that can be stored in and retrieved from a computer. It is a structured format that enables standard bibliographic records in book and other catalogue formats to be manipulated by computer in a standard way to facilitate the exchange of records between libraries.

Specifically, the MARC (Machine-Readable Cataloguing) format, now in almost universal use for automated library catalogues, originated in the deliberations of the LIBRARY OF CONGRESS on the possibility of using automated techniques for its catalogue provision in the early 1960s. After several pilot programmes by the Library of Congress and the BRITISH LIBRARY, the MARC format became the universal standard for catalogue records worldwide. As more countries began to use MARC, various national variations emerged. The UNIMARC format is an attempt to gather national variations into one universal exchange format. In recent years, with the development of appropriate software, it has become relatively easy to convert from one MARC format to another.

Normal database structure involves holding data in records and fields, and the MARC format is an attempt to do this for standard cataloguing records, at present incorporating data in ANGLO-AMERICAN CATALOGUING RULES (AACR).

A UKMARC record is made up of two sections. The first consists of (1) the record label, which includes processing instructions and information such as the total length of the record, the format (book etc.), (2) the directory, which is an index to the control and data fields within a record, and (3) the control fields, which are fixed-length fields input by the cataloguer and consist of data such as country of publication, language, etc.

The second section comprises content designators, which hold the bibliographic data of the item concerned. The content designators structure the data into particular fields and subfields. The fields are identified by a three-digit tag representing the elements of the bibliographic record and the access points:

001–009	Control fields
010–099	Coded and numeric data
100–244	Main-entry access points
245–299	Titles and title paragraph (title, edition, imprint)
300–399	Physical description
400–499	Series statements
500–599	Notes
600–699	Subject access points
700–799	Added-entry access points
800–899	Series access points
900–948	References
949–999	Reserved for local implementation

Along with tags, each field includes two field indicators that distinguish particular cataloguing cases such as added entries.

Within each field the data is further broken

down into subfields. These are signalled by a series of subfield codes that are defined for each field. Within the personal author field, the most common subfields are $a indicating surname, $h first name, $c dates, e.g. 100 10$aRobinson$h-John$-c1919–1980.

Use of MARC format

Most large centralized databases use MARC format, which means that it is the predominant, widespread standard for catalogue records. It was, however, developed solely for catalogues that, although computerized, were not accessible online. With the proliferation of online public-access catalogues (OPACS) there are considerable doubts as to whether or not the format is still appropriate. This debate centres around two considerations: first, MARC format is solidly linked with AACR and includes fields for main entry, uniform titles, etc., which may no longer be suitable in online searching, and, second, many other information databases of periodical articles are now available that do not use MARC format yet suffer no loss of searching power. Indeed, some would argue that the record structure of these databases gives better retrieval possibilities, especially in subject searching. However, for the moment MARC remains largely unchallenged as the standard format for catalogue records.

Further reading

Gredley, E. and Hopkinson, A. (1990) *Exchanging Bibliographic Data: MARC and Other International Formats*, Library Association.
Hagler, R. (1991) *The Bibliographic Record and Information Technology*, 2nd edn, Adamantine Press.
Hill, R.W. (1994) *Setting the Record Straight: Understanding the MARC Format*, 2nd edn, The British Library.
Rowley, J. and Farrow, J. (2000) *Organizing Knowledge: An Introduction to Managing Access to Information*, 3rd edn, Gower.
UNIMARC Manual (1987) IFLA UBCIM (2nd edn 1990, British Library Bibliographic Services Division).

SEE ALSO: bibliographic control; catalogues; East Asia

ANN O'BRIEN

MACHINE TRANSLATION

The translation of text from one natural (i.e. human) language to another using computers. The machine translation (MT) process may be fully automatic or involve different levels of human intervention such as pre-editing (preparation of input texts), post-editing (revision of output texts) and interactive MT.

Historical perspective

Historically, MT research can be traced to the late 1940s. The success of cryptanalysis using computers during the Second World War led some scientists to believe that translation could be treated as a cryptography problem. The early researchers were generally very optimistic and thought that MT would be achieved in the near future. A turning point that ended the early enthusiasm was the publication of the ALPAC report in 1964 by the Automatic Language Processing Advisory Committee of the National Academy of Science in the USA. The report effectively regarded the MT work as an expensive failure. In the wake of the ALPAC report MT research continued on a much-reduced scale. MT gradually came out of recession around the mid-1970s, which were marked by the development of SYSTRAN for the Commission of the European Communities (CEC). Since the 1980s MT has enjoyed increasing interest and progress in both academia and industry. Geographically, the USA and the Soviet Union were once the most important countries contributing to MT, mainly Russian–English MT. Current key players are the European Union (EU), the USA and Japan. The historical advancement of MT is reviewed in Hutchins (1986). A good introductory text is Arnold *et al.* (1994).

MT system architecture

MT systems are generally classified into three categories or generations according to their architecture, i.e. direct translation systems (first generation), indirect translation systems (second generation) and AI (ARTIFICIAL INTELLIGENCE)-based systems (third generation). At present most experimental MT systems are of second-generation design and most commercial ones are effectively of first-generation architecture.

The direct translation system is designed specifically for a particular pair of languages. It operates in one stage by translating a source-language (SL) text directly into a target-language (TL) text. The MT process employs a bilingual

SL–TL dictionary. The earliest direct translation systems were the 'word-for-word' systems with or without minimal analysis of word structure (morphology) and sentence structure (syntax) of the languages. Later systems tended to apply some form of syntactic analysis. The analysis of morphology and syntax, or more generally computational linguistics, is now a separate discipline (though it stemmed from MT), but MT is still heavily based on the theories and techniques of computational linguistics (Grishman 1986). The aforementioned SYSTRAN used by CEC for English–French translation is an example of the direct translation system.

The indirect translation approach consists of two subcategories: 'interlingual' systems and 'transfer' systems. The former operate in two stages: analysis and synthesis. An SL text is first analysed into interlingual representations, which are then synthesized to a TL text. The interlingua is an artificial language with a set of semantic primitives common to all languages, or a more abstract syntax free of the morphological and syntactic constraints of natural languages. To create such an interlingua has, however, proved difficult. In fact, some of the systems initially adopting the 'interlingual' approach, e.g. METAL of the University of Texas, later switched to the 'transfer' architecture. Presently, almost all the indirect translation systems use the 'transfer' method, which operates in three stages: analysis, transfer and synthesis. An SL text is first analysed into SL representations, which are then transferred into TL representations, to be finally synthesized to a TL text. The EU's multilingual MT system EUROTRA is such an example. An important characteristic of the second-generation architecture is modularity, albeit absorbed to some extent into the first-generation systems. In fact, to separate the MT process into several stages is a reflection of modularity. Other aspects of modularity mainly include the separation of grammar formalisms from linguistic analysis algorithms, and the stratificational bottom-up analyses of morphology to syntax. The major advantage of modularity is that part of the system can be modified or enhanced without changing the rest of the system. For example, an indirect translation system can be extended from a bilingual to a multilingual system, whereas a direct translation system can hardly achieve that.

The first- and second-generation MT systems are generally linguistics-oriented. The third-generation ones are largely based on AI techniques. An important characteristic of these systems is the emphasis on semantics or the development of models that capture domain knowledge. While the second-generation MT systems (mainly 'transfer' systems) may also involve some semantic analyses, these are usually very limited and serve as constraints on the syntactic analysis. For the AI-based systems, semantics becomes the central focus. Some knowledge-representation methods, such as preference semantics and conceptual dependency, have been experimented with alongside MT. The knowledge-based MT (KBMT) at Carnegie Mellon University, an example of AI-based MT, investigates discourse pragmatics and the use of domain knowledge to resolve ambiguities in translation.

MT has had many achievements in the past but still faces difficult challenges. Some researchers have pointed out the limitations of current second-generation architecture and the application of AI to MT (Nirenburg 1992–3). For example, the current second-generation MT systems are largely based on syntactic theories but these linguistic models sometimes break down in a real environment. Use of sophisticated theories does not necessarily enhance the effectiveness of MT. Another difficult problem for MT has been the resolution of ambiguities in natural languages. The ambiguities occur at all levels of linguistic analyses, from morphology and syntax to semantics. For example, at the morphological level there is the problem of the homograph, i.e. words of the same spelling but different meaning, e.g. 'can' meaning able to and 'can' meaning metal container. Anaphora, i.e. pronoun reference, is another instance of ambiguity, as illustrated in the following sentences.

The men created the translation machines. *They* worked well.
The men created the translation machines. *They* worked hard.

Due to these complexities, some of the more recent research suggested approaches that transcend the second- and third-generation systems (Arnold *et al.* 1994). One notable proposal is the example-based translation that stores a corpus of bilingual example phrases; then the translation copies the closest example that is selected using a best-match algorithm. Another approach applies statistical techniques to calculate the probability of occurrence of words and phrases. Many researchers envisage that future high-quality MT systems require an integration of these empirical techniques with the orthodox linguistic and AI methods.

The problem of computer translation of human language remains so complicated that even the best current MT systems cannot provide a perfect translation. However, they have a number of practical uses. The best MT systems can get the main idea of a text across to someone who would otherwise understand nothing of it at all. Content scanning in bodies like the European Community is thus made possible by the creation of a rough draft containing the general gist of a text. MT can also aid professional translators, particularly when they are translating highly repetitive texts, such as technical documentation. It is particularly useful for translating Web pages, e-mail and chat, since it not only translates the text, but preserves links, pictures and other non-textual features.

References

Arnold, D., Balkan, L., Meijer, S., Humphreys, R.L. and Sadler, L. (1994) *Machine Translation: An Introductory Guide* (http://clwww.essex.ac.uk/MTbook/).

Grishman, R. (1986) *Computational Linguistics: An Introduction*, Cambridge: Cambridge University Press.

Hutchins, W.J. (1986) *Machine Translation: Past, Present, Future*, Chichester: Ellis Horwood.

Nirenburg, S. (ed.) (1992–3) 'Machine translation', *Current Research in Machine Translation* (forum issue) 7(4): 229–322.

Further reading

Machine Translation (1986–) Kluwer. Quarterly journal that publishes articles on all major aspects.

SEE ALSO: communication; computer science; expert systems; translations

ZIMIN WU, REVISED BY EDITORS

MACHLUP, FRITZ (1902–83)

Economist.

Born near Vienna, in the Austro-Hungarian Empire, and was taught at the University of Vienna by the most distinguished economists of the Austrian School. He held academic posts at the University of Buffalo, Johns Hopkins University, Princeton University and New York University. He was an extremely prolific author in fields including international finance, methodology of the social sciences and microeconomic problems. His eminence as a writer and teacher was recognized by many formal honours, including the presidencies of the American Association of University Professors (1962–4), the American Economic Association (1966) and the International Economic Association (1971–4).

In 1962 he published the seminal *Production and Distribution of Knowledge in the United States*, a work that brought the full intensity of a powerful economic intelligence to play on the area of knowledge and information for the first time. Machlup perceived very clearly the scope and importance of this new field, particularly in the light of the knowledge explosion of the late twentieth century. In the 1970s he began a much larger assignment, the projected ten volumes of *Knowledge; Its Creation, Distribution and Economic Significance*, the first volume of which appeared in 1980. Although the series had only reached three volumes by the time of his death, he fully deserves to be regarded as the founder of the study of the ECONOMICS OF INFORMATION.

Further reading

Dryer, J.S. (ed.) (1978) *Breadth and Depth in Economics. Fritz Machlup – the Man and His Ideas*, D.C. Health.

SEE ALSO: information society

MAGNETIC STORAGE

Introduction

The predominant form of computer-based storage technology, as the permanent data-retention capability of magnetic media ensures reliable storage. The ability to write and rewrite to the same device an unlimited number of times substantially increases the utility of magnetic storage over non-rewriteable technologies. The large marketplace for computer-based storage has resulted in significant R&D effort being deployed, which has successfully reduced the cost per bit of storage.

Tape-based storage

Magnetic storage was first used widely in early voice recorders, which originally utilized an iron-based (ferrite) wire for storage and later a thin tape, coated with a magnetic oxide, which revolved around a tape head. The head could either apply an electric field, which would magnetize the material under the head at that instant in a particular orientation to write data, or, alternatively, sense an electric field induced by the previously magnetized material passing close to a coil of wire, to read the data.

This tape-based storage was widely used for data retention in early computer systems. However, the spool-based nature of tapes means that the access time for information is a function of the current position of the tape and the location of the data. Where information is located close to the current tape position, data is much more quickly accessed than information stored further away. This time difference can be a matter of minutes. Where the order of access to data is not known in advance, this results in slow and unpredictable operating speeds as the tape is wound forwards and backwards. Furthermore, this rapid acceleration and deceleration can lead to tape stretching or even snapping, both of which affect reliability.

For archival storage, tape offers an attractive combination of low cost and high data-storage capacity and is widely used in this application area.

Magnetic disks

The precursor of the magnetic disk was the drum. Obsolete today, the drum provided the first device where the speed of data access was largely independent of its location. A drum comprised a cylinder of magnetic coated material mounted on a spindle and rotating at up to several hundred revolutions per minute. Close to the outer surface of the drum is a line of read–write heads. Each head is associated with one slice of the drum, known as a track, and reads/writes data on that track only. Since the drive is continuously rotating, it takes only a few milliseconds for a piece of data to be accessed. This is in marked contrast to tapes, where spooling from one end of a tape to another may take minutes. However, the cost and complexity of drum-based storage meant that originally only the largest computer systems could make use of it.

The benefits of drum-based storage led to a demand for a lower-cost method of storage for mass-market applications. The magnetic disk was developed in response to this demand. As its name implies, a disk is a single flat circular sheet of material coated with a magnetic layer, once again organized as concentric tracks. Each track comprises a number of sectors with intersector gaps to permit easy determination of where the head is.

The disk spins horizontally and a single head moves across its surface to read/write data. The single head reduces costs. Furthermore, since the disk is lighter than the drum it could be rotated more quickly, hence reducing access time. It is this essential approach, developed in the 1960s, to using a disk (or sometimes a platter of vertically stacked disks) that contemporary disk-based systems use.

Developments since the 1960s have been many, but the essential structure has been retained. Storage density has been improved by using materials with much more powerful magnetic properties, permitting more bits per unit area to be stored. Disk heads have moved closer to the disk platter (sometimes only a fraction of a millimetre away) in order to pick up the weaker currents induced by high-density storage. This latter development has necessitated hermetically sealing the disk and head within a dust-free environment. Such an encapsulated storage device is often known as a 'Winchester disk'. These disks are the most widely used today in contemporary information storage systems.

The floppy disk, a device that uses flexible plastic coated with magnetic material for the disk, has been widely used since the mid-1970s as a low-cost, low-density, portable storage medium.

Future developments

By the early 1990s the predominance of magnetic disk storage was coming to an end. The text-based nature of information storage was challenged by MULTIMEDIA data Such databases required orders of magnitude more storage than text. Consequently, the demand for storage capacity rapidly increased. Second, new materials with superior magnetic characteristics proved to be expensive and difficult to manufacture. For applications where data is read-only or for applications such as archiving where data is only written once, compact-disc (CD) technology was rapidly adopted. The development of writeable and erasable OPTICAL-DISK technology in the mid-1990s changed the whole data storage process.

Further reading

McLeod, J. (1983) *Winchester Disks in Microcomputers*, Elsevier Publications.

Patterson, D.A. and Hennesy, J.L. (1990) *Computer Architecture: A Quantitative Approach*, Morgan Kaufmann Publishers.

SEE ALSO: information and communication technology

S. JONES

MAILING LIST

An INTERNET discussion forum in which messages on some subject area, contributed by subscribed members, are sent by e-mail to all other members. Mailing lists are distinct from Usenet newsgroups because of the requirement to subscribe.

MAINFRAME COMPUTER

A large centralized computer system, which was the normal means of handling large volumes of data processing in the late 1970s and early 1980s. The early 1990s saw a move away from reliance on a central mainframe computer towards distributed computing using networked PERSONAL COMPUTERS and SERVERS.

SEE ALSO: information and communication technology; networks

MANAGEMENT SUPPORT SYSTEMS

Management support systems (MSS) can be defined as 'systems that involve the use of information technologies to support managerial decision-making' (Scott Morton 1984). Consequently, management support systems are a generic category that includes management information systems (MIS), DECISION SUPPORT SYSTEMS (DSS) and EXPERT SYSTEMS, which are applied to managerial tasks. It should be noted that the term management support systems does not cover all the computer-based systems typically found within a library. For example, OFFICE AUTOMATION systems or systems that solely automate the process of issuing and returning books without explicitly supporting the decision-making process would not typically be classified as management support systems.

References

Scott Morton, M. (1984) 'The state of art of research', in F. McFarlan (ed.) *The Information Systems Research Challenge*, Harvard Business School Press, pp 13–45.

Further reading

Turban. E. (1993) *Decision Support and Expert Systems: Management Support Systems*, 3rd edn, Macmillan.

SEE ALSO: information management; information systems

MANUSCRIPT

Literally a document of any kind that is written by hand, but more particularly the original version, before it has been printed, of a literary or musical composition in handwritten or typescript form. Information professionals distinguish between manuscripts, which typically form part of a library collection, and official documents or records, which are regarded as ARCHIVES.

MANUSCRIPT LIBRARIES

Whilst the narrow definition of a manuscript is self-evident, many manuscript collections in RESEARCH LIBRARIES contain a diversity of materials, not least because of the way in which research materials find their way into libraries. Perhaps a wider definition of these collections would be that they contain the unpublished materials of an author, first and subsequent drafts, notes, letters and non-book materials. Some would refer to these artefacts as archival material, and in many university, state and national libraries this would be the case. Whilst there is no doubt about what Eastern manuscripts and Western mediaeval and Renaissance manuscripts are, where modern Western manuscript material is concerned, in most cases a wider definition now obtains.

In the Western hemisphere, manuscripts continued to be produced after the introduction of printing from movable type. The Vatican Library, the BIBLIOTHÈQUE NATIONALE DE FRANCE and the Escorial Library were founded in the fifteenth and sixteenth centuries; these and similar foundations were central to the transmission of knowledge considered important enough to the maintenance and improvement of civilization. The manuscript copy was central to this, and it is largely due to those early librarians and their careful custodianship, often in times of political uncertainty, that the great works of classical and Arab authors are accessible to present-day readers. Manuscript librarians have been developing their special skills over a long period of time. This body of carefully built-up expertise is currently under threat.

The skills demanded of custodians of manuscript collections are primarily those of anyone engaged in COLLECTION MANAGEMENT, i.e. the acquisition (see ACQUISITIONS), organization, maintenance and exploitation of such materials. Those involved in acquisitions need to possess a sensitivity to important and relevant collections, an ability to negotiate with, on the one hand, prospective donors and vendors and, on the other, those who are responsible for financing such transactions in order to bring about a satisfactory outcome. In the case of living authors, making arrangements concerning the eventual transfer of ARCHIVES can be tortuous and require great tact, often in the face of competition from other, possibly richer, institutions.

The organization of such collections is also well documented. Effort has been brought to bear on the computerization of records, many libraries now having purpose-built software for accessioning and cataloguing. In the United Kingdom, that developed for the BRITISH LIBRARY has been made generally available.

Since the mid-1970s there has been increasing concern regarding maintenance, deterioration and accident. In Europe and North America there have been many conferences highlighting CONSERVATION issues. As a result many libraries have written disaster preparedness plans (see DISASTER PREPAREDNESS PLANNING) that can be implemented swiftly when serious damage by fire or flood is threatened. Preventative maintenance now enjoys a higher profile than in the recent past.

Traditionally, keepers of manuscript collections have been responsive to scholarly enquiry rather than active in promoting the use of their materials, save through their scholarship in publishing catalogues and articles highlighting important acquisitions. However, in the United Kingdom during the 1980s, as a result of political focus upon the public funding of museums and libraries, librarians have had to enter the marketplace. Those responsible for archival, rare-book and manuscript collections have not been excepted from this trend. In addition to actively promoting the use of their materials, staff have had to engage in fundraising through, for example, the publication of greetings cards and other reproductions from the collections. There is now a growing demand that the need to maintain and increase such collections within the public domain should be justified in terms of cold commercial criteria. This is no isolated example of cultural insanity, however, but is set in the context of a widespread and continuous review of government policy on expenditure on public services. Here there is cause for concern, for those seeking answers to such questions point to the rapid advance and increasingly economical availability of INFORMATION AND COMMUNICATION TECHNOLOGY.

While LIBRARY BUILDINGS and conservation of materials have high profiles and continue to attract funds, long-term staffing issues are largely ignored. Possibly the biggest threat to manuscript and rare-book collections is that in many large academic libraries there are now few qualified specialists to oversee the collections. Although manuscript materials and rare-book collections can be found in large PUBLIC LIBRARIES, specialists are rarely employed. As yet there has been no focus on the problem that will arise when the existing experts retire from the scene and there are no replacements available with that local knowledge acquired through years of on-the-job training.

The state of uncertainty felt in the mid-1990s by those engaged in rare-book and manuscript librarianship was not only engendered by government indifference to libraries and a lack of public awareness and esteem, but also by professional neglect. In public libraries the focus is on community librarianship, and in ACADEMIC LIBRARIES a focus on the provision of textbooks for a growing and more financially insecure undergraduate population has resulted largely in a weakening of the position of manuscript and rare-book librarians. In public libraries rare materials are often seen as elitist, and in academic circles specialists are frequently seen as luxury appointments that, increasingly, heavily used libraries can no longer afford. The fashion for flexible staff has had a knock-on effect on professional education. During the last twenty-five years there has been a steady decline in the teaching of book and manuscript skills within degree and postgraduate courses in librarianship. The decreasing number of posts open to those interested in rare-book and manuscript librarianship could result in such remaining professional elements disappearing altogether from the syllabus.

The impact of information technology on libraries is also changing the traditional outlook on manuscript and rare-book collections. This concern was voiced at an international symposium held at Harvard University in September 1992. Twenty-three papers on this topic were delivered to many of the foremost experts in the field. The ability to digitize and thus make generally available to anyone with the appropriate equipment access, not only to bibliographic databases but also to full texts, will undoubtedly raise questions concerning the cost of maintaining collections of old manuscripts, possibly transferring this responsibility from library funding to heritage funding. Keepers of manuscripts and rare books will have to justify their policies when questioned on the need to acquire and keep such materials when they can be so easily digitized and accessed by a greater number of individuals. In the mid- to late 1990s, however, the digitization of manuscripts themselves, and the increasing availability of manuscript catalogues on the World Wide Web, has perhaps eased some of these concerns. By 2000, another symposium on manuscripts in libraries, held at the Harry Ransom Center at the University of Texas at Austin, took a more optimistic view. The relevant papers can be found in *Libraries and Culture*, vol. 37, part 1 (winter 2002).

In the case of modern manuscript materials, where authors' preliminary notes, letters, variant scripts and final texts form the basis of a huge scholastic industry, the impact of new technology is already being felt by the rare-book and manuscript trade. Generation of text through word-processing software means that, for the most part, only the author's final text will remain extant. It is scarcely likely that writers will wish to preserve variant material. Whilst this means that there will be less hard copy for librarians to acquire in the future, there will also be a diminution in material available for postgraduate study and research.

Further reading

Association of College and Research Libraries (1999) 'Guidelines for the security of rare books, manuscripts and other special collection', *College and Research Libraries News* 60: 3–19.

Bibliographic Access to Medieval and Renaissance Manuscripts (1992) Haworth Press.

British Manuscript Collections (1989) *Automated Cataloguing: A Manual*, British Library.

Brindley, L. (2002) 'The future of libraries and humanities research', *Libraries and Culture* 37: 26–36.

DeWitt, D.L. (1994) *Guides to Archives and Manuscript Collections in the United States: A Bibliographical Guide*, Greenwood Press.

Duckett, K.W. (1975) *Modern Manuscripts*, American Association for State and Local History.

Reiman, D.H. (1993) *The Study of Modern Manuscripts: Public, Confidential and Private*, Johns Hopkins University Press.

Royal Commission on Historical Manuscripts (1994) *Surveys of Historical Manuscripts in the United Kingdom: A Select Bibliography*, 2nd edn, HMSO.

Stockdale, R. (2000) 'The retrospective conversion of the British Library manuscripts' catalogue: A description of the project', *Journal of the Society of Archivists* 21: 199–213.

Wendhof, R. (1993) *Rare Book and Manuscript Libraries in the Twenty-First Century*, Harvard University Library.

SEE ALSO: digitization; national archives; rare-book libraries

IAN ROGERSON

MAP

A graphic representation of all or some part of the earth's surface, showing physical features and human aspects such as political boundaries etc., usually drawn to scale. Maps rely for their ability to represent geographical space on a number of technical devices, such as the projection, scale, grid system and sets of symbols to represent particular features. Their content can be indexed and the information presented in a GAZETTEER, and a collection of maps can be published as an atlas. Great numbers of maps are compiled and published by national cartographic agencies, such as the UK Ordnance Survey, and there are also commercial specialist map publishers. The peculiar storage, cataloguing and interpretation problems presented by maps mean that they are often kept in a separate MAP LIBRARY and looked after by specially trained map librarians. Much mapping data is nowadays assembled from remote sensing devices conveyed by satellites and held in the form of electronic databases of geographical information. GEOGRAPHIC INFOR-MATION SYSTEMS supplement the scope of printed maps, but have not replaced them.

MAP LIBRARY

A library in which a major component of the collection is cartographic material – maps, charts, atlases, globes, relief models, remotely sensed imagery and digital data.

Within this definition, map libraries – in terms of size, organization and the material held – form a very disparate group. In some collections only current mapping is valued, while in others super-seded maps are kept as valued historical docu-ments. A map library may be a major entity in its own right or it may form a very small part of a larger organization, perhaps without full-time staffing. Map libraries exist, for example, in academic (see ACADEMIC LIBRARIES), historical and research institutions (see RESEARCH LI-BRARIES), in NATIONAL LIBRARIES and COPY-RIGHT libraries, in government departments and local authorities, in mineral and oil exploration companies, military organizations, cartographic and survey organizations. The maps are used as working tools or as a historical resource, the latter also providing an archive of cartographic activity.

Maps and the library user

Although requests for maps can be generic, for example – all skiing maps or Braille maps – or be defined by cartographer (especially for antiquar-ian maps) or publishing house, most queries are area-specific. A major use for maps in historical collections is as a record of the landscape through time: to locate places now disappeared or renamed; to plot land use through time; to help interpret written documents; to identify administrative or property boundaries, and so on.

Depending on the scale and its intended purpose, a map may cover an area in one sheet (a single sheet map) or in a series of sheets – a map series, defined by Parry and Perkins (1987) as 'a set of map sheets drawn to a common specification which when assembled in their correct relative positions cover a large area of land and which together may be regarded as constituting a single map'. The relationship of the sheets can be shown on a graphic index or

cover diagram. This shows the sheet lines and the name or number of the individual sheets, and can also be marked up with the libraries' holdings.

In most general map libraries, staff need to spend considerably more time helping users than is required in many other libraries. Not only are requests complicated by map series and the concept of scale, but the very act of compiling a map, involving generalization from reality and its representation as symbols on a flat surface, means that interpretation of maps must be done cautiously. Even the intended purpose of the map or, for example, a political sponsor, can influence the type of information included or excluded or the accuracy of its portrayal.

From a purely practical point of view, maps are usually large and therefore the library must be equipped with large tables plus weights to prevent curling, long rulers and magnifying glasses.

Storage

Maps may be printed or manuscript. They may be available on stone, vellum, paper, cloth and a variety of other materials. The variety of formats and the generally large size of cartographic items results in map libraries requiring many different types of storage. The vast majority of maps in collections are on paper. These may be stored folded, rolled or flat. Flat maps may be stored horizontally in drawers, perhaps folded in half, or vertically, in suspended folders or on strips of paper or plastic attached to the map and in turn suspended.

Cataloguing and classification

A primary means of access to a map collection is through the area covered by the map or map series. Geographical systems of CLASSIFICATION may be of three types: alphabetic, alphanumeric and numeric (Larsgaard 1998). All libraries using geographical classifications need to address the problem of how to deal with places that change their name or countries that change their bor-ders. Widely used alphanumeric systems are Library of Congress, DDC, and that devised by the UK Ministry of Defence, GSGS 5307 (Minis-try of Defence 1978). Non-geographic classifica-tions, for example by issuing body or provenance, are widely used in ARCHIVES and record offices.

It is not uncommon for map library collections to be uncatalogued, retrieval relying on the classification scheme or staff knowledge. In many institutions maps are seen as 'difficult' and/or ephemeral material. Automation of map CATALO-GUES has trailed behind that of their book-based equivalents, with maps often being added to systems essentially designed for books as an uncomfortable afterthought. Nevertheless, increasing numbers of map catalogues are automated, resulting in much greater powers of retrieval. MARC format is used in, for example, the BRITISH LIBRARY and LIBRARY OF CONGRESS map libraries, allowing ONLINE access and much greater potentiality for co-operative cataloguing. There are also many home-grown automated map catalogues in use.

Map series can be catalogued at the series level, resulting in one catalogue entry for many sheets; or at the sheet level, providing many entries for each series. The latter option requires a considerably greater amount of time but potentially provides easier access to the collection, particularly if geographic co-ordinates are included on a suitable automated system. A graphics interface can combine catalogue entries with graphic indexes.

An International Standard Bibliographical Description has been published for cartographic materials – ISBD(CM) (1987) – and a manual of interpretation for the ANGLO-AMERICAN CATALO-GUING RULES, AACR2 (1982), for cartographic materials is also available.

Apart from geographical coverage other fundamental elements in a cartographic catalogue are scale, authorship (more often an organization than an individual and frequently equated with the publisher, at least for modern maps), date of publication and of information, format (map, globe, printed, manuscript), subject (geological, administrative, etc.) and size.

Digital data

Increasingly maps are being produced in digital form – often without a paper counterpart. Depending on the sophistication of the DATA-BASE, this offers many advantages to the map user – it may be possible to view only selected data, to incorporate it into a Geographic Information System (see GEOGRAPHIC INFORMATION SYSTEMS), to centre a map on a particular site and therefore to ignore the sheet lines necessary

with paper maps. Such products are found in map libraries and the role of the map librarian is consequently changing, but they may equally be found in computer departments or in people's offices. The archiving of this information is something that is being addressed (Board and Lawrence 1994). Should the digital product or some hard copy, perhaps microform (see MICRO-FORMS), output be preserved? At present digital products are not subject to LEGAL DEPOSIT in the copyright libraries – How are we to provide access to the data and archive it for future generations? Is this the role of the map library?

References

Board, C. and Lawrence, P. (eds) (1994) *Recording Our Changing Landscape*, Royal Society and the British Academy in association with the British Cartographic Society.
Cartographic Materials: A Manual of Interpretation for AACR2 (1982) American Library Association.
ISBD(CM): International Standard Bibliographic Description for Cartographic Materials (1987) IFLA Universal Bibliographic Control and International MARC Programme.
Larsgaard, M.L. (1998) *Map Librarianship: An Introduction*, 3rd edn, Libraries Unlimited.
Ministry of Defence (1978) *Manual of Map Library Classification and Cataloguing*, GSGS 5307.
Parry, R.B. and Perkins, C.R. (eds) (1987) *World Mapping Today*, Butterworths.

Further reading

Dubreuil, L. (ed.) (1993) *World Directory of Map Collections*, 3rd edn, compiled by the Section of Geography and Map Libraries of the International Federation of Library Associations and Institutions, Saur.
Perkins, C.R. and Parry, R.B. (eds) (1990) *Information Sources in Cartography*, Bowker-Saur.

SEE ALSO: digital library; national archives; special libraries

ANNE TAYLOR

MARC

The acronym invariably used for the standard format for MACHINE-READABLE CATALOGUING.

SEE ALSO: UKMARC; UNIMARC; USMARC

MARK-UP LANGUAGES

Mark-up is information embedded within an electronic document, in order to control the processing of that document by computer programs. It makes explicit for computer processing things that are implicit for the human reader. Mark-up is usually in the form of encoding tags. A mark-up language can be a specific set of encoding tags or a method for defining encoding tags.

Mark-up for display

Documents created by WORD-PROCESSING programs contain mark-up that controls the appearance of portions of the document, for example centred text or text in italics. Normally this mark-up is not easily visible to the user who sees only the effect of the mark-up when the document is displayed. Before the widespread use of word processing, text formatting systems used visible mark-up to control the appearance of documents, for example with formatting instructions such as *.ce* to cause the next portion of text to be centred. The formatting program processed the document to produce a version suitable for display or printing. The typesetting system TeX, still widely used in COMPUTER SCIENCE and related disciplines, operates in this way.

Mark-up for analysis

Other forms of mark-up are used with computer programs that manipulate or analyse documents in some way. Document retrieval systems usually require features such as author, title and keywords to be inserted in a particular format within a document. In the humanities more detailed mark-up systems have been developed to handle different types of primary texts such as verse, drama, manuscripts, transcriptions of conversations and dictionaries. These languages are used to identify each word that has been retrieved by page number, act, scene, line number or whatever unit is the most appropriate for the text.

Generalized mark-up

Mark-up languages for formatting and for analysis developed more or less independently of each other. However, formatting languages can be ambiguous for any other form of computer processing where, for example, something in italic might be a title or a foreign word or an emphasized word. Furthermore, most mark-up languages were designed for use with only one

program, making it necessary to perform some kind of conversion on the document for use with other programs. It made sense to develop a machine-independent mark-up scheme that could be used with many different programs without making changes to a document.

This is the basic principle underlying the Standard Generalized Mark-up Language (SGML). SGML became an international standard in 1986, but it has now largely been superseded by a simpler version called the Extensible Mark-up Language (XML), which became a recommendation of the World Wide Web Consortium (W3C) in 1998. Both are metalanguages. They provide a framework for creating a mark-up system according to certain rules. Mark-up tags within SGML and XML are descriptive rather than prescriptive. They specify components within a document rather than what a computer program is to do with those components. *Pride and Prejudice* would be encoded thus: < title > Pride and Prejudice < /title > . With this mark-up in place one computer program could make an index of all titles, while another could display titles in italic and a third could make the titles into HYPERTEXT links, all without making any changes to the document.

The set of mark-up tags defined for any group of documents is called an SGML or XML application. The tags are defined in a process known as document analysis where sample documents are examined and features within the documents and the relationships between the features are specified in detail. Documents are assumed to be hierarchical in structure with tags nested within each other. A formal specification of the document structure can be defined in a Document Type Definition (DTD) or, for XML only, a schema. The DTD or schema can then used by a computer program to validate the mark-up or to control the processing in other ways.

SGML and XML applications

The HyperText Markup Language (HTML) is a simple application of SGML. Other SGML and XML applications have been developed for digital libraries (see DIGITAL LIBRARY) and for electronic publishing. One of the best known is the Text Encoding Initiative (TEI), an international project that defined an SGML application for the humanities. Humanities primary source texts are particularly complex and the TEI developed specifications for encoding many features within them from editorial annotations to linguistic analysis to transcriptions of oral archives. The TEI guidelines are publicly available and are used by many digital library projects. They are now being converted to XML.

XML is just as useful for encoding METADATA or for the text that needs to be associated with images in order for those images to be searchable. The Resource Description Framework (RDF) now being promoted by the W3C as a general-purpose metadata system is based on XML as is the Encoded Archival Description (EAD). XML is now being widely adopted in industry and many new applications are being developed. Up till now most effort has concentrated on defining XML applications but there is a steady development of software for desktop tools and for use by programmers comfortable with Unix. The W3C also has other activities associated with XML including style sheet languages and a method of linking across documents that is much more powerful than that provided by HTML.

Mark-up theory

Such has been the recent interest in mark-up languages that a whole new research area of mark-up theory has developed in the last few years. Within it, questions have been raised about the distinction between descriptive and prescriptive mark-up, about the relationship between mark-up and ontologies (see ONTOLOGY), and on the problems of representing documents as hierarchies.

Further reading

Burnard, L. (1995) 'What is SGML and how does it help?', *Computers and the Humanities* 29: 41–50.

Coombs, J.H., Renear, A.H. and DeRose, S.J. (1987) 'Markup systems and the future of scholarly text processing', *Communications of the ACM* 30: 933–47.

Encoded Archival Description (2001) (http://lcweb.loc.gov/ead/) [official website for the EAD].

Hockey, S. (2000) *Electronic Texts in the Humanities. Principles and Practice*, Oxford University Press.

Text Encoding Initiative (2001) (http://www.tei-c.org/) [introductory and advanced material about the TEI].

The XML Cover Pages (1994–) (http://www.oasis-open.org/cover/) [comprehensive source of information about XML and related activities].

SEE ALSO: image retrieval; informatics; standards specifications

SUSAN HOCKEY

MARKET RESEARCH

Systematic investigation of the type, quality and quantity of services required by users (sometimes also referred to as clients or customers) is the basis of MARKETING in the context of library and information services provision. The concept of a 'market' for library and information services emerged in the 1960s and early 1970s when studies of user requirements started to be taken more seriously. Prior to this time it would be fair to say that service provision was professionally determined and systems-led rather than customer-driven.

Pioneering investigations by Groombridge (1964), Luckham (1971) and Totterdell and Bird (1976) all focused on British public library services. Cronin (1984a, 1984b), who has contributed significantly to the marketing literature, suggests that these earliest studies were attempts to explore the relationship between the thinking of service providers and the perceptions of disparate communities of users. He suggests that the majority of USER STUDIES since then 'have been relatively unsophisticated in terms of the conceptualisation, methodologies and statistical rigour'.

In spite of these shortcomings, some of which were addressed by the setting up of the Centre for User Studies at Sheffield University, the library profession has begun to understand the need for market research to support the design and planning of services and products. The concept of medium- to long-term strategic planning was a 1980s phenomenon that encouraged feasibility studies, surveys of various types and community profiling. The Cheshire survey (Cheshire Libraries and Museums 1985) was an important milestone in this respect. Market research has, however, not been restricted to public libraries, and many commercial institutions, who provide an in-house library service, and academic bodies now undertake market research exercises to determine the type and amount of library support activity that may be needed in order that the organization may function effectively.

Techniques

Techniques used in library market research are largely drawn from those employed within the commercial sector and may be designed to assess both the quantitative and the qualitative aspects of service provision and use. They are tests of both fact and opinion. Various methodologies may be used, such as questionnaires, completed by either the recipient or an interviewer; 'user panels' or 'focus groups', in which the views of a larger number of people are collected through a discussion under the direction of a neutral facilitator; or using analysis of data collected as part of library housekeeping – reservations, enquiry failure rates. There is also an increasing use of a survey technique, 'Priority Search', in which participants indicate their preferences.

Telephone surveys provide a simple way of obtaining both quantitative and qualitative data from users and non-users. Fax and ELECTRONIC MAIL can also be used where time-scales are short, but in such cases response rates are sometimes variable. Postal surveys, in which a printed questionnaire is sent to the participant, are quite commonly used. But this method generally suffers from a low response rate and the additional difficulty that respondents are self-selecting – they choose whether to respond or not, and results are often biased. Response rates can sometimes be improved by offering an incentive, such as participation in a prize draw, or by reducing the inconvenience and cost of responding by providing pre-paid postal envelopes or a Freephone telephone number.

Sampling

To avoid the bias that a non-representative group may impose, proper structuring of the sample is one of the critical factors in market research studies. For some surveys it is feasible to examine the whole population under study, but usually some sort of sample is constructed. Random sampling, which involves selecting participants at will or using random number tables, is commonly used by libraries, as is systematic sampling. This requires examining or interviewing, for example, every tenth person entering the library or every fifth record in a file. Two other methods of sampling are occasionally used within library market research. These are structured sampling, in which records/participants are chosen according to some predetermined criteria

(e.g. age, sex), and cluster sampling, where participants are chosen by some other collective factor (e.g. those entering the library during some predetermined time period).

Data analysis

Results can be processed manually, but it is more usual to make use of one of the proprietary software packages, such as SPSS or SNAP, which are specifically designed to handle large amounts of information and present it graphically.

Most of the market surveys undertaken in the library and information sector are locally focused, but national surveys have been undertaken, of which the most notable is the British Public Library Review of 1994, which was carried out by ASLIB on behalf of the UK Department of Heritage (Myers 1994).

References

Cheshire Libraries and Museums (1985) *The Cheshire Library Survey: New Town, New Library*, Cheshire Libraries and Museums, BLRDD Report no. 5838 [a study on the use of and attitudes to Runcorn Library before and after its opening].

Cronin, B. (1984a) 'The marketing of public library services in the UK – practical applications', *European Journal of Marketing* 18(2): 45–55.

—— (1984b) 'The marketing of public library services in the United Kingdom – the rationale for a marketing approach', *European Journal of Marketing* 18(2): 33–44.

Groombridge, B. (1964) *The Londoner and His Library*, Research Institute for Consumer Affairs.

Luckham, B. (1971) *The Library in Society: A Study of the Public Library in an Urban Setting*, Library Association.

Myers, J. (1994) 'Stable, quiet retreats, or bustling with innovation', *Library Association Record* 96(8): 426–7.

Totterdell, B. and Bird, J. (1976) *The Effective Library: A Report on the Hillingdon Project on Public Library Effectiveness*, Library Association.

Further reading

Durcan, A. (1984) 'A reference library talks to its users', *European Journal of Marketing* 18(2): 65–71.

Jackson, A. and Martin, P. (1991) 'The non-use of Manchester's library service: An investigation', *Public Library Journal* 6(4): 109–13.

Line, M.B. (1972) *Library Surveys*, C. Bingley.

Local Government Training Board (1987) *Getting Closer to the Public – Part 1: What it Means*, LGTB.

National Consumer Council (1986) *Measuring Up*, NCC.

Reid, C. and Webster, K. (1993) 'Business needs and supply in Scotland', *Business Information Review* 10(2): 36–47.

Rowlands, J. (1992) *The Cuckoo Factor: An Investigation into the Effects of Transient Populations on the Development of Library Services*, Humberside County Council Leisure Services.

Sugg, A. (1998) *Consulting the Customer: Using Market Research in Libraries*, Capital Planning Information.

SEE ALSO: libraries; marketing

DON KENNINGTON

MARKETING

Marketing is commonly associated with high-budget advertising campaigns designed to sell, influence and persuade people to buy things they do not want or need. This is not surprising in light of the fact that the average person experiences thousands of advertising impressions per day through print, broadcast, the WORLD WIDE WEB, product packaging and event sponsors. But marketing is much more than advertising, selling, persuasion or PROMOTION. Marketing is a tried and true systematic approach that relies heavily on designing the service or product in terms of consumers' needs and desires, with consumer satisfaction as its goal.

Brief history of marketing

Marketing was popularized after the Second World War. Prior to that time emphasis was placed on producing products without any special regard for consumer needs or demand, coupled with the intent to sell that same product to an undefined market for a profit. Demand at this time was far greater than supply and the customer usually sought out the producer. Eventually this trend reversed and consumers realized they could make choices as well as demands of the producers. Hence was born marketing.

MARKETING FOR NON-PROFIT ORGANIZATIONS

Marketing for non-profit is defined as the voluntary exchange of values (e.g. books for knowledge) with targeted markets (e.g. university age library users), built upon organizational goals and objectives (e.g. increase university age registrations by 25 per cent in one year), that achieve customer satisfaction (higher grade point average based upon productive library use).

Non-profit sectors rapidly adopted marketing practices in the late 1970s as changes in the external environment created competition, and more limited funding sources. Agencies such as libraries, museums, hospitals and zoos were suddenly faced with diverse and demanding clientele who were no longer satisfied with the status quo.

Introduction to marketing activities

By describing the elements of a marketing model, its application to libraries can be further illustrated. A model is simply a step-by-step emulation of a process that illuminates important components or variables that are imperative to the success of the process. The four steps include MARKET RESEARCH, market segmentation, marketing mix and marketing evaluation.

1 Market research is finding out all relevant data regarding the library's market. A market is all the people who have some stated interest in a particular product or service or could be expected to do so. The market research process is continuous, identifying markets and opportunities, and gathering and processing relevant data needed to successfully serve those markets.

2 Market segmentation is based upon the fact that markets are heterogeneous. A market segment is a group of potential users who are identified through the market research process as sharing similar wants and needs. It is imperative for library managers to define and understand various markets in order to allocate resources efficiently and to provide services effectively.

3 Marketing mix is comprised of product, price, place and promotion, the 4 Ps. While the mix is the most visible part of the model, it is not exclusively the most important. Librarians historically participate heavily in the promotion arm of the mix. Less explicit regard has been given by the library profession to aspects of price, place and product when considering which segments to prioritize service to.

Product is defined as anything that can be offered to a market to satisfy a need. A large assortment of materials, services and programmes constitute the library's product lines. A library offers goods, either tangible (e.g. books and Internet access) or intangible (e.g. personal assistance, or value of the library as a premier community institution).

Price is defined as the actual charge made by an organization as well as the toil and trouble of acquiring it. Library services are not free. Although the library may or may not charge specific prices for its products, the user incurs costs in obtaining service. Time spent preparing to go to the library, travelling there or online searching time has a price. Unless the user expects to be rewarded with information worth more than the cost of obtaining it, the user will forego library use.

Place is defined as how the organization makes its products and services available and accessible to markets. Location of facilities and optimum accessibility is critical to library success. GEOGRAPHIC INFORMATION SYSTEMS are facilitating optimal library facility location (Koontz 1997: 85–108).

Promotion articulates what the library is doing and what it is. The four groups of promotion tools include advertising, sales promotion, personal selling and PUBLICITY.

4   Marketing evaluation is a formalized activity, often called the marketing audit, which can occur before an organization markets, during the marketing process and after marketing begins. It takes a comprehensive and systematic review of the organization's internal and external environment, strategies and activities, identifying problem areas and opportunities, and recommending a plan for improvement.

SUMMARY

Marketing represents an organized way of offering library services cost-effectively and efficiently, based upon user interests, communication methods, imaginative design of service and products, and feedback that improves what the library is doing.

References

Koontz, C. (1997) *Library Facility Siting and Location Handbook*, Greenwood [an introduction to Geographic Information Systems (GIS) for market analysis].

Further reading

Hart, K. (1999) *Putting Marketing Ideas into Action*, Library Association Publishing [an introduction to

marketing techniques that can be put into action by libraries].
Kotler, P. (1996) *Strategic Marketing for Nonprofit Organizations*, Prentice Hall [extends private-sector concepts of marketing to the non-profit marketing environment, and develops a framework of utilizing marketing for strategic planning].

CHRISTINE M. KOONTZ

McKERROW, RONALD BRUNLESS (1872–1940)

Bibliographer and literary scholar.

After Harrow and Cambridge, McKerrow taught English in Japan and became interested in hand printing. When he returned to Britain he was persuaded by A.H. Bullen to edit the work of Thomas Nashe, which began a lifetime's interest in the printing, publication and textual transmission of Elizabethan and Jacobean literature. McKerrow was Secretary of the Bibliographical Society from 1912 to 1934, and, as such, negotiated the transfer of *The Library* from the Library Association to the Society.

He is best remembered for his *Introduction to Bibliography* (1927, and subsequent editions), which until the 1970s was a standard work for students of literature and, to a lesser extent, librarianship. He also compiled and edited an important dictionary of members of the English book trade from 1557 to 1640 (1910), which is still valuable; was the founder and first editor of the *Review of English Studies*, which introduced new standards into English literary scholarship; and was a major contributor to many bibliographical enterprises of the period including the pre-1640 *Short-Title Catalogue*.

Further reading

Greg, W.W. (1940) 'Ronald Brunless McKerrow', *Proceedings of the British Academy* 26: 488–515.

SEE ALSO: bibliography

McLUHAN, (HERBERT) MARSHALL (1911–80)

Canadian sociologist and writer on communications.

Educated at the universities of Manitoba and Cambridge, from 1946 to 1966 he taught in the English department at the University of Toronto, as Director of the Centre for Culture and Technology at the University of Toronto and, in 1967, was appointed Albert Schweitzer Professor in the Humanities at Fordham University, New York. He first examined the effects of technology and the media on society in his book *The Mechanical Bride: Folklore of Industrial Man* (1952), in which he analysed the socio-psychological impact of mass communication and interpreted it as an extension of the human nervous system. This thesis he reinforced and expanded in works including *The Gutenberg Galaxy* (1962) and *The Medium is the Massage* (1967). The title of the latter is a play on the slogan with which his work is identified: 'the medium is the message'.

His provocative and deliberately outrageous formulations of his ideas received wide attention and he became one of the most well-known public figures of the 1960s. His thesis was that as society switched its attention from the printed word towards electronic media of communication, books would disappear and the characteristics of a particular medium would influence the individual more than the content it carried. He argued that electronic communication would create a world of instant awareness, 'the global village' in which a sense of private identity would be impossible. Much of his commentary is still valid, but the attention-grabbing style in which he expressed it has dated badly and this has led to an eclipse of his reputation.

Further reading

Marchand, P. (1998) *Marshall McLuhan: The Medium and the Messenger*, MIT Press.

SEE ALSO: communication; mass media

MASS MEDIA

Organizations using INFORMATION AND COMMUNICATION TECHNOLOGY to manufacture and distribute public messages, in the form of information and entertainment, to large, dispersed and anonymous audiences. The key characteristics of such organizations are that the communication process is normally one-way, not interactive or reciprocal, and that the flow is from the few to the many, who are anonymous from the perspective of the producers. In normal usage the mass media are understood to include book PUBLISHING, newspapers and magazines,

FILM, radio and television. Other technologies, including records (vinyl, cassette and compact disc) and video recordings, are sometimes included in what is unavoidably an imprecise, umbrella term. The INTERNET is now sometimes described as a mass medium, but both common sense and pedantry suggest it is better conceived of as a new technology and system by which mass-media organizations and others distribute or access information. The size of the audience is not the defining criterion. In many countries in recent years cinema-going has become a habit largely restricted to a minority (mostly young) section of the population. While cinema retains some of the characteristics of a mass medium, the majority of film viewing is on television screens, either from broadcasting or videotapes.

While essentially a plural phrase, in recent decades the term mass media has commonly, if irritatingly to many ears, been used in the singular. Raymond Williams (1976) notes that the term incorporates three converging senses. First, it denotes an agency or intervening substance. Thus newspapers are the means by which news is distributed to their readers. Second, the term media refers to the technologies. Third, as they have evolved in capitalist societies, the media are the carrier of some other material than originally intended. Thus broadcasting or newspapers become the media for the transmission of advertising to consumers. It is in this sense that it is sometimes suggested that the economic function of commercial television is to rent its viewers to its advertisers.

All mass media develop from small-scale beginnings, often lacking at least one of the defining characteristics. Newspapers, for example, evolve from the provision of newsletters for private patrons, through the evolution of printing after the late fifteenth century, into pamphlet accounts of single events and the corantos of seventeenth-century Europe providing general news of a short period for a wider readership. These only become the full-blown newspapers of the eighteenth century, published daily and with a miscellaneous content, with the establishment of joint stock companies to provide the financial basis for their production. In the nineteenth century, population increases and urbanization provided a new audience, while technological innovation (steam printing, the rotary press, wood-pulp-based paper) provided the means for large-scale production. The growth of consumer markets, the 'retail revolution', and with it the advertising industry, provided the basis for the commercial expansion of the newspaper industry into its twentieth-century form.

As this example illustrates, the mass media are first and foremost industries, whose form and social function can best be understood by their relation to the wider economy and to changing social conditions. In the twentieth century the media grew into a major industrial sector, occupying a key place in most advanced economies. They also provide the main means by which people occupy their leisure time. This has led to five features of their recent growth. First, the media are dominated by multinational businesses such as News Corporation, Disney, Viacom and AOL Time Warner. Such companies operate across most media sectors. Second, the provision of entertainment and information has become increasingly mixed, with popular newspapers in particular significantly driven by entertainment objectives, while the film and television industries are largely integrated. Third, the introduction of new technologies has made the definition of mass media much less certain. Cable, video and satellite have changed the character of BROAD-CASTING, while the rapid evolution of computing and TELECOMMUNICATIONS has revolutionized newspaper production. Fourth, the growth of pay-television and the massive expansion of broadcast material available on increasing numbers of diverse channels have begun to create a differentiated audience for broadcasting. This, coupled with the 'digital divide', which has led to a major gap in access to and experience of new technologies between low- and high-income countries, and between low- and high-income groups within countries, is beginning to create a fragmented and varied experience of mass media that questions the very definition of the term. Finally, the previous developments have all posed new questions about state and international policy, and regulation of the mass media.

All states have sought to control the media, from the earliest licensing of printers. This regulation attempts to control two aspects of the media: their industrial and organizational form on the one hand, and the content of what they distribute on the other. Growing diversity of distribution technologies allied to the increasing power of multinational media companies have changed the ability and, in many cases, the desire of nation-states to regulate the media. In parti-

cular, public broadcasting organizations, notably in Europe, have seen their centrality challenged by the expansion of the private sector. In some countries concern about the content of the media (particularly relating to sex and violence, or, notably in Third World countries, the impact of imported material on cultural sovereignty and integrity) has conflicted with a desire to encourage their industrial development. The intrinsic conflict between industrial and cultural policy is likely to continue to be a feature of mass-media regulation.

References

Williams, R. (1976) *Keywords: A Vocabulary of Culture and Society*, London: Fontana

Further reading

Garnham, N. (2000) *Emancipation, the Media, and Modernity*, London: Oxford University Press. [A theoretical discussion of the modern media opposing arguments for post-modernism or information societies as useful descriptions of recent changes. Despite polemic and a theoretical style, a valuable and insightful account of key issues.]

McQuail, D. (2000) *McQuail's Mass Communication Theory: An Introduction*, 4th edn, London: Sage. [The most widely used and authoritative textbook reviewing a broad range of research and debate.]

Thussu, D.K. (2000) *International Communication: Continuity and Change*, London: Arnold. [Critical and informed account, mainly of broadcasting, telecommunications and related sectors, with relevant theoretical and empirical material.]

Tunstall, J. and Machin, D. (1999) *The Anglo-American Media Connection*, London: Oxford University Press. [A clear descriptive account of the recent development of the USA and UK media worlds, and their global expansion, connections and rivalries.]

SEE ALSO: book trade; broadcasting; film; knowledge industries; telecommunications

PETER GOLDING

MEDICAL INFORMATICS

Introduction

Medical INFORMATICS can be described as the scientific field that combines biomedical information with COMPUTER SCIENCES, psychology, epidemiology and engineering. To understand the concept of medical informatics it is first necessary to understand how medical data is compiled and the various uses and communication of that information.

Medical data is primarily derived from patient activity, e.g. the amount of time a patient spends on a waiting list prior to visiting the consultant, the length of stay of a patient in a hospital bed, the type and amount of drug used to treat a specific condition and the trialing of drugs or devices with patients prior to use in the medical field. Vast amounts of data are generated by patient activity and biomedical research. Medical information is used to plan, control, manage and monitor healthcare services. The efficient collection, collation and dissemination of information and, subsequently, resources is crucial to the effective management of health services, hence a robust and sophisticated approach to the use of computer and communications systems is required to be adopted in the medical arena.

Ted Shortliffe of Columbia University, New York, is quoted as saying:

[T]hat the emergence of Medical Informatics as a new discipline is due in a large part to the rapid advances in computing and communications technology, to an increasing awareness that the knowledge base of biomedicine is essentially unmanageable by traditional paper based methods, and to a growing conviction that the process of informed decision making is as important to modern biomedicine as is the collection of facts upon which clinical decisions or research plans are made.
(Quoted at www.cs.man.ac.uk/mig/links/what.-medinfo.html)

Evidence-based medicine

The need to support clinical decisions with evidence in a structured way rather than relying upon personal experience or the oral exchange of information from peers is a relatively new concept in medicine. It is of course an obvious step and one that has been long overdue for the patient. David Sackett developed the principles of evidence-based medicine (EBM) in Canada. To provide information for clinical decision-making demands an infrastructure of INFORMATION AND COMMUNICATION TECHNOLOGY, trained personnel and systems for the provision of textual and statistical information. It also requires acceptance of the concept from the clinical staff. The Sackett principles dictate that the best evidence is found.

Evidence is graded according to clearly defined rules. This can be controversial as one clinician may accept a set of research findings as definitive and yet another colleague may disagree.

An international perspective

The history of medical informatics is rooted in the North American model of healthcare services, where healthcare is provided for a specified fee and the patient must provide an assurance of method of payment to the healthcare provider prior to treatment. This almost invariably involves the use of insurance schemes. The patient is usually insured by his or her employer, thus guaranteeing payment for healthcare service. To manage such health schemes, which generate a great volume of patient data that has to be linked to financial data, specialized computer systems are used. This was the origin of the interest from the late 1970s onwards in the development of systems that did more than merely allocate a fee for the treatment of a specific condition.

The use of information in management of patients by using EBM is clearly an active and developing use of medical informatics by medical and nursing staff and by other practitioners of professions allied to medicine, exemplified in the work of the NHS Centre for Reviews and Dissemination, housed at the University of York, UK. The Centre has established a database of international reputation for Randomized Control Trials (RCT) known as the Cochrane Collaboration. The RCT is often regarded as the pivotal information in clinical decision-making.

The United Kingdom experience

The National Health Service (NHS) in the UK is a multimillion pound organization employing nearly 1 million people; therefore it is essential that all data be managed efficiently. The NHS will need to invest in a substantially improved infrastructure of computing provision within the service until 2005 to meet current demands and future expectations.

One of the major developments in the use of medical informatics in the UK is the establishment of NHS Direct (www.nhsdirect.nhs.uk). This is a health information service for the use of the general public. The service is nurse-led and activated by telephone; each enquiry from the public is answered by nursing staff using a controlled protocol. The decision tree process contained in the protocol is designed to reassure the enquirer and provide basic advice, prior to contacting a doctor and /or seeking medical treatment.

NHS Direct can also be accessed via the Internet. This version contains decision trees for searching for specific enquiries, general language can be used and specialized medical knowledge is not always required. The advantage of using the Internet application is that the enquirer can investigate in his or her own time without a third party and view or print the material immediately. The Internet service is planned to be fully interactive in the next few years.

Although many similar services can be found on the Internet, NHS Direct is probably uniquely authoritative as an information system intended for patients rather than service providers.

A major component of the NHS's informatics development is the Electronic Patient Record (EPR), which can be seen as the backbone of the medical informatics concept in the NHS. The EPR is designed to capture all of the data about an individual patient in a single record, rather than allowing many to exist in various agencies. This is a major paradigm shift in the recording of patient information in the NHS. The focus is on the patient not the condition or disease and it is a holistic approach to the management of information about the patient in the NHS. The EPR is being developed and has six levels of data specification. The use of the EPR demands the strategic and standardized provision of ICT facilities throughout the NHS. It also demands a culture shift in the staff's approach to using information. The use of the EPR will necessitate sharing of patient information by healthcare professionals within the same organization and also between primary and secondary sectors of the service. The benefits of improved access to patient-centred data via the EPR for all healthcare professionals will be subsequently measured in the improvement for patients in both ease and speed of treatment and information provision.

Conclusions

Medical informatics is an invaluable tool for the future use of the vast amounts of patient and biomedical information generated by both medical services and the pharmaceutical industry, enabling it to be managed and used for the benefit of the patient and the services. However, international standards for the creation, access and dissemination need to be understood and accepted, and are still awaiting development despite the work that has been done at York.

Further reading

Shortliffe, E.H. (ed.) (2000) *Medical Informatics: Computer Applications in Health Care and Biomedicine*, New York: Springer-Verlag.
Wyatt, J.C. (2000) *Clinical Knowledge and Practice in the Information Age: A Handbook for Health Professionals*, London: RSM Press.

SEE ALSO: evidence-based healthcare; health science libraries

JANET HARRISON

MEGABYTE

One million BYTEs of digital data; usually written as Mb.

SEE ALSO: informatics; information and communication technology

MENU

A list of choices in a computer system, presented on screen by a program that allows the user to select a particular option and indicate it in one of a number of ways such as pressing the 'Return' key or the mouse button. Menus range from very simple text lists occupying the entire screen, to pull-down or pop-up menus that appear from a menu bar or icon.

METADATA

Metadata are structured information used to find, access, use and manage information resources, primarily in a digital environment. A metadata scheme consists of a pre-defined set of elements that contain information about a resource. Two major factors influenced the development of metadata schemes: the need for systematic discovery and retrieval of networked resources; and the ability to embed metadata in the digital object.

The term 'metadata' is a late entry in the vocabulary of the organization of information, but the concept is not. Librarians, information specialists and archivists used 'bibliographic data' to organize and produce a variety of retrieval tools, including CATALOGUES, INDEXES and FINDING AIDS. In the 1980s, computer scientists began to use the term 'metadata' to describe information that documented the characteristics of the data contained in DATABASE MANAGEMENT SYSTEMS (DBMS). This use in DBMS popularized the definition of metadata as 'data about data' and began association of the term with a computer environment. The various methods of information organization converged in the network environment of the 1990s, and 'metadata' became the common term for information about a resource.

As the number of digital resources increased, information organizers questioned the practicality of applying detailed, labour-intensive bibliographic standards to volatile electronic resources. Some information communities abandoned library standards such as the ANGLO-AMERICAN CATALOGUING RULES (AACR) and the MACHINE-READABLE CATALOGUING (MARC) format to develop simpler systems for digital resource discovery and retrieval. This resulted in the development of a wide variety of metadata schemes.

Some metadata schemes, such as the DUBLIN CORE Metadata Element Set (DCMES), are general in nature and are designed to accommodate information about digital resources in a wide variety of formats and disciplines. Other metadata schemes, such as the Categories of Description for Works of Art (CDWA), are specialized and apply to information in a specific medium or within a specific discipline. Common to all metadata schemes is a set of defined data elements that describe the resource. Beyond that, each scheme varies as to the number, definition and content of data elements.

Metadata functions

Metadata assist both humans and computers in a variety of descriptive, structural or administrative functions. Descriptive metadata, like traditional bibliographic data, identify a resource, describe its attributes, characterize its relationships to other resources and provide location and evaluative data for the resource. Structural metadata provide information that links together the separate files of a composite resource and provides the computer with architectural guidelines for storage, navigation, sequence and presentation of the resource. Administrative metadata are often divided into subcategories, including technical,

provenance, preservation and rights management information. Technical metadata supply information about the digitization process, file format details, technical aspects of images or sound, or migration data. PROVENANCE metadata provide information about the original source of a digitized object and track its authenticity. PRESERVATION metadata help ensure that the digital object exists and is technically accessible over the long term and include information about encryption techniques, file modification history and operating-system environment. Rights management metadata include information on INTELLECTUAL PROPERTY, reproduction and access rights. The creation and maintenance of metadata is often a collaborative effort that takes place over the life cycle of a resource, with a variety of individuals and organizations contributing to the process.

Metadata characteristics and standards

Characteristics common to all metadata include semantics, syntax and structure. Semantics refers to the number, type and content of metadata elements, and can vary from simple metadata sets with two or three data elements, to complex schemes with many data elements and content prescribed by standards and rules. Syntax refers to the way in which content is structured according to a specified grammar. Metadata syntax may range from an undefined syntax like the original DCMES to a complex coding system such as a mark-up language (see MARK-UP LANGUAGES) like Standard Generalized Mark-up Language (SGML). Structure refers to the overall architecture that contains the metadata content and syntax. The structure is based on standards and technology that form the foundation for the metadata's storage, transmittal and use. Metadata may be embedded in the digital object they describe and extracted as needed, or they may reside in a separately indexed database. The data can be contained in a variety of architectural structures, including Z39.50-compliant library catalogues, proprietary databases or the Resource Description Framework (RDF) standard.

Interoperability and extensibility are desirable characteristics of metadata schemes. Interoperability refers to the ability to transfer metadata among different schemes and information systems. A core element set that is common to all metadata schemes will facilitate the exchange and use of metadata at a general level of description and retrieval. Extensibility allows expansion of the core element set to provide more precise description and retrieval. Element qualifiers are used to narrow the meaning of an element. Encoding scheme qualifiers are used to identify the standards used and to help interpret the content of a metadata element. Extensibility provides greater specificity in description and retrieval, but creates a more complex syntax for interoperability.

Standards are critical for successful metadata interoperability and may be applied to data content, formal syntax or parsing rules and metadata architectures. Crosswalks map data elements from one metadata set to another to assist data conversion across information systems and to facilitate interoperability. Successful crosswalk mapping requires standardized elements, syntax and structure.

Research

Ongoing research aims to test and improve many aspects of the metadata process. Projects cover areas such as assessment of subject-specific metadata needs; development of tools to automate metadata creation; and design of new architectures to support the efficient and accurate exchange of data among different systems and communities.

Further reading

Baca, M. (ed.) (1998) *Introduction to Metadata: Pathways to Digital Information*, Getty Information Institute.

Dempsey, L. and Heery, R.M. (1998) 'Metadata: A current view of practice and issues', *Journal of Documentation* 52(4): 145–72.

Hudgins, J., Agnew, G. and Brown, E. (1999) *Getting Mileage out of Metadata: Applications for the Library*, American Library Association.

Vellucci, S.L. (1999) 'Metadata', *Annual Review of Information Science and Technology* 33: 187–222.

SEE ALSO: bibliographic description; digital library; informatics; information retrieval; markup languages; organization of knowledge; standards specifications

SHERRY L. VELLUCCI

MICROFORMS

Miniaturized graphic communications media, generally on film, but also on paper or card, and containing for the most part print, but occasionally diagrams, drawings and other illustrations also. Some equipment or device for enlarging the image is required in order to 'read' the medium.

There are several types of microform, distinguished by their format and other characteristics. They may be broadly categorized into roll microfilm, microfiche, micro-opaques and miniaturized print, but there are other variants.

Roll microfilm is customarily available in standard widths of 35 mm or 16 mm and is generally supplied on open reels. The 35 mm format, with its relatively large frame size, is particularly suitable for recording newspaper pages, engineering drawings, charts and plans. The 16 mm format is useful for recording periodicals and has found a role in special applications such as recording correspondence and business ARCHIVES. Alternatives to the open reel, employing permanent housing of the film within a container, such as a cassette (with two built-in reels or cores) or a cartridge (with a single reel or core), have been developed to overcome some of the basic inconvenience and risk of damage associated with handling loose film and threading it into viewers.

Several systems have been developed for coding roll film to identify individual frames to facilitate document image retrieval.

An adaptation of roll microfilm is unitized microfilm, in which short lengths of cut film are used for image storage. In this way small documents, or single periodical articles can be individually treated, although there are some attendant handling difficulties. A further development, which was of some significance when punched cards were popular for sorting and retrieval, was the use of unitized microfilm in aperture cards. These incorporated a piece of microfilm as an insert in a 'window' in a standard punched card.

Microfiche is basically a flat rectangle of sheet film upon which images are recorded. Several sizes of microfiche may be encountered but the most common currently available is equivalent to the international A6 paper size. Superfiche and Ultrafiche are variants created by more sophisticated and precise technology. Superfiche images are reduced by seventy-five times to provide about 1,000 frames per sheet. Ultrafiche images are reduced by 150 times to provide about 3,200 frames per sheet. Jacketed fiche, which may be regarded as an extension of unitized microfilm, features the use of transparent carriers or 'jackets' into which short lengths of film are inserted to facilitate storage and protection when handling.

Both roll microfilm and microfiche are available in monochrome (black and white) or colour, though the latter is quite expensive and consequently scarcer in libraries. Monochrome film may be either negative (white print on a black background) or positive (black print on a white background).

Computer Output Microfilm (COM) is a term that does not strictly describe a microform format but rather the means by which information is recorded on the medium. Information from computer processing is directly output and recorded on to microfiche rather than paper (or screens), utilizing special equipment to produce it.

Micro-opaques, also called microcard or microprint, are sheets of opaque flat card on which images are recorded, either photographically or by photolithography. Partly because of the need for specialized viewers and because of the difficulty of achieving quality of enlarged images comparable to microfilm and microfiche, their appeal is not great.

Miniaturized print represents the transition from true microform to conventional print. For this format material is reduced by two or four times from the original and produced photolithographically. It can just be read with the naked eye, although it is more usual and comfortable to use a hand-magnifier. This format allows a significant reduction in the volume of material to be accomplished but without the need for sophisticated equipment. Miniaturized print has found a particularly useful application for otherwise bulky reference books, of which the *Oxford English Dictionary* and the *British Museum Catalogue of Printed Books* are examples.

Microforms have fulfilled an important role in COLLECTION DEVELOPMENT in library and information services, and in the broad area of administrative processes also. The use of microforms as a document publishing medium for a variety of material, including books, pamphlets, periodicals, theses, papers and manuscripts, has had a significant impact on library collection-building. They have brought economy in terms of production and duplication, storage and transportation of both original and republished material. They have also contributed to increasing the availability of copies of important and scarce items, and at the same time contributed towards the preservation of material. Microform document publishing practices may be divided into categories: original or primary publishing, where material makes its first appearance in microform; parallel publishing, where paper and microform versions appear simultaneously; and retrospective publishing, where previously published paper material is produced or 'reprinted' in microform. Microform is also used as a tool of PRESERVATION; users are required to consult films of rare, valuable or damaged documents in order to protect the originals.

In addition to their potential for general administrative applications, such as the filming and storage of correspondence and financial records or the copying and distribution of local reports and documents, microforms have featured in more specialized areas of library and information service management. They formed an important stage in the evolution of the library catalogue (see CATALOGUES) with the introduction of COM for the production and distribution of catalogues, although this phase of development is now largely superseded by Online Public-Access Catalogues (OPACS).

Microforms are a medium dependent on equipment, together with a certain level of user skill. The design and quality of microforms and equipment are therefore critical to their successful exploitation, as is the provision of a suitable reading environment. The availability of viewing and printing machines goes some way to overcoming the user resistance to reading microforms for sustained periods, although much of the technology that is available is still of old-fashioned and inconvenient design.

Microform material has established a very useful niche in library and information services and it is now a feature of services and collections in libraries of various types and sizes. In the 1940s there was speculation that microforms would rapidly displace paper and print material for many purposes. More recently the speedy eclipse of microform by the newer electronic media, particularly CD-ROM, has been forecast. The current reality encompasses neither of these scenarios. Though early claims for the popularity of microforms were undoubtedly exaggerated, a role emerged for them. They will continue for some time to provide a useful and inexpensive means of archiving and distributing specialized documentation.

Further reading

British Standards Institution *Micrographics – Vocabulary*, BS ISO 6196 (all parts in the series).
Davies, J.E. (1982) 'Why microforms? Management experience in a modern university library', *International Journal of Micrographics and Video Technology* 1(4): 183–98.
Teague, S.J. (1985) *Microform, Video and Electronic Media Librarianship*, London: Butterworths.

SEE ALSO: informatics; knowledge industries

J.E. DAVIES, REVISED BY THE EDITORS

MIDDLE EAST

The Middle East includes all the Arab countries and Turkey, Iran, Afghanistan and Israel. All the Arab countries have Arabic as a native language. English, French and German are widely known among educated people throughout the region.

Egypt, Turkey and Iran are the biggest countries in terms of population (60 million). Sudan, Saudi Arabia, Algeria and Mauritania are the biggest in terms of total area (2–2.5 million sq. km). In terms of national income Saudi Arabia is the richest country in the region. Generally speaking, more than half of the population in the Middle East are illiterate. Book publishing is modest. Annual income per capita varies drastically from one country to another. In petroleum countries the average is $100,000. In non-petroleum countries the average is only $1,000.

The library situation is affected by local conditions, so it differs greatly from one country to another. This account tries to illustrate the general picture of the library movement in the region as a whole.

National libraries

The majority of countries in the region have NATIONAL LIBRARIES or libraries playing the role of a national library; for example in Israel and Afghanistan, where the university library is the national library as well. These are the Hebrew University Library in Israel and Kabul University Library in Afghanistan. Some national libraries play a dual role as national and public libraries. The oldest and biggest national library in the Middle East is the Egyptian National Library (Dar Al Kutub Al Misryyah), with its 3 million printed books and 80,000 manuscripts. It holds also a great quantity of papyri and coins. It was founded in 1870 and in 2002 was joined by the new Library of Alexandria as an Egyptian national and regional library. The youngest and smallest national library in the region is that of the United Arab Emirates (1984). The national library in the majority of countries is responsible for the NATIONAL BIBLIOGRAPHY, as in Egypt, Tunisia, Algeria, Iraq and Qatar. The Egyptian National Bibliography is the oldest in the region (1955). Countries without national libraries are Oman, Bahrain, Jordan and Kuwait.

Table 17 illustrates the dates of foundation of the major national libraries in the region.

Public libraries

The public library movement in the Middle East is very weak if compared with Europe or North America, and in respect of the total population of the region. In countries like Egypt and Iran there are only 300 PUBLIC LIBRARIES for 60 million people in each country. In Saudi Arabia there are

Table 17 National libraries in the Middle East

Egypt	1870	Iraq	1963
Syria	1880	Qatar	1963
Tunisia	1885	Mauritania	1965
Morocco	1920	Saudi Arabia	1968
Lebanon	1921	Yemen	1968
Iran	1935	Libya	1972
Turkey	1946	United Arab Emirates	1984
Algeria	1963		

Source: Shaban A. Khalifa (1991) *Egyptian National Library, Cairo*, Al Arabi Publishing House [in Arabic]

only thirty libraries for 10 million inhabitants. In Iraq, seventy-seven libraries serve 20 million people. In Turkey, however, the situation is much better, with 600 public libraries.

Holdings of public libraries vary from several hundreds of volumes to several hundreds of thousands. The main library materials to be found in these libraries are books and periodicals. Some libraries in Turkey, Egypt, Morocco and Iran hold manuscripts; a very few public libraries hold audiovisual materials in Egypt, Tunisia and Saudi Arabia.

The majority of public libraries in the region use traditional methods in controlling their collections. There are few libraries using automated integrated systems; they include Greater Cairo Public Library, Guiza Public Library and Heliopolis Public Library in Egypt, and Jeddah Public Library in Saudi Arabia.

Public libraries in Middle Eastern countries are operated by various agencies; among these we can distinguish:

1 National libraries, where many of them run a system of public libraries as branches. This is found in countries like Egypt, Qatar and Tunisia.
2 Ministries of Culture, as in Tunisia, Morocco, Syria and Turkey.
3 Ministries of Education, as in Turkey, Iran, Egypt, Lebanon and Bahrain.
4 Ministries of Endowments. Since almost all countries of the region are Muslim, these ministries operate many public libraries.
5 Ministries of Mass Communications, as in Qatar, Iraq and other countries.
6 Municipalities. In many countries of the region municipalities run some public libraries, as in Iran, Egypt and Turkey. According to the Iranian Library Act of 1965, each municipality has to allocate 1.5 per cent of its revenue to public libraries. In some countries we find different agencies operating public libraries of their own.

The total number of public libraries in the region does not exceed 2,000 libraries for more than 400 million inhabitants.

School libraries

Generally speaking, education before university is divided into three stages: elementary (primary), preparatory and secondary. There are three kinds of schools in the region: government schools, private schools and foreign schools.

Elementary SCHOOL LIBRARIES are only collections of not more than a few hundred books, often uncatalogued and unclassified. These books are put there only for circulation among pupils and are held without change for many years.

The majority of preparatory and secondary schools have real libraries, with collections ranging from 3,000 to 15,000 volumes. Few school libraries hold periodicals and audiovisual materials; very few school libraries hold machine-readable data files or optical disks. Catalogues are still in card form in the majority of these libraries. Some libraries, as in Qatar, Iraq, Egypt, Tunisia, Iran, Turkey and Syria, do not have any kind of catalogues. School libraries are often open access.

Library services are limited to lending and simple reference services. These libraries are usually run by unqualified persons.

University libraries

All the countries of the Middle East have institutions of higher education. The oldest universities are to be found in Egypt: Al Azhar University (a religious institution) was founded more than 1,000 years ago; Cairo University was founded in 1908.

Some countries of the region have upwards of fifteen universities, as do Turkey and Egypt; some have only one university, as do Qatar, Bahrain, Tunisia and Oman. Independent colleges are widespread in many countries.

There are different levels of UNIVERSITY LIBRARIES in Middle Eastern countries. Some universities have only one library for all faculties to serve both undergraduates and postgraduates, and for both students and staff. This situation is found in Saudi Arabia, Qatar and Bahrain, for example. Some universities have two libraries, one for staff members and postgraduate students, the other for undergraduate students. Some universities do not have a main central library, but only faculty libraries. On the other hand some universities have three levels of libraries, i.e. a central library, faculty libraries and departmental libraries. The central library offers service to all faculties, all departments, all students and all staff members. The faculty library is used only by students and staff members of that particular faculty. The departmental library is used only by students and staff members of that particular department.

Some universities are very big, for example Cairo University with its 100,000 undergraduate students, 20,000 postgraduate students and 16,000 staff members. Some universities are very small, for example Qatar University with its 5,000 students and 300 staff members.

Collections of university libraries range from 150,000 volumes to over 1 million volumes. Faculty libraries' collections range from 15,000 volumes to 100,000 volumes. Departmental libraries' collections are usually small because they serve a narrow area; they range around 1,000–2,000 volumes. Periodicals, microforms, audio-visual materials, machine-readable data files and optical laser disks form an important part of university libraries' collections in many countries. Some university libraries are still primitive in handling library materials and services. Some are fully automated, such as Qatar University and the Saudi universities. Services in the majority of university libraries are limited to lending materials. Only a few libraries offer advanced services such as CURRENT AWARENESS, SDI, reference services or ONLINE searches.

Seating capacity is very low in respect of the users' community in many of the libraries; for example, Cairo University Library has only 200 seats for 150,000 users. Seating capacity is adequate in Saudi libraries, at Qatar University, and in Oman, the Emirates, Bahrain and Kuwait.

Some libraries are overstaffed, e.g. Cairo University Library with its 550 workers. On the other hand some are understaffed, as in Afghanistan and Tunisia. Generally speaking, there is a shortage of qualified and professional staff.

Special libraries

SPECIAL LIBRARIES in the Middle Eastern countries belong to different agencies:

Parliamentary agencies.
Justice departments and law courts.
Government departments.
Research centres.
Armed forces.
Scientific societies.
Guilds and professional societies.
Special clubs.

The work of a special library is determined by the brief of the agency of which it is part. The library of the Ministry of Agriculture works in the field of agriculture; the library of a bank deals with money, economics and banking. So special libraries cover a wide range of specializations. There is a great number of these libraries in many countries of the region. In Egypt, for example, there are more than 5,000 special libraries, and in Turkey more than 3,000 libraries.

Some countries are very poor in special libraries, for example Afghanistan, Mauritania, Algeria and Sudan. Some special libraries are very rich, for example NIDOC (National Information and Documentation Centre) in Egypt with its 300,000 volumes and 1,000 periodical titles. Some are fully automated but the majority are still primitive in handling materials and services.

Many of these libraries are run by unqualified persons without even a specialized background in the field of the library.

Cataloguing and classification in Middle Eastern libraries

DDC is widespread among the libraries of the region either in the original form or in an adapted version and translation. UDC is used only in some special libraries. LC is used in a few university libraries. Many still use local classifications and artificial classifications by size or accession number. ANGLO-AMERICAN CATALOGUING RULES (AACR2) are adopted either in the original version or in an adapted, modified and translated version.

Library education

Many countries in the Middle East have formal library and information education. Some of them have more than one school. In Egypt there are ten schools offering undergraduate and postgraduate studies. In Saudi Arabia there are five schools at both levels. In Iraq there are five schools. Turkey, Israel, Tunisia, Morocco, Libya, Lebanon, Syria, Qatar, Kuwait, Bahrain, Algeria, Sudan and Jordan all have formal LIBRARY EDUCATION. Qatar, Bahrain and Jordan offer only postgraduate education.

Degrees obtained are Bachelor's, Diploma, Master's and Doctorate. Some schools follow the credit hours system, while some follow the full academic-year system. The oldest and biggest school in the region is the one at Cairo

University, with 1,200 students in both levels and sixty staff members. This school was opened in 1950/1.

Library associations

There is a regional library association for the Arab countries called the Arab Federation for Libraries and Information (AFLI). This federation was set up in January 1986. Not all countries of the Middle East have national LIBRARY ASSOCIA-TIONS. Countries with library associations are Egypt, Tunisia, Syria, Iraq, Jordan, Iran, Turkey and Lebanon. In Egypt there are several library associations: the Egyptian Association for Libraries, Information and Archives; the School Library Association; the Society of Microforms and Information; the Society of Information Systems. The oldest and biggest in the region is the Egyptian Association for Libraries, Information and Archives. It was set up in 1948 and membership has now reached 20,000.

Professional publications

There are several current periodicals issued in the region in Arabic and English. The most famous are *Modern Trends in Library and Information Studies*, *School Library Journal* (both in Egypt), *Arab Journal for Librarianship and Information Science* (Saudi Arabia) and *Library Journal* (Jordan). In addition, there are subject headings lists, classification schemes and authority lists of names. There are plenty of monographs, research papers, seminars and conference papers. It is estimated that fifty new titles are issued every year in the region dealing with librarianship and information either in Arabic or in English, or translated.

Further reading

Sardar, Z. (1988) *Information and the Muslim World: A Strategy for the Twenty-First Century*, Mansell.
Sernikli, A. (1995) 'National libraries in Turkey, Middle East and Central Asia', *Newsletter of the IFLA Section of National Libraries*' (June): 29–43.
Wise, M. and Olden, A. (eds) (1994) *Information and Libraries in the Arab World*, Library Association Publishing.

SHABAN A. KHALIFA

MIDDLEWARE

Software that connects NETWORKS with computer applications, sometimes referred to as 'glue'. Rather than requiring applications to provide their own identification, authentication, authorization, directories and security, these can be provided through the agency of middleware. This promotes standards and improves interoperability across networks, allowing applications to function more effectively in a resource-sharing environment.

Further reading

NSF Middleware Initiative (www.nsf-middleware.org).

MILITARY INTELLIGENCE

The increasing importance and use of information in human activity is nowhere more visible than in the field of military intelligence. The revolutions in information practice and technology that occurred in the twentieth century, first manual in nature and later automated, were reflected in the gradually increasing status that has been awarded to military intelligence in the planning of warfare and state security.

In the context of military affairs and state security, intelligence is an activity that has to perform a series of informational functions: appropriate data about opponents has to be identified, acquired, confirmed, organized, correlated and interpreted, and the resultant information made available to those who need it. Good intelligence may be succinctly defined as up-to-date information about the enemy that has been distilled by experts from raw data.

Information about other countries is now recognised as an indispensable resource for the well-being of the sovereign nation state. Such information can be economic, scientific, technological, diplomatic, political or military in character, but each are interlinked and overlap, meaning that any effective effort to gather and analyse military information inevitably takes account of intelligence drawn from other spheres of activity. This holistic view of military intelligence makes sense when one examines the definition of 'intelligence' *per se*: the ability not only to acquire but also apply knowledge. Intelligence, derived from the Latin '*intelligere*' (to understand), entails the processing and analysing of data, which is best achieved when contextual or impinging knowledge is utilised. In this respect, the term 'military intelligence' might easily be replaced by 'military information', in recognition of the argument that information in its modern meaning is the result of raw data having been worked upon and appropriately organized for consumption by the human mind.

There are essentially three types of military intelligence – to be distinguished from methods used to obtain it, such as reconnaissance (discontinuous, mobile observation), SURVEILLANCE (stationary, continuous observation) and signals interception and decryption (codebreaking). *Strategic intelligence* comprises information obtained about the aims and capabilities of other nations and is at a premium before battle arises. There are any number of examples in history of the importance of strategic intelligence to those collecting it. In the third century BC, in all the battles that the Carthaginian general Hannibal fought in Italy he was significantly outnumbered and was thus forced to rely heavily on strategic intelligence to help him decide when and where he engaged the enemy. In late 1941 Stalin's spies were able to tell him that Japan's strategic ambitions lay in the direction of the Pacific, thereby enabling him to transfer troops trained in winter warfare from the Far East to protect the beleaguered cities of Moscow and Leningrad. One of the most celebrated events in the history of military intelligence is the success of the British in the Second World War in breaking the German military code with the help of a captured Enigma machine designed for mechanical enciphering, thereby giving the Allies access to German plans at the strategic as well as the tactical level.

Tactical intelligence comprises information at the operational, combat level that is sought after by commanders whose aim it is to direct forces to accomplish strategic objectives. Before the era of modern warfare, obtaining and exploiting intelligence on the battlefield was chiefly a communications problem. The speed of communication, by such means as written reports delivered by messenger, was slow. However, with the development of telegraph, telephone radio and radar (and now satellite technology), communications within the arena of battle became 'real time'. Although this has guaranteed neither the accuracy of the information being transmitted nor, because easier communication vastly increased the volume of information being carried, its speedy processing and analysis, instantaneous transmission of information has arguably

nonetheless enhanced the ability of leaders to make effective decisions. It has also improved the status of intelligence in the operational arena, where historically reliance was mostly on material superiority and the genius and intuition of commanders.

The third form of military intelligence – *counter-intelligence* – is essentially defensive in nature. It relates to information about the intelligence capability of an opponent and is essentially about neutralizing the threat posed by foreign spies and internal insurgents. The development of counter-intelligence in the United Kingdom in the twentieth century shows how modern military intelligence is less about adventure and intrigue than about intellectual sweat and the mundane construction of systems for information collection and retrieval. Founded in 1909, the Security Service, which became known as MI5, was given the task of countering sabotage, ESPIONAGE and subversion at home and across the British Empire. The vast amount of information that flowed into the organization before and during the First World War forced it to construct a relatively efficient manual information management system. The hub of MI5's information activity was its registry, where documents were arranged by hundreds of clerks in subject and personal files, backed up by detailed indexing and cross-referencing in a card catalogue. At the start of the Second World War, MI5's information management system virtually collapsed due to years of neglect and a tidal wave of data flooding the system. This crisis led to informational renewal in the form of the appointment of a small army of civilian, professional knowledge workers drawn from the law, banking and the universities, and the introduction of punched-card machines, microfilming and improved card indexing.

Since the Second World War, intelligence organizations around the world like MI5 have made successful use of computers and new technologies of surveillance to gather, organize and evaluate data. This has increased dramatically the contribution of intelligence to the conduct of military affairs, although the rise of international terrorism since the 1970s has shown that even the most sophisticated information systems cannot prevent 'intelligence failure' resulting in devastating surprise attacks.

Throughout most of human history it has been possible to conduct warfare without intelligence, however ineffective the result may have been. But to go to war without armed forces has until now been impossible. With the advent of information warfare, however, where theoretically victory can be claimed without recourse to bomb, bullet or missile by targeting the information infrastructure of the enemy, the importance of information capability in the military sphere has never been more important.

Further reading

Aldrich, R.J. (1998) *Espionage, Security and Intelligence in Britain 1945–1970*, Manchester University Press.

Black, A. and Brunt, R. (2000) 'MI5, 1909–1945: And information management perspective', *Journal of Information Science* 26(3): 185–97.

Handel, M.I. (ed.) (1990) *Intelligence and Military Operations*, Frank Cass.

Hinsley, F.H. (1993) *British Intelligence in the Second World War*, abridged edn, HMSO.

House, J.M. (1993) *Military Intelligence, 1870–1991: A Research Guide*, Greenwood Press.

Sebag-Montefiore, H. (2000) *Enigma: The Battle for the Code*, Weidenfeld & Nicolson.

Sheldon, R.M. (1986) 'Hannibal's spies', *International Journal of Intelligence and Counterintelligence* 1(3): 53–70.

ALISTAIR BLACK

MINITEL

A French videotex system, based on low-cost terminals, in conjunction with a central VIDEOTEX computer system. It was introduced as a means of promoting information technology in France by making a specific aspect of it available in virtually every home, and, as such, it was a notable success. Initially it provided an electronic telephone directory service, but has subsequently carried a variety of other information and communication services. It is the largest videotex network in the world. However, its ubiquity and predominantly French-language content has arguably inhibited French take-up of the Internet, which is seen by some French commentators as over-reliant on the English language.

SEE ALSO: electronic public information services

MOBILE COMMUNICATIONS

Communications systems and devices that can be used in any location, and do not need to be physically connected to a NETWORK in order to

access it. The earliest examples were radios used for two-way COMMUNICATION in the middle of the twentieth century, chiefly for military purposes, and usually known as 'walkie-talkies'. The devices were very heavy, were normally carried in backpacks and often had to be put on the ground before they could be used. Truly mobile devices became comparatively common in civilian life only in the 1970s, with the development of Citizens' Band Radio, for which a small number of short-wave frequencies were allocated for private use. Lorry drivers warning each other of police speed traps are said to have been the most frequent users.

These early station-to-station devices, which were limited in range and in portability, have been almost entirely displaced by the now ubiquitous mobile telephone, sometimes called the 'cellular telephone', or 'cell phone'. Mobile phones became available in the 1970s in the USA (so-called 'first generation', or 'G1'), but it was not until the mid-1990s that cheap lightweight devices made them into a normal accessory of business and personal life in the developed world. This was a result of the introduction of digital services ('G2'), developed in Europe during the 1980s, and introduced commercially in 1992.

When a call is initiated, the phone sends a signal to the nearest receiving station, which then transmits that signal through a series of interlinked 'cells' until it finds the intended recipient (identified by a unique number). Whenever a mobile phone is switched on, it can be found by the nearest transmitter, although there are still areas with a small population or topographical difficulties (such as high mountains), even in North America and Western Europe, where the cellular network has not yet reached. There are links between the cellular networks and the conventional cable-based TELECOMMUNICATIONS networks. In effect, a mobile phone gives unlimited access to all the voice communications systems that can be accessed through a conventional hard-wired telephone. Perhaps the greatest single breakthrough for mobile communications, however, was the addition to the networks of the facility for text messaging (technically, Short Messaging Service, or SMS), which seems to have become the normal medium of communication for many younger (and not a few older) people throughout the Western world. At the same time, the installation of cellular networks in some parts of the developing world, and especially in SOUTHEAST ASIA, has begun to overcome some of the problems encountered by traditional PTTs, especially in rural areas.

The next phase of development will be the further digitization of the cellular networks, a process that has already begun with the hybrid 'G2.5' devices. These offer both voice communication facilities and some INTERNET access, although this is limited in functionality and very slow. At present it is normally achieved by linking the instrument to a portable computer, but the next generation ('3G') of phones will be *de facto* computers. The 3G services have been introduced in Japan, and will be gradually introduced elsewhere from late 2002 onwards. These will offer full mobile Internet facilities. Indeed, the capacity for voice communications seems likely to be one of the less commonly used functions of 3G devices; they will be networked personal computers with all the normal facilities, as well as being the equivalent of a personal stereo (often, no doubt, playing music downloaded from the Internet) and having a full range of MULTIMEDIA functionality.

Mobile devices will continue to supplement and displace conventional fixed-location hard-wired devices for the foreseeable future, and become a key element in the application of INFORMATION AND COMMUNICATION TECHNOLOGY in social and economic life. Their impact on the provision of information services can only be a matter of speculation at this stage in their development, but it seems likely to be very significant.

MOBILE LIBRARY

Variously referred to as book bus (or, in French, *bibliobus*), 'mobile library', 'bookmobile' or merely 'mobile', the term tends to be applied to motor vehicles that are used to transport collections of library materials for the benefit of users whose access to libraries is limited by distance or other impediment. More accurately applied, the term describes the collections rather than the vehicles. The distinction is worth making because the forms of transport can vary greatly, including book boats for remote coastal communities in Scandinavia, a railway coach in Mali, a donkey cart in Zimbabwe (Tate 2002b), pack camels in Kenya (Tate 2002a), pack mules in the Andes

and bicycle bags in Mozambique. The mobile-library concept improves on earlier ideas such as the itinerating libraries inaugurated by Samuel Brown (1779–1839) in early nineteenth-century Scotland. Brown's itinerating libraries were small collections of books, transported in specially constructed boxes to designated centres, where they were left for local use for a period of months, until exchanged with different collections that had been left in other participating communities. Similar book box service is still provided to rural areas in some developing countries.

In contrast a mobile library service addresses similar problems by bringing a much larger collection to a target location for a much briefer period (a few hours or less) at more frequent intervals (weekly or monthly, for instance) with only the books that have been borrowed remaining in the community until a future visit. Because of the high proportion of stock on loan, the total number of volumes available from a mobile library is normally about three times that carried on the vehicle. The content of the collection can be exchanged frequently from the base library resources and this ensures that a good range of stock is available to a regular user over a period of time.

History

The British experience can be used as an example of early development and advanced practice. The first known British travelling library was set up in Warrington in 1859. Others were then developed by the Mechanics Institutes (community self-help educational and leisure organizations invariably providing library services) during the second half of the nineteenth century. In 1904 Glasgow Public Libraries purchased a library delivery vehicle and by 1920 horse-drawn mobile libraries were replaced by motor vehicles. British county libraries were developed in the mid-twentieth century to extend library service to rural areas. They tended to rely first on book boxes sent to community centres in villages and small towns, but subsequently they developed extensive mobile library networks. By 1955 the great majority of British counties had mobile fleets.

The 1950s saw the introduction of mobile libraries into urban areas. These urban services recognized that sheer distance from fixed library service points is not the only factor isolating potential library users. People can be isolated within a larger community because of a lack of public transport, particularly if they are too frail to walk, they live in sheltered accommodation, they have a physical handicap or mental illness that does not allow them to venture out alone, they are carers for people in these categories or they are in some other way housebound. Whilst urban mobiles take the public lending library service to whole districts, in the same way that rural services do, mobile services are also provided direct to families with housebound members, or groups of people living in care institutions.

Vehicles

Without forgetting that mobile libraries are not exclusively provided using motor vehicles, it is the case, in countries where they are used extensively, that the vehicles can be used to define the types of service. The vehicles are almost always custom-built by specialist body-builders on standard chassis types. Typically there can be a number of sizes and specifications, on a variety of chassis.

HOUSEBOUND VEHICLES

These are small vehicles, normally of 6 to 7 m. Their stock generally consists of leisure reading, frequently geared to older people, e.g. large-print and spoken-word materials. They make visits at fortnightly or monthly intervals.

RURAL MOBILE LIBRARIES

Their size is larger: 8–10 m. Their stock of 2,000–3,000 volumes can include a full range of leisure material, plus audiovisual items. They provide service primarily to adult users, but include books for pre-school children on a regular basis and junior books during school holiday periods. They visit frequently, usually on a fortnightly basis.

URBAN MOBILE LIBRARIES

A typical size is 10–12 m with a stock of up to 4,500 items. In addition to a substantial collection of popular books, a representation of more advanced or scholarly works is possible. They tend to offer a good range of audio and video material, plus some reference and information resources. Mobiles of this size generally have

telephone links so as to offer information service. They visit weekly or fortnightly.

TRAILER LIBRARIES

Their size is 12 m and upwards. Their stock of 4,000 and upwards includes a range of titles comparable to that of a small- to medium-sized branch library. A networked computer can be provided in a vehicle of this size. They serve large villages and suburban communities, and visit weekly or twice a week.

SCHOOL MOBILE LIBRARIES

Vehicles, typically of 8–10 m, are used by many British public library systems to provide central support for the services provided by individual schools. They will stock 2,000–3,000 junior titles, and a school library will be able to exchange a substantial number of volumes to refresh its own collections and obtain materials on topics currently being studied by the pupils. They will normally visit each term or semester.

Technical features

The development of mobile libraries has been rapid since the mid-1970s. In Britain this has owed a great deal to regular UK Mobilemeets. Such events were organized by the Branch and Mobile Libraries Group of the Library Association and attendance by in excess of fifty mobile libraries of all varieties and 300 delegates was typical. Major improvements to be found on mobile libraries are in three categories.

1   Disabled access, including lifts, step lights, low-profile steps and improved handrails.
2   User/crew comfort and safety, with features such as automatic reversing stops, automatic doors, air curtains, carpeting, video reversing equipment, coach heating and ventilation, and opaque roof and side windows.
3   Improved stock and information provision, including adjustable shelving, paperback spinners and carousels, kinderboxes, computer circulation control, photocopiers, networked computers and CD-ROMs for information.

References

Tate, T. (2002a) *Camel Library Services in Kenya*, IFLA Professional Report 73.

—— (2002b) *The Donkey Drawn Mobile Library Services in Zimbabwe*, IFLA Professional Report 72.

Further reading

Orton, G.I.J. (1980) *An Illustrated History of Mobile Library Services in the UK*, Branch and Mobile Libraries Group.

Pybus, R.L. (1990) *The Design and Construction of Mobile Libraries*, 2nd edn, Branch and Mobile Libraries Group.

—— (1985) *Mobile Libraries in England and Wales: A Guide to Their Construction and Use*, 2nd edn, Branch and Mobile Libraries Group.

SEE ALSO: public libraries; rural library services; school libraries; services for visually impaired people; social exclusion and libraries; Southeast Asia

BILL WEBB, REVISED BY THE EDITORS

MODEM

Modulator-Demodulator: the device that links computers to the telephone network and thus permits access to NETWORKS. The modem works by enabling digital data to be modulated so that it is compatible with the analogue signals carried by the telephone system. Signals are sent to the modem of a remote computer, where they are demodulated and the original data restored.

SEE ALSO: informatics; information and communication technology

MONASTIC LIBRARY

Christian monasteries have a tradition of libraries that goes back to their origins. The Rule of St Benedict required monks to read and to copy manuscripts. Monastic libraries were the principal means of the preservation and transmission of ancient texts, and many medieval texts, before the invention of printing. The type of librarianship practised was essentially curatorial and many did not have library premises as such, only a series of storage places within the monastery. The collections of many monastic libraries were dispersed after events such as the Dissolution of the Monasteries, in sixteenth-century England, or the French Revolution. However, richly stocked monastic libraries do still survive in some parts of Europe.

SEE ALSO: ecclesiastical libraries; history of libraries

MONITORING

In business and industry, describes the regular overseeing of a process, or activity, which seeks to establish the extent to which inputs, work schedules, other required actions and targeted outputs are proceeding according to plan, so that action can be taken to correct any deficiencies detected. Also an aspect of a broader SURVEILLANCE practised in modern society by government, security agencies, corporations and other bodies, generally using technology such as closed-circuit television and the interception of electronic communication. Workplace monitoring tracks employee activity, using the technical capacities of the computer systems in use so as to establish that targets are met, activity is directed towards the objectives of the organization and that theft and wastage do not occur. Monitoring of network use is a prerequisite for the FILTERING of Internet use that is applied by those who – whether in the home, workplace, educational institution, or library – provide Internet access and fear the 'harmful' or distracting capacity of the content available.

MONOGRAPH

A separate treatise that is concerned with a single, distinct subject, usually giving a detailed and thoroughly researched treatment of the topic. The monograph is the most respected means of SCHOLARLY COMMUNICATION in many humanities disciplines. However, in cataloguing, and therefore in the parlance of some libraries, it is used to mean any publication that is not a serial, thus losing the full resonance of the term.

MORAL RIGHTS

The rights of authors to have their creations respected. They are not property rights, in the way that COPYRIGHT is. Moral rights derive from continental European traditions of INTELLECTUAL PROPERTY law, and have subsisted in some countries (e.g. France) for a century or more. A number of moral rights can be found in various civil jurisdictions, but the fundamental one is the right to be acknowledged as the author of a work (the right of paternity) and the right not to have a work subject to derogatory treatment (the right of integrity). Common-law countries have only recently adopted the concept. In the UK the Copyright, Designs and Patents Act 1988 introduced the moral rights of paternity and integrity, and extended the right to object to false attribution of authorship. The exercise of the right of integrity is a problem for those who indulge in parody, for humorous or satirical purposes. In the past, such activities were not curtailed by a copyright law that concentrated on preventing infringement of the economic rights of authors.

MOREL, EUGÈNE (1869–1934)

French promoter of the idea of free public libraries.

A librarian at the BIBLIOTHÈQUE NATIONALE DE FRANCE, he was impressed by the PUBLIC LIBRARIES he saw on a visit to England and systematically gathered data on library development, publishing a number of articles and books based on this subject. His 1910 book *La Librairie publique* was not merely the first French book to be devoted entirely to public libraries; it also sought to substitute the word '*librairie*' for '*bibliothèque*' and all its antiquarian associations.

He became the dominant figure in French librarianship, and much of the twentieth-century modernization of the French library world can be traced back to his advocacy. His achievements included the first application of decimal classification in a French public library, the organization of the first course of lectures on modern librarianship in France (1910–14) and the reform of the French copyright deposit law in 1925. He also had a strong interest in technical improvements such as film strips, microfilm and mechanical processes for the duplication of catalogue cards. His reputation outside France was considerable, and his book *Bibliothèques* was the inspiration for the Belgian law of 1921, which has been described as the first compulsory library law in continental Europe. He was an active member of the predecessor of FID, the International Institute of Bibliography.

MULTIMEDIA

Literally meaning 'many media', the term is commonly used to describe digital objects that use a combination of text, graphics, sound and video. Such objects may be stored on OPTICAL DISKS, or downloaded from the World Wide Web. More loosely, the term has also come to be used somewhat imprecisely, especially by librarians, to replace the term 'AUDIOVISUAL MATERIALS', i.e. films, videos, audio CDs, records, tapes, slides, etc.

MULTIMEDIA LIBRARIANSHIP

Defining MULTIMEDIA is difficult. This is its strength: it is all-pervasive, a force that is improving the presentation and application of information, and one of the elements leading to new organizational forms and alliances in information services management. At one level it refers to an electronic presentation of information in a range of forms: text, visual images and sound, and also in a number of formats. This information will be digital, specifically designed to exploit, and capitalize on, the special features offered by this medium. In the information technology sense the term can also refer to the automated systems that take care of the housekeeping aspects: the creation, storage, management, retrieval and preservation of the multimedia artefacts.

At an organizational level, it is applied to collections of material in different formats. These are organized as a coherent whole and complement each other, containing traditional and electronic material as well as three-dimensional objects. Examples of this are to be found in hybrid libraries, such as the AGORA project, making available images of all types, bibliographic records, URLs and full text.

The role of multimedia

Taking this together, all libraries, if they are to discharge their proper functions, are now multimedia libraries. They embrace the INTERNET, electronic DOCUMENT DELIVERY, IT services and user support. They also adopt the principle of access and the resulting cross-sectoral, public–private and cross-border partnerships. In the multimedia field, this approach has led to major developments offering massive collections of text and multimedia resources – multidisciplinary and cross-sectoral in that they link libraries, museums, archives and other sources.

The significant influence is obviously technology. One of the disadvantages of using multimedia was the poor quality of this technology, now changing so fast that comment will be out of date before publication. An example of this is broadband video streaming, making available high-quality film, video and music for a very wide range of interests. As well as the expected areas of sport, drama, travel and music there are also examples of high quality in academic disciplines including education, and also in training. There are still limitations imposed by the standard of the end-user's equipment, but this is also changing. There have also been significant advances in downloading technology, thus beginning to overcome the difficulties of streaming. Technological developments are now providing cheap, powerful and widely available computers.

Some applications

Communications technology is making this power available to a larger audience, undermining to some degree a view, when the electronic revolution was gathering force, that it would produce an information-starved, underprivileged underclass. The potential of WAP (wireless application protocol), allowing MOBILE COMMUNICATIONS devices to connect to purpose-built websites, is apposite. In spite of indications that the technology is not delivering, examples like the relaunching of websites carrying railway timetables indicate that it can succeed, and can fulfil a useful purpose. Current technological limitations still mean that the multimedia content of these sites is crude. However, if the plans of governments and industry come to fruition, it will deliver sophisticated multimedia presentations to any location.

The reverse comment can be made about interactive television. Here the technology has been available for many years, but use is depressed by low or uneven programme quality. Even here, organizations like the UK Department of Health are considering it as a medium for disseminating health information.

Alongside this, the information profession is becoming increasingly confident in its technical management of multimedia. Web catalogues are common, not only within but also between institutions. Many of these systems have considerable potential for handling multimedia.

There is now also a growing sophistication in the ways in which content is described, and this enriches the use of the artefacts themselves. There is an increased emphasis on content development. The libraries that will hold the keys to multimedia are pushing for a shift from physical ownership to the management of access to distributed resources. This involves partnerships with other information providers, and commercial interests are becoming major players. It is now possible to buy a complete education – pre-school to postgraduate – from a commercial supplier.

It is no surprise that in this environment multimedia has made a wide-ranging impact. The technological revolution described briefly above has gone hand in hand with social and educational change that has made lifelong learners of us all.

The influence of multimedia

The strengths of multimedia are the ability to command and hold interest, and to tell a story in a way that promotes learning and enhances leisure experiences. Because of this, multimedia is now well established as a learning and training medium. Here there is some evidence that the delivery mechanism is now changing from CD to online, and it is clear that a properly designed interactive multimedia presentation has an impact that other formats do not, and offers learning opportunities that match the learner's strengths and inclinations. Multimedia is also a strong element in Web-based corporate learning portals (see PORTALS AND GATEWAYS) offering on-demand learning. It is especially effective where a message has to be conveyed with a minimum of text, but also in change situations, reskilling and winning or retaining a competitive edge, where traditional methods may be less effective. E-learning is also cheaper to deliver, but not to produce. The influence of multimedia specialists is evident in the development of standards for online learning resources, with a number of projects, and formal research, now providing an impetus towards the proper design of Web resources and the layout of Web pages. It is also notable that the standards of multimedia publishing are improving in general, as the characteristics of the Internet and the traditional qualities of the printed page are married with the requirements of user-friendly on-screen reading.

Further reading

AGORA (www.hosted.ukoln.ac.uk/agora).

Ariadne (http://www.ariadne.ac.uk).

DLib Magazine (www.dlib.org).

Journal of Academic Media Librarianship (www. wings.buffalo.edu/publications/mcjrnl/v8n1/index. html).

Landoni, M., Wilson, R. and Gibb, F. (2000) 'From the visual book to the Web book: The importance of good design', Fourth European Conference on Research and Advanced Technology for Digital Libraries, Lisbon, Portugal, 18–20 September 2000.

Thompson, A.H. (2001) 'Library Association reference awards: Electronic media', *MmIT* 27(3) (August): 260–3.

SEE ALSO: digital library; electronic books; picture libraries

LYNDON PUGH

MUSEOLOGY

That part of information science concerned with the identification, preservation and communication of the museality of material testimonies of culture and nature (primarily museum objects) to ensure the protection of human heritage and the proper interpretation and transmission of their messages. Museology also concerns itself with forms of organized and institutionalized human activity (mostly in MUSEUMS) designed to further these objectives.

The divisions of museology

Museology is divided into general museology, which is the central discipline, and a number of special museologies that surround it. Historical museology studies the historical development of the discipline. Theoretical museology lays the theoretical foundations of the discipline and links it with different epistemological views. Special museology relates general museology to other disciplines studying the material evidence of mankind's heritage. Applied museology deals with practical implications of museological principles (van Mensch 1989). The New Museology movement (since 1983) extends the museological parameters from collections, institutions and audiences to heritage, territory and population.

Museological methodology

Museological methodology acts as a link between theoretical and applied museology. It is based on four parameters: scope of heritage, museological functions, museological institutions and society's attitude towards its heritage. Its key concepts are the following: field, form, pattern, object and purpose of museological activity (van Mensch 1994).

The subject of museology

The subject of museology is the study of the process of discovery and transmission of information stored in individual objects or complexes of human heritage, thus reducing the field of museal indefiniteness of a given museum object, collection or system of cultural or natural heritage. Equally, museology also studies the manner and history of their PRESERVATION and the transmission of their messages. The range of museological interests covers the social, cultural, scientific, organizational and technological aspects of museological work in the course of information and communication processes.

Museality

The material and form of the object are the carriers of museality. Museality is a qualitative property of a given object, which defines its significance as a document of a given reality determined by space, time or social setting. These determinants may participate in the identification of museality synchronously, asynchronously or in different combinations (Maroević 1994).

The museum object

The museum object is a heritage item worthy of being preserved. In the museal reality it becomes a document of the reality from which it has been isolated. A heritage object is a physical object whose material and form carry rich layers of meaning to be communicated as messages from the past to the present and to be preserved for the future. The specific aspects of meaning of museum objects are the following: practical, aesthetic, symbolical and metaphysical (van Mensch 1994). The museum object is the source, carrier and transmitter of information. It is a link between museology and a fundamental discipline. While the fundamental discipline focuses on one aspect of the object and remains confined to the documentational and partly communicational approach, museology develops an open approach to the object as an unlimited source of information to be preserved and communicated. The consequence of this approach is an analytical study of different identities of the museum object, whereby it becomes a source of information. Its conceptual identity is that which its maker had in mind before making it; its factual identity is its shape at the moment when it was made; its functional identity reflects and follows its changing uses; and its structural identity reflects its changing material structure in the course of its lifetime; finally, its actual identity is a changeable property reflecting the object's actual state at present (van Mensch 1989).

The museum

The museum is a permanent institution that holds collections of objects as corporeal documents and generates knowledge about these documents. The key functions of the museum include PRESERVATION, study and COMMUNICATION. Preservation involves the transfer of selected objects to a museological institution or their preservation *in situ*; the preservation – preventive or remedial – of the object's material substance, form and meaning, respecting the prescribed procedural ethics; preparation of MUSEUM DOCUMENTATION; and socialization of preservation. Research and study is directed towards the analysis, description, cultural, social and other comparative evaluation of the object in its own (original or artificial) setting; applied research has to do with the CONSERVATION, restoration and presentation of museum objects. Communication takes the form of exhibitions of different kinds, publication of museum documentation and research results, and presentation of cultural heritage.

References

Maroević, I. (1994) 'The museum object as a document', *ICOFOM Study Series (ISS)* 23: 63–70.
van Mensch, P. (1994) 'Towards a methodology of museology', *ICOFOM Study Series (ISS)* 23: 111–22.
—— (ed.) (1989) *Professionalising the Muses*, Amsterdam: AHA Books [on the theoretical approach to museology].

Further reading

Hooper-Greenhill, E. (ed.) (1994) *Museum, Media, Message*, Routledge [conference proceedings].
Maroević, I. and Edson, G. (1998) *Introduction to Museology: The European Approach*, Verlag Dr. C. Mueller Straten.
Pearce, S. (ed.) (1990) *Objects of Knowledge*, Leicester University Press [new research in museum studies].
Stransky, Z.Z. (1980) 'Museology as a science', *Museologia* 15: 33–40.

IVO MAROEVIĆ

MUSEUM

Definitions

Depending on the definition, the term 'museum' can cover a wide variety of organizations. Most definitions include traditional institutions holding collections such as natural history or archaeology and collection-holding art galleries and historic buildings. Some definitions go further: the American Association of Museums (AAM) also includes institutions that may not have collections – such as art centres, children's museums, planetariums and science and technology centres; or may have 'living collections' – such as nature centres, aquariums, arboreta, botanical gardens and zoos. The International Council of Museums (ICOM) definition includes, among other things, 'natural, archaeological and ethnographic monuments and sites and historical monuments and sites of a museum nature', non-profit art exhibition galleries, nature reserves, and cultural centres 'that facilitate the preservation, continuation and management of tangible or intangible heritage resources (living heritage and digital creative activity)' (ICOM 2001).

Purposes and functions

The United Kingdom tends to adopt a narrower definition of museums, but one that sets out their purpose quite well: 'Museums enable people to explore collections for inspiration, learning and enjoyment. They are institutions that collect, safeguard and make accessible artefacts and specimens, which they hold in trust on behalf of society' (MA 2002). From this definition there flows a series of values, which are common to most concepts of museums throughout the world. Museums are not-for-profit, they regard their collections as held on behalf of society, they are fundamentally educational, they offer and encourage wide public access for reasons ranging from enjoyment to scholarship, they regard their collections as to be held permanently in the public domain (some US art museums sell items from their collections, but this is the exception rather than the rule), they safeguard their collections and aim to transmit them in good condition to future generations.

Museums have a number of core functions. They acquire items for the collection – by gift, purchase or fieldwork (while expensive paintings catch the headlines, most items acquired by museums have low financial value); they preserve items, by ensuring they are secure from theft or damage and through conservation, with a growing emphasis on preventive CONSERVATION; they catalogue (see CATALOGUES) and document items (see MUSEUM DOCUMENTATION); they display a selection of items and interpret them in galleries regularly open to visitors; they undertake research, or facilitate research; many museums offer extra educational services. Museums throughout the West are seeking to increase access, for example through outreach work; and in some countries, such as the UK, many museums have a growing focus on work aiming to improve social inclusion.

The importance of public service, access and education cannot be overstated: a collection that did not offer wide public access would not be regarded as a museum. AAM's first code of ethics, published in 1925, states in its preface:

> Museums…hold their possessions in trust for mankind and for the future welfare of the [human] race. Their value is in direct proportion to the service they render the emotional and intellectual life of the people. The life of a museum worker is essentially one of service.

The revised Code of Ethics of the UK Museums Association states similarly 'Museums belong to everybody. They exist to serve the public. They should enhance the quality of life of everyone, both today and in the future. They are funded because of their positive social, cultural, educational and economic impact' (MA 2002: para. 2.0).

History and governance

The first organization recognizable as a museum in modern times is probably the Ashmolean Museum at the University of Oxford, opened in 1683. Some key national museums opened in the eighteenth century, the British Museum in 1753 and the Louvre in 1793 (in the USA the Smithso-nian Institution's first building, the Castle, was completed in 1855). The nineteenth century saw the founding of many great museums by, for example, local authorities in the great British industrial cities. Increasing numbers of museums were established in the twentieth century, with many new types being created in large numbers in the latter part of the century, such as children's museums in the USA, ecomuseums in France and museums of industrial and social history in the United Kingdom.

Governance structures of museums vary. Some are directly run departments of central governments, although this model is increasingly falling from favour and in many countries governments are increasingly introducing 'arm's-length' arrangements in which responsibility for the museum is vested by government in a board of trustees. Many museums are directly run by local government; others, particularly in the USA, but elsewhere too, are non-profit organizations (such as charitable trusts) that may receive a large (or negligible) part of their income from public sources, but are fully independent. Still others are run by universities or the armed forces.

Some current trends and problems

Perhaps the greatest challenge facing museums in the early twenty-first century is to increase knowledge and use of their collections, especially those that are not normally on public display. This includes the need to fully document and digitize them, as well as to make them physically accessible. While a few museums have good storage and extensive digital records of their collections, many collections are under-used, badly stored or inadequately documented.

Museums continue to grow. New museums open regularly and existing ones routinely extend their buildings. They play an increasing role in tourism and economic regeneration strategies. One trend is for internationalization, with the Guggenheim and the Hermitage opening branches outside their home countries. Another trend is for museums to return items to their original owners or place of origin. This is true of, particularly, human remains and related artefacts in the USA, Canada, Australia and New Zealand, and also of artworks seized from their rightful owners by the Nazis during the Holocaust. There have been a few isolated examples of the return of material from European museums to once-colonized countries, but it is not yet clear whether this will be a major trend.

Museums are increasingly focusing on their relationships between their collections and people – both individuals and communities. People regard museums as trusted, relatively neutral, institutions and a reliable source of balanced information and informal education. They are often described as society's new cathedrals and they can play a role in public life greater than their value as information sources, with key items in collections sometimes having iconic significance for a community and museum buildings being a notable part of the public realm (particularly if they offer free admission).

References

ICOM (2001) *International Council of Museums, Statutes*, 2001 edn, Paris
MA (2002) *Museums Association, Code of Ethics*, 2002 edn, London: Museums Association (www.museumsassociation.org).

Further reading

American Association of Museums (www.aam-us.org).
International Council of Museums (www.icom.org) [includes access to the Virtual Library Museum Pages, an extensive reference site with links to many museum websites worldwide].
Museums and Galleries Yearbook (Museums Yearbook before 2002), 2 vols, published annually, London: Museums Association [the most comprehensive listing of UK museums].
Museums of the World (2001) 2 vols, München: K.G Saur [the most comprehensive listing of museums worldwide].
The Official Museum Directory, 2 vols, published annually, New Providence NJ: National Register Publishing [the most comprehensive guide to museums in the USA; published in association with the American Association of Museums].
UK Museums Association (www.museumsassociation.org).
Network of European Museum Organisations (www.ne-mo.org) [includes links to European museums associations].

SEE ALSO: museology

MAURICE DAVIES

MUSEUM DOCUMENTATION

This refers to all the recorded information a MUSEUM holds about the items in its care. It also describes the activity of gathering, storing, manipulating and retrieving that information. Documentation is guided by an ACQUISITIONS and disposals policy and by a detailed COLLECTION MANAGEMENT policy. It provides the basis for good collection and information management, enabling people to find the information they need.

Documentation systems

Museums and museum collections vary enormously in their structure and organization, and deal with material ranging from works of art through to natural science specimens and archaeological finds. Documentation systems are therefore very specialized at the information level but they do employ a number of common procedures. Used in relation to one another these procedures form an integrated system, which can be both manual and/or computerized.

Standard documentation procedures

The process as outlined in *SPECTRUM: The UK Documentation Standard* (see Cowton 1997) comprises some twenty procedures. Of these procedures, the Museums and Galleries Commission (MGC, now Re:source: the Council for Museums Archives and Libraries) has identified eight primary ones. Attainment of the minimum SPECTRUM standard in all eight ensures compliance with the documentation requirement of MGC's Museum Registration Scheme (1995).

Object entry

The process normally begins when an object – e.g. a painting, a button, a ceramic, etc. – enters the museum as an enquiry, a gift or a loan. Object entry is 'the management and documentation of the receipt of objects that are not currently part of the collections' (*SPECTRUM Interactive* 1997). This procedure establishes the terms and conditions under which objects will be received, uniquely identifies new objects and ensures that the museum can account for all objects left in its care. It covers issue of a receipt and recording of key information about the object including the reason for its arrival. The procedure also helps establish legal title if the object is subsequently accepted into the permanent collection.

Loans in

This procedure is defined as 'managing and documenting the borrowing of objects for which the institution is responsible for a specific period of time and for a specified purpose, normally display, but including research, education or photography' (*SPECTRUM Interactive* 1997). It covers areas such as loan agreements and records, security, environmental control and condition of borrowed objects, insurance and indemnity.

Acquisition

Objects offered to the museum via the object entry procedure are reviewed against the museum's acquisitions policy (a policy governing the types and range of objects the museum collects) as well as any relevant laws treaties and codes of practice. If they are accepted, the acquisition procedure is invoked. Acquisition refers to 'documenting and managing the addition of objects to the permanent collections of the institution' (*SPECTRUM Interactive* 1997). It involves the process of transfer of legal title from the donor to the museum, the assigning of a unique permanent identity number (the accession number) to the object and the completion of an entry in the museum registers. The accession number is then marked on to the object and this becomes the key link between the object and its associated information.

Cataloguing

Once the object has been formally acquired it is catalogued. The procedure is defined as 'the compilation and maintenance of primary information describing, formally identifying or otherwise relating to objects' (*SPECTRUM Interactive* 1997). Catalogue information (see CATALOGUES) can be created and maintained by documenting the continuing research into an object and its contexts and/or by access to collections management documentation, e.g. loans, acquisition, conservation. It is within cataloguing that most recording diversity is found, due to the types of information recorded for different types of collection and for different purposes. Within a manual system for example, the cataloguing process will result in a core record, plus a number of card indexes ordered by, for example, donor, location, number or object type. Within a computer system, retrieval is obviously more flexible.

Location and movement control

Once it is within the museum collection, procedures are established so the object can be easily located whether on display, in store, being conserved, etc. The procedure deals with 'documentation and management of information concerning the current and past locations of all objects or groups of objects in the institution's care' (*SPECTRUM Interactive* 1997).

Loans out

This procedure mirrors the Loans in procedure, facilitating the borrowing of objects, usually by another museum. Again, it involves the creation of a loans agreement, obtaining assurances as to security and care, insurance or indemnity details and a change to the location record.

Dispatch

This procedure covers the 'management and documentation of objects leaving the institution's premises' (*SPECTRUM Interactive* 1997). The purpose is to ensure that the institution's legal and policy requirements are met when objects leave the museum, that the institution is able to account for all objects dispatched, that location information is maintained, and that proper authorization and a receipt is obtained. A deaccession and disposal procedure covers accessioned objects permanently removed from collections although there is always a presumption against this (MA 2002)

Retrospective documentation

Documentation not completed according to the procedures above is treated as a backlog. Retrospective documentation enables 'the improvement of the standard of information and the production of new information for an existing collection' (*SPECTRUM Interactive* 1997). This involves having a policy and stated time-scale for eliminating backlogs.

Other procedures

There are a number of other procedures that form either offshoots or subroutines within a documentation system. These include inventory control, conservation and collections care, valuation control, insurance, indemnity, reproduction, risk management and object condition checking.

References

Cowton, J. (ed.) (1997) *SPECTRUM: The UK Museum Documentation Standard*, 2nd edn, Cambridge: The Museum Documentation Association.

Museums Association (2002) *Code of Ethics for Museums*, London: Museums Association.

Museums and Galleries Commission. (1995) *Registration Scheme for Museums and Galleries in the United Kingdom: Registration Guidelines*, London, MGC.

SPECTRUM Interactive, the UK Documentation Standard (1997) 2nd edn, Museum Documentation Association [the electronic version of the standard as a Windows help file].

Further reading

Ashby, H., McKenna, G. and Stiff, M. (eds) (2001) *SPECTRUM Knowledge: Standards for Cultural Information Management*, Cambridge: MDA.

Holm, S. (2002) *Cataloguing Made Easy: How to Catalogue your Collections*, 2nd edn Cambridge, Museum Documentation Association.

—— (1998) *Facts and Artefacts: How to Document a Museum Collection*, 2nd edn, Cambridge: MDA.

Stiff, M. and McKenna, G. (ed.) (2000) *Standards In Action: SPECTRUM IT Guide Book 2*, Cambridge, MDA.

SPECTRUM documentation fact sheets are available to from the MDA website (www.mda.org.uk).

DIANE LEES, REVISED BY SANDE NUTTALL

MUSEUM PROFESSIONAL

Someone involved in professional aspects of the running of a MUSEUM, whose expertise might broadly relate either to the care of the collections or to communication with the user community. The term deliberately leaves reference to the particular skills of the individual concerned open to further definition.

The term usually used in the past for those responsible for museum work was curator. Not only does this fail to express the modern, outward-looking trend of museums all over the world, but it also does not comprehend all those aspects of museum work that are not curatorial. One broad division of museum work does consist of those with specialists skills relating to the collections, which would include curators as such, information specialists documenting the collections, often called registrars, and conservators with skills relating to a host of relevant materials and genres. A second division includes those whose skills are in education, communication, interpretation, exhibition design and related matters. The balance of professionals within and between these divisions in a given museum will vary greatly according to the nature of the museum's specialty. Education for museum work is complicated by the range of skills needed, and it is difficult for a professional association such as the Museums Association (founded 1889) in Britain to serve all its potential constituencies effectively. The existence of specialist associations such as the Museums Documentation Association is thus quite natural.

SEE ALSO: information professions; museum documentation

MUSIC LIBRARIES AND DOCUMENTATION

A sector of the information profession encompassing the provision and bibliographic control of books on music, printed and manuscript music, audiovisual materials and online resources.

Range and scope of music libraries

A number of broad categories of music library supply different services to specific groups. PUBLIC LIBRARIES make available material for education and leisure to a particular community; ACADEMIC and *conservatoire* LIBRARIES provide material for students, researchers and lecturers, and often house important collections of source materials; NATIONAL LIBRARIES offer research facilities and access to unique and valuable heritage collections; BROADCASTING libraries provide materials for live and recorded performances; Music Information Centres give access to scores and recordings of the music of a particular country (usually specializing in contemporary works); and specialist societies hold collections covering, for example, the works of a specific composer, instrument, genre or aspect of music.

Characteristics of the materials

Music, as one of the performing arts, does not truly exist other than at the moment of performance. Printed music and multimedia materials are therefore media that allow the re-creation of the originals which they represent. It is this performance aspect that gives music materials their particular characteristics and special needs in their provision. For example, they must be delivered in time to meet specific deadlines for rehearsals, examinations, concerts or recordings, and must be in the format exactly as specified. An alternative edition or arrangement or a piece similar in character cannot be offered as a substitute. Music is thus both time- and repertoire-specific, and library and information services must be structured to reflect this (Foreman 1992).

Bibliographic control and resource discovery

The difference between printed music and monographs must be appreciated in order to understand the difficulties inherent in the former's BIBLIOGRAPHIC CONTROL. Music is unique in that the same composition can be published in many different physical formats and editions, each suited to a particular purpose. Examples of such formats are full score, vocal score, orchestral parts, piano reductions and arrangements, and only one of these formats will satisfy a user's particular requirements. For example, a string quartet cannot perform from a miniature score of the work; each member of the quartet requires an individual part.

Lack of effective bibliographic control means that identifying known items and discovering their availability for loan or purchase can be time-consuming and difficult. Specialized knowledge of publishers' output and library holdings is often essential. A significant proportion of contemporary music is available only on hire from publishers and this, coupled with the problems of other types of undocumented 'fugitive' material such as publishers' archives, popular music ephemera and other special collections, means that access to a significant amount of material is denied simply because its existence is unknown to most people. Access via the INTERNET to the catalogues of many large academic and national libraries, including the BRITISH LIBRARY's current catalogue of printed music, is gradually improving the situation, but search techniques are varied, often cumbersome and can be time-consuming.

The introduction in 1993 of the International Standard Music Number (ISMN) (ISO 1993), after a decade of development, should do much to improve bibliographic control of printed music. It is now possible to provide each published physical format of a piece of music with a unique control number. As music publishers apply these numbers to their back catalogues of available material, cataloguers can add them to existing records in library databases, thus enabling the benefits of automated data-processing to be enjoyed by printed music as well as monographs and serials.

The development of online resources over the past few years has given rise to a number of initiatives designed to improve music resource discovery. For example, in the UK, there are: the online union catalogue of performance sets, *Encore!*; the collection description database *Cecilia*; Music Libraries Online using Z39.50 to search across UK *conservatoire* catalogues; and *Ensemble*, a programme of retrospective conversion of music catalogue records then added to the CURL database. Many libraries have developed programmes of digitization of some of their music holdings and so are able to provide access to materials via the INTERNET. Examples include the Library of Congress, the Bodleian Library at Oxford University and the National Library of Australia.

Sound recordings

SOUND RECORDINGS are another broad category of material collected by music libraries, and, as with printed music, they have their own characteristics. Storage and display of audio materials is inextricably linked with considerations of their security, militating against ease of access. The multiplicity of physical formats of sound carriers must be recognized and catered for. Bibliographic control of the sound carriers themselves is hampered by the lack of a universally adopted control numbering system (although there exists the International Standard Recording Number (ISRN), which applies to the recording itself), and information on availability relies even more heavily on record companies' catalogues and commercially produced discographies than it does for printed music.

Early printed music, manuscripts, periodicals and music literature

There are four major international projects concerned with the documentation of source materials in music librarianship. RISM (Répertoire

Internationale des Sources Musicales, begun in 1953) provides details of music printed before 1800 and manuscript source materials, together with a directory of libraries in which items are held (Lesure 1989). RILM (Répertoire Internationale de Littérature Musicale) lists writings on music from monographs and periodicals, plus other sources such as conference proceedings and Festchriften (Brook 1989). The database is available as a CD-ROM called MUSE (Music Search). RIPM (Répertoire Internationale de la Presse Musicale) has as its flagship a series of indexes to nineteenth-century music periodicals. Finally RIdIM (Répertoire Internationale d'Iconographie Musicale) is concerned with the encouragement of the study of music in art. All projects enjoy the support of the International Association of Music Libraries (see below) and the International Musicological Society. In addition, consideration is beginning to be given to ways in which access to information held in collections of concert programmes can be achieved.

Specialized associations

The International Association of Music Libraries (IAML), Archives and Documentation Centres was founded in 1951 for the express purpose of providing a forum for the discussion and development of aspects of music librarianship and the documentation of music materials at an international level. Many countries have since formed their own national branches, for example the United Kingdom (United Kingdom and Ireland from 2002), Germany, France, Spain, Italy and Estonia, which, in addition to contributing to international projects and initiatives such as outreach to assist the information poor or the development of bibliographic standards, concentrate on specific domestic issues. For example, the United Kingdom branch published proposals for a Music Library and Information Plan designed to improve access through co-operation (Woodhouse 1993), and in 1991 the French branch published a study of how French libraries should react to the increase in the use of music as a leisure pursuit in France (Hausfater 1991). There are two parallel organizations, the International Association of Music Information Centres (IAMIC) and the International Association of Sound Archives (IASA), covering music information centres and sound archives, respectively. The other major specialized association in the music field is the (American) Music Library Association (MLA). This was founded in 1931 to provide a focus for the interests and concerns of music librarians in the USA, who had, until then, been represented through the AMERICAN LIBRARY ASSOCIATION (ALA). The MLA is active in music library education and has published a considerable body of material on music libraries, has its own periodical, *Notes*, and an electronic bulletin board, MLA-L, accessible via the Internet.

References

Brook, B.S. (1989) 'The road to RILM', *Modern Music Librarianship: Essays in Honour of Ruth Watanabe*, Barenreiter, Pendragon, pp. 85–94.
Foreman, L. (1992) *Lost and Only Sometimes Found*, British Music Society.
Hausfater, D. (1991) *La Médiathèque musicale publique: evolution d'un concept et perspectives d'avenir*, AIBM.
International Standards Organization (ISO) (1993) *ISO 10957: International Standard Music Number*, ISO.
Lesure, F. (1989) 'Les Debuts du RISM', *Modern Music Librarianship: Essays in Honour of Ruth Watanabe*, Barenreiter, Pendragon, pp. 79–83.
Woodhouse, S. (1993) *Library and Information Plan for Music: Written Statement*, IAML (UK).

Further reading

Bradley, C.J. (1990) *American Music Librarianship: A Biographical and Historical Survey*, Greenwood Press.
—— (1973) *Reader in Music Librarianship*, Indian Head.
Jones, M. (1979) *Music Librarianship*, Bingley.

SUSI WOODHOUSE

N

NATIONAL ARCHIVES

The central ARCHIVES in a national archival administration.

The Archives Nationales de France were the first national archives to be formally established (12 September 1790). Since that time, almost all countries of the world have developed national archives. They normally operate under legislation. The size, structure and level of competence of national archives vary greatly from country to country. Countries with federal systems of government have also a central archives administration – the equivalent of national archives – and several have state archives, as in the USA, Germany and Canada.

Reasons for establishment

There are several reasons why countries find it necessary to establish national archives. First, governments need to have a mechanism through which non-current records are selected for permanent PRESERVATION while valueless records are destroyed in a systematic and regular manner. The development and implementation of such RECORDS MANAGEMENT programmes will naturally require the existence of a central archives administration, often called national archives. In this regard, it is the responsibility of this institution to develop policies, standards and procedures for the efficient management of government records and archives. The existence and implementation of such policies, standards and guidelines is especially important in that when valueless records are allowed to glut public offices, they hamper the efficient conduct of business and occupy valuable office space and equipment.

Second, records are the main administrative tools through which the work of a government is carried out. They contain evidence and commitments that must be preserved to protect the government itself. Furthermore, the records also contain vital information on the rights and privileges of the citizens that are derived from the citizens' relationship with the government. Since this immense concentration of official information is later transferred and preserved in the national archives, it therefore serves as the memory of the nation. There is no doubt that the governments would, just like persons without memory, find it quite difficult to function without this memory, the national archives.

From 1790 when the first national archive was established, a citizen's right to have access to public archives has been recognized. This need would have been very difficult to fulfil if there were no central places where members of the public and research scholars could have the necessary facilities to inspect documents that have been selected for preservation. Available evidence shows that research needs are now the most significant force leading to expansion and improvement of national archival services all over the world. It must, however, be pointed out that not all documents may be made accessible to researchers. Some records may contain sensitive information that may, for some time, need to be restricted from public inspection. National archives must therefore find a balance between the requirements of the government to keep some restriction to certain documents, and the needs of the users. But, as a general principle, documents should be open to public inspection to the maximum extent that is consistent with the interest of the citizens.

The holdings and subject coverage

The public service in any given country creates and receives an immense wealth of documentation in the course of business. The data and information contained in these public records cover an extremely wide range of subjects. The record, documents and publications are also in different formats and sizes. When these records are no longer needed for administrative and other purposes by the creating departments, the valuable ones are transferred to the national archives. It therefore follows that a national archive will contain records, documents and publications with an equally wide variety of subjects, which may range, for example, from leisure to nuclear energy, from education to defence, and from agriculture to industry. It must be noted, however, that the size, complexity and subject coverage of the holdings will differ from one national archives to another, depending on various factors, which include the geographical size of the country, population and the level of development.

Requirements

A national archive must meet certain requirements if it is to function efficiently. One such requirement is a building, preferably purpose-designed with controlled temperature and humidity. This is especially necessary for storage areas for audiovisual records, moving images and other materials that are sensitive to high and fluctuating temperatures and humidity. Even conventional paper records need appropriate storage conditions if they are to be preserved for a long time. It will also be necessary for the building to have sufficient safeguards against fire, floods and other similar dangers. The need for appropriate and adequate storage space can, of course, never be emphasized enough since it is a basic requirement for every national archive.

It is not enough for a national archive just to have a building. The building should have the necessary facilities to preserve archives, documents and publications. These include such things as archival shelves, reprographic facilities and well-equipped conservation workshops. In addition, a national archive should have adequate facilities and capabilities for arrangement, description and indexing of records and archives. These facilities should include the use of information technology.

A national archive will also need to have adequate personnel, who must be well qualified and experienced. This requirement has become more complicated in that the range of experts needed for records and archives management has greatly increased. Apart from general archivists, national archives now need information technology experts, preservation chemists and other experts with diverse academic backgrounds. For example all national archives need experts to manage electronic records throughout the entire life cycle. Most other non-paper records also need such specialized personnel. The total number of personnel and the type of experts required will vary from country to country, of course depending on the size and complexity of the particular national archive.

And finally, a national archive should have adequate financial resources for its recurrent and development budgets. Money is needed, for example, for staff salary, procurement and maintenance of equipment, as well as for the maintenance of the archive building itself. It is mainly the inadequate provision of personnel and financial resources in developing countries that make their national archives so different from those of developed countries in terms of performance.

SEE ALSO: freedom of information; National Archives of the United States; Public Record Office

MUSILA MUSEMBI

NATIONAL ARCHIVES OF THE UNITED STATES

The National Archives is the repository of the official government records of the USA and the home of the nation's 'Charters of Freedom': the Declaration of Independence, the US Constitution and the Bill of Rights. Its Office of the Federal Register edits and publishes important legal and rule-making publications of the federal government. Its grant-making body, the National Historical Publications and Records Commission, subsidizes printed publications series and provides grants for the care of historical records.

The research collections of the National Archives encompass the nation's civil, military and diplomatic activities. They are enormous and include many different formats. At its facilities in Washington, DC, the records total more than

4 billion pieces of paper and 10 million still pictures; more than 90,000 reels of motion pictures, reaching back to the inauguration of President McKinley in 1897; 164,000 sound and video recordings, including Congressional hearings, Supreme Court arguments and the Nuremberg trials; 2.5 million maps and charts; nearly 3 million architectural and engineering plans; and nearly 16 million aerial photographs. This documentary record of the US people includes genealogical and census records, military service and pension records, and ship-passenger lists recording the arrival of immigrants.

The USA was relatively late in establishing such a repository. The Department of State and the LIBRARY OF CONGRESS were the principal repositories of government records before 1934, when a long campaign led by the historian J. Franklin Jameson culminated in the establishment of the National Archives of the United States, which is known formally as the National Archives and Records Administration (NARA).

The Act of Congress establishing the National Archives, signed by President Franklin Delano Roosevelt on 19 June 1934, stipulated that all archives or records belonging to the Government of the United States would be placed under the charge of an Archivist of the United States, who would be appointed by the President of the United States with the consent of the US Senate. A National Archives Council was established to advise the Archivist, particularly regarding the transfer of documents from other government agencies. President Roosevelt appointed R.D.W. Connor of North Carolina, who had been nominated for the post by the American Historical Association, to be the first Archivist of the United States.

Personally interested in history, President Roosevelt supported Connor and his early efforts to define and build the National Archives. The activist Roosevelt administration also created a substantial number of records to be housed in the new National Archives Building, then being constructed adjacent to the Mall in central Washington, DC, under the supervision of architect John Russell Pope. This colossal structure, located between 7th and 9th Streets and bounded by Constitution Avenue to the south and Pennsylvania Avenue to the north, occupies a strategic place in the group of buildings known as the Federal Triangle. It opened in 1935. A second major National Archives building was opened in

1994 in College Park, Maryland, near Washington, DC, on the University of Maryland campus.

In its early days, the National Archives emphasized identifying and ensuring the preservation of those records of the US government that have permanent historical value. However the growth of US government during the Second World War brought with it a boom in the production of federal records and a new role for the National Archives: archives management. The need to manage (and dispose of) current records had become an overriding concern, and regional records centres were created throughout the USA under the Archives' supervision.

The Administrative Services Act of 1949 established a new National Archives and Records Service within the government's General Services Agency, a step that many people felt undermined the independence of the National Archives. The Federal Records Act of 1950 established procedures for the creation, maintenance and retirement of federal records. It also provided the legal basis for the transfer in 1952 of the Declaration of Independence and the US Constitution to the National Archives from the Library of Congress, where the documents had resided since 1921 and been on public display since 1924.

President Roosevelt was responsible for an important new function of the National Archives that was spelled out in the 1949 Administrative Services Act: administration of the Franklin D. Roosevelt Library in Hyde Park, New York. In 1938 he had revealed a plan for dedicating his personal and presidential papers to the federal government and housing them in a separate research centre that would be built with private funds. Previously, most presidents had been content to leave their papers to the Library of Congress. A national committee raised the necessary funds, then title to the site transferred to the government, accepted by Congress and placed under the care of the National Archives.

Today the National Archives operates and maintains ten PRESIDENTIAL LIBRARIES and two presidential materials projects that preserve and make available to the public the papers and other historical materials of twelve US presidents. They are: Herbert Hoover Library, West Branch, Iowa; Franklin D. Roosevelt Library, Hyde Park, New York; Harry S. Truman Library, Independence, Missouri; Dwight D. Eisenhower Library, Abilene, Kansas; John F. Kennedy Library, Boston, Massachusetts; Lyndon B. Johnson Library, Austin, Texas; Gerald R. Ford Library, Ann Arbor, Michigan; Jimmy Carter Library, Atlanta, Georgia; Ronald Reagan Library, Simi Valley, California; George Bush Library, College Station, Texas; Nixon Presidential Materials Project, College Park, Maryland (The Nixon Library, located in Yorba Linda, California, is not part of the National Archives Presidential library system); and the Clinton Presidential Materials Project, Little Rock, Arkansas.

The National Archives administers nineteen regional records facilities in various cities throughout the USA. These centres store the non-permanent records of the agencies in their regions, and they preserve and make accessible to researchers materials that document the actions of the federal government in their regions. The records range from court cases relating to the sinking of the Titanic and farm foreclosures during the Great Depression, to naturalization papers for Hollywood movie stars and Chinese immigration files.

John W. Carlin was sworn in as the eighth Archivist of the United States on 1 June 1995. A major renovation of the original National Archives Building began in February 2000. The research side of the building, located on Pennsylvania Avenue, is open for business throughout the renovation. The exhibition side, on Constitution Avenue, closed on 5 July 2001, and will reopen in 2003. The exhibition Rotunda is being remodelled and expanded, and new encasements and exhibition cases are being designed for the Charters of Freedom.

Further reading

McCoy, D. (1978) *The National Archives: America's Ministry of Documents, 1934–1968*, University of North Carolina.
National Archives website (www.nara.gov).

SEE ALSO: archives

JOHN Y. COLE

NATIONAL BIBLIOGRAPHY

In the very broadest sense, this means the listing of information products relating to a particular nation. In practice it encompasses a very diverse range of such activities, and offering too specific a definition would almost certainly risk accidentally excluding some facet or other. It most commonly deals with books and pamphlets, but should ideally also list the whole national documentary heritage (other than that which is properly the domain of the NATIONAL ARCHIVES). Ideally, its scope should include serials, printed music, maps, MULTIMEDIA materials, government publications (see GOVERNMENT PUBLISHING) and electronic information products. In most cases this means material produced within the national territory, but is often broadened to include material on the subject of the nation, or some specific feature of the nation; material produced by members of the nation, originating wheresoever it might; and material in the national language. It is generally subdivided into retrospective bibliography and current bibliography.

Retrospective national bibliography has usually been achieved by the publication of the catalogue of the national library (see NATIONAL LIBRARIES), usually relying on the institution's collections that result from the exercise of LEGAL DEPOSIT rights. The published *Library of Congress Catalog* exemplifies this. However, this does not fully sum up the scope of retrospective national bibliographic activity, since the work of a project like the *Eighteenth-Century Short Title Catalogue* expands the information on past published output far beyond the limitations of the national library's holdings, however close to comprehensiveness those holdings may seem to approach.

Current national bibliographic listing was originally undertaken by the book trade as an aid to commerce in books, and this activity still survives in publications like the *Cumulative Book Index* in the USA. However, since the UNESCO Conference on the Improvement of Bibliographic Services in 1951, regular listing of books and other documents has been seen as a function of a national agency, often, but not exclusively, forming part of the national library. The degree of currency actually achieved by the many national bibliographies that are now published varies greatly from country to country, but long time-lags between the appearance of a document and the appearance of a listing are the rule rather than the exception. The aim today is to create not simply a serial bibliography published on paper, but an electronic national bibliographic database in machine-readable format (MARC was created for this purpose). Such a database can be used to generate bibliographic products in paper or card form, and made available online and via the Internet.

SEE ALSO: bibliographic control; bibliography

NATIONAL INFORMATION SYSTEMS

A national system that systematically exploits information providers and resources in a co-ordinated way, for the benefit of users. The rudimentary idea of a national library system (see NATIONAL LIBRARIES) dates back to the nineteenth century and even earlier, in the USA and Europe, with the feasibility of interlibrary loans. The Kenyon Report of 1929 proposed the establishment of the UK National Central Library (1930) to organize a national system. The Second World War (1939–45) provided new perspectives for research work and therefore the need for a national network of broadly based literature resources in a wide range of subjects but, above all, science, engineering and technology.

In the late 1960s the International Council of Scientific Unions was concerned about the growth of scientific literature, and with UNESCO it organized an intergovernmental conference in 1971 on a World System of Information in Science and Technology (UNISIST). In 1974 the Documentation, Library and Archives Department of UNESCO (DBA) organized an Intergovernmental Conference on the Planning of National Documentation Library and Archives Infrastructures (the NATIS Conference). The conference discussions were based on five papers: (1) recommendations of previous regional meetings of experts; (2) integrated planning of overall documentation library and archives structures; (3) UNIVERSAL BIBLIOGRAPHIC CONTROL AND INTERNATIONAL MARC (UBCIM); (4) planning for information technology; (5) planning information manpower. Little consideration had been given to the systematic organization and dissemination of information, one of the vital resources of any country. The Conference advocated a strong national information policy, while UBC was conceived as a long-term programme for a worldwide system for the control and exchange of bibliographical information, through the establishment of an international centre, later set up at the BRITISH LIBRARY. The manpower

planning paper examined trends in education and training, and proposed an internationally agreed core curriculum for documentation, library and archives programmes.

The objectives of the Conference were: (1) the formulation of a national policy; (2) the stimulation of user awareness; (3) promotion of the reading habit; (4) assessment of user needs; (5) analysis of existing information resources; (6) analysis of manpower resources; (7) planning the organizational structure; (8) supplying manpower for NATIS; (9) planning the technological needs of NATIS; (10) establishing a legislative framework for NATIS; (11) financing NATIS; (12) UBC; (13) assistance to Member States, especially in proposing suitable methodologies, application of INFORMATION TECHNOLOGY and the development of professional education and training; (14) promotion of UBC; (15) a long-term programme of action in planning coherent national information systems; and (16) convening a further conference in 1978 (actually 1979). Following the Conference there was a meeting of experts to design a plan of action for UBC in 1975 and a general conference on UBC in 1978.

The NATIS concept was further outlined in the first NATIS newsletter (later subsumed in the UNISIST *Newsletter*), which proposed to governments the need to establish national systems to facilitate access to information through documentation, library and archive services, as well as assuming responsibility for the education of citizens in this area. Focal points were established in a number of countries, usually in national libraries, though in many countries they did not provide for the development of information services on the scale expected.

The conference hardly justified its long-term aims. The notion of a national INFORMATION POLICY was frustrated in industrialized countries by established vested interests and in developing countries by petty jealousies. Only Jamaica really set up a NATIS programme, though there were other tentative attempts. UNISIST and NATIS programmes were seen as rival programmes, respectively, for the industrialized and the developing world (and not as complementary programmes). But the Conference resulted in the development of UBC and the better organization of international cataloguing. It stimulated the organization of professional education and training, and provided the foundation for the library and information profession as an international profession. The Conference resulted in a considerable amount of literature (1970s and 1980s). With the rivalries within UNESCO, the withdrawal of the USA and the United Kingdom from UNESCO in 1984–5, and the world recession, the effort put in by UNESCO to continue the programme has been minimized. In 1978 UNISIST and NATIS were amalgamated to become the General Information Programme (PGI; Programme Général de l'Information). The British Library's PGI Committee, active in the late 1970s, faded out in the early 1980s. In 1988 PGI and the UNESCO library, documentation and archives were merged to become the Office of Information Programmes and Services. Gradually NATIS was omitted in favour of UNISIST. In later medium-term plans of UNESCO, all reference to UNISIST was dropped. A book by Michael Hill, which took a broader view of the concept of NATIS and which replaced 'systems' with 'policies', effectively reshaped the idea into an acceptable form for a decentralized, flexible, evolving information environment (Hill 1994). Vitiello (2000) provides detail of many national information policies.

References

Hill, M.W. (1994) *National Information Policies and Strategies*, Bowker Saur.
Vitiello, G. (2000) 'National information policy and planning', in M. Line *et al.* (eds) *Library and Information Work Worldwide 2000*, Bowker Saur, pp. 139–65.

Further reading

Anderson, D. (1974) *Universal Bibliographical Control*, UNESCO (COM 74/NATIS/REF.3).
Annuar, H. (1977) *The Integration of Library, Documentation and Archives Services in Southeast Asia. Proceedings of the Third Conference of Southeast Asia Librarians (CONSAL)*, Pusat Dokumentasi llmiat Nasional.
Burchinal, L.G. and Becker, J. (1974) *Planning for Information Technology*, UNESCO (COM 74/NATIS/REF.4).
Foskett, D.J. (1976) *NATIS: Preliminary Survey of Education Training Programmes at University Level*, UNESCO.
Havard-Williams, P. and Franz, E.G. (1975) 'Planning information manpower', *UNESCO Bulletin for Libraries* (February): 2–15.
MacMurdoch, A. (1976) 'Workshop on the planning of NATIS', *Guyana Library Association Bulletin* 5(2): 1–4.
Regional Meetings of Experts on the National Planning of Documentation and Library Services (Arab Republic of Egypt, 1974: Uganda, 1970; Sri Lanka, 1967; Ecuador, 1966). Summary of the Main Recommendations, UNESCO (COM 74/NATIS/REF.1).
Zaher, C.R. (1976) *National and International Library Planning in UNESCO and National Library Planning: Key Papers Presented at the 40th Session of the IFLA General Council*, Verlag Dokumentation, pp. 15–19.

SEE ALSO: Caribbean; information policy

PETER HAVARD-WILLIAMS
REVISED BY EDITORS

NATIONAL LIBRARIES

National libraries vary widely in their origins and functions. In one or another form they are found in more than a hundred countries. At its meeting in Bangkok in 1999 the CDNL (Conference of Directors of National Libraries) defined a national library as:

> [A]n institution, primarily funded (directly or indirectly) by the state, which is responsible for comprehensively collecting, bibliographically recording, preserving and making available the documentary heritage (primarily published materials of all types) emanating from or relating to its country; and which may also be responsible for furthering the effective and efficient functioning of the country's libraries through such tasks as the management of nationally significant collections, the provision of an infrastructure, the coordination of activities in the country's library and information system, international liaison, and the exercise of leadership. Normally these responsibilities are formally recognised, usually in law. For the purpose of this definition a country is defined as a sovereign independent state.

Institutions termed national libraries also occur in non-sovereign national entities such as Catalonia, Québec and Wales.

Origins and orientations

The origins of national libraries are closely linked to those of LEGAL DEPOSIT and the acquisitions of bibliophile monarchs and wealthy individuals. The earliest national libraries originated during the Renaissance as royal or private libraries. In several European countries (e.g. the Netherlands) the national library is still called the royal library. Over time royal libraries became more generally accessible and they were eventually designated as national libraries as a result of political upheavals (e.g. France) or more gradual constitutional development (e.g. Sweden). At the risk of over-simplification three main national library orientations can be distinguished.

The older national libraries can be considered to exemplify the heritage orientation, characterized by an emphasis on the nation's documentary heritage, the management, preservation and exploitation of rich collections of old, rare and valuable materials ('treasures') and service to learned scholars and researchers.

A second group arose in the nineteenth and twentieth centuries in response to nationalistic and modernizing movements (e.g. South Africa, Thailand, Venezuela). They place emphasis on the development of a national infrastructure (e.g. a NATIONAL BIBLIOGRAPHY, national union catalogues, national INTERLIBRARY LENDING schemes) to support the work of the nation's libraries and information agencies. Today most national libraries in the developed world combine the characteristics of these two orientations. This is illustrated most notably by the merging and rationalisation of formerly distinct institutions in the UK to form the BRITISH LIBRARY (1973) and in France to form the BIBLIOTHÈQUE NATIONALE DE FRANCE (1994).

A third group arose in developing countries (e.g. Namibia, Papua New Guinea), where the national library is often called a 'national library service'. These offer services to the general population through a network of PUBLIC LIBRARIES, SCHOOL LIBRARIES and other (e.g. hospital and prison) libraries, much as a metropolitan or county public library service would in a developed country.

Most national libraries experience a tension between the functional demands of two or more of these orientations, which imply diverse client groups. This is compounded in the case of dual-purpose national libraries that also serve as PARLIAMENTARY LIBRARIES (e.g. the US LIBRARY OF CONGRESS), UNIVERSITY LIBRARIES (e.g. Helsinki University Library in Finland) or other.

Current developments and issues

National libraries face challenges posed by political and socio-economic conditions in their countries, rapid developments in INFORMATION AND COMMUNICATION TECHNOLOGY (ICT) and globalization.

They have taken advantage of ICT to make their catalogues and national bibliographies available online, on CD-ROM and on the WORLD WIDE WEB. Many, foremost among them the Library of Congress, have embarked on digitization projects for purposes of PRESERVATION and access. In some countries legal deposit has been extended to audiovisual, broadcast and electronic media. Their national libraries are grappling with the legal and technological problems of acquiring, organizing, preserving and providing long-term access to born-digital materials such as online and CD-ROM databases, electronic journals and websites. The Internet has opened up opportunities for the creation of national library websites and portals. The European Union has funded a number of cooperative R&D projects aimed at exploiting such opportunities.

Preservation of print and other analogue materials remains a major challenge for national libraries; the new technologies notwithstanding, microfilm remains the technology of choice for long-term preservation.

In many developing countries national libraries are underfunded and lead a precarious existence. Even in developed countries they face many constraints. Of necessity they are being managed more professionally, with emphasis on identifying and understanding the national library's environment and clients, the rethinking of missions, functions and collections policies, the development of strategic partnerships, the relevance, timeliness and quality of products and services, the efficiency and costs of operations, cost-recovery, promotion and marketing. In some countries management reviews and reorganizations have taken place. More attention is given to formal evaluation of outputs and impacts, strategic planning and the development of coherent corporate plans.

The future of national libraries in their present form cannot be taken for granted. It has been suggested that they may develop into, or be replaced by, virtual or hybrid (analogue/virtual) libraries. Nevertheless there have been significant investments in national library buildings during the 1990s. These include not only the striking and controversial buildings of the British Library and the Bibliothèque Nationale de France, but also those of national libraries in countries ranging from Denmark to Estonia, Mexico and Namibia. If this is anything to go by, there can be little doubt that well-managed national libraries can survive – if they adapt to their rapidly changing environment.

Further reading

Alexandria: The Journal of National and International Library and Information Issues (1989–). [The foremost journal dealing with national libraries. It contains an annual survey on the world literature on national libraries.]
Cornish, G.P. (1991) *The Role of National Libraries in the New Information Environment*, PGI-91/WS/3, UNESCO.
Gabriel: gateway to Europe's national libraries (2001) (www.bl.uk/gabriel/en/welcome.html).
Line, M.B. (1990) 'Do we need national libraries, and if so what sort? An assessment in the light of an analysis of national library and information needs', *Alexandria* 2: 27–38.
Line, M.B. and Line, J. (eds) (1995) *National Libraries 3; A Selection of Articles on National Libraries, 1986–1994*, ASLIB.
Lor, P.J. (1997) *Guidelines for Legislation for National Library Services*, CII-97/WS/7, UNESCO.
Mchombu, K.J. (1983) 'Alternatives to the national library in less developed countries', *Libri* 35: 227–49.

PETER JOHAN LOR

NAUDÉ, GABRIEL (1600–53)

Librarian to Cardinal Mazarin and author of one of the first significant treatises on librarianship, *Advis pour dresser une bibliothèque* (1627).

Born in Paris and originally a student of medicine, he became librarian in succession to several great book collectors, including Cardinal Richelieu and Queen Christina of Sweden. For Mazarin, whose librarian he became in 1643, he assembled a library of over 40,000 books, collected from all over Europe. In this library he was able to put into practice many of the ideas expressed in the *Advis*. He believed that a scholarly library should contain books that are valuable for their content, rather than their rarity or beauty. He advocated the arrangement of library collections by subject and argued that the owners of great libraries should make their collections freely accessible to scholars. His ideas on the internal environment of the library were progressive, showing attention to natural lighting and precautions against dampness and intrusive noise. Although his book was never widely available, it was influential, reaching Gottfried Wilhelm LEIBNIZ and John Durie, author of the *Reformed Librarie-Keeper* (1650).

SEE ALSO: librarian

NAVIGATION

Finding ways to move from one web page to another. Like the use of the word surf for unstructured Web use (see SURFING), navigation is a maritime metaphor intended to reflect the enormous extent and changeability of the INTERNET. Navigation can mean using a WEB BROWSER to view new sites, or moving between pages within a website. A website can be expected to provide a navigation bar consisting of links to its main sections for easy internal navigation. SEARCH ENGINES and hyperlinks will provide the means to move from one site to another.

SEE ALSO: hypermedia; information theory

NETIQUETTE

Codes of behaviour for INTERNET users, developed by users themselves. They concern how to deal with insults (flaming), uncontrolled messaging (SPAM) and the running of Internet games, chatrooms, newsgroups and special-interest websites.

Further reading

Shea, V. (1994) *Netiquette*. San Francisco: Albion Books.

NETWORK

A system of physically separate computers with telecommunication links through which they can exchange information and share resources. Also used in the abstract sense to mean modes of interaction between people.

NETWORKS

Computers linked by a TELECOMMUNICATIONS system. Networks offer two resources. First, they offer access to the people who use computers on the network, by means of ELECTRONIC MAIL, conferencing or chat facilities. Second, networks permit the use of files (text, graphics, sounds and video), software, databases and peripherals (like printers or fax machines) stored on, or attached to, computers on the network.

Types of network

A critical limiting factor on the operation of any network is the speed of the telecommunications system that links computers on the network. Some networks use the public telephone system to link computers. A MODEM is needed to translate digital data into analogue form for transmission and then back into digital form when received. Most networks use some form of digital link, ranging from a simple serial connection to a leased line connection. Because networks link a variety of computers and software packages over different telecommunications lines, telecommunications standards like TCP/IP (Transmission Control Protocol/Internet Protocol) are vital.

Originally networks operated PEER TO PEER, with no one computer controlling significant resources that other computers on the network depended on. However, many networks now operate on the client–server principle, which, in hardware terms, means that one central computer (the server) supports the other computers (the clients). For software there is a corresponding split between functions carried out on the server computer and those on a client computer. Functions can thus be divided between two completely different software packages, one acting as server, the other as client. Topologies determine how computers in a network are connected and there are a variety of models (e.g. bus, star and ring) that have implications for the functions and management of a network.

The computers owned by an organization at one site can be networked. Such a network is known as a LOCAL-AREA NETWORK (LAN). As well as supporting standard applications LANs allow new applications. One such is groupware, software that enables people to share information and communicate over the LAN. A network that is not limited to one organization and one site is known as a WIDE-AREA NETWORK (WAN).

There are different types of WAN. One such is a co-operative network where costs are supported by a group of separate institutions or individuals. An example is Fidonet, which is a network of BULLETIN BOARD systems (BBS) run on ordinary microcomputers owned by private individuals who use special software to set up menus of services. Other people access a BBS by telephone from their computer.

Another type of WAN is a commercial (for-profit) network, available to the public at large, or to closed user groups, on a fee-paying basis. One such is CompuServe, which in 2001 had over 1 million subscribers worldwide. There are other commercial networks that compete with CompuServe.

Academic networks are WANs financed by public money, usually to support research. One such is JANET (the Joint Academic NETwork) in the UK. Research institutions like universities pay flat-rate annual fees to maintain their INTERNET connection.

The final type of WAN are metanetworks – these are 'networks of networks' encompassing any or all of the above types; the Internet is the prime exemplar of a metanetwork – it is a vast conglomerate of interconnected computer networks that brings together people, information and computer resources from across the globe. Virtual private networks (VPNs) are extensions of LANs across a WAN, which hide private data from the public network(s) it travels across.

Virtual communities

Networks bring people together, either as co-workers connected by LANs (and sometimes VPNs) or as what Rheingold (1994) calls virtual communities, people who use a WAN to communicate regarding a common, shared interest. For example, the oldest virtual community is the INVISIBLE COLLEGE of scientists on the Internet, who have long seen themselves as an international community, where ideas are more important than national origin.

The basic communication tool a network offers is ELECTRONIC MAIL (e-mail), an asynchronous, textual messaging system by which individuals send and receive messages. Conferencing is similar to e-mail except that messages are not sent to individuals but to named, topic-based forums or discussion areas, which individuals access to read and post messages. Synchronous communication is possible using chat or instant messaging facilities, in which text messages are exchanged instantaneously between individuals, or by videoconferencing, in which video pictures and sounds of participants are synchronized. Voice alone may be transmitted over a computer network, for example using VOIP (Voice Over IP) on the Internet. Most of these facilities are provided by groupware over a LAN, to which are added shared diaries and calendars, and also workflow management, the tracking of progress on shared tasks.

There are PRIVACY issues to communicating over a network, since all communications can be intercepted and recorded without participants being aware. ENCRYPTION technologies, especially public key encryption systems, can help by keeping communications coded and readable only by the intended participants. There are also PRESERVATION issues in networked communication, since much important communication may never be recorded, and, conversely, much unimportant material may be stored for posterity (for example the archive of Internet newsgroup postings currently available on Google), although the research potential of this material may prove great.

Information resources

Information on networks is stored in computer files. Computer files can be of two types: data files and software files. The latter are applications (like word processors) that users can run from a network. An advantage of a network is that it promotes resource sharing, for example ten users might share one copy of an application that is only needed rarely. Obviously, software use on a network should not violate purchase restrictions and limits often have to be set on how many copies of a software application can be running at any one time.

Data files have two problems on a network. First, there is the problem of how to find them, and, second, how to view/use them. The WORLD WIDE WEB started out as a LAN application at CERN in Switzerland, which used hypertext links to locate files on CERN's network. Hypertext though becomes unmanageable with large numbers of files, and SEARCH ENGINES, which are searchable databases of files on a network, are needed. Once a data file is found it needs to be viewed, a task that the potential variety of machines on a network complicates. Usually a file format has an associated viewer (software that just opens the data file and does not change it). For example, HTML (HyperText Mark-up Language) files use Web browsers like Internet Explorer as viewers. Each data file format has its

own viewer, and it can be problematic assembling the collection of viewers needed. This problem gets more acute if data files containing MULTIMEDIA (images, sounds and video) are used.

Files do not just appear on a network: someone must publish them. Typically, files will either be published via some centralized server, or via a decentralized INTRANET, a local implementation of Web technologies, which can allow individuals to publish files. If the audience for those files includes authorized individuals outside the organization that owns the intranet then it becomes an extranet. Content management software aids the publication of files in a form suitable for intra- and extranets.

Finally the storage of files on a network might take up large volumes of disk space. Disk mirrors and RAID (Random Array of Inexpensive Disks) are devices for automatically backing up (making copies of) files. Optical media (like writeable CDs) or magnetic tape might be used for long-term preservation of files.

Conclusion

Networks should not be seen as consisting solely of computers nor existing solely to support an organization. Mobile telephones, hand-held devices, televisions and even domestic equipment like fridges are now all potentially connectable to a network. Sitting at a desk in the office is no longer the only place one can use a network: small devices, like for example 3G (third generation) mobile phones, will enable network use on the move. Broadband technologies are delivering faster access via cables while wireless networking protocols like 802.11B and Bluetooth give freedom from cables (see WIRELESS APPLICATIONS). While the functional foundations of networks will persist, their physical limitations in terms of reach and flexibility are quickly evaporating.

References

Rheingold, H. (1994) *The Virtual Community: Home-Steading on the Electronic Frontier*, Secker.

Further reading

Comer, D. and Droms, R. (2001) *Computer Networks and Internets*, 3rd edn, Prentice Hall.
Pool, I. De Sola (1990) *Technologies without Bound-*

aries: On Telecommunications in a Global Age, Harvard University Press

SEE ALSO: communication; informatics; information and communication technology; information policy

ALAN POULTER

NEURAL NETWORK

A method of designing a computer system that attempts to mimic some functions of the human brain. Like the brain, neural network computers are made up of large numbers of simple processing elements (called 'neurons'), which receive incoming data in parallel, then map this into a pattern representing an acceptable solution. They are particularly good at analysing problems with many variables. They do not depend on programming in the conventional sense, but derive their abilities from 'learning' about the problem with which they are to deal. They are used in a wide variety of commercial applications, including speech and image recognition, financial analysis, medical diagnosis, database management systems, and image and signal processing.

SEE ALSO: informatics

NEWSPAPER

A publication issued periodically, usually daily or weekly, traditionally containing the most recent news. Because radio, television, teletext and other media can now offer immediate news coverage, newspapers in many industrialized countries are increasingly dominated by feature material. The newspaper industry is large, multinational and to an increasing extent cross-owned with other media industries; in some countries it is severely constrained by state censorship.

SEE ALSO: communication; knowledge industries

NEWSPAPER LIBRARY

A library provided for the needs of the staff of a newspaper; sometimes affectionately referred to as the 'morgue'. Although such a library will usually contain some reference books and other published materials, its chief content will be cuttings files, notes assembled by staff members and photographs and other illustrations. Electro-

nic access to information is increasingly used in an industry dependent on the speed at which it can assemble and disseminate information, so the conventional newspaper library is effectively being replaced by a swifter and more comprehensive form of access.

SEE ALSO: mass media

NORDIC COUNTRIES

The Nordic countries, Denmark, Finland, Iceland, Norway and Sweden, are often also known by the geographical term 'Scandinavia'. These countries have managed to develop co-operation in all aspects of life – professional, political and social – that is unique in the world. Nordic co-operation takes multiple forms in this region of more than 1 million sq. km where 25 million inhabitants move freely without passports. All the countries have common history although that history has often been of the ruler and the ruled. Nowadays Nordic co-operation is led by the Nordic Council, which is a Nordic parliament (established in 1952), and its executive counterpart, the Nordic Council of Ministers (established in 1971). Each government appoints one of its ministers as the Minister of Nordic Affairs to co-ordinate actions on the highest level of government. Supported by a Nordic budget, co-operation is practised by means of about thirty institutions that are mostly small and scattered around the Nordic region, covering all aspects of society including women's issues, Asian studies, volcanology, theoretical physics, drug and alcohol issues, to name but a few.

Nordic library co-operation

Nordic co-operation in the field of library development has existed for close to a century. The birth of formal co-operation was in 1914 when the first Nordic library journal, *Nordisk tidskrift för bok- och biblioteksväsen* (Nordic journal for book and library issues), was published with editors from four of the five countries (Iceland was not included). This journal is still published. Informal co-operation among the national librarians existed even before that. Large co-operative projects were launched in the 1950s including a common acquisition plan, the Scandia Plan, and a Nordic union catalogue of serials, NOSP. During the 1970s, library co-operation became more formal with financial support from the Nordic coffers and the establishment of the first Nordic institution within this field in 1970, called NORDDOK. That was later superseded by NORDINFO, the Nordic Council for Scientific Information, founded in 1976, which co-ordinates co-operation among research and special libraries in the Nordic region. NORDINFO, which is located in Helsinki, Finland, finances common projects where there are obvious benefits beyond what can be achieved at the national level. Financial support covers research and development, courses, conferences and summer schools as well as information activities where efforts are made to pool specialist knowledge in all the countries and make advances that can be of use to most of the region. Actual projects have included three centres of excellence, one on electronic publishing, one on networking and one on digitization. These centres actually exist in different countries but they received additional funding from NORDINFO for new developments during a period of three years. Presently emphasis has been placed on Nordic developments related to the electronic library.

A separate committee, NORDBOK, the Nordic Literature and Library Committee, was established in 1989. NORDBOK is located in Copenhagen, Denmark. It was founded to encourage and support the distribution of Nordic literature among the Nordic countries as well as to strengthen co-operation between Nordic PUBLIC LIBRARIES. NORDBOK gives grants to translations of Nordic works from one language to another. It also finances courses and projects related to public library development. Both NORDINFO and NORDBOK are administered by boards that include members from all the Nordic countries.

Library organization and management

In spite of great difference in population from the 8 million Swedes as contrasted with less than 300 thousand Icelanders, all the countries adhere to similar economic and social systems and services, and hence their library services are quite comparable and well developed, although from the organizational point of view they differ.

In Denmark Biblioteksstyrelsen (The Danish National Library Authority) is the Danish government's central administrative and advisory body to public as well as research libraries and

is an independent agency under the Ministry of Culture. In Sweden, BIBSAM (The Royal Library's Department for National Co-ordination and Development) has the main task to co-ordinate and develop the provision of information for higher education and research and development, primarily by taking measures to handle issues related to research libraries and Statens kulturråd (The Swedish National Council for Cultural Affairs), which leads the public library development.

As of 2002 Norway has a new directorate for libraries, ARCHIVES and MUSEUMS that is to take over three former authorities, Statens bibliotek-tilsyn (Norwegian Directorate for Public Libraries), Riksbibliotektjenesten (The National Office for Research Documentation, Academic and Special Libraries) and Norsk museumsutvik-ling (Norwegian Museum Authority). In Iceland and Finland the largest libraries, the combined National and University Library in each country, have assumed much of the leading functions on the national level.

Electronic library development

All the Nordic countries have emphasized the development of digital libraries (see DIGITAL LIBRARY) to facilitate the citizen's access to information. In most cases the research libraries have been at the forefront of these developments but in some cases, such as in Denmark, the public libraries have also formed a part of the national electronic library. Each country has selected their own form for this development, although it has been possible to create developmental projects that have served all the Nordic region.

In Denmark the Denmark Electronic Research Library (DEF) was set up as a five-year project, 1998–2002, funded by the Ministries of Culture, Research and Education. It forms a part of the information technology plan 'Info 2000' issued by the Danish government. DEF has as its main objective to provide users with relevant research information, regardless of where the researcher or the information is located. Through the website of the DEF the user can access subject groups, library catalogues and electronic journals, as well as the homepages of participating libraries and links. The participants are most of the Danish research libraries that in one way or another are involved with the development of a comprehensive national virtual library.

In Finland the Finnish National Electronic Library, (FinELib) was formally launched in 1998. The development of FinELib is in line with the national information policy that the Finnish Ministry of Education has published, called 'Education, training and research in the information society. A National Strategy 2000–2004', where there is an emphasis on content production and on developing learning environments. FinELib has three main goals, which are (1) to increase the amount of information available to users, (2) to improve information retrieval from the Internet, and (3) to develop a graphical user interface to facilitate user access to heterogeneous information sources. FinELib is a consortium of universities, trade schools, research institutes and public libraries. The consortium is financed partly by the government and partly by the libraries themselves. The electronic library forms a part of the National Library that is also the Library of the University of Helsinki and is operated as an integral part of that library but all developments are done in co-operation with the consortium partners. It has mainly been active in acquiring and making accessible a variety of electronic material (licences) such as journals and databases.

The National and University Library of Iceland is the country's largest – and in fact the only – research library with substantial collections. It has been in a leading position in developing the electronic library and has been very active in digitizing old, unique Icelandic material, including maps and manuscripts (Saganet). The country has chosen a common automated library system, Aleph, which is to be used in all libraries of the country. Nationwide contracts have been signed with international vendors. Everybody in the whole country with access to the Internet has access to the licensed electronic journals and databases.

One of the most important national digital projects in Norway is Cultural Network Norway (Kulturnett). This project aims at strengthening co-operation and development among libraries, archives and museums, as well as educational and research institutions. Library Network Norway is a project that is administered by the Norwegian Directorate for Public Libraries but linked to the Cultural Network. Its purpose is to serve as a gateway to all Norwegian libraries.

In Sweden, SVEBIB, the Swedish Electronic Research Library, is administered by BIBSAM. SVEBIB is expected to include all types of electronic resources that are relevant to the Swedish research and higher-education communities, and make these available to all students, teachers, scientists and scholars of the Swedish university system. SVEBIB has been defined as a collection of Web-based electronic resources used in research and higher education that are made available as broadly as possible within a country via the Internet.

All the countries carry out their own developmental projects aimed at the digital library, some of which have become Nordic and received Nordic financial support through NORDINFO. One can mention Tiden, the Nordic Digital Newspaper Library, i.e. newspapers from the eighteenth and nineteenth centuries that have been digitized from microfilms. Another project is NORDVEST, the digitization of old printed material from Iceland, Greenland and the Faeroe Islands. This is considered to be unique material that requires the development of new technical solutions due to the different languages. SVUC, the Scandinavian Virtual Union Catalogue, is a project partially financed by NORDINFO with the ultimate goal to provide a virtual single point of access to the union catalogues and national bibliographies in the Nordic countries.

Library education

Nordic library education is undergoing radical changes. In Sweden, Norway and Denmark the former largest library schools are being transferred to the university levels and are hiring their first professors. Finland and Iceland have had their library education on a university level for a long time. In this area the Nordic countries have established a network, NordISNET (Nordic Information Studies Research Education Network), with representation from all the library schools. The aim of the network is to enhance Nordic and Baltic research education in information studies by pooling the mentoring expertise for specific supervision and teaching, and by creating a critical mass of doctoral students for organizing courses and by exchanging doctoral students. By organizing courses, workshops and supervision, and by publicizing and supporting participation in the national research courses, the network assists the participating institutions to form more comprehensive, specialized and tailored doctoral programmes for their own doctoral students.

Library associations

Although all the Nordic countries have their own LIBRARY ASSOCIATIONS, often divided according to types of libraries, there is also much activity at Nordic level. The Nordic Federation of Research Libraries Associations (NVBF) was founded in 1947 and has been very active ever since. Today the following national research library associations are affiliated to the Federation and the members of all of them are automatically attached to the Federation: Foreningen af Medarbejdere ved Danmarks Forskningsbiblioteker (Association of Staff Members of Research Libraries in Denmark); Suomen Tieteellinen Kirjastoseura (The Finnish Research Library Association); Upplýsing – Félag bókasafns-og upplýsingafræða (Information – the Icelandic Library and Information Science Association); Norsk fagbibliotekforening (The Norwegian Association of Special Libraries); Svensk Biblioteksförening (The Swedish Library Association). The main objective of NVBF is to strengthen the co-operation between staff members of the Nordic research libraries and in this way also to improve the contact between their libraries as institutions. This objective is encouraged by the holding of joint Nordic library meetings, conferences and summer schools in each of the member countries. A general conference for all members is organized every three years, the aim of which is professional briefing through lectures and discussions that will enable the participants to take a stand on library matters of current interest.

On the international level, Nordic librarians have been very active in IFLA as well as FID and EBLIDA where they have been strong advocates of Nordic values in library services.

The most important common feature of library services in the Nordic countries is the concept of free and equal access to documents and information, both for the present and the future population. This policy is supported by national information policies and national legislation including legislation on copyright and legal deposits. In all the Nordic countries the library system is instrumental in guaranteeing active participation in the democratic processes.

Further reading

Nordic websites:
www.nordinfo.helsinki.fi/index.htm.
www.dpb.dpu.dk/df/nvbf_eng.html#intro.
www.bs.dk/index.ihtml.
www.info.uta.fi/informaatio/nordisnet/.
Denmark:
www.bs.dk/index.ihtml.
www.deflink.dk/.
Finland:
www.lib.helsinki.fi/english/index.htm.
hul.helsinki.fi/finelib.
www.jyu.fi/~library/virtuaalikirjasto/engvirli.htm.
Iceland:
www.bok.hi.is/english/third.htm.
Norway:
www.rbt.no/.
www.bibtils.no/index.htm.
Sweden:
www.kb.se/bibsam/.
www.kb.se/svebib/.

SEE ALSO: library co-operation; library education; national libraries

SIGRÚN KLARA HANNESDÓTTIR

NORTH AMERICAN LIBRARIES AND LIBRARIANSHIP

The changing environment of libraries and librarianship in the USA and Canada

North American libraries have been adapting to a rapidly changing technological environment for the last quarter of a century. Complicating revolutionary changes in information and communication technologies have been burgeoning amounts of information, changes in the publishing industry, rising costs, competition for financial resources and changing demographics, both within the field and in the general population. Digital information production and delivery, especially the Web, has provided new sets of challenges and opportunities. Whilst the virtual library has grown by leaps and bounds, the library as place is being reaffirmed.

The digital environment

As the twenty-first century begins, libraries of all types have been transformed by the pervasiveness of information and communication technologies. The Web, which made its debut in the early 1990s, has revolutionized most library functions.

Some SPECIAL LIBRARIES rely solely on information accessible through the Internet.

Library users now can check library holdings (both of their local and of remote libraries), request INTERLIBRARY LENDING items, receive documents, access reserve reading materials for college courses and sometimes gain access to entire ELECTRONIC BOOKS without leaving their homes or dormitories.

Librarians select and digitize resources to post on the specially designed sites on the World Wide Web for sharing with users anywhere in the world, making unique or fragile materials widely available. They select digital resources created by others and make them available to their users through subject-specific or audience-specific Web guides, applying traditional skills to a new format. Some librarians respond to reference questions posed by ELECTRONIC MAIL or through the Web, while a few offer a real-time electronic reference service. Some ACADEMIC LIBRARIES now measure the number of 'hits' to their various databases and Web pages as well as the number of people who enter through their physical doors. More than 95 per cent of all public libraries in the USA and virtually all academic libraries provide public access Internet connections, according to government reports by McClure and Bertot. Many have Internet rooms or computer laboratories where users can have assistance in locating and using digital resources. The proliferation of information of questionable value has prompted a movement to provide instruction in INFORMATION LITERACY, or how to be a skilful and critical consumer of information, not just in academic and SCHOOL LIBRARIES, but also in PUBLIC LIBRARIES.

It has also prompted a movement, in the USA strengthened by a series of legislative enactments, to place software 'filters' (see FILTERING) on Internet browsers in public and school libraries in an effort to protect minors from exposure to pornographic materials. The US Communications Decency Act was struck down, and the Children's Internet Protection Act has been challenged in court by the American Library Association and its allies. The ALA maintains that filters limit adults to reading suitable for children and deny access to valuable materials even for children, and, furthermore, that they are not effective at screening out undesirable materials. It recommends Internet use policies, also adopted by many Canadian libraries, as an alternative. Nevertheless, significant numbers of libraries offer filtering software on computers intended for use by children, and some small percentage have installed it on all computers.

The vulnerability of children to people who might glean information about them through their interactions with the World Wide Web has also highlighted the issue of PRIVACY in the digital world. Not only do Web-based companies gather personally identifiable information from users for their own purposes, but also some have sold this information to others without users' knowledge. In addition, the ease of compiling personal information through Web SEARCH ENGINES has made privacy a major concern of librarians and others. Especially in the wake of terrorist attacks on the USA in September 2001, librarians have had to re-examine and re-affirm their policies on confidentiality of library records, especially since some of the alleged terrorists were said to have used library computers to carry out their planning.

Although free access to Internet-connected computers poses problems at times, the high price of desirable materials that can be accessed through the Web also is problematic. The huge costs associated with the many electronic INDEXes, ABSTRACTs and full-text, numeric, or even image databases made available to library users have added shared licence (see LICENCES) agreements to the many extant types of resource sharing – such as reciprocal borrowing privileges; regional union lists; shared cataloguing through OCLC, RLIN and the National Library of Canada; and courier and document delivery services. Licensing of databases by state-wide or regional library consortia has become commonplace, and librarians have had to learn skills of contract and licence negotiation as part of their materials acquisitions practices.

The economic, political and legal environments

These databases pose other problems for librarians, however, as content aggregators continue to try to replace COPYRIGHT law with contract law, subverting the 'fair use' doctrine. Copyright, 'click-through' or 'shrink-wrap' licences for digital products, and issues surrounding cost-per-use, are very much in contention, especially in the USA, where the Digital Millennium Copyright Act (DMCA) and the Sonny Bono Copyright Act, which extends copyright to the life of the creator plus ninety years, are being challenged in the courts. Librarians contend that these revisions of copyright, and the use of 'digital rights management' technologies to enforce these rights, will lead to ever more commodification of information, thereby widening the 'digital divide' and inhibiting the creation of new knowledge. Both the ALA and the Canadian Library Association have adopted policies to help ensure equitable and universal access to information.

Content aggregators – publishers – and librarians continue also to be at odds over the costs of library materials. During the last two decades of the twentieth century, many book and journal publishers merged with media and entertainment companies, forming huge multinational corporations, whose perspectives differ widely from traditional publishers, thus reducing effective competition. The historic co-operative relationship of librarians and publishers has become increasingly strained; perhaps only in the areas of children's literature and opposition to censorship does it survive in relatively good health.

Serials prices, in particular those in science and technology, but in other areas as well, have continued to increase at a rate much greater than the rate of inflation. At the same time, publishers have tried to impose contract limitations on the use of their journals. Librarians, however, have not simply reacted, but – in addition to the necessary cancellations of many titles based on use of sophisticated management data such as cost-per-use of individual titles – have utilized new digital technologies to launch competitor journals. The Association for Research Libraries' Scholarly Publications and Academic Resources Coalition (SPARC), the largest such initiative, is an example of the way in which libraries are trying to use new technologies to seize the initiative to provide the best information at the lowest possible cost.

Providing more with less has become a fact of life for most North American libraries. Although the 1990s were a period of relative prosperity, competition for revenues and a public generally unsympathetic to increased taxes has meant continued constraints for many libraries. The early twenty-first century saw an economic downturn that put additional duress on both privately and publicly funded libraries. Under pressure to improve the bottom line, corporations have asked their libraries to document their

value. Public or academic libraries have for several years sought collaborations with other community agencies or corporate funders, a trend that concerns some who prefer that libraries not be allied with any particular viewpoint or brand. Training librarians for advocacy on behalf of libraries has become increasingly important. In spite of scarce resources, however, many communities have raised revenues to build or renovate public libraries or to add branches in new city neighbourhoods, as Chicago, Illinois, has done.

In fact, the library as place seems to have gained in importance, in spite of librarians' fears that it would become obsolete. Vendors of electronic books and other library resources appear to be less of a threat, at least to date, than initially perceived. The bankrupt e-book company netLibrary was acquired by the non-profit library co-operative OCLC in January 2002. Questia, a fee-based library-like vendor of books and articles that went live in January 2001, had laid off three-fourths of its workforce by November of that same year. While many young people turn first to the World Wide Web for information, and while the online bookstores, Amazon.com and Barnes and Noble.com have raised a good deal of concern and given librarians different models of service, libraries are heavily used. Americans check out an average of seven books per person annually; reference librarians in academic and public libraries answer more than 7 million questions weekly, according to statistics gathered by ALA's Office for Research and Statistics. Libraries and librarians continue to play their traditional role of providing access to information, but now use new skills and new technologies to do so – and serve much different populations than in the past.

Changing library workforce

Continuing professional development opportunities to enable librarians to keep up with the ever-changing skills needed in today's library has become a major issue throughout North America. Schools of library and information science, consortia and professional associations, as well as various commercial vendors, all provide courses aimed at the library profession. Technology, advocacy and change management courses are much in demand.

Helping librarianship look more like the

diverse populations libraries serve has become a major focus of the ALA and of library education. Since 1998 Spectrum scholarships have assisted students of colour to attend ALA-accredited schools in the USA and Canada. In addition to trying to meet the need for librarians of colour, the profession is facing an ageing workforce: more than 25 per cent of US librarians will reach sixty-five by 2009; the median age of librarians was forty-seven, the highest for any occupation, according to 2000 US Census figures. Already academic and public libraries face critical shortages in some areas. In 2001 the ALA placement centre at annual conference posted 831 position openings and had only 260 applicants. Although the worsening economy has slowed hiring in some areas, it is clear that the shortage persists and will worsen.

Although a number of library schools closed in the 1980s, school closings cannot be blamed for the shortage. The vast majority survived and reinvented themselves as schools of library and information science, with curricula embedded firmly in information and communication technologies. Most are thriving and some, like Florida State University and Washington University, have grown quite dramatically. Some have dropped the name 'library' in order to communicate that their graduates are not bound to a particular type of institution and possess a wide array of information technology skills and per-spectives. Several are delivering courses to distant learners through Web-based technologies. A number have instituted undergraduate 'information studies' degrees. All are coping with the need for graduates to have both traditional library skills of materials selection, cataloguing, reference provision and the like, and the new skills connected with the digital library – not only Internet searching skills, but skills of digitization, Web design and so on. Graduates with such skills, however, are often able to get more lucrative non-library positions with the government, technology firms and other kinds of corporations. In addition, in the digital environment, libraries, archives and museums are converging. The new US Institute for Museum and Library Services reflects that convergence through its funding priorities. Skills applicable to the selection and digitization of library materials can be put to good use in archives and museum settings. The number of schools providing students with opportunities to specialize in archival or museum studies is increasing. Thus, while schools of library and information science enrol more students than ever before, the combination of a greying workforce and a wide array of positions to choose from both within and outside libraries and other cultural institutions has created a growing shortage of librarians to cope with an increasingly complicated library environment.

LOUISE S. ROBBINS

O

OBJECT-ORIENTED TECHNOLOGY

Objects store computerized data. However, unlike standard computer record and field structures, which store only data, objects store both data and the set of procedures that can operate on that data. Storage of data and procedures together is known as encapsulation. Data stored in objects can only be manipulated by means of messages to the stored procedures for that data. A class is a group of objects that store identical procedures and data. A subclass of objects derived from an object class inherits the procedures and data for that object class and can add procedures and/or data of its own.

Origins

Object-oriented technology appeared in COMPUTER SCIENCE in the early 1980s as a better means of developing software. Encapsulation could produce reliable, fully documented objects that could be used by more than one piece of software. Object classes, and the hierarchy of subclasses that could be constructed using them, helped programmers organize and develop the functions and routines that habitually appeared in their software. Object-oriented technology was also ideal for handling the complexity of building a GRAPHIC USER INTERFACE for software. Most PROGRAMMING LANGUAGES now handle objects either natively or through extensions (e.g. C++ is an extension of C which includes objects).

Applications

More recently object-oriented technology has moved into two areas that have implications for computerized information management. The first area is object-oriented databases and the structured documents they can store. The second area is the change in focus of operating-systems function, from giving primacy to supporting applications like word processors or spreadsheets that manipulate data, to giving primacy to the data itself. This data is typically stored in an object-oriented manner. Operating systems that do this are known as 'document-centred systems'. These two areas are converging.

STRUCTURED DOCUMENTS

STANDARDS SPECIFICATIONS exist for structured documents. The two most notable ones are Open Document Architecture (ODA), typically used in OFFICE AUTOMATION and Standard Generalized Mark-up Language (SGML), used in electronic publishing. Both these standards concentrate on describing document content rather than appearance. Neither standard is particularly suited to implementation using relational databases, as these databases use records and fields to store data. However, object-oriented databases appear to be not only much better suited to handling TEXT RETRIEVAL functions on structured documents, but also able to integrate MULTIMEDIA data (e.g. images) and HYPERMEDIA links (Heather and Rossiter 1989).

DOCUMENT-CENTRED SYSTEMS

Object-oriented databases are just beginning to make a commercial impact. Structured document handling is still in its infancy. By contrast, document-centred capabilities are already present in many leading operating systems, for example, Object Linking and Embedding (OLE) in Microsoft Windows. There is intense commercial competition to improve the object-orientation of basic operating-system functions (Lu 1992). There is a vendor-neutral standards body, the Object Management Group (OMG), but this has not stopped vendors from fostering their own standards.

References

Heather, M.A. and Rossiter, B.N. (1989) 'Theoretical structures for object-based text', in *WOODMAN '89: Workshop on Object-oriented Document Manipulation*, AFCET, pp. 178–92.
Lu, C. (1992) 'Objects for end users', *Byte* (December): 143–52.

Further reading

Bhalla, N. (1991) 'Object-oriented data models: A perspective and comparative view', *Journal of Information Science* 17: 145–60 [a good introduction to object-oriented technology in general and object-oriented databases in particular].
Furuta, R. (1989) 'An object-based taxonomy for abstract structure in document models', *Computer Journal* 32(6): 494–504 [a wide-ranging paper addressing the theoretical aspects of applying objects to structured document handling].

SEE ALSO: informatics

ALAN POULTER

OCLC

An enormous networked database consisting of records from US and UK MARC, and records created by member libraries for material not covered by the MARC files. It began as Ohio College Library Centre, founded in 1967, but, in recognition of its much expanded membership outside Ohio, has since 1981 been known as Online Computer Library Center. Over the years it has provided a wide range of services, including a microcomputer-based serials control system, a circulation control system and an online public-access catalogue (see OPACS) system. OCLC is a major source of catalogue data for libraries throughout the world.

SEE ALSO: Kilgour, Frederick Gridley

OCR

OCR (optical character recognition) is a technique for machine recognition of printed or typed characters based on their appearance. The characters to be identified are electronically scanned; the image of each character is analysed and, if recognizable, is then converted into the equivalent internal character code. OCR technology successfully permits the reading of documents containing a mixture of fonts in different sizes and styles. The output is a digital file that can be handled by the computer as if it had been keyboarded.

SEE ALSO: informatics

OFFICE AUTOMATION

Office automation has been defined as the 'planned integration of new technologies with office processes to increase the productivity and effectiveness of all knowledge workers' (Hicks 1995). In this context, knowledge workers are those employees, including managers, professionals, secretaries and clerks, whose responsibilities largely focus upon the processing of text and data. Office automation is a generic term that covers all aspects of text, image and even voice processing supported by communications software within the office environment.

Background

The use of INFORMATION AND COMMUNICATION TECHNOLOGY and INFORMATION SYSTEMS to support the effective management of libraries is now commonplace throughout the world. One area that computer-based technology can be most productively applied in is the area of automating all of a library's many clerical and office-based procedures. The office is a particularly appropriate area for computerization because of the huge quantities of paperwork that are routinely processed. The long-term objective of office automation is to replace many of the office functions that required reams of paper and filing cabinets full of documents with the creation of an office that is largely paperless (Sedacca 1991). Although much progress has been made in the development of office automation software, the creation of a paperless office is still a long way off. The remainder of this article examines the principal technologies involved in office automation and then identifies the major organizational issues relating to its implementation.

Primary office automation technologies

There is currently a wide variety of computer-based applications available that may support the automation of office activities in most types of organizations, including libraries. Each of the major technologies is briefly reviewed below.

WORD PROCESSING

Word processing refers to the software and hardware required to create, store, edit and print documents. Such systems are the single most common application of information technology to office work. Word processing greatly simplifies the task of creating and revising documents, as they need to be typed in only once, and may then be revised as many times as necessary. One of the most important facilities available within word-processing packages is their ability to merge text and data. This facility, for example, allows data such as a library member's name, address and details of overdue books to be merged with text in a standard recall letter.

DESKTOP PUBLISHING (DTP)

DESKTOP PUBLISHING packages are ones that can support the integration of text, data, charts and graphics in order to design, display and print high-quality documents comparable to those produced by professional typesetters.

ELECTRONIC MAIL

ELECTRONIC MAIL systems such as e-mail (Horten 1992) are used for the transmission, storage and distribution of text material in electronic form over a communications network. Electronic mail therefore facilitates organizational communications as it enables managers to communicate effectively with large groups of employees in a cost-effective manner. More sophisticated forms of electronic mail are now becoming available, in which the sender records a spoken message that is digitized before being transmitted to the recipient. The recipient may then command the message to be reconverted into a spoken form when ready to hear it. Such systems are known as voice mail systems (VMS).

FACSIMILE

The facsimile, or fax, is where the telephone system is used for the transmission and receipt of hard-copy documents, in a fast and relatively cheap manner.

ELECTRONIC CALENDARS

Typically electronic calendars, or diaries, keep track of appointments for individuals. However, electronic calendars are increasing in sophistication, and they can now be used to organize meetings automatically by searching the individual diaries of all required attendees to determine when a mutually satisfactory meeting can be initiated.

CONFERENCING SOFTWARE

Meetings requiring the attendance of many individuals from a variety of locations can be difficult, time-consuming and costly to arrange and conduct. Consequently, much effort has been directed towards finding ways of utilizing information technology to allow conferences to take place without the attendees leaving their own offices. Automated conferences can take place on a number of levels, from the fairly basic, where electronic mail is used to exchange ideas and data with regard to a specific issue, to the very sophisticated, where a two-way, full-motion video and audio link is activated. The latter type of conferencing is known as video-conferencing.

DOCUMENT IMAGE PROCESSING (DIP)

This is where information technology is applied to the task of capturing, storing, processing and retrieving images that may include data, text, graphics, documents, photographs and even handwriting. Document image processing offers the potential to use optical scanners, mass storage devices and PC networks to replace the office paper mountain (Bird 1993).

The integration of office automation software

The various text, voice and image-processing tools are typically run on personal computers using 'off the shelf' packaged software. To operate most effectively, these applications are then interconnected, typically using a LAN, which is a TELECOMMUNICATIONS system that encompasses a relatively small area such as a building or group of buildings. Originally, office automation systems were largely isolated from other commercial systems. Most users and suppliers of office automation software now recognize that its full potential can only be realized if it is fully integrated with other information systems applications, so that an organization's data may be directly incorporated into reports, documents and correspondence (Lawrence 1990). Furthermore, office applications may be directly linked to online information services, so that up-to-date information may be directly incorporated into documents.

The utilization of office automation software, integrated with other applications, offers organizations the opportunity greatly to increase the efficiency and productivity of their office operations. Libraries are prime candidates for the introduction of such technologies because of the large quantities of paperwork that are generated and processed within their offices.

References

Bird, J. (1993) 'Going for a DTP', *Computer Weekly* (19 August): 21–2.

Hicks, G.W. (1995) *Information Systems for Managers*, West.

Horten, M. (1992) 'Mail models', *Computing* (18 June): 24–5.

Lawrence, A. (1990) 'Office practices that need integrated architectures', *Computing* (15 November): 30–2.

Sedacca, B. (1991) 'Desk bound systems', *Network* (June): 125–34.

Further reading

Thorne, T.J. (1991) *Office Automation: The Barriers and Opportunities*, Touche Ross [a good introductory text].

SEE ALSO: computer science; informatics; records management

NEIL F. DOHERTY

OFFICIAL PUBLICATIONS

A document that has to be produced in multiple copies in an appropriate reprographic process by an organization considered to be an official body that is making it available to a wider public. If an 'official body' comprises any organization funded by or accountable to government, then any consideration of official publications must include GREY LITERATURE. Similarly, because international organizations and local or state governments are funded by national governments, they too must be considered to be official publishers. After defining an official body, IFLA (in Johansson 1982) stated that 'An official publication is defined by the status of the issuing source regardless of the subject matter or content'.

The effect of this definition has been to include many thousands of documents once judged to be too transitory to be included in the opus of a country's national publishing. This category of document is now universally defined as grey literature. Since the definition was originally drafted, an unforeseen development has been the diversity of publication and the format of publication. Government information is routinely sold in microform (see MICROFORMS) or on CD-ROM databases: free information is published on the INTERNET or as photocopies.

Range

Official publications include not only those that disseminate legislative, regulatory and statistical information but also those that propose, state and review policy and which publish the results of government research. Legislative documents normally exclude works specifically for legal practitioners but include primary and secondary legislation, bills and debates (like Hansard in the UK). Regulatory documents like treaties, circulars and guidelines comprise a large proportion of official publishing. The EC publishes much of its detailed regulatory and legislative information not as individual documents but in a multipart serial, *Official Journal of the European Communities*. Policy documents cover the entire range of government activity. The most influential of these are reviewed on an annual basis in the sixth issue of each volume of the *Journal of Government Information*.

Publishers

The size and variety of official publishers repeatedly cause a problem for the citizen who wishes to access official information. Normally, each country has its own government publisher (like the Government Printing Office in the USA and HMSO in the UK). Such publishers will usually provide subscription services to enable libraries to buy their whole output or publications on a specific subject. These documents will normally cross government departmental boundaries. Smaller government publishers, however, may only disseminate documents from a single government department or agency of, quite often, a single office. These documents are known as 'departmental publications' and often do not conform to normal bibliographical or book-trade standards. For the librarian, access, BIBLIO-GRAPHIC CONTROL and availability of departmental publications is a greater challenge than the control of central government publishing. Departmental publications have been described as 'fugitive publications' because of their transitory nature. The publications of international organizations and local or state authorities have many of the features of departmental publications. Some organizations like the United Nations have a catalogue of all their published and semi-published documents. Obviously, many organizations work over a wide geographical area and so central sales offices cannot be established. These bodies may have sales agencies with other commercial or government publishers, but the lack of comprehensive catalogues of publications and the divergent number of small publishers within an organization make it impossible to expect a comprehensive service.

Electronic publication

Electronic access to government information during the 1970s and 1980s was only through online databases. Relevant ones were normally bibliographies of particular publishers. The important subject databases (with the notable exception of ERIC) excluded any coverage of official publications. CD-ROM databases brought the advantages of low-cost electronic storage, access and distribution for the more esoteric datasets. Initially CD-ROMs containing bibliographical or statistical databases were published, but slowly official publishers started to produce full-text databases. At about the same time, in the early 1990s, access to online databases started to decline and some services were discontinued.

The development of Internet databases is an indicator of future trends. Although full-text documents are regularly made available, it remains to be seen whether they will remain permanently so. The purpose of posting information on a network will vary between individual agencies: some will use it to draw attention to new information or publications; others will use it as a public relations tool; and some will try to transmit neutral and necessary information to their public. The quality and purpose of these home pages is variable, with a few of them providing effective links to a wide range of other information providers. The White House page (www.whitehouse.gov/) in the USA and those of the Open Government initiative (www.open.gov. uk/) in the UK are good examples. The LIBRARY OF CONGRESS pages (lcweb.loc.gov/) are arguably the best pages for government information in the world.

Resources

In the USA, the Depository Library Program ensures that over 1,400 public and academic libraries receive, free of charge, the entire publishing output, or a selection of it, from the Government Printing Office. This is to ensure citizen access to all government publishing. There is no equivalent system in the UK and the only library with a collection that comprehensively covers both the grey as well as the mainstream publishing is the BRITISH LIBRARY. All NATIONAL LIBRARIES profess to have a comprehensive collection of their national official output, but the increasing amount of departmental publishing, grey literature and electronic products is making success hard to achieve. The primary journals in the field are published in the USA, the *Journal of Government Information* is published by Elsevier and JAI Press publish *Government Information Quarterly*; both are international in scope.

References

Johansson, E. (1982) 'The definition of an official publication', *IFLA Journal* 8: 393–5.

Further reading

Butcher, D. (1991) *Official Publications in Britain*, 2nd edn, LAPL.
Cherns, J.J. (1979) *Official Publishing: An Overview*, Pergamon.
Hernon, P. and McClure, C.R. (1988) *Public Access to Government Information*, 2nd edn, Ablex.

SEE ALSO: e-government; government publishing

ALASTAIR J. ALLAN

OFFICIAL SECRECY

The practice of governments everywhere of denying their citizens, and, by the same means, the citizens of other countries, access to certain information, in government possession or already circulating, which they allege will be harmful to the state, the government, the nation or some particular part of any of these.

Secrecy in totalitarian states

The security apparatus of the totalitarian or dictatorial state not only extends to suppression of comment and discussion amongst its citizens, so as to hinder or prevent the development of effective opposition, but also includes the protection of secrets, both within and without its frontiers. Typically, a proliferation of secret service agencies and units, answerable only to a president, a junta or a political party, will pursue suspected dissidents with an apparatus of informers and surveillance procedures, sometimes operating within the framework of the law, but frequently recognizing no limitation on their ability to detain, torture and kill those they suspect of offences or who threaten their power. They will also combat the agents of other powers that are seen to threaten the security of the state and, in turn, seek to obtain MILITARY INTELLIGENCE and other information about these rivals. The whole ESPIONAGE and counter-espionage operation has spawned a massively popular genre of books, films and TV programmes, so that genuine agencies such as the CIA, KGB, Mossad or MI5 are merged in the popular consciousness with a host of other fictional ones. Real examples of the action of government agencies in the protection of official secrecy and suppression of dissent can be drawn from all over the world, very frequently despite the explicit provisions of their constitution and laws (Article Nineteen 1991).

Secrecy in the USA

The association of official secrecy and dictatorship should not be allowed to mask the importance of official secrecy in democracies too. Arguably the least secretive government in the world is that of the USA, where the First Amendment to the Constitution prohibits Congress from 'abridging the freedom of speech, or of the press'. However, the USA does have laws on libel, obscenity, national security and access to government information that limit this constitutional freedom. The 1966 Freedom of Information Act (FOIA) provides mechanisms for the citizen to gain access held by government and its agencies, but if the government does not wish some aspect of its work to be subject to public scrutiny, it is able to put into effect the National Security Decision Directive (NSDD). During the Reagan presidency, for instance, this form of secret decree was used approximately 300 times. Additionally, the classes of documents exempt from the FOIA were expanded during this period, and security classification of documents about agencies such as the FBI and the CIA became more usual. On occasion this was extended to documents already held in libraries and until then regarded as being in the public domain (Bamford 1983).

Secrecy in Britain

Even more secretive, and perhaps the most secretive of all democratic states, is the UK, which has a strongly established culture of official secrecy. British legislation is pervaded by restrictions on access to one category of information or another, and government agencies routinely withhold information, the release of which might not be considered harmful, but which, in their judgement, would not be helpful to the enquirer. Government ministers can suppress information that they are advised may be damaging to national interests by the use of Public Interest Immunity Certificates (PIICs). The media, in turn, operate under a number of restrictions, including the attention of the Defence, Press and Broadcasting Committee, which seeks out forthcoming books, articles and broadcasts with defence implications. If the Committee feels an item is likely to be damaging to national security, it can then issue a 'D Notice' to prevent its appearance. Additionally, the law courts have the power to postpone or ban publication of information that they feel might threaten the administration of justice. Most notoriously, the UK Home Secretary in 1988 banned the broadcasting of words spoken by the representatives of Irish 'terrorist' organizations. Archives are also affected, and documents are not opened to researchers for a period after deposit: the British PUBLIC RECORD OFFICE imposes a standard thirty years, but as much as 3 per cent of the documentation received by the PRO is restricted indefinitely or for specified periods such as 100 years. The general tendency towards concealment was scarcely dented by the government Code of Practice on Access to Information, which came into effect in April 1994. Its replacement, the Freedom of Information Act 2000, is not scheduled to come into full operation until 2005.

At the apex of the system of secrecy in Britain is the Official Secrets Act, the current version of which was passed in 1989. The Act applies to members of the security and intelligence services, and other government employees and contractors who might possess potentially damaging information. It binds them to secrecy for life on a whole range of official information, but most particularly defence, the secret service and international relations. Also amongst those covered can be librarians in British government employ. The Act tends to be enforced as strictly as possible. Thus, for instance, in 1997 a former MI5 official, David Shayler, felt obliged to leave the country to avoid prosecution when he made public allegations that the agency regularly exceeded its powers. Whilst Shayler was being pursued under the law, details of his allegations were published in other countries and distributed via the Internet. Unable to obtain his extradition under the criminal law provisions of the Act, the government turned to actions under the civil law (infringement of copyright, breach of contract and of confidence) as alternatives. Whilst the actions against Shayler dragged on, information service providers and providers of Internet access (such as libraries) were forced to calculate the risk involved in making available the information that was the source of the dispute. The situation was similar to the earlier case of *Spycatcher* by Peter Wright (1987), which had made similar revelations to those of Shayler. Although published in Australia, the book allegedly offended against British official secrecy law. The British government sought through the law courts not merely to prevent publication in Britain, but to suppress it in Australia, and stop copies entering the country (Turnbull 1988). Whilst the government's ultimately unsuccessful actions were in progress, librarians who placed it on their shelves had reason to feel that they too were at risk. Such cases show up the tension between secrecy and concealment in a country with notionally uncensored media and libraries free from outside interference.

References

Article Nineteen (1991) *Information, Freedom and Censorship*, Library Association.
Bamford, J. (1983) *The Puzzle Palace: A Report on America's Most Secret Agency*, Viking.
Turnbull, M. (1988) *The Spycatcher Trial*, Heinemann.
Wright, P. (1987) *Spycatcher: The Candid Autobiography of a Senior Intelligence Officer*, Viking.

Further reading

Rogers, A. (1997) *Secrecy and Power in the British State: A History of the British Official Secrets Act 1911–1989*, Pluto Press.

SEE ALSO: freedom of information

PAUL STURGES

ONE-PERSON LIBRARY

The term used to describe a library or information service run by one individual, often with little or no assistance. Other terms used to describe this include the solo librarian, the singleton post and the one-man band. The last mentioned was not seen as being a sexist term by those who use it in the UK, according to representatives of ASLIB's One-Man Band (OMB) special interest group. It has its origins in entertainment terminology, describing a person who carried and played a multitude of musical instruments. It has also been applied more broadly to describe anyone running a small business without supporting staff. The Special Libraries Association of the USA defines 'solo librarians' as 'information managers without professional peers in the same organization'. The term 'singleton post' is used in UK government libraries and is seen as 'one in which the postholder is the only professional in the library' (Burge 1995).

Employing organizations

The term 'one-person library' (OPL) is used largely to refer to those library or information units that exist within what are commonly described as SPECIAL LIBRARIES, e.g. within commercial and industrial organizations; professional practices; membership associations; government departments or agencies; voluntary bodies and other types of organization, excluding public libraries. Around 95 per cent of the membership of ASLIB's OMB group works in special libraries. Although there are probably many small branches within public library services that are operated by a single member of staff, that individual would not be likely to be the only library worker within the parent organization, as is often the case in special libraries. He or she would be part of the overall staffing within the network of units that make up each area's public library service, thereby having access to other colleagues and probably working as part of a team.

Staff support

Single operators, more than any other group of information workers, seem to be strongly aware of the importance of professional contact and interaction in combating the feeling of professional isolation (Shuter 1984). Membership of interest groups such as the ASLIB one already mentioned or, in the USA, the Solo Librarians' Division of the Special Libraries Association, provides such contact in the form of a network of like-minded LIS workers. In addition to the groups set up specifically with the solo operator in mind, formal and informal subject interest groups are also likely to have a number of solo librarians among their membership. Those employed in OPLs find networking invaluable, providing considerable stimulus for new thinking, with the chance to test new ideas and seek solutions to problems, as well as to establish reciprocal arrangements for the exchange of, and access to, additional sources of information. Newsletters are also seen as a valuable element in networking and are used to draw attention to relevant events and developments, e.g. members of ASLIB's OMB group receive a newsletter as part of membership. In the USA there is a commercially produced newsletter, *One-Person Library*, available on subscription from SMR International of New York.

As is suggested by the above definition, the OPL presents its incumbent with a range of tasks to perform and priorities to meet, usually without the possibility of delegating any of these to a colleague. Some posts are held by professionally qualified librarians or information scientists, while others are not. Burge (1995) notes that, in the case of singleton posts in UK government libraries, the postholder is professionally qualified and in the majority of cases will have some form of clerical support. In many other OPLs the grading of the post, the requirement for qualifications and the provision of clerical support will vary considerably. In some cases an OPL will have been created as such; in others it may have come into being through overall reductions in staffing levels.

OPLs may also operate on a part-time basis or involve a postholder running units at more than one site within the same organization. Some small libraries may not have permanent staff but contract out the running of their OPL to an independent operator.

Management and personal skills required

Given the demands made on the solo operator, frustration may be experienced, but so may a considerable amount of personal development. A positive attitude will certainly help in turning what could be perceived as potential obstacles into opportunities, as is illustrated by several personal case studies in the chapter 'On your own' in *Personal Development in Information Work* (Webb 1991). Motivation, the use of initiative and a generally entrepreneurial approach, as well as skills in communication and work organization, are all seen to play a vital part in running an effective OPL. Investment of a little time in keeping up to date with professional developments can lead to considerable savings of time in the long run. Making sensible use of information technology can not only improve the library or information service, but also enhance its status and its ability to feature as a central and essential part of the organization's own development. The successful operation of an OPL or information services is dependent on the librarian having established clear objectives in line with organizational needs, supported by appropriate procedures and systems. Effective ways of setting about this by taking a systematic approach to the planning and development of such a service is set out in *Creating an Information Service* (Webb 1996).

References

Burge, S. (1995) *Broken Down by Grade and Sex: The Career Development of Government Librarians*, Library Association, Government Libraries Group.

Shuter, J. (1984) *The Information Worker in Isolation: Problems and Achievements*, MCB University Press.

Webb, S.P. (1996) *Creating an Information Service*, ASLIB.

—— (1991) *Personal Development in Information Work*, ASLIB.

SEE ALSO: information professions

SYLVIA P. WEBB

ONLINE

Access to a computer system via TELECOMMUNI-
CATIONS links. The particular significance of the
term for LIS is as a means of remote access to
databases of information, particularly bibliographic information. It is used, therefore, in
distinction to access to information on paper,
CD-ROM or any other format where a copy of
the original is held by the user.

SEE ALSO: information retrieval

ONLINE SERVICES

The key technological components of online
systems are computers that can act in time-
shared mode and teleprocessing systems with
terminal equipment. Online services employ online systems technology to provide remote users
with access to information organized in databases with greater flexibility, precision and speed
than comparable print resources can.

Technological development

Online systems developed rapidly from the 1960s
through the convergence of several streams of
technological advances: time-sharing computers
that permit large numbers of users to conduct
simultaneous interactions with systems that may
be located far from the central computer and its
information store; increasingly efficient interactive computer programmes, powerful and user-
friendly; rapid-access storage devices that grew in
capacity and decreased in data storage costs;
computer terminals and compact, inexpensive
PERSONAL COMPUTERS that can transmit, receive
and display information; telecommunications
networks that provide fast, cheap data transmission; growing volumes of numerical, textual and
graphical information (DATABASES) created by
publishers and other organizations in computer-
readable form. Local-area networks permit online access over a limited site (e.g. a university
campus). Wide-area networks operate nationally
and internationally, and may themselves be
linked together in a network of networks (the
INTERNET).

Functions of online services

Most database producers, particularly those compiling bibliographic databases, license their data-

bases to other organizations called 'online
services' or 'host computer services' or simply a
host, which provide the computer, software and
TELECOMMUNICATIONS support that enables remote users to access the databases. The larger
hosts provide access to several hundreds of
databases in a wide range of subject areas (they
are sometimes called 'supermarket' hosts). The
operation of such services requires large investments in hardware and software. The functions
of hosts are structuring, loading and subsequently updating the databases into large time-
sharing computers; maintaining 24-hour access;
connecting their computers to national and international networks; maintaining user-friendly programmes so that the databases can be
interrogated easily and efficiently; offering downloading facilities enabling users to store and
display retrieved information locally; providing
gateway access that permits users to switch to
other hosts; connecting to DOCUMENT DELIVERY
services by means of which the full texts of
retrieved references are delivered electronically
(ELECTRONIC MAIL, fax) or by post. Hosts market
their services at exhibitions and conferences, and
provide systems and database manuals, newsletters, 'help desk' services and training courses.

Service charging

The main components of most charging systems
relate to telecommunications rates; the elapsed
time a user is connected to a host computer;
storage of regular search routines; downloading
and printing fees for retrieved information. The
latter are often components of the royalty
charges paid by hosts to database producers,
with whom the copyright of the database usually
resides. Some hosts charge a fixed annual subscription to their specialized services that allows
unlimited access over a 12-month period.

End-user access

In the earlier years of online services, connecting
to hosts and searching databases was a complex,
expensive activity and the task was often dele-
gated to specialist 'intermediaries' (librarians and
information officers). More recently the trend
has been towards encouraging the individuals
actually seeking the information – the 'end-users'
– to do their own searching. Staff and students at
British universities can search, by means of
terminals in offices, laboratories and libraries,

databases relating to science, engineering, medicine and the social sciences that are accessible through a joint academic network (JANET). Each university supports the services with annual subscriptions, enabling academic end-users to have free and unrestricted access to the database at the point of use. Users can download the results of their searches into an e-mail service. Complementary document delivery services have been implemented through which an end-user can request (and pay for by credit card transfer) copies of original documents.

Localized online search services

Databases recorded on CD-ROMs, though originally intended to be searched on 'stand-alone' personal computers, are increasingly being made available for simultaneous search for a number of online users by means of local area networks. Such services are popular on university campuses as they are cheap to operate and the search software provided by the CD-ROM producers is usually very user-friendly. As the capacity of hard disks is increasing (and the unit costs of storage declining) some organizations are beginning to load relatively large databases on their own computers – bypassing commercial hosts – to provide networked online services for closed communities of end-users.

Further reading

Armstrong, C.J. and Hartley, R.J. (1997) *Online and CD-ROM Database Searching*. 2nd edn, Mansell.
Vigil, P.J. (1988) *Online Retrieval: Analysis and Strategy*, Wiley.
Walker, G. and Janes, J. (1999) *Online Retrieval: A Dialogue of Theory and Practice*, Libraries Unlimited.

SEE ALSO: computer science; electronic public-information services; informatics; information policy

HARRY EAST

ONTOLOGY

A term from the discipline of philosophy appropriated by the ARTIFICIAL INTELLIGENCE (AI) community. Whilst in philosophy it signifies a systematic account of existence, in AI it is used in a more limited sense as a specification, or a set of definitions, of a conceptualization. A knowledge-based system, or AI agent, is necessarily com-

mitted to some conceptualization of the domain within which it is to operate. In practice an ontology sets out the concepts and relationships that make up the formal vocabulary used in building an AI agent. Ontologies are an essential component of the SEMANTIC WEB.

Further reading

Gruber, T.R. (1993) 'A translation approach to portable ontologies', *Knowledge Acquisition* 5: 199–220.

SEE ALSO: information theory

OPACS

An OPAC (Online Public-Access Catalogue) is a DATABASE of bibliographic records describing the holdings usually of one particular library. It allows searching by name, title and subject, and offers online access through public terminals.

Online catalogues were developed in the late 1970s and since then have become widely accepted as the contemporary form of catalogue (see CATALOGUES) in the developed world. Since their advent, vast numbers of bibliographic records have been converted into computer format, using the MAchine-Readable Cataloguing (MARC) format, although public use of catalogues was often still in printed form, by cards, or in microform (see MICROFORMS). A number of major US libraries pioneered online access and developed the first online catalogues. Gradually, bibliographic agencies, co-operatives and commercial companies developed LIBRARY AUTOMATION systems that included OPAC. During the 1980s, most academic libraries and an increasing number of public libraries (especially in the USA, the UK, Australia and Europe) installed online catalogues. One of the major advantages of an online catalogue (apart from enhanced access to library materials) is that if linked to an automated circulation system it can indicate the current status of an item, e.g. on loan, available for borrowing, etc., in an integrated system.

The database

An online catalogue database normally consists of bibliographic records describing mainly monographs, compiled according to international standards such as ANGLO-AMERICAN CATALOGUING RULES (AACR) and MARC format, commonly used classification codes such as Library of

Congress and DDC, and standard subject headings such as LCSH. This approach replicates the standard inner form of early manual catalogues, and online catalogues have been criticized for simply transferring the flat, linear structure of manual catalogues into an online environment, rather than taking the opportunity to rethink the internal structure of the bibliographic record itself.

Methods of access

Early online catalogues were 'command-driven', i.e. it was necessary for the user to learn a set of commands in order to type in a search. Current systems usually offer a 'menu-based' approach where the user makes a choice of access points from a menu. As graphical user interfaces become more common, more catalogues offer this method of access, and Web-type access is becoming standard.

Access points

Access points in online catalogues generally echo those of manual catalogues but offer supplementary access that greatly enhances retrieval. The ability to search by 'keyword' or 'freetext' liberates the user from the need to have full author or title information. However, many online catalogues do not incorporate full authority control over authors and subjects, and this lack can result in inaccurate and imprecise searching, as opposed to the best practice in manual catalogues.

Subject searching

The most problematic area of searching is that of subject access. In the USA, the traditional subject access system, LCSH, has been incorporated online, but whereas in manual catalogues the onus was on the user to find the correct subject heading, it was then possible to browse though lists/cards for relevant books. In some online catalogues, it is necessary to input the full or partial subject heading string. This can make subject searching much more difficult. Many systems now offer keyword searching on subject headings, which allows users to use natural language in searching but undermines the power of a highly structured system such as LCSH. In the UK, where LCSH has not been common in manual catalogues, a few libraries have now

adopted this system; some others have transferred online their own subject index, usually developed in-house, while other libraries have no formal subject system and rely on keyword searching of title and other fields for subject access. Overall, there is some evidence that where both are available there has been a move from strict subject searching to keyword searching (Larson 1991).

Traditionally, monographs have been poorly indexed in online catalogues and although keyword access has improved retrieval by subject, online catalogues are badly served in comparison with the amount of subject information available in databases of journal articles. An attempt to reduce this anomaly is the move to add extra subject-rich data, such as contents pages, extra keywords and terms from back-of-the-book-indexes. This has the effect of increasing the exhaustiveness of the indexing but frequently results in an excessive number of items being retrieved.

Current considerations

As online catalogues become the norm, some of the initial euphoria that characterized their arrival has been replaced with a more measured view of their worth. Early online catalogues were difficult to use and often led to no items being retrieved in searches of any complexity. Recent emphasis has been on simplifying search procedures, but in some cases the result of this has been excessive reliance on keywords, which can lead to excessive numbers of items retrieved. Online catalogues increasingly include non-monographic and other special materials such as music, manuscripts, etc. Once again the standard access points facilitate general retrieval but are often inadequate for highly specific requests.

The increasing ability to access information via networks such as the INTERNET is having an increasing effect on the role of catalogues as an essential requirement in any library. Many libraries make the catalogues of remote libraries readily available and readers have access to databases of journal articles alongside them. Copies of documents may be requested and delivered by post, fax and, increasingly, by electronic means. Although there is a diversity of interfaces and retrieval languages, it is increasingly possible to access the resources of remote libraries using the commands of the home cata-logue. Developments such as these have increas-ingly impinged on the role of the catalogue in individual libraries. As yet, however imperfect, the online catalogue is the most popular and successful way of indicating the holdings and status of items in a library.

References

Larson, R.R. (1991) 'The decline of subject searching: Long-term trends and patterns of index use in an online catalog', *Journal of the American Society for Information Science* 42(3): 197–215.

Further reading

Buckland, M.K. (1992) *Redesigning Library Services: A Manifesto*, American Library Association.
Hildreth, C.R. (1991) 'Advancing towards E3OPAC: The imperative and the path', in N. Van Pulis (ed.) *Think Tank on the Present and Future of the Online Catalog: Proceedings, 1991, January 11–12*, Amer-ican Library Association, Reference and Adult Ser-vices Division, pp. 39–48.
Hughes, J.E. (2001) 'Access, access, access! The new OPAC mantra', *American Libraries* 32: 62–4.
O'Brien, A. (1994) 'Online catalogs: Enhancements and developments', in M.E. Williams (ed.) *Annual Re-view of Information Science and Technology*, vol. 29, Learned Information, pp. 219–42.

SEE ALSO: bibliographic description; catalogues; indexing; online services; user studies

ANN O'BRIEN

OPEN ACCESS

A system of access to library materials in which users have the freedom to move around the collection and make their own selection of material to consult on the premises or to borrow. The term is used in distinction to CLOSED ACCESS and is a distinguishing feature of modern librar-ianship. During the twentieth century it has replaced closed access virtually everywhere ex-cept in archival and research collections or the remnants of the library systems of totalitarian states. Because it lays the collections open to the risk of theft and damage, it can call for higher levels of library security (see SECURITY IN LI-BRARIES). Despite the enhanced autonomy of the user, it does not remove the need for reader assistance services and creates a strong need for user instruction programmes.

OPEN SOURCE

A term coined in 1998 to describe what had until then been described as free software or freeware. It represents a radically different, non-proprietor-ial view of software from that generally held by the major software companies. Most commer-cially available software is supplied only in compiled versions (that is, the source code in which the developer originally created it has been translated into a form that the computer can understand). This is not only necessary for practical purposes, but reinforces the control that companies have over the INTELLECTUAL PROP-ERTY in the product and enables them to protect the code from commercial rivals. In contrast, open-source software is available free of charge, and includes both the source code and the compiled version. Developers who accept the open-source concept believe that software is a common good that should be shared rather than sold for profit, and that it can best be adapted, improved and de-bugged by its users. To make this possible the users need access to the source code.

Although Linus Torvalds's release of his Linux operating system in 1991 predates the use of the term it is, nevertheless, the best exemplar of the principle. Linux has been improved over the years as a result of the co-operative efforts of large numbers of enthusias-tic users. The difficulty with Linux and other open-source products is that when problems occur the user is obliged to be more knowledge-able and resourceful than normal. To counter this difficulty it is accepted that versions of open-source products can be sold rather than supplied free, but when users buy open-source products they are actually paying for the war-ranty and technical support that can then be offered. Thus Red Hat Software sells Official Red Hat Linux on precisely this basis. The open-source movement now includes a non-profit company, the Open Source Initiative, which certifies open-source products on the basis of a nine-point definition.

Further reading

Fitzgerald, B. and Keller, J. (2002) *Understanding Open Source Software Development*, Addison-Wesley.
Opensource.org, *The Open Source Definition* (www.opensource.org/docs/definition_plain.html).

OPEN-SYSTEMS INTERCONNECTION

OSI is the term adopted by the International Standards Organization (ISO) to describe manufacturer-independent standards for interconnecting computer equipment. It is a response to the problem of mixing computer systems and terminals supplied by different manufacturers in a single network. The standards are guided by a framework, known as the OSI reference model, which defines the relationships between the hardware and software components within a communications network.

SEE ALSO: information and communication technology

OPERATING SYSTEM

The essential program loaded into a computer whenever it starts up, which controls access to all the resources of the computer and to its peripherals, and supervises the running of other programs. In the past it was usually supplied as if it were part of the computer hardware, but operating systems such as MS-DOS, Unix and Microsoft Windows were developed independently of hardware design and manufacture. The various types of operating systems are referred to as *platforms*.

SEE ALSO: information and communication technology

OPERATIONS RESEARCH

Used to enable rational decision-making in many professional, official, business and industrial contexts through prediction of the behaviour of complex systems, with the aim of improving or optimizing system performance. The approach is interdisciplinary and experimental, encompassing managerial decision-making, mathematical and computer modelling, and the use of information technology. Operations research professionals address a wide variety of design and operational issues in communication and data networks; computer operations; and many areas relating to business productivity and efficiency. A typical area for the use of operations research would be to assist in deciding how best to employ resources in a search for information so as to minimize the costs associated with the search and yet avoid the errors that inadequate information might produce.

SEE ALSO: economics of information; information systems; management support systems

OPTICAL DISK

A storage medium for digital data that is written to, and read, by lasers. The storage capacity for optical disks is much greater than that of magnetic disks and their durability is greater. For the user, they behave in three main ways:

- Read only – audio CDs and CD-ROMs come with data already encoded on them, and this cannot be modified.
- Write once – data can be written on WORM (write once, read many) disks, but after that they perform as a read-only disks.
- Erasable – data can be written, erased and replaced with new data. With the availability of reasonably priced CD burners and the improvement of access speed, they are increasingly popular as a data storage or back-up medium.

ORAL TRADITIONS

Found in all societies, but particularly significant where the main method of exchanging information is through oral communication. This is the case in developing societies, where print culture is a recent innovation and oral culture is dominant for the majority of people.

Present status

Before the invention of writing and printing, communication was based on oral traditions. When writing and printing became well established in Western countries and strong economies permitted the establishment of viable publishing industries, there was a steady replacement of oral culture by a written culture – that is, one based on the written word. In contrast, in most Third World countries, with high levels of illiteracy coupled with weak economies that cannot support a viable publishing industry, oral traditions still dominate in the exchange of information.

The evolution from an oral to a print-based

culture has led to the conclusion that oral culture is a stage before the invention of writing or the acquisition of literacy (Ndiaye 1988). Rehnema has called the above conclusion an ethnocentric view of history and points out that 'it is wrong to suppose that a society must necessarily move in linear progression from the oral stage associated with a primitive form of expression, to that of writing, seen as a higher form of mental development' (Rehnema 1982).

The fear that oral culture will be weakened by a culture based on the written word has led to a rejectionist approach whereby calls have been made for libraries in the Third World to reject printed materials and develop oral librarianship. This stems from a perceived conflict between oral traditions and print-based information systems (Amadi 1981). The possibility that oral traditions could make a major contribution to Third World librarianship if libraries are reformed has been raised (Durrani 1985).

Aspects of oral traditions

Various terms, which are often used interchangeably with oral tradition, but which are in actual fact distinct aspects of it, are briefly explored below.

ORAL LITERATURE

Oral traditions have been viewed as a rich source of contemporary literature in Third World societies because most of their literature is not found in the written form (Finnegan 1970). Oral literature is subdivided into several forms. The folk tale is perhaps the best known. This form, often of high creativity, contains various themes and aims at bringing the lessons of life to its audience. Poetry and songs constitute another well-known form. These include praise poems and elegiac, religious and political poems. Proverbs are short sayings encapsulating the experiences of members of society in a brief and memorable statement full of imagery and succinct expression. Good examples include this proverb from the Fulani of Nigeria: 'You will not see an elephant moving on your own head, only a louse moving on another's'; or this Swahili proverb from East Africa: 'Heavy silence has a mighty noise.'

The various forms of oral literature add up to a vast information resource base and suggestions have been made that libraries have a section that consists of oral literature resources (Oyeoku 1975). UNESCO has initiated several programmes to promote research and create awareness for the preservation of oral literature (UNESCO 1974).

ORAL HISTORY

The value of oral traditions is perhaps most evident as a primary source of history. Such recognition arises from the effort of Third World countries to write their history from their own perspective rather than that of colonial administrators (Mbaye 1990). To achieve this aim, interviews are conducted with elderly people and recorded on tape and later transcribed. A good example of this aspect of oral traditions was the General History of Africa Project sponsored by UNESCO, which was launched in the mid-1970s and aimed at producing a text reflecting the past of Africa from an African point of view.

There have also been several oral history programmes based in the national archives of countries in developing and developed countries. Interest in oral history has resulted in Oral History Associations dedicated to research and general scholarship in a number of countries (Starr 1977).

ORAL COMMUNICATION

Another functional dimension of oral traditions is their role as a communication channel. Oral traditions are a medium of communication that can be used to disseminate information to rural people and other disadvantaged groups to speed up national development (Aboyade 1984). There are also groups of professional people who prefer oral communication to written forms of communication when seeking work-related information (Allen 1969).

An innovation attempted in Southeast Asia involved the use of a video medium by ordinary people within an oral culture to communicate messages to government officials and transfer information to people in other parts of the world, and this met with great success (Stuart 1987). In some cases, the dominance of oral traditions has been condemned and is regarded as the main hindrance to the use of print-based information systems in the Third World (Reddy and Sandeep 1979).

INDIGENOUS KNOWLEDGE

Oral traditions contain a vast unrecorded KNOWLEDGE base of people not yet drawn into a print and electronic media culture. Such knowledge, which has enabled tribal people to survive, is passed from one generation to the next through a chain of oral communication, involving folk tales, ritual, ceremonies, myth and rites of passage (Chambers 1983). The realization that tribal societies possess valuable knowledge, sometimes superior to its Western counterpart, arises from the disastrous mismanagement of the environment using modern scientific methods (Linden 1991). There are several areas where traditional knowledge has gained wide recognition. In medicine, the WHO has advised Third World countries to incorporate traditional medicine into their health services. Tribal healers are helping scientists in their search for plants with useful medicinal properties. In agriculture and environmental management, tribal practices are being re-examined for possible wider adoption. There are several issues to be addressed before use of indigenous knowledge can be re-established. Many Third World government agencies still regard all forms of indigenous knowledge as an impediment to development. The oral nature of this type of knowledge means that, as elders who possess it die, valuable information disappears. Western education and urban migration have alienated the youth from their culture, so that they are unwilling to learn and inherit this knowledge from the older generation.

References

Aboyade, B.O. (1984) 'Oral tradition as a medium for information transfer in rural communities', *Nigerian Journal of Library and Information Studies* 2(2): 69–75.

Allen, T. (1969) 'Information needs and uses', in C. Cuadra (ed.) *Annual Review of Information Science and Technology*, vol. 4, William Benton, pp. 1–29.

Amadi, A.O. (1981) *African Libraries: Western Tradition and Colonial Brainwashing*, Scarecrow Press.

Chambers, R. (1983) *Rural Development: Putting the Last First*, Longmans.

Durrani, S. (1985) 'Rural information in Kenya', *Information Development* 1(3): 149–57.

Finnegan, R. (1970) *Oral Literature in Africa*, Clarendon Press.

Linden, E. (1991) 'Lost tribes, lost knowledge', *Times International* (23 September): 44–54.

Mbaye, S. (1990) 'Oral records in Senegal', *American Archivist* 53(4): 566–74.

Ndiaye, R. (1988) 'Oral culture in libraries', *IFLA Journal* 14(1): 40–6.

Oyeoku, K.K. (1975) 'Publishing in Africa: Breaking the development barrier', in E. Oluwasanmi, E. Maclean and H. Zell (eds) *Publishing in Africa in the Seventies*, University of Ife Press, pp. 277–88.

Reddy, E. and Sandeep, P. (1979) *Communication for Adult Education and Development in Rural Context*, Department of Non-Formal Adult Continuing Education.

Rehnema, M. (1982) 'The sound library, a simple but revolutionary tool for development', *UNESCO Journal of Information Science, Librarianship and Archives Administration* 4(3): 151–8.

Starr, L. (1977) 'Oral history', in A. Kent, H. Lancour and J. Daily (eds) *Encyclopedia of Library and Information Science*, vol. 20, Marcel Dekker, pp. 440–65.

Stuart, S. (1987) 'The village video network: Video as a tool for local development and South to South exchange', *Convergence* 20(2): 63–8.

UNESCO (1974) *African Oral Tradition: Selection and Formulation of Some Themes*, UNESCO.

SEE ALSO: Africa; communication; rural library services

KINGO MCHOMBU

ORGANIZATION OF KNOWLEDGE

The description (INDEXING) and organization (CLASSIFICATION) for retrieval of messages representing knowledge, texts by which KNOWLEDGE is recorded, and documents in which texts are embedded. Knowledge itself resides in minds and brains of living creatures. Its organization for retrieval via short- and long-term memory is a principal topic of COGNITIVE SCIENCE. Library and information science deals with the description and organization of the artefacts (messages, texts, documents) by which knowledge (including feelings, emotions, desires) is represented and shared with others. These knowledge resources are often called information resources as well. Thus 'knowledge organization' in the context of library and information science is a short form for 'knowledge resources organization' or 'knowledge representations organization'. It is often called 'information organization'.

The organization of knowledge in library and information science consists of several aspects: identification of messages (often called works); identification of texts in which messages (works) are represented; description of documents in which texts are presented; and description of the content, features and meaning of messages. The resulting identifications and descriptions are organized into indexes, catalogues, databases, digital libraries and other information retrieval systems for access by searchers. The creation and organization of these identifications and descriptions are called INDEXING, abstracting, cataloguing (see CATALOGUES), BIBLIOGRAPHIC CLASSIFICATION, BIBLIOGRAPHY, RECORDS MANAGEMENT and KNOWLEDGE MANAGEMENT, in various contexts.

Although language texts often predominate in organization of knowledge activities, the procedures apply to every form or format of message, text and document: artistic and musical creations, visual images and three-dimensional objects (sculpture), scientific and mathematical formulations, performances, as well as works represented in spoken or written language. Likewise every sort of medium is encompassed by the organization of knowledge: paper, film, video, clay tablets, three-dimensional objects, electronic digital media, and combinations of formats and media, now called 'MULTIMEDIA'.

This article addresses the major procedures for the description and organization of knowledge resources in library and information science: indexing, cataloguing and classification, including document and content description, vocabulary control and the methods, both automatic and intellectual, for performing these functions. It then turns to the products of knowledge organization – CATALOGUES, indexes, DATABASES and digital libraries (see DIGITAL LIBRARY), and addresses the fundamental attributes of these INFORMATION RETRIEVAL systems: scope and domain, presentation media, documentary units, analysis base, indexing exhaustivity, vocabulary specificity, indexing methods, syntax for index headings and search statements, vocabulary management, document surrogation, and SURROGATE and index display.

Role in library and information science

If the provision of information on demand, or in anticipation of demand in response to perceived need, is the major function of librarianship, and if the study of information retrieval is the major focus of INFORMATION SCIENCE, then the organization of knowledge resources to facilitate information access and retrieval is a central concern of both fields. It is a fundamental contribution of library and information science to society. Its history is as old as writing and the development of the first documents. This article focuses on current methods.

Indexing, cataloguing and classification

Indexing, cataloguing and classification are three methods, often confused, for organizing knowledge resources. Indexing (that is, indicating) involves methods for providing access to document collections, single documents and parts of documents without regard to the location of these documents. Cataloguing is the indexing of documents in particular collections. Classification is the grouping and arrangement of index (or catalogue) categories and entries in accordance with relations among them, as opposed to alphabetical or numerical arrangement based on entry terms.

Because cataloguing and classification depend on indexing – indeed they represent special cases of indexing – indexing itself is the fundamental method for organizing knowledge resources. Therefore, this article will emphasize types and attributes of indexing and indexes.

DOCUMENT DESCRIPTION

Indexing always involves the description of documents that contain messages of interest, unless the document is self-evident, as in back-of-the-book indexes. Document description usually involves noting the creator(s) of the message and its text, the name(s) given to the text, the version of the text, the name of the document's publisher, distributor and/or manufacturer, the size, shape, format and medium of the document, and similar notable characteristics.

There is an enormous literature guiding the description of messages (works), texts and documents of all formats and media. The most widely used rules for description and non-topical access are the *Anglo-American Cataloguing Rules* (AACR) (1998), but there are many specialized guides, such as *Standard Citation Forms for Published Bibliographies and Catalogs Used in Rare Book Cataloging* (VanWingen and Urquiza 1996), *Descriptive Cataloging of Rare Books* (Library of Congress, Office for Descriptive Cataloging Policy 1991), *Map Cataloging Manual* (Library of Congress, Geography and Map Division 1991), *Archival Moving Image Materials: a Cataloging Manual* (Library of Congress, AMIM Revision Committee 2000), *Archives, Personal Papers, and Manuscripts: a Cataloging Manual for Archival Repositories, Historical Societies, and Manuscript Libraries* (Hensen

1989) and *Sheet Music Cataloging and Processing: a Manual* (Shaw and Shiere 1984), as well as innumerable style guides for citing documents in various contexts. According to Wellisch (1980), building on work by Wilson (1968), there are no major theoretical problems in the description of texts and documents, apart from their content or meaning. We know how to do it, and we have plenty of guidance for doing it properly. This does not mean that it is easy, because messages, texts and documents come in an enormous variety of shapes, sizes, media and formats, from many types of publishers and producers, with little standardization. Unresolved theoretical issues lie largely in the realm of identification and description of content and meaning.

With the onset of electronic documents, the WORLD WIDE WEB and the INTERNET, the definition and description of documents have become unsettled, leading to discussions about revising the Anglo-American Cataloguing Rules (Weihs 1998; Schottlaender 1998). In the meantime, specialized guides for indexing and cataloguing electronic resources have appeared, such as *Cataloging Internet Resources: a Manual and Practical Guide* (Olson 1997).

DOCUMENT IDENTIFIERS

Also in the context of electronic knowledge resources, there has been increased interest in extending concise document identifiers, patterned after ISBN for books and ISSN for serials, to many other types of resources. Examples include DOI (Digital Object Identifier), SICI (Serial Item and Contribution Identifier), PII (Publisher Item Identifier), BICI (Book Item and Component Identifier), ISMN (International Standard Music Number), ISRC (International Standard Recording Code), ISAN (International Standard Audiovisual Number), ISWC (International Standard Work Code), URN (Uniform Resource Name) and PURL (Persistent Uniform Resource Locator). Good summaries of these efforts have been provided by Green and Bide (1997), and Paskin (1997).

IDENTIFICATION OF MESSAGES (WORKS)

For at least 100 years, cataloguing codes have emphasized the need to identify the underlying message or work that is represented in a text and recorded in a document. The purpose of this work identification has been to enable users to find, in one place, all versions of a particular work, regardless of its particular text or manifestation (translations, reproductions, new printings under various titles, etc.). Thus, records and descriptions for all versions of Shakespeare's *Hamlet* or books of the Bible or a Beethoven symphony or a Van Gogh painting can be gathered together, regardless of the many different titles such works may have been given.

The traditional method used to identify works has been to assign to every work a single 'main entry heading' and, if a work has appeared under various titles (e.g., in various languages or the same language), a standard or uniform title as well. Traditionally, the main entry heading has been the first or chief author (if there are more than one), or if a chief author cannot be identified, the original title of the work. Together, the main entry heading and title of the work (a uniform title if needed) have identified the work.

'Main entry heading' has been one of the most misunderstood (and misleading) terms in library cataloguing. The misunderstanding stems from its former association with printed book catalogues in which there was a 'main' full entry, with many less complete secondary entries referring to the complete entry. This complete entry was placed under the main entry heading. This pattern of publication has continued in many printed indexing and abstracting services, where brief author and subject entries lead to a full entry with full citation and abstract.

But the fundamental and continuing purpose of the main entry heading has not been to provide a full entry. Library catalogues have generally made every entry complete since the development of the unit card or unit entry in the second half of the nineteenth century. Similarly, in modern OPACS (online public-access catalogues) and information retrieval databases, every access point can lead to as full a record as the user desires. The purpose of the main entry heading is not access to particular records or documents – every access point given to a record or document is equal in this regard. The main entry heading, together with a title, is used to identify a work and to gather together all its manifestations.

Anyone who suggests that the main entry heading is no longer needed in the electronic environment either does not understand the function of the main entry heading or does not believe the capability of gathering together all manifestations of the same message or work is worth preserving. Of course there are other ways to identify messages and to link or gather them in electronic indexes and catalogues. Unfortunately many persons who advocate the elimination of main entry headings do not seem to understand their purpose.

CONTENT DESCRIPTION

Much more problematic than the identification of messages, texts and documents is the description of the content, meaning, purpose and related features of messages (representations of knowledge) found in documents, document collections and parts of documents. Some type of subject description or indexing, subject cataloguing or classification is required in order to organize and provide access to messages in documents whenever particular documents are not known in advance. In contrast to document description, there is no consensus within the library and information science community on how this should be done, and many methods compete with or complement each other. This is the major research area in information science, often referred to as information retrieval. Most of the rest of this article will therefore focus on content description.

VOCABULARY CONTROL

After documents and their content have been described, these descriptions must be stated in terms that will match the query terms of searchers. This requires some sort of vocabulary control or management. The traditional approach has been to require the use of a restricted set of terms, with occasional provision of cross-references from alternative terms. This method has been applied to every aspect of indexing, including names of authors and other persons (Blair, Eric, *see* Orwell, George), titles of messages (The tragicall historie of Hamlet, Prince of Denmarke, *see* Hamlet), names of topics (informatics, *see* information science) and features, such as intellectual level (juvenile literature, *see* children's books).

Names of persons and messages are standardized, in traditional practice, on the basis of detailed rules for their establishment, such as *Anglo-American Cataloguing Rules* (1998). Names of topics and features have been standardized over the past century through the production of large lists of approved headings, such as *Library of Congress Subject Headings* (Library of Congress, Subject Cataloging Division 2001). In the later decades of the twentieth century, information retrieval thesauri emphasizing single-concept terms rather than complex subject headings were created to standardize indexing terminology for many disciplines and subject fields. The *Art and Architecture Thesaurus* (1994) is a prominent example.

Research in psychology and information science has repeatedly demonstrated the enormous variability in the use of language by humans describing or seeking information (Collantes 1995). This is true for searchers as well as for indexers (Saracevic *et al.* 1988). Study after study indicates that indexers and searchers agree on terms about 25 per cent of the time. Most of the variability appears to be due to differences in choices for terms, and the remainder to differences in perception or conceptualization of topics or features (Iivonen 1994). Furnas *et al.* (1987) suggest that a good information retrieval system needs to provide as many as fifteen ways to express a topic or feature in order to accommodate up to 80 per cent of the search statements submitted by users.

With the growing use of automatic indexing techniques and the increasing need to search across multiple databases where even controlled vocabularies can be extremely diverse, information scientists have begun to suggest and experiment with searching thesauri (as opposed to indexing thesauri). Searching thesauri do not list required preferred terms that indexers must use, but rather attempt to map the vocabulary of a subject field, linking variant terms for single concepts as well as related broader, narrower and associated terms. Their purpose is to facilitate searches regardless of the vocabulary used in indexes, rather than control or restrict indexing vocabulary.

Recently there has been increased interest in 'ontologies' (see ONTOLOGY) to facilitate vocabulary management and conceptual NAVIGATION in the context of electronic searching and machine manipulation. Ontology, of course, is a basic branch of philosophy devoted to the understanding of being, existence and reality. The term was borrowed by researchers in ARTIFICIAL INTELLIGENCE and knowledge engineering to represent attempts to describe, in a formal, machine-manipulable way, the characteristics of reality or 'the real world' in small domains. These ontologies have taken on the characteristics of classified thesauri.

According to Hjerppe (1996), the main difference between the usual information retrieval THESAURUS and an ontology is that thesauri are designed for direct use by humans who are seeking help with terminology and access, while ontologies are designed for integration into software operations. As a result, the rules for constructing categories and hierarchies in ontologies tend to be much more rigorous. Modern thesauri, such as the *Unesco Thesaurus* (Unesco 1995) and *Eurovoc* (European Communities 1995), display associated terms in clusters called microthesauri, without regard to formal relationships among terms. When end-users are seeking information about marital status, for example, *Eurovoc* displays such terms as 'cohabitation' and 'divorced person' together in the same microthesaurus cluster. In contrast, the typical ontology would be careful to distinguish between the activity of 'cohabitation' from the property of being 'divorced' or the entity of 'divorced person'. These differences reflect the differing requirements for a human–machine interface compared to a machine–machine interface. For a discussion of ontological categories, see Poli (1996). Vickery (1997) provides an excellent overview of ontologies in information retrieval.

Automatic and intellectual methods

There are two fundamental approaches to the description of the content, meaning and possible applications of messages for the purposes of information retrieval: human intellectual analysis and machine analysis on the basis of computer algorithms. Human indexing is often erroneously referred to as 'manual' indexing, but it is performed by the mind, not the hands. Increasingly, these two approaches to the analysis of messages are being combined in order to take advantage of the strengths of each approach, and to counterbalance their weaknesses. An overview of human and machine methods with suggestions for effective allocation of the two approaches are provided by Anderson and Pérez-Carballo (2001).

AUTOMATIC INDEXING

Automatic indexing has been used almost exclusively for the analysis of linguistic text messages (Belkin and Croft 1992; Salton *et al*. 1994).

Research has only just begun to apply automatic techniques to images (Fidel *et al*. 1994), especially to the content of visual messages, as opposed to features such as shapes, colour and contrast. Similarly, only limited attention has been focused on the application of automatic techniques to the description of documents, as in descriptive cataloguing, as opposed to the description of the content of messages (e.g. Knutson 1993; Molto and Svenonius 1991; Weibel 1992).

Automatic techniques usually rely on statistical analysis of the occurrence of words in texts. To this basic technique are often added methods for isolating word roots. Syntactic parsing is sometimes attempted to identify word phrases that should be treated as a unit. Semantic aspects can be added to automatic indexing by matching words or phrases against comprehensive thesauri, in order to establish uniform terminology and to link related terms.

Co-occurrence of words, terms, phrases and bibliographic citations has long been exploited to help locate related terms or documents. In the associative interactive dictionary developed by Doszkocs (1978), terms are ranked according to frequency of co-occurrence with terms in, or assigned to, retrieved texts, so that the most closely related terms are presented first. For example, this procedure listed terms like 'postnatal', 'gestational' and 'foetus' as most closely related to the initial search terms 'pre-natal' and 'toxicity'.

More recently, co-occurrence of phrases has been used to create innovative browsable interfaces for digital libraries (Gutwin *et al*. 1998).

Co-occurrence of bibliographic citations is the basis for citation indexes, which help searchers to track authors and documents that cite previous work of interest. Bibliographic coupling can be used to cluster groups of documents that share the same citations (Kessler 1963). Co-citation is used to identify clusters of new documents that tend to get cited together, helping to identify emerging patterns of research (Small 1973).

Latent semantic analysis is an example of advanced methods of automatic indexing. Here, messages are described not by means of individual terms, which can be quite diverse even when the same topic is discussed, but on the basis of clusters of terms that, through statistical analysis, have been identified as closely related through co-occurrence across large numbers of texts.

Latent semantic analysis attempts to overcome the challenge of diverse terminology by using these clusters of terms, which tend to be more stable than individual terms (Deerwester *et al.* 1990).

Some of the most advanced methods for knowledge representation and organization are found in expert systems. Based on research in artificial intelligence and natural-language processing, EXPERT SYSTEMS are increasingly important for decision support, management support systems, MEDICAL INFORMATICS systems, and spatial and GEOGRAPHIC INFORMATION SYSTEMS (Gluck 1994). Unlike the information retrieval systems described in this article, which point to and retrieve existing texts, expert systems create new texts in ways that permit a variety of inference and control operations on knowledge representations so as to suggest answers to problems. To permit these operations, expert knowledge is represented in the form of rules, frames, classes, hierarchies, attributes, propositions, constraints, procedures, certainty factors, possibility intervals and fuzzy variables (Hayes-Roth and Jacobstein 1994). Ontologies, discussed above under 'Vocabulary control', grew out of these efforts.

HUMAN INTELLECTUAL INDEXING

The process of human indexing is much more difficult to describe. The procedures used by humans to perceive and identify significant topics, features, meaning or possible applications of linguistic texts, images or other types of messages are rooted in the cognitive processes of the mind and brain. These processes are not well understood and constitute a major focus of fields like cognitive psychology, cognitive science and artificial intelligence. We know that human indexing consists of at least two major steps: identification of topics and features, and description of these topics and features in terms appropriate for retrieval. We also know that indexers, both experienced experts and inexperienced novices, will perform the indexing process in wildly varying ways (Leonard 1977). This variability is reduced with use of controlled vocabularies (Iivonen 1994). Fugmann (1993) believes that indexing variability can be reduced significantly by increasingly rigorous guides or rules for identification of topics and assignment of terms. Human methods are discussed in detail in Anderson and Pérez-Carballo (2001).

COMPUTER-ASSISTED TECHNIQUES

Increasingly, systems for knowledge organization are taking advantage of both human and automatic indexing techniques. Automatic indexing tends to be more exhaustive, with more specific terminology. (Exhaustivity and specificity are discussed below.) Human indexing tends to be much more selective and evaluative, often using more generic and more consistent terminology, and it may also be more successful in identifying messages of interest when the topic of interest is not explicitly mentioned or discussed in the text.

Even when automatic indexing is eschewed, computer techniques are used frequently to facilitate human indexing.

INDEXING SOFTWARE

Indexing software is widely used by human indexers, not only to analyse text directly and suggest indexing terms, but also to provide a variety of tools and techniques to assist the human indexer in performing such routine tasks as formatting and arranging entries, creating and verifying cross-references, checking terminology against a thesaurus, suggesting terms that often co-occur with terms already designated, suggesting classification categories based on co-occurrence of terms and copying headings previously assigned to other documents. Fetters (1995) has surveyed such programs designed for back-of-the-book indexers. Hodge and Milstead (1998) have discussed the application of computer-assisted techniques by large-scale indexing and abstracting services.

STRING INDEXING ALGORITHMS

One of the earliest applications of computers to indexing was the creation of algorithms for creating complex headings, each beginning with a different access term, from a set or 'string' of terms associated with a document (Craven 1986). PRECIS, the Preserved Context Indexing System, developed under the direction of Derek Austin for the British National Bibliography, was an early and widely influential example (Austin and Dykstra 1984). String algorithms were also used to create the earliest automatic indexes, KWIC (KeyWord in Context), KWOC (KeyWord out of Context) and KWAC (KeyWord and Context). These types of indexes will be described in more detail below under 'Syntax'.

FRAME-BASED PROMPTING SYSTEMS

One of the more sophisticated attempts to provide computer-based aids to improve human indexing is the MedIndEx project of the US National Library of Medicine (Humphrey 1993). Indexers are provided with a frame in which relevant categories of terms are suggested. Because in practice terms are often assigned in clusters, the assignment of one term may call forth suggestions of other terms that are frequently associated with the first term. The hope is that systems such as this will contribute to more thorough and more consistent indexing.

Catalogues, indexes, databases, digital libraries

The results of knowledge organization are presented in catalogues, indexes, bibliographies, digital libraries and even back-of-the-book indexes for monographic treatises, all of which may be subsumed under the term 'information retrieval databases' (IR databases). These are sometimes called textual databases or textbases, but in this case 'text' refers to any type of organized set of symbols used to convey a message (visual, aural, verbal), not just linguistic texts. Also, this sense of IR database is not limited to any particular medium. It includes print databases of all types as well as electronic. An older, traditional term for IR databases was 'bibliographic databases', because all IR databases retrieve information about messages, texts and documents described in bibliographic terms. Older IR databases tended to be 'reference' databases, retrieving only references to messages, texts and documents; many modern IR databases are 'full-text', retrieving the entire text of a message in various formats.

IR databases, including the procedures and components for making them accessible to users, are the systems through which the results of knowledge organization are presented to persons who wish to search for messages, texts, documents or the information that they may offer.

Just as tools and machines may be seen as extensions of human muscles, enabling us to perform tasks with considerably more power, IR databases may be seen as an extension of our minds, especially of our memories, and of the IR techniques of the mind (Anderson 1985). Our IR databases, then, are artificial tools we have created to extend the organizing power of the mind.

The remaining sections discuss the attributes of these IR databases.

SCOPE AND DOMAIN

There are thousands of IR databases available for searching. The first step in any effective search is to select the appropriate databases. Succinct description of scope and domain will assist in this initial selection process.

Scope refers to characteristics of documents that are covered by a database. Domain refers to characteristics of the anticipated user community (subject or user domain) and of the sources of information about these documents (documentary domain), including the territory covered to locate them (Bates 1976).

Subject scope and domain

An effective statement of subject scope specifies, in broad strokes, which categories of topics are indexed, and by implication the kinds of topical questions or searches that are appropriate for the database. Similarly, the subject domain describes the kinds of user communities for whom the database is intended. It is not sufficient simply to name the overall subject area or discipline, such as 'medicine'. Such a skimpy description does not tell potential users whether databases can respond to questions about therapies or drugs or types of medical personnel or particular physicians or varieties of medical institutions or the economics of health insurance. Also, medical databases could be designed for very different user domains – researchers, practising healthcare professionals, patients, the general public or even children. The user domain will have an important impact on the kinds of indexing and terminology that are appropriate (Hjørland 1997).

A thorough statement of subject scope provides a list of categories of indexed topics, and this same list can serve as a guide for database producers in selecting appropriate documents and for indexers as they attempt to indicate topics of potential importance to users. Such a list can help promote indexing that responds to known interests as opposed simply to the content of documents. Soergel (1985) calls this 'request-oriented' indexing as opposed to document or 'entity-oriented' indexing. He gives an example of a document on the 'percentage of children of blue-collar workers attending college'. Request-oriented indexing might use a term like 'intergenerational social mobility', even though this topic is not discussed directly.

Examples of subject scope categories are concrete entities, such as persons (individuals or groups), artefacts and natural objects; abstract entities, such as institutions, movements, disciplines, belief systems, theories, hypotheses and imaginary entities (fictional characters, mythological animals); attributes and properties; raw materials or constituent elements; operations, processes and events; places or environments; time and historical periods. The subject scope list should be more specific for narrower fields, so that for literature, for example, the following categories of topics might be indexed: individual persons, such as authors and critics, literary works, groups of persons, movements, languages, places, genres, performance media, stylistic and structural features, themes, sources, influences, processes, methodological approaches, theories, devices and tools (*MLA International Bibliography* 2000).

Documentary scope and domain

While the subject scope and domain defines the topics of documents that should be indexed and the user community for whom the indexing is performed, the documentary scope and domain defines the characteristics of the actual documents that are sought for and admitted into the database and the documentary features that should be noted for retrieval (that is, indexed). Important non-topical features almost always include authors, titles and dates of publication or creation. Other documentary features will vary by medium. For print-on paper documents, they usually include such attributes as format or genre, periodicity (monographs versus serials of various types), audience or intellectual level, language or other textual system (e.g. musical notation), place of publication, publisher, presence of illustrations and size.

Sometimes the documentary scope of a database can be described simply by listing the names of documents being indexed. This would apply to a database covering articles appearing only in a select list of periodicals. Back-of-the-book indexes fall into this category as well, because their documentary scope is obvious.

Additional documentary criteria can include quality or appropriateness for particular clientele or purposes. Such criteria should be specified to the extent possible.

Documentary domain refers to the territory whence came the documentary data for the database. First of all, is the database based on primary sources? Are documents described and indexed on the basis of direct inspection and analysis, versus secondary sources, where data about documents are gathered from other sources, such as other indexing and abstracting tools, library catalogues or publishers' announcements? The second aspect of domain is the geographical territory covered in seeking to find documents that fit the subject scope and domain, and the documentary scope. A database that is limited to documents found only in a single library collection, for example, is very different from a database that includes documents located through extensive searches all over the world.

Catalogues, by definition, are databases whose domain is limited to a single collection, or, in the case of union catalogues, to several collections.

DATABASE MEDIA

The medium of the database will determine many other options. The principal media are print-on-paper, including card files, and electronic media, including online and CD-ROM databases, and the WORLD WIDE WEB (WWW). In the past MICROFORMS were important media for IR databases, but they have been largely supplanted by ELECTRONIC INFORMATION RESOURCES.

Electronic databases

Electronic media permit electronic searches of database records and texts without actually viewing index entries. Search terms may be entered into a search programme, and document records containing these terms can then be retrieved and listed. Indexes that are searched electronically rather than through visual inspection are called 'non-displayed' indexes (Anderson 1997). Of course, indexes can also be displayed for visual inspection and browsing in electronic media.

The principal advantages of electronic databases are potentially faster updating (especially for online and WWW databases), elimination of bulky physical volumes and the increasing expense of producing them, and marked augmented search options and flexibility. Whereas in print databases index entries are fixed and one can only search index headings that have been previously established, and only in the form and order in which they are printed, in electronic indexes using electronic search techniques it is possible to search for any word or sequence of characters, or several words in any order. Thus the search unit is no longer the complete, pre-established, pre-arranged heading, but individual words or parts of words, which can be combined in any order. Also, entire records, sometimes entire texts, can be searched, rather than only the terms and headings that have been placed in a searchable index.

Print databases

In print media databases, indexes must be displayed, because it is only through visual inspection of arrays of index entries that a user can access the database.

The principal advantages of print databases are their portability (assuming they are not too large and bulky), the capability of searching without an electronic intermediary, much greater visual resolution and clarity of typography, and the larger layout of arrays of entries that is possible. Also, it is often easier for users to apprehend the structure and arrangement of print indexes simply by looking at them. It is often difficult to comprehend the structure and content of electronic databases, especially those that are searched unseen via electronic algorithms. Even when indexes are displayed in electronic media, they rarely provide the large-scope display that is possible in well-designed print databases.

Searchable, browsable displays are rapidly becoming more and more sophisticated in electronic media, and for many purposes their advantages outweigh those of print media, especially in economic terms. Nevertheless, there will probably always be a need for well-designed print databases as well. If nowhere else, all texts important enough to publish in the form of a print-on-paper book probably deserve a well-designed print-on-paper back-of-the-book index!

DOCUMENTARY UNITS

The size of documentary units that are identified, indexed and organized for retrieval will determine the size of units that can be retrieved. This is one of the few 'causal laws' in library and information science. Size of documentary unit is the principal variable that underlies distinctions that are sometimes made (in error) between 'information' retrieval systems and 'document'

or 'bibliographic' retrieval systems. It is not the case that 'information' retrieval systems retrieve direct answers to questions, while 'document' or 'bibliographic' retrieval systems only retrieve whole documents, or reference citations to whole documents. The real difference is the size of documentary units that are analysed, described, organized and retrieved. In all cases, these are documents, or parts of documents, because messages must always be represented by text encoded in media. This is precisely what documents are – the combination of the text of a message and its medium (Anderson 1997). The related distinction between 'full-text' and 'reference' databases will be discussed below, under 'Surrogates'.

The size of documentary units can vary from very small – single statements for example – to very large: whole monographs, whole series, complete runs of periodicals, or even large collections and entire libraries. Whatever is analysed, described and organized is the documentary unit that will be retrieved or pointed to by the IR database.

Traditionally, documentary units have consisted of complete documents in library catalogues, and in most indexing and abstracting services complete monographs or complete periodical articles. Some SPECIAL LIBRARIES and many ABSTRACTING AND INDEXING SERVICES analyse, describe and organize individual chapters in books, especially in collections of separate essays or papers in proceedings. In these cases, the documentary unit matches the documentary scope of the database.

But there is no necessary connection between the types of documents defined for coverage in the documentary scope and the documentary unit for analysis, organization and retrieval. Periodical articles, for example, can be analysed on a page-by-page or paragraph-by-paragraph basis, and if this is done searchers can be led to particular pages or paragraphs.

Smaller units of analysis are becoming common in full-text databases. No one wants to search the complete text of a document and then be referred to the complete text, or even to a large section. Full-text searches should lead one directly to the segment of text most relevant to the search, and this is exactly what happens in good full-text retrieval systems. The documentary unit is each unit of text, such as, in the case of linguistic texts, the sentence or paragraph.

Back-of-the-book indexes have traditionally used the page as the unit of analysis, or documentary unit, so that back-of-the-book indexes refer searchers to pages, using page numbers. The technical report on indexing from the US National Information Standards Organization (NISO) (Anderson 1997) suggests that such indexes might better use natural or inherent units of text, such as paragraphs. This is especially important as more and more books are published in both paper and electronic media. For the great majority of books the page is not an element of the text, but only of the print-on-paper medium in which the text is presented. Pages of printed books do not travel with the text to electronic media unless they are artificially imposed. If pages were used for the documentary unit in a back-of-the-book index, the index becomes useless when the text is moved to electronic media, where there are no pages. But if the index points to paragraphs rather than pages, the index can be used in electronic media, and it also saves time for users who no longer have to search for particular paragraphs on dense pages of text. This new documentary unit for back-of-the-book indexes does, however, present a challenge to book designers to come up with a discreet and unobtrusive method for numbering paragraphs!

ANALYSIS BASE/INDEXABLE MATTER

Once the documentary unit has been established for a particular IR database, the analysis base within the documentary unit must be determined. The analysis base is the segment or portion of a documentary unit that is analysed (by humans or by machines) in order to place the unit into the system of organization and on which retrieval will be based. The analysis base can be quite brief, such as the title of a document or an abstract, or it can extend to the complete documentary unit. The analysis base consists of the textual matter to be indexed, so it is sometimes called 'indexable matter'.

The size of the analysis base should relate to the exhaustivity of indexing. If only a few terms are assigned or extracted to represent documentary units, a smaller analysis base, such as title and/or abstract, may be adequate for most purposes. Obviously, however, the suitability of the title alone as analysis base will depend on the extent to which the title is an accurate summary of the content and meaning of a text. We all know of cases where this is far from the case.

Such titles can be 'enriched' with an explanatory phrase.

More exhaustive indexing will need a larger analysis base, which for periodical articles might include introductory and concluding paragraphs in addition to titles and abstracts, or the entire article.

EXHAUSTIVITY

Exhaustivity of indexing refers to the level of detail with which the content, meaning, purpose or features of messages and their texts are described for retrieval. In quantitative terms, it is the number of terms assigned to or extracted from texts.

Highly selective indexing, with low exhaustivity, is based on a high threshold of importance that must be met before terms are assigned. As a result, retrieved documents are likely to be highly relevant to a search using their index terms, because only central topics or dominant features are indexed. Thus, at least in theory, low-exhaustivity indexing can lead to high-precision search results, with fewer non-relevant documents retrieved. On the other hand, many documents that may treat a desired topic in passing and may therefore be relevant to someone wanting everything on a topic will not be retrieved, resulting in a loss of desired recall.

High-exhaustivity indexing sets a low threshold of importance for terms to be assigned or extracted, resulting in potentially greater recall, because more of the documents in which a particular topic is addressed will be retrieved. But these documents will include those in which the topic is not central, but only peripheral. Users wanting only documents focusing directly on the topic may judge such peripheral treatments to be irrelevant, therefore lowering the precision of a search.

Automatic indexing tends to operate at very high exhaustivity levels, often resulting in higher recall but lower precision. A principal challenge in automatic indexing is the development of techniques to lower the exhaustivity of indexing by identifying the central topics or dominant features of messages and texts in order to make indexing more selective.

Human intellectual indexing tends to be quite selective, with a high threshold of importance for topics and features, and therefore a low exhaustivity level. It is for this reason that many databases combine both types of indexing, relying on human indexing for certain types of high-precision searches and automatic, often full-text, indexing for certain types of high-recall searches.

The influence of exhaustivity does not operate in a vacuum. The specificity of vocabulary, type of syntax and the linking of vocabulary to indicate broader, narrower and other relationships can counteract or augment the potential effects of exhaustivity. The highly specific vocabulary that is typical of automatic indexing, for example, can in some cases lead to highly precise search results, contradicting the general tendency of high-exhaustivity indexing.

VOCABULARY SPECIFICITY

The specificity of vocabulary used to describe topics and features will influence the types of searches that an IR database can support and the results of these searches. Specificity refers to the exactness with which a term describes a topic or feature. If a message discusses Labrador retrievers but the index term is 'dogs', the term is generic rather than specific. This will mean that a person desiring documents on Labrador retrievers must search for 'dogs' and then examine many irrelevant documents or document surrogates. The precision, or exactness, of the search will suffer. On the other hand, if the index term is 'Labrador retrievers', the term is specific and the search should be more precise, but recall may suffer because there may be discussions of Labrador retrievers, along with other dogs, that were indexed with the terms 'dogs' rather than 'Labrador retrievers'.

Indexing standards call for more, rather than less, specificity in indexing terminology, because good vocabulary management can help expand searches to more generic levels when needed. On the other hand, the more specific the vocabulary, the more terms there will be. Larger controlled vocabularies are more expensive to maintain and can be harder to use than smaller vocabularies. Indexing that is based directly on terms used in linguistic texts, as is the case for most automatic indexing methods, will use terms as specific as those used in the text.

Indexing systems that rely on both controlled vocabulary assigned on the basis of intellectual analysis and automatic indexing based on terms found in the text can take advantage of the differences in specificity to balance the advantages and disadvantages of each approach.

METHOD OF INDEXING

The method of indexing – human intellectual analysis, machine algorithmic analysis or combinations of these fundamental approaches – has already been discussed. It is mentioned again here to emphasize that it constitutes an important attribute of IR databases.

SYNTAX

Syntax refers to the grammar of indexing and searching – the method for combining terms into headings and subheadings for entries in print indexes or displayed indexes in electronic media, or for creating search statements for electronic searches of non-displayed indexes. It also includes techniques for modifying terms in searches, such as stemming and truncation, as well as specifying variable weights, proximity requirements or the use of links and operators, such as the Boolean 'and', 'or' and 'not'.

Syntax for electronic searches

The two basic methods for combining terms for electronic searches are (1) BOOLEAN LOGIC and (2) weighted term vectors, sometimes based on probabilistic criteria. Both of these methods may be combined with techniques for stemming, truncation and specification of term proximity or location.

Boolean searching divides a database into two mutually exclusive segments – those records whose terms match the search statement and those whose terms do not. Unless some method of giving weights to terms is used, retrieved records all have the same value or weight. There is no inherent method for ranking records in terms of potential relevance to the search statement.

The lack of ranked retrieval is the biggest disadvantage of Boolean searching. As databases get larger and larger, retrieved sets also get larger and larger, or else search statements are made more and more restrictive in order to reduce the number of retrieved records, thereby increasing the risk of missing important documents.

Term vector or probabilistic searching simply matches a set of search terms with document records, then, on the basis of this matching, the database is rearranged into a ranked list based on predicted (or probable) relevance.

In describing documents, weights can also be given to index terms, based on their importance in relation to topics or features of a text. In automatic indexing this can be based on frequency of occurrence in the text, either of the term itself (perhaps after stemming) or of the term and equivalent or closely related terms determined by reference to a thesaurus or co-occurrence clusters. These weights can be modified by the relative frequency of a term across all documents in the database. A term that occurs frequently in many documents is not a good discriminator in searching, so it can be given a lower weight, while a term occurring infrequently in the database as a whole would get a higher weight (inverse document frequency).

Boolean searching became a *de facto* standard in electronic databases in the early decades of their development because it was in use prior to the coming of the computer to information retrieval, but it is now frequently replaced by or complemented with term vector or probabilistic techniques, which have become the standard for electronic searches on the Web.

Syntax for browsable displayed indexes

Displayed indexes, especially those presented in print databases, must be created in advance of presentation to searchers. Such indexes are often called 'pre-co-ordinate' because terms are co-ordinated – put together into index headings – in advance of publication. In contrast, in electronic searching it is the searcher who combines terms for the search *after* the index has been prepared, so indexing designed specifically for electronic searching is often called 'post-co-ordinate'.

Pre-co-ordinate syntax has become increasingly important for electronic IR databases in recent years as researchers and database producers have come to recognize the importance of browsing for many users (Rice *et al*. 2001; Marchionini 1995). Electronic searches of non-displayed indexes are very appropriate for users who know what they want and know what terms to use to describe it. But for many users who are unsure of what they want or what terms to use, browsing displayed indexes can be very helpful. It is much easier to recognize terms or headings that might be relevant, than to try to think of terms or combinations of terms when the user is uncertain what these might be. Searchers often suffer from 'ASK' – an 'ANOMALOUS STATE OF KNOWLEDGE' – because they are searching for answers in topical areas that are unfamiliar to them (Belkin *et al*. 1982). Browsable displayed

indexes, whether arranged in alphabetical or classified arrays, require headings that are created by indexers or by computer algorithm in advance of presentation to the user.

The many types of syntax for browsable displayed indexes can be divided into six categories: *ad hoc* syntax, subject heading syntax, classification syntax, natural-language syntax, permuted syntax and string syntax.

Ad hoc syntax

When a displayed index is created for a single document, such as a back-of-the-book index, or a one-time index is created for a collection of documents, terms are often combined into headings and subheadings on an *ad hoc* basis rather than according to a pre-established syntax system or list of headings. The indexer selects terms based on the vocabulary of the text (if it is linguistic text, in the same language as the index) and the anticipated vocabulary of potential users, and creates heading–subheading combinations designed to describe the topics and features of documentary units.

It is customary in English language indexes to use nouns or noun phrases as terms, with plural forms for discrete objects that can be counted. Prepositions are used sparingly to clarify relationships among terms. A good index will provide a sufficient variety of subheadings so that no heading or heading–subheading combination will point to too many documentary units. The NISO technical report on indexing (Anderson 1997) suggests that no more than five documentary units should share the same heading–subheading combination, so that in the compiled index no more than five locators would follow any heading or heading–subheading combination. Modern practice prefers direct, natural language order for multiword terms ('fire insurance' rather than 'insurance, fire') except for names of persons, which are usually inverted and entered under family names. The NISO technical report also suggests that only proper nouns be capitalized and that the use of articles be minimized. Terms that have different meanings should be qualified, as in 'mercury (planet)', 'mercury (chemical element)'.

Many of these conventions are used with other forms of indexing syntax as well.

Subject heading syntax

Subject headings were developed in the mid- and late nineteenth century in order to provide consistent headings for library subject catalogues. The largest and most famous general compilation of subject headings is that of the US LIBRARY OF CONGRESS (Library of Congress, Subject Cataloging Division 2001). One of the most famous specialized lists is *MeSH: Medical Subject Headings* of the US National Library of Medicine (2001).

The Library of Congress list contains hundreds of thousands of headings consisting of single terms, multiple terms in heading–subheading combinations ('Animals – Diseases – Nutritional aspects') or phrases ('Telephone assistance programmes for the poor'). In earlier years, many terms were inverted ('Students, Foreign'), but current practice prefers direct natural language order. However, because LIBRARY OF CONGRESS SUBJECT HEADINGS have been developed over many decades, different patterns have been used over the years, and today they co-exist. This lack of consistent syntactic patterns is one of the chief complaints levelled against traditional subject headings. It is difficult to predict, for example, whether a place-name heading should precede or follow a topical heading. Both 'Archives – United States' and 'United States – Library resources' are used. Similarly, the use of adjectival versus noun forms or heading–subheading combinations versus phrases is inconsistent, as in 'Animal films' but 'Animals – Folklore' and 'Animals in literature'.

In addition to pre-co-ordinated heading–subheading combinations and phrase headings, subject heading lists provide 'standard' subheadings that may be combined with other headings. Pattern headings for people, cities, nations and many other categories of topics provide models for the creation of new heading–subheading combinations. Strings of headings, subheadings and sub-subheadings can become quite long, and maintaining consistency among many different cataloguers is a big challenge, necessitating large manuals of procedure (Library of Congress, Subject Cataloging Division 1996).

Despite an enormous literature critical of subject headings, they are the most widely used method for indexing library collections. In the USA, for example, they are used by every general library of any consequence, so that they provide a consistent form of access in thousands of libraries. They are especially useful as the catalogues of many of the largest libraries have become available on the Internet.

Some indexing and abstracting services use subject headings for main headings but create '*ad hoc*' subheadings based on topics and features of documents being indexed.

Classification syntax

The syntax of classification systems has been very similar to that of subject heading systems. Earlier systems have been largely enumerative, in which classes (with captions or headings and notation) for complex topics have been pre-co-ordinated and laid out (enumerated) in the desired order. The LIBRARY OF CONGRESS CLASSIFICATION is one of the most enumerative of the major systems of classification. The DEWEY DECIMAL CLASSIFICATION, and even more its offshoot, the UNIVERSAL DECIMAL CLASSIFICATION, have adopted many synthetic features, by which classes for complex topics, with captions and notation, can be synthesized from various categories or facets within the classification scheme. This style of classification is often called 'analytico-synthetic,' because topics are first analysed into their components, then a composite class is synthesized from the components. The most modern classifications, beginning with RANGANATHAN's famous COLON CLASSIFICATION and exemplified by the new edition of the Bliss Classification (Bliss 1977), are more fully faceted. Topics and features are listed in facets according to basic characteristics. Ranganathan referred to the most basic facet categories with the initials 'PMEST', representing 'personality' (i.e. entities), 'material' (i.e. constituent elements and attributes), 'energy' (i.e. operations, processes, events, etc.), 'space' (i.e. places) and 'time'. Classes, with captions and notation, are built up from segments from individual facets (Ranganathan 1965).

Fully FACETED CLASSIFICATIONS are most appropriate for display and browsing in electronic environments because users may choose the order of facets – in effect they may create their own classifications to suit their purposes. In more traditional environments, such as arranging items on shelves or displaying classifications in static media such as print-on-paper, the order of facets must be chosen in advance and cannot be changed. Topics on literature, for example, might be classed according to this sequence of facets: nationality, language, genre, period, writer, work, theme. But in the HYPERTEXT-based electronic environment, facets such as these can be displayed to users, and users may choose to browse facets of greatest interest, and in the order they prefer. A user might choose, for example, to browse facets for theme, genre and nationality, in that order. All headings for particular themes would come together, whereas in traditional fixed classifications where theme is considered much later in the 'citation order of facets', themes would be scattered among nationalities, genres, periods and other facets. Pollitt and his research team at Huddersfield University in the UK have been leaders in designing faceted browsable classification displays for users in hypertext environments (Pollitt *et al.* 1997).

CHAIN INDEXING is a technique for converting the 'chains' or strings of classification headings or captions into a set of headings for display in alphabetical indexes, so that users have access to a classified display via each distinct term in the classification heading.

Natural language syntax

In natural language indexes, the syntax of natural-language text segments, such as titles or key sentences, is preserved in order to create browsable index entries consisting of a KEYWORD or key phrase, plus a contextual subheading or string of text consisting of all or part of the text segment. The three most common examples of natural language displayed indexes are KWIC (KeyWord in Context, in which the keyword or phrase remains in its original context), KWOC (KeyWord out of Context, in which the keyword is pulled out of its context for display) and KWAC (KeyWord and Context, in which the keyword is pulled out of its context, but words following the keyword are placed next to it). These indexes are usually created by computer algorithm. As noted under 'Automatic indexing', innovative digital libraries have used the KWIC format to display key sentences containing key phrases identified by co-occurrence and frequency criteria.

Permuted syntax

Permuted syntax was developed to provide maximum access through the combination of all possible word pairs. Permutations can be based on assigned terms or on keywords from natural-language segments, such as titles. In principle, permuted syntax could be used to create all possible combinations of three or more words, but because the number of unique entries expands very quickly (exponentially) as the number

of words in each heading increases, permutations of more that two words are not practical.

The INSTITUTE FOR SCIENTIFIC INFORMATION (2001) has used permuted indexes (called 'Permuterm Indexes') to complement its citation indexes for many years.

String syntax

String indexing makes use of computer algorithms to create multiple entries from a single set or 'string' of terms. The terms themselves may be assigned and coded for manipulation by human indexers (Craven 1986).

The simplest form of string indexing is simply to list the terms associated with a document in alphanumeric order within the string, but to rotate each term, in turn, to the lead position. Thus in an a browsable alphabetical index, the complete string will appear under every term in the string, and, after each lead term, all other terms will be displayed in alphanumeric order. This technique, sometimes called 'rotated-term syntax', has been used successfully for many years by ABC-Clio (2001) in its databases *America History and Life* and *Historical Abstracts*.

More sophisticated forms of string indexing attempt to arrange terms under a lead term in a conceptually meaningful order, in contrast to the simple alphanumeric order used in rotation syntax. In faceted indexing, terms are labelled or tagged with facet or role indicators and the order of terms is determined by their facets or roles. One of the earliest and most sophisticated systems of faceted indexing was PRECIS (Preserved Context Indexing System) (Austin and Dykstra 1984).

In general systems like PRECIS, facets and roles consist of very general categories, such as location, key entity or system, modifier, action and agent or instrument. A computer algorithm uses these categories to create index headings, such as:

England
    Korean automobiles. sales. effects of advertising.

When faceted indexing is used for a particular discipline or subject field, facets tend to be much more specific. Here is an example from the MLA International Bibliography (1981), based on the CIFT (Contextual Indexing and Faceted Taxonomy) system (Anderson 1979):

[literature]
   English literature
[genre]
   short story
[period]
   1900–1999
[author]
   Forster, E.M.
[work]
   'Dr Woolacott'
[stylistic technique]
   symbolism
[theme]
   salvation; homosexuality

These terms, along with their facet codes, result in index headings such as:

Salvation
   English literature. short story. 1900–1999. Forster, E.M.

   'Dr Woolacott'. symbolism. treatment of SALVATION; homosexuality

The lead term is repeated, in full capitals, in its contextual position in the headings.

NEPHIS (Nested Phrase Indexing System), developed by Timothy Craven (1986), provides a method for coding a subject statement in order to create multiple entries. The statements can be created by indexers or they can be existing text segments, such as titles. Four coding symbols are used: angular brackets (< >) indicate words or phrases under which entries should be created; the 'at' sign (@) negates an automatic entry under the first word of a statement or phrase; and the question mark (?) marks connectives between terms and phrases, usually prepositions. As an example, the following coded statement would produce the following entry:

effects? of < advertising > ? on < sales? of Korean
   < automobiles > > ? in < England > >

automobiles
   Korean –. sales in England. effects of advertising

Similar entries would also be created for each term preceded by ' < ' in the string.

VOCABULARY MANAGEMENT

The importance of vocabulary control was discussed earlier in this article. Here the emphasis is on methods for integrating vocabulary management into the design of IR databases.

Because of the enormous variability in the human use of language, some sort of vocabulary management is essential in the overall information retrieval process. If an IR database does not provide it, then users will have to provide it by trying to think of the various ways in which is particular concept might be expressed.

The purpose of vocabulary management systems is to provide links among terms that are synonymous or essentially equivalent in the context of the IR database (e.g. 'lawyer', 'attorney', 'barrister', 'solicitor') and to point to other terms that are narrower in scope or share some other type of relationship. Some systems also provide pointers to broader terms as well. (In some contexts, 'barrister' and 'solicitor' will be considered narrower terms rather than equivalent terms for 'lawyer' or 'attorney'.)

Vocabulary management should be integrated into the searching system itself, whether it is an electronic search interface or displayed browsable alphabetical or classified indexes. Users should not have to consult a separate thesaurus or list of subject headings, follow up cross-references, then return to the search interface. For displayed indexes, this means that cross-references should be built into the index display. For indexes that are searched electronically, the display of alternative or related vocabulary should appear as soon as initial search terms are chosen.

Thus if a user enters the search term 'lawyers' into an electronic search interface, linked terms should be displayed. A window can be used to list equivalent terms ('attorneys', 'solicitors', 'barristers'), narrower terms, if any ('trial lawyers', 'defence attorneys', 'tax attorneys'), broader terms ('legal system personnel') and related terms ('crime', 'law', 'justice', 'courts'). If a controlled vocabulary is used, users should be informed that the initial term 'lawyers' is being converted to the established term 'attorneys' (or vice versa). Users should have the option of adding any of the other terms to the search or substituting displayed terms for the original terms. It should also be possible to consult the thesaurus record for any of the displayed terms to see their narrower, broader and related terms as well. All terms selected should be added to the search directly. The user should not have to re-key any of them.

Linked vocabulary terms can be displayed in similar ways in browsable displays.

By using the vocabulary management component of an IR database, users can narrow the search by substituting narrower terms that may be more specific to the objective of the search; the search can be broadened by adding additional terms or substituting broader terms.

Vocabulary management can be based on a formal thesaurus or on term relationships based on term co-occurrence in texts. This later approach displays terms that frequently co-occur in the database with the initial search terms. In an early example of this approach by Doszkocs (1978), mentioned previously under 'Automatic indexing', the following related terms were displayed for a search on 'pre-natal' and 'toxicity', ranked according to the frequency of co-occurrence: post-natal, gestational, foetus, gestations, teratogenicity, embryocidal, peri-natal, placental, mothers, clefts, retardation, foetuses, stillbirths, resorptions, rubratoxins, developmental, palates, organogenesis, foetal, pregnant. Such a list gives searchers the opportunity to consider the relevance of a term they may not have thought of.

SURROGATES AND LOCATORS

Documentary units that are indexed and organized for retrieval by an IR database must be represented in some manner. The process of representation is called 'surrogation' and the results are called 'surrogates'. Even in full-text databases, where the entire text is present, users often want to examine much briefer representations than the full text, in order to decide whether the text is relevant for their purposes. In 'reference databases', which refer to documents not included within the database, surrogates are the only representations of documents within the database. Surrogates usually consist of citations to, or descriptions of, documentary units, and sometimes also include summaries or abstracts of contents and features. Descriptors or index terms assigned to documentary units are also included.

Part of a surrogate is the locator, which is the device used to locate the document itself, whether it is contained within the database or is only outside the database, as in reference databases. Reference databases use citations for

locators that can be used to locate documents in the larger documentary universe, including library collections or the World Wide Web. Also used as locators are the growing number of identifiers, as discussed previously under 'Document identifiers'.

Within full-text databases, including books with back-of-the-book indexes, a system of internal locators is required. For example, a back-of-the-book index often uses page or paragraph numbers to refer to the documentary units within the full text of the document. In electronic databases, internal locators generally consist of hypertext links leading from brief surrogates to fuller surrogates or full texts.

SURROGATE DISPLAY

The display of surrogates is an important aspect of INTERFACE design. In different stages of a search, users can best be served by different portions of surrogates. The arrangement and summarization of multiple surrogates are also important. Surrogates not only serve to represent single documents, but also provide data for overviews of the contents of the entire database (Greene *et al.* 2000). Overviews can include a variety of graphical depictions of the topical strengths of a database.

During a subject search, users may only want to see brief subject-oriented descriptions of documents, such as a string of descriptors, so that multiple descriptions can be examined easily and quickly. These brief topical surrogates should be arranged by topic, either in alphabetical or classified displays, or ranked by potential relevance. In author searches, brief surrogates should consist of authors and titles of documents. Eventually users may want to see full surrogates, and here the arrangement of elements should relate to the kind of search. In subject searches, subject elements, such as subject descriptors and brief summaries, should be placed at the top of the full surrogate. This could be followed by a fuller abstract and citation with authors, titles and publication details. On the other hand, in author or title searches, these elements should be placed first.

INDEX DISPLAY

Browsable index displays are absolutely essential in print databases, because they provide the only access to the terms and headings representing topics and features of documentary units. Browsable index displays are increasingly important in electronic environments, permitting users to browse categories, facets or headings prior to or during a search. Psychological research has long confirmed that human beings find it easier to recognize relevant terms than to recall them from their memories. This is especially true for topics or areas with which the searcher is not familiar. Effective index displays suggest alternative options for a search. Vocabulary management displays can also be very helpful for this purpose as well.

Indexes can be displayed in two fundamentally different ways – alphanumerically, based on the letters and numerals that make up index headings, and relationally in classified arrays so that closely related topics or features are grouped together.

Relational classification displays

As discussed under 'Classification syntax', classified displays can be based on existing classification systems, such as the Universal Decimal Classification (UDC), Dewey Decimal Classification (DDC), Library of Congress Classification (LCC) and many others. In electronic environments, however, faceted classifications in which the user has control over the selection and ordering of facets of interest are appropriate.

Within facets, topics can be arranged alphabetically, but this will scatter closely related topics, such as, for example, antelopes and zebras. In order to bring together closely related topics within a facet, hierarchical, chronological, genealogical or geographical arrangements are often more appropriate. For example, in the facet for languages, the thousands of human languages could be arranged in alphabetical order, but browsers may be better served by grouping them into language families, such as Indo-European, Uralic, Semitic, etc. These families can then be arranged by subfamilies, such as Germanic, Indic, Romance and Slavic within Indo-European, until individual languages are reached. Such a classification will place French, Spanish, Italian and other Romance languages together.

Alphanumeric displays

Many displayed indexes are arranged in alphabetical or alphanumeric order. At first glance, alphanumeric order appears to be straightforward and non-problematic, but instead it is an area of extreme disagreement among information professionals. It is also an example of an area where opinions, strongly held, are not based on empirical research.

The major controversies are about whether to consider the space and various punctuation marks as sorting characters, the treatment of numerals and the use of sorting criteria other than the characters in headings. Depending on the choices adopted, very different arrangements can result. Users who do not understand the principles of arrangement can miss a sought-after entry by a great distance.

If the space is considered, the arrangement is called 'word-by-word' rather than 'letter-by-letter', because headings that begin with the same word will come together. Thus, in word-by-word arrangement, 'New York' will come before 'Newark,' but in letter-by-letter arrangement, 'Newark' will come before 'New York'.

Older standards called for numbers to be arranged as if spelled out in words, whereas modern standards call for numbers to be arranged according to numerical value, preceding alphabetic letters. But, even here, there is disagreement about whether arrangement should be based on the actual characters present or the mathematical value of the characters. For example, should '1/4' be placed with '0.25' or should it be arranged on the basis of its characters, '1', '/' and '4'. Both the American Library Association Filing Committee (1980) and the Library of Congress Processing Department (1980) opt for the latter option, not only for fractions, but also for decimals, so that headings with fractions or decimals can be wildly out of numerical value order. Roman numerals are usually arranged by their numerical value rather than on the basis of their alphabetical letters.

One of the most controversial areas is arrangement based on extra-alphanumeric criteria. The Library of Congress, for example, still insists that headings beginning with the same word should be arranged not on the basis of the following word, but on the basis of the nature of the entity represented and the form of the heading in the following order: persons entered under forenames, persons entered under family names, places, corporate body names and topical headings, and titles of texts. This means that a title like 'Paris after the war' will come long after a person named 'Paris, Virginia', or an entry for 'Paris (France)'. These principles are rarely explained to users.

Such classified sequences within alphanumeric

arrays can be useful for browsing, but only if the arrangement is made clear to users, using such techniques as search trees, as advocated by Drabenstott and Vizine-Goetz (1994).

References

ABC-Clio (2001) *America: History and Life; Historical Abstracts.*

American Library Association, Filing Committee (1980) *ALA Filing Rules.* ALA.

Anderson, James D. (1979) 'Contextual indexing and faceted classification for databases in the humanities', *American Society for Information Science, 42nd annual meeting, Minneapolis, Oct. 14–18, 1979. Proceedings, vol. 16*, Knowledge Industry Publications, pp. 194–201.

—— (1985) 'Indexing systems: extensions of the mind's organizing power', *Information and Behavior*, vol. 1, pp. 287–323.

—— (1997) *Guidelines for Indexes and Related Information Retrieval Devices*, NISO Press (National Information Standards Organization, Technical Report; 2)

Anderson, James D.; Pérez-Carballo, José (2001) 'The nature of indexing: how humans and machines analyze messages and texts for retrieval, Part I: Research, and the nature of human indexing; Part II: Machine indexing, and the allocation of human versus machine effort', *Information Processing & Management*, vol. 37, pp. 231–77.

Anglo-American Cataloguing Rules (1998) 2ᵈ edn, American Library Association.

Art and Architecture Thesaurus (1994) 2ᵈ edn, Oxford University Press/J. Paul Getty Trust.

Austin, Derek; Dykstra, Mary (1984) *PRECIS: A Manual of Concept Analysis and Subject Indexing*, 2ⁿᵈ edn, British Library.

Bates, Marcia J. (1976) 'Rigorous systematic bibliography', *RQ*, vol. 16, pp. 7–26.

Belkin, Nicholas J.; Oddy, R.N.; Brooks, H.M. (1982) 'Ask for information retrieval: part I. background and theory', *Journal of Documentation*, vol. 38(2), pp. 61–71; 'Part II. results of a design study', *Journal of Documentation*, vol. 38(3), pp. 145–64.

Belkin, Nicholas; Croft, W. Bruce (1992) 'Information filtering and information retrieval: two sides of the same coin?', *Communications of the ACM*, vol. 35(12), pp. 29–38.

Bliss, Henry Evelyn (1977) *Bliss Bibliographic Classification*, 2ᵈ edn, J. Mills and Vanda Broughton (eds), Butterworths.

Collantes, Lourdes Y. (1995) 'Degree of agreement in naming objects and concepts for information retrieval', *Journal of the American Society for Information Science*, vol. 46, pp. 116–32.

Craven, Timothy C. (1986) *String Indexing*, Academic Press.

Deerwester, Scott C.; Dumais, Susan T.; Furnas, George W.; Landauer, Thomas K.; Harshman, Richard (1990) 'Indexing by latent semantic analysis', *Journal of the American Society for Information Science*, vol. 41, pp. 391–407.

Doszkocs, Tamas E. (1978) 'An associative interactive dictionary (AID) for online bibliographic searching', *American Society for Information Science. 41st Annual Meeting, New York, Nov. 13–17, 1978. Proceedings, vol. 15*, Knowledge Industry Publications, pp. 105–9.

Drabenstott, Karen Markey; Vizine-Goetz, Diane (1994) *Using Subject Headings for Online Retrieval: Theory, Practice, and Potential*, Academic Press.

European Communities (1995) *Thesaurus Eurovoc*, Office for Official Publications of the EC.

Fetters, Linda K. (1995) *A Guide to Indexing Software*, 5ᵗʰ edn, American Society of Indexers.

Fidel, Raya; Hahn, Trudi; Rasmussen, Eddie M.; Smith, Philip J. (eds) (1994) *Challenges in Indexing Electronic Text and Images*, American Society for Information Science/Learned Information.

Fugmann, Robert (1993) *Subject Analysis and Indexing: Theoretical Foundation and Practical Advice*, Indeks Verlag.

Furnas, George W.; Landauer, Thomas K.; Gomez, Louis M.; Dumais, Susan T. (1987) 'The vocabulary problem in human-system communication', *Communications of the ACM*, vol. 30(11), pp. 964–71.

Gluck, Myke (1994) 'Special topic issue: spatial information', *Journal of the American Society for Information Science*, vol. 45, pp. 639–717.

Green, Brian; Bide, Mark (1997) *Unique Identifiers: a Brief Introduction*, Book Industry Communication/EDItEUR, http://www.bic.uk/uniquid.html.

Greene, Stephan; Marchionini, Gary; Plaisant, Catherine; Shneiderman, Ben (2000) 'Previews and overviews in digital libraries: designing surrogates to support visual information seeking', *Journal of the American Society for Information Science*, vol. 51(4), pp. 380–93.

Gutwin, Carl; Paynter, Gordon; Witten, Ian H.; Nevill-Manning, Craig G.; Frank, Eibe (1998) *Improving Browsing in Digital Libraries with Keyphrase Indexes*. Technical report 98–1, Computer Science Department, University of Saskatchewan, http://www.cs.usask.ca/faculty/gutwin/1998/keyphind-tech-report/html/keyphind-9.html.

Hayes-Roth, Frederick; Jacobstein, Neil (1994) 'The state of knowledge-based systems', *Communications of the ACM*, vol. 37(3), pp. 27–39.

Hensen, Steven L. (1989) *Archives, Personal Papers, and Manuscripts: a Cataloging Manual for Archival Repositories, Historical Societies, and Manuscript Libraries*, Society of American Archivists.

Hjerppe, Roland (1996) 'Go with the flow, or abide by the side, or watch the wave? Challenges of change for knowledge organization', in Green, Rebecca (ed.), *Proceedings of the Fourth International ISKO Conference, 1996 July 15–18, Washington, DC*, Indeks Verlag, pp. 10–25.

Hjørland, Birger (1997) *Information Seeking and Subject Representation: an Activity-Theoretical Approach to Information Science*, Greenwood Press.

Hodge, Gail M.; Milstead, Jessica L. (1998) *Computer Support to Indexing*, National Federation of Abstracting and Information Services.

Humphrey, Susanne M. (1993) 'The MedIndEx prototype for computer assisted MEDLINE database indexing', *American Society of Indexers. 25th Annual Meeting. Proceedings*, ASI, pp. 45–54.

Iivonen, Mirja (1994) 'Consistency in the selection of search concepts and search terms', *Information Processing & Management*, vol. 31(2), pp. 173–90.

Institute for Scientific Information (2001) *Arts and Humanities Citation Index; Science Citation Index; Social Science Citation Index; Current Contents*, ISI.

Kessler, M.M. (1963) 'Bibliographic coupling between scientific papers', *American Documentation*, vol. 14, pp. 10–25.

Knutson, Gunnar (1993) 'The year's work in descriptive cataloging, 1992', *Library Resources and Technical Services*, vol. 37, p. 263.

Leonard, Leonard E. (1977) *Inter-indexer Consistency Studies, 1954–1975: a Review of the Literature and Summary of Study Results*, Occasional papers no. 131, University of Illinois, Graduate School of Library Science.

Library of Congress, AMIM Revision Committee (2000) *Archival Moving Image Materials: a Cataloging Manual*, 2nd edn, LC.

Library of Congress, Geography and Map Division (1991) *Map Cataloguing Manual*, LC.

Library of Congress, Office for Descriptive Cataloging Policy (1991) *Descriptive Cataloging of Rare Books*, 2nd edn, LC.

Library of Congress, Processing Department (1980) *Library of Congress Filing Rules*, prepared by J.C. Rather and S.C. Biebel, LC.

Library of Congress, Subject Cataloging Division (1996) *Subject Cataloging Manual: Subject Headings*, 5th edn, LC.

—— (2001) *Library of Congress Subject Headings*, LC.

Marchionini, Gary (1995) *Information Seeking in Electronic Environments*, Cambridge University Press.

MLA International Bibliography (1981, 2000) Modern Language Association of America.

Molto, Mavis; Svenonius, Elaine (1991) 'Automatic recognition of title page names', *Information Processing and Management*, vol. 27, pp. 83–95.

National Library of Medicine (2001) *Medical Subject Headings*, NLM.

Olson, Nancy B. (ed.) (1997) *Cataloging Internet Resources: a Manual and Practical Guide*, 2nd edn, OCLC, http://www.purl.org/oclc/cataloging-internet.

Paskin, Norman (1997 'Information identifiers', *Learned publishing*, vol. 10(2), pp. 135–56.

Poli, Roberto (1996) 'Ontology for knowledge organization', in Green, Rebecca (ed.) *Proceedings of the Fourth International ISKO Conference, 1996 July 15–18, Washington, DC.*, Indeks Verlag, pp. 313–19.

Pollitt, A. Steven; Smith, Martin P.; Braekevelt, Patrick A.J. (1997) *View-based Searching Systems – a New Paradigm for Information Retrieval Based on Faceted Classification and Indexing Using Mutually Constraining Knowledge-based Views*, Centre for Database Access Research, School of Computing and Mathematics, University of Huddersfield, http://www.hud.ac.uk/schools/cedar/bcshci.htm.

Ranganathan, S.R. (1965) *The Colon Classification*, Graduate School of Library Service, Rutgers, the State University.

Rice, Ronald E.; McCreadie, Maureen; Chang, Shan-Ju L. (2001) *Accessing and Browsing: Information and Communication*, MIT Press.

Salton, Gerard; Allan, James; Buckley, Chris (1994) 'Automatic structuring and retrieval of large text files', *Communications of the ACM*, vol. 37(2), pp. 97–108.

Saracevic, Tefko; Kantor, Paul; Chamis, Alice Y.; Trivison, Donna (1988) 'A study of information seeking and retrieving', *Journal of the American Society for Information Science*, vol. 39, pp. 161–216.

Schottlaender, Brian E.C. (ed.) (1998) *The Future of the Descriptive Cataloging Rules: Papers from the ALCTS Preconference, AACR2000, American Library Association Annual Conference, Chicago, June 22, 1995*, ALA.

Shaw, Sarah J.; Shiere, Lauralee (1984) *Sheet Music Cataloging and Processing: a Manual*, Music Library Association.

Small, Henry G. (1973) 'Co-citation in the scientific literature: a new measure of the relationship between two documents', *Journal of the American Society for Information Science*, vol. 24, pp. 265–9.

Soergel, Dagobert (1985) *Organizing Information: Principles of Data Base and Retrieval systems*, Academic Press.

Unesco (1995) *Unesco Thesaurus*, Unesco.

VanWingen, Peter M. and Urquiza, Belinda D. (1996) *Standard Citation Forms for Published Bibliographies and Catalogs Used in Rare Book Cataloging*, 2nd edn, Library of Congress.

Vickery, Brian C. (1997) 'Ontologies', *Journal of Information Science*, vol. 23, pp. 277–86.

Weibel, S. (1992) 'Automated cataloging: implication for libraries and patrons', in F.W. Lancaster and Linda C. Smith (eds) *Artificial Intelligence and Expert Systems: Will They Change the Library?*, Clinic on Library Applications of Data Processing (1990), Graduate School of Library and Information Science, University of Illinois at Urbana-Champaign, pp. 67–80.

Weihs, Jean (ed.) (1998) *The Principles and Future of AACR: International Conference on the Principles and Future Development of AACR, 1997, Toronto*, Canadian Library Association.

Wellisch, Hans H. (1980) 'The cybernetics of bibliographic control: toward a theory of document retrieval systems', *Journal of the American Society for Information Science*, vol. 31, pp. 41–50.

Wilson, Patrick (1968) *Two Kinds of Power: An Essay on Bibliographical Control*, University of California Press.

Further reading

Aitchison, Jean; Gilchrist, Alan; Bawden, David (1997) *Thesaurus Construction and Use: a Practical Manual*, 3rd edn, ASLIB.

Allen, Bryce L. (1996) *Information Tasks: Toward a User-Centered Approach to Information Systems*, Academic Press.

Bates, Marcia J. (1998) 'Indexing and access for digital libraries and the internet: human, database, and domain factors', *Journal of the American Society for Information Science*, vol. 49(13), pp. 1185–205.

Bean, Carol A.; Green, Rebecca (2001) *Relationships in the Organization of Knowledge*, Kluwer Academic Publishers.

Berman, Sanford (1993) *Prejudices and Antipathies: a Tract on the LC Subject Headings Concerning People*, McFarland.

Carpenter, M. and Svenonius, E. (eds) (1985) *Foundations of Cataloging: A Sourcebook*, Libraries Unlimited.

Chan, Lois Mai (1995) *Library of Congress Subject Headings: Principles and Applications*, 3rd edn, Libraries Unlimited.

—— (1999) *A Guide to the Library of Congress Classification*, 5th edn, Libraries Unlimited.

—— (1985) *Theory of Subject Analysis: a Sourcebook*, Libraries Unlimited.

Chowdhury, G.G. (1999) *Introduction to Modern Information Retrieval*, Library Association.

Frohmann, Bernd (1990) 'Rules of indexing: a critique of mentalism in information retrieval theory', *Journal of Documentation*, vol. 46(2), pp. 81–101.

Gilchrist, Alan; Strachan, David (ed.) (1990) *The UDC: Essays for a New Decade*, ASLIB.

Hutchins, W.J. (1975) *Languages of Indexing and Classification: a Linguistic Study of Structures and Functions*, Peregrinus.

Korfhage, Robert R. (1997) *Information Storage and Retrieval*, Wiley Computer Publishing.

Kowalski, Gerald (1997) *Information Retrieval Systems: Theory and Implementation*, Kluwer Academic Publishers.

Lancaster, F.W. (1998) *Indexing and Abstracting in Theory and Practice*, 2nd edn, Graduate School of Library and Information Science, University of Illinois/Library Association.

Langridge, D.W. (1992) *Classification: Its Kinds, Elements, Systems and Applications*, Bowker-Saur.

Miksa, Francis L. (1989) *The DDC, the Universe of Knowledge, and the Post-Modern Library*, OCLC.

Milstead, Jessica L. (1984) *Subject Access Systems: Alternatives in Design*, Academic Press.

Mulvany, Nancy C. (1994) *Indexing Books*, University of Chicago Press.

O'Connor, Brian C. (1996) *Explorations in Indexing and Abstracting: Pointing, Virtue, and Power*, Libraries Unlimited.

Salton, Gerard (1989) *Automatic Text Processing: The Transformation, Analysis, and Retrieval of Information by Computer*, Addison-Wesley.

Sparck-Jones, Karen (ed.) (1981) *Information Retrieval Experiment*, Butterworths.

Stone, Alva T. (ed.) (2000) 'The LCSH century: one hundred years with the Library of Congress subject headings system', *Cataloging and Classification Quarterly*, vol. 29(1–2), pp. 1–234.

Strzalkowski, Tomek (ed.) (1999) *Natural language Information Retrieval*, Kluwer Academic Publishers.

Svenonius, Elaine (2000) *The Intellectual Foundation of Information Organization*, MIT Press.

Taylor, Arlene G. (1999) *The Organization of Information*, Libraries Unlimited.

Vickery, B.C. (1966) *Faceted Classification Schemes*, Graduate School of Library Service, Rutgers, the State University.

Weinberg, Bella Hass (ed.) (1988) *Indexing: the State of Our Knowledge and the State of Our Ignorance: Proceedings of the 20th Annual Meeting of the American Society of Indexers, 1988 May 13, New York*, Learned Information.

Wellisch, Hans H. (1995) *Indexing from A to Z*, 2nd edn, H.W. Wilson.

SEE ALSO: communication; taxonomies

JAMES D. ANDERSON

ORGANIZATIONAL INFORMATION POLICIES

Organizational information policies parallel national information policies – though they probably stand a better chance of being implemented – and encouragement of them can form part of national policies (Moore 1998). Within organizations, they belong to the same category as MARKETING or research and development (R&D) policies – an expression of what overall corporate objectives mean in terms of a specific area of activity that is essential for achieving them. Like other organizational policies, they often form the basis for a strategy (see definitions listed below).

Interest in organizational information policies developed from the late 1970s. A Diebold Research Programme report from that period cited by Fried (1979) suggested that top US corporations were 'groping in the dark' because over 80 per cent of them lacked an overall information policy. The impact of computerization and management information systems probably provided the stimulus for such policies. Karmi (1983), for example, presents an information policy matrix, and a case study that was certainly motivated by questions about computerization. The related concept of INFORMATION MANAGEMENT also started to become current at about this time (see for example Lewis and Martyn 1986: 33).

Some definitions, based on Orna (1999) are:

- Organizational information policy.
- Founded on the organization's overall objectives, defines at a general level.
- The objectives of information use in the organization.
- What 'information' means in the context of whatever the organization is in business for.
- The principles on which it will manage information.

- Principles for the use of human resources for managing information.
- Principles for the use of technology to support information management.
- Principles it will apply in relation to establishing the value added by information and knowledge.
- Organizational information strategy.

The detailed expression of information policy is in terms of objectives, targets and actions to achieve them, for a defined period ahead. It provides a supportive framework for information management, and, supported by appropriate systems and technology, is the 'engine' for:

- Maintaining, managing and applying the organization's information resources.
- Supporting its essential knowledge base and all who contribute to it, with strategic intelligence, for achieving its key business objectives.

Why do organizations need an information policy? How can they benefit? The short answer is that they need it to ensure that the KNOWLEDGE that they need to survive and prosper is kept fed with information that nourishes it, so that it is fit for successful action to achieve their objectives.

The benefits that organizations can expect from serious application of an information policy can be summarised as:

- Integration of all information activities, allowing information to contribute fully to meeting organizational objectives.
- Objective criteria for allocating resources to information activities, based on their contribution to organizational goals, allowing effective deployment of resources, and promoting long-term planning and continuity in developing the use of information.
- Enriched use of knowledge and information through interfunctional and interdisciplinary co-operation; discovery of new possibilities for productive use of knowledge and information.
- Enhanced chances of successful innovation and competition, with potential for increased return on R&D investment, increased market share, better competitive position.
- Sound criteria for decisions on investment in information technology and systems, leading to productive developments in information

use, support for essential internal and external information interactions.

- Monitoring the organization's internal and external environment for significant intelligence makes it possible to anticipate change and respond to it effectively, and to take productive change initiatives.
- Risks it helps to avoid include: missed opportunities; loss of customers/clients; failures of legal compliance; loss of reputation because of lack of vital information; failures of innovation because of poor information interchange; poor return on systems and IT investment; failure to identify threatening change.

Steps towards organizational information policy

Before deciding on an information policy it is necessary to understand the organization for which it is to be designed: what it seeks to achieve; how it manages; how it sees itself and its outside world (organizational 'culture' and business values); its history; its structure; its business processes. That will help in defining and 'selling' a policy that has a chance of being accepted and implemented.

While, in order to survive and prosper, all organizations need certain kinds of knowledge, and appropriate information resources to 'feed' that knowledge (no organization, for example, can survive without self-knowledge, and knowledge of what is going on in the outside world on which it depends for its livelihood), the content of the life-sustaining knowledge and information is highly specific for each individual organization.

The next step for any organization that is serious about developing an information policy should therefore be to define what constitutes its essential knowledge and information – though very few actually do so as yet. A useful practical approach is to ask and answer these questions:

- What does the organization, and the people who make it up, need to know to achieve its objectives?
- What resources of information does it need to maintain the required knowledge?

Information achieves nothing for organizations until it reaches the people who need it, so that they can absorb what they require, and act on it. A third vital question is therefore:

- How does the necessary information need to flow around within the organization and between it and its outside world? How do people need to interact with each other in getting and using information? In its simplest terms – who needs to tell whom about what?

These initial steps make a light demand on resources – they require mainly desk research and thinking time, preferably by a small group of those responsible for managing information resources, and information systems/IT, with senior management sponsorship. The results indicate the important issues that the organization's information policy should address, and can lead to a first formulation of it.

It is of course not enough just to have an information policy statement. It is essential to gain senior management commitment and guaranteed resources for implementing it, and the understanding and support of all who are concerned with managing any resources of information and of the systems/technology infrastructure. For examples of organizational information policies, see Orna (1990: 167–77, 1999: 106–8).

From information policy to information strategy

Information policy expresses aspirations – what should be. To translate it into a working strategy that delivers the goods, it is first necessary to have an accurate picture of the existing situation: What resources of information and knowledge does the organization actually have? Where are they? Who is responsible for them? How are they used? What information interactions take place inside the organization, and with its outside world?

That makes it possible to compare the existing situation with the aspiration, and see how the two diverge or converge – the essential basis for developing an information strategy. This process is usually called an INFORMATION AUDIT. The results of the audit should lead to:

- Refinement of the information policy.
- Development and implementation of information strategy.

Conclusion

The impact of information technology was probably responsible for the initial interest in organizational information policies. It is worth noting in conclusion that recent developments in business-to-business electronic commerce (e-commerce) raise once again the need for business-wide information policies to protect businesses from uninformed technology investment driven by fear of being left behind and unjustified hopes of a large return on investment.

References

Fried, L (1979) *Practical Data Processing Management*, Reston Publishing Co. Inc.

Karmi, R. (1983) 'A methodological framework for formulating information policy', *Information and Management* 6: 269–80.

Lewis, D.A. and Martyn, J. (1986) 'An appraisal of national information policy in the United Kingdom', *ASLIB Proceedings* 38(1): 25–34.

Moore, N. (1998) 'The British national information strategy', *Journal of Information Science* 24(5): 337–44.

Orna, E. (1999) *Practical Information Policies*, 2nd edn, Gower.

—— (1990) *Practical Information Policies*, Gower.

Further reading

Davenport, T.H. *et al.* (1998) *Working Knowledge, How Organizations Manage What They Know*, Harvard Business School Press.

—— (1997) *Information Ecology*, Oxford University Press.

—— (1992) 'Information politics', *Sloan Management Review*, Fall, pp. 53–65.

Drucker, P. (1995) *Managing in a Time of Great Change*, Butterworth Heinemann.

—— (1995) 'The information executives truly need', *Harvard Business Review* (Jan–Feb): 54–62.

Farkas-Conn, I. (1989) 'Information as a corporate resource', *Information Services and Use* 9: 205–15.

Itami, H. with Roehl, T. (1987) *Mobilizing Invisible Assets*, Harvard University Press.

Marchand, D.A. (1997) 'Competing with information: Know what you want', *FT Mastering Management Reader*, July/August: 7–12.

—— (1997) 'Managing strategic intelligence', in *Financial Times Mastering Management*, Financial Times/ Pitman, pp. 346–50.

Nonaka, I. and Takeuchi, H. (1995) *The Knowledge-Creating Company: How Japanese Companies Create the Dynamics of Information*, Oxford University Press.

Owens, I. and Wilson, T. with Abell, A. (1996) *Information and Business Performance. A Study of Information Systems and Services in High Performing Companies*, Bowker-Saur.

Reponen, T. (1994) 'Organizational information management strategies', *Information Systems Journal* 4: 27–44.

SEE ALSO: information policy; knowledge management; management support systems

ELIZABETH ORNA

OTLET, PAUL-MARIE-GHISLAIN (1868–1944)

Bibliographer and internationalist whose collaboration with Henri LaFontaine produced the International Federation for Information and Documentation (FID), the Union of International Associations (UIA) and the UNIVERSAL DECIMAL CLASSIFICATION (UDC). He popularized and gave its specialized contemporary meaning to the word 'documentation'.

Born in Brussels, he obtained a law degree, but was more inspired by bibliography. When he became aware of the DEWEY DECIMAL CLASSIFICATION (DCC), he saw its potential for the subject organization of a universal catalogue of publications. An International Institute of Bibliography (IIB) was formed in 1895 for this purpose and a documentary union of governments was proposed to support it. The Belgian government provided a headquarters for the Institute, where the principles of decimal classification were used to list the bibliographical citations that began to be collected in enormous numbers. Increasing divergence from Dewey's system led to the formal constitution of UDC. Although the universal bibliographical project eventually collapsed under the pressures of lack of finance and the size of the task, the Institute survived, after reconstitution in 1937, as FID.

In 1910 Otlet and LaFontaine organized the first World Congress of International Associations, at which the UIA was founded. Otlet taught librarianship and documentation in Brussels, and many of his ideas on documentation were summed up in *Traité; de la documentation* (1934).

OUTREACH SERVICE

Services provided by a library outside its usual location, particularly those intended to attract new users or to appeal to groups in the community who do not make full use of conventional services. Target groups are typically the housebound, ethnic minorities and people in districts of socio-economic deprivation.

SEE ALSO: mobile library; social exclusion and libraries

P

PACKET SWITCHING

A method of handling messages transmitted across a NETWORK. A packet-switching network consists of a number of exchanges interconnected by high-speed transmission lines. The exchanges are responsible for routing the packets across the network, choosing the best route based on the traffic on the network at the time; storing packets temporarily until a transmission path is available; and ensuring that packets arrive at their destination uncorrupted and in the same sequence as they were sent. Packet switching makes efficient use of transmission capacity where a large number of computer systems and terminals wish to share transmission paths between one another.

SEE ALSO: informatics; information and communication technology

PALAEOGRAPHY

Palaeography, a word coined from the Greek *palaios* and *graphein*, meaning ancient writing, is the study of the past through the forms of handwriting. Though regarded as a science ancillary to history, it is in fact vital to our knowledge of any literate society before the invention of printing. In studying the medieval West, palaeography is concerned first with the scripts in which Latin was written and then with their adaptation to the vernacular languages of Europe, but the history of Latin writing and its derivatives refers back to the Greeks, from whom the Romans directly and indirectly acquired both the alphabet itself and the habits of LITERACY.

The alphabet descended to the West through the Phoenicians from a Semitic script, the first symbols of which, *aleph*, ox, and *beth*, house, have given their names to the whole sequence. The Greeks adapted the letters variously to their own dialects, but their great contribution was to add distinctive vowels, which allowed the script to be applied freely to other languages. The standard form of the Greek alphabet emerged from Ionic speech, but the Romans acquired their version from the Greek settlement at Cumae, which is why the consonant r is represented by R in Western Europe, instead of P as in modern Greek and Russian.

The earliest forms of writing in both Greek and Latin are inscriptions cut in stone, to which the square forms of majuscule, or capital, letters were readily suited. The Latin capitals themselves were soon modified in writing to the more flowing shapes called Rustic. In both cultures the spread of literacy produced cursive scripts in minuscule, and a new formal script, known as Uncial, was then concocted from a mixture of majuscule and minuscule letters. Solemn texts, such as Virgil's poetry or biblical and patristic works in the early Church, were usually written in capitals or Uncial, which are distinguished as book-hands. The texts introduced to Anglo-Saxon England by the missionaries led by St Augustine of Canterbury, in AD 597, were of that kind, and so were the copies of them that the English converts first made.

Meanwhile late Roman cursive, visually an unattractive script, remained current in Italy and Merovingian France. From the eighth century, however, the missionary efforts of the Carolingian church, powerfully impelled by clergy from England and Ireland, called for a reformed and standardized script. The result, carefully developed in the abbeys of the Loire and northern France from the best available Roman exemplars, was the handsome, simple and eminently legible hand known as Carolingian minuscule. In central Italy, notably at Monte Cassino, a similarly fine hand known as the Beneventan script evolved, but the Carolingian hand was adopted, with local variations, in most of Western Europe. It survives today in every book printed in the Roman alphabet, as well as on visual display units.

For several hundred years written texts were shaped primarily if not exclusively to meet the needs of the church. There was a constant demand for Bibles and service books, but also for a great variety of other texts. The Church itself was a literate society, and in lending its skills to secular authority it promoted literacy amongst the laity also. Writing did not for some centuries revert to the casual uses common in the classical world, but cursive scripts, systematically abbreviated, were evolved for administrative and literary work. The medieval administrative scripts are sometimes known as court hands, and their resemblances from one country to another are often more striking than the differences between them.

With the revival of interest in classical learning that began in Italy in the thirteenth century, scholars searched for reliable texts of Roman authors. Although the Italians then coined the phrase *il medio aevo*, the Middle Ages, for the period from which they believed themselves to have emerged, they had little sense of the layers of the past. They therefore supposed that the beautifully legible Carolingian minuscule was a product of antiquity, and they revived it together with the works that it preserved. Their own particular refinement of the script is with us still as Italic. More important, the minuscule was perpetuated on its merits by the early Italian printers, such as Aldus Manutius (*c.* 1450–1515), and by their successors down to the present day.

The advent of printing transformed the reproduction of literary texts, and formal writing – calligraphy – became a matter of individual taste. However, administrative documents were generally handwritten, and in styles in which speed and economy of effort were more important than appearance. In England the so-called secretary-hand, derived from court hand, long held its own against the Italian humanist scripts. The outcome

was an odd one, for both eventually gave way to a contrived cursive script known, from the manuals that promoted it, as copperplate, which spread into offices everywhere with British commercial supremacy.

The critical study of palaeography has advanced with other historical sciences, notably in the work of Jean Mabillon, OSB (1632–1707), and the Maurists, and later of professional institutes such as the French École des Chartes. Photography, as in the collotype plates published by the Palaeographical Society (1873) and the New Palaeographical Society (1903), greatly advanced the discipline. Much work has also been done since the late nineteenth century in papyrology, the elucidation of texts, mainly Greek, preserved on papyrus in the deserts of the Middle East.

Palaeography is now inseparably associated with codicology, the critical assessment of manuscript books, which in England began with the work of Humfrey Wanley (1672–1726). It extends, by the detailed physical examination of manuscripts, from the close dating of individual texts to the reconstruction of lost libraries.

Further reading

Boyle, L.E. (1995) *Medieval Latin Palaeography: A Bibliographic Introduction*, 2nd edn, University of Toronto Press.

Jenkinson, C.H. and Johnson, C. (1927) *Later Court Hands in England*, Cambridge University Press.

—— (1915) *English Court Hand*, Cambridge University Press.

Parkes, M.B. (1992) *Pause and Effect: An Introduction to the History of Punctuation in the West*, Scolar Press.

Reynolds, I.D. and Wilson, N.G. (1974) *Scribes and Scholars: A Guide to the Transmission of Greek and Latin Literature*, 2nd edn, Clarendon Press.

Sharpe, R. (1997) *A Handlist of the Latin Writers of Great Britain and Ireland before 1540*, Brepols.

Thompson, E.M. (1912) *Greek and Latin Palaeography*, Clarendon Press.

SEE ALSO: archives; manuscript libraries

GEOFFREY MARTIN

PAMPHLET

A short publication, sometimes defined as having at least five but not more than forty-eight pages, but which is not a part of a serial. An older sense of the word suggests a polemical content, so that a pamphleteer was one who disseminated political comment in the form of small printed documents.

SEE ALSO: book trade

PANIZZI, SIR ANTONY (1797–1879)

Librarian of the British Museum who, if anyone does, probably deserves to be referred to as a great librarian. The concept of what a national library could and should be was enormously advanced by Panizzi's example at the British Museum.

Born at Brescello, in the (then) Austrian part of Italy, he became a political refugee in England. In 1831 he joined the staff of the British Museum. Its book and manuscript collections were rich but ill-organized, and access was difficult. As Panizzi moved up the hierarchy of the Museum he succeeded in transforming most aspects of the library for the better. LEGAL DEPOSIT was vigorously enforced to provide for current British literature, and government was persuaded to provide funds to acquire older material and foreign publications. He was responsible for the planning of the great Round Reading Room, with its surrounding stack areas, which gave readers proper conditions in which to work. A new cataloguing code, the famous 91 Rules, and an alphabetical name catalogue in manuscript form were developed under his direction. In 1856 he was appointed Principal Librarian and held the post until his retirement in 1866. His achievements were officially recognized by the award of a knighthood.

Further reading

Miller, E. (1967) *Prince of Librarians: The Life and Times of Antonio Panizzi of the British Museum*, London: Deutsch.

SEE ALSO: British Library; history of libraries; national libraries

PAPER

Exists in many different forms, but the common underlying feature is that they all consist of fibrous elements bonded to one another.

Although in the late twentieth century there were rapid advances in the electronic storage of information, there is no doubt that paper will continue to be widely used because of its relative cheapness and convenience. As important, if not more so, is the fact that much of our existing stock of information and other aspects of our cultural heritage is in the form of print on paper, which needs care, PRESERVATION and CONSERVATION (Priest 1987).

Structure and properties

COMPOSITION OF PAPER

A paper-like sheet can be made from many different types of fibre, but virtually all the paper encountered in libraries and archives will be made from naturally occurring vegetable fibres. The single, central and most important unifying feature of such conventional papers is as follows: on dispersion in water, cellulose-based fibres absorb moisture and become swollen and pliant. When a mat is formed by draining the suspension through a fine, flat wire mesh, the wet fibres tend to be aligned in layers parallel to the plane of the wire, but otherwise in more or less, but not quite, random directions. On drying this wet web, a profound change takes place. As water is lost, the fibres are drawn into close contact and a special type of chemical bond, the hydrogen bond, forms in the regions where fibres overlap and make contact. This self-bonding is the key to producing a coherent, strong, stiff sheet of paper. No extra adhesive is necessary and paper can be made simply by draining wet cellulosic fibre and allowing the web to dry.

In the Western world, before the introduction of papermaking machines in the first half of the nineteenth century, paper was made largely from fibres derived from cotton or linen, mostly from rags, i.e. discarded textiles. Today at least 95 per cent of the paper produced in the world contains fibres derived from wood. The remainder is mostly made from vegetable fibres such as bagasse (from sugar cane), straw or bamboo. However, very small quantities of special grades of paper are still made from plant fibres such as cotton, linen and hemp, including currency papers, artists' papers, high-grade printing and writing papers, and papers especially made for conservation work.

PREPARATION OF FIBRES FOR PAPERMAKING

The first step in making paper is to separate the fibres from their original matrix in the wood. This is known as pulping, of which there are two distinct types. In mechanical pulping processes, intense mechanical action is employed to fragment the wood and break it up into fibrous particles. In the other major type, known as chemical pulping, wood chips are treated with various chemical compounds under heat and pressure. The yield is substantially less than in mechanical pulping but the fibres are recovered in a virtually undamaged state and so can be made into much stronger paper. There are now pulping processes that contain elements of both of these basic types. Bleaching may also be involved if the product is to be a white paper.

A key aspect of papermaking is the process in which the fibres, dispersed in water, are subjected to an intense mechanical shearing action. The effect of beating or refining is to affect markedly the mechanical properties of the paper. For example, increasing the extent of treatment increases tensile and burst strength, and also the apparent density. The net effect on the fibres, which is complex in detail, is that they become more flexible and are able to bed down together to give increased surface area in contact and enhanced interfibre bond strength.

NON-FIBROUS COMPONENTS IN PAPER

Printing and writing papers usually contain a proportion of filler. The outcome, amongst other things, is an increase in opacity, smoothness and general uniformity of appearance. Materials in most common use are clay or chalk (calcium carbonate). Papers may contain significant proportions of these materials, typically around 10–15 per cent by weight.

Most types of paper are treated in some way to control their interaction with water and other aqueous fluids. A paper made only from beaten cellulosic fibres is by its nature extremely hydrophilic and very readily absorbs water. Such paper is completely unsuitable, for example, for writing on with pen and ink. Moreover, in many common commercial processes, paper needs to resist wetting to a greater or lesser degree. The procedure by which paper is given water resistance is known as sizing. Internal sizing, as it is known, is widely used and involves the addition of sizing agents to the aqueous suspension of fibres before the paper is formed. The traditional material is wood rosin, augmented by aluminium sulphate (known as 'alum' by papermakers), which acts to fix the rosin on to the surfaces of the fibres. Unfortunately this means that the paper is made in an acidic environment because of the use of the alum. The acidity remains in the paper, and this is the chief cause of the slow loss of strength that takes place in much paper upon storage. In recent years economically competitive neutral or alkaline internal sizing methods have been introduced, which should largely avoid the ageing problem (Priest 1989). Internal sizing needs to be distinguished carefully from surface and tub sizing, which involve treatment with starch or gelatine, or similar materials, principally to give surface cohesion.

Although these are usually present in much smaller proportions, papers can also contain a wide range of different additives that perform various functions, often related to the particular type of paper. Examples are wet strength agents, optical brightening agents and dyes to control the shade or precise hue of the paper.

COATINGS AND SURFACE TREATMENTS

Coatings and surface treatments represent an important class of non-fibrous components in paper. An example is the glossy coated papers used for magazines and increasingly for books. The coatings, which are normally based on powdered mineral pigments, typically clay or calcium carbonate, are applied as a distinct process not to be confused with fillers. The basic result is to produce a very much enhanced printing surface.

PROPERTIES OF PAPER

Like any other material, paper has a set of important properties that need measurement and control if the paper is to meet its functional requirements. In essence, there are three important categories: properties of the bulk material, such as strength, grammage (mass per unit area) and apparent density; properties relating to the surface of the paper, such as smoothness, which are of key importance in conversion processes such as printing; and optical properties, principally colour, brightness and opacity.

When used in books, paper clearly needs to be strong enough for the purpose and have acceptable colour and brightness. On the preservation side, a major problem is undoubtedly the loss of strength on ageing. The matter of colour and how it changes with ageing is also important, but will relate in different ways to different types of artefact, e.g. it may be more important in works of art on paper.

A basic method of studying the mechanical properties of paper is by means of a load elongation curve. The load at the break point represents the tensile strength of the paper under test, whilst the elongation at break is a measure of the toughness, or the capability to absorb energy before breaking.

There are many other tests for mechanical properties, several of which have been based on some kind of simulation of the forces the paper is required to withstand in use. Examples are tear strength, measured by the energy required to propagate a tear in a sample of paper in which a slit has been made; burst strength (the force required to burst a hole through paper using an inflated rubber diaphragm); and folding endurance, measured as the number of times a strip can be folded to and fro before breaking. As mentioned above, in addition to mechanical properties colour is probably of greatest interest to those concerned with paper as an information carrier. Discolouration, normally to a yellowish brown on exposure to light, is the usual problem. A familiar example is the yellowing seen in old paperback books, especially the edges of leaves. A key factor here is the presence or absence of lignin, because paper containing it quickly turns yellow on exposure to light.

The future: standards for permanent paper

In the light of the huge problems facing libraries, ARCHIVES and other repositories, it is vital that collections now being created should be as free as possible from the defects that have caused our present difficulties. In effect, in an ideal world all documents and books should be on paper that is as durable and long-lasting as deemed necessary. One way of moving towards this goal is by means of agreed standards that specify how such paper can be produced.

Standards for especially long-lasting archival grades of paper have been in existence for some time, but as such papers are usually purchased in relatively small quantities they are much more expensive to purchase than ordinary grades, and hence their use is restricted to specific applications where permanence is of special importance. This situation has changed profoundly in recent years by the introduction into conventional papermaking of the neutral or alkaline sizing systems. This now makes it possible to set standards for long-life paper intended for more widespread use in books and other general publications where longevity is of importance. This has brought about a pivotal change in the prospects for the future preservation of books and documents being produced at the present time. However, it is vital that the requirements of standards should be practicable and economic for the manufacturer, otherwise they will fall into disrepute.

An important step forward was the publication by the American National Standard Institution of ANSI Z39.48–1984, *Permanence of Paper for Printed Library Materials*, which has recently been updated. The ISO has produced its own standard for similar types of paper, ISO 9706. Its aim is to enable book printers, publishers and others to use a specified paper economically for all types of document, record or publications that are likely to be stored in libraries or archives for a prolonged period. The specification is set up entirely in terms of stipulated test results. It remains to be seen whether or not this new standard will meet with approval and be used as a basis for longer-lasting books and documents. One thing is now quite clear – the way is open for the production of inexpensive paper that more than adequately meets the normal life expectancy for many archival and similar applications.

References

Priest, D.J. (1989) 'Permanence and neutral/alkaline papermaking', in S.H. Zeronian and H.L. Needles (eds) *Historic Textile and Paper Materials, Conservation and Characterisation II*, American Chemical Society.

—— (1987) 'Paper and its problems', *Library Review* 36 (part 3).

Further reading

Casey, J.P. (ed.) (1983) *Pulp and Paper: Chemistry and Chemical Technology*, Wiley-Interscience, 4 vols [a comprehensive and widely used text on all aspects of the subject].

Hunter, D. (1978) *Papermaking: The History and Technique of an Ancient Craft*, Dover Publications Inc. [this book, which is an unabridged republication of the 2nd edn of 1947 (Alfred A. Knopf), gives a very good account of early and oriental papermaking].

Smook, G.A. (1982) *Handbook for Pulp and Paper Technologists*, TAPPI and Canadian Pulp and Paper

Association [a good introductory text, dealing particularly well with the technology].

DEREK J. PRIEST

PAPERLESS SOCIETY

A term that expresses the vision of a future society wholly committed to electronic communication. The phrase is usually said to have been coined by F.W. LANCASTER and countered by Maurice Line, who said he could no more imagine a paperless society than he could a paperless lavatory. At the beginning of the twenty-first century, whilst the enormous growth of electronic communication has curtailed the use of postal services for serious communication (as opposed to junk mail), it does not seem to have otherwise moderated the output of paper documentation.

SEE ALSO: information management

PARAPROFESSIONAL

A term used to describe staff in libraries and other information service providers who are trained to understand and use a range of specific techniques, procedures and services that can be undertaken according to a set of predetermined rules, thus enabling them to be assigned high-level support responsibilities specific to libraries and information services but which do not require the exercise of professional judgement.

Roles, tasks and responsibilities

Paraprofessionals (sometimes correctly called library technicians, incorrectly support or non-professional staff) undertake aspects of professional work formerly performed by professionals but now perceived as suitable to be carried out at a subprofessional level (compare paramedics, legal assistants). Commonly these tasks are technology-based, involving technical library skills and requiring low-level decision-making. Examples include ACQUISITIONS, original and copy cataloguing, periodicals control, first-line enquiries, administration, and supervising and training others in the delivery of services direct to users. Other less common tasks include planning programmes for children, staff selection interviewing, budget planning, online searching, USER EDUCATION (both classroom and indivi-

dual), book selection and INTERLIBRARY LENDING (Burgin and Hansel 1991; Oberg 1992; Oberg *et al.* 1992).

PARAPROFESSIONALS AS MANAGERS

Higher-level responsibility may be given to paraprofessionals by employing them as managers of staff, services and systems, carrying out such tasks as reviewing staff performance, delivering services at local level and managing workflows. Many of these tasks are perceived by professionals as professional. Supporters of paraprofessionals see them as relieving professionals of low-level routine; opponents, as encroachment leading to replacement (Pantazis 1978). The AMERICAN LIBRARY ASSOCIATION identified only sixteen out of sixty tasks as more likely to be assigned to a professional than to a paraprofessional (Mugnier 1980).

Skills

Skills required are wide-ranging, and include: planning, budgeting, decision-making, problem-solving, time management, supervision, and interpersonal and communication skills (managerial); operating equipment, systems, health and safety (technical); enquiries, empathy with client groups (client-based).

Training and educational qualifications

Education and training for paraprofessionals was evident in Germany from 1906, the former USSR in 1929, and developed in North America and Australia in the 1950s and 1960s. The Library Association of Australia guidelines aimed to minimize divergence and maximize portability of training programmes (Library Courses (Vocational) Standing Committee 1976). Common in-service training practice in the USA and the United Kingdom is to treat professionals and paraprofessionals similarly, allowing study time to enhance qualifications and paying for tuition, courses and conferences.

QUALIFICATIONS

Many paraprofessionals in the United Kingdom hold a City and Guilds of London Institute 737 Library Assistant's Certificate or a Business and Technician Education Council (BTEC) National Certificate or Diploma in Business Studies (which includes a double module in library and information studies). National Vocational Qualifications

(NVQs) in the United Kingdom provide a framework for all library and information workers to acquire certificated skills and competences. In South Africa, Botswana, Zimbabwe and other African countries, courses run at polytechnics/technikons lead to the award of a National Diploma in Library and Information Studies.

Employment

Strong economic pressure to drive down staff costs has led to the deletion of many professional posts. Significant numbers of paraprofessional posts are filled by professionally qualified librarians unable to find suitable professional posts.

SALARIES AND GRADES

In the United Kingdom and the USA there is some overlap between salaries on professional and paraprofessional grades. Confusion (and sometimes disadvantage) is caused by placing paraprofessionals, support and other clerical staff on similar grades. Many paraprofessionals stay in a post for upwards of ten years, but a clear career progression (where it exists) tends to be evident only in large organizations.

STATUS

Some professionals denigrate paraprofessionals because they see them as a threat to their position. Paraprofessionals are often dissatisfied with being paid less than professionals for doing (as they see it) the same work, by a lack of recognition and by poor or unclear career prospects. However, many paraprofessionals are better motivated than professionals to improve their performance through training, having particularly positive attitudes to new technology (Burgin and Hansel 1991).

GENDER

Research in the USA found that, in academic libraries, women paraprofessionals outnumbered men by four to one (see WOMEN IN LIBRARIAN-SHIP). In libraries where there were some men as well as women in paraprofessional posts, there was a tendency for the salary structure to be better, for more professional tasks to be assigned to paraprofessionals, for more release time and funded conference attendance, for post holders to have better overall educational qualifications and for there to be a higher turnover (Oberg *et al.* 1992).

SUPPORT

Support mechanisms for paraprofessionals operate through affiliate membership of the Library Association of the United Kingdom, a separate membership category of the Association of College and Research Libraries (ACRL) in the USA and journals such as *Library Mosaics*.

References

Burgin, R. and Hansel, P. (1991) 'Library management: A dialogue', *Wilson Library Bulletin* 66 (September): 66–8.

Library Courses (Vocational) Standing Committee (1976) *Guidelines for the Education of Library Technicians: Report of the National Workshop*, Melbourne, 24–7 May 1976.

Mugnier, C. (1980) *The Paraprofessional and the Professional Job Structure*, American Library Association.

Oberg, L.R. (1992) 'The emergence of the paraprofessional in academic libraries: Perceptions and realities', *College and Research Libraries* 53(2): 99–112.

Oberg, L.R., Mentges, M.E., McDermott, P.N. and Harusadangkul, V. (1992) 'The role, status and working conditions of paraprofessionals: A national survey of academic libraries', *College and Research Libraries* 53(3): 215–38.

Pantazis, F. (1978) 'Library technicians in the hierarchy', *Canadian Library Journal* 35(2): 77–85, 87.

Further reading

Canadian Library Association (1981) *Guidelines for the Education of Library Technicians*, CLA.

Davidson-Arnott, F. and Kay, D. (1998) 'Library technician programs: Skills-oriented paraprofessional education', *Library Trends* 46: 540–63.

Howarth, L.C. (1998) 'The role of the paraprofessional in technical services in libraries', *Library Trends* 46: 526–39.

Johnson, C.P. (1996) 'The changing nature of jobs: A paraprofessional time series', *College and Research Libraries* 57: 59–67.

Library Mosaics (1989–) Yenor Inc. (bi-monthly).

Library Support Staff.com (www.librarysupportstaff.com).

Nettlefold, B.A. (1989) 'Paraprofessionalism in librarianship', *International Library Review* 21: 519–31 [a good overview of the main issues].

Ostertag, J.K. (1992) 'Annotated bibliography', in J.K. Ostertag and K.M. Heim (eds) *Library Support Staff: Challenges for the 90s*, American Library Association, Office for Library Personnel Resources [an excellent source of references].

Owen, L.J. (1997) 'Paraprofessional groups and associations', *Library Trends* 46: 348–72.

SEE ALSO: information professions

ROBERT E. OLDROYD

PARLIAMENTARY LIBRARIES

Parliamentary libraries make an important contribution to informing the legislature at the national or state level. Publicly funded, most parliamentary libraries exclusively serve the legislature, its members, committees and staff. Organizationally, the library may report directly to the political leadership of the legislature, or its chief executive officer, or a special committee.

Roles and objectives

The parliamentary library is a key component in a legislature obtaining the knowledge and information it needs to function effectively. In an environment dominated by advocacy, legislators need immediate access to information that is objective, timely, authoritative, targeted at their unique needs and presented in a form that is easily accessible to non-experts. Information may be provided in print, via the Internet (through parliamentary websites), e-mail, telephone, fax or in-person briefings.

History

France launched its National Assembly library in 1796, soon followed by the creation of the US LIBRARY OF CONGRESS in 1800. The second chamber of the Netherlands began a parliamentary library in 1815, and in 1818 the first Parliamentary Librarian of the UK House of Commons was appointed. Parliamentary libraries proliferated widely in the nineteenth century, reaching all continents by the early twentieth century. Parliaments in CENTRAL AND EASTERN EUROPE and RUSSIA AND THE FORMER SOVIET UNION reinvigorated their libraries in the 1990s. Today, nearly every active legislature has a parliamentary library.

Staff and organization

Functioning as a highly specialized library requires staff with excellent reference and information research skills, and knowledge of pertinent resources – particularly electronic sources. As the scale of library activity increases from providing information to conducting research, the skills of lawyers, economists, political scientists or other programme specialists are added. Library staff need to be service-oriented problem-solvers, with high energy and a commitment to meeting deadlines. They should also be proactive, building their information bases in anticipation of parliamentary questions.

Most parliamentary libraries are relatively modest in scale. The median number of staff is approximately fifteen for libraries in Western Europe, ten for Latin America and four or five staff for the rest of the world. A few parliamentary libraries are quite large. The US Congressional Research Service (CRS) (part of the Library of Congress) has a staff of over 740, including over 370 specialized researchers. Library staffs of 200 or more are found in Australia, Canada, India, South Korea and the UK House of Commons.

The organization of the library follows its functions. In some cases, traditional library services are aligned with research. In a few cases, integrated information services combine library, research, documentation, archives and information technology functions. Where research activity and library services are not directly joined, special efforts should be made to create co-operative linkages to avoid member confusion and duplication of effort.

Services, collections and technology

Most parliamentary libraries offer traditional library services (collections of books, periodicals and electronic resources; databases; lending services; bibliographies; clipping services; and reference services). Some also provide current awareness services, access to parliamentary documents, research support and seminars and briefings. The demand for and rapid development of computer-based services to the parliament in the last decade is noteworthy. After CRS launched its website on the congressional intranet in 1996, the percentage of requests answered by direct access to the website grew astronomically in the course of five years – from roughly 33 per cent of total requests in 1997 to nearly 80 per cent in 2001. Through the CRS website, congressional users can access the current status of legislation (including the text of bills and reports), track legislative issues, access all active CRS reports, make requests and use electronic 'briefing books' on topics of key legislative interest.

The spread of such technology is impressive. Today, roughly 70 per cent of legislatures have access to e-mail, and two-thirds have a parliamentary website. Parliamentary libraries have access to both e-mail and the Internet through the parliament itself, and over 20 per cent of the libraries either have their own website or have information about the library accessible to clients through the main parliamentary website. With the march of globalization and advent of the electronic revolution, the interest in and ability to do comparative research on the practices of other countries has been both amplified and accelerated.

The international dimension

Parliamentary librarians actively exchange information needed to inform their legislatures, but also share ideas on how to serve their clients more effectively. In an effort to increase the opportunities for face-to-face contact, a number of regional library associations have been created. The oldest is that for Nordic librarians, which was created in 1922. Virtually every continent now has such a regional forum. The most comprehensive is the European Centre for Parliamentary Research and Documentation (ECPRD) created in 1977. It brings together librarians, researchers, document specialists and INFORMATION TECHNOLOGY staff. Finally, IFLA provides an international venue for its Section on Library and Research Services for Parliaments to share ideas and technology. In addition to a full IFLA program, the Section also offers two special day-long workshops (on library management and parliamentary research). Finally, the Section has its own Web page (through the IFLA website) and listserv to enhance exchange of information and facilitate communication.

Conclusion

In today's complex world, the key to an effective legislature is the knowledge and information that will help make individual policy decisions efficacious, and enhance the role that the legislature can play in the policy process of the nation. The parliamentary library serves as the parliament's principal information broker between the world of ideas and the world of action.

Further reading

Brian, R. (ed.) (1997) *Parliamentary Libraries and Information Services of Asia and the Pacific*, IFLA Publications no. 83, K.G. Saur.
Englefield, D. (ed.) (1993) *Guidelines for Legislative Libraries*, IFLA Publications no. 64, K.G. Saur.
German Bundestag website (2002) *World Directory of Parliamentary Libraries* (www.bundestag.de/datbk/library/alpha.htm).
Robinson, W. (1998) 'Parliamentary libraries', in *World Encyclopedia of Parliaments and Legislatures*, Congressional Quarterly, Inc., pp. 815–29.
Robinson, W. and Gastelum, R. (eds) (1998) *Parliamentary Libraries and Research Services in Central and Eastern Europe*, IFLA Publications no.87, K.G. Saur.
Tanfield, J. (ed.) (2001) *Parliamentary Library, Research and Information Services of Western Europe*, ECPRD.

WILLIAM H. ROBINSON

PATENTS

When an inventor makes a new and useful invention – that is, a technical idea embodied in a process or product – a patent allows them to develop and market this within the protection of a limited time monopoly, usually of sixteen to twenty years. In return the inventor has to deposit in a public place a description of the invention in such detail that experts in the art could reproduce that invention. The protection given is a type of INTELLECTUAL PROPERTY.

Application for protection is normally made by submitting a written specification to national patent offices. There are provisions in most patent systems for a literature search and a substantive examination of the contents of the application. The specification, modified where necessary, will be published. It discloses the technical content of the invention and the limits of its legal protection. Patents spread information about technological inventions and also reward the inventors and developers of products derived from these inventions.

International protection

Patents permit a high degree of international uniformity to facilitate technology transfer across, as well as within, national boundaries. Since patents must be new, taken at its most literal this would require that all applications worldwide would have to be made simultaneously. Instead, the Paris Convention for the Protection of Industrial Property, 1883, defines the priority date as the date of first application in any convention country. One then has up to twelve months to apply anywhere else and still claim the original priority date, application number and country. These details on the specification identify families of equivalent patents, which give the extent of protection worldwide and indicate the distribution of likely markets. The descriptions are unlikely to be identical as national patent laws dictate what is put in.

The patent specification

Each specification is introduced by a front page with bibliographic information. This includes a title, abstract, names of inventors and applicants, dates and numbers relating to the application and publications, classifications – both national, if used, and international – and a diagram, if relevant. Then there is the body of the specification, which outlines reasons for the invention and gives a technical description with examples and variations. The last section is made up of the claims, where what is new is set out to delineate the legal scope of protection. A list of citations of documents found in the literature search may also be given, either listed on the front page or as a separate report.

Information content of patents

TECHNOLOGICAL INFORMATION

The result of the patent bargain is that libraries, websites and electronic information services both online and CD-ROM can build up collections of documents giving full details of particular inventions. The totality of services allows access via indexes, abstracts and full text. The information remains useful indefinitely as problems can recur in related technologies and in analogous form in other areas. Many inventions have to be 'remade' because of the natural compartmentalization of human endeavours. Patent Office classifications help to monitor resemblances as they are designed to focus on the invented technology and to distinguish it from applications. In electronic form, patents are also searchable by means of text words, but to search effectively, the complexity of patentable subject matter normally requires full text (Bryant and Stein 1983; Bryant *et al.* 1986). Patents are of great value to the industries of less developed countries, which come to need inventions at a later date than most developed countries. It is unlikely that one invention will fit a new need precisely, but a set of patents can show the scope of what was done and problems encountered. Using these can help

find a new solution for a new situation (OTAF 1979).

COMMERCIAL APPLICATIONS

The information in patents databases can be used to check, by means of statistical manipulations, what a particular company is working on, who are the productive inventors, what line of problems is being solved in the industry as a whole, and so on. These techniques are used by managers, strategic planners, accountants and even national governments.

Information services

Each country will usually hold a central collection of national patents in print, and many patent offices also mount websites. Many countries have also established regional patent collections and advice services to encourage and help with use of the documentation (Auger 1992; Newton 2000; van Dulken 1998) and many industrial companies hold relevant patent documents internally.

For technical awareness, many journals covering chemistry, engineering, etc. also cover the more accessible patents in the discipline. To find all relevant patents, one needs to look at specialized patent services, which may be in print, online or CD-ROM. Some of these are for single countries. In particular, there are a number covering the USA, such as CLAIMS. There are two main multicountry services. Derwent's World Patents Index covers forty current countries and authorities with titles and abstracts created in-house by staff. Its strengths are the deep indexing in chemistry and electronics, and its tailored abstracts and specialized topic groupings. World Patents Index is online on several hosts, including DIALOG, QUESTEL.ORBIT and STN (Derwent 2002). The European Patent Office (EPO) has information services that are collectively named EPIDOS and include the ESPACE series of full texts and indexes on CD-ROM. It also includes the INPADOC files that cover seventy current countries, giving bibliographic information contributed by patent offices. Its strengths are the wide country coverage and currency of the information. Output is online on QUESTEL.ORBIT, DIALOG and EPIDOS, and on CD-ROM (EPIDOS 2002). To keep track of country coverage and services, it is best to monitor the relevant websites.

References

Auger, P. (1992) *Information Sources in Patents*, Bowker Saur.

Bryant, J.H. and Stein, D.P. (1993) 'Automated patent searching', *World Patent Information* 5: 226–9.

Bryant, J.H., Terapane, J. and Kiron, A. (1986) 'Study of automated text searching', *World Patent Information* 8: 4–7.

Derwent (2002) (www.derwent.com).

EPIDOS (2002) (www.european-patent-office.org).

Newton, D. (2000) *How to Find Information: Patents on the Internet*, London: British Library.

OTAF (1979) *Patent Technology Transfer to Developing Countries*, 9th Report, Organization of Technology Assessment and Forecast, US Congress.

Van Dulken, S. (1998) *Introduction to Patents Information*, 3rd edn, London: British Library.

SEE ALSO: information policy; transfer of technology

TAMARA EISENSCHITZ

PEER TO PEER

Peer to peer (P2P) is file sharing by Internet users with fellow users (their peers) whose computers have an IP address and can be used as SERVERS. In the mid-1990s PERSONAL COMPUTERS that were not constantly connected to the INTERNET were not accessible in a way that allowed their resources of processing power and memory to be fully exploited. After 1996 intermittently connected PCs became directly addressable by other users, and files could be downloaded from them. The chief symbol of P2P has been Napster, which facilitated the exchange of music held in MP3 compression format through a centralized server that could store and resolve addresses. The legal actions for copyright infringement that resulted in Napster's closure as a free service did not effect systems such as Gnutella and Freenet, which were technically more truly P2P in that they did not rely on a centralized resource. The exchange of music, video and other formats in great quantities, without regard to their copyright status, represents arguably the greatest challenge yet to the world intellectual property regime.

Further reading

O'Reilly P2P (www.openp2p.com).

SEE ALSO: informatics; information and communication technology

PERFORMANCE MEASUREMENT IN LIBRARIES

Performance is generally considered to be the accomplishment of something or the manner in which something is carried out. Library performance can include the performance of the library as a whole, of individual services provided, of specific functions or activities or of specific resources within the library (the staff, the collection, the automated systems, the facilities, etc.). Through the years, library performance has been described as the delivery of library services in a variety of ways. Because there are several considerations associated with library performance measurement, there is sometimes confusion as to the perspective from which performance is measured. A librarian's view of performance should, but may not, be the same as that of the user of the services provided; similarly, the perspective of the funders of the library may differ from those of the library users and library staff. Further difficulty can be experienced in defining the object of the performance assessment.

Performance measurement can be used to support planning, communication of services performed and improvements achieved, decision-making, monitoring of progress and resource allocation.

The evolution of library performance measurement

The measurement of library performance has been much discussed in the literature over the last thirty-five years. In a review of the literature, Goodall (1987) refers to Morse (1968) as being the pioneering work on library effectiveness in which both outputs as well as inputs are considered. Soon after, King and Bryant (1971) produced a textbook on the evaluation of information services and products. This concentrated on document transfer systems and covered all the functions and processes necessary to transfer documents from authors to users. Both books relied on operations research techniques. Whereas Morse used a highly mathematical approach, King and Bryant presented easily followed tutorials on statistical methods, user surveys and market research, and experimental design. Unfortunately, neither was widely adopted by the library community, although both covered library services.

In 1973, the Public Library Association (an organization within the AMERICAN LIBRARY ASSOCIATION) performed an extensive review of previous efforts to determine library effectiveness and performance, and an analysis of existing library statistics gathered at the federal, state and local levels (deProspo *et al*. 1973). The report recommended a new approach to public library measurement and evaluation: the measurement of the outputs of a library and of library services. The report demonstrated that it is possible to gather data that describe the services a library provides to its users and establish a basis for selecting 'meaningful indicators'. Following publication of the *Performance Measures* report, two state-wide projects were initiated to test the measures (Clark 1976; Powell 1976). Both projects recommended changes in procedures for gathering data and suggested additional measures. Several other adaptations of the original *Performance Measures* reports were reported (Ramsden 1978).

Academic librarians have also shown concern for library outputs, although it was not until the mid-1970s that a movement to study library users and uses began to build in the academic library environment. Issues and concerns voiced at the 1976 Conference on Resource Sharing in Libraries (Kent and Galvin 1977) included as priorities:

- The study of use of collections and relationship to cost.
- Study of user requests, user demand, user needs.
- Research on attitude adjustment of users, librarians and administrators.

The Pittsburgh conference acted as a catalyst in bringing to the attention of academic librarians the need for better and more relevant performance criteria and measures. Soon after, the Committee on Statistics began to explore the use of performance measures and funded Kantor to develop performance measures for academic and research libraries. Four measures were tested by several ARL libraries and a manual for implementing the measures was produced by Kantor (1984).

Knightly (1979) identifies four different classes of evaluation relevant to libraries: inputs (resources), processes (capability), outputs (utilization) and impacts (benefits). Knightly surveyed

managers in sixty-two academic, public and special libraries to determine the extent to which the performance criteria proposed in the literature were actually in use and to develop guidelines for future criteria selection. Seven types of performance criteria were described, including assessment on the basis of user opinion, expert opinion, ideal standards, comparison with other organizations, quantifiable outputs, quantifiable processes, and costs or unit costs. The study found that nearly 60 per cent of the performance criteria cited in the annual reports of libraries were quantifiable, with about half concerning process evaluation and half concerning output evaluation.

In parallel with the above developments in approaches to library performance and measurement, there was also a trend away from the use of national standards for library service towards local determination of library needs because they:

- Focused on library inputs rather than on the services that resulted.
- Were used both as minimum standards and as levels of excellence.
- Had no empirical base.
- Imposed an inappropriate uniformity on public libraries.

In 1978, the prevailing thought regarding public library performance measurement was that public libraries should use a community-based planning process to determine local needs for service. In 1981, ALA funded King Research Inc. to develop such a process and a manual for use by local librarians. The manual (Palmour *et al*. 1980) recommends the measurement of output both as a part of the data gathering that precedes the setting of goals and objectives, and as essential to providing a baseline against which progress towards the objectives can be assessed.

Soon after the publication of the *Planning Process for Public Libraries* the Public Library Association Goals Guidelines and Standards Committee decided to produce a 'how-to' guide to public library performance measurement. The Committee assembled a set of output measures from the *Planning Process* and other relevant documents and from the experience of its members. The objective of the exercise was to provide the public library profession with consistent and standardized methods of collecting output data. The manual (Zweizig and Rodger 1982) contains procedures for collecting and reporting results on twelve output measures. These measures were selected after field-testing in five public libraries. A brief conceptual explanation is given for each measure, data collection measure and interpretation results. This manual became the major performance measurement tool for public libraries in the USA.

Both the *Planning Process* and *Output Measures* manuals have been updated (McClure *et al.* 1987; Van House *et al.* 1987). The main difference between the new and the original editions is the addition of two further considerations in planning and evaluation. The first is the role of the public library in the community it is intended to serve. This concept was introduced in the original planning process, but was not dealt with in detail, particularly not in terms of the multiplicity of roles that public libraries seemed to be adopting. The concept of library roles was based on observations that public libraries were trying to be 'all things to all people' and that they found it difficult to provide all the levels of service desired. It was further recommended that libraries select a subset of roles upon which they would focus their efforts. The manuals also stated the desirability of providing comparative data. Because the original manuals did not provide such useful comparisons, the Public Library Data Service was established to collect and make accessible a selective set of data from public libraries in the USA. Meanwhile, Moore (1989) prepared an extended version of these measures for the international library community.

Subsequent to the development of output measures and the production of several manuals, the general literature reflected the concentration on satisfying user needs. This paralleled the concept of the 'user-friendly' system. Reporting on a study initiated in 1977, Chweh (1981) reviewed the criteria that 209 library users indicated as the ten most important criteria in judging a 'good' library. The sample of library users was drawn from public, academic and school libraries in the Los Angeles area. A total of 1,249 different criteria were identified. The ten highest ranked were:

- Availability of books.
- Availability of periodicals.
- Quality of reference service.
- Good reference collection.
- Keeping the library quiet.
- Integrity of the catalogue.
- Friendly service.
- Copying facilities.
- Non-book materials.
- Helpful librarians.

A model questionnaire was proposed but results do not distinguish among users of each type of library separately as it is likely that different sets of criteria would emerge.

A somewhat similar approach to library evaluation was taken by Hannabuss (1983). He explores the relationship between the perceived value of a library and the marketing of library services. The article discusses a number of concepts related to value assessments such as effectiveness, efficiency, benefits, cost benefits and cost-effectiveness. The most interesting aspect of Hannabuss's paper is its recognition that evaluation and promotion are two interrelated functions.

User satisfaction as a measure of public library performance was further explored by D'Elia and Walsh (1983) as a subjective indicator of public library performance. It had been used to:

- Evaluate the performance of various services within a library.
- Measure a given library's overall level of performance.
- Compare this level of performance with those reported for other libraries.

Results of a survey of public library patrons shows that user satisfaction is:

- Potentially useful for evaluating the performances of services within a library.
- Influenced by the demographic characteristics of the users; it should not be used to compare presumed levels of performance for libraries serving different communities.
- Not related to the user's degree of use (a result contradicted by subsequent King Research studies in all types of libraries).

In response to a growing interest on the part of librarians in identifying techniques to use in evaluation of library services, Lancaster (1977) prepared a basic text for courses on library evaluation. Lancaster sets forth a framework for describing library operations and services. The book focuses on a review and synthesis of the literature to date. In 1988, Lancaster published a complementary book that was intended as a practical guide to the conduct of evaluation within libraries. A second edition of *If You Want to Evaluate Your Library* was published in 1993 and included a new chapter on evaluation of bibliographic instruction and on expansion of cost-effectiveness, cost–benefit evaluation and resource-sharing.

In 1990 and 1991, Griffiths and King prepared two manuals. The *Keys to Success* manual (1990), prepared for the British Library Research and Development Department, defines in detail a process by which performance, effectiveness, cost-effectiveness and impact indicators can be developed for library and information services. A conceptual framework is presented and examples of measures, indicators and models are developed and each is discussed as to how they can be interpreted presented to management, funders and users. The Advisory Group for Aerospace Research and Development (AGARD) manual (Griffiths and King 1991), in contrast, focuses much more on the underlying evaluation methods. There are three major distinctions between the approach developed by Griffiths and King and other prior work. The first is the comprehensiveness of their approach: it addresses inputs, outputs and various levels of outcomes. Second, it recognizes that measures of inputs, outputs and outcomes cannot be considered in isolation from each other. Third, by developing a process for performance measure and indicator development they provide a tool that can be used by libraries of all types to address both current and future services.

The *Keys to Success* manual was evaluated by Bloor (1991) to determine whether the measures could be applied in practice and whether they could be incorporated into a decision support system for libraries. The study concluded that:

- *Keys to Success* can provide a simple and effective means of analysing library data. The manual's calculations are straightforward and the results easy to understand. This means it can be used constructively at all levels, providing useful information for decision-making within the library, and also for communicating with the people that it serves and those responsible for its funding.
- Because the main principles of the manual are

general, it is relevant to academic and other types of libraries, as well as public libraries.
- The measures and performance indicators described in the manual offer a framework for collecting and analysing data about how a library is working, how it is being used and how far it is meeting the needs of the people it was set up to serve.

Since the *Keys to Success* framework was considered a useful part of a library decision support system, it was integrated into operational decision support systems for academic libraries, further developed by Adams *et al.* (1993).

In 1992, Griffiths and King received a Special Libraries Association research grant to summarize evidence derived from twenty-seven independent studies performed over a ten-year period, including over 10,000 survey responses. The book (Griffiths and King 1993) provides measures of library service performance (e.g. productivity, unit costs, etc.) and effectiveness (e.g. indicators of the extent to which service attributes and other factors affect service use). The book also presents abundant evidence of the usefulness, value and impact of information, and of the substantial contribution that corporate and government libraries make.

Adaptation, adoption and acceptance of library performance measures

The years 1992–2001 have seen tremendous growth in the application and use of library performance measures through greater geographic penetration and adoption by libraries in all sectors and of all types. As might be expected, performance measures evolved to address electronic information services and products.

This phase in the evolution of library performance measures can be characterized by the adaptation of measures and the development of handbooks and manuals geared to specific types of library, followed by the development of guidelines and standards reaching across library types. This evolution builds ownership in the various sets of performance measures through design, development, testing, adoption and routine use. The knowledge gained in these activities can then be used to share experiences with different professional groups, leading to the development of common sets of measures or standards.

In the UK, noteworthy publications during this

phase include the Follett Report (Joint Funding Council 1993), which focused on traditional input measures followed two years later by a framework for measuring the effectiveness of academic libraries (Joint Funding Council 1995); the development of a collection of service-level agreements (Revill and Ford 1994). In the USA, library performance measures expanded to address public library services to children and young adults (Walter 1992 and 1995), a 'lite' manual for evaluating library performance, which focuses on how to design useful evaluation (Zweizig *et al.* 1996). A further indicator of the geographic diffusion of library performance measures was the selection and adaptation of performance measures for the set of International Federation of Library Associations (IFLA) international guidelines for performance measurement in academic libraries (Poll and te Boekhorst 1996). From an original list of thirty indicators drawn from a review of the literature, seventeen are included in the guidelines, each focusing on library effectiveness. In 1998, the International Organization for Standardization published ISO 11620 (1998), a standard on Library Performance Indicators. It specifies twenty-nine indicators grouped into three areas: user satisfaction, public services and technical services, with particular emphasis on cost-effectiveness. The standard includes suggestions on data collection methods as well as guidelines for accurately interpreting each indicator.

Using a stakeholder method to design a set of user-chosen library performance measures, a comprehensive comparative study (Crawford *et al.* 1998) of several sets of indicators was performed by Glasgow Caledonian University. This study demonstrated clearly that different stakeholders have differing performance priorities, confirming the importance of understanding the audiences for the performance measurement activities.

While performance measures and indicators were proliferating and being applied by many more libraries than ever before, questions returned to issues of the usefulness of the measures and the whole measurement process. Two meta-indicators were proposed (D'Avigdor 1997) relating the effort involved in measurement and evaluation against both the effort needed to produce the services being evaluated, and the decisions and actions taken by library management.

Most recently, attention has turned to the proliferation of electronic and digital library services. Several performance measures aimed specifically at these services have been developed for academic and public libraries (McClure and Lopata 1996; Bertot *et al.* 2001). As more and more technology is applied to information systems and library services delivery, the tendency has been to use the technology to produce a variety of statistics. Gilbert (2000) identified several categories of problems with electronically generated statistical reports. The problem categories include problems with definitions, responsibility, information generated from job tracking systems and the generation of web statistics. Gilbert concludes with a set of recommendations on ensuring the electronic generation of meaningful statistics, especially the importance of being sure about what is being measured.

In February, 2001 the National Information Standards Organization (NISO) sponsored a forum on performance measures and statistics, in preparation for a review of the Library Statistics Standard (Z39.7–1995). A broad spectrum of the library and business (vendor) community gathered to discuss issues related to the management of library services and electronic resources. The full proceedings of the meeting and a resource webography can be found on the NISO website (2001) (www.web.syr.edu/jryan/infopro/stats.html).

Conclusions

Only since 1980 has there been a concerted effort on the part of libraries and library organizations to formalize the process of performance evaluation.

A major change in emphasis from input measures to output measures occurred in the mid- to late 1970s. A similar shift from outputs to outcomes assessments occurred in the early 1990s. Performance cannot be measured solely in terms of inputs or outputs or outcomes. Rather, it is the set of relationships among all three types of measures that yields results that can be interpreted and actions that can be taken to improve performance.

There has been a concentration on quantifying library performance, sometimes to the exclusion of any recognition of qualitative and non-quantifiable aspects of library services. Again, a balanced approach, including quantitative measures and non-quantitative approaches, is needed.

Finally, the definition and adoption of performance criteria and measures tend to reflect the political and societal values of the time. Recently, productivity was a focus of international concern. This was followed by a shift in emphasis to the issue of competitiveness. In the mid-1990s quality became the predominant criterion and today we see increasing concerns for return on investment or value received.

References

Adams, R. *et al.* (1993) *Decision Support Systems and Performance Assessment in Academic Libraries*, Bowker Saur.

Bertot, J.C., McClure, C.R. and Ryan, J. (2001) *Statistics and Performance Measures for Public Library Networked Services*, American Library Association.

Bloor, I. (1991) *Performance Indicators and Decision Support Systems for Libraries: A Practical Application of 'Keys to Success'*, British Library Research Paper 93, British Library Research and Development Department.

Chweh, S.S. (1981) 'User criteria for evaluation of library service', *Journal of Library Administration* 2(1): 35–46.

Clark, P.M. (1976) *A Study to Refine and Test New Measures of Library Service and Train Library Personnel in Their Use*, Rutgers University, Bureau of Library and Information Science Research.

Crawford, J., Pickering, H. and McLelland, D. (1998) 'The stakeholder approach to the construction of performance measures', *Journal of Librarianship and Information Science* 30(2): 87–112.

D'Avigdor, R. (1997) 'Indispensable or indifferent? The reality of information service performance measurement at UNSW library', *AARL Australian Academic and Research Libraries* 28(4): 264–80.

D'Elia, G. and Walsh, S. (1983) 'User satisfaction with library service – a measure of public library performance?', *Library Quarterly* 53(2): 109–33.

deProspo, E.R. *et al.* (1973) *Performance Measures for Public Libraries*, American Library Association.

Gilbert, C. (2000) 'Problems with the electronic generation of library statistics', *LASIE* 31(1): 18–23.

Goodall, D.L. (1987) *Twenty Years of Performance Measurement*, Loughborough University, Library and Information Statistics Unit.

Griffiths, J.-M. and King, D.W. (1993) *Special Libraries: Increasing the Information Edge*, Special Libraries Association.

—— (1991) *A Manual on the Evaluation of Information Centers and Services*, NATO/AGARD.

—— (1990) *Keys to Success: Performance Indicators for Public Libraries*, Office of Arts and Libraries.

Hannabuss, S. (1983) 'Measuring the value and marketing the service: An approach to library benefit', *ASLIB Proceedings* 35(10): 418–27.

ISO 11620 (1998) *Information and Documentation –*

Library Performance Indicators, International Organization for Standardization (ISO).

Joint Funding Councils Library Review Group (1995) *The Effective Academic Library: A Framework for Evaluating the Performance of UK Academic Libraries*, Higher Education Funding Council for England.

—— (1993) *Report*, Higher Education Funding Council for England (Follett Report).

Kantor, P.B. (1984) *Objective Performance Measures for Academic and Research Libraries*, Association of Research Libraries.

Kent, A. and Galvin, T.J. (1977) *Library Resource Sharing. Proceedings of the 1976 Conference on Resource Sharing in Libraries, Pittsburgh, Pennsylvania*, Marcel Dekker, Inc.

King, D.W. and Bryant, E.C. (1971) *The Evaluation of Information Services and Products*, Information Resources Press.

Knightly, J.J. (1979) 'Overcoming the criterion problem in the evaluation of library performance', *Special Libraries* 70(4): 173–7.

Lancaster, F.W. (1977) *The Measurement and Evaluation of Library Services*, Information Resources Press.

McClure, C.R. *et al.* (1987) *Planning and Role Setting for Public Libraries. Prepared for the Public Library Development Project*, American Library Association.

McClure, C.R. and Lopata, C.L. (1996) *Assessing the Academic Networked Environment: Strategies and Options*, Coalition for Networked Information.

Moore, N. (1989) *Measuring the Performance of Public Libraries: A Draft Manual*, UNESCO.

Morse, P.M. (1968) *Library Effectiveness: A Systems Approach*, MIT Press.

NISO (2001) *Forum on Performance Measures and Statistics* (www.niso.org/stats.html).

—— (2001) *Measure the Information Age Webography* (www.niso.org/stats.html#webography).

Palmour, V.E. *et al.* (1980) *A Planning Process for Public Libraries. Prepared for the Public Library Association of the American Library Association*, American Library Association.

Poll, R. and te Boekhorst, P. (1996) *Measuring Quality: International Guidelines for Performance Measurement in Academic Libraries*, IFLA publications 76, K.G. Saur.

Powell, R.R. (1976) 'An investigation of the relationship between reference collection size and other reference service factors and success in answering reference questions', Doctoral dissertation, University of Illinois, Graduate School of Library Science.

Ramsden, M.J. (1978) *Performance Measurement of Some Melbourne Public Libraries*, Library Council of Victoria.

Revill, D.H. and Ford, G. (eds) (1994) *Working Papers on Service Level Agreements*, SCONUL.

Van House, N.A. *et al.* (1987) *Output Measures for Public Libraries. Prepared for the Public Library Development Project*, American Library Association.

Walter, V.A. (1995) *Output Measures and More: Planning and Evaluating Public Library Services for Young Adults*, American Library Association.

—— (1992) *Output Measures for Public Library*

Service to Children: A Manual of Standardized Procedures, American Library Association.

Zweizig, D. and Rodger, E.J. (1982) *Output Measures for Public Libraries: A Manual of Standardized Procedures*. Prepared for the Public Library Association of the American Library Association, American Library Association.

Zweizig, D., Johnson, D.W., Robbins, J. with Besant, M. (1996) *The TELL IT! Manual: The Complete Program for Evaluating Library Performance*, American Library Association.

SEE ALSO: academic libraries; libraries; management support systems; public libraries; quality in library and information services; statistics on libraries; strategic planning

JOSÉ-MARIE GRIFFITHS

PERIODICAL

A publication appearing at regular and fixed intervals of time under a distinctive title, which the publishers intend should continue so to appear, without any anticipated cessation. Its contents are usually some mixture of articles, reviews, stories or other writings by several contributors. The magazine would be a classic example of a periodical. Although some cataloguers may not include the newspaper and the learned journal under this heading, there is no logical, as opposed to practical, reason not to do so. Serial is a slightly broader near-synonym that is generally taken to include some regularly appearing reference works that would not usually be included under the term periodical.

SEE ALSO: communication

PERSONAL COMPUTER

A computer designed for individual use, rather than to be shared by a number of users concurrently. The term entered common use when IBM introduced its own best-selling product called by this name, and is often abbreviated to PC. Microcomputer was the earlier generic term used for computers of this description, and is still used in this sense, although microcomputers appear in more forms than just personal computers. The term PC is often used to distinguish an IBM-compatible microcomputer from an Apple Macintosh, often referred to as a Mac. The PC is normally understood to be a desktop device, although the term is also applied to laptop and palmtop computers that have similar functionality.

SEE ALSO: informatics; information and communication technology

PHILOSOPHIES OF SCIENCE

Philosophy of science consists of epistemological problems as well as other kinds of philosophical problems related to science. EPISTEMOLOGY is an important philosophical subdiscipline concerned with the nature, sources and limits of KNOWLEDGE. Because scientific knowledge is often taken as a model for knowledge in general the two areas are strongly overlapping. A crude classification of basic epistemologies is:

- Rationalism stresses the role of *a priori* theorising.
- Empiricism (see EMPIRICISM AND POSITIVISM) stresses observation.
- Historicism stresses the role of background knowledge.
- Pragmatism stresses the role of analysing values and goals.

The difference between them is thus related to the relative role they ascribe to those different elements and methods in getting information and producing knowledge. In this way they constitute the basic theories about information seeking and thus information science. The two extremes in the range of approaches are empiricism/POSITIVISM and HERMENEUTICS.

It is important to realize that each of the epistemological positions mentioned above produces very strong arguments against the other positions. The classical rationalist argument against empiricism is that observation cannot play the sole role (or even the major role) in acquiring knowledge because we cannot experience anything that is not already anticipated in our in-born capacity to sense and form concepts. This argument is as strong today as ever. Our knowledge about, for example, colours cannot come from experience alone because the ability to discriminate colours is a prerequisite to experiencing them.

The inherent weakness in the epistemological positions may lead to scepticism or methodological anarchism. Our common sense shows us, however, that science is successful in producing knowledge. Thus it is possible to produce valuable knowledge, and some principles and methods simply are better than others to describe how this is done.

Epistemology has been dominated by Plato's view of knowledge as 'justified true belief' related to rationalism and empiricism. However, the pragmatic view is probably the most relevant to information science. This sees living and acting in the world as constituting the *a priori* of human knowledge. Knowledge is constructed in such a way that an application of well-constructed knowledge will directly or indirectly serve living and acting. When knowledge becomes part of an acting system, it functions as an internal action determinant. There is a continuous interaction between knowledge and action so that knowledge is created in and through action, and so that experiences that the actor acquires through action influence subsequent actions. Value-knowledge, factual knowledge and procedural knowledge are three types of knowledge connected to the three types of internal action determinants. Having value-knowledge means knowing what fulfils the criteria of good values. Having factual knowledge means having true beliefs about the three worlds in which one is living. Having procedural knowledge means knowing how to carry out a specific act or act sequence. Knowledge can be unarticulated or articulated. Unarticulated knowledge is, for instance, tacit knowledge, familiarity, knowledge by acquaintance. Knowledge can be articulated in everyday language, science and art. (Sarvimäki 1988: 58–9).

One example of the pragmatic view is feminist epistemology. The impact of feminism on epistemology has been to move the question 'Whose knowledge are we talking about?' to a central place in epistemological inquiry. Hence feminist epistemologists are producing conceptions of knowledge that are quite specifically contextualized and situated, and of socially responsible epistemic agency (Code 1998). This can be seen as a specific case of the pragmatic epistemology emphasizing goals and values, and regarding social aspects of knowledge. The pragmatic view of knowledge is of special importance to Library and Information Science (LIS) because it is connected to the societal role of LIS institutions, whether they are scientific or commercial, or public libraries serving democracy and enlightenment.

Different views of knowledge underlie different approaches or paradigms in all fields of knowledge (including LIS itself). Especially in the social sciences there exist many different approaches or paradigms. Such approaches are ultimately connected to different epistemological views. Hjørland (1997) demonstrates how the facet–analytic tradition in classification research is connected to rationalism, while the experimental INFORMATION RETRIEVAL tradition and BIBLIOMETRICS have mainly been dominated by empiricism/positivism. He tries to base information science on activity theory that is related to both pragmatism and (critical) forms of realism.

Epistemology is not only important for LIS in relation to the research methods adapted. Because LIS is about communicating knowledge, LIS can essentially be seen as applied epistemology. Any kind of activity concerning selecting, organizing, seeking or communicating knowledge is basically an epistemological activity.

In LIS as in other social sciences our view of knowledge tends to be dominated by empiricism/positivism. There are, however, attempts to inform the field by, for example, activity theory, feminist epistemology, hermeneutics, post-modernism and social constructionism. Such attempts are very necessary. There is, however, a danger that they remain in a meta-theoretical position without sufficient connection to specific LIS problems. Hjørland (1998) has suggested that the methods of classification inside and outside LIS are basically connected to the above four presented epistemological positions, and that epistemological knowledge helps us to identify strengths and weaknesses in different approaches to classification. Other problems in LIS have similar relations to epistemology.

References

Code, L. (1998) 'Feminist epistemology', in *Routledge Encyclopedia of Philosophy, Version 1.0*, London: Routledge

Hjørland, B. (1998) 'The classification of psychology: A case study in the classification of a knowledge field', *Knowledge Organization* 24(4): 162–201.

—— (1997) *Information Seeking and Subject Representation. An Activity-Theoretical Approach to Information Science*, Westport & London: Greenwood Press.

Sarvimäki, A. (1988) *Knowledge in Interactive Practice Disciplines: An Analysis of Knowledge in Education and Health Care*, Helsinki: University of Helsinki, Department of Education.

Further reading

Chalmers, A.F. (1999) *What is This Thing Called Science? An Assessment of the Nature and Status of Science and Its Methods*, 3rd edn, Cambridge, Indianapolis: Hackett Publishing Company, Inc.

Routledge Encyclopedia of Philosophy. Vol. 1–10 (1998) [also on CD-ROM], London: Routledge. [Many different articles on specific epistemologies. All articles have short 'abstracts' providing basic information and user-friendly annotated bibliographies.]

SEE ALSO: research in library and information science; sociology of knowledge

BIRGER HJØRLAND

PHILOSOPHY OF LIBRARIANSHIP

The identification and articulation of the main principles underlying the practical operations of LIBRARIES and information services, in particular those relating to collection policies, conservation, access, functions and the role of libraries in society. These principles have evolved over a period of more than 2,500 years and fall broadly into three historical phases: early period, nineteenth century and twentieth century.

Early period

The earliest libraries were founded primarily on the principle of systematic and comprehensive acquisition, as exemplified by the great clay tablet library in Nineveh created by Ashurbanipal, king of Assyria, 668–624 BC, and the Alexandrian Library of papyrus rolls established by Ptolemy Soter around 300 BC. However, during the 1,000 years after the fall of the Roman Empire, collections (of writings on parchment in codex form) were typically small, but guarded and conserved with fervour. Even as collections began to grow again with the advent of the printed book, the philosophy of accretion and retention remained dominant. In relation to society, libraries were associated with power, temporal or ecclesiastical, as shown by their being housed either in palaces or in monasteries and cathedrals.

Nineteenth century

The principle of systematic and comprehensive acquisition persisted triumphantly throughout the nineteenth century, manifesting itself most notably in the growth of national libraries, in particular of the British Museum Library under the direction of Antony PANIZZI from 1837, and of the LIBRARY OF CONGRESS under its first great librarian, Ainsworth Rand Spofford. Both Panizzi and Spofford sought to enforce LEGAL DEPOSIT, and both concentrated on acquisition. However, the second priority, certainly for Panizzi, was access for all who required it to the collections so amassed. An important part of access was the organization of libraries for use rather than primarily for retention and conservation. Here the great pioneers were American: Melvil DEWEY, Charles Ammi CUTTER and William Frederick Poole.

The coming together of the era of the printed book, the rise of democracy and the spread of popular education also resulted in the creation in the second half of the nineteenth century of PUBLIC LIBRARIES in Britain and the USA, a development which demonstrated that libraries are created by society, reflecting what society requires. Some of the founders of American librarianship – Dewey, John Cotton Dana, Sam Walter Foss – saw the library as an extension of the public educational system and were chiefly concerned about its administration as a public institution (McCrimmon 1975).

Twentieth century

The principle of comprehensive acquisition faltered in the latter half of the twentieth century, as library collections of millions of volumes, particularly in university libraries, proliferated, and the resulting combination of economic, spatial and organizational problems brought with it the realization that such indefinite growth was no longer sustainable. Ironically, after a long period of neglect CONSERVATION was revived as a curatorial issue, triggered by the widespread and obvious deterioration of a large proportion of library holdings. What, however, really came into its own in the twentieth century was the philosophical concept that libraries cannot just be storehouses of knowledge, but must also disseminate that knowledge and information. Hence emphasis increased on access and use.

Early in the century one of the most influential thinkers in the field, S.R. RANGANATHAN, formulated his *Five Laws of Library Science*, the very first of which encapsulated this spirit of the time:

'Books are for use' (Ranganathan 1931). The emphasis on use and service was also reflected in the development and refinement of the techniques and methods of library and information work: from the 'library economy' of the late nineteenth century to the 'library science' and 'information science' of present times. Instrumental in this respect, both in the matter of the prosecution of research and the education and training of information work personnel, have been the library schools, from that founded by Melvil Dewey in 1887 at Columbia College onwards.

Access to libraries as a principle is now taken for granted, and has been further reinforced in the closing decades of the century by the matchless possibilities of electronic access. What has also evolved is a clearer and fuller concept of the societal role of libraries. The simple recognition in the late nineteenth century of the educational function of libraries, along with a belief in the power of education to promote general welfare, which in turn would ideally lead to social stability and good citizenship (McCrimmon 1975), was endorsed well into the twentieth century by outstanding public librarians such as Lionel McColvin, who argued strongly that libraries 'help in the making of whole individuals' able to 'contribute to and benefit from the constructive life of the community' (McColvin 1942). In the wake of the Second World War, and conditioned by international experience of a widespread variety of tyrannical regimes, even greater value, however, was placed on the free exchange of ideas, unhindered access and freedom from CENSORSHIP (Broadfield 1949). In sum, libraries are now perceived as sources of power, deriving initially from the fact that they are the storehouses of knowledge, the repositories of the records of mankind's achievements and discoveries. As a consequence they conserve and transmit culture; they underpin education, both individual and formal; they are important to economic welfare; they are crucially related to all other intellectual, artistic and creative activities; they are instruments of social and political change; and they are the guardians of the freedom of thought (Thompson 1974).

References

Broadfield, A. (1949) *A Philosophy of Librarianship*, Grafton.

McColvin, L.R. (1942) *The Public Library System of Great Britain*, Library Association.
McCrimmon, B. (ed.) (1975) *American Library Philosophy: An Anthology*, Shoe String Press.
Ranganathan, S.R. (1931) *Five Laws of Library Science*, Madras Library Association.
Thompson, J. (1974) *Library Power*, Bingley.

Further reading

De Beer, F. (1999) 'A proposed philosophico-ethical approach to the information era', *Mousaion* 17: 2–16.
McCook, K.P. (2001) 'Social justice, personalism and the practice of librarianship', *Catholic Library World* 72: 80–4.
Nitecki, J.E. (1998) 'Conceptual aspects of bibliothecal communication: Philosophical legacy of twentieth century American librarianship', *Public Library Quarterly* 17: 27–36.
Steinerova, J. (2001) 'Human issues of library and information work', *Information Research* 6 (www.shef.ac.uk/is/publications/infres/6–2/paper95.html).
Thompson, J. (1977) *A History of the Principles of Librarianship*, Bingley.

SEE ALSO: history of libraries; information professions; librarianship

JAMES THOMSON

PICTURE LIBRARIES

Though picture libraries, by definition, exist to house and to make available visual documents, they vary substantially in the relative importance they assign to these functions. This results in a diversity of establishments that differ in their methods of acquisition (see ACQUISITIONS), CLASSIFICATION and retrieval, the conditions whereby the pictures are made available, and the procedures whereby they are accessed. A collection of medieval manuscripts and a sports photo agency will have little in common apart from the basic fact that they both hold pictures. The manuscripts will be kept, in rigorously controlled conditions, hopefully forever; the majority of sports photographs will lose their interest tomorrow. Students will pore over the manuscripts at leisure; the evening papers need their photos of this afternoon's match in minutes rather than hours. And between these extremes are pictures gathered into libraries of all sorts and sizes.

Private picture libraries are, typically, in-house collections serving the specific needs of an institution. Thus an art college will maintain its own slide collection of art reference material, available to lecturers and students for study purposes but not normally to outsiders. Such collections rarely hold original material, and what they hold will rarely be of reproduction quality. The needs of the users will dictate the scope of the collection and consequent acquisition: access and retrieval will be planned to integrate with other activities of the establishment. Perceived as providing a service, private libraries are not expected to be economically self-supporting.

Public picture libraries are headed by the major national archives – the British Library, the BIBLIOTHÈQUE NATIONALE DE FRANCE and their equivalents elsewhere. These are supplemented by specifically oriented collections such as the National Maritime Museum, by regional libraries holding material relating to a specific area and by libraries dedicated to a particular subject such as science, transport, theatre or costume. Then there are collections acquired by academic institutions, such as the John Johnson EPHEMERA collection acquired by the Bodleian Library, Oxford, or built up by cultural institutions such as the Shakespeare Centre at Stratford-on-Avon. Regarded as a national heritage, such collections are maintained at public expense.

PUBLIC LIBRARIES and ACADEMIC LIBRARIES, while recognizing an obligation to make their material available to the public, are primarily archives so far as their picture collections are concerned; their holdings constitute a unique record whose safekeeping takes priority over any other function. This concern affects procedures at every stage: security (see SECURITY IN LIBRARIES) may dictate that users comply with stringent requirements before being allowed access, and the material itself may be scattered in dozens of separate collections, each of which must be accessed in its own right.

Though modern technology has greatly enhanced the ability of public institutions to respond to the needs of individual users, their sheer size means that it is not practicable to anticipate every user's need by having every item immediately available in borrowable form. However, the growing demand for visual material means that the picture holdings of these institutions constitute not only a valuable heritage but also a useful source of income, and increasingly MUSEUMS such as the Natural History Museum are setting up their own picture libraries. What this generally means in practice is that a library will make copies of its most popular items, for hire or purchase, while others must be ordered, with an unavoidable time-lag. Nevertheless, despite the practical obstacles, the fact that they possess unique material of the highest quality ensures that public picture libraries remain a primary source of visual documentation.

Commercial picture libraries receive no institutional sponsorship or state patronage, and are consequently dependent on such income as they can generate from the use of their material, usually in the form of reproduction fees. They fall into three main categories:

- Agencies hold material supplied by contributing photographers, whose work they handle in return for a percentage of the income derived from marketing it. The most important are the Press Agencies, which deal in current affairs: they have little interest in building up a library as such, since their material will look old-fashioned within a year or two. However, the more far-sighted will transfer their out-of-date material to a 'morgue' to await rediscovery by posterity. General stock photo agencies, which have proliferated over recent decades, hold contemporary photographs of subjects likely to interest editors or advertisers – family and lifestyle scenes, evocative landscapes and the like. These too can hardly be said to constitute libraries *per se*, with the exception of those, such as Getty Images, created before World War Two to service the needs of a publishing house, which possesses important archive material in addition to its current photo stock. While such libraries depend for survival on making their material commercially available, some are aware of constituting important resources in their own right and may conceive their function in a wider sense than simply that of short-term profitability.
- Individual photographers or associations of photographers who have accumulated a sufficient body of work may make it available in a formal library. Here again most are likely to be ephemeral but a few will survive to achieve archive status along with 'name' photographers of yesteryear such as Brassai or Cartier-Bresson.
- Collections are libraries holding material that is their own property but the bulk of which they have not produced themselves, acquiring it by purchase, commission or donation. They

are likely to be devoted to specific activities or particular interests: thus important libraries are maintained by industrial companies such as Shell, religious organizations such as the Mormons or Shakers, social institutions such as the Women's Library, or professional bodies such as the Institution of Civil Engineers. At these libraries, with their strong incentive to encourage use, user convenience is a priority.

In addition, there are many hundreds of smaller, specialist collections. These range from the world-famous Mander and Mitchenson Theatre Collection, to Michael Ochs's showbiz portraits, the Advertising Archive, the Dickens House Museum, or the Mary Evans Picture Library where history is documented by old engravings and modern photographs, postcards and other ephemera.

Of the tens of thousands of picture libraries that exist throughout the world, only some 1,400 (those listed in Evans and Evans 2001) represent significant resources readily accessible by the public or potential users. Distribution globally is uneven. While every country maintains a national archive and press agencies are universal, specialist collections are comparatively rare outside the USA and the UK. Stock photograph agencies are international in scope and widely syndicated, with the consequence that the same images are available worldwide from a variety of sources: an agency in Portugal may possess no original material of its own but act as local agent for companies in the USA or Japan. Thanks to the Internet, pictures can be transmitted instantly round the globe, and the larger companies such as Corbis and Getty make a growing proportion of their stock instantly available on searchable websites, where the customer can view, select and download what he or she wants without needing to have any direct contact with the company. Such establishments scarcely deserve to be classified as picture libraries, yet some do indeed house collections of original material together with their syndicated stock.

Such procedures are already the norm for clients who need their pictures immediately – libraries specializing in sports and current affairs need to make their pictures instantly available to the media. How soon this will come to be the norm for users who are not in such a hurry it is impossible to predict, but sooner or later it will

surely happen. At present, the enormous investment involved in digitizing pictures and offering them online, especially in high resolution suitable for reproduction, is affordable only to large and wealthy organizations, and the future of the small specialist library is at risk until the cost of technology drops substantially.

That picture libraries will continue to exist is certain, as the use of visual materials becomes wider. But the economics of the matter are such that those libraries that are dependent on revenue may become non-viable unless subsidized or taken over by a wealthier company. Even public institutions may find that the revenue derived from their picture library does not justify the cost of maintaining it. It is ironic that the technology that makes pictures so much more easily available may have the effect of making it uneconomical to do so.

References

Evans, H. and Evans, M. (2001) *The Picture Researcher's Handbook*, 7th edn, Pira International [an international guide to picture resources].

Further reading

Evans, H. (1992) *Practical Picture Research*, Blueprint.
—— (1980) *Picture Librarianship*, K.G. Saur/Clive Bingley [a guide to the practical aspects of planning and running a library].

SEE ALSO: image retrieval; multimedia librarianship

HILARY EVANS

PIRACY

The systematic appropriation of INTELLECTUAL PROPERTY, whether in the form of print, disk, CD or other format with the intention of marketing unauthorized copies for profit. The practice is widespread in all regions of the world, but the publishing and related industries of a number of countries that have not acceded to the international intellectual property agreements have traded in pirated products on a particularly large scale.

Further reading

Gleason, P. (2001) 'Copyright and electronic publishing: Background and recent developments', *Acquisitions Librarian* 26: 5–26.
Graybisch. A.J. (2001) 'Bootlegs: Intellectual property

and popular culture', *Journal of Information Ethics* 10: 35–50.

SEE ALSO: copyright; knowledge industries

PIXEL

An approximate abbreviation for 'picture element', and originally meaning the elements that are used to create a television picture. Now it is also used to refer to the smallest element of a bitmapped visual display, or a scanned image, which can be distinguished by a computer.

SEE ALSO: information and communication technology

PORAT, MARC URI (1947–)

Communications technology entrepreneur whose early academic work put forward an immensely influential redefinition of the information sector in the US economy.

Born Ramat Gan, Israel, he obtained a BA in psychology and sociology from Columbia and turned to the economics of information for his MA thesis at Stanford. His PhD, also from Stanford, in 1976, was the original statement of his views on the information economy. His subsequent career has involved the development and marketing of various communication system projects. From 1983–8 he was Chairman and CEO of Private Satellite Network, 1990–5 Chairman and CEO of General Magic, and since 1998 Chairman of Perfect Commerce Inc.

His contribution to ideas on the information society is set out in *The Information Society* (Washington: Government Printing Office, 1977). This extended the argument that society has moved from an initial agricultural phase, first to an industrial phase, then to an economy based on services, to define the modern economy as an information economy. If, as Porat did, we add to employment in the INFORMATION PROFESSIONS and the KNOWLEDGE INDUSTRIES a host of other occupations that predominantly involve the collecting, processing and use of information, as opposed to working with more tangible products and services, it becomes easy to see information as the central focus of modern society. His contribution is generally cited alongside that of Fritz MACHLUP as a cornerstone of thinking on the INFORMATION SOCIETY.

PORTABILITY

The ability of computer software, programming languages and operating systems to operate independently of any one specific type of platform, and thus to be 'carried' over from one to another. Portability is achieved by including the software within a 'shell' that can easily be modified to accommodate the peculiarities of the computer on which it is run. The distinction is made between source portability, meaning that the source program must be recompiled on the receiving computer, and binary portability, meaning that recompilation is unnecessary.

PORTALS AND GATEWAYS

Introduction

The terms 'gateway' and 'portal' tend to be used interchangeably and often in combination to denote a service providing browser-based access to information resources and applications. In data networking a gateway is a device that translates a data stream from one protocol to another, without adding any additional value in the translation process. More recently the term has been used within the Common Gateway Interface (CGI) through which an HTML call can be converted to a script that can access a database or other non-HTML resource. The concept of a portal is something more than a simple switch or exchange, and usually provides a higher level of integration and personalisation. A portal has been likened to a medieval fair (Stewart 1998).

Portal evolution

The earliest use of the term portal was probably by Jerry Yang and David Filo, who founded Yahoo! in 1993 as a service that would organise Internet sites into categories. Yahoo! is an acronym for Yet Another Hierarchical Officious Oracle! (Schlender 2002). Yahoo! not only brought to the Web the concept of a hierarchical directory structure for Web resources, but also a business model that used advertising to generate the revenues needed to support the very substantial team of indexers that were required to index websites. Strictly speaking this was not the first hierarchical index to the Web, as the WWW

Virtual Library had been initiated at CERN in 1993 under the direction of Arthur Secret.

The competition was from search engine sites such as Alta Vista, Lycos, Hotbot and others (see SEARCH ENGINES). They also needed to generate revenues, saw the benefits of the Yahoo! model and started to introduce advertising themselves. However there were other consumer information services in existence, such as America Online and The Source, using PC technology instead of Internet protocols at this stage. This was the beginning of what are often referred to as the portal wars, as AOL, MSN (Microsoft Network), Excite, Walt Disney and NBC amongst others added content and services to their sites in order to be the first point of entry onto the Web.

It was Yahoo! that made the next important step in portal evolution, and that was the introduction in 1996 of myYahoo!, which gave users the ability to create a personal homepage of links to the Web resources. In 1997 Michael McNulty, Michael Hagan and Mark Walsh, the founders of VerticalNet, developed the concept of the vertical portal. Sometimes this concept has been referred to as a vortal, though the term has never really become established. VerticalNet established industry-specific websites, providing information resources, buyer's guides, discussion forums and recruitment services, and also the ability to transact business on the site.

The corporate world

In November 1998 two Merrill Lynch analysts published a report (Shilakes and Tylman 1998) that identified a developing market for Enterprise Information Portal (EIP) software that enabled companies to 'unlock internally and externally stored information and provide users a single gateway to personalised information needed to make informed business decisions'. In fact implicit in this definition is that an EIP provides access both to information resources and applications, and this is a boundary (albeit a rather fuzzy boundary) between a gateway and a portal. Over the period from 1998 to 2000 well over a hundred EIP vendors entered the market in the USA and in Europe, using XML and Java programming to provide companies with links to internal databases and display them on a multiple-windowed screen. By 2001 the down-

turn in the business economy, and significant investment in product development by IBM, Microsoft, SAP and other major IT companies, was starting to catalyse a shakeout in the market (White 2001).

Gateways

The use of the term 'gateway' has tended to be predominantly amongst the academic and library communities. The definition used by the Social Science Information Gateway (SOSIG) is that it is '[a] freely available Internet service which aims to provide a trusted source of selected, high quality Internet information for students, academics, researchers and practitioners in the social sciences, business and law'. SOSIG is part of the Resource Discovery Network, a co-operative network of Internet resource catalogues providing access to descriptions of resources selected for their quality and accuracy by subject specialists throughout the UK academic community.

Gateways tend to be funded through grants from the public sector, or as a spin-off of work being conducted by an academic institution, such as the Legal Web Sites Library of the University of Dundee. Increasingly, gateway sites offer personal account facilities, so that a user can be alerted to new resources in their particular area of interest.

Portal developments

The initial concept of the EIP has now been further developed by both software vendors for the purposes of product differentiation, and also by consulting companies (notably the Gartner Group, the Delphi Group, Ovum and International Data Corporation) trying to help their customers make sense of the portal marketplace. The use of 'corporate portal' as the top-level generic term is starting to emerge, and beneath that there are now knowledge portals, employee portals, ERP's (Enterprise Resource Portals) (notably mySAP) and many others. The common features are that these applications provide linkages to existing and new corporate resources through a very flexible browser-based desktop that usually enables users to customize the desktop by a 'drag and drop' process. This is one significant difference between current corporate portal applications and gateways, as most gateways are designed to be used in low-technology environments worldwide whereas portals are optimized for the high-bandwidth enterprise sector.

References

Schlender, B. (2002) 'How a virtuoso plays the Web', *Fortune* (March): F29–F36.
Shilakes, C.C. and Tylman, J. (1998) *Enterprise Information Portals*, New York: Merrill Lynch & Co.
Stewart, T.A. (1998) 'Internet portals: No one-stop shop', *Fortune* (December): 121–2.
White, M. (2001) 'Reality check for the EIP market', *EContent* 24: 54–5.

Further reading

Collins, H. (2001) *Corporate Portals*, Amacom [a division of American Management Association].
Dias, C. (2001) 'Corporate portals: A literature review of a new concept in information management', *International Journal of Information Management* 21: 269–87.
White, M. (2000) 'Corporate portals: Realising their promise, avoiding costly failure', *Business Information Review* 17: 177–84.

SEE ALSO: electronic information resources; information management; online services; Web browser

MARTIN WHITE

POSITIVISM

Positivism refers to a broad attitude about science and philosophy that in particular is ascribed to Auguste Comte (1798–1857) and to twentieth-century logical positivism. In its purest form, positivism argues that there is a single scientific method that can be applied to all forms of sciences and philosophy, and that all metaphysical claims are pseudoscientific. It thus opposes the approach of empiricism (see EMPIRICISM AND POSITIVISM) that characterizes much RESEARCH IN LIBRARY AND INFORMATION SCIENCE.

SEE ALSO: hermeneutics; information theory

POSTAL SERVICES

Systems, usually provided by government, which enable people to send letters and parcels to other people, whether within the country or abroad. Postal services have been, and still are, vital infrastructural elements of a modern society, despite the proliferation of alternative methods of communication over distance. Effective busi-

ness and national administration could scarcely operate without the facilities they offer, and it sometimes seems to be forgotten that the aspects of E-COMMERCE that deal with the sale of goods could not function without delivery services, a large proportion of which are provided by postal services. The removal of the monopoly status of state postal services has in many countries produced a proliferation of parcel delivery and courier services in competition. State postal services have frequently taken on extra, non-postal, functions. Their nationwide networks of post offices can, for instance, provide basic banking services in areas in which it is uneconomic for commercial banks to operate. The payment of social security benefits or collection of certain forms of taxation are also common functions of post offices.

SEE ALSO: communication; PTT; rural library services

PREPRINT

This can refer either to a portion of a work, most commonly a journal article, printed and issued before the publication of the complete work, or a paper to be submitted at a conference that is printed for circulation prior to the holding of the conference. The circulation of preprints amongst interested persons is a common function of the INVISIBLE COLLEGE and is considerably facilitated by use of the Internet, to the extent that it is now common to talk of e-prints. This type of circulation of texts is important in disciplines where the currency of information is vital and the need to claim priority of discovery is strong.

SEE ALSO: communication

Further reading

Garner, J. *et al* (2001) 'The place of eprints in scholarly information delivery', *Online Information Review* 25: 250–6.
Harter, S.P. and Park, T.K. (2000) 'Impact of prior electronic publication on manuscript consideration policies of scholarly journals', *JASIS* 51: 940–8.

PRESERVATION

The processes and activities that stabilize and protect objects so that they will be permanent and durable, or as long-lasting as it is possible to make them. For PAPER-based materials, preservation is achieved through appropriate selection, housing, care and handling, security, climate control, repair and CONSERVATION treatment. Increasingly, libraries and archives must also preserve the far more fugitive digital materials. DIGITAL PRESERVATION refers to the processes and activities that stabilize and protect both reformatted and 'born digital' electronic materials in forms that are retrievable, readable and usable over time. In order to achieve this, it is necessary to begin preserving an item at the point of its creation. This is accomplished by creating preservation METADATA, and by regularly refreshing and reformatting information. Digital preservation entails a preventive rather than a remedial approach. The longevity of the medium on which information is stored is a combination of its physical make-up and the technology of its hardware and software.

Preservation is an umbrella term that applies to the overall responsibilities of caring for collections. Regardless of the format – print, non-print or digital – all library and archival materials require protection. In some institutions, preservation is carried out as part of collection management responsibilities. Preservation is considered from the point of accession to deaccession – when materials are discarded. In RESEARCH LIBRARIES materials are usually maintained until they are too fragile to be used or until they have outlived their usefulness. Fragile books and manuscripts are often replaced with new copies or SURROGATE copies such as reprints or microform (see MICROFORMS), or are duplicated through other reformatting technologies. Sometimes a hybrid approach is used. For example, a book may be microfilmed and later scanned, or else a book may be filmed and scanned simultaneously. In archives, there is usually a retention schedule for records. Although digitizing paper or film may provide users with increased access, digitization is not a preservation measure.

Decision-making for preservation is part of an integrated programme. The first question on the part of a preservation manager must be, 'Should this item be retained in the collection?' The answer is usually determined by the criteria set forth in the library's collection development policy. If the answer is 'yes', the next question will relate to the value of the item. If it has artefactual or historical value, repair, extensive treatment, rebinding or the use of protective housing might be appropriate solutions. If the

item is not deemed to have such value, the solution might be to purchase a reprint or microfilm. There is no consensus in the library community as to what constitutes artefactual or historical value. Strategic preservation decision-making must take into account a number of considerations. Each institution must evaluate its own priorities and values.

Preservation ensures that when an item has been purchased and catalogued, it will be available when users want to consult or examine it. Until the nineteenth century, much of the emphasis in libraries was on preservation of materials. Patrons were not given access to library stacks, access was limited and so was wear-and-tear on the books. Since books were not handled as much as they are today, deterioration took place at a slower rate. With the development of the modern profession of librarianship in the late nineteenth century and an egalitarian emphasis on access to collections, preserving collections became less of a concern.

At the same time, librarians and archivists began to realize that modern books and paper were less stable than older materials. The Industrial Revolution led to poor air quality that in turn contributed to the decay of leather and paper. The need to deal with the problem of deteriorating collections was recognized, but it was not until the 1950s that serious investigations into the causes of deterioration of paper and bindings began to take place in the USA and Europe. It was clear that many library collections had deteriorated and that drastic measures needed to be taken if these collections were to be preserved for immediate as well as future use.

Deterioration is inherent in all organic materials; by the middle of the nineteenth century machine-made paper was manufactured with wood pulp containing lignin and other acidic components that caused paper to deteriorate relatively quickly. The development and use of alum rosin sizing compounded the problem. Leather also contained harmful acidic ingredients that caused deterioration. The deterioration of books was hastened by environmental factors such as high temperature and relative humidity, exposure to light, air pollution and careless handling by increased numbers of users in open-access repositories. By the 1960s efforts were under way to identify causes of deterioration and to seek ways of retarding it.

The flooding of the Arno River in Florence,

Italy, in November 1966 served as a catalyst, for it brought bookbinders and paper conservators to the city, first to salvage the books and manuscripts from the Laurentian Library and other collections, and later to develop new treatments. As the books and manuscripts were cleaned, repaired and, in many instances, rebound, conservators learned a great deal about book, leather, vellum and paper structure and longevity. These conservators returned to their respective countries (or moved to other countries) with a new understanding of book and paper conservation. The relationships fostered by the Florence experience led to further research and training, and the establishment of new conservation laboratories in Europe and the USA.

Preservation of library and archival materials was not taught as a separate subject in schools of library, information and archival science until the early 1970s, but by the late 1960s librarians and archivists began to specialize in the preservation of collections, learning through seminars and workshops, often from conservators who had been active in Florence. Today most schools of information offer specific courses in preservation, and preservation issues and concerns are included in courses on collection development, management and new media.

Co-operation is the key to successful preservation initiatives. No one library or archive can preserve everything. Through co-operation, mass treatment techniques, such as the de-acidification of books and papers, are being developed. Co-operative programmes to preserve valued collections on microfilm have been successful in North America and Europe; today countries are working together to preserve their documentary heritage through such efforts as the European Register of Microfilm Masters (EROMM) and increased bibliographic control, assisted by the Internet. At the same time, librarians and archivists around the world are developing principles for basic digital preservation strategies. Refreshing, migration, emulation, technology preservation and digital archaeology are current strategies in use. Though none of these can as yet be considered permanent solutions, with continued international co-operation in the development of principles, standards and techniques, solutions may be forthcoming.

Preservation is necessary to ensure that people, in the present and future, will have access to the information that constitutes our documentary heritage. Increasingly in this new electronic age, the preservation of text and images will depend on the ongoing refreshing and migration of data. Soon preservation will be the responsibility not just of librarians and archivists, but also of ordinary citizens who will need to become cultural custodians if their own digital photographs and documents are to become part of the overall documentary heritage.

Further reading

Banks, P.N. and Pilette, R. (eds) (2000) *Preservation: Issues and Planning*, American Library Association.

Feather, J. (1996) *Preservation and the Management of Library Collections*, 2nd edn, Library Association Publishing.

Jones, M. and Beagrie, N. (2002) *Preservation Management of Digital Materials: A Handbook*, The British Library.

Swartzburg, S.G. (1995) *Preserving Library Materials: A Manual*, 2nd edn, Scarecrow.

COnservation On Line website (COOL) (http//palimpsest.stanford.edu). [An invaluable source of information about developments, recent and forthcoming events, and people.]

SEE ALSO: digitization

SUSAN G. SWARTZBURG,
REVISED BY MICHÈLE VALERIE CLOONAN

PRESIDENTIAL LIBRARIES

The papers of each US President since Herbert Hoover have been placed in separate research libraries operated and maintained by the NATIONAL ARCHIVES OF THE UNITED STATES. Fundraising for the buildings and facilities, which tend to be on a lavish scale, is undertaken by friends and admirers, and the libraries are a substantial set of monuments to the presidents.

Further reading

Hyland, P. (1996) *Presidential Libraries and Museums: An Illustrated Guide*, Congressional Quarterly Books.

'Symposium on Presidential Libraries and Materials' (1994–5) *Government Information Quarterly* 11: 7–69; 12: 15–125.

PRIMARY LITERATURE

To the historian this means original manuscripts, contemporary records or documents that are used by an author in researching a book or article, which in its turn would form part of the

SECONDARY LITERATURE. To the scientist and the librarian it means the monograph or journal literature itself, as opposed to the bibliographic or secondary literature.

SEE ALSO: communication; economics of information

PRIVACY

The quality of protection for aspects of the life, and information about the life, of an individual or a group, from the intervention or knowledge of others. Respect for the privacy of certain aspects of information is a counterbalance to the principle of FREEDOM OF INFORMATION. Not all societies have a highly developed concept of privacy, and social, as opposed to private, life may be the dominant human mode. However, in industrialized societies, a sense of the need for privacy for the individual, and legitimate business secrecy for the organization, is well established.

Constitutional and legal protection

International agreements, most notably the United Nations' Universal Declaration of Human Rights, 1948, invariably recognize privacy as a right. In the European Convention on Human Rights, Article 8 expresses it as: 'Everyone has the right to respect for his private and family life, his home and his correspondence.' The constitutions of many countries also offer protection for privacy. The Constitution of Portugal that was enacted in 1989, for instance, has an Article 35 providing for the protection of information about individuals. Some countries, such as France, have privacy laws designed to protect individuals from media intrusion into their private lives. Many countries – Sweden, Germany and France, to name only a few – have specific legislation on DATA PROTECTION. These govern access to, and protect the integrity of, the information about individuals that is legitimately collected by official and commercial bodies of all kinds. General data protection laws are only one aspect of this approach to the protection of privacy. The US Driver's Privacy Protection Act, 1993, is an example dealing with a specific category of information. Because in a few much-publicized cases criminals had located their victims by looking up their car registration details in the publicly available records of state motor vehicle

agencies, such records were closed to access. The USA also has a Privacy Act of 1974, which is concerned specifically with information gathered by the federal government concerning individuals.

Rather in contrast to most industrialized countries, until recently there was little or no actual privacy law in Britain. The tort law on breach of confidence did protect certain types of information, both within the domestic environment and the workplace, from being divulged to third parties. Today this tends to be cited in the law courts mainly in relation to business confidentiality. Britain also passed Data Protection Acts in 1984 and 1998. However, curbing the country's highly intrusive media was avoided for various reasons, including the fear that such law would hinder investigative journalism. With the inclusion of the European Convention on Human Rights into British law in 2000, as the Human Rights Act, this changed, and the principle of the protection of privacy immediately began to be cited in the courts.

Interception of communications

Electronic communication introduces a new dimension into questions of the protection of privacy. It is particularly vulnerable to interference and penetration by those with the necessary skills and equipment. It is often argued that the only real means of protecting the privacy of electronic communications is to code messages or, to use the more usual term, employ ENCRYPTION techniques. Within an organization it is very easy for electronic mail to be read by persons other than those to whom it was sent, particularly the system administrators who have to have access to all parts of the system. Employees have been dismissed from companies when the records of their e-mail have shown that they were involved in disloyal communications or were circulating pornography. The distinctive thing about interference with electronic communication, however, is that those who do it include people, usually referred to as hackers, or crackers, who do so for reasons of mischief. Their activities are usually described as COMPUTER CRIME. Official surveillance of networks has emerged in response not only to the activities of hackers, but also criminal gangs, political subversives, terrorists (especially since 11 September 2001) and even football hooligans.

Privacy in libraries

Since libraries hold and have access to substantial quantities of information about their users as a group, they need to be alert to privacy issues. Membership records are common to most types of library and they offer obvious marketing opportunities (Estabrook 1996). This would also be attractive to companies wanting to target advertising at sectors of the reading public. Many types of library CIRCULATION SYSTEMS, particularly computerized ones, result in a record of transactions that is capable of being referred to at a later date. Some libraries choose not to develop a fully fledged archiving facility in their systems because they do not wish to accumulate records that could be used for police surveillance of library users. If the use of library files to investigate and take action against users seems possible but unlikely in practice, the US 'Library Awareness Programme' is evidence that this is a genuine concern. In 1988 it was revealed that the FBI was in the habit of demanding that librarians reveal the names and reading habits of library users who could be considered 'hostile to the USA' (Foerstel 1991).

References

Estabrook, L. (1996) 'Sacred trust or competitive opportunity: Using patron records', *Library Journal* 121: 48–9.
Foerstel, H. (1991) *Surveillance in the Stacks: The FBI's Library Awareness Program*, Greenwood Press.

Further reading

Branscomb, A.W. (1994) *Who Owns Information? From Privacy to Public Access*, Basic Books.
Reid, B.C. (1986) *Confidentiality and Law*, Waterlow.
Sterling, B. (1992) *The Hacker Crackdown*, Viking.
Sturges, P., Teng, V. and Iliffe, U. (2001) 'User privacy in the digital library environment: A matter of concern for information professionals', *Library Management* 22: 364–70.

SEE ALSO: freedom of information; information policy; official secrecy

PAUL STURGES

PRIVATE LIBRARIES

Collections of books accumulated by individuals for their own use and enjoyment. The term can be used to embrace both large and small collections, and the books may be gathered for a variety of reasons, such as use, display or merely for the pleasure of owning them. Private libraries differ from institutional ones in that they reflect the interests of an individual rather than a community of users, but there is a long tradition of absorbing private libraries into public ones after the death of the owner. Big private collections have played a major part in shaping many national and academic libraries: the manuscripts of Sir Robert Cotton (1571–1631) and the books of Sir Hans Sloane (1660–1753) became foundation collections of the BRITISH LIBRARY; the bequest of Martin Routh's 15,000 books to Durham University Library in 1854 effectively created an instant library for that recently founded institution. Owners of major private collections have often allowed access to friends and scholars, a privilege that was especially important in earlier centuries, before the development of a network of publicly funded libraries.

Importance

Private libraries offer important insights into the history of books and the development of taste, and they have been extensively documented and studied. If we know the titles of the books on a person's shelves, we can go at least some way towards knowing what they read and what texts are likely to have influenced their thinking. When the books survive and can be identified, they may contain marginalia or other annotations that offer first-hand evidence of the reaction of the reader to the ideas contained in the books. Volumes annotated by celebrated scholars have long been valued, and various studies based on the importance of such marginalia have been published. By looking at the contents of private libraries of a particular period, we can discover which books were considered important and worth owning, and which were not; interests change over the centuries.

History

The history of private libraries is as old as that of books. There are references to private collections in the writings of the ancient Greeks – Euripides, for example, is reputed to have had a fine book collection – and there is also plentiful evidence to show that the Romans valued private libraries. The books have not often survived, but a collection of about 800 papyrus rolls forming the library of a villa in AD 79 was preserved in the volcanic ruins of Herculaneum.

The history of private book ownership in Europe during the medieval period is not easy to trace in detail, as much of the evidence has disappeared. The significant book collections were generally attached to ecclesiastical institutions and the spread of books in private hands was restricted by their high cost, at a time when they all had to be individually written, and by the limited extent of LITERACY. Studies of wills suggest that book ownership in medieval England, even among the educated classes, often amounted to no more than a few standard theological or devotional texts, although there are odd exceptions: a thirteenth-century London priest, Geoffrey de Lawath, had a library of at least forty-eight volumes. The big medieval private collections were usually associated with senior ecclesiastics such as Archbishop Simon Langham, who bequeathed ninety-four books to Westminster Abbey in 1376, or Cardinal Adam Easton (d. 1398), whose books filled six barrels after his death. Most of these collections were modest in size by post-Renaissance standards, with the notable exception of the library of Richard de Bury, Bishop of Durham (d. 1345), comprising over 1,000 volumes.

The introduction of printing in the second half of the fifteenth century, combining mass-production techniques with a lowering of prices at a time of steadily increasing literacy, greatly facilitated the development of private libraries. Book ownership became much more widespread, and dedicated collectors with appropriate means came to acquire bigger and bigger libraries. Thomas Cranmer, Archbishop of Canterbury (1489–1556), is thought to have had about 400 books; fifty years later one of his successors, Archbishop Richard Bancroft (1544–1610), was able to bequeath a collection of about 6,000 volumes. In 1649 Richard Holdsworth, Master of Emmanuel College, Cambridge, died leaving a collection of over 10,000 books; John Moore, Bishop of Ely (1646–1714), was able to build a library of nearly 30,000 volumes; Thomas Rawlinson (1681–1725) managed to amass over 200,000 volumes in his short lifetime. These men had the biggest private libraries of their generations, but book ownership was no longer restricted to a senior elite, and significant collections could be formed by people of relatively modest means who had the will to acquire them;

for example, Robert Burton (1577–1640), the author of *The Anatomy of Melancholy*, who left about 1,800 books when he died.

Motives for collecting

Private libraries have varied in character as well as size, influenced by the motives for acquiring them. Working scholars have always needed ready access to a range of texts – more and more as the centuries have passed – and this has long been a major driving force behind book buying. The development of antiquarian interests from the late sixteenth century onwards led men like Cotton to collect pre-Reformation manuscripts in a spirit of preserving that which would otherwise be lost; Matthew Parker (1504–75), another manuscript collector, was further motivated by a desire to use early texts in political debate. Private collections have also been formed with the deliberate intention of donating the end product to an institution, such as the library that John Cosin built up to give to the diocese of Durham on his death in 1672. Bibliophilia has also played a major part in the development of private libraries – the wish to collect not so much for practical working needs, but because books are desirable and interesting objects that reflect the taste of the owner. Collecting for reasons of connoisseurship is often reckoned to have begun around the beginning of the eighteenth century, when a number of British aristocrats developed a passion for buying INCUNABULA.

Tracing information

Research into private libraries can be approached from various angles. Many historic collections are preserved more or less intact, having passed into institutional libraries. However, many more have been dispersed and their history can only be pieced together from individual books carrying inscriptions or other marks of ownership. Some collections were documented at the point of dispersal through the compilation of a sale catalogue, and such catalogues offer invaluable information on the contents of private libraries from the late seventeenth century onwards (in Britain, the earliest book auction was in 1676).

Further reading

De Ricci, S. (1930) *English Collectors of Books and Manuscripts*, Cambridge University Press [historical survey of major English collectors from the sixteenth century onwards].

Pearson, D. (1994) *Provenance Research in Book History: A Handbook*, British Library [reference work with extensive guidance on further sources for the history of private libraries].

SEE ALSO: bibliomania; history of libraries; provenance; rare-book libraries

DAVID PEARSON

PRIVATE PRESS

A range of printing and publishing activities different from those in the commercial book world, used to categorize a subset of books and other publications produced outside conventional trade channels.

Mallinckrodt's *De Ortu ac Progressu Artis Typographicae* (Cologne, 1639) celebrated the invention of printing and discussed the work of great scholar printers such as Aldus, Froben and Plantin. It also included notes on some individuals 'who had sometimes their hired printers and set up their peculiar and private presses'.

Until the late eighteenth century, private presses were usually controlled by the powerful and wealthy, and used to print such documents as they chose. Of these earlier private presses, some were used to:

- Facilitate private circulation of a book to scholars for their comment, in advance of regular publication. In Elizabethan England, Archbishop Parker used the method for his *De Antiquitate Britannicae Ecclesiae*; the French theologian Bossuet's *Exposition de la doctrine de l'église catholique* was similarly circulated.
- Produce books to a higher standard of textual accuracy than commercial publishers. The work of early astronomers such as Regiomontanus, Tycho Brahe and Johann Hevelius was issued in this way.
- Issue books to higher production standards than commercial printing/publication would allow; private printing permitted extensive use of mathematical illustrations and of volvelles in the *Instrument Buch* (1533) and other books by Petrus Apianus.
- Print books in exotic languages. Much early printing in Arabic types used types cast for and owned by Arabic scholars, not printers.
- Extend printing/book production into new areas. The earliest printing in Iceland, for

example, was procured through a patron's recruitment of printers. The mission presses that introduced printing to many countries and tongues beyond Europe had a similar purpose, and many missionaries became amateur printers.

- Maximize profits by excluding middlemen. Some authors have found they could make more money by personalized production. In the eighteenth century profits from Charles Viner's *General Abridgement of Law and Equity* helped endow an Oxford Professorship, and the eminent surgeon John Hunter made substantial profits from issuing his own medical works.
- Get 'unpublishable' works into print, when authors unable to place a book with commercial printers/publishers produced it themselves (e.g. William Davy, a Devon clergyman, who printed his *System of Divinity*, in twenty-six volumes, 1795–1807).

Work unpublishable because it is politically unacceptable, blasphemous, libellous or (most often) pornographic has sometimes been printed by private presses. Private presses also contributed powerfully to the resistance movements in France, Poland and the Netherlands during the Second World War, but such illicit production is usually clandestine rather than private work.

Adam Lackman's *Annalium Typographicorum* (Hamburg, 1740) recorded the work of many private presses, but the eighteenth century saw new growth. Portable presses were developed; nineteenth-century iron presses (some designed for an amateur market) made the spread of printing easier.

Many were negligible, but some presses usefully reprinted scarce early works: those issued by the Lee Priory Press and the Auchinleck Press were of this kind, anticipating the Early English Text Society – or today's reprinters of rare books in microfiche or CD-ROM form. But being outside the book trade, private press books were (and are) difficult to procure; as many are technically not published, they are still often not caught by legal deposit or included in national bibliographical records. The best bibliographical control is through the Private Libraries Association's *Private Press Books* (1959–).

Modern private presses developed at the end of the nineteenth century as a reaction to technological innovations, because late Victorian books were markedly inferior in design and execution to, for example, Italian books of 1500. At his Kelmscott Press, William Morris sought to rediscover how to make books perfect reading machines; most later private presses in the period up to the Second World War had a similar idealism about them, seeking the form of the ideal book.

Kelmscott medievalized; the Doves Press used one 'ideal' typeface and a severe unillustrated format for all its work. Golden Cockerel Press books provided vehicles for the revival of wood engraving and the integration of text and illustration; the Nonesuch Press had a more eclectic approach, using a variety of designs and seeking the best for a particular text. In the USA and in Europe there were similar experiments in fine book production. Private press books (published at prices often ten to fifteen times higher than trade books) set a model of excellence. The influence of the 'private press movement' on commercial book design was marked.

Changes in printing technology have reduced the connections between fine printing and commercial production. Contemporary private presses keep the old crafts of letterpress printing alive, as a form of industrial archaeology; with few exceptions, they show little interest in the design possibilities presented by DESKTOP PUBLISHING. Their connection with commercial production is now very tenuous, though much desktop publishing work would be improved by consulting their example. Aiming for perfect production, using the best materials on texts they consider worthy, private presses in Britain, Japan, Germany, the Netherlands and the USA still provide an effective (if expensive) alternative aesthetic. Reviewed in such journals as *Private Library, Bookways, Fine Print* or *Matrix*, private presses will still continue to print traditional books from metal types when other production is entirely digitized.

Further reading

Cave, R. (2001) *Fine Printing and Private Presses. Selected Papers*, The British Library.
—— (1983) *The Private Press*, 2nd edn, Bowker.
Franklin, C. (1969) *The Private Presses*, Studio Vista.
Ransom, W. (1929) *Private Presses and Their Books*, Bowker.
Rodenberg, J. (1925) *Deutsche Pressen*, Harrasowitz.

SEE ALSO: book trade

RODERICK CAVE

PROFESSIONALISM

The combination of qualities and conduct that distinguish a particular profession. A process of professionalization can be observed in process in many occupations whereby the characteristics expected of a profession are identified and nurtured by practitioners, usually under the guidance of a society or association.

Professions and professionalism

Professionalism involves the exercising of professional judgement to meet the needs of clients or users. In some professions, such as medicine or law, the professional is dealing with the client on an individual basis, where there is a clear understanding of what services are to be provided to meet the needs of the individual. For the librarian/information scientist, meeting the needs of users may on occasion conflict with the policy of the organization that funds the library/information service. This may come about in various ways, for example through financial restrictions on the purchase of specialized materials or constraints on use for particular groups of users.

In some circumstances more serious difficulties may arise, with issues such as CENSORSHIP and lack of FREEDOM OF INFORMATION that limit users' awareness of what is available relevant to their needs. Librarians/information scientists may then find that their professionalism brings them into conflict with political or funding organizations of considerable power and authority.

The concepts of professions and professionalism form the basis of a substantial body of literature. There are arguments that the words are used too liberally and that too many occupations claim to be professions. In relation to the library and INFORMATION PROFESSIONS it has also been argued that the traditional definition of professionalism is too restrictive (Cronin and Davenport 1988).

Regulation of professions

Acquisition of an identifiable body of knowledge and range of specific skills is generally regarded as essential for a profession. Individuals are required to demonstrate in some way to a peer group that they have reached the appropriate level of professional development and competence required for practice.

In most countries certain professions, such as medicine and law, are subject to legislation. Other professions, including librarianship and information science, are, to a greater or lesser degree, self-regulated through professional associations. The two kinds of regulation are referred to as being statutory and non-statutory.

Whichever form of regulation applies, most professions have some sort of professional code for the guidance of their members. These codes are usually binding on members. There are normally formal disciplinary proceedings to which members of the profession may be subject if they are in breach of the code.

The AMERICAN LIBRARY ASSOCIATION has had a Code of Professional Ethics since 1939 (latest revision 1981). The LIBRARY ASSOCIATION (United Kingdom) adopted a Code of Professional Conduct in 1982. Both codes emphasize the responsibility of the member to maintain professional competence.

Professional associations

In the United Kingdom and elsewhere in the British Commonwealth it is an accepted role for professional associations to award professional qualifications. These qualifications place emphasis on the need for candidates to demonstrate professional competence and commitment as well as provide proof of having acquired appropriate underpinning knowledge through appropriate awards from academic institutions. For example, CILIP (formerly the Library Association) and the Australian Library and Information Association both require evidence of professional competence and judgement for the award of their qualifications. The qualifications of professional bodies are dependent upon continuing personal membership of the awarding body.

Outside the United Kingdom and British Commonwealth it is unusual for a professional association to award qualifications. A notable exception to this generalization is the Medical Library Association (USA), which introduced a code for the certification of medical librarians after the Second World War. This was revised in the 1970s and a system of compulsory recertification every five years was introduced, based on evidence of a minimum number of hours of continuing professional development.

Continuing professional development

In the United Kingdom there has been a general move in recent years for professional bodies to place increasing importance on the need for their members to maintain the currency of their qualifications through continuing professional development (CPD). In a number of professions there is now as much emphasis on CPD as on initial professional education. In some professions CPD is compulsory for the retention of the qualifications needed to practice.

Technological developments have made most information professionals aware that professional knowledge and practical skills are in need of constant updating. The arrival of the INFORMATION SOCIETY requires regular reconsideration of issues surrounding the right of access to information. National and international legislation in fields such as copyright and issues of personal and professional liability all increase the need for CPD to be taken seriously.

The Library Association (United Kingdom) drew up a Framework for Continuing Professional Development that was issued to all members and is designed to support and encourage CPD. The Framework has been licensed to the American Library Association for use in the USA. It has been argued that this voluntary approach is no longer sufficient and that CPD should become mandatory for the profession (Roberts and Konn 1991).

References

Cronin, B. and Davenport, E. (1988) *Post-Professionalism: Transforming the Information Heartland*, Taylor Graham.

Roberts, N. and Konn, T. (1991) *Librarians and Professional Status: Continuing Professional Development and Academic Libraries*, Library Association.

SEE ALSO: library associations; library education

KATE WOOD

PROGRAMMING LANGUAGE

A language used to write programs, either for computer systems or for other types of programmable machine: COBOL, BASIC, FORTRAN, etc. Computer languages evolved from basic machine code, which was difficult to write in and hard to debug, into 'high-level' languages such as C++, Hyper Talk and Lingo.

SEE ALSO: information and communication technology; machine language

PROMOTION

Promotion is the fourth component of the MARKETING mix. The marketing mix is comprised of product, price, place and promotion, often called the 4 Ps. While the mix is the most visible part of the marketing model, it is not exclusively the most important. Librarians historically participate heavily in the promotion arm of the mix. More material is written on promotion (primarily PUBLICITY) than any other single aspect of the marketing mix. Promotion is often confused with public relations, which is often called the 5th P. Public relations is a two-way communication depending on feedback. Promotion is a targeted, planned information and persuasion campaign that invites user action. To achieve the best results, the promotional plan must match the market, the product, the media and the appeal to users.

Promotion tools

There are two ways to activate the market – promotion, and professional assistance and advice. Promotion is more than publicity and public relations. Promotion includes advertising, sales promotion, personal selling and publicity. Advertising is any paid form of communication through web, print or broadcast by an identified sponsor. Sales promotion could be point of purchase displays, samples such as bookmarks or special library cards, prizes, coupons or library website offers. Personal selling is best encapsulated in staff communication, i.e. the responsiveness of the reference librarian over the desk or through e-reference via the Internet.

Publicity is a non-paid-for presentation, generally via some medium (broadcast, print, in person, online) that communicates information about the library or its services and materials. Publicity in concept is problematic for the library and information profession as it is often considered synonymous with marketing. While publicity is a very effective and powerful tool when based upon market research and targeted to a particular audience, it is only one facet of the marketing process.

The most effective promotional tool

The most effective and flexible promotional tool available is the professional advice and assistance that staff members can give users (personal selling). It is somewhat analogous to salesmanship in business in that it is instructive and shows the user how the library product will benefit the user. In other words professional assistance tailors the product offered to the unique demand of the user. When the need for assistance is low, help can be given by impersonal and relatively impersonal means – such as signs or displays. When a more complex decision is necessary for the user, more personal assistance is required to help the user make a selection. When detail is of ultimate importance and extensive, authoritative information is necessary and valuable. This is where the librarian's most important service, expertise, is rendered. This is the ultimate promotion tool.

Benefits of market-based promotion

The library needs to communicate actively with potential users about the wealth of information offered from and stored there. To do less is to under-utilize or waste organization or community resources. Most potential users are not aggressive in pursuit of such information. Users must be activated with continuous generation and DISSEMINATION OF INFORMATION, to explain what is available to them, how they can access it and – often – why they need it. This information must be communicated in terms that capture the user's interest and induce them to try and adopt the products for regular use. The promotional message must appeal to potential users' needs and motives for using library resources. Successful promotion can boost market share and increase use of the library's resources. Every material or service going unused costs the library money in personnel, storage, facility and maintenance expense, and creates no user satisfaction.

Further reading

Hart, K. (1999) *Putting Marketing Ideas into Action*, Library Association Publishing [this offers an introduction to promotion tools within the broader marketing environment through exercises and interpretation of jargon].

CHRISTINE M. KOONTZ

PROPAGANDA

A term, invariably used with pejorative intent, to describe an organized programme for the DIS-SEMINATION OF INFORMATION (true or false) and doctrine, in order to change opinion, with the intention of bringing about political and social change. It is characteristic of propaganda that it consciously selects methods and content to ma-nipulate the responses and subsequent actions of its recipients. Public speaking was a traditional medium of propaganda, but the MASS MEDIA are ideally suited to this purpose.

SEE ALSO: information policy

PROTOCOL

A set of specifications that are used for commu-nication across a network between computer systems that may be dissimilar from each other. The most significant are the TCP/IP protocols (Transmission Control Protocol/Internet Proto-col) that are the means by which the various networks that make up the INTERNET are made transparently accessible to users.

PROVENANCE

The history of the previous ownership and custody of a document. The concept is particu-larly important in archive science, since the integrity of a group of records, or FONDS, from a particular source is a central principle in the care of ARCHIVES. Archive materials are orga-nized and described according to the principle of provenance; the way in which they were created and originally used by an institution or indivi-dual is paramount. The originating entity of a document and information concerning the suc-cessive changes of ownership or custody can both be referred to as its provenance. In RARE BOOK LIBRARIES a special binding, book plate or inscription may be used to suggest a book's provenance.

SEE ALSO: private libraries

PTT

Originally an abbreviation of Post, Telephone, Telegraph and still frequently used in Europe to refer to the national TELECOMMUNICATIONS authority, even though POSTAL SERVICES and telecommunications responsibilities have been separated in many countries. PTT is used to some extent to signify the concept, as opposed to the practicality, of an institution that provides ser-vices and regulatory functions in this area. The term National Telecommunications Agency (NTA) is also sometimes used.

SEE ALSO: information and communication technology; information policy

PUBLIC DOMAIN

Material for which COPYRIGHT is not exercised, as when a state agency deliberately relinquishes copyright to make information more widely available; or which falls outside the realm of copyright, by virtue of being too commonplace or trivial for authorship to be claimed; or for which copyright has expired.

SEE ALSO: intellectual property

PUBLIC LENDING RIGHT

Public Lending Right (PLR) is a right that enables authors to receive payment for the use of their works in publicly funded libraries.

The most usual form relates to the free lending of books by PUBLIC LIBRARIES, but PLR can extend to loans of other works (e.g. audio-cassettes and videos) and to the use of authors' works in ACADEMIC LIBRARIES and SCHOOL LIBRARIES.

In practice the right is largely supported by legislation, or is recognized as part of wider COPYRIGHT law. For example the United King-dom has its own Public Lending Right Act (1979) that recognizes PLR as a separate IN-TELLECTUAL PROPERTY right; in other countries (e.g. Germany and the Netherlands) PLR oper-ates as part of the wider copyright system. There are also a few instances (e.g. New Zealand and Canada) where PLR systems have no basis in statute, but operate under adminis-trative subsidy arrangements similar to artists' grant awards.

Historical development

By the end of the nineteenth century authors were making the case for some form of monetary compensation for the lending out of their books by libraries. But it was not until the end of the Second World War that the first lending right system – in Denmark – was established. This was followed by Norway (1947), Sweden (1954) and Finland (1963). More recently PLR systems have been established in Australia (1974), Israel (1986) and Canada (1988).

In the UK, the 1979 Public Lending Right Act gave authors a legal right to receive payment for the loan of their books by public libraries. The Act came after a thirty-year struggle by authors. Early campaigners like John Brophy and A.P. Herbert established the legitimacy of the PLR case, but it fell to the authors Maureen Duffy and Brigid Brophy, supported by the Writers' Action Group, to carry the day in 1979. The PLR Act recognized the legal right of authors to be remunerated for library loans of their books, and made provision for the appointment of a Registrar to manage the new lending right system with funding from central government. Secondary legislation (the PLR Scheme) in 1982 provided more detailed rules for loans data collection, payment calculation and author and book eligibility.

Currently fifteen countries have working PLR systems; a further twelve (mainly European) have passed legislation recognizing lending rights in principle, but have yet to set up PLR systems. Differences in approach characterize the existing PLR systems, but in terms of 'philosophy' they can be divided broadly into two categories:

'CULTURAL' SCHEMES

In these cases PLR forms part of the state's support for the arts and culture where the primary aim is to provide financial support for the country's writers and to help protect minority languages. In Sweden, Denmark and Norway eligibility for PLR is restricted to authors writing in each country's national language(s). This ensures that PLR payments go on the whole to native writers while ensuring that the eligibility criteria of each scheme do not discriminate against other European Union (EU) citizens on grounds of nationality.

'EQUITY' SCHEMES

These aim to relate payment directly to use, and, in principle at least, are open to authors regardless of nationality or linguistic background. The most developed systems are in Germany and the United Kingdom. Both systems make provision for payment to authors from other European countries. The EU's 1992 Lending and Rental Right Directive adopted the 'equity' approach at European level by recognizing a copyright-based lending right.

Although the Directive includes a number of flexibilities to take account of the variety of approach in existing PLR systems, it provides a template particularly for countries in CENTRAL AND EASTERN EUROPE seeking to develop new PLR systems as part of their preparations for membership of the EU.

PLR features

In addition to writers, PLR can be paid to translators, illustrators and (literary) editors. The EU's Lending Right Directive extended to all categories of loaned material, including audio and music cassettes, and as a result composers and performers are increasingly qualifying for payment. Generally books qualify for PLR if they appear in national bibliographies or carry an ISBN. Deciding relative shares between joint authors, editors and illustrators can be a complex and difficult task. Having established which authors and which books qualify, there is then the task of assessing payment. For this task statistical sampling is generally used. It can be based on a count of stock, loans or acquisitions, or conceptually on more than one of these factors. Counts of bookstock or loans are the most common. The UK system is based on the latter, and since the 1980s loans sampling through automated public library circulation systems has been technically feasible. In the UK the clever manipulation of software and a close working relationship between the Registrar and public libraries has enabled coverage of the PLR sample to be increased to 15 per cent of national loans.

There is usually a maximum limit set for any author's annual payment (£6,000 in the UK) and frequently payment systems are weighted to favour the less prolific author. There are various arrangements to determine whether payments continue after an author's death, and some schemes fund pensions. Apart from the financial rewards, which for most authors are quite small, there is a sense of just reward and satisfaction felt from the evidence of readership that is genuinely appreciated by many authors.

Further reading

Brophy, B. (1983) *A Guide to Public Lending Right*, Gower [detail now outdated, but an excellent lively account of the historical perspective and political arguments in the UK and in Europe].

International PLR Network website (www.plrinternational.com).

Parker, J. (ed.) (1999) *Whose Loan is it Anyway? Essays in Celebration of PLR's Twentieth Anniversary*, Registrar of Public Lending Right [entertaining accounts by prominent British authors and politicians of their contribution to the achievement of PLR in 1979].

Sumsion, J. (1991) *PLR in Practice*, 2ⁿᵈ edn, Registrar of Public Lending Right.

3ʳᵈ International Public Lending Right Conference: The Right to Culture and a Culture of Rights, Ottawa, 1–4 October 1999, [Canadian] Public Lending Right Commission.

SEE ALSO: book trade; cultural industries; European Union information policies; information policy

JIM PARKER

PUBLIC LIBRARIES

Libraries that are provided through public funding for public use and the public good. Public libraries make use of materials in printed, audiovisual and electronic formats in order to collect, preserve, organize, retrieve, disseminate and communicate information, ideas and the creative product of the human imagination.

History

Many libraries in Britain and elsewhere were open to the public in the seventeenth and eighteenth centuries, but the first truly public libraries were established in the USA and Britain in the middle of the nineteenth century with the aim of introducing education, culture and, according to some, morality to working people. According to Kelly, the term public library:

> [F]irst appeared in its Latin form (*bibliotheca publica*) as a technical term to distinguish the general university libraries of Oxford and Cambridge from those of the colleges, [but] was frequently used in its more modern sense with reference to endowed libraries from the seventeenth century onwards.
>
> (Kelly 1973: 4)

For many years public libraries had a working-class image, but in the 1930s this began to change as they increasingly attracted members of the middle class. In the 1960s and 1970s many within the profession felt that the service was failing to respond to the social issues of the time. They set about changing this by introducing community-based policies and services for disadvantaged and minority groups. This approach was modified in the 1980s and 1990s by a much greater emphasis on market forces and the financing and costing of services. Since then, in many parts of the world, and at varying rates of progress, library authorities have invested time and money to provide access to INFORMATION AND COMMUNICATION TECHNOLOGY. At the same time there has been a renewal of interest in reading and reader development. Research has shown public libraries to be one of the most highly regarded and heavily used of local public services. Although the figures vary from place to place it is estimated that about 60 per cent of Britons and 53 per cent of Americans use a public library at some time.

Functions

Most modern statements of purpose suggest that the public library makes an essential contribution to democracy and citizenship. It is also vital to a nation's literacy and productivity. There have been many successful literacy schemes based on public libraries in both the more and the less-developed world, and business information (see BUSINESS INFORMATION SERVICE) and other services have made a significant contribution to economic development at both the local and national levels. In addition, public libraries provide the opportunity for personal and community development and artistic and scientific achievement through the selection, preservation and dissemination of materials for education, lifelong learning, research, leisure and recreation. The emphasis given to any one of these roles will vary according to the place and time.

Public library services include lending and reference collections. Services may be housed in dedicated buildings, in the premises of other organizations such as prisons and social care homes, and/or taken to rural and other communities by MOBILE LIBRARY and outreach services of various kinds. Increasingly services are also available via the Internet. Services to children and young people are regarded as especially important. In principle all libraries, including mobile libraries, should provide access for disabled people, including those with wheelchairs. All services should reflect the needs of the communities they serve. The local library should also provide access to national and international collections by participating in co-operative schemes and networking activities. It is increasingly recognized that public libraries 'are frequently the only point of access to information and learning that is available to the deprived, the excluded or the disaffected' (Re:source 2001).

Finance and control

In some countries, but not all, the public library is a statutory service. For example, in England and Wales the Public Libraries and Museums Act, 1964, places a statutory obligation on local authorities to provide 'a comprehensive and efficient service for all persons desiring to make use thereof'. On the other hand there is no such national legislation in the USA.

The service is financed and controlled by local and/or national governments. However, in the wake of the new models of management, which have been adopted by or imposed on the public sector, there have been moves to enter into alliances with the private and voluntary sectors. In some countries partnerships with other 'memory institutions' such as museums, archives and galleries are being encouraged.

An increased emphasis on the managerial accountability of public services has resulted in a variety of official statements that make explicit what users can expect from a modern public library. For example, government-backed public library standards for England were published in 2001 while, at an international level, the revised IFLA (2001) Guidelines, endorsed by UNESCO, were officially launched at the IFLA conference of the same year. These identify the key roles for the public library as education, information and personal development.

The core functions should be provided free of direct charge for the user. This principle is central to the public service values of professionals in the field, and is emphasized in legislative documents across the world. It has been criticized by the New Right (White 1983; Adam Smith Institute 1986), but calls for the introduction of charges have received little public or political support. Indeed their introduction would seem to run contrary to the spirit of the UNESCO Public Library Manifesto, which states that 'the public library shall in principle be free of charge' and that services 'should be provided on the basis of equality of access for all regardless of age, race, gender, religion, nationality, language or social status' (UNESCO 1995).

The spread of information and communications technology together with changing social priorities have led some to question the future of public libraries. Opportunities and dangers are on the horizon but the service will survive, and thrive, if it continues to meet the needs of individuals and communities, and maintains the values that distinguish it from much of the mass media, and some electronic providers of infotainment.

References

Adam Smith Institute (1986) *Ex Libris*.

IFLA/UNESCO (2001) *Guidelines for Development. The Public Library Service*, prepared by a working group chaired by Philip Gill, on behalf of the Section of Public Libraries, IFLA Publications vol. 97, K.G. Saur.

Kelly, T. (1973) *A History of Public Libraries in Great Britain 1845–1965*, Library Association.

Re:source (2001) *Building on Success. An Action Plan for Libraries* (draft for consultation) (www.resource. gov.uk/information/bosucc.pdf) [accessed 13 August 2001].

UNESCO (1995) 'Public library manifesto 1994', *IFLA Public Library News, Newsletter of the Section of Public Libraries* (January), no. 12.

White, L.J. (1983) *The Public Library in the 1980s*, Lexington Books.

Further reading

Building the New Library Network (1998) *A Report to Government*, Library and Information Commission (www.lic.gov.uk/publications/policyreports/ building/).

Comprehensive, Efficient and Modern Public Libraries – Standards and Assessment (2001) Department for Culture, Media and Support.

Kinnell, M. and Sturges, P. (eds) (1996) *Continuity and Innovation in the Public Library*, Library Association Publishing.

Usherwood, B. (1996) *Rediscovering Public Library Management*, Library Association Publishing.

SEE ALSO: children's libraries; information policy; lending libraries; libraries; Public Lending Right; reference libraries; rural library services; social exclusion and libraries

BOB USHERWOOD

PUBLIC RECORD OFFICE

The Public Record Office (PRO), which houses the NATIONAL ARCHIVES of the United Kingdom, is the official repository of the records of the British Crown. It was established in 1838 as a department of state, and became an executive agency in 1992. In 2001 its holdings amounted to some 100 shelf-miles of records.

The archive is exceptionally rich, reflecting the operations of the central government, first of England and then of the United Kingdom, both at home and abroad. Its contents derive exclusively from the routine of public administration, but they contain much matter of unexpected kinds, including an accumulation of more than 500,000 original photographs.

The Public Records Act of 1838 (1 & 2 Vict., c. 94) followed upon six Royal Commissions (1800–37) and a long debate on the security of the records. The Act placed the public records in the charge and superintendence of the Master of the Rolls, the judge who was titular guardian of the records of the Court of Chancery. At that time the ancient records of the Crown were held in some fifty separate repositories in London and Westminster, including the Tower of London, the chapter house of Westminster Abbey and the chapel of Rolls House, in Chancery Lane, the Master's official residence.

It was decided to concentrate the records in a new repository, in the grounds of Rolls House. The first director of the Office, styled the Deputy Keeper because he was subordinate to the Master of the Rolls, was Sir Francis Palgrave (1788–1861), formerly keeper of the records in the chapter house at Westminster. The new repository, designed by James Pennethorne and opened to the public in 1860, was subsequently extended to provide some twenty miles of shelving in 120 fireproof strong-rooms. It remained the principal home of the records until the opening of the repository at Kew in 1977.

The PRO owes much to the self-inculcated professionalism of Palgrave, a historical scholar with a natural sense of the value of ARCHIVES. His first care was for the physical safety of the records, and the Chancery Lane repository was built to the highest standards of the day. He also, however, appreciated the historical potential of modern papers, and in 1851 he moved to secure the enumerators' books from the decennial census, a decision that might seem to their many later users to be his principal achievement. One of his last actions in office was to sanction the photographing of the Domesday Book by the Ordnance Survey, to make a facsimile edition published in 1861–3.

The contents of the PRO, ranging over nine centuries, exemplify the principle that ARCHIVES are accumulated for the sake of the information which they record and that the archivist's business is both to preserve them and to facilitate access to them. Until the PRO was established the various departments of state kept their own records, which in the Exchequer began with Domesday Book (1086). From the sixteenth century the multifarious business of the secretaries of state and the sovereign's council was recorded in the state papers, which had their own keeper until 1783, when the secretaries' functions were formally divided between foreign and domestic affairs. The newly designated Foreign and Home Offices were the first modern departments of government, which in turn accumulated archives of their own.

It was the government's decision in 1861 to demolish the State Paper Office in Whitehall and lodge its extensive holdings in the PRO that produced the first crisis of accommodation in the new central archives. By the end of the nineteenth century the Chancery Lane building was full, despite two extensions, and the Office was seeking space in ancillary repositories. It had also established, under two Acts (40 & 41 Vict., c. 55, 1877; and 61 & 62 Vict., c. 12, 1898), routines for the selective destruction of departmental records, from which only material earlier than 1660 was exempt.

In the meantime, however, the volume of contemporary records continued to grow. It was then vastly increased by the First and Second World Wars, which extended the concerns of government into every aspect of life, and again by the legislation attendant upon social and economic change after 1945. Eventually the management and preservation of departmental records was discussed by a ministerial committee chaired by Sir James Grigg, and the committee's report, published in 1954, was followed by the Public Records Act of 1958 (6 & 7 Eliz. 2, c. 51).

The Act placed the PRO under the direction of a Keeper of Public Records, answerable to the Lord Chancellor as minister. It placed all public records within the PRO's purview, ordering that any record chosen for permanent preservation should be made available to the public fifty years after its creation. That rule was immediately waived to allow the early release of records relating to the First World War, and then replaced by a thirty-year rule under the Public Records Act of 1967 (1967, c. 44).

The range and intensity of public interest in archives has grown with the records themselves, but it would clearly be impossible to preserve the 100 shelf-miles of documents that the 200 departments of government generate every year (a figure that excludes machine-readable records, in magnetic storage). Since 1958 departments have been free to destroy only ephemeral papers: those dispensable within five years of their creation. All others are then retained for a consultative review after twenty years, when approximately 1 per cent (comprising some 2,000 yards of boxed documents) are selected for permanent preservation. Accessions to the PRO have been listed by computer since the 1960s, and the older means of reference, which include manuscript lists several centuries old, are being incorporated into a single automated system and made accessible on the Internet.

A new repository for modern records was opened at Kew in 1977, and in the 1990s was extended to receive the contents of the building in Chancery Lane. The enlarged Office is still, as it was in the nineteenth century, a notable focus of traditional scholarship, but one-fifth of the 560,000 documents consulted there each year are produced at the request of government departments. A great number of readers pursue genealogical and allied inquiries, both at Kew and at the Family Records Centre in Finsbury. The Centre, opened in 1997, contains the indexes to the Registrar General's records of births, marriages and deaths, and the returns of the decennial census of population from 1841 to 1901. It is used annually by almost 170,000 readers. Those are changes familiar to archivists in all industrialized countries. What distinguishes the PRO is the antiquity of its oldest holdings and the continuity of the institutions that it reflects.

Further reading

Cantwell, J.D. (1991) *The Public Record Office, 1838–1958*, HMSO.

Galbraith, V.H. (1934) *An Introduction to the Use of the Public Records*, Oxford University Press.

Kitching, C.J. (1988) 'The history of record keeping in the United Kingdom to 1939: A select bibliography', *Journal of the Society of Archivists* 9: 8–100.

Martin, G.H. and Spufford, P. (eds) (1990) *The Records of the Nation: The Public Record Office, 1838–1988; The British Record Society, 1888–1988*, Boydell Press.

PRO website (www.pro.gov.uk).

Report of the Committee on Departmental Records (1954) (Cmd 9163 of 1954), HMSO.

Report of the Keeper of Public Records on the Work of the Public Record Office, HMSO (annual).

SEE ALSO: information policy; records management

GEOFFREY MARTIN

PUBLICITY

The process of making the services of a library known to its clients and potential clients, as a key aspect of the MARKETING of its services. Publicity is effected by the use of all types of media: printed material, the World Wide Web, AUDIOVISUAL MATERIALS, display, signing and guiding (see GUIDING AND SIGNS), USER EDUCATION, point of use instruction and the press. It involves all staff, not just those with specific responsibility for their organization. Each form of PROMOTION identifies the organization and makes a statement about its attitude.

Historical development

Once given a low priority, publicity is now an essential part of any modern library service. This change has been manifested by two factors. First, the public has become accustomed to sophisticated forms of commercial promotion and, second, there is a real need for libraries to promote the value of their service. The public rightly expects quality, and librarians as professional information providers should complement services with quality support and promotional material.

Before the mid-1970s there was a reluctance to promote library services. This was viewed as something relevant to the commercial world that could be left to the large advertising agencies. (Indeed there are great benefits to be gained by observing closely commercial practice in promotional work.) The majority of library material was produced by staff with artistic flair given limited resources. The result was a quality that ranged from average to unacceptable, rarely matching the professionalism of the services that it aimed to promote.

Improving standards

The trend towards effective publicity and public relations was led by PUBLIC LIBRARIES, with special and academic libraries slow to follow. The need to 'sell' services became apparent when libraries began to fight against other services for a share of budgets. During the 1980s some of the larger authorities began to employ staff with specific responsibility for library promotion. Gradually the standard of design could be seen to improve, demonstrating the benefits of investment in specialist staff.

Well-planned programmes bring together expertise from a range of industries: design, print, display, photography, the mass media, copy writing and marketing, to name but a few. Contacts within these industries should be acknowledged as professionals in their own right. The time spent talking with them to gain a basic insight into their industry is a sound investment that will lead to a better end-product.

The availability of word processing and graphic packages on personal computers and DESKTOP PUBLISHING (DTP) provides the opportunity to develop creativity. Unfortunately, technology does not always bring benefits. Operated by trained staff, DTP is a powerful design tool; operated by untrained staff, the results can be disastrous. It should be remembered that the range and scope of facilities offered by DTP do not give the librarian the skills of a designer or typesetter. The expedience of technology becomes apparent only when equipment is operated by skilled staff. Increasingly, a well-designed and informative website is seen as the key to effective promotion and publicity.

The statement of attitude that promotion makes about the organization, coupled with the creativity which is enabled by technology, can lead to inconsistent representation of an organization's image. Industry and commerce have long recognized the value of corporate identity as a method of ensuring consistency of image, and without exception library authorities have followed this trend. A well-organized authority will publish a style manual that will give specific instructions in the use of colour, typefaces and the representation of the logo on a variety of formats. On face value this may seem restrictive but the advantages are realized in a standard approach to professional presentation. Libraries must follow their authority's manual but may need to negotiate the development of sections specific to their needs.

A cost-effective approach

The investment in staff resources and production is considerable. It is therefore wise to consider methods of production that are both cost-effective and flexible. The use of standard ranges of stationery for overprinting, quality photocopying for short print runs and devising flexible systems for signing and guiding are practices that ensure expedient use of budget and resources. Similar care should be exercised when selecting service providers. Librarians may be encouraged to use in-house departments as opposed to commercial enterprise to deliver the service or product. It is important to assess the advantages and disadvantages of each. Ultimately, a quality product or service delivered on schedule is the measure of value for money.

Planning

Irrespective of investment and an informed selection of service providers, publicity programmes will only meet their stated aims if the approach is researched, planned and sustained. A clear profile of the needs, interests and levels of users and non-users is the foundation on which effective promotion rests. Project leaders must be clear about what they are saying, why they are saying it, to whom, where and when. These questions must be answered if publicity is to attract the attention and interest of its defined audience effectively.

As discussed earlier, promotional projects draw on a wide range of services and therefore require careful management. The relationship between conventional publicity media and the use of the WORLD WIDE WEB now takes an important place in the planning process. Schedules need to be planned bearing in mind that when a range of contributors are involved things can go wrong. An allowance for slippage has to be built in to any schedule. It is considered best practice that the person responsible for planning the schedule assumes responsibility for ensuring that deadlines are met.

Professional organizations

Staff with specific responsibility for library promotion represent a small percentage of the profession. In Britain, they were served by the Publicity and Public Relations Group (PPRG) of the LIBRARY ASSOCIATION, which will continue to function in CILIP. The PPRG encourages the raising of standards in library promotion and provides a forum for the exchange of ideas through its courses and its newsletter *Public Eye*. It also takes an active role in the organization and judging of the Library Association/T.C. Farries Public Relations and Publicity Awards, which have made a great impact on standards of library promotion.

Publicity and public relations have been slow to evolve within library and information services, and there is an urgent need to develop this aspect of professional work. The technology exists to facilitate creativity and impact with ease. The onus is on librarians to make a strong case for adequate resources to exploit its use to the full.

Further reading

Ashcroft, L. and Hoey, C. (2001) 'PR, marketing and the Internet: Implications for information professionals', *Library Management* 22: 68–74.

Dworkin, K.D. (2001) 'Library marketing: Eight ways to get unconventionally creative', *Online* 25: 52–4.

Jacso, P. (2001) 'Promoting the library by using technology', *Computers in Libraries* 21: 58–60.

Kinnell, M. (ed.) (1989) *Planned Public Relations for Libraries – A PPRG Handbook*, Taylor Graham.

Quinn, P. (1992) *Effective Copy Writing for Librarians*, PPRG.

SEE ALSO: strategic planning

LINDA M. SMITH, REVISED BY THE EDITORS

PUBLISHING

The trade of making and selling books, and other knowledge products such as music, art reproductions, photographs and maps. It includes commissioning manuscripts, negotiations with authors or their agents, design of books, book production, publicity, and sales through book wholesalers and retailers. Electronic publishing is in the process not merely of changing the production of print products (through the submission, editing and printing of books from disk), but also of vastly extending the range of 'non-print' publishing, to include MULTIMEDIA and DATABASE publishing on CD-ROM and disk, and ONLINE and networked publishing.

Publishing is a global industry, increasingly dominated by multinational media companies (such as News Corporation and Vivendi) that also have interests in BROADCASTING, the creation of audiovisual products (such as film and music on video), newspapers and magazines, and Internet Service Providers.

Further reading

Feather, J. (2002) *Publishing: Communicating Knowledge in the 21st Century*. K.G. Saur.

SEE ALSO: book trade; economics of information; information policy; knowledge industries; licences

PUSH TECHNOLOGY

Updating systems by which users of the INTERNET, or INTRANETS, can receive news and other information through periodic and unobtrusive transmissions. Also referred to more specifically as webcasting, or netcasting, push technology informs users about material relevant to their interests before any specific request is made, on the basis of pre-selected topics. The websites selected are referred to as channels, and this choice of terminology suggests the way in which push technology imposes more order on the flow of information than can be obtained through individual searches. Although push technology is aimed strongly at the corporate market, individual users can also benefit. Looked at in the context of information science, it adds a new technical dimension to the practice of DISSEMINATION OF INFORMATION.

Further reading

Herther, N. (1998) 'Push and the politics of the Internet', *Electronic Library* 16: 109–16.

Pedley, P. (1999) *Intranets and Push Technology: Creating an Information Sharing Environment*, London: ASLIB.

Q

QUALITY ASSURANCE

Quality assurance is an approach to the entire manufacturing or service provision effort, which focuses upon the potential suppliers' capabilities and reliability. Through quality assurance the organization seeks to reduce human error in the manufacture of a product or provision of a service. It is now widely applied to library and information service provision, as well as to the production of knowledge products such as books and software.

Further reading

St. Clair, G. (2000) *Total Quality Management*, Bowker Saur.

SEE ALSO: performance measurement in libraries; quality in library and information services

QUALITY IN LIBRARY AND INFORMATION SERVICES

'Conformance to the requirements of the user' and 'fitness for the user's purpose' are the classic definitions of quality found in the literature of quality management. Work by 'quality gurus' such as Deming (1986), Juran (1989), Crosby (1986) and Feigenbaum (1983) has demonstrated the importance of quality management in a wide variety of fields. Although the initial work took place in the industrial sector, quality management has spread to services, including those in the public sector, and is now widely applied in almost every field. Libraries and information services are no exception.

Earlier approaches that emphasized quality control, usually involving the inspection of products and services to see that they conform to a specification and then rejecting those which do not, have largely given way to QUALITY ASSURANCE, with a much greater emphasis on using quality failures as opportunities to improve the underlying processes so that the same fault does not occur again. Systematic approaches to quality assurance include the International Standard ISO 9000, known in the UK prior to 1995 as BS5750. Its applications to libraries have been documented (Ellis and Norton 1993; Brophy 1993).

Total Quality Management (TQM) emphasizes that quality is a holistic concept that, if it is to succeed, must be applied to every aspect of an organization's activities. TQM is concerned with cultural change, so that every individual in the organization becomes fully committed to providing quality products and services: some writers go so far as to call for an 'obsession' with quality. Barnard (1993) describes a model for TQM in libraries developed by the US Association of Research Libraries' Office of Management Services and involving a ten-stage process of implementation.

Quality chains, consisting of sequences of internal customer–supplier relationships between individuals, sections and departments, are as important as the final relationship with the end-user, external customer or client. The cost of quality, perhaps more accurately termed the cost of quality failure, has been found to be very significant in every type of organization, leading as it does to reworking, lost customers and poor customer perceptions of the product or service. Yet quality failures can be prevented, providing they are seen as the responsibility of managers, who can tackle them through the systematic introduction of better procedures, better training, empowerment of 'front-of-house' workers and clarity of purpose.

An important distinction must be made between quality and grade. Customers will often be willing to pay extra for a higher-grade service – such as a first-class seat in an aircraft or train – but the quality issues are the same for all grades: good, efficient, relevant services and products that meet or exceed the specification that has been agreed, implicitly or explicitly, with the customer.

In librarianship and information science quality issues have come to the fore partly as a result of earlier and continuing emphasis on PERFORMANCE MEASUREMENT IN LIBRARIES, partly through the influence of writers on general management issues such as Peters and Waterman (1982) and Garvin (1988), and partly in response to external pressures. This last influence includes the adoption of TQM or other quality approaches by parent bodies such as corporations or universities, and external audit of public-sector services by bodies such as the UK Audit Commission, which has a statutory role in overseeing public library services and their quality. The influence of the 'Customer's Charter' in the UK has been very significant, and has included a system of Charter Marks for what are judged to be quality services.

Key concepts of quality for services, including libraries and information services, have emerged from work by Zeithaml *et al.* (1990), who suggest that attention needs to be paid to five aspects of service, the RATER categories:

1   Reliability: does the service meet set or implied standards consistently?
2   Assurance: do staff give the impression of being knowledgeable about their jobs, of being trustworthy and confident? Are they courteous to each customer?
3   Tangibles: do the premises appear tidy, well designed, suitable for their purpose? Does equipment work? Are staff appropriately dressed? Do leaflets communicate information that is needed?
4   Empathy: do customers get individual attention that meets *their* needs? Do staff appear to care about customers' real needs?
5   Responsiveness: is the service prompt? Are staff willing to go out of their way to help customers?

Within the RATER categories can be found those 'softer' aspects of service that are so often ignored by management and review processes that rely on hard, statistical evidence. The library assistant who greets each user with eye contact and a smile projects far more quality to most users than the dry, efficient yet impersonal service that older approaches to management have so often suggested.

Perhaps it is in the pursuit of excellence in these soft attributes of service that quality management has most to offer library and information science. At the end of the day, customer satisfaction, and hence quality, is more often achieved through these personal touches than in any other way.

References

Barnard, S.B. (1993) 'Implementing total quality management: A model for research libraries', *Journal of Library Administration* 18(1/2): 57–70.

Brophy, P. (1993) 'Towards BS5750 in a university library', in M. Ashcroft and D. Barton (eds) *Quality Management: Towards BS5750: Proceedings of a Seminar Held in Stamford, Lincolnshire, on 21st April 1993*, Capital Planning Information, pp. 3–11.

Crosby, P.B. (1986) *Running Things: The Art of Making Things Happen*, McGraw-Hill.

Deming, W.E. (1986) *Out of the Crisis: Quality, Productivity and Competitive Position*, MIT Press.

Ellis, D. and Norton, B. (1993) *Implementing BS5750/ISO 9000 in Libraries*, ASLIB.

Feigenbaum, A.V. (1983) *Total Quality Control*, 3rd edn, McGraw-Hill.

Garvin, D.A. (1988) *Managing Quality*, Free Press.

Juran, J.M. (1989) *Juran on Leadership for Quality: An Executive Handbook*, Free Press.

Peters, T. and Waterman, R.J. (1982) *In Search of Excellence: Lessons from America's Best Run Companies*, Warner Bros.

Zeithaml, V.A., Parasuraman, A. and Berry, L.L. (1990) *Delivering Quality Service: Balancing Customer Perceptions and Expectations*, Collier Macmillan.

Further reading

Brophy, P. and Coulling, K. (1996) *Quality Management for Information and Library Managers*, Gower.

Masters, D.G. (1996) 'Total quality management in libraries: ERIC Digest' (www.ed.gov/datanases/ERIC_digests/ed396759.html).

Nitecki, D.A. (1997) 'SERVQUAL: Measuring service quality in academic libraries' (www.arl.org/newsltr/191/servqual.html).

SEE ALSO: libraries

PETER BROPHY

R

RANDOM-ACCESS MEMORY

Random-access memory (RAM) is memory in a computer organized so that every location used is given a unique address and can be accessed in the same amount of time. It is the most widely used memory technology for computing.

SEE ALSO: information and communication technology

RANGANATHAN, SHIYALI RAMAMRITA (1892–1972)

Librarian, creator of the COLON CLASSIFICATION and of the Five Laws of Library Science.

Born in Madras State, India, he studied Mathematics at Madras Christian College. In 1924 he was appointed as the first Librarian of the University of Madras, and then studied Librarianship at University College, London. He also served as University Librarian and Professor of Library Science at Benares Hindu University (1945–7), Professor of Library Science at the University of Delhi (1947–54) and Honorary Professor and Head of the Documentation Research and Training Centre, Bangalore. In 1965 the Indian government appointed him National Research Professor in Library Science.

The COLON CLASSIFICATION, although not much used outside India, has had a very wide influence on the development of other CLASSIFICATION and indexing systems. Ranganathan also contributed to cataloguing through his codes of rules for dictionary and classified catalogues. His vision extended beyond the cataloguing room, and he proposed a national library network for India and outlined a thirty-year programme for libraries. His Five Laws still provide a good basis for discussion of the principles behind the management and organization of libraries. He was revered as a guru in India and his work won great respect throughout the world. He was President of the Indian Library Association (1944–53) and of the Madras Library Association (1958–67), Vice-President of FID (1953–6 and 1958–61) and an Honorary Vice-President of the UK Library Association.

SEE ALSO: library education; philosophy of librarianship; organization of knowledge; South Asia

RARE BOOK

Literally, a book of which copies are scarce and hard to obtain. The term has various secondary implications concerning the age, research content, production values and financial value of a book. The term originates in the BOOK TRADE, where there are rare-book dealers, but carries over into librarianship, where RARE BOOK LIBRARIES, departments and librarians are sometimes identified. SPECIAL COLLECTIONS and the ARCHIVAL LIBRARY are naturally extensively stocked with rare books.

Further reading

Lieberman, R. (1995) 'What makes a rare book rare? A primer for the enthusiastic but hesitant librarian', *College and Undergraduate Libraries* 2: 139–45.

RARE BOOK LIBRARIES

Rare book libraries exist for the same reasons and have the same functions as other libraries.

They acquire, preserve, describe and provide reference and access to the materials – in this case, 'rare books' – for which they care. However rare books are defined – and their definition is complex, uncertain and changing – they require unusually intensive attention in their use and storage. The closed stacks and supervised reading rooms characteristic of rare book libraries are thought to encourage such attention, whereas the looser conditions that characterize general reference or circulating collections do not.

Contents

At one time, a widely held consensus about the definition of 'rare books' may have made rare book libraries appear to be more similar in their holdings than the subsequent spread of rare book libraries and growing uncertainties about rarity and value now permit. In general, the contents of rare book libraries in that earlier (perhaps somewhat mythical) period would have consisted, first, primarily of older imprints that, second, would most often have been the product of writers widely agreed to possess some distinction, and that were, third, demonstrably 'rare' (as, for example, in the case of books printed in limited runs by a PRIVATE PRESS).

Even so vague a consensus about the nature and definition of rare books is no longer possible. Librarians and scholars recognize that it conceals a multitude of unconscious biases. 'Old' in Buenos Aires, Perth or Winnipeg is not the same as 'old' in Manchester, Padua or Seville. Notions of literary or other forms of distinction are increasingly under interrogation in many disciplines. The supposed rarity of any individual publication may matter less, for some purposes, than the agglomeration of large collections in which books, common or rare, function to support pedagogy and research in new ways. In this environment, the institutional administrators of rare book libraries – in the USA more commonly called 'special collections' – increasingly regard them as repositories for any primary materials that, if collected in depth, can be used by researchers in the historical humanities. These libraries have a function similar to that of MANU-SCRIPT LIBRARIES – in fact, they are often organizationally related to or identical with them.

The increasing complication of and uncertainty about what constitutes a rare book affects rare book librarians whether they work in departments that are part of large general libraries, independent institutions responsible for whatever materials or subjects they make their speciality or institutions that collect manuscripts as well as printed books. Formerly concerned with materials primarily 'old', 'distinguished' or 'rare', rare book librarians now acquire, preserve, describe and make accessible materials that may be old or new, distinguished in an almost incalculable variety of ways or merely constitutive of a vast collection devoted to a special author, subject, chronological era or geographical region.

Rare book libraries collect printed books in a variety of forms and for a variety of reasons. Age (date of imprint) has always been, as it continues to be, a major criterion, but is now a relative rather than an absolute criterion. INCUNABULA (that is, books printed in Europe between the beginning of printing from movable type, which occurred c. 1455 in Mainz, and the end of the year 1500) are almost always located in a rare-book library. With a frequency that tends to decrease the more recently they were produced, sixteenth-, seventeenth- and eighteenth-century imprints are also placed in rare book libraries. Even nineteenth-century imprints now seem more historical than was true earlier in the twentieth century, when they still seemed 'recent', and are considered for inclusion in rare book libraries. Exemplars of early printing from Asia, where printing long antedated its development in Europe, are also normally located in rare book libraries.

First or early editions of great or influential works in the history of literature or thought, good or bad, old or new, are commonly placed in rare book libraries. But many institutions now disregard 'greatness' or 'influence' altogether. They move to rare book libraries all printed books whose imprints antedate a certain arbitrarily selected year. The arbitrariness of this criterion is indicated by a lack of consensus about dates: for example, in some libraries many eighteenth-century imprints remain in circulation, while in others they are housed with the rare books.

Early imprints from a specific place – for instance, eighteenth-century British printing in India; evangelical printing from mission presses in the Pacific during the mid-nineteenth century; the first imprints of Alberta – are often located in rare book libraries. Here, too, consensus is not general: thus libraries in Alberta specifically and Canada generally are more likely to notice early Alberta imprints than libraries in other areas of the world.

Many other criteria influence the decision to locate a book in a rare book collection. Its current market price, if known, may be a determinant: no one wants to have to replace an expensive book that a reader has inadvertently damaged, so exceptionally expensive books are located where their use can be supervised. The same is true of books that can be demonstrated to be absolutely rare (no other copies are reported anywhere at all, or only a limited number of copies was issued). Because a replacement copy may be simply unavailable, no matter what one is willing to pay for it, such books also require supervised use. What might be called the 'iconic' value of some books also apparently justifies locating them in rare book libraries, whether they are common or rare (e.g. the 1611 King James Bible or the 1623 Folio of Shakespeare's plays, neither one especially uncommon although each is expensive). Books illustrated by famous artists; covered in spectacularly beautiful or historically significant bindings; with a famous PROVENANCE; presented by their author to a close relative, friend or lover; signed, annotated or corrected by an author, a friend, a contemporary or a later person of some note: all such books are typically located in rare book libraries. The sheer physical fragility of a book thought to have some permanent merit as an intellectual entity in its original condition can justify its inclusion in a rare book library. Sometimes the presence of a dust-wrapper, or of a map, will justify that location. Any of these factors can work to locate in a rare book library an imprint of the 1990s as well as one from the 1490s.

In addition, rare book libraries also often collect broadsides, playbills, promptbooks, drawings, prints, maps or photographs. Under some circumstances, they may even hold MICRO-FORMS or other reproductions, as well as reference books and secondary sources that enumerate, define, describe or otherwise illuminate the library's specialities. They may also house objects (for example, a portrait of a writer or person represented in the collections; a lock of a poet's hair; a writer's desk or grandfather clock; the gun with which a political leader was assassinated).

Rationale

Like all libraries, rare book libraries exist in order to provide access to sources of information and knowledge. To this overarching goal, however, they add a second imperative. Regarding their collections as essential to teaching and research in, and advancement of, the historical humanities, rare book libraries concern themselves to an unusual degree with the CONSERVATION and PRESERVATION of the material embodiments of the subjects in which they specialize. Collections, far from being ephemeral, are acquired in the belief that they cannot be 'used up'; decisions to acquire are thus decisions to retain, so far as possible, for posterity. The effort to achieve an appropriate balance between the two values of access and preservation – often harmonious but occasionally in conflict – is, in one sense, the story of rare book librarianship.

Rare book libraries gather materials for use under supervision, a first line of defence to preserve the books in such collections. For many Western librarians, the concept of 'supervision' conflicts with another ingrained professional value: respect for readers' privacy. Library materials ordinarily circulate without supervision outside a library's physical premises to any reader with permission to use that library; or, in noncirculating reference libraries, they are consulted, with a minimum of staff mediation, in large reading rooms that permit at best only marginal invigilation. Most of the time, when books are actually in use, neither they nor their users receive any supervision at all. A principled aversion to any oversight over readers and their interest is one of the profession's cherished means of ensuring free inquiry and thought. By contrast, rare book libraries require readers to consult books within the precincts of their own reading rooms where staff can observe them at will. They permit readers to use only pencils (or laptop computers) for notes; photography, photocopying, tracing, scanning or chemical testing of rare book materials without curatorial intervention are not allowed. Records of the books' readers' use are carefully maintained.

Such supervision is justified, despite considerable aversion to it from both readers and librarians, on several grounds. Basic is a conception of the primacy of the objects that rare-book libraries collect and of the desirability of prolonging their physical existences as long as possible. The convenience of today's reader is less important than the continued existence of the object for tomorrow's reader. Without some such conception, rare book libraries would not have been called into existence in the first place.

In addition, the sheer age of some materials, their uniqueness and virtual irreplaceability at any price or projected replacement cost, all are thought to justify supervising readers who use rare books. It really makes no difference, for instance, that the 1623 Shakespeare Folio – whose location in rare book libraries is also a function of its iconic value, mentioned above, as an embodiment of 'English literature' – is not especially rare. Its price (measured in US dollars) hovers in the high six figures and is pushing at seven. Most librarians would feel it an abandonment of their fiduciary responsibilities to their institutions were the book to circulate like a modern novel.

Fragility – often associated, of course, with age – may also require supervision of the use of materials. Bindings may be on the verge of or already disintegrating; PAPER may be inherently weak or assaulted by acidic inks; illustrations may be vulnerable to illicit removal or damage from over-exposure to light. A host of related problems may require that materials be used only with great care – if they can be used at all. In addition, a binding may be not only fragile, but also fine; illustrators may be collectible in their own right; a famous person may have signed a book or, better yet, annotated it in some way; an unfamous person may have left extensive handwritten commentary in the text of an important writer; a playscript may be marked up for theatrical presentation. Unchecked reader carelessness is felt likely to prove more dangerous to the survival of objects possessing such characteristics than deliberate malice. Moreover, all of the primary materials in rare book libraries may at some time require, and presumably have been judged to deserve, conservatorial attention. Tight supervision as they are used improves the chances that they will receive such attention while they can still benefit from it.

Even ordinary reference books or modern books supplemental to a special subject, author or other collection, or the ordinary books from the library of a writer or scientist whose literary remains constitute a special collection, may function in a rare book library environment. Clearly, the number of reasons for locating books in such a place is almost without limit. All boil down to a judgement that the objects merit preservation.

Materials are placed in rare book libraries for more than increased supervision of their use and an eye on their preservation. To such protective goals, rare book libraries add the expansive goal of trying to make their holdings more accessible than the ordinary author, title and – in modern cataloguing – subject access points that most libraries regard as sufficient actually permit. Some forms of research may require, for example, access to all books known to have been in somebody's library, printed in a certain city between 1675 and 1701, written by a Latin poet with marginal annotations by a seventeenth-century Italian classicist, or bound in a specific shop or with metal clasps or foredge paintings. Many rare book libraries attempt to provide such specialized forms of access by creating files for provenance, imprint, chronology or bindings. They may also produce internal or published guides to large and complex collections, or annotate published reference tools to indicate their own holdings of particular authors or subjects. These services attempt to promote easy access through non-standard as well as standard approaches, compensating for the fact that rare book libraries normally disallow browsing in stack or storage areas. Provision of numerous access points in addition to author, title and subject seems essential if such departments are to be fully usable by the readers they hope to serve.

Institutional contexts

All of these generalizations are complicated by the varied natures not only of the materials that rare book libraries collect but also of the institutional contexts in which they exist. In one place, rare books may be collected and serviced by a rare book library that also includes commonplace materials not brought together elsewhere in such a unified way. In another, rare books may be housed with general (perhaps even circulating) collections and nonetheless include materials rarely found anywhere else in the country. Both extremes, and most conceivable variations on them, are exemplified in practice somewhere at the present time.

Rare books are found in NATIONAL LIBRARIES, UNIVERSITY LIBRARIES, SCHOOL LIBRARIES, PUBLIC LIBRARIES, governmental, independent and even some SPECIAL LIBRARIES, each with distinctive missions and programmes. They may themselves be libraries of enormous or small size, or part of big or little libraries. Generalizations must always be qualified by exceptions. Practices, institutional contexts and histories are not truly congruent even within type of library; they differ from country to country as well. The pattern of royal libraries eventually passing to state control and becoming either the basis for or part of major rare book collections – a pattern, for example, varyingly characteristic of both France and the United Kingdom – can have no analogue in countries without indigenous royal collectors, such as Canada, New Zealand or the USA. The vastly different histories of the growth of rare book collections at the BRITISH LIBRARY and the LIBRARY OF CONGRESS reflect national styles that differ far more than libraries alone. Within a centralizing British context it is, for instance, almost unimaginable to suppose that the national library would not be the repository of record for the vast bulk of English imprints. In the decentralized USA, by contrast, the *de facto* national library does not have that role. It was ceded long ago (at least for the period up to the end of the American Civil War) to an entirely independent, non-federal – indeed, non-state and non-copyright deposit – library in a small city in eastern Massachusetts (the American Antiquarian Society in Worcester).

Despite this caveat about generalizations, it remains fair to say, in general, that rare book libraries developed historically from 'reserve' collections of materials moved for safekeeping within an institution away from locations permitting public access or from collections that originated in private hands. Over time, such collections, assisted by private philanthropy – especially donations of collections created by individuals – formed the basis upon which modern rare book libraries, both within larger institutions and as independent institutions in their own right, developed and flourished.

In the early history of rare book libraries, closets in library directors' offices often figure: these were the places where rare books were kept. As the contents and interest in them increased, libraries found it useful to display them to potential benefactors. 'Treasure rooms' housing these books became the first departmental administrative structures devoted to their care. Particularly in institutions that began to

ape Germanic research-supporting models, treasure rooms were gradually transformed into rare-book libraries. Major growth followed the end of the Second World War, when university and other research-supporting institutions underwent vast expansion in many North American and European, and some South American, Asian and Pacific, countries. As the definition of topics on which research could profitably be undertaken expanded to include more recent as well as older subjects and authors, large and comprehensive collections of materials not intrinsically rare began to seem of sufficient intellectual (and sometimes monetary) value to warrant location in departments charged to facilitate research and to preserve its material basis. Rare book libraries, in fact if not in title, often expanded to become 'special collections' – that is, congeries of old books, rare books, new books and various more or less distinct author, subject and reference collections that could include any combination of printed books, periodicals and related, or separate, codices and archival collections of modern manuscripts.

Individuals had long gathered their own collections, whether to support their curiosity, scholarship, vanity or sense of public need. These collections tended over time to gravitate towards or become the basis of public institutions. Sir Robert Cotton's collection already served a quasi-public function in seventeenth-century England; it is now one of the older constituents of the British Library. This trend quickened during the eighteenth century and received an additional impetus following the French Revolution. University and other libraries similarly benefited from the work of collectors and philanthropists. Some established independent libraries based on their own holdings (e.g. the Folger Shakespeare Library in Washington, DC) or endowed libraries with funds sufficient to allow them to create major rare book resources *ex nihilo* (e.g. the Newberry Library in Chicago, Illinois). Others founded research libraries to augment the programmes of already extant libraries (e.g. Mrs Kenneth Spencer's gift establishing the University of Kansas's Kenneth Spencer Research Library). Others still gave materials they possessed as creators of or participants in the subjects of their collections. Harriet Monroe's gift of her modern poetry collection to the University of Chicago and H.L. Mencken's gifts from his manuscripts and books to Baltimore's Enoch Pratt Library and the New York Public Library exemplify this kind of gift. Many collectors simply gave their collections to an institution; thus the Bodleian Library at Oxford University acquired the John Johnson Collection of printed ephemera.

Undirected and unco-ordinated, these patterns of growth yielded many different kinds of institutions with rare book libraries. Universities and colleges, independent research libraries, great public institutions, historical societies, local, state, county or provincial and national libraries, some business and foundation libraries, art, history and natural history museums, genealogical societies: all sorts of institutions actively collect and make accessible materials through rare book departments. Some, although not all, are use- and programme-driven: they exist solely to support teaching and research. Others, viewing themselves as repositories only, restrict access unless specifically directed to grant it by some authority. Still others must balance individual research needs against broad educational objectives. They may, for example, periodically display selections from their collections in public exhibitions that prevent materials from being used. Some, although they may tolerate research, regard special collections as merely ancillary to their main collecting needs, assuming that most of their readers require modern books and periodicals to support their teaching and studies. Rare book libraries in such institutions may function only for exhibition or to impress visiting dignitaries. Some institutions may make almost no use of such materials at all, keeping them as necessary to their institution's self-image or prestige, because their retention is mandated by some authority or other, or because divestiture seems legally impossible, intimidatingly difficult or bad public relations. How an institution defines its mission is central to the use it makes of its rare books. Indeed, redefinition of that mission may occasionally lead to the dispersal of all or parts of such collections.

In general, and admitting the variability of the institutional contexts in which special collections function, the promotion of research, broadly conceived, and the preservation of its primary tools in a condition as close as possible to the condition in which they were issued, are the fundamental justifications for creating and maintaining rare book libraries. Normally expensive to operate, they need justification: not only do they require substantial expenditures for environmental and physical security of their contents; they are in addition staff-intensive, especially relative to the number of users they normally receive. A large library may receive more readers on a single day than its rare book department or analogue may serve in an entire year. Yet the staff of such a department may need to include, *inter alia*, specialists in reader services, preservation and conservation, exhibitions, early printed books, modern and privately printed books, original cataloguing of rare books and, perhaps, staff for any number of conceivable subspecialities significant to the collections for which the department cares. Language skills are an obvious prerequisite; so, too, is familiarity with a market geared to serve the needs of specialists. In addition, reading room supervisory staff must be provided.

As the kinds of materials collected by such departments become increasingly specialized, staff with correspondingly specialized educational backgrounds become necessary in order to interpret collections to their potential users and build them knowledgeably. Such staff tend to command somewhat higher salaries than staff in other departments, a sign not only of the complexity of special collections but also of the growing professionalism of the field itself. Originally handled by private collectors, with or without hired librarians, or by librarians who cared for them with their left hand, so to speak, while reserving their right hands for their 'real' work, special collections then often became the purview of the gentlemen librarians – the gendered word is used deliberately here – able to treat institutional collections as extensions of or analogues to their own. Now, with research a predominant if not a universal value in the world most libraries exist to support, staffing in special collections reflects a growing emphasis on both librarianship and subject expertise. Professional degrees in librarianship and advanced degrees in academic subject fields relevant to those represented in the collections are now commonly demanded of those aspiring to work in rare book libraries. This emphasis on credentials is complemented, as creation of this professional subspeciality proceeds, by the institutionalization of specialized professional organizations and the establishment of professional journals. These developments are typical of the self-definition modern professions undergo.

As the century and the millennium drew to a close, electronic and other high-technology forms of communication complemented the once-dominant printed book. Simultaneously, libraries and higher education have both entered a period of significant change. Speculation about the future of rare book libraries in such times is hazardous. Preservation of significant monuments from the printed records of the present is nonetheless likely to continue to appeal to many people, including scholars and collectors. Antiquarian and historical research may become less significant than they have been but, barring large-scale reversals in both research practices and the institutional base of the university itself, rare book libraries seem an entrenched part of the academic and library landscape. Some institutions that entered the field relatively late, which are uncertain in their commitments or that lack sufficient financial resources, will leave the field or retrench. Tradition and bureaucratic inertia, on the one hand, and a persistent interest in charting the past of most forms of human endeavour and creation, on the other, will likely provide for the growth, perhaps even the strengthening, of rare book libraries despite the intellectual changes and economic difficulties that persistently characterize intellectual and academic life in the modern era.

Further reading

Belanger, T. (ed.) (1983) 'Rare book librarianship: A special intensity', *Wilson Library Bulletin* 58: 96–119.

Cave, R. (1982) *Rare Book Librarianship*, 2nd edn, Library Association.

Cloonan, M.V. (ed.) (1987) 'Recent trends in rare book librarianship', *Library Trends* 36 (special issue).

'Guidelines for the security of rare books, manuscripts and other special collections' (1999) *College and Research Library News* 60: 741–8.

Ryan, M.T. (1991) 'Developing special collections in the '90s: A *fin-de-siècle* perspective', *Journal of Academic Librarianship* 17: 288–93.

Traister, E.D. (1992) 'What good is an old book?', *Rare Books and Manuscripts Librarianship* 7: 26–42.

Wendorf, R. (ed.) (1993) *Rare Book and Manuscript Libraries in the Twenty-first Century*, Cambridge, MA: Harvard University Library.

SEE ALSO: history of libraries; private libraries; provenance; research libraries

DANIEL TRAISTER

READ-ONLY MEMORY

Read-only memory (ROM) is a computer memory facility from which data can be retrieved, but which cannot be erased, altered or updated.

READING ROOM

A room set aside for the reading of books, periodicals and other materials in a library or information centre. Such facilities are necessarily provided in CLOSED-ACCESS libraries, but in practice reading rooms, or analogous study areas, exist in almost all libraries. The term is also used for a community facility independent of a library in which, whilst little or no reading material is provided, people may use their own study materials. Such facilities are particularly valuable in less developed countries, where a space with tables, chairs and artificial light in which students can work may be of very high community value.

READING RESEARCH

Research into the acquisition of reading skills and the reading habits of both young people and adults.

Reading is a key area of research in the field of education, and in other disciplines such as psychology, linguistics and the social sciences, including librarianship. The US National Reading Panel (1999) estimated that 100,000 research studies on reading had been published in the English language between 1996 and 1999. Teaching methods and the role of the new technologies were predominant research themes across these disciplines in the 1990s.

Teaching methods

Within the pedagogy of reading, research frequently focuses on initial reading instruction, and on the learning methods known as code emphasis (systematic instruction of alphabetic 'code' using phonics) and meaning emphasis (reading instruction that stresses comprehension and teaches skills as part of students' reading for meaning). Such research has indicated that systematic phonics instruction is a successful method of reading instruction, provided that it is embedded in a programme that provides meaningful encounters with text (US National Reading Panel 1999).

The role of the new technologies

Although the implications of electronic resources on reading have been the subject of considerable research and debate in the UK, this topic seems less prevalent in other countries. A consistent finding, however, is that INFORMATION AND COMMUNICATION TECHNOLOGY is no substitute for the teacher or the librarian in person (Hawes 1998).

Reading research is not only concerned with the acquisition of reading skills and the cognitive processes underlying the process of reading, but also with the sociology of reading. This incorporates the investigation of the reading habits of both adults and young people, and their preferences and attitudes towards reading.

The reading public

Statistical evidence collected within the library profession indicates that the public library service makes a major contribution to the reading habits of the general public. In the UK, 501,000,000 books are loaned each year, 260,000,000 (52 per cent) of which are FICTION (Davidson *et al.* 1998). In 2001, Euromonitor (2001) reported that, at any given moment, over 40 per cent of British adults are in the process of reading a book, with 78 per cent of adults purchasing new books in 2000.

> There has been a growth of research providing new evidence of the impact of imaginative literature on individuals and groups in society. Library service users, whatever their literacy level, are increasingly expecting the library to act as intermediary in the reading experience.
> (Toyne and Usherwood 2001)

Two major strands of sociological research are family LITERACY and reader development. The significant growth of these areas took place in the UK as a direct consequence of government initiatives since the beginning of the Labour administration in 1997. A large proportion of government funds has been allocated both to raising literacy standards in schools, via the National Literacy Strategy, and to promoting reading as a leisure activity, via PUBLIC LIBRARIES (DCMS 2001).

> A key aim of the National Year of Reading in the UK (September 1998–August 1999) was to raise the reading standards of both adults and young people, by involving the whole of

society in a wide-ranging campaign to encourage and promote reading.
> (National Literacy Trust 2000)

Research in this area is also conducted in developing countries: for example, UNESCO research into improving reading skills in Uganda examined how the home environment affects the reading capabilities of children in primary schools. The findings revealed that attitudes of parents affected children's reading, and that children from homes where parents were literate were more likely to enjoy reading and to be encouraged to read than in homes where parents were illiterate. In addition, the language used as a medium of instruction and the availability of reading materials in the local language were identified as factors influencing students' future interest in reading (Obua-otua 1997).

Reader development

Reader development, and adult readers in particular, experienced a dramatic growth in the UK at the turn of the twenty-first century, yet definitions of the term are sometimes unclear. Whereas reading development focuses on the acquisition of reading skills, reader development focuses on the reading experience itself. Forrest (2001) defines the concept in terms of audience development.

Because of the essentially practical nature of reader development, research within this area has been largely reported in non-refereed, professional documentation rather than through academic literature. The majority of texts are intended to be read by practitioners (librarians, booksellers and teachers), to provide transferable models of good practice in reading promotion.

Research methodologies

It has been illustrated that reading research is moving outwards from literacy learning in a formal, educational context to broader, society-based settings. Inevitably, this paradigm shift has affected research methodologies. For example, there has been a movement away from smaller-scale, controlled experimental studies of reading skills acquisition to more broadly conceived investigations of reading habits, adopting an ethnographic approach to document the roles of reading and writing in people's lives (Barton and Hamilton 1998).

Although it has generally been the case that policy makers placed a greater reliance on quantitative as opposed to qualitative data, there may be indications that they are starting to be more willing to use qualitative data in order to inform political decisions. Research conducted for programmes such as the National Year of Reading and the three-year Branching Out initiative (1998–2001) has provided data with which to link key initiatives on the government agenda, such as lifelong learning and social inclusion (Train and Elkin 2001).

It seems inevitable that research into the social aspects of literacy and reading will continue to be an area of significant future growth.

References

Barton, D. and Hamilton, M. (1998) *Local Literacies: Reading and Writing in One Community*, Routledge.

Davidson, J., Hicks, D. and McKearney, M. (1998) *The Next Issue: Reading Partnerships for Libraries*, The Arts Council of England and the Library Association.

DCMS (2001) *DCMS/Wolfson Public Libraries Challenge Fund: Annual Report 1999–2000*, The Department for Culture, Media and Sport (www.culture.gov.uk/heritage/index).

Euromonitor (2001) *Books in the UK 2001*, Euromonitor International.

Forrest, T. (2001) 'Who's afraid of those declining adult issues?', *Library Association Record* 103(3): 168–9.

Hawes, K. (1998) 'Reading the Internet', *Journal of Adolescent and Adult Literacy* 41(7): 563–5.

National Literacy Trust (2000) *Building a Nation of Readers: A Review of the National Year of Reading*, National Literacy Trust for the Department for Education and Employment.

Obua-otua, Y. (1997) *Improving Reading Skills in Primary Schools in Uganda*, UNESCO.

Toyne, J. and Usherwood, B. (2001) *Checking the Books: The Value and Impact of Public Library Book Reading*, University of Sheffield.

Train, B. and Elkin, J. (2001) *Branching Out: Overview of Evaluative Findings*, University of Central England in Birmingham.

US National Reading Panel (1999) *Teaching Children to Read*, US Department of Education.

Further reading

Book Marketing Limited (2000) *Reading the Situation: Book Reading, Buying and Borrowing Habits in Britain*, Book Marketing Limited, Library and Information Commission Report 34.

Eco, U. (1984) *The Role of the Reader – Explorations in the Semiotics of Texts*, Indiana University Press.

Hatt, F. (1976) *The Reading Process: A Framework for Analysis and Description*, Bingley.

McKearney, M. (1990) *Well Worth Reading*, Well Worth Reading.

Van Riel, R. and Fowler, O. (1996) *Opening the Book*, Bradford Libraries.

SEE ALSO: book trade; research in library and information science

BRIONY TRAIN

RECOMMENDER SYSTEMS

Electronic systems that are, in spirit, the same as published consumer reports. They draw together input from people with experience of particular products or services so as to help other potential buyers. An electronic recommender system can help people select INTERNET content by gathering recommendations that users supply, or, alternatively, by gathering the implicit recommendations in people's use of content (in the form of references to URLs in Usenet postings, personal favourites lists or the amount of time people spend with a site). The software can take into account factors such as past agreement between recommenders, or combine evaluations and content analysis to produce a recommendation.

Further reading

Resnick, P. and Varian, H. (eds.) (1997) 'Recommender systems', *Communications of the ACM* 40: 56–89, special section.

RECORD

Has a number of quite distinct and important meanings in LIS. In ARCHIVES and RECORDS MANAGEMENT it chiefly refers to a DOCUMENT arising from some transaction that preserves an account of the fact of the matter in permanent and discrete form. In a catalogue (see CATALOGUES) it is the data relating to a document that forms the substance of a catalogue or other entry. In computing it means a collection of related items of data, which for the purposes of operating systems is treated as representing a unit of information. In popular parlance, it can mean a gramophone record: a sound recording made on a vinyl disc.

SEE ALSO: organization of knowledge

RECORD OFFICE

A repository for the safekeeping of ARCHIVES and the deposit of contemporary official records. The record office, sometimes known as the 'archives' or archive office, cares for the preservation of the material deposited there, and organizes it for intellectual and physical access by administrators, researchers and interested members of the public.

SEE ALSO: information professions

RECORDS MANAGEMENT

A RECORD is a discrete item of transactional information captured on a recording medium and maintained by an organization for current and future need. Records management represents a systematic, ongoing, organization-wide managerial effort to control all records – regardless of medium – created or received in the normal course of an organization's affairs. These normally unpublished documents include correspondence, reports, printed forms, memoranda and directives. Sometimes called records and information management, records management – like archives management and corporate librarianship – is a discipline within the larger domain of INFORMATION MANAGEMENT. However, unlike the educational, research and cultural values of traditional LIBRARIANSHIP and archives management, the records management paradigm focuses on managerial issues, such as cost reduction and avoidance, improving productivity in information handling and the reduction of obsolete and unnecessary records.

Records management applies management principles and information technology techniques to the various stages of an information life cycle: creation, storage, retrieval, maintenance (for the amount of time required by a retention schedule) and final disposition (either transfer to an institutional archive – *c.* 5 per cent – or destruction – *c.* 95 per cent). A variation on the life cycle concept is the records continuum, which is gaining wide acceptance in Commonwealth countries. This precept takes a higher-order intellectual view of records, follows an integrated model rather than one made up of stages and stresses the need for records professionals to be more involved in the earliest planning stage of INFORMATION SYSTEMS.

History

Historically, the impetus to create records precedes the emergence of documents of literary value. For 10,000 years, in fact, records have been created as the information necessary for day-to-day operations of all organizations. As early as 8,000 BCE in the Tigris–Euphrates Valley, clay tokens of various shapes and sizes were created, organized and used to record complex business and administrative transactions. In fact, 90 per cent of all clay-based documents as yet recovered are administrative or commercial in nature.

In the modern period, the life cycle concept and the occupational title 'records manager' first emerged at the NATIONAL ARCHIVES OF THE UNITED STATES. An archivist, Emmett J. Leahy (1910–64), applied records management practices on a large scale for the US Navy during the paperwork explosion of the Second World War and created the first records centres used to store inactive records. Leahy tirelessly promoted expansion of the field and made a successful career of records management.

Objectives of records management

Records management programmes have numerous objectives; among them are:

- Cost reduction and avoidance in operating expenses (e.g. space, equipment, personnel time).
- Reduction of obsolete records.
- Improved efficiency and productivity by quick access to needed records.
- Protection of vital records, those needed for resumption of business in case of disaster.
- Reduction of incidents of lost information.
- Assimilation of information technologies appropriate to specific business processes.
- Protection of sensitive records from inappropriate access or use.
- Preservation of the organization's archival documents (those having permanent value for research, supporting legal requirements, long-term financial accountability and informational purposes).
- Enhanced litigation avoidance and support.
- Increased audit compliance.
- Protection of the rights of customers, staff and the organization as a whole.

PRIMARY FUNCTIONS
Records inventory

Upon completion of a needs assessment survey, an inventory or INFORMATION AUDIT of all records created and stored by an organization is the necessary first step in instituting records management. From the inventory is learned, for example, the locations of all information resources, the volume of inactive records to be transferred to a records centre each year and the identity of records needing special treatment (e.g. conversion to other media such as microform (see MICROFORMS) or OPTICAL DISK). Data from the inventory is the foundation for the organization's records retention schedules.

Records retention schedules

There are legal and economic reasons not to retain records any longer than necessary, and records retention policies and practices are central to any records management programme. Just as many other expensive resources have schedules for acquisition, maintenance and disposition, records are appraised for their retention value. Records management software applies the retention schedules and generates lists of inactive records for continuous removal from expensive office space to low-cost, high-volume records centres. In addition to managing the period of retention, the schedules spell out other features of each records type; e.g. whether the records are vital in character (needing special protection in the event of disaster), archival (having permanent value for historical, legal, financial or information purposes) or confidential and thus requiring special handling.

Electronic records

The principles of records management apply to AUDIOVISUAL MATERIALS, MULTIMEDIA and other forms of electronic records. Records managers, however, have been challenged by the mercurial nature of electronic records (e.g. ELECTRONIC MAIL, DATABASE records) and the difficulty in treating these records in groups rather than as discrete items. Records managers sometimes find their values at odds with those of information technologists. The records manager, for example, is concerned about the timely application of retention schedules to electronic records where the technology specialist sees little point in deleting records when digital media is so widely and inexpensively available.

Records standards

Two international standards – ISO 9000 and ISO 15489 – have drawn the attention of senior managers to the importance of effective records systems. ISO 9000 focuses on issues of quality; it sets numerous requirements for the creation and maintenance of records, particularly those related to maintaining standards of quality in manufacturing and services. ISO 15489 brings together the best practices in records management on an international level and adds greater credibility to records management as a global management discipline.

Further reading

Penn, I.A., Pennix, G.B. and Coulson, J. (1994) *Records Management Handbook*, 2nd edn, Gower.
Robek, M.F., Brown, G.F. and Stephens, D.O. (1995) *Information and Records Management: Document-Based Systems*, 4th edn, Glencoe-McGraw-Hill.

SEE ALSO: archives; information management; information professions; microforms; optical disk; preservation

J. MICHAEL PEMBERTON

REFERENCE BOOK

Defined in the *Oxford English Dictionary* (OED) as the type of book 'intended to be or suitable for being, referred to or consulted'. People who regularly go to libraries are inclined to define a reference book as any that cannot be checked out of the library. Today the INTERNET is a ubiquitous, unruly digital type of reference book that offers answers found previously only in print.

In the crush of some 1,400 to 1,600 reference works published each year in the USA, and approximately the same number in each Western country, the tradition is to include in the assemblage well-known forms. The generic 'reference book', designed to be consulted for bits of information rather than to be read consecutively, normally includes almanacs, bibliographies, biographical sources, dictionaries, directories, encyclopedias, geographical sources, handbooks, indexes, manuals and yearbooks. Government documents may cover all of these types.

Reference books, in print or on the Internet, are a means to the end of accurate, usually succinct responses to trivial or earth-shaking queries. Unquestionably, from South Africa to Alaska, from 3000 BC to the present, there have been people with questions and reference works in which to find the answers. Organization, format and certainly audiences have changed drastically, yet the need for either superficial or philosophical absolutes in response to questions remains the same.

What is different is the revolutionary change in format. Few librarians in the Western world today rely only on print. They turn to the Internet, as does a good portion of the population. Here can be found traditional reference works, from ABSTRACTING AND INDEXING SERVICES to encyclopedias and directories. What only a few years ago was available exclusively in print may now be only online, particularly indexes and current information sources. Indeed, it is likely that within the next decade or so all basic reference books will be in digital form. Only the more popular and heavily used (such as dictionaries and ready reference titles) will still be available in print. Ironically, the early, pioneering CD-ROM digital format has rapidly been replaced by its online junior. In the future, CD reference works will be less popular than print. The implications of all this for reference services, more or less reference books, is not clear. What is certain, though, is that online questions and answers are now a major part of today's reference world, both inside and outside the library.

The cuneiform tablet and the online database afford a seamless reminder of the orderly, laudable and durable nature of reference titles. One may turn to the standard bibliographies of primarily English-language reference books (e.g. the latest editions of *Guide to Reference Books*, *Guide to Reference Materials* or *Gale Directory of Databases*) for what title to buy, lease or desire. The latter bibliography will, if only indirectly, spell out the delights of sitting at a computer keyboard and punching in questions that will search scores of indexes and other reference works for answers.

The migration from print to digital is justified by simple economics. It costs less to put a reference work online. Paper, binding, distribution and similar traditional business expenses associated with the reference book all disappear. More important, the format switch and the flood of information that this made available have altered the role of the reference librarian. He or she must now, as never before, be a mediator between the masses of data and the needs of the individual, and particularly of the person unable to discriminate the good from the poor, the best from the better.

In the whirlwind of argument about future reference books, there remain some constants. Librarian or layperson must decide whether to buy or not to buy a title. Here one calls up traditional judgements suitable for a home with a dozen or so titles, to a library with 20,000 or more reference works, as well as access to hundreds of thousands of online sources, especially those dealing with current affairs, consumer queries and celebrated individuals from Maradona to Madonna. The evaluation, while differing in particulars, holds for both print and new technological formats. Essentially, one must ask: (1) 'What is the purpose of the work, and has the compiler, author or editorial board fulfilled that purpose?' The table of contents, introduction, preface or index will indicate, for example, whether or not a reference work on general environment actually is about that, or limited to political arguments concerning global warming. (2) 'Is the work authoritative and objective?' Here one looks to the publisher and to the qualifications of the person(s) who wrote the book by checking accuracy of facts, handling of minorities, debatable theories, discussions of questionable historical data and the like. (3) 'What does/doesn't the book cover?' This is important for libraries, where the scope of a reference work may do little more than duplicate similar titles on the shelves. Is there something new, different or added that gives this work an edge over earlier titles? (4) 'For whom is the work intended – the amateur, expert; young person, adult; or a combination?' This should be evident by reading a paragraph or two at random. (5) Other deciding points include cost, ease of use, illustrations, indexes, paper, size of type and related items.

Much of the aforementioned evaluation map is also employed to chart the success or failure of online services, CD-ROMs and new media. Obviously, there are added considerations, such as: the success or failure of the software; how often the material is updated; and how much or how little of the printed version is found in the new format. Authority and accuracy of data online are especially important to evaluate.

The reference book demands a disproportionate degree of evaluation because it is such an important source of information. Regardless of its future form, readers will turn to it for answers to questions and valuable insights in the chores of everyday living. In the realm of the personal or the public library, the reference book is an intellectual triumph that can take one from weighty matters of human fate to trivia. So it has been, and so it will be tomorrow.

References

Balay, R. (1996) *Guide to Reference Books*, American Library Association.
Gale Group (2000) *Gale Directory of Databases*, Gale.
Walford, A.J. (2000) *Guide to Reference Material*, 8th edn, Facet Publishing.

Further reading

Katz, W.A. (2001) *Introduction to Reference Work*, 2 vols, 8th edn, McGraw Hill (available online at www.mhhe.com/primis; also updated at www.mhhe.com/katz).
—— (1998) *Cuneiform to Computer: A History of Reference Sources*, Scarecrow Press.

W.A. KATZ

REFERENCE INTERVIEW

The dialogue between user and information worker that is intended to refine an original enquiry to the point at which potential sources of an answer can be identified. It is at this point of contact that the effect of a complex of preparatory activities, such as collection development and cataloguing, can be achieved, but the quality of the reference interview largely governs the extent of their effect. The reference interview was memorably described to his students by Roy Stokes (of the Loughborough Library School and the University of British Columbia) as 'sheer librarianship'.

Further reading

Jennerich, E.Z. and Jennerich, E.J. (1998) *The Reference Interview as Creative Art*, Englewood, NJ: Libraries Unlimited.

REFERENCE LIBRARIES

Traditionally, the providers of books meant to be referred to rather than read continuously, a selection of newspapers and periodicals, a local collection, quiet accommodation for private study and a specialist staff.

Reference libraries mainly developed in the nineteenth century. In the United Kingdom, following the adoption of the 1850 Public Libraries Act, a small number of public reference libraries were established. These libraries initially struggled for resources but in time some of those based in the larger cities such as Manchester and Birmingham became outstanding examples of their type, serving as regional as well as local centres. Many smaller local authorities also developed reference services, often separated from lending departments or as special sections within a single room, as space allowed.

Ideally, the modern reference library should provide an easily accessible, up-to-date, regularly edited stock supported by an adequate, if not generous, budget. The collection, for quick reference and for more in-depth study, should be available in varied formats, including all types of printed sources, such as books, periodicals, secondary services, GREY LITERATURE, EPHEMERA and AUDIOVISUAL MATERIALS. There should be access to ONLINE SERVICES, CD-ROM publications and the INTERNET, resources much more common in libraries in the USA than in the United Kingdom. All subjects should be encompassed, with an emphasis on local specialist needs such as those of the business community or local studies researchers (see LOCAL STUDIES COLLECTIONS).

The staff should consist of well-trained, well-established personnel, numerous enough to provide continuous availability of service and adequate supervision of trainee staff. They should be skilled in negotiating reference enquiries and familiar with the resources. The reference process should be efficiently and professionally undertaken using well-established procedures. The answers to enquiries should be provided speedily and, above all, accurately.

The accommodation should be appropriate both in layout and size, providing space for study and a clearly signed and continuously staffed enquiry point.

Although many excellent libraries strive to meet these standards, in reality a compromise usually has to be accepted. Few reference libraries can afford to be the embodiment of *Walford's Guide to Reference Material*. Few have a budget that supports the constant updating of stock necessary for an efficient service, and few do not experience the frustrations of limited access to outside resources because of financial restraints.

Staffing is rarely totally satisfactory. It is far from easy to keep together a team of trained, experienced professionals to provide continuity of service to the public. Too often, untrained clerical personnel are required to staff enquiry points. Even in reference libraries staffed by professionals, a patron may only have a 55 per cent chance of receiving a correct answer to an enquiry, according to the findings of a number of unobtrusive studies (Hernon and McClure 1986). With appropriate training this figure can be increased considerably although few libraries seem able or willing to invest in the time and expense of this practice.

One of the most significant developments in the 1990s was the trend towards integrating the reference and lending services into a single department or into subject departments such as business or commercial services. A major survey was carried out in 1992 by the LIBRARY ASSOCIATION Information Services Group (1993) on the provision of information services in British public libraries. The results showed that only one in ten libraries reported having a separate and separately staffed reference library or department.

The integrated department may possess a separate section for reference material, usually concentrating on quick-reference sources. Alternatively the reference and lending stock may be shelved together. The other most notable feature is that the reference librarian's desk would be replaced by a central enquiry point. The 'Enquiry' or 'Information desk' would normally be staffed by professional librarians, who may have to provide various services as well as assistance in subject and bibliographical enquiries, from both lending and reference stock, and, more commonly, provide community information.

The change of emphasis from reference work to 'information' work has not passed without its critics. Although commendable in assuming a service of better quality and efficiency, it more probably results from a desire to reduce staffing levels and save money in many instances.

There can be no doubt that technological developments, such as the advent of online services, have enhanced the quality of reference work in providing information from local databases and services from the major international hosts. Print-based stock, although still the main source of reference answers, has major weaknesses, such as its lack of currency. This is particularly exacerbated when financial resources do not allow the latest annual volume or edition of a quick reference book to be purchased to replace out-of-date stock. Electronic publications are able to complement the printed works, providing access to an enormous store of information previously inaccessible to most libraries and often far more up to date than that in the printed equivalents.

Online services, where direct costs can be measured, and political influences have been the twin catalysts for a further threat to the reference library, which has traditionally provided free service to its patrons. The 1980s saw the start of a contentious 'free versus fee' debate, with the implication that a possible two-tier type of service be created with a higher-quality reference/information service provided to those with the resources to pay for it. The business community and genealogical researchers have been the main targets of this policy where it has been implemented.

The future role of the reference library is brought into question with the advent of the Information Superhighway, which gives access to many traditional published information sources (e.g. *Encyclopaedia Britannica*) as well as previously unpublished information, much of spurious origins. The growth of the Internet, accessible from home computers, is signalling changes in the publishing infrastructure of the ways information is communicated. Although the technology for the 'VIRTUAL LIBRARY' is already in existence, the pace at which reference libraries will be connected to networked information sources will inevitably be cautiously slow. Reference librarians and library users have been slow to move from print to electronic information, which suggests that total dependency on a 'virtual library' is a far-off reality.

References

Library Association Information Services Group (1993) *Information Matters*, Library Association.

Walford, A.J. *Guide to Reference Material* (2000), 8th edn, Facet Publishing.

Further reading

Hernon, P. and McClure, C.R. (1986) 'Unobtrusive reference testing: The 55 percent rule', *Library Journal* 111: 37–41.

Koutnik, C. (1997) 'The World Wide Web is here: Is the end of printed reference sources near?', *RQ* 36: 422–9.

Lea, P.W. and Day, A.E. (1996) *Reference Information Sources*, Library Association.

Norton, B. (1988) *Charging for Library and Information Services*, Library Association.

Whittaker, K.A. (1990) 'Unobtrusive testing of reference enquiry work', *Library Review* 39: 50–4.

SEE ALSO: fee-based services; literature search; public libraries; reference book

PETER W. LEA

REFERRAL SERVICE

A service that directs enquirers to an appropriate source for the information or data that they require. Referral may be to libraries and documentation centres, or to appropriate agencies and individuals. A referral centre, as such, does not supply data or documents, but most commonly this area is referred to as information and referral, rather than referral alone.

RELATIONAL DATABASE

A DATABASE that uses the mathematical theory of relations and is structured as a series of two-dimensional tables. These can be manipulated by mathematical and algebraic operations, the latter using BOOLEAN LOGIC. Each record or entry in the database is made up of a list of connected items (such as a person's name, address, age, gender, etc.), and any subset of these can be easily retrieved.

REMOTE SENSING

The use of a variety of satellite-borne sensors, operating in the visible and infrared areas of the electromagnetic spectrum, to collect data about the earth's surface and transmit it to a host computer. This data is used in a considerable variety of applications, from weather and agricultural forecasting to land use, mineral surveying and pollution monitoring. Remote sensing has proved to be a powerful tool for accurate recording and forecasting of weather. The current mapping work of agencies such as the UK Ordnance Survey is now heavily dependent on remote sensing, the results of which are fed into databases of map information, from which various geographical information products, such as printed maps, can be produced.

SEE ALSO: Geographic Information Systems

RENTAL RIGHT

An INTELLECTUAL PROPERTY right, introduced in the UK 1988 Copyright Act, by which any rental to the public of COPYRIGHT materials, such as sound recordings or software, is restricted to the copyright owner. In practice, rental rights tend to be enforced through licence agreements (see LICENCES).

REPORT LITERATURE

Reports are identified as a distinct form of documentation because of their volume and significance in scientific and technical fields. This classic form of GREY LITERATURE contains information that may or may not eventually appear in some conventionally published form, but that, because of its currency, must be available to practitioners in the field. The definition adopted by a library or information service may include technical notes and memoranda, preprints, conference proceedings and papers, and research and development reports. Increasingly, report literature is also to be found on the WORLD WIDE WEB.

Further reading

Moody, M.K. (1996) 'Technical report literature on the World Wide Web', *Internet Reference Services Quarterly* 1: 7–21.

REPROGRAPHY

Reprography is an all-embracing term coined in the early 1960s to describe, according to the *Oxford English Dictionary*, 'The branch of technology concerned with the copying and reproduction of documentary and graphic material'. A succinct yet comprehensive definition was created by the Institute of Reprographic Technology (established in 1961 and later subsumed into the Institute for Administrative Management): 'The technology of producing and reproducing two-dimensional visual communication media in business and administrative operations.' The spectrum of reprography ranges from limited-volume facsimile copying (or photocopying), through quantity duplication, to small-scale print production. The ubiquity of INFORMATION AND COMMUNICATION TECHNOLOGY (ICT) has not served to reduce the importance of reprography, as organizations and individuals continue to require immense volumes of photocopies and document reproduction in other forms. Indeed, because reprography plays a part in capturing and transforming the output of ICT operations, its importance has arguably been enhanced.

Several different types of technical methods for facsimile copying have been developed in the past and some, though not all, are now relegated to history. Modern copiers embody clean, speedy, flexible, economical and easy operation with very high copy quality. Selected technologies are described briefly below. They may be divided into camera methods, incorporating optical devices for imaging, and non-camera methods, or contact methods, where document and copy material are placed together for imaging. Camera methods include electrophotographic and photostat processes.

The electrophotographic transfer technique (featured, for example, in Xerox machines) relies on the photosensitive properties of certain materials, selenium being the most usual, although some organic materials exhibit the same tendency. The document to be copied is scanned and its image projected on to a photosensitive drum that has already been electrostatically charged. Where white light falls on the drum the charge is dispersed; the dark areas representing the print remain charged. Toner in the form of fine black powder is introduced on to the drum and adheres to the charged (print) areas. The powder is then transferred on to plain paper by pressure and is subsequently 'fused' or fixed to the paper by heat. The finished copy on plain paper emerges instantly usable and permanent.

Some machines employ liquid toners, which are colloidal suspensions of toner material in a dispersant or solvent, to perform the print 'developing' function. Recent developments include machines that employ a laser to describe the image on the drum and scanners that digitize document images, thus enabling them to be extensively manipulated and the output relayed to different machines. Colour copiers are also available.

Less frequently encountered now is the electrophotographic direct technique, which uses special coated paper that is electrostatically sensitive. The copy image is projected directly on to the coated paper, which has already been charged. The charge on the paper is dispersed where light falls and is retained in the dark (print) areas. The paper is fed through a toner bath, where the 'developer' adheres to the charged areas. The solvent or dispersant quickly evaporates – sometimes with the aid of a heated air current – to leave the toner image on the paper. Coated paper has a characteristic 'feel' and appearance, and is less acceptable than plain paper for many applications. The process therefore has fewer supporters.

Far less widely used nowadays is the once popular photostat process, which employed a camera containing sensitized paper instead of film to 'photograph' the material to be copied. The paper received chemical processing using conventional photographic developing methods. As a true photographic process it offered the facility of enabling variable-sized copies of originals to be made long before rival processes were available.

Examples of non-camera methods include the dyeline or diazo process and the thermographic process.

The dyeline process relies on the translucency of the original to be copied and is not therefore suitable for material printed on both sides. It uses special copying paper coated with diazonium salts. The original is placed over the copy paper and exposed to ultraviolet light, which breaks down the salts in the areas subjected to light. Where print has shielded the light the salts remain. The copy is 'developed' by exposure to ammonia vapour or heat, which renders the salts visible. The image has the characteristic mauve appearance. The dyeline process was a common method for copying plans, charts and drawings, as well as documents. The hazards and special handling required for ammonia developers have greatly reduced the convenience and appeal of this process.

The thermographic process uses special copying material that is heat-sensitive. The original and copy material are placed together and exposed to infrared radiation, which strikes the carbon in the print, producing heat that is then absorbed by the copy material to form an image. This is frequently encountered in copiers for making overhead transparency acetates, as well as in document copiers. The copy material remains heat-sensitive and copies can be damaged by careless storage near heat sources. Not all original material can be copied by this process because some inks and colours do not contain sufficient carbon.

There are several duplicating technologies and they vary considerably in sophistication, complexity, cost and quality of output. Some are briefly outlined below.

Electrophotographic photocopiers, though primarily regarded as machines for creating individual facsimile copies of documents, have, because of their reliability and convenience, encroached into copy duplicating. They are capable of producing very high-quality work in a range of quantities economically and without the need for specialist and skilled operation.

The spirit duplicating or hectographic process involves the creation of a master by writing or typing on a sheet placed against a wax-coated backing card. The master, once prepared, is attached to a roller in a machine that has a mechanism for introducing alcohol spirit on to the master from a reservoir. Copy paper is fed through the machine. For each copy, a small amount of spirit dissolves a little wax on the master and the image is transferred on to the copy paper. The process is suitable for a fairly limited number of copies (up to 300 perhaps) before the wax is exhausted. Copies are generally of indifferent quality and appearance. A variety of copy colours can be achieved by using different wax backings.

Stencil duplicating – also eponymously termed Roneo or Gestetner duplicating, after two prominent equipment suppliers in the field – is another technique. The duplicating master is formed from a sheet or membrane that is coated to resist ink. The text or image to be duplicated is 'cut' on to the sheet with a typewriter set on the 'stencil' setting or with a scratching tool or stylus. Electronically cut stencil masters can also be created from existing typescript or similar copy. The cut portions in the master will allow ink to permeate through on to copy paper.

The master is attached to a roller in a machine with an ink reservoir. Paper is fed through the machine. For each copy a small amount of ink is 'squeezed' through the master on to the copy paper. Fairly porous paper is normally used to absorb the ink rapidly. Copy quality is tolerable and the process can produce moderate quantities (several hundreds) of copies. The whole operation is quite messy, however, especially for the inexperienced.

Small offset is a highly refined process that employs as its basis the art of lithography. Lithography is dependent upon the various properties of water, grease and ink. A printing plate has an image created on it in a greasy medium. It is then 'washed' with water. Water stays on the plain areas of the plate, but is repelled by the 'greasy' parts. Ink is now introduced and adheres to the greasy parts but not to the 'wet' areas. Paper is placed on the plate and a print taken off.

In a small offset machine this basic process is embodied in a rotary machine for speed and economy. A printing plate is prepared photographically from camera-ready copy. The plate contains a right-reading positive image and can be easily proof-checked. The plate is placed on a roller in the machine that has fluid and ink reservoirs. Ink on the plate is transferred (offset) to an intermediate roller to reverse the image and subsequently to paper. Printing plates can be metal, plastic or even paper.

The process allows for very high-quality print production and is economic from about 30 copies to upwards of 5,000. It is also speedy once the plate has been prepared. A variety of text and images can be copied. The capital cost for equipping a small offset operation is, however, relatively high and it requires skilled operation.

To conclude, modern reprographic technology has greatly assisted the management and delivery of library and information services, and has facilitated fundamental improvements in the nature of services offered, ranging from speedy on-demand facsimile copying to quality newsletter production. Alongside ELECTROCOPYING it is a key technology for modern information work.

SEE ALSO: informatics

J.E. DAVIES

RESEARCH IN LIBRARY AND INFORMATION SCIENCE

Goldhor defines research as 'any investigation which seeks to increase one's knowledge of a given situation' (1972: 7) and in these changing times for library and information science (LIS), a broad spectrum of research continues. There is a healthy tension between what Brophy (2001: 15) highlights as a predominance of 'practice-based (LIS) research in the UK' and the more theoretical approaches, and there is activity in both areas. The conjunction of CONSULTANCY (e.g. the UK group Comedia) and research is demonstrated in some of the work in the UK and Australia on public libraries.

Methodologies

Williamson's (2000) text outlines many of the methodologies and techniques in use, though by its own admission omits the important research facets of BIBLIOMETRICS, content analysis and ethics. Bibliometrics and its subsets, including CITATION ANALYSIS, continue to draw activity and debate. Some international trends in LIS research are reported by Rochester and Vakkari who found, in their examination of LIS research up until 1994/5 in Scandinavia, Australia, China, Spain, Turkey and the UK, 'a remarkable degree of variation of emphases and trends in research in the countries examined' (in prep.: 22). They found conceptual method and surveys amongst the popular methodologies, with historical method following; experimental and qualitative methods were little used. Other analyses of LIS research confirm the diversity, a rise in qualitative methodologies, the popularity of the survey and the multidisciplinarity in methods used. Quantitative analyses, although not as common, are seen in work on transaction and Web log analyses, cost-effectiveness studies, and cost–benefit analyses. The use of the electronic domain to assist in research projects brings with it ethical monitoring of the validity of the data sought and received. The reflections of editors Hernon and Schwartz in the journal *Library and Information Science Research* provide a useful commentary on the validity of some methods.

Topics

Research topics discussed at the Library Theory and Research Section's contributions to the last eight IFLA conferences could be seen as indicative of the work underway worldwide. They cover a wide range: teaching research methods, LIS research for social development, bibliometrics, digital libraries (see DIGITAL LIBRARY), professional communication, LIS research in Asia and the EU, library history, LIS research itself, codes of ethics, multicultural library service provision and collaboration between theory and practice. Research into issues of scholarly communication and the sub-issues of copyright and publication licensing have occupied the more practical research projects of large research libraries around the world. The public library's role in society has underpinned the research in that area.

Communication

The major ways of communicating LIS research are through conferences, journals, websites and theses, of which there are many. As examples, the 8th International Conference on Scientometrics and Informetrics held in Sydney, Australia, in July 2001 drew an international collection of seventy-two full and twenty-six poster papers. Research into information-seeking and its context within information retrieval is closely followed by the electronic journal *Information Research* (http://informationr.net/ir/) and the conference series ISIC (Information Seeking in Context). Journals from various parts of the world should not be forgotten, even though much of the LIS journal literature is paper, English-language and UK- and USA-based, and some content analyses of LIS research have shown a heavy reliance on the literature from the USA and UK. The rise of the electronic journal as a research publication medium is recognised in LIS, with the journals *LIBRES* (http://libres.curtin.edu.au) and *Information Research* being two of the longer standing publications. The steady production of Master's and Doctoral theses is captured by services like *Current Research in Library and Information Science* and *Dissertation Abstracts*. They are also listed on some LIS School Web pages. Research-in-progress and more substantial work can also be found on many information-oriented Web pages (e.g. the EC's Information Society Web page: http://europa.eu.int/information_society/services/sitemap/index_en.htm).

Funding

There have been some significant funding initiatives including the European Commission's research projects on the information society, and the Follett Committee's Report inspired a number of research initiatives in the UK: the Electronic Libraries Programme (eLib) being one. UK funding for LIS research was mainly through the British Library's Research and Development Department (and its successor the British Library Research and Innovation Centre) whose role, in 1999, was taken over by the Library and Information Commission (LIC), that being subsumed in 2000 by Re:source – a merger of LIC and the Museums and Galleries Commission. This could be the end of a 'long and distinguished history for. . .library R&D' (Brophy 2001: 17). Funding in the USA is various and includes government funding, and consortia-based and grant initiatives. The recent interest in public library research, e.g. in the UK and Australia, has often been funded at the local government level.

References

Brophy, P. (2001) 'The historical context of eLib: Practice-based library research in the UK', *Library Management* 22(1/2): 15–18.

Goldhor, H. (1972) *An Introduction to Scientific Research in Librarianship*, University of Illinois Graduate School of Library Science.

Rochester, M.K. and Vakkari, P. (in prep.) *International Library and Information Science Research: A Comparison of National Trends*, IFLA Professional Report.

Williamson, K. (2000) *Research Methods for Students and Professionals: Information Management and Systems*, Centre for Information Studies, Charles Sturt University. [Textbooks on library research appear infrequently. This is the latest.]

Further reading

Goodall, D. (1996) 'It ain't what you do, it's the way that you do it', *Public Library Journal* 11(3): 69–76.

Hamilton, J.C. (1999) 'The ethics of conducting social-science research on the Internet', *The Chronicle of Higher Education* XLVI: B6–B7.

Klasson, M. (1997) 'Public library research in Sweden', *Scandinavian Public Library Quarterly* 3: 29–33.

Pettigrew, K.E. and McKechnie, L.E.F. (2001) 'The use of theory in information science research', *Journal of the American Society for Information Science and Technology* 52(1): 62–73.

Powell, R.R. (1999) 'Recent trends in research: A methodological essay', *Library and Information Science Research* 21(1): 91–119.

SEE ALSO: code of professional conduct; electronic journals; European Union information policies; information ethics

KERRY SMITH

RESEARCH LIBRARIES GROUP

Research Libraries Group (RLG) is a consortium of major universities and research institutions in the USA. Its members collaborate on a number of projects and ongoing programmes, of which RLG's automated information network, RLIN, is probably the most generally known. It combines databases and computer systems to serve the materials-processing and public-service requirements of RLG's members and of many non-member institutions.

RESEARCH LIBRARIES

Libraries that provide materials and facilities for research, usually in the humanities. The words 'research' and 'library' have become tightly linked in a commonly used phrase only since the formation of the Association of Research Libraries in 1932. The goal of that organization was to provide a framework for co-operation among large libraries that were seen as being similar even though sources of support – university, municipality or nation – differed. 'Research libraries' began, therefore, as an umbrella term of practical utility rather than as a concept, and it has so continued in the USA.

The phrase has also been used in the UK, though not in the name of an organization. On the European continent the term 'research library' has rarely been used, though there are exceptions, as in the Swedish catalogue of accessions of foreign works in Swedish research libraries (*Accessionskatalog over utländsk litteratur i svenska forsknings-bibliotek*), begun in 1956, as well as in the name or description of two German libraries. In the name of the European Consortium of Research Libraries, which was formed in 1992 to create a catalogue of early printed books, we see the same pattern as in the USA.

The word 'research' has had such positive connotations in US society that institutions other than the very largest libraries have wished to dwell under its reflected light. Thus, even before the decade of the 1930s was out – in 1939 – the journal *College and Research Libraries* began publication, even though its parent body was then the College and Reference Section, only later renamed the Association of College and Research Libraries. Later, in 1952, that association published a monograph about staffing in a 'small research library'. Examples of grossly inflationary usage exist.

College libraries, as well as specialized but small libraries, are, of course, employed by researchers, but in them the scholar cannot carry out the type of investigations that merit use of the term 'research library'. Those libraries to which the phrase can justly be applied have been best described by Fabian (1983).

The research library, writes Fabian, is the humanist's laboratory, a place where the scholar, beginning with a thesis or with a question, can pursue it wherever it leads, among both primary and secondary materials. At the same time that the humanist's laboratory allows the researcher to follow – with efficiency – an idea that spontaneously arises, it also permits accidental discovery, as, for instance, through exploring on the spot a large body of material in search of the relevant.

More than a large stock of books is, as Fabian notes, ideally part of the research library. This began to be explicitly recognized in the USA in the 1920s and 1930s. Herbert Putnam, Librarian of Congress, pioneered in delivering a paper on *American Libraries in Relation to Scholarly Studies and Research* (1929); Louis Round Wilson, in his 'The service of libraries in promoting scholarship and research' (Wilson 1933), described in considerable detail the direction in which many US libraries would move. Wilson's paper was stimulated by the dedication in 1932 of two libraries devoted exclusively to scholarship and research: the Furness Memorial Library of Shakespeareana of the University of Pennsylvania and the Folger Shakespeare Library, the latter one of the independent research libraries that became ever more active in fostering scholarship – and ever more influential as models.

Wilson, besides emphasizing the accumulation of materials, wrote of making them available: through the organization of space for readers, by means of catalogues, by provision for INTER-LIBRARY LENDING and for reproduction. Under 'Personal assistance to scholars', Wilson wrote of the need for availability of specialists who could assist researchers, and he also commented on the role of the librarian as preserver. For Wilson the librarian also had the role of teacher, as well as that of compiler, editor and publisher. Wilson's last section was devoted to international cooperation, through international associations and by means of exchanges and international loans. He concluded by mentioning the function of libraries as stimulators of 'scholarly interests and attitudes' (Wilson 1933).

What Wilson in 1933 described and advocated has recently been noted as characteristic of a true research library, by Fabian as well as by Knoche (1993) in his 'Die Forschungsbibliothek: Umrisse eines in Deutschland neuen Bibliothekstyps'. Knoche's twelve characteristics include a more or less independent large library devoted to humanistic scholarship that uses historical materials and is capable of supplying from its own resources significant quantities of primary as well as secondary literature; a good catalogue; work-

places for scholars and fellowships to aid in their support, conservation and preservation activities; scholarship on the history of the library itself; headquarters for large scholarly projects; and sponsorship of symposia and conferences.

Fabian carried the key elements of the concept of research library one step further – universal collections and access to them – when he proposed to create complete collections of German imprints, in the original and in microform. This is being done in Germany, as it has been in the Anglo-American world, with short-title catalogues and the microfilming based on them. DIGITIZATION may further foster comprehensiveness, though no one knows to what extent the mass of millions of early printed materials will ever actually be available as an electronic research collection.

The concept of the research library, based as it is on the way scholars work (or ideally should be able to work), has continuing utility in an era of networked libraries and information. It reminds us that large numbers of researchers continue to need access to quantities of physical objects from the past, not merely to texts. Even more importantly, it holds up the ideal of universality – that is, of the desired work being immediately to hand rather than being obtainable only with delay from a distributed national research collection.

References

Fabian, B. (1983) *Buch, Bibliothek und geisteswissenschaftliche Forschung*, Vandenhoeck and Ruprecht.

Knoche, M. (1993) 'Die Forschungsbibliothek: Umrisse eines in Deutschland neuen Bibliothekstyps', *Bibliothek. Forschung und Praxis* 17: 291–300.

Wilson, L.W. (1933) 'The service of libraries in promoting scholarship and research', *Library Quarterly* 3: 127–45.

Further reading

Kyrillidou, M. (2000) 'Research library trends: ARL statistics', *Journal of Academic Librarianship* 26: 427–36.

SEE ALSO: academic libraries; rare-book libraries

KENNETH E. CARPENTER

RESERVE COLLECTION

Has two quite contradictory meanings. It is used either to refer to library materials for which there is infrequent demand and which consequently are not kept on open shelves. Alternatively it can mean material in academic libraries for which there is great demand, because of being placed on reading lists, which is therefore held in a separate short-loan collection.

SEE ALSO: information management

REVIEW ARTICLE

A substantial article, usually published in a periodical, which reviews the literature on a particular topic, evaluating an extensive range of materials and drawing attention to the most significant publications. As such, it is distinct from a book review or a review of any other single document.

SEE ALSO: dissemination of information; scholarly communication

RIDER, ARTHUR FREMONT (1885–1962)

University librarian and innovator in librarianship.

Born in Trenton, New Jersey, he spent his earlier years as a writer and editor. In 1933 he became Librarian of Wesleyan University's Olin Library. The collections more than doubled in number while he was librarian, and he took the opportunity to experiment with catalogues, cooperative arrangements and the shelving of the books. His compact shelving programme for little-used books was new and controversial. Amongst his many writings, *The Scholar and the Future of the Research Library: A Problem and its Solution* (1944) very clearly reveals both his achievement and his failure. The book analysed research library growth and concluded that collections doubled in size approximately every sixteen years. This, coupled with the observation that most research materials were infrequently used, led Rider to advocate the use of microcards as a cost-effective means of information storage. Although his solution has been overtaken by technological developments, and some of his pronouncements about the future of microform (see MICROFORMS) now seem slightly ridiculous, his analysis of the problem is still a significant contribution to the literature of INFORMATION SCIENCE. Appropriately, the National Microfilm

Association awarded him its annual medal in 1961.

SEE ALSO: research libraries

ROYALTY

Payment made to an AUTHOR, or other creator, by the publisher of a book or other knowledge product, normally calculated as a percentage of the retail price of the copies sold. It can also mean the fee paid in respect of a licence for the use of copyright material (see LICENCES).

SEE ALSO: intellectual property

RURAL LIBRARY SERVICES

Rural library services operate in an environment of geographical remoteness, characterized by small population units and consequent modest financial support. The first PUBLIC LIBRARIES were established in urban areas, where large populations are concentrated into relatively small areas. Rural communities live in areas of low population density: definitions of 'rural' vary from areas with less than 100 persons (New Zealand), to those with less than 500 persons (Canada) or 10,000 persons (USA).

Whereas all rural communities tend to be dispersed, agricultural-based and relatively unsophisticated, a great disparity also exists between such societies from country to country, according to political, administrative, historical and cultural factors. In the Third World, rural communities have the added problems of low levels of LITERACY, multiplicity of languages and lack of a communications infrastructure. The percentage of the population living in rural areas of developed countries is decreasing and can be as low as below 10 per cent. On the other hand, sub-Saharan AFRICA has the most rural of the world's populations, with an estimate of over 80 per cent living in rural areas. The nature of a rural library service differs between countries, so as to be able to satisfy different information needs.

Origins and development of rural library services

Public library services were already a well-established feature of urban local government when the reading needs of rural populations in the USA were first addressed at the beginning of the twentieth century. This interest was part of a broader concern for improving the conditions of rural life. The chosen solution was to set up county libraries, i.e. large-area public library services. The first county library was established in 1898 in Ohio, and subsequently two approaches were used: either an existing city library was contracted to serve the county or a library service was set up that was directly responsible to the county government. Enabling legislation was at the state level. By 1914, fifty-seven such libraries had been established. In Great Britain it was not until 1919 that legislation was passed permitting county councils to set up libraries. By 1931 there were county libraries in all counties of Great Britain. The basic components of a county library service were a central library, branch libraries and mobile libraries (see MOBILE LIBRARY). In both countries, the system was strengthened in post-war years by federal and national legislation (the Library Services Act of 1956 in the USA and the Public Libraries Act of 1964 in the UK) encouraging consolidation of smaller independent libraries into the large-unit services and incorporating the rural library services into national public library services through resource- and system-sharing.

Similar systems became the pattern for rural library services in those countries that were part of the Anglo-American library tradition, e.g. the NORDIC COUNTRIES, Canada, South Africa, Australia, New Zealand. Even in the USSR, it was a US county library organizer who visited Russia in 1920 to advise the new government on rural library service. The Carnegie Corporation was particularly instrumental in the setting up of rural library services. It was a report of the Carnegie United Kingdom Trust that led to the 1919 legislation in the UK and it was the Carnegie Corporation that provided the impetus for rural library services in the southern Dominions during the 1930s. New Zealand in 1938 set up community libraries with regular loans of books through the County Library Service. In South Africa and the former Rhodesia, similar services were financed for both white and non-white populations. In Kenya a circulating library scheme for Europeans was started in 1931 and the African Library Service in 1950. The national library services set up in the newly independent countries of Africa and Asia aimed to serve rural areas in much the same way, through a central library, branch libraries, book boxes, mobile libraries and books by mail.

New directions

COMMUNITY INFORMATION

In the second half of the 1970s, in the UK and other developed countries, there were several reviews of information services in general which revealed that rural areas were inadequately covered and that libraries played little part in the rural information system. There was a rediscovery of the role of the library as a community information centre. Rural library services now look beyond traditional book-based reference and loan services.

INFORMATION FOR RURAL DEVELOPMENT

In the developing world, it was obvious by the 1980s that there had been little progress in rural development and that the centralized national library services (see NATIONAL LIBRARIES) set up at independence had failed to establish services to rural areas. Since the mid-1980s research has been carried out into the identification of information needs for rural development and into the most appropriate channels of communication, including the role of indigenous information systems. There has been renewed activity within the library sector. Many national library systems have set up rural library projects aimed at meeting community needs and advancing literacy in a more dynamic way. Communities have also been helped to start their own resource centres or set up an information service aimed at satisfying a specific need.

INFORMATION AND COMMUNICATION TECHNOLOGY

In the 1990s, the potential of INFORMATION AND COMMUNICATION TECHNOLOGY (ICT) to provide access to information in rural communities has been recognized. Multipurpose community TELECENTRES have been established in both the developed and developing world, not only providing access to ICT-based services but also including libraries, training facilities and seminar rooms. Evaluation of ownership and operating models is in progress.

SOURCES OF INFORMATION

In developed countries, many national libraries, public libraries and library associations have undertaken projects on rural information services. In the developing world, UNESCO, IFLA, IDRC and the Commonwealth Secretariat have financed initiatives in rural library services since the early 1990s, and information can be found in their publications.

Further reading

Rural Libraries. (1980–) Vol. 1–. Center for Rural Library Services, Department of Library Science, Clarion University of Pennsylvania [a semi-annual journal].

SEE ALSO: Russia and the former Soviet Union; social exclusion and libraries; telecentres

DIANA ROSENBERG

RUSSIA AND THE FORMER SOVIET UNION

With the collapse of the USSR, the vast library system established by the Soviet state faced tremendous challenges. Indeed, the problems and successes of the Russian library system can be understood only in the context of the Soviet past.

The Soviet system

One of the most cherished clichés of the Soviet era was to call the USSR 'the world's foremost nation of readers'. Indeed, the country's BOOK TRADE had few rivals worldwide either in the number of titles published or in their print runs. Thanks to a planned and co-ordinated development of librarianship, a state-run network was formed that included 326,000 libraries of all types with an aggregate stock of more than 5.6 billion volumes. (These are summarized data for the fifteen republics of the former Soviet Union.) The Soviet library network was one of the world's biggest and played a crucial part in the progress of Soviet culture, research and education. More than half of the population were library users. Library services were provided to rural populations; millions of first-generation readers gained access to books. Under Soviet rule, illiteracy was eradicated throughout the country, while dozens of smaller ethnic groups were granted books in their own languages.

The network of mass libraries accounted for over one-third of the total libraries and held about 40 per cent of the country's aggregate book stock. The mass-library concept was used by the Soviet state as an instrument of ideological education. This type of library, while displaying all the external features of Western-style PUBLIC LIBRARIES, differed from them in essence. Perhaps the one principle that these mass libraries had in common with their Western counterparts was that of service which is free at the point of use. Most of the other universally recognized principles either proved to be empty declarations (such as general availability, maximum satisfaction of users' interests, etc.) or were not recognized at all (freedom of reading, or freedom of exchange of information).

Fundamental documents that determined libraries' activities started with their basic task – the education of Soviet people in the spirit of Marxist-Leninist ideas. Access to information, especially social, political, economic and humanitarian information, was limited and strictly controlled by Soviet ideologists. Thus there were 'special storage departments', actually libraries within libraries holding 'closed' literature (ideologically suspect titles in the main) accessible to a select few, CENSORSHIP in book publishing and in BOOK SELECTION, and compilation of so-called recommendatory bibliographies. Reading guidance theory constituted the leading dogma of library service. The underlying assumption was that the librarians were in a position to 'teach' users because of their superior knowledge of what was good for them, and librarians were accountable to the state rather than to the public. The library was regarded as a state-run production unit and was required to fulfil planned assignments for numbers of users and book issues (most importantly, for the loan of socio-political literature). According to different surveys, the satisfaction rate averaged 50 to 60 per cent.

The post-Soviet changes

With the disintegration of the Soviet Union and the breakdown of the former socio-economic order, libraries found themselves free of the ideological diktat of the state and for the first time were able to determine the content of their work.

The last decade of the twentieth century was a period of considerable change and development in the Russian library scene. Inevitable tensions and losses in some areas were set off by real achievements in others. Library funding suffered severe cuts (the funds provided by the state were barely enough to cover salary costs); libraries found it increasingly difficult to cover the costs of acquisition, preservation and access. As the country went through the hard times of political and economic reforms, progressing from totalitarian state towards democracy and open society, the demand was growing for books on law, economics, management, ecology, electronics, computers, for textbooks and language courses. The change in reading requirements influenced the publishing trade; new publishers emerged, while the established houses revised their priorities. In 1990 censorship was abolished. Libraries opened up their 'special storage departments' and patrons were free to access previously banned books. Thus, a religious literature reading room has been in operation for several years in the Library for Foreign Literature, as have two reading rooms devoted to overseas Russian authors in that library and in the Russian State Library.

The number of new publications accessioned by the Russian Ministry of Culture libraries in 1995 was less than half of the 1990 figure. The situation in libraries of other affiliations (academic, school and research) was even worse, with village libraries the most adversely affected. Since the old book trade infrastructure has effectively collapsed and the new one is still in the making, as many as 90 per cent of newly printed publications never find their way into bookstores in many regions of the country.

Decentralization of administration and government, and increasing regionalization of all spheres of life, resulted in great disparities in the funding of libraries from region to region, broadening the divide between the possibilities and level of access to information locally and centrally. In 1995 the acquisition expenditures of general research libraries in the constituent members of the Russian Federation differed greatly, some being fifteen times the size of others. 'Information poor' areas appeared, another obstacle to the stabilization of society.

POSITIVE TRENDS

For the vast majority of the Russian population, public libraries remained the main resource to meet growing information requirements. Use of state-supported public libraries, primarily the larger ones, rose appreciably, mostly due to young patrons. Although the number of public libraries was down 15 per cent from 1985, their use was up by the same 15 per cent. The rates of use of central universal libraries in the constituent members of the Russian Federation went up more than 30 per cent since 1993.

The total number of libraries decreased slightly over the years of economic reform in Russia. Numerous Communist Party libraries and trade-union reading rooms ceased to exist. Some small rural and municipal libraries were closed and their holdings turned over to larger regional libraries. At the same time, new libraries appeared that were affiliated to new government bodies, e.g. presidential administration, parliament, etc. In addition, libraries were set up by various foundations, movements and organizations. A unique library of Russian literature from abroad was established in Moscow in 1996. Some Russian regions, with their industry almost at a standstill, saw the construction of large modern facilities (e.g. in such cities as Rostov-on-Don, Omsk, Krasnoyarsk, Ryazan). Therefore the overall number of libraries remains large.

THE PATTERN OF PROVISION

As of 1 January 1999, there were approximately 150,000 libraries in Russia, including more than 54,000 public libraries (down from over 62,000 in 1990). The biggest libraries in the country are the two national libraries: the Russian State Library in Moscow (formerly the V.I. Lenin State Library), with a collection of 42 million items, and the National Library of Russia in St Petersburg, with a collection of 32 million; and also the Library of the Russian Academy of Sciences, with a collection of 20 million. The network of public libraries is the most diverse and extensive. They have 60 million users who annually borrow nearly 1.5 billion items. Nationwide, there is one fixed-point library for every 3,000 people.

The great majority of libraries serving the general public are part of a network subordinated to the Ministry of Culture of the Russian Federation. They include nine federal libraries, 282 central libraries in all the eighty-nine constituent members of the Russian Federation (general research libraries, children's and youth libraries, and libraries for the blind) and 49,700 public municipal libraries, with 39,400 libraries in rural communities and 10,300 in towns and cities. In the 1970s such libraries were incorporated into centralized library networks headed by the central libraries of cities, districts and rural areas.

The system of higher and vocational education operates approximately 3,000 libraries of universities, academies, institutes and colleges. The general education system runs over 63,000 school libraries. The Russian Academy of Sciences has a large network of 375 RESEARCH LIBRARIES. There are also numerous SPECIAL LIBRARIES set up by the ministries during the Soviet period. For example, there are over 3,500 sci-tech libraries in industry and in the transportation and communication sectors; more than 700 special libraries in agriculture; nearly 1,500 libraries in healthcare and medicine.

Modern Russian librarianship has retained some characteristics of the Soviet library system. Library services and information resources of Russian libraries are organized on the basis of two main principles, territorial and disciplinary. In practically every sector of the national economy there is a federal-level central library serving as the main library of the special libraries network and funded by the parent ministry. In addition, a central regional library with a comprehensive collection that also includes scientific literature is in operation in each of the constituent members that make up the Russian Federation. These libraries are financed from regional budgets and serve as centres of methodology for all public libraries of their respective area (republic, territory or region).

A special bibliographic utility – the Russian Book Chamber – is responsible for national BIBLIOGRAPHIC CONTROL of Russian publications, which represents a different model from other countries, where national bibliographies are usually handled by NATIONAL LIBRARIES.

Radical political and economic reforms in Russia caused sweeping changes in government information and cultural policies that had a great influence on libraries. Two federal laws were enacted in 1994: *Library Law* and *Legal Deposit Copy Law*. Statutory force was given to the principles of library work, guaranteeing the right of individuals, public organizations, nations and ethnic groups to have free access to information, free spiritual development, access to the values of national and global culture, and to cultural, scientific and educational activities. Never before had this conception of the role and tasks of libraries been stated at a government level.

Federal professional laws fostered the enactment of respective regional laws by constituent members of the Russian Federation. At present almost all of them have already adopted or are elaborating local legislation on libraries and local legal deposit, which develops the respective federal acts.

By 1995 priorities had been defined for the national policy of modernization of librarianship pursued by the Ministry of Culture of the Russian Federation. Automation of library services topped the list. In 1995 another relevant federal law was passed – *On Information, Informatization, and Information Protection*. This law identifies library holdings and information products as universally accessible national information resources so as to enable libraries to be responsible for the satisfaction of public information needs as fully as possible.

AUTOMATION

LIBRARY AUTOMATION began in the majority of Russian libraries in the late 1980s and early 1990s. Over the past ten years, many Russian libraries automated cataloguing procedures and started building electronic catalogues. They have accumulated some experience in ELECTRONIC DOCUMENT DELIVERY. Some of the larger research libraries developed high-capacity Online Public-Access Catalogues (OPACS) and DATABASES, which are in wide use. Hundreds of libraries (many federal and over half of the regional libraries) have gained access to the Internet via dial-up and dedicated lines, and made themselves known in the information world by their own Web servers. The merging of library catalogues into co-operative systems and the development of digital libraries (see DIGITAL LIBRARY) is on the agenda today.

LIBNET, the programme to develop Russia's national information and library computer network, addresses a major social problem – providing Russian citizens with free access to the distributed information resources of Russian and foreign libraries. The development and implementation of this federal library networking programme has been supervised by the Inter-departmental Board of Experts on the Informatization of Russian Libraries under the Ministry of Culture of the Russian Federation. Board members include leaders and library automation professionals from some of the largest Russian libraries of different affiliations. The LIBNET programme plans to develop, between 1998 and 2001, the core component of the national library and computer network incorporating 150 libraries – all the larger libraries of Russia as well as the central research libraries of the Russian Federation constituent members. However, economic instability in the country hampers implementation of both library laws and the LIBNET programme.

FUNDING

Many accomplishments in the last ten years were made possible by the active efforts of top- and medium-level managers of libraries, rather than government policy. Fundraising became one of their primary concerns. The easiest way out for some libraries is to rent their premises to private businesses. Many others have extended the assortment of FEE-BASED SERVICES by using technology (photocopying, scanning, modelling) and providing some complex information services that go beyond the scope of conventional free services. Some libraries also offer printing, photographic and microfilming services; bind and restore books; teach foreign languages; and prepare and hold conferences, seminars and expositions. Organizations take an active interest in these services. It should be emphasized that free library service, as guaranteed by the law, remains unchanged. The paid services usually provide only a small income and represent a small contribution to libraries' budgets.

Therefore, the main source of funding to support many library projects has become the programmes and projects of different charitable foundations and organizations, such as the Open Society Institute, the Russian Foundation for Basic Research and others. The megaproject named 'Pushkin Library' is an example of this kind of initiative. The project, planned for three years, obtained support of $100 million from the Open Society Institute. Under the project, 3,500 Russian libraries can purchase up to 1,000 books every year on preferential terms.

NEW IDEAS

In the new Russia, the social role of libraries is evolving. In seeking a new identity for itself the library profession is increasingly turning to international librarianship for concepts and values, trying to develop a new world outlook and a new service model. In addition to their traditional functions of education, preservation and extension of the cultural heritage, libraries are acquiring new roles as information centres that provide public access to national and global information networks and databases. The librarian's role is being revised: no longer the user's teacher, but an intermediary between user and information. The concept of reading guidance, long established in the Soviet librarianship, is fast losing adherents. Traditional technologies change inside libraries, as do the forms of public library services and the patterns of interaction with ruling bodies.

Libraries in today's Russia – and by no means only the largest and richest ones, but also ordinary municipal and district libraries – can no longer imagine living without an extensive exhibition area, a linguistics reading room, a mediatheque and an Internet class.

THE PROFESSION

Liberation from the ideological diktat and the centralized control of the state furthered development of a professional movement among librarians and other members of the INFORMATION PROFESSIONS. In the late 1980s and early 1990s several LIBRARY ASSOCIATIONS were formed. The first ones appeared in Moscow and St Petersburg – the Moscow Library Association and the St Petersburg Library Society (1989). They were followed by more than thirty regional associations and societies. In October 1994 the Russian Library Association (RLA) was formally constituted in Moscow. It is the largest library association in Russia, which unites more than 130 institutional members, including libraries of different levels and departments, regional library associations and societies. In 1995 the RLA was admitted to IFLA as a national associated member. The number of Russian institutional IFLA members is steadily growing as Russian libraries strive to become active members of the international library community.

In conclusion, during the ten years since the break-up of the Soviet system tremendous changes have taken place in Russian librarianship. Libraries have assumed a totally new ideological orientation. They have completely revised their professional activities and are building a new model of the library: a genuine institution of culture, education and information.

Further reading

A variety of material on the subject is to be found in Russia's three leading library journals, *Bibliotekovedenie* (until 1993 *Sovetskoe bibliotekovedenie*), *Bibliografiya* (until 1992 *Sovetskaya bibliografiya*) and *Biblioteka* (until 1992 *Bibliotekar*).

Chubaryan, O.S. (1976) *Obshchee bibliotekovedenie* [General library science], 3rd edn, Kniga, pp. 47 –9.

Genieva, E.Yu. (2000) 'Kuda dvizhets'a Rossija? Rol' bibliotek v transformatsii gosudarstva' [Which direction is Russia going? The role of libraries in transforming the state], *Biblioteka* 8: 6 –9.

Kuzmin, E.I. (1999) *Bibliotechnaja Rossija na rubezhe tis'acheletij* [Library Russia at the turn of the millennium], Libereja, p. 224.

EKATERINA GENIEVA

S

SCHELLENBERG, THEODORE R. (1903–70)

Widely regarded as responsible for defining the content of modern archival knowledge and practice (along with Hilary JENKINSON).

Born to a Mennonite family in Kansas, he took his AB in 1928 and his MA in 1930 at the University of Kansas, and a PhD in History at the University of Pennsylvania. He was appointed to a post at the National Archives in 1935, and returned there in 1948 after war service and other archival employment, retiring in 1963. His career at the National Archives was one of turbulent relationships with colleagues, but outstanding professional success.

Arguably Schellenberg's greatest specific contribution to archive science was his systematic statement of appraisal principles, criteria and guidelines. He wrote his *Modern Archives: Principles and Techniques* (Chicago: University of Chicago Press, 1956) as a replacement for Jenkinson's *Manual of Archive Administration*, then the most authoritative work, but regarded by Schellenberg as outdated and unreadable. His second major work was the controversial *Management of Archives* (Washington, DC: National Archives, 1965), which was the fruit of a retirement in which he taught and advised all over the world. The most contentious proposition in the book was that archive science should be taught in library schools, both because the schools were concerned with methodological training, and because librarians were responsible for the care of so much archive material. Together the books are still consistently cited, and are read as basic texts for programmes of archival studies.

Further reading

Smith, Jane F. (1981) 'Schellenberg: Americanizer and popularizer', *American Archivist* 44: 313–26.

SCHOLARLY COMMUNICATION

The word 'scholarly' is generally used of activities that entail research or investigation, especially in an academic environment. As such, it covers any topic that appears in the higher-education curriculum, from science, through the social sciences, to the humanities. Scholarly communication typically occurs between researchers, but can also involve COMMUNICATION between a researcher and someone who wishes to apply the research (e.g. in an industrial process, in the production of a play), or between a researcher and a general audience.

The growth of scholarly communication

Down the centuries, research has typically been communicated in parallel by speech and writing. Such scholarly communication originated with the Greeks in the last few centuries BC. So 'academic discussions' hark back to the Academy in Athens, while the works of Greek scholars, especially those of Aristotle, established the tradition of written research. The appearance of modern research depended particularly on developments in Western Europe during the sixteenth and seventeenth centuries. By the nineteenth century, the volume of research being produced was such that individual researchers were forced to become more and more specialized in their interests. Correspondingly, the communication of research became concentrated on a series of more restricted audiences. This has been reflected in the growth of both specialized societies and specialized journals over the past century and a half. Nowadays, most research is done by professionals (i.e. people who are paid to do research), though amateur contributions continue to be valuable in some disciplines, especially in the humanities. The main motivation for doing research is to aid the development of the subject and to obtain personal recognition. (For professionals, the latter point is connected with advancement in their career.) Both of these entail the communication of research, especially via print.

Quality control

The ways in which research is communicated naturally tend to follow the course of the research itself. While the research is still under way, most communication about it is informal. This may involve discussions with colleagues, or, later, presentation at a departmental seminar. As the research nears completion, it may be presented at national or international conferences. Finally, when complete, the research is submitted for formal publication. For scholarly research, most publication is via journals or books, though reports are also favoured in some research fields.

One of the key questions in this publication process is whether the research is of acceptable quality. The mechanism for deciding this is most clearly defined for journals. Journal editors typically rely on external referees for assistance in assessing submitted material. Their suggestions frequently make recommendations for improving submissions, rather than for immediate acceptance or rejection. Assessing the quality of books is less well organized. Although publishers employ expert readers to vet submitted manuscripts, much of the quality assessment occurs after publication in the form of book reviews. There is no standard system for evaluating reports. Research appearing in these is, however, often summarized for submission to journals, or extended into books.

Differences between subjects

The nature of scholarly communication often depends on the subject concerned. One external factor that can affect communication is the financial status of the research discipline.

Many science subjects are of major importance in industry and for defence, so they attract considerable funding. Many humanities subjects do not. More money is therefore available to support the publication and dissemination of research in the sciences than in the humanities. Expectations regarding communication also differ. Science is generally expected to attract a global audience, both within universities and outside; the same is not always true of humanities research. Scientists often expect their research to be published rapidly, whereas there is usually less urgency in the need to publish humanities research. Factors such as these lead to differing communication emphases in different subjects.

A comparison of journals in the sciences and in the humanities reveals that the former, on average, contain more material, appear more frequently and have a larger and/or wider circulation than the latter. Less obviously, the rejection rate for articles submitted to humanities journals is usually appreciably higher than for science journals. This difference in success rate can be related to economic factors – a lack of finance to support humanities journals – and the nature of the subject, not least the greater ease of reaching agreement between referees in the sciences. These factors tend to favour journal publishing in the sciences; conversely, they favour book publishing in the humanities. It follows that interaction with publishers differs. For much of its history, scientific research has typically been publicized in learned society journals. Commercial publishers now compete successfully with these, but many high-prestige journals continue to be produced by learned societies. Although some learned societies in the humanities publish research monographs of considerable excellence, many of the most important books in the humanities have been produced by independent publishers (including, under this heading, university presses).

Electronic communication

The continual growth in research publication, especially via journals, has led to problems of access. The proportion of the research literature that a university library, for example, can afford to acquire is continually decreasing. The growth of electronic publishing has been seen as one way of alleviating this problem. How it might best do this is currently unclear, not least because of uncertainties regarding COPYRIGHT. However, significant progress has been made in some subjects. In physics, for example, where speed of publication is important, a highly organized system of rapid electronic publication of research already exists. This bypasses the normal process of quality control, but, like much science, physics research is typically a team effort. In consequence, informal refereeing usually occurs within the group.

Electronic communication actually introduces some generic differences as compared with print-based communication. Two aspects, in particular, may affect scholarly communication. The first is that networking blurs the traditional dividing line between formal and informal communication. Though, say, ELECTRONIC MAIL and ELECTRONIC JOURNALS may appear to be two separate activities, it is actually possible to create a continuum of communication possibilities between the two. The second point is that networking evens out the communication opportunities between disciplines. The same subsidized NETWORKS are available to all academics, and researchers in the humanities seem to be using them with almost as much enthusiasm as scientists. Overall, all disciplines are likely to develop a new flexibility as regards scholarly communication in the future.

Further reading

Harnad, S. (www.cogsci.soton.ac.uk/harnad) [presents an ongoing discussion of possible changes due to the electronic publishing of research].
Meadows, A.J. (1998) *Communicating Research*, Academic Press [looks in detail at the points raised here].
Tenopir, C. and King, D.W. (2000) *Towards Electronic Journals*, Special Libraries Association Publishing [is particularly good on usage and economics].
Weller, A.C. (2001) *Editorial Peer Review*, American Society for Information Science and Technology [provides a detailed discussion of quality control].

SEE ALSO: communication; digital library; electronic-journal archives; hybrid libraries

JACK MEADOWS

SCHOOL LIBRARIES

The school library, perhaps known as the school library media centre or the school library resource centre, is found in schools at all educational phases. It supports the needs of teachers, other school staff and pupils in all areas of the curriculum – literacy and reading; information skills and independent learning – and gives equality of opportunity for all.

The role of the school library

The IFLA/UNESCO manifesto for school libraries (IFLA 2000), defines the role and goals as follows:

> The school library provides information and ideas that are fundamental to functioning successfully in today's society, which is increasingly information and knowledge-based. The school library equips students with lifelong learning skills and develops the imagination, enabling them to live as responsible citizens.

Goals of the school library

The school library is integral to the educational process.

The following are essential to the development of literacy, information literacy, teaching, learning and culture, and are core school library services:

- Supporting and enhancing educational goals as outlined in the school's mission and curriculum.
- Developing and sustaining in children the habit and enjoyment of reading and learning, and the use of libraries throughout their lives.
- Offering opportunities for experiences in creating and using information for knowledge, understanding, imagination and enjoyment.
- Supporting all students in learning and practising skills for evaluating and using information, regardless of form, format or medium, including sensitivity to the modes of communication within the community.
- Providing access to local, regional, national and global resources and opportunities that expose learners to diverse ideas, experiences and opinions.
- Organizing activities that encourage cultural and social awareness and sensitivity.
- Working with students, teachers, administrators and parents to achieve the mission of the school.
- Proclaiming the concept that intellectual freedom and access to information are essential to effective and responsible citizenship and participation in a democracy.
- Promoting reading and the resources and

services of the school library to the whole school community and beyond.

- The school library fulfils these functions by developing policies and services, selecting and acquiring resources, providing physical and intellectual access to appropriate sources of information, providing instructional facilities and employing trained staff.

In order to achieve these goals school libraries need certain attributes:

- Sufficient resources to support the curriculum and pupils' reading for pleasure, wide-ranging in format, print, non-print and electronic, and subject matter to cater for all tastes and interests.
- Accommodation that is attractive, suitable, accessible with adequate study, reading and display areas, appropriately furnished; a programme of promotional activities; access to the library at all times; adequate and appropriate staffing; good partnerships and relationships with other facilities and organizations, including public libraries.

All of this should be within a well thought out, published policy ensuring effective library management

School libraries around the world

There is an inequality of library provision in schools between countries and within countries, and there are school libraries everywhere that are greatly in need of improvement.

Issues, which affect the development of good school libraries universally, are the inadequate training programmes for school librarians; the employment of non-qualified staff in school libraries; and the low status of the school librarian within the school and the wider library community. And yet there is evidence from research in several places, but particularly in the USA, which links good-quality library provision with higher levels of pupil achievement. The importance of appropriate staffing is illustrated by the studies. However, even in countries where school library provision is good, there are problems in relation to the recruitment and retention of school library personnel.

There are excellent school libraries, fully staffed with professionally qualified librarians and support personnel, which are well resourced, but there are many that give an inadequate service to the teachers and pupils. They have too few books and other materials, and those that they have are poor, in terms of physical condition, being outdated and irrelevant to the curriculum and needs of the children. In some countries the lack of available quality resources and/or insufficient funding means that this situation cannot be improved. The development of school libraries is often hampered by a poor understanding by a school's senior management and teaching staff of the part the library can play in school life, especially in the delivery of the curriculum. This does not lead to good co-operation and partnership between teacher and librarian. The lack of national policies, standards and guidelines in many countries stifles improvement.

School libraries all over the world are being transformed by the technological developments that are enabling global communication and transforming learning opportunities. The need for learners to be information literate, as well as literate in a traditional sense, is self-evident. School libraries have the potential to give all children and young people equal access to electronic resources and print, visual and aural sources. Some schools do not recognize the need for the library to be integral to information and communication technology developments in the school, so the school library cannot fulfil that potential. In some countries, the technology is not available in many schools, and there is an increasing gap between those who have and those who have not.

Despite all of these drawbacks, there is a widespread belief in the efficacy of school libraries throughout formal education, and guidelines and standards are being produced and shared. There is an awareness that the role of the library in the educational process and providing a foundation for using libraries throughout life will need to be promulgated at all levels, from Ministries of Education to schools themselves, continuously.

The dissemination of the IFLA/UNESCO School Library Manifesto provides the tools to undertake this promotion.

References

IFLA/UNESCO (2000) *The School Library in Teaching*

and Learning for All: The School Library Manifesto, International Federation of Library Associations and Institutions.

Further reading

Bernhard, P. (ed.) (1997) *Resource Book for School Libraries and Resource Centres*, IFLA Publication 79, K.G. Saur.

Information Power: Building Partnerships for Learning (1998) American Library Association.

Primary School Library Guidelines (2000) The Library Association.

Tilke, A. (ed.) (1998) *Library Association Guidelines for Secondary School Libraries*, The Library Association.

Williams, D. and Wavell, C. (2001) *The Impact of the School Library Resource Centre on Learning*, Library and Information Commission research report 112, Robert Gordon University for Re:source: The Council for Museums, Archives and Libraries.

GLENYS WILLARS

SCIENTOMETRICS

This term achieved prominence with the foundation of the journal *Scientometrics* in 1977. Scientometrics forms part of the sociology of science and is often applied to issues of science policy-making. It involves quantitative studies of scientific activities including, significantly, publication. For this reason, it overlaps with BIBLIOMETRICS. It aims, through the revelation of objective quantitative regularities, to determine the stage reached by an intellectual domain and suggest possible lines of future development.

SEE ALSO: informetrics

SCRIPT

A means of expressing language in graphic form, whether it be alphabetic, syllabic or ideographic. It usually refers to handwritten rather than printed characters. The term also has other more specialized meanings, such as the text of a play, film or broadcast. In computing, a script indicates a section of program code associated with a particular event or condition and which, when the event or condition occurs, is executed so that an appropriate reaction takes place.

SEE ALSO: communication

SEARCH

The act of a user, an information worker on the user's behalf, or an automated system activated by the user or the intermediary, in making a systematic investigation to obtain data or information. Information professionals will be expected to devise a coherent search strategy for this purpose. In database software, the process of seeking out an entry, keyword or phrase is called the search and may, for instance, use several keywords strung together and qualified by BOOLEAN LOGIC operators such as 'AND', 'OR' and 'NOT'.

SEARCH ENGINES

A search engine is a computer program that allows the user to search the INTERNET and find particular terms or phrases. The software allows this search to be made at very high speed, so that search engines have become an essential tool in Internet usage, and particularly in searching the WORLD WIDE WEB.

The current Internet search engines evolved in the early 1990s along with the use of the suite of Internet protocols enabling communication, using public domain software (FREEWARE), between computers across the globe. The emergence of the World Wide Web, has led to the creation of a vast number of documents, for the most part coded with HyperText MARK-UP LANGUAGE (HTML), stored on computers around the world. Search engines are very much a part of this distributed and dynamic information environment and are designed to help people locate information. The information that they locate is contained in the form of Web pages and a collection of these located at a UNIFORM RESOURCE LOCATOR (URL) is referred to as a 'website'. Currently, there are several hundred search engines: some are specific to particular regions or countries, others claim to be international and some help to retrieve specific subject matter or media or cater to a particular age group such as children. There are three main types of search engine: single search engines, metasearch engines and subject indexes. Lastly it is also necessary to discuss intelligent agents briefly.

SINGLE SEARCH ENGINES

The single search engines are also known as 'key word indexes'. These search engines are the most common. One element to the search engine is the 'crawler' software (also known as 'bots', 'robot' or 'spiders'). The crawler automatically navigates the Internet identifying websites. Once it finds a site it will retrieve enough data to index that site within its central database. When using a search engine it is the index that is searched. The extent of the indexing varies between search engines. In addition the extent a search engine explores the links and indexes the various levels of a website also varies. This is known as the 'depth of the crawl'. Search engines will often retrieve information by retrieving the terms held within key portions of a HTML document. These may be METADATA stored within a certain part of the document. The frequency with which the crawler updates the search engine's index also varies. Hence the data stored on one search engine's database may not be as up to date as on others. Search engines also vary in terms of their geographic coverage and the number of websites that they index. Search engines also tend to concentrate on different types of material. Some, for example, will explicitly index files that contain images. Others will index newsgroup material, for example, 'Google Groups'. The number of sites indexed, material indexed, depth of indexing, frequency of update and depth of crawl, therefore, all form key evaluation criteria. It should be noted, however, that not all websites indexed by search engines will have been found by the crawler software. In some cases people will have alerted the search engine organization to a particular site and may have paid to get their site indexed by the search engine. Search engines that accept this alerting method include Alta Vista, Google, Fast and Lycos. The players, however, keep changing as search engines compete with each other by developing algorithms that improve relevance of retrieved items ('hits'), indexing new material and adding output and information management features. New arrivals as from 2001 include Wisenut, Teoma and Daypop.

A key aspect of the single search engine is its search functionality. The amount of functionality varies between search engines and often a basic and advanced search interface is provided. The advanced search interface allows the user to be more specific and use a wider range of criteria to construct his or her search. Most single search engines allow Boolean searching, that is, to be able to combine terms using AND, OR and NOT. In addition they may offer proximity searching, where terms must be within a defined number of words of each other. They also offer truncation and various forms of stemming either at the beginning of, end of or within the term. Field searching is enabled by some search engines, and searchers can limit their search to particular parts of the document, such as the title, the URL and HYPERTEXT links to and from a website. In addition the language, geographic area and file type (examples include graphic files (JPEG, GIF), portable document format (PDF) and HTML) can be specified.

Once the search engine has conducted a search it will prioritize the 'hits' using algorithms to rank the output, hopefully putting the more relevant hits at the top of the list. As mentioned above, one of the ways search engines compete with each other is the relevance of the items the user sees within the first two screens of hits. Generally users do not browse more than two screens of hits and it is therefore important to get the most relevant first. The ranking of hits is achieved through 'best-match' algorithms. In the past databases worked on 'exact-match' algorithms, that is, if the terms that were requested were in the text it was considered relevant. Single search engines use the 'best-match' principle where they use the terms in the search to prioritize hits using statistical calculations. Commonly these are based on the frequency of search terms occurring in the item, the frequency of terms occurring next or near each other and where those terms occur. If, for example, the search terms appear near the beginning of the document or in the title then that document will be ranked highly and displayed near the start of the list. Other criteria may also be used. The frequency of a search term appearing in the entire index can also be a factor. A term that is common across the index, in other words found in many items, may be given a low weighting since it is not discriminatory. Recently search engines have incorporated other criteria in their relevance judgements. For example some search engines, such as Google and Lycos, rank more highly those sites that have many hypertext links pointing to them from other sites. The assumption here is that, if a site has been 'pointed to' by others, people are recommending that site.

The presentation of the hits on the screen will vary between search engines. Search engines will provide varying amounts of data. In general they will show the URL and portions of text that contain the search terms. Web pages from the same site may be clustered together and in some cases search engines, such as Wisenut, will cluster retrieved hits under broad subjects. Features such as this have increased over the years along with functionality, and are designed to help the user to find material that is related to their needs. Other features utilize relevance feedback technology where users can indicate that they want to search for more items similar to a particular hit. The search engine will then reformulate the search algorithm based on the original query and characteristics of the hit that the user has indicated as relevant.

Single search engines have evolved over the years, gradually catering to the needs of different users. When they were first developed the search entry box and ranking algorithms were seen as a searcher's panacea. However this perception was largely that of the technical developers who were relatively new to large-scale information retrieval and had not experienced the development of online databases and CD-ROM technologies. This was apparent from the lack of help systems, limited functionality and the 'one solution for all'.

METASEARCH ENGINES

The metasearch engines are similar to the single search engines. They enable the user, however, to search the index of more than one single search engine. For example, Dogpile, Mamma or Surfwax enable the user to search in the common single search engines simultaneously. The advantage of this is that the user only has to learn the functionality of one search engine and does not have to repeat the search in more than one search engine. The disadvantage is that the metasearch engine will only use the functionality that applies to all the single search engines and the unique characteristics of individual search engines will be lost. Metasearch engines will vary in terms of the number of search engines they search, the functionality offered and the output. Certain metasearch engines, for example Surfwax, give summaries of websites retrieved, enabling one to decide whether or not it is worth further investigation. Generally metasearch engines will de-duplicate the hits retrieved from the various search engines.

SUBJECT INDEX SEARCH ENGINES

The third main type of search engine is the 'subject index', also known as 'subject directories'. Subject indexes evolved because people wanted to bring order to the Internet and help others find good information. These search tools are, in a sense, portals (see PORTALS AND GATEWAYS) in that they gather material together from the Web and make it available to the user in one place. Subject indexes, such as Yahoo!, tend to use both search engines and people to search the Web, and then organize what has been found under subject headings. Yahoo!, for example, uses UNIVERSAL DECIMAL CLASSIFICATION to organize the websites that it has found. The advantage of the subject index is that the initial search has been done for the user and sites found on topics. This process generally involves some kind of review process that implies that the websites in a subject index are of good quality. However fewer items will be found via the subject search engine than via a single search engine. Users can either browse the site, clicking on subject headings, and eventually will be provided with a list of websites, or they can use the search engine to search the subject index site. In the event of no items being retrieved, either users will be asked if they wish the search to be broadened, or the system will automatically search the index of a search engine that indexes the wider Web.

Again, as with single search engines, the purpose, the subject content, geographic coverage, number of items indexed, functionality and output will vary between subject indexes. Some subject indexes focus on specific subject areas. These tend to be called portals. However, portals tend to provide access to a wider range of data than a subject index. They give, for example, access to software or subject-specific discussion lists or collections of primary data. These distinctions are becoming increasingly blurred. Vortals are a variation of the portal. These tend to provide access to data concerning a vertical market and usually offer opportunities for E-COMMERCE and recruitment.

INTELLIGENT AGENTS

Lastly a new development, but compared to the above three categories of search engine of relatively minor significance, are what have been termed 'intelligent agents'. These are a form of crawler but cater to the individual. An intelligent agent enables the user to set up a search strategy and then this will be automatically run on a regular basis so that when the user opens up their e-mail account, if the agent has found new items, they will be shown. Agents can be general or concentrate on a specific media such as news. The latter are known as 'newsbots'. Crayon, for example, will create your own newspaper depending on your profile and what it has found. These agents need to be 'trained', that is, a profile needs to be set up. Some, such as Autonomy Knowledge Update, can be modified over time so that depending on the headlines one reads the search algorithm will change. In addition it is possible for the user to indicate items that they want more of using relevance feedback technology.

Further reading

Internet.com (2002) Search engine watch (http://search-enginewatch.com/).

Search Engine Showdown (2002) (http://searchengine-showdown.com/).

Search Tools Consulting (2002) (www.searchtools.com/) [search tools for websites and intranets].

MARK HEPWORTH AND IAN MURRAY

SECONDARY LITERATURE

For the librarian this refers to the bibliographic sources in which books, articles and other PRIMARY LITERATURE are listed. However, for the historian it refers to the books and articles that are written using historical record material as sources, these sources being regarded as the primary literature.

SECURITY IN LIBRARIES

Ensuring security in libraries depends on designing out or minimizing the potential for crime and disruptive activity.

The security of library users, staff and resources is a crucially important consideration that demands close attention, yet has received, and generally continues to receive, little systematic treatment from library managers worldwide. Security measures have been enforced erratically and neglected in varying degrees. The *raison d'être* of libraries is to collect, promote and encourage access to resources, but in doing so

they can create a milieu in which crime can readily flourish and security be compromised. The trend towards CRIME IN LIBRARIES is rising and it is no longer wise to conclude that libraries can be exempted from these global considerations. Librarians and information managers are having to come to terms with the uncomfortable reality that security is a paramount consideration that cannot be ignored if resources are to be protected.

The key to success has been the raising of security consciousness through the creation of a security plan or policy within the context of the STRATEGIC PLANNING process. In this way, security consciousness becomes integral to, rather than being grafted on to, an existing framework. The most successful adoption and implementation of security plans seem to have been where staff have been closely involved in the audit and proposal mechanisms. Each library organization will place its own unique emphasis on the level and nature of security to be adopted and these will be related to local circumstances. Examples and guidelines are contained in Chaney and MacDougall (1992), Lund (1993), Chavez (1993) and Ewing (1994). The subject of security is typically considered under the headings of staff, materials (including equipment) and buildings.

Security of staff includes the issues of verbal abuse and threats, violence and assault. An increasing number of organizations are taking these issues into account in their security planning procedures. Various organizations perceive, and some have identified through a security audit, that there is a need to establish training programmes which help staff to handle conflict situations, even to the extent of giving advice on self-defence (Bahr 1989; Chaney and MacDougall 1992). Others, however, prefer to keep the matter low-key, on the basis that giving the subject undue attention might instil more fear, when in practice the likelihood of assault is remote in many libraries. Nonetheless, general courses on customer care increasingly introduce the subject and are useful channels for a discussion of the problem. However, the need for more tangible assistance in the form of back-up facilities is being acknowledged and introduced into libraries, including the installation of additional telephone lines and panic button alarms at the counter, regular patrols inside and outside the building, and employment of attendants at entry points. All these methods give a degree of reassurance. There is also evidence to suggest (Chaney and MacDougall 1992) that the community rather than an individual library approach to the problem of abuse, assault and violence can be of positive assistance. This process would normally involve discussion between customers, library staff and local community people (for example, social workers, community workers and police) to evolve an agreed course of action (Hinks 1989).

The second general heading associated with security is that of materials. It is one that has been of concern from the early days of manuscripts, when volumes were chained to the library shelf. Numerous articles in the professional literature attest to the fact that theft and mutilation continue to be a major problem. It has become necessary to install detection devices to protect material. These devices are no more than deterrents and mainly remind the forgetful; they catch the careless user, rather than the determined thief. Indeed, the view has been advanced that these devices only encourage the most determined thief to attempt to beat the system by removing pages of text that are less likely to have security tags. This adds to the increase in mutilated material left in the library.

The most calculating criminal intent on building collections or obtaining rare items for personal gain is much harder to deter unless very systematic, stringent and restrictive security policies are put into place (Huntsberry 1992). The deployment of closed-circuit television (CCTV) is being used on a more regular basis in libraries, especially where it is demonstrated to be cost-effective. The acquisition of increasing amounts of expensive technology, such as CD-ROM equipment and workstations, begins to make CCTV more attractive, although physically securing equipment to work surfaces is often used as a simple form of deterrent.

In recent times there has also been the added complication of ensuring the security of information stored in electronic form. COMPUTER SECURITY is a subject that will be of ever increasing concern as more and more data are stored both in-house and remotely but need to be accessible to the library clientele. This calls into question the ability to protect files of electronic information from unauthorized use, whether it be in the form of obtaining confidential informa-

tion, altering existing files or implanting viruses into software (Riley 1992; Wilkinson 1992). In many countries there is also an additional legal responsibility to ensure confidentiality of computer-stored information about an individual's personal details under DATA PROTECTION acts (Chaney and MacDougall 1992). The need for library policy and plans about such matters cannot be overemphasized; it is not just a matter of cost-effective protection but of possible prosecution.

The third major heading associated with security is that of the building, in terms both of the protection of users from assault or threat and of the protection of the materials and equipment. Attention is now being given to designing out, or at least minimizing, criminal acts (Jones and Larkin 1993). One inherent problem is that the larger the building, the greater the problem of attempting to minimize or design out crime. Certain principles need to be considered, such as the need to have good sightlines from staff vantage points and, by implication, to reduce hidden corners and, where feasible, to integrate office and other administrative areas into public areas so as to encourage random surveillance by staff. It is often suggested that a high level of staff presence in the library, where finance permits, will reduce the level of crime. Many libraries have employed attendants at the front desk or have deployed card access machines to enable entrance to the buildings. Better lighting levels both inside and outside are also being deployed. Toilets, also, have been singled out as a possible security threat and are now being sited outside the library entrance rather than inside it.

The need for concerted action to ensure that the resources continue to be kept available for users is one of the biggest challenges to library and information managers. The requirement for availability and accessibility, the feasibility of applying legal sanction, and economics have to be balanced and assessed. More control could lead to a fortress mentality and to an attendant reduction in use (one public library in the UK has already had to close over crime issues). This notwithstanding, the library manager cannot afford the luxury of ignorance; a coherent security strategy and plan is a *sine qua non* for protecting resources for continued use in the twenty-first century.

References

Bahr, A.H. (1989) 'Library, security, training, sources', *Library and Archival Security (US)* 9(1): 37–44.

Chaney, M. and MacDougall, A.F. (eds) (1992) *Security and Crime Prevention in Libraries*, Ashgate Publishing Co.

Chavez, A.M. (1993) 'Library crime and security in academic libraries in Texas', *Library and Archival Security (US)* 12(1): 55–78.

Ewing, D. (1994) 'Library security in the UK. Are our libraries safe?', *Library Management* 15(2): 18–26.

Hinks, J. (1989) 'Behaviour problems: The youth worker option', *Assistant Librarian* 82(2): 29–31.

Huntsberry, J.S. (1992) 'Library security', *Journal of Information Ethics* 1: 46–50.

Jones, D. and Larkin, G. (1993) 'Securing a good design: A library building consultant and an architect consider library security', *Australasian Public Libraries and Information Services* 6(4): 164–70.

Lund, R. (1993) 'Library security', *CAPE Librarian* 37(6): 34–6.

Riley, G. (1992) 'Managing microcomputer security', *Library and Archival Security (US)* 11(2): 1–22.

Wilkinson, D.W. (1992) 'CD-ROM workstation security: Context of risk and appropriate responses', *CD-ROM Librarian* 7(1): 20–5.

Further reading

Arndt, D.A. (2001) 'Problem patrons and library security', *Legal Reference Services Quarterly* 19: 19–40.

Lincoln, A.J. and Lincoln, C.Z. (1987) *Library Crime and Security: An International Perspective*, Haworth Press.

Quinsee, A.G. and McDonald A.C. (1991) *Security in Academic and Research Libraries*, proceedings of three seminars organised by SCONUL and the British Library, held at the British Library 1989–90, Newcastle upon Tyne University Library.

SEE ALSO: crime in libraries

ALAN MACDOUGALL

SEMANTIC WEB

A project designed to make the WORLD WIDE WEB more capable of being 'understood' by computers so as to deliver up relevant, processable material to users. The idea was originally proposed by Tim BERNERS-LEE, who was responsible for the creation of the Web itself. He outlines it as follows: 'The Semantic Web is an extension of the current web, in which information is given well-defined meaning, better enabling computers and people to work in cooperation' (Berners-Lee *et al.* 2001: 31). The technologies behind this are XML (eXtensible Mark-up Language), which allow descriptive tags to be attached to content, and the RDF (Resource Description Framework), which provides METADATA platforms that can use XML tags in triple-based structures to represent data. Links to specified ontologies (see ONTOLOGY) will provide the means by which this is interpreted by computers.

References

Berners-Lee, T. *et al.* (2001) 'The Semantic Web', *Scientific American* (May): 29–37.

SEE ALSO: informatics

SEMIOTICS

The science of signs and sign systems; it is built round the distinction between the signifier, the sign and the signified. The discipline is often divided into three main subdivisions: semantics, syntactics and pragmatics, each of which can be pure, descriptive or applied. The significance of semiotics for INFORMATION THEORY is its ability to provide an analytic framework for forms of documentation and modes of COMMUNICATION.

SERENDIPITY

Described as the knack of making unexpected discoveries by accident, it really refers to the ability to perceive the potential or immediate utility of information encountered whilst not actively being sought at that time. BROWSING permits serendipity and is a traditional (and sometimes very effective) way of using a library.

SEE ALSO: search

SERIAL

The broadest term, and the one favoured in US usage, to describe a publication issued in successive parts and intended to be continued indefinitely. It includes PERIODICALS, annuals, numbered monographic series and other categories of this description. SERIALS LIBRARIANSHIP is frequently recognized as a distinct professional specialization.

SEE ALSO: collection development

SERIALS LIBRARIANSHIP

Serials librarianship is concerned with the overall management and administration of a serials collection regardless of the format of the items within it. The range is wide, because a serial is any publication that is published on a continuing basis, either regularly or irregularly. The term thus encompasses a wide range of printed materials, for example PERIODICALS, NEWSPAPERS, annuals, society proceedings and transactions, and national and international government publications. The term also covers material in audiovisual format, for example MICROFORMS and audio tapes, and increasingly importantly ELECTRONIC JOURNALS, delivered for example on CD-ROM or via the INTERNET (Woodward 1990).

The importance of serials

Because of the nature and role of serials as carriers of SCHOLARLY COMMUNICATION, most medium to large serials collections are located in academic and RESEARCH LIBRARIES, government and NATIONAL LIBRARIES, and larger commercial and industrial libraries. For many academics and researchers, the serials to which a library subscribes are the most important and useful elements of its stock. Articles in serials are published much more rapidly than books and thus serials constitute a vital flow of up-to-date information. This is particularly important in rapidly developing areas of science and technology. Furthermore, articles in serials frequently discuss in-depth, highly specialized topics and include information that may never appear in book form.

Problems of serials management

Three major problems confront the librarian in the management of serials collections. The first is the extent, diversity and growth of the serials literature. The 1993/4 edition of *Ulrich's International Periodicals Directory* contains information on over 140,000 titles. Davinson (1978) estimates that between 1 and 5 million serial titles have been published. Newspapers, too, are a category of serial and it has been estimated that over 300,000 newspapers are recorded as having been published at one time or another in the USA alone. Moreover, new serial titles are regularly being launched and old titles are dying, while others are merging and splitting. By nature, serials are far from static and as a result those statistics that do exist can only be approximate. The second problem is that of serial prices, which for a number of decades have increased annually far in excess of the general rate of inflation. The problem of serial pricing is a complex one. Publishers claim that price increases are due to the increased cost of production, an increase in the total number of articles published and falling subscriptions. Whilst acknowledging the truth of some of these claims, the librarian is nonetheless faced with the dilemma of how to continue acquiring important research-related serials that are constantly escalating in price. As this is combined with the third major problem of static or declining library budgets, there are only two possible courses of action: either cancel serials or acquire fewer monographs. In reality most libraries have been forced to do both, and as subscription cancellations lead to higher prices this downward spiral looks set to continue until viable alternatives to serials as carriers of scholarly information become widely accepted (Woodward and Pilling 1993).

The role of the serials librarian

Managing a serials collection differs in significant respects from managing a monographs collection. The nature of the material is voluminous and diverse, and decisions regarding selection and retention need to be made on a regular basis. Receipt and claiming missing issues are complex, and detailed and accurate financial control and budgeting are difficult and time-consuming. The main objectives of the serials librarian are to ensure the collection is, and remains, relevant to the needs of the user community, by acquiring an appropriate range of print and electronic journals; to ensure prompt and uninterrupted receipt of serial issues; to conserve and preserve materials; to facilitate access to up-to-date information about the range, scope and location of materials within the collection; to facilitate access to current and back issues of serials; to exploit the collection by alerting users to the range of serial acquisitions (Woodward 1991).

HOUSEKEEPING

Such objectives translate into a major aspect of the serials librarian's job, namely the establishment and maintenance of effective and efficient housekeeping routines. This is of fundamental importance: if basic housekeeping activities are not carried out well, then the collection will not meet the needs of library users to maximum effect. Thus, procedures for the accurate and timely ordering and checking in of serial parts must be devised, introduced and supervised, together with routines for claiming missing issues, binding completed volumes and reshelving and tidying the collection.

FINANCIAL CONTROL

Financial control and budgeting are also of paramount importance. Most medium to large libraries purchase the bulk of their serials through subscription agents. A major advantage of using an agent (as opposed to purchasing titles directly from publishers) is the reduction in the number of invoices requiring checking and payment, and the standardization of layout and content of invoices in a library-determined format. Other benefits can also accrue from the use of agents, for example discounts for co-operative purchasing and/or early payment of invoices, access to bibliographical and pricing data from the agent's database, discounts on automated systems and detailed local management and financial reports. Unlike books, which are paid for as and when published, serials are paid for well in advance of publication. Budget formulation takes place even earlier, thus most serial budgets in the past have been derived from the previous year's figures, with an amount added on for inflation. More recently this dilemma has eased somewhat with the commitment of major journal publishers to guaranteeing firm prices at a much earlier date and the efforts of subscription agents (working closely with publishers) to forecast future price trends.

AUTOMATION

Automation can play a major part in serials management. Once installed, a serials management system can materially advance the librarian's control of the serials collection through superior public access to information, improved claiming of missing issues, circulation facilities, enhanced binding control and a far wider range of financial and management reports. Automated links between libraries and suppliers can also significantly enhance the efficiency of a serials department by providing faster receipt of orders and claims, facilities for feedback and database connections.

The future of serials librarianship

The tremendous growth in the volume of scholarly information, escalating journal prices and cuts in library acquisition budgets are beginning to change the nature of serials collections in libraries. Although currently collections remain dominated by printed journals, many librarians are now looking towards electronic information as an alternative to print. Significant developments are taking place in the area of electronic document supply – article provision rather than journal provision. Many mainstream publishers are now either investigating or providing electronic versions of their printed journals and the number of electronic journals (both free and subscription-based) on the Internet is growing rapidly. The impact of this trend towards electronic information provision on libraries is still uncertain; more certain is that it will continue unabated.

References

Davinson, D. (1978) *The Periodicals Collection*, rev. edn, Westview Press, p. 4.
Woodward, H.M. (1991) 'Management of serials collections', in C. Jenkins and M. Morley (eds) *Collection Management in Academic Libraries*, Gower, pp. 163–84.
—— (1990) 'Periodicals', in P.W. Lea (ed.) *Printed Reference Material*, 3rd edn, Library Association, pp. 159–82.
Woodward, H. and Pilling, S. (1993) 'The international serials industry: An overview', in H. Woodward and S. Pilling (eds) *The International Serials Industry*, Gower, pp. 1–22.

Further reading

Graham, M.E. and Buettel, F. (eds) (1990) *Serials Management: A Practical Handbook*, ASLIB/United Kingdom Serials Group.

HAZEL WOODWARD

SERVER

A computer attached to a network, whether the INTERNET or an INTRANET, so as to manage resources and services. The term may be made more specific by the addition of a qualifying adjective. Thus, a file server will store files on behalf of any user of the particular network and serve them to users, a print server will manage a printer or printers, a network server will manage network traffic, and a database server will provide access to a database. Servers are often dedicated wholly to their server tasks, but it is also possible for a multiprocessing computer to perform the function of a server alongside other tasks. In this case, 'server' would refer to the program that is managing resources rather than the entire computer.

SERVICES FOR VISUALLY IMPAIRED PEOPLE

Visually impaired people (VIP), whether blind or with some residual sight, require library services adapted to meet their need for information and reading material that they find difficult to access in traditional print formats. This includes joining procedures that can be accomplished independently, and staff with a commitment to meeting needs and trained in visual awareness, as well as the provision of accessible reading materials and specialist equipment. The overwhelming majority of VIP are elderly, and may be housebound, or have other age-related impairments, which affect their use of library services. Further, there are wide variations in the degree of impairment, so that some VIP can read very effectively using large print or a simple magnifier, while others require tactile formats or recordings. Among younger VIP in particular, the use of INFORMA-TION AND COMMUNICATION TECHNOLOGY, with appropriate software, is growing. As the proportion of people with access to ICT and appropriate skills increases in the population at large, it is likely that the proportion of VIP wishing to use adapted technologies will also grow. This has implications for the future development of library and information services for VIP.

A range of alternative information formats, and adaptive technologies, are available, including large-print materials, Braille and other tactile formats, talking books, reading machines and specialist software. There is also a wide range of providers of library services to VIP, with different arrangements in various countries. In the UK, the Disability Discrimination Act (1995) required that public library (see PUBLIC LIBRARIES) services be made fully accessible to all disabled people, including VIP. The Royal National Institute for the Blind Talking Books service is available to anyone who cannot read standard type comfortably, with the best possible spectacles. Books are recorded, unabridged, onto multi-track cassettes, and played on machines specially adapted for people with sight loss. The Calibre Cassette Library provides a postal lending service using standard cassettes and commercially available audio books. The National Library for the Blind provides a postal lending service of material transcribed into Braille and Moon, and has an extensive website providing an array of electronic services. The Talking Newspaper Association of the UK provides national newspapers and magazines on audio tape, computer disk, e-mail or CD-ROM, and is the umbrella group for local talking newspapers. The Share the Vision programme, funded by Re:source: the Council for Museums, Archives and Libraries, has been instrumental in developing services, and has produced a manual of best practice.

In the USA library services for VIP are delivered through an extensive library network headed by the LIBRARY OF CONGRESS National Library Service for the Blind and Physically Handicapped. As well as directly producing around 2,000 titles each year in alternative formats, it is responsible for developing and disseminating policies at national level, and aims to support a uniform quality of service. The majority of the NORDIC COUNTRIES provide state-funded services for VIP, delivered through special libraries, responsible for both production and delivery of alternative format materials. Public libraries are generally seen as a major local access point to these services.

While the majority of library services to VIP are concentrated on provision of general services through public libraries and/or specialist agencies, similar considerations apply to ACADEMIC LIBRARIES. All respondents to a recent survey of higher-education libraries in the UK offered some level of support to students and staff with visual impairment, although the levels of service available varied considerably between institutions. Almost half the respondents had plans to further develop their services and one-fifth were keeping the situation under review (Brophy and Craven, 1999: 38–9).

VIP as users of library services

A survey of VIP in the UK (Davies *et al.* 2001) carried out in 1999–2000 looked at the views of users of a range of services for VIP. This found that VIP preferred different formats for different types of information – magnifiers or someone reading aloud was preferred for information seeking, for example from small items such as leaflets, and for non-fiction materials, while sound recordings were most popular for 'recreational' reading – fiction, magazines and newspapers. Use of tactile formats such as Braille and Moon was often restricted by insufficiently sensitive fingers to learn and maintain the skills required.

The overwhelming majority of VIP surveyed had used a public library at some time, but less than one-third had used the service within the previous six months. There was a lack of awareness of the range of facilities and services available. Most users visited their local branch library, or made use of the housebound service. While large-print and spoken-word materials were widely available throughout the branch network, specialist equipment was more likely to be found at central libraries (Kinnell *et al.* 2000: 41).

Thirty per cent of respondents to the survey did not use any of the primary library services available. More than half used other sources of information and reading material, most commonly small collections held locally at drop-in centres and social services departments. A key finding of the report was that many VIP were unaware of the services available to them, which leads to the conclusion that appropriately targeted promotion is necessary. All service providers attracted very positive responses in terms of customer satisfaction with the services used, although there were issues of communication and consultation that remain to be addressed.

References

Brophy, P. and Craven, J. (1999) *The Integrated Accessible Library: A Model of Service Development for the 21st Century*, Centre for Research in Library and Information Management.
Davies, J.E., Wisdom, S. and Creaser, C. (2001) *Out of Sight but Not out of Mind: Visually Impaired People's Perspectives of Library and Information Services*, Library and Information Statistics Unit.
Kinnell, M., Yu, L. and Creaser, C. (2000) *Public Library Services for Visually Impaired People*, Library and Information Statistics Unit.

Further reading

A number of these publications contain further extensive bibliographies relevant to this topic.
Craddock, P. (1997) 'Share the vision', paper presented at the 63rd IFLA General Conference (www.ifla.org/IV/ifla63/63crap.htm).
Machell, J. (1996) *Library and Information Services for Visually Impaired People: National Guidelines*, Library Association Publishing.
Re:source (2000) *Library Services for Visually Impaired People: A Manual of Best Practice* (www.nlbuk.org/bpm/index.html).

CLAIRE CREASER

SHANNON, CLAUDE ELWOOD (1916–2001)

The originator of information theory, the mathematical theory of COMMUNICATION.

Born in Gaylord, Michigan, and a graduate of Michigan University and of MIT. He was a student of Vannevar BUSH. He worked first at Bell Laboratories and held a chair at MIT. His theory was announced in the article 'The mathematical theory of communication' in the *Bell System Technical Journal* (1948). He took information to include the messages occurring in communications media, in information technology systems and in the nerve networks of humans and other animals. He analysed a communication system in terms of an information source, a transmitter, a communication channel, a receiver and a destination. He then sought to discover mathematical laws governing such systems. Whilst his results have been of most interest to communication engineers, some of the concepts have been adapted in such fields as psychology and linguistics. Information theory overlaps to a considerable extent with communication theory but is most concerned with limits to the processing and communication of information.

SEE ALSO: communication; economics of information; informatics; information and communication technology; information theory

SHAREWARE

COPYRIGHT SOFTWARE that is offered to users in finished or evaluation versions so that they can assess whether it meets their needs before buying. If users try software offered by this method and decide to continue using it, they are expected to register as users and pay for the licence to do so (see LICENCES). The ways in which the developers of shareware handle the process vary greatly. Some merely request that users register while others require it. What is offered with registration varies from the simple right to continue using the product to an updated program with a manual and support facilities. Because the shareware sector is comparatively informal and the developer's costs are low, the prices asked are also low. Although developers of shareware intend to profit from their creations, their ethos is quite distinct from that of the major software corporations and much more akin to that of the suppliers of FREEWARE, and the OPEN-SOURCE movement.

SHELL

In COMPUTER SCIENCE, a program providing an interface between a user and an operating system; in ARTIFICIAL INTELLIGENCE, an EXPERT SYSTEMS package that can be used in conjunction with a knowledge base produced by a user.

SHERA, JESSE HAUK (1903–82)

Philosopher and theoretician of librarianship.

Born in Oxford, Ohio, and studied at Miami University, Yale and the University of Chicago. In 1944 he became Associate Director of the University of Chicago Libraries and began to teach in the Graduate Library School. In 1952 he was appointed Dean of Western Reserve's School of Library Science, where he set up the Center for Documentation and Communication Research (CDCR) to develop a programme of teaching and research in information retrieval. In his teaching and writing, he consistently upheld the position that documentation and INFORMATION SCIENCE are an integral part of librarianship. In his view, information science contributes a theoretical and intellectual underpinning for the work of the librarian. Perhaps his major achievement was his work on the theoretical and practical basis for education for librarianship. This received funding from the Carnegie Corporation and appeared in 1972 as *Foundations of Education for Librarianship*.

SEE ALSO: library education

SOCIAL EXCLUSION AND LIBRARIES

Combating social exclusion has been one of the main policy drivers of social democratic governments in Europe since the 1980s. In Britain the New Labour government established a Social Exclusion Unit within the Cabinet Office in 1997.

Social exclusion encompasses concepts such as class, poverty, discrimination, equal opportunities and racism. Many initiatives to tackle social exclusion have been focused on combating poverty. While poverty is a key underlying cause of social exclusion, some individuals and groups are affluent, but can still experience social exclusion. Gay, lesbian and transgendered people fall into this category. Most of the government initiatives to tackle social exclusion are targeted on getting unemployed people into jobs. This focus has both economic and moral motivations. However, a job alone does not guarantee social inclusion. Low-paid and casual work may not be sufficient to overcome economic exclusion, for example. Black people in jobs still experience other forms of exclusion, including prejudice and discrimination. Social exclusion, therefore, has a mixture of social, economic and political dimensions.

Political exclusion is to do with the lack of power among working-class, black and other communities. In a capitalist market economy social exclusion cannot be eradicated, because it is based on differences of power and class. However, social exclusion can be ameliorated, and this has been the main thrust of government policy. While each socially excluded community is different, a number of generic causes, effects, and solutions can be identified for all excluded communities. This paper will focus on the social exclusion from library and information services of black communities, by reasons of ethnicity and language. Examples are drawn mostly from the UK and from PUBLIC LIBRARIES.

Historical review, 1978–98

The *Assistant Librarian* carried a number of radical articles on racism and libraries in the 1970s. Topics included social class and race relations (Jordan, March 1972), black studies (Martin, August 1972) and libraries, culture and blacks (Dawes, July 1973). Black images also appeared in the *Assistant Librarian*, including two covers featuring photographs of leaders of the Black Panther Party: Angela Davis and Eldridge Cleaver. The key text to emerge from the 1970s was Clough and Quarmby (1978). This was the first major research project to study public libraries and ethnic minorities nationally. Clough and Quarmby had only partial success in influencing the profession.

During the 1980s race had a high profile in the national press (for example, the Brixton and Toxteth riots) but was mostly absent from professional journals, with the exception of Rait (1984), Elliott (1984) and a seminar organised by the Community Services Group of the Library Association, September 1984, on Library and Race. Elliott's research focused on the relationship between public libraries and ethnic communities. Few of Elliott's recommendations were implemented by library services.

The situation remained bleak through much of the 1990s until New Labour came to power in 1997 and established the Social Exclusion Unit. This opened the floodgates to a great deal of research into the causes and effects of, and approaches to, tackling, social exclusion. This activity was reflected in the library world via Roach and Morrison (1998a, 1998b). Roach and Morrison's key findings were that the public library service had not engaged with black communities and that a social distance existed between libraries and black communities. There was a lack of vision and leadership on black issues and there were no strategies to identify and track the changing needs of black communities. The public library was not central to or supportive of black communities and the structure, culture and ethnic profile of public libraries excluded black people. The public library service had failed to account for lack of progress in race equality, and the resource pressure on the public library service would present further challenges to black engagement and exclusion.

Institutional racism

Many of the points made by Roach and Morrison had been expressed twenty years earlier by Clough and Quarmby. Nothing had changed in terms of library services to black communities, and nothing changed as a result of Roach and Morrison – their recommendations were ignored and their baseline for good practice (Roach and Morrison 1998b) was not implemented. This prompted a statement by Durrani that: 'In LIS it is the White middle class that holds the stick which is used to marginalise Black and working

class people and their information, education, and cultural services' (1999).

The catalyst for change with regard to race and libraries was the publication of the report on the inquiry into the murder of Stephen Lawrence (Macpherson 1999). This report, which defined institutional racism, made recommendations for a wide range of public services. These recommendations were placed in the public library context by *Libraries for All – Social Inclusion in Public Libraries* (DCMS 1999). This policy guidance included a six-point plan for tackling social exclusion, which can be applied to black communities or any other excluded group:

- Identify the people who are socially excluded and their geographical distribution.
- Engage them to establish their needs.
- Assess and review current practice; develop a strategy and prioritise resources.
- Develop the services, and train the library staff to provide them.
- Implement the services and publicise them.
- Evaluate success, review and improve.

Libraries for All was combined with *Centres for Social Change* (DCMS 2000), a social inclusion policy for museums, galleries and archives, to produce *Libraries, Museums, Galleries and Archives for All* – co-operating across the sectors to tackle social exclusion (DCMS 2001). The main recommendations were that social inclusion should be mainstreamed as a policy priority, and there should be library policy objectives with regard to access, outreach and libraries as agents of social change.

Open to all?

Muddiman (2000) suggested that, if libraries are to become agents of social change, they need to be transformed by the mainstreaming of provision for socially excluded groups and communities, and the establishment of standards of service and their monitoring. Resourcing strategies need to be adopted that prioritise the needs of excluded people and communities. A recasting of the role of library staff is required to encompass a more socially responsive and educative approach. Staffing policies and practices should be developed to address exclusion, discrimination and prejudice. Excluded social groups and communities should be targeted, alongside the development of community-based approaches to library provision, which incorporate consultation and partnership with local communities. INFORMATION AND COMMUNICATION TECHNOLOGY (ICT) and networking developments should actively focus on the needs of excluded people. A recasting of the image and identity of the public library is needed to link it more closely with the cultures of excluded communities and social groups.

The *Open to All?* research project produced a series of working papers on aspects of social exclusion. Durrani (2000) suggested that a partnership of black communities, black library workers, senior librarianship and information science (LIS) managers and other stakeholders is needed to prepare a vision of a library service that is at ease with diversity. A Charter of Rights for black library workers and service users should be developed to move the question of equality from the realm of desire and goodwill to a legal requirement. A National Race Council is required to address race issues, conduct formal investigations and secure legally enforceable agreements to end discrimination. A DCMS Black LIS Rights Agency should be set up to ensure that LIS policies respond to the needs of black communities and that they are put into practice. An affirmative/positive action policy framework should ensure that black LIS staffing and services reflect the black community. Black Workers Groups at workplace and national levels are needed so that black LIS workers can articulate their concerns and make policy recommendations.

Black communities should be empowered to ensure that there is a meaningful involvement of black communities in library service policy and practice. Roach and Morrison, *Libraries for All, Open to All?* and the Stephen Lawrence report should be fully implemented. Library management must create an environment that reflects commitment to change so that black communities and workers receive fair and equal services. CILIP must ensure that issues and concerns of black LIS workers and communities are properly addressed. Libraries must respond to a multicultural Britain through recruitment and development of black staff, changes in organisational culture, funding and management commitment. Research into the needs of black communities and recruitment of black LIS workers should be carried out within the Best Value Framework. In the final analysis, elimination of racism is a matter of human rights.

Change at last

There is evidence to suggest that some of the recommendations made by *Libraries for All, Open to All?* and *Struggle against Racial Exclusion* are being implemented. This evidence includes Best Value inspection reports, Annual Library Plans, Public Library Standards, the Library Association Policy Action Group on Social Exclusion, the Diversity Council, the Social Exclusion Action Planning Network and the Quality Leaders Programme for black library workers.

Best Value, a key New Labour vehicle to reform local Government, requires a review and external inspection of all council services every five years. The published Best Value inspection reports of public library reviews suggest that racial equality is being taken seriously by some library authorities. Further evidence of this can be found in Annual Library Plans, which require library services to plan their services to black communities. A key element of Annual Library Plans are Public Library Standards, which strongly encourage library authorities to adopt and implement the principles contained in *Libraries for All*. The LIBRARY ASSOCIATION established a Policy Action Group on Social Exclusion, which made recommendations regarding racial diversity. CILIP now also intends to establish a Diversity Council to consider issues such as racial exclusion.

Two key outcomes of the *Open to All?* research were the Social Exclusion Action Planning Network (a network of library authorities committed to tackling social exclusion) and the Quality Leaders Programme for black library workers. This latter programme seeks to simultaneously develop black library workers and create new or improved library services to black communities. The programme was developed and tested by Merton and Birmingham library services, and the management school at the University of North London.

There is now a real momentum building within the UK public library movement for social change and to address issues such as racial diversity. However, these efforts remain patchy and very few library authorities have the appropriate strategies, structures and cultures in place for effectively tackling social exclusion. In the last resort, this is the responsibility of individual library workers. As Durrani has said:

The struggle against racial exclusion should be waged in every workplace, every policy forum, every community meeting, every library shelf. It is a struggle not only for those excluded, but also for those who benefit, knowingly or unknowingly, from the exclusion of some people, some communities, some countries. Just as slavery is unacceptable to us today, so should be racism and all the exploitation and social oppression that goes under its name. The challenge to eliminate racism is for each one of us.

(Durrani 2000)

References

Clough, E and Quarmby, J. (1978) *A Public Library Service for Ethnic Minorities in Great Britain*, Library Association.

Dawes, L. (1973) 'Libraries, culture and blacks', *Assistant Librarian* July 66: 106–9.

DCMS (2001) *Libraries, Museums, Galleries and Archives for All*, Department of Culture, Media and Sport.

—— (2000) *Centres for Social Change*, Department of Culture, Media and Sport.

—— (1999) *Libraries for All – Social Inclusion in Public Libraries*, Department of Culture, Media and Sport.

Durrani, S. (2000) *Struggle against Racial Exclusion in Public Libraries*, Leeds Metropolitan University.

—— (1999) 'Black communities and information workers in search of social justice', *New Library World* 100: 265–78.

Elliott, P. (1984) *Public Libraries and Self Help Ethnic Minority Organisations*, Polytechnic of North London.

Jordan, P. (1972) 'Social class, race relations and the public library', *Assistant Librarian*, March.

Macpherson, Sir W. (1999) *Stephen Lawrence Inquiry*, The Home Office.

Martin, W.J. (1972) 'Black studies and the British librarian', *Assistant Librarian*, August: 122–4.

Muddiman, D. (2000) *Open to All?*, Leeds Metropolitan University.

Rait, S.K. (1984) 'Public libraries and racism', *Assistant Librarian* (October): 123.

Roach, P. and Morrison, M. (1998a) *Public Libraries, Ethnic Diversity and Citizenship*, University of Warwick.

—— (1998b) *Public Libraries and Ethnic Diversity: A Baseline for Good Practice*, University of Warwick.

SEE ALSO: digital library; lesbigay librarians; telecentres

JOHN PATEMAN

SOCIOLOGY OF KNOWLEDGE

A branch of sociology that is concerned with the study of the influence of social factors on the evolution of knowledge. Its programme is to correlate ideas, theories and intellectual products in general with the social locations of their producers. It is a basic hypothesis of the sociology of knowledge that all knowledge is socially constructed.

Concepts

Three questions have traditionally been raised in the field, showing that three different concepts are present. First, can knowledge be considered universally valid if it is subject to social conditions of production? Second, should all types of knowledge be studied (i.e. ideology, myth, philosophy, belief, political doctrines, theological thought, science and commonsense ideas) or only ideology – that is, the part of knowledge which is implied by social life and human relations? Third, what should be studied: the social conditions of knowledge construction, acquisition, organization, communication, popularization and use?

In the field of library and INFORMATION SCIENCE the third concept of the sociology of knowledge is important because it concerns elements that help us to understand fundamental phenomena.

Origins

At the beginning of the seventeenth century, Francis Bacon, looking for the origin of false notions and of obstacles to true knowledge, which both depend on social factors, outlined the general territory of the relations between society and thought. Then, Condorcet enquired about the social preconditions for different types of knowledge. Saint-Simon, asserting the existence of a necessary relation between feudal systems and theological thought, and between industrial systems and positive and socialist thought, sketched the problematics developed further by Auguste Comte, the founder of sociology, in his 'law of three stages' (theological, metaphysical and positive) and then by Marx and Durkheim. But knowledge in Marx's view and in the view of Mannheim, who defined in 1929 the programme of the sociology of knowledge, was restricted to ideology, that is philosophy, religion, politics: the sociology of knowledge was a theory of ideologies. Mathematics and the natural sciences were considered exempt from the direct influence of the social structures. So, sociology of knowledge and EPISTEMOLOGY were considered as complementary disciplines.

In the European tradition, attention tended to be centred upon the construction of ideas; US research was more concerned with the use of ideas. The empirical Anglo-Saxon pragmatism tried to define concrete and precise problems, and to study them with the help of statistical methods.

Trends

The present field of the sociology of knowledge is no longer limited to the traditional studies of religion and political ideologies. Three orientations have extended the field of investigations to include sociology of science and technology, sociology of education, and sociology of MASS MEDIA and public opinion. Mead (1974) insisted on the importance of communication in the development of thought: the progress of knowledge is only conceivable through social relations. Znaniecki's (1940) work seems an excellent example of contributions to the study of the communication of messages through social structures, where the role of 'men of knowledge' and social circles appear to shape audiences and publics. Important notions such as opinion leaders in communication science and GATEKEEPERS in information science are direct applications of these results. The last notion is important in the strategic information sector of science and technology monitoring.

Sociology of science and technology

Starting in 1940 with Merton (1973), the sociology of science and technology, on account of the development of scientific and technical knowledge, and its impact on social and cultural changes, has become a part of the sociology of knowledge and is for library and information science a priority domain. The main objectives of research in this sector are better understanding of the social conditions of intellectual innovation and the social structure of science institutions. The effects of research communication on social and economic structures are also studied. Sciences (including social sciences) are considered

as social realities. So, scientific work is studied: scientists as social actors participate in co-operative activities, but in the pursuit of professional recognition, and pressed by the motto 'publish or perish', often engage in bitter quarrels over claims for priority. First Bernal (1939) and then Price (1963) insisted on the possibility of an excess of information due to the exponential growth rates for different aspects of science. Research on the relations between science, technology and society (STS) has dealt with the social consequences, as yet not fully understood, of the massive and continuing changes induced by scientific and technological progress. And recently, whilst Merton refused to analyse scientific contents, the social mechanisms determining these contents have been analysed.

Sociology of scientific and technological knowledge

This new orientation started during the 1970s and implies extending the sociology of knowledge to include scientific and technological knowledge. It is considered as the 'maximalist' form of the sociology of knowledge because it states that no intellectual product can be excluded from social influences. The core of the 'constructivist' programme is based on the postulate that scientific facts do not result from the observation of nature but are social constructions (Bloor 1976). Although somewhat excessive, this programme has allowed the study of 'science in action' (Latour 1987) and renewed the study of knowledge construction. Scientific creativity (Feeney and Merry 1990), controversies and social interaction processes have been studied to better understand how scientists elaborate on scientific facts. It results in a better understanding of the qualitative and quantitative (BIBLIOMETRICS and INFORMETRICS) aspects of the social processes of construction, communication and use of scientific and technological knowledge that are basic for information science and technology.

References

Bernal, J.D. (1939) *The Social Function of Science*, Routledge & Kegan Paul.
Bloor, D. (1976) *Knowledge and Social Imagery*, Routledge & Kegan Paul.
Feeney, M. and Merry, K. (eds) (1990) *Information Technology and the Research Process*, Bowker Saur.

Latour, B. (1987) *Science in Action*, Open University Press.

Mead, G.H. (1974) *Mind, Self and Society: From the Standpoint of a Social Behaviourist*, ed. C.W. Morris, University of Chicago Press.

Merton, R. (1973) *The Sociology of Science*, University of Chicago Press.

Price, D.J. de Solla (1963) *Little Science, Big Science*, Columbia University Press.

Znaniecki, F. (1940) *The Social Role of the Man of Knowledge*, Columbia University Press.

Further reading

Kuhn, T.S. (1962) *The Structure of Scientific Revolutions*, University of Chicago Press.

Machlup, F. (1962) *The Production and Distribution of Knowledge in the United States*, Princeton University Press.

Mendelssohn, E., Weingart, P. and Withley, R. (eds) (1997) *The Social Production of Scientific Knowledge*, D. Reidel Publishing Company.

SEE ALSO: communication

YVES F. LE COADIC

SOFT SYSTEMS METHODOLOGY

Soft systems methodology (SSM) is an approach aimed at helping its users to uncover and resolve the deep 'soft' issues, which are embedded in purposeful action in real-world (often organizational) situations. SSM was developed at Lancaster University (UK) in a thirty-year programme of action research in real situations conducted by Professor Peter Checkland and his colleagues in many different settings in organizations large and small, in both public and private sectors. It is widely used in relation to the study of INFORMATION SYSTEMS.

SSM derived from the failure of the systems engineering (SE) approach to cope with the subtleties of human situations of the kind with which managers, of all kinds and at all levels, have to cope. SSM takes as central the fact that any perceived 'problem' in the world is always subjective. This means that it does not focus on *the* problem or *the* system that needs to be fixed. Rather, its focus is on the worldviews, which cause people to see some aspects of their situations as problematical, and on a process to enable coherent purposeful action to be taken.

SSM is best used participatively. It creates a well-structured discussion/debate in which worldviews are surfaced and examined in the historical, political and cultural context of the problem situation. The aim is to tease out the accommodations between conflicting views that will enable purposeful 'action to improve' to be taken. Thus the methodology does not seek to 'solve' problems whose existence is taken as given, but to achieve action through better understanding of the situation in which issues and problems are perceived.

A significant benefit of using SSM is the learning which participants can derive from their engagement in the methodological process. For this reason SSM can also be described as a learning system: it learns its way to the 'action to improve'.

The methodology can be expressed as the four stages depicted in Figure 19: the situation in which problems are perceived; the creation of models of pure purposeful activity constructed on the basis of declared worldviews; the use of the models to structure debate about the situation by questioning the perceived 'real world'; and the accommodations that enable action to be taken. Progress through the stages is iterative as insight is gained, and much recycling will normally occur with willing participants.

The essential ideas that underlie this process are: the construction of human (purposeful) activity models, not as would-be descriptions of real-world action, but as devices to structure debate, and the use of these devices in an organized process of learning. These ideas were illustrated in the first version of the methodology, which was expressed as the seven-stage process shown in Figure 20. This is the form in which most people learn the methodology and it will be useful for explanatory purposes to describe those stages here.

Stages 1 and 2: expression

These are stages where SSM user(s) are engaged in the discovery of the richest possible insights into the situation and are articulating these perceptions in the most useful form – rich pictures. These are called rich pictures because SSM users are free to use any technique, method, tool or format in order to give rise to the best expression of the understanding gained. This is not a one-off exercise, and it may go through a number of revisions, if necessary based on continuous deepening of knowledge gained from the situation. There is a deliberate attempt to dis-

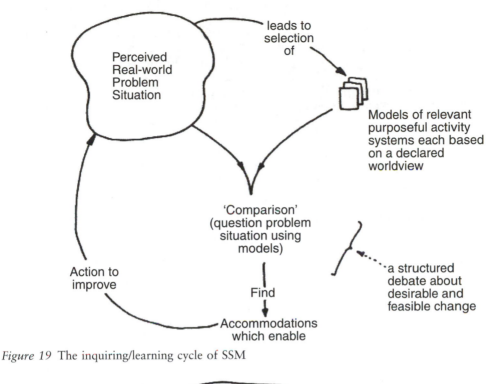

Figure 19 The inquiring/learning cycle of SSM

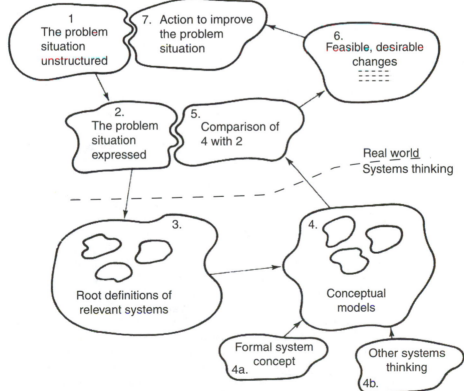

Figure 20 Seven-stage process (Checkland, 1999)

courage SSM users from identifying *the* systems or *the* problems here in order to free up their thinking.

Stages 3 and 4: root definitions of relevant systems and making models

Users select some purposeful activities thought 'relevant' to gaining insight into the problem situation and build human activity system models that consist of linked activities connected to make a purposeful whole, together with a monitoring and control system. The models represent pure activity from the viewpoint of a declared worldview. For example, the purposeful action institutionalised in a real-world prison could be modelled as punishment, or rehabilitation, or protecting society, or training criminals (the 'university of crime' worldview). Each worldview would yield a different activity model. Of course, whether any particular model turns out actually to be relevant will emerge when the models are used in the next stage.

Stage 5: comparing models with reality – structuring debate

In this stage the models are used as a source of questions, which are addressed to the real situation. Answering these questions will increase insights into the real situation and also draw attention to the previously unexamined worldviews held by participants in the process. It will also lead to new ideas for more relevant 'relevant systems'. The models are thus a device for enabling a deeper discussion to occur than normally takes place in the everyday hurly-burly.

Stages 6 and 7: defining and implementing 'feasible and desirable' changes

In the course of Stage 5 ideas for change will emerge. The craft skill involved at this stage of the methodological process is to move the discussion from the comparison of model activities with real-world action to a discussion of changes, which would constitute improvements to the real situation. Such changes might be structural, procedural or attitudinal – often a combination of all three – and of course what counts as 'improvement' will depend upon the worldviews surfaced in the course of the debate. What is sought is possible change, which meets

two criteria simultaneously. It must be 'desirable', given *this* debate based on *these* relevant models, and also 'feasible' for these particular people in their particular situation with its particular history; that is to say it must be *culturally* feasible. Hence the focus is on finding accommodations that will enable 'action to improve' to be taken.

Introducing change will of course modify or transform the problem situation and so the whole methodological cycle can in principle begin again. In this sense SSM is a methodology for managing change.

Refinements

Although the methodology was first expressed in the seven-stage form of Figure 20, and this is how most people learn about it and begin to use it, experienced users soon internalize the approach and do not follow a sequence of stages mechanically. Rather they engage with a problem situation on its terms (and using its language) while retaining Figure 19 as a sense-making device as the intervention unfolds. This provides a map that enables the intervention to be structured, a means of ensuring that the intervention remains coherent as the full complexity of a human situation is explored.

Checkland's books describe many applications of the use of SSM in different situations, and their 'family resemblances' all stem from the principles that underpin Figure 19.

Although SSM emerged from the failure of the SE approach in management (rather than technical) situations, in fact in its mature form it *subsumes* SE as an occasional special case. Experience has shown that in a particular situation it may well be appropriate to take some part of the real world to be 'a system' and to engineer it to achieve its objectives using all the techniques of SE. This demonstrates that the 'hard' systems thinking of SE is itself a special case of the 'soft' systems thinking of SSM in which the focus is on the process of inquiry set up as a *learning system*.

The thirty-year action research programme that produced SSM has generated a methodology of great practicality, as is shown by its use in organizations around the world and by its being taught in colleges and universities in many different countries. That is the measure of Checkland's contribution.

Further reading

Checkland, P. (1981 and 1999) *Systems Thinking, Systems Practice*, J Wiley and Sons. [Note that the 1999 version also contains Checkland's 30-year retrospective on the development of SSM.]
Checkland, P. and Holwell, S. (1988) *Information, Systems and Information Systems*.
Checkland, P. and Scholes, J. (1990 and 1999) *Soft Systems Methodology in Action*, J. Wiley and Sons.

NIMAL JAYARATNA

SOFTWARE

The components of a computer system that are programmed rather than manufactured. It is the programmable elements of computer systems that enable computers to be matched to particular sets of user requirements. There are three main categories: the operating software (in the past invariably provided by the computer system manufacturer, but not necessarily so today) that controls the operation of the hardware and of the other software components that the system runs; applications programmes and applications packages that do the particular work required of a system; the system building tools and compilers that are used to help build the applications programs and packages. In popular usage, the term is much more likely to be used in relation to off-the-shelf applications packages than to the other two categories, or even to custom-made applications systems.

SEE ALSO: informatics; information and communication technology; information management; information technology

SOUND ARCHIVES

Collections of SOUND RECORDINGS held in libraries, by broadcasting and record companies, and in specialist organizations created for that purpose.

Definitions and scope

Sound recordings are collected for three discrete but overlapping reasons: first, they provide archival material for future research and playback; second, sound recordings provide support for teaching in both formal academic and non-academic studies; and, third, sound recordings can be of recreational interest for the general public. Collections of recordings are found in the full range of libraries, though the content of collections will differ. PUBLIC LIBRARIES generally limit their collections to popular music and spoken-word recordings. ACADEMIC LIBRARIES face the dual task of providing materials for both teaching and research whilst collecting and preserving archival sound recordings. Special collections are limited to collecting materials for one specific content area or genre. For example, record companies generally keep archives of all their own releases. Some academic libraries specialize in a particular genre; notable examples include the University of Exeter's collection of US jazz and blues recordings.

Sound recording archives and technological advances

Sound archives have been kept since Edison's first successful experiments with the 'Phonograph' in 1877. One of the first archives to provide an almost comprehensive collection of sound recordings was set up by the British Broadcasting Corporation (BBC) in 1900. Sound archives available to the public became commonplace in the 1920s and 1930s following advances in sound recording techniques. Sound recordings were viewed as being supplementary resources to books, and charges were made for individual playback. The development of different recording formats after the Second World War and the rise of popular music from the 1950s onwards have presented both advantages and problems for the development of sound archives. New methods of sound recording, notably the compact cassette (early 1960s) and the compact disc (1983), have allowed easier and better-quality recordings. Notable COPYRIGHT problems faced by archives have included pirated recordings (commonly from the MIDDLE EAST and SOUTHEAST ASIA) and the illegal recording of master copies. Collection and PRESERVATION of sound recordings has also presented challenges. Deterioration of early recordings on wax cylinders, magnetic tape and shellac has made controlled environments and careful handling necessary. It is becoming apparent that digital recordings are also subject to deterioration over time, presenting further problems for archive collections.

Access to sound archives

Unlike the complete printed collections of national deposit libraries, there has never been a LEGAL DEPOSIT requirement for sound recordings in many countries; the USA is an important exception. Accordingly, sound archives have generally developed in a piecemeal fashion during the twentieth century. One of the most comprehensive archives of recorded material includes the BBC sound archive. Developments following the Second World War include the setting up of the British Institute of Recorded Sound (BIRS) in 1948, which concentrated on collecting classical recordings. The Institute first received public funding in the early 1960s to establish a national (but not a legal deposit) archive of sound recordings. BIRS became a department of the British Library in April 1983, its name being changed to the National Sound Archive (NSA). The NSA provides the most comprehensive collection in the UK of Western art music, international music, jazz, popular music, wildlife recordings and spoken-word collections. International recognition of sound archives has officially existed since 1969, when the UNESCO-affiliated International Association of Sound Archives (IASA) was founded. Members of IASA include most of the national sound archives in the world, including the NSA, the Association for Recorded Sound Collections (USA) (ARSC) and the French Association for Sound Archives (AFAS).

Further reading

Johansen, T. (2001) 'Preservation of AVA heritage: Strategies of development and audiovisual archives', *Library Review* 50: 417–20.
Ward, A. (1990) *A Manual of Sound Archive Administration*, Gower.

SEE ALSO: audiovisual materials; multimedia librarianship

JAMES DEARNLEY

SOUND RECORDINGS

The process of transcribing vibrations perceptible as sound on to a storage medium. Sound reproduction reverses this process by converting the stored vibrations into sound waves.

Sound recording has, historically, used a variety of storage media for recording and reproduction. Three media have been particularly successful: mechanical (phonograph); magnetic (recorded tape); and digital (compact disc, MP3).

Mechanical and electrical sound recording

A photograph disc stores a replica (or analogue) of sound waves as a series of undulations in a groove. The first successful demonstration of sound recording and reproduction is attributed to Thomas Edison's 'Phonograph' in 1877. His analogue system stored sounds on indented tinfoil wrapped around a cylinder, played back via a stylus. Other methods of sound recording were experimented with at this time, most notably Bell and Sumner-Tainter's Wax Cylinder Phonograph in 1885. The first attempt at producing flat phonographic discs is credited to Emil Berliner in the early 1890s. Berliner's hand-cranked, flat disc 'Gramophone' eventually became the standard format for mechanical sound recording and reproduction.

By the 1920s, flat discs had virtually replaced cylinders, and records were made from natural thermoplastic ('shellac'). The introduction of electrical recording in 1925 by Western Electric allowed better sound recording and reproduction. The year 1948 saw the introduction of 33 rpm (revolutions per minute) long-playing records (LPs) by Columbia and the 45 rpm 'single' by RCA-Victor. Both these new formats used vinylite. This was later complemented by the development of multichannel recording in Britain and the USA. Multichannel recording allowed two separate channels of information to be recorded in the same groove and could then reproduce sound with spatial perspective. 'Stereophonic' records (as opposed to single-channel 'Monophonic' records) were eventually mass-produced in 1958. The introduction of stereophonic records and improvements in sound quality and systems quickly consigned the shellac 78 rpm disc format to obsolescence. In the 1980s, sales of magnetic and digital sound recordings overtook sales of phonograph records.

Magnetic sound recording

Audio tape decks electromagnetically impose or detect various magnetic patterns that correspond to sound waves on a moving magnetizable surface. As with mechanical recording, magnetic recording is an analogue system aiming to preserve an accurate correspondence between variations of sound waves and storing replicas of original sounds. Unlike compact disc, magnetic systems both allow playback and are recordable.

The first successful device to store information magnetically by magnetizing areas of steel wire was Poulsen's 'Telegraphone' of 1898. Major developments took place in the 1930s. Magnetic systems were developed to help synchronize sound and film; in 1936, the German Magnetophon Company demonstrated the uses of its 'Magnetophon' tape recorder by recording a performance of the London Philharmonic Orchestra. Commercial developments of tape recording remained limited until the development of the compact cassette by Philips in 1963. The compact cassette (universally known simply as 'cassette') was designed originally as a dictation device for business. The cassette allowed high-fidelity recording and playback. Its commercial success meant that the format effectively replaced reel-to-reel tape recorders during the 1970s. By 1983, sales of pre-recorded music cassettes exceeded those of phonograph records.

Digital sound recording

Digital sound recording samples sound waves at set intervals; the value of each sampled sound wave is a series of pulses. The main vehicle for digital recording is still the read-only compact disc (CD), but compression formats (notably MP3, see below) have proved successful, if controversial, since the late 1990s. CDs were developed jointly by Philips and Sony in the 1970s, and introduced commercially in 1983. Data is stored on a disc protected by a plastic cover. A laser beam optically converts a digital recording for playback. By 1988, unit sales of CDs exceeded those of records. Other formats introduced in the late 1980s and early 1990s for digital recording (apart from digital recordings available on analogue systems) proved less successful. Digital Audio Tape (DAT) was introduced commercially in 1988, allowing digital playback and offering a recording facility. Digital Compact Cassette (DCC) and MiniDisc (MD), both introduced commercially in 1992, failed to complement or replace CDs as the primary digital medium.

The success of CDs paved the way for the introduction of another optical disk format – the Digital Video Disc (DVD, now more commonly referred to as Digital *Versatile* Disc). DVD applications were introduced commercially in 1996, and offered superior data capacity to the CD. They have proved particularly successful for film (DVD-Video), and also for computer-based multimedia applications (DVD-ROM). The DVD-Audio format was introduced commercially in 2000, allowing high-quality sound reproduction and surround sound. DVD applications have proved commercially successful since 1996, though it remains to be seen whether DVD-Audio will supplant the CD.

Although CD and DVD represent the primary digital media for commercial sound recordings, the growth of Internet usage since 1993 has had impacts on sound recording and copyright holders. Compression formats, such as the Moving Picture Experts Group Audio Layer III (commonly referred to as MP3), allow sound recordings to be compacted for fast download times. The success of MP3 was due to the ready availability of playback devices, both as hardware and software. Additionally, Shawn Fanning's Napster software (introduced commercially in 1999) allowed straightforward downloading of MP3 recordings from users' computers around the world. The MP3 phenomenon has raised serious questions regarding copyright, with computers and the Internet giving the ability to copy and distribute digital sound recordings easily. Napster and MP3 can be seen as the beginnings of a PEER TO PEER (P2P) movement in which intellectual property, including recorded sound, is exchanged between individuals over the Internet in preference to purchase within the commercial system.

Further reading

Eargle, J.M. (1990) *Music, Sound and Technology*, Van Nostrand Reinhold [a good introduction to all aspects of sound recording].
Pierce, J.R. (1992) *The Science of Musical Sound*, rev. edn, W.H. Freeman & Company.
Schoenherr, S.E. (2002) *Recording Technology History* (http://history.sandiego.edu/gen/recording/notes.html) [accessed 10 May 2002].

SEE ALSO: copyright; informatics; information society; Internet; World Wide Web

JAMES DEARNLEY

SOUTH AMERICA

South American countries show a wide range of levels of development in library and information service. On the one hand, there are libraries that are totally automated, connected to international information databanks and which use the most modern electronic information systems; on the other hand, there is the great majority of libraries of the continent, still at the most rudimentary level of development, in which the minimal services are totally manual.

Many factors contribute to the almost general failure of information services in South America: high illiteracy rates, geographical environment, communication difficulties and political instability. But most of all, the general underestimation of the value of libraries, both by the authorities and by society itself, can be seen as the main reason for libraries not receiving adequate support in the region. Nevertheless, it is important to acknowledge that since the 1970s library and information centres have been generally increasing their services on the South American continent, although this development varies from country to country and between sectors. The impact of technological advances is bringing many improvements to the field, accelerating the process of change.

University libraries

UNIVERSITY LIBRARIES have achieved great progress, but much still remains to be done. In general, they have reached a higher level of development than other libraries, incorporating new INFORMATION TECHNOLOGY. Most countries have undertaken activities in favour of university libraries, encouraging the creation of NETWORKS as well as concentrating and co-ordinating activities and processes within each university. This has been evident in Brazil since the University Reform Act of 1972 and the establishment of the National Plan for University Libraries, which has greatly increased the systematization and use of information in higher education. In Venezuela, university libraries are co-ordinated by the National System of Library Information (SINASBI). In Argentina a National Network of University Libraries (RENBU) has been established and in Colombia the Colombian Institute for the Development of Higher Education (ICFES) is responsible for the co-ordination of university libraries. In recent years, many consortia directed to

rationalizing the acquisitions and use of information products in university libraries have been developed in different countries in South America, as, for example, the Consortium of University Libraries in Chile and The Program Electronic Library (PROBE) in Brazil. Consortia initiatives involving university libraries in several countries at the same time have also been established in South America, as the Agricultural Information and Documentation System for America (SIDALC), the Consortium for the Development of the Andes Eco-region (CONDESAN) and the Ibero-American Science and Technology Education Consortium (ISTEC).

School and public libraries

SCHOOL LIBRARIES have not developed effectively in South America. Schools that can count on effective library services are exceptions on the continent. Most education institutions do not have libraries: students are supposed to use PUBLIC LIBRARIES to complete their formal education. This peculiar environment has forced public libraries to develop in a particular way. In many countries, public libraries have a double role, functioning at the same time both as public and school libraries.

The lack of effective policy and a permanent lack of financial resources constitute serious problems for library managers. Although there is great demand for materials in public libraries, a large percentage of their customers are primary and secondary school students who use library services in order to obtain support for their formal education. These students come principally from state schools, where the quality of education is poorer than in private ones.

Financial limitations have normally obliged public libraries to concentrate their stocks on basic learning materials and to restrict their services to those related to educational purposes, thus limiting the library's ability to maintain a diverse collection. Leisure materials, even when representing a significant percentage of stock, have been relegated to passive use. In general, public libraries are seen as places where young people go to study because they do not have a suitable room at home. Figures for loans of books and for the relationship between the size of the community and the number of volumes in public libraries are very poor when compared to other regions of the world. Colombia, Venezuela,

Argentina and Brazil have developed relatively efficient public libraries, but the other countries have not yet managed to provide adequate services. Public libraries have improved noticeably in Brazil, where the activities of the Public Library System and the National Library Foundation have given special support to them. They are also increasing their services in Venezuela due to co-ordination by the Autonomous System of Library Services. In Colombia the growth of public libraries has received push with the organization of the National Network of Public Libraries, created in 1997, and the activities of the Foundation for the Support to Reading, a private institution founded by the Colombian graphic industry.

Special libraries and information centres

Advancements of science and technology imperatives have made SPECIAL LIBRARIES in South America expand greatly. In order to give support to social and economic development, countries have generally established systems to co-ordinate the supply of scientific and technological information, trying to link together the efforts of all their libraries and information centres. The Centre of Scientific Documentation in Argentina, the National Bolivian Centre of Scientific and Technological Documentation, the Brazilian Institute for Information in Science and Technology (IBICT) and the National Centre for Information and Documentation (CENID) in Chile are just a few examples of national organizations with the objective of incorporating all information resources in the worldwide network. It is also important to mention that many South American special libraries, principally those in the fields of medicine, agriculture, electricity and nuclear energy, can sometimes equal their counterparts in more developed countries, using all the resources technological progress provides, like CD-ROM, electronic communication and access to international databases, to provide their users with access to countless scientific and technological products and services.

Status of the librarian

The number of librarians has grown in South America, but the status of the profession is improving only slowly. Librarians' salaries are normally not very high, especially when compared with those received by other professionals.

There has always been a predominance of WO-MEN IN LIBRARIANSHIP, which is probably responsible for the low salaries. Cultural prejudices are still found, with a tendency to see librarians as a negative stereotype. The majority of countries in South America have legislation that tries to provide recognition for the profession. In countries such as Colombia and Brazil the library profession is regulated by a special law, giving support to professionals who attended library schools. Although the status of librarians has been improving in several countries where the professional image is slowly changing, it must be admitted that there is still a long way to go before it can be considered satisfactory.

Professional associations

The need to increase their status is a principal reason why almost all countries have organized their professionals into associations. Although cultural attitudes and an unfavourable economic environment can threaten their survival, South American professional associations organize congresses, seminars, continuing education courses, publish professional literature, encourage the exchange of ideas and promote unity. Again, Brazil and Argentina, with twenty-five and eighteen LIBRARY ASSOCIATIONS, respectively, are outstanding examples of countries that have presented greater development in the field. Many South American associations are affiliated to IFLA.

Information science education

The development of human resources for libraries has received reasonable attention in South America. The great majority of countries have at least one library school, with several of them providing postgraduate courses. Brazil, with thirty-two Bachelor's courses, six courses for Master's degrees and three for the Doctorate, followed by Argentina, with seven Bachelor's courses, are the countries where library education and information science education are most developed. Bachelor's courses normally take four years to complete. The Master's degree, generally covering both library and information sciences, takes about three years to complete. The scarcity of professional literature in native languages and the scarce number of full-time teachers are probably the worst problems faced by library schools.

Prospects for the future

The emergence of a global market economy in the beginning of the twenty-first century is making countries look for a means of reducing the gap between developed and less-developed countries. Looking at what library professionals in South America have achieved, it seems clear they are trying to contribute to that objective by making their best efforts to improve the services they provide to their communities. Additionally, in spite of having to acknowledge the limitations of libraries and information centres, the speed at which they have been upgrading their infrastructure and activities may be an indication that South American national policy formulators have become aware of the importance of information in an increasingly technological world. In Brazil in 2000, for example, the federal government launched the Information Society Programme, which aims to guarantee the benefits of the information technology to all the Brazilian population.

Further reading

Fernandez de Zamora, R.M. (1991) 'Library resources in Latin America: A general panorama', *IFLA Journal* 17: 45–54.

WALDOMIRO VERGUEIRO

SOUTH ASIA

The Indian subcontinent, with its history dating back to 4000 BC, was divided into India (Bharat) and Pakistan on 14 August 1947 when the British left India. The erstwhile East Pakistan, separated by 1,000 miles of Indian territory, became an independent country, in 1971, with the name of Bangladesh. The subcontinent thus split into three separate and independent countries.

Libraries in India

EARLIER DAYS TO TRANSFER OF POWER

India has a rich library heritage. Libraries at Taxila (558–30 BC; Punjab, now in Pakistan) and Nalanda University (Middle Ages; Bihar, India) attracted foreign travellers. The Muslim rulers of 1290–1707 had established libraries but their modernization began during British rule (1757–1947) with the arrival of British and US librarians in India after the Mutiny of 1857. First came

John Macfarlane, of the British Museum Library, in 1903, who served until his death in 1906 as Librarian of the Imperial Library, Calcutta (now Kolkata founded in 1902) on the nucleus of the Calcutta Public Library (1836), one of a number of such libraries established by the mid-1850s throughout the country. The next arrival was William Alanson Borden, who was selected by Maharaja Sajirao Gaekwad III on his US tour in 1910. He had been impressed by the US public libraries and wanted to establish a free public library system in Baroda, as a part of primary education provision. The third librarian, Asa Don Dickinson, a former student of Melvil DEWEY at New York State Library School (1903), was appointed University Librarian of the Punjab University, Lahore, which was one of the eight early universities of the country. The post was advertised in the USA by the Vice-Chancellor, Dr C.R. Ewing, who was originally a US missionary.

The influence of the British Museum Library through Macfarlane was confined to the Imperial Library, but that of Borden's free public library system, established in Baroda between 1910 and 1913, with a supporting journal and training programme, had a wider impact. The library system progressed so well that Borden's departure (1913) and even the death of the ruler (1939) did not deter it. The collection had increased to 1 million volumes by 1941 and library services were available to 83 per cent of the population of the state. Its influence on the Indian library movement – from the All-India Conference in the post-1918 period to the founding of the Indian Library Association (ILA) in 1933, aimed at dispelling British influence on libraries – and Baroda's echo abroad has been fully documented by Nagar (1969).

By contrast, Dickinson was uncertain about his success in the British setting in which he was to work. But on arrival in Lahore he was able to adjust, and started work with the missionary zeal of his teacher, Dewey, both at the Library and in the library education class, which like that of Borden included (besides graduates) some non-graduate practising librarians. This practice of undergraduate admission continued from 1918 to 1928, when the course was suspended for two years. From 1935 to 1945 the course was held on alternate years to make room for the Imperial Library's undergraduate Diploma course at Calcutta (Kolkata). In 1923 the book-based lectures by experts increased from twenty-two to seventy-six.

Dickinson wrote an easy-to-understand textbook for students that was published by Punjab University (1916). Based on Dewey's classnotes, this was the type of textbook that C.C. Williamson wanted for library schools (Kaser 1992). The two earlier books by Borden (1911) and his associate B.H. Mehta (1913), published from Baroda, are no match. The spread of the DEWEY DECIMAL CLASSIFICATION in India was his other contribution, which he hoped, in his letter to Dewey (1931), would increase with the appointment of his student, K.M. Asadullah, as Librarian of the Imperial Library (Comaromi and Satija 1985).

S.R. RANGANATHAN's return, as Madras University Librarian (1925), after London training, changed the library situation much faster. He founded the Madras Library Association (MALA) and started a certificate course that his university later took over (1931) and changed to a full-time postgraduate Diploma course (1937). Of his sixty books, *Colon Classification* (1933) produced the greatest impact. He became a one-man library movement (Shera 1962). His influence on the subcontinent is apparent from the institutions founded by him. After 1945 Ranganathan prepared a library development plan at the government's request. The Congress Ministries formed in various provinces (1937) opened village and travelling libraries as a follow-up to the Baroda experiment and Fyzee Committee recommendations for Bombay (now Mumbai) State. The IFLA New Delhi Conference (1992), to synchronize with the centenary of his birth, is a good example of his global impact.

The Calcutta University Commission (1917–19) also had its impact on university libraries. Libraries were opened where they had not existed. Librarians were appointed in teacher's grades, as recommended by the Commission. Madras University was a good example of this change.

India, Republic of (Bharat)

India gained independence in 1947, but without the Muslim majority states, three of which were divided to make them part of India. Mass migration and riots resulted, which affected libraries and the ILA. The Association's journal (1942–) was suspended from 1946–9. India has a population of 944 million (1996 estimate), 52.1 per cent of whom are literate, and is over 3,165,596 sq. km in size, divided into twenty-five states and seven union territories.

NATIONAL LIBRARIES

The Imperial Library became the country's national library (see NATIONAL LIBRARIES) by an Act (1948), as a subordinate institution under the Department of Culture in the Ministry of Human Resources Development. This 600-seat Library (collection: over 2 million volumes, 17,650 current periodicals and 800 newspapers, 1992) with free lending facilities for Calcutta (Kolkata) was opened in 1958. The Library receives all-language Indian publications including newspapers and periodicals (along with three other libraries) by LEGAL DEPOSIT under the Book Delivery Acts, 1954 and 1956, and publishes the *Indian National Bibliography*.

There are two other national libraries, located in New Delhi. The Central Medical Library (1961) was raised to the status of National Medical Library (NML) in 1966. Holding a collection of 250,000 books/reports and 2,300 current serials, the NML serves as a national focal point for MEDLARS ON-LINE (MEDLINE), publishes a quarterly bibliography of medical literature and updates a union catalogue of medical journals. The National Science Library (NSL) was founded in 1964 as part of the Indian National Scientific Documentation Centre (INSDOC), which had been founded in 1952. The Library holds 200,000 volumes and subscribes to 5,000 current periodicals.

PUBLIC LIBRARIES

The Madras (now Tamil Nadu) State enacted Ranganathan's draft bill in 1948, with some amendments, to support its public library system (see PUBLIC LIBRARIES). The Delhi Public Library (1951), a UNESCO demonstration pilot library, developed into a viable network for free public library services to the city, but without any enabling act. This Library now has a bookstock of 1,484,000 volumes, with five mobile vans and nineteen deposit stations. The Sinha Report (1957) also recommended legislative support for its proposed library system for the country. These developments resulted in the enactment of library acts in nine states, by 1989, to support their public libraries. Some 7,180 public libraries, including twenty-six central libraries, hold a collection of 35.9 million volumes. Kaula (1985) points out anomalies in various public library systems. The Raja Ram Mohan Roy Foundation (RRMRF) (1972) also helps to develop public library networks. The Punchayet Raj Bodies (PRB) were created to promote rural libraries under a constitutional amendment in 1992. A model public library act for this purpose was approved in a national seminar organized by ILA and RRMRF in New Delhi (1990). Some 44,200 further libraries are estimated (1993) to exist in India. The fund's outlay in the Eighth Plan (1992–7) has also been increased (Jambhekar 1995; Raju 1997).

ACADEMIC LIBRARIES

At the time of independence, ACADEMIC LI-BRARIES were deficient; the library allocation was only 1.8 per cent of the higher education budget. The Radhakrishnan Commission report (1948) recommended 6.25 per cent of university budget should be for this purpose, but by 1955 most of the university libraries were spending less than 1 per cent. The $5 million grant to the University Grants Commission (UGC), India (1953), from the US Wheat Loan, made a real difference. Library budgets and bookstocks increased; new buildings were constructed. More importantly, librarians were sent to the USA for study tours and on their return workshops were organized. The twenty universities in 1947 have increased to 200 universities, and twenty-two institutes and learned bodies with university status, with collections varying from 1,029,700 (Delhi University, f. 1922) to 10,000 volumes (Bundelkhand University, f. 1975). In all 7,112 academic libraries and their constituent branches hold 188,200,000 volumes (1989). The Agricultural Research Institute, New Delhi (600,000 vols and 5,000 current serials), publishes a monthly bibliography as well. Resource sharing in academic and research libraries gradually increased in India in 1991 with the establishment of UGC-supported National Information Network (INFLIBNET) with its base in Ahmedabad. As a result eight metropolitan areas and university towns started working together until 1995 to establish a LOCAL-AREA NET-WORK (LAN). Delhi started DELNET in 1991. Now 190 local libraries are participating in it with online catalogue access. The opening of CALINET at Calcutta (Kolkata), 1993, with the present participation of thirty-eight science and technology libraries, a 'high-tech' database and

co-operation with DELNET for global searching has changed the automation scenario in India altogether (Vyas 1997; Kar 1999).

INFLIBNET has brought this about with the help of the National Information System for Science and Technology (NISSAT), the National Information Centre (NICNET), ILA and the Indian Association of Special Libraries and Information Centres (IASLIC), among others. The Convention of Automation in Libraries (CALI-BER) has been held annually since 1994. The Ninth Plan proposes to computerize the rest of the university libraries in the country.

SPECIAL LIBRARIES

The industrialization of the country, the establishment of Institutes (1950–61) and the founding of INSDOC (1952) with centres at Bangalore, Calcutta (Kolkata) and Madras (Chinnoy), with supportive and commendable services, speeded up the growth of SPECIAL LIBRARIES; 2,500 special libraries (collection: 50 million volumes in 2,000 libraries; 1989) in the country, mostly in science, are supported by NSL with INSDOC's depository report collection and bibliographic access to India's science literature and its periodical holdings. Social science libraries (600 in number) also receive back-up services from the Indian Council of Social Science Centre, New Delhi, and its documentation centre. NISSAT co-ordinates with other systems in the country. Computer access in libraries is increasing. Inputs from India are also made to foreign databases.

SCHOOL LIBRARIES

The Secondary Education Commission (1952–3) noted the lack of urgency in developing SCHOOL LIBRARIES in India and recommended well-equipped libraries with a yearly intake of two books per student in the library collection and a trained librarian paid as a teacher to look after it. A 1981 survey found these libraries in a very poor condition. There are 62,240 school libraries in the country, with a total bookstock of 64,240,000 volumes (1989), manned by 25,000 librarians with certificates of library training etc. Some high schools, however, possess good libraries.

LIBRARY EDUCATION

Delhi University, under Ranganathan's direction, started the Commonwealth's first degree course in Library Science (BLibSc, 1948, changed later to

MLibSc, 1949). The PhD programme began in 1952, with the degree first awarded in 1957. In 1947 four universities offered Diploma courses. The Government of India Libraries Association (1951–60) and Women's Polytechnics (1961–) also started similar courses; the latter was of two-years duration. The Aligrah Muslim University started a shorter certificate course (1959) but replaced it with BLibSc. By 1995 seventy-five universities offered one-year Bachelor degree courses; fifty-five also offered a one-year MLibSc/MLIS programme. Only two had a two-year Master's programme. Two or three universities had an MPhil programme, while twenty-five had a Doctoral programme. Five universities offered an informal distance-education programme in BLibSc/Diploma, while two of them had similar Master's programmes. Satija (1992) gives an output of 100 PhDs by the early 1990s, with an annual output of ten, but the research is rarely cited. Mangla (1997) reports more than sixty PhDs by 1997. INSDOC and the Documentation Research and Training Centre (DRTC) offer an Associateship in Documentation and in Information Science, respectively, recognized by the government as a Master's degree. A number of associations, institutes and organizations offer certificate courses. IASLIC and other documentation centres offer short-term special courses too. In addition, Information Science and Technology courses are presently included in the curricula of Bombay, Delhi and Nagpur Universities. The degrees are badged as Library and Information Science.

LIBRARY ASSOCIATIONS

ILA is the largest association that holds its conference every year and has published proceedings and a journal regularly since 1955. IASLIC is the second largest association and publishes two journals, including *Indian Science Abstracts* (1967). Almost all the states/territories have their local LIBRARY ASSOCIATIONS; some offer courses and publish journals. The oldest association is Andhra Pradesh Library Association (1914), which has published its Telgu-language journal since 1915, with a few gaps.

Pakistan, Islamic Republic of

LIBRARIES IN THE EARLY YEARS

Pakistan was carved out of British India but East Bengal/East Pakistan was separated from West Pakistan by 1,000 miles of Indian territory. Pakistan has a population of 130.6 million (1998), of whom 26 per cent were literate in 1985; the country extends over 796,096 sq. km divided into four provinces. Riots in 1947–8 damaged libraries in Lahore, known for their rich resources. In East Pakistan, Dacca (Dhaka) University, founded as a model for pre-partition India, had an edge over the others because of the library's rich holdings on ancient history. Mass migration dislocated educational activities and those of libraries. The Punjab Library Association of pre-partition days was suspended. Its journal was discontinued in 1946. Dickinson's School was closed. The homecoming of Asadullah, a dynamic library leader in India, also could not save the declining situation of libraries in this new country. He died in 1949 without having made any impact on Pakistan. Indian libraries were not divided because of bureaucratic indifference, while Pakistan had to start from scratch and problems abounded; no clear-cut policy on education and libraries could be developed. The Pakistan Education Conference (1947), however, made some decisions. Consequently, the Directorate of Archives and Libraries was established (1951) with a national library under its control, which changed name and status from time to time. The Pakistan Bibliographical Working Group (PBWG) was formed in 1950. Local library associations were also organized in Lahore (1948); Karachi (1949); and in East Pakistan EPLA was founded in Dhaka in 1956. EPLA was well organized and published a journal, *Eastern Librarian*, until 1978. The *Modern Librarian* was revived in 1949 by the Association in Lahore, which called itself a national body, but the journal was discontinued in 1950. A certificate course was started by Punjab University (1950) but without book-based technical lectures. The arrival of foreign consultants after 1950, and L.C. Key's four-year plan for thirty-six model libraries of almost all types and two library schools, resulted in brisk activities although the plan itself remained shelved. The country's first postgraduate library course was at Karachi University in 1956, before the Key Report. The establishment of the Pakistan National Scientific and Technical Documentation Centre (PANSDOC) in 1956 in Karachi and, more importantly, the founding of the Pakistan Library Association (PLA) in 1957 and the inauguration of its first Conference by the then-President of Pakistan (1958), made a great difference.

NATIONAL LIBRARY

The national library – called Liaquat Memorial Library (LML) – eventually only performed *ad hoc* functions of that role. The Central Library of Pakistan rented premises in Dhaka (1968) and started collecting local publications, under the Delivery of Books and Newspapers Ordinance, 1962. Another library of the LML type was demanded for Dhaka in 1971, but the separation of East Pakistan closed that chapter. As a result of separation, the Department of Libraries was also divided in 1974, and it was transferred to Islamabad in 1981. The *Pakistan National Bibliography* (PNB; 1962–; annual/irregular), published since 1966 by LML, was taken over by the Department. The LML itself was transferred to the Sindh provincial government in 1986. In 1993 the 500-seat National Library of Pakistan was formally opened to the public in its grand new building in Islamabad with 130,000 volumes and 600 manuscripts. A computer centre has been established for automation of its services. The latest *PNB* was published in 1996 but the last fascicule of the retrospective *Bibliography* (1947–61) for subjects 500–900 compiled by PBWG was at long last published in 1999. Revised according to DEWEY DECIMAL CLASSIFI-CATION (19th edn) and AACR2 (see ANGLO-AMERICAN CATALOGUING RULES) and ISBD rules, this BIBLIOGRAPHY is of more than 560 pages, with an index.

ACADEMIC LIBRARIES

The growth in the number of libraries from three in 1947 to twenty-three (with collections of 2,899,400 volumes) in 1990 made up the gap caused by the loss of six libraries to East Pakistan. The Education Policy (1992) proposed to designate the Quaid-e-Azam University, Islamabad, as a Science University, and its Library (collection: 155,000 volumes, 1994) as the National Science Library, but political change made it otherwise. The President's Ordinance, 1994, established the National University of Science and Technology as a decentralized multicampus complex comprising the military colleges and institutes of Rawalpindi and Riasalpur. Some libraries have automated their operations and have Internet access. The Aga Khan University of Health Sciences Library (AKUHSL) started a resource-sharing consortium of eleven local medical libraries. This facility is extended abroad to Arab Gulf Co-operation Council Medical Libraries (AGCCML). AKUHSL College of Physicians and Surgeons of Pakistan Library, Karachi, and Lahore University of Management Sciences (LUMS) provide access to CD-ROM databases. The College is also a national focal point for MEDLINE. Lahore Business and Economics Libraries Network (LABELNET) was established by LUMS with a union catalogue/list of the books and periodicals of participating libraries.

During 1980–7, UGC and the British Council organized seminars/workshops in the country and follow-up training at Loughborough University, to remedy manpower deficiencies in academic libraries. Smith (1991) documents the good results of the programme. The Netherlands Library Development Project-Pakistan (NLDP) started orientation and training in Holland in 1991, but unlike the earlier programme it was not confined to academic librarians. There were fifty-eight universities and degree-awarding institutions in the country (thirty-seven public and twenty-one private universities in 2001). In 1994 their main and constituent libraries held a collection of 3,296,500 vols (Fazil Khan 1996). College libraries are poor in resources and services: 435 colleges (out of 680, 1988) reported (1990) 3,640,000 volumes, ranging from 35,000 volumes at DJ Science College, Karachi (founded in 1887) to 115,000 volumes at Government College, Lahore (founded in 1864). The latter is the only college in the country to reach six figures in its collection.

PUBLIC LIBRARIES

The 229 public libraries of Pakistan (1970) included 116 libraries, along with three city libraries of the Key Report, in East Pakistan. By 1989 the number of libraries in Pakistan had increased to 281 (collection: over 2.1 million volumes), along with 4,373 box libraries in villages, with over 1 million books, distributed by the Ministry of Local Self-Government and Rural Development as a joint partner of the proposed Technical Working Group (TWG) system. This was a result of continued campaigning by the PLA and the Society for the Promotion and Improvement of Libraries, founded in 1960. Free public library services are provided by committees and the country's oldest library, Frere Hall Public Library (opened 1951), now under

Karachi Metropolitan Corporation; collection: 48,600 vols (total collection in the City 300,000 vols). Fifty-one Karachi Municipal Committee Libraries under Zonal Committees are also due to their efforts. The TWG's report to the government (1984/published 1985), the establishment of the Public Libraries Directorate in Punjab (1981) and the Punjab Library Foundation (1985) have their share too in development. The TWG report, however, does not reflect anybody else's opinion but those of the public and the professional librarians with whom they made contact during their sittings in various cities and interviews, and questionnaires answered by those who influence public opinion in this regard. This has fully been explained in the summary of the report published in Anis Khurshid (2000). Thus, while its draft recommendations were discussed in a two-day National Seminar, Karachi, in September 1993 and slightly modified, the system did not materialize due to political change.

SPECIAL LIBRARIES

The Scientific Commission (1960) and PANS-DOC's Symposium (1963) promoted the need for better organized science libraries in the country. Herman H. Henkle's recommendation for a science library in each part to support the country's documentation services was examined by experts in 1972–6. PANSDOC was shifted to Islamabad to become an Information Centre attached to Pakistan Science Foundation in 1973. PASTIC, as it is now called, with branches in various cities, produced a computerized union catalogue of the science periodicals of local libraries in 1987. In 1989 there were 331 special libraries, with 2.5 million volumes.

SCHOOL LIBRARIES

School libraries are, however, somewhat better. A Gallup Pakistan survey in 1987 reported the existence of school libraries in 60 per cent of villages, with an average of 600 books in each. Students do use these books. Efforts were made by various associations and the Hamdard Foundation to improve their condition, with no result. Even a government-appointed subcommittee's recommendation (1981) did not produce any results. A school library system for the city schools in Karachi, Hyderabad and Quetta (forty-six libraries, the largest number in Karachi) has been computerized in a central catalogue in the Head Office at Karachi.

LIBRARY EDUCATION

Punjab University was a trendsetter on the subcontinent but its academic indifference to raising its certificate course to a higher level continued even after the foundation of Pakistan. A breakthrough was made in 1956 by Karachi University, when it started a postgraduate Diploma course, first as an evening programme but later, after availability of trained manpower, as a full-time Master's programme in 1962, with a PhD programme in 1967. Karachi University also helped Dhaka University, to some extent, in instituting a Master's programme in 1962. Seven universities offer a full-time Postgraduate Diploma in Library Science (PG DLIS). The BLIS is a separate degree course at Karachi University along with a one-year MLIS course. Punjab University also offers it as an evening programme. AIOU is the seventh university to start a one-year MLIS in its distance education programme, with ten papers spread over four semesters. Its earlier BLIS is an undergraduate programme of four courses in Urdu spread over two semesters. It also offers a certificate course in Urdu consisting of two papers that are also included in BLIS. The Air Force College is the only college in Karachi to teach BLIS degree courses with affiliation to Karachi University.

Sindh University was the first to start an MPhil programme and award a degree in 1980. Starting a direct PhD programme as early as 1969, the university has been able to award a PhD to two candidates. Islamia University awarded a PhD degree in 1984. An MPhil programme based on a year's seminar courses was approved in 1985 with a thesis in the second year or thereafter. However, it did not progress because of the indifference of senior teachers. It was never intended to be a substitute for the PhD programme nor has it abolished it, as it would appear from the award of a PhD in 1995. Information science teaching is supported by access to computers.

Intermediate and BA (Minor) optional courses have also been taught or approved in various cities in the country but largely as the use of books and libraries. Universities have begun to give preference to students seeking admission in library courses who had taken such courses in their undergraduate programme. Sindh University has approved such a minor course of BSc and BCom (Hons) as well.

There are still differences between DLIS papers

in various universities. There are as many as fifteen papers in Islamia University, which has a combined two-year MLIS programme to twelve papers and an eight-week Practicum in a selected Lahore library as a compulsory requirement, while some other universities following a two-year programme have just ten or twelve papers. This disparity has resulted from various curriculum revisions commissioned by UGC in the post-1980 period that were not uniformly adopted in the country as the UGC first revision (1980) had been. The last National Revision Committee met in Karachi (October 2001) to finalize the 4th or 5th draft revision, which has not been made public. Some criticism was made recently in the literature. Khalid Mahmood (1997) says that the 1991 revision for the first time recognized the importance of Information Technology, which is not true. He does not, however, mention the dropping of one paper, although this had not been demanded. The fact that expansion that took place in the subject of Information Science and its technology, which was made a compulsory paper in the 1980 syllabus, meant that far more time was now required to cover developments in the subject. Another critic, after relinquishing an important responsibility in a university, finds faults in the library education programme itself but he does not say why those deficiencies highlighted were not removed.

LIBRARY ASSOCIATIONS

PLA and PBWG are the two national associations that are active. The former has zonal branches, some of which established computer training centres with the assistance of NLDP (but it has now discontinued this programme) and none of the centres have funds to maintain their equipment. PLA holds conferences and publishes the proceedings, and also publishes a journal irregularly. It rotates its headquarters every two or more years to zonal headquarters. The Punjab University Library Science Alumni Association revived its activities by holding two conferences in the early 1990s.

Bangladesh, People's Republic of

East Pakistan separated in 1971, and Bangladesh became an independent country. New institutions were established; some old ones were upgraded. Migration started once again. The EPLA became the Library Association of Bangladesh (LAB).

Eastern Librarian, which was its organ, was discontinued in 1978. Bangladesh (area 143,998 sq. km) has a population of 125 million (1997), with 38.9 per cent adult literacy (1997). There are five administrative divisions.

NATIONAL LIBRARIES

The CPL (collection: 112,400 volumes, 1968) became the National Library of Bangladesh (NLB) in 1975, under the Directorate of Archives and Libraries. The Education Commission (1974) had recommended this status for CPL and a separate directorate to look after libraries. The NLB (collection: 2,000,000 volumes, 1999) receives the country's publications under a new LEGAL DEPOSIT act, and has published the *Bangladesh National Bibliography* annually since 1979. Funds, however, delayed the publication of the *Bibliography* from 1990.

Ahmed (1985) names three more national libraries located in Dhaka: (1) National Health Library and Documentation Centre, under the Directorate General of Health Services (collection: 14,000 volumes and 300 current periodicals), with national focal point for MEDLINE etc.; (2) National Science Library, established in 1981 by merging with the National Bangladesh Scientific Documentation Centre (BANSDOC; 1963 as a branch, 1972); and (3) National Agricultural Library and Documentation Centre (present collection: 12,000), under the Bangladesh Agricultural Research Council (BARC).

ACADEMIC LIBRARIES

No new university has been opened since independence. Six university libraries hold a bookstock of over 1.1 million volumes (1990). Dhaka University Library is the country's oldest and richest library (collection: 651,200 volumes and 30,000 manuscripts, 1994). The latest edition of *World of Learning* lists nine university libraries, whereas Rahman (1997) gives eleven in addition to eighteen private university libraries. Half-a-dozen such libraries are foreign-sponsored specialized subject libraries mostly opened (1992) in Dhaka, in business, engineering and computer science, with relatively small collections compared to public universities. They, however, provide specialized reference services and even outside access to much larger databases and Internet services (Foote 1995). There were 600 colleges in 1978, with collections ranging from 35,000 to 58,300 volumes in 1981.

PUBLIC LIBRARIES

The CPL (collection: 112,400 volumes) is the country's major public library; it administers four divisional libraries, with collections of 32,100 to 69,100 volumes in each (originally opened as model city libraries), and sixty-three district libraries, with a bookstock of 4,000 volumes each. These libraries do not lend books. The Public Libraries Department (1983) supervises them. Rahman (1997) mentions about fifty-seven non-government district libraries, 245 libraries and sixty-four small libraries but no library legislation exists in the country. The National Book Policy has recommended such legislation for public libraries.

The Centre for Integrated Rural Development for Asia and the Pacific (CIRDAP), an inter-government organization of eleven countries with the headquarters in Bangladesh, established the Information Network on Rural Development (INRD). Some forty libraries in the area partici-pate in this and exchange information. LAB has prepared a format for the Network. 'It enjoys materials and working conditions which most of the colleagues can only dream of' (Wanasundera 1994).

SPECIAL LIBRARIES

Fifty-seven special libraries (in 1970), with col-lections ranging from 750 to 37,500 volumes, have increased to 125 libraries since the estab-lishment of Bangladesh (Rahman 1997). Their resources and services, in some cases, are ahead of other libraries in the country. Most libraries are part of scientific, research and governmental organizations. The libraries of BARC and the International Centre for Diarrhoeal Disease Re-search, Bangladesh (collection: 34,500 volumes and 525 periodicals), represent the most sophis-ticated operations in the country. They are specialized libraries opened by foreign agencies with ample funds and access to foreign experts, the latest journals, online and offline databases, and CD-ROM facilities (Foote 1995).

SCHOOL LIBRARIES

The Education Commission (1974) found school libraries in bad condition. Where they exist they are locked in the headteachers' offices or tea-chers' common rooms. In the mid-1980s a programme of training for librarians and supply of AUDIOVISUAL MATERIALS to schools was un-dertaken.

LIBRARY EDUCATION

Dhaka University has offered MPhil and PhD programmes since 1976 and 1979, respectively, in addition to MA (LIS) (1962) a two-year MA in LS in 1975–6 and a three-year BA Honours in LIS (1988). Its Diploma course has been taken over by the LAB (1989), which already offers a four-month certificate course twice a year with a second centre in Rajshahi (1973). Rajshahi Uni-versity also started a Diploma course in 1991 and a three-year BA (Hons) in 1993.

LIBRARY ASSOCIATIONS

The LAB has restarted publication of *Eastern Librarian*. There are three more separate associa-tions for college/medical librarians and informa-tion specialists.

References

Ahmed, Z. (1985) 'The national libraries of Bangla-desh: Their present status and future role', *Eastern Librarian* 11: 36–50.

Comaromi, J.P. and Satija, M.P. (1985) 'History of Indianization of the Dewey Decimal Classification', *Libri* 35: 7–11.

Fazil Khan, M. (1996) 'Information society and its status in Pakistan', *Pakistan Library Bulletin* 27: 1–9.

Foote, J.B. (1995) *Third World Libraries* [now *World Libraries*] 5: 58–66 [on Bangladesh].

Jambhekar, N. (1995) 'National policy on public libraries in India', *Third World Libraries* [now *World Libraries*] 5: 8–21

Kar, P. (1999) 'XML: towards efficient searching', in P.S.G. Kumar and C.P. Vashisth (eds), *CALIBER 1999: Academic Libraries in the Internet Era. Proceedings of the Sixth National Convention for Automation of Libraries in Education and Research, Nagpur, India, 18–20 February 1999*, pp. 451–8

Kaser, D. (1992) 'Asa Don Dickinson', in Sajjad-ur-Rehman *et al.* (eds), *Library Education in Pakistan*, Punjab University Library Science Alumni Associa-tion, pp. 3–10.

Kaula, P.N. (1985) 'Librarianship – a career', *Herald of Library Science* 24: 312–16.

Khurshid, A. (2000) *Planning and Management of Library and Information Services in Pakistan*, Kar-achi: Library and Information Services Group.

Mahmood, K. (1997) 'Information technology and library education in Pakistan: recent developments in the curriculum', *Education for Information* 15: 197–205.

Mangla, P.B. (1997) 'National policies on libraries, information systems and services in India: an over-view', *New Review of Library and Information Research* 3: 155–74.

Nagar, M. (1969) 'Public library movement in Baroda', unpublished PhD dissertation, Columbia University.

Rahman, Afifa (1997) 'Library development in Bangla-desh', *Herald Lib. Sc.* 36: 52–9.

Raju, K.A. (1997) 'Decentralised development and the role of public libraries in India', *Public Library Quarterly* 16: 39–57.

Satija, M.P. (1992) 'Library science research in India', Indo-US Conference of Library and Information Professionals, pre-IFLA Conference, New Delhi, 27–28 August 1992, unpublished paper.

Shera, J.H. (1962) 'S.R. Ranganathan; One American view', *Pakistan Library Review* 4: 6–8.

Smith, I.A. (1991) 'International co-operation in professional development of academic librarians: A Pakistan–British Council success story', in N. Qureshi *et al.* (eds) *Trends in International Librarianship*, Royal Book Co., pp. 105–32.

Vyas, S.D. (1997) 'Management of backlog cataloguing in university libraries in Rajasthan', *Annals of Library Science and Documentation* 44: 1–17.

Wanasundera, L. (1994) 'The information network on rural development, Bangladesh', *Third World Libraries* 5: 11–16.

Further reading

Banerjee, D.N. (1997) 'India's National Library', *Herald of Library Science* 33: 230–8.

Khurshid, Anis (1969) *Standards for Library Education in Burma, Ceylon, India, and Pakistan*, University of Pittsburgh [describes library development from the early days to 1969].

SEE ALSO: distance learning; library education

ANIS KHURSHID

SOUTHEAST ASIA

Southeast Asia, or ASEAN as it is more popularly known in the international arena, is a region comprising Brunei, Cambodia, Indonesia, PDR Lao (Laos), Malaysia, Myanmar (formerly Burma), the Philippines, Singapore, Thailand and Vietnam. All ten nations are now members of ASEAN (Association of Southeast Asia Nations) and comprise some 500 million residents. The economies of these countries are quite disparate, but, through the ASEAN mechanism, they collaborate on a variety of socio-economic programmes and initiatives including reading, culture and librarianship to ensure that the region as a whole makes progress. A strong alliance and a collaborative spirit has also been forged among libraries and librarians in this region. They work closely through a parallel mechanism – the Congress of Southeast Asian Libraries or CONSAL.

CONSAL was founded in Singapore in 1970 in response to a growing sense of a Southeast Asian identity. The initiative in forming CON-SAL was taken by the Library Associations of Singapore and Malaysia, due to their common origin and long history of close co-operation. Representatives from the LIBRARY ASSOCIATIONS of Cambodia, Indonesia, Malaysia, the Philippines, Singapore, Thailand and South Vietnam ratified the constitution and became the founding members of CONSAL. CONSAL focuses on promoting co-operation in the fields of librarianship, bibliography, documentation and related activities. Membership is open to national library associations, NATIONAL LIBRARIES and other related organizations in the region. CONSAL holds a conference once every three years with each member country taking turns to host the event.

CONSAL XI was held in Singapore in April (Yit and Foo 2002). This was a landmark event as it resulted in the admission of the two remaining ASEAN countries, Myanmar and PDR Lao, as CONSAL members and the formation of the CONSAL Secretariat. Singapore was appointed to host the Secretariat for a period of three years and manage the collaborative projects that were endorsed. Among the projects approved at CONSAL XI were resource sharing and LEGAL DEPOSIT to facilitate access to national bibliographic resources including acquisitions and exchange; COPYRIGHT to explore the guidelines for fair use of various types of materials, especially digital transmission and to explore setting up a rights management system; PRESERVATION and CONSERVATION of library materials for member countries; translation of materials for the main purpose of making available the cultural heritage of each country; and a training and development plan to co-ordinate training of librarians in the region.

Investing in libraries

There is a growing demand for more sophisticated library and information services in the region, propelled by technological advances, environmental changes and a more technologically aware and affluent user community. As a result, governments in the region have been reviewing and investing in the PUBLIC LIBRARIES to promote reading, info-literacy, learning and innovation among the people, and to provide community-based institutions. The region shares the common goal of promoting social inclusion and bridging the divide by ensuring equal access to content and services available at the libraries as well as through the INTERNET. The mission statements of the national libraries or authorities overseeing libraries reflect the scope of most libraries in the region. The roles of libraries seem to revolve around the twin strategies of supporting lifelong learning through access to information and preserving the nation's intellectual capital. To illustrate, the mission of the National Library Board, the government agency spearheading public library development in Singapore, is 'to expand the learning capacity of the nation so as to enhance national competitiveness and to promote a gracious society', and the corporate philosophy of the National Library of Malaysia, which is 'ensuring that Malaysia's intellectual heritage [is] collected for the...reference of present and future generations'. These are reflective of the ambitious goals of the nation's publicly funded libraries.

A review of developments in the ASEAN libraries revealed the quantum changes occurring, especially in Malaysia, Singapore and Thailand, and the newer economies such as Vietnam. Vast improvements have been seen in the collections with an increase also in digital collections, library education, automation and going digital, co-operative projects, manpower training and service improvements. The newly emerging economies of Cambodia, PDR Lao, Myanmar and Vietnam are slowly making attempts, in some cases with foreign aid, to restore much of what was destroyed through years of war and neglect.

Overview of libraries in ASEAN

The information needs of the citizens are collectively served by a constellation of national, public, academic and special libraries. They provide the same basic services as those in the more developed world. However, these libraries may lack depth and comprehensiveness because of budgetary and other resource constraints. The publicly funded libraries are managed by the appropriate government agencies; for instance, ACADEMIC LIBRARIES are usually under the education agency and public libraries are under culture or information-related agencies. The launch of *Library 2000: Investing in a Learning Nation* by the Singapore Ministry of Information and the Arts in April 1994 spurred other countries in the region and the world to reinvent and position libraries as key pillars supporting life-

long learning. Many are developing their own strategic plans and/or revamping library and information services (see Quick tour, below). Emphasis has also been placed on LIBRARY AUTOMATION, linking the libraries and creating digital content so that the users can seamlessly access the nation's information resources.

The national libraries in the region have the usual functions of providing a reference and information service, and acting as the legal deposit libraries in their respective countries. As such, most of the national libraries have embarked on DIGITIZATION programmes to make available their treasures online. They are also the INTERNATIONAL STANDARD BOOK NUMBER agencies. The National Library of the Philippines acts as the Copyright Office while Singapore has plans to take on this role. The major developments in the last decade include the move, in 1992, of the National Library of Malaysia to its new expanded premises with enhanced services including catering to the disadvantaged, and the major renovation of Singapore's National Library, in 1997, to include multimedia facilities and a café. Singapore has commenced work on a brand new National Library building that will be at least five times larger than the existing facility. The new library has been named National Library SINGAPORE and will open its doors in 2004. The national libraries typically provide the leadership in library matters in most ASEAN countries, except Brunei (where there is no national library) and Singapore where the National Library Board was set up in 1995 to spearhead public library development.

The public libraries in the region focus on the provision of lending and basic reference services to the public at large. A typical configuration of the public library system is one comprising a network of state and local public libraries supported by mobile libraries (see MOBILE LIBRARY) and a wide array of USER EDUCATION and outreach programmes. Countries such as Indonesia, Malaysia, Thailand and Vietnam place emphasis on providing RURAL LIBRARY SERVICES, and conduct various library programmes such as storytelling and reading. The developments in Singapore demonstrate the vast improvements made in the region. Public libraries in Singapore have been transformed into lifestyle experiences. This transformation resulted in the doubling and tripling of loans and visitors at the libraries, with some 25 million loans and 21 million visitors a year in 2000 compared to 14 million loans and 7.3 million visitors in 1995. The *Library 2000 Report* had recommended an adaptive three-tier public library system with quality services through market orientation to reach out to the target communities and raise usage. Libraries in Singapore have adopted new merchandising techniques and technology to improve both business operations and service quality. Borrowing and returning books has been simplified through the implementation of the RFID-enabled self-check system for borrowing and returning stations. Fines can be paid using cashcards at the borrower enquiry stations. RFID-enabled systems allow for immediate cancellation of loans upon return at book drops at the libraries. The first remote book drop (perhaps in the world) is located at the premises of a bank in the busy central business district, allowing library users working in the area to drop off books in the city.

Public libraries in Singapore are now not just stand-alone libraries in residential neighbourhoods but are brought to where the people are, and hence are located in shopping malls and civic and community centres. To reach out to young adults, the largest population group that is not using libraries, a trendy new library was opened at a busy shopping mall in the heart of the city. Called the 'Library Orchard', it has proven to be a crowd puller and also stimulated Ngee Ann Polytechnic to design a 'lifestyle library' and play its part in inculcating reading habits in the young adult student population at the polytechnic. In addition to general lending libraries, Singapore is also beginning to roll out thematic libraries, while the performing arts library ('Library Esplanade') will open at the new Theatres at the Bay Performing Arts Centre in late 2002. Singapore may make another first when it opens its 'Library Sengkang', a community library in the northeast of the island, which will be unstaffed. It will be a self-help library, with no librarians on-site but in touch through a 'cybrarian' service.

Vast changes have been made or are being made at the public libraries, but the developments in the academic libraries have been somewhat less colourful. These libraries continue to place priority on serving the needs of the academic community and in some cases extending their services to industry. Through the collaborations between the academic institutions and overseas partners, the academic libraries are forging links with overseas academic libraries. This is particularly the case in Singapore. In academic libraries COLLECTION DEVELOPMENT, information technology, involvement in the academic curriculum, co-operation and responding to the national aspirations are common themes. These libraries also recognize the implicit role of the academic and research library in supporting the transformation of the economy and human resource development.

The academic libraries of Malaysia, the Philippines, Singapore and Thailand seem comparatively more developed in terms of the collections and services offered to the user. Many are moving towards adopting the digital path to delivery of services by creating digital libraries (see DIGITAL LIBRARY) as part of the campus-wide e-strategy. In the less developed ASEAN countries, such as Myanmar, Cambodia, PDR Lao and Vietnam, budgetary constraints hamper developments. Many are seeking assistance from international agencies to assist them in the development of collections and exploitation of technology.

Some interesting developments in the region can be seen in Singapore at Nanyang Technological University, Ngee Ann Polytechnic and the newly formed third university, the Singapore Management University. Nanyang Technological University transformed its main library into an e-library with some 450 computers allowing students to access a vast variety of information services and resources. The Ngee Ann Polytechnic introduced a 'lifestyle library' with a café to complement its academic library, and the Singapore Management University decided to outsource the development and operations of its library to the National Library Board. This, the SMU said, allows for it to focus on its core business of teaching and research while leaving the non-core business to partners who have the core competencies. It also addressed the issue of career development of library staff, as the university did not have to worry about the specialized team's career development needs.

School libraries

The development of SCHOOL LIBRARIES in the region is still at an early stage. For example, in Brunei Darussalam, the school library is a recent social phenomenon. However, all newly built schools now have libraries or resource centres. In most of the ASEAN countries, teachers manage the school libraries as an added responsibility to the teaching load. Student librarians then assist the teacher in running the library. The national libraries and the library associations assist by organizing training programmes for teachers. It has been recognized in Malaysia and Singapore that there is a need for integration of the resource centre into the educational process and professional involvement in developing generic information handling skills and INFORMATION LITERACY. The Ministry of Education in Singapore is exploring working with the National Library Board to set in place school media resource centres. The National Library Board's Student Virtual Community supports the needs of students. It encourages continuous learning and sharing of ideas among students. Malaysia has explored Bill Gates's concept of a Connected Learning Community (CLC) Project. It provides a three-way connectivity between schools, libraries/learning resources and parents, and facilitates equal access and opportunity for the students and community to learn. The project involves the NLM, fourteen state libraries and others.

Special libraries

The majority of SPECIAL LIBRARIES in the region are in the government sector. In Indonesia, for example, it is estimated that there are 620 special libraries of which 81 per cent are in government organizations. Malaysia, although it has fewer special libraries than Indonesia, has a broader selection of different types of special library with some offering substantial services; the situation is similar in Thailand. Singapore has some 200 special libraries with the government libraries being managed by librarians or library officers seconded from the National Library. Most special libraries offer a range of services customized to meet the needs of their clientele and they were among the early adopters of electronic information services. Another emerging trend being witnessed is the expanded role the special libraries play in KNOWLEDGE MANAGEMENT, with the librarian playing the role of the knowledge steward or officer, especially in Singapore and Malaysia.

An innovative special library service can be seen at the Kuala Lumpur Stock Exchange (KLSE) Library in Malaysia. The KLSE Library offers a comprehensive and consolidated securities information service both through its main library at the exchange, and also through its branches and the WORLD WIDE WEB. The service suite includes daily alerts, information searches, creating digital library and CD-ROM products, electronic publishing and running the Publications Unit and a shop. It also boasts of a state-of-the-art 'Info Gallery' showcasing various services such as access to securities databases, a simulation room allowing users to try their hands at investment and a gallery on the history of the KLSE. The library staff also conduct user education programmes including travelling roadshows across the states of Malaysia to promote awareness of KLSE and securities investment. The Singapore Press Holding's Library is another state-of-the-art special newspaper library that has come a long way. It has unique and vast historical archives that date back to 1845, when *The Straits Times* was first published. The newspaper collection from 1989 is now available through the Newslink database. Unlike other libraries, it houses a precious collection of 20 million photographic negatives and 5 million photographs, which are available in hard copy and in online databases, some of which were never published. These collections rival even those in the National Archives. What is interesting is that with its move to brand new modern premises, these massive historical information sources are being made available for anyone and everyone, from the inquisitive secondary school student to the serious doctoral researcher.

Quick tour

BRUNEI

One of the newer CONSAL members, it opened its first library in 1953, which was operated by the information services department with only an attendant to run it. Brunei has since come a long way and now has a network of public libraries and special libraries in government agencies. Brunei does not have a national library but the Dewan Bahasa dan Pustaka (DBP), established in 1963 (opened in 1970), serves as the main source of information for the public and researchers with lending, reference and enquiry services. The DBP comprises a network of four branch libraries and forty-three mobile library service points. The library plays a leadership role in publishing the *Directory of Libraries in Brunei Darussalam* and *Directory of Librarians*.

CAMBODIA

Though war-torn for years, the country now boasts some seventy libraries, with the National Library of Cambodia (NLC) playing a pivotal role. The NLC is managed by the Department of Books and Reading of the Ministry of Culture and the Fine Arts, and acts as the legal deposit library maintaining the national filing and documentation centre. Various international organizations such as the UNDP, UNESCO and UNICEF have set up libraries in Cambodia. It has a unique collection of national written heritage documents published in French between 1925–70 and those in the Khmer language between 1955–75, and a collection of works written on palm leaves.

INDONESIA

Indonesia is prolific in provision, with some 157 public libraries serving 314 districts, 500 academic libraries, 1,600 special libraries and 219,000 school libraries. The National Library's Indonesiana collection provides a wealth of information on the history and culture of each region including rare manuscripts written in a variety of formats – palm leaves, barks, bamboo and so on, and mainly in the Dutch language. To reach the dispersed communities living in isolated areas, there is a need for mobile libraries. To encourage reading and library use, the libraries have proclaimed the month of September as the 'Reading Habit Month' and 'Visit Library Day'.

PDR LAO

Traditional libraries were found in, for instance, the Laotian Buddhist temples, which were usually small and windowless. There are some 1,700 such libraries in the seventeen provinces. The collections date back to the sixteenth and seventeenth centuries CE, many on palm leaves and stored in beautifully lacquered wooden manuscript caskets. These precious materials were saved from damage and loss by the generosity of a German foundation that funded a preservation project in 1992–2002. The National Library of Lao (NLL) is being rebuilt and receives book donations from other countries, including, in the past, the Soviet Union. It also houses national manuscript collections. The NLL co-ordinates library development throughout Laos. The public libraries are branches of the NLL. Bookmobiles serve regions without a library. School libraries are widely distributed and largely supported by the Ecoles Sans Fron-

tières (ESC); bookcases containing children's books circulate between libraries. NLL is trying its best to get connected to the world and to make available Internet and online services.

MALAYSIA

Malaysia's Perpustakaan Negara Malaysia (National Library Malaysia, NLM) was established as a unit of the National Archives in 1966. However, in 1972, the National Library Act was passed and the National Library was separated from the National Archives, becoming a federal government department. The Deposit of Library Material Act was passed in 1986 and the National Library Act amended in 1987. It also hosts a virtual exhibition of Malaysia's history, culture and heritage. The Library moved to its current premises in 1992 and the building is a cultural landmark known for its unique architecture; the architectural concept is that of a Tengkolok, the customary Malay headgear used by royalty and commoners on special occasions to cover the head, reflecting the country's intellectual and cultural achievements. The National Policy for Library and Information Services was approved in 1989. NLM aspires to be a world-class library in the provision of excellent information services, and it contributes to the realization of Malaysia's vision of becoming an industrialized and developed nation by 2020 in line with the national *Vision 2020*. It is also developing a strategic plan and setting in place a competency development plan for all professional staff. It places emphasis on administrative reforms for better quality services and is ISO 9000 certified.

THE PHILIPPINES

The origin of the National Library of the Philippines (NLP) dates back to 1900 when Museo Biblioteca de Filipinas was established. The practice of librarianship did not start till 1901 when the American Circulating Library was donated and that formed the nucleus of NLP, which comes under the jurisdiction of the National Commission of Culture and the Arts (NCCA) in the Office of the President. NLP has the dual function of being both the national library and central node for the public library system. The public libraries operate under the aegis of the NLP. The Philippines has some 861 public libraries and fourteen bookmobiles. It also provides assistance to local government units in the establishment, development and maintenance of libraries in provinces, with the goal of narrowing social and economic divides, especially in the rural communities. Library Day and National Book Week are held on 9 March and 24–30 November annually. The NLP carries a rich array of printed material in various Filippina dialects such as Tagalog, Cebuano and Bikol. Historical materials from the Spanish to the Japanese periods, and the precious manuscripts of the national hero José P. Rizal's novels *Noli Me Tangere* and *El Filibusterismo*. The NLP also takes on the additional role of a copyright registration office and administers the registration of copyright by authors.

SINGAPORE

The National Library, established in 1958, serves as the national and public library of Singapore. Its roots, however, go back in time to the establishment of the Singapore Institution (Raffles Institution, as it is known today) in 1823, by Singapore's founder – Sir Stamford Raffles. The National Library was officially opened by the Yang di Pertuan Negara Inche Yusoff bin Ishak on 12 November 1960. However, in 1992 the government carried out a major library review resulting in the formation of the National Library Board (NLB) on 1 September 1995. Its service philosophy is to provide a convenient, accessible, affordable and usable service to the public. It has innovatively exploited technology to enhance its services and operations, thereby creating an enriching experience for the user. The Board oversees the management of the National Library itself, two regional libraries, eighteen community libraries and forty-six community children's libraries. Through these libraries and those of its partners, the NLB ensures that users have access to a rich array of information services to support lifelong learning. Its public library services include loans, community information services, reference and information services, audiovisual services and the organizing of talks and programmes for adults, young people and children. The academic and special libraries complement the public library services. All these libraries work closely together to meet the nation's information needs. The libraries in Singapore have become an integral part of the national learning infrastructure, having been positioned as key pillars to support learning, discovery and exploration. Through its numerous programmes, the Library helps to contribute tremendously in creating the 'digital dividend'. For instance, mass training is carried out at the One Learning Place (OLP) to inculcate new information technology and information literacy skills in young and old alike, in both English and other languages. The NLB was appointed to coordinate the National IT Literacy Training Programme in Singapore. In addition, some 800 computers in the libraries are a boon to those who do not own a computer, offering them a great opportunity to experience life on the Information Highway and access virtual resources at nominal, affordable rates. The NLB has made available a rich array of information sources in print and digital media in the libraries and contributed in bridging the digital divide.

THAILAND

The National Library of Thailand (NLT) was established in 1905 by the amalgamation of three older royal libraries, though in reality the library's history dates back to the fourteenth century CE. It moved to its current premises in 1966, within the precinct of the Grand Palace in Bangkok. About eighteen branches located in various provinces support the main library. It was Internet-enabled in 1999. Two major policy documents have influenced developments. These are the *National Information Policy* and the *National IT Policy*. Both policies place emphasis on developing information as an integral part of national and economic development. A wide network of public and academic libraries supports the national library. The academic libraries are quite well developed and offer a good range of services. Two official government agencies, the Non-Formal Education Department and the Bangkok Metropolitan Administration, also play their part in the library arena by managing mobile library services. The mobile libraries take many forms depending on the specific sites they have to reach. For instance, in one case the mobile library was a book basket. There are also motorboat mobiles and book packages. The future plans for mobile libraries include reaching out to the disadvantaged and including electronic services. The Thai National Information System project (Thai NATIS) was initiated in the late 1980s and the Library acts as the Secretariat. There are also a number of other dedicated specialized networks for medicine, the humanities, economics, and science and technology, amongst others. Chulalongkorn

University offers a digital library service. The government-funded university libraries have established an Inter-University Network (Uni-Net) for sharing of library databases. The Thai Academic Libraries Network and the Thai Library Integrated System have moved to the second phase, with emphasis on digital content and electronic document delivery services.

VIETNAM

Vietnam is a small country; two-thirds of its area is mountainous and its economy is ranked among the poorest in the world. The library landscape of Vietnam consists of the National Library of Vietnam (NLV), sixty-one provincial libraries, 540 district libraries, 7,500 commune and village libraries, 250 academic libraries, 13,500 school libraries, 300 special libraries and 1,000 military libraries. Vietnam does not have a library association but the NLV is required by the Ordinance of Librarianship to act as the Central Library with several responsibilities. These include exploiting domestic and foreign resources to meet readers' needs; collecting publications under legal deposit; preserving the National Collection; compiling the national and general bibliographies; providing library services; co-operating, and exchanging materials, with foreign libraries and agencies; and improving competencies. In recent years, some 1,500 new libraries have been established. These take the shape of Cultural Village Bookcases and Bookcases of Commune Cultural Post Offices. Though the Vietnamese government has made great efforts, millions of people in the mountains and other remote areas do not have access to books and newspapers because of economic and geographical difficulties. With encouragement from IFLA and the support of the government, more than 150 mobile libraries have been established in the past decade. The mobile libraries have been adapted to suit different areas and include models such as Libraries on Cultural Boats; Book Bags of Border Guards; Bookcases of Commune Cultural Post Offices. Vietnam foresees that, in the twenty-first century, it will continue to face difficulties, and it will have great problems in overcoming poverty and backwardness. Mobile libraries have been an effective means of promoting culture and information in the poor regions Thus, the government continues to advocate the development of mobile libraries as a strategic move to improve the cultural life of the population. It is also interesting to note that, in December 2000, the Vietnam National Assembly issued an ordinance on libraries and approved support for the programme of district libraries and school libraries in the 2001–5 plan. The ordinance, which consists of seven chapters and thirty-one articles, covers provisions to develop library resources and to increase efficiency in management of library activities such as the rights and responsibilities of organizations and individuals in library activities; library organization and operation; library investment and development; state management on library development; reward and handling violation in library activities; and other implementation provisions.

The library's e-strategies

Despite being seen as a developing region, ASEAN has made a great deal of progress in embracing technology and launching digital library initiatives. The proliferation of the Internet has propelled the libraries in the region to place equal emphasis on evolving the virtual libraries (see VIRTUAL LIBRARY), and other online provision. These take the form of a variety of digital libraries, portals (see PORTALS AND GATEWAYS) and virtual communities, all sharing the common goal of increasing access round-the-clock to content and services in a more personalized and customized manner.

The adoption of technology can be traced back to the 1970s when countries like Malaysia made modest beginnings in exploiting technology to improve business operations. Malaysia's MAL-MARC project that simplified and promoted shared cataloguing was initiated in 1970, and Singapore libraries tapped this service. MAL-MARC now forms the core of the Malaysian Bibliographic Network. In the 1980s, Singapore developed its equivalent of MALMARC, called SILAS (Singapore Integrated Library Automation Service), which promotes shared cataloguing as well as maintaining the national union catalogue. The Singapore National Bibliography (SNB) is now available in CD-ROM format with plans to be made available on the Internet.

From the early 1980s, libraries started looking into LIBRARY AUTOMATION with academic libraries taking the lead. Since then, computerization has taken on a number of forms, including the automation of catalogues and circulation systems, the installation of CD-ROMs as stand-alones or on a network, access to overseas online databases such as DIALOG, Reuters and some specialized databases (but often controlled), the development of local databases, information retrieval systems (often initially developed in-house) and use of the Internet. Library automation itself has taken place to a greater or lesser extent throughout the region, varying from micro/mini-based solutions for staff use, running, for example, CDS/ISIS provided by UNESCO, to mini/mainframe solutions with end-user OPACS access, running, for example, DRA, Innopac, URICA, CARL, V-LIB and more recently Ex-Libris systems.

Other developments include the Thai Computer Network Project that links all the science and technology databases created by eleven universities. THAIPOPIN is a national population information network linking eighteen institutes. There is also the Provincial University Library Network (PULINET), as well as the Documentation Centre of the Asian Institute of Technology, which has created the Thailand Inter-University Network (ATUNET) and seventeen other databases. These developments are also reflected in the more recent implementation of Internet applications.

Developments in Malaysia, Singapore and ASEAN as a unified entity articulate well with the huge steps being taken to make the region a presence in the new Net Economy. Singapore's IT 2000 Masterplan is transforming the country into an Intelligent Island where INFORMATION AND COMMUNICATION TECHNOLOGY is exploited to the fullest to enhance the quality of life of the population at home, work and play. *Singapore ONE* is a major milestone in the realization of this vision. Singapore ONE is one of the world's pioneering national MULTIMEDIA, BROADBAND networks that delivers a new level of interactive multimedia applications and services to homes, schools and businesses. The implementation of IT 2000 and Singapore ONE has enabled Singapore to lay a solid foundation in ICT and paves the way for the Infocomm 21 strategic plan, which will guide ICT development over the next ten years. Infocomm 21, launched in 2000, articulates various strategies aimed at creating a vibrant ICT industry – which will transform Singapore into a dynamic and vibrant global ICT capital with a thriving and prosperous net economy by the year 2010.

The IT 2000 initiative laid the foundation and infrastructure upon which various applications could be built. The Digital Library Initiative was one such application aimed at bringing information to the people of Singapore. It was championed by two government agencies with the involvement of the major academic and special libraries. In 1996, Singapore was among the pioneering nations to launch their first nation-wide digital library service. Christened TIARA (Timely Information for All, Relevant and Affordable), it offered a suite of services including seamless access to the catalogues of libraries in Singapore, a reference enquiry service called Ask TIARA and access to major information databases such as DIALOG, Gartner Group, Cambridge Scientific Abstracts and Engineering Index, among others. Singapore had then successfully negotiated 'national' LICENCES so that citizens could gain access to these reservoirs of information in a more cost-effective manner. It also acted as a co-ordinated gateway to Internet resources that were organized to facilitate easier retrieval. Since then, Singapore libraries have dabbled in a variety of e-library initiatives such as the creation of portals, virtual communities for students, ethnic communities and so on.

The most recent iteration of the digital library is the eLibraryHub. Launched in September 2001, the eLibraryHub is a one-stop integrated digital library that offers users a 'personalized' experience of having a library of their own. An initiative by the National Library Board, eLibraryHub provides immediate reach to vast information resources from the world's leading libraries and content providers – via a single point of access, anywhere and at any time. The eLibraryHub allows the individual, or a community or corporation, to create a personalized library. Using personal e-tools, e-mails, discussion forums, online chats, photo albums, bookshelves and research rooms can be organized for effective retrieval. The eLibraryHub will also alert the user to book recommendations from peers based on his/her reading habits. It will also serve as a portable learning companion that is accessible using any appliance (personal computers, MOBILE COMMUNICATIONS devices and so on). It includes a cybrarian service (remote librarians online to assist users) and an electronic payment system. The eLibraryHub hopes to serve each user as 'MY LIBRARY' and 'MY LEARNING COMPANION', and support personal and professional as well as learning and leisure information needs.

Similarly, the academic libraries have developed their own versions of the digital library to serve the needs of staff and students. The National University of Singapore, for instance, placed emphasis on developing digital content and the delivery of personalized services. Its Library InfoGate – a document management and retrieval system that provides access to examination papers and a periodicals index to articles on Singapore, Malaysia, Brunei and ASEAN (PERIND) – and Video-On-Demand services were launched campus-wide in 1995 and thereafter it developed at a much faster pace to include access to ELECTRONIC JOURNALS and DATABASES. In 1999, the Nanyang Technological University Library launched the i-Gateway to Educational and Media Services (iGEMS), a portal offering a rich array of personalized, timely and relevant information for each individual user. In addition, the NLB's libraries and the number of academic libraries are embracing the RFID technologies to make borrowing and return of books easy.

Malaysia, the other more advanced nation in ASEAN, also has plans that are just as ambitious and aligned to that of its Multimedia Super Corridor (MSC). The Malaysian National Digital Library, or PERDANA as it is popularly known, is a major MSC project aimed at catalysing the planned transformation of Malaysia into a knowledge-based society. The objectives of the project include establishing a platform to encourage local online services and content as part of the MSC initiative; accelerating the local information content industry; and providing affordable online information services to the whole nation. A pilot digital library project (MyLib) was launched in June 2000. MyLib is aimed at promoting the economical and efficient delivery of information and knowledge, especially databases and local content, on the Net to all levels of the Malaysian society. MyLib is a collaborative project involving the NLM, the Multimedia Development Corporation, government libraries and state public libraries, among others. All libraries were encouraged to share their public domain databases and digitize their institutions' publications (such as theses, annual reports, directories, cultural and intellectual heritage documents, and so on). Libraries are also encouraged to make their bibliographic records, in-

dexes, abstracts, bibliographies, tables of contents and so on accessible. MyLib is seen as a logical extension of the Jaringan Ilmu (JI) project that was launched in January 1994. JI was a strategic alliance between the NLM and MIMOS, a government agency. Amongst its objectives were to establish a national network of libraries; to encourage libraries to create databases containing text, graphics and bibliographic information; and to encourage the creation of local public-domain databases. The JI project has enabled special libraries and state libraries to be linked via the Internet, made possible by NLM funding, which provided the hardware, software and training. The academic libraries were not directly involved in the pilot project.

The other ASEAN countries, eager not to be left behind, are making modest attempts to embark on the digital journey. Indonesia, for instance, is beginning to develop the Indonesian Digital Library Network. The Indonesian government, through the Ministry of Technology and Research, is building the national information technology framework, IPTEKNET (Science and Technology Information Networking), a nationwide network connected to the Internet. The Petra Christian University is also developing its own digital library system. The software will be installed at the Christian universities that have joined the Indonesian Christian Universities Virtual Library (InCU-VL). The Philippine Library Information Network (PHILIN) is an integrated library management and information system. In Vietnam, the government has approved the National Library's ICT development project, which includes a library management system, scanners, servers and so on, and the creation of a website. The French government is also working with the NLV to set up a digital laboratory to digitize rare collections of the NLV.

Recognizing the gap amongst the more developed and less developed ASEAN member countries, the ASEAN governments initiated the e-ASEAN strategy to ensure that ASEAN as a whole can get the socio-economic benefits of networking. One such initiative is that of the proposed ASEAN Information Network (AINet). AINet aims to bridge the information gap among ASEAN member countries by establishing a rich shared information resource base. It is an outcome of the growing interest among ASEAN member countries in sharing information, not just for business and research but also to build a greater understanding of the diverse cultural heritage among its citizens. AINet will link a wide spectrum of socio-economic and cultural resources in the region to enable libraries, governments, businesses and citizens to access and exchange a wide-range of information and knowledge. The successful implementation of AINet will allow the 500 million residents of ASEAN nations to access some 40 million titles available in the national libraries, and Web-based and multimedia resources. The information provided will be in English and the indigenous languages. Four CONSAL member countries (Brunei, Malaysia, the Philippines and Singapore) have taken the lead to develop digital content for AINet. The remaining six countries will be phased into the project over the next few years. In March 2001, the lead countries deliberated on collaborative DIGITIZATION strategies to present Southeast Asian digital content online as a showcase for the region. This project is the second phase of the Resource Sharing and Legal Deposit initiative approved by the CONSAL Executive Board in April 2000. Ultimately, it is envisaged that the disparate digitization efforts in the ASEAN countries can be consolidated and made available through AINet in a more concerted manner.

Dramatic changes are taking place to make available cultural heritage and memories. Libraries are beginning to invest in preserving the past so that future generations can experience the past, live the present and explore the future. Emphasis is placed by the national libraries on the PRESERVATION of these treasures, and many are embarking on digitizing their more important collections. Funding is a major constraint and many try to collaborate with industry and seek various sources of funding to preserve these fragile treasures. For instance, the Philippines was awarded US$10,000 for the 'Philippine-American Project on Historic Photograph Collection' from the Ambassador's Fund for Cultural Preservation 2001 Award. Cambodia was awarded US$15,000 for the project on 'Preservation of Ancient Books and Manuscripts' from the Ambassador's Fund for Cultural Preservation 2001 Award. Laos was awarded US$10,000 for the project 'A Stonehenge in Laos: Mapping, Archiving, Exhibiting' from the Ambassador's Fund for Cultural Preservation 2001 Award.

In Singapore, the National Archives is the major content provider for Singapore history, and has made its content accessible via the Internet. Its information portal Archives and Artefacts Online (a2o) allows for a seamless search across various databases for social, economic, cultural and political developments within the country. This includes various independent databases and selected photographs, maps and plans, oral history interview samplers and snippets of audiovisual recordings. In addition, a2o also provides information on materials recently acquired by NAS, online exhibitions and student programmes. Other heritage services include: Picture Archives Singapore (PICAS), a text and IMAGE RETRIEVAL system on the Web; Knowledge Net: Singapore, a multimedia content-rich website on Singapore history to foster a community that understands the significance of their past by the sharing of knowledge; and 1942 – Battlefield Singapore, which reminds Singaporeans of the past and honours those who fought for the country. This last site exploits the latest virtual-reality technology to allow users to experience the 1942 battle and provides comprehensive information on the Second World War and the Japanese occupation.

Copyright

Many historical factors have influenced the development of copyright in Asia. British legal traditions influenced the copyright system of a number of ASEAN countries, notably Singapore, Malaysia, Brunei and Myanmar, while the Dutch and Americans exerted influence on the system in Indonesia and the Philippines respectively. These colonial influences are reflected in current legislation. International agreements such as TRIPS (Trade-Related Aspects of Intellectual Property Rights) have also had an impact on laws in the region.

For instance, the explanatory note to the Bill introducing amendments to the Singapore Copyright Act of 1998 highlighted that the 'bill seeks to amend the Copyright Act (cap 63), primarily to enable Singapore to meet its obligations in regard to copyright under the Agreement on Trade Related aspects of Intellectual Property Rights (TRIPS)'. Subsequently, the Act was once again amended to extend protection to works in CYBERSPACE. The explanatory note states that the amendments were *inter alia* to give full effect to the TRIPS agreement. Malaysia's 1997 amendments were a move towards the standards of the WIPO Copyright Treaty (WCT). Thus the insertion of a new definition of 'communication to public' to mean:

> [T]he transmission of a work through wire or wireless means to the public, including the making available of a work to the public in such a way that members of the public may access the work from a place and at a time individually chosen by them.

The general view was that these changes were timely as Malaysia was at that time attracting investments into the MSC Project.

Indonesia was the first ASEAN country to accede to the WCT and made the appropriate changes in 1997 but it is not yet TRIPS-compliant. Thailand amended its law in 1995 and the Philippines in 1998; both are TRIPS-compliant. Thailand also enacted a law to establish an Intellectual Property and International Trade Court with the hope of speeding up the implementation and enforcement of copyright laws. Brunei has developed a Copyright Act and Vietnam has the most recent copyright law but it is also not TRIPS-compliant yet. Cambodia and Laos have yet to enact any copyright legislation, while Myanmar still uses the 1911 UK Imperial Copyright Act but is working on a new law.

The challenge that libraries face is in maintaining a balance between protecting the interests of the copyright owners while allowing fair use in the interests of social, economic, educational and cultural good, including preservation of the literary works for posterity.

Training and education

Historically, in the early years of development and even into the early 1990s, the region relied on overseas institutions and programmes to train its librarians. These included sending staff to overseas universities and distance education. With the emphasis placed on libraries as key pillars supporting lifelong learning, there is a need for more trained and competent staff especially equipped with new and emerging skills such as digital libraries, organization of information, information searching and packaging, digitization, preservation and knowledge management. The staff also need to enhance their planning, negotiation and marketing skills.

A multipronged approach has been used to develop the professional talent pool through formal and professional development short courses, certification programmes and even in-service training programmes to ensure librarians are equipped with new skills and remain relevant in the knowledge economy. Formal training at certificate, diploma and degree levels is now available at the universities and polytechnics but they still send a small number overseas on scholarships. Many programmes are found in Indonesia, the Philippines and Thailand. Malaysia and Singapore have more focused training. Singapore recently launched a Master's programme in knowledge management. Informal training and continuing-education programmes have been organized by the educational institutions, libraries and library associations, at local, regional and international levels. Libraries also send their staff overseas on knowledge acquisition trips.

With the formation of the CONSAL Secretariat, the region has identified the need for a co-ordinated training plan as a priority. CONSAL conducts various training programmes. For instance, CONSAL librarians attend training in Singapore under the Singapore Co-operation Programme twice a year. CONSAL has also experimented by hosting two online conferences via the CONSAL Web and plans to host more virtually. One discussed 'Librarianship in the New Millennium' and the other 'Consultation on Higher Library Education'. Under the auspices of ASEAN, the ASEAN COCI initiates various exchange programmes that allow librarians in the region to meet and learn from each other. One such programme, hosted in Bangkok, looked at library education in the region. The NLB, Singapore, has also invested in setting up an NLB Institute that looks into the training needs of its staff and extends these to librarians in Singapore and the region. The Institute places emphasis on inculcating information and IT skills in librarians and works with local and international experts to conduct training in new areas of interest.

Funding libraries

The disparity in the progress made by libraries in ASEAN can be attributed to the disparities between the national economies. In the less developed ASEAN countries, seeking funding for library development has been a challenge due to conflicting priorities that the governments have to tackle. Though libraries play an important role in inculcating reading habits, supporting basic literacy training (including in English) and in making available information and reading materials, funding has been limited. Hence, many ASEAN countries seek funding from world organizations and industry to raise the information literacy of its population and to bridge the information gap. Indonesia, for instance, successfully obtained US$4.2 million from the International Development Association to fund its Library Development Project, which aims to develop innovative approaches to increase the use of reading materials in community and primary school libraries, to motivate students and communities alike to make use of valuable information, and to develop a supportive strategy among communities, non-governmental organizations (NGOs) and local government. Cambodia, meanwhile, has submitted a proposal to the World Bank Group for funding for the project on 'Rejuvenation of the National Library of Cambodia', estimated to cost US$117,850 per year.

Conclusion

The libraries in the region have – despite the socio-economic situation – made good progress over the years and implemented various innovative services and programmes. The library world can learn from these countries because despite constraints, but with dedication, passion and drive, the librarians in the region have made waves in the library arena. Visitors to international meetings and conferences and exhibitions in the region can bear witness to this statement. The fruits are seen in the IFLA mirror site being hosted in Singapore, a noted Malaysian Librarian chairing IFLA's Asia/Oceania Grouping and Asian international meetings being held in the region.

References

Yit, C.C. and Foo, S. (2002) 'Development of libraries of the Congress of Southeast Asian Librarians (CONSAL): 1996–1999', *LIBRES* 12 (http://libres-curtin.edu.au/libres12n1/Index.htm).

Further reading

Abdoulaye, K. and Majid, S. (2000) 'Use of the Internet for reference services in Malaysian academic libraries', *Online Information Review* 24: 381–8.

Chaudhry, A.S. and al-Hawamdeh, S. (1999) 'Libraries and the Internet in Singapore', *Journal of Global Information Management* 7: 12–17.

Chia, C. (2001) 'Transformation of libraries in Singapore', *Library Review* 50: 343–8.

Cordeiro, C.M. and al-Hawamdeh, S. (2001) 'National information infrastructure and the realisation of Singapore IT2000 initiative', *Information Research* 6 (www.shef.ac.uk/is/publications/infres/6–2/paper96. html).

Cornish, G.P. (1996) 'Developing document delivery in South East Asia now and in future', *Interlending and Document Supply* 24: 19–24.

Dean J.F. (1999) 'Burma, Cambodia, Laos and Vietnam: The road to recovery for library and archival collections after war and civil unrest', in P. Sturges and D. Rosenberg (eds) *Disaster and After: The Practicalities of Information Services in Times of War and Other Catastrophes*, Taylor Graham, pp. 29–50.

Fahmi, I., Mahmudin, O.W.P., Hasanah, N. and Suwandi, S. (1999) 'The library network in Indonesia', *LASIE* 30: 24–8.

Gould, S. and Watkins, J. (1995) *From Palm Leaves to PCs: Library Development in South East Asia*, IFLA.

Hee, Y.K. (2000) 'Multimedia library services on Singapore "One" network', *Herald of Library Science* 39: 224–31.

Hernandez, V.S. (2001) 'Trends in Philippine library history', *Libraries and Culture* 36: 329–44.

Krebs, V. (2001) 'The impact of the Internet on Myanmar', *First Monday* 6 (www.firstmonday.dk/issues/issue6_5/krebs/).

Lam, V.-T. (1999) 'Issues for library development in Vietnam', *Asian Libraries* 8: 182–90.

Premsmith, P. (1999) 'Library and information service in Thailand', *IFLA Journal* 25: 137–42.

Reid, E. (1999) 'Malaysia's Multimedia Super Corridor and role of information professionals', *IATUL Proceedings*, New Series, 8 (www.iatul.org/conference/pretpap/reid.html).

Samad, R.A. (2001) 'The double edged sword: A brief comparison of information technology and Internet development in Malaysia and some neighbouring countries', *IFLA Journal* 27: 314–18.

See, C.K. (2001) 'Government information and information about government in Southeast Asia: A new era? An overview', *Inspel* 35: 120–36.

Tran, L.A. (1999) 'Recent library developments in Vietnam', *Asian Libraries* 8: 17–28.

Tung, L.L. (1999) 'The implementation of information kiosks in Singapore: An exploratory study', *International Journal of Information Management* 19: 237–52.

Van Koert, R. (2002) 'The impact of democratic deficits on electronic media in rural development', *First Monday* 7 (www.firstmonday.dk/issues/issue7_4/koert/) [Indonesia and Vietnam].

Yusof, Z.M. and Chell, R.W. (1999) 'Managing

business records in Malaysia: Awareness and attitudes among business managers', *Information Development* 15: 228–34.

SEE ALSO: information society; library education; social exclusion and libraries

JULIE SABARATNAM, WITH THE COLLABORATION OF COLLEAGUES AND REVISED BY THE EDITORS

SOUTHERN EUROPE

A geo-political concept, Southern Europe only exists as an abstract entity in librarianship. During the twentieth century, Portugal, Spain and Greece went through harsh dictatorships that were anything but interested in libraries and access to information. With its rich cultural history, Italy has considered libraries for long as mere heritage institutions. The movement for public libraries, buoyant in Northern European countries and in the USA since the nineteenth century, has become reality in the Mediterranean region only in the last decade of the twentieth century. As a result, the Library Programme launched by the European Commission at the beginning of the 1990s classified Southern European countries as LFR (Less Favoured Regions). Not only political correctness made the acronym fade away. Improvements in librarianship and information science have been genuine and have helped to remove, or at least to lessen, the gap with other Western European countries.

Portugal

With the name of *Mesa Censoria* (Censorship Desk), a public library was opened in Lisbon in 1791 and became Biblioteca Nacional in 1836. It was only at the beginning of the twentieth century, with librarians such as Raoul Proença, that services were improved and cataloguing of old Portuguese collections was triggered. The Golden Age of the National Library came to an end with the Salazar dictatorship. The return to democracy in 1974 and full membership of the European Union in 1985 brought new life to the major Portuguese library. Its mandate includes not only legal deposit of the Portuguese publishing output and the publication of the national bibliography, but also the maintenance and development of PORBASE, the union catalogue of Portuguese libraries. Although resources are relatively limited (7 million euros in 1999), the national bibliography of print publications has good coverage and a satisfactory rate of effectiveness. Under legal deposit, publishers are compelled to send thirteen copies of their publications to the NL, which shares this task with twelve other institutions. Reform in this field is urgently needed.

The bulk of university libraries in Portugal are gathered around the PORBASE union catalogue, which provides for 85 per cent of the bibliographic records they need. PORBASE is also used as a source for interlibrary loan and document supply. It is not, however, the only pillar of library development. The most accomplished achievement is the growth of public libraries – a success story in Europe. After the Carnation revolution (1974), adult illiteracy in Portugal was of the order of 25 per cent. Started in 1986, the national scheme intended to support libraries, Programa de Apoio às Bibliotecas Municipais, was enacted as an effective way to combat illiteracy. The programme is still underway and combines financial aid with technical assistance. A general framework is provided by the Ministry of Culture with a well-established set of technical specifications for library size and related performance. Municipalities have to initiate the project and commit themselves to maintain the candidate library, while the state intervenes with 50 per cent of the global funds needed for its creation and development. Thanks to the Support Programme, 209 municipalities have received funds and ninety-nine new libraries have been inaugurated in the last ten years. The successful scheme is now being applied to school libraries, still underdeveloped in Portugal.

Spain

Created in 1711, the National Library of Spain was settled in its actual premises in Madrid in 1894. Underdeveloped during the nineteenth century, it was reformed twice in the twentieth century, the last regulation being adopted in 1986, more than a decade after democracy was re-established. Legal deposit reaches relatively satisfactory rates of effectiveness thanks to a complex, but effective, system: legal deposit offices are situated in practically all Spanish regions and monitor the publishing output locally. With its many series, the Spanish National Bibliography has gone through some turbulence during the 1990s, but its work has recently improved thanks also to an agreement passed with REBIUN (Red de Bibliotecas universitarias), the university library network.

Mainly devoted to its Catalan collection – Catalan is the second most spoken Spanish official language – is the National Library of Catalunya, founded in 1907 and based in Barcelona. As almost half of the Spanish publishing houses are settled in Catalunya, the National Library has a rich legal deposit intake and also publishes the bibliography of Catalan publications.

The creation and the maintenance of public libraries in Spain is the responsibility of municipalities that have a legal obligation to set up a library when the area they control has more than 5,000 inhabitants. Due to the Spanish federal system, Comunidades autonomas (Spanish regions) have legislated on their own and set up parameters for library performances in almost each region. Official statistics identify over 3,700 public libraries, but most of them are inadequately equipped, with no acceptable standards of performance. The average number of documents per capita in public libraries was 0.79 in 1999 (by comparison, 2.23 documents are circulated in the United Kingdom libraries and 6 in some Nordic countries). In the same year, expenses for acquisitions in Spanish public libraries amounted to 0.46 euros yearly per capita (by comparison, France and the United Kingdom allocate, respectively, 1.98 and 3.73 euros yearly). Fifty-two important public libraries are directly within the state remit. Great expectations have been raised by a Support Plan for Spanish Public Libraries, launched in 2000, with a view to creating interconnection to the Internet for the whole of the public library system.

With the academic sector booming after the end of the Franco regime, Spanish university libraries also thrived and made important strides The number of library administrative units increased by 29 per cent from 1981 to 1990, and service points expanded at a rate of 7.5 per cent every year. For example, in Catalunya alone five universities out of eight were founded in the 1980s! In the academic library field, co-operation between university libraries has eventually led to the setting up, in 2000, of the academic union catalogue REBIUN, which is permanently incorporated in the Conference of Rectors of Spanish universities. With its 6 million records and its services shared among fifty-four university libraries, REBIUN has emerged as one of the most interesting library resources in Spain.

Italy

When Italy was unified, the first Decree on libraries (1869) designated no less than three national libraries, with that of Florence having the privilege of being depository for all Italian publications. Such idiosyncrasy still features in the Italian library system. According to a Decree approved in 2001, the term 'national' is assigned to nine libraries, although only two, Florence and Rome, are considered 'central national' and benefit from legal deposit legislation. The central national library of Florence issues the national bibliography, which is produced within the framework of the Italian union catalogue (SBN, Servizio Bibliotecario Nazionale). Reform of legal deposit is desperately needed in Italy: according to the current law, promulgated for censorship purposes during fascist rule (1939), publications are sent to the local prefectures (regional governmental offices). As a result, only 65–70 per cent of printed publications are collected by both national libraries.

In Italy, competence for public libraries has been devolved to regions. Some of them have taken advantage of the devolution movement and set up appropriate library policies. This is the case, for instance, for the Region Lombardia where, in 2000, 2.15 documents per inhabitant were loaned from public libraries and 1.11 euros per capita is spent for library acquisitions. Other regions, too, in northern and central Italy have provided momentum to the development of library policies. Disparities, however, are conspicuous and especially affect southern Italian regions. Co-operation between the state, the regions and the universities is enacted through the national union catalogue, SBN, which includes 4 million bibliographic records and offers integrated library services such as shared cataloguing and bibliographic search, as well as access to other national and international DATABASES.

A recent bill has given autonomy to local Italian universities but not to university libraries, in spite of the creation of a position of a central 'co-ordinator' in charge of steering the work of libraries in university departments and schools. An inquiry carried out in 1999 showed that resources are adequate for acquisitions and personnel. The high number of access points

(2,227), however, contributes to the dispersion of library services and is a major hindrance to the rationalization of the university library system in Italy.

Greece

Founded in 1832, the National Library of Greece was established in its own premises in Athens in 1903. Greek publications are collected by legal deposit and recorded in a national bibliography. Both tasks are strenuously pursued, but difficulties are great and performance is less than satisfactory.

Greek university libraries were pictured in a dismal way in a collection of essays published in 1992. The list of problems included organization, infrastructure, collection development and personnel. Poorly funded, libraries were dispersed among faculties and departments, and were considered more the personal commodity of university professors than as centres providing services for the whole academic community. By the end of the decade the situation had changed, but more by fits and starts than as a result of a homogeneous process. Libraries of the University of Athens still have dispersed collections and no overall co-ordinated policy. Things are different in Thessaloniki, where collections have been transferred to a new, purpose-designed building, and at the University of Crete, where there is a central library fully automated since its inception.

Under the general term of 'popular' libraries are included Greek libraries belonging to municipalities and civic and private associations oriented towards the public. An enquiry carried out in 1998 gave a figure of some 1,000 libraries of this kind in Greece; among these, the 'central public' libraries are established in the regional capital cities, and also provide mobile library services to the surrounding districts. The size of library collections rarely goes beyond 20,000 volumes. According to a recent report, public library development in Greece is hampered by a series of factors such as the lack of a framework legislation – which would define funding rules and service standards – an old-fashioned image and collections housed in old buildings, which are poorly furnished and equipped. At least on a regional basis, the importance of libraries is recognized and there are serious attempts to create a regional infrastructure.

Education

Education in library and information science is a relatively recent development in Southern European countries. In Spain, since 1974, some ten universities provide specialized courses divided into three cycles. The first lasts three years eventually leading to a Diploma in Librarianship and Documentation. The second implies a greater degree of specialization and grants a student a Licence. In the third cycle, students are enabled to prepare a PhD. The same scheme is now implemented in Italy after a general reform of higher education studies that took place in 2000. Courses on Librarianship are organized within the framework of the Departments of Science of Cultural Assets, present in some fifteen Italian universities. Library education in Portugal and Greece has benefited from the assistance of Anglo-Saxon education institutes but a national framework is still to be established with standards that would correspond to library needs and would be given adequate consideration by cultural and educational administrators.

Library networks

Library networks in Southern European countries have been established according to the different paths of development of library infrastructure. In Portugal and Italy, there are main, although not exclusive, library union catalogues, respectively PORBASE and SBN. Such networks act as bibliographic utilities and facilitate interlibrary loans and the exchange of records. The advantage is that resources are concentrated around a single initiative, thus avoiding overlapping among bibliographic utilities. Nevertheless, rules governing the two networks lead to no clear task-sharing schemes. In Spain, networking is following three sectoral paths of development: the union catalogue of state public libraries (gathered around the REBECA database), the academic library network (with the already mentioned REBIUN) and the networks existing on a given territory (e.g. Catàleg Col.lectiu de Catalunya (CCC)).

Library associations

Portugal and Italy each have a single library association: respectively BAD (Bibliotecarios, Arquivistas e Documentalistas) and AIB (Associazione Italiana Biblioteche). Spain has some fifteen professional associations for librarians and documentalists, on a regional or sectoral basis, most of them members of FESABID, the Spanish Federation of Library Associations. The Greek member of EBLIDA, the European Board of Library Associations, is the Enosis Ellenon Bibliothekarion.

Digital libraries

Plans for developing digital libraries exist in most Southern European countries. In Portugal, such plans aim at setting up projects concerning digitally published works of Portuguese authors, and theses, dissertations and reports, as well as preserving heritage works in digital form. In Spain the National Library has launched the Memoria Ispanica project; other projects include the availability of publications in full text. In Italy, developments are focused on the existing rich cultural heritage and its digitization as a form of support for research.

Useful websites

SOUTHERN EUROPEAN LIBRARIES: STATISTICS
www.libecon.org/.

SOUTHERN EUROPEAN NATIONAL LIBRARIES
http://portico.bl.uk/gabriel/
The National Library of Catalunya (www.gencat.es/bc/).

SOUTHERN EUROPEAN PUBLIC LIBRARIES
Greece (www.culture.gr/2/22/221/22101/book.html).
Portugal (www.iplb.pt/redes/redes.html).
Spain (www.mcu.es/guia/pagina35c.html and www.mcu.es/lab/bibliote/plan/index.html).
Italy – Lombardia (www.biblioteche.regione.lombardia.it/regsrc/tabella.htm).

SOUTHERN EUROPEAN UNIVERSITY LIBRARIES
Greece (www.hri.org/nodes/grlib.html).
Italy (www.miur.it/osservatorio/ricbibl.htm).

SOUTHERN EUROPEAN LIBRARY NETWORKS
Portugal (http://porbase.bn.pt/org/).
Spain (www.crue.org/cgi-bin/rebiun).
Italy (www.sbn.it/).

Further reading

Borbinha, J.L. (1998) 'Digital libraries: A perspective from Portugal', *LIBER Quarterly* 8: 81–5.
Colodron, V. (2000) 'Libraries in Spain', *Information Europe* 2 (summer): 26–8.
Keller, D. (ed.) (1993) *Academic Libraries in Greece: The Recent Situation and Future Prospectus*, New York: Haworth Press.
Ministério da Cultura, Instituto da Biblioteca Nacional e do Livro (1996) *Guia da Biblioteca Nacional*, Lisboa: Instituto da Biblioteca Nacional e do Livro.
National Book Centre of Greece, Book Monitoring Unit (1998) *Survey of Greek Libraries*, Athens (www.culture.gr/2/22/221/book.html).
Moscoso, P. and Malo de Molina, T. (1999) 'And after automation, what? Spanish libraries and the challenge of modernization', *Journal of Librarianship and Information Science* 31(2) (June): 111–19.
Petrucciani, A. (2001) 'La laurea in biblioteconomia: Finalità e prospettive dei nuovi ordinamenti universitari', *Bollettino AIB* 41(2) (June): 145–55.
Raptis, P. and Sitas, A. (1996) 'Academic libraries in Greece: A new perspective', *Libri* 46: 100–12.
Ubieto, A.P., Sanchez Casabon, A. and Ubieto, I. (1996) 'Studies of librarianship and documentation in Spain (1978–1994)', *Education for Information, IOS Press* 14: 47–54.
Vitiello, G. (in press) *Alessandrie d'Europa. Storie e visioni di biblioteche nazionali*, Milano: Sylvestre Bonnard.

SEE ALSO: European Union information policies

GIUSEPPE VITIELLO

SPAM

Unsolicited e-mail messages or newsgroup postings sent seemingly at random across the network, usually containing advertisements. The origin of the name is said to be a reference to the Monty Python song 'Spam', the words of which are mainly mindless repetition of the word spam, sung by a group of Vikings. Spam is the equivalent of junk mail and junk fax. Even though many online service providers do attempt to protect their subscribers from this wasteful and selfish use of network BANDWIDTH, their attempts tend to be as unsuccessful as attempts to prevent junk mail.

SPECIAL COLLECTIONS

A collection of documents connected with some subject, or the original collector of the material, or gathered on the basis of some other specific rationale in a library that is otherwise general in character. The term is often used as a generic term for RARE BOOK LIBRARIES and MANUSCRIPT LIBRARIES.

SPECIAL LIBRARIES

Information resource centres located in corporations, private businesses, government agencies, museums, colleges, hospitals, associations and other organizations with specialized information needs. Using the latest advances in computer and telecommunications technology, such as online databases, compact discs and Internet access, special librarians collect, monitor, organize, analyse, evaluate, package and disseminate resource material for their parent or client organizations.

According to William Esrey, Chairman of Sprint, an international telecommunications company, the special librarian is the one 'who monitors a river of information, identifies and selects key data that decision makers should see, then channels it to the right people – before it becomes necessary to ask'.

Technological advances are transforming the special library from a finite collection of books, periodicals and documents stored on shelves and in drawers to an infinite collection of information stored in bytes. COMPUTERS have grown in efficiency more than a million-fold during the past thirty years, and FIBRE OPTICS have enhanced the efficiency of telecommunications as much as a million-fold. Today, information can be transmitted at a rate of 6.6 gigabits per second. That is the equivalent of 60,000 books per minute.

Computerization and automation are impacting on every aspect of the library profession. MULTIMEDIA and imaging, once novelties, have become serious technologies. Card catalogues have been replaced by software packages. Online searching can be done by knowbots. The physical retrieval of material is being accomplished by robotics. Knowledge engineering and EXPERT SYSTEMS are being employed in libraries for everything from inputting information to billing.

Some alarmists contend that the proliferation of computers and computer networks will result in special librarians becoming little more than antique dealers of outdated knowledge and curators of dusty books in an electronic age. However, special librarians have begun making changes in their traditional functions in response to changing demands and technology.

For example, special librarians have become more proactive than ever. They have become involved in the vision, values and goals of their patrons and the organizations for which they work. They anticipate their information needs and help meet their personal and professional objectives. PUSH TECHNOLOGY is now widely employed in special libraries, and special librarians are frequently involved in a broader KNOWLEDGE MANAGEMENT within the organization. For example, at *Newsday*, a major US daily newspaper, the members of the corporate library staff do not sit at their desks waiting for reporters to call. They attend editorial staff meetings. They make themselves part of the reporting teams.

A second way that special librarians' traditional role is changing is that they are learning to add value to information. They do not just collect information and pass it on. They begin by constantly evaluating the vast quantity of sources available to them. For example, the number of online DATABASES has grown from hundreds to thousands, and an important responsibility of information managers is determining which ones are best for their users.

As a vital part of the collection process for a particular request, special librarians also evaluate the information. They examine it for timeliness and assess its accuracy, based on their knowledge of the field in which they are working. Many special librarians have an undergraduate or advanced degree in the speciality area of the organization for which they work as well as a Master's degree in library or information science.

Then, the required next step in adding value to the material is arranging it to increase its ease of use. Sometimes special librarians find it beneficial to arrange identical material in several ways for the various users' benefit. The ultimate objective is to convert data into information and then convert that information into knowledge that will benefit the organizations' users.

Further reading

Dossett, P. (ed.) (1992) *Handbook of Special Librarianship and Information Work*, 6th edn, ASLIB.

Griffiths, J.-M. (1993) *Special Libraries: Increasing the Information Edge*, Special Libraries Association.

Mount, E. and Massoud, R. (1999) *Special Libraries and Information Centers*, 4th edn, Special Libraries Association.

Opitz, H. and Richter, E. (1995) *World Guide to Special Libraries*, 3rd edn, Saur.

SEE ALSO: online services

DAVID R. BENDER

SPREADSHEET

An applications program (usually a package) that helps users to build up two-dimensional tables of numeric and text information. Spreadsheets are widely used for budgeting and financial modelling. As well as entering information, the user can also create formulae that will, for example, compute column or row totals or work out variances. When fresh data is entered, the spreadsheet software automatically recalculates any other values that are affected.

SEE ALSO: software

STANDARDS SPECIFICATIONS

Documents that recommend or prescribe terminology; classification; attributes (such as dimensions, quality or performance) of materials, products, processes or systems; or methods of measurement or testing. They are available to the public, developed with the approval of representatives of interested parties and approved by a recognized body.

Technical requirements

Standards specifications (also referred to simply as standards where the context provides no risk of ambiguity) are part of a range of technical requirements that include the mandatory technical regulation which contains legislative or administrative rules, as well as the voluntary consensus standard.

The development and adoption of standards is essential to many aspects of modern life. Their adoption ensures protection from hazard at work or in the use of products. They ensure compatibility and interchangeability of products such as electrical connectors and fasteners. They reduce costs in industry by providing a means of communication for functions such as design, purchasing and production.

Scope

Standards can be characterized by their scope and by their issuing body. Classifying them by their scope or purpose, we can distinguish: dimensional standards (e.g. for the sizes of paper used in printing); performance standards, which specify the minimum performance so that a product is fit for its purpose (e.g. for the optical properties of paper for optical character recognition); test methods, which specify procedures and tools (e.g. for determining the grammage of paper); terminology or graphic symbols (e.g. a glossary of terms relating to paper); codes of practice, which specify standard procedures for installation, operation, maintenance or other operations (e.g. for the storage and exhibition of paper and other archival documents). Any particular standard may include elements from more than one purpose (e.g. performance requirements and the performance tests).

Issuing bodies

Standards can be produced by trade associations and professional societies, government agencies, national standardization bodies and international standardization bodies. In addition, other bodies such as testing organizations and insurance companies produce specifications that are significant because of the extent of their use and their status. The bulk of standards-making is carried out by only a few of the many organizations involved.

ASSOCIATIONS AND SOCIETIES

Trade associations and professional societies are particularly important producers of standards in the USA, where there is less centralization of standards-making by government than in European and other countries. Often the standard made by these bodies is approved as a national standard by the national standardization body. For example, a number of American Petroleum Institute (API) standards are approved by the American National Standards Institute (ANSI).

GOVERNMENT AGENCIES

Some standards are published as OFFICIAL PUBLICATIONS. For example, a large number of standards are produced in the military field, by the (US) Department of Defense or the (UK) Ministry of Defence. In addition, in the USA the government General Services Administration issues federal standards.

NATIONAL STANDARDIZATION BODIES

Over seventy countries have national standardization bodies, though they operate in differing administrative, regulatory and legal circumstances. The most significant in Western Europe are the British Standards Institution (BSI), the Deutsches Institut für Normung (DIN) and the Association Française de Normalisation (AFNOR). ANSI has a corresponding though less influential position in the USA. There are significant bodies also in Australia, Canada, Japan and New Zealand.

INTERNATIONAL STANDARDIZATION BODIES

The two most important international bodies are the International Organization for Standardization (ISO) and the International Electrotechnical Commission (IEC). ISO covers most subject fields other than electrical and electronic engineering, which is covered by the IEC. In addition, there are about thirty other international agencies concerned with standardization, such as the International Telecommunications Union (ITU).

There are a number of standardization bodies at the regional level, the most significant being the Joint European Standards Organization (CEN/CENELEC).

It is increasingly the case that standards-making at the regional or international level is replacing the development of purely national standards. This reflects both the importance of international work on information technology and communications standards (Spring 1991), and the emphasis placed on harmonization of standards across international markets. Of particular note is the set of standards for QUALITY ASSURANCE (QA) systems (the ISO 9000 series), which is being adopted widely as a set of national and regional standards.

Bibliographic control

A number of printed and electronic sources exist for the BIBLIOGRAPHIC CONTROL of standards. The majority of standardization bodies produce an annual catalogue; the *BSI Standards Catalogue* is a particularly good example. They also usually produce a regular newsletter that lists new, withdrawn and changed standards. Often they maintain extensive collections of their own and other standards that they are able to use to answer bibliographic enquiries; BSI and the (US) National Bureau of Standards have important SPECIAL LIBRARIES.

A number of bibliographic DATABASES exist for standards information, both online and on CD-ROM. Currency and completeness are important as standards are subject to constant revision, and the updating of the databases is therefore often frequent.

A number of European bodies have collaborated on *PERINORM*, a CD-ROM database of national, European and international standards. There are similar databases for Canada, the NORDIC COUNTRIES and some US bodies. There are also databases produced by commercial companies, notably Information Handling Services (Technical Indexes in the UK).

In addition, a number of standards bodies, such as ISO and the (US) National Information Standards Organization (NISO), are making their standards information available on the INTERNET.

Electronic publishing

Some standards bodies are developing systems for electronic publishing. BSI, for example, is using such a system for 'on-demand' publishing (in order to avoid the need to hold large stocks of standards). The full text of British, French, German and International Standards is available on CD-ROM as *NormImage*, as are the standards of the American Society for Testing and Materials (ASTM) and US military standards.

References

Spring, M.B. (1991) 'Information technology standards', in *Annual Review of Information Science and Technology*, Learned Information, pp. 79–111.

Further reading

Abell, A.M. (1985) 'Standards and engineering', in *Information Sources in Engineering*, Butterworth, pp. 35–55 [describes standardization bodies in an important field of standards activity].
Pantry, S. (1985) *Health and Safety: A Guide to Sources of Information*, Capital Planning Information.
Ward, S. (1994) 'Standards: Their relevance to scientific and technical information', *ASLIB Proceedings* 46(1): 3–14 [looks at standards of importance to library and information services].
Widdowson, J.S. (1989) 'Standards – worldwide', in R.T. Adkins, *Information Sources in Polymers and Plastics*, Bowker-Saur, pp. 64–90 [includes general sections on the role of standardization, particularly its relation to quality assurance, and on bibliographic control].

ALAN COOPER

STATISTICS ON LIBRARIES

Statistics to describe a library and information service in whole or in part

Traditionally, statistics have focused on inputs, holdings and expenditure to record changes over time and for comparison with others. In recent years they have extended to cover outputs, use and availability; there are also interesting projects to quantify aspects of quality and some bold attempts at impact.

LIS statistics have three principal functions: (1) to monitor operational effectiveness, (2) to provide a base for STRATEGIC PLANNING and (3) to demonstrate the value obtained by users – including the potential value to users in future generations. While the form of statistics varies between academic, public, school and special libraries – and between closed-, open- and remote-access situations – their objectives are the same.

Generally the value of statistics such as these is to point to particular problems and achievements – and to quantify their significance – rather than to provide answers or explanations. Statistics, being essentially historical, can only provide information after the event. However they may form the basis for OPERATIONS RESEARCH or mathematical modelling and so contribute to prediction.

Input and resource statistics

These measure the stock of physical resources, annual changes and the expenditure involved. Stock and ACQUISITIONS comprise: books, periodicals (current and back runs), newspapers, maps, music, other printed materials (GREY LITERATURE, standards, OFFICIAL PUBLICATIONS, etc.), AUDIOVISUAL MATERIALS, electronic data (CD-ROMs) and other items such as visual art, craft objects, toys and realia. Most frequently back runs of periodicals are counted with the bookstock. Microform and microfiche materials may be counted with books (by content) or as electronic materials (by format). Bookstock is often measured in length of shelving (linear metres) rather than in volumes to avoid misleading results when slight leaflets and thick tomes count as equal units. Statistics for separate categories of stock are valuable: the most common in PUBLIC LIBRARIES distinguish adult from children's, fiction from non-fiction, and lending from reference.

In future where access to ELECTRONIC JOURNALS, DATABASES and ELECTRONIC BOOKS is acquired for the benefit of users this will be included as an extra element of both stock and acquisitions.

Statistics of space include floor area, length of shelving used and unused, number of sites, reserve storage and the number of seats and study places provided. The number, proportion and usage of workstations connected to the INTERNET and with other ICT facilities are increasingly important.

Statistics of staff should distinguish between information professionals (see INFORMATION PROFESSIONS), specialist staff in other professions, library assistants (or PARAPROFESSIONALS) and manual/security personnel. Normally they should be expressed as FTE (full-time equivalent) so that the presence of part-time staff is correctly treated. Staff engaged in binding and PRESERVATION are usually counted separately. The amount of time spent by staff in training users is an increasingly popular statistic as networked facilities become more widespread and complex.

Expenditure statistics are appropriate for all the above items. Spending on capital – distinguished from annual recurrent expenditure – is mostly concerned with premises, furniture and equipment but includes computer systems, hardware and software. Materials should generally be included as operating expenditure, though large purchases for new library buildings are often treated as capital.

There is important variation in the way and extent that libraries are charged with the cost of premises and central institution services. This can have a substantial effect in calculating the proportion of the institutional budget allocated to library services and in comparing different libraries' results. Other significant variations can arise from the questions of whether income-generating activities are netted in the accounts and to what extent the library retains such income.

Expenditure is either gross or net: 'net expenditure' is calculated after deducting income that the library has generated from specific services and charges.

Output statistics

Availability is measured principally by opening hours: location features, although very important, are better described on a map than by statistics.

There are many measures of activity: material issued for loan, material on loan, material consulted on the premises, personal enquiries, information provided to remote users, visits, seat occupancy and photocopying. Borrowing statistics need to be qualified by the duration of loan permitted and by any maximum limit to items borrowed.

Access to material and information available in other libraries is an increasingly important function. INTERLIBRARY LENDING is counted in units received and units supplied.

In the provision of electronic information, data from remote online DATABASES are best quantified by cost – likewise the (declining) provision of stand-alone CD-ROMs. Measuring the use of electronic materials accessed via the Internet is a rapidly developing field (Bertot 2001) where, typically, the most useful data are provided by the publisher or database provider rather than collected from library sources. Activities to be counted include: database sessions, database searches, the number of items examined and the number items downloaded. The remote electronic use of library services is measured by virtual visits and by virtual reference transactions.

Several statistics pertain to users. Most common are registered users, active borrowers and visiting users. For many performance ratios it is essential to know the number of potential users – the target user population – which may also be expressed as primary and secondary user groups.

Quality and performance

Timeliness of service can be measured (1) in days or weeks taken to acquire and catalogue material, and to supply material from elsewhere, (2) in hours or minutes taken to answer enquiries and to obtain material from closed-access or reserve stocks, and (3) in seconds or microseconds to interrogate computer files. Generally it is more appropriate to use the median rather than the arithmetic mean to calculate average times taken. Sampling is appropriate for these statistics.

Quality of service is only susceptible in part to quantitative analysis. Statistical sampling is used

to measure the availability to users of particular titles or of books appropriate to a particular need. In the best-known methodology these are known as 'title & author/subject needs fill rates' (Van House *et al.* 1987). Other uses measured by sampling cover success or failure of users in searching the catalogue and in seeking information. Availability of material and information may also be sampled by the use of prepared lists. Questionnaires seeking users' appraisal of particular services typically use a 1–5 scale (unsatisfactory to very good), with results expressed as a percentage.

Such user statistics are termed output performance measures (see PERFORMANCE MEASUREMENT IN LIBRARIES). The term performance indicators – the two are sometimes used interchangeably – refers more specifically to the ratio where an output statistic is expressed per user, per target population, per unit of stock or per quantity of expenditure. Some common examples are issues per capita, materials spend as a proportion of total expenditure, materials spend per capita, stock turn (average annual issues per item of stock), proportion of stock on loan and professional staff per capita.

Statistics of output related to cost form the basis of cost–benefit analysis. Here it is important to compare only those costs associated with the output in question.

Prospects

In many countries statistics are collected and published nationally in excellent and comprehensive collections. This is usually done separately for national, academic and public libraries; it is rare for them to cover special and school libraries to the same degree. In other countries national statistics are rudimentary or non-existent, as can be seen from inspection of United Nations and UNESCO compilations.

There are two important developments at the turn of the century. First, the LIBECON Project has assembled a complete database of European countries' national statistics (LIBECON2000 Millennium Report) and is extending this collection to several countries in the rest of the world. Second, a major revision of the international standard ISO 2789 is well advanced and should be published in 2002. Many traditional statistical headings and definitions are being revised. Sampling techniques are accepted in the new standard and an Annexe was introduced to list and define optional measures applicable only to some library sectors. To cover electronic services and the Internet statistics of expenditure, access provision and facilities are being fitted into the existing structure. Measuring use is less clear-cut – but definitions are emerging for virtual visits, database sessions, searches, electronic journals, etc.

Presentation and use

Computer facilities have revolutionized the presentation and accessibility of library statistics. It is now common for statistical data to be collected, compiled and presented in formats such as Excel. Not only does this facilitate data collection, but it also allows easy transmission of, and access to, the results. Some statistical websites have advanced to interactive presentation where the user can build up a custom-made statistical report (see *IFLA Journal* 27(4) (2001)).

Locally published statistics can form a valuable part of the annual report, but are of more direct value in informing management decision-making and planning. Computer systems and statistical sampling techniques extend much further the scope and use of statistics in management. However, qualitative analysis will always be necessary to supplement the quantitative. Provision of information and materials can usually be measured: attempts to measure its relevance and value to the user are still developing and are not yet standard.

References

Bertot, J.C. (2001) 'Measuring service quality in the networked environment: Approaches and considerations', *Library Trends* 49(4) (spring): 758–75.

IFLA Journal (2001) 27(4), special number, 'Library Statistics to Enjoy – Measuring Success' (also at www.ifla.org/V/iflaj/index.htm).

International Standard ISO 2789, 2nd edn, 1991–05–01, *Information and Documentation – International Library Statistics*, International Standards Organization.

LIBECON2000 Millennium Report on Economics (Statistics) of European Libraries (www.libecon2000.org/millenniumstudy/default.htm) [LIBECON future developments are described and updated at www.libecon.org.].

Van House *et al.* (1987) *Output Measures for Public Libraries*, American Library Association.

Further reading

In-progress research (and annual statistical reports) at www.arl.org/stats/newmeas/emetrics/index.html.

Bertot, J.C., McClure, C.R. and Ryan, J. (2001) *Statistics and Performance Measures for Public Library Networked Services*, Chicago, IL: American Library Association.

Keys to Success: Performance Indicators for Public Libraries; A Manual of Performance Measures and Indicators (1990) King Research Ltd [the comprehensive description of particular measures and techniques is more valuable than the theoretical methodology].

Lancaster, F.W. (1993) *If You Want to Evaluate Your Library*, 2nd edn, Library Association Publishing.

Library Trends (2001) 49(4), special number 'Measuring Service Quality'.

Poll, R. and Boekhorst, P. (1996) *Measuring Quality: International Guidelines for Performance Measurement in Academic Libraries*, Munich: K.G. Saur (IFLA Publications 76 – prepared by IFLA Section of University Libraries and Other General Research Libraries).

Proceedings of the Northumbria International Conferences on Performance Measurement in Libraries and Information Services (1995, 1997 and 1999) ed. P. Wressell and associates, Newcastle upon Tyne: Information North.

Van House *et al.* (1990) *Measuring Academic Library Performance: A Practical Approach*, American Library Association.

Ward, S. *et al.* (1995) *Library Performance Indicators and Library Management Tools (PROLIB/PI)*, Luxembourg: European Commission, DG XIII-E3, 'EUR 16483 EN' [often referred to as 'The Toolbox Study'].

SEE ALSO: performance measurement in libraries; quality assurance; research in library and information science; user studies

JOHN SUMSION

STOCK EDITING

The process of maintaining the bookstock of a library in good condition and ensuring that the latest and most useful titles are available in adequate quantities. It is an essential element of COLLECTION MANAGEMENT and may in some libraries be performed by a librarian whose post is designated as that of stock editor.

STRATEGIC PLANNING

A process and framework for relating an organization to its environment, defining its scope and direction, and deciding actions needed to achieve specified goals. This involves gathering and processing information, identifying and evaluating options, deciding and refining objectives, formulating and implementing plans, monitoring and reviewing progress.

Strategic planning originated in the USA during the 1960s and spread to Europe and beyond in the 1970s and 1980s to become an accepted part of managerial thinking and practice in the business world and public sector. It differs from traditional long-range planning in its focus on environmental forces and concern with fundamental questions about where an organization is going and how it will get there. Strategic planning is about the systematic management of discontinuous change, requiring continuous monitoring of a changing environment and frequent review of organizational priorities in line with environmental factors. There is considerable overlap between corporate/business strategy and marketing strategy, and many of the models and tools used in strategic planning are concerned with MARKETING variables. However, strategic planning is essentially about defining the business (or businesses) of an organization and setting overall objectives, while marketing plans elaborate strategies to achieve these objectives. Nevertheless, MARKET RESEARCH is an essential aspect of the environmental analysis that underpins strategic planning.

The adoption of strategic planning concepts and techniques by library and information service managers has followed the general trend, with US libraries acting as pioneers from the 1970s onwards, and libraries in other countries gradually following their lead. In the United Kingdom, the BRITISH LIBRARY was among the first to produce and publish a formal strategic plan in 1985, but was quickly emulated by academic and government libraries. In both the USA and the UK PUBLIC LIBRARIES also began to adopt formal planning processes during the 1980s.

There have been some centralized initiatives to encourage formal planning in libraries, notably the process developed by the Public Library Association, a division of the AMERICAN LIBRARY ASSOCIATION (Palmour et al. 1980), the manual produced by the UK Library and Information Services Council Working Group on Public Library Objectives (1991) and the programme offered by the Association of Research Libraries Office of Management Studies (Jurow and Webster 1991). The contribution of professional associations is also evident at international level in papers presented at the General Conference of IFLA where representatives of national libraries

have pointed to the value of strategic planning for developing countries as well as richer nations in raising awareness and opening debate on their function and role with government, users, the general public and the professional community (Ferguson 1992; Donlon and Line 1992). Developments in special libraries are less well documented but the Special Libraries Association promoted the concept by publishing a practical guide (Asantewa 1992).

Approaches and terminology used in strategic planning vary but common elements include a statement of purpose or mission, the articulation of values or principles, a vision of the desired future, a set of goals and targets, and an action plan with a timetable. Early examples of library plans were often developed over eighteen months or longer, but planning processes have gradually been streamlined, evidenced by the later Public Library Association recommendation of a four- to five-month timeline to complete a plan (Nelson 2001). From the mid-1990s, the trend has been away from extensive documentation of environmental factors and service characteristics to concise presentation of key issues, proposed strategies and intended results. Time spans covered have also shortened with plans typically limited to five years or less. Some library managers have extended the scope of their planning processes by using more sophisticated techniques such as scenario development (Giesecke 1998) or developing broader plans for interorganizational activity (Bolt and Stephan 1998).

The impetus for strategic planning may come from within a library or information unit, but some form of plan is usually required by the parent body or funding authority. Library planning needs to be related to general organizational objectives and strategies for particular units or functions, especially those concerned with information provision. The nature and scope of library plans will also be affected by the development of enterprise-wide information or knowledge strategies, which are often associated with the convergence and restructuring of library and information technology services, and the adoption of formal approaches to KNOWLEDGE MANAGEMENT.

Despite the time and effort required for strategic planning, published accounts point to significant benefits, including new perspectives on services, strengthened cases for funding, easier delegation of decisions, more ownership of changes and a shared sense of purpose, especially where staff and users have participated in the planning process. Strategic planning also helps managers to identify critical issues and is a prerequisite for PERFORMANCE MEASUREMENT IN LIBRARIES.

References

Asantewa, D. (1992) *Strategic Planning Basics for Special Libraries*, Special Libraries Association.

Bolt, N.M. and Stephan, S.S. (1998) *Strategic Planning for Multitype Library Cooperatives: A Planning Process*, American Library Association.

Donlon, P. and Line, M. (1992) 'Strategic planning in national libraries', *Alexandria* 4(2): 83–94.

Ferguson, S. (1992) 'Strategic planning for national libraries in developing countries: An optimist's view', *IFLA Journal* 18(4): 339–44.

Giesecke, J. (ed.) (1998) *Scenario Planning for Libraries*, American Library Association.

Jurow, S. and Webster, D. (1991) 'Building new futures for research libraries', *Journal of Library Administration* 14(2): 5–19.

Library and Information Services Council Working Group on Public Library Objectives (1991) *Setting Objectives for Public Library Services: A Manual of Public Library Objectives*, HMSO.

Nelson, S. (2001) *The New Planning for Results: A Streamlined Approach*, American Library Association.

Palmour, V.E., Bellassai, M.C. and DeWath, N.V. (1980) *A Planning Process for Public Libraries*, American Library Association.

Further reading

Corrall, S. (2000) *Strategic Management of Information Services: A Planning Handbook*, ASLIB/IMI [comprehensive guide with practical examples and annotated bibliographies covering general management and information services].

Favret, L. (1995) 'Local government change and strategic management: An historical perspective and a case study', *Public Library Journal* 10(4): 95–101 [case study of the London Borough of Bromley, relating library developments to organizational strategies].

Hughes, A. (2000) 'Information strategies', in J. Elkin and D. Law (eds) *Managing Information*, Open University Press, pp. 49–64 [discussion of strategy development in higher education including speculation about future migration to knowledge management].

Hussey, D. (1999) *Strategy and Planning: A Manager's Guide*, John Wiley [concise introduction with separate chapters on marketing, financial and human resource planning].

Jacob, M.E.L. (1990) *Strategic Planning: A How-to-do-it Manual for Librarians*, Neal Schuman.

SEE ALSO: information management; organizational information policies

SHEILA CORRALL

STRING INDEXING

A form of document indexing characterized by a 'string' or set of indexing terms for each entry. The terms within each string are connected by relationships to each other according to a set of rules for the particular scheme. The idea is that a basic string will be generated by a human indexer and then manipulated by a computer to produce a multiple-access index to the documents. PRECIS is a highly developed example of a string-indexing system.

SEE ALSO: organization of knowledge

SUBJECT CATALOGUE

CATALOGUES that offer the facility for tracing documents on a particular subject (as opposed to tracing documents by their author), whether it does so by virtue of arrangement in alphabetical order of subject terms or some form of classified subject order.

SEE ALSO: organization of knowledge

SUBJECT HEADING

The word or group of words under which books and other material on a subject are entered in any catalogue or BIBLIOGRAPHY in which the entries are arranged in alphabetical order. In a classified catalogue (see CLASSIFIED CATALOGUES), a classification symbol is substituted for the verbal subject denominator. Standard lists of subject headings, such as the LIBRARY OF CONGRESS SUBJECT HEADINGS, are used in the preparation of some catalogues to aid the cataloguers in making a choice of subject headings so as to preserve uniformity of practice.

SEE ALSO: organization of knowledge

SUBJECT INDEX

An INDEX through which the user can trace references to material on a particular topic. Published subject indexes are available for many topic areas, and subject indexes are provided for

CLASSIFIED CATALOGUES to direct users to the class number under which entries for books or other documents on some required subject will be found.

SEE ALSO: organization of knowledge

SUBJECT LIBRARIAN

A librarian with special knowledge of, and responsibility for, a particular subject or subjects. This may include work on ACQUISITIONS, STOCK EDITING and services to users. In the USA this is often known as a bibliographer, and in some continental European countries as a research librarian, in the latter case having an explicit duty to carry on research, usually bibliographical, in their subject area.

SEE ALSO: academic libraries; information professions

SUBSCRIPTION LIBRARIES

Libraries that charge a subscription of readers or borrowers; now applied usually to libraries with permanent collections and a regular membership, but can also cover commercial circulating libraries (see CIRCULATING LIBRARY). The history of subscription libraries and circulating libraries can be traced back to the eighteenth century, well before the concept of free PUBLIC LIBRARIES became common.

Circulating libraries

Commercial circulating libraries developed from the early eighteenth century onwards, as an offshoot of the bookselling business, when booksellers began to hire out their surplus stock. Later, collections were built up specifically for lending. Libraries of this kind, usually meeting popular demand for novels and less serious material, spread rapidly throughout Britain, the USA and the continent of Europe; they were open to anyone, not restricted to members of a club.

The pattern in Britain was diverse. Most towns of any size had a number of such libraries, usually linked to bookshops, and they were an accepted feature of spas and seaside resorts. By the nineteenth century some had become very large, with sizeable premises; some, for example Mudie's Select Library, provided a postal service

on a national scale. Some catered for specialized needs, for example supplying books in French or German, or music or plays. Chain stores such as W.H. Smith and Boots developed libraries in their many branches, and which survived until the 1960s; most other large circulating libraries had closed earlier in the century because of changes in taste and the rise of public libraries. Others remained small; the very smallest, which survived well into the twentieth century, operated from the back of newsagents or grocers' shops, with the latest books supplied by specialized agencies. (The commercial video library is perhaps the modern equivalent.)

Surviving printed catalogues of circulating libraries, which are known from the 1730s or earlier, provide valuable evidence of contemporary reading taste; though very few records of loans survive; such libraries had to cater to their readers' wishes and their stock therefore reflects what was in demand. The largest libraries, however, had a strong influence on the policies of fiction publishers through the later nineteenth century, because of their domination of the market and their insistence on certain types and formats for the novels they bought. This led to changes in publishing and book-pricing, another factor in the disappearance of circulating libraries.

Subscription libraries

The subscription library movement was a parallel development, providing permanent collections, often of more serious material and sometimes of significant scholarly value, and offering more club-like facilities. (Their origin can be traced back to BOOK CLUBS, which bought books for a small number of members who read them in turn but which did not build up permanent collections.)

Subscription libraries were established in many towns and cities of Britain from the mid-eighteenth century onwards (Liverpool in 1758, Leeds in 1768) to provide for the needs of their subscribers; these were usually members of the professional and middle classes, though amongst the earliest such libraries are those established by the mining communities in Wanlockhead and Leadhills in Scotland. In many cases the libraries were owned jointly by the subscribing 'proprietors' and had elaborate constitutions designed to control abuse. Many soon acquired their own premises, often specially built; other activities often took place alongside the library, such as lectures, classes or indoor games like cards or chess.

The libraries thus became notable social centres, and in many cases provided services later taken over – on a wider scale – by the public libraries. This was even more true of the parallel Mechanics' Institute movement, which had much in common with subscription libraries but was particularly concerned with adult education and aimed to serve a rather lower social class. Specialized subscription libraries for law or medicine also developed in larger towns.

Indeed, subscription libraries in provincial cities often took the lead in developing literary and scientific culture, and their printed catalogues permit the study of the spread of new ideas. Their role in the development of urban society is consequently very significant. (They did, however, also provide FICTION and some lighter reading, sometimes supplied by the large circulating libraries, supplementing the services of the local commercial libraries.)

In London there were various smaller subscription libraries but, perhaps because of the presence of large circulating libraries, nothing on a large scale before 1841, when the London Library was founded on the initiative of Thomas Carlyle. This represents the culmination of the subscription library in Britain; it now has well over 1 million volumes and is a major resource for writers and scholars in the humanities. As with other subscription libraries, one of its attractions is the generous loan of books that are otherwise unavailable.

The present day

The growth of public libraries, and other changes in society, has led to the disappearance of most of the old subscription libraries. The Association of Independent Libraries, founded in 1989, now links about twenty surviving libraries throughout the British Isles. They continue to serve an enthusiastic membership that finds in such institutions something lacking in public libraries. Most remain sturdily independent, though some are developing links with other local libraries, for example to give wider access to their collections of older literature; the very collections of the London Library are a notable example. Others, such as the Linen Hall Library in Belfast, have a

very significant local role and receive some public funding. In the USA some important subscription libraries survive, but they have largely disappeared from the European scene.

Further reading

Gerard, D.E. (1980) 'Subscription libraries (Great Britain)', in *Encyclopedia of Library and Information Science*, vol. 29, pp. 205–21 [covers both proprietary and circulating libraries; useful bibliography].

Griest, G.L. (1970) *Mudie's Circulating Library and the Victorian Novel*, Indiana University Press.

Killen, J. (1990) *A History of the Linen Hall Library, 1788–1988*, Linen Hall Library.

Martino, A. (1990) *Die deutsche Leihbibliothek*, Harrassowitz [comprehensive study of commercial circulating libraries in German-speaking countries, with references to activity elsewhere].

Wells, J. (1991) *Rude Words: An Informal History of the London Library*, Macmillan.

PETER HOARE

SURFING

Surfing is a widely used term to describe a kind of unfocused BROWSING of the INTERNET that has become a popular pastime. The hyperlinks between pages and the listings provided by SEARCH ENGINES offer almost infinite possibilities for whiling away the hours, just as, at the same time, they permit highly focused and effective searching on specific topics.

SURROGATE

Surrogates, or substitutes, are used for various purposes in LIS. In PRESERVATION, a surrogate can be a copy of a document created to protect the original, created by photography or DIGITIZATION, which is offered to all users other than those for whom direct examination of the original is unavoidable. In special librarianship and information science, it could be an ABSTRACT or other summary of a document, which is capable of satisfying user requirements in a proportion of cases.

SEE ALSO: organization of knowledge

SURVEILLANCE

The close observation of people for any one of a variety of reasons. Originally it tended to refer to policing, or MILITARY INTELLIGENCE. It now frequently refers to other uses, such as work on the incidence and spread of diseases for health-care purposes, or flows of traffic for transport management and development. Modern surveillance relies on the availability of a range of technologies that, until recently, were only used by the state, for instance, businesses practice surveillance for marketing purposes through the collection of information from credit cards and retailing loyalty cards. Data from customer surveys and extended warranty applications can also be fed into consumer DATABASES. Employers engage in MONITORING of the actions and performance of their workers, by searching employee computer files, voice mail, e-mail or other networked communications. Public spaces are overlooked by closed-circuit television cameras, controlled by police, traffic authorities, householders and corporate property owners. It is frequently alleged that a surveillance society has developed in which PRIVACY is a concept that has become seriously limited.

Further reading

Lyon, D. (2001) *Surveillance Society: Monitoring in Everyday Life*, Open University Press.
Lyon, D. and Zureik, E. (eds) (1996) *Computers, Surveillance and Privacy*, University of Minnesota Press.
Surveillance and Society (www.surveillance-and-society. org/journal.htm).

SYSTEMS ANALYSIS

Analysis that can suggest how best an automated system might be introduced into a particular area of an organization's operations. When the desirability and feasibility of introducing a new system have been established, existing systems and procedures are investigated in detail. From this analysis, the alternative ways that the system might be designed can be considered and the best option decided upon. For this, a functional specification can then be designed, so as to make clear, both to potential users and to development staff, how the new system should operate, in functional rather than technical terms.

SEE ALSO: information systems; information theory; organizational information policies; systems theory

SYSTEMS THEORY

Systems theory is concerned with the co-ordination of complex systems, both technical and social. The dominant paradigm for the application of systems theory to practical human problems has evolved from the classical scientific method derived from the physical sciences and has led to the search for overarching concepts and 'general laws' that govern all systems, living organisms, societies, economics and languages. The proponents of systems theory reject the reductionist approach of classical science as the understanding of a phenomenon based upon the disassembly and study of its constituent parts. Instead they propose to explain a phenomenon in terms of the properties that are emergent from the relationship between its components. This holistic approach allows for the study of these emergent properties of a system that are independent of its constituent elements. Thus from the perspective of systems theory valid knowledge and meaningful understanding reflects the adage that 'the whole is often greater than the sum of its parts'.

In the development of systems theory a key idea borrowed from the study of systems under the natural sciences is the assumption that social phenomena are real systems and that the social world therefore comprises many inter-related social systems. In demonstrating this Ludwig Von Bertalanffy (1981), one of the founders of the general systems theory movement, observes that concepts of reductionism are inadequate for the appreciation of the dynamics of both natural and social phenomena. Von Bertalanffy identifies that systems interact with their environments and in doing so acquire new qualitative properties. He suggests that these same principles of systemic organization are transferable to the understanding of different disciplines and proposes that this open systems view of the world must replace the scientific perspectives of the nineteenth and early twentieth centuries and their reductionist philosophies. Von Bertalanffy's contribution, together with later work by Ross Ashby (1956) on CYBERNETICS theory, was to allow the establishment of a series of principles and insights, and the identification of their potential application to a variety of fields, most notably those of managerial and organisational analysis. Thus, although systems theory has a history independent of organizational and industrial theories, it has nonetheless evolved in managerial and policy circles as a methodology suited to providing analysts with the tools and frameworks required for decision-making and control in complex and uncertain environments.

In terms of the development and applications of systems theory, while many of its concepts are traceable to the ideas of Von Bertalanffy and Ashby (and the earlier ideas of the nineteenth-century *philosophes* Auguste Comte and Henri Saint-Simon), in its recent manifestations in management and COMPUTER SCIENCE, the practical use of systems theory can be understood to be the product of a series of converging developments that have taken place both during and after the Second World War. The military needs of this period in terms of managing scarce resources efficiently and effectively, and planning and controlling military strategies and tactics, resulted in the formation of multidisciplinary scientific groups working on tactical and logistical problems concerning the war effort. These Operational Research groups, as they were known, were characterized by the use of mathematical techniques and models to assist decision-makers in solving their problems. After the war many of these groups were maintained and developed as research centres concerned with the perceived threat of nuclear war and the development of space technology (e.g. The Research and National Development [RAND] Corporation in the USA). Early RAND research, like wartime operations research, dealt with the mathematical and statistical treatment (largely through linear programming techniques) of well-defined, low-level, often military, tactical decision problems (e.g. radar operator response to target tracking). By the early 1950s RAND projects had begun to incorporate and develop work in various disciplines including biology, computer sciences, IN-FORMATION THEORY, linguistics, economic game theory, political science, COMMUNICATION theory, cybernetics and OPERATIONS RESEARCH. The 'systems approach', as this convergence of methodologies came to be called in the managerial and policy sciences, consists of a set of techniques for the diagnosis, design, evaluation and control of complex configurations of people, technologies and organizations. Because of its use in the planning and evaluation of complex tasks associated with NASA's space programme, the systems approach became described as the 'Space-Age technology' for problem solving and was

often described as the most valuable spin-off of the aerospace programme (Churchman 1979). In this aspect Churchman portrays it as revolutionizing management and planning in government, business and human problems.

The success of systems theory in military and space programmes led to the belief among planners that similar 'scientific' thought processes can be applied equally to getting a person to the moon and to solving problems of the inner city or drought-stricken areas in Africa. In attempting to deal with economic and social problems that have less clearly defined objectives, systems analysis was adopted as one of the subdisciplines of the general systems theory movement. Systems analysis, for this reason, tended to rely less on rigorous quantitative techniques, reserving their use for selected aspects of particular problems. Its practitioners sometimes describe it as an attempt to supply systematic reasoning to the structuring of complex or 'wicked' problems. The seminal ideas rested upon the theory of information feedback as a means of evaluating business and other organizational and social contexts. This form of control could be either positive or negative. Negative feedback or balanced loop control exists where the conditions of an organism move out of a range of control parameters, and then action is taken to reestablish normal conditions. Positive feedback, or amplifying loop control, emphasizes dynamic growth and trends. An example of this is the system dynamics model of Jay Forrester (1971), which is concerned with creating models of real-world systems, studying their dynamics and improving problematic system behaviour. As such, systems analysis is a way of thinking that came to emphasize the technical side of problems over their social and political dimensions. Thus systems theory, particularly in the USA, became considered as a viable means to address the social problems surrounding the redesign of cities, the elimination of poverty and the improvement of education.

Systems theory continues to be a central tenet of more recent developments in the study of complexity in organizational environments. Examples include work by Senge (1990), who describes the important contribution of 'systems thinking' to the understanding and development of organizational learning and who continues to be of major influence for researchers in the managerial and social sciences.

References

Ashby, W.R. (1956) *An Introduction to Cybernetics*, London: Chapman & Hall.

Bertalanffy, L. Von (1981) *A Systems View of Man*, ed. P.A. La Violette, Boulding, CA: Westview.

Churchman, C.W. (1979) *The Systems Approach and Its Enemies*, New York: Basic Books.

Forrester, J.W. (1971) *World Dynamics*, Cambridge, MA: MIT Press.

Senge, P. (1990) *The Fifth Discipline*, New York: Doubleday.

SEE ALSO: military intelligence

FRANCIS WILSON

T

TAUBE, MORTIMER (1910–65)

Information scientist and library consultant.

Born in Jersey City, New Jersey, and, after studying at Harvard and Berkeley, held various library posts, including senior posts at the Library of Congress. In 1952 Taube founded Documentation, Inc., and was its Chairman for the rest of his life. It was arguably the first ever INFORMATION SCIENCE company and it undertook innovative studies for government agencies, including the US Air Force and National Institutes of Health. It also undertook information facilities management, administering the first contract-operated national information programme at NASA (1962–8).

Taube pioneered the use of co-ordinate indexing through the application of uniterms. This was not only effective when applied to manual retrieval systems, but also forms the basis of search strategies that are effective with electronically held information.

He passed on his ideas through teaching at the Universities of Chicago and Columbia, and through his articles and books. These include the six volumes of *Studies in Coordinate Indexing* (1953–65) and *Computers and Common Sense: The Myth of Thinking Machines* (1961).

SEE ALSO: organization of knowledge

TAXONOMIES

The word taxonomy is normally understood to mean CLASSIFICATION, and is used mainly in the life sciences. It is not clear where or when the word was given a different slant in the general area of information retrieval and so, perhaps not surprisingly, there is no clearly agreed definition of the term as it is now being used. This has led to some confusion as to whether they are the same as a classification or a THESAURUS; but while they are clearly related to these retrieval tools, they usually display different characteristics, and since they are mostly used on the Internet, intranets or extranets, they may be closely associated with the new generation of information retrieval software.

The reasons for taxonomies

There are perhaps three main reasons to explain why taxonomies have attracted interest:

- Information overload. It was estimated in 2000 that the surface (as opposed to the invisible) Web contained some 2.5 billion documents and was growing at the rate of 7.3 million pages per day. Large organizations like British Telecom and Microsoft have 3 million documents on their intranets. Conventional SEARCH ENGINES are often incapable of dealing effectively with such large databases, and users need complementary search aids.
- INFORMATION LITERACY. Research has shown that the majority of end-users have severe problems in knowing how to search for information, leading to wasted time and the missing of useful information.
- Organizational terminology. Published classifications and thesauri do not reflect the particular languages of organizations, in which, typically, 80 per cent of the information held has been created internally.

These three factors are addressed separately or in combination by different taxonomic approaches.

Types of taxonomies

WEB DIRECTORIES

These are in common use on the Web and are, in fact, a form of classification. A menu of top terms is offered to the user, and clicking on a selected term will display a second level, and so on for perhaps six or seven levels. The searcher will perhaps arrive finally at some information or references, or the option of offering the last selected term to one or more search engines. Each level does not have to be hierarchical in the normally accepted sense, and terms may be repeated at different levels, providing alternative pathways for the searcher. Common Web directories most, or perhaps all, of which are manually created include Yahoo! (www.yahoo.com) and the Open Directory (www.dmoz.com).

TAXONOMIES CREATED BY AUTOMATIC CATEGORIZATION

A growing number of software packages are now available, using a range of techniques such as statistical analysis of occurrence and co-occurrence of terms, and which purport to be able to analyse text, to automatically create categories from that analysis and to classify the analysed documents according to the categories created. These categories may then be displayed as Web directories (see above) and/or as two-dimensional maps, where related terms are linked to the selected term, which appears in the middle of the map. Selection of a related term will then move that term to the centre and introduce a new set of related terms. In practice, these packages are only effective when dealing with relatively large collections of conceptually homogeneous material, and when seeded at the beginning of the operation with relevant terminologies or glossaries. They also normally require a significant amount of human editing and maintenance.

TAXONOMIES TO SUPPORT AUTOMATIC INDEXING

In this case, what the user sees is a shallow classification of typically two levels and perhaps 1,000 to 4,000 terms in all. What the user does not see is the rules base behind the classification, in which each term has associated with it synonyms and quasi-synonyms, related terms, word stems and weights. All of these are used to extract appropriate index terms automatically. These may, or may not, appear in the documents to which they refer. This approach is particularly attractive where throughputs are so large as to negate the possibility of manual indexing. Nevertheless, the compilation of the rules bases is very labour intensive, often taking four or five hours per term.

CORPORATE TAXONOMIES

Many organizations, particularly the larger multinationals, are expending considerable resources on tackling the three problems listed above in the implementation of their INTRANET or portal (see PORTALS AND GATEWAYS). They are also employing a wide range of techniques and associated software, many of which are referred to, rather loosely, as taxonomies. The generic term often applied to this activity is INFORMATION ARCHITECTURE – a coherent set of strategies and plans for information access and delivery inside organizations. These architectures will often employ one or more of the types of taxonomies described above, or adaptations and elaborations of existing corporate classifications and thesauri. Some manifestations include a super-thesaurus, wherein a number of existing thesauri have been loosely merged and each term carries the addresses of any corporate information repositories using that term; a corporate macrothesaurus containing terms common to the whole enterprise, and to which are hooked microthesauri for specialist areas; a METADATA registry made available to portal owners and information providers, containing tagging standards supported by generic terminologies; knowledge maps for the location of relevant repositories, with guidelines on their contents and access paths and protocols; expertise databases supporting knowledge-sharing through person-to-person connections, often supported by the facility to annotate shared documents or a process of collaborative filtering. A particular problem facing the corporate enterprise is the mapping of internal and external information retrieval languages.

Finally, in an increasingly global and dynamic world, there is a lot of interest in the use of taxonomies to ameliorate mergers and acquisitions; to share information between organizations through extranets; and to support the work of virtual COMMUNITIES OF INTEREST or practice. Some of these applications collect not only the terminologies of the topics of interest to the organization, but also the organizational terminologies relating to their structures, business processes, and standards and rules in operation.

Further reading

Adams, K.C. *Word Wranglers* (www.intelligentkm.com/feature/010101/feat1.shtml).

Gilchrist, A. and Kibby, P. (2000) *Taxonomies for Business: Access and Connectivity in a Wired World*, TFPL Ltd.

ALAN GILCHRIST

TELECENTRES

Telecentres have quickly become a major concern of governments and civil society organizations looking for ways to broaden access to INFORMATION AND COMMUNICATION TECHNOLOGY (ICT). A telecentre may be roughly defined as a facility for providing public access to ICT-based services. Telecentres appeared in the mid-1980s in industrialized countries and spread over most of these. From the early 1990s the concept was introduced in the so-called developing countries, mostly as isolated experiments. A few years later, large schemes for the implantation of telecentres were becoming commonplace, especially in Latin America.

A number of different names are given to these facilities such as telecottage (Europe), community technology center (US), multipurpose community telecentre (AFRICA), infocentro (El Salvador), computer club (Cuba), public Internet cabin (Peru), etc. Some consider the cybercafé as a particular type of telecentre. Somewhat artificial distinctions try to characterize one or another name as corresponding more to a community-driven, or conversely a commercially driven, endeavour. In fact there is no real reason why the same name cannot be used to describe radically different endeavours with the same fundamental character.

The groundwork of telecentres

The provision of public access to ICT is seen as a policy requirement when geographic or socio-economic conditions make private access excessively expensive or difficult. Location-wise, telecentres tend to be associated with isolated communities and low population density areas (rural and mountainous districts or small islands), but also poor neighbourhoods in urban areas. In terms of socio-economic conditions, they are directed at low-income, underprivileged and minority groups. Telecentres are expected to contribute to community development programmes of whatever kind. They are thus strongly associated with a range of projects, in particular those geared at the reduction of the so-called digital divide (the ratio of the population that cannot use ICT for lack of access and basic skills). They enhance community participation in, and effectiveness of, local government. They further represent an alternative to the individual equipment and consumption model upon which ICT industries have relied so far.

The nature of telecentres is shaped by tensions between contradictory forces: not-for-profit, or even free, services versus financial self-sustainability; private ownership and management versus community ownership; and collective management, consumer use of ICT and existing electronic services versus empowerment orientation (endogenous development). It is their goals and the means they use to achieve them, rather than a name or any identifiable practical characteristics, which distinguish telecentres as a type of business from telecentres as community development tools.

Many telecentres, especially in the so-called developing countries, are established through international co-operation projects or governmental programmes. Unless they are deeply rooted in their community and, from the inception, implement a plan to secure an appropriate level of self-sustainability they face serious risks of disruption when programmes terminate.

Telecentre functions

Telecentres are expected to provide affordable basic telecommunication services such as telephone, fax, access to the Internet for electronic mail, the World Wide Web and chat. A photocopying service is often a popular feature. Other office services such as binding, document protection and local computer-based office applications (text processing, spreadsheet, printing) can be offered as well as educational and entertainment facilities (use of CD-ROMs and educational software; videotapes, DVDs, film). A powerful addition to the arsenal is the use of local radio or Internet radio for broadcast information as well as the use of various types of conventional media (posters, newspapers) and communication opportunities (community meetings, visits by extension agents, etc.). When operated by public libraries, telecentres benefit from the complement of the traditional services that libraries provide. Those housed within schools may take advantage of the school libraries and media centres. Others may build a basic reference collection of print materials.

In addition most telecentres do offer opportunities for acquiring the basic computer and information literacy skills that are required for using them. This may be expanded to include opportunities to learn about the production of Web pages and creation of local information content. Training activities in community development-driven telecentres may encompass a wide range of skills, in particular those required for the promotion of local business and teleworking. Eventually a room for the meetings of community groups and for courses may be available. A telecentre may also operate advice services, or these can be provided by other organizations using its premises. In conjunction with tele-medicine schemes, a telecentre may become a primary healthcare centre. Distance education resources may further strengthen the role of telecentres in supporting educational efforts in a community.

TELECENTRE DEVELOPMENT

The idea that a new stage in human history has been reached with the general diffusion of computer networks and effective access to, and use of, ICT, by themselves, is questionable. But there is ample evidence that these technologies can be powerful tools to open up avenues for development. By enabling groups otherwise left out to get connected to the rest of the world, express themselves and develop ties, leverage their unique skills and heritage, they create unprecedented conditions for change, even when basic social constraints, such as the power structure, gender, ethnic and age group relationships, welfare, etc., remain as they are.

Telecentres face many challenges to their continuing success. Telecommunications companies are reluctant to provide them with cost-effective conditions of connectivity, even if they are not tempted simply to take them over and eliminate competition. Technical and management skills among telecentre staff and the maintenance of proactive community participation need constant strengthening. Sharing of experience through a representative international movement of telecentres, as initiated by SomosTelecentros in Latin America, appears a necessary response.

Further reading

The Commonwealth of Learning (www.col.org/Tele-centres/telecentre_intro.htm).
Community Technology Centers' Network (2001) (www.ctcnet.org/publics.html).
Gómez, R. and Hunt, P. (eds) (1999) *Telecentre Evaluation: A Global Perspective*, Ottawa: IDRC (www.idrc.ca/telecentre/evaluation/html/main.html).
Latchem, C. and Walker, D. (eds) (2001) *Telecentres: Case Studies and Key Issues*, Vancouver.
Miller, J. (ed.) (2000) *CentraTEL Telecentre CD-Rom*, version 1.0, Hout Bay, Rep. of South Africa: CentraTEL (www.centratel.com).
Murray, W. and Cornford, D. (1999) 'Telecottage and Telecentre Survey 1998 [UK and Ireland]' (www.itu.int/ITU-D/Univ-Access/telecentres).
SomosTelecentros (2001) (www.tele-centros.org).
Telecommons Development Group (2001) (www.tele-commons.com/reports.cfm).
Telework, Telecottage and Telecentre Association (TCA) (2001) (www.tca.org.uk).
Wilcox, D. (2001) *Making the Net Work* (www.ma-kingthenetwork.org/).

SEE ALSO: community information; information society

MICHEL J. MENOU

TELECOMMUNICATIONS

The transmission of data from one point and reception at a remote point, using wires, FIBRE-OPTICS, radio waves, microwaves or another medium of transmission. In association with computing, it forms the defining technology of the information age. Although traditionally associated with the transmission of voice data (as conventional telephone calls), telecommunications systems (telecoms, or telecomms, in the jargon) are now universally used for transmitting digitized data of all kinds.

SEE ALSO: communication; informatics; information and communication technology; information management; information policy; knowledge industries; mobile communications; PTT

TELECOMMUTING

Describes the increasingly common practice of employing people to carry out office work in the home rather than in premises provided by the organization. It depends on using INFORMATION TECHNOLOGY and a telecommunications link to maintain contact, and once the physical link with the office is broken there is theoretically no limit to the distance from which it can be carried out. Although it has been presented by some commentators as the working mode for the twenty-first century, and some telecommuters thrive on the scope it offers for a less pressured lifestyle, ingrained organizational cultures often mean that it does not always prove to be as effective as anticipated.

SEE ALSO: economics of information

TELETEXT

A generic term for broadcast information services that are received by an adapted television, and which use the spare lines of the television picture to form frames consisting of text and simple block graphics. In the UK, where the earliest work was done on such systems, CEEFAX and ORACLE provide continuously updated news services by this means. It can also be used to provide closed captions for aurally handicapped viewers of television programmes because of its ability to be superimposed on the normal transmissions. Despite its crudity, it is still widely used by those searching for simple up-to-date information on topics such as the weather, travel conditions and sports results.

SEE ALSO: electronic public-information services; information and communication technology; knowledge industries

TEXT

In common parlance (and in most information science contexts), a text is a coherent assemblage of words. This might take the form of continuous prose (or indeed verse), or it may be a list of words (as in an index), or a short phrase, possible even grammatically and syntactically incomplete (as in some advertising slogans), or indeed may be numerical as well as verbal. In a highly specialized sense, the word is used by literary critics and theorists (and with greater caution in HISTORICAL BIBLIOGRAPHY) to describe the work of an author.

TEXT RETRIEVAL

The form of INFORMATION RETRIEVAL in which the files that are searched consist of free-form text,

such as documents, reports or abstracts, rather than structured data found, for example, in a SPREADSHEET or a structured DATABASE. The user uses either specified keywords (keyword retrieval) or any combination of words contained in the text (full-text retrieval) as search criteria to identify the records required. The user is provided with a printout or display of the whole or part of the relevant documents, instead of merely references to them. This is essentially the form of retrieval used by SEARCH ENGINES, as opposed to searching METADATA specifically provided for that purpose.

SEE ALSO: informatics

TEXTBASE

A DATABASE of textual records, which may range in terms of structure from a simple datastream of characters to a highly structured database management system. Bibliographic databases tend to be in the middle of this range, having structure at the level of fields (e.g. author, title, abstract) but with the content of fields remaining largely unstructured. A textbase does not set out to provide exact responses to queries, but rather to leave the interpretation of the meaning of the data largely to the user.

SEE ALSO: information management

THESAURUS

A lexicon in which words are grouped by concept, thus providing a grouping or classification of synonyms or near-synonyms, and a set of equivalent classes of terminology. Thesauri of the most commonly used terms in various fields have been published so as to permit a harmonizing of indexing terminology in these fields.

SEE ALSO: organization of knowledge

TOUCH SCREEN

A visual display screen that has sensors (either infrared or capacitance-sensitive) superimposed on the display. Menu options, icons and other interface buttons are overlaid with touch-sensitive areas (see HOT SPOT) so the user can choose an option directly, with a finger, rather than using a mouse or other pointing device. The potential of touch screen facilities in public information service kiosks and interactive MU-SEUM displays has been explored and is increasingly exploited. They are also used in some commercial applications, forming, for example, the interface with self-operated ticketing facilities at airports and railways stations.

Further reading

Internet Studies Research Group (ISRG) (2001) *ASLIB Proceedings* 53: 110–11.

TRADE BIBLIOGRAPHY

Bibliographies issued by or for the book trade as a guide to currently available publications, such as *British Books in Print*. Trade bibliographies are typically published serially (perhaps as frequently as weekly), and cumulated. The cumulated versions are normally available online to subscribers.

TRADE LITERATURE

Material prepared in hard copy and on websites with varying degrees of technical specification by companies to describe their products or services to potential customers and which Lowe (1999) considers to include the term 'product literature'. Examples include catalogues, technical data sheets, price lists, product brochures and technical literature. Some commentators also specifically include directories, house journals and annual company reports in the definition, while Kaye (1991) precludes directories and further limits the definition solely to the companies that are manufacturers or suppliers of parts. As a marketing tool, trade literature is often subject to deliberate attempts to avoid uniformity of format and series in the belief that variety will enhance the chance of sales. Thus, it can be considered to be a type of GREY LITERATURE, with all the problems associated with that category of material, but exacerbated by overlap, duplication and currency problems between paper and online versions.

The range, frequency of change, variations of format and limited BIBLIOGRAPHIC CONTROL make trade literature one of the least easy types of information to collect, catalogue, store and retrieve. It is often issued for free, or with the nominal cost waived, and customers usually view it as a transitory, but very necessary, form of information. It is subject to such frequent revision that the need to maintain a comprehensive collection is easily challenged. Nevertheless, trade literature often contains the latest information about new technology, chemical compounds, processes or service provisions, and is often available before a patent specification appears. As such it can be a useful source of competitor intelligence to monitor the activities of other companies.

Lowe (1999: 191) describes efforts to standardize BIBLIOGRAPHIC CONTROL in industries such as construction using the Uniclass system. Specialist companies such as Technical Indexes Ltd and Barbour Index Ltd organize, classify and index manufacturers' literature in online, CD-ROM, binder or microfile format, covering high-demand, complex areas such as construction and chemical engineering industries. These 'package libraries' are available for hire, are regularly maintained and can be tailored to a customer's requirements. Otherwise, directories can be used to identify certain products or possible companies as they provide comprehensive coverage usually by product or geographic area; examples include the Kompass series, Kelly's Manufacturers' and Merchants' Directory and the Thomas Register of American Manufacturers.

Websites, mailing lists, advertising, exhibitions and trade fairs are used to disseminate information, and consequently different versions of trade information may be tailored to target different audiences of customers, such as consumers and professional buyers. Specialist trade journals, such as the *Grocer* or *Metal Bulletin*, often contain pricing information for their markets.

PUBLIC LIBRARIES and ACADEMIC LIBRARIES tend to amass collections in an uneven manner, usually in response to specific pressure from interested users, direct mailings from companies or donations from various projects. Certain companies may be targeted for information in a systematic manner, but this is usually the exception. The sheer volume of material makes a collection policy difficult and libraries tend to prefer to concentrate on the usual directories such as those produced by Kompass to enable, and indeed encourage, enquirers to contact the companies direct.

While the importance of the technical detail is often given less prominence than the advertising copy included, trade information has been described by Auger as 'eventually becoming of great interest to historians, especially those working in the fields of technology and social studies' (1994: 157). Researchers in the US (Connor 1990; Ratner 1990) have reviewed trade literature and related it to aspects of social history and the graphic arts. Certainly the cultural value of the drawings and photos is of value to historians and designers. In the mean time the opportunities to examine and access sizeable collections are limited to those in the hands of special libraries, usually associated with major companies, trade or professional associations, some research related organizations, the National Art Library and the BRITISH LIBRARY Science Reference Information Service, which maintains an extensive collection of product-related literature.

The advent of the availability of trade literature via the Web from organizations advertising their services and products, such as software, will lead to a broadening of the current definition. As information is updated electronically at a very rapid rate the appearance of 'electronic ephemera' will make the task of cataloguing trade information even more difficult. Indeed some organizations have turned to libraries to service their COLLECTION (Gartrell 1999).

References

Auger, C.P. (1994) *Information Sources in Grey Literature*, Bowker-Saur.

Connor, B.M. (1990) 'Trade catalogs in the Los Angeles Public Library', *Science and Technology Libraries* 10: 9–14.

Gartrell, E.G. (1999) 'Some things we have learned: Managing advertising archives for business and non-business users', *American Archivist* 60(1): 56–70.

Lowe, M. (1999) *Business Information at Work*, ASLIB/IMI.

Kaye, D. (1991) *Information and Business: An Introduction*, Library Association Publishing.

Ratner, R.S. (1990) 'Historical research in trade catalogs', *Science and Technology Libraries* 10: 15–22.

Further reading

Wall, R.A. (1986) (ed.) *Finding and Using Product Information: From Trade Catalogues to Computer System*, Gower.

SEE ALSO: business information service; special libraries

DEREK STEPHENS

TRADE MARKS

Signs that identify and distinguish the goods or services of particular enterprises and that are protectable by registration or other legal means. According to the UK Trade Marks Act 1994, which was enacted primarily to harmonize United Kingdom trade mark law with that of other European Union countries, a trade mark may consist of words (including personal names), designs, letters, numerals or the shape of goods or their packaging. This definition is wide enough to include slogans, colours, sounds and other sensory marks such as scents. The term 'trade mark' originally referred only to goods, but modern trade mark law also encompasses services, for example banking, TELECOMMUNICATIONS and transport. Trade marks, popularly known as 'brand names' or 'brands', fulfil a number of distinct though related functions: they indicate in commercial terms the origin or source of goods or services; they distinguish the goods or services of one enterprise from those of its competitors; they identify particular goods or services, thus assisting and informing consumer choice; and they provide for consumers an assurance of quality. Examples of enduring and successful trade marks include Coca-Cola, Kleenex, Kodak and Sony.

Although trade mark law varies from country to country, in general two broad aims are evident: the protection of consumers against confusion or deception and the protection of traders against acts of unfair competition by commercial rivals. Trade marks are valuable commercial assets and can be legally safeguarded in a number of ways. The strongest protection results from registration, which gives the owner an exclusive property right in the mark itself and the right to sue for trade mark infringement should a competitor use an identical or similar mark on the same or similar goods or services. Remedies for trade mark infringement range from monetary compensation to confiscation of the offending goods.

Trade mark proprietors always take care to alert competitors and consumers to the existence of their trade marks by emphasizing their special status in a variety of ways, including typography and colour. The symbol ® is widely used to indicate that a trade mark is registered; and the symbol ™ is also frequently used to indicate that trade mark rights are claimed in the mark, although it may not be formally registered. Registers of Trade Marks are normally maintained by the national patent or trade marks office: in the United Kingdom this is the Patent Office. It is also possible to register trade marks internationally or on a European-wide basis (Community Trade Marks). In theory, registered trade mark rights can continue indefinitely: in European Union countries the initial period of registration is ten years, renewable thereafter for further ten-year periods. Trade mark rights may also be revoked, on certain grounds, and the mark removed from the Register. Trade mark rights can be lost, for example as a result of non-use over a certain period of time or if the mark becomes generic, i.e. comes to mean the product itself rather than the brand name for the product. Examples of trade marks that have suffered this fate include aspirin, cellophane and linoleum. Some trade mark owners face a constant battle to ensure that their trade marks are not endangered in this way. Trade marks are commercially exploitable and may be bought and sold, often changing hands for vast sums of money, as well as licensed for use by third parties, for example in product merchandising. Counterfeiting of registered trade marks is in most countries a criminal offence and in the United Kingdom is punishable by fine and/or imprisonment.

Not all marks qualify for registration, and those which are not registered may be protected under other forms of action, depending on national laws. Additionally, all countries that are signatories to the Paris Convention for the Protection of Industrial Property have an obligation to protect well-known marks. In the United Kingdom and in other countries whose laws have been influenced by the English legal system, unregistered marks may be protected by the non-statutory form of action known as 'passing-off', provided that the owners have acquired goodwill and reputation in the marks and the marks have become distinctive of their goods or services.

Specialist advice on trade mark matters can be obtained from professional trade mark agents or suitably qualified lawyers. Enterprises that have large trade mark portfolios usually employ their own legally qualified staff to manage their trade marks, keep a watchful eye on the activities of competitors and initiate any necessary legal action.

Further reading

Annand, R. and Norman, H. (1994) *Blackstone's Guide to the Trade Marks Act 1994*, Blackstone Press.

Firth, A. (1995) *Trade Marks: The New Law*, Jordans.

Gyngell, J. and Poulter, A. (1998) *A User's Guide to Trade Marks and Passing Off*, 2nd edn, Butterworths.

Kerly, D.M. and Kitchin, D. (2001) *Kerly's Law of Trade Marks and Trade Names*, 13th edn, Sweet & Maxwell.

United Kingdom Trade Mark Handbook (1991–) FT Law and Tax, for the Chartered Institute of Patent Agents and the Institute of Trade Mark Agents, 2 vols [continuously updated].

SEE ALSO: information policy; intellectual property

ELLEN GREDLEY

TRANSBORDER DATA FLOW

The movement of electronic data between computer systems across national frontiers to be stored, processed, retrieved or otherwise utilized by the receiving system.

The nature of transborder data flow (TDF)

Data have been transferred across national frontiers for centuries, but the advent of instantaneous, mutable, invisible electronic data transmissions marks a fundamental change from the paper-based transfers of the past. Transmitting electronic information or messages involves many parties. There is the provider of the communication infrastructure by cable or satellite. Value-added networks (VANs) provide services along the route, packet switching, data storage, data processing and so on. Computer service companies can provide hardware and software on their own, or leased, networks. Online systems and services (see ONLINE SERVICES) will involve the information providers and the database host. Many national frontiers may be crossed. An online database may collect information in countries A, B and C, key it by low-cost labour in country D into a computer in country E, to be transmitted eventually to a user in country F. Possibilities for corruption of data are considerable; allocation of responsibility is difficult. Security and authentication of business messages can involve encryption to prevent unauthorized access, checks to show up corruption en route, and electronic 'signatures' to authenticate origin, all of which have had to be evolved.

Applications of TDF

Online databases are the most familiar application of TDF to the information professional. Multinational corporations with world-wide operations are the major users of TDF: data collected in other countries form the basis of management decisions at headquarters subsequently transmitted back to foreign branches for implementation. The travel industry needs hotel reservations and airline bookings; airline operations depend on TDF. International financial transactions are conducted by TDF, with ELECTRONIC FUND TRANSFERS ranging from small invoice settlements to multimillion-pound transfers. The Society for Worldwide Interbank Financial Communications (SWIFT) handles over 1 million electronic messages a day. International use of credit cards involves TDF. Currency trading and international stock markets depend on TDF for information and implementation of trades. ELECTRONIC DATA INTERCHANGE (EDI) or Electronic Commerce can involve the whole of a commercial transaction being documented by electronic communication obviating paper-based documentation. Shipping documents can be replaced by TDF. Academic and research communication on the INTERNET is well developed and the information superhighway can handle anything from electronic shopping to films, news and books.

Cultural, political and social concerns

Free flows of information are important to defenders of FREEDOM OF INFORMATION as well as to multinational corporations, whose operations are highly sensitive to any restrictions. Free flows may, however, be restricted by governments for various reasons. States can be concerned about their vital economic or other data being held in foreign computers. In times of crisis a nation could be cut off from its essential information sources or they could be misused by an enemy. Cultural dilution is a menace to, for example, France, fighting against the dominance of the Anglo-American language, or Singapore, seeking to preserve Asian values whilst aiming to be a global communications centre. Electronic data flows from abroad pose greater problems for a country seeking to preserve its cultural

identity than older, more controllable, media. International division of labour facilitated by TDF can disadvantage developing countries. Multinational companies can centralize managerial functions at headquarters, communicating instructions to, and collecting information from, lower-grade personnel in distant developing countries. Inputting data into online databases is often performed in low-wage countries, for utilization in the developed world.

Legal aspects

Legal issues raised by TDF concern, first, controls imposed by governments for reasons of public policy or national security and, second, legal rights and responsibilities of individuals and corporate bodies that form part of all legal systems but which involve particular problems in the context of TDF. Public policy often demands controls on TDF for reasons of personal PRIVACY. Many states attempt to regulate international transfers of personal data, especially to countries with inadequate protection. Two international agreements prescribe rules for DATA PROTECTION: the Council of Europe Convention is binding on signatory states; the guidelines of the Organization for Economic Co-operation and Development (OECD) are advisory only. In the UK, the Data Protection Registrar has statutory powers to forbid overseas transfers of personal data. National sovereignty, security, economic interests or suppression of crime may require control of TDF. Banking and financial law may restrict data flows.

PRIVATE LAW

Copyright infringement is a serious problem given the ease with which data can be transmitted worldwide, downloaded, reformatted and republished illegally. Pirated software is available on the Internet. Defamation on the Internet and release of confidential information are further problems. In the criminal field international electronic banking fraud is almost commonplace. Fraudulent investment schemes have appeared on the Internet.

DIFFICULTY OF CONTROL

The nature of TDF, mutable, invisible and instantaneous, transiting national frontiers without hindrance and involving many different parties, makes conventional legal solutions inadequate. Identifying the party at fault, whether fraudulent or simply negligent, is complicated. There are formidable problems of proof when a permanent paper-based evidential trail has been replaced by evanescent digital signals. Even if the point in the transmission can be identified where crime, breach of contract or tortious act occurred, which country's law applies? Conventional conflict of principles of law cannot be applied to a communications satellite transiting seventy countries in as many minutes.

Further reading

Collier, H. (1988) *Information Flow across Frontiers: The Question of Transborder Data*, Learned Information.

SEE ALSO: informatics; information policy

PAUL MARETT

TRANSFER OF TECHNOLOGY

The processes whereby new technologies generated by invention and innovation are dispersed across national boundaries. The transfer of technology is the international diffusion of information and is governed by many of the same forces that determine the diffusion of information within an economy. Broader definitions of technology allow the phrase to refer to the transfer of knowledge.

Context

While the processes of invention and innovation are critical to the development of new technologies, without the diffusion of those technologies they will not enhance the growth of an economy. Consequently the diffusion of technology has long been recognized as a critical determinant of growth, and the rate of technological change as a major determinant of an economy's growth rate (Denison 1967). Thus it is argued that developing countries can raise their growth rates and catch up if the technological gap is reduced by the transfer of more advanced technologies from developed economies. The technological gap is therefore presumed to be synonymous with developing countries. Although research has cast doubts upon the completeness of this argument, it remains generally accepted that transfers of technology will have a positive impact on growth rates.

Processes

Economists have sought to understand the diffusion process from a range of theoretical perspectives. Two key considerations have been prominent in the literature: the extent to which the processes of diffusion represent shifting equilibria or are disequilibrium processes, and what the determinants of the availability of information are and how these affect potential adopters. Equilibrium models use firm-specific characteristics to explain differential adoption paths, both when there is full information and when acquiring information is costly. In contrast, disequilibrium models argue that technological advances are inherently disequilibrating, and thus current technologies generally lag behind the optimal choices either because firms are not fully adjusted to new technologies and/or there are limitations upon knowledge (Metcalfe 1988). The ECONOMICS OF INFORMATION literature has emphasized the costs of information. These costs are incurred both in acquisition and assimilation of information, and reduce the potential benefits of adopting new technologies.

MARKET TRANSFERS

A major justification for patent schemes is that developers of new technologies, in a market economy, must be able to profit from the technology. Thus if developers can sell rights to use their technologies they have incentives to engage in inventive and innovative activities. Moreover, potential users, particularly those in competitive industries, have an incentive to adopt the technology so as to remain competitive and to realize additional profits. However, if the new technology is a product, then PATENTS may inhibit the diffusion of technologies but stimulate attempts at imitation. Since imitation is likely to be less costly than innovation, its importance as a means of technology transfer is potentially important.

MARKET FAILURE

The market mechanism may produce socially suboptimal transfers of technology, i.e. there may be market failures. Such failures can arise for a multitude of reasons, although two are particularly important. First, if the technologies and/or the structure of an industry proscribe the private realization of all the benefits of new technologies transfers will be socially suboptimal.

This situation is common in agriculture, and the transfer of Green Revolution technologies, largely through funding from the Ford and Rockefeller Foundations, has often been explained in these terms. Second, the acquisition of information is costly and this may inhibit the diffusion of technologies. This may be offset by the public provision of LIBRARIES, DATABASES and ARCHIVES since there are potential economies of scale in the provision of information. Moreover, since entrepreneurial time is severely limited in developing countries, information systems that save time and increase information flows are valuable.

MULTINATIONAL COMPANIES

Although technological innovation remains heavily concentrated in the developed countries, it is increasingly firm- rather than nation-specific: hence new technologies are often simultaneously exploited in several economies. This implies the existence of economies of scale in R&D that can be exploited by the transfer of technology. The extent to which this happens between developed and developing economies depends in part upon transfer costs. If the technology can be readily embodied in new capital equipment without the need for sophisticated co-factors, then the cost of transfer may be relatively low, whereas a lack of local expertise, e.g. an unskilled labour force, may severely restrict the transfer of technology.

Information

The pure (neo-classical) theory of international trade presumes that the technologies available in economies are identical, and thereby ignores the issue of the transfer of technology, whereas technology gap theories allow for international differences in technology. Early explanations of the transfer of technology were modelled on the idea that technologies were initially exported in commodities. Then, as the technology became older, the technology was exported embodied in capital goods and ultimately the technology itself became available to overseas economies (Vernon 1966). Developments in the economics of information have indicated the extent to which the costs of acquiring information and market failures in the provision of information place substantive constraints upon economic performance. These developments have indicated that rational agents may engage in socially suboptimal trans-

fers of technology. Advances in INFORMATION TECHNOLOGY may not reduce the costs of assimilating information but should reduce the costs of acquiring information. Economic theory would therefore suggest that, other things being equal, transfers of technology will become more rapid as information systems become more comprehensive and less expensive. The shift in policy emphasis from invention and innovation to diffusion (Stoneman and Diederen 1994) is consistent with growing recognition of the potential benefits of increasing the flows of information.

References

Denison, E.F. (1967) *Why Growth Rates Differ: Post-War Experience in Nine Western Countries*, Brookings Institute.

Metcalfe, J.S. (1988) 'The diffusion of innovations: An interpretive survey', in G. Dosi, C. Freeman, R. Nelson, G. Silverberg and L. Soete (eds) *Technical Change and Economic Theory*, Pinter.

Stoneman, P. and Diederen, P. (1994) 'Technology diffusion and public policy', *Economic Journal* 104: 918–30.

Vernon, R. (1966) 'International investment and international trade in the product cycle', *Quarterly Journal of Economics* 80: 190–207.

Further reading

Dosi, G., Freeman, C., Nelson, R., Silverberg, G. and Soete, L. (eds) (1998) *Technical Change and Economic Theory*, Pinter.

SEE ALSO: information policy; information society

SCOTT MCDONALD

TRANSLATIONS

A written work expressed in a language other than the language in which it was originally composed. The purpose of a translation is to make a document accessible to those who have insufficient knowledge of a language to be able to comprehend the text in its original form.

Types of translation

SUBJECT MATTER

A distinction can be made here between translations of literary works, scientific and technical documents, legal documents, business reports, etc.

Published translations are accessible to a wide audience through conventional outlets such as libraries and booksellers. A translation can be published in the same form as the original (e.g. book, report, journal) or incorporated into a collective publication such as a translation journal. Translation journals contain a selection of translations from either the same source or multiple sources, usually in the same subject field. A cover-to-cover translation journal is a full translation of a journal originally published in another language. *Ad hoc* (unpublished) translations are translations that have been privately commissioned by an individual, commercial or government organization for in-house use. Some organizations make their scientific and technical translations available through the World Translations Index (WTI) database to give other researchers the benefit.

Methods of translation

HUMAN TRANSLATION

The most common method of translation is that of human translation performed by someone with a good knowledge of both the subject and the source and target languages.

MACHINE TRANSLATION

Since the 1960s it has been possible, to a varying extent, to employ computers to generate translations. This is known as MACHINE TRANSLATION (MT). A machine translation is a translation generated by a computer, with or without the assistance of a human (Lawson 1989). MT provides translations of entire sentences or texts but can offer translations that are unacceptable. For this reason, human assistance may be necessary. This may be given in the form of pre-, interactive, or post-editing. A translation produced without any human intervention is known as a raw machine translation.

MACHINE-AIDED TRANSLATION (MAT) OR COMPUTER-ASSISTED TRANSLATION (CAT)

This is translation generated by a human with the help of a computer. This help can be in the form of: word processing; terminology banks or dictionaries; other computerized databanks; spelling, grammar or style checkers; electronic publishing, etc.

Translation indexes

These can cover translations produced by a single organization or a country, or translations pertaining to a specific subject field. The recent history of translation indexes, and the enterprise of translation itself, is illustrated by the story of the World Translations Index (WTI). This major source cited Western language translations of foreign research reports, papers and theses, conference proceedings and patents. The files 1979–97, still available online (WTI 2002), are a considerable information resource. They covered engineering and aeronautics and aerospace technology, biological and marine sciences, chemistry, earth sciences and oceanography, agriculture, physics, maths, energy, and nuclear science and technology. The existing records contain bibliographic references to both the original and the translated documents. Included in the file are translations that were published in journals and other publications, and translations that were prepared by translating organizations. Significantly, more than 65 per cent relate to translations into English. Half of the English translations were originally published in Russian, while another 30 per cent were from Japanese and German originals.

The index was produced by the not-for-profit foundation International Translations Centre (ITC), which was dissolved at the end of 1997 after thirty-six years of business. Subscriptions to the WTI had declined steadily over the years to a point at which it was no longer economic to continue. The fall in demand for WTI was a reflection of the changes that had taken place in the field of translation since the centre's foundation in 1961. The increasing acceptance of English as the lingua franca for scholarly communication had, along with other factors, resulted in a significant decline in the number of translations that needed to be made, so that material for citation in WTI became increasingly scarce. Whilst translation continues to be an important activity, in the scientific and technical field it is more commonly undertaken as a result of demand for a specific document than as, in the past, an offering of whole categories and groupings of literature in translated form.

References

Lawson, V. (1989) 'Machine translation', in C. Picken

(ed.) *The Translator's Handbook*, ASLIB, pp. 203–13.

WTI (2002) (http://library.dialog.com/bluesheets/html/bl0295.html/).

Further reading

Benefits of Computer Assisted Translation to Information Managers and End-Users (1990) Agard lecture series no.171.

Risseeuw, M. (1993) 'Translations, a darker shade of grey: Their value and accessibility', in *Conference Proceedings First International Conference on Grey Literature GL '93*, pp. 107–13.

Risseeuw, M. and Smits, G.N. (1989) 'Indexes of translations', in C. Picken (ed.) *The Translator's Handbook*, ASLIB, pp. 215–30.

Risseeuw, M., Wilde, D.U. and Cooper, N.R. (1992) 'Global awareness boosts productivity', *Proceedings of the Thirteenth National Online Meeting*, pp. 307–13.

SEE ALSO: book trade; communication

MICKEY RISSEEUW, REVISED BY THE EDITORS

TURING, ALAN MATHISON (1912–54)

Mathematician and computer pioneer.

Born in London and educated at Cambridge. He developed the idea of the 'Turing Machine', which would be capable of modelling the process of human computation. When during the Second World War he was assigned to the task of deciphering German codes, he was able to demonstrate the importance of logical machines in solving otherwise intractable problems. After the war he joined the staff of the National Physical Laboratory at Teddington to work on the development of ACE (Automatic Computing Engine), moving in 1948 to Manchester University to work on MADAM (Manchester Automatic Digital Machine). Whilst there he published a widely read paper, 'Computing machinery and intelligence' (1950), which argued the essential similarities between computers and intelligent minds.

Turing was one of the major intellectual pioneers of computer science and of electronic computing but obtained little of the official support that his work deserved. His premature end was tragic: he committed suicide after having been arrested for a homosexual act, which was at that time in Britain a criminal offence.

Further reading

Hodges, A. (1983) *Alan Turing, the Enigma*, Simon & Schuster.

Turing Digital Archive (www.turingarchive.org).

SEE ALSO: informatics

U

UKMARC

The British version of the MARC format, developed by the BRITISH LIBRARY.

UNESCO

United Nations Educational, Scientific and Cultural Organization, an international body that exists to further work in these fields among the member states of the United Nations, and particularly in less-developed countries. UNESCO supports many of the activities of IFLA and the INTERNATIONAL COUNCIL ON ARCHIVES, and has also developed its own information-related activities, including the General Information Programme (*Programme Générale d'Information* or PGI) (Roberts 1989; Tocatlian and Abid 1986). As an initiator and funder of projects and programmes in the information field it proved extremely influential in the past and is still looked on as a source of leadership in the cultural sphere, having recovered from the political difficulties it encountered in the 1980s and early 1990s. Important statements include its *Manifestos* on PUBLIC LIBRARIES and SCHOOL LIBRARIES, which are significant general statements of policy objectives in their respective domains. Other areas of activity include COPYRIGHT and other aspects of INTELLECTUAL PROPERTY, PRESERVATION of the heritage (through its *Memory of the World* programme) (Abid 2001) and archives (Records and Archives Management Programme, or RAMP) (Cox 1990; Couture and Lajeunesse 1993). UNESCO has been particularly active in supporting the revival of libraries and librarianship in CENTRAL AND EASTERN EUROPE, and in RUSSIA AND THE FORMER SOVIET UNION, and in helping libraries in the successor states to Yugoslavia to recover from war damage.

UNESCO is also an important source of STATISTICS ON LIBRARIES, although these are derived from national statistics and are therefore only as reliable as their various sources, and are often in arrears. They are to be found in the Culture and Communications section of the *UNESCO Statistical Yearbook*, of which the most recent edition is available at www.uis.unesco.org/en/stats/stats0.htm. This invaluable resource also includes data on the book trade, and other aspects of the knowledge industry (see KNOWLEDGE INDUSTRIES) and CULTURAL INDUSTRIES.

References

Abid, A. (2001) 'Memory of the world: Preserving and sharing access to our documentary heritage', *Focus* 2: 5–25.

Couture, C. and Lajeunesse, M. (1993) 'Statues principles et statues fonctions archivistiques: historique du programme RAMP et analyse des études RAMP: origine, développement et synthèse analytique', *Archives Québec* 25: 17–43.

Cox, R.J. (1990) 'RAMP studies and related UNESCO publications: An international source for archival administration', *American Archivist* 53: 488–95.

Roberts, K.H. (1989) 'The General Information Programme of UNESCO', *IATUL Quarterly* 3: 165–72.

Tocatlian, J. and Abid, A. (1986) 'The development of library and information services in developing countries: Unesco/PGI's role and activities', *IFLA Journal* 12: 280–5.

Further reading

Full details of UNESCO's activities can be found on its website at www.unesco.org.

SEE ALSO: informatics; information ethics; information policy; national information systems

UNIFORM RESOURCE LOCATOR

The Uniform Resource Locator (URL) is the address that a WEB BROWSER uses to locate an INTERNET file. It indicates the site that holds the file, and the file pathname.

UNIMARC

The most comprehensive version of the MARC format, developed under the auspices of IFLA. UNIMARC (Universal Machine-Readable Cataloguing) specifies the tags, indicators and subfields to be assigned to bibliographic records in machine-readable form. Its primary purpose is to facilitate the international exchange of bibliographic data in machine-readable form between the agencies responsible for national bibliographies (see NATIONAL BIBLIOGRAPHY).

UNION CATALOGUES

A catalogue (see CATALOGUES) that contains not only a listing of bibliographic records from more than one library, but also locations to identify holdings of the contributing libraries.

Union catalogues must be considered in the context of shared cataloguing, NETWORKS and BIBLIOGRAPHIC CONTROL. Mid-nineteenth-century attempts at compiling a union catalogue, such as those of Charles Coffin Jewett of the Smithsonian Institution Library, were unsuccessful due to technical difficulties and also problems of lack of standardization and quality control.

One of the most important union catalogues is the *National Union Catalog* (NUC), published by the LIBRARY OF CONGRESS (1953–83 in book form and subsequently on microfiche; see also the Library of Congress website at www.loc.gov). The NUC is a continuation of the *Library of Congress Catalog: A Cumulative Catalog of Books Represented by Library of Congress Printed Cards* (published 1942–7), and its name change indicates an extension of scope to encompass records, many including location information, from contributing libraries in North America. Many Western European countries followed suit in an attempt to exert national bibliographic control. Current online bibliographic databases, such as those of the Online Computer Library Center (OCLC), and other

bibliographic co-operatives (utilities) function, in part, as union catalogues in this way.

The role of union catalogues

The usefulness of a catalogue is limited if it includes the holdings of only one library. It is a decided advantage if readers can inspect the holdings of several institutions, especially on a national or regional basis. This was the rationale of developing such catalogues, especially if printed or otherwise made widely available, so that, for example, a scholar anywhere could see all the books or periodicals held by various libraries and, more importantly, could find the most suitable location for access. The impetus for this approach was the increasing climate of co-operation and the growth of INTERLIBRARY LENDING. Similarly, the development of shared cataloguing NETWORKS resulted in large national and regional union catalogues.

Another reason for their development was as a result of direct policy, for example the co-ordination of library resources on a national, regional or local basis. Unnecessary duplication is avoided if the strengths of particular collections are known and available to all. In a similar way, gaps and weaknesses in provision can be dealt with by focusing resources in an appropriate manner.

The future of union catalogues

As access to online public-access catalogues (OPACS) and other information databases becomes common, the potential of union catalogues is stimulated but may also be called into question. To ascertain the location of specific items, it is increasingly possible to access most major catalogues in a region or country individually. However, at present this can be time-consuming and unsystematic. A good regional, national or indeed international union catalogue still has an important role to play in offering more effective access to such information.

INESE A. SMITH

UNION LIST

A listing, typically with less complete bibliographic records than a union catalogue (see

UNION CATALOGUES), of the holdings of two or more libraries. It is typically confined to a particular genre of documents (newspapers, manuscripts, materials on a particular place, subject or person, and so on), and a well-defined group of libraries or archives (such as those in a particular city or country, or of a certain type). Such lists are still valuable, especially to researchers in the humanities seeking unique or fugitive material scattered among many libraries and archives.

UNIVERSAL AVAILABILITY OF PUBLICATIONS

Universal Availability of Publications (UAP), a programme sponsored by IFLA, supported by UNESCO, aimed to ensure the widest possible availability of published materials. It is now incorporated into IFLA's programme for UNIVERSAL BIBLIOGRAPHIC CONTROL AND INTERNATIONAL MARC.

UNIVERSAL BIBLIOGRAPHIC CONTROL AND INTERNATIONAL MARC

Universal Bibliographic Control and International MARC (UBCIM) is a complementary programme to the UNIVERSAL AVAILABILITY OF PUBLICATIONS (UAP) that seeks to create a worldwide system for the control and exchange of bibliographic information in an internationally acceptable form. Launched in 1974 by IFLA, as the Universal Bibliographic Control project, it relies on efficient national BIBLIOGRAPHIC CONTROL. For this, each national bibliographic agency has to ensure that it has access to all new publications issued in its country so as to establish a definitive record. Then it can, in turn, distribute this to other countries and receive their data. IFLA has produced international standards for the presentation of the bibliographical data incorporating, for example, the international numbering schemes such as ISBN and ISSN. The International MARC Programme was amalgamated in 1986 with the UBC Programme, as UBCIM.

UNIVERSAL DECIMAL CLASSIFICATION

The Universal Decimal Classification (UDC) is essentially an elaborate expansion of the DEWEY DECIMAL CLASSIFICATION, using various symbols in addition to Arabic numerals to create long and expressive notations for particular documents. This makes it particularly appropriate for use in specialist libraries and collections, and its adoption by the International Organization for Standardization (ISO) has ensured its use worldwide. It was developed by the FID, under the direction of Paul OTLET and Henri la Fontaine.

SEE ALSO: bibliographic classification; organization of knowledge

UNIVERSITY LIBRARIES

The library, or LIBRARIES, of a university, which obtains and maintains collections of books and other media and provides information services to users. The two objectives have frequently clashed, but from the mid-nineteenth century onwards the second has become more important in most institutions. By the late twentieth century the university library without its own collections appears a distinct possibility; certainly the development of digital libraries (see DIGITAL LIBRARY) and virtual libraries (see VIRTUAL LIBRARY) gives relatively easy access to users outside the universities to many services and information resources formerly only available in the library building itself.

Like the universities, libraries reflect the communities they serve. The university exists for the advancement of learning by teaching and research. When that simple objective is put in the context of thirteenth-century Paris, Renaissance Florence, seventeenth-century England, nineteenth-century Germany or twentieth-century America, all times and places where universities flourished, the outcomes are very different. The university may serve an elite, whether secular or religious, or be a vehicle for mass education. Its funding, and thereby largely its autonomy, may or may not be independent of state or Church. Similarly, the aims and problems of university libraries are superficially the same, independent of time and place. Culturally, however, differences between institutions are most marked, even within one country and in one century.

Patterns of service

The common themes of university libraries may be classified under seven headings.

USERS

Teachers and students of the university are those normally served, but there have been many examples where students were excluded. In some parts of the world, for example in Germanic and some NORDIC COUNTRIES, a university library is also the national library (see NATIONAL LIBRARIES) or has a state-defined role outside its parent university. The relationship between the support of research and the support of teaching is frequently uneasy. In contrast to other areas of academe, however, the library has long been a service-oriented organization.

FINANCE

Early university libraries suffered from the almost total absence of reliable income streams, and Sir Thomas BODLEY's endowment with money as well as with books of the Bodleian Library in Oxford in the seventeenth century was amongst his most significant innovations. In no age has any individual library been adequately funded in the eyes of its keepers. A university library is, however, almost the administrator's financial bottomless pit! It is also a temple of learning, a material symbol of scholarship and an essential adjunct to teaching. Funding varies between these extreme views.

STAFFING

Book handling is labour-intensive. As all libraries are always underfunded, so they are always understaffed. In the twentieth-century university, LIBRARIANSHIP became a profession but remained an ill-paid one, with a largely female workforce, save in positions of library director.

THE COLLECTIONS

Medieval and Renaissance libraries, as well as many later foundations, were stocked almost entirely by donation (see DONATIONS TO LIBRARIES). Another method was the imposition of LEGAL DEPOSIT in approved libraries, enforced on publishers by the state. In the mid-twentieth century, libraries were better funded than ever

before. They grew exponentially but still failed to keep pace with the growth in the output of publications. Selectivity and specialization replaced aspirations to universality. Policies of providing access to information, rather than owning and storing books, have become inevitable for most universities.

BUILDINGS

The library needs to provide space for books, readers, staff and, increasingly, equipment. Most early libraries were small, rooms within buildings rather than entire structures. In the nineteenth century and later, large dedicated LIBRARY BUILDINGS became the norm, frequently conceived more with a view to form than function. Size (with consequent problems of lighting and ventilation), changing ideas concerning good service (e.g. open and closed access), the need to adapt to updated technology (such as networking by cable) and, above all, growth in user numbers and collection size have led to frequent extensions and new structures.

TECHNOLOGY

Contrary to popular reputation libraries have always been good at exploiting new technology. The card catalogue and its arrangement were developed in the nineteenth century and reached incredible size and sophistication in the twentieth. Developments in linguistic as distinct from numeric data processing were led by the needs of libraries. The physical forms of recorded information (manuscript, printed, photographic, electronic, etc.) have been exploited by librarians. The reverse of the coin is that libraries also must preserve past scholarship, sometimes to the detriment of the needs of most users.

CO-OPERATION

Libraries have been far more successful at co-operating amongst themselves than most faculties of universities. Co-operation has taken many forms: local and national consortia; provision of services centrally, and sometimes even internationally, by both national libraries (LIBRARY OF CONGRESS) and commercial enterprises (OCLC).

Past and future

The university library reached its apotheosis in mid-twentieth-century North America. The University of Toronto library system grew from less than half a million volumes in 1947 to 8 million in 1981. The University of Texas assembled in Austin the greater part of the manuscripts of all 'significant' twentieth-century writers from all over the world. It is probably safe to assume that these days are passing forever. Scale, complexity and electronic technology require university libraries to be different beasts in the future.

Further reading

Corrall, S. (2001) *The SCONUL Vision: Academic Information Services in the Year 2005*, SCONUL.
Cummings, A.M. *et al.* (1992) *University Libraries and Scholarly Communication. A Study Prepared for the Andrew W. Mellon Foundation*, Association of Research Libraries.
Hamlin, A.T. (1981) *The University Library in the United States: Its Origins and Development*, University of Pennsylvania Press.
Higher Education Funding Councils' Libraries Review Group (1993) *Report* (Chairman: Sir Brian Follett).
Philip, I. (1983) *The Bodleian Library in the Seventeenth and Eighteenth Centuries*, Oxford University Press.

SEE ALSO: academic libraries; information professions; women in librarianship

CHRISTOPHER J. HUNT, REVISED BY THE EDITORS

URQUHART, DONALD JOHN (1909–94)

Librarian and innovator in DOCUMENT DELIVERY services.

Born in Whitley Bay, England, he studied at Sheffield University then joined the Science Museum Library in 1938, under S.C. BRADFORD. Service during the Second World War in government departments concerned with the supply of scientific and industrial information convinced him that information services generally were in need of modernization and improvement. His solution to the lack of an adequate system of scientific libraries in the UK was to advocate the establishment within the Department of Scientific and Industrial Research (DSIR), by which he was employed after the war, of a so-called Lending Library Unit.

This was then set up as the National Lending Library for Science and Technology (NLLST), later the BRITISH LIBRARY Document Supply Centre. The location of the Library in Boston Spa, Yorkshire, was very much Urquhart's choice. He argued that the functions of the

library could be carried out anywhere within normal (i.e. next-day delivery) postal reach of all parts of the country. The institution that he set up there was very self-consciously the antithesis of the conventional library. Since it was there to supply other libraries with documents they did not themselves hold, the NLLST stored its holdings in the very crudest way, alphabetical order by title, and demanded that requesting libraries put in the bibliographical work needed to establish accurate details of the requested document. Within the NLLST's warehouse-like walls, Urquhart delighted in introducing devices, such as conveyor belts, to speed up its operation. His clarity of vision and determination gave Britain a service that was respected and emulated throughout the world and has remained at the forefront of document delivery work since.

Further reading

Urquhart, D.J. (1990) *Mr Boston Spa*, Wood Garth.

USENET

The network of tens of thousands of discussion groups, the first of which were set up in 1979 using ARPANET, the original network from which the INTERNET evolved. Usenet is categorized into areas such as recreation, the sciences and social issues, and within these categories there are groups that deal with an enormous number of specific subjects. These newsgroups provide discussion and news items that are held for a specified time by receiving computers so that users can access them, respond and download. Archives of Usenet postings (such as Dejanews) are also made available for consultation.

USER EDUCATION

User education (UE) is training in how to use a library, so as to be able to find out where information is available, why to use a particular search strategy, what other sources can help and how to exploit them further. Formal programmes of user education have tended to be regarded as essential for all library and information services and facilities, and in the 1970s and 1980s a very considerable literature was generated on the topic. More recently, the area has been subsumed within the more versatile and inclusive concept of INFORMATION LITERACY.

Programmes dedicated to helping users make the best advantage of library services are still, however, provided by great numbers of institutions and the principles and practices of user education remain an important aspect of the skills of the librarian.

Introduction

Library users are heterogeneous, and information-seeking is a complex activity. User education has to be a continuous process for two reasons: first, because of some characteristics of the library system, such as the use of jargon, lack of strategy and professionalism in marketing, complexities and perplexities in catalogues, preconceived ideas of user needs and self-centred librarians; second, the deficiencies in communication between the user and the library, such as attitudes of users towards the library as a last resort, the image of the librarian and intricacies in information-seeking patterns in the idea plane and in the verbal plane.

The term UE is used interchangeably with 'library instruction', 'library orientation' and 'bibliographic instruction'. Neelameghan (1985) distinguishes user education, user orientation and user assistance. Roberts and Blandy (1989) prefer a broad term: library instruction. User education (1) is a comprehensive service and a process of making the user self-reliant in locating, sorting and repacking information; (2) is an inspirational and informational link between the 'book' and the user, essential for a new user and desirable for an experienced one; and (3) prepares the user for self-evaluation of information. This process may require two strategies: for general exposure, and for specific subject-oriented – bibliographic instruction. The first visit to the library is mostly casual and in a sense this requires more frequent meetings with the user. Thus UE is at first impersonal and gradually becomes personal.

History

By the 1850s, US librarians instructed patrons on library use. Samuel Green's attempt to initiate a reference desk in the public library in the 1870s, Louis Shore's library-college movement in the 1920s and Patricia Knapp's Montieth College programme in the 1960s are all significant. In 1949 the three-stage user education programme proposed by the UK LIBRARY ASSOCIATION's University and Research Section was a landmark. RANGANATHAN (1940) prescribed the role of an intermediary as a user-friendly reference librarian. Boon (1960), Fjallbrant and Stevenson (1978), Hopkins (1982), Roberts and Blandy (1989) and others have made extensive historical assessments. Progress was slow, partly due to the problem of defining its place in the services; it was lost in the informational function or reference service.

While lectures, tours and seminars are traditional methods, programmed learning, teaching machines, audiovisual tools and computer-assisted learning (CAL) are the recent advances. User education is not merely a library tour or a brochure, it includes searching databases (local and global) and generally making the user less dependent on others.

Practice

MEDIA

A variety of media are used. One-to-one instruction is simple but expensive. Orientation by informal tour is traditional and effective, but it is time-consuming and too general, and can cause boredom. Printed materials (leaflet, handout) describe services, tools and search strategies, but need frequent revision and may not be used. Displaying of posters, diagrams, etc. can teaching skills, but requires a mediator. In workbooks, the audience is involved, which enables learning at the individual's pace and the educator can know the effect of learning. But some users may hesitate to write and even feel shy. In course-related education, library assignments become part of the course, but this is cumbersome in terms of staff and materials, and consumes much staff time.

AUDIOVISUAL MATERIALS are useful and effective, but they are not easily prepared, economical or simple to use. Programmed instruction includes multimedia, and CAL is one example (see COMPUTER-ASSISTED LEARNING IN LIBRARY AND INFORMATION SCIENCE). CAL can be a costly product as it needs computers and still depends on other methods, but it has the advantage that it allows networking.

For groups, lectures, seminars and tutorials, and audiovisuals, CAL and tour methods can be used. For individuals, printed guides, pathfinders, practical exercises, programmed instruction and personal assistance are helpful.

APPLICATIONS

Among the existing general purpose tools some are highly useful, for instance the video developed by the Learning Resource Centre, Ohio State University: *Battle of the Library Superstars* (1981). It gives coverage of specific tools – catalogues, manual and automated, indexes, etc. – and is professionally produced.

Model user education programmes include the person-to-person approach (University of Sussex), the systematic approach (Chalmers University of Technology) and the project-oriented approach (Roskilde University Centre). User education has been a popular theme for seminars, conferences and workshops. For example, the Library Orientation Instruction Exchange's (LOEX) Clearing House (Eastern Michigan University) has conducted many programmes and an annual meeting since the 1970s. The ALA's Library Instruction Round Table is involved in many such meetings and ACRL's Bibliographic Instruction Section has a Think Tank that is very active. In Britain the Standing Conference of National and University Libraries (SCONUL) has encouraged co-operative production of audiovisual materials since the 1970s, and many public libraries and special libraries have taken up the task.

The future

Though user education has come of age, many issues are yet to be resolved – a major one is that it is not always well integrated with other aspects of library services and with programmes in information literacy. Assessment of needs, clear goals and objectives, and involvement of staff in the development of user education programmes are still much needed.

References

Boon, G.S. (1960) 'Training laymen in the use of the library', in *The State of the Library Art*, Rutgers University Press.

Fjallbrant, N. and Stevenson, M. (1978) *User Education in Libraries*, Clive Bingley.

Hopkins, F.L. (1982) 'A century of bibliographic instruction: The historical claim to professional and academic legitimacy', *College and Research Libraries* 43: 192–8.

Neelameghan, A. (1985) 'User orientation', in 'Library and information studies curriculum: Some aspects with special reference to developing countries', *Journal of Library and Information Science* 10: 53–65.

Ranganathan, S.R. (1940 [1992]) 'Initiation of freshmen', in *Reference Service*, UBS Publishers.

Roberts, A.F. and Blandy, S.G. (1989) *Library Instruction for Librarians*, 2nd rev. edn, Libraries Unlimited.

Further reading

Aluri, D.R. (1981) 'Application of learning theories to library user instruction', *Libri* 31(2): 41.

Cox, A. (1997) 'Using the World Wide Web for user education: A review article', *Journal of Librarianship and Information Science* 29: 39–43.

Dewey, B.I. (2001) *Library User Education: Powerful Learning, Powerful Partnerships*, Scarecrow.

George, M.W. (1993) 'Information literacy: A selective review of recent literature', *New Jersey Libraries* 26: 3–4 (bibliographical essay).

Green, S. (1876) 'Desirableness of establishing personal intercourse and relations between librarians and readers in public libraries', *Library Journal* 1: 74–81.

Kokkonen, O. (1992) *User Education Around the World: The UNESCO Survey of Library and Information User Education Programmes in Some Developing Countries*, 58th IFLA General Conference, New Delhi.

Kumar, G. and Kumar, K. (1983) *Philosophy of User Education*, Vikas.

Prorak, D. *et al.* (1994) 'Teaching method and psychological type in bibliographic instruction: Effect on student learning and confidence', *RQ* 33: 484–95.

Shirato, L. (1993) *What is Good Instruction Now? Library Instruction for the 1990s*, 20th LOEX Library Instruction Conference, Pierian Press.

Van Vuren, A.J. and Henning, J. (1999) 'User education in a flexible learning environment: An opportunity to stay relevant in the 21st century', *IATUL Proceedings*, new series vol. 8, at www.iatul.org/conference/pretpap/vuren.html.

White, H.S. (1991) 'Bibliographic instruction and library school curriculum', *Journal of Education for Library and Information Science* 32: 194–202.

MOHAMED TAHER

USER STUDIES

In a narrow sense, the study of the characteristics of users of libraries and/or information; in practice, most so-called user studies consider use as well as users. In contrast to use studies, however, user studies are more concerned with people and what they do than with libraries and other information organizations *per se*. Studies that take the form of market or community analyses also collect information about non-users.

Background

User studies, however defined, have reflected a variety of emphases and perspectives. They have examined information needs, INFORMATION-SEEKING BEHAVIOUR and more personal characteristics of users. The proceedings of a series of Information Seeking in Context conferences, for example Wilson and Allen (1999), illustrate this type of investigation very effectively.

Specific user-related characteristics or variables that have been measured include:

1 Frequency of library/information use.
2 Reasons for use.
3 Types of library/information use.
4 Attitudes and opinions regarding libraries.
5 Reading patterns.
6 Level of satisfaction.
7 Demographic data.
8 Personality.
9 Lifestyle.
10 Awareness of library services.

The scope of user studies has varied from investigations of broad communities (e.g. US physicians), through studies of individuals within a single organization, to studies of the use of a particular service or resource. Some studies focus on a single type of library; others consider all library and information use of certain individuals.

User studies have been conducted for a number of purposes and have realized a variety of benefits. In general, they have been used to provide data for evaluations of libraries and other information agencies and to facilitate planning for collection development, programmes and services. More recently, user studies have been utilized in some of the attempts to measure how the use of libraries and information affects the user. There is a growing consensus that if libraries are to be truly effective they must be most concerned with their ultimate performance, and that the most meaningful indicators of performance are user-oriented.

The literature of user studies is considerable and ranges from reports of generalizable basic research to descriptions of situation-specific projects. Some of the reports represent nationwide studies; others are limited to small, in-house studies.

Also, there is a substantial body of literature on how to design and conduct user studies. Baker and Lancaster (1991), in their standard work on the measurement and evaluation of library services, present a useful overview of user studies. An article by Butler and Gratch (1982) provides some helpful suggestions for planning a user study. Texts on research methods for library and information science professionals (Powell 1991; Simpson 1988; Busha and Harter 1980; and others) provide more detailed information on a variety of research methods and techniques applicable to user studies.

Methods

User studies can be designed as basic research or as applied/action research. In the latter case, they often are used to gather evaluative data. In either case, user studies can employ quantitative or qualitative methods, direct or indirect methods.

Quantitative research methods involve a problem-solving approach that is highly structured in nature and that relies on the quantification of variables for purposes of measurement and analysis. Qualitative research methods are less reliant on quantitative measurement and give more attention to the subjective aspects of human experience and behaviour.

Direct methods rely on obtaining information directly from the user. Indirect methods involve examining some evidence of user behaviour, such as circulation records, and deducing something about the user accordingly. Both direct and indirect methods can be quantitative or qualitative in nature.

The bulk of user studies continues to take the form of surveys and is usually designed to collect data from a sample rather than from an entire population. The questionnaire, interview and observation remain common data-collection techniques for surveys. Here again, these techniques can take a qualitative or quantitative approach to the measurement process. An increasingly popular type of interview used to evaluate library use is the focused or focus group interview.

In contrast to the typical survey, critical-incident techniques concentrate on a single recent event. Case studies focus on a small number of individuals or organizations but gather comprehensive data. In diary-type studies, users are asked to collect their own data over a period of time. Techniques involving the examination of documents include citation and content analyses. Modelling has found some applications in user studies.

Summary and conclusions

User studies can provide information about the populations using libraries, user awareness of services, levels of and reasons for user satisfaction and dissatisfaction, unmet needs, types of information used, reasons why individuals use particular resources, and even help to predict library/information usage. User studies also can measure the actual impact of library/information use, i.e. how such use affects or benefits the life of the user. But user studies cannot provide any of these benefits if careful attention is not given to their design. They must be as valid, reliable and scientifically rigorous as is possible. User studies must reflect the best and latest knowledge on how to design and conduct sound research. Only then can such studies provide the kind of user-based information needed to determine the real effectiveness of libraries and other information agencies.

References

Baker, S.L. and Lancaster, F.W. (1991) *The Measurement and Evaluation of Library Services*, 2nd edn, Information Resources Press.

Busha, C.H. and Harter, S.P. (1980) *Research Methods in Librarianship*, Academic Press.

Butler, M. and Gratch, B. (1982) 'Planning a user study: The process defined', *College and Research Libraries* 43(4): 320–30.

Powell, R.R. (1991) *Basic Research Methods for Librarians*, 2nd edn, Ablex Publishing.

Simpson, I.S. (1988) *Basic Statistics for Librarians*, 3rd edn, Library Association.

Wilson, T. and Allen, D. (1999) *Exploring the Contexts of Information Behaviour. Proceedings of the Second International Conference on Research in Information Needs, Seeking and Use in Different Contexts, Sheffield 13–15 August 1998*. Taylor Graham.

Further reading

Siatri, R. (1999) 'The evolution of user studies', *Libri* 49: 132–41.

Wilson, T.D. (2000) 'Recent trends in user studies: Action research and qualitative methods', *Information Research 5*, at www.shef.ac.uk/is/publications/infres/paper76.html.

SEE ALSO: performance measurement in libraries; quality assurance; research in library and information science

RONALD R. POWELL

USMARC

The US version of the MARC format, developed by the LIBRARY OF CONGRESS.

V

VALUE ADDED

A term from the business field used in LIS to describe the enhancement of existing information products and services for the benefit of users. In particular, it is used to refer to networks that lease TELECOMMUNICATIONS links from a public utility, supplement these with additional services, specialized features, etc. and market the improved resulting network to customers.

VIDEOCONFERENCE

The use of TELECOMMUNICATIONS networks and video technology to permit people in remote locations to participate in meetings where all or some of the participants are 'present' in the form of an interactive video link. Videoconferencing is an attractive alternative to 'real' meetings when the costs of air travel and hotel accommodation are considered, though set-up costs can be high, and a reasonable quality of transmission can only be achieved when BROADBAND networks are accessible.

SEE ALSO: informatics

VIDEOTEX

Generic term for interactive information retrieval services designed for adapted television receivers. It was originally called viewdata, and was invented by Sam Fedida, UK Post Office engineer, in 1970. A special decoder enabled the display of pages of information, retrieved from a remote computer system, on the television screen. The system could also be accessed via a conventional visual display terminal or a personal computer running special software. A number of countries established public videotex services, such as the UK's Prestel, but the technology was put to best effect in successor versions such as France's MINITEL (a distributed system that was much more popular than Prestel). Some companies established private videotex services, for example to distribute corporate information internally or to give customers details of their current product range. The crudity of the technology and the limited range of resources to which it gave access led to its swift eclipse when public access to the Internet became widely available during the 1990s.

SEE ALSO: electronic public information services; information and communication technology; knowledge industries

VIRTUAL LIBRARY

A user-accessible network of computer-based information resources, also referred to as digital libraries (see DIGITAL LIBRARY) or electronic libraries (see ELECTRONIC LIBRARY). Access through a subject gateway or portal (see PORTALS AND GATEWAYS) creates the sense of a single library of resources. To be distinguished from a VIRTUAL REALITY library, which is effectively a new form of OPAC built using virtual reality technology so as to create the illusion that the user is searching the shelves of an actual library to retrieve information about resources.

SEE ALSO: libraries

VIRTUAL REALITY

A computer-generated world, around which a person can move, interacting with items encountered. Special software is required to control the visual, audio and tactile presentation of the virtual world. Devices such as head-mounted displays and data gloves may be required for immersion and interaction in the virtual world. Desktop virtual reality systems eschew immersion and similar devices, using instead a conventional computer monitor and control devices such as joysticks or keyboards.

History

Virtual reality is a recent development in COMPUTER SCIENCE that promises a new form of HUMAN–COMPUTER INTERACTION. Because of its immaturity, virtual reality technology is expensive and not particularly effective in creating realistic virtual worlds. It has found applications in areas that either can bear the huge expense of creating realistic virtual worlds (e.g. military flight simulators) or benefit from less intensive computer-controlled renderings of physical phenomena (e.g. architecture, medicine).

Applications

There is a potential for using virtual reality technology to create information spaces, visual representations of information to aid INFORMATION RETRIEVAL.

One approach sees virtual reality as a way of emulating by computer the retrieval by browsing that users carry out in the real world. Users would browse an image of items in an information collection using a virtual reality system, in much the same way as they browse physical shelf orderings of items. Since browsing depends solely on a person's innate ability to recognize and recall item orderings, a virtual reality-based retrieval system ought to be simpler to use than the current generation of textual, query-based online public access catalogues (OPACS) (Poulter 1993, Koh 1995, Beheshti 1997).

Another approach harnesses the ability of virtual reality to create on computers visual representations of information that would not be possible in the real world. This is known as information visualization, as these representations seek to enrich a user's perception of available information. One does not have to use virtual reality technology to create information spaces, but rather conventional three-dimensional computer graphics.

References

Beheshti, J. (1997) 'The evolving OPAC', *Cataloguing and Classification Quarterly* 24(1/2): 163–85.

Koh, G. (1995) 'Options in classification available through modern technology', *Cataloguing and Classification Quarterly* 19(3/4): 195–211.

Poulter, A. (1993) 'Towards a virtual reality library', *ASLIB Proceedings* 45(1): 11–17.

Further reading

Hearst, M. (1999) 'User interfaces and visualization', in R. Baeza-Yates and B. Ribeiro-Neto, *Modern Information Retrieval*, Addison Wesley, pp. 257–323.

Newby, G.B. (1993) 'Virtual reality', *Annual Review of Information Science and Technology* 28: 187–229.

SEE ALSO: informatics

ALAN POULTER

VISUAL DISPLAY TERMINAL (VDT)

Sometimes also called a visual display unit (VDU). This is a terminal, equipped with keyboard and screen, which is capable of connection to a computer system for the exchange of data between the terminal and the computer. Often referred to as a dumb terminal.

VON NEUMANN, JOHN (1903–57)

Mathematician who made important contributions to a number of disciplines, including COMPUTER SCIENCE.

A Hungarian-born German-American who studied in Berlin and Zurich, in 1929 he received a PhD in mathematics from the University of Budapest, with a dissertation about set theory. He was appointed professor at Princeton in 1931 and after 1933 was attached to the Institute for Advanced Study there, until his death. His book on quantum mechanics, *The Mathematical Foundations of Quantum Mechanics* (1932), remains a standard treatment of the subject, and, although his papers were mainly in physics and pure and applied mathematics, his ideas were influential and much cited in a diverse range of disciplines.

In computer science, Von Neumann did much of the pioneering work in logic design, in the problem of obtaining reliable answers from a machine with unreliable components, the function of memory, machine imitation of randomness and the problem of constructing automata that can reproduce their own kind. His work on the theory of competitive games has been much used in applying mathematical analysis to social, industrial and business situations, including those concerned with information.

SEE ALSO: economics of information; information theory

W

WAPLES, DOUGLAS (1893–1978)

Educationalist whose efforts established the importance of research in librarianship and education for librarianship.

Waples was born in Philadelphia and educated at Haverford College, Harvard and the University of Pennsylvania (1920). He taught as Assistant Professor of Psychology and Education at Tufts University, and moved to the University of Pittsburgh in 1923 and the University of Chicago in 1925. At the Chicago Graduate Library School his work centred on public COMMUNICATION, in particular the international exchange of ideas. He was acutely aware of the need for a research-based body of knowledge for librarianship and was largely responsible for the dominant influence of research on the Graduate Library School. His book on research methods for librarianship, *Investigating Library Problems* (1939), was for long the chief text on the topic.

He, himself, did important work on reading behaviour in a series of books and articles that explored different methods and approached research questions from different perspectives. Perhaps his outstanding contribution was the research report (with Bernard Berelson and Franklyn Bradshaw) *What Reading Does to People* (1940), which contained a summing up of research on the social effects of reading and important methodological recommendations.

SEE ALSO: reading research; research in library and information science

WEB BROWSER

Also referred to as simply 'browser', this is a software application that is used to locate and display pages on the WORLD WIDE WEB. The two most widely used browsers, Netscape Navigator and Internet Explorer, are able to display both text and graphics. Sound and video can also be presented by browsers, though it may be necessary to use additional plug-in software, sometimes referred to as viewers, for certain formats.

WEBMASTER

The individual responsible for setting up, inputting content to and maintaining a website.

WIDE-AREA NETWORK (WAN)

A NETWORK, or part of a network, that interconnects computer resources at sites and/or buildings, over large distances (regionally, nationally or internationally). JANET is an example of a WAN.

SEE ALSO: information and communication technology

WIENER, NORBERT (1894–1964)

Mathematician and a founder of cybernetics.

Wiener studied at Tufts (graduating in Mathematics at the age of fourteen) and Harvard. He also studied at Cambridge and Göttingen. He then taught mathematics at Massachusetts Institute of Technology. The theoretical developments arising from his wartime work on mathematical theory applied to artillery fire led to valuable statistical methods for control and communications engineering, and, in turn, led to Wiener's formulation of the concept of CYBERNETICS.

Further reading

Wiener, N. *et al.* (1997) *The Legacy of Norbert Wiener: A Centennial Symposium*, Providence: American Mathematical Society.

SEE ALSO: information theory

WINDOWS

Both the generic term for overlaid screens and the proprietary name of Microsoft's GRAPHIC USER INTERFACE, of the kind that was developed by Xerox and featured on Macintosh computers from 1984. It has since become the normal form of interface across the range of computer types.

WIRELESS APPLICATIONS

Originally the term 'wireless' was used in computing to refer to the use of radio communication to connect computers within a network, but now it includes other methods of transmission, such as infrared and ultraviolet. The convergence of cellular phone and network technology increases the scope for wireless applications to contribute to the informatization of society. The Wireless Application Protocol is the technical basis for the use of mobile telephones for INTERNET access.

SEE ALSO: mobile communications

WOMEN IN LIBRARIANSHIP

Overview: historical, comparative and theoretical issues

Women have held full-time positions in LIBRARIES for more than a century and a half, but it was during the fifty-year period between the 1870s and the 1920s that they were actively encouraged to pursue library careers in North America and Europe. Although not always welcomed in the great university and research libraries, well-educated women on both sides of the Atlantic were recruited by public library leaders who presented a dynamic, new image of the profession. For example, in 1910 a US vocational guide for women stated that the public librarian:

> [H]as the opportunity of making her library the centre of educational and intellectual life of the community....There is in this work scope for the exercise of all a woman's powers, executive ability, knowledge of books, social sympathies, knowledge of human nature.
>
> (Rathbone 1910)

Library careers opened to women in continental Europe later than in the USA (1850s) or Britain (1870s); in 1888 the first two Italian women passed the state library examination and in 1895 the first German woman librarian was employed in a public library in Berlin. Although female public librarians in Germany had founded the Association of Women Working in Libraries by 1907, few women were employed in academic libraries prior to the end of the Second World War. The earliest reference to a French woman holding a full-time library post dates from 1903, but it was between 1920 and 1945 that the rapid feminization of the field occurred in France.

Following the Russian Revolution, many women were recruited into librarianship at the instigation of Lenin's wife, Nadezha Krupskaja, who became a central figure in the movement to centralize Soviet library services and set up public library collections throughout the USSR. In Latin America a few women emerged as library leaders during the interwar period, and by the 1930s the first women were named to library posts in India. In Africa it was not until the 1940s and 1950s that a few expatriate women librarians came from France and England to participate in the establishment of new libraries and in the training of African librarians. In the decade following the independence movement a small number of African women rose to positions of leadership in libraries; however, by the end of the century men still accounted for a large majority of the trained librarians in Francophone Africa, and even in Nigeria, where more women held library credentials, male librarians greatly outnumbered women in academic and special libraries.

Looking at the experience of women librarians from an international perspective, it is clear that their career opportunities have differed significantly, due to social and cultural norms in each country as well as the economic and political conditions that influenced their access to education and employment. To understand the nature of women's employment in librarianship, it is useful to combine a 'gender role' perspective with a broader 'structural perspective'. In such a socio-historical approach the 'gender role perspective' allows for analysis based on gender socialization as the primary determinant of women's workforce status, while the 'structural perspective' emphasizes the structural features of the workplace and other social institutions. Although these two perspectives are often considered mutually exclusive, it is only through a synthesis of the two that a comparative analysis of women's careers is possible.

In addition it is important to identify constraints, barriers and restraints that influenced women's career choices and advancement. In the context of library careers *barriers* are defined as external variables that make entry or advancement in a field more difficult for women than for men (e.g. laws and regulations barring their access to higher education and professional practice, and discrimination against women in appointment or promotion). In addition, laws that bar married women from working also proved significant barriers to women's persistence and advancement. *Restraints* relate to social expectations and family responsibilities placed on women that may limit their career potential, and *constraints* are the internalized patterns of behaviour and attitudes that result from gender socialization. For each of these inhibiting factors, there are other factors that motivate women to seek careers in fields previously occupied by men. Thus women may be motivated to overcome various kinds of *barriers* when new *opportunities* for employment exist; they are more likely to overcome *social restraints* when there are strong *incentives* (such as the need to become self-supporting). Lack of confidence and other *self-imposed constraints* are less inhibiting for those women who have *socio-psychological support* from family, friends, teachers, mentors or colleagues. Barriers and opportunities are seen as structural variables because they are largely determined by the legal, political and educational system and by

the economic structure of the workforce. Restraints and incentives can be viewed from both a structural and a gender socialization perspective, whereas constraints relate to the degree to which individual women have internalized gender norms that limit their achievements outside the home.

Historical research in Europe and North America suggests that large numbers of women entered librarianship at times when great social change affected the longstanding structure of gender relations. Other incentives were, of course, economic; for example women have been drawn to librarianship as vacancies occurred – either because of economic expansion (as in the USA in the 1870s), or at times when there was a shortage of men to fill new and/or existing posts (e.g. Britain and France after the First World War). In many cases, the feminization of librarianship occurred simultaneously with the growing professionalization of the field. In both France and the USA the feminization of librarianship was relatively rapid, occurring within twenty-five to forty years. Britain meanwhile experienced a much slower influx of women into the library field, and nearly sixty years elapsed before women made up the majority of librarians. The contrast between Britain and the other two countries is even more striking in regard to professional leadership. In France and the USA, the election of the first woman as library association president occurred approximately one generation after the admission of female librarians to the national association, whereas nearly ninety years passed in Britain before the LIBRARY ASSOCIATION elected a woman to its highest office. Although no woman was appointed to the professional ranks of the British Museum Library until 1931, Britain was the first of the three countries to name a woman as head of its national library. However, a number of leading women librarians have held senior posts in the LIBRARY OF CONGRESS and the BIBLIOTHÈQUE NATIONALE DE FRANCE (BN), and the first two women presidents of the French library association were drawn from the staff of the BN.

Regardless of their nationality, women were often barred or discouraged from becoming directors of major libraries. Although a number of US women held library directorships or headed library schools at the end of the nineteenth century, historians have documented a backlash that began prior to the First World War when some of these leading women were replaced by men or were denied promotion to director. Nonetheless, certain outstanding women became what feminist scholars have termed 'non-positional leaders', serving as change agents and as opinion leaders even though they did not hold high-ranking posts. In many countries women librarians played a crucial role in the development of children's services, outreach services and bookmobiles; in other areas, such as reference work and cataloguing, women have also left an important legacy and the AMERICAN LIBRARY ASSOCIATION (ALA) has named awards in honour of women in these two specialities. Throughout Europe women have been acknowledged as leaders in all aspects of librarianship, including the closely related fields of documentation and bibliography. In Britain, women played a significant role in the county libraries set up by the legislation of 1919 and in France during the interwar years non-positional leadership was demonstrated by a number of female librarians whose work greatly influenced the reform of French public libraries following the liberation (Maack 1983).

Research and publication

Although all aspects of librarianship have benefited from contributions by women, until recently their accomplishments were often overlooked by biographers and historians. In 1979 Kathleen Weibel and Kathleen M. Heim published *The Role of Women in Librarianship 1876–1976*, a ground-breaking book that included an anthology of forty-four selections from the library literature of Great Britain and the USA, and an international bibliography of over 1,000 items arranged chronologically. The bibliography has been updated in five-year supplements, each entitled *On Account Of Sex: An Annotated Bibliography on the Status of Women in Librarianship*; these four supplementary volumes now contain over 2,500 additional entries of works ranging from dissertations and research monographs to book reviews, letters and opinion pieces. Although historical and biographical works make up nearly 40 per cent of the entries in the latest volume, the publications listed cover all aspects of women's experience in librarianship, from contemporary research on salaries and

placement to articles on leadership, pay equity, career development and sexual harassment. An anthology of earlier articles on women in librarianship (similar to Weibel and Heim 1979) was published in Germany by Helga Ludtke (1992), who also included an extensive bibliography. There is a small but growing body of research literature from Australia and Canada that deals with a wide range of topics, from non-sexist cataloguing to women in management and the impact of technology on women's careers. In Britain two important studies were published by Dr Gillian Burrington (1987, 1993) and in 1994 the Library Association (LAUK) commissioned a research study of career barriers and progression of woman in senior management (Poland 1996). In France there have been a number of scholarly biographical studies of women library leaders, including academic theses and oral history interviews; the most notable publication is a recent monograph on the history of documentation in France that features a number of important women librarians (Fayet-Scribe 2000). Earlier, a special issue of a French library journal (Lemaître 1983) was devoted to articles on and interviews with the first French women to work as librarians.

Special issues of journals have also been an important means to disseminate feminist research in other countries including Canada, Britain and the USA (*Canadian Journal of Information Science* (1992), *Journal of Library History* (fall 1983) and *Library Trends* (fall 1985)). In addition, several collections of papers from special meetings devoted to women in librarianship have been published. Examples include a collection of papers from ALA Library History Research Forum (Grotzinger 1994) and the proceedings of an international conference entitled 'Gendering Library History', which have been recently issued as a monograph (Kerslake and Moody 2000).

Gender issues and activism

In response to the second feminist movement, both researchers and library activists have organized special sessions offering managerial or assertiveness training to help empower women with the confidence and skills they needed to advance their careers. In a number of countries feminist librarians also called meetings to examine issues such as pay equity and advancement, and in Japan a Feminist Library Network was formed. Although there are a few autonomous organizations for women librarians, more often gender interest groups operate within professional associations (e.g. the Task Force on the Status of Women of the Canadian Library Association; the ALA Committee on the Status of Women in Libraries; and the Status of Women in Librarianship Special Interest Group of the Library Association of Australia). In Britain, a group called Women in Libraries was created and the Library Association published a special manual entitled *Training and Development for Women* (Morris 1993). The International Federation of Library Associations and Institutions (IFLA) has sponsored conference programmes on women in libraries since 1988 when eighty librarians attended a pre-conference seminar on 'Women and the Power of Managing Information' in Australia; in 1993 the Round Table on Women's Issues was formally recognized by IFLA.

Another significant outcome of feminist activism has been the publication of placement, salary and advancement statistics broken down by gender. First gathered in the 1970s or early 1980s, these statistics clearly showed a pattern of employment called 'hierarchical segregation' or gender stratification where women were systematically denied the highest-level posts. Library women have, to some degree, also experienced what feminist scholars term 'territorial discrimination' – that is they have been more concentrated in certain kinds of libraries or in certain types of work than in others. Important surveys done in the early 1980s showed that the proportion of male librarians was 16 per cent in France; 19 per cent in the USA; and 38 per cent in Britain; however, in all three countries there was a pattern of greater concentration of men in high-prestige academic and research libraries. For example, in 1981 men accounted for 38 per cent of the professionals in the 120 largest US and Canadian libraries that belong to the Association of Research Libraries (ARL); this figure (which was double the proportion of men in the field at large) fell slightly by 2001 when men occupied 35 per cent of ARL positions. In regard to type of work within ARL libraries, women are somewhat more concentrated in both cataloguing and reference where they hold 78 per cent of the positions, but less concentrated in rare-book librarianship (54 per cent); men outnumber women in computer systems work (they hold 65

per cent of the positions) and they still account for 54 per cent of the library directors (ARL 2001).

During the last thirty years considerable progress has nonetheless been made in women's advancement to top positions in Britain and in North America. ARL statistics clearly show that it is in the directorship category where women have made the greatest gains; according to a 1980 survey women held only 27 per cent of the directorships in all academic libraries (Heim 1982), whereas in 2001 they headed 46 per cent of the ARL libraries and, as a group, earned slightly more than their male counterparts. Women in ARL libraries also made salary gains overall – going from 87 per cent of the salary earned by male librarians in 1981 to 93 per cent in 2001. While this is definite progress towards pay equity, at that rate of change it would take another two decades before parity is reached (ARL 2001). Salary statistics from Britain also show that the gender gap in advancement to top positions and in pay equity has begun to narrow. Overall there has been a growth in the percentage of women in management positions, from 5 per cent in 1971, to 11 per cent in 1981 to 25 per cent a decade later (Morris 1993); however, by 1996 a survey of senior library managers showed that 20 per cent of the men librarians earned over £27,000 as compared with only 9 per cent of the women (Poland 1996).

References

ARL Annual Salary Survey 2000–2001 (2001) Association of Research Libraries.

Burrington, G.A. (1993) *Equally Good: Women in British Librarianship?*, Association of Assistant Librarians.

—— (1987) *Equal Opportunities in Librarianship?*, Library Association.

Fayet-Scribe, S. (2000) *Histoire de la documentation en France*, Paris: CNRS Editions.

Grotzinger, L. (ed.) (1994) *Women's Work: Vision and Change in Librarianship*, Occasional Papers of the Graduate School of Library and Information Science, University of Illinois, no. 196.

Heim, K. (1982) 'The demographic and economic status of librarians in the 1970s with special reference to women', *Advances in Librarianship* 12: 1–45.

Kerslake, E. and Moody, N. (eds) (2000) *Gendering Library History*, John Moores University Press.

Lemaître, R. (ed.) (1983) *Bulletin d'Information de l'Association des Diplomés de l'Ecole de Bibliothé-*

caires *Documentalistes. Numéro Special Femmes Bibliothécaires* 22 (Novembre): 3–16

Ludtke, H. (1992) *Leidenschaft und Bildung: zur Geschichte der Frauenarbeit in Bibliotheken*, Berlin: Orlanda Frauenverlag.

Maack, M.N. (ed.) (1983) 'Women librarians in France: The first generation', *Journal of Library History* 18(4): 407–49.

Morris, B. (1993) *Training and Development for Women*, Library Association.

Poland, F. (1996) *Women and Senior Management: A Research Study of Career Barriers and Progression in the Library and Information Sector*, Library Association.

Rathbone, J. (1910) 'Library work', in *Vocations for the Trained Woman*, New York: Longmans, Green and Co.

Weibel, K. and Heim, K. (eds) (1979) *The Role of Women in Librarianship 1876–1976: The Entry, Advancement and Struggle for Equalization in One Profession*, Phoenix, AZ: Oryx Press [this work is updated by four supplements, each entitled: *On Account of Sex: An Annotated Bibliography on the Status of Women in Librarianship*, vol. 1, 1977–81 (1984); vol. 2, 1982–6 (1989); vol. 3, 1987–92 (1993); vol. 4, 1993–7 (2000).

Further reading

Dumont, R. (ed.) (1985) 'Women and leadership in the library profession', special issue, *Library Trends* 34(2)

Harris, R. (1992) *Librarianship: The Erosion of a Woman's Profession*, Norwood, NJ: Ablex.

Hildenbrand, S. (ed.) (1996) *Reclaiming the American Library Past: Writing the Women In*, Norwood, NJ: Ablex.

Kenady, C. (1989) *Pay Equity: An Action Manual for Library Workers*, Chicago: American Library Association.

Maack, M.N. and Passet, J. (1994) *Aspirations and Mentoring in an Academic Environment: Women Faculty In Library and Information Science*, Westport, CT: Greenwood Press.

Passet, J. (1994) *Cultural Crusaders: Women Librarians in the American West, 1900–1917*, Albuquerque, NM: University of New Mexico Press.

Williams, C. (1995) *Still a Man's World: Men Who Do Women's Work*, Berkeley, CA: University of California Press.

SEE ALSO: history of libraries; information professions; public libraries

MARY NILES MAACK

WORD PROCESSING

A computer application program that enables the user to enter text, edit it, format it, manage it and print out documents consisting of text and simple graphics and tables. The contrast, which has meant that it has more or less replaced the typewriter, is that changes to the text can be made easily, at any stage, whilst the typewriter produces a hard-copy version at the same time as text is entered. Word processing has transformed not merely office practice, but the whole act of writing; literary composition has become a much more fluent activity.

SEE ALSO: office automation

WORKSTATION

A powerful desktop COMPUTER system, usually having a high-resolution display screen and the ability to integrate text and graphics. A workstation would be expected both to process and store information locally, and to exchange information with other systems. The performance gap and the price differential between products marketed as workstations and the standard PERSONAL COMPUTERS widely used in offices have gradually narrowed. In practice, most workstations are now networked PCs.

SEE ALSO: informatics; information and communication technology; information management

WORLD WIDE WEB

The World Wide Web (WWW), or just 'the Web', is a HYPERMEDIA information service on the INTERNET, which has been in place since 1991. It began as a distributed hypertext-based information system developed at CERN (the European particle physics research centre in Geneva, Switzerland) by Tim BERNERS-LEE, but found its true home on the Internet, becoming almost a synonym for Internet itself. It interfaces with most other Internet services (FTP, telnet, NNTP, etc.). It allows the easy production of documents containing MULTIMEDIA as well as text and hyperlinks by means of a simple MARK-UP LANGUAGE, HTML (HyperText Mark-up Language). Web documents, typically referred to as pages, are stored on SERVERS and retrieved by client software known as WEB BROWSERS (for example Microsoft's Internet Explorer). A page is retrieved by quoting its URL (UNIFORM RESOURCE LOCATOR) in a browser, which then fetches a copy of the page from its server using the HTTP (HyperText Transfer Protocol). Pages tend to be stored in linked local groups, termed a website, on a server.

Popularity has a price. Nobody knows for sure how many web pages there are. Current estimates range from 2 billion upwards. Thus the practice of exploring links to see where they lead, known as SURFING, can be fun but is not for the serious information seeker. There are two types of search engine (see SEARCH ENGINES). One type stores URLs of hand-picked pages under a hierarchical subject listing. The other type employs software known as a spider or a robot to copy pages into a searchable database. Examples of these two types are Yahoo! and AltaVista, respectively. Most search engines are commercially funded but some are publicly funded, e.g. those in the UK Resource Discovery Network. Some search engines search just agglomerations of other search engines (e.g. Ixquick) and are known as metasearch engines. However no one search engine is comprehensive and not all information resources on the Internet (e.g. the 'invisible Web') are directly accessible via the Web.

The invisible Web consists of DATABASES accessible via Web servers, but indirectly. A Web server can access a database either by server-side scripts (special programs accessible to a Web server) or by MIDDLEWARE, software which connects Web servers to other facilities. Server-side scripting comes in many forms from standard CGI (Common Gateway Interface) scripts written in PROGRAMMING LANGUAGES like Perl or PHP to proprietary server extensions like Microsoft's ASP (Active Server Pages). It allows the addition of new features to the web such as the ability to create 'dynamic' pages in response to user input via a Web form or to track users by means of 'COOKIES', short identifying strings. Dynamic Web pages can also be produced by embedding client-side scripts in pages, using languages like JavaScript or Java (a powerful cross-platform language). These scripts work in the browser on the user's machine.

This functional and technical extensibility of the Web has enabled it to become a platform for E-COMMERCE on the Internet. Sites like Amazon use Web-based 'shopping cart' systems to sell books and other products. Other sites like MSN (MicroSoft Network) are portals (see PORTALS AND GATEWAYS) offering many Web-based services to users (e-mail, chat, searching, etc.) in order to create audiences for advertising. Within organizations, intranets can access a variety of Web-based and legacy information systems and services, and deliver the results via Web browsers to employees.

Because the Web is now so vital globally and in so many arenas, its technical development is controlled by an international organization representing governments, business and academia, the World Wide Web Steering Consortium (W3C). The most important new direction headed by W3C is the replacement of HTML by XML (eXtensible Mark-up Language), which will enable the encoding not just of the display of content but of the meaning of content on Web pages, what Tim Berners-Lee refers to as the 'semantic Web'. The Web appears to be the premier information management tool for the foreseeable future.

Further reading

Berners-Lee, T. (1999) *Weaving the Web: The Past, Present and Future of the World Wide Web by Its Inventor*, Orion Business Books.

Poulter, A., Tseng, G. and Sargent, G. (1999) *The Information and Library Professional's Guide to the World Wide Web*, Library Association Publishing.

SEE ALSO: information and communication technology; information technology; knowledge industries; networks

ALAN POULTER

Z

ZIPF, GEORGE KINGSLEY (1902–50)

Psychologist and philologist who applied statistical and linguistic theories to human communication.

Born in Freeport, Illinois, he graduated from Harvard in 1924, also studied in Bonn and Berlin, and took a Harvard PhD in Comparative Philology in 1930. He taught German at Harvard for the rest of his life.

Zipf pioneered the study of word frequencies, not so as to apply this to questions of style, but as a means of throwing light on the nature of COMMUNICATION. From these studies he developed a theory of word frequencies that paralleled that of LOTKA for research papers and which is referred to as Zipf's Law. His use of ranking also relates to the study of the distribution of papers across a range of journals described by BRADFORD. In *The Psychobiology of Language* (1935) he related his linguistic ideas to human communication generally, and in *Human Behaviour and the Principle of Least Effort* (1949) he brought together semantic, psychological, sociological and geographical elements into a broader theoretical basis for his statistical observations.

Further reading

Tuchinsky, P.M. (1980) *Zipf's Law and His Efforts to Use Infinite Series in Linguistics*, Cambridge, MA: Birkhauser Boston.

Index

Notes: **Bold** page numbers indicate main entries. Abbreviations, *see also* detailed list on pages xxiii to xxxii.